Human Development: A Life-Span View,
Eighth Edition
Robert V. Kail and John C. Cavanaugh

Product Director: Marta Lee-Perriard

Product Team Manager: Star Burruto

Product Manager: Andrew Ginsberg

Content Developer: Nedah Rose

Product Assistant: Leah Jenson

Digital Content Specialist: Allison Marion

Content Project Manager: Ruth Sakata Corley

Production and Composition Service:
SPi Global

Intellectual Property Analyst: Deanna Ettinger

Intellectual Property Project Manager:
Kathryn Kucharek

Art Director: Vernon Boes

Text and Cover Designer: Cheryl Carrington

Cover Image: (top to bottom) FatCamera/
Getty Images, Mike Kemp/Blend Images/
Getty Images, Hero Images/Getty Images,
Mireya Acierto/Getty Images, John Lund/
Getty Images, Knauer/Johnston/Getty Images,
Maskot/Getty Images, andipantz/iStock/
Getty Images

Library of Congress Control Number: 2017950383

Student Edition:
ISBN: 978-1-337-55483-1

Loose-leaf Edition:
ISBN: 978-1-337-56365-9

Cengage
20 Channel Center Street
Boston, MA 02210
USA

Cengage is a leading provider of customized learning solutions with employees residing in nearly 40 different countries and sales in more than 125 countries around the world. Find your local representative at **www.cengage.com.**

Cengage products are represented in Canada by Nelson Education, Ltd.

To learn more about Cengage platforms and services, visit **www.cengage.com.**

Printed in the United States of America
Print Number: 02   Print Year: 2018

8e

Human Development

A Life-Span View

Robert V. Kail
Purdue University

John C. Cavanaugh
Consortium of Universities of the Washington Metropolitan Area

✺ CENGAGE

Australia • Brazil • Mexico • Singapore • United Kingdom • United States

To Dea and Chris

About the Author

ROBERT V. KAIL is Distinguished Professor of Psychological Sciences at Purdue University. His undergraduate degree is from Ohio Wesleyan University and his PhD is from the University of Michigan. Kail is editor of *Child Development Perspectives* and editor emeritus of *Psychological Science*. He received the McCandless Young Scientist Award from the American Psychological Association, was named the Distinguished Sesquicentennial Alumnus in Psychology by Ohio Wesleyan University, is a fellow of the Association for Psychological Science, and is an honorary professor at the University of Heidelberg, Germany. Kail has also written *Children and Their Development* and *Scientific Writing for Psychology*. His research focuses on cognitive development during childhood and adolescence. Away from the office, he enjoys photography and working out.

JOHN C. CAVANAUGH is President and CEO of the Consortium of Universities of the Washington Metropolitan Area. He received his undergraduate degree from the University of Delaware and his PhD from the University of Notre Dame. Cavanaugh is a fellow of the American Psychological Association, the Association for Psychological Science, and the Gerontological Society of America, and has served as president of the Adult Development and Aging Division (Division 20) of the APA. Cavanaugh has also written (with the late Fredda Blanchard-Fields) *Adult Development and Aging*. His research interests in gerontology concern family caregiving as well as the role of beliefs in older adults' cognitive performance. For enjoyment, he backpacks, enjoys photography and cooking, and is an avid traveler.

Brief Contents

Contents

1 The Study of Human Development   3

part 1   Prenatal Development, Infancy, and Early Childhood   38

2 Biological Foundations: Heredity, Prenatal Development, and Birth   39

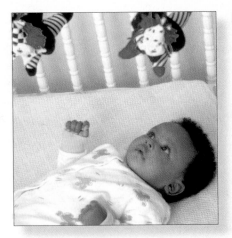

3 Tools for Exploring the World: Physical, Perceptual, and Motor Development   79

part 2   School-Age Children and Adolescents   189

6   Off to School: Cognitive and Physical Development in Middle Childhood   189

9 Moving into the Adult Social World: Socioemotional Development in Adolescence 289

12 Working and Relaxing 387

15 Social Aspects of Later Life: Psychosocial, Retirement, Relationship, and Societal Issues   501

16 Dying and Bereavement 541

Preface

" What do you want to be when you grow up?" "Where do you see yourself in the next 5 or 10 years?" "What kind of person do you want to become?" These and other questions about "becoming" confront us across our lives. Answering them requires us to understand ourselves in very thorough ways. It requires us to understand how we develop.

Human development is both the most fascinating and the most complex science there is. *Human Development: A Life-Span View*, Eighth Edition, introduces you to the issues, forces, and outcomes that make us who we are.

Contemporary research and theory on human development consistently emphasize the multidisciplinary approach needed to describe and explain how people change (and how they stay the same) over time. Moreover, the great diversity of people requires an appreciation for individual differences throughout development. *Human Development: A Life-Span View*, Eighth Edition, incorporates both and aims to address three specific goals:

- To provide a comprehensive, yet highly readable, account of human development across the life span.
- To provide theoretical and empirical foundations that enable students to become educated and critical interpreters of developmental information.
- To provide a blend of basic and applied research, as well as controversial topics and emergent trends, to demonstrate connections between the laboratory and life and the dynamic science of human development.

ORGANIZATION

A Modified Chronological Approach

The great debate among authors and instructors in the field of human development is whether to take a *chronological approach* (focusing on functioning at specific stages of the life span, such as infancy, adolescence, and middle adulthood) or a *topical approach* (following a specific aspect of development, such as personality, throughout the life span). Both approaches have their merits. We have chosen a modified chronological approach that combines the best aspects of both. The overall organization of the text is chronological: We trace development from conception through late life in sequential order and dedicate several chapters to topical issues pertaining to particular points in the life span (such as infancy and early childhood, adolescence, young adulthood, middle adulthood, and late life).

Because the developmental continuity of such topics as social and cognitive development gets lost with narrowly defined, artificial age-stage divisions, we dedicate some chapters to tracing their development over larger segments of the life span. These chapters provide a much more coherent description of important developmental changes, emphasize the fact that development is not easily divided into "slices," and provide students with understandable explications of developmental theories.

Balanced Coverage of the Entire Life Span

A primary difference between *Human Development: A Life-Span View*, Eighth Edition, and similar texts is that this book provides a much richer and more complete description of adult development and aging. Following the introductory chapter, the remaining

15 chapters of the text are evenly divided between childhood, adolescence, adulthood, and aging. This balanced treatment reflects not only the rapid emergence of adult development and aging as a major emphasis in the science of human development but also recognizes that roughly three-fourths of a person's life occurs beyond adolescence.

As a reflection of our modified chronological approach, *Human Development: A Life-Span View*, Eighth Edition, is divided into four main parts. After an introduction to the science of human development (Chapter 1), Part One includes a discussion of the biological foundations of life (Chapter 2) and development during infancy and early childhood (Chapters 3–5). Part Two focuses on development during middle childhood and adolescence (Chapters 6–9). Part Three (Chapters 10–13) focuses on young and middle adulthood. Part Four examines late adulthood (Chapters 14 and 15) and concludes with a consideration of dying and bereavement (Chapter 16).

CONTENT AND APPROACH: The Biopsychosocial Emphasis

Our text provides comprehensive, up-to-date coverage of research and theory from conception to old age and death. We explicitly adopt the biopsychosocial framework as an organizing theme, describing it in depth in Chapter 1, then integrating it throughout the text—often in combination with other developmental theories.

An Engaging Personal Style

On several occasions, we communicate our personal involvement with the issues being discussed by providing examples from our own experiences as illustrations of how human development plays itself out in people's lives. Additionally, every major section of a chapter opens with a short vignette, helping to personalize a concept just before it is discussed. Other rich examples are integrated throughout the text narrative and showcased in the *Real People* features.

Emphasis on Inclusiveness

In content coverage, in the personalized examples used, and in the photo program, we emphasize diversity—within the United States and around the world—in ethnicity, gender, race, age, ability, and sexual orientation.

CHANGES IN THE EIGHTH EDITION

The eighth edition has been updated with new graphics and several hundred new reference citations to work from the past 3 years. Of particular note are these content additions, updates, and revisions:

Chapter 1

- New *Real People* feature on Muhammad Ali

Chapter 2

- Much revised *What Do You Think?* feature on conception in the 21st century
- Much revised coverage of the period of the fetus
- Much revised coverage of nutrition during pregnancy
- New material about noninvasive prenatal testing

Chapter 3

- Much revised coverage of co-sleeping
- Much revised coverage of breastfeeding
- New *Spotlight on Research* feature on infant reaching
- Much revised coverage of handedness

Chapter 4

- Much revised description of young children's naïve theories of biology
- New *Spotlight on Research* on preschool children's essentialist thinking
- Much revised description of memory
- Much revised description of infants' number skills
- Much revised coverage of infant-directed speech
- New coverage on the benefits of touchscreen devices for children's word learning

Chapter 5

- Much revised coverage of pretend play and solitary play
- Much revised coverage of father–infant relationships
- Much revised coverage of the impact of child care
- Much revised coverage of emotion regulation

Chapter 6

- New *Spotlight on Research* feature on impaired reading comprehension
- Much revised coverage of ADHD
- New material on children's mastery of conceptual and procedural knowledge of math

Chapter 7

- New coverage of impact of quality of sibling relationships
- New coverage of open adoptions
- Much revised coverage of divorce
- Much revised coverage of maltreatment
- Much revised coverage of groups
- Much revised coverage of bullying
- Much revised coverage of electronic media, including new *Spotlight on Research* feature

Chapter 8

- Much revised material on evaluating Kohlberg's theory, including new material on adolescents' balancing of fairness with group loyalty
- Much revised coverage of analytic and heuristic solutions in problem-solving

Chapter 9

- Revised coverage of adolescent storm and stress
- Much revised coverage of dating violence
- Much revised coverage of sexual minority youth
- New material on social cognitive career theory
- Much revised coverage of adolescent depression, including new *Spotlight on Research* feature

Chapter 10

- Revised Emerging Adulthood section that now includes subsections on Neuroscience, Behavior, and Emerging Adulthood; and Achieving Milestones: Education, Workforce, and Erikson's Intimacy
- Expanded discussion of relation between educational attainment and employment
- Expanded discussion of quarter-life crisis, including Robinson's reframing of Erikson's intimacy-isolation to commitment-independence and the addition of an emerging adult transition phase.
- Revised discussion on binge drinking, sexual assault, and alcohol use disorder.
- Revised nutrition discussion to reflect new dietary guidelines and work with Native American tribes
- New discussions of emotional intelligence and impression formation

Chapter 11

- Discussion of Social Baseline Theory to explain how the brain activity reveals how people seek social relationships to mitigate risk
- New *Real People* feature on James Obergefell and John Arthur
- Inclusion of millennial generation lifestyles, including their likely much lower rates of marriage and likelihood of being less well off than their parents
- Rewritten discussion of LGBTQ adults
- New *What Do You Think?* feature on paid family leave

Chapter 12

- New chapter introduction focusing on the shift to the "gig economy" and its impact on the meaning of work
- Differentiation of mentoring and coaching
- Mention of burnout effects on the brain
- Reduced redundancy in parenting and work–family conflict sections
- New *Spotlight on Research* feature on the long-term health effects of leisure activities
- New *Real People* feature on the politics of unemployment

Chapter 13

- Revised discussion of treatments for arthritis
- Revised discussion of the effects of stress on physical health
- Addition of the TESSERA (Triggering situations, Expectancy, States/State Expressions, and Reactions model in the discussion of personality traits

Chapter 14

- Expanded discussion of international demographics of older adults
- Reorganized and revised section on biological theories of aging
- Revised discussion of the role of beta-amyloid protein in brain aging and as a biomarker of Alzheimer's disease
- New *Real People* feature on the "Angelina Jolie effect" on breast cancer screening
- Revised discussion on divided attention
- Expanded discussion of neuroimaging research on creativity and aging
- New *What Do You Think?* feature on the question of whether creativity exists
- Revised discussions about genetics and dementia, and about the beta-amyloid cascade hypothesis

Chapter 15

- Revised discussion of healthy aging and connection with selective optimization with compensation framework
- New discussion of the preventive and corrective proactivity model
- New *Real People* feature on Katherine Johnson
- Revised discussion of spirituality in later life
- Revised discussion on LGBT long-term relationships
- Expanded and revised discussion of frailty and disability in late life, especially related to socioeconomic factors, and global issues
- Revised discussion of financial exploitation of older adults and the role of financial institutions in preventing it

Chapter 16

- Table with most frequent causes of death by age
- Discussion of updated brain death criteria and implementation issues
- New *What Do You Think?* featuring the Brittany Maynard case
- Discussion of death doulas
- New *Real People* feature with focus on Randy Pausch's last lecture
- Discussion of the model of adaptive grieving dynamics
- Discussion of disenfranchised grief
- Added discussion of ambiguous grief

SPECIAL FEATURES

Three special features are a significant reason why this textbook is unique. These features are woven seamlessly into the narrative—not boxed off from the flow of the chapter. Each box appears in nearly every chapter. The three features are:

Spotlight on Research	These features emphasize a fuller understanding of the science and scope of life-span development.
What Do *You* Think?	These features ask students to think critically about social and developmental issues.
Real People Applying Human Development	These features illustrate the everyday applications of life-span development issues.

PEDAGOGICAL FEATURES

Among the most important aspects of *Human Development: A Life-Span View*, Eighth Edition, is its exceptional integration of pedagogical features, designed to help students maximize their learning.

- *Section-by-Section Pedagogy.* Each major section of a chapter (every chapter has four or five) has been carefully crafted: It opens with a set of learning objectives, a vignette, typically includes one or more *Think About It* questions in the margin encouraging critical thinking, and ends with a set of questions called *Test Yourself* that reinforces key elements of the section. For easy assignment and to help readers visually organize the material, major units within each chapter are numbered.
- *Chapter-by-Chapter Pedagogy.* Each chapter opens with a table of contents and concludes with a bulleted, detailed *Summary* (broken down by learning objective within each major section), followed by a list of *Key Terms* (with page references).

In sum, we believe that our integrated pedagogical system will give the student all the tools she or he needs to comprehend the material and study for tests.

MINDTAP®

MindTap® for *Human Development: A Life-Span View* engages and empowers students to produce their best work—consistently. By seamlessly integrating course material with videos, activities, apps, and much more, MindTap® creates a unique learning path that fosters increased comprehension and efficiency.

For students:

- MindTap® delivers real-world relevance with activities and assignments that help students build critical thinking and analytic skills that will transfer to other courses and their professional lives.
- MindTap® helps students stay organized and efficient with a single destination that reflects what's important to the instructor, along with the tools students need to master the content.
- MindTap® empowers and motivates students with information that shows where they stand at all times—both individually and compared to the highest performers in class.

Additionally, for instructors, MindTap® allows you to:

- Control what content students see and when they see it with a learning path that can be used as-is or matched to your syllabus exactly.
- Create a unique learning path of relevant readings and multimedia and activities that move students up the learning taxonomy from basic knowledge and comprehension to analysis, application, and critical thinking.
- Integrate your own content into the MindTap® Reader using your own documents or pulling from sources such as RSS feeds, YouTube videos, websites, Googledocs, and more.
- Use powerful analytics and reports that provide a snapshot of class progress, time in course, engagement, and completion.

In addition to the benefits of the platform, MindTap® for *Human Development: A Life-Span View* includes:

- Formative assessments at the conclusion of each chapter.
- Interactive activities drawn from the *What Do You Think?* and *Real People* text features that foster student participation through polls, photo shares, and discussion threads.
- Illustrative video embedded in the MindTap® Reader to highlight key concepts for the students.
- Investigate Development enables students to observe, evaluate, and make decisions about human development so they see the implications of research on a personal level. Students interact with simulated case studies of milestones in a person's development, observing and analyzing audiovisual cues, consulting research, and making decisions. Instead of rote memorization of isolated concepts, Investigate Development compels students to think critically about research and brings human development to life.

SUPPLEMENTS FOR THE INSTRUCTOR

Online PowerPoint® Slides

These vibrant Microsoft® PowerPoint® lecture slides for each chapter assist you with your lecture by providing concept coverage using images, figures, and tables directly from the textbook.

Online Instructor's Manual

This detailed manual provides sample syllabi, course guidelines, in-class exercises, and chapter objectives to assist instructors in teaching the course.

Cengage Learning Testing, powered by Cognero®
Instant Access

Cengage Learning Testing Powered by Cognero® is a flexible, online system that allows you to: import, edit, and manipulate content from the text's test bank or elsewhere, including your own favorite test questions; create multiple test versions in an instant; and deliver tests from your LMS, your classroom, or wherever you want.

ACKNOWLEDGMENTS

Textbook authors do not produce books on their own. We owe a debt of thanks to many people who helped take this project from a first draft to a bound book. Thanks to Jim Brace-Thompson, for his enthusiasm, good humor, and sage advice at the beginning of this project; to Nedah Rose for taking the reins and guiding the eighth edition; and to Andrew Ginsberg, Product Manager; Ruth Sakata-Corley, Content Production Manager; and Vernon Boes, Art Director, for their work in bringing this edition to life.

We would also like to thank the many reviewers who generously gave their time and effort to help us sharpen our thinking about human development and, in so doing, shape the development of this text.

Past Reviewers of *Human Development: A Life-Span View*

GARY L. ALLEN
University of South Carolina

POLLY APPLEFIELD
University of North Carolina at Wilmington

ANN M. B. AUSTIN
Utah State University

KENNETH E. BELL
University of New Hampshire

DANIEL R. BELLACK
Trident Technical College

MAIDA BERENBLATT
Suffolk County Community College

L. RENÉ BERGERON
University of New Hampshire

BELINDA BEVINS-KNABE
University of Arkansas at Little Rock

DAVID BISHOP
Luther College

ELIZABETH M. BLUNK
Southwest Texas State University

JOSETTE BONEWITZ
Vincennes University

JANINE P. BUCKNER
Seton Hall University

CYNTHIA B. CALHOUN
Southwest Tennessee Community College

LANTHAN D. CAMBLIN, JR.
University of Cincinnati

PAUL ANDERER CASTILLO
State University of New York, Canton

LISA DAVIDSON
Northern Illinois University

CATHERINE DEERING
Clayton College and State University

CHARLES TIMOTHY DICKEL
Creighton University

JUDITH DIETERLE
Daytona Beach Community College

SHELLEY M. DRAZEN
SUNY, Binghamton

SANDY EGGERS
University of Memphis

KENNETH ELLIOTT
University of Maine, Augusta

MARTHA ELLIS
Collin County Community College

NOLEN EMBRY
Lexington Community College

WILLIAM FABRICIUS
Arizona State University

STEVE FINKS
University of Tennessee

LINDA FLICKINGER
St. Clair County Community College

DOUGLAS FRIEDRICH
University of West Florida

REBECCA GLOVER
University of North Texas

J. A. GREAVES
Jefferson State Community College

TRESMAINE R. GRIMES
Iona College

PATRICIA GUTH
Westmoreland County Community College

LANA-LEE HARDACRE
Conestoga College

JULIE A. HASELEU
Kirkwood Community College

PHYLLIS HEATH
Central Michigan University

MYRA HEINRICH
Mesa State College

BRETT HEINTZ
Delgado Community College

SANDRA HELLYER
Indiana University–Purdue University at Indianapolis

SHIRLEY-ANNE HENSCH
University of Wisconsin Center

THOMAS HESS
North Carolina State University

HEATHER M. HILL
University of Texas, San Antonio

SUSAN HORTON
Mesa Community College

ALYCIA M. HUND
Illinois State University

KATHLEEN HURLBURT
University of Massachusetts–Lowell

JENEFER HUSMAN
University of Alabama

KAREN IHNEN
St. Cloud Technical and Community College

HEIDI INDERBITZEN
University of Nebraska at Lincoln

ERWIN J. JANEK
Henderson State University

WAYNE JOOSE
Calvin College

RICHARD KANDUS
Mt. San Jacinto College

MARGARET D. KASIMATIS
Carroll College

MICHELLE L. KELLEY
Old Dominion University

JOHN KLEIN
Castleton State College

WENDY KLIEWER
Virginia Commonwealth University

AMY LANDERS
Old Dominion University

KIRSTEN D. LINNEY
University of Northern Iowa

BLAKE TE-NEIL LLOYD
University of South Carolina

SANFORD LOPATER
Christopher Newport University

NANCY MACDONALD
University of South Carolina, Sumter

SUSAN MAGUN-JACKSON
University of Memphis

MARION G. MASON
Bloomsburg University of Pennsylvania

MICHAEL JASON MCCOY
Cape Fear Community College

LISA MCGUIRE
Allegheny College

JULIE ANN MCINTYRE
Russell Sage College

BILL MEREDITH
University of Nebraska at Omaha

EDWARD J. MORRIS
Owensboro Community College

MARTIN D. MURPHY
University of Akron

JANET D. MURRAY
University of Central Florida

MARY ANNE O'NEILL
Rollins College Hamilton Holt School

JOHN W. OTEY
Southern Arkansas University

SHANA PACK
Western Kentucky University

MARIBETH PALMER-KING
Broome Community College

ELLEN E. PASTORINO
Valencia Community College

IAN PAYTON
Bethune-Cookman College

JOHN PFISTER
Dartmouth College

BRADFORD PILLOW
Northern Illinois University

GARY POPOLI
Hartford Community College

ROBERT PORESKY
Kansas State University

JOSEPH M. PRICE
San Diego State University

HARVE RAWSON
Franklin College

To the Student

Human Development: A Life-Span View is written with you, the student, in mind. In the next few pages, we describe several features of the book that will make it easier for you to learn. Please don't skip this material; it will save you time in the long run.

Learning and Study Aids

Each chapter includes several distinctive features to help you learn the material and organize your studying.

- Each chapter opens with an overview of the main topics and a detailed outline.
- Each major section within a chapter begins with a set of learning objectives. There is also a brief vignette introducing one of the topics to be covered in that section and providing an example of the developmental issues people face.
- When key terms are introduced in the text, they appear in bold, orange type and are defined in the margin. This should make key terms easy to find and learn.
- Key developmental theories are introduced in Chapter 1 and are referred to throughout the text.
- Critical thinking questions appear in the margins. These *Think About It* questions are designed to help you make connections across sections within a chapter or across chapters.
- The end of each section includes a feature called *Test Yourself*, which will help you check your knowledge of major ideas you just read about. The Test Yourself questions serve two purposes. First, they give you a chance to spot-check your understanding of the material. Second, the questions will relate the material you have just read to other facts, theories, or the biopsychosocial framework you read about earlier.
- Text features expand or highlight a specific topic. This book includes the following three features:
    - *Spotlight on Research* elaborates a specific research study discussed in the text and provides more details on the design and methods used.
    - *What Do You Think?* offers thought-provoking discussions about current issues affecting development.
    - *Real People: Applying Human Development* is a case study that illustrates how an issue in human development discussed in the chapter is manifested in the life of a real person.
- The end of each chapter includes several special study tools. A *Summary* organized by learning objective within major section headings provides a review of the key ideas in the chapter. Next is a list of *Key Terms* that appear in the chapter.

We strongly encourage you to take advantage of these learning and study aids as you read the book. We have also left room in the margins for you to make notes to yourself on the material, so you can more easily integrate the text with your class and lecture material.

Your instructor will probably assign about one chapter per week. Don't try to read an entire chapter in one sitting. Instead, on the first day, preview the chapter. Read the introduction and notice how the chapter fits into the entire book; then page through the chapter, reading the learning objectives, vignettes, and major headings. Also read the italicized sentences and the boldfaced terms. Your goal is to get a general overview of the entire chapter—a sense of what it's all about.

Now you're ready to begin reading. Go to the first major section and preview it again, reminding yourself of the topics covered. Then start to read. As you read, think about what you're reading. Every few paragraphs, stop briefly. Try to summarize the main ideas in your own words; ask yourself if the ideas describe your own experience or that of others you know; tell a friend about something interesting in the material. In other words, read actively—get involved in what you're reading. Don't just stare glassy-eyed at the page!

Continue this pattern—reading, summarizing, thinking—until you finish the section. Then answer the Test Yourself questions to determine how well you've learned what you've read. If you've followed the read-summarize-think cycle as you worked your way through the section, you should be able to answer most of the questions.

The next time you sit down to read (preferably the next day), start by reviewing the second major section. Then complete it with the read-summarize-think cycle. Repeat this procedure for all the major sections.

When you've finished the last major section, wait a day or two and then review each major section. Pay careful attention to the italicized sentences, the boldfaced terms, and the Test Yourself questions. Also, use the study aids at the end of the chapter to help you integrate the ideas in the chapters.

With this approach, it should take several 30- to 45-minute study sessions to complete each chapter. Don't be tempted to rush through an entire chapter in a single session. Research consistently shows that you learn more effectively by having daily (or nearly daily) study sessions devoted to both reviewing familiar material *and* taking on a relatively small amount of new material.

Terminology

A few words about terminology before we embark. We use certain terms to refer to different periods of the life span. Although you may already be familiar with the terms, we want to clarify how they will appear in this text. The following terms will refer to a specific range of ages:

> *Newborn:* birth to 1 month
> *Infant:* 1 month to 1 year
> *Toddler:* 1 year to 2 years
> *Preschooler:* 2 years to 6 years
> *School-age child:* 6 years to 12 years
> *Adolescent:* 12 years to 20 years
> *Young adult:* 20 years to 40 years
> *Middle-age adult:* 40 years to 60 years
> *Young-old adult:* 60 years to 80 years
> *Old-old adult:* 80 years and beyond

Sometimes, for the sake of variety, we will use other terms that are less tied to specific ages, such as babies, youngsters, and older adults. However, you will be able to determine the specific ages from the context.

Organization

Authors of textbooks on human development always face the problem of deciding how to organize the material into meaningful segments across the life span. This book is organized into four parts: Prenatal Development, Infancy, and Early Childhood; School-Age Children and Adolescents; Young and Middle Adulthood; and Late Adulthood. We believe this organization achieves two major goals. First, it divides the life span in ways that relate to the divisions encountered in everyday life. Second, it enables us to provide a more complete account of adulthood than other books do.

Because some developmental issues pertain only to a specific point in the life span, some chapters are organized around specific ages. Overall, the text begins with conception and proceeds through childhood, adolescence, adulthood, and old age to death. But because some developmental processes unfold over longer periods of time, some of the chapters are organized around specific topics.

Part One covers prenatal development, infancy, and early childhood. Here we will see how genetic inheritance operates and how the prenatal environment affects a person's future development. During the first two years of life, the rate of change in both motor and perceptual arenas is amazing. How young children acquire language and begin to think about their world is as intriguing as it is rapid. Early childhood also marks the emergence of social relationships, as well as an understanding of gender roles and identity. By the end of this period, a child is reasonably proficient as a thinker, uses language in sophisticated ways, and is ready for the major transition into formal education.

Part Two covers the years from elementary school through high school. In middle childhood and adolescence, the cognitive skills formed earlier in life evolve to adult-like levels in many areas. Family and peer relationships expand. During adolescence, there is increased attention to work, and sexuality emerges. The young person begins to learn how to face difficult issues in life. By the end of this period, a person is on the verge of legal adulthood. The typical individual uses logic and has been introduced to most of the issues that adults face.

Part Three covers young adulthood and middle age. During this period, most people achieve their most advanced modes of thinking, achieve peak physical performance, form intimate relationships, start families of their own, begin and advance within their occupations, manage to balance many conflicting roles, and begin to confront aging. Over these years, many people go from breaking away from their families to having their children break away from them. Relationships with parents are redefined, and the pressures of being caught between the younger and older generations are felt. By the end of this period, most people have shifted focus from time since birth to time until death.

Part Four covers the last decades of life. The biological, physical, cognitive, and social changes associated with aging become apparent. Although many changes reflect decline, many other aspects of old age represent positive elements: wisdom, retirement, friendships, and family relationships. We conclude this section, and the text, with a discussion of the end of life. Through our consideration of death, we will gain additional insights into the meaning of life and human development.

We hope the organization and learning features of the text are helpful to you—making it easier for you to learn about human development. After all, this book tells the story of people's lives. Understanding the story is what it's all about.

Neuroscience Index

Diversity Index

The Study of Human Development

Jeanne Calment was one of the most important people to have ever lived. Her amazing achievement was not made in sports, government, or any other profession. When she died in 1996 at age 122 years and 164 days, she set the world record that still stands for the longest verified human life span. Jeanne lived her whole life in Arles, France. She met Vincent Van Gogh and experienced the inventions of the light bulb, automobiles, airplanes, space travel, computers, and all sorts of everyday conveniences. She survived two world wars. Longevity ran in her family: her older brother François lived to 97, her father to 93, and her mother to 86. Jeanne was extraordinarily healthy her whole life, rarely being ill. She was also active; she learned fencing when she was 85, and she was still riding a bicycle at age 100. She lived on her own until she was 110, when she moved to a nursing home. Her life was documented in the 1995 film *Beyond 120 Years with Jeanne Calment*. Shortly before her 121st birthday, Musicdisc released *Time's Mistress*, a CD of Jeanne speaking over a background of rap and hip-hop music.

Did you ever wonder how long you will live? The people you will meet and the experiences you will have? Did you ever think about how you managed to go from being a young child to the more experienced person you are now? Or what might lie ahead over the next few years or decades? Would you like to

Jeanne Calment experienced many changes in society during her 122-year life span.

Georges GOBET/Agence France Presse/Newscom

break Jeanne Calment's longevity record? What do you think other people would want? The What Do *You* Think? feature provides the results of a poll of Americans, as well as provocative questions about extending life radically.

Consider your life to this point. Make a note to yourself about—or share with someone else—your fondest memories from childhood or the events and people who have most influenced you. Also make a note about what you think you might experience during the rest of your life. Put your notes in a safe place (if it's stored online, don't forget your password). Then many years from now, retrieve it and see if you were right.

Thinking about your past and future experiences is the beginning of an exciting personal journey. Remember major moments or experiences you've had. What happened? Why do you think things happened the way they did? What major forces have shaped your life?

Likewise, look ahead. What future story do you want to write about yourself? Think about the forces that may shape the course of your life years from now—about those forces that you can influence and those that you cannot. Think about how the changes you experience will affect your future.

In this course, you will have the opportunity to ask some of life's most basic questions: How did your life begin? How did you go from a single cell—about the size of the period at the end of a sentence in this text—to the fully grown, complex adult person you are today?

What Do *You* Think?　Would You Want to Live to Be 142?

Humans may be on the brink of fundamentally redefining the typical life span. The May 2013 issue of *National Geographic* magazine showed a baby with the caption "This baby will live to be 120." Topping that, the February 23/March 2, 2015, double issue of *Time* magazine devoted its main feature to the possibility the baby on their front cover could live to 142 years (or longer). As you will learn in this book, our knowledge of the factors determining the length of the human life span is extensive, and we have in our grasp the ability to dramatically lengthen the number of years people live. But just because science enables us to think about extending life considerably, the key question is whether people will *want* to live to be 142 (or even 120).

The Pew Research Center (2013a) asked a representative sample of 2,012 U.S. adults whether they would want to live decades longer, to at least 120 years. Interestingly, when people answered from their own perspective, 56% said they would not want to live that long. But when asked what they thought other people would do, 68% said they thought other people would choose to live to at least 120. We will take a closer look at other aspects of this poll in later chapters,

but in general, the results showed that people are optimistic about their own aging and the scientific advances that will enable them to enjoy a better quality of life in old age.

A dramatic extension of the human life span to 120 years or more would likely raise ethical and moral questions, such as how to define a full and purpose-driven life, especially with respect to how we should handle the end of life. For questions such as these, many people turn to religious leaders for guidance. As part of their survey research project, the Pew Research Center (2013b) also looked at how 18 major American religious groups might approach radical life extension. Because no major religious group in America has taken a formal position on this issue, Pew researchers looked at what bioethicists (people who focus on ethics within health areas, for instance), clergy, and other scholars have said about how their respective traditions might approach the matter.

The Pew report contains links to related writings in the various religious traditions that, as you might imagine, vary across denomination. Buddhists may see longer life as providing more opportunities to learn wisdom and compassion and to achieve nirvana. Catholics may see longer lives as diminishing the search

for the transcendent. Hindus may welcome longer life, as their normal blessing is "Live long." Muslims and Jews may view longer life as a reflection of God's plan for humanity. For many Protestants, the key factor would be whether longer life spans are seen as a way to avoid death, which would likely lead them to oppose it. These views reflect different perspectives that result from interpreting both individual and collective experiences that are influenced in turn by various biological, psychological, and sociocultural forces (explored later in this chapter).

As we move along our journey through the human life span, questions that take us to the intersection of science and personal belief will occur frequently. Later in this chapter, we will encounter the rules by which scientific research is conducted, so you will better understand what the Pew Research Center did in conducting their poll. In Chapter 16, when we encounter the complex personal issues relating to the end of life, you will have a thorough grounding in how people use (or ignore) research findings in their own lives.

Back to the question posed here—would *you* like to live to 120? 142? Longer? What do *you* think?

Will you be the same or different later in life? How do you influence other people's lives? How do they influence yours? How do the various roles you play throughout life—child, teenager, partner, spouse, parent, worker, grandparent—shape your development? How do you deal with the thought of your own death and the death of others?

These are examples of the questions that create the scientific foundation of human development, *the multidisciplinary study of how people change and how they remain the same over time.* Answering these questions requires us to draw on theories and research in the physical and social sciences, including biology, genetics, neuroscience, chemistry, allied health and medicine, psychology, sociology, demography, ethnography, economics, and anthropology. The science of human development reflects the complexity and uniqueness of each person and each person's experiences as well as commonalities and patterns among people. As a science, human development is firmly grounded in theory and research as it seeks to understand human behavior.

Before our journey begins, we need to collect some things to make the trip more rewarding. In this chapter, we pick up the necessary GPS coordinates that point us in the proper direction: a framework to organize theories and research, common issues and influences on development, and the methods developmental scientists use to make discoveries. Throughout the book, we will point out how the various theories and research connect to your own experience. Pack well and bon voyage.

human development

The multidisciplinary study of how people change and how they remain the same over time.

1.1 Thinking About Development

LEARNING OBJECTIVES

- What fundamental issues of development have scholars addressed throughout history?
- What are the basic forces in the biopsychosocial framework? How does the timing of these forces affect their impact?
- How does neuroscience enhance our understanding of human development?

Hassan Qabbani smiled broadly as he held his newborn grandson for the first time. So many thoughts rushed into his mind: What would Mohammad experience growing up? Would the poor neighborhood they lived in prevent him from reaching his potential? Would he inherit the family genes for good health? How would his life growing up as an Arab American in the United States be different from Hassan's experiences in Syria?

Like many grandparents, Hassan wonders what the future holds for his grandson. The questions he asks are interesting in their own right, but they are important for another reason: They bear on general issues of human development that have intrigued philosophers and scientists for centuries. In the next few pages, we introduce some of these issues, which surface when any aspect of development is being investigated.

Recurring Issues in Human Development

What factors shaped the *you* that you are right now? You might suspect such things as your genetic heritage, your family or neighborhood, the suddenness of some changes in your life and the gradualness of others, and the culture(s) in which you grew up or now live. You also might have noticed that you are like some people you know—and very much unlike others. So you might suspect that everyone's life is shaped by a complex set of factors.

Your speculations capture three fundamental characteristics of human development: nature and nurture, continuity and discontinuity, and universal and context-specific development. A person's development is a blend of these characteristics; for example, some of your characteristics remain the same through life (continuity) and others change (discontinuity). Because these characteristics apply to all the topics in this book, we'll examine each one.

Nature and Nurture

Think about a particular feature that you and several people in your family have, such as intelligence, good looks, or a friendly and outgoing personality. Why is this feature so prevalent? Did you inherit it from your parents and they from your grandparents? Or is it mainly because of where and how you and your parents were brought up? *Answers to these questions illustrate different positions on the* nature–nurture issue, *which involves the degree to which genetic or hereditary influences (nature) and experiential or environmental influences (nurture) determine the kind of person you are.* The key point is that development is always shaped by both: Nature and nurture are mutually interactive influences.

For example, in Chapter 2, you will see that some individuals inherit a disease that leads to intellectual disability if they eat dairy products. However, if their environment contains no dairy products, they develop normal intelligence. Similarly, in Chapter 10, you will learn that one risk factor for cardiovascular disease is heredity but that lifestyle factors such as diet and smoking play important roles in determining who has heart attacks.

As these examples illustrate, a major aim of human development research is to understand how heredity and environment jointly determine development. For Hassan, it means his grandson's development will surely be shaped both by the genes he inherited and by the experiences he will have.

Continuity and Discontinuity

Think of some ways in which you are still the same as you were as a 5-year-old. Maybe you were outgoing and friendly at that age and remain outgoing and friendly today. Such examples suggest a great deal of continuity in development. From this perspective, once a person heads down a particular developmental path—for example, toward friendliness or intelligence—he or she tends to stay on that path throughout life, other things being equal. From a continuity perspective, if Mohammad is a friendly and smart 5-year-old, then he should be friendly and smart as a 25-year-old and a 75-year-old.

The other view is that development is not always continuous. In this view, people can change from one developmental path to another and perhaps several times in their lives. Consequently, Mohammad might be smart and friendly at age 5, smart but obnoxious at 25, and wise but aloof at 75.

The continuity–discontinuity issue *concerns whether a particular developmental phenomenon represents a smooth progression throughout the life span (continuity) or a series of abrupt shifts (discontinuity).* Of course, on a day-to-day basis, behaviors often look nearly identical, or continuous. But when viewed over the course of many months or years, the same behaviors may have changed dramatically, reflecting discontinuous change. For example, your face may look nearly identical in "selfies" taken on successive days (continuity) but change dramatically in photos taken years apart (discontinuity).

Throughout this book, you will find examples of developmental changes that represent continuities and others that are discontinuities. For example, in Chapter 5, you will see evidence of continuity: Infants who have satisfying emotional relationships with their parents typically become children with satisfying peer relationships. But in Chapter 15, you will see an instance of discontinuity: After spending most of adulthood trying to ensure the success of the next generation and to leave a legacy, older adults turn to evaluating their own lives in search of closure and a sense that what they have done has been worthwhile.

Universal and Context-Specific Development

In many native and indigenous cultures, mathematical concepts are mastered by young children not through formal education about numbers but through everyday tasks such as picking berries and selling goods in street markets (Kisker et al., 2012; Sleeter, 2016). In contrast, children in the United States are formally taught at home or school to identify numbers and to perform the abstract arithmetic operations needed to handle these tasks.

Can one theory explain development in both groups of children? *The universal and context-specific development issue concerns whether there is one path of development or several.* Some theorists argue that despite what look like differences in development, there is only one fundamental developmental process for everyone. According to this view, differences in development are simply variations on the same fundamental process in much the same way cars as different as a Chevrolet, a Honda, and a Lexus are all products of fundamentally the same manufacturing process.

The alternative view is that differences among people are not simply variations on a theme. Advocates of this view argue that human development is inextricably intertwined with the context within which it occurs. A person's development is a product of complex interaction with the environment, and that interaction is *not* fundamentally the same in all environments. Rather, each environment has its own set of unique procedures that shape development, just as the "recipes" for different cars yield vehicles as different as a Smart car and a stretch limousine.

As is the case for the nature–nurture and continuity–discontinuity issues, the result is a blend; individual development reflects both universal and context-specific influences. For example, the order of development of physical skills in infancy is essentially the same in all cultures. But how those skills are focused or encouraged in daily life differs.

Putting all three issues together and using personality to illustrate, we can ask how the development of personality is shaped by interactions between heredity and environment, is continuous or discontinuous, and develops in much the same way around the world. To answer these kinds of questions, we need to look at the forces that combine to shape human development.

Even with little formal education, this Brazilian boy has well-developed mathematical skills. This is an example of cultural contextual forces shaping development.

Basic Forces in Human Development: The Biopsychosocial Framework

When trying to explain why people develop as they do, scientists usually consider four interactive forces:

- Biological forces *that include all genetic and health-related factors that affect development.*
- Psychological forces *that include all internal perceptual, cognitive, emotional, and personality factors that affect development.*
- Sociocultural forces *that include interpersonal, societal, cultural, and ethnic factors that affect development.*
- Life-cycle forces *that reflect differences in how the same event affects people of different ages.*

Each person is a unique combination of these forces. To see why each force is important, think about whether a mother decides to breast-feed her infant. Her decision will be based on biological variables (e.g., the quality and amount of milk she produces), her attitudes about the virtues of breast-feeding, the influences of other people (e.g., the father, her own mother), and her cultural traditions and societal norms about appropriate ways to feed infants. In addition, her decision will reflect her age and stage of life. Only by focusing on all of these forces can we have a complete view of the mother's decision.

One useful way to organize the biological, psychological, and sociocultural forces on human development is with the biopsychosocial framework. As you can see in ▶ Figure 1.1, the biopsychosocial framework emphasizes that each of the forces interacts with the others to make up development. Let's look at the different elements of the biopsychosocial model in more detail.

universal and context-specific development issue
Concerns whether there is one path of development or several.

biological forces
All genetic and health-related factors that affect development.

psychological forces
All internal perceptual, cognitive, emotional, and personality factors that affect development.

sociocultural forces
Interpersonal, societal, cultural, and ethnic factors that affect development.

life-cycle forces
Differences in how the same event affects people of different ages.

biopsychosocial framework
Useful way to organize the biological, psychological, and sociocultural forces on human development.

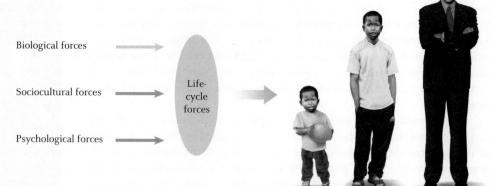

© 2019 Cengage

▶ **Figure 1.1**
The biopsychosocial framework shows that human development results from interacting forces.

Biological Forces: Genetics and Health

Prenatal development, brain maturation, puberty, and physical aging may occur to you as outcomes of biological forces. Indeed, major aspects of each process are determined by our genetic code. For example, many children resemble their parents, which shows biological influences on development. But biological forces are not only genetic; they also include the effects of such things as diet and exercise. Collectively, biological forces can be viewed as providing the raw material necessary and as setting the boundary conditions (in the case of genetics) for development.

Psychological Forces: Known by Our Behavior

Psychological forces seem familiar because they are the ones used most often to describe the characteristics of a person. For example, think about how you describe yourself to others. Most of us say that we have a nice personality and are intelligent, honest, self-confident, or something similar. Concepts such as these reflect psychological forces.

In general, psychological forces are all the internal cognitive, emotional, personality, perceptual, and related factors that help define us as individuals and that influence behavior. Psychological forces have received the most attention of the three main developmental forces, and their impact is evident throughout this text. For example, we will see how the development of intelligence enables individuals to experience and think about their world in different ways. We'll also see how the emergence of self-esteem is related to the beliefs people have about their abilities, which in turn influence what they do.

Sociocultural Forces: Race, Ethnicity, and Culture

People develop in the world, not in a vacuum. To understand human development, we need to know how people and their environments interact and mutually influence each other. That is, we need to view an individual's development as part of a much larger system in which any individual part influences all other aspects of the system. This larger system includes one's parents, children, siblings, extended family, as well as important individuals outside the family, such as friends, teachers, and coworkers. The system also includes institutions that influence development, such as schools, media, and the workplace. At a broader level, the society in which a person grows up plays a key role.

All of these people and institutions fit together to form a person's culture: the knowledge, attitudes, and behavior associated with a group of people. Culture can be linked to a particular country or people (e.g., French culture); to a specific point in time (e.g., popular culture of the 2010s); or to groups of individuals who maintain specific, identifiable cultural traditions (e.g., Native American tribes, Muslims). Knowing the culture from which a person comes provides some general information about important influences that become manifest throughout the life span.

Understanding the impact of culture is particularly important in the United States, one of the most culturally diverse countries in the world. Hundreds of different languages are spoken, and in many states, no single racial or ethnic group constitutes a majority. The many customs of people from different cultures offer insights into the broad spectrum of human experience and attest to the diversity of the U.S. population.

Although the U.S. population is changing rapidly, much of the research we describe in this text was conducted on middle-class European Americans. Accordingly, we must be careful *not* to assume that findings from this group necessarily apply to people in other groups. Indeed, there is a great need for research on different cultural groups. Perhaps as a result of taking this course, you will help fill this need by becoming a developmental researcher yourself.

Another practical problem that we face is how to describe racial and ethnic groups. Terminology changes over time. For example, the terms *colored people*, *Negroes*, *black Americans*, and *African Americans* have all been used to describe Americans of African ancestry. In this book, we use the term *African American* because it emphasizes their unique cultural heritage. Following the same reasoning, we use *European American* (instead of *Caucasian* or *white*), *Native American* (instead of *Indian* or *American Indian*), *Asian American*, and *Latino American* (rather than *Hispanic*).

These labels are not perfect. In some cases, they blur distinctions among ethnic groups. For example, people from both Puerto Rico and Mexico may be described as Latinos. However, their cultural backgrounds vary on several important dimensions, so we should not view them as a homogeneous group. Similarly, the term *Asian American* blurs variations among people whose heritage is, for example, Japanese, Chinese, or Korean. Throughout this text, whenever researchers have identified the subgroups in their research sample, we will use the more specific terms in describing results. When we use the more general terms, remember that conclusions may not apply to all subgroups within the group described by the more general term.

Life-Cycle Forces: Timing Is Everything

Consider the following two females. Jacqui, a 32-year-old, has been happily married for six years. She and her husband have a steady income. They decide to start a family, and a month later Jacqui learns that she is pregnant. Jenny, a 17-year-old, lives in the same neighborhood as Jacqui. She has been sexually active for about six months but is not in a stable relationship. After missing her period, Jenny takes a pregnancy test and discovers that she is pregnant.

The culture in which you grow up influences how you experience life.

Although both Jacqui and Jenny became pregnant, the outcome of each pregnancy will certainly be affected by factors in each woman's situation, such as her age, her financial situation, and the extent of her social support systems. The example illustrates life-cycle forces: The same event can have different effects depending on when it happens in a person's life. In the scenarios with Jacqui and Jenny, the same event—pregnancy—produces happiness and eager anticipation for one woman but anxiety and concern for the other.

The Forces Interact

So far, we've described the four forces in the biopsychosocial framework as if they were independent. But as we pointed out, each force mutually shapes the others. Consider eating habits. When the authors of this text were growing up, a "red meat and potatoes" diet was common and thought to be healthy. Scientists later discovered that high-fat diets may lead to cardiovascular disease and some forms of cancer. Consequently, research changed dietary recommendations, and social pressures changed what people eat, the advertisements they saw, and the different foods restaurants began to serve. Thus, the biological forces of the consequences of fat in the diet were influenced by the social forces of the times, whether in support of or in opposition to eating beef every evening. As your authors became more educated about diets and their effects on health, the psychological forces of thinking and reasoning also influenced their choice of diets. (We confess, however, that dark chocolate remains a passion for one of us.) However, research on the effects of fat sometimes collided with centuries of cultural food traditions and with the ability to afford healthier alternatives, meaning that some folks were able to change their diets more easily than were others. Finally, the age of the person when this research became widely known mattered, too. Young children eat what their parents provide, whereas adults may have the ability to make choices.

This example illustrates that no aspect of human development can be fully understood by examining the forces in isolation. All four must be considered in interaction. In fact, we'll see later in this chapter that integration across the major forces of the biopsychosocial framework is one criterion by which the adequacy of a developmental theory can be judged.

Combining the four developmental forces gives a view of human development that encompasses the life span yet appreciates the unique aspects of each phase of life. From this perspective we can view each life story as a complex interplay among the four forces. Try this for yourself. Read the short biography of Muhammad Ali in the Real People: Applying Human Development feature; then think about how each of the developmental forces would explain how he accomplished as much as he did.

Neuroscience: A Window into Human Development

Understanding that the four developmental forces interact is one thing. But what if, like the comic book hero Superman, you could use your X-ray vision and actually *see* these forces interact? That's what is possible in the field of neuroscience. *Applied to human development,* neuroscience *is the study of the brain and the nervous system, especially in terms of brain–behavior relationships.* Neuroscientists use several methods to do this, from molecular analyses of individual brain cells to sophisticated techniques that yield images of brain activity.

Neuroscientific approaches are being applied to a wide range of issues in human development, especially those involving memory, reasoning, and emotion (e.g., Linden, 2016; Sugiura, in press). For example, neuroscientists are unlocking relations between developmental changes in specific regions of the brain to explain well-known developmental phenomena such as adolescents' tendency to engage in risky behavior and older adults' short-term memory problems.

neuroscience

The study of the brain and the nervous system, especially in terms of brain–behavior relationships.

Neuroscience brings an important perspective to human development. Identifying patterns of brain activity helps to reveal interactions between biological, psychological, sociocultural, and life-cycle forces, which allows a better understanding of how each person is a unique expression of these forces.

Real People | Applying Human Development

Muhammad Ali

Muhammad Ali never left any doubt about how he perceived himself: "I am the greatest." And he backed up his claim, becoming one of the most important, controversial, inspiring, and respected figures of the 20th century. Born Cassius Marcellus Clay, Jr. in 1942, he changed his name from what he referred to as his "slave name" to Muhammad Ali to reflect both his religious conversion to Sunni Islam and his support of the civil rights movement in the 1960s.

Ali was the dominant boxer of his generation and remains the only fighter to win the heavyweight title three separate times. His epic bouts against Sonny Liston, Joe Frazier, and George Foreman have become legendary. He aimed to "float like a butterfly and sting like a bee" in the ring, and his "rope-a-dope" tactic gave him a way to tire his opponents.

Ali craved the limelight and media. His verbal skills, in particular his poetry, made him a star, and his recordings earned him two Grammy Award nominations. At a time when most boxers, and most sports figures, shied from politics, he made a point to be provocative and even outlandish.

In 1966, two years after winning his first heavyweight title, Ali refused to be drafted into the U.S. military, stating his religious beliefs and opposition to the Vietnam War as his reasons for being a conscientious objector. He was arrested, convicted of draft evasion, and stripped of his title. Although the U.S. Supreme Court overturned his conviction in 1971, Ali had lost four years of his prime fighting career.

Ali retired from boxing in 1981 and devoted the remainder of his life to charitable and religious work. He was one of the most recognized figures globally, and was recognized by U.S. Presidents Bill Clinton and George W. Bush, as well as the United Nations and numerous other organizations.

Diagnosed with Parkinson's disease in 1984 as a consequence of boxing-related brain injuries, Ali made fewer public appearances in the last decades of his life. Most notably, he lit the Olympic flame at the 1996 Atlanta Games. His family provided care for him until his death on June 3, 2016, at the age of 74.

Muhammad Ali's life demonstrates all of the developmental forces. His phenomenal boxing prowess and his later succumbing to Parkinson's disease were the result of biological forces. His high self-confidence and quick verbal skills reflect psychological forces. His choice not to serve in the Vietnam War and his very strong support for civil rights reflected the sociocultural forces of the times. The arc of his boxing success and his later move to religious and charitable work indicate the action of life-cycle forces. Ali was both a man of his times, and a figure for all times.

Muhammad Ali

Featureflash Photo Agency/Shutterstock.com

TEST YOURSELF 1.1

Recall

1. The nature–nurture issue involves the degree to which _____ and the environment influence human development.

2. Azar remarked that her 14-year-old son has been incredibly shy ever since he was a baby. This illustrates the _____ of development.

3. _____ forces include genetic and health factors.

4. Neuroscience examines _____ relations.

Interpret

- How does the biopsychosocial framework provide insight into the recurring issues of development (nature–nurture, continuity–discontinuity, universal–context-specific)?

Apply

- How does your life experience reflect the four developmental forces?

Check your answers to the Recall Questions at the end of the chapter.

LEARNING OBJECTIVES

- What is a developmental theory?
- How do psychodynamic theories account for development?
- What is the focus of learning theories of development?
- How do cognitive-developmental theories explain changes in thinking?

- What are the main points in the ecological and systems approach?
- What are the major tenets of life-span and life-course theories?

Marcus has just graduated from high school, first in his class. For his proud mother, Betty, this is a time to reflect on her son's past and to ponder his future. Marcus has always been a happy, easygoing child—a joy to rear. And he's been interested in learning for as long as she can remember. Betty wonders why he is so perpetually good-natured and so curious. If she knew the secret, she laughed, she could write a best-selling book and be a guest on *The Late Show with Stephen Colbert*.

theory

An organized set of ideas that explains development.

To answer Betty's questions about her son's growth, developmental researchers need to provide a theory of his development. Theories are essential because they provide the "why's" for development. What is a theory? *In human development, a **theory** is an organized set of ideas that explains development.* For example, suppose friends of yours have a baby who cries often. You could imagine several explanations for her crying. Maybe the baby cries because she's hungry; maybe she cries to get her parents to hold her; maybe she cries because she's a cranky, unhappy baby. Each of these explanations is a very simple theory: It tries to explain why the baby cries so much. Of course, actual theories in human development are more complicated, but the purpose is the same—to explain behavior and development.

There are no truly comprehensive theories of human development to guide research (Newman & Newman, 2015). Instead, five general perspectives influence current research: psychodynamic theory; learning theory; cognitive theory; ecological and systems theory; and theories involving the life-span perspective, selective optimization with compensation, and the life-course perspective. Let's consider each approach briefly.

Psychodynamic Theory

psychodynamic theories

Hold that development is largely determined by how well people resolve conflicts they face at different ages.

Psychodynamic theories *hold that development is largely determined by how well people resolve conflicts they face at different ages.* This perspective traces its roots to Sigmund Freud's theory that personality emerges from conflicts that children experience between what they want to do and what society wants them to do.

Building on Sigmund Freud's ideas, Erik Erikson (1902–1994) proposed his psychosocial theory, the first comprehensive life-span view, which still remains an important theoretical framework.

Erikson's Theory

psychosocial theory

Erikson theory that personality development is determined by the interaction of an internal maturational plan and external societal demands.

*In his **psychosocial theory**, Erikson proposed that personality development is determined by the interaction of an internal maturational plan and external societal demands.* He proposed that the life cycle is composed of eight stages and that the order of the stages is biologically fixed (the eight stages shown in ▶ Table 1.1). The name of each stage reflects the challenge people face at a particular age. For example, the challenge for young adults is to become involved in a loving relationship. Challenges are met through a combination of inner psychological influences and outer social influences. When challenges are met successfully, people are well prepared to meet the challenge of the next stage.

The sequence of stages in Erikson's theory is based on the epigenetic principle, *which means that each psychosocial strength has its own special period of particular importance.* The eight stages represent the order of this ascendancy, and it takes a lifetime to acquire all of the psychosocial strengths. Moreover, Erikson realizes that present and future behavior must have its roots in the past because later stages are built on the foundation laid in previous stages.

The psychodynamic perspective emphasizes that the trek to adulthood is difficult because the path is strewn with challenges. Outcomes of development reflect the manner and ease (or difficulty) with which people surmount (or fail to overcome) life's barriers. When children easily overcome early obstacles, for example, they are better able to handle the later ones. A psychodynamic theorist would tell Betty that her son's cheerful disposition and his academic record suggest that he has handled life's early obstacles well, which is a good sign for his future development.

© 2019 Cengage

Erik Erikson

Learning Theory

In contrast to psychodynamic theory, learning theory concentrates on how learning influences a person's behavior. This perspective emphasizes the role of experience, examining whether a person's behavior is rewarded or punished. This perspective also emphasizes that people learn from watching others around them. Two influential theories in this perspective are behaviorism and social learning theory.

Behaviorism

Early in the 20th century, John Watson (1878–1958) believed that infants' minds were essentially "blank slates" and argued that learning alone determines what people will become. He assumed that with the correct techniques, almost anyone could learn anything. In Watson's view then, experience was about all that mattered in determining the course of development.

Watson did little research to support his claims, but B. F. Skinner (1904–1990) filled this gap. *Skinner studied* operant conditioning, *in which the consequences of a behavior determine whether a behavior is repeated in the future.* Skinner showed that two kinds of consequences were especially influential. *A* reinforcement *is a consequence that increases the likelihood of the behavior that it follows.* Positive reinforcement consists of giving a reward such as chocolate, gold stars, or paychecks to increase the likelihood of a behavior. A father who wants to encourage his daughter to help with chores may reinforce her

epigenetic principle

Means by which each psychosocial strength has its own special period of particular importance.

operant conditioning

Technique in which the consequences of a behavior determine whether a behavior is repeated in the future.

reinforcement

A consequence that increases the likelihood of the behavior that it follows.

Table 1.1

The Eight Stages of Psychosocial Development in Erikson's Theory

PSYCHOSOCIAL STAGE	AGE	CHALLENGE
Basic trust vs. mistrust	Birth to 1 year	To develop a sense that the world is safe, a "good place"
Autonomy vs. shame	1 to 3 years	To realize that one is an independent person who can make decisions and doubt
Initiative vs. guilt	3 to 6 years	To develop the ability to try new things and to handle failure
Industry vs. inferiority	6 years to adolescence	To learn basic skills and to work with others
Identity vs. identity confusion	Adolescence	To develop a lasting, integrated sense of self
Intimacy vs. isolation	Young adulthood	To commit to another in a loving relationship
Generativity vs. stagnation	Middle adulthood	To contribute to younger people through child rearing, child care, or other productive work
Integrity vs. despair	Late life	To view one's life as satisfactory and worth living

B. F. Skinner

punishment

A consequence that decreases the likelihood of the behavior that it follows.

imitation or observational learning

Learning by simply watching those around them.

■
_____

Think About It

How could you use the basic ideas of operant conditioning to explain how children create theories of the physical and social world?

self-efficacy

People's beliefs about their own abilities and talents.

Albert Bandura

with praise, food treats, or money whenever she cleans her room. Negative reinforcement consists of rewarding people by taking away unpleasant things. The same father could use negative reinforcement by saying that whenever his daughter cleans her room, she doesn't have to wash the dishes or weed the garden.

A punishment *is a consequence that decreases the likelihood of the behavior that it follows.* Punishment suppresses a behavior either by adding something aversive or by withholding a pleasant event. Should the daughter fail to clean her room, the father may punish her by nagging (adding something aversive) or by not allowing her to FaceTime her friends (withholding a pleasant event).

Skinner's research was done primarily with animals, but human development researchers showed that the principles of operant conditioning could be extended readily to people, too (Baer & Wolf, 1968). Applied properly, reinforcement and punishment are powerful influences on children, adolescents, and adults; however, compared with punishment, reinforcement tends to result in quicker and longer-lasting learning.

Social Learning Theory

People sometimes learn without reinforcement or punishment. *People learn much by simply watching those around them, which is known as* imitation or observational learning. Imitation is the reason one toddler throws a toy after seeing a peer do so or when a school-age child offers to help an older adult carry groceries because she's seen her parents do the same.

Perhaps imitation makes you think of "monkey see, monkey do," in which people simply mimic what they see. Early investigators had this view, too, but subsequent research showed that this was wrong. People do not always imitate what they see around them. People are more likely to imitate if the person they see is important, popular, smart, or talented. They're also more likely to imitate when the behavior they see is rewarded than when it is punished. Findings like these imply that imitation is more complex than sheer mimicry. People are not mechanically copying what they see and hear; instead, they look to others for information about appropriate behavior. When peers are reinforced for behaving in a particular way, this encourages imitation. This is one explanation for why groups of friends tend to behave, talk, and think similarly.

Albert Bandura (1925–) based his social cognitive theory on this more complex view of reward, punishment, and imitation. Bandura's theory is "cognitive" because he believes people actively try to understand what goes on in their world; the theory is "social" because, along with reinforcement and punishment, what other people do is an important source of information about the world.

Bandura also argues that experience gives people a sense of self-efficacy, *which refers to people's beliefs about their own abilities and talents.* Self-efficacy beliefs help to determine when people will imitate others. A child who sees himself as not athletically talented, for example, will not try to imitate LeBron James dunking a basketball despite the fact that LeBron is obviously talented and popular. Thus, whether an individual imitates others depends on who the other person is, on whether that person's behavior is rewarded, and on the individual's beliefs about his or her own abilities.

Bandura's social cognitive theory is a far cry from Skinner's operant conditioning. The operant conditioned person who responds mechanically to reinforcement and punishment has been replaced by the social cognitive person who actively interprets these and other events. Nevertheless, Skinner, Bandura, and all learning theorists share the view that experience propels people along their developmental journeys. These theorists would tell Betty that she can thank experience for making Marcus both happy and successful academically.

Cognitive-Developmental Theory

Another way to approach development is to focus on thought processes and a person constructing knowledge actively. In cognitive-developmental theory, the key is how people think and how thinking changes over time. Three distinct approaches have developed.

One approach postulates that thinking develops in a universal sequence of stages; Piaget's theory of cognitive development (and its extensions) is the best-known example. The second approach proposes that people process information as computers do, becoming more efficient over much of the life span; information-processing theory is an example of this view. The third approach emphasizes the contributions of culture on thinking and cognitive growth.

Piaget's Theory

The cognitive-developmental perspective began with a focus on how children construct knowledge and how their constructions change over time. Jean Piaget (1896–1980), the most influential child and adolescent developmental psychologist of the 20th century, proposed the best known of these theories. Piaget believed that children naturally try to make sense of their world. Throughout infancy, childhood, and adolescence, individuals want to understand the workings of both the physical and social world. For example, infants want to know about objects: "What happens when I push this toy off the table?" And they want to know about people: "Who is this person who feeds and cares for me?"

As children try to comprehend their world, Piaget believed that they act like scientists, creating theories about the physical and social worlds. Children try to weave all that they know about objects and people into a complete theory, which is tested daily by experience because their theories lead children to expect certain things to happen. As with real scientific theories, when the predicted events do occur, a child's belief in her theory grows stronger. When the predicted events do not occur, the child must revise her theory.

Imagine an infant whose theory of objects includes the idea that "Toys pushed off the table fall to the floor." If the infant pushes some other object—a plate or an article of clothing—she finds that it, too, falls to the floor, and she can then make the theory more general: "Objects pushed off the table fall to the floor."

Piaget also believed that children begin to construct knowledge in new ways at a few critical points in development. When this happens, they revise their theories radically. These changes are so fundamental that the revised theory is, in many respects, brand-new. Piaget claimed that these changes occur first at about age 2 years, again at about age 7, and a third time just before adolescence. These changes mean that children go through four distinct stages in cognitive development. Each stage represents a fundamental change in how children understand and organize their environment, and each stage is characterized by more sophisticated types of reasoning. For example, the first or *sensorimotor* stage begins at birth and lasts until about 2 years of age. As the name implies, sensorimotor thinking refers to an infant's constructing knowledge through sensory and motor skills. This stage and the three later stages are shown in ❱ Table 1.2.

Jean Piaget

© 2019 Cengage

Table 1.2		
Piaget's Four Stages of Cognitive Development		
STAGE	**APPROXIMATE AGE**	**CHARACTERISTICS**
Sensorimotor	Birth to 2 years	Infant's knowledge of the world is based on senses and motor skills; by the end of the period, uses mental representation
Preoperational thought	2 to 6 years	Child learns how to use symbols such as words and numbers to represent aspects of the world but relates to the world only through his or her perspective
Concrete operational thought	7 years to early adolescence	Child understands and applies logical operations to experiences provided they are focused on the here and now
Formal operational thought	Adolescence and beyond	Adolescent or adult thinks abstractly, deals with hypothetical situations, and speculates about what may be possible

Piaget's theory has had an enormous influence on how developmentalists and practitioners think about cognitive development during childhood and adolescence. The theory has been applied in many ways—from the creation of discovery learning toys to the ways teachers plan lessons. In Chapter 4, we'll see how Piaget explained thinking during infancy and the preschool years; in Chapters 6 and 8, we'll learn about his description of thinking in school-age children and adolescents.

Information-Processing Theory

Information-processing theorists draw heavily on how computers work to explain how thinking develops through childhood, adolescence, and adulthood. *Just as computers consist of both hardware (disk drives, random-access memory, and the central processing unit) and software (the programs the computer runs),* information-processing theory *proposes that human cognition consists of mental hardware and mental software.* Mental hardware refers to cognitive structures, including different memories where information is stored. Mental software includes cognitive processes that enable people to complete specific tasks such as reading a sentence, playing a video game, or hitting a baseball. For example, an information-processing psychologist would say that for students to do well on an exam, they must encode the information as they study, store it in memory, and then retrieve it during the test.

To explain developmental changes in thinking, information-processing psychologists believe that like computers, adolescents and adults have better hardware and better software than do younger children, who have less powerful and sophisticated processors. For example, adolescents typically solve math word problems better than younger children do because adolescents have greater memory capacity to store the facts in the problem and because their methods for performing arithmetic operations are more efficient.

Some researchers also point to deterioration of the mental hardware—along with declines in the mental software—as explanations of cognitive aging. In Chapter 14, we will see, for example, that normative aging brings with it significant changes in people's ability to process information.

Rob Marmion/Shutterstock.com

Information-processing theory helps explain how this girl learns, stores, and retrieves information as she is studying for an exam.

information-processing theory
Proposes that human cognition consists of mental hardware and mental software.

Vygotsky's Theory

Lev Vygotsky (1896–1934) was one of the first theorists to emphasize that children's thinking is influenced by the sociocultural context in which they grow up. A Russian psychologist, Vygotsky believed that because all societies aim to help children acquire essential cultural values and skills, every aspect of a child's development must be considered against this backdrop. For example, most parents in the United States want their children to work hard in school and go to college because earning a degree is a key to finding a good job. However, in Mali (an African country), Bambara parents want their children to learn to farm, herd animals such as cattle and goats, gather food such as honey, and hunt because these skills are key to survival in their environment. Vygotsky's key insight was to view development as an apprenticeship in which children develop as they work with skilled adults, including teachers and parents, to learn what is valued in their culture.

For Piaget, information-processing theorists, and Vygotsky, children's thinking becomes more sophisticated as they develop. Piaget explained this change as resulting from the more sophisticated knowledge that children actively construct; information-processing psychologists attribute it to improved mental hardware and mental software; Vygotsky claimed learning and thinking developed as a result of and as part of cultural context. What would these theorists say to Betty about Marcus's good nature? Vygotsky would point out that Betty communicated key aspects of the culture to Marcus, which influenced his good nature. Neither Piaget nor information-processing theorists would have much to say because their theories do not handle personality issues very well. What about Marcus's academic success? That's a different story. Piaget would explain that all

© 2019 Cengage

Lev Vygotsky

children naturally want to understand their world; Marcus is simply unusually skilled in this regard. An information-processing psychologist would point to superior hardware and superior software as the keys to his academic success. Vygotsky would again emphasize Betty's influence in cultural transmission.

The Ecological and Systems Approach

Most developmentalists agree that the environment is an important force in many aspects of development. However, only ecological theories (which get their name from the branch of biology dealing with the relation of living things to their environment and to each other) have focused on the complexities of environments and their links to development. *In ecological theory, human development is inseparable from the environmental contexts in which a person develops.* The ecological approach proposes that all aspects of development are interconnected, much like the threads of a spider's web, so that no aspect of development can be isolated from others and understood independently. An ecological theorist would emphasize that to understand why adolescents behave as they do, we need to consider the many different systems that influence them, including parents, peers, teachers, media, the neighborhood, and social policy.

We will consider two examples of the ecological and systems approach: Bronfenbrenner's theory and the competence–environmental press framework.

Bronfenbrenner's Theory

The best-known advocate of the ecological approach was Urie Bronfenbrenner (1917–2005), who proposed that the developing person is embedded in a series of complex and interactive systems. Bronfenbrenner (1995) divided the environment into the four levels shown in ❱ Figure 1.2: the microsystem, the mesosystem, the exosystem, and the macrosystem.

© 2019 Cengage

Urie Bronfenbrenner

ecological theory
Theory that views human development as inseparable from the environmental contexts in which a person develops.

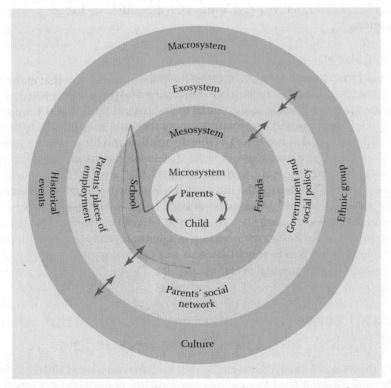

SOURCE: Kopp, C. B., Krakow, J. B. (Eds.). (1982). *The Child: Development in a Social Context* (p. 648). Reading, MA: Addison-Wesley. Reprinted by permission of Pearson Education.

❱ **Figure 1.2**
Bronfenbrenner's ecological approach emphasizes the interaction across different systems in which people operate.

microsystem

The people and objects in an individual's immediate environment.

mesosystem

Provides connections across microsystems because what happens in one microsystem is likely to influence others.

exosystem

Social settings that a person may not experience firsthand but that still influence development.

macrosystem

The cultures and subcultures in which the microsystem, mesosystem, and exosystem are embedded.

competence

People's abilities.

environmental press

The demands put on people by the environment.

The microsystem consists of the people and objects in an individual's immediate environment. These are the people closest to a person, such as parents or siblings. Some people may have more than one microsystem. For example, a young child might have the microsystems of the family and of the day-care setting. A retired adult might have the microsystems of a spouse and close friends. As you can imagine, microsystems strongly influence development.

Microsystems themselves are connected to create the mesosystem. *The mesosystem provides connections across microsystems because what happens in one microsystem is likely to influence others.* Perhaps you've found that if you have a stressful day at work or school, you're often grouchy at home. This indicates that your mesosystem is alive and well; your microsystems of home and work are interconnected emotionally for you.

The exosystem refers to social settings that a person may not experience firsthand but that still influence development. For example, changes in government policy regarding welfare may mean that economically disadvantaged children have fewer opportunities for enriched preschool experiences. Although the influence of the exosystem is indirect, its effects on human development can be quite strong.

The broadest environmental context is the macrosystem, the cultures and subcultures in which the microsystem, mesosystem, and exosystem are embedded. A mother, her workplace, her child, and the child's school are part of a larger cultural setting, such as Chinese Americans living in San Francisco or Italian Americans living in Brooklyn. Members of these cultural groups share a common identity, a common heritage, and common values. The macrosystem evolves over time; each successive generation may develop in a unique macrosystem.

Bronfenbrenner's ecological theory emphasizes the many levels of influence on human development. People are affected directly by family members and friends and indirectly by social systems such as neighborhoods and religious institutions—which, in turn, are affected by the beliefs and heritage of one's culture.

Competence–Environmental Press Theory

Another view of the influence of environments on human development comes from Lawton and Nahemow's (1973) competence–environmental press theory. *According to this theory, people adapt most effectively when their competence, or abilities, match the environmental press, or the demands put on them by the environment.* This theory was originally proposed to account for the ways in which older adults function in their environment, but it applies throughout the life span. For example, the match between an adult's social skills and her work group's demands can determine whether she is accepted by the group. As with Bronfenbrenner's theory, competence–environmental press theory emphasizes that to understand people's functioning, it is essential to understand the systems in which they live.

Ecological theorists would agree with learning theorists in telling Betty that the environment has been pivotal in her son's amiable disposition and his academic achievements. However, the ecological theorist would insist that environment means much more than the reinforcements, punishments, and observations that are central to learning theory; such a theorist would emphasize the different levels of environmental influence on Marcus. Betty's ability to balance home (microsystem) and work (mesosystem) so skillfully (which meant that she was usually in a good mood herself) contributed positively to Marcus's development, as did Betty's membership in a cultural group (exosystem) that emphasized the value of doing well in school. Marcus was also competent enough to handle the external demands (environmental press) put on him.

Life-Span Perspective, Selective Optimization with Compensation, and Life-Course Perspective

Most of the theories of human development that we have considered so far pay little attention to the adult years of the life span (Erikson's theory is the main exception). Historically, adulthood was downplayed, owing to the belief that it was a time when abilities had reached a plateau (rather than continuing to develop) and that adulthood was followed by inevitable decline in old age. However, modern perspectives emphasize the importance of viewing human development as a lifelong process. These perspectives view development in terms of where a person has been and where he or she is heading.

Life-Span Perspective and Selective Optimization with Compensation

We can only understand adults' experiences by understanding their childhood and adolescence. Placing adults' lives in this broader context is what the life-span perspective does.

According to the life-span perspective, *human development is multiply determined and cannot be understood within the scope of a single framework.* The basic premise of the life-span perspective is that aging is a lifelong process of growing up and growing old, beginning with conception and ending with death. No single period of a person's life (such as childhood, adolescence, or middle age) can be understood apart from its origins and its consequences. To understand a specific period, we must know what came before and what is likely to come afterward (Riley, 1979). In addition, how one's life is played out is affected by social, environmental, and historical change. Thus, the experiences of one generation may not be the same as those of another.

Paul Baltes (1939–2006) and colleagues provide many of the main approaches to human development from a life-span perspective (Baltes, Lindenberger, & Staudinger, 2006) in a model that has influenced a wide range of research, especially on adult development and aging. They identify four key features of the life-span perspective as follows.

life-span perspective
View that human development is multiply determined and cannot be understood within the scope of a single framework.

- *Multidirectionality* Development involves both growth and decline; as people grow in one area, they may lose in another. For example, people's vocabulary tends to increase throughout life, but their memory skills weaken.
- *Plasticity* One's capacity is not predetermined or carved in stone. Many skills can be learned or improved with practice, even in late life. For example, people can learn better ways to remember information, which may help them deal with declining memory. There are limits to the degree of potential improvement, though, as described in later chapters.
- *Historical context* Each of us develops within a particular set of circumstances determined by the historical time in which we are born and the culture in which we grow up. For example, living in a middle-class suburb in 1980s Atlanta has little in common with living in a poor Latino neighborhood in 2000s Texas.
- *Multiple causation* Development reflects the biological, psychological, sociocultural, and life-cycle forces that we mentioned previously. For example, children's success in school will depend on their heredity, their cognitive skills, their culture's emphasis on achievement, and whether their parents are teenagers, young adults, or middle aged.

selective optimization with compensation (SOC) model
View that selection, optimization, and compensation form a system of behavioral action that generates and regulates development and aging.

Taken together, the principles of the life-span perspective describe and explain the successful adaptation of people to the changes that occur with aging by proposing an interaction between three processes: selection, compensation, and optimization (Baltes, 1997; Baltes et al., 2006; Baltes & Carstensen, 1999; Baltes & Heydens-Gahir, 2003). Selection processes serve to choose goals, life domains, and life tasks, whereas optimization and compensation concern maintaining or enhancing chosen goals. *The basic assumption of the* selective optimization with compensation (SOC) model *is that the three processes form a system of behavioral action that generates and regulates development and aging.*

As people mature and grow old, they select from a range of possibilities or opportunities. This selection occurs for two main reasons. *Elective selection* occurs when people reduce their involvement to fewer domains as a result of new demands or tasks, such as when a college student drops out of some organizations because of the amount of work required in the courses he is taking that term. *Loss-based selection* occurs when real or anticipated losses in personal or environmental resources cause people to reduce their involvement, such as when an older person stops going to church because he can no longer drive. In either case, selection sometimes means continuing previous goals on a lesser scale or substituting with new goals.

© 2019 Cengage

Paul Baltes

Compensation occurs when people's skills have decreased so they no longer function well in a particular domain. When people compensate, they search for an alternate way to accomplish the goal. For example, if an older adult can no longer drive because she has a broken leg, she might compensate by taking the bus. Sometimes, compensation requires learning a new skill; for example, an older adult experiencing short-term memory problems might compensate by learning to use a smartphone app for lists. Thus, compensation differs from selection in that the task or goal is maintained but achieved through other means.

Optimization involves minimizing losses and maximizing gains. The main idea is to find the best match possible between one's resources (biological, psychological, and sociocultural) and one's desired goals. Because people cannot achieve optimal outcomes in everything, development becomes a dynamic process of selecting the right goals and compensating when possible to help maximize the odds of achieving them.

One can see the SOC model at work in many situations. For example, aging musicians who want to continue to play concerts may reduce the number of pieces they play (selection), rehearse them more often (optimization), and sing them in a lower key (compensation). A college athlete who excels at ice hockey and baseball may decide to concentrate on hockey (selection), work on training all year (optimization), and develop a wicked wrist shot to make up for a mediocre slap shot (compensation).

The life-span perspective and the SOC model have provided important approaches to the contemporary study of human development. The emphasis on the need for a using multidisciplinary approach and for recognizing many interactive forces will be developed throughout this text.

Life-Course Perspective

Adults often describe their lives as a story that includes several key life events and transitions (e.g., going to school, getting a first job, getting married, having children). Such stories show how people move through their lives and experience unique interactions of the four forces of development.

The **life-course perspective** *describes the ways in which various generations experience the biological, psychological, and sociocultural forces of development in their respective historical contexts.* Specifically, it lets researchers examine the effects of historical time on how people create their lives (Dannefer & Miklowski, 2006; Hagestad & Dannefer, 2001; Hareven, 1995, 2001; Mayer, 2009). A key feature of the life-course perspective is the dynamic interplay between the individual and society. This interplay creates three major dimensions, all involving timing and underlying the life-course perspective:

- *The individual timing of life events in relation to external historical events* This dimension addresses the question: How do people time and sequence their lives (e.g., getting a first job, having their first child, entering retirement) in the context of changing historical conditions (e.g., economic good times or recession)?
- *The synchronization of individual transitions with collective familial ones* This dimension addresses the question: How do people balance their own lives (e.g., work obligations) with those of their family (e.g., children's soccer games)?
- *The impact of earlier life events, as shaped by historical events, on subsequent ones* This dimension addresses the question: How does experiencing an event earlier in life (e.g., a male turning 18 years old) at a particular point in history (e.g., when there is a military draft) affect one's subsequent life (e.g., choosing a particular career)?

Research from the life-course perspective has shown that major life transitions such as marriage, childbearing, starting and ending a career, and completing one's education occur at many different ages across people and generations. These differences first appear after adolescence, when people begin to have more control over the course of their lives. Research has also shown that life transitions are more continuous and multidirectional than previously thought. For example, completing an education was relegated to early adulthood in traditional models, yet current realities of returning adult students and life-long learning make this view obsolete. Finally, research shows that the various domains of

life-course perspective

Describes the ways in which various generations experience the biological, psychological, and sociocultural forces of development in their respective historical contexts.

At age 93, cellist Pablo Casals said he still practiced three hours a day because he was "beginning to notice some improvement."

people's lives are highly interdependent; for example, the decision to have a child is often made in the context of where one is in one's career and education.

The emphasis in the life-course perspective on interrelations between the individual and society with reference to historical time has made it a dominant view in the social sciences. In particular, this approach is useful in helping researchers understand how the various aspects of people's experiences (work, family, education) interact to create unique lives.

Overall, life-span and life-cycle theories have greatly enhanced developmental theory by drawing attention to the role of aging in the broader context of human development (Gilleard & Higgs, 2016). These theories have played a major role in conceptualizing adulthood and have greatly influenced the research we consider in Chapters 10 through 15. Theorists espousing a life-span or life-course perspective would tell Betty that Marcus will continue to develop throughout his adult years and that this developmental journey will be influenced by biopsychosocial forces, including his own family.

The Big Picture

As summarized in ❱ Table 1.3, each of the theories provides ways of explaining how the biological, psychological, sociocultural, and life-cycle forces create human development. But because no single theory provides a complete explanation of all aspects of development, we must rely on the biopsychosocial framework to piece together an account based on many different theories. Throughout the remainder of this text, you will read about many theories that differ in focus and in scope. To help you understand them better, each theory will be introduced in the context of the issues that it addresses.

One criterion for a theory is that it be testable. The next section describes the methods by which developmentalists conduct research and test their theories.

Table 1.3				
Theoretical Perspectives on Human Development				
PERSPECTIVE	**EXAMPLES**	**MAIN IDEA**	**EMPHASES IN BIOPSYCHOSOCIAL FRAMEWORK**	**POSITIONS ON DEVELOPMENTAL ISSUES**
Psychodynamic	Erikson's psychosocial theory	Personality develops through sequence of stages	Psychological, social, and life-cycle forces crucial; less emphasis on biological	Nature–nurture interaction, discontinuity, universal sequence but individual differences in rate
Learning	Behaviorism (Watson, Skinner)	Environment controls behavior	In all theories, some emphasis on biological and psychological, major focus on social, little recognition of life cycle	In all theories, strongly nurture, continuity, and universal principles of learning
	Social learning theory (Bandura)	People learn through modeling and observing		
Cognitive	Piaget's theory (and extensions)	Thinking develops in a sequence of stages	Main emphasis on biological and social forces, less on psychological, little on life cycle	Strongly nature, discontinuity, and universal sequence of stages
	Information-processing theory	Thought develops by increases in efficiency at handling information	Emphasis on biological and psychological, less on social and life cycle	Nature–nurture interaction, continuity, individual differences in universal structures
	Vygotsky's theory	Development influenced by culture	Emphasis on psychological and social forces	Nature–nurture interaction, continuity, individual differences

[Continued on next page]

			EMPHASES IN BIOPSYCHOSOCIAL	POSITIONS ON DEVELOPMENTAL
PERSPECTIVE	EXAMPLES	MAIN IDEA	FRAMEWORK	ISSUES
Ecological and Systems	Bronfenbrenner's theory	Developing person embedded in a series of interacting systems	Low emphasis on biological, moderate on psychological and life cycle, heavy on social	Nature–nurture interaction, continuity, context-specific
	Competence–environmental press (Lawton and Nahemow)	Adaptation is optimal when ability and demands are in balance	Strong emphasis on biological, psychological, and social, moderate on life cycle	Nature–nurture interaction, continuity, context-specific
Life-Span Perspective/SOC	Baltes's life-span perspective and selective optimization with compensation (SOC)	Development is multiply determined; optimization of goals	Strong emphasis on the interactions of all four forces; cannot consider any in isolation	Nature–nurture interaction, continuity and discontinuity, context-specific
Life-Course Perspective	Life-course theory	Life-course transitions decreasingly tied to age; increased continuity over time; specific life paths across domains are interdependent	Strong emphasis on psychological, sociocultural, life cycle; less on biological	Nature–nurture interaction, continuity and discontinuity, context-specific

Theoretical Perspectives on Human Development (Continued)

TEST YOURSELF 1.2

Recall

1. _____ organize knowledge to provide testable explanations of human behaviors and the ways in which they change over time.

2. The _____ perspective proposes that development is determined by the interaction of an internal maturational plan and external societal demands.

3. According to social cognitive theory, people learn from reinforcements, from punishments, and through _____.

4. Piaget's theory and Vygotsky's theory are examples of the _____ perspective.

5. According to Bronfenbrenner, development occurs in the context of the _____, mesosystem, exosystem, and macrosystem.

6. A belief that human development is characterized by multidirectionality and plasticity is fundamental to the _____ perspective.

Interpret

- How are the information-processing perspective and Piaget's theory similar? How do they differ?

Apply

- Using three different developmental theories, explain how LeBron James or Lady Gaga achieved their success.

Check your answers to the Recall Questions at the end of the chapter.

1.3 Doing Developmental Research

LEARNING OBJECTIVES

- How do scientists measure topics of interest in studying human development?

- What research designs are used to study human development?

- How do researchers integrate results from multiple studies?

- What ethical procedures must researchers follow?

- How do investigators communicate results from research studies?

- How does research affect public policy?

Leah and Joan are mothers of 10-year-old boys. Their sons have many friends, but the basis for the friendships is not obvious to the mothers. Leah believes "opposites attract"—children form friendships with peers who have complementary interests and abilities. Joan doubts this; her son seems to seek out other boys who are near clones of himself in their interests and abilities.

Suppose Leah and Joan know that you're taking a course in human development, so they ask you to settle their argument. Leah believes complementary children are more often friends, whereas Joan believes similar children are more often friends. You know that research could show whose ideas are supported under which circumstances, but how?

Human development researchers start their search for knowledge by asking good questions such as these. Once the questions are framed, they make several important decisions as they prepare to study a topic. They need to decide how to measure the topic of interest, they design their study, they choose a method for studying development, and they decide whether their plan respects the rights of individuals participating in the research. In practice, all of these steps occur simultaneously; for example, the selection of a measure or method is done in the context of the rights of research participants. But for simplicity, we'll describe each of these steps in sequence.

Measurement in Human Development Research

The first step in doing developmental research is deciding how to measure the topic or behavior of interest. So the first step toward answering Leah and Joan's question would be to decide how to measure friendships.

Human development researchers use one of four approaches: observing systematically, using tasks to sample behavior, asking people for self-reports, and taking physiological measures.

Systematic Observation

As the name implies, systematic observation *involves watching people and carefully recording what they do or say.* Two forms of systematic observation are common.

In naturalistic observation, *people are observed as they behave spontaneously in a real-life situation.* There's a catch with observation, though. Researchers can't keep track of everything that someone does, so beforehand they must decide what specific variables to record. For example, researchers studying friendship might decide to observe children as they start their first year in middle school (chosen because this is a time when many children will be making new friends). They could decide to record where children sit in the lunchroom and who talks to whom.

Structured observations *differ from naturalistic observations in that the researcher creates a setting that is likely to bring out the behavior of interest.* Structured observations are particularly useful for studying behaviors that are difficult to observe naturally, such as how people respond to emergencies. An investigator relying on natural observations to study people's responses to emergencies wouldn't make much progress with naturalistic observation because emergencies don't occur at predetermined times and locations. However, using a structured observation, an investigator might stage an emergency—perhaps cooperating with authorities to simulate an accident—to observe people's responses.

Some behaviors are difficult for researchers to observe because they occur in private, not public, settings. For example, sexual activity tends to occur in private, where it is difficult for investigators to observe unobtrusively. However, researchers could ask couples to come to the researcher's laboratory, which might be furnished to resemble a typical bedroom. The researchers would then observe the friends' activity by watching from another room, watching through a one-way mirror, or videotaping them. Later in this book, we will consider findings from research such as this that has greatly helped us understand human behavior, such as providing insights into how people provide consent for engaging in sexual activity.

systematic observation

Watching people and carefully recording what they do or say.

naturalistic observation

Observing people as they behave spontaneously in a real-life situation.

structured observations

Method in which the researcher creates a setting that is likely to bring out the behavior of interest.

Structured observations are valuable in enabling researchers to observe behavior(s) that would otherwise be difficult to study. But there are limits. For example, observing couples engaging in sexual activity in a mock bedroom has many artificial aspects to it: The couples are not in their rooms, they were told in general terms what to do, and they know they're being observed. Any of these factors may cause couples to behave differently than they would in the real world. Researchers must be careful that their method does not make the behavior they are observing unnatural or unrealistic.

Sampling Behavior with Tasks

When investigators can't observe a behavior directly, an alternative is to create tasks that are thought to sample the behavior of interest. One task often used to measure older adults' memory is "digit span": Adults listen as a sequence of digits is presented aloud. After the last digit is presented, they try to repeat the digits in order.

Another example is shown in ❱ Figure 1.3. To study the ability to recognize emotions, the child has been asked to look at the photographs and point to the face that looks happy. A child's answers on this sort of task are useful in determining his or her ability to recognize emotions. This approach is popular and convenient; however, a potential problem is that the task may not provide a realistic sample of the behavior of interest. For example, asking children to judge emotions from photographs may not be valid because it underestimates what they do in real life. Why might this be the case? We mention several reasons on page 34, just before Test Yourself.

Self-Reports

self-reports

People's answers to questions about the topic of interest.

Self-reports represent a special case of using tasks to measure people's behavior. Self-reports *are people's answers to questions about the topic of interest.*

When questions are posed in written form, the self-report is a questionnaire; when questions are posed orally, the self-report is an interview. Either way, questions are created that probe different aspects of the topic of interest. For example, if you believe that adults are more often friends when they have interests in common, then you might tell your research participants the following:

> Tom and Dave just met each other at work. Tom likes to read, plays the clarinet, and is not interested in sports; Dave likes to tweet his friends, enjoys tinkering with his car, and watches sports all weekend. Do you think Tom and Dave will become friends?

The participants would then decide, perhaps using a rating scale, whether the men are likely to become friends.

Self-reports are useful because they can lead directly to information on the topic of interest. They are also relatively convenient, particularly when they can be administered to groups of participants or administered online.

However, self-reports are not always a good measure of people's behavior because not all answers are accurate. Why? When asked about past events, for example, people may not remember them accurately. For example, an older adult asked about adolescent friends may not remember those friendships well. Sometimes people answer incorrectly as a result of "response bias": For many questions, they are more likely to respond in a socially acceptable manner (e.g., they may be reluctant to admit they had no friends). As long as investigators remain aware of these potential biases, though, self-reports can be a valuable tool for research in human development.

Physiological Measures

One less common but potentially powerful form of measurement is measuring people's physiological responses. Earlier we saw that brain activity is used in neuroscience research to track certain behaviors, such as memory.

❱ **Figure 1.3**

In this example of sampling behavior with tasks, the child is to select the face that looks happy.

© 2019 Cengage

▶ Figure 1.4 shows an image that researchers might use in such research. Another measure is heart rate, which often slows down when people are paying close attention to something interesting. Consequently, researchers often measure heart rate to determine a person's degree of attention. As another example, the hormone cortisol is often secreted in response to stress. By measuring cortisol levels in saliva, scientists can determine when people are experiencing stress.

As these examples suggest, physiological measures are usually specialized—they focus on a particular aspect of a person's behavior (in these examples, memory, attention, and stress). What's more, they're often used with behaviorally oriented methods. A researcher studying stress might observe several people for overt signs of stress, ask parents/partners/friends to rate the target person's stress, and measure cortisol in the target person's saliva. If all three measures lead to the same conclusions about stress, then the researcher can be more confident about those conclusions.

As we have discussed, there are strengths and weaknesses in each of the four approaches to measurement. These are summarized in ▶ Table 1.4. Which approach a researcher takes will depend on which one best matches the research questions as well as the feasibility and appropriateness of use with particular research participants.

Reliability and Validity

After researchers choose a method, they must show that it is both reliable and valid. *The reliability of a measure is the extent to which it provides a consistent index of a characteristic.* A measure of friendship, for example, is reliable if it consistently estimates a person's friendship network each time you administer it. Reliability of a measure is essential, but it isn't enough. A measure must also be valid to be useful.

The validity of a measure refers to whether it actually measures what researchers think it measures. For example, a measure of friendship is valid if it actually measures friendship and not, for example, popularity. Validity is often established by showing that the measure in question is closely related to another measure known to be valid.

Representative Sampling

Valid measures also depend on the people who are tested. *Researchers are usually interested in broad groups of people called* populations. Examples of populations are all American 7-year-olds or all African American grandparents. *Virtually all studies include only a* sample *of people, which is a subset of the population.* Researchers must take care that their sample represents the population of interest because an unrepresentative sample

Think About It

If you were studying middle-aged adults caring for their aging parents, what would be the relative advantages of systematic observation, sampling behavior with tasks, and self-reports?

▶ **Figure 1.4**

Brain imaging techniques provide a physiological measure that helps researchers understand brain–behavior relations.

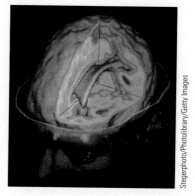

Stegerphoto/Photolibrary/Getty Images

reliability

The extent to which a measure provides a consistent index of a characteristic.

validity

Whether a measure actually measures what researchers think it measures.

populations

Broad groups of people that are of interest to researchers.

sample

A subset of the population.

Table 1.4		
Measuring Behaviors of Interest in Human Development Research		
METHOD	**STRENGTH**	**WEAKNESS**
Systematic Observation		
Naturalistic observation	Captures people's behavior in its natural setting	Difficult to use with behaviors that are rare or that typically occur in private settings
Structured observation	Can be used to study behaviors that are rare or that typically occur in private settings	May be invalid if structured setting distorts the behavior
Sampling Behavior with Tasks	Convenient—can be used to study most behaviors	May be invalid if the task does not sample behavior as it occurs naturally
Self-Reports	Convenient—can be used to study most behaviors	May be invalid because people answer incorrectly (due to either forgetting or response bias)
Physiological Measures	Provide a more direct measure of underlying behavior	Highly specific in what they measure and thus cannot be applied broadly

can lead to invalid conclusions. For example, if a study of friendship in older adults tested only people who had no siblings, you would probably decide that this sample is not representative of the population of older adults and question its validity.

As you read on, you'll soon discover that much of the research we describe was conducted with samples that consist mostly of middle-class European American people. Are these samples representative of all people in the United States? Of all people in the world? No. To make samples more representative, some U.S. federal agencies now require researchers to include certain groups (e.g., ethnic minorities, women, children) or explain in detail why they are not, a policy that has resulted in a broader view of developmental processes. But until we have representative samples in all developmental research, we cannot know whether a particular phenomenon applies only to the group studied or to people more generally.

General Designs for Research

Having selected a way to measure the topic or behavior of interest, researchers embed this measure in a research design that yields useful, relevant results. Human development researchers rely on two primary designs in their work: correlational studies and experimental studies.

Correlational Studies

correlational study

Investigation looking at relations between variables as they exist naturally in the world.

In a correlational study, *investigators look at relations between variables as they exist naturally in the world.* Imagine a researcher who wants to test the idea that smart people have more friends. To find out, the researcher would measure two variables for each person—the number of friends the person has and the person's intelligence—and then see whether the two variables are related.

The results of a correlational study are usually measured by calculating a correlation coefficient, *which expresses the strength and direction of a relation between two variables.* Correlations can range from −1.0 to 1.0. The correlation coefficient reflects one of three possible relations between intelligence and the number of friends:

correlation coefficient

An expression of the strength and direction of a relation between two variables.

- People's intelligence is unrelated to the number of friends they have, reflected in a correlation of 0.
- People who are smart tend to have more friends than people who are not as smart. That is, *more* intelligence is associated with having *more* friends. In this case, the variables are positively related and the correlation is between 0 and 1.
- People who are smart tend to have fewer friends than people who are not as smart. That is, *more* intelligence is associated with having *fewer* friends. In this case, the variables are negatively related and the correlation is between −1 and 0.

In interpreting a correlation coefficient, you need to consider both the sign *and* size of the correlation. The sign indicates the *direction* of the relation between variables: A positive sign means that larger values of one variable are associated with larger values of the second variable, whereas a negative sign means that larger values of one variable are associated with smaller values of the second variable.

The *size* or *strength* of a relation is measured by how much the correlation differs from 0, either positively or negatively. A correlation of 0.9 between intelligence and number of friends would indicate a very strong relation: Knowing a person's intelligence, you could accurately predict how many friends the person has. If instead the correlation was only 0.3, then the link between intelligence and number of friends would be weaker: Although more intelligent people would have more friends on average, there would be many exceptions. Similarly, a correlation of −0.9 would indicate a strong negative relation between intelligence and number of friends, whereas a correlation of −0.3 would indicate a weak negative relation.

Although a correlational study can determine whether variables are related, it doesn't address the question of cause and effect between the variables. For example, a correlation of 0.7 between intelligence and number of friends indicates that people who are smarter have more friends than people who are not as smart. This correlation has three possible interpretations, shown in ❯ Figure 1.5: (1) Being smart causes people to have more friends; (2) having more friends causes people to be smarter; or (3) neither variable causes the other; instead, both intelligence and number of friends are caused by a third variable (such as parents who are supportive) that was not measured in the study. Any of these interpretations could be true, but they cannot be distinguished in a correlational study. Investigators who want to track down causes must resort to a different design, called an experimental study.

Experimental Studies

In an experiment, *investigators systematically manipulate the factor(s) that they think causes a particular behavior. The factor being manipulated is called the* independent variable; *the behavior being observed is called the* dependent variable. In human development, an experiment requires that the investigator begin with one or more independent variables (usually treatments, interventions, experiences, or events) that are thought to affect the behavior of interest. People are then assigned randomly to conditions that differ in the amount of the independent variable. Finally, an appropriate measure (the dependent variable) is taken of all participants to see whether the treatment or treatments had the expected effect. Because each person has an equal chance of being assigned to each treatment condition (the definition of random assignment), any differences between the groups can be attributed to the differential treatment people received in the experiment rather than to other factors.

Suppose, for example, that an investigator believes that older adults perform better in a driving simulator when they are not talking on a mobile phone. The photo on page 28 shows how we might test this hypothesis. Older adults come to the laboratory equipped with a driving simulator. Some are randomly assigned to a condition in which they drive while talking on a mobile phone, but others are assigned to a condition in which they drive but do not talk on a mobile phone.

All participants drive under circumstances that are held as constant as possible—except for the presence or absence of talking on the mobile phone. If on average older adults drive better in the "no phone" condition than in the "mobile phone" condition, then the investigator could say with confidence that the mobile phone has a harmful effect on driving skill. Conclusions about cause and effect are possible because the direct manipulation occurred under controlled conditions.

Human development researchers usually conduct experiments in laboratory-like settings because this allows better control over the variables that may influence the outcome of the research. Thus, a shortcoming of laboratory experiments is that the behavior of interest is not studied in its natural setting. For example, driving in a simulator may

experiment
A systematic way of manipulating the key factor(s) that the investigator thinks causes a particular behavior.

independent variable
The factor manipulated in an experiment.

dependent variable
The behavior being observed in an experiment, used to evaluate the impact of the independent variable.

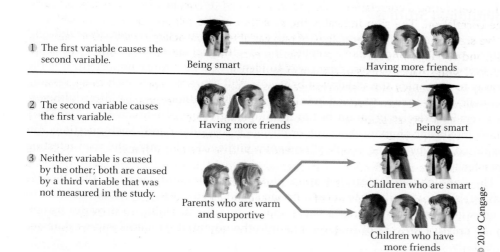

1. The first variable causes the second variable.
   Being smart → Having more friends

2. The second variable causes the first variable.
   Having more friends → Being smart

3. Neither variable is caused by the other; both are caused by a third variable that was not measured in the study.
   Parents who are warm and supportive → Children who are smart / Children who have more friends

© 2019 Cengage

❯ **Figure 1.5**
There are three basic interpretations of a correlation coefficient because there is no direct way to assess cause and effect.

An experiment using a driving simulator to examine skills of older drivers. In this "no phone" condition, the driver is not talking on a mobile phone.

qualitative research

Method that involves gaining in-depth understanding of human behavior and what governs it.

not be the same as driving on a highway. Consequently, there is always the potential problem that the results may be invalid because they are artificial—specific to the laboratory setting and not representative of the behavior outside of the laboratory.

Each research design used by developmentalists has both strengths and weaknesses. There is no one best method. Consequently, no single investigation can definitively answer a question. Researchers rarely rely on one study or even one method to reach conclusions. Instead, they prefer to find converging evidence from as many different kinds of studies as possible.

Qualitative Studies

Suppose you live near a children's playground. Each day, you watch the children play various games with each other and on the swings and sliding board. Because you are interested in learning more about how children go about playing, you decide to watch more carefully. With the parents' permission, you video the children's play each day for several weeks. You then watch the videos and notice whether there are specific patterns that emerge.

What you have done is to conduct one type of qualitative research, *which involves gaining in-depth understanding of human behavior and what governs it.* Because qualitative research typically involves intensive observation of behavior over extended periods of time, the need is for smaller but focused samples rather than large random samples. Frequently used techniques include video recording and detailed interviews, from which qualitative researchers categorize the data into patterns as the primary basis for organizing and reporting results. In contrast, quantitative research relies on numerical data and statistical tests as the bases for reporting results.

Qualitative research can be conducted for its own sake, as a preliminary step, or as a complement to quantitative research. Research reports of qualitative research are usually richer and provide more details about the behavior being observed.

Designs for Studying Development

Research in human development usually concerns differences or changes that occur over time. In these cases—in addition to deciding how to measure the behavior of interest and whether the study will be correlational or experimental—investigators must also choose one of three designs that allow them to examine development: longitudinal, cross-sectional, or sequential.

Longitudinal Studies

longitudinal study

A research design in which the same individuals are observed or tested repeatedly at different points in their lives.

In a longitudinal study, *the same individuals are observed or tested repeatedly at different points in their lives.* As the name implies, the longitudinal approach examines development over time. It is the most direct way to identify change. More important, it is the only way to determine the stability of behavior: Will characteristics such as aggression, dependency, or mistrust observed in infancy or early childhood persist into adulthood? Will a regular exercise program begun in middle age have benefits in later life? Does people's intelligence remain the same or change across adulthood? Such questions can be explored only by testing people at one point in their development and then retesting them later.

The Spotlight on Research feature illustrates a longitudinal study that focuses on the stability of intelligence across the life span. As you read, pay close attention to the questions and how the researchers approached them. Doing so provides insight into the creative process of research and into the potential strengths and weaknesses of the study.

The Stability of Intelligence from Age 11 to Age 90 Years

Who were the investigators, and what was the aim of the study? A long-standing issue in human development is the degree to which personal character-istics, such as intelligence, remain stable or change over one's life. Ian Deary, Alison Pattie, and John Starr (2013) addressed this issue by examining the stability and validity of individual differences based on the same intelligence test (the Moray House Test) given to the same people at ages 11 and 90. This is one of the few studies of a personal characteristic over such a long period of time in the same people.

How did the investigators measure the topic of interest? The primary assessment of intelligence was the Moray House Test, which mainly tests verbal reasoning, along with some numerical and other items. Participants were also given the National Adult Reading Test, Mini-Mental State Examination (a screening test for dementia), Raven's Progressive Matrices (a measure of nonverbal reasoning), and the Wechsler Logical Memory Test (a test of verbal recall of stories).

Who were the participants in the study? The participants were members of the 1921 Lothian (Scotland) Birth Cohort. In 1932, at roughly age 11, almost every member of the cohort was given the Moray House Test in school. Between 1999 and 2001, 550 survivors were tested between ages 78 and 80. In 2011 and 2012, 106 survivors were tested as close to their 90th birthday as possible. Because of the long period that had elapsed since initial testing, many of the original participants were unable to be retested due to death, mental or physical incapacity, or other reasons.

▶ Figure 1.6 depicts the various reasons why participants were not retested.

What was the design of the study? The study used a longitudinal design.

Were there ethical concerns with the study? All participants were provided infor-mation about the purpose of the study and the tests they would take. Parents provided informed consent for their children; each adult participant provided informed consent. Participants were screened for signs of mental impairment that may have interfered with either their ability to understand the purpose of the study and provide consent or their ability to understand and complete the tasks.

What were the results? The correlation between raw scores on the Moray House Test at age 11 and age 90 was 0.67. Scores correlated 0.73 between ages 79 and 90. In other words, 11-year-olds with high scores tended to have high scores at 79 and 90. Importantly, scores on the Moray House Test correlated with the other cognitive measures, evidence of the Moray House Test's validity. Although the sample showed evidence of several physical health problems, there was no evidence that mental ability in childhood predicts individual differences in norma-tive cognitive aging or with the likelihood of dementia.

What did the investigators conclude? Deary, Pattie, and Starr concluded that individual differences in intelligence in middle childhood as measured by the Moray House Test showed reasonably high stability at age 90. In other words, smart 11-year-olds tend to be smart 90-year-olds and not-so-smart 11-year-olds tend to be not-so-smart 90-year-olds.

What converging evidence would strengthen these conclusions? Because the sample included only Scottish participants, it would be necessary to study people from other cultures to find out whether the results generalize across cultures. In addition, the use of only one test in the assessment of the participants at age 11 provides a narrow view of intelligence.

▶ **Figure 1.6**

Number and mean age of participants and causes of attrition at each wave of testing in the Lothian Birth Cohort of 1921.

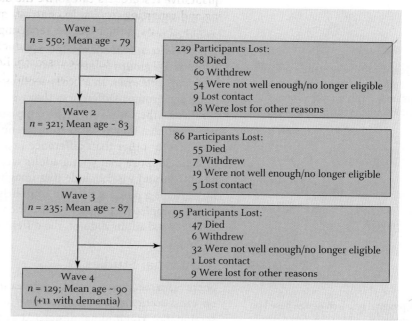

NOTE: "Withdrew" refers to participants who did not wish to continue to participate. "Not well enough/no longer eligible" refers to participants who withdrew for health reasons, including being too frail to travel, and participants who had severe visual impairments or dementia (except at Wave 4, when 11 people with dementia were examined at home by a physician, but not given tests of cognitive functioning). "Other reasons" for leaving the study include, for example, living too far away to travel to the testing site, caring for a spouse, refusal by the participant's general medical practitioner, and missing an appointment.

SOURCE: Deary, I. J., Pattie, A., & Starr, J. M. (2013). The stability of intelligence from age 11 to age 90 years: The Lothian birth cohort of 1921. *Psychological Science, 24,* 2361–2368. doi: 10.1177/0956797613486487.

As powerful as it is in identifying what does—or does not—change over time, the longitudinal approach has disadvantages that frequently offset its strengths. One is cost: The expense of keeping up with a large sample of individuals can be staggering. A related problem is the need to keep the sample together over the course of the research. Maintaining contact with people over years or decades can be challenging. Even among those who do not move away, some lose interest and choose not to continue; others may die. These "dropouts" often differ significantly from their peers, and this fact may also distort the study's outcome. For example, a study may seem to show that a group of older adults shows intellectual stability late in life. What may have happened, however, is that those who found earlier testing most difficult quit the study and thereby raised the group average on the next round. Even when the sample remains constant, taking the same test many times may make people "test-wise." Improvement over time may be attributed to development when it actually stems from practice with a particular test. Changing the test from testing session to testing session solves the practice problem but raises a new question: how to compare responses to different tests.

Because of these and other problems with the longitudinal method, human development researchers often use cross-sectional studies instead.

Cross-Sectional Studies

cross-sectional study

Study in which developmental differences are identified by testing people of different ages.

In a cross-sectional study, *developmental differences are identified by testing people of different ages.* Development is charted by noting the differences between individuals of different ages at the same point in calendar time. The cross-sectional approach avoids the problems of repeated testing and the costs of tracking a sample over time. But cross-sectional research has its own weaknesses. Because people are tested at only one point in their lives, we learn nothing about the continuity of development. Consequently, we cannot tell whether an aggressive 14-year-old remains aggressive at age 30 because the person would be tested either at age 14 or age 30 but not both.

cohort effects

A problem with cross-sectional designs in which differences between age groups (cohorts) may result from environmental events not from developmental processes.

Cross-sectional studies are also affected by cohort effects, *meaning that differences between age groups (cohorts) may result as much from environmental events as from developmental processes.* In a cross-sectional study, we typically compare people from two or more age groups. Differences that we find are attributed to the difference in age, but this needn't be the case. Why? The cross-sectional study assumes that when the older people were younger, they resembled the people in the younger age group. This isn't always true. Some factor other than difference in age may be responsible for differences between the groups. Suppose that young adults were found to be more imaginative than middle-aged adults. Should we conclude that imagination declines between these ages? Not necessarily. Perhaps a new curriculum to nourish creativity was introduced after the middle-aged adults completed school. Because the younger adults experienced the curriculum but the middle-aged adults did not, the difference between them is difficult to interpret.

Sequential Studies

sequential design

Developmental research design based on cross-sectional and longitudinal designs.

Some researchers use a more complex approach, called a sequential design, *that is based on cross-sectional and longitudinal designs.* A sequential design begins with a cross-sectional or longitudinal design. At some regular interval, the researcher then adds more cross-sectional or longitudinal studies, resulting in a sequence of these studies. For example, suppose a researcher wants to learn whether adults' memory ability changes with age. One way to do this would be to start with a typical cross-sectional study in which 60- and 75-year-olds are tested. Then the two groups would be retested every three years, creating two separate longitudinal studies.

Although sequential designs are rare because they are so expensive, they are powerful because they allow researchers to distinguish age-related change from other effects (e.g., cohort effects, participant dropout). We will encounter examples of sequential designs when we consider some of the large studies examining the normal processes of aging in Chapters 10 and 14.

▶ Table 1.5 summarizes the strengths and weaknesses of the general research designs and the developmental designs. You'll read about each of these designs throughout this book, although the two cross-sectional types (cross-sectional experimental and cross-sectional correlational) occur more frequently than the other combinations of general and developmental designs. Why? The relative ease of conducting cross-sectional studies more than compensates for their limitations.

Integrating Findings from Different Studies

Several times in the past few pages, we've emphasized the value of using different methods to study the same phenomenon. The advantage of this approach is that conclusions are most convincing when the results are consistent regardless of method.

However, sometimes findings are inconsistent. For example, suppose many researchers find that people often share highly personal information with friends on social media, some researchers find that people share occasionally with friends, and a few researchers find that people never share with friends. What should we conclude? Meta-analysis *allows researchers to synthesize the results of many quantitative studies to estimate actual relations between variables* (Schmidt & Hunter, 2014). In conducting a meta-analysis, investigators find all studies published on a topic over a substantial period of time (e.g., 10 to 20 years) and then record and analyze the results and important methodological variables.

The usefulness of meta-analysis is illustrated in a study by Kojima and colleagues (2016). After identifying 5,145 potential studies on the association between frailty and the quality of life of older adults living in the community, they focused on 11 cross-sectional and two longitudinal studies that used comparable measures. This meta-analysis indicated that frail older adults had lower quality of life. As a result, Kojima and colleagues suggest that interventions aimed at helping older adults deal with frailty may also improve their quality of life.

meta-analysis
A tool that enables researchers to synthesize the results of many studies to estimate relations between variables.

Table 1.5

Designs Used in Human Development Research

TYPE OF DESIGN	DEFINITION	STRENGTHS	WEAKNESSES
General Designs			
Correlational	Observe variables as they exist in the world and determine their relations	Behavior is measured as it occurs naturally	Cannot determine cause and effect
Experimental	Manipulate independent variable and determine effect on dependent variable	Control of variables allows conclusions about cause and effect	Work is often laboratory-based, which can be artificial
Developmental Designs			
Longitudinal	One group of people is tested repeatedly as they develop	Only way to chart an individual's development and look at the stability of behavior over time	Expensive, participants drop out, and repeated testing can distort performance
Cross-sectional	People of different ages are tested at the same time	Convenient—solves all problems associated with longitudinal studies	Cannot study stability of behavior; cohort effects complicate interpretation of differences between groups
Sequential	Multiple groups of people are tested over time, based on either multiple longitudinal or cross-sectional designs	Best way to address limitation of single longitudinal and cross-sectional designs	Very expensive and time consuming; may not completely solve limitations of longitudinal and cross-sectional designs

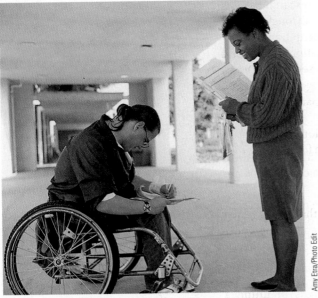

Informed consent is a necessary aspect of any research effort in human development.

Meta-analysis is a particularly powerful tool because it allows scientists to determine whether a finding generalizes across many studies. In addition, meta-analysis can reveal the impact of different methods on results and further the development of specific theories of behavior.

Conducting Research Ethically

Choosing a good research design involves more than just selecting a method. Researchers must determine whether the methods they plan to use protects the rights of people who participate. To verify that every research project incorporates these protections, local panels of experts and community representatives, called the Institutional Review Board, evaluate proposed studies before any data are collected. Only with the approval of this panel can scientists begin their study. If the review panel objects to some aspects of the proposed study, then the researcher must revise those aspects and present them anew for the panel's approval.

To guide review panels, professional organizations (e.g., the American Psychological Association and government agencies (e.g., the National Institutes of Health) have codes of ethical conduct that specify the rights of research participants as well as procedures to protect these participants. The following essential guidelines are included in all of these codes:

- *Minimize risks to research participants* Use methods that have the least potential for causing harm or stress for research participants. During the research, monitor the procedures to ensure avoidance of any unforeseen stress or harm.
- *Describe the research to potential participants so that they can determine whether they want to participate* Prospective participants must be told the purpose of the project, what they will be asked to do, whether there are any risks or potential harm or any benefits they may receive, that they are free to discontinue participation at any time without penalty, and that, after they have participated, the project will be described. After the study has been explained, each *participant* signs a document stating that he or she understands what he or she will do in the study. Special caution must be exercised in obtaining consent for the participation of children and adolescents, as well as people who have conditions that affect intellectual functioning (e.g., Alzheimer's disease, severe head injury). In these cases, consent from a parent, a legal guardian, or another responsible person—in addition to consent of the participant—is necessary.
- *Avoid deception; if participants must be deceived, provide a thorough explanation of the true nature of the experiment as soon as possible* Providing complete information about a study in advance sometimes biases or distorts a person's responses. Consequently, investigators may provide participants with partial information about the study or even mislead them about its true purpose. As soon as it is feasible—typically, just after the experiment—any false information that was given to research participants must be corrected and the reasons for the deception must be provided.
- *Results should be anonymous or confidential* Research results should be anonymous, which means that people's data cannot be linked to their name. When anonymity is not possible, research results should be confidential, which means that the identity of participants is known only to the investigator(s) conducting the study.

Conducting research ethically is an obligation of every investigator. If you conduct a project, you should submit your procedures for review. If you are a participant in someone else's project, make sure you are given complete information and read it thoroughly.

Communicating Research Results

When the study is complete and the data have been analyzed, researchers write a report of their work that describes what they did and why, their results, and the meanings of their results. The researchers will submit the report to one of several scientific journals that specialize in human development research. Some of these are *Child Development, Developmental Psychology, Psychology and Aging,* and the *Journals of Gerontology.* If the journal editor accepts the report, it will appear in the journal, where other human development researchers can learn of the results.

These reports of research are the basis for virtually all the information we present in this book. You have already encountered many citations of research in the format of names in parentheses, followed by a date, like this:

(Smith & Jones, 2015)

This indicates the last name(s) of the person(s) who did the research and the year in which the research was published. By looking in the Reference section at the end of the book, which is organized alphabetically by the first author's last name, you can find the title of the article and the journal in which it was published.

All of these steps in research may seem tedious and involved to you. However, for a human development researcher, much of the fun of research is planning a study that no one has done before and that will provide information useful to other specialists. This is one of the most creative and challenging parts of human development research.

Applying Research Results: Social Policy

Some people question whether research really matters. Actually, research on human development has a strong influence on policy makers and politicians. For example, every state in the United States and many countries around the world have laws against child abuse and laws that govern child labor practices. Many countries have laws setting minimum ages for certain activities, such as consuming alcohol, voting, and driving. Some states in the United States are changing the way older drivers are screened when they renew their driver's licenses. Human development research played a role in establishing all of these laws and regulations.

Other examples of how developmental research affects social policy include the elimination of mandatory retirement, the Americans with Disabilities Act, many educational reform laws, indices courts use to decide whether an adolescent offender should be tried as a juvenile or an adult, and whether a person is mentally competent. Clearly, the research done by developmentalists influences many aspects of daily life that are governed by laws and societal rules.

At several points in the text, we will describe important connections between human development research and social policy. As you will see, these connections are broad-ranging and include areas that you may take for granted. For example, lead-based paint and lead water pipes can no longer be used in the United States, mainly because research by developmentalists showed that infants and young children who were exposed to lead (and who sometimes ate paint chips when they flaked off or drank water containing lead) suffered brain damage and learning problems. Research on human development not only provides many insights into what makes people tick but also can provide ways to improve the quality of life.

However, the views of scientists, ethicists, public citizens, and government sometimes collide in ways that result in significant debate concerning research. Such is the case with stem cell research, a hotly debated topic. We will consider controversial topics such as this throughout this text.

Problems with Using Photographs to Measure Understanding of Emotions

© 2019 Cengage

On page 24, we invited you to consider why asking children to judge emotions from photos may not be valid. Children's judgments of the emotions depicted in photographs may be less accurate than they would be in real life because in real life (1) facial features are usually moving—not still as in the photographs—and movement may be one of the clues children naturally use to judge emotions; (2) facial expressions are often accompanied by sounds, and children use both sight and sound to judge emotions; and (3) children most often judge facial expressions of people they know (parents, siblings, peers, teachers), and knowing the "usual" appearance of a face may help children judge emotions accurately.

▶ **Figure 1.7**

TEST YOURSELF **1.3**

1. In _____, people are observed as they behave spontaneously in a real-life setting.

2. A(n) _____ is a group of individuals thought to be representative of some larger population of interest.

3. The _____ variable is measured in an experiment to evaluate the impact of the variable that was manipulated.

4. Problems of longitudinal studies include the length of time to complete the work, loss of research participants over time, and _____.

5. Human development researchers must submit their plans for research to a review board that determines whether the research _____.

Interpret

- How could a longitudinal design be used to test Piaget's theory?

Apply

- While at work, you notice that some people advance faster in their careers than other people do. How could you determine what factors might be responsible for or related to such success?

Check your answers to the Recall Questions at the end of the chapter.

SUMMARY

1.1 Thinking About Development

What fundamental issues of development have scholars addressed throughout history?

- Three main issues are prominent in the study of human development. The nature–nurture issue involves the degree to which genetics and the environment influence human development. Researchers view nature and nurture as mutually interactive influences; development is shaped by both. The continuity–discontinuity issue concerns whether the same explanations (continuity) or different explanations (discontinuity) must be used to explain changes in people over time. Continuity approaches emphasize quantitative change; discontinuity approaches emphasize qualitative change. In the issue of universal versus context-specific development, the question is whether development follows the same general path in all people or fundamentally depends on the sociocultural context.

What are the basic forces in the biopsychosocial framework? How does the timing of these forces make a difference in their impact?

- Development is based on the combined impact of four primary forces. Biological forces include all genetic and health-related factors that affect development. Many of these biological forces are determined by our genetic code.

- Psychological forces include all internal cognitive, emotional, perceptual, and personality factors that influence development. Collectively, psychological forces explain the most noticeable differences in people.

- Sociocultural forces include interpersonal, societal, cultural, and ethnic factors that affect development. Culture consists of the knowledge, attitudes, and behavior associated with a group of people. Overall, sociocultural forces provide the context or backdrop for development.

- Life-cycle forces provide a context for understanding how people perceive their current situation and what effects it has on them.

- The biopsychosocial framework emphasizes that the four forces are mutually interactive; development cannot be understood by examining the forces in isolation. Furthermore, the same event can have different effects, depending on when it happens.

How does neuroscience enhance our understanding of human development?

- Neuroscience is the study of the brain and the nervous system, especially in terms of brain–behavior relationships. Identifying patterns of brain activity helps demonstrate how developmental forces interact.

1.2 Developmental Theories

What is a developmental theory?

- Developmental theories organize knowledge so as to provide testable explanations of human behaviors and the ways in which they change over time. Current approaches to developmental theory focus on specific aspects of behavior. At present, there is no single unified theory of human development.

How do psychodynamic theories account for development?

- Psychodynamic theories propose that behavior is determined by the way people deal with conflicts they face at different ages. Erikson proposed a life-span theory of psychosocial development consisting of eight universal stages, each characterized by a particular struggle.

What is the focus of learning theories of development?

- Learning theory focuses on the development of observable behavior. Operant conditioning is based on the notions of reinforcement, punishment, and environmental control of behavior. Social learning theory proposes that people learn by observing and interpreting others' behavior.

How do cognitive-developmental theories explain changes in thinking?

- Cognitive-developmental theory focuses on thought processes. Piaget proposed a four-stage universal sequence based on the notion that throughout development, people create theories to explain how the world works. According to information-processing theory, people deal with information like a computer does; development consists of increased efficiency in handling information. Vygotsky emphasized the influence of culture on development.

What are the main points in the ecological and systems approach?

- Bronfenbrenner proposed that development occurs in the context of several interconnected systems of increasing complexity. The competence–environmental press theory postulates that there is a "best fit" between a person's abilities and the demands of the person's environment.

What are the major tenets of life-span and life-course theories?

- According to the life-span perspective, human development is characterized by four critical developmental forces: multidirectionality, plasticity, historical context, and multiple causation.

- Selective optimization with compensation refers to the developmental trends to focus one's efforts and abilities in successively fewer domains as one ages and to acquire ways to compensate for normative losses.

- The life-course perspective refers to understanding human development within the context of the historical time period in which a generation develops, which creates unique sets of experiences.

1.3 Doing Developmental Research

How do scientists measure topics of interest in studying human development?

- Research typically begins by determining how to measure the topic of interest. Systematic observation involves recording people's behavior as it takes place, in either a natural environment (naturalistic observation) or a structured setting (structured observation). Researchers sometimes create tasks to obtain samples of behavior. In self-reports, people answer questions posed by the experimenter. Physiological measures provide a way to examine body–behavior relationships.

- Researchers must determine that their measures are reliable and valid; they must also obtain a sample representative of a larger population.

What research designs are used to study human development?

- In correlational studies, investigators examine relations among variables as they occur naturally. This relation is often measured by a correlation coefficient, which can vary from -1 (strong inverse relation) to 0 (no relation) to $+1$ (strong positive relation). Correlational studies cannot determine cause and effect, so researchers do experimental studies in which an independent variable is manipulated and the impact of this manipulation on a dependent variable is recorded. Experimental studies allow conclusions about cause and effect, but the required strict control of other variables often makes the situation artificial. The best approach is to use both experimental and correlational studies to provide converging evidence. Qualitative research permits more in-depth analysis of behavior and is often used as a preliminary step for, or in conjunction with, quantitative research.

- To study development, some researchers use a longitudinal design in which the same people are observed repeatedly as they grow. This approach provides evidence concerning actual patterns of individual growth but is time-consuming, some people drop out of the project, and repeated testing can affect performance.

- An alternative, the cross-sectional design, involves testing people of different ages. This design avoids the problems of the longitudinal design but provides no information about individual growth. Also, what appear to be age differences may be cohort effects. Because neither design is problem-free, the best approach involves using both to provide converging evidence.

- Sequential designs are based on multiple longitudinal or cross-sectional designs.

How do researchers integrate results from multiple studies?

- Meta-analysis provides a way for researchers to look for trends across multiple studies to estimate the relations among variables.

What ethical procedures must researchers follow?

- Planning research also involves selecting methods that preserve the rights of research participants. Experimenters must minimize the risks to participants, describe the research so that candidates can make an informed decision about participating, avoid deception, and keep results anonymous or confidential.

How do investigators communicate results from research studies?

- Once research data are collected and analyzed, investigators publish the results in scientific outlets such as journals and books. Such results form the foundation of knowledge about human development.

How does research affect public policy?

- Research results are sometimes used to inform and shape public policy. The ban on lead-based paint is an example.

Test Yourself: Recall Answers

1.1 1. genetics **2.** continuity **3.** Biological **4.** brain–behavior **1.2 1.** Theories **2.** psychosocial **3.** observing others **4.** cognitive-developmental **5.** microsystem **6.** life-span **1.3 1.** naturalistic observation **2.** sample **3.** dependent **4.** influence of repeated testing on a person's performance **5.** preserves the rights of research participants

Key Terms

human development (5)
nature–nurture issue (6)
continuity–discontinuity issue (6)
universal and context-specific
   development issue (7)
biological forces (7)
psychological forces (7)
sociocultural forces (7)
life-cycle forces (7)
biopsychosocial framework (7)
neuroscience (10)
theory (12)
psychodynamic theories (12)
psychosocial theory (12)
epigenetic principle (13)
operant conditioning (13)
reinforcement (13)

punishment (14)
imitation or observational learning (14)
self-efficacy (14)
information-processing theory (16)
ecological theory (17)
microsystem (18)
mesosystem (18)
exosystem (18)
macrosystem (18)
competence (18)
environmental press (18)
life-span perspective (19)
selective optimization with compensation
   (SOC) model (19)
life-course perspective (20)
systematic observation (23)
naturalistic observation (23)

structured observations (23)
self-reports (24)
reliability (25)
validity (25)
populations (25)
sample (25)
correlational study (26)
correlation coefficient (26)
experiment (27)
independent variable (27)
dependent variable (27)
qualitative research (28)
longitudinal study (28)
cross-sectional study (30)
cohort effects (30)
sequential design (30)
meta-analysis (31)

Biological Foundations: Heredity, Prenatal Development, and Birth

2

If you ask parents to name the most memorable experiences of their lives, many immediately mention the events associated with the birth of their children. From the initial exciting news that a woman is pregnant through birth 9 months later, pregnancy and birth evoke awe and wonder.

The period before birth is the foundation for all human development and the focus of this chapter. Pregnancy begins when egg and sperm cells unite and exchange hereditary material. In the first section, you'll see how this exchange takes place and, in the process, learn about inherited factors that affect development. The second section of the chapter traces the events that transform sperm and egg into a living, breathing human being. You'll learn about the timetable that governs development before birth and, along the way, get answers to common questions about pregnancy. We talk about some of the problems that can occur during development before birth in the third section of the chapter. The last section focuses on birth and the newborn baby. You'll find out how an expectant mother can prepare for birth and what labor and delivery are like.

LEARNING OBJECTIVES

- What are chromosomes and genes? How do they carry hereditary information from one generation to the next?

- What are common problems involving chromosomes, and what are their consequences?

- How is children's heredity influenced by the environment in which they grow up?

Leslie and Glenn are excited at the thought of starting their own family. At the same time, they're nervous because Leslie's grandfather had sickle-cell disease and died when he was just 20 years old. Leslie is terrified that her baby may inherit the disease that killed her grandfather. She and Glenn wish that someone could reassure them that their baby will be okay.

How can we reassure Leslie and Glenn? For starters, we need to know more about sickle-cell disease. Red blood cells carry oxygen and carbon dioxide to and from the body. When a person has sickle-cell disease, the red blood cells are long and curved like a sickle. These stiff, misshapen cells cannot pass through small capillaries, so oxygen cannot reach all parts of the body. The trapped sickle cells also block the way of white blood cells that are the body's natural defense against bacteria. As a result, many people with sickle-cell disease are often tired, may experience acute pain for hours or days, and are prone to infections. About 10% of people with the disease die by age 20 and 50% die by age 50 (Kumar et al., 2010). Sickle-cell disease is inherited, and because Leslie's grandfather had the disorder, it runs in her family. Will Leslie's baby inherit the disease? To answer that question, we need to examine the mechanisms of heredity.

Mechanisms of Heredity

chromosomes

Threadlike structures in the nuclei of cells that contain genetic material.

autosomes

First 22 pairs of chromosomes.

sex chromosomes

23rd pair of chromosomes; these determine the sex of the child.

At conception, egg and sperm unite to create a new organism that incorporates some characteristics of each parent. *Each egg and sperm cell has 23* chromosomes, *threadlike structures in the nucleus that contain genetic material.* When a sperm penetrates an egg, their chromosomes combine to produce 23 pairs of chromosomes. *The first 22 pairs of chromosomes are called* autosomes. *The 23rd pair determines the sex of the child, so these are known as the* sex chromosomes. When the 23rd pair consists of an X and a Y chromosome, the result is a boy; two X chromosomes produce a girl.

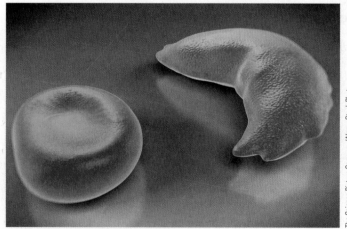

Red blood cells like the one on the left carry oxygen throughout the body. However, in sickle-cell disease, sickle-shaped cells like the one on the right cannot pass through the body's small blood vessels.

The Science Picture Company/Alamy Stock Photo

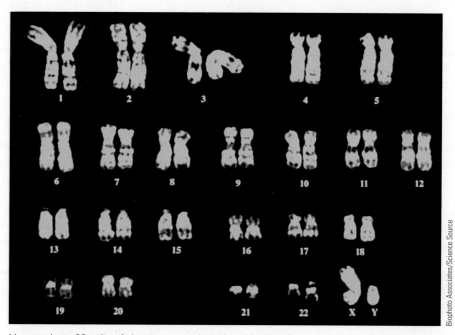

Humans have 23 pairs of chromosomes, including 22 pairs of autosomes and 1 pair of sex chromosomes.

deoxyribonucleic acid (DNA)

Molecule composed of four nucleotide bases that is the biochemical basis of heredity.

gene

Group of nucleotide bases that provides a specific set of biochemical instructions.

genotype

Person's hereditary makeup.

phenotype

Physical, behavioral, and psychological features that result from the interaction between one's genes and the environment.

alleles

Variations of genes.

homozygous

When the alleles in a pair of chromosomes are the same.

heterozygous

When the alleles in a pair of chromosomes differ from each other.

▶ **Figure 2.1**

DNA is organized in a double helix, with strands of phosphates and sugars linked by nucleotide bases.

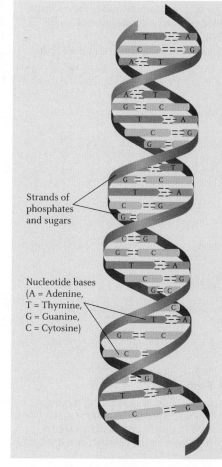

Strands of phosphates and sugars

Nucleotide bases (A = Adenine, T = Thymine, G = Guanine, C = Cytosine)

© 2019 Cengage

Each chromosome actually consists of one molecule of deoxyribonucleic acid— DNA *for short.* To understand the structure of DNA, imagine four different colors of beads placed on two strings. The strings complement each other precisely: Wherever a red bead appears on one string, a blue bead appears on the other; wherever a green bead appears on one string, a yellow one appears on the other. DNA is organized this way, except that the four colors of beads are four different chemical compounds: adenine, thymine, guanine, and cytosine. The strings, which are made up of phosphates and sugars, wrap around each other, creating the double helix shown in ▶ Figure 2.1.

The order in which the chemical compound "beads" appear is a code that causes the cell to create specific amino acids, proteins, and enzymes—important biological building blocks. For example, three consecutive thymine "beads" make up the instruction to create the amino acid phenylalanine. *Each group of compounds that provides a specific set of biochemical instructions is a* gene. Thus, genes are the functional units of heredity because they determine the production of chemical substances that are, ultimately, the basis for all human characteristics and abilities.

Altogether, a person's 46 chromosomes include roughly 20,500 genes. Chromosome 1 has the most genes (nearly 3,000), and the Y chromosome has the fewest (just over 200). Most of these genes are the same for all people—fewer than 1% of genes cause differences between people (Human Genome Project, 2003). Through biochemical instructions that are coded in DNA, genes regulate the development of all human characteristics and abilities. *The complete set of genes makes up a person's heredity and is known as the person's* genotype. *Genetic instructions, in conjunction with environmental influences, produce a* phenotype, *an individual's physical, behavioral, and psychological features.*

How do genetic instructions produce the misshapen red blood cells of sickle-cell disease? *Genes come in different forms that are known as* alleles. For example, in the case of red blood cells, two alleles can be present on chromosome 11. One allele has instructions for normal red blood cells; another allele has instructions for sickle-shaped red blood cells. *The alleles in the pair of chromosomes are sometimes the same, which is known as being* homozygous. *The alleles sometimes differ, which is known as being* heterozygous. Leslie's baby would be homozygous if it had two alleles for normal cells *or* two alleles for sickle-shaped cells. The baby would be heterozygous if it had one allele of each type.

How does a genotype produce a phenotype? With sickle-cell disease, how do genotypes lead to specific kinds of blood cells? The answer is simple if a person is homozygous. When both alleles are the same—and therefore have chemical instructions for the same phenotype—that phenotype usually results. If Leslie's baby had an allele for normal red blood cells on both of its 11th chromosomes, then the baby would almost be guaranteed to have normal cells. If, instead, the baby had two alleles for sickle-shaped cells, then it would almost certainly suffer from the disease.

When a person is heterozygous, the process is more complex. *Often one allele is* **dominant**, *which means that its chemical instructions are followed, while those of the other* **recessive** *allele are ignored.* In sickle-cell disease, the allele for normal cells is dominant and the allele for sickle-shaped cells is recessive. This is good news for Leslie: As long as either she or Glenn contributes the allele for normal red blood cells, their baby will not develop sickle-cell disease.

▶ Figure 2.2 summarizes what we've learned about sickle-cell disease: *A* denotes the allele for normal blood cells, and *a* denotes the allele for sickle-shaped cells. Depending on the alleles in Leslie's egg and in the sperm that fertilizes that egg, three outcomes are possible. Only if the baby inherits two recessive alleles for sickle-shaped cells is it likely to develop sickle-cell disease. But this is unlikely in Glenn's case: He is positive that no one in his family has had sickle-cell disease, so he almost certainly has the allele for normal blood cells on both of the chromosomes in his 11th pair.

Even though Glenn's sperm will carry the gene for normal red blood cells, this doesn't guarantee that their baby will be healthy. Why? *Sometimes one allele does not dominate another completely, a situation known as* **incomplete dominance**. In incomplete dominance, the phenotype that results often falls between the phenotype associated with either allele. This is the case for the genes that control red blood cells. *Individuals with one dominant and one recessive allele have* **sickle-cell trait**: *In most situations they have no problems, but when seriously short of oxygen, they suffer a temporary, relatively mild form of the disease.* Thus, sickle-cell trait is likely to appear when the person exercises vigorously, becomes dehydrated, or is at high altitudes (Fidler, 2012). Leslie and Glenn's baby would have sickle-cell trait if it inherits a recessive gene from Leslie and a dominant gene from Glenn.

dominant

Form of an allele whose chemical instructions are followed.

recessive

Allele whose instructions are ignored in the presence of a dominant allele.

incomplete dominance

Situation in which one allele does not dominate another completely.

sickle-cell trait

Disorder in which individuals show signs of mild anemia only when they are seriously deprived of oxygen; occurs in individuals who have one dominant allele for normal blood cells and one recessive sickle-cell allele.

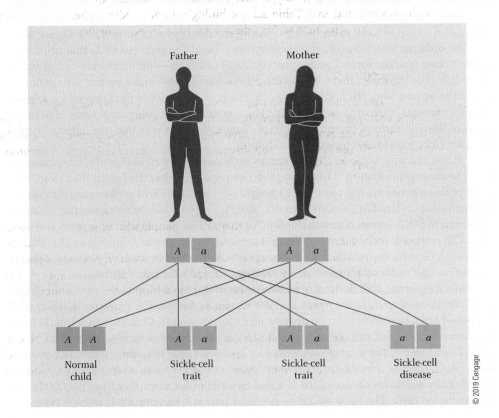

▶ **Figure 2.2**

In single-gene inheritance, a heterozygous father and a heterozygous mother can have a healthy child, a child with sickle-cell trait, or a child with sickle-cell disease.

© 2019 Cengage

Table 2.1

Some Common Phenotypes Associated with Single Pairs of Genes	
DOMINANT PHENOTYPE	**RECESSIVE PHENOTYPE**
Curly hair	Straight hair
Normal hair	Pattern baldness (men)
Dark hair	Blond hair
Thick lips	Thin lips
Cheek dimples	No dimples
Normal hearing	Some types of deafness
Normal vision	Nearsightedness
Farsightedness	Normal vision
Normal color vision	Red–green color blindness
Type A blood	Type O blood
Type B blood	Type O blood
Rh-positive blood	Rh-negative blood

Source: McKusick, 1995.

The simple genetic mechanism responsible for sickle-cell disease—which involves a single gene pair with one dominant allele and one recessive allele—is also responsible for numerous other common traits, as shown in ▶ Table 2.1. In each of these instances, individuals with the recessive phenotype have two recessive alleles, one from each parent. Individuals with the dominant phenotype have at least one dominant allele.

Most of the traits listed in ▶ Table 2.1 are biological and medical phenotypes. This same genetic mechanism can cause serious disorders, as we'll see in the next section.

Genetic Disorders

Genetics can derail development in two ways. First, some disorders are inherited. Sickle-cell disease is one example of an inherited disorder. Second, sometimes eggs or sperm do not include the usual 23 chromosomes but have more or fewer chromosomes instead. In the next few pages, we'll see how inherited disorders and abnormal numbers of chromosomes can alter a person's development.

Inherited Disorders

You know that sickle-cell disease is a disorder that affects people who inherit two recessive alleles. *Another disorder that involves recessive alleles is* phenylketonuria (PKU), *a disorder in which babies are born lacking an important liver enzyme.* This enzyme converts phenyl-alanine—an amino acid found in dairy products, bread, diet soda, and fish—into tyrosine (another amino acid). Without this enzyme, phenylalanine accumulates and produces poisons that harm the nervous system, resulting in mental retardation (Diamond et al., 1997; Mange & Mange, 1990).

Most inherited disorders are like sickle-cell disease and PKU in that they are carried by recessive alleles. Few serious disorders are caused by dominant alleles. Why? If the allele for the disorder is dominant, every person with at least one of these alleles would have the disorder. Individuals affected with these disorders typically do not live long enough to reproduce, so dominant alleles that produce fatal disorders soon vanish

phenylketonuria (PKU)
Inherited disorder in which the infant lacks a liver enzyme.

Huntington's disease

Progressive and fatal type of dementia caused by dominant alleles.

from the species. *An exception is* Huntington's disease, *a fatal disease characterized by progressive degeneration of the nervous system.* Huntington's disease is caused by a dominant allele found on chromosome 4. Individuals who inherit this disorder develop normally through childhood, adolescence, and young adulthood. However, during middle age, nerve cells in the brain begin to deteriorate; by this time, many adults with Huntington's have already had children, many of whom will develop the disease themselves.

Abnormal Chromosomes

Sometimes individuals do not receive the normal complement of 46 chromosomes. If they are born with extra, missing, or damaged chromosomes, development is disturbed. The best example is Down syndrome. People with Down syndrome have almond-shaped eyes and a fold over the eyelid. Their head, neck, and nose are usually smaller than normal. During the first several months of life, development of babies with Down syndrome seems to be normal. Thereafter, their mental and behavioral development lags behind that of the average child. For example, a child with Down syndrome might first sit up without help at about 1 year, walk at 2, and talk at 3, reaching each of these developmental milestones months or even years behind children without Down syndrome. By childhood, most aspects of cognitive and social development are seriously retarded.

Rearing a child with Down syndrome presents special challenges. During the preschool years, children with Down syndrome need special programs to prepare them for school. Educational achievements of children with Down syndrome are likely to be limited, and their average life expectancy is about 50 years (Coppus, 2013). Nevertheless, as you'll see in Chapter 6, many individuals with Down syndrome lead full, satisfying lives.

Children with Down syndrome typically have upward slanting eyes with a fold over the eyelid, a flattened facial profile, and a smaller than average nose and mouth.

What causes Down syndrome? Individuals with Down syndrome typically have an extra 21st chromosome that is usually provided by the egg (Vraneković et al., 2012). Why the mother provides two 21st chromosomes is unknown. However, the odds that a woman will bear a child with Down syndrome increase markedly as she gets older. For a woman in her late 20s, the risk of giving birth to a baby with Down syndrome is about 1 in 1,000; for a woman in her early 40s, the risk is about 1 in 50. Why? A woman's eggs have been in her ovaries since her own prenatal development. Eggs may deteriorate over time as part of aging or because an older woman has a longer history of exposure to hazards in the environment, that may damage her eggs (e.g., X-rays).

An extra autosome (as in Down syndrome), a missing autosome, or a damaged autosome always has far-reaching consequences for development because the autosomes contain huge amounts of genetic material. In fact, nearly half of all fertilized eggs abort spontaneously within two weeks—primarily because of abnormal autosomes. Thus, most eggs that cannot develop normally are removed naturally (Moore & Persaud, 1993).

Abnormal sex chromosomes can also disrupt development. ▶ Table 2.2 lists four of the more frequent disorders associated with atypical numbers of X and Y chromosomes. Frequent is a relative term; although these disorders are more frequent than PKU or Huntington's disease, most are uncommon. Notice that no disorders consist solely of Y chromosomes. The presence of an X chromosome appears to be necessary for life.

Fortunately, most of us receive the correct number of chromosomes and do not inherit life-threatening illnesses. For most people, heredity reveals its power in creating a unique individual—a person unlike any other.

Now that you understand the basic mechanisms of heredity, we can learn how heredity and environment work together to produce behavioral and psychological development.

Table 2.2

Common Disorders Associated with the Sex Chromosomes			
DISORDER	**SEX CHROMOSOMES**	**FREQUENCY**	**CHARACTERISTICS**
Klinefelter's syndrome	XXY	1 in 500 male births	Tall, small testicles, sterile, below-normal intelligence, passive
XYY complement	XYY	1 in 1,000 male births	Tall, some cases apparently have below-normal intelligence
Turner's syndrome	X	1 in 2,500–5,000 female births	Short, limited development of secondary sex characteristics, problems perceiving spatial relations
XXX syndrome	XXX	1 in 500–1,200 female births	Normal stature but delayed motor and language development

Heredity, Environment, and Development

Many people mistakenly view heredity as a set of phenotypes unfolding automatically from the genotypes that are set at conception. Nothing could be further from the truth. Although genotypes are fixed when the sperm fertilizes the egg, phenotypes are not. Instead, phenotypes depend both on genotypes and on the environment in which individuals develop.

To begin our study of heredity and environment, we need to look first at the methods that developmental scientists use.

Behavioral Genetics: Mechanisms and Methods

Behavioral genetics *is the branch of genetics that deals with inheritance of behavioral and psychological traits.* Behavioral genetics is complex, in part, because behavioral and psychological phenotypes are complex. Traits controlled by single genes are usually "either-or" phenotypes. A person either has dimpled cheeks or not; a person either has normal color vision or red–green color blindness; a person's blood either clots normally or it does not. In contrast, most important behavioral and psychological characteristics are *not* of an "either-or" nature; rather, a range of different outcomes is possible. Consider extraversion as an example. You probably know a few extremely outgoing individuals and a few intensely shy persons, but most of your friends and acquaintances are somewhere in between; extroversion forms a continuum ranging from extreme extroversion at one end to extreme introversion at the other.

Many behavioral and psychological characteristics, including intelligence and aspects of personality, are distributed in this fashion, with a few individuals at the ends of the continuum and most near the middle. *Phenotypes distributed like this often reflect the combined activity of many separate genes, a pattern known as* polygenic inheritance. Because so many genes are involved in polygenic inheritance, we cannot trace the effects of each gene. But we can use a hypothetical example to show how many genes work together to produce a behavioral phenotype that spans a continuum. Suppose that four pairs of genes contribute to extroversion, that the allele for extroversion is dominant, and that the total amount of extroversion is simply the sum of the dominant alleles. If we continue to use uppercase letters to represent dominant alleles and lowercase letters to represent the recessive allele, then the four gene pairs would be Aa, Bb, Cc, and Dd.

These four pairs of genes produce 81 different genotypes and nine distinct phenotypes. For example, a person with the genotype AABBCCDD has eight alleles for extroversion (the proverbial party animal). A person with the genotype aabbccdd has no alleles for extroversion (the proverbial wallflower). All other genotypes involve some combination of dominant and recessive alleles, so these are associated with phenotypes

behavioral genetics
The branch of genetics that studies the inheritance of behavioral and psychological traits.

Think About It

Introversion–extroversion is an example of a psychological characteristic that defines a continuum. Think of other psychological characteristics like this, in which outcomes are not "either–or" but are distributed across a range.

polygenic inheritance
When phenotypes are the result of the combined activity of many separate genes.

representing intermediate levels of extroversion. In fact, ❱ Figure 2.3 shows that the most common outcome is for people to inherit four dominant and four recessive alleles, and 19 of the 81 genotypes (e.g., AABbccDd, aaBbcCDd) produce this pattern. A few extreme cases (very outgoing or very shy), when coupled with many intermediate cases, produce the familiar bell-shaped distribution that characterizes many behavioral and psychological traits.

Remember, this example is hypothetical. Extroversion is *not* based on the combined influence of eight pairs of genes. However, the example shows how several genes working together *could* produce a continuum of phenotypes. Something like our example is probably involved in the inheritance of numerous human behavioral traits, except that many more pairs of genes are involved and the environment also influences the phenotype (Plomin, 2013).

If many behavioral phenotypes involve countless genes, how can we hope to unravel the influence of heredity? Twins and adopted children provide some important clues to the role of heredity. In twin studies, researchers compare identical and fraternal twins. *Identical twins are called* monozygotic twins *because they come from a single fertilized egg that splits in two.* Because identical twins come from the same fertilized egg, the same genes control their body structure, height, and facial features, which explains why identical twins look alike. *In contrast, fraternal or* dizygotic twins *come from two separate eggs fertilized by two separate sperm.* Genetically, fraternal twins are just like any other siblings—on average, about half their genes are the same. In twin studies, scientists compare identical and fraternal twins to measure the influence of heredity. When identical twins are more alike than fraternal twins, this implicates heredity.

Adopted children are another important source of information about heredity. They are compared with their biological parents, who provide the children's genes, and their adoptive parents, who provide the children's environment. If an adopted child's behavior

monozygotic twins

The result of a single fertilized egg splitting to form two new individuals; also called identical twins.

dizygotic twins

The result of two separate eggs fertilized by two sperm; also called fraternal twins.

❱ **Figure 2.3**

Many behavioral phenotypes represent a continuum (with many people falling at the middle of the continuum), an outcome that can be caused by many genes working together.

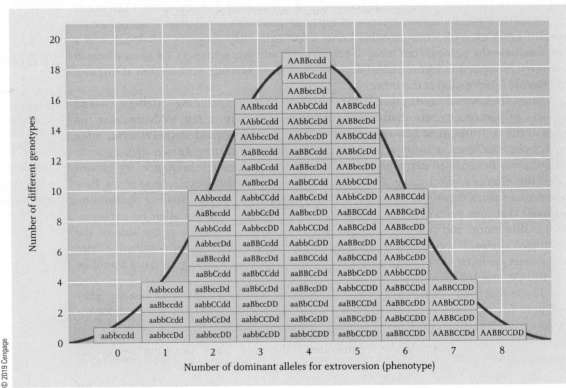

resembles that of his or her biological parents, this shows the impact of heredity; if the adopted child's behavior resembles his or her adoptive parents, this shows the influence of the environment.

These and other methods are not foolproof. A potential flaw in twin studies is that parents and others may treat monozygotic twins more similarly than they treat dizygotic twins. This would make monozygotic twins more similar than dizygotic twins in their experiences as well as in their genes. Each method of study has its unique pitfalls, but if different methods converge on the same conclusion about the influence of heredity, then we can be confident of that result. Throughout this book, you'll see many instances where twin studies and adoption studies have pointed to genetic influences on human development.

Behavioral geneticists are now moving beyond twin and adoption studies to connect behavior to molecular genetics (Plomin, 2013; Trzaskowski et al., 2014). Today, researchers can obtain DNA by gathering cheek cells from inside a child's mouth. A solution containing the DNA is placed on a microarray—a "chip" about the size of a postage stamp—that contains thousands of known sequences of DNA. Every match between the child's DNA and the known sequences is recorded, creating a profile of the child's genotype. Researchers then look to see if the genotype is associated with behavior phenotypes. For example, recent research has identified candidate genes that are linked to children's disability in reading and mathematics (Petrill, 2016).

This kind of molecular genetics research is challenging, in part because detecting the tiny effects of individual genes requires samples of thousands of children. But this research has the promise of linking individual genes to behavior. And when used with traditional methods of behavioral genetics (e.g., adoption studies), the new methods promise much greater understanding of how genes influence behavior and development (Plomin, 2013).

Identical twins are called monozygotic twins because they came from a single fertilized egg that split in two; consequently, they have identical genes.

Throughout the rest of this book, you'll encounter many instances that show the interactive influences of heredity and environment on human development. In the next few pages, however, we want to mention some general principles of heredity—environment interactions.

Paths from Genes to Behavior

How do genes work together—for example, to make some children brighter than others and some more outgoing than others? That is, how does the information in strands of DNA influence a person's behavioral and psychological development? In the next few pages, we'll discover some general properties of the paths linking genes to behavior.

1. *Heredity and environment interact dynamically throughout development.* A traditional but simple-minded view of heredity and environment is that heredity provides the clay of life and experience does the sculpting. In fact, genes and environments constantly interact to produce phenotypes throughout a person's development (LaFreniere & MacDonald, 2013). Although we often think there is a direct link between a genotype and a phenotype—given a certain genotype, a specific phenotype occurs, necessarily and automatically—in fact, the path from genotype to phenotype is more complicated and less direct than this. A more accurate description would be that a genotype leads to a phenotype but only if the environment "cooperates" in the usual manner.

   A good example of this genotype–phenotype link is seen in the disease phenylketonuria (PKU for short). As we saw on page 43, PKU is a homozygous recessive trait in which phenylalanine accumulates in the child's body, damaging the nervous system and leading to retarded mental development. Phenylalanine is abundant in many foods that most children eat regularly—meat, chicken, eggs, cheese—so that the environment usually provides the input (phenylalanine) necessary for the phenotype (PKU) to emerge. However, in the middle of the 20th century, the biochemical basis for PKU was discovered, and now newborns are tested for the disorder. Infants who have the genotype for the disease are immediately placed on a diet that limits phenylalanine, and the disease does not appear; their nervous system develops normally. In more general terms, a genotype is expressed differently (no disease) when it is exposed to a different environment (one lacking phenylalanine).

The effect can work in the other direction, too, with the environment triggering genetic expression. That is, people's experiences can help to determine how and when genes are activated. For instance, when infant girls who do not have a strong emotional attachment with their mothers also experience a stressful childhood, they begin to menstruate at a younger age (Sung et al., 2016). The exact pathway of influence is unknown (although it probably involves the hormones that are triggered by stress and those that initiate ovulation), but this is a clear case in which the environment advances the genes that regulate the developmental clock (Ellis, 2004).

We've used a rare disease (PKU) and a once-in-a-lifetime event (onset of menstruation) to show intimate connections between nature and nurture in human development. These examples may make it seem as if such connections are rare, but nothing could be further from the truth. At a biological level, genes always operate in a cellular environment. Genetic instructions interact constantly with the nature of the immediate cellular environment, which can be influenced by a host of much broader environmental factors (e.g., hormones triggered by a child's experiences). This continuous interplay between genes and multiple levels of the environment (from cells to culture) that drives development is known as epigenesis.

Returning to the analogy of sculpting clay, an epigenetic view of molding would be that new and different forms of genetic clay are constantly being added to the sculpture, leading to resculpting by the environment, which causes more clay to be added, and the cycle continues. Hereditary clay and environmental sculpting are continuously interweaving and influencing each other.

Research in molecular genetics has begun to reveal ways in which experiences get "under the skin." Sometimes experiences change the expression of DNA—the genetic code is preserved but some genes are "turned off." This process is known as methylation because the chemical silencer is a methyl molecule (van IJzendoorn, Bakermans-Kranenburg, & Ebstein, 2011). To illustrate, adversity early in life has been linked to increased methylation of a gene that helps regulate the body's response to stress (Boyce & Kobor, 2015; Conradt, 2017). In other words, an experience (early adversity) led to changes in heredity (a gene linked to stress regulation was "turned off").

Because of the epigenetic principle, you need to be wary when you read statements such as "X percent of a trait is due to heredity." In fact, *behavioral geneticists often use correlations from twin and adoption studies to calculate a* heritability coefficient, *which estimates the extent to which differences between people reflect heredity*. For example, intelligence has a heritability coefficient of about 0.5, which means that about 50% of the differences in intelligence between people are due to heredity (Bouchard, 2004).

Why be cautious? One reason is that many people mistakenly interpret heritability coefficients to mean that 50% of *an individual's* intelligence is due to heredity; this is incorrect because heritability coefficients apply to groups of people, not to a single person.

A second reason for caution is that heritability coefficients apply only to a specific group of people living in a specific environment. They cannot be applied to other groups of people living in the same environment or to the same people living elsewhere. For example, a child's height is certainly influenced by heredity, but the value of a heritability coefficient depends on the environment. When children grow

heritability coefficient

A measure (derived from a correlation coefficient) of the extent to which a trait or characteristic is inherited.

in an environment that has ample nutrition—allowing all children to grow to their full genetic potential—heritability coefficients are large. But when some children receive inadequate nutrition, this aspect of their environment will limit their height and, in the process, reduce the heritability coefficient.

Similarly, the heritability coefficient for cognitive skill is larger for parents who are well educated than for parents who aren't (Tucker-Drob, Briley, & Harden, 2013). Why? Well-educated parents more often provide the academically stimulating environment that fosters a child's cognitive development; consequently, cognitive skill in this group usually reflects heredity. In contrast, less educated parents less often provide the needed stimulation; thus, cognitive skill reflects a mixture of genetic and environmental influences.

This brings us back to the principle that began this section: *"Heredity and environment interact dynamically throughout development."* Both genes and environments are powerful influences on development, but we can understand one only by considering the other, too. This is why it is essential to expand research beyond the middle-class, European American participants who have dominated the samples of scientists studying human development. Only by studying diverse groups of people can we understand the many ways in which genes and environments propel children along their developmental journeys (Tucker-Drob et al., 2013).

2. *Genes can influence the kind of environment to which a person is exposed.* In other words, "nature" can help to determine the kind of "nurturing" that a child receives (Scarr, 1992; Scarr & McCartney, 1983). A person's genotype can lead others to respond in a specific way. For example, imagine someone who is bright and outgoing as a result, in part, of her genes. As a child, she may receive plenty of attention and encouragement from teachers. In contrast, someone who is not as bright and is more withdrawn (again, due in part to heredity) may be easily overlooked by teachers. In addition, as children grow and become more independent, they actively seek environments that fit their genetic makeup. Children who are bright may actively seek peers, adults, and activities that strengthen their intellectual development. Similarly, people who are outgoing may seek the company of other people, particularly extroverts like themselves. *This process of deliberately seeking environments that fit one's heredity is called* niche-picking. Niche-picking is first seen in childhood and becomes more common as children grow older and can control their environments. Through niche-picking, the environment amplifies genetic differences as, for example, bright children seek intellectually stimulating environments that make them even smarter and extroverted children seek socially stimulating environments that make them even more outgoing (Tucker-Drob et al., 2013). The Real People feature on page 50 shows niche-picking in action.

3. *Environmental influences typically make children within a family different.* One of the fruits of behavioral genetic research is greater understanding of the manner in which environments influence people (Harden, 2013). Traditionally, scientists considered some environments beneficial and others detrimental for people. This view has been especially strong in regard to family environments. Some parenting practices are thought to be more effective than others, and parents who use these effective practices are believed to have children who are, on average, better off than children of parents who don't use these practices. This view leads to a simple prediction: Children within a family should be similar because they all receive the same type of effective (or ineffective) parenting. However, dozens of behavioral genetic studies show that, in reality, siblings are not very much alike in their cognitive and social development (Plomin & Spinath, 2004).

niche-picking
Process of deliberately seeking environments that are compatible with one's genetic makeup.

Children who are outgoing often like to be with other people and deliberately seek them out; this is an example of niche-picking.

iStock.com/track5

Ben and Matt Pick Their Niches

Ben and Matt Kail were born 25 months apart. Even as a young baby, Ben was always a "people person." He relished contact with other people and preferred play that involved others. From the beginning, Matt was different. He was more withdrawn and was quite happy to play alone. The first separation from parents was harder for Ben than for Matt because Ben relished parental contact more. When they entered school, Ben enjoyed increasing the scope of his friendships; Matt liked all the different activities that were available and barely noticed the new faces. Although brothers, Ben and Matt are quite dissimilar in terms of their sociability, a characteristic known to have important genetic components (Braungart et al., 1992).

As Ben and Matt have grown up (they're now adults), they have consistently sought environments that fit their different needs for social stimulation. Ben was involved in team sports and now enjoys teaching. Matt took art and photography classes and now is happy working at his computer. Ben and Matt have chosen very different niches, and their choices have been driven in part by the genes that regulate sociability.

---

nonshared environmental influences

Forces within a family that make siblings different from one another.

Children's experiences within a family typically make them different from one another, not more alike.

Peter Cade/The Image Bank/Getty Images

Does this mean that family environment is not important? No. *These findings point to the importance of* nonshared environmental influences, *the forces within a family that make children different from one another.* Although the family environment is important, it usually affects each child in a unique way, making siblings different. Each child is likely to have different experiences in daily family life. For example, parents may be more affectionate with one child than another, they may use more physical punishment with one child than another, or they may have higher expectations for school achievement by one child than another. All these contrasting parental influences tend to make siblings different, not alike (Liang & Eley, 2005). Family environments are important, but—as we describe their influence throughout this book—you should remember that families create multiple unique environments, one for each person in the family.

Much of what we have said about genes, environment, and development is summarized in ❱ Figure 2.4 (Lytton, 2000). Parents are the source of children's genes and, at least for young children, the primary source of children's experiences. Children's genes also influence the experiences they have and the impact of those experiences on them. However, to capture the idea of nonshared environmental influences, we would need a separate diagram for each child, reflecting the fact that parents provide unique genes and a unique family environment for each of their offspring.

Most of this book explains the links between nature, nurture, and development. We can see the interaction of nature and nurture during prenatal development, which we examine in the next section of this chapter.

❱ **Figure 2.4**

Parents influence their children by providing genes and experiences; children's genes and their environments work together to shape development.

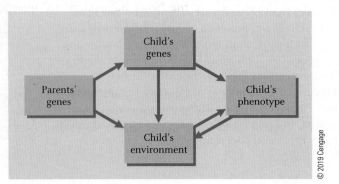

© 2019 Cengage

Recall

1. The first 22 pairs of chromosomes are called _____.

2. _____ reflects the combined activity of a number of distinct genes.

3. Individuals with _____ have an extra 21st chromosome, usually inherited from the mother.

4. When a fertilized egg has defective autosomes, the usual result is that _____.

5. Nonshared environmental influences tend to make siblings _____.

Apply

- Leslie and Glenn, the couple concerned that their baby could have sickle-cell disease, are already charting their baby's life course. Leslie, who has always loved to sing, is confident that her baby will be a fantastic musician and imagines a routine of music lessons, rehearsals, and concerts. Glenn, a pilot, is just as confident that his child will share his love of flying; he is already planning trips the two of them can take together. What advice might you give to Leslie and Glenn about factors they are ignoring?

Interpret

- Explain how niche-picking shows the interaction between heredity and environment.

Check your answers to the Recall Questions at the end of the chapter.

2.2 From Conception to Birth

LEARNING OBJECTIVES

- What happens to a fertilized egg in the first two weeks after conception?

- When do body structures and internal organs emerge in prenatal development?

- When do body systems begin to function well enough to support life?

Eun Jung has just learned that she is pregnant with her first child. Like many other parents-to-be, she and her husband are ecstatic. But they also realize how little they know about "what happens when" during pregnancy. Eun Jung is eager to visit her obstetrician to learn more about the timetable of events during pregnancy.

The many changes that transform an egg fertilized by a sperm cell into a newborn human constitute prenatal development. Prenatal development takes an average of 38 weeks, which are divided into three periods: the period of the zygote, the period of the embryo, and the period of the fetus.* Each period gets its name from the scientific term used to describe the baby-to-be at that point in its prenatal development.

In this section, we'll trace the major developments of each of these periods. As we do, you'll learn the answers to the "what happens when" question that intrigues Eun Jung.

prenatal development

The many changes that turn a fertilized egg into a newborn human.

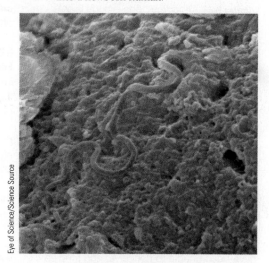

Eye of Science/Science Source

In this photo, the tail of the sperm can be seen clearly but the sperm has burrowed so deeply that the head is barely visible.

Period of the Zygote (Weeks 1–2)

The teaspoon or so of seminal fluid produced during a fertile male's ejaculation contains from 200 to 500 million sperm. Of the sperm released into the vagina, only a few hundred complete the six- or seven-inch journey to the fallopian tubes.

*Perhaps you've heard that pregnancy lasts 40 weeks and wonder why we say that prenatal development lasts 38 weeks. The reason is that the 40 weeks of pregnancy are measured from the start of a woman's last menstrual period, which typically is about 2 weeks before conception.

zygote

Fertilized egg, created when a sperm cell penetrates an egg.

in vitro fertilization

Process by which sperm and an egg are mixed in a petri dish to create a zygote, which is then placed in a woman's uterus.

preimplantation genetic screening (PGS)

A procedure used to test the heredity of an egg fertilized with assisted reproductive technology, typically to determine the presence of genetic disorders.

eugenics

Effort to improve the human species by letting only people whose characteristics are valued by a society mate and pass along their genes.

An egg arrives there monthly, hours after it is released by an ovary. If an egg is present, many sperm simultaneously begin to burrow their way through the cluster of nurturing cells that surround the egg. When one sperm finally penetrates the cellular wall of the egg, chemical changes occur in the wall immediately, blocking out all other sperm. Then the nuclei of the egg and sperm fuse, and the two independent sets of 23 chromosomes are interchanged. The development of a new human being is under way.

For nearly all of history, sexual intercourse was the only way for egg and sperm to unite and begin the development that results in a human being. This is no longer the only way, as we see in the What Do *You* Think? feature.

Whether by artificial means or by natural means, fertilization begins the period of the zygote, *the term for the fertilized egg.* This period ends when the zygote implants itself in the wall of the uterus. During these two weeks, the zygote grows rapidly through cell division. ❱ Figure 2.5 traces the egg cell from the time it is released from the ovary until the zygote becomes implanted in the wall of the uterus. The zygote travels down the fallopian tube toward the uterus. Within hours, the zygote divides for the first time; it then continues to do so every 12 hours. Occasionally, the zygote separates into two clusters that develop into identical twins. Fraternal twins, which are more common, are created when two eggs are released and each is fertilized by a different sperm cell.

What Do *You* Think?   Conception in the 21st Century

About 40 years ago, Louise Brown captured the world's attention as the first test-tube baby—conceived in a petri dish instead of in her mother's body. Today, assisted reproductive technology is no longer experimental; it is used nearly 200,000 times annually with American women, producing more than 65,000 babies (Centers for Disease Control and Prevention, 2015). Many new techniques are available to couples who cannot conceive a child through sexual intercourse. *The best-known technique,* in vitro fertilization, *involves mixing sperm and egg in a petri dish and then placing several fertilized eggs in the mother's uterus, with the hope that they become implanted in the uterine wall.* Other methods include injecting many sperm directly into the fallopian tubes or a single sperm directly into an egg (Ramalingam, Durgadevit, & Mahmood, 2016).

The sperm and egg usually come from the prospective parents, but sometimes they are provided by donors. Typically, the fertilized eggs are placed in the uterus of the prospective mother, but sometimes they are placed in the uterus of a surrogate mother who carries the baby to term. This means that a baby could have as many as five "parents": the man and woman who provided the sperm and egg; the surrogate mother who carried the baby; and the mother and father who rear the baby.

New reproductive techniques offer hope for couples who have long wanted a child but have been unable to conceive, and studies of the first generation of children conceived

via these techniques indicates that their social and emotional development is normal (Golombok, 2013). But there are difficulties. For women under 35, about 40% of attempts at in vitro fertilization succeed; for older women, success is less likely. What's more, when a woman becomes pregnant, she is more likely to have twins or triplets because multiple eggs are transferred to increase the odds that at least one fertilized egg will implant in the mother's uterus (Ramalingam et al., 2016). She is also at greater risk for giving birth to a baby with low birth weight (Luke et al., 2016) or birth defects. Finally, the procedure is expensive—the average cost in the United States of a single cycle of treatment is between $10,000 and $17,000—and often is not covered by health insurance.

These problems emphasize that although technology has increased the alternatives for infertile couples, pregnancy on demand is still in the realm of science fiction. At the same time, the new technologies have led to much controversy because of complex ethical issues associated with their use. One concerns the prospective parents' right to select particular egg and sperm cells; another involves who should be able to use this technology.

Designer embryos? Today, parents can ask that the genes of a fertilized egg be analyzed before it is implanted in a woman's uterus. This procedure, known as preimplantation genetic screening (PGS), is usually used with couples known to be at risk for genetic disorders (e.g., sickle-cell anemia). But PGS

can also be used to determine a child-to-be's gender or, for that matter, hair color (Ethics Committee of the American Society for Reproductive Medicine, 2015). If parents aren't pleased with the test results, they can have the embryo discarded.

Some claim that prospective parents have a right to be fully informed about the properties of the embryo that will be implanted in the woman's uterus. *Others argue that this amounts to* eugenics, *which is the effort to improve the human species by allowing only certain people to mate and pass along their genes.*

Available to all? About 75% of women who use assisted reproductive technology are in their 30s, but about 1% involve women who are 45 and older and cannot conceive naturally because they have gone through menopause. The American Society for Reproductive Medicine (2016) recommends that women older than 55 be discouraged from using reproductive technology because pregnancy could pose risks to their health. But what about 45- to 55-year-old women? Some argue that it is unfair for a child to have parents who may not live until the child reaches adulthood. Others point out that people are living longer and that middle-aged (or older) adults make better parents. (We discuss this issue in more depth in Chapter 13.)

What do you think? Should prospective parents be allowed to "pick and choose" their embryos? Should new reproductive technologies be available to all, regardless of age?

▶ **Figure 2.5**

The period of the zygote spans 14 days, beginning with fertilization of the egg in the fallopian tube and ending with implantation of the fertilized egg in the wall of the uterus.

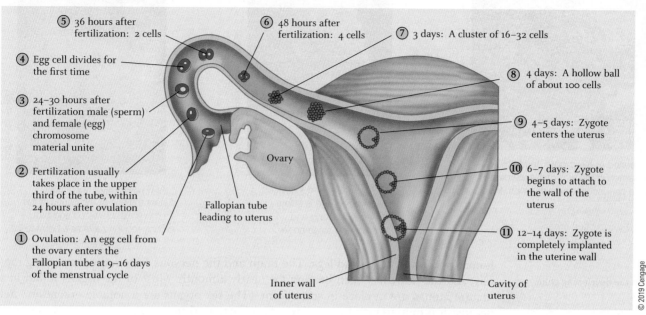

⑤ 36 hours after fertilization: 2 cells

⑥ 48 hours after fertilization: 4 cells

⑦ 3 days: A cluster of 16–32 cells

④ Egg cell divides for the first time

③ 24–30 hours after fertilization male (sperm) and female (egg) chromosome material unite

② Fertilization usually takes place in the upper third of the tube, within 24 hours after ovulation

① Ovulation: An egg cell from the ovary enters the Fallopian tube at 9–16 days of the menstrual cycle

Ovary

Fallopian tube leading to uterus

⑧ 4 days: A hollow ball of about 100 cells

⑨ 4–5 days: Zygote enters the uterus

⑩ 6–7 days: Zygote begins to attach to the wall of the uterus

⑪ 12–14 days: Zygote is completely implanted in the uterine wall

Inner wall of uterus

Cavity of uterus

© 2019 Cengage

After about four days, the zygote includes about 100 cells and resembles a hollow ball. The inner part of the ball is destined to become the baby. The outer layer of cells will form a number of structures that provide a life-support system throughout prenatal development.

By the end of the first week, the zygote reaches the uterus. *The next step is* implantation, *in which the zygote burrows into the uterine wall and establishes connections with the woman's blood vessels.* Implantation takes about a week to complete and triggers hormonal changes that prevent menstruation, letting the woman know that she has conceived.

The implanted zygote is less than a millimeter in diameter, yet its cells have already begun to differentiate. *A small cluster of cells near the center of the zygote, the* germ disc, *eventually develop into the baby.* The other cells become structures that support, nourish, and protect the developing organism. *The layer of cells closest to the uterus becomes the* placenta, *a structure through which nutrients and wastes are exchanged between the mother and the developing organism.*

Implantation and differentiation of cells mark the end of the period of the zygote. Sheltered in the uterus, the zygote is well prepared for the remaining 36 weeks of the journey to birth.

Period of the Embryo (Weeks 3–8)

After the zygote is completely embedded in the uterine wall, it is called an embryo. This new period typically begins the third week after conception and lasts until the end of the eighth week. During the period of the embryo, body structures and internal organs develop. At the beginning of this period, three layers form in the embryo. *The outer layer, or* ectoderm, *becomes hair, the outer layer of skin, and the nervous system; the middle layer, or* mesoderm, *forms muscles, bones, and the circulatory system; the inner layer, or* endoderm, *forms the digestive system and the lungs.*

A dramatic way to see these changes is to compare a 3-week-old embryo with an 8-week-old embryo. The 3-week-old embryo is about 2 millimeters long and looks more like a salamander than a human being. But growth and specialization proceed so rapidly that the 8-week-old embryo shown in the right photo on page 54 looks distinctively

implantation

Step in which the zygote burrows into the uterine wall and establishes connections with the woman's blood vessels.

germ disc

Small cluster of cells near the center of the zygote that eventually develop into the baby.

placenta

Structure through which nutrients and wastes are exchanged between the mother and the developing child.

embryo

Term given to the zygote once it is completely embedded in the uterine wall.

ectoderm

Outer layer of the embryo, which becomes the hair, outer layer of skin, and nervous system.

mesoderm

Middle layer of the embryo, which becomes the muscles, bones, and circulatory system.

endoderm

Inner layer of the embryo, which becomes the lungs and digestive system.

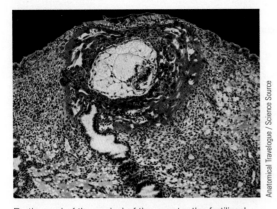

By the end of the period of the zygote, the fertilized egg has been implanted in the wall of the uterus and has begun to make connections with the mother's blood vessels.

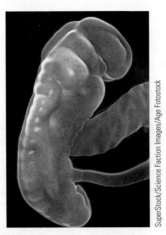

At 3 weeks after conception, the fertilized egg is about 2 millimeters long and resembles a salamander.

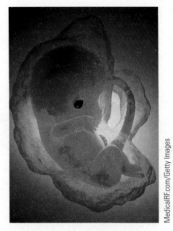

At 8 weeks after conception near the end of the period of the embryo, the fertilized egg is obviously recognizable as a baby-to-be.

amnion

Inner sac in which the developing child rests.

amniotic fluid

Fluid that surrounds the fetus.

umbilical cord

Structure containing veins and arteries that connects the developing child to the placenta.

cephalocaudal principle

A principle of physical growth that states that structures nearest the head develop first.

proximodistal principle

Principle of physical growth that states that structures nearest the center of the body develop first.

human with eyes, arms, and legs. The brain and the nervous system are developing rapidly, and the heart has been beating for nearly a month. Most of the organs found in a mature human are in place in some form. (The sex organs are a notable exception.) Yet because it is only an inch long and weighs a fraction of an ounce, the embryo is too small for the mother to feel its presence.

The embryo's environment is shown in ▶ Figure 2.6. *The embryo rests in a sac called the* amnion, *which is filled with* amniotic fluid *that cushions the embryo and maintains a constant temperature.* The embryo is linked to the mother via two structures, the placenta and the umbilical cord. *The* umbilical cord *houses blood vessels that join the embryo to the placenta.* In the placenta, the blood vessels from the umbilical cord run close to the mother's blood vessels, allowing nutrients, oxygen, vitamins, and waste products to be exchanged between mother and embryo.

Growth in the period of the embryo follows two important principles. First, the head develops before the rest of the body. *Such growth, from the head to the base of the spine, illustrates the* cephalocaudal principle. Second, arms and legs develop before hands and feet. *Growth of parts near the center of the body before those that are more distant illustrates the* proximodistal principle. Growth after birth also follows these principles.

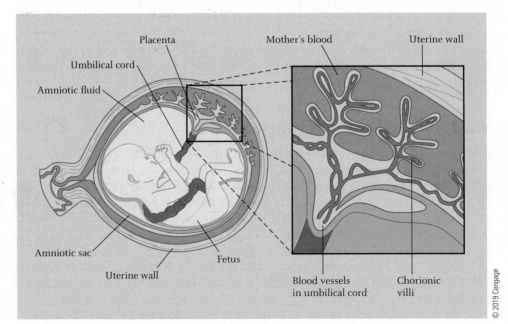

▶ **Figure 2.6**

The fetus is wrapped in the amniotic sac and connected to the mother by the umbilical cord.

Period of the Fetus (Weeks 9–38)

The final and longest phase of prenatal development, the period of the fetus, *begins at the ninth week and ends at birth.* During this period, the baby-to-be becomes much larger and its bodily systems begin to work. The increase in size is remarkable. At the beginning of this period, the fetus weighs less than an ounce. At about 4 months, the fetus weighs roughly 4 to 8 ounces, which is large enough for the mother to feel its movements. In the last 5 months of pregnancy, the fetus gains an additional 7 or 8 pounds before birth. ▶ Figure 2.7, which depicts the fetus at one-eighth of its actual size, shows these incredible increases in size.

During the fetal period, the finishing touches are placed on the many systems essential to human life, such as respiration, digestion, and vision. Some highlights of this period include the following:

- At 4 weeks after conception, a flat set of cells curls to form a tube. One end of the tube swells to form the brain; the rest forms the spinal cord. By the start of the fetal period, the brain has distinct structures and has begun to regulate body functions. *During the period of the fetus, all regions of the brain grow—particularly the* cerebral cortex, *the wrinkled surface of the brain that regulates many important human behaviors.*
- Near the end of the embryonic period, male embryos develop testes and female embryos develop ovaries. In the third month, the testes in a male fetus secrete a hormone that causes a set of cells to become a penis and scrotum; in a female fetus, this hormone is absent, so the same cells become a vagina and labia.
- By about 4 months after conception, the fetus moves: it stretches, yawns, swallows, and moves its limbs. Initially, these movements are global and uncoordinated. But over the last few months of pregnancy, they become more differentiated and fluid. However, fetuses differ in their level of activity: Some seem to be moving constantly but others are much less active (DiPietro, Costigan, & Voegtline, 2015).
- During the fifth and sixth months after conception, eyebrows, eyelashes, and scalp hair emerge. *The skin thickens and is covered with a thick greasy substance, or* vernix, *that protects the fetus during its long bath in amniotic fluid.*
- Perceptual systems begin to work during the period of the fetus. The fetus responds to touch at 14 weeks after conception and responds to light at 26 weeks after conception.

period of the fetus

Longest period of prenatal development, extending from the 9th until the 38th week after conception.

cerebral cortex

Wrinkled surface of the brain that regulates many functions that are distinctly human.

vernix

Substance that protects the fetus's skin during development.

▶ **Figure 2.7**

The baby-to-be becomes much larger during the period of the fetus, and its bodily systems start to work.

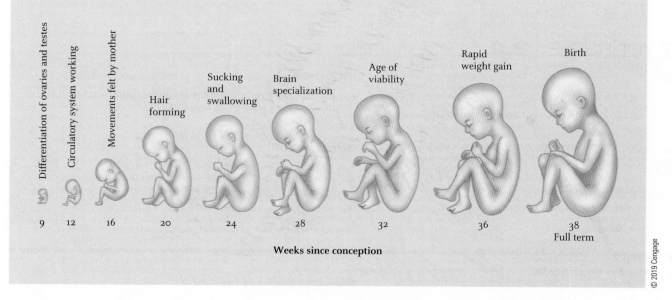

© 2019 Cengage

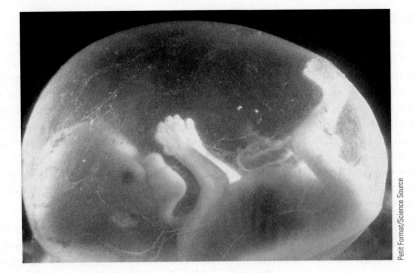

At 22 to 28 weeks after conception, the fetus has achieved the age of viability, meaning that it has a chance of surviving if born prematurely.

Most impressive, however, is the fetus's sensitivity to sound. The fetus responds to sound at 29 weeks after conception and by 34 weeks can distinguish different speech sounds, including different vowel sounds and different languages (Hepper, 2015; Kisilevsky, 2016).

- The fetus can learn and remember. When a fetus is exposed repeatedly to distinct sounds (e.g., its mother's voice) or distinct tastes (e.g., its mother eats garlic), the fetus recognizes those stimuli after birth (Hepper, 2015). For example, after women drank carrot juice frequently during the last month of pregnancy, as 5- and 6-month-olds, their infants preferred cereal flavored with carrot juice (Mennella, Jagnow, & Beauchamp, 2001). These skills are adaptive in helping newborns to recognize mother (by her voice and smell) and in helping them to learn language (because the sounds are familiar).

With these and other rapid changes, by 22 to 28 weeks, most systems function well enough that a fetus born at this time has a chance to survive, which is why this age range is called the age of viability. By this age, the fetus has a distinctly baby-like look, but babies born this early have trouble breathing because their lungs are not yet mature. Also, they cannot regulate their body temperature very well because they lack the insulating layer of fat that appears in the eighth month after conception. With modern neonatal intensive care, infants born this early can survive, but they face other challenges, as we'll see later in this chapter.

Think About It

Healthcare professionals often divide pregnancy into three 3-month trimesters. How do these three trimesters correspond to the periods of the zygote, embryo, and fetus?

age of viability

age at which a fetus can survive outside the womb because most of its bodily systems function adequately; typically at 7 months after conception

TEST YOURSELF 2.2

Recall

1. The period of the zygote ends _____.
2. Body structures and internal organs are created during the period of the _____.
3. _____ is called the age of viability because this is when most body systems function well enough to support life.
4. Behaviors that emerge in the fetal period include movement, perception of touch, light, and sound, and _____.

Interpret

- Compare the events of prenatal development that precede the age of viability with those that follow it.

Apply

- In the last few months before birth, the fetus has some basic perceptual and motor skills; a fetus can hear, see, taste, and move. What are the advantages of having these skills in place months before they're needed?

Check your answers to the Recall Questions at the end of the chapter.

Influences on Prenatal Development

LEARNING OBJECTIVES

- How is prenatal development influenced by a pregnant woman's age, her nutrition, and the stress she experiences while pregnant?

- How do diseases, drugs, and environmental hazards sometimes affect prenatal development?

- What general principles affect the ways that prenatal development can be harmed?

- How can prenatal development be monitored? Can abnormal prenatal development be corrected?

Chloe was 2 months pregnant at her first prenatal checkup. As her appointment drew near, she began making a list of questions to ask her obstetrician. "I use my cell phone a lot. Is radiation from the phone harmful to my baby?" "When my husband and I get home from work, we have a glass of wine to help us unwind from the stress of the day. Is moderate drinking like that okay?" "I'm 38. I know older women are more likely to give birth to babies with mental retardation. Will I be able to find out if my baby is mentally retarded?"

Each of Chloe's questions concerns the possibility of harm befalling her baby-to-be. She worries about the safety of her cell phone, about her nightly glass of wine, and about her age. Chloe's concerns are well founded. Many factors influence the course of prenatal development, and they are the focus of this section. If you can answer *all* of Chloe's questions, then skip this section and go directly to page 66. Otherwise, read on to learn about problems that sometimes arise in pregnancy.

General Risk Factors

As the name implies, general risk factors can have widespread effects on prenatal development. Scientists have identified three general risk factors: nutrition, stress, and a mother's age.

Nutrition

The mother is the developing child's sole source of nutrition, so a balanced diet that includes foods from each of the five major food groups is vital. Most pregnant women need to increase their intake of calories by about 10% to 20% to meet the needs of prenatal development. In addition, pregnant women need to be sure to consume key nutrients: *folic acid* (found in green leafy vegetables) is essential for the spinal cord to develop properly; *iron* (found in beef, chicken, beans, spinach, and tofu) is necessary to make additional hemoglobin, which carries oxygen to the body's cells, and *calcium* (found in milk, yogurt, and cheese) is required to develop strong teeth and bones as well as a healthy heart, muscles, and nerves.

A diet that lacks these nutrients can harm the developing child. *For example, if mothers do not consume adequate amounts of folic acid, their babies are at risk for* spina bifida, *a disorder in which the embryo's neural tube does not close properly during the first month of pregnancy.* When the neural tube does not close properly, the result is permanent damage to the spinal cord and the nervous system; consequently, many children with spina bifida use crutches, braces, or wheelchairs (National Institute of Neurological Disorders and Stroke, 2013). To ensure that pregnant women receive adequate amounts of folic acid and other nutrients, health care providers often recommend a vitamin/mineral supplement (Kohn, 2015).

spina bifida
Disorder in which the embryo's neural tube does not close properly.

Stress

stress

Physical and psychological responses to threatening or challenging conditions.

Does a pregnant woman's mood affect the zygote, embryo, or fetus in her uterus? Is a woman who is happy during pregnancy more likely to give birth to a happy baby? Is a harried office worker more likely to give birth to an irritable baby? *These questions address the impact on prenatal development of chronic* stress, *which refers to a person's physical and psychological responses to threatening or challenging situations.* Women who report greater anxiety during pregnancy more often give birth early or have babies who weigh less than average (Staneva et al, 2015; Tegethoff et al., 2010). What's more, when pregnant women are anxious, their children are less able to pay attention and more prone to behavioral problems as preschoolers (Grizenko et al., 2015). Similar results emerged from studies of pregnant women exposed to disasters, such as the September 11 attacks on the World Trade Center: Their children's physical, cognitive, and language development was affected (Engel et al., 2005; King et al., 2012). Finally, the harmful effects of stress are not linked to anxiety in general but are specific to worries about pregnancy, particularly in the first few months (Davis & Sandman, 2010; DiPietro et al., 2006).

Increased stress can harm prenatal development in several ways. First, when a pregnant woman experiences stress, her body secretes hormones that reduce the flow of oxygen to the fetus while increasing its heart rate and activity level (Monk et al., 2000). Second, stress can weaken a pregnant woman's immune system, making her more susceptible to illness (Cohen & Williamson, 1991) that can, in turn, damage fetal development. Third, pregnant women under stress are more likely to smoke or drink alcohol and are less likely to rest, exercise, and eat properly (DiPietro et al., 2004). Fourth, stress may produce epigenetic changes (described on page 48) in which genes that help children regulate their behavior are made less effective (Monk, Spicer, & Champagne, 2012). All these behaviors endanger prenatal development.

We want to emphasize that the results described here apply to women who experience prolonged, extreme stress. Virtually all women become anxious or upset sometime during their pregnancy. Occasional, relatively mild anxiety is not thought to have any harmful consequences for prenatal development.

Mother's Age

Traditionally, the 20s were thought to be the prime childbearing years. Teenage women as well as women who were 30 and older were considered less fit for the rigors of pregnancy. Is being a 20-something really important for a successful pregnancy? Let's answer that question separately for teenagers and older women. Compared with women in their 20s, teenage girls are at greater risk to give birth early and to give birth to babies low in birth weight (Khashan, Baker, & Kenny, 2010). This is largely because pregnant teenagers are more likely to be living in poverty and do not receive good prenatal care.

Nevertheless, even when a teenager receives adequate prenatal care and gives birth to a healthy baby, all is not rosy. Children of teenage mothers generally do less well in school and more often have behavioral problems (D'Onofrio et al., 2009; Fergusson & Woodward, 2000). For example, as adolescents, they're more likely to be convicted of crimes (Coyne et al., 2013).

Of course, not all teenage mothers and their infants follow this dismal life course. Some teenage mothers finish school, find good jobs, and have happy marriages; their children do well in school academically and socially. These "success stories" are more likely when teenage moms live with a relative—typically, the child's grandmother (Gordon, Chase-Lansdale, & Brooks-Gunn, 2004). However, teenage pregnancies with "happy endings" are the exception; for most teenage mothers and their children, life is a struggle.

When pregnant women experience chronic stress, they're more likely to give birth early or have smaller babies. This may be because women who are stressed are more likely to smoke or drink and less likely to rest, exercise, and eat properly.

Zurijeta/Shutterstock.com

And teen parenthood may become even more challenging: In the U. S., the safety net for teen parents has been shrinking, which means they have fewer resources than before. In addition, the average age at first birth is increasing, so teenage moms are becoming increasingly dissimilar to the typical U. S. mom and perhaps more likely to be stigmatized (Mollborn, 2017).

Are older women better suited for pregnancy? That is an important question because today's American woman is waiting longer than ever to have her first child. Completing an education and beginning a career often delay childbearing. In fact, the birth rate in the early 2000s among 40- to 44-year-olds was at its highest rate since the 1960s (Hamilton, Martin, & Ventura, 2010).

Traditionally, older women were thought to have more difficult pregnancies and more complicated labor and deliveries. Today, we know that older women have more difficulty getting pregnant and are less likely to have successful pregnancies. Women in their 20s are twice as fertile as women in their 30s (Dunson, Colombo, & Baird, 2002), and past 35 years of age, the risks of miscarriage and stillbirth increase rapidly. For example, among 40- to 45-year-olds, pregnancies are much more likely to result in miscarriage or in babies with low birth weight (Khalil et al., 2013). What's more, women in their 40s are more likely to give birth to babies with Down syndrome. However, as mothers, older women are quite effective. For example, they are just as able to provide the sort of sensitive, responsive caregiving that promotes a child's development (Bornstein et al., 2006).

In general then, prenatal development is most likely to proceed normally when women are between 20 and 35 years of age, are healthy and eat right, get good health care, and lead lives that are free of chronic stress. But even in these optimal cases, prenatal development can be disrupted, as we'll see in the next section.

For teenage mothers and their babies, life is often a struggle because the mothers are unable to complete their education and often live in poverty.

Teratogens: Drugs, Diseases, and Environmental Hazards

In the late 1950s, many pregnant women in Germany took thalidomide, a drug that helped them sleep. Soon, however, came reports that many of these women were giving birth to babies with deformed arms, legs, hands, or fingers. *Thalidomide is a powerful* teratogen, *an agent that causes abnormal prenatal development.* Ultimately, more than 7,000 babies worldwide were harmed before thalidomide was withdrawn from the market (Kolberg, 1999).

Prompted by the thalidomide disaster, scientists began to study teratogens extensively. Today, we know a great deal about many teratogens that affect prenatal development. Most teratogens fall into one of three categories: drugs, diseases, or environmental hazards.

teratogen

An agent that causes abnormal prenatal development.

Drugs

Thalidomide illustrates the harm that drugs can cause during prenatal development. ▶ Table 2.3 lists several other drugs that are known teratogens. Most of the drugs in the list are substances you may use routinely—Accutane (used to treat acne), alcohol, aspirin, caffeine, and nicotine. Nevertheless, when consumed by pregnant women, they present special dangers (Behnke & Eyler, 1993).

Cigarette smoking is typical of the potential harm from teratogenic drugs (Cornelius et al., 1995; Espy et al., 2011). The nicotine in cigarette smoke constricts blood vessels and thus reduces the oxygen and nutrients that can reach the fetus through the placenta. Therefore, pregnant women who smoke are more likely to miscarry (abort the fetus spontaneously) and to bear children who are smaller than average at birth (D'Onofrio et al., 2014). Most of these harmful effects depend on degree of exposure—heavy smoking is more

Table 2.3

Teratogenic Drugs and Their Consequences	
DRUG	**POTENTIAL CONSEQUENCES**
Alcohol	Fetal alcohol syndrome, cognitive deficits, heart damage, retarded growth
Aspirin	Deficits in intelligence, attention, and motor skills
Caffeine	Lower birth weight, decreased muscle tone
Cocaine and heroin	Retarded growth, irritability in newborns
Marijuana	Lower birth weight, less motor control
Nicotine	Retarded growth, possible cognitive impairments

fetal alcohol spectrum disorder (FASD)

Disorder affecting babies whose mothers consumed large amounts of alcohol while they were pregnant.

When pregnant women drink large amounts of alcohol, their children often have fetal alcohol syndrome; these children tend to have a small head and a thin upper lip as well as retarded mental development.

Betty Udesen KRT/Newscom

harmful than moderate smoking—and on the fetal genotype: Some children inherit genes that are more effective in defending, in utero, against the toxins in cigarette smoke (Price et al., 2010).

Even secondhand smoke is harmful: When pregnant women don't smoke but their environment is filled with tobacco smoke, their babies tend to be smaller at birth, to be born early, and to be at risk for birth defects such as cleft palate or spina bifida (Hoyt et al., 2016; Meeker & Benedict, 2013). These harmful effects are reduced when smoking is banned in public places and workplaces (Bakolis et al., 2016).

Alcohol also carries serious risk. *Pregnant women who regularly consume alcoholic beverages may give birth to babies with* fetal alcohol spectrum disorder (FASD). The most extreme form, fetal alcohol syndrome (FAS), is most likely in pregnant women who are heavy drinkers—for example, they drink 15 or more cans of beer over a weekend (May et al., 2013). Children with FAS usually grow more slowly than normal and have heart problems and misshapen faces. Like the child in the photo, youngsters with FAS often have a small head, a thin upper lip, a short nose, and widely spaced eyes. FAS is the leading cause of developmental disabilities in the United States, and children with FAS have serious attentional, cognitive, and behavioral problems (Davis et al., 2013).

Is there any amount of drinking that's safe during pregnancy? Maybe, but scientists have yet to determine one. This inconclusiveness stems from two factors. First, drinking is often estimated from women's responses to interviews or questionnaires. These replies may be incorrect, leading to inaccurate estimates of the harm associated with drinking. Second, any safe level of consumption is probably not the same for all women. Based on their health and heredity, some women may be able to consume more alcohol safely than others.

These factors make it impossible to offer guaranteed statements about safe levels of alcohol or any of the other drugs listed in ❱ Table 2.3. For this reason, the best policy is for women to avoid all drugs during pregnancy.

Diseases

Sometimes women become ill while pregnant. Most diseases, such as colds and many strains of the flu, do not affect the fetus. However, many bacterial and viral infections can be harmful; several are listed in ❱ Table 2.4.

Table 2.4

Teratogenic Diseases and Their Consequences	
DISEASE	**POTENTIAL CONSEQUENCES**
AIDS	Frequent infections, neurological disorders, death
Chlamydia	Premature birth, low birth weight, eye inflammation
Chicken pox	Spontaneous abortion, developmental delays, mental retardation
Cytomegalovirus	Deafness, blindness, abnormally small head, mental retardation
Genital herpes	Encephalitis, enlarged spleen, improper blood clotting
Rubella (German measles)	Mental retardation; damage to eyes, ears, and heart
Syphilis	Damage to the central nervous system, teeth, and bones
Toxoplasmosis	Damage to the eyes and brain; learning disabilities

Some of these diseases pass from the mother through the placenta to attack the embryo or fetus directly. They include cytomegalovirus (a type of herpes), rubella, and syphilis. Other diseases attack during birth: The virus is present in the lining of the birth canal, and babies are infected as they pass through the canal. AIDS and genital herpes are two such diseases.

The only way to guarantee that these diseases will not harm prenatal development is for a woman not to contract them before or during her pregnancy. Medicines that may help to treat a woman after she becomes ill do not prevent the disease from damaging the fetus.

Environmental Hazards

As a by-product of life in an industrialized world, people are often exposed to toxins in food they eat, fluids they drink, and air they breathe. Chemicals associated with industrial waste are the most common form of environmental teratogens. The quantity involved is usually minute; however, as with drugs, amounts that go unnoticed in an adult can cause serious damage to the fetus.

Polychlorinated biphenyls (PCBs) illustrate the danger of environmental teratogens. These were used in electrical transformers and paints until the U.S. government banned them in the 1970s. However, PCBs (like many industrial by-products) seeped into the waterways, where they contaminated fish and wildlife. The amount of PCBs in a typical contaminated fish does not affect adults, but when pregnant women ate large numbers of PCB-contaminated fish, their children's cognitive skills and reading achievement were impaired (Jacobson & Jacobson, 1996; Winneke, 2011).

Several environmental hazards that are known teratogens are listed in ▶ Table 2.5. In developed nations, the most common teratogen is polluted air. Exposure to highly polluted air is associated with greater risk for premature births and lower birth weight (Currie, 2013). For example, in a clever natural experiment (Currie & Walker, 2011), researchers studied pregnant women living near highway toll plazas. When devices are installed that allow drivers to pay tolls electronically without stopping, air pollution drops substantially (because cars neither wait to pay nor accelerate back to highway speed). Collecting tolls electronically produced a 10% drop in prematurity and low birth weight among pregnant women living near the toll plazas.

You may be wondering about one ubiquitous feature of modern environments that doesn't appear in ▶ Table 2.5: cell phones. Is the use of a cell phone by a pregnant woman hazardous to the health of her fetus? Although the radiofrequency radiation that cell phones generate has sometimes been linked to health risks in adults (e.g., cancer), the findings for pregnant women are inconsistent. Some studies reported greater risk for behavioral problems in children whose mothers used cell phones frequently during pregnancy (Divan et al., 2012), but other studies find no harm associated with using cell phones during pregnancy (Baste et al., 2015). Of course, one way in which cell phones represent a

Think About It

A pregnant woman reluctant to give up her morning cup of coffee and nightly glass of wine says, "I drink so little coffee and wine that it couldn't possibly hurt my baby." What do you think?

Table 2.5

Environmental Teratogens and Their Consequences	
HAZARD	**POTENTIAL CONSEQUENCES**
Air pollution	Low birth weight, premature birth, lower test scores
Lead	Mental retardation
Mercury	Retarded growth, mental retardation, cerebral palsy
PCBs	Impaired memory and verbal skills
X-rays	Retarded growth, leukemia, mental retardation

huge risk for pregnant women is talking while driving, which increases the odds of being in an accident by more than 50% (Asbridge, Brubacher, & Chan, 2013). So while we wait for research to provide more information, the best advice for a pregnant woman is to keep a cell phone at a distance when it's not being used and never use it while driving.

Environmental teratogens are treacherous because people are unaware of their presence in the environment. For example, the women studied by Jacobson, Jacobson, and Humphrey (1990) did not realize they were eating PCB-laden fish. The invisibility of some environmental teratogens makes it more difficult for a pregnant woman to protect herself from them. Pregnant women need to be particularly careful of the foods they eat and the air they breathe. They should clean all foods thoroughly to rid them of insecticides and should avoid convenience foods, which often contain chemical additives. And they should stay away from air that's been contaminated by household products such as cleansers, paint strippers, and fertilizers. Women in jobs that require contact with potential teratogens (e.g., housecleaners, hairdressers) should switch to less potent chemicals. For example, they should use baking soda instead of more chemically laden cleansers. They also should wear protective gloves, aprons, and masks to reduce their contact with potential teratogens. Finally, because environmental teratogens continue to increase, pregnant women should check with a health care provider to learn if they should avoid other materials.

How Teratogens Influence Prenatal Development

By assembling all the evidence on the harm caused by drugs, diseases, and environmental hazards, scientists have identified five important general principles about how teratogens usually work (Hogge, 1990; Jacobson & Jacobson, 2000; Vorhees & Mollnow, 1987).

1. *The impact of a teratogen depends on the genotype of the organism.* A substance may be harmful to one species but not to another. To determine its safety, thalidomide was tested on pregnant rats and rabbits, and their offspring had normal limbs. Yet when pregnant women took the same drug in comparable doses, many had children with deformed limbs. Moreover, some women who took thalidomide gave birth to babies with normal limbs, whereas others who took comparable doses of thalidomide at the same time in their pregnancies gave birth to babies with deformed arms and legs. Apparently, heredity makes some individuals more susceptible to a teratogen.

2. *The impact of teratogens changes over the course of prenatal development.* The timing of exposure to a teratogen is very important. ◗ Figure 2.8 shows how the consequences of teratogens differ for the periods of the zygote, embryo, and fetus. During the period of the zygote, exposure to teratogens usually results in spontaneous abortion of the fertilized egg. During the period of the embryo, exposure to teratogens produces major defects in bodily structure. For instance, women who took thalidomide during the period of the embryo had babies with ill-formed or missing limbs, and women who contract rubella during the period of the embryo have babies with heart defects. During the period of the fetus, exposure to teratogens either produces minor defects in bodily structure or causes body systems to

function improperly. For example, when women drink large quantities of alcohol during this period, the fetus develops fewer brain cells.

Even within the different periods of prenatal development, developing body parts and systems are more vulnerable at some times than others. The orange shading in the chart indicates a time of maximum vulnerability; yellow shading indicates a time when the developing organism is less vulnerable. The heart, for example, is most sensitive to teratogens during the first half of the embryonic period. Exposure to teratogens before this time rarely produces heart damage, and exposure after this time results in relatively mild damage.

3. *Each teratogen affects a specific aspect (or aspects) of prenatal development.* Teratogens do not harm all body systems; instead, damage is selective. When women contract rubella, their babies often have problems with their eyes, ears, and heart but have normal limbs. When mothers consume PCB-contaminated fish, their babies typically have normal body parts and normal motor skills but below-average verbal and memory skills.

4. *The impact of teratogens depends on the dose.* Just as a single drop of oil won't pollute a lake, small doses of teratogens may not harm the fetus. In research on PCBs, for example, cognitive skills were affected only among children who had the greatest prenatal exposure to these by-products. In general, the greater the exposure, the greater the risk for damage (Adams, 1999). An implication of this principle is that researchers should be able to determine safe levels for a teratogen. In reality, this is extremely difficult because sensitivity to teratogens is not the same for all people (and it's not practical to establish safe amounts for each person). Hence, the safest rule is zero exposure to teratogens.

5. *Damage from teratogens is not always evident at birth but may appear later in life.* In the case of malformed limbs, the effects of a teratogen are obvious immediately. Sometimes, however, the damage from a teratogen becomes evident only as the

▶ **Figure 2.8**
The effects of a teratogen on an unborn child depend on the stage of prenatal development.

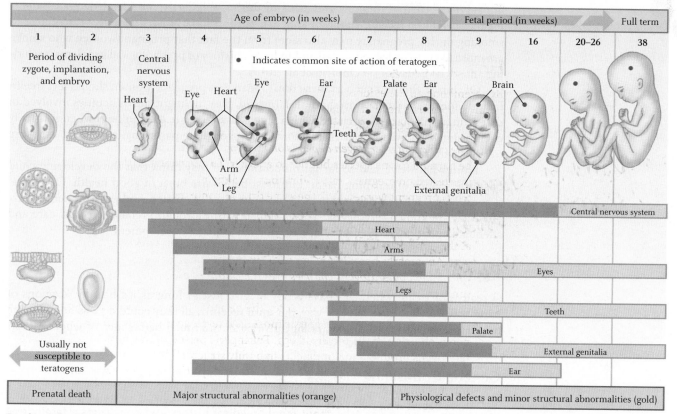

Based on *Before We Are Born*, 4th ed., by K. L. Moore and T. V. N. Persaud, p. 130.

child develops. For example, when women ate PCB-contaminated fish, their babies were normal at birth. Their below-average cognitive skills were not evident until several months later.

An even more dramatic example of the delayed impact of a teratogen involves the drug diethylstilbestrol (DES). Between 1947 and 1971, many pregnant women took DES, a synthetic version of the female hormone estrogen, to prevent miscarriages. Their babies were apparently normal at birth. As adults, however, daughters of women who took DES are more likely to have breast cancer or a rare cancer of the vagina. And they sometimes have abnormalities in their reproductive tract that make it difficult to become pregnant. Sons of women who took DES are at risk for testicular abnormalities and for testicular cancer (National Cancer Institute, 2006). In this case, the impact of the teratogen is not evident until decades after birth.

The Real World of Prenatal Risk

We have discussed risk factors individually as if each factor were the only potential threat to prenatal development. In reality, infants are sometimes exposed to multiple general risks and multiple teratogens. Pregnant women who drink alcohol often smoke and drink coffee (Baron et al., 2013). Pregnant women who are under stress often drink alcohol and may self-medicate with aspirin or other over-the-counter drugs. Many of these same women live in poverty, which means that they may have inadequate nutrition and receive minimal medical care during pregnancy. When all the risks are combined, prenatal development is rarely optimal (Yumoto, Jacobson, & Jacobson, 2008).

This pattern explains why it's often challenging for human development researchers to determine the harm associated with individual teratogens. Cocaine is a perfect example. You may remember stories in newspapers and magazines about "crack babies" and their developmental problems. Children exposed to cocaine during prenatal development suffer from a range of problems in physical growth, cognitive development, behavioral regulation, and psychopathology (e.g., Buckingham-Howes et al., 2013; Schuetze, Molnar, & Eiden, 2012). However, many of the problems associated with cocaine reflect, in part, the impact of concurrent smoking and drinking during pregnancy and the inadequate parenting these children receive (Lambert & Bauer, 2012). Similarly, harmful effects attributed to smoking during pregnancy may also stem from the fact that pregnant women who smoke are more likely to be less educated and to have a history of psychological problems, including antisocial behavior (D'Onofrio et al., 2013).

Of course, findings such as these don't mean that pregnant women should feel free to light up (or for that matter, to shoot up). Instead, they highlight the difficulties involved in determining the harm associated with a single risk factor (e.g., smoking) when it usually occurs alongside many other risk factors (e.g., inadequate parenting, continued exposure to smoke after birth).

From what we've said so far in this section, you may think that the developing child has little chance of escaping harm. But most babies *are* born in good health. Of course, a good policy for pregnant women is to avoid diseases, drugs, and environmental hazards that are known teratogens. This, coupled with thorough prenatal medical care and adequate nutrition, is the best recipe for normal prenatal development.

Prenatal Diagnosis and Treatment

"I really don't care whether I have a boy or girl, just as long as it's healthy." Legions of parents worldwide have felt this way, but until recently, all they could do was hope for the best. However, advances in technology give parents a much better idea of whether their baby is developing normally.

Genetic Counseling

Often the first step in deciding whether a couple's baby is likely to be at risk is genetic counseling. A counselor asks about family medical history and constructs a family tree for each parent to assess the odds that their child will inherit a disorder. If the family tree suggests that a parent is likely to be a carrier of the disorder, blood tests can determine the parent's genotype. With this information, a genetic counselor then advises prospective parents about their choices. A couple might go ahead and attempt to conceive a child "naturally," use sperm or eggs from donors, or adopt a child.

Prenatal Diagnosis

After a woman is pregnant, how can we know whether prenatal development is progressing normally? Traditionally, obstetricians tracked the progress of prenatal development by feeling the size and position of the fetus through a woman's abdomen. This technique was not very precise and couldn't be done at all until the fetus was large enough to feel. However, several new techniques have revolutionized our ability to monitor prenatal growth and development. *A standard part of prenatal care in the United States is* ultrasound, *in which sound waves are used to generate a picture of the fetus.* In this procedure, a tool about the size of a hair dryer is rubbed over the woman's abdomen, and the image appears on a nearby computer monitor. The pictures generated are hardly portrait quality; they are grainy, and it takes an expert's eye to distinguish what's what. Nevertheless, parents are often thrilled to see their baby and to watch it move.

Ultrasound typically can be used as early as 4 or 5 weeks after conception; prior to this time, the embryo is not large enough to generate an interpretable image. Ultrasound pictures are useful for determining the position of the fetus within the uterus and, at 16 to 20 weeks after conception, its sex. Ultrasound is also helpful in detecting twins or triplets. Finally, ultrasound is used to identify gross physical deformities, such as abnormal growth of the head.

In pregnancies where a genetic disorder is suspected, three other techniques are particularly valuable because they provide a sample of fetal cells that can be analyzed. *In* amniocentesis, *a needle is inserted through the mother's abdomen to obtain a sample of the amniotic fluid that surrounds the fetus.* As you can see in ❱ Figure 2.9, ultrasound is used to guide the needle into the uterus. The fluid contains skin cells that can be grown in a laboratory and then analyzed to determine the genotype of the fetus.

A procedure that can be used much earlier in pregnancy is chorionic villus sampling (CVS) *in which a sample of tissue is obtained from part of the placenta.* ❱ Figure 2.10

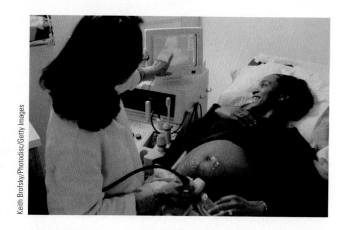
Keith Brofsky/Photodisc/Getty Images

A standard part of prenatal care is ultrasound, in which sound waves are used to generate an image of the fetus that can be used to determine its position in the uterus.

ultrasound

Prenatal diagnostic technique that uses sound waves to generate an image of the fetus.

amniocentesis

Prenatal diagnostic technique that uses a syringe to withdraw a sample of amniotic fluid through the mother's abdomen.

chorionic villus sampling (CVS)

Prenatal diagnostic technique that involves taking a sample of tissue from the placenta.

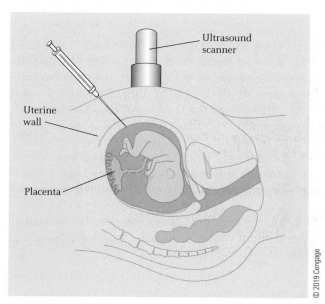

❱ **Figure 2.9**
In amniocentesis, a sample of fetal cells is extracted from the fluid in the amniotic sac.

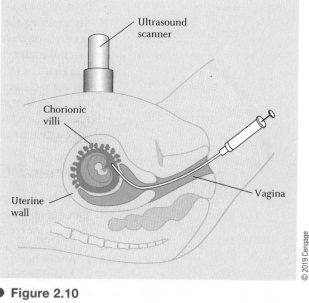

❱ **Figure 2.10**
In chorionic villus sampling, fetal cells are extracted from the placenta.

shows that a small tube—typically inserted through the vagina and into the uterus but sometimes through the abdomen—is used to collect a small plug of cells from the placenta. This procedure can be used within 9 to 12 weeks after conception, much earlier than amniocentesis.

With the samples obtained from either technique, roughly 200 different genetic disorders, including Down syndrome, can be detected. These procedures are virtually free of errors but miscarriages are slightly—1% or 2%—more likely after amniocentesis or chorionic villus sampling (Wilson, 2000). However, a new test is available to help women evaluate the value of these procedures. The placenta releases genetic material that circulates in a pregnant woman's blood stream, genetic material that reflects the fetal genotype. *In non-invasive prenatal testing (NIPT), this genetic material is analyzed in a routine sample of blood from a pregnant woman.* Genetic disorders such as hemophilia and cystic fibrosis can be detected; any findings suggesting genetic disorders are confirmed via amniocentesis or CVS (American College of Obstetricians and Gynecologists, 2015).

non-invasive prenatal testing (NIPT)
A prenatal diagnostic technique that analyzes genetic material released from the placenta that circulates in a pregnant woman's blood stream.

■
Think About It
Imagine that you are 42 years old and pregnant. Would you want to have amniocentesis or chorionic villus sampling to determine the genotype of the fetus? Why or why not?

fetal therapy
Field of medicine concerned with treating prenatal problems before birth.

Fetal Medicine

Ultrasound, amniocentesis, chorionic villus sampling, and noninvasive prenatal testing have made it much easier to determine whether prenatal development is progressing normally. But what happens when it is not? Traditionally, a woman's options have been limited: She could continue the pregnancy or end it. Today, the list of options is expanding. *A new field called fetal therapy is concerned with treating prenatal problems before birth.* Many tools are now available to solve problems that are detected during pregnancy (Rodeck & Whittle, 2009). One approach is to treat disorders medically by administering drugs or hormones to the fetus. For example, in fetal hypothyroidism, the fetal thyroid gland does not produce enough hormones. This can lead to retarded physical and mental development, but the disorder can be treated by injecting the necessary hormones directly into the amniotic cavity, resulting in normal growth.

Another way to correct prenatal problems is fetal surgery (Warner, Altimier, & Crombleholme, 2007). For instance, spina bifida can be corrected with fetal surgery in the seventh or eighth month of pregnancy. Surgeons cut through the mother's abdominal wall to expose the fetus and then cut through the fetal abdominal wall; the spinal cord is repaired, and the fetus is returned to the uterus. However, the procedure is far from foolproof: The best techniques and the ideal times to use them are still unknown (Deprest et al., 2016).

Yet another approach is genetic engineering. A new technique called CRISPR allows scientists to edit hereditary material: genes can be removed, turned off, or replaced off. Consider sickle-cell disease as an example. Recall from page 42 that when a baby inherits the recessive allele for sickle-cell disease from both parents, the child has misshaped red blood cells that can't pass through capillaries. In principle, CRISPR could edit the genome, replacing the recessive alleles from the 11th pair of chromosomes with dominant genes. CRISPR is still experimental. The first clinical trial is underway to determine whether CRISPR can be used to edit cancer-causing genes; many scientific, technical, and ethical answers need to be addressed before gene-editing becomes a routine part of prenatal care (Reardon, 2016). Nevertheless, CRISPR offers hope for prospective parents who fear that their offspring may suffer fatal or debilitating diseases (Hayden, 2016).

Answers to Chloe's Questions. Now you can return to Chloe's questions in the section-opening vignette (page 57) and answer them. If you're not certain, here are the pages in this chapter where the answers appear:

- About her cell phone—page 61
- About her nightly glass of wine—page 60
- About giving birth to a baby with mental retardation—page 44

Recall

1. General risk factors in pregnancy include a woman's nutrition, _____, and her age.

2. _____ are some of the most dangerous teratogens because a pregnant woman is often unaware of their presence.

3. During the period of the zygote, exposure to a teratogen typically results in _____.

4. Three techniques used to determine whether a fetus has a hereditary disorder are amniocentesis, chorionic villus sampling, and _____.

Interpret

- Explain how the impact of a teratogen changes over the course of prenatal development.

Apply

- What would you say to a 45-year-old woman who is eager to become pregnant but is unsure about the risks associated with pregnancy at this age?

Check your answers to the Recall Questions at the end of the chapter.

2.4 Labor and Delivery

LEARNING OBJECTIVES

- What are the different phases of labor and delivery?

- What are "natural" ways of coping with the pain of childbirth? Is childbirth at home safe?

- What adjustments do parents face after a baby's birth?

- What are some complications that can occur during birth?

- What contributes to infant mortality in developed and least developed countries?

Dominique is 6 months pregnant; soon she and her partner will begin childbirth classes at the local hospital. She is relieved that the classes are finally starting because this means that her pregnancy is nearly over. But all the talk she has heard about "breathing exercises" and "coaching" sounds mysterious to her. Dominique wonders what's involved and how the classes will help her during labor and delivery.

As women such as Dominique near the end of pregnancy, they find that sleeping and breathing become more difficult, that they tire more rapidly, and that their legs and feet swell. Women look forward to birth, both to relieve their discomfort and, of course, to meet their baby. In this section, you'll see the different steps involved in birth, review different approaches to childbirth, and look at problems that can arise. Along the way, we'll look at classes like those Dominique will take and the exercises she'll learn.

Stages of Labor

Labor is an appropriate name for childbirth, which is the most intense, prolonged physical effort that humans experience. Labor is usually divided into the three stages shown in ▶ Figure 2.11.

- In stage 1, which may last from 12 to 24 hours for a first birth, the uterus starts to contract. The first contractions are weak and irregular. Gradually, they become stronger and more rhythmic, enlarging the cervix (the opening from the uterus to the vagina) to approximately 10 centimeters.

- In stage 2, the baby passes through the cervix and enters the vagina. The mother helps push the baby along by contracting muscles in her abdomen. *Soon the top of the baby's head appears, an event known as* crowning. Within about an hour, the baby is delivered.

crowning
Appearance of the top of the baby's head during labor.

Labor includes three stages, beginning when the uterus contracts and ending when the placenta is expelled.

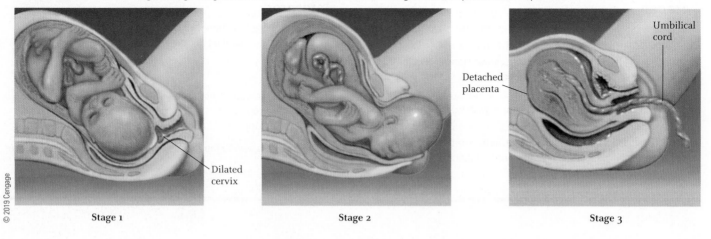

© 2019 Cengage

Stage 1 — Dilated cervix

Stage 2

Stage 3 — Detached placenta, Umbilical cord

- In stage 3, which lasts only minutes, the mother pushes a few more times to expel the placenta (also called, appropriately, the *afterbirth*).

The times given for each of the stages are only approximations; the actual times vary greatly among women. For most women, labor with their second and subsequent children is more rapid; stage 1 may last 4 to 6 hours, and stage 2 may be as brief as 20 minutes.

Approaches to Childbirth

When your authors were born in the 1950s, women in labor were admitted to a hospital and administered a general anesthetic. Fathers waited anxiously in a nearby room for news of the baby. These were standard hospital procedures, and virtually all American babies were born this way.

But childbirth has changed. In the middle of the 20th century, two European physicians—Grantly Dick-Read (1959) and Fernand Lamaze (1958)—criticized the traditional view in which labor and delivery had come to involve elaborate medical procedures that were often unnecessary and often left women afraid of giving birth. This fear led them to be tense, thereby increasing the pain they experienced during labor. These physicians argued for a more "natural" or prepared approach to childbirth, viewing labor and delivery as life events to be celebrated rather than medical procedures to be endured.

Today, many varieties of prepared childbirth are available to pregnant women. However, most share some fundamental beliefs. One is that birth is more likely to be problem-free and rewarding when mothers and fathers understand what's happening during pregnancy, labor, and delivery. Consequently, prepared childbirth means going to classes to learn basic facts about pregnancy and childbirth (like the material presented in this chapter).

A second common element is that natural methods of dealing with pain are emphasized over medical procedures, which involve possible side effects and complications. For example, the most common procedure in the United States is epidural analgesia, in which drugs are injected into the space below the spinal cord. These reduce the pain of childbirth but sometimes cause women to experience headaches or decreased blood pressure (American College of Obstetricians and Gynecologists, 2011b). One key to reducing birth pain without drugs is relaxation. Because pain often feels greater when a person is tense, pregnant women learn to relax during labor by deep breathing or by visualizing a reassuring, pleasant scene or experience. Whenever they begin to experience pain during labor, they use these methods to relax.

During childbirth preparation classes, pregnant women learn exercises that help them relax and reduce the pain associated with childbirth.

James Marshall/The Image Works

A third common element of prepared childbirth is the involvement of a supportive adult, who may be the father-to-be, a relative, a close friend, or a trained birth assistant (known as a doula). These people provide emotional support, act as advocates (communicating a woman's wishes to health care personnel), and help a woman use techniques for managing pain. When pregnant women are supported in this manner, their labor tends to be shorter, they use less medication, and they report greater satisfaction with childbirth (Hodnett. et al., 2012).

Another element of the trend to natural childbirth is the idea that birth need not take place in a hospital. Virtually all babies in the United States are born in hospitals, with only 1% born at home (Martin et al., 2013). For Americans accustomed to hospital delivery, home delivery can seem like a risky proposition and some medical professionals remain skeptical (Declercq, 2012). However, many women are more relaxed during labor at home, and they enjoy the greater control they have over labor and birth in a home delivery. That said, women should consider birth at home only if they are healthy, their pregnancy has been problem-free, labor and delivery are expected to be problem-free, a trained healthcare professional is present to assist, and comprehensive medical care is readily available should the need arise (Wax, Pinette, & Cartin, 2010).

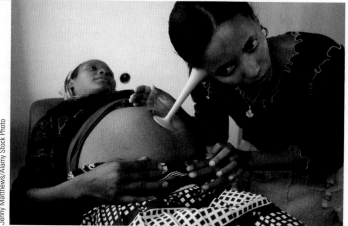

In many countries around the world, a midwife delivers the baby.

Adjusting to Parenthood

For parents, the time immediately after a trouble-free birth is full of excitement, pride, and joy—the much-anticipated baby is finally here! But it is also a time of adjustments for parents. A woman experiences many physical changes after birth. Her breasts begin to produce milk, and her uterus gradually becomes smaller, returning to its normal size in five or six weeks. And levels of female hormones (e.g., estrogen) drop.

Parents must also adjust psychologically. They reorganize old routines, particularly for first-born children, to fit the young baby's sleep–wake cycle. In the process, fathers sometimes feel left out when mothers devote most of their attention to the baby.

Becoming a parent can be a huge adjustment, so it's not surprising that roughly half of all new mothers find that their initial excitement gives way to irritation, resentment, and crying spells—the so-called baby blues. These feelings usually last a week or two and probably reflect both the stress of caring for a new baby and the physiological changes that take place as a woman's body returns to a nonpregnant state (Brockington, 1996).

For 10% to 15% of new mothers, however, irritability continues for months and is often accompanied by feelings of low self-worth, disturbed sleep, poor appetite, and apathy—a condition known as postpartum depression. Postpartum depression does not strike randomly. Biology contributes: Change in hormonal levels following birth place some women at risk for postpartum depression (O'Hara & McCabe, 2013). Experience also contributes: Women are more likely to experience postpartum depression when they are single, were depressed before pregnancy, are coping with other life stresses (e.g., dealing with the death of a loved one or moving to a new residence), did not plan to become pregnant, or lack other adults (e.g., the father) to support their adjustment to motherhood (Edwards et al., 2012; O'Hara, 2009).

Women who are lethargic and emotionless do not mother warmly and enthusiastically. They don't touch and cuddle their new babies much or talk to them. And depressed moms are less effective in the common but essential tasks of feeding and sleep routines (Field, 2010). When postpartum depression persists over years, children's development is affected (Goodman et al., 2011). In the Spotlight on Research feature, for example, you'll see how maternal depression can lead children to have behavioral problems.

Findings like those in the Spotlight on Research feature show that postpartum depression should not be taken lightly: If a mother's depression doesn't lift after a few weeks, she should seek help. Home visits by trained health care professionals can be valuable

Links Between Maternal Depression and Children's Behavior Problems

Who were the investigators, and what was the aim of the study? When mothers are depressed, they don't parent effectively. However, this might not be due to depression per se because the same factors that put women at risk for experiencing postpartum depression—for example, being single, lacking social support, and experiencing stress—may contribute to their ineffective parenting. Edward Barker and his colleagues (Barker et al., 2012) hoped to better understand how maternal depression affects children's development.

How did the investigators measure the topic of interest? Barker and colleagues were interested in three variables: maternal depression, maternal risk factors associated with depression that might impair children's development, and children's behavioral problems. They measured the first two with questionnaires: When children were 1½ years old, moms completed a depression questionnaire; at various points between birth and their child's second birthday, moms completed questionnaires measuring exposure to risk factors such as being single, being exposed to stressful events such as cruelty from a partner, and having an inadequate support network. When children were 7 or 8 years old, their behavioral problems were diagnosed by experienced clinicians from teachers' and parents' reports of children's behavior.

Who were the participants in the study? The sample was drawn from the Avon Longitudinal Study of Parents and Children, a project conducted in England that investigates children's health and development. Data on all three variables were available for 7,429 mothers and children.

What was the design of the study? The study was correlational because the investigators were interested in the relation that existed naturally among depression, risk factors, and children's problem behaviors. The study was longitudinal because children and parents were tested multiple times (and are still being tested as the study is ongoing).

Were there ethical concerns with the study? No. The measures were ones commonly used with parents and children; they posed no known risks. The investigators obtained permission from the parents and their children to participate.

What were the results? Using the mothers' replies to the depression questionnaire, Barker and his colleagues distinguished moms who had been depressed when their child was 1½ years old from moms who were not depressed. Then they compared rates of behavioral problems in children of the two groups of moms; those results are shown in ▶ Figure 2.12. For each of the five disorders, 7- and 8-year-olds were more likely to have behavioral problems if their mom had been depressed; overall, they were 2.56 times more likely to have problems. Next, Barker and his colleagues confirmed that, as expected, risk rates were greater for depressed moms. For example, depressed moms were five times more likely to have experienced cruelty from a partner and four times more likely to have inadequate support. Nevertheless, when these differences in exposure to risk were equated statistically, children with depressed moms were still 1.92 times more likely to have behavioral problems.

What did the investigators conclude? The depression that some women experience following childbirth influences children in two ways. One is that depression symptoms per se are harmful for children: Depressed moms are less able to parent effectively, and this may lead to behavioral problems. A second path is that the same factors that put moms

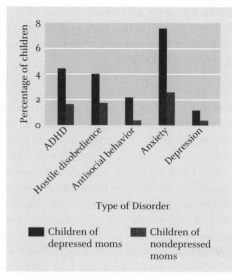

▶ **Figure 2.12**
When mothers are depressed, their children are at risk for ADHD, disobedient and antisocial behavior, anxiety, and depression.

at risk for depression (e.g., inadequate support) can impair a child's development, perhaps because they lead moms to parent less effectively.

What converging evidence would strengthen these conclusions? These findings are based largely on mothers' reports of their depression, their risk factors, and their children's behavior. It would be valuable to have independent estimates of these variables (e.g., observation of children's antisocial behavior that contributes to the diagnosis of conduct disorder). In addition, nearly one-third of the mothers dropped out of the study and those dropping out were more likely to have been exposed to risk. The present findings would be strengthened if they were replicated in a sample that was more stable over time.

(O'Hara & McCabe, 2013). During these visits, the visitors show mom better ways to cope with the many changes that accompany her new baby. They also provide emotional support by being a caring, sensitive listener, and they can refer the mother to other community resources if needed. Finally, one simple way to reduce the risk of postpartum depression is worth mentioning—breast-feeding. Moms who breast-feed are less likely to become depressed, perhaps because breast-feeding releases hormones that act as antidepressants (Gagliardi, 2005).

Birth Complications

Women who are healthy when they become pregnant usually have a normal pregnancy, labor, and delivery. When women are not healthy or don't receive adequate prenatal care, problems can surface during labor and delivery. (Of course, even healthy women can have problems, but not as often.) The more common birth complications are listed in ▶ Table 2.6.

Some of these complications, such as a prolapsed umbilical cord, are dangerous because they disrupt the flow of blood through the umbilical cord. *If this flow of blood is disrupted, then infants do not receive adequate oxygen, a condition known as* hypoxia. Hypoxia sometimes occurs during labor and delivery because the umbilical cord is pinched or squeezed shut, cutting off the flow of blood. Hypoxia is serious because it can lead to mental retardation or death (Hogan et al., 2006).

To guard against hypoxia, fetal heart rate is monitored during labor by ultrasound or with a tiny electrode that is passed through the vagina and attached to the scalp of the fetus. An abrupt change in heart rate can be a sign that the fetus is not receiving enough oxygen. If the heart rate does change suddenly, a health care professional will try to confirm that the fetus is in distress, perhaps by measuring fetal heart rate with a stethoscope on the mother's abdomen.

When a fetus is in distress or when the fetus is in an irregular position or is too large to pass through the birth canal, a physician may decide to remove it from the mother's uterus surgically (American College of Obstetricians and Gynecologists, 2011a). *In a* cesarean section (*or* C-section), *an incision is made in the abdomen to remove the baby from the uterus.* A C-section is riskier than a vaginal delivery for mothers because of increased bleeding and greater danger of infection. A C-section poses little risk for babies, although they are often lethargic briefly from the anesthesia the mother receives before the operation. And mother–infant interactions are much the same for babies delivered vaginally or by planned or unplanned C-sections (Durik, Hyde, & Clark, 2000).

Birth complications are hazardous not just for a newborn's health; they have long-term effects, too. When babies experience many birth complications, they are at risk for becoming aggressive or violent and for developing schizophrenia (de Haan et al., 2006; Fazel et al., 2012). This is particularly true for newborns with birth complications who later experience family adversity, such as living in poverty (Arseneault et al., 2002). These outcomes underscore the importance of excellent health care for the mother through pregnancy and labor and the need for a supportive environment throughout childhood.

Problems also arise when babies are born too early or too small. Normally, a baby spends about 38 weeks developing before being born. *Babies born before the 36th week are called* preterm *or* premature. In the first year or so, premature infants often lag behind full-term infants in many facets of development. However, by 2 or 3 years of age, such differences have vanished, and most premature infants develop normally (Greenberg & Crnic, 1988).

hypoxia
A birth complication in which umbilical blood flow is disrupted and the infant does not receive adequate oxygen.

cesarean section (C-section)
Surgical removal of an infant from the uterus through an incision made in the mother's abdomen.

Think About It

A friend of yours has just given birth six weeks prematurely. The baby is average size for a baby born prematurely and seems to be faring well, but your friend is concerned nonetheless. What would you say to reassure your friend?

preterm or premature
Babies born before the 36th week after conception.

Table 2.6	
Common Birth Complications	
COMPLICATION	**FEATURES**
Cephalopelvic disproportion	The infant's head is larger than the pelvis, making it impossible for the baby to pass through the birth canal.
Irregular position	In shoulder presentation, the baby is lying crosswise in the uterus and the shoulder appears first; in breech presentation, the buttocks appear first.
Preeclampsia	A pregnant woman has high blood pressure, protein in her urine, and swelling in her extremities (due to fluid retention).
Prolapsed umbilical cord	The umbilical cord precedes the baby through the birth canal and is squeezed shut, cutting off oxygen to the baby.

Prospects are usually not as bright for babies who are "small for date." These infants are most often born to women who smoke or drink alcohol frequently during pregnancy or who do not eat enough nutritious food (Chomitz, Cheung, & Lieberman, 1995). *Newborns who weigh 2,500 grams (5.5 pounds) or less are said to have* low birth weight, *newborns weighing less than 1,500 grams (3.3 pounds) are said to have* very low birth weight, *and those weighing less than 1,000 grams (2.2 pounds) are said to have* extremely low birth weight.

Babies with very or extremely low birth weight do not fare well. Many do not survive, and those who live often lag behind in the development of intellectual and motor skills (Kavsek & Bornstein, 2010). Newborns who weigh more than 1,500 grams have better prospects if they receive appropriate care. These babies are placed in special sealed beds where temperature and air quality are regulated carefully. These beds isolate infants, depriving them of environmental stimulation. Consequently, they often receive auditory stimulation, such as a recording of soothing music or their mother's voice, or visual stimulation from a mobile placed over the bed. Infants also receive tactile stimulation—they are "massaged" several times daily. These forms of stimulation foster physical and cognitive development in small-for-date babies (Field, Diego, & Hernandez-Reif, 2010).

This special care should continue when infants leave the hospital to go home. Consequently, intervention programs for small-for-date babies typically include training programs designed for parents of infants and young children. In these programs, parents learn to respond appropriately to their child's behaviors. For example, they are taught the signs that a baby is in distress, overstimulated, or ready to interact. Parents also learn how to use games and activities to foster their child's development. In addition, children are enrolled in high-quality child care centers where the curriculum is coordinated with parent training. This sensitive care promotes development in low birth weight babies; for example, sometimes they catch up to full-term infants in terms of cognitive development (Hill, Brooks-Gunn, & Waldfogel, 2003).

Small-for-date babies often survive, but their cognitive and motor development usually is delayed.

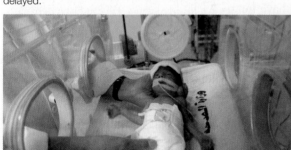

Abid Katib/Getty Images News/Getty Images

Long-term positive outcomes for these infants depend critically on providing a supportive and stimulating home environment. Unfortunately, not all at-risk babies have these optimal experiences. Many experience stress or disorder in their family lives. In these cases, development is usually affected (Poehlmann et al., 2011).

The importance of a supportive environment for low birth weight babies is underscored by the results of a 30-year longitudinal study by Werner (1989, 1995) covering all children born on the Hawaiian island of Kauai in 1955. When low birth weight children grew up in stable homes—defined as having two mentally healthy parents throughout childhood—they were indistinguishable from children born without birth complications. However, when low birth weight children experienced an unstable family environment—defined as including divorce, parental alcoholism, or parental mental illness—they lagged behind their peers in intellectual and social development.

Thus, when both biological and sociocultural forces are harmful—low birth weight *plus* inadequate medical care or family stress—the prognosis for babies is grim. The message to parents of low birth weight newborns is clear: Do not despair because excellent caregiving can compensate for all but the most severe birth problems (Werner, 1994; Werner & Smith, 1992).

Infant Mortality

If you were the proud parent of a newborn and a citizen of Afghanistan, the odds are 1 in 6 that your baby would die before his or her first birthday—worldwide, Afghanistan has the highest infant mortality *rate, defined as the percentage of infants who die before their first birthday.* In contrast, if you were a parent and a citizen of the Czech Republic, Iceland, Finland, or Japan, the odds are less than 1 in 300 that your baby would die within a year because these countries have some of the lowest infant mortality rates.

The graphs in ▶ Figure 2.13 put these numbers in a global context, depicting infant mortality rates for 15 developed nations as well as for 15 least developed countries. Not surprisingly, risks to infants are far greater—about 20 times, on average—in the least developed nations compared with developed nations (Central Intelligence Agency, 2013). In fact, the differences are so great that the graphs for the two groups of nations must be drawn on different scales.

If you're an American, you may be surprised to see that the United States ranks near the bottom of the list of developed nations. The difference is small, but if the United States were to reduce its infant mortality rate to the 4% that's common in European countries, this would mean that 8,000 American babies who now die annually before their first birthday would live.

What explains these differences in infant mortality rates? The United States has more babies with low birth weight than virtually all other developed countries, and we've already seen that low birth weight places an infant at risk. Low birth weight can usually be prevented when a pregnant woman gets regular prenatal care, but many pregnant women in the United States receive inadequate or no prenatal care because they have no health insurance (Cohen, Martinez, & Ward, 2010). Virtually all countries that rank ahead of the United States provide complete prenatal care at little or no cost. Many of these countries also provide for paid leaves of absence for pregnant women (OECD, 2006).

In least developed countries, inadequate prenatal care is common and mothers often have inadequate nutrition. After birth, infants in these countries face the twin challenges of receiving adequate nutrition and avoiding disease. However, with improved prenatal care and improved health care and nutrition for infants, the global infant mortality has been cut in half since 1990 (UNICEF, 2007).

▶ **Figure 2.13**

The infant mortality rate in least developed countries is much greater than in developed countries.

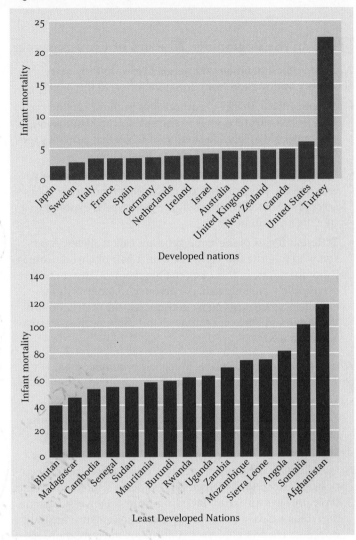

SOURCE: Data from Central Intelligence Agency 2013.

TEST YOURSELF 2.4

Recall

1. In the third stage of labor, the _____ is delivered.
2. Prepared childbirth includes communicating basic facts of labor and delivery, minimizing the use of medication to relieve pain, and _____.
3. Home delivery is safe when a pregnant woman is healthy, has had a problem-free pregnancy, and expects to have a problem-free delivery and when _____.
4. When the supply of oxygen to the fetus is disrupted because the umbilical cord is squeezed shut, _____ results.

Interpret

- Explain why some at-risk newborns develop normally but others do not.

Apply

- Lynn is pregnant with her first child and would like to give birth at home. Her husband is against the idea, claiming that it's much too risky. What advice would you give them?

Check your answers to the Recall Questions at the end of the chapter.

SUMMARY

2.1 In the Beginning: 23 Pairs of Chromosomes

What are chromosomes and genes? How do they carry hereditary information from one generation to the next?

- At conception, the 23 chromosomes in the sperm merge with the 23 chromosomes in the egg. Each chromosome is one molecule of DNA; a section of DNA that provides specific biochemical instructions is called a gene.

- All of a person's genes make up a genotype; the phenotype refers to the physical, behavioral, and psychological characteristics that develop when the genotype is exposed to a specific environment.

- Different forms of the same gene are called alleles. A person who inherits the same allele on a pair of chromosomes is homozygous; in this case, the biochemical instructions on the allele are followed. A person who inherits different alleles is heterozygous; in this case, the instructions of the dominant allele are followed and those of the recessive allele ignored.

What are common problems involving chromosomes, and what are their consequences?

- Most inherited disorders are carried by recessive alleles. Examples include sickle-cell disease and phenylketonuria, in which toxins accumulate and cause mental retardation.

- Sometimes fertilized eggs do not have 46 chromosomes. Usually they are aborted spontaneously soon after conception. An exception is Down syndrome, in which individuals typically have an extra 21st chromosome. Down syndrome individuals have a distinctive appearance and are mentally retarded. Disorders of the sex chromosomes are more common because these chromosomes contain less genetic material than do autosomes.

How is children's heredity influenced by the environment in which they grow up?

- Behavioral and psychological phenotypes that reflect an underlying continuum (such as intelligence) often involve polygenic inheritance. In polygenic inheritance, the phenotype reflects the combined activity of many distinct genes. Traditionally, polygenic inheritance has been examined by studying twins and adopted children and, more recently, by identifying DNA markers.

- The impact of heredity on a child's development depends on the environment in which the genetic instructions are carried out, and these heredity–environment interactions occur throughout a child's life. A child's genotype can affect the kinds of experiences the child has; children and adolescents often actively seek environments related to their genetic makeup. Family environments affect siblings differently (nonshared environmental influence); parents provide a unique environment for each child in the family.

2.2 From Conception to Birth

What happens to a fertilized egg in the first two weeks after conception?

- The first period of prenatal development lasts two weeks. It begins when the egg is fertilized by the sperm in the fallopian tube and ends when the fertilized egg has implanted itself in the wall of the uterus. By the end of this period, cells have begun to differentiate.

When do body structures and internal organs emerge in prenatal development?

- The second period of prenatal development begins two weeks after conception and lasts until the end of the eighth week. This is a period of rapid growth in which most major body structures are created. Growth in this period is cephalocaudal (the head develops first) and proximodistal (parts near the center of the body develop first).

When do body systems begin to function well enough to support life?

- The third period of prenatal development begins nine weeks after conception and lasts until birth. The highlights of this period are a remarkable increase in the size of the fetus and changes in body systems that are necessary for life. By 7 months, most body systems function well enough to support life.

2.3 Influences on Prenatal Development

How is prenatal development influenced by a pregnant woman's age, her nutrition, and the stress she experiences while pregnant?

- The woman's age can affect prenatal development. Teenagers often have problem pregnancies, mainly because they rarely receive adequate prenatal care. After age 35, pregnant women are more likely to have a miscarriage or to give birth to a child with mental retardation. Prenatal development can also be harmed if a pregnant mother has inadequate nutrition or experiences considerable stress.

How do diseases, drugs, and environmental hazards sometimes affect prenatal development?

- Teratogens are agents that can cause abnormal prenatal development. Many drugs that adults take are teratogens. For most drugs, scientists have not established amounts that can be consumed safely.

- Several diseases are teratogens. Only by avoiding these diseases entirely can a pregnant woman escape their harmful consequences.
- Environmental teratogens are particularly dangerous because a pregnant woman may not know that these substances are present in the environment.

What general principles affect the ways that prenatal development can be harmed?

- The impact of teratogens depends on the genotype of the organism, the period of prenatal development when the organism is exposed to the teratogen, and the amount of exposure. Sometimes the effect of a teratogen is not evident until later in life.

How can prenatal development be monitored? Can abnormal prenatal development be corrected?

- Many techniques are used to track the progress of prenatal development. A common component of prenatal care is ultrasound, which uses sound waves to generate a picture of the fetus. This picture can be used to determine the position of the fetus; its sex; and gross physical deformities, if any.
- When genetic disorders are suspected, amniocentesis, chorionic villus sampling, and noninvasive prenatal testing are used to determine the genotype of the fetus.
- Fetal therapy is a new field in which problems of prenatal development are corrected medically via surgery or genetic engineering.

2.4 Labor and Delivery

What are the different phases of labor and delivery?

- Labor consists of three stages. In stage 1, the muscles of the uterus contract. The contractions, which are weak at first and gradually become stronger, cause the cervix to enlarge. In stage 2, the baby moves through the birth canal. In stage 3, the placenta is delivered.

What are "natural" ways of coping with the pain of childbirth? Is childbirth at home safe?

- Natural or prepared childbirth is based on the assumption that parents should understand what takes place during pregnancy and birth. In prepared childbirth, women learn to cope with pain through relaxation, imagery, and the help of a supportive coach.
- Most American babies are born in hospitals, but home delivery can be safe when the mother is healthy, when pregnancy and birth are trouble-free, and when a health care professional is present to deliver the baby.

What adjustments do parents face after a baby's birth?

- Following the birth of a child, a woman's body undergoes several changes: her breasts fill with milk, her uterus becomes smaller, and hormone levels drop. Both parents also adjust psychologically, and sometimes fathers feel left out. After giving birth, some women experience postpartum depression: they are irritable, have poor appetite and disturbed sleep, and are apathetic.

What are some complications that can occur during birth?

- During labor and delivery, the flow of blood to the fetus can be disrupted because the umbilical cord is squeezed shut. This causes hypoxia, a lack of oxygen to the fetus. Some babies are born prematurely, and others are "small for date." Premature babies develop more slowly at first but catch up by 2 or 3 years of age. Small-for-date babies often do not fare well, particularly when they weigh less than 1,500 grams at birth and their environment is stressful.

What contributes to infant mortality in developed and least developed countries?

- Infant mortality is relatively high in many countries around the world, primarily because of inadequate care before birth and disease and inadequate nutrition after birth.

Test Yourself: Recall Answers

2.1 1. autosomes 2. Polygenic inheritance 3. Down syndrome 4. the fertilized egg is aborted spontaneously 5. different from each other 2.2 1. at two weeks after conception (when the zygote is completely implanted in the wall of the uterus) 2. embryo 3. Between 22 and 28 weeks 4. learning and remembering 2.3 1. prolonged stress 2. Environmental hazards 3. spontaneous abortion of the fertilized egg 4. non-invasive prenatal testing 2.4 1. placenta 2. the presence of a supportive adult 3. trained health care professionals are present to deliver the baby 4. Hypoxia

Key Terms

chromosomes (40)
autosomes (40)
sex chromosomes (40)
deoxyribonucleic acid (DNA) (41)
gene (41)
genotype (41)
phenotype (41)
alleles (41)
homozygous (41)
heterozygous (41)
dominant (42)
recessive (42)
incomplete dominance (42)
sickle-cell trait (42)
phenylketonuria (PKU) (43)
Huntington's disease (44)
behavioral genetics (45)
polygenic inheritance (45)
monozygotic twins (46)
dizygotic twins (46)
heritability coefficient (48)

niche-picking (49)
nonshared environmental influences (50)
prenatal development (51)
zygote (52)
in vitro fertilization (52)
preimplantation genetic screening
  (PGS) (52)
eugenics (52)
implantation (53)
germ disc (53)
placenta (53)
embryo (53)
ectoderm (53)
mesoderm (53)
endoderm (53)
amnion (54)
amniotic fluid (54)
umbilical cord (54)
cephalocaudal principle (54)
proximodistal principle (54)
period of the fetus (55)

cerebral cortex (55)
vernix (55)
age of viability (56)
spina bifida (57)
stress (58)
teratogen (59)
fetal alcohol spectrum disorder
  (FASD) (60)
ultrasound (65)
amniocentesis (65)
chorionic villus sampling (CVS) (65)
non-invasive prenatal testing (NIPT) (66)
fetal therapy (66)
crowning (67)
hypoxia (71)
cesarean section (C-section) (71)
preterm (premature) (71)
low birth weight (72)
very low birth weight (72)
extremely low birth weight (72)
infant mortality (72)

Tools for Exploring the W...

Physical, Perceptual, and Motor Development

Think about what you were like 2 years ago. Whatever you were doing, you probably look, act, think, and feel in much the same way today as you did then. Two years in an adult's life usually doesn't result in profound changes, but two years makes a big difference early in life. The changes that occur in the first few years after birth are incredible. In less than two years, an infant is transformed from a seemingly helpless newborn into a talking, walking, havoc-wreaking toddler. No changes at any other point in the life span come close to the drama and excitement of these early years.

In this chapter, our tour of these two years begins with the newborn and then moves to physical growth—changes in the body and the brain. The third section of the chapter examines motor skills. You'll discover how babies learn to walk and how they learn to use their hands to hold and then manipulate objects. In the fourth section, we'll examine changes in infants' sensory abilities that allow them to comprehend their world.

As children begin to explore their world and learn more about it, they also learn more about themselves. They learn to recognize themselves and begin to understand more about their thoughts and others' thoughts. We'll explore these changes in the last section of the chapter.

...lp newborns interact with the world?

...rmine whether a baby is healthy and
...e outside the uterus?

- What behavioral states are common among newborns?
- What are the different features of temperament? Do they change as children grow?

Lisa and Steve, proud but exhausted parents, are astonished at how their lives revolve around 10-day-old Dan's eating and sleeping. Lisa feels as if she is feeding Dan around the clock. When Dan naps, Lisa thinks of many things she should be doing but usually naps herself because she is so tired. Steve wonders when Dan will start sleeping through the night so that he and Lisa can get a good night's sleep.

The newborn baby who thrills parents like Lisa and Steve is actually rather homely. Newborns arrive covered with blood and vernix, a white-colored "wax" that protected the skin during the many months of prenatal development. In addition, the baby's head is temporarily distorted from its journey through the birth canal, and the newborn has a beer belly and is bowlegged.

What can newborns like Dan do? We'll answer that question in this section, and as we do, you'll learn when Lisa and Steve can expect to get a full night's sleep again.

The Newborn's Reflexes

reflexes
Unlearned responses triggered by specific stimulation.

Most newborns are well prepared to begin interacting with their world; they are endowed with a rich set of reflexes, *unlearned responses that are triggered by a specific form of stimulation*. Table 3.1 shows the variety of reflexes commonly found in newborn babies.

Some reflexes pave the way for newborns to get the nutrients they need to grow: The rooting and sucking reflexes ensure that the newborn is prepared to begin a new diet of life-sustaining milk. Other reflexes protect the newborn from danger in the environment. The eye blink, for example, helps newborns avoid unpleasant stimulation.

Still other reflexes are the foundation for larger, voluntary patterns of motor activity. For example, the stepping reflex motions look like precursors to walking, so it's not surprising that babies who practice the stepping reflex often learn to walk earlier than those who don't practice (Zelazo, 1993).

Reflexes are also important because they can help determine whether the newborn's nervous system is working properly. For example, infants with damage to the sciatic nerve, which is found in the spinal cord, do not show the withdrawal reflex. Infants who have problems with the lower part of the spine do not show the Babinski reflex. If these or other reflexes are weak or missing altogether, a thorough physical and behavioral assessment is necessary. Similarly, many of these reflexes normally vanish during infancy; if they linger, this, too, indicates the need for a thorough physical examination.

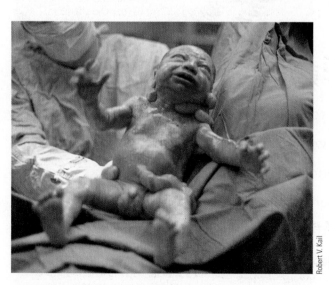

Robert V. Kail

This newborn baby (Ben Kail at 20 seconds old) is covered with vernix and is bow-legged; his head is distorted from the journey down the birth canal.

Assessing the Newborn

Imagine that a mother has just asked you if her newborn baby is healthy. How would you decide? You would probably check to see whether the baby seems to be breathing and if the baby's heart seems to be beating.

Table 3.1

Some Major Reflexes Found in Newborns

NAME	RESPONSE	AGE WHEN REFLEX DISAPPEARS	SIGNIFICANCE
Babinski	A baby's toes fan out when the sole of the foot is stroked from heel to toe	8–12 months	Perhaps a remnant of evolution
Blink	A baby's eyes close in response to bright light or loud noise	Permanent	Protects the eyes
Moro	A baby throws its arms out and then inward (as if embracing) in response to loud noise or when its head falls	6 months	May help a baby cling to its mother
Palmar	A baby grasps an object placed in the palm of its hand	3–4 months	Precursor to voluntary walking
Rooting	When a baby's cheek is stroked, it turns its head toward the stroking and opens its mouth	3–4 weeks (replaced with voluntary head turning)	Helps a baby find the nipple
Stepping	A baby who is held upright by an adult and is then moved forward begins to step rhythmically	2–3 months	Precursor to voluntary walking
Sucking	A baby sucks when an object is placed in its mouth	4 months (replaced with voluntary sucking)	Permits feeding

In fact, breathing and heartbeat are two vital signs included in the Apgar score, which provides a quick assessment of the newborn's status by focusing on the body systems needed to sustain life. The other vital signs are muscle tone, presence of reflexes such as coughing, and skin tone. Each of the five vital signs receives a score of 0, 1, or 2, where 2 is optimal. For example, a newborn whose muscles are completely limp receives a 0; a baby who moves arms and legs vigorously receives a 2. The five scores are summed, with a total score of 7 or more indicating that a baby is in good physical condition. A score of 4 to 6 means that a newborn needs special attention and care. A score of 3 or less signals a life-threatening situation requiring emergency medical care (Apgar, 1953).

For a comprehensive evaluation of the newborn's well-being, pediatricians and other child development specialists sometimes administer the Neonatal Behavioral Assessment Scale, or NBAS (Brazelton & Nugent, 1995). The NBAS includes 28 behavioral items (e.g., the baby's response to light, sound, and touch) along with 18 items that test reflexes such as those we just described. The baby's performance is used to evaluate the functioning of these four systems:

- *Autonomic:* the baby's ability to control body functions such as breathing and temperature regulation
- *Motor:* the baby's ability to control body movements and activity level
- *State:* the baby's ability to maintain a state (e.g., staying alert or staying asleep)
- *Social:* the baby's ability to interact with people

The NBAS is based on the view that newborns are remarkably competent individuals who are well prepared to interact with the environment. Reflecting this view, examiners go to great lengths to bring out a baby's best performance by making a baby feel comfortable and secure during testing. And if an infant does not at first succeed on an item, the examiner assists (Alberts, 2005).

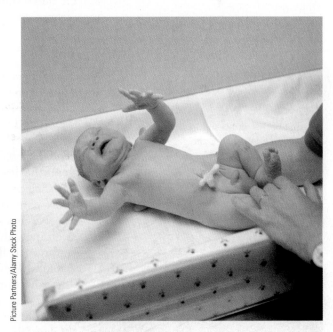

Picture Partners/Alamy Stock Photo

Newborns exhibit the Moro reflex, opening their arms and then bringing them inward in response to loud noise or when their head falls.

Think About It

Newborns seem to be extremely well prepared to begin to interact with their environment. Which of the theories described in Chapter 1 predict such preparedness? Which do not?

Besides the NBAS being useful to clinicians in evaluating the well-being of individual babies, researchers also have found it a valuable tool. Sometimes performance on the NBAS is used as a dependent variable. For example, infants whose mothers were depressed during pregnancy have lower scores on the NBAS (e.g., Suri et al., 2014). Researchers also use scores on the NBAS to predict later development; for example, in one study infants with greater scores on the NBAS were, as 10-year-olds, more empathic and less prone to accidents (Feldman, 2015).

The Newborn's States

Newborns spend most of each day alternating between four different states (St. James-Roberts & Plewis, 1996; Wolff, 1987):

- Alert inactivity—*The baby is calm with eyes open and attentive; the baby seems to be deliberately inspecting the environment.*
- Waking activity—*The baby's eyes are open, but they seem unfocused; the arms or legs move in bursts of uncoordinated motion.*
- Crying—*The baby cries vigorously, usually accompanied by agitated but uncoordinated motion.*
- Sleeping—*The baby alternates between being still and breathing regularly to moving gently and breathing irregularly; eyes are closed throughout.*

Of these states, crying and sleeping have captured the attention of parents and researchers alike.

Crying

Newborns spend two to three hours each day crying or on the verge of crying. If you've not spent much time around newborns, you might think that all crying is pretty much alike. In fact, scientists and parents can identify three distinctive types of cries (Snow, 1998). *A* basic cry *starts softly and gradually becomes more intense; it usually occurs when a baby is hungry or tired. A* mad cry *is a more intense version of a basic cry; a* pain cry *begins with a sudden, long burst of crying followed by a long pause and gasping.* Thus, crying represents the newborn's first venture into interpersonal communication. By crying, babies tell their parents that they are hungry or tired, angry or hurt. By responding to these cries, parents are encouraging their newborn's efforts to communicate.

Parents are naturally concerned when their baby cries, and if they can't quiet a crying baby, their concern mounts and can easily give way to frustration and annoyance. It's no surprise then that parents develop little tricks for soothing their babies. Many Western parents lift a baby to the shoulder and walk or gently rock the baby. Sometimes they also sing lullabies, pat the baby's back, or give the baby a pacifier. Yet another method is to put a newborn in a car seat and go for a drive; this technique was used once, as a last resort, at 2 a.m. with Ben Kail when he was 10 days old. After about the 12th time around the block, he finally stopped crying and fell asleep.

Another useful technique is swaddling, in which an infant is wrapped tightly in a blanket. Swaddling is used in many cultures around the world, including Turkey and Peru, as well as by Native Americans. Swaddling provides warmth and tactile stimulation that usually works well to soothe a baby (Delaney, 2000).

Parents are sometimes reluctant to respond to their crying infant for fear of producing a baby who cries constantly. Yet they hear their baby's cry as a call for help that they shouldn't ignore. What to do? Should parents respond? Yes, until their baby is about 3 months old. However, with older babies, parents should consider why their infant is crying and the intensity of the crying (St. James-Roberts, 2007). When an older baby wakes during the night and cries quietly, a parent should wait before responding, giving the baby a chance to calm herself. Of course, if parents hear a loud noise from an infant's bedroom followed by a mad cry, they should respond

---

alert inactivity

State in which a baby is calm with eyes open and attentive; the baby seems to be deliberately inspecting the environment.

waking activity

State in which a baby's eyes are open but seem unfocused while the arms or legs move in bursts of uncoordinated motion.

crying

State in which a baby cries vigorously, usually accompanied by agitated but uncoordinated movement.

sleeping

State in which a baby alternates between being still and breathing regularly to moving gently and breathing irregularly; the eyes are closed throughout.

basic cry

Cry that starts softly and gradually becomes more intense; often heard when babies are hungry or tired.

mad cry

More intense version of a basic cry.

pain cry

Cry that begins with a sudden long burst, followed by a long pause and gasping.

Eye Ubiquitous/Newscom

In many countries worldwide, infants are wrapped tightly in blankets as a way to keep them calm.

immediately. Parents need to remember that crying is the newborn's first attempt to communicate. They need to decide what the infant is trying to tell them and whether that warrants a quick response or whether they should let the baby soothe herself.

Sleeping

Crying may get parents' attention, but sleep is what newborns do more than anything else. They sleep 16 to 18 hours daily. The problem for tired parents is that newborns sleep in naps taken around the clock. Newborns typically go through a cycle of wakefulness and sleep about every four hours. That is, they will be awake for about an hour, sleep for three hours, and then start the cycle anew. During the hour when newborns are awake, they regularly move between the different waking states several times. Cycles of alert inactivity, waking activity, and crying are common.

As babies grow older, the sleep–wake cycle gradually begins to correspond to the day–night cycle (St. James-Roberts & Plewis, 1996). By 3 or 4 months, many babies sleep for 5 to 6 hours straight, and by 6 months, many are sleeping for 10 to 12 hours at night, a major milestone for bleary-eyed parents such as Lisa and Steve.

By 6 months, most North American infants are sleeping in a crib in their own room. Although this practice seems "natural" to North American parents, in much of the rest of the world (and for much of human history), children sleep with their parents throughout infancy and the preschool years. Such parent–child "co-sleeping" is more common in Africa and in Asia than in Europe and North America—a regional split that coincides approximately with cultures where people are seen as interdependent (Africa, Asia) versus cultures that see people as independent and self-reliant (Mileva-Seitz et al., 2016; Tan, 2009).

How does co-sleeping work? Infants may sleep in a cradle placed next to their parents' bed or in a basket that's in their parents' bed. When they outgrow this arrangement, they sleep in the bed with their mother; depending on the culture, the father may sleep in the same bed, in another bed in the same room, in another room, or in another house altogether.

Perhaps you're skeptical about co-sleeping because you've heard reports about babies who died while sleeping with their parents. In fact, research suggests that co-sleeping is dangerous only when parents smoke, drink, or sleep with babies in sofas or chairs, and with babies who were born prematurely or with low birth weight (Fleming & Blair, 2015). And one advantage of co-sleeping is that it facilitates breastfeeding: moms who breastfeed often decide to co-sleep and this simplifies breastfeeding (Mileva-Seitz et al., 2016).

Beyond safety and breastfeeding, scientists, healthcare professionals, and parents have wondered how co-sleeping affects whether babies sleep well, become emotionally attached to their mothers, and become autonomous. Unfortunately, research provides no solid answers to these questions. They're difficult to answer, in part, because researchers must consider whether co-sleeping is a well-established cultural practice or just a "new trend" and whether parents choose to co-sleep because they believe in its benefits or if they resort to co-sleeping to address a baby's sleep-related problems (Mileva-Seitz et al., 2016).

Roughly half of newborns' sleep is irregular *or* rapid-eye-movement (REM) sleep, *a time when the body is quite active.* During REM sleep, newborns move their arms and legs; they may grimace, and their eyes may dart beneath their eyelids. Brain waves register fast activity, the heart beats more rapidly, and breathing is more rapid. *In* regular *or* nonREM sleep, *breathing, heart rate, and brain activity are steady and newborns lie quietly without the twitching associated with REM sleep.* Newborns spend about equal amounts of time in REM and non-REM sleep. REM sleep becomes less frequent as infants grow: By the first birthday, REM sleep drops to about 33%, not far from the adult average of 20% (Lushington et al., 2013).

Think About It

When Mary's 4-month-old son cries, she rushes to him immediately and does everything possible to console him. Is this a good idea?

Per-Anders Pettersson/Getty Images News/Getty Images

Co-sleeping, in which infants and young children sleep with their parents, is common in many countries around the world.

irregular or rapid-eye-movement (REM) sleep

Irregular sleep in which an infant's eyes dart rapidly beneath the eyelids while the body is quite active.

regular or nonREM sleep

Sleep in which heart rate, breathing, and brain activity are steady.

The function of REM sleep is still debated. Older children and adults dream during REM sleep, and brain waves during REM sleep resemble those of an alert, awake person. Consequently, many scientists believe that REM sleep provides stimulation for the brain that fosters growth in the nervous system (Halpern et al., 1995; Roffwarg, Muzio, & Dement, 1966).

By the toddler and preschool years, sleep routines are well established. Most 2-year-olds spend about 13 hours sleeping, compared to just under 11 hours for 6-year-olds. By age 4, most youngsters give up their afternoon nap and sleep longer at night to compensate. This can be a challenging time for parents and caregivers who use naptime as an opportunity to complete some work or to relax.

Following an active day, most preschool children drift off to sleep easily. However, most children have an occasional night when bedtime is a struggle. Furthermore, for approximately 20% to 30% of preschool children, bedtime struggles occur nightly (Lozoff, Wolf, & Davis, 1985). More often than not, these bedtime problems reflect the absence of a regular bedtime routine. The key to a pleasant bedtime is to establish a nighttime routine that helps children to "wind down" from busy daytime activities. This routine should start at about the same time every night ("It's time to get ready for bed.") and end at about the same time (when the parent leaves the child and the child tries to fall asleep). This nighttime routine may be anywhere from 15 to 45 minutes long, depending on the child. Also, as children get older, parents can expect them to perform more of these tasks independently. A 2-year-old will need help all along the way, but a 5-year-old can do many of these tasks alone. But parents must remember to follow the routine consistently; this way, children know that each step is getting them closer to bedtime and falling asleep.

Sudden Infant Death Syndrome

For many parents of young babies, however, sleep is a cause of concern. *In* sudden infant death syndrome (SIDS), *a healthy baby dies suddenly for no apparent reason.* Approximately 2 of every 1,000 American babies die from SIDS. Most of them are between 2 and 4 months of age (Wegman, 1994).

Scientists don't know the exact causes of SIDS, but one idea is that 2- to 4-month-old infants are particularly vulnerable to SIDS because many newborn reflexes are waning during these months and thus infants may not respond effectively when breathing becomes difficult. They may not reflexively move their head away from a blanket or pillow that is smothering them (Lipsitt, 2003).

Researchers have also identified several risk factors associated with SIDS (Carpenter et al., 2013; Sahni, Fifer, & Myers, 2007). Babies are more vulnerable if they were born prematurely or with low birth weight. They are also more vulnerable when their parents smoke. SIDS is more likely when a baby sleeps on its stomach (face down) than when it sleeps on its back (face up). Finally, SIDS is more likely during winter, when babies sometimes become overheated from too many blankets and sleepwear that is too heavy (Carroll & Loughlin, 1994). Evidently, SIDS infants, many of whom were born prematurely or with low birth weight, are less able to withstand physiological stresses and imbalances that are brought on by cigarette smoke, breathing that is temporarily interrupted, or overheating (Simpson, 2001).

In 1992, based on mounting evidence that SIDS occurred more often when infants slept on their stomachs, the American Academy of Pediatrics (AAP) began advising parents to put babies to sleep on their backs or sides. In 1994, the AAP joined forces with the U.S. Public Health Service to launch a national program to educate parents about the dangers of SIDS and the importance of putting babies to sleep on their backs. The "Back to Sleep" campaign was widely publicized through brochures, posters like the one in ▶ Figure 3.1, and videos.

Since the "Back to Sleep" campaign began, the incidence of SIDS has been cut in half, but it still remains the leading cause of death in 1- to 12-month-olds (Hakeem et al., 2015). Consequently, in the 21st century, the National Institutes of Health (NIH) focused on groups in which SIDS is more common, including African Americans and Native

sudden infant death syndrome (SIDS)

When a healthy baby dies suddenly for no apparent reason.

▶ **Figure 3.1**

This poster is one part of an effective campaign to reduce SIDS by encouraging parents to put their babies to sleep on their backs.

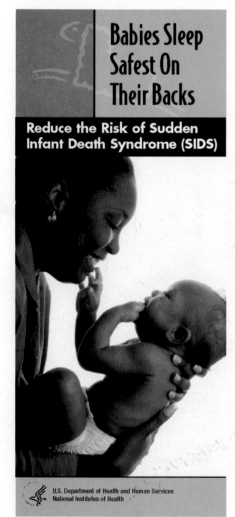

Babies Sleep Safest On Their Backs

Reduce the Risk of Sudden Infant Death Syndrome (SIDS)

U.S. Department of Health and Human Services
National Institutes of Health

National Institute of Child Health and Human Development.

Americans. The NIH developed ways to convey the "Back to Sleep" message in a culturally appropriate manner to African American communities (NICHD, 2004). In addition, the NIH developed educational programs for nurses and pharmacists. In 2012, the campaign was named Safe to Sleep and included additional recommendations to keep infants safe while asleep. Through these policies, the NIH hopes to spread the word to parents and others who care for infants: The keys to safe sleeping include keeping babies away from smoke, putting them on a firm mattress on their backs to sleep, and not overdressing them or wrapping them too tightly in blankets.

Temperament

So far, we've talked as if all babies are alike. But if you've seen a number of babies together, you know that isn't true. Perhaps you've seen some babies who were quiet most of the time alongside others who cried often and impatiently? Maybe you've known infants who responded warmly to strangers next to others who seemed shy? *These characteristics of infants indicate a consistent style or pattern to an infant's behavior, and collectively they define an infant's* temperament.

temperament
Consistent style or pattern of behavior.

Alexander Thomas and Stella Chess (Thomas & Chess, 1977; Thomas, Chess, & Birch, 1968) pioneered the study of temperament with the New York Longitudinal Study, in which they traced the lives of 141 individuals from infancy through adulthood. Thomas and Chess interviewed parents about their babies and had individuals unfamiliar with the children observe them at home. From these interviews and observations, Thomas and Chess suggested that infants' behavior varied along nine temperamental dimensions. One was activity, which referred to an infant's typical level of motor activity. A second was persistence, which referred to the amount of time an infant devoted to an activity, particularly when obstacles were present.

The New York Longitudinal Study launched research on infant temperament, but today we know that Thomas and Chess overestimated the number of temperamental dimensions. Instead of nine dimensions, scientists now propose from two to six dimensions. For example, Mary K. Rothbart (2011) devised an influential theory of temperament that includes three different dimensions:

Twin studies show the impact of heredity on temperament: If one identical twin is active, the other one usually is, too.

- *Surgency/extroversion* refers to the extent to which a child is generally happy, active, and vocal and regularly seeks interesting stimulation.
- *Negative affect* refers to the extent to which a child is angry, fearful, frustrated, shy, and not easily soothed.
- *Effortful control* refers to the extent to which a child can focus attention, is not readily distracted, and can inhibit responses.

These dimensions of temperament emerge in infancy, continue into childhood, and are related to dimensions of personality that are found in adolescence and adulthood (Gartstein, Knyazev, & Slobodskaya, 2005). However, the dimensions are not independent: Infants who are high on effortful control tend to be high on surgency/extroversion and low on negative affect. In other words, babies who can control their attention and inhibit responses tend to be happy and active but not angry or fearful.

Hereditary and Environmental Contributions to Temperament

Temperament reflects both heredity and experience. The influence of heredity is shown in twin studies and adoption studies. For example, the three dimensions of Rothbart's model—surgency, negative affect, and effortful control— are strongly influenced by heredity; if one identical twin is skilled at effortful control, the odds are that the other twin will also be skilled (Saudino & Micalizzi, 2015).

Stuart Monk/Fotolia

The environment also contributes to children's temperament. Positive emotionality—youngsters who laugh often, seem to be generally happy, and express pleasure often—seems to reflect environmental influences (Goldsmith, Buss, & Lemery, 1997). What's more, infants are less emotional when parents are responsive (Gudmundson & Leerkes, 2012; Leerkes, Blankson, & O'Brien, 2009). Conversely, infants become increasingly fearful when their mothers are depressed (Gartstein et al., 2010). And some temperamental characteristics are more common in some cultures than in others. For example, compared with toddlers from North America and Europe, toddlers in Asia often have greater effortful control but lower levels of positive emotion (Krassner et al., 2017).

Of course, in trying to determine the contributions of heredity and environment to temperament, the most likely explanation is that both contribute (Henderson & Wachs, 2007). In fact, one view is that temperament may make some children particularly susceptible to environmental influences—either beneficial or harmful (Belsky, Bakermans-Kranenburg, & van IJzendoorn, 2007). For example, in one study (Kochanska, Aksan, & Joy, 2007), emotionally fearful children were more likely to cheat in a game when their parents' discipline emphasized asserting power (e.g., "Do this now and don't argue!"). Yet these children were least likely to cheat when parents were nurturing and supportive. In other words, temperamentally fearful preschoolers can become dishonest or honest, depending on their parents' disciplinary style.

There's no question that heredity and experience cause babies' temperaments to differ, but how stable is temperament? We'll find out in the next section.

Stability of Temperament

Do calm, easygoing babies grow up to be calm, easygoing children, adolescents, and adults? Are difficult, irritable infants destined to grow up to be cranky, whiny children? In fact, temperament is moderately stable throughout infancy, childhood, and adolescence (Janson & Mathiesen, 2008; Wachs & Bates, 2001). For example, 6-month-olds who laugh and smile often tend to become 12-month-olds who laugh and smile often (Bornstein et al., 2015). In addition, when inhibited toddlers are adults, they respond more strongly to unfamiliar stimuli (Schwartz et al., 2003).

Thus, evidence suggests that temperament is at least somewhat stable throughout infancy and the toddler years (Lemery et al., 1999). Of course, the links are not perfect. Sam, an emotional 1-year-old, is more likely to be emotional as a 12-year-old than Dave, an unemotional 1-year-old. However, it's not a "sure thing" that Sam will still be emotional as a 12-year-old. Instead, think of temperament as a predisposition. Some infants are naturally predisposed to be sociable, emotional, or active; others *can* act in these ways, too, but only if the behaviors are nurtured by parents and others.

Although temperament is only moderately stable during infancy and toddlerhood, it can still shape development in important ways. For example, an infant's temperament may determine the experiences that parents provide. Parents may read more to quiet babies but play more physical games with their active babies. These different experiences, driven by the infants' temperament, contribute to each infant's development despite the fact that the infants' temperament may change over the years. Thus, although infants have many features in common, temperament characteristics remind us that each baby also seems to have a unique personality from the very start.

Richard Lord/The Image Works

Children's temperament influences the way that adults treat them; for example, parents engage in more vigorous play when their children are temperamentally active.

Recall

1. Some reflexes help infants get necessary nutrients, other reflexes protect infants from danger, and still other reflexes _____.

2. The _____ is based on five vital functions and provides a quick indication of a newborn's physical health.

3. A baby lying calmly with his or her eyes open and focused is in a state of _____.

4. Newborns spend more time asleep than awake, and about half this time asleep is spent in _____, a time thought to foster growth in the central nervous system.

5. The campaign to reduce SIDS emphasizes that infants should _____.

6. Research on the stability of temperament in infants and young children typically finds that _____.

Interpret

- Compare the Apgar and the NBAS as measures of a newborn baby's well-being.

Apply

- Based on what you know about the stability of temperament, what would you say to a parent who's worried that her 15-month-old seems shy and inhibited?

Check your answers to the Recall Questions at the end of the chapter.

3.2 Physical Development

LEARNING OBJECTIVES

- How do height and weight change from birth to 2 years of age?

- What nutrients do young children need? How are nutrients best provided?

- What are the consequences of malnutrition? How can it be treated?

- What are nerve cells, and how are they organized in the brain?

- How does the brain develop? When does it begin to function?

While crossing the street, 4-year-old Martin was struck by a passing car. He was in a coma for a week but then gradually became more alert. Now he seems to be aware of his surroundings. Needless to say, Martin's mother is grateful that he survived the accident, but she wonders what the future holds for her son.

For parents and children alike, physical growth is a topic of great interest and a source of pride. Parents marvel at the speed with which babies add pounds and inches, and 2-year-olds proudly proclaim, "I bigger now!" In this section, we examine some of the basic features of physical growth, see how the brain develops, and discover how the accident affected Martin's development.

Growth of the Body

Growth is more rapid in infancy than during any other period after birth. Typically, infants double their birth weight by 3 months of age and triple it by their first birthday. This rate of growth is so rapid that if continued throughout childhood, a typical 10-year-old boy would be nearly as long as a jumbo jet and weigh almost as much (McCall, 1979).

Average heights and weights for young children are represented by the lines marked 50th percentile in ▶ Figure 3.2. An average girl weighs about 7 pounds at birth, about 21 pounds at 12 months, and about 26 pounds at 24 months. If perfectly average, she would be 19 to 20 inches long at birth and grow to 29 to 30 inches at 12 months and 34 to 35 inches at 24 months. Figures for an average boy are similar, but weights are slightly greater at ages 12 and 24 months.

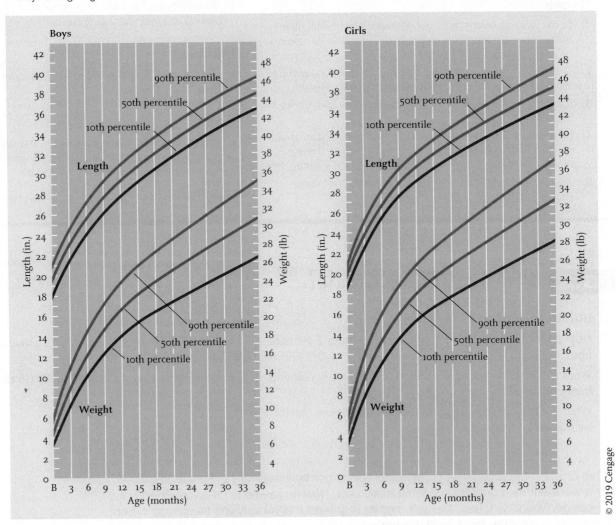

These charts also highlight how much children of the same age vary in weight and height. The lines marked 90th percentile in ▶ Figure 3.2 represent heights and weights for children who are larger than 90% of their peers; the lines marked 10th percentile represent heights and weights for children who are smaller than 90% of their peers. Any heights and weights between these lines are considered normal. At age 1, for example, normal weights for boys range from about 19 to 27 pounds. This means that an extremely light but normal boy weighs only two-thirds as much as his extremely heavy but normal peer.

The important message here is that average height and normal height are not one and the same. Many children are much taller or shorter than average but are still perfectly normal. This applies to all of the age norms that we mention in this book. Whenever we provide a typical or average age for a developmental milestone, remember that the normal range for passing the milestone is much wider.

Whether an infant is short or tall depends largely on heredity. Both parents contribute to their children's height. In fact, the correlation between the average of the two parents' heights and their child's height at 2 years of age is about 0.7 (Plomin, 1990). As a general rule, two tall parents will have tall offspring, two short parents will have short offspring, and one tall parent and one short parent will have offspring of medium height.

So far we have emphasized the quantitative aspects of growth, such as height. This ignores an important fact: Infants are not simply scaled-down versions of adults. ▶ Figure 3.3

Think About It

In Chapter 2, we explained how polygenic inheritance is often involved when phenotypes form a continuum. Height is such a phenotype. Propose a simple polygenic model to explain how height might be inherited.

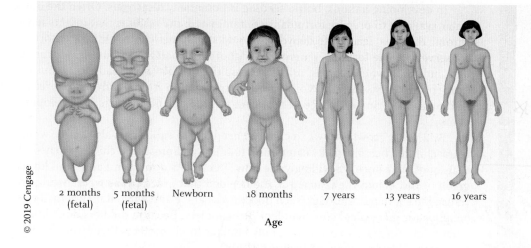

2 months (fetal) 5 months (fetal) Newborn 18 months 7 years 13 years 16 years

Age

▶ **Figure 3.3**
The head and trunk develop before the hips, legs, and feet, which gives young children a top-heavy appearance.

shows that compared with adolescents and adults, infants and young children look top-heavy because their heads and trunks are disproportionately large. As growth of the hips, legs, and feet catches up later in childhood, their bodies take on more adult proportions. This pattern of growth, in which the head and trunk develop first, follows the cephalocaudal principle introduced in Chapter 2 (page 54).

Growth of this sort requires energy. Let's see how food and drink provide the fuel to grow.

"You Are What You Eat": Nutrition and Growth

In a typical 2-month-old, roughly 40% of the body's energy is devoted to growth. Most of the remaining energy is used for basic bodily functions such as digestion and respiration. A much smaller portion is consumed in physical activity. Because growth requires so much high energy, young babies must consume about 50 calories per pound of weight (compared with 15 to 20 calories per pound for an adult).

Breastfeeding is the best way to ensure that babies get the nourishment they need. Human milk contains the proper amounts of carbohydrates, fats, protein, vitamins, and minerals for babies. Breastfeeding also has several other advantages compared with bottle-feeding. First, breastfeeding has short- and long-term health-related benefits for babies. In the short-term, they are less likely to be ill (because breast milk contains a mother's antibodies) and less likely to die (because they are less prone to diarrhea, a leading cause of death for infants in developing countries). In the long-term, breastfed babies are less prone to become obese or to develop diabetes (Victora et al., 2016). Second, breastfed babies typically transition to solid foods more easily, apparently because they are accustomed to changes in the taste of breast milk that reflect a mother's diet. Third, breast milk cannot be contaminated, which is a significant problem in developing countries when formula is used to bottle-feed babies.

Experts recommend that children be breastfed until they are 2 years old and that they be breastfed exclusively for the first six months (UNICEF, 2016). In fact, in many developing nations in African, Asia, and Latin America, mothers approximate these guidelines, but in the United States and other developed nations, most mothers stop breastfeeding by 12 months, often because it is inconvenient when they return to full-time work (Victora et al., 2016). Consequently, health experts have devised interventions to encourage mothers to breastfeed from birth through 2 years of age. These interventions (e.g., guidance from a lactation counselor) are effective (Rollins et al., 2016). If they were successful worldwide in meeting guidelines for breastfeeding, this would reduce childhood mortality by more than 800,000 deaths annually (Victora et al., 2016).

David Page Photography/Photolibrary/Getty Images

Toddlers and preschool children often become picky eaters. This can be annoying but should not concern parents.

In developing nations, bottle-feeding is potentially disastrous. Often the only water available to prepare formula is contaminated; the result is that infants have chronic diarrhea, leading to dehydration and sometimes death. Or in an effort to conserve valuable formula, parents may ignore instructions and use less formula than indicated when making milk; the resulting "weak" milk leads to malnutrition. For these reasons, the World Health Organization strongly advocates breast-feeding as the primary source of nutrition for infants and toddlers in developing nations.

By 2 years, growth slows; so children need less to eat. This is also a time when many children become picky eaters, and toddlers and preschool children may find that foods they once ate willingly are now "yucky." As a toddler, Laura Kail loved green beans. When she reached 2, she decided that green beans were awful and refused to eat them. Although such finickiness can be annoying, it may actually be adaptive for increasingly independent preschoolers. Because toddlers don't know what is and isn't safe to eat, eating only familiar foods protects them from potential harm (Aldridge, Dovey, & Halford, 2009).

Parents should not be overly concerned about this finicky period. Although some children eat less than before (in terms of calories per pound), virtually all picky eaters get adequate food for growth. Nevertheless, several methods can be used to encourage youngsters to eat more healthfully:

- Reward children when they eat healthy foods; in one study (Cooke et al., 2011), when 4- to 6-year-olds received a sticker after they tasted a vegetable, consumption increased sixfold and persisted for 3 months after rewards were dropped.
- Parents can model eating unfamiliar foods; when parents seem to be enjoying novel fruits and vegetables, young children are more willing to try them (Edelson, Mokdad, & Martin, 2016).
- Teach children about nutrition, emphasizing that different body functions require a diverse diet that includes a variety of nutrients; in one study (Gripshover & Markman, 2013), preschoolers taught these concepts from story books ate twice as many vegetables.
- Offer children new foods over several meals, in small amounts; encourage but don't force children to eat new foods; and when children reject a new food, continue to offer it over several meals so that it will become familiar (Lam, 2015).

Collectively, these methods can help children receive the nutrition they need to grow.

Malnutrition

malnourished

Being small for one's age because of inadequate nutrition.

An adequate diet is only a dream to many of the world's children. *Worldwide, about one in four children under age 5 is* malnourished, *as indicated by being small for their age.* Many, like the children in the photo on page 91, are from developing countries in Southern Asia (e.g., Bangladesh, India, Pakistan) and Africa (UNICEF-WHO-The World Bank, 2016). But malnutrition is regrettably common in industrialized countries, too. Many American children growing up homeless and in poverty are malnourished. Approximately 13% of American households have difficulty at some point in providing adequate food for all family members (Coleman-Jensen et al., 2016).

Malnourishment is especially damaging during infancy because growth is rapid during these years. By the school-age years, children with a history of infant malnutrition are easily distracted in school. Malnutrition during rapid periods of growth apparently damages the developing brain, affecting a child's abilities to pay attention and learn (Nyaradi et al., 2013).

Malnutrition would seem to have a simple cure—an adequate diet. But the solution is more complex than you might expect. Malnourished children are often listless and inactive, behaviors that are useful because they conserve limited energy. Unfortunately, when children are routinely unresponsive and lethargic, parents often come to believe that their actions have little impact on the children. Over time, parents tend to provide fewer experiences that foster their children's development. In other words, a biological influence (lethargy stemming from insufficient nourishment) causes a profound change in the experiences (parental teaching) that foster a child's development (Aboud & Yousafzai, 2015).

Thus, to counter the effects of malnutrition, children need more than an improved diet. Parents must be taught how to foster their children's development and must be encouraged to do so. Programs that combine dietary supplements with parent training offer promise in treating malnutrition. Children in these programs often improve their physical and intellectual growth, showing that the best way to reduce the effect of malnutrition on psychological forces is by addressing both biological and sociocultural forces (Yousafzai et al., 2016).

The Emerging Nervous System

The physical changes we see as infants grow are impressive. Even more awe-inspiring are the changes we cannot see—those involving the brain and the nervous system. An infant's feelings of hunger or pain, the infant's smiles or laughs, and his or her efforts to sit upright or to hold a rattle all reflect the functioning of the brain and the rest of the emerging nervous system.

How does the brain accomplish these many tasks? To answer this question, we need to look at the organization of the brain. *The basic unit in the brain and the rest of the nervous system is the* neuron, *a cell that specializes in receiving and transmitting information.* Neurons have the basic elements shown in ▶ Figure 3.4. *The* cell body, *in the center of the cell, contains the basic biological machinery that keeps the neuron alive. The receiving end of the neuron, the* dendrite, *looks like a tree with its many branches.* This structure allows one neuron to receive input from thousands of other neurons (Morgan & Gibson, 1991). *The tubelike structure that emerges from the other side of the cell body, the* axon, *transmits information to other neurons. At the end of the axon are small knobs called* terminal buttons, *which release chemicals called neurotransmitters.* These neurotransmitters are the messengers that carry information to nearby neurons.

With 50 to 100 billion neurons such as these, you have the beginnings of a human brain. An adult's brain weighs a little less than 3 pounds and easily fits in your hands. *The wrinkled surface of the brain is the* cerebral cortex; *made up of 10 billion neurons, the*

Many children around the world are malnourished.

neuron

Basic cellular unit of the brain and nervous system that specializes in receiving and transmitting information.

cell body

Center of the neuron that keeps the neuron alive.

dendrite

End of the neuron that receives information; it looks like a tree with many branches.

axon

Tubelike structure that emerges from the cell body and transmits information to other neurons.

terminal buttons

Small knobs at the end of the axon that release neurotransmitters.

neurotransmitters

Chemicals released by the terminal buttons that allow neurons to communicate with each other.

cerebral cortex

Wrinkled surface of the brain that regulates many functions that are distinctly human.

▶ **Figure 3.4**

A nerve cell includes dendrites that receive information; a cell body that has life-sustaining machinery; and for sending information, an axon that ends in terminal buttons.

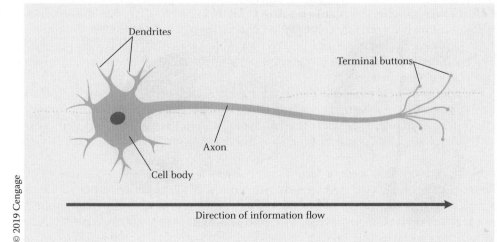

hemispheres

Right and left halves of the cortex.

corpus callosum

Thick bundle of neurons that connects the two hemispheres.

frontal cortex

Brain region that regulates personality and goal-directed behavior.

cortex regulates many of the functions that we think of as distinctly human. The cortex consists of left and right halves, called hemispheres, *linked by a thick bundle of neurons called the* corpus callosum. The characteristics you value the most—your engaging personality, your "way with words," or your uncanny knack for "reading" others' emotions— are all controlled by specific regions in the cortex (◗ Figure 3.5). *For example, your personality and your ability to make and carry out plans are largely centered in an area in the front of the cortex called the* frontal cortex. For most people, the ability to produce and understand language is mainly housed in neurons in the left hemisphere of the cortex. When you recognize that others are happy or sad, neurons in your right hemisphere are usually at work.

Now that we know how the mature brain is organized, let's look at how it grows and begins to function.

Emerging Brain Structures

The brain weighs only 12 ounces at birth, which is roughly 25% of the weight of an adult brain. But the brain grows rapidly during infancy and the preschool years. However, brain weight doesn't tell us much about the fascinating changes that take place to create a working brain. Instead, we need to look back at prenatal development.

The beginnings of the brain can be traced to the period of the zygote. *At roughly three weeks after conception, a group of cells form a flat structure known as the* neural plate. At four weeks, the neural plate folds to form a tube that ultimately becomes the brain and spinal cord. When the ends of the tube fuse shut, neurons are produced in one small region of the neural tube. Production of neurons begins about 10 weeks after conception, and by 28 weeks, the developing brain has virtually all the neurons it will ever have. During these weeks, neurons form at the incredible rate of more than 3,000 per second. Surprisingly, many of these newly formed neurons are short-lived: they are programmed to die, creating space for nearby neurons to form connections (Stiles, 2008).

From the neuron-manufacturing site in the neural tube, neurons migrate to their final positions in the brain. The brain is built in stages, beginning with the innermost layers. Neurons in the deepest layer are positioned first, followed by neurons in the second layer, and so on. This layering process continues until all six layers of the mature brain are in place, which occurs about seven months after conception (Rakic, 1995).

In the fourth month of prenatal development, axons begin to acquire myelin—*the fatty wrap that speeds neural transmission.* This process continues through infancy into childhood and adolescence (Paus, 2010). Neurons that carry sensory information are the first to acquire myelin; neurons in the cortex are among the last. You can see the effect of more

neural plate

Flat group of cells present in prenatal development that becomes the brain and spinal cord.

myelin

Fatty sheath that wraps around neurons and enables them to transmit information more rapidly.

◗ **Figure 3.5**

The brain on the left, viewed from above, shows the left and right hemispheres. The brain on the right, viewed from the side, shows the major regions of the cortex and their primary functions.

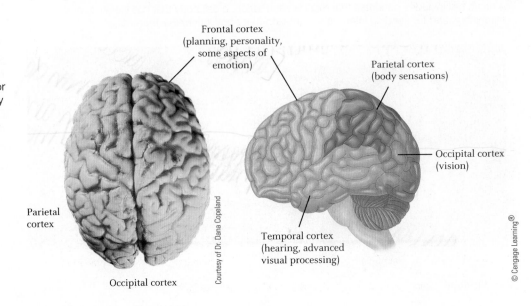

Frontal cortex
(planning, personality,
some aspects of
emotion)

Parietal cortex
(body sensations)

Occipital cortex
(vision)

Parietal cortex

Occipital cortex

Temporal cortex
(hearing, advanced
visual processing)

Courtesy of Dr. Dana Copeland

© Cengage Learning®

myelin in improved coordination and reaction times. The older the infant and (later) the child, the more rapid and coordinated his or her reactions.

In the months after birth, the brain grows rapidly. Axons and dendrites grow longer, and like a maturing tree, dendrites quickly sprout new limbs. As the number of dendrites increases, so does the number of synapses, reaching a peak at about the first birthday. *Soon after, synapses begin to disappear gradually, a phenomenon known as* synaptic pruning. Thus, beginning in infancy and continuing into early adolescence, the brain goes through its own version of "downsizing," weeding out unnecessary connections between neurons. This pruning depends on the activity of the neural circuits: Synapses that are active are preserved, but those that aren't active are eliminated (Webb, Monk, & Nelson, 2001). Pruning is completed first for brain regions associated with sensory and motor functions. Regions associated with basic language and spatial skills are completed next, followed by regions associated with attention and planning (Casey et al., 2005).

synaptic pruning

Gradual reduction in the number of synapses, beginning in infancy and continuing until early adolescence.

Growth of a Specialized Brain

Because the mature brain is specialized, with different psychological functions localized in particular regions, developmental researchers have had a keen interest in determining the origins and time course of the brain's specialization. For many years, the only clues to specialization came from children who had suffered brain injury. The logic linked the location of the injury to the resulting impairment: If a region of the brain regulates a particular function (e.g., understanding speech), then damage to that region should impair the function.

Fortunately, relatively few children suffer brain injury. But this meant that scientists needed other methods to study brain development. *One of them,* electroencephalography, *involves measuring the brain's electrical activity from electrodes placed on the scalp, as shown in the photo* at the top of page 94. If a region of the brain regulates a function, then the region should show distinctive patterns of electrical activity while a child is using that function. *A newer technique,* functional magnetic resonance imaging (fMRI), *uses magnetic fields to track the flow of blood in the brain*. With this method, shown in the photo at the bottom of page 94, the research participant's brain is literally wrapped in an incredibly powerful magnet that can track blood flow in the brain as participants perform different cognitive tasks (Casey et al., 2005). The logic is that active brain regions need more oxygen, which increases blood flow to those regions.

electroencephalography

The study of brain waves recorded from electrodes that are placed on the scalp.

functional magnetic resonance imaging (fMRI)

Method of studying brain activity by using magnetic fields to track blood flow in the brain.

None of these methods is perfect; each has drawbacks. For example, fMRI is used sparingly because it's expensive and participants must lie still for several minutes at a time. Despite these limitations, the combined outcome of research using these different approaches has identified some general principles that describe the brain's specialization as children develop.

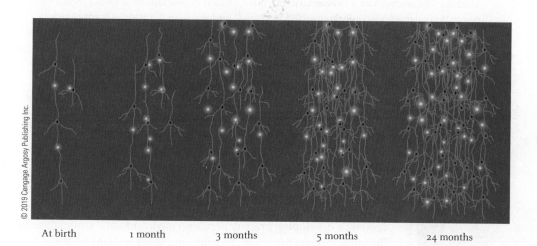

At birth   1 month   3 months   5 months   24 months

From birth to 2 years, neurons grow and create many new synapses with other neurons.

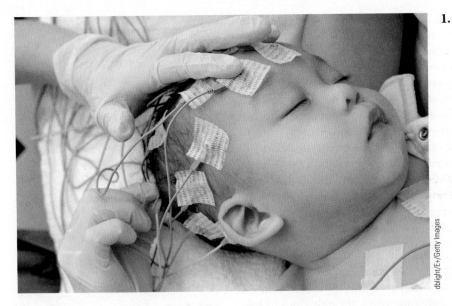

Electrodes placed on an infant's scalp can detect electrical activity that is used to create an electroencephalogram, a pattern of the brain's response to stimulation.

experience-expectant growth

Process by which the wiring of the brain is organized by experiences that are common to most humans.

In fMRI, a magnet is used to track the flow of blood to different regions of the brain as children and adults perform cognitive tasks.

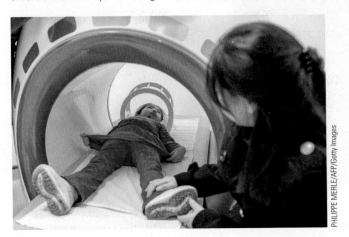

1. *Specialization is evident early in development.* Maybe you expect the brain to be completely unspecialized? In fact, many regions are already specialized very early in infancy. For example, early specialization of the frontal cortex is shown by the finding that damage to this region in infancy results in impaired decision making and abnormal emotional responses (Anderson et al., 2001). Similarly, studies using electroencephalography show that a newborn infant's left hemisphere generates more electrical activity in response to speech than does the right hemisphere (Maitre et al., 2014). Thus, by birth, the cortex of the left hemisphere is already specialized for language processing. As we'll see in Chapter 4, this specialization allows language to develop rapidly during infancy. Finally, studies tracking the flow of blood in the infant's brain indicate a region in the right hemisphere—the parietal cortex, which is directly behind the frontal cortex—that responds to changes in number (Edwards et al., 2016).

2. *Specialization takes two specific forms.* First, with development, the brain regions active during processing become more focused, much like the difference between a weak thunderstorm that covers a large areas versus a more powerful storm that covers a smaller region (Haist et al., 2013). Second, the kinds of stimuli that trigger brain activity shift from being general to being specific (Johnson, Grossman, & Cohen Kadosh, 2009). Processing of facelike stimuli by the brain shows both trends: It becomes focused in a particular area (the fusiform gyrus) and becomes tuned narrowly to faces (Cohen Kadosh et al., 2013; Haist et al., 2013).

3. *Different brain systems specialize at different rates.* Think of a new housing development involving construction of many multistory homes. In each house, the first floor is completed before higher floors, but some houses are finished before others are even started. In this same way, brain regions involving basic sensory and perceptual processes specialize well before those regions necessary for higher-order processes (Fox, Levitt, & Nelson, 2010). Similarly, some brain systems that are sensitive to reward (especially to rewards from peers) may reach maturity in adolescence, but the systems responsible for self-control aren't fully specialized until adulthood (Casey & Caudle, 2013; Galván, 2013).

4. *Successful specialization requires stimulation from the environment.* To return to the analogy of the brain as a house, the newborn's brain is perhaps best conceived as a partially finished, partially furnished house: A general organizational framework is present, with preliminary neural pathways designed to perform certain functions. The left hemisphere has some language pathways, and the frontal cortex has some emotion-related pathways. However, completing the typical organization of the mature brain requires input from the environment (Greenough & Black, 1992). *In this case, environmental input influences* experience-expectant growth—*over the course of evolution, human infants have typically been exposed to some forms of stimulation that are used to adjust brain wiring, strengthening some circuits and eliminating others.* For example, under normal conditions, healthy human infants experience moving visual patterns (e.g., faces) and varied sounds (e.g., voices). Just as a newly planted seed depends on a water-filled environment for growth, a developing brain depends on environmental stimulation to fine-tune circuits for vision, hearing, and other systems (Black, 2003). And when this expected stimulation is missing, brain

development can go awry: For example, young children reared in institutions receive far less of the cognitive and social stimulation that most parents provide; this often leads to underdevelopment of the brain regions that support processing of complex cognitive and social information (McLaughlin, Sheridan, & Lambert, 2014).

Of course, experiences later in life also sculpt the brain (and we'll see this in several chapters later in this book). *Experience-dependent growth* denotes changes *in the brain that are not linked to specific points in development and that vary across individuals and across cultures.* Experience-dependent growth is illustrated by a preschool child's learning of a classmate's name, an elementary school child's discovery of a shortcut home from school, and an adolescent's mastery of the functions of a new cell phone. In each case, brain circuits are modified in response to an individual's experiences. With today's technology, we can't see these daily changes in the brain. But when they accumulate over many years—as when individuals acquire expertise in a skill—brain changes can be detected. For example, skilled cellists have extensive brain regions devoted to controlling the fingers of the left hand as they are positioned on the strings (Elbert et al., 1995). And years of driving a taxicab produces changes in the hippocampus, a region of the brain implicated in navigation and way-finding (Maguire, Woollett, & Spiers, 2006).

5. *The immature brain's lack of specialization confers a benefit—greater plasticity.* Just as the structures in a housing development follow a plan that specifies the location of each house and its design, brain development usually follows a predictable course that reflects epigenetic interactions (page 48) between the genetic code and required environmental input. Sometimes, however, the normal course is disrupted. A person may experience events harmful to the brain (e.g., injured in an accident) or may be deprived of some essential ingredients of successful "brain building" (e.g., necessary experiences).

Research that examines the consequences of these atypical experiences shows that the brain has some flexibility: It is plastic. Remember Martin, the child in the vignette whose brain was damaged when he was struck by a car? His language skills were impaired after the accident. This was not surprising because the left hemisphere of Martin's brain had absorbed most of the force of the collision. But within several months, Martin had completely recovered his language skills. Apparently other neurons took over language-related processing from the damaged neurons. This recovery of function is not uncommon—particularly for young children—and shows that the brain is plastic. In other words, young children often recover more skills after brain injury than older children and adults, apparently because functions are more easily reassigned in the young brain (Kolb & Teskey, 2012; Demir, Levine, & Goldin-Meadow, 2010).

experience-dependent growth
Process by which an individual's unique experiences over a lifetime affect brain structures and organization.

Think About It
What's an example of experience-expectant growth for U.S. 3-year-olds? What's a common type of experience-dependent growth at this age?

TEST YOURSELF 3.2

Recall

1. Compared to older children and adults, an infant's head and trunk are _____.

2. Because of the high demands of growth, infants need _____ calories per pound than do adults.

3. The most effective treatment for malnutrition is improved diet and _____.

4. The _____ is the part of the neuron that contains the basic machinery to keep the cell alive.

5. The frontal cortex is the seat of personality and regulates _____.

6. Human speech typically elicits the greatest electrical activity from the _____ of an infant's brain.

7. A good example of brain plasticity is that although children with brain damage often have impaired cognitive processes, _____.

Interpret

• Compare growth of the brain before birth with growth of the brain after birth.

Apply

• How does malnutrition illustrate the influence on development of life-cycle forces in the biopsychosocial framework?

Check your answers to the Recall Questions at the end of the chapter.

LEARNING OBJECTIVES

- What are the component skills involved in learning to walk? At what age do infants master them?

- How do infants learn to coordinate the use of their hands?

Nancy is 14 months old and a world-class crawler. Using hands and knees, she can go just about anywhere she wants. Nancy does not walk and seems uninterested in learning how. Nancy's dad wonders whether he should be doing something to help Nancy progress beyond crawling. Deep down, he worries that perhaps he was negligent in not providing more exercise for Nancy when she was younger.

Do you remember what it was like to learn to type, to drive a car with a stick shift, to play a musical instrument, or to play a sport? *Each of these activities involves* motor skills: *coordinated movements of the muscles and limbs*. Success demands that each movement be done precisely, in exactly the right sequence, and at exactly the right time. For example, in the few seconds that it takes you to type *human development*, if you don't move your fingers in the correct sequence to the precise location on the keyboard, you might get *jinsj drveo;nrwnt*.

These activities are demanding for adults, but think about similar challenges for infants. *Infants must learn to move about in the world, to* locomote. Newborns are relatively immobile, but infants soon learn to crawl, stand, and walk. Learning to move through the environment upright leaves the arms and hands free, which allows infants to grasp and manipulate objects. *Infants must learn the* fine motor skills *associated with grasping, holding, and manipulating objects*. In the case of feeding, for example, infants progress from being fed by others, to holding a bottle, to feeding themselves with their fingers, to eating with utensils.

Together, locomotion and fine motor skills give children access to an enormous variety of information about shapes, textures, and features in their environment. In this section, we'll see how locomotion and fine motor skills develop. As we do, we'll see whether Nancy's dad should worry about her lack of interest in walking.

motor skills
Coordinated movements of the muscles and limbs.

locomote
To move around in the world.

fine motor skills
Motor skills associated with grasping, holding, and manipulating objects.

Locomotion

Advances in posture and locomotion transform the infant in little more than a year. ❯ Figure 3.6 shows the age by which most infants achieve important milestones in motor development. By about 5 months of age, most babies have rolled from back to front and can sit upright with support. By 7 months, infants can sit alone, and by 10 months, they can creep. A typical 14-month-old is able to stand alone briefly and walk with assistance. *This early, unsteady form of walking is called* toddling (*hence the term* toddler). Of course, not all children walk at the same age. Some walk before their first birthday; others—like Nancy, the world-class crawler in the vignette—take their first steps as late as 18 or 19 months of age. By 24 months, most children can climb steps, walk backward, and kick a ball.

Researchers once thought these developmental milestones reflected maturation (e.g., McGraw, 1935). Walking, for example, emerged naturally when the necessary muscles and neural circuits matured. However, today locomotion—and, in fact, all of motor development—is viewed from a new perspective. *According to* dynamic systems theory, *motor development involves many distinct skills that are organized and reorganized over time to meet the demands of specific tasks*. For example, walking includes maintaining balance, moving limbs, perceiving the environment, and having a reason to move. Only by understanding each of these skills and how they are combined to allow movement in a specific situation can we understand walking (Thelen & Smith, 1998).

toddling
Early, unsteady form of walking done by infants.

toddler
Young children who have just learned to walk.

dynamic systems theory
Theory that views motor development as involving many distinct skills that are organized and reorganized over time to meet specific needs.

Locomotor skills improve rapidly in the 15 months after birth, and progress can be measured by many developmental milestones.

Fetal posture
0 months

Chin up
1 month

Chest up
2 month

Reach and miss
3 month

Sit with support
4 month

Sit on lap;
grasp object
5 month

Sit on high chair;
grasp dangling object
6 months

Sit alone
7 months

Stand with help
8 months

Stand holding
furniture
9 months

Creep
10 months

Walk when led
11 months

Pull to stand
by furniture
12 months

Climb stair steps
13 months

Stand alone
14 months

Walk alone
15 months

Based on Bayley, 1969; Shirley, 1931.

Posture and Balance

The ability to maintain an upright posture is fundamental to walking. But upright posture is virtually impossible for newborns and young infants because of they are top-heavy. Consequently, as soon as a young infant starts to lose her balance, she tumbles over. Only with growth of the legs and muscles can infants maintain an upright posture. After infants can stand upright, they adjust their posture to avoid falling down, relying on visual cues to stay upright (Adolph & Berger, 2015).

Balance is not, however, something that infants master just once. Instead, infants must relearn balancing for sitting, crawling, walking, and other postures. Why? The body rotates around different points in each posture (e.g., the wrists for crawling versus the ankles for walking), and different muscle groups are used to generate compensating motions when infants begin to lose their balance. Consequently, it's hardly surprising that infants who easily maintain their balance when sitting still topple over time after time when crawling. And after they walk, infants must adjust their posture further when they carry objects because these affect balance (Garciaguirre, Adolph, & Shrout, 2007). Infants must recalibrate the balance system as they take on each new posture, just as basketball players recalibrate their muscle movements when they move from dunking to shooting a three-pointer (Adolph, 2000, 2002).

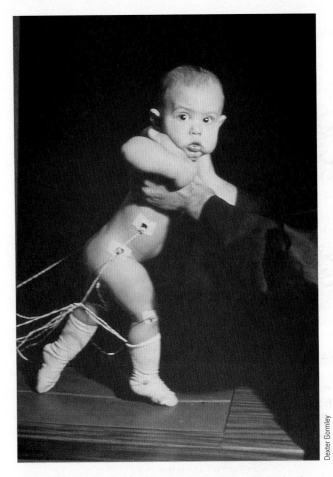

Infants are capable of stepping—moving the legs alternately—long before they can walk alone.

Stepping

Another essential element of walking is moving the legs alternately, repeatedly transferring the weight of the body from one foot to the other. Children don't step spontaneously until approximately 10 months because they must be able to stand in order to step.

Can younger children step if they are held upright? Thelen and Ulrich (1991) devised a clever procedure to answer this question. Infants were placed on a treadmill and held upright by an adult. When the belt on the treadmill started to move, infants could respond in one of several ways. They might simply let both legs be dragged rearward by the belt. Or they might let their legs be dragged briefly, then move them forward together in a hopping motion. Many 6- and 7-month-olds demonstrated the mature pattern of alternating steps on each leg. Apparently, the alternate stepping motion that is essential for walking is evident long before infants walk alone. Walking unassisted is not possible, though, until other component skills are mastered.

Environmental Cues

Many infants learn to walk in the relative security of flat, uncluttered floors at home. But they soon discover that the environment offers a variety of surfaces, some more conducive to walking than others. Infants use cues in the environment to judge whether a surface is suitable for walking. For example, they are more likely to cross a bridge when it's wide and has a rigid handrail than when it is narrow and has a wobbly handrail (Berger, Adolph, & Lobo, 2005; Kretch & Adolph, 2013b). And when walking down stairs, if a step is too large to descend safely, novice walkers often continue (and fall), but older experienced walkers either stop or slide down on their backs; only experienced walkers recognize the cues that signal steps are safe for walking (Kretch & Adolph, 2013a). Finally, expert walkers use a parent's social cues ("Come on!" "No, stop!") but mainly when they can't decide for themselves if a surface is safe (Karasik, Tamis-LeMonda, & Adolph, 2016). Results like these show that infants use cues from the environment to decide whether a surface is safe for walking.

Coordinating Skills

Dynamic systems theory emphasizes that learning to walk demands orchestration of many individual skills. Each component skill must first be mastered alone and then integrated with the other skills (Werner, 1948). That is, *mastery of intricate motions requires both* differentiation *(mastery of component skills) and* integration—*combining the motions in proper sequence into a coherent, working whole.* In the case of walking, not until 12 to 15 months of age have children mastered the component skills to be coordinated and so allow independent, unsupported walking.

Mastering individual skills and coordinating them well does not happen overnight. Novice walkers take nearly 1,500 steps per hour, covering about one-fifth of a mile, and falling more than 30 times; infants obviously get much natural practice (along with feedback from falls) as they master walking (Adolph et al., 2012).

These findings from laboratory research are not the only evidence that practice promotes motor development; cross-cultural research points to the same conclusion. In Europe and North America, most infants typically walk alone near their first birthday. But infants in other cultures often begin to walk (and reach the other milestones listed on page 97) at an earlier age because childcare practices allow children to practice their emerging motor skills. For example, in some traditional African cultures, infants sit and walk at younger ages. Why? Infants are commonly carried by their parents piggyback style, which helps develop muscles in the infants' trunk and legs.

differentiation
Distinguishing and mastering individual motions.

integration
Linking individual motions into a coherent, coordinated whole.

Some cultures even go a step further. They believe that practice is essential for motor skills to develop normally, so they (or siblings) provide daily training sessions. For example, the Kipsigis of Kenya help children learn to sit by having them sit while propped up (Super, 1981). Among the West Indians of Jamaica, mothers have an exercise routine that allows babies to practice walking (Hopkins & Westra, 1988). Not surprisingly, infants with these opportunities learn to sit and walk earlier, findings that are confirmed by experimental work in which parents participate in activities that let babies practice controlling their bodies (Lobo & Galloway, 2012).

You may be surprised that some cultures do just the opposite—they have practices that *discourage* motor development. The Ache, an indigenous group in Paraguay, protect infants and toddlers from harm by carrying them constantly (Kaplan & Dove, 1987). In Chinese cities, parents often allow their children to crawl only on a bed surrounded by pillows, in part because they don't want their children crawling on a dirty floor (Campos et al., 2000). In both cases, infants reach motor milestones a few months later than the ages listed in the chart on page 97.

In many African cultures, infants are routinely carried piggyback style; this strengthens the infant's legs, which allows them to walk at a younger age.

Even European and North American infants are reaching motor milestones at older ages today than did previous generations (Miller et al., 2011). This difference reflects the effectiveness of the Back to Sleep campaign described on page 84. Because today's babies spend less time on their tummies, they have fewer opportunities to discover that they can propel themselves by creeping, which would otherwise prepare them for crawling.

Thus, cultural practices can accelerate or delay the early stages of motor development, depending on the nature of practice that infants and toddlers receive (Adolph & Robinson, 2013). In the long run, however, the age of mastering various motor milestones is not critical for children's development. All healthy children learn to walk, and whether this happens a few months before or after the "typical" ages shown on page 97 has no bearing on children's later development (Lung & Shu, 2011).

Beyond Walking

If you can recall the feeling of freedom that accompanied your first driver's license, you can imagine how the world expands for infants and toddlers as they learn to move independently. The first tentative steps soon are followed by others that are more skilled. With more experience, infants take longer, straighter steps. Like adults, they begin to swing their arms, rotating the left arm forward as the right leg moves, then repeating with the right arm and left leg (Ledebt, 2000; Ledebt, van Wieringen, & Savelsbergh, 2004).

Children's growing skill is evident in their running and hopping. Most 2-year-olds have a hurried walk instead of a true run; they move their legs stiffly (rather than bending them at the knees) and are not airborne as is the case when running. By 5 or 6 years, children run easily, quickly changing directions or speed.

Infants use their new walking skills to get distant objects—a favorite toy that's in a different room of the house—and carry them to share with other people (Karasik, Tamis-Lemonda, & Adolph, 2011). In the next section, we'll see how infants' fine motor skills allow them to grasp objects.

Think About It

How does learning to hop on one foot demonstrate differentiation and integration of motor skills?

Locomotor skills develop rapidly in preschool children, making it possible for them to play vigorously.

A typical 4-month-old grasps an object with fingers alone.

Fine Motor Skills

A major accomplishment of infancy is skilled use of the hands. Newborns have little apparent control of their hands, but 1-year-olds are extraordinarily talented.

Reaching and Grasping

At about 4 months, infants can successfully reach for objects (Bertenthal & Clifton, 1998). These early reaches often look clumsy, because infants don't move their arm and hand smoothly to the desired object. Instead, the infant's hand follows a zigzag path: It moves a short distance, slows, then moves again in a slightly different direction—a process that's repeated until the hand finally contacts the object. As infants grow, their reaches have fewer movements, although they still are not as continuous and smooth as reaches by older children and adults (Adolph & Berger, 2015).

Reaching requires that an infant move the hand to the location of a desired object. Grasping poses a different challenge: Now the infant must coordinate movements of individual fingers to grab an object. Over the first year, infants become more skilled in orienting their hand and positioning their fingers to grasp an object. For example, if trying to grasp a long thin rod, infants place their fingers perpendicular to the rod, which is the best position for grasping. And babies learn when to grip for power (using all fingers) versus when to grip for precision (using only the thumb and forefinger). By 12 months, babies have become skilled at grasping, an accomplishment that allows them to enjoy playing with objects.

Infants' growing control of each hand is accompanied by greater coordination of the two hands. Although 4-month-olds use both hands, their motions are not coordinated; rather, each hand seems to have a mind of its own. Infants may hold a toy motionless in one hand while shaking a rattle in the other. At roughly 5 to 6 months of age, infants can coordinate the motions of their hands so that each hand performs different actions that serve a common goal. So a child might, for example, hold a toy animal in one hand and pet it with the other (Karniol, 1989). These skills continue to improve after the child's first birthday: One-year-olds reach for most objects with one hand; by 2 years, they reach with one or two hands, as appropriate, depending on the size of the object (van Hof, van der Kamp, & Savelsbergh, 2002).

These gradual changes in fine motor coordination are well illustrated by the ways children feed themselves. Beginning at roughly 6 months of age, many infants experiment with "finger foods" such as sliced bananas and green beans. Infants can easily pick up such foods, but getting them into their mouths is another story. The hand grasping the food may be raised to the cheek, then moved to the edge of the lips, and finally shoved into the mouth. Mission accomplished, but only after many detours along the way! However, infants' eye–hand coordination improves rapidly, and foods varying in size, shape, and texture are soon placed directly in the mouth.

At about the first birthday, many parents allow their children to try eating with a spoon. Youngsters first play with the spoon, dipping it in and out of a dish filled with food or sucking on an empty spoon. Soon they learn to fill the spoon with food and place it in their mouth, but the motions are awkward. For example, most 1-year-olds fill a spoon by first placing it directly over a dish. Then they lower the spoon until its bowl is full. In contrast, 2-year-olds typically scoop food from a dish by rotating their wrist, which is the same motion adults use.

As preschoolers, children become more dexterous and are able to make many precise and delicate movements with their hands and fingers. Greater fine motor skill means that preschool children begin to care for themselves. No longer must they rely primarily on parents to feed and clothe them; instead, they become increasingly skilled at feeding and dressing themselves. A 2- or 3-year-old, for example, can put on simple clothing and use zippers but not buttons; by 3 or 4 years, children can fasten buttons and take off their clothes when going to the bathroom; and most 5-year-olds can dress and undress themselves—except for tying shoes, which children typically master at about age 6.

All these actions illustrate the principles of differentiation and integration that were introduced in our discussion of locomotion. Complex acts involve simple movements that must be performed correctly and in the proper sequence. Development involves first mastering the separate elements and then assembling them into a smoothly functioning whole. And, as we'll see in the Spotlight on Research feature, having infants practice these movements can have long-lasting consequences.

Handedness

Before birth, most children are emergent right handers: fetuses are more likely to suck their right thumb than their left, to move the right arm than the left, and to turn the head to the right rather than to the left. After birth, babies reach more often and more accurately with their right hand than with the left (Fagard, 2013). By the first birthday, most youngsters use their left hand to steady the toy while the right hand manipulates the object.

Spotlight | On Research

Benefits of Training Babies to Grasp

Who were the investigators, and what was the aim of the study? By 4 to 6 months, babies can reach and grasp objects, actions that allow them to explore objects and, in the process, foster their cognitive, social, and linguistic skills. Before 4 months, babies have little success when trying to grasp objects. If they were better able to grasp, would they benefit from exploring objects? Answering this question was the aim of research by Klaus Libertus and his colleagues, Amy Joh and Amy Needham (2010, 2016).

How did the investigators measure the topic of interest? Libertus and colleagues created "sticky" mittens for 3-month-olds. The mittens were covered with Velcro® as were interesting toys. Wearing the mittens, any contact allowed babies to "grasp" and explore the object. For 2 weeks, the babies wore the mittens daily for 10 minutes. In one control condition, babies wore mittens that had no Velcro®; these babies played with toys and, during the daily play sessions, parents held the toys against the mittens (simulating the experience of babies wearing sticky mittens). After 2 weeks of training, babies came to the researchers' lab, where a colorful rattle was placed within their reach; the researchers recorded babies' efforts to grasp the rattle. About one year later, the procedure was repeated, with the rattle replaced by a bead maze. In two other control conditions, babies received no training at all but were just tested in the laboratory, either as 3-month-olds or as 15-month-olds.

Who were the participants in the study? The study included 55 3-month-olds and 15 15-month-olds.

What was the design of the study? This study was experimental. The independent variable was the nature of the training experience (sticky mittens, regular mittens, no training). The dependent variable was the percentage of time that the babies tried to grasp the novel toys. The study included a longitudinal component (babies in the mitten conditions who were tested as 3-month-olds *and again* as 15-month-olds) as well as cross-sectional component (babies who received no training and were tested as 3-month-olds *or* as 15-month-olds).

Were there ethical concerns with the study? No. There was no obvious harm associated with wearing the mittens or playing with toys.

What were the results? The researchers calculated the percentage of time that babies reached for the toys. As you can see in ▶ Figure 3.7, at 3 and 15 months, babies who wore the sticky mittens were more likely than babies in the other groups to grasp objects. In contrast, wearing regular mittens did not affect babies' reaching.

What did the investigators conclude? Training babies to reach had immediate and long-term benefits: Babies who wore the sticky mittens were more likely to reach immediately after training and approximately one year later. Training may have affected babies directly—they learned the benefits of reaching and grasping—and may have affected them indirectly—when parents see babies interested in objects around them,

▶ **Figure 3.7**
When babies were trained to reach using "sticky" mittens, they were more likely to reach for objects, both immediately after training and one year later.

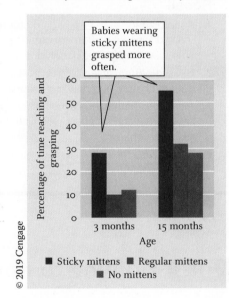

they more often engage their children in object-oriented play.

What converging evidence would strengthen these conclusions? One useful extension of this work would be to see if the impact of training persists beyond 15 months and if it extends to domains beyond grasping (e.g., learning the names of objects). Another extension would be to determine whether the training affects parent-child play, particularly play that involves objects.

By age 5, fine motor skills are developed to the point that most youngsters can dress themselves.

This early preference for one hand becomes stronger and more consistent during the preschool years and is well established by kindergarten (Marschik et al., 2008; Nelson, Campbell, & Michel, 2013).

What determines whether children become left- or right-handed? Not surprisingly, heredity and environment both contribute. Scientists believe that as many as 30 to 40 different genes may play a role in determining whether children are left or right handed (Ocklenburg, Beste, & Güntürkün, 2013). But experience also contributes. Many cultures have traditionally viewed left-handedness as evil and have punished children for using their left hand to eat or write. Not surprisingly, left-handed children are rare in these cultures. Similarly, in many developed nations, elementary school teachers used to urge left-handed children to write with their right hands. As this practice was abandoned, the percentage of left-handed children has increased (Provins, 1997). Thus, handedness is influenced by both heredity and environment.

TEST YOURSELF 3.3

Recall

1. According to _____, motor development involves many distinct skills that are organized and reorganized over time, depending on task demands.

2. Skills important in learning to walk include maintaining upright posture and balance, stepping, and _____.

3. Akira uses both hands simultaneously, but not in a coordinated manner; each hand seems to be "doing its own thing." Akira is probably _____ months old.

4. At one year, most infants use their left hand to steady a toy and their right hand to _____.

Interpret

- Compare and contrast the milestones of locomotor development in the first year with the fine motor milestones.

Apply

- Describe how the mastery of a fine motor skill—such as learning to use a spoon or a crayon—illustrates the integration of biological, psychological, and sociocultural forces in the biopsychosocial framework.

Check your answers to the Recall Questions at the end of the chapter.

3.4 Coming to Know the World: Perception

LEARNING OBJECTIVES

- Are infants able to smell, taste, and experience pain?
- How well do infants hear?
- How well can infants see? Can they see color and depth?
- How do infants coordinate information between different sensory modalities, such as between vision and hearing?

Darla is mesmerized by her newborn daughter, Olivia. Darla loves holding Olivia, talking to her, and simply watching her. Darla is certain that Olivia is already getting to know her and is coming to recognize her face and the sound of her voice. Darla's husband, Steve, thinks she is crazy: "Everyone knows that babies are born blind, and they probably can't hear much either." Darla doubts Steve and wishes someone could tell her the truth about Olivia's vision and hearing.

To answer Darla's questions, we need to define what it means for an infant to experience or sense the world. Humans have several kinds of sense organs, each receptive to a different kind of physical energy. For example, the retina at the back of the eye is sensitive to some types of electromagnetic energy, and sight is the result. The eardrum detects changes in air pressure, and hearing is the result. Cells at the top of the nasal passage detect the passage of airborne molecules, and smell is the result. In each case, the sense organ translates the physical stimulus into nerve impulses that are sent to the brain. *The process by which the brain receives, selects, modifies, and organizes these impulses is known as* perception. This is the first step in the complex process of accumulating information that eventually results in "knowing."

Darla's questions are really about her newborn daughter's perceptual skills. By the end of this section, you'll be able to answer her questions because we're going to look at how infants use different senses to experience the world.

Smell, Taste, and Touch

Newborns have a keen sense of smell. Infants respond positively to pleasant smells and negatively to unpleasant smells (Mennella & Beauchamp, 1997). They have a relaxed and contented facial expression when they smell honey or chocolate, but they frown or turn away when they smell rotten eggs or ammonia. Young babies also recognize familiar odors. Newborns look in the direction of a pad that is saturated with their own amniotic fluid (Schaal, Marlier, & Soussignan, 1998). They also turn toward a pad saturated with the odor of their mother's breast or her perfume (Porter & Winberg, 1999).

Newborns also have a highly developed sense of taste. They readily differentiate salty, sour, bitter, and sweet tastes (Schwartz, Issanchou, & Nicklaus, 2009). Most infants prefer sweet and salty substances—they react to them by smiling, sucking, and licking their lips (Beauchamp & Mennella, 2011) but grimace when fed bitter or sour substances (Kaijura, Cowart, & Beauchamp, 1992). Infants are also sensitive to changes in the taste of breast milk that reflect a mother's diet and will nurse more after their mother has consumed a sweet-tasting substance such as vanilla (Mennella & Beauchamp, 1996).

Newborns are sensitive to touch. As we saw earlier in this chapter, many areas of the newborn's body respond reflexively when touched. Touching an infant's cheek, mouth, hand, or foot produces reflexive movements, documenting that infants perceive touch. What's more, babies' behavior in response to apparent pain-provoking stimuli suggests that they experience pain. Look, for example, at the baby in the photo who is receiving an inoculation. She's opened her mouth to cry, and although we can't hear her, the sound of her cry is probably the unique pattern associated with pain. The pain cry begins suddenly, is high-pitched, and is not easily soothed. Her heart rate has jumped; and she's trying to move her hands, arms, and legs (Warnock et al., 2014). Collectively, these signs strongly suggest that babies experience pain.

Perceptual skills are extraordinarily useful to newborns and young babies. Smell and touch help them recognize their mothers. Smell and taste make it much easier for them to learn to eat. Early development of smell, taste, and touch prepares newborns and young babies to learn about the world.

Hearing

We saw in Chapter 2 that the fetus can hear at seven or eight months after conception. As you would expect from these results, newborns typically respond to sounds in their surroundings. If a parent is quiet and then coughs, an infant may startle, blink his eyes, and move his arms or legs. These responses may seem natural, but they indicate that infants are sensitive to sound.

Overall, adults can hear better than infants, but infants eliminate much of the gap by 6 months, particularly for higher-pitched sounds. Infants can pick out a sound from

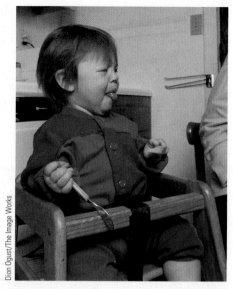

Infants and toddlers do not like bitter and sour tastes!

perception

Processes by which the brain receives, selects, modifies, and organizes incoming nerve impulses that are the result of physical stimulation.

An infant's response to an inoculation—a distinctive facial expression coupled with a distinctive cry—clearly suggests that the baby feels pain.

background noise, though not as skillfully as adults (Litovsky, 2015). More interesting, infants best hear sounds that have pitches in the range of human speech: neither very high-pitched nor very low-pitched. Infants can distinguish speech sounds, such as vowels from consonant sounds, and by 4 or 5 months, they can recognize their own names (Jusczyk, 1995; Mandel, Jusczyk, & Pisoni, 1995).

Infants also can distinguish different musical sounds. They can distinguish different melodies and prefer melodies that are pleasant-sounding over those that are unpleasant-sounding or dissonant (Trainor & Heinmiller, 1998). And infants are sensitive to the rhythmic structure of music: After hearing a sequence of notes, 5-month-olds notice when the rhythmic structure of the notes changes (Hannon, Soley, & Levine, 2011). This early sensitivity to music is remarkable but perhaps not so surprising when you consider that music is (and has been) central in all cultures.

Thus, by the middle of the first year, infants respond to much of the information that is provided by sound. In Chapter 4, we will reach the same conclusion when we examine the perception of language-related sounds.

Seeing

If you've ever watched infants, you probably noticed that they spend much of their waking time looking around. Sometimes they scan their environment, and sometimes they focus on nearby objects. What do they see as a result? Perhaps their visual world is a sea of confusing gray blobs. Or maybe they see the world as adults do. Actually, neither of these descriptions is entirely accurate, but the second is closer to the truth.

The various elements of the visual system—the eye, the optic nerve, and the brain—are relatively well developed at birth. Newborns respond to light and can track moving objects with their eyes. How well do infants see? *The clarity of vision, called* visual acuity, *is defined as the smallest pattern that can be distinguished dependably.* You've undoubtedly had your acuity measured, probably by being asked to read rows of progressively smaller letters or numbers from a chart. To assess newborns' acuity, researchers use a similar approach, testing infants' looking at patterns (e.g., stripes). This work reveals that newborns and 1-month-olds see at 20 feet what normal adults would see at 200 to 400 feet, but 1-year-olds have the acuity of an adult with normal vision (Kellman & Arterberry, 2006). This improvement reflects changes in the eye: receptors move to the center of the eye and become longer, allowing them to collect more light (Johnson, 2013).

visual acuity

Smallest pattern that one can distinguish reliably.

Color

Infants not only see the world with greater acuity during the first year, they also begin to see it in color! How do we perceive color? The wavelength of light is the basis of color perception. In ❱ Figure 3.8, light that we see as red has a relatively long wavelength, whereas violet (at the other end of the color spectrum) has a much shorter wavelength. *Concentrated in the back of the eye along the retina are specialized neurons called* cones. Some cones are sensitive to short-wavelength light (blues and violets). Others are sensitive to medium-wavelength light (greens and yellows), and still others are sensitive to long-wavelength light (reds and oranges). These different kinds of cones are linked by complex circuits of neurons, and this circuitry is responsible for our ability to see the world in colors.

cones

Specialized neurons in the back of the eye that sense color.

These circuits gradually begin to function in the first few months after birth. Newborns and young babies can perceive few colors, but by 3 months, the three kinds of cones and their associated circuits are working and infants are able to see the full range of colors (Kellman & Arterberry, 2006). In fact, by 4 to 6 months, infants' color perception seems similar to that of adults: Like adults, infants see categories of color. They see the spectrum as a group of reds, a group of yellows, a group of greens, and the like (Yang et al., 2016).

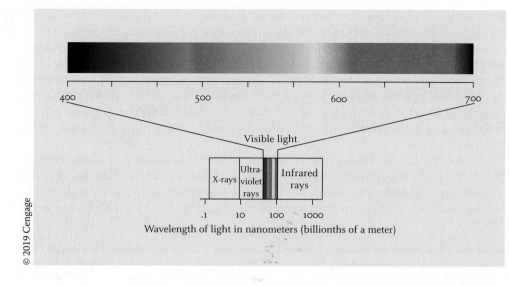

© 2019 Cengage

Figure 3.8
The visible portion of light ranges from a wavelength of about 400 nanometers (which looks violet) to nearly 700 nanometers (which looks red).

Depth

People see objects as having three dimensions: height, width, and depth. The retina of the eye is flat, so height and width can be represented directly on its two-dimensional surface. But the third dimension, depth, cannot be represented directly on this flat surface; so how do we perceive depth? We use perceptual processing to *infer* depth.

Depth perception tells us whether objects are near or far, which was the basis for some classic research by Eleanor Gibson and Richard Walk (1960) on the origins of depth perception. In their work, *babies were placed on a glass-covered platform, a device known as the* visual cliff. On one side of the platform, a checkerboard pattern appeared directly under the glass; on the other side, the pattern appeared several feet below the glass. The result was that the first side looked shallow but the other looked deep, like a cliff.

Mothers stood on each side of the visual cliff and tried to coax their infants across the deep side or the shallow side. Most babies willingly crawled to their mothers when they stood on the shallow side. In contrast, babies refused to cross the deep side, even when the mothers called them by name and tried to lure them with an attractive toy. Clearly, infants can perceive depth by the time they are old enough to crawl.

What about younger babies who cannot yet crawl? When babies as young as 6 weeks are placed on the visual cliff, their hearts beat more slowly when they are placed on the deep side of the cliff. Heart rate often decelerates when people notice something interesting, so this would suggest that 6-week-olds notice that the deep side is different. At 7 months, infants' heart rates accelerate, a sign of fear. Thus, although young babies can detect a difference between the shallow and deep sides of the visual cliff, only older crawling babies are afraid of the deep side (Campos et al., 1978).

How do infants infer depth on the visual cliff or anywhere else? They use several kinds of cues. *Among the first are* kinetic cues, *in which motion is used to estimate depth.* Visual expansion *refers to the fact that as an object moves closer, it fills an ever-greater proportion of the retina.* Visual expansion is why we flinch when someone unexpectedly tosses a soda can toward us, and it's what allows a batter to estimate when a baseball will arrive over the plate. *Another cue,* motion parallax, *refers to the fact that nearby moving objects move across our visual field faster than those at a distance.* Motion parallax is in action when you look out the side window in a moving car: Trees next to the road move rapidly across the visual field, but mountains in the distance move more slowly. Babies use these cues in the first weeks after birth; for example, a 1-month-old baby will blink if a moving object looks as if it's going to hit him in the face (Nánez & Yonas, 1994).

visual cliff
Glass-covered platform that appears to have a "shallow" and a "deep" side; used to study infants' depth perception.

kinetic cues
Cues to depth perception in which motion is used to estimate depth.

visual expansion
Kinetic cue to depth perception that is based on the fact that an object fills an ever-greater proportion of the retina as it moves closer.

motion parallax
Kinetic cue to depth perception based on the fact that nearby moving objects move across our visual field faster than do distant objects.

Mark Richards/PhotoEdit

Despite their mother's coaxing, infants avoid the "deep side" of the visual cliff, indicating that they perceive depth.

binocular disparity

Way of inferring depth based on differences in the retinal images in the left and right eyes.

pictorial cues

Cues to depth perception that are used to convey depth in drawings and paintings.

linear perspective

A cue to depth perception based on the fact that parallel lines come together at a single point in the distance.

texture gradient

Perceptual cue to depth based on the fact that the texture of objects changes from distinct for nearby objects to finer and less distinct for distant objects.

Think About It

Psychologists often refer to "perceptual-motor skills," which implies that the two are closely related. Based on what you've learned in this chapter, how might motor skills influence perception? How could perception influence motor skills?

Another cue becomes important at about 4 months. Binocular disparity *is based on the fact that the left and right eyes often see slightly different versions of the same scene.* You can demonstrate binocular disparity by touching your nose with your finger. If you look at your finger with one eye (closing the other eye), each eye has a very different view of your finger. But if you hold your finger at arm's length from your nose and repeat the demonstration, each eye has similar views of your fingers. Thus, greater disparity in retinal images signifies that an object is close. By about 4 months, infants use binocular disparity as a depth cue, correctly inferring that objects are nearby when disparity is great (Kavšek & Braun, 2016).

By about 6 months, infants use several cues for depth that depend on the arrangement of objects in the environment (Kavšek, Yonas, & Granrud, 2012). *These are sometimes called* pictorial cues *because they're the same cues that artists use to convey depth in drawings and paintings.* Here are two examples of pictorial cues that 7-month-olds use to infer depth.

- Linear perspective: *Parallel lines come together at a single point in the distance.* Thus, we use the space between the lines as a cue to distance and consequently decide that the tracks close together are farther away than the tracks far apart.
- Texture gradient: *The texture of objects changes from distinct for nearby objects to finer and less distinct for distant objects.* We judge that distinct flowers are close and that blurred ones are distant.

Infants not only use visual cues to judge depth but also use sound. Infants correctly judge quieter objects to be more distant than louder objects. Given such an assortment of cues, it is not surprising that infants gauge depth so accurately.

Perceiving Objects

Perceptual processes enable us to interpret patterns of lines, textures, and colors as objects. That is, our perception actually creates an object from sensory stimulation. This is particularly challenging because we often see only parts of objects—nearby objects often obscure parts of more distant objects. Nevertheless, we recognize these objects despite this complexity in our visual environment.

Perception of objects is limited in newborns, but it develops rapidly in the first few months after birth (Johnson, 2001). By 4 months, infants use a number of cues to determine which elements go together to form objects. One important cue is motion: Elements

Linear perspective is one cue to depth: We interpret the railroad tracks that are close together as being more distant than the tracks that are far apart.

Texture gradient is used to infer depth: We interpret the distinct flowers as being closer than the flowers with the blurry texture.

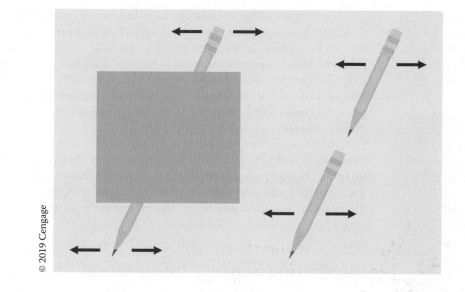

© 2019 Cengage

Figure 3.9
After infants have seen the pencil ends moving behind the square, they are surprised to see two pencils when the square is removed; this shows that babies use common motion as a way to determine what makes up an object.

that move together are usually part of the same object (Kellman & Arterberry, 2006). For example, at the left of ▶ Figure 3.9, a pencil appears to be moving back and forth behind a colored square. If the square were removed, you would be surprised to see a pair of pencil stubs, as shown on the right side of the diagram. The common movement of the pencil's eraser and point leads us to believe that they're part of the same pencil.

Young infants, too, are surprised by demonstrations such as this. If they see a display such as the moving pencils, they will then look briefly at a whole pencil, apparently because they expected it. In contrast, if after seeing the moving pencil they're shown the two pencil stubs, they look much longer—as if trying to figure out what happened (Amso & Johnson, 2006; Eizenman & Bertenthal, 1998). Babies use common motion to identify objects, and given the right conditions, newborns do, too (Valenza & Bulf, 2011).

Motion is one clue to object unity, but infants use others, including color, texture, and aligned edges. As you can see in ▶ Figure 3.10, infants more often group features together (i.e., believe they're part of the same object) when they're the same color, they have the same texture, and their edges are aligned (Bremner et al., 2013; Johnson, 2001).

Perceiving Faces

Babies depend on other people to care for them, so it's not surprising that young babies are attuned to human faces. For example, newborns prefer (1) faces with normal features over faces in which features are scrambled (Easterbrook et al., 1999), (2) upright faces over inverted faces (Mondloch et al., 1999), and (3) attractive faces over unattractive faces (Slater et al., 2000). Findings such as these lead some scientists to claim that babies are innately attracted to moving stimuli that are facelike (e.g., consist of three high-contrast blobs close together). In other words, newborns' face perception may be reflexive based on primitive circuits in the brain. At about 2 or 3 months of age, different circuits in the brain's cortex begin to control infants' looking at faces, allowing infants to learn about faces and to distinguish different faces (Morton & Johnson, 1991).

Through the first few months after birth, infants have a very general prototype for a face—one that includes human and nonhuman faces (Pascalis, de Haan, & Nelson, 2002). However, over the first year, infants fine-tune their prototype of a face so that it reflects faces that are familiar in their environments. For example, 3-month-olds prefer to look at faces from their own race, but they can recognize faces from other races (and other species). In contrast, 6-month-olds often fail to recognize faces of individuals from other unfamiliar races (Anzures et al., 2013). And by 9 months, infants lump together faces from all other races: For example, European American babies create an "other race" category that includes Asian and African faces (Quinn et al., 2016).

Think About It
When 6-month-old Sebastian watches his mother type on a keyboard, how does he know that her fingers and the keyboard are not simply one big unusual object?

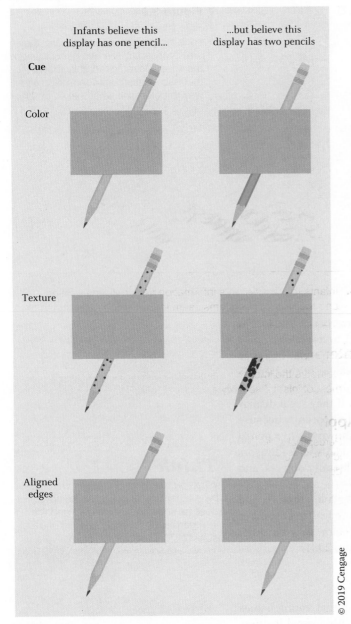

Infants believe this display has one pencil...

...but believe this display has two pencils

Cue

Color

Texture

Aligned edges

© 2019 Cengage

▶ **Figure 3.10**

In addition to common motion, infants use common color, common texture, and aligned edges as clues to object unity.

intersensory redundancy

Infants' sensory systems are attuned to information presented simultaneously to different sensory modes.

Apparently, older infants' greater familiarity with faces of their own race leads to a more precise configuration of faces, one that includes faces of familiar racial and ethnic groups. Consistent with this interpretation, infants born in Asia but adopted by European parents recognize European faces better than Asian faces (Sangrigoli et al., 2005). What's more, if older infants receive extensive experience with other-race faces, they can learn to recognize them (Anzures et al., 2012).

These changes in face-recognition skill show the role of experience in fine-tuning infants' perception, a theme that will emerge again in the early phases of language learning (Chapter 4). And these improved face-recognition skills are adaptive, for they provide the basis for social relationships that infants form during the rest of the first year, which we'll examine in Chapter 5.

Integrating Sensory Information

So far, we have discussed infants' sensory systems separately. In reality, most infant experiences are better described as "multimedia events." For example, a nursing mother provides visual and taste cues to her baby. A rattle stimulates vision, hearing, and touch. In fact, much stimulation is not specific to one sense, but spans multiple senses. Temporal information, such as duration or tempo, can be seen or heard. For example, you can detect the rhythm of a person clapping by seeing the hands meet or by hearing the sound of hands striking. Similarly, the texture of a surface—whether it's rough or smooth—can be detected by sight or by feel.

Infants readily perceive many of these relations. For example, infants can recognize visually an object that they have only touched previously (Sann & Streri, 2007). Similarly, they can detect relations between information presented visually and auditorily. Babies look longer when an object's motion matches its sound (it makes higher-pitched sounds while rising but lower-pitched sounds while falling) than when it doesn't (Walker et al., 2010). And they can link the temporal properties of visual and auditory stimulation, such as duration and rhythm (Lewkowicz, 2000). Finally, they link their own body movement to their perceptions of musical rhythm, giving new meaning to the phrase "feel the beat, baby!" (Gerry, Faux, & Trainor, 2010).

Traditionally, coordinating information from different senses (e.g., vision with hearing, vision with touch) was thought to be a challenging task for infants. But a new view is that cross-modal perception is *easier* for infants because regions in the brain devoted to sensory processing are not yet specialized in infancy. For example, regions in an adult's brain that respond only to visual stimuli respond to visual *and* auditory input in the infant's brain (Spector & Maurer, 2009). *And some researchers have argued that the infant's sensory systems are particularly attuned to* intersensory redundancy—*that is, to information that is presented simultaneously to different sensory modes* (Bahrick & Lickliter, 2002; 2012). Perception is best when information is presented redundantly to multiple senses. When an infant sees and hears the mother clapping (visual, auditory information), he focuses on the information conveyed to both senses and pays less attention to information that's only available in one sense, such as the color of the mother's nail polish or the sounds of her humming along with the tune (Bahrick et al., 2015). Or the infant can learn that the mom's lips are chapped from seeing the flaking skin and by feeling the roughness as the mother kisses him. According to intersensory redundancy theory, it's as if infants follow the rule "Any information that's presented in multiple senses must be important, so pay attention to it!"

Integrating information from different senses is yet another variation on the theme that has dominated this chapter: Infants' sensory and perceptual skills are impressive. Darla's newborn daughter, from the opening vignette, can smell, taste, and feel pain. She can distinguish sounds. Her vision is a little blurry now but will improve rapidly; in a few months, she'll see the full range of colors and perceive depth. In short, Darla's daughter, like most infants, is exceptionally well prepared to begin to make sense out of her environment.

A mother who breastfeeds provides her baby with a multimedia event: the baby sees, smells, hears, feels, and tastes her!

Nancy Ney/Photodisc/Getty images

TEST YOURSELF 3.4

Recall

1. Infants respond negatively to substances that taste sour or _____.

2. Infants respond to _____ with a high-pitched cry that is hard to soothe.

3. Infants' hearing is best for sounds that have the pitch of _____.

4. At age _____, infants' acuity is like that of an adult with normal vision.

5. _____ are specialized neurons in the retina that are sensitive to color.

6. _____ refers to the fact that images of an object in the left and right eyes differ for nearby objects.

7. When elements consistently move together, infants decide that they are _____.

8. Infants readily integrate information from different senses, and their sensory systems seem to be particularly attuned to _____.

Interpret

- Compare the impact of nature and nurture on the development of infants' sensory and perceptual skills.

Apply

- Perceptual skills are quite refined at birth and mature rapidly. What evolutionary purposes are served by this rapid development?

Check your answers to the Recall Questions at the end of the chapter.

3.5 Becoming Self-Aware

LEARNING OBJECTIVES

- When do children begin to realize that they exist?
- What are toddlers' and preschoolers' self-concepts like?
- When do preschool children begin to acquire a theory of mind?

When Ximena brushes her teeth, she puts her 20-month-old son, Christof, in an infant seat facing the bathroom mirror. She's been doing this for months, and Christof enjoys looking at the images in the mirror. Lately, he seems to pay special attention to his own reflection. Ximena thinks that sometimes Christof deliberately frowns or laughs just to see what he looks like. Is this possible, Ximena wonders, or is her imagination simply running wild?

Not until 15 to 18 months of age do babies recognize themselves in the mirror, which is an important step in becoming self-aware.

As infants' physical, motor, and perceptual skills grow, they learn more and more about the world around them. As part of this learning, infants and toddlers begin to realize that they exist independently of other people and objects in the environment and that their existence continues over time. In this last section, you'll see how children become self-aware and learn what Christof knows about himself.

Origins of Self-Concept

When do children begin to understand that they exist? Measuring the onset of this awareness is not easy. Obviously, we can't simply ask a 3-year-old, "So tell me, when did you first realize you existed and weren't just part of the furniture?" Investigators need a less direct approach, and a mirror offers one route. Babies sometimes touch the face in the mirror or wave at it, but none of their behaviors indicate that they recognize themselves in the mirror. Instead, babies act as if the face in the mirror is simply a very interesting stimulus.

How would we know that infants recognize themselves in a mirror? One clever approach is to have mothers place a red mark on their infant's nose; they do this surreptitiously, while wiping the baby's face. Then the infant is returned to the mirror. Many 1-year-olds touch the red mark on the mirror, showing that they notice the mark on the face in the mirror. By 15 months, however, an important change occurs: Babies see the red mark in the mirror, then reach up and touch their own noses. By age 2, virtually all children do this (Bullock & Lütkenhaus, 1990; Lewis & Brooks-Gunn, 1979). When these older children notice the red mark in the mirror, they understand that the funny-looking nose in the mirror is their own!

Other features of young children's behavior suggest that self-awareness emerges between 18 and 24 months. During this same period, toddlers look more at photographs of themselves than at photos of other children. They also refer to themselves by name or with a personal pronoun, such as *I* or *me*, and sometimes they know their age and gender. These changes often occur together and they suggest that self-awareness is well established in most children by age 2, although it develops faster in cultures that encourage toddlers to be independent (Lewis, 2011; Ross et al., 2016).

Soon toddlers and young children begin to recognize continuity in the self over time; the "I" in the present is linked to the "I" in the past (Nelson, 2001). Awareness of a self that is extended in time is fostered by conversations with parents about the past and the future. Through such conversations, a 3-year-old celebrating a birthday understands that she's an older version of the same person who had a birthday a year ago.

Children's growing awareness of a self extended in time is also revealed by their understanding of ownership (Fasig, 2000). When a toddler sees his favorite toy and says "mine," this implies awareness of continuity of the self over time: "In the past, I played with that." And when toddlers say "Mine," rather than being selfish, they're indicating ownership as a way of defining themselves. They are not trying to deny the toy to another, but simply asserting that playing with this toy is part of who they are (Levine, 1983).

Once children fully understand that they exist, they begin to wonder who they are. They want to define themselves. Throughout the preschool years, possessions continue to be one of the ways in which children define themselves. Preschoolers are also likely to mention physical characteristics ("I have blue eyes"), their preferences ("I like spaghetti"), and their competencies ("I can count to 50"). What these features have in common is a focus on a child's characteristics that are observable and concrete (Harter, 2006).

As children enter school, their self-concepts become even more elaborate (Harter, 1994), changes that we'll explore in Chapter 9.

Theory of Mind

As youngsters gain more insights into themselves as thinking beings, they begin to realize that people have thoughts, beliefs, and intentions. They also understand that thoughts, beliefs, and intentions often cause people to behave as they do. Amazingly, even infants understand that people's behavior is often intentional—designed to achieve a goal. Imagine a father who says "Where are the crackers?" in front of his 1-year-old daughter and then begins opening kitchen cabinets, moving objects to look behind them. Finding the box of crackers, he says, "There they are!" An infant who understands intentionality would realize how her father's actions (searching, moving objects) were related to the goal of finding the crackers.

Many clever experiments have revealed that 1-year-olds do indeed understand intentionality (Baillargeon, Scott, & Bian, 2016). For example, in one study, infants observed a woman who consistently seemed interested in one of two stuffed animals: she looked at it intently and seemed happy. Next, the woman picked up either that stuffed animal or another one that she had ignored. By 12 months, infants were surprised to see the woman pick up the animal that she had ignored instead of that animal that had seemed interesting. Infants apparently inferred from the women's looking that she intended to pick up one animal and were surprised when she picked up the other instead (Dunphy-Lelii et al., 2014).

From this early understanding of intentionality, young children's naïve psychology expands rapidly. *Between 2 and 5 years of age, children develop a* theory of mind, *a naïve understanding of the relations between mind and behavior*. One of the leading researchers on theory of mind, Henry Wellman (2014), believes that children's theory of mind moves through several phases during the preschool years. In the earliest phase, preschoolers understand that people can have different desires: One child might want raisins for a snack while another child wants crackers. In the next phase, children know that people can have different beliefs: In trying to find a missing shoe, one child might believe that the shoe is in the kitchen while another child believes that it's in the car. In the third phase, children understand that different experiences can lead to different states of knowledge: A child who has seen a toy hidden in a drawer knows what's in the now-closed drawer, but a child who did not see the toy hidden does not.

The next phase represents a fundamental shift in children's theory of mind: Children understand that behavior is based on a person's beliefs about events and situations, *even when those beliefs are wrong*. Children's understanding of the influence of such false beliefs is revealed in tasks such as the one shown in ▶ Figure 3.11. Anne knows that the marble has been moved to the box, but Sally believes that the marble is still in the basket. Not until 4 years of age do most children correctly say that Sally will look for the marble in the basket (acting on her false belief); 4-year-olds understand that Sally's behavior is based on her beliefs even though her belief is wrong.

In the final phase, children understand that people may feel one emotion but show another. For example, a child who is disappointed by a birthday present smiles anyway because she doesn't want her parents to know how she really feels.

Thus, children's theory of mind becomes more sophisticated over the preschool years. This general pattern is found for children around the world, with one twist: The five-phase sequence we described here is common in many Western nations, but in China and Iran, preschoolers typically understand differences in knowledge (phase 3) before differences in beliefs (Shahaeian et al., 2011; Wellman, Fang, & Peterson, 2011). One explanation for this difference is that compared to Western parents, parents in China and Iran emphasize

This is Sally. Sally has a basket.

This is Anne. Anne has a box.

Sally puts her ball in her basket.

Sally goes out for a walk.

Anne takes the ball from the basket and puts it into the box.

Now Sally comes back. She wants to play with her ball. Where will she look for her ball?

© 2019 Cengage

▶ **Figure 3.11**

In a false-belief task, most 3-year-olds say that Sally will look for the ball in the box, showing that they do not understand how people can act on their beliefs (where the ball is) even when those beliefs are wrong.

theory of mind

Ideas about connections between thoughts, beliefs, intentions, and behavior that create an intuitive understanding of the link between mind and behavior.

"Seeing Is Believing ..." for 3-Year-Olds

Preschoolers gradually recognize that people's behavior is sometimes guided by mistaken beliefs. We once witnessed an episode at a day care center that documented this growing understanding. After lunch, Karen, a 2-year-old, saw ketchup on the floor and squealed, "blood, blood!" Lonna, a 3-year-old, said in a disgusted tone, "It's not blood—it's ketchup." Then Shenan, a 4-year-old, interjected, "Yeah, but Karen *thought* it was blood." A similar incident took place a few weeks later on the day after Halloween. This time Lonna put on a monster mask and scared Karen. When Karen began to cry, Lonna said, "Oh stop. It's just a mask." Shenan broke in again, saying, "You know it's just a mask. But she *thinks* it's a monster." In both cases, only Shenan understood that Karen's behavior was based on her beliefs (that the ketchup is blood and that the monster is real) even though her beliefs were false.

knowledge to their young children ("knowing the right things") and are less tolerant of different beliefs (Wellman, 2012).

You can see preschool children's growing understanding of false belief in the Real People feature.

The early stages of children's theory of mind seem clear. But just *how* this happens is a matter of debate. One view emphasizes the contribution of language, which develops rapidly during the same years that theory of mind emerges (as we'll see in Chapter 4). Some scientists believe that children's language skills contribute to growth of theory of mind, perhaps reflecting the benefit of an expanding vocabulary that includes verbs describing mental states, such as *think, know,* and *believe* (Pascual et al., 2008). Or the benefits may reflect children's mastery of grammatical forms that can be used to describe a setting where a person knows that another person has a false belief (Farrant, Maybery, & Fletcher, 2012).

A different view is that a child's theory of mind emerges from interactions with other people, interactions that provide children with insights into different mental states (Dunn & Brophy, 2005; Slaughter, 2015). Through conversations with parents and older siblings that focus on other people's mental states, children learn facts of mental life, and this helps children to see that others often have different perspectives than they do. In other words, when children frequently participate in conversations that focus on other people's moods, feelings, and intentions, they learn that people's behavior is based on their beliefs, regardless of the accuracy of those beliefs.

These different views are also used to explain why theory of mind develops very slowly in children with autism, which is our last topic in this chapter.

Think About It

Suppose you believe that a theory of mind develops faster when preschoolers spend much time with other children. What sort of correlational study would you devise to test this hypothesis? How could you do an experimental study to test the same hypothesis?

Children with autism master language later than usual and are often more interested in objects than in people.

Sean Sprague/Alamy Stock Photo

Theory of Mind in Children with Autism

Autism is the most serious of a family of disorders known as autism spectrum disorders (ASD). Individuals with ASD acquire language later than usual, and their speech often echoes what others say to them; also, they sometimes become intensely interested in objects (e.g., making the same actions with a toy over and over). In addition, they often seem uninterested in other people, and when they do interact, those exchanges are often awkward, as if individuals with ASD aren't following the rules that govern social interactions. Symptoms usually emerge early in life, typically by 2 years of age. Roughly 8% of children worldwide are diagnosed with ASD; about 80% of them are boys (Baxter et al., 2015). ASD has many possible causes, including genetics, being born prematurely or to older mothers, and being exposed prenatally to toxins (Lyall et al., 2017). Many studies point to atypical brain functioning, perhaps due to an imbalance in excitatory and inhibitory neurotransmitters (Robertson, Ratai, & Kanwisher, 2016).

Children with ASD grasp false belief very slowly, and this performance leads some researchers to conclude that the absence of a theory of mind—sometimes called "mind-blindness" (Baron-Cohen, 2005)—is the defining characteristic of ASD (Leekam, 2016). Other scientists aren't convinced. Although no one doubts that autistic children find false-belief tasks puzzling, some scientists say that mindblindness is a by-product of other deficits and not the cause of the symptoms associated with ASD. One idea is that ASD reflects problems in inhibiting irrelevant actions and in shifting smoothly between actions (Pellicano, 2013). Another idea emphasizes a focused processing style that is common in ASD. For example, children with ASD find hidden objects faster than typically developing children do (Chen et al., 2012). But this emphasis on perceptual details usually comes at the expense of maintaining a coherent overall picture. Consequently, in social interactions, children with ASD may focus on one facet of another person's behavior (e.g., gestures) but ignore other verbal and nonverbal cues (e.g., speech, facial expressions, body language) that collectively promote fluid interactions. Research to evaluate these claims is still ongoing; the answers will likely indicate that multiple factors contribute to ASD.

ASD can't be cured. However, therapy can be used to improve language and social skills in children with autism. In addition, medications can be used to reduce some of the symptoms, such as compulsive behavior and depression (National Institutes of Health, 2015). When ASD is diagnosed early and autistic children grow up in supportive, responsive environments and receive appropriate treatments, they can lead satisfying and productive lives.

TEST YOURSELF 3.5

Recall

1. Apparently children are first self-aware at age 2 because this is when they first recognize themselves in a mirror and in photographs and when they first use _____.

2. During the preschool years, children's self-concepts emphasize _____, physical characteristics, preferences, and competencies.

3. Unlike 4-year-olds, most 3-year-olds don't understand that other people's behavior is sometimes based on _____.

Interpret

- Compare and contrast different explanations of the growth of theory of mind during the preschool years.

Apply

- Self-concept emerges over the same months that toddlers show rapid gains in locomotor skills. How might changes in locomotor skill contribute to a toddler's emerging sense of self?

Check your answers to the Recall Questions at the end of the chapter.

SUMMARY

3.1 The Newborn

How do reflexes help newborns interact with the world?

- Babies are born with a number of different reflexes. Some help them adjust to life outside the uterus, some help protect them from danger, and some serve as the basis for later voluntary motor behavior.

How do we determine whether a baby is healthy and adjusting to life outside the uterus?

- The Apgar scale measures five vital signs to determine a newborn baby's physical well-being. The Neonatal Behavioral Assessment Scale provides a comprehensive evaluation of a baby's behavioral and physical status.

What behavioral states are common among newborns?

- Newborns spend their day in one of four states: alert inactivity, waking activity, crying, and sleeping. A newborn's crying includes a basic cry, a mad cry, and a pain cry. The best way to calm a crying baby is to put the baby on the shoulder and rock him or her.

- Newborns spend approximately two-thirds of every day asleep and go through a complete sleep–wake cycle once every four hours. By 3 or 4 months, babies sleep through the night. Newborns spend about half of their time asleep in REM sleep, an active form of sleep that may stimulate growth in the nervous system.

- Some healthy babies die from sudden infant death syndrome (SIDS). Factors that contribute to SIDS are prematurity, low birth weight, and smoking. Also, babies are vulnerable to SIDS when they sleep on their stomach and when they are overheated. The Back to Sleep campaign was designed to prevent SIDS by encouraging parents to have infants sleep on their backs.

What are the different features of temperament? Do they change as children grow?

- Temperament refers to a consistent style or pattern to an infant's behavior. Modern theories list two to six dimensions of temperament, including, for example, extroversion and negative affect. Temperament is influenced by both heredity and environment and is a reasonably stable characteristic of infants and young children.

3.2 Physical Development

How do height and weight change from birth to 2 years of age?

- Physical growth is particularly rapid during infancy, but babies of the same age differ considerably in their height and weight. Size at maturity is largely determined by heredity.

- Growth follows the cephalocaudal principle, in which the head and trunk develop before the legs. Consequently, infants and young children have disproportionately large heads and trunks.

What nutrients do young children need? How are nutrients best provided?

- Infants must consume a large number of calories relative to their body weight, primarily because of the energy required for growth. Breast-feeding is the best way to provide infants with nourishment and has several other advantages compared with bottle-feeding (e.g., health benefits).

- Malnutrition is a worldwide problem that is particularly harmful during infancy, when growth is so rapid. Treating malnutrition adequately requires improving children's diets and training their parents to provide stimulating environments.

What are nerve cells, and how are they organized in the brain?

- A nerve cell, called a neuron, includes a cell body, a dendrite, and an axon. The mature brain consists of billions of neurons organized into nearly identical left and right hemispheres connected by the corpus callosum. The cerebral cortex regulates most of the functions we think of as distinctively human. The frontal cortex is associated with personality and goal-directed behavior; the left hemisphere of the cortex, with language; and the right hemisphere of the cortex, with nonverbal processes such as perceiving emotions.

How does the brain develop? When does it begin to function?

- Brain specialization is evident in infancy; further specialization involves more focused brain areas and narrowing of stimuli that trigger brain activity. Different systems specialize at different rates. Specialization depends on stimulation from the environment. The relative lack of specialization in the immature brain makes it better able to recover from injury.

3.3 Moving and Grasping: Early Motor Skills

What component skills are involved in learning to walk? At what age do infants master them?

- Infants acquire a series of locomotor skills during their first year, culminating in walking a few months after the first birthday. Like most motor skills, learning to walk involves differentiation of individual skills, such as maintaining balance and using the legs alternately, and then integrating those skills into a coherent whole.

How do infants learn to coordinate the use of their hands?

- Infants first use one hand at a time; then both hands independently; then both hands in common actions; and finally, at about 5 months of age, both hands in different actions with a common purpose.

- Most people are right-handed, a preference observed in prenatal development that becomes stronger during the preschool years. Handedness is determined by heredity but can also be influenced by cultural values.

3.4 Coming to Know the World: Perception

Are infants able to smell, taste, and experience pain?

- Newborns are able to smell, and some can recognize their mother's odor; they also taste, preferring sweet substances and responding negatively to bitter and sour tastes.

- Infants respond to touch. They probably experience pain because their responses to painful stimuli resemble those of older children.

How well do infants hear?

- Babies can hear. More importantly, they can distinguish different speech sounds and different musical sounds.

How well can infants see? Can they see color and depth?

- A newborn's visual acuity is relatively poor, but 1-year-olds can see as well as an adult with normal vision.

- Color vision develops as different sets of cones begin to function, a process that seems to be complete by 4 to 6 months of age. Infants perceive depth based on kinetic cues, binocular disparity, and pictorial cues. They also use motion to recognize objects.

- Infants are attracted to faces, and experience leads infants to form a prototypic face based on faces they see often.

How do infants process and combine information from different sensory modalities, such as between vision and hearing?

- Infants coordinate information from different senses. They can recognize by sight an object they felt previously. Infants are often particularly attentive to information presented redundantly to multiple senses.

3.5 Becoming Self-Aware

When do children begin to realize that they exist?

- Beginning at about 15 months, infants begin to recognize themselves in the mirror, which is one of the first signs of self-recognition. They also begin to prefer looking at

pictures of themselves, begin referring to themselves by name (or using personal pronouns), and sometimes know their age and gender. Evidently, by 2 years of age, most children are self-aware.

What are toddlers' and preschoolers' self-concepts like?

- Preschoolers often define themselves in terms of observable characteristics such as possessions, physical characteristics, preferences, and competencies.

When do preschool children begin to acquire a theory of ind?

- During the preschool years, children's theory of mind becomes progressively more sophisticated. One landmark is the understanding that people's behavior is based on beliefs about events and situations, even when those beliefs are wrong. Children with autism have a limited theory of mind.

Test Yourself: Recall Answers

3.1 1. serve as the basis for later motor behaviors **2.** Apgar score **3.** alert inactivity **4.** REM sleep **5.** sleep on their backs **6.** temperament is moderately stable in these years **3.2 1.** disproportionately large **2.** more **3.** parent training **4.** cell body **5.** planning **6.** left hemisphere **7.** they often regain their earlier skills over time **3.3 1.** dynamic systems theory **2.** using perceptual information **3.** 4 **4.** manipulate the toy **3.4 1.** bitter **2.** pain **3.** human speech **4.** 1 year **5.** Cones **6.** binocular disparity **7.** part of the same object **8.** information presented redundantly to multiple senses **3.5 1.** personal pronouns such as *I* and *me* **2.** possessions **3.** false beliefs

Key Terms

reflexes (80)
alert inactivity (82)
waking activity (82)
crying (82)
sleeping (82)
basic cry (82)
mad cry (82)
pain cry (82)
irregular or rapid-eye-movement (REM) sleep (83)
regular or nonREM sleep (83)
sudden infant death syndrome (SIDS) (84)
temperament (85)
malnourished (90)
neuron (91)
cell body (91)
dendrite (91)
axon (91)

terminal buttons (91)
neurotransmitters (91)
cerebral cortex (91)
hemispheres (92)
corpus callosum (92)
frontal cortex (92)
neural plate (92)
myelin (92)
synaptic pruning (93)
electroencephalography (93)
functional magnetic resonance imaging (fMRI) (93)
experience-expectant growth (94)
experience-dependent growth (95)
motor skills (96)
locomote (96)
fine motor skills (96)
toddling (96)

toddler (96)
dynamic systems theory (96)
differentiation (98)
integration (98)
perception (103)
visual acuity (104)
cones (104)
visual cliff (105)
kinetic cues (105)
visual expansion (105)
motion parallax (105)
binocular disparity (106)
pictorial cues (106)
linear perspective (106)
texture gradient (106)
intersensory redundancy (108)
theory of mind (111)

The Emergence of Thought and Language

Cognitive Development in Infancy and Early Childhood

4

On the TV show *Family Guy*, Stewie is a 1-year-old who can't stand his mother (Stewie: "Hey, mother. I come bearing a gift. I'll give you a hint. It's in my diaper, and it's not a toaster.") and hopes to dominate the world. Much of the humor, of course, turns on the idea that babies are capable of sophisticated thinking and just can't express it. But what thoughts actually lurk in the mind of an infant who is not yet speaking? How does cognition develop during infancy and early childhood? What makes these changes possible?

These questions provide the focus of this chapter. We begin with what has long been considered the definitive account of cognitive development, Jean Piaget's theory, as well as a later variant, the core knowledge approach. The next two sections of the chapter concern alternative accounts of cognitive development. One account, the information-processing perspective, traces children's emerging cognitive skills in many specific domains, including memory skills. The other, Lev Vygotsky's theory, emphasizes the cultural origins of cognitive development and explains why children sometimes talk to themselves as they play or work.

Throughout development, children express their thoughts in oral and written language. In the last section of this chapter, you'll see how children master the sounds, words, and grammar of their native language.

4.1 The Onset of Thinking: Piaget's Account

LEARNING OBJECTIVES

- According to Piaget, how do schemes, assimilation, and accommodation provide the foundation for cognitive development throughout the life span?

- How does thinking become more advanced as infants progress through the sensorimotor stage?

- What are the distinguishing characteristics of thinking during the preoperational stage?

- What are the strengths and weaknesses of Piaget's theory?

- How have contemporary researchers extended Piaget's theory?

Three-year-old Jamila loves talking to her grandmother ("Gram") on the telephone. Sometimes these conversations don't succeed because Gram asks questions and Jamila replies by nodding her head "yes" or "no." Jamila's dad has explained that Gram (and others on the phone) can't see her nodding—that she needs to say "yes" or "no." But Jamila invariably returns to head-nodding. Her dad can't understand why such a bright and talkative child doesn't realize that nodding is meaningless over the phone.

Why does Jamila insist on nodding her head when she's talking on the phone? This behavior is quite typical according to the famous Swiss psychologist Jean Piaget (1896–1980). In Piaget's theory, children's thinking progresses through four qualitatively different stages. In this section, we'll begin by describing some of the general features of Piaget's theory, then examine Piaget's account of thinking during the first two stages (those spanning infancy and the preschool years), and finally consider some of the strengths and weaknesses of the theory.

Basic Principles of Cognitive Development

Piaget believed that children are naturally curious. They constantly want to make sense of their experience and, in the process, construct their understanding of the world. For Piaget, children at all ages are like scientists in creating theories about how the world works. Of course, children's theories are often incomplete but they are valuable in making the world seem more predictable to children.

schemes

According to Piaget, mental structures that organize information and regulate behavior.

According to Piaget, children understand the world with schemes, *psychological structures that organize experience.* Schemes are mental categories of related events, objects, and knowledge. During infancy, most schemes are based on actions. Infants group objects based on the actions they can perform on them. For example, infants suck and grasp, and they use these actions to create categories of objects that can be sucked and objects that can be grasped.

Schemes are just as important after infancy, but they are now based primarily on functional or conceptual relationships, not action. For example, preschoolers learn that forks, knives, and spoons form a functional category of "things I use to eat." And they learn that dogs, cats, and goldfish form a conceptual category of "pets."

Like preschoolers, older children and adolescents have schemes based on functional and conceptual schemes. But they also have schemes that are based on increasingly abstract properties. For example, an adolescent might put fascism, racism, and sexism in a category of "ideologies I despise."

Thus, schemes of related objects, events, and ideas are present throughout development. But as children develop, their rules for creating schemes shift from physical activity to functional, conceptual, and, later, abstract properties of objects, events, and ideas.

Assimilation and Accommodation

Schemes change constantly, adapting to children's experiences. In fact, intellectual adaptation involves two processes working together: assimilation and accommodation. Assimilation *occurs when new experiences are readily incorporated into existing schemes.* Imagine a baby who has the familiar grasping scheme. The baby soon discovers that the grasping scheme also works well on blocks, toy cars, and other small objects. Extending the existing grasping scheme to new objects illustrates assimilation. Accommodation *occurs when schemes are modified based on experience.* Soon the infant learns that some objects can only be lifted with two hands and that some can't be lifted at all. Changing the scheme so that it works for new objects (e.g., using two hands to grasp heavy objects) illustrates accommodation.

Assimilation and accommodation are easier to understand when you remember Piaget's belief that infants, children, and adolescents create theories to try to understand events and objects around them. An infant whose theory is that objects can be lifted with one hand finds the theory confirmed when she tries to pick up small objects, but she's in for a surprise when she tries to pick up a heavy book. The unexpected result forces the infant, like a good scientist, to revise her theory to include this new finding.

The Real People feature shows how accommodation and assimilation allow young children to understand their worlds.

assimilation
According to Piaget, taking in information that is compatible with what one already knows.

accommodation
According to Piaget, changing existing knowledge based on new knowledge.

Equilibration and Stages of Cognitive Development

Assimilation and accommodation are usually in balance, or equilibrium. Children find that they can readily assimilate many experiences into their schemes but that they sometimes need to accommodate their schemes to adjust to new experiences. This balance between assimilation and accommodation was illustrated by our infant with a theory about lifting objects. However, periodically this balance is upset, producing a state of disequilibrium. That is, children discover that their schemes are not adequate because they are spending too much time accommodating and much less time assimilating. *When disequilibrium occurs, children reorganize their schemes to return to a state of equilibrium, a process that Piaget called* equilibration. To restore the balance, current but outmoded ways of thinking are replaced with a qualitatively different, more advanced set of schemes.

equilibration
According to Piaget, the process by which children reorganize their schemes to return to a state of equilibrium when disequilibrium occurs.

Real People | Applying Human Development

Learning about Butterflies: Accommodation and Assimilation in Action

When Ethan, an energetic 2½-year-old, saw a monarch butterfly for the first time, his mother, Kat, told him, "Butterfly, butterfly; that's a butterfly, Ethan." A few minutes later, a zebra swallowtail butterfly landed on a nearby bush and Ethan shouted in excitement, "Butterfly, Mama, butterfly!" A little later, a moth flew out of another bush; with even greater excitement in his voice, Ethan shouted, "Butterfly, Mama, more butterfly!" As Kat was telling Ethan, "No, honey. That's

a moth, not a butterfly," she marveled at how rapidly Ethan seemed to grasp new concepts with so little direction from her. How was this possible?

Piaget's explanation would be that when Kat named the monarch butterfly for Ethan, he formed a simple theory, something like "butterflies are bugs with big wings." The second butterfly differed in color but was still a bug with big wings, so it was readily *assimilated* into Ethan's new theory of butterflies. However,

when Ethan referred to the moth as a butterfly, Kat corrected him. Ethan was forced to *accommodate* to this new experience. He changed his theory of butterflies to make it more precise; the new theory might be something like "butterflies are bugs with thin bodies and big, colorful wings." He also created a new theory, something like "a moth is a bug with a bigger body and plain wings." Accommodation and assimilation work together to help Ethan make sense of his experiences.

This baby will learn that many objects can be grasped easily with one hand—illustrating assimilation—but will also discover that bigger, heavier objects can be grasped only with two hands—illustrating accommodation.

One way to understand equilibration is to return to the metaphor of the child as a scientist. As we discussed in Chapter 1, good scientific theories readily explain some phenomena but usually must be revised to explain others. Children's theories allow them to understand many experiences by predicting, for example, what will happen ("It's morning, so it's time for breakfast") or who will do what ("Mom's gone to work, so Dad will take me to school"), but the theories must be modified when predictions go awry ("Dad thinks I'm old enough to walk to school, so he won't take me").

Sometimes scientists find that their theories contain critical flaws that can't be fixed simply by revising; instead, they must create a new theory that draws on the older theory but differs fundamentally. For example, when the astronomer Copernicus realized that the earth-centered theory of the solar system was fundamentally wrong, his new theory built on the assumption that the sun is the center of the solar system. In much the same way, periodically children reach states in which their current theories seem to be wrong much of the time, so they abandon these theories in favor of more advanced ways of thinking about their physical and social worlds.

According to Piaget, these revolutionary changes in thought occur three times over the life span, at approximately 2, 7, and 11 years of age. This divides cognitive development into the following four stages:

PERIOD OF DEVELOPMENT	AGE RANGE
Sensorimotor period	Infancy (0–2 years)
Preoperational period	Preschool and early elementary school years (2–7 years)
Concrete operational period	Middle and late elementary school years (7–11 years)
Formal operational period	Adolescence and adulthood (11 years and up)

The ages listed are only approximate. Some youngsters move through the periods more rapidly than other children do. However, the only route to formal operations—the most sophisticated type of thought—is through the first three periods, in sequence. Sensorimotor thinking always gives rise to preoperational thinking; a child cannot "skip" preoperational thinking and move directly from the sensorimotor to the concrete operational period.

In the next few pages of this chapter, we consider Piaget's account of sensorimotor and preoperational thinking, the periods from birth to approximately 7 years of age. In Chapter 6, we will return to Piaget's theory to examine his account of concrete and formal operational thinking in older children and adolescents.

Sensorimotor Thinking

sensorimotor period

First of Piaget's four stages of cognitive development, which lasts from birth to approximately 2 years.

Piaget (1951, 1952, 1954) believed that the first two years of life form a distinct phase in human development. *The sensorimotor period, from birth to roughly 2 years of age, is the first of Piaget's four periods of cognitive development.* In the 24 months of this stage, infants' thinking progresses remarkably along three important fronts.

Adapting to and Exploring the Environment

Newborns respond reflexively to many stimuli, but between 1 and 4 months, reflexes are first modified by experience. An infant may inadvertently touch his lips with his thumb, thereby initiating sucking and the pleasing sensations associated with sucking. Later, the infant tries to re-create these sensations by guiding his thumb to his mouth. Sucking no longer occurs only reflexively when a mother places a nipple at the infant's mouth; instead, the infant can initiate sucking.

At about 8 months, infants reach a watershed: the onset of deliberate, intentional behavior. For the first time, the "means" and "end" of activities are distinct. For example, if a father places his hand in front of a toy, an infant will move his father's hand to be able to play with the toy. "The moving the hand" scheme is the means to achieve the goal of "grasping the toy." Using one action as a means to achieve another end is the first indication of purposeful, goal-directed behavior during infancy.

Beginning at about 12 months, infants become active experimenters. An infant may deliberately shake a number of different objects, trying to discover which produce sounds. Or an infant may decide to drop different objects to see what happens. An infant will discover that stuffed animals land quietly, whereas bigger toys often make a more satisfying "clunk" when they hit the ground. These actions represent a significant extension of intentional behavior; now babies repeat actions with different objects solely for the purpose of seeing what will happen.

Understanding Objects

The world is filled with animate objects such as dogs, spiders, and college students, as well as inanimate objects such as cheeseburgers, socks, and this book. But they all share a fundamental property—they exist independently of our actions and thoughts toward them. *Piaget's term for this understanding that objects exist independently is* object permanence. And Piaget made the astonishing claim that infants lacked this understanding for much of the first year. He proposed that an infant's understanding of objects could be summarized as "out of sight, out of mind." For infants, objects exist when in sight and no longer exist when out of sight.

Piaget showed that 4- to 8-month-olds will grasp for an interesting object that is placed in front of them. However, if the object is then hidden by a barrier or covered with a cloth, the infant will neither reach nor search. Instead, the infant seems to lose all interest in the object, as if the now hidden object no longer exists. Paraphrasing the familiar phrase, "out of sight is out of existence."

Beginning at about 8 months, infants search for an object that an experimenter has covered with a cloth. In fact, many 8- to 12-month-olds enjoy playing this game: An adult covers the object, and the infant sweeps away the cover, laughing and smiling all the while! But despite this accomplishment, their understanding of object permanence remains incomplete, according to Piaget. If 8- to 10-month-olds see an object hidden under one container several times and then see it hidden under a second container, they usually reach for the toy under the first container. Piaget claimed that this behavior shows fragmentary understanding of objects because infants do not distinguish the object from the actions they use to locate it, such as reaching for a particular container.

Piaget argued that not until approximately 18 months do infants have full understanding of object permanence. However, in a few pages, we'll see that infants know more about objects than Piaget claimed.

Using Symbols

By 18 months, most infants have begun to talk and gesture, evidence of their emerging capacity to use symbols. Words and gestures are symbols that stand for something else. When a baby waves, it's a symbol that's just as effective as saying "good-bye" to bid farewell. Children also begin to engage in pretend play, another use of symbols. At 20 months, children may move their hand back and forth in front of their mouth, pretending to brush their teeth.

Once infants can use symbols, they can anticipate the consequences of actions mentally instead of having to perform them. Imagine that an infant and a parent construct a tower of blocks next to an open door. Leaving the room, a 12- to

object permanence
Understanding, acquired in infancy, that objects exist independently of oneself.

Toddlers frequently gesture, a sign of their growing competence at using symbols.

David Young-Wolff/PhotoEdit

18-month-old might close the door, knocking over the tower because he cannot foresee this outcome of closing the door. But an 18- to 24-month-old can anticipate the consequence of closing the door and move the tower beforehand.

In just 2 years, the infant progresses from responding reflexively to actively exploring the world, understanding objects, and using symbols. These achievements are remarkable and set the stage for preoperational thinking, which we'll examine next.

Preoperational Thinking

Once young children have crossed into preoperational thinking, the magical power of symbols is available to them. Of course, mastering this power is a lifelong process; the preschool child's efforts are tentative and sometimes incorrect. Piaget identified a number of characteristic shortcomings in preschoolers' symbolic skills. Let's look at three.

Egocentrism

egocentrism

Difficulty in seeing the world from another's point of view; typical of children in the preoperational period.

Preoperational children typically believe that others see the world—literally and figuratively—exactly as they do. Egocentrism *is difficulty in seeing the world from another's outlook.* When youngsters stubbornly cling to their own way, they are not simply being contrary. Preoperational children do not comprehend that other people differ in their ideas, convictions, and emotions.

One of Piaget's famous experiments, the three-mountains problem, demonstrates preoperational children's egocentrism (Piaget & Inhelder, 1956, Chap. 8). Youngsters were seated at a table like the one shown in ▶Figure 4.1. When preoperational children were asked to choose the photograph that corresponded to another person's view of the mountains, they usually picked the photograph that showed their own view of the mountains, not the other person's. Preoperational youngsters evidently suppose that the mountains are seen

▶ **Figure 4.1**

Egocentrism: When asked to select the photograph that shows the mountains as the adult sees them, preschool children often select the photograph that shows how the mountains look to them.

© 2019 Cengage

the same way by all; they presume that theirs is the only view, not one of many possible views. According to Piaget, only concrete operational children fully understand that all people do not experience an event in exactly the same way.

In the vignette, 3-year-old Jamila nods her head during phone conversations with her grandmother. This, too, reflects preoperational egocentrism. Jamila assumes that because she is aware that her head is moving up and down (or side to side), her grandmother must be aware of it, too. Because of this egocentrism, preoperational youngsters often attribute their own thoughts and feelings to others. *They may even credit inanimate objects with life and lifelike properties, a phenomenon known as* animism (Piaget, 1929). A preschool child may think that the sun is unhappy on a cloudy day or that a car hurts when it's in an accident. Caught up in their egocentrism, preoperational youngsters believe that inanimate objects have feelings just as they do.

animism
Phenomenon of crediting inanimate objects with life and lifelike properties such as feelings.

Centration

A second characteristic of preoperational thinking is that children seem to have the psychological equivalent of tunnel vision: They often concentrate on one aspect of a problem but ignore other, equally relevant aspects. Centration *is Piaget's term for this narrowly focused thought that characterizes preoperational youngsters.*

centration
According to Piaget, narrowly focused type of thought characteristic of preoperational children.

Piaget demonstrated centration in his experiments involving conservation. In these experiments, Piaget wanted to determine when children realize that important characteristics of objects (or sets of objects) stay the same despite changes in their physical appearance. Some tasks that Piaget used to study conservation are shown in ❯ Figure 4.2. Each begins with identical objects (or sets of objects). Then one of the objects (or sets) is transformed, and children are asked if the objects are the same in terms of some important feature.

A typical conservation problem involves conservation of liquid quantity. Children are shown identical beakers filled with the same amount of juice. After children agree that the two beakers have the same amount of juice, the juice is poured from one beaker into a taller, thinner beaker. The juice looks different in the tall, thin beaker—it rises higher—but of course the amount is unchanged. Nevertheless, preoperational children claim that the tall, thin beaker has more juice than the original beaker. (And if the juice is poured into a wider beaker, they believe it has less.)

What is happening here? According to Piaget, preoperational children center on the level of the juice in the beaker. If the juice is higher after it is poured, preoperational children believe that there must be more juice now than before. Because preoperational thinking is centered, these youngsters ignore the fact that the change in the level of the juice is always accompanied by a change in the diameter of the beaker.

Appearance as Reality

A final feature of preoperational thinking is that preschool children believe that an object's appearance tells what the object is really like. For instance, many a 3-year-old has watched with fascination as an older brother or sister put on a ghoulish costume only to erupt in frightened tears when their sibling put on scary makeup. The scary made-up face is reality, not just something that looks frightening but really isn't.

Confusion between appearance and reality is not limited to costumes and masks. It is a general characteristic of preoperational thinking. Consider the following cases where appearances and reality conflict:

- A boy is angry because a friend is being mean but smiles because he's afraid the friend will leave if he reveals his anger.
- A glass of milk looks brown when seen through sunglasses.
- A piece of hard rubber looks like food (e.g., a piece of pizza).

In conservation problems, preschool children typically do not believe that the quantity of a liquid remains the same when it is poured into a taller, more slender beaker.

Lew Merrim/Science Source

▶ **Figure 4.2**

Children in the preoperational stage of development typically have difficulty solving conservation problems, in which important features of an object (or objects) stay the same despite changes in physical appearance.

Type of conservation	Starting configuration	Transformation	Final configuration
Liquid quantity	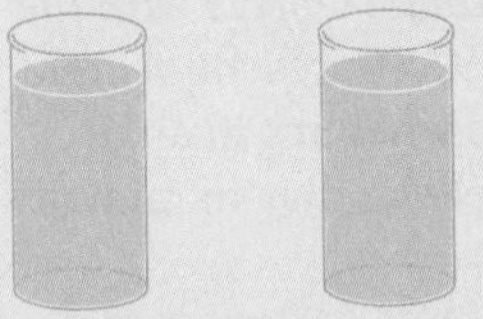 Is there the same amount of water in each glass?	Pour water from one glass into a shorter, wider glass.	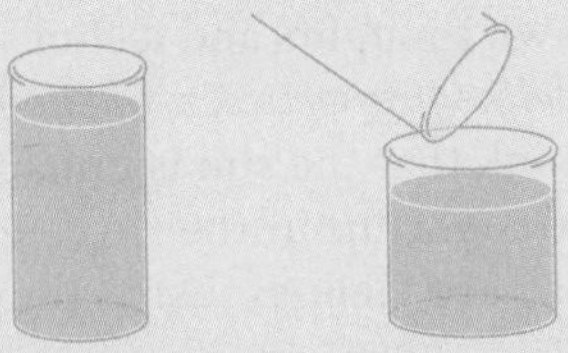 Now is there the same amount of water in each glass, or does one glass have more?
Number	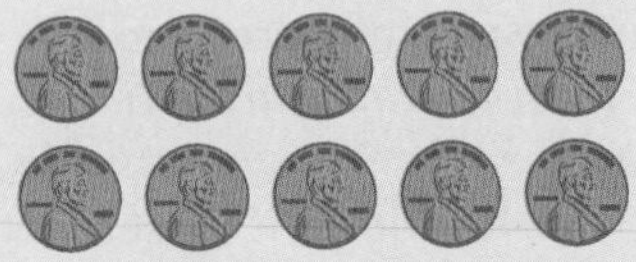 Are there the same number of pennies in each row?	Stretch out the top row of pennies, push together the bottom row.	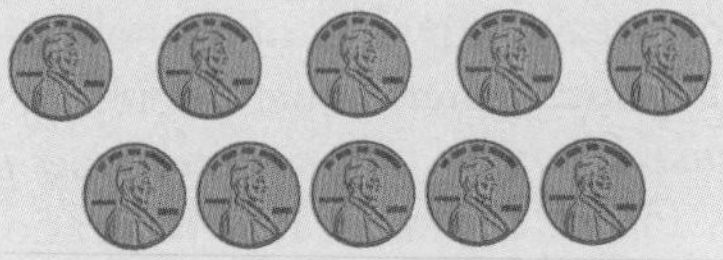 Now are there the same number of pennies in each row, or does one row have more?
Length	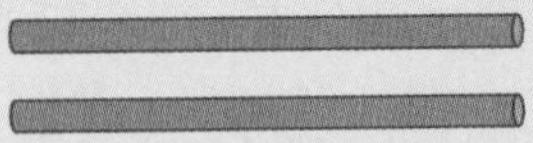 Are these sticks the same length?	Move one stick to the left and the other to the right.	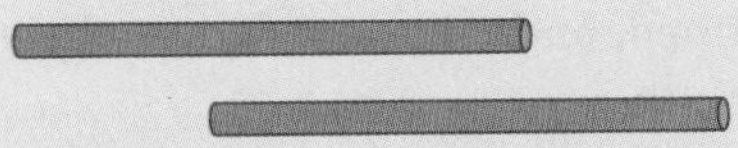 Now are the sticks the same length, or is one longer?
Mass	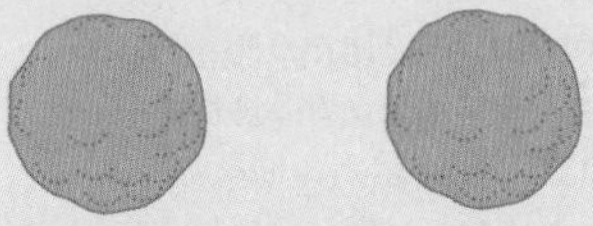 Does each ball have the same amount of clay?	Roll one ball so that it looks like a sausage.	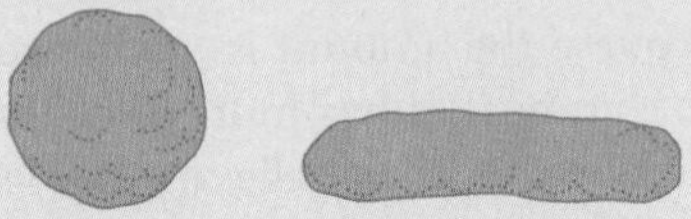 Now does each piece have the same amount of clay, or does one have more?
Area	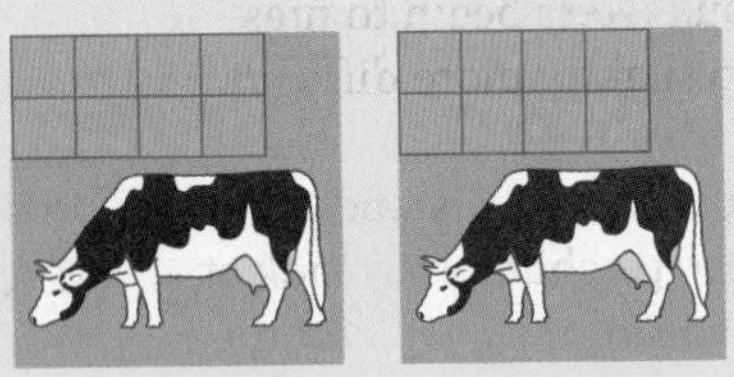 Does each cow have the same amount of grass to eat?	Spread out the squares in one field.	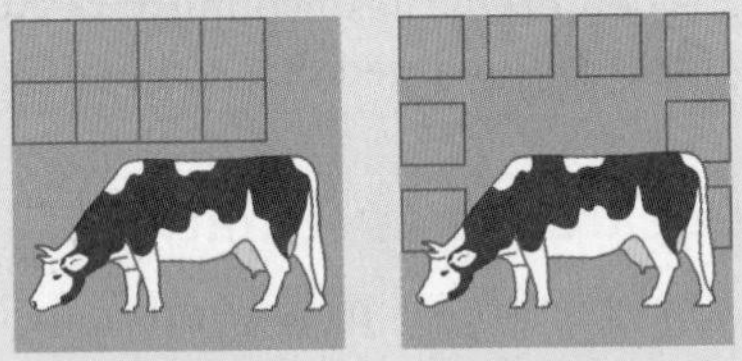 Now does each cow have the same amount to eat, or does one cow have more?

© 2019 Cengage

Older children and adults know that the boy looks happy, the milk looks brown, and the object looks like food but that the boy is really angry, the milk is really white, and the object is really rubber. In contrast, preoperational children confuse appearance and reality, thinking the boy is happy, the milk is brown, and the piece of rubber is edible.

The defining characteristics of preoperational thought are summarized in ▶ Table 4.1.

Table 4.1

Characteristics of Preoperational Thinking		
CHARACTERISTIC	**DEFINITION**	**EXAMPLE**
Egocentrism	Child believes that all people see the world as he or she does	A child gestures during a telephone conversation, not realizing that the listener cannot see the gestures
Centration	Child focuses on one aspect of a problem or situation but ignores other relevant aspects	In conservation of liquid quantity, child pays attention to the height of the liquid in the beaker but ignores the diameter of the beaker
Appearance as reality	Child assumes that an object really is what it appears to be	Child believes that a person smiling at another person is really happy even though the other person is being mean

Evaluating Piaget's Theory

Because Piaget's theory is so comprehensive, it has stimulated much research. Much of this work supports Piaget's view that children actively try to understand the world around them and to organize their knowledge and that cognitive development includes major qualitative changes (Brainerd, 1996; Flavell, 1996). One important contribution of Piaget's theory is that many teachers and parents have found it a rich source of ideas about ways to foster children's development.

Guidelines for Fostering Cognitive Development

Piaget's theory has several straightforward implications for conditions that promote cognitive growth.

- Cognitive growth occurs as children construct their own understanding of the world, so the teacher's role is to create environments where children can discover how the world works. A teacher shouldn't simply try to tell children how addition and subtraction are complementary, but should provide children with materials that allow them to discover the complementarity themselves.
- Children profit from experience only when they can interpret the experience with their current cognitive structures. Consequently, the best teaching experiences are slightly ahead of the children's current level of thinking. As youngsters begin to master basic addition, don't jump directly to subtraction, but go to slightly more difficult addition problems.
- Cognitive growth can be particularly rapid when children discover inconsistencies and errors in their own thinking. Therefore, teachers should encourage children to look at the consistency of their thinking, but then let children take the lead in sorting out the inconsistencies. If a child is making mistakes in borrowing on subtraction problems, a teacher shouldn't correct the error directly, but should encourage the child to look at a large number of these errors to discover what he or she is doing wrong.

According to Piaget's theory of cognitive development, children need to learn by doing.

Criticisms of Piaget's Theory

Although Piaget's contributions to child development are legendary, some elements of his theory have held up better than others (Miller, 2011; Newcombe, 2013; Siegler & Alibali, 2005).

- *Piaget's theory underestimates cognitive competence in infants and young children and overestimates cognitive competence in adolescents.* In Piaget's theory, cognitive development is steady in early childhood but not particularly rapid. In contrast, a main theme of modern child development science is that infants and toddlers are extraordinarily competent. By using more sensitive tasks than Piaget's, modern investigators have shown that infants and toddlers are vastly more capable than expected based on Piaget's theory. For example, in a few pages, we'll see that infants have a much greater understanding of objects than Piaget believed. However, Piaget overestimated cognitive skill in adolescents, who often fail to reason according to formal operational principles and revert to less sophisticated reasoning.

- *Piaget's theory is vague concerning processes and mechanisms of change.* Many of the key components of the theory, such as accommodation and assimilation, are too vague to test scientifically. Consequently, scientists abandoned them in favor of other cognitive processes that could be evaluated more readily and hence could provide more convincing accounts of children's thinking.

- *Piaget's stage model does not account for variability in children's performance.* In Piaget's view, each stage of intellectual development has unique characteristics that leave their mark on everything a child does. For example, preoperational thinking is defined by egocentrism and centration. Consequently, children's performance on different tasks should be consistent. On the conservation and the three-mountains tasks, for instance, according to Piaget, 4-year-olds should always respond in a preoperational way: They should say that the water is not the same after pouring and that another person sees the mountains the same way they do. In fact, children's thinking is not this consistent. A child's thinking may be sophisticated in some domains but naïve in others (Siegler, 1981). This inconsistency does not support Piaget's view that children's thinking should always reflect the distinctive imprint of their current stage of cognitive development.

- *Piaget's theory undervalues the influence of the sociocultural environment on cognitive development.* Returning to the metaphor of the child as scientist, Piaget describes the child as a lone scientist, constantly trying to figure out by herself how her theory coordinates with data. In reality, a child's effort to understand her world is far more social than Piaget described. Her growing understanding of the world is profoundly influenced by interactions with family members, peers, and teachers, and it takes place against the backdrop of cultural values. Piaget did not ignore these social and cultural forces entirely, but they are not prominent in his theory.

These criticisms do not mean that Piaget's theory is invalid or should be abandoned. As noted previously, it remains the most complete account of cognitive development. However, in recent years, researchers have attempted to round out our understanding of cognitive development using other theoretical perspectives, such as the information-processing approach examined later in this chapter.

Extending Piaget's Account: Children's Naïve Theories

Piaget believed that children, like scientists, formulate theories about how the world works. Children's theories are usually called "naïve theories" because, unlike real scientific theories, they are not created by specialists and are rarely evaluated by real experiments. Nevertheless, naïve theories are valuable because they allow children (and adults) to understand new experiences and predict future events.

In Piaget's view, children formulate a grand, comprehensive theory that attempts to explain an enormous variety of phenomena—including reasoning about objects, people, and morals, for example—within a common framework. More recent views retain the idea of children as theorists but propose that children, like real scientists, develop specialized theories about much narrower areas. For example, *according to the* core knowledge hypothesis, *infants are born with rudimentary knowledge of the world; this knowledge is elaborated based on children's experiences* (Newcombe, 2013; Spelke & Kinzler, 2007). Some of the theories young children first develop concern physics, psychology, and biology. That is, infants and toddlers rapidly develop theories that organize their knowledge about properties of objects, people, and living things (Wellman & Gelman, 1998).

core knowledge hypothesis
Infants are born with rudimentary knowledge of the world, which is elaborated based on experiences.

We examined children's developing theory of mind in Chapter 3; in the next few pages, we'll look at children's naïve theories of physics and biology.

Naïve Physics

As adults, we know much about objects and their properties. For example, we know that if we place a coffee cup on a table, it will remain there unless another person moves it; it will not move by itself or disappear. And we don't release a coffee cup in midair because we know that an unsupported object will fall. Child development researchers have long been interested in young children's understanding of objects, in part because Piaget claimed that understanding of objects develops slowly and takes many months to become complete. However, by devising some clever procedures, other investigators have shown that babies understand objects much earlier than Piaget claimed. Renée Baillargeon (1987, 1994), for example, assessed object permanence by using a procedure in which infants first saw a silver screen that appeared to be rotating back and forth. After an infant became familiar with this display, one of two new displays was shown. In the "realistic" event, a red box appeared in a position behind the screen, making it impossible for the screen to rotate as far back as it had previously. Instead, the screen moved away from the infant until it made contact with the box, then moved back toward the infant. In the "unrealistic" event, shown in ❱ Figure 4.3, the red box appeared but the screen continued to move as before. The screen moved away from the infant until it was flat, then moved forward, again revealing the red box. The illusion was possible because the box was mounted on a movable platform that allowed it to drop out of the way of the moving screen. However, from the infant's perspective, the box seemed to vanish behind the screen, only to reappear.

❱ **Figure 4.3**

Object permanence in 3½- and 4½-month-old infants. Infants are surprised to see the silver screen rotate flat, which suggests that they understand the "permanence" of the red box. box (Baillargeon, R., 1987).

1. The silver screen is lying flat on the table and the red box is fully visible.

2. The silver screen has begun to rotate, but the red box is largely visible.

3. The silver screen is now vertical, blocking the red box.

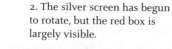

4. The silver screen continues to rotate, blocking the red box, which has started to drop through the trap door.

5. The silver screen is completely flat, apparently having "rotated through" the red box which is actually now under the table.

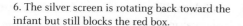

6. The silver screen is rotating back toward the infant but still blocks the red box.

7. The silver screen is again flat and the box fully visible to the infant.

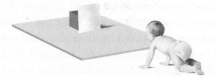

Toddlers distinguish animate objects, such as goats, from inanimate objects, such as furniture and tools.

The disappearance and reappearance of the box violates the idea that objects exist permanently. Consequently, an infant who understands that objects are permanent should find the unrealistic event a novel stimulus and look at it longer than the realistic event. Baillargeon found that 4½-month-olds consistently looked longer at the unrealistic event than at the realistic event. Infants apparently thought that the unrealistic event was novel, just as we are surprised when an object vanishes from a magician's scarf. Evidently, infants have some understanding of object permanence early in the first year of life.

Of course, infants' understanding of objects is rudimentary and research has begun to reveal the specific features of events that lead infants to believe that objects do not vanish (Bremner, Slater, & Johnson, 2015). And infants know more about objects than permanence. They know that objects move continuously on a path, not magically moving from one spot to another; they know that objects are solid and that objects cannot "pass through" each other; they know that one object must contact another to cause movement; and they know that unsupported objects will fall (Hespos & vanMarle, 2012; Wang, Zhang, & Baillargeon, 2016). In short, infants rapidly create a simple but useful theory of basic properties of objects, a theory that helps them expect that objects such as toys will act predictably.

Naïve Biology

Fundamental to adults' naïve theories is the distinction between living and nonliving things. Adults know that living things, for example, are made of cells, inherit properties from parents, and move spontaneously. Adults' theories of living things begin in infancy, when youngsters first distinguish animate objects (e.g., people, insects, other animals) from inanimate objects (e.g., rocks, plants, furniture, tools). Motion is critical in infants' understanding of the difference between animate and inanimate objects. That is, by about 9 months, infants have determined that animate objects are self-propelled, sometimes move in irregular paths, and act to achieve goals (Opfer & Gelman, 2011).

During the preschool years, children's naïve theories of biology expand to include many specific properties associated with living things, particularly when they have daily contact with animals (Geerdts, Van de Walle, & LoBue, 2015). Many 4-year-olds' theories of biology include the ideas that only animals can grow, become ill, and heal when damaged (Legare, Wellman, & Gelman, 2009; Margett & Witherington, 2011). And their understanding is so sophisticated that children aren't fooled by lifelike robots: 4-year-olds know that robots are machines that (a) do not eat or grow and (b) are made by people and can break (Jipson & Gelman, 2007). Nevertheless, preschoolers believe that robots represent a special kind of machine because youngsters attribute humanlike traits to robots, such as being friendly (Kahn, Gary, & Shen, 2013).

A fundamental part of young children's theory of living things is a commitment to **teleological explanations**: *Children believe that livings things, including their parts and their actions, exist for a purpose.* For example, young children believe that lions exist so that people can see them in a zoo (Kelemen, 2003). And they believe that a child's pet ran away to teach the child to be more responsible (Banerjee & Bloom, 2015). Teleological thinking resembles animism (described on page 123) and may reflect a child's tendency to extend to animals the knowledge that objects such as tools are made for a specific purpose (Kelemen & DiYanni, 2005).

Young children's theories of living things are also rooted in **essentialism**: *Children believe that many living things have an essence that can't be seen but gives a living thing its identity.* Specifically, essentialism assumes that certain natural categories (e.g., turtles, girls) have sharp boundaries that can't be changed, that members of these categories share many features, and that these shared features are caused by an underlying essence present in all category members (Gelman, 2003). For example, essentialism says that birds form a category that is clearly distinguishable from other categories (i.e., there are no animals that

teleological explanations
Children's belief that living things, including their parts and their actions, exist for a purpose.

essentialism
Children's belief that all living things have an essence that can't be seen but gives a living thing its identity.

are part bird and part squirrel), they share many features (e.g., they fly, sing, and lay eggs), and they have an underlying essence—"birdness"—that is responsible for the shared features. Young children's essentialism explains why 4-year-olds believe that a baby kangaroo adopted by goats will still hop and have a pouch and why they believe that a watermelon seed planted in a cornfield will produce watermelons (Solomon & Zaitchik, 2012).

One way to see children's essentialism in action is through "transplant studies" in which children are told about internal parts transplanted from one person to another and children are asked whether the organ recipient takes on the properties of the organ donor. One of these studies is the subject of the Spotlight on Research feature.

Spotlight On Research

Have a Heart! Preschoolers' Essentialist Thinking

Who were the investigators, and what was the aim of the study? Imagine that your heart is failing and that you need a transplant to live. The only heart available is Adolf Hitler's. Would you take it? Many adults would not because they fear that organ recipients might take on the properties of the organ donor, even though there is no evidence that transplanting a heart would transfer properties of the donor. This shows essentialism: The heart is seen as part of the essence of "human-ness" so a transplant transfers other properties to the recipient. Would preschool children show this sort of essentialism? Meredith Meyer and her colleagues, Susan Gelman, Steven Roberts, and Sarah-Jane Leslie, conducted a study to find out (2016).

How did the investigators measure the topic of interest? Meyer and colleagues created scenarios in which children were described as being nice, mean, smart, or not smart. They also included scenarios that described pigs and monkeys acting naturally. Children participating in the study were asked to imagine that they had received $1 from the child or animal in the scenario or that they had received a heart from the child or animal in the scenario. Then they were asked if they had received $1 or a heart, whether they would become like the child or animal in the scenario (i.e., become nice, mean, smart, not smart, piglike, monkeylike).

Who were the children in the study? The researchers tested preschool children and elementary school children. For simplicity, we describe only the findings for the 4- and 5-year-olds.

What was the design of the study? This study was experimental: Meyers and

colleagues manipulated the kind of transfer—heart versus money—and examined its impact on children's judgments that they would take on characteristics of the donor. The study was cross-sectional, but we're only considering the findings from the younger children.

Were there ethical concerns with the study? No. The tasks posed no danger to the children.

What were the results? The results are shown in ❱ Figure 4.4. A score of 0 corresponds to "no transfer"—in other words, children judged that they would not take on the characteristics of the donor. Scores greater than 0 indicate ever greater judgments that children would take on the features of the donor. The left bars of Figure 4.4 show that overall preschoolers believed they would be unaffected by receiving $1 but would be affected by receiving a heart.

One potential problem is that nice people are sometimes referred to as "warm hearted" and mean people are sometimes described as "cold hearted," so children's responses might not reflect essentialist thinking. Consequently, to provide a more stringent test of children's essentialist beliefs, the researchers repeated the analyses but excluding nice and mean (i.e., including only smart, not smart, piglike, and monkeylike). The results, shown in the right bars, are nearly identical to the full analyses. Children do not believe that they would become not smart or monkeylike if they were to receive $1, but they think it would be possible if they were to receive a heart.

What did the investigators conclude? The findings illustrate a key element of essentialism: "children appeal to an internal . . . essence when making

predictions about outward features" (p. 15). In other words, children seem to view the heart as an internal essence that could cause a recipient of that heart to take on properties of the donor, such as being nice, smart, or like a monkey.

What converging evidence would strengthen these conclusions? Meyer and her colleagues examined transfer of a single internal organ: It would be useful to extend the work to other internal organs such as the stomach or the lungs. And researchers, by asking children about transplants involving hair or skin (biological but not internal) or a pacemaker (internal but not biological), could describe more precisely what preschool children consider to be essences.

❱ **Figure 4.4**

Preschool children believe that they might take on the features of a heart donor, a finding that reveals essentialist thinking.

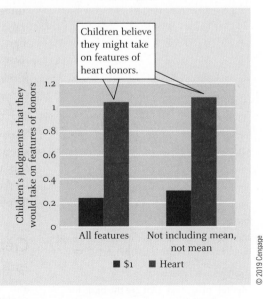

Children believe they might take on features of heart donors.

© 2019 Cengage

Of course, although preschoolers' naïve theories of biology are complex, their theories have some flaws. The most striking is that although preschoolers know that plants grow and heal, they don't consider plants to be living things, apparently because they see goal-directed motion as a key property of living things (Opfer & Siegler, 2004). Nevertheless, children's naïve theories of biology, when joined with their naïve theory of physics, provide powerful tools for making sense of their world and for understanding new experiences.

TEST YOURSELF 4.1

Recall

1. The term _____ refers to modification of schemes based on experience.

2. According to Piaget, _____ are psychological structures that organize experience.

3. Piaget believed that infants' understanding of objects could be summarized as _____.

4. By 18 months, most infants talk and gesture, which shows that they have the capacity _____.

5. Preschoolers are often _____, meaning that they are unable to take another person's viewpoint.

6. Preoperational children sometimes attribute thoughts and feelings to inanimate objects; this is called _____.

7. One criticism of Piaget's theory is that it underestimates cognitive competence in _____.

8. Most 4-year-olds know that living things move, _____, become ill, and heal when injured.

Interpret

- Piaget championed the view that children participate actively in their own development. How do the sensorimotor child's contributions differ from the formal-operational child's contributions?

Apply

- Based on what you know about Piaget's theory, what would his position have been on the continuity–discontinuity issue discussed in Chapter 1?

Check your answers to the Recall Questions at the end of the chapter.

4.2 Information Processing During Infancy and Early Childhood

LEARNING OBJECTIVES

- What is the basis of the information-processing approach?
- How well do young children pay attention?
- What kinds of learning take place during infancy?
- Do infants and preschool children remember?
- What do infants and preschoolers know about numbers?

When Claire, a bubbly 3-year-old, is asked how old she'll be on her next birthday, she proudly says, "Four!" while holding up five fingers. Asked to count four objects, whether they're candies, toys, or socks, Claire usually says, "1, 2, 6, 7 . . . SEVEN!" Claire's older brothers find this very funny, but her mother thinks that, the mistakes notwithstanding, Claire's behavior shows that she knows a great deal about numbers and counting. But what exactly does Claire understand? That question has her mother stumped!

Today, many developmentalists borrow from computer science to formulate their ideas about human thinking and how it develops (Plunkett, 1996). As you recall from Chapter 1, this approach is called information processing. In this section, we'll see what information processing has revealed about young children's thinking and, along the way, see what to make of Claire's counting.

mental hardware

Mental and neural structures that are built in and allow the mind to operate.

mental software

Mental "programs" that are the basis for performing particular tasks.

General Principles of Information Processing

In the information-processing view, human thinking is based on both mental hardware and mental software. Mental hardware *refers to mental and neural structures that are built in and allow the mind to operate.* Mental software *refers to mental "programs" that are the basis for performing particular tasks.* Information-processing psychologists claim that as children develop, their mental software becomes more complex, more powerful, and more efficient.

In the next few pages, we'll look at the development of information-processing skills in infants, toddlers, and preschoolers, beginning with attention.

Attention

Hannah was only 3 days old and was often startled by the sounds of traffic outside her family's apartment. Hannah's parents worried that she might not get enough sleep. Yet within a few days, traffic sounds no longer disturbed Hannah; she slept blissfully. Why was a noise that had been so troubling no longer a problem? *The key is* attention, *a process that determines which sensory information receives additional cognitive processing.*

Hannah's response was normal not only for infants but also for children and adolescents. *When presented with a strong or unfamiliar stimulus, an* orienting response *usually occurs: A person startles, fixes the eyes on the stimulus, and shows changes in heart rate and brain-wave activity.* Collectively, these responses indicate that the infant has noticed the stimulus. Remember, too, that Hannah soon ignored the sounds of traffic. When a stimulus is presented repeatedly, people recognize it as familiar and the orienting response gradually disappears. Habituation *is the diminished response to a stimulus as it becomes familiar.*

The orienting response and habituation are both useful to infants. Orienting makes the infant aware of potentially important or dangerous events in the environment. However, responding constantly to insignificant stimuli is wasteful, so habituation keeps infants from devoting too much energy to insignificant events (Rovee-Collier, 1987).

Preschool children gradually learn how to focus their attention, but when compared with older children and adults, they are often not very attentive (Hatania & Smith, 2010). In the meantime, teachers and parents can help young children pay attention better. For example, Tools of the Mind is a curriculum for preschool and kindergarten children that uses pretend play to improve attentional processes (Diamond & Lee, 2011). Pretend play may seem like a surprising way to improve attention, but staying "in character" while pretending teaches children to inhibit inappropriate "out-of-character" behavior. And it encourages thinking flexibly as children respond to their playmates' improvisation. Teachers also contribute by providing visual reminders of the need to pay attention, such as showing a drawing of an ear to remind children to listen. Tools of the Mind improves attention, particularly in children who are at risk for problems in school (Blair, 2016).

Parents can also help promote their children's attentional skills. In one study (Neville et al., 2013), parents and their preschool children attended an after-school program that included activities designed to improve children's attention. For example, in one task, children were taught how to color carefully while being distracted by nearby peers playing with balloons. Parents were taught ways to support their children's attention, for example by monitoring how they spoke to their children. After children participated in this program, their attention improved.

Learning

From birth, babies rapidly learn about the people and the objects in their environment. This learning reflects several processes:

- You may recall experiments in which dogs learned to salivate when they heard a bell. *This learning represents* classical conditioning, *in which a neutral stimulus (a bell) elicits a response (salivation) that was originally produced by another stimulus (food).* Similarly, when infants repeatedly hear a tone just before sugar water is placed in their mouth with a dropper, they learn to suck when they hear the tone (Lipsitt, 1990). Classical conditioning gives infants a sense of order in their

attention
Processes that determine which information will be processed further by an individual.

orienting response
An individual views a strong or unfamiliar stimulus, and changes in heart rate and brain-wave activity occur.

habituation
Act of becoming unresponsive to a stimulus that is presented repeatedly.

classical conditioning
A form of learning that involves pairing a neutral stimulus and a response originally produced by another stimulus.

Infants (and older children) pay attention to loud stimuli at first but then ignore them if they aren't interesting or dangerous.

LIU JIN/AFP/Getty Images

Toddlers who have fun playing in the water will welcome the sound of the bathtub being filled.

operant conditioning
Form of learning that emphasizes the consequences of reward and punishment.

environment; they learn that a stimulus is a signal for what will happen next. For example, a toddler may smile when she hears the family dog's collar because she knows the dog is coming to play with her.

- *Operant conditioning focuses on the relation between the consequences of behavior and the likelihood that the behavior will recur.* When a child's behavior leads to pleasant consequences, the child will probably behave similarly in the future; when the child's behavior leads to unpleasant consequences, the child will probably not repeat the behavior. When a baby smiles, an adult may hug the baby in return; this pleasing consequence makes the baby more likely to smile in the future. When a baby grabs a family heirloom, an adult may become angry and shout at the baby; these unpleasant consequences make the baby less likely to grab the heirloom in the future.

- In *imitation*, children, adolescents, and young adults learn much simply by watching others behave. For example, children learn new sports moves by watching pro athletes, they learn gender roles by watching TV, and they learn new computer games by watching peers. Some scientists believe that imitation begins at birth (Meltzoff & Moore, 1994) but the evidence is inconsistent and open to different interpretations (Oostenbroek et al., 2013, 2016). However, by 6 months, infants definitely imitate (Barr & Hayne, 1999). For example, a baby may imitate an adult waving her finger.

Processes like classical conditioning, operant conditioning, and imitation allow babies to make sense of the world around them.

Memory

Several days after infants learn that kicking moves a mobile, they kick when they see the mobile, showing that they remember the connection between kicking and the mobile's movements.

Young babies remember events for days and even weeks at a time, an ability that was revealed by experiments in which a ribbon from a mobile is attached to a 2- or 3-month-old's leg (Rovee-Collier, 1997, 1999). Within minutes, the baby learns to kick to make the mobile move. When the ribbon is attached several days or a couple of weeks later, babies would still kick to make the mobile move. However, after several weeks passed, most babies forgot that kicking moved the mobile. But when babies were reminded—a researcher moved the mobile without attaching the ribbon to the baby's foot—the next day most kicked to move the mobile. Thus, this work shows that three important features of memory exist by 2 and 3 months of age: (1) an event from the past is remembered, (2) over time, the event can no longer be recalled, and (3) a cue can serve to retrieve a memory that seems to have been forgotten.

From these humble origins, memory improves rapidly in older infants and toddlers. Youngsters require fewer exposure to information to remember it and they can remember it longer (Lukowski & Bauer, 2014). When shown novel actions with toys and later asked to imitate what they saw, compared with infants, toddlers require fewer exposures to the actions to remember them and remember them longer. As children master language and are asked to describe past events aloud, older preschoolers provide more elaborate descriptions and often highlight the unique features of events (e.g., a birthday party with a Star Wars theme).

These improvements in memory can be traced, in part, to growth in the brain regions that support memory (Lukowski & Bower, 2014; Olson & Newcombe, 2014). The hippocampus, a brain structure that plays a key role in storing information in memory, develops rapidly during the first year although some regions are not mature until about two years. The prefrontal cortex, a structure responsible for retrieving these stored memories, develops more slowly, into the preschool and elementary school years. Thus, development of memory during the first two years reflects growth in these two different brain regions.

Autobiographical Memory

Do you remember the name of your teacher in fourth grade or where your high school graduation was held? In answering those questions, you searched memory, just as you would to answer questions such as "What is the capital of Canada?" and "Who invented the sewing machine?" However, answers to questions about Canada and sewing machines are based on general knowledge that you have not experienced personally; in contrast, answers to questions about your fourth-grade teacher and your high school graduation are based on knowledge unique to your own life. Autobiographical memory *refers to people's memory of the significant events and experiences of their own lives.* Autobiographical memory is important because it helps people construct a personal life history. In addition, autobiographical memory allows people to relate their experiences to others, creating socially shared memories.

Asian parents are less likely than Europeans or North Americans to talk to their children about events that foster autobiographical memory.

autobiographical memory
Memories of the significant events and experiences of one's own life

Autobiographical memory originates early. Infants and toddlers have the basic memory skills that enable them to remember past events, but they forget so rapidly that many experiences are not represented in long-term memory. However, preschoolers' memories are more robust, supporting autobiographical memory (Bauer, 2015). Layered on top of these memory skills is a child's sense of self (Howe, 2014). Toddlers come to understand that they exist independently in space and time, an understanding that provides coherence and continuity to children's experience. Children realize that the self who went to the park a few days ago is the same self who is now at a birthday party and is the same self who will read a book with dad before bedtime.

Also contributing to autobiographical memory are young children's improved language skills, skills that allow children to converse with parents about past and future events (Fivush, 2014). Parents may talk about what the child did today at day care or remind the child about what she will be doing this weekend. Children's autobiographical memories are richer when parents talk about past events in detail and, specifically, when they encourage children to expand their description of past events by asking open-ended questions such as "Where did Mommy go last night?" (Fivush, 2014). The elaborative style is more common among European American parents than Asian parents, a finding that explains why European American children often report more specific details of events than Chinese children do (Wang, 2014).

Preschoolers as Eyewitnesses

Research on children's autobiographical memory has played a central role in cases of suspected child abuse. When abuse is suspected, the victim is usually the sole witness. To prosecute the alleged abuser, the child's testimony is needed. But can preschoolers accurately recall these events? Sometimes. One obstacle to accurate testimony is that young children are often interviewed repeatedly, a practice that can cause them to confuse what actually happened with what others suggest may have happened. When the questioner is an adult in a position of authority, children often believe that what is suggested by the adult actually happened (Candel et al., 2009; Ceci & Bruck, 1998). They will tell a convincing tale about "what really happened" simply because adults have led them to believe things must have happened that way. Young children's storytelling can be so convincing that professionals often cannot distinguish true and false reports (Gordon, Baker-Ward, & Ornstein, 2001).

Preschool children are particularly suggestible. Why? One idea is that preschool children are more suggestible because they don't remember the sources of information that they remember (Poole & Lindsay, 1995; Roberts, Evans & Duncanson, 2016). For example, they may know that a cousin dressed as a ghost for Halloween, but they can't remember whether they actually saw the cousin in her costume or learned about the costume from a parent. When confused in this manner, preschoolers frequently assume they must have experienced something personally. Consequently, when preschool children are asked leading questions (e.g., "When the man touched you, did it hurt?"), children store this information but later have trouble distinguishing what they actually experienced from what interviewers imply that they experienced (Ghetti, 2008).

Although preschoolers are easily misled, they can provide reliable testimony if interviewers follow several guidelines derived from research on children's memory. Specifically, interviewers should:

- Interview children as soon as possible after the event in question.
- Encourage children to tell the truth, to feel free to say "I don't know" to questions, and to correct interviewers when they say something that's incorrect.
- Avoid nonverbal cues such as gestures or facial expressions because these may lead children to believe they should respond in a certain way. Also, avoid selectively reinforcing responses that are consistent with allegations.
- Start by asking children to describe the event in their own words ("Tell me what happened after school."), follow up with open-ended questions ("Can you tell me more about what happened while you were walking home?"), and avoid yes/no and multiple-choice questions (because they lead to fewer details as well as more mistakes and inconsistencies).
- Allow children to understand and feel comfortable in the interview format by beginning with a neutral event (e.g., a birthday party or holiday celebration) before moving to the event of interest.
- Ask questions that consider other explanations of the event (i.e., explanations that don't involve abuse).

Following guidelines such as these can foster the conditions under which children are likely to recall past events more accurately and thereby be better witnesses (Brown & Lamb, 2015; Cleveland, Quas, & Lyon, 2016; Poole & Bruck, 2012).

Learning Number Skills

Powerful learning and memory skills allow infants and preschoolers to learn much about their worlds. This rapid growth is well illustrated by research on children's understanding of the concept of number. Basic number skills originate in infancy, long before babies learn the names of numbers. Many babies experience daily variation in quantity. They play with two blocks and see that another baby has three; they watch as a father sorts laundry and finds two black socks but only one blue sock; and they eat 6 grapes for lunch while an older brother eats 15.

From these experiences, babies apparently come to appreciate that quantity or amount is one of the ways in which objects in the world can differ. In fact, infants may represent number using two distinct systems (Mussolin et al., 2016). One system is used for sets of one to four objects and is very precise; it allows babies to distinguish one object from two and two objects from three (Opfer & Siegler, 2012).

This system also allows babies to perform simple addition and subtraction. In experiments using the method shown in ▶ Figure 4.5, infants view a stage with one mouse. A screen hides the mouse and then a hand appears with a second mouse, which is placed behind the screen. When the screen is removed and reveals one mouse, 5-month-olds look longer than when two mice appear. Apparently, 5-month-olds expect that one mouse plus another mouse should equal two mice, and they look longer when this expectancy is violated (Wynn, 1992). Likewise, when the stage first has two mice and one of them is removed, infants are surprised when the screen is removed and two mice are still on the stage.

The other system—known as the approximate number system (ANS)—estimates quantities and is used to distinguish larger sets. This system allows babies to distinguish 8 objects from 16 but not 8 objects from 12, because the ANS isn't sufficiently precise (Opfer & Siegler, 2012). Representations of number in the ANS become sharper with development and this allows 6-year-olds to discriminate larger sets (e.g., 50 teddy bears

> **Figure 4.5**

Infants are surprised when they see objects added or removed but the original number of objects is still present when the screen is removed; this pattern suggests some basic understanding of addition and subtraction.

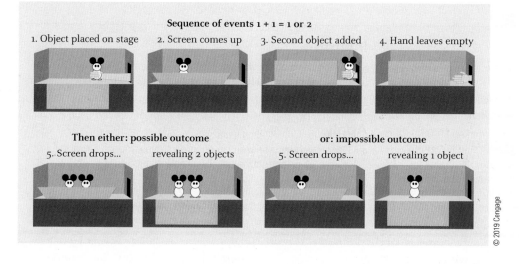

versus 60 teddy bears) that 3-year-olds cannot (Halberda & Feigenson, 2008). And number representations in the ANS have been linked to a specific region in the brain's parietal lobe (Emerson & Cantlon, 2015).

Learning to Count

By 2 years of age, most youngsters know some number words and have begun to count. However, this counting is usually full of mistakes. They might count "1, 2, 6, 7"—skipping 3, 4, and 5. Gelman and Meck (1986) charted preschoolers' understanding of counting. They simply placed several objects in front of a child and asked, "How many?" By analyzing children's answers to many of these questions, Gelman and Meck discovered that by age 3, most children have mastered three basic principles of counting—at least for counting up to five objects.

- **One-to-one principle**: *There must be one and only one number name for each object that is counted.* A child who counts three objects as "1, 2, a" understands this principle because the number of names matches the number of objects to be counted, even though the third name is a letter.
- **Stable-order principle**: *Number names must be counted in the same order.* A child who counts in the same sequence—for example, consistently counting four objects as "1, 2, 4, 5"—understands this principle.
- **Cardinality principle**: *The last number name differs from the previous ones in a counting sequence by denoting the number of objects.* Typically, 3-year-olds reveal their understanding of this principle by repeating the last number name, often with emphasis: "1, 2, 4, 8 . . . EIGHT!"

During the preschool years, children master these basic principles and apply them to ever-larger sets of objects. By age 5, most youngsters apply these counting principles to as many as nine objects. And children are more likely to master counting principles when parents mention numbers in their speech, such as counting objects with their children or simply stating the number of objects present (Gunderson & Levine, 2011). By age 4, most youngsters know the numbers to 20, and some can count to 99 (Siegler & Robinson, 1982).

one-to-one principle
Counting principle that states that there must be one and only one number name for each object counted.

stable-order principle
Counting principle that states that number names must always be counted in the same order.

cardinality principle
Counting principle that states that the last number name denotes the number of objects being counted.

By age 5, children have mastered the three counting principles and can apply them to large sets of objects.

Thus far, we have not considered the impact of social context on children's thinking. In the next section, we'll examine a theory developed by Vygotsky, who believed that cognitive development has its roots in social interactions.

TEST YOURSELF 4.2

Recall

1. One way to improve preschool children's attention is to have them engage in _____ play.

2. Four-month-old Tanya has forgotten that kicking moves a mobile. To remind her of the link between kicking and the mobile's movement, we could _____.

3. Preschoolers may be particularly suggestible because they are less skilled at _____.

4. When a child who is counting a set of objects repeats the last number, usually with emphasis, this indicates the child understands the _____ principle of counting.

Interpret

- Do the developmental mechanisms in the information-processing perspective emphasize nature, nurture, or both? How?

Apply

- Describe how research on children's eyewitness testimony illustrates connections among emotional, cognitive, and social development.

Check your answers to the Recall Questions at the end of the chapter.

4.3 Mind and Culture: Vygotsky's Theory

LEARNING OBJECTIVES

- What is the zone of proximal development? How does it help explain how children accomplish more when they collaborate with others?

- Why is scaffolding a particularly effective way of teaching youngsters new concepts and skills?

- When and why do children talk to themselves as they solve problems?

Victoria, a 4-year-old, enjoys solving jigsaw puzzles, coloring, and building towers with blocks. While busy with these activities, she often talks to herself. For example, once as she was coloring a picture, she said, "Where's the red crayon? Stay inside the lines. Color the blocks blue." These remarks were not directed at anyone else—Victoria was alone. Why did she say these things? What purpose did they serve?

Human development is often referred to as a journey that takes people along many different paths. For Piaget and for information-processing psychologists, children make the journey alone. Other people (and culture in general) influence the direction that children take, but fundamentally the child is a solitary adventurer-explorer, boldly forging ahead. Lev Vygotsky (1896–1934), a Russian psychologist, proposed a very different account: Development is an apprenticeship in which children advance when they collaborate with others who are more skilled. According to Vygotsky (1978), children rarely make much headway on the developmental path when they walk alone; they progress when they walk hand in hand with an expert.

For Vygotsky and other sociocultural theorists, the social nature of cognitive development is captured in the concept of intersubjectivity, *which refers to mutual, shared understanding among participants in an activity.* For example, when parents and children play board games together, they share an understanding of the goals of their activity and of their roles in playing the games. Such shared understanding allows parents and children to work together in complementary fashion on the puzzles. *Such interactions typify* guided participation, *in which cognitive growth results from children's involvement in structured activities with others who are more skilled than they.* Through guided

intersubjectivity

Mutual, shared understanding among participants in an activity.

guided participation

Children's involvement in structured activities with others who are more skilled, typically producing cognitive growth.

participation, children learn from others how to connect new experiences and new skills with what they already know (Rogoff, 2003). Guided participation is shown when a child learns a new video game from a peer or an adolescent learns a new karate move from a partner.

Vygotsky died when he was only 37 years old, so he did not develop his theory fully. However, his ideas are influential, largely because they fill some gaps in the Piagetian and information-processing accounts. In the next few pages, we'll look at three of Vygotsky's most important contributions—the zone of proximal development, scaffolding, and private speech—and learn more about why Victoria talks to herself.

The Zone of Proximal Development

Four-year-old Ian and his father often solve puzzles together. Although Ian does most of the work, his father encourages him, sometimes finding a piece that he needs or showing Ian how to put parts together. When Ian tries to assemble the same puzzles by himself, he rarely can complete them. *The difference between what Ian can do with assistance and what he does alone defines his* zone of proximal development. That is, the zone is the area between the level of performance a child can achieve when working independently and a higher level of performance that is possible when working under the guidance or direction of more skilled adults or peers (Daniels, 2011; Wertsch & Tulviste, 1992). For example, many elementary school children have difficulty solving arithmetic story problems because they don't know where to begin. By structuring the task for them—"first decide what you're supposed to figure out; then decide what information you're told in the problem"— teachers can help children accomplish what they cannot do by themselves. Thus, just as training wheels help children learn to ride a bike by allowing them to concentrate on certain aspects of bicycling, collaborators help children perform more effectively by providing structure, hints, and reminders.

The idea of a zone of proximal development follows naturally from Vygotsky's basic premise: Cognition develops first in a social setting and only gradually comes under the child's independent control. What factors aid this shift? This leads us to the second of Vygotsky's key contributions.

Scaffolding

Have you had the good fortune to work with a master teacher, one who knew exactly when to say something to help you over an obstacle but otherwise let you work uninterrupted? Scaffolding *is a style in which teachers gauge the amount of assistance they offer to match the learner's needs.* Early in learning a new task, children know little; so teachers give much direct instruction about how to do all the different elements of a task. As the children catch on, teachers need to provide less direct instruction; they are more likely to give reminders.

Worldwide, parents scaffold their children's learning, but not always using the same methods. In cultures that value children's independence (e.g., many countries in North America and Europe), parents allow children to play at a distance (to encourage their independence) and thus parents rely on language to scaffold their children. In contrast, in cultures that value children's interdependence with other people (e.g., many countries in Latin America and Asia), parents keep children close physically and rely on gesture and touch to scaffold (Kuhl & Keller, 2008; Luo & Tamis-LeMonda, 2016).

zone of proximal development
Difference between what children can do with assistance and what they can do alone.

scaffolding
A style in which teachers gauge the amount of assistance they offer to match the learner's needs.

Young children can often accomplish far more with some adult guidance than they can accomplish alone; Vygotsky referred to this difference as the zone of proximal development.

John Birdsall / The Image Works

Young children often regulate their own behavior by talking to themselves, particularly while performing difficult tasks.

The defining characteristic of scaffolding—giving help but not more than is needed—clearly promotes learning (Cole, 2006). Youngsters do not learn readily when they are constantly told what to do or when they are simply left to struggle through a problem unaided. However, when teachers collaborate with children, allowing them to take on more and more of a task as they master its different elements, they learn more effectively (Murphy & Messer, 2000). Scaffolding is an important technique for transferring skills from others to the child, both in formal settings such as schools and in informal settings such as the home and playground (Bernier, Carlson, & Whipple, 2010).

■

Think About It

Vygotsky emphasized cognitive development as collaboration. How could such collaboration be included in Piaget's theory? In information processing?

private speech

A child's comments that are not intended for others but are designed to help regulate the child's own behavior.

Private Speech

Remember Victoria, the 4-year-old in the vignette who talked to herself as she colored? *Her behavior demonstrates* **private speech**: *comments that are not intended for others but are designed to help children regulate their own behavior.* Thus, Victoria's remarks are simply an effort to help her color the picture.

Vygotsky viewed private speech as an intermediate step toward self-regulation of cognitive skills (Fernyhough, 2010). At first, children's behavior is regulated by speech from other people that is directed toward them. When youngsters first try to control their own behavior and thoughts without others present, they instruct themselves by speaking aloud. Private speech seems to be children's way of guiding themselves, of making sure they do all the required steps in solving a problem. Finally, as children gain ever greater skill, private speech becomes *inner speech*, which was Vygotsky's term for thought.

If private speech functions in this way, then children should use private speech more often on difficult tasks than on easy tasks because children are most likely to need extra guidance on harder tasks. Also, children should be more likely to use private speech after a mistake than after a correct response. These predictions are supported by research (Berk, 2003), findings that suggest the power of language in helping children learn to control their own behavior and thinking.

Thus, Vygotsky's work has characterized cognitive development not as a solitary undertaking, but as a collaboration between expert and novice. His work reminds us of the importance of language, which we'll examine in detail in the last section of this chapter.

TEST YOURSELF 4.3

Recall

1. The _____ is the difference between the level of performance that youngsters can achieve with assistance and the level they can achieve alone.

2. The term _____ refers to a style in which teachers adjust their assistance to match a child's needs.

3. According to Vygotsky, _____ is an intermediate step between speech from others and inner speech.

Interpret

- How would scaffolding appropriate for infants differ from the scaffolding appropriate for preschool children?

Apply

- Review Piaget's description of the conditions that foster cognitive development (on page 125). How would an analogous list derived from Vygotsky's theory compare?

Check your answers to the Recall Questions at the end of the chapter.

LEARNING OBJECTIVES

- When do infants first hear and make speech sounds?
- When do children start to talk? How do they learn word meanings?
- How do young children learn grammar?
- How well do youngsters communicate?

Nabina is just a few weeks away from her first birthday. For the past month, she has seemed to understand much of her mother's speech. If her mom asks, "Where's Garfield?" (the family cat), Nabina scans the room and points toward Garfield. Yet Nabina's own speech is still gibberish: She "talks" constantly, but her mom can't understand a word of it. If Nabina apparently understands others' speech, why can't she speak herself?

Soon after the first birthday, most children say their first word, which is followed in the ensuing months by hundreds more. This marks the beginning of a child's ability to communicate orally with others. Through speech, youngsters impart their ideas, beliefs, and feelings to family, friends, and others.

The first spoken words represent the climax of a year's worth of language growth. To tell the story of language acquisition properly and explain Nabina's seemingly strange behavior, we begin with the months preceding the first words.

The Road to Speech

When a baby is upset, a concerned mother tries to console him. Unable to talk, the infant conveys his unhappiness by crying. The mother uses both verbal and nonverbal measures to cheer her baby. In this situation, do babies understand any of the speech directed at them? And how do infants progress from crying to more effective methods of oral communication, such as speech? Let's start by answering the first question.

Perceiving Speech

Even newborn infants hear remarkably well (page 103); the left hemisphere of a newborn's brain is particularly sensitive to language (page 94); and babies prefer to listen to speech over comparably complex nonspeech sounds (Vouloumanos et al., 2010). Critically, babies can distinguish consonant sounds, such as the sound of *t* in *toe* and *tap*, as well as vowel sounds, such as the sound of *e* in *get* and *bed* (Cristia et al., 2016; Galle &McMurray, 2014).

The Impact of Language Exposure. Not all languages use the same set of language sounds, phonemes, so a distinction that is important in one language may be ignored in another. For example, Japanese does not distinguish the consonant sound of *r* in *rip* from the sound of *l* in *lip*, and Japanese adults trying to learn English have great difficulty distinguishing these sounds. At about 6 to 8 months, Japanese and American infants can distinguish these sounds equally well. However, by 10 to 12 months, perception of *r* and *l* improves for American infants—presumably because they hear these sounds frequently—but declines for Japanese babies (Werker & Hensch, 2015).

Thus, young babies can distinguish a range of sounds but, as babies are more exposed to a particular language, they only notice the linguistic distinctions that are meaningful in that language. In other words, specializing in one language apparently comes at the cost of making it more difficult to hear sounds in other languages. And this pattern of greater specialization in speech perception resembles the profile for face perception described on page 108.

A baby's first form of communication—crying—is soon joined by other language-based ways of communicating.

With greater exposure to human faces, babies develop a more refined notion of a human face, just as they develop a more refined notion of the sounds (and signs) that are important in their native language (Pascalis et al., 2014).

Identifying Words. Of course, identifying language sounds is just the first step in perceiving speech. One of the biggest challenges for infants is identifying words. Imagine, for example, an infant overhearing this conversation between a parent and an older sibling:

SIBLING: Jerry got a new *bike*.
PARENT: Was his old *bike* broken?
SIBLING: No. He'd saved his money to buy a new mountain *bike*.

An infant listening to this conversation hears *bike* three times. Can the infant learn from this experience? Yes. When 7- to 8-month-olds hear a word repeatedly in different sentences, they later pay more attention to this word than to words they haven't heard previously (Houston & Jusczyk, 2003; Saffran, Aslin, & Newport, 1996). By 6 months, infants pay more attention to content words (e.g., nouns, verbs) than to function words (e.g., articles, prepositions), and they look at the correct parent when they hear "mommy" or "daddy" (Shi & Werker, 2001; Tincoff & Jusczyk, 1999).

In normal conversation, there are no silent gaps between words, so how do infants pick out words? Stress is one important clue. English contains many one-syllable words that are stressed and many two-syllable words that have a stressed syllable followed by an unstressed syllable (e.g., *dough'-nut, tooth'-paste, bas'-ket*). Infants pay more attention to stressed syllables than unstressed syllables, which is a good strategy for identifying the beginnings of words (Bortfeld & Morgan, 2010; Thiessen & Saffran, 2003). And infants learn words more readily when they appear at the beginnings and ends of sentences, probably because the brief pause between sentences makes it easier to identify first and last words (Seidl & Johnson, 2006).

Another way to identify words in speech is statistical. Infants notice syllables that go together frequently (Jusczyk, 2002). For example, in many studies, 8-month-olds heard the following sounds, which consisted of four 3-syllable artificial words, said over and over in random order:

pa bi ku *go la tu* *da ro pi* *ti bu do* *da ro pi* *go la tu* *pa bi ku* *da ro pi* . . .

We've underlined the words and inserted gaps between them so that you can see them more easily, but in the studies, there were no breaks—just a steady flow of syllables for three minutes. Later, infants listened to these words less than to new words that were novel combinations of the same syllables. They had detected *pa bi ku, go la tu, da ro pi*, and *ti bu do* as familiar patterns and hence listened to them less than to new "words" such as *tu da ro* even though the latter were made up from syllables they'd already heard (Aslin, 2017).

Yet another way that infants identify words is through their emerging knowledge of how sounds are used in their native language. For example, *s* followed by *t* and *s* followed by *d* are quite common at the end of one word and the beginning of the next: bu*s t*akes, ki*ss t*ook; thi*s d*og, pa*ss d*irectly. However, *s* and *t* occur frequently within a word (*st*op, li*st*, pe*st*, *st*ink) but *s* and *d* do not. Consequently, when *d* follows an *s*, it probably starts a new word. In fact, 9-month-olds follow rules such as this one: When they hear novel words embedded in continuous speech, they're more likely to identify the novel word when the final sound in the preceding word occurs infrequently with the first sound of the novel word (Mattys & Jusczyk, 2001).

Another strategy that infants use is to rely on familiar function words, such as the articles *a* and *the*, to break up the speech stream. These words are common in adults' speech; by 6 months, most infants recognize these words and use them to determine the onset of a new word (Shi, 2014). For example, for infants familiar with *a*, the sequence *aballabata-glove* becomes *a ball a bat a glove*. The new words are isolated by the familiar ones.

Thus, infants use many powerful tools to identify words in speech. Of course, they don't yet understand the meanings of these words; at this point, they simply recognize a word as a distinct configuration of sounds. Nevertheless, these early perceptual skills are important because infants who are more skilled at identifying words within the speech stream know more words as toddlers (Newman, Rowe, & Ratner, 2016).

Parents (and other adults) often help infants master language sounds by talking in a distinctive style. *In* infant-directed speech, *adults speak slowly with exaggerated changes in pitch and loudness.*[1] If you listen to a mother talking to her baby, you will notice that she speaks slowly, in a higher and more variable pitch, and with exaggerated facial expressions, and her sentences are brief. Infant-directed speech is common in most cultures that have been studied, although the specific features often vary with the language (Saint-Georges et al., 2013).

Babies benefit from infant-directed speech, for two reasons. First, the higher pitch, the variability in pitch and the exaggerated facial expressions, of infant-directed speech grab a baby's attention. In short, babies pay more attention to the speech they're hearing when it's expressed in infant-directed speech. Second, infant-directed speech has features that help babies to learn language. The slow pace and variable pitch of infant-directed speech seems to help babies to segment the speech stream. In addition, infant-directed speech is beneficial in providing excellent examples of language sounds, examples that help babies to learn different language sounds (Golinkoff et al., 2015).

When mothers and other adults talk to young children, they often use infant-directed speech in which they speak slowly with exaggerated changes in pitch and loudness.

infant-directed speech

Speech that adults use with infants that is slow and has exaggerated changes in pitch and volume; it helps children master language.

cooing

Early vowellike sounds that babies produce.

babbling

Speechlike sounds that consist of vowel–consonant combinations; common at about 6 months.

Steps to Speech

As any new parent can testify, newborns and young babies make many sounds—they cry, burp, and sneeze. Language-based sounds don't appear immediately. *At 2 months, infants begin to produce vowellike sounds such as "ooooooo" and "ahhhhhh," a phenomenon known as* cooing. Sometimes infants become quite excited as they coo, perhaps reflecting the joy of simply playing with sounds.

After cooing comes babbling, *speechlike sound that has no meaning.* A typical 6-month-old might say "dah" or "bah," utterances that sound like a single syllable consisting of a consonant and a vowel. Over the next few months, babbling becomes more elaborate as babies apparently experiment with more complex speech sounds. Older infants sometimes repeat a sound, as in "bahbahbah," and begin to combine different sounds, such as "dahmahbah" (Hoff, 2014).

Babbling is not just mindless playing with sounds; it is a precursor to real speech. We know this, in part, from video records of people's mouths while speaking. When an adult speaks, the mouth opens somewhat wider on the right side than on the left side, reflecting the left hemisphere's control of language and muscle movements on the body's right side (Graves & Landis, 1990). Infants do the same when they babble but not when making other nonbabbling sounds, which suggests that babbling is fundamentally linguistic (Holowka & Petitto, 2002).

Other evidence for the linguistic nature of babbling comes from studies of developmental change in babbling: At roughly 8 to 11 months, infants' babbling sounds more like real speech because infants stress some syllables and vary the pitch of their speech (Snow, 2006). In English declarative sentences, for example, pitch first rises and then falls toward the end of the sentence. However, in questions the pitch is level and then rises toward the end of the question. Older babies' babbling reflects these patterns: Babies who are brought up by English-speaking parents have both the declarative and question patterns of intonation in their babbling. Babies exposed to a language with different patterns of intonation, such as Japanese and French, reflect their language's intonation in their babbling (Levitt & Utman, 1992).

[1]Infant-directed speech was once known as *motherese* because this form of speaking was first noted in mothers, but we know now that most caregivers talk this way to infants.

Think About It

Compare and contrast the steps in learning to make speech sounds with Piaget's account of the sensorimotor period.

The appearance of intonation in babbling indicates a strong link between perception and production of speech: Infants' babbling is influenced by the characteristics of the speech that they hear (Goldstein & Schwade, 2008). Beginning in the middle of the first year, infants try to reproduce the sounds of language that others use in trying to communicate with them (or in the case of deaf infants with deaf parents, the signs that others use). Hearing *dog*, an infant may first say "dod" and then "gog" before finally saying "dog" correctly. In the same way that beginning typists gradually link movements of their fingers with particular keys, through babbling, infants learn to use their lips, tongue, and teeth to produce specific sounds, gradually making sounds that approximate real words (Poulson et al., 1991).

These developments in production of sound, coupled with the 1-year-old's advanced ability to perceive speech sounds, set the stage for the infant's first true words.

First Words and Many More

Recall that Nabina, the 1-year-old in the vignette, looks at the family cat when she hears its name. This phenomenon is common in 10- to 14-month-olds. They appear to understand what others say despite the fact that they have yet to speak. In response to "Where is the book?" children will find the book. They grasp the question even though their own speech is limited to advanced babbling (Fenson et al., 1994; Hoff-Ginsberg, 1997). Evidently, children have linked speech sounds and particular objects even though they cannot yet manufacture the sounds themselves. As fluent adult speakers, we forget that speech is a motor skill requiring perfect timing and tremendous coordination.

A few months later, most youngsters utter their first words. In many languages, those words are similar (Nelson, 1973; Tardif et al., 2008) and include terms for mother and father, greetings (*hi, bye-bye*), and foods and toys (*juice, ball*). By age 2, most youngsters have a vocabulary of a few hundred words, and by age 6, a typical child's vocabulary includes more than 10,000 words (Bloom, 2000). Worldwide, nouns are common in children's early vocabularies, perhaps because they refer to objects that infants can perceive easily; verbs are less common than nouns, but this difference is smaller (and sometimes disappears) in languages such as Korean and Chinese, perhaps because verbs are more prominent in these languages or because East Asian cultures emphasize actions more than objects (Waxman et al., 2013).

The Grand Insight: Words as Symbols

To make the transition from babbling to real speech, infants need to learn that speech is more than just entertaining sound. They need to know that particular sounds form words that can refer to objects, actions, and properties. Put another way, infants must recognize that words are symbols—entities that stand for other entities. By the first birthday, children's experiences cause them to form concepts such as "round, bouncy things" and "furry things that bark." With the insight that speech sounds can denote these concepts, infants begin to identify a word that goes with each concept (Reich, 1986).

If this argument is correct, then we should find that children use symbols in other areas, not just in language. They do. Gestures are symbols, and infants begin to gesture shortly before their first birthday (Goodwyn & Acredolo, 1993). Young children may open and close their hands to request an object or wave "bye-bye" when leaving. Infants' vocabularies of gestures and spoken words expand at about the same rate, consistent with the idea that words and gestures reflect the infant's emerging understanding of symbols (Caselli et al., 2012).

What's more, gestures sometimes pave the way for language. Before knowing an object's name, infants often point to it or pick it up for a listener, as if saying, "I want this!" or "What's this?" In one study, youngsters first referred to nearly 50% of objects by gesture and, about three months later, by word (Iverson & Goldin-Meadow, 2005). Given this connection between early gestures and first spoken words, it's not surprising that toddlers who are more advanced in their use of gesture tend to have, as preschoolers, more complex spoken language (Kuhn et al., 2014; Rowe, Raudenbush, & Goldin-Meadow, 2012).

What's What? Fast Mapping of Words

After children know that a word can symbolize an object or action, their vocabularies grow, but slowly at first. A typical 15-month-old, for example, may learn about 10 words each month. However, between 18 and 24 months, many children experience a naming explosion during which they learn new words—particularly names of objects—much more rapidly than before. Children now learn 25 to 30 new words each month (Samuelson & McMurray, 2017).

This rapid rate of word learning is astonishing when we realize that most words have many plausible but incorrect referents. To illustrate, imagine what's going through the mind of a child whose mother points to a flower and says, "Flower. This is a flower. See the flower." This all seems crystal clear to you and incredibly straightforward. But what might the child learn from this episode? Perhaps the correct referent for "flower." But a youngster could conclude that "flower" refers to a petal, to the color of the flower, or to the mother's actions in pointing at the flower.

Surprisingly, though, most youngsters learn the proper meanings of simple words in just a few presentations. *Children's ability to connect new words to referents so rapidly that they cannot be considering all possible meanings for the new word is termed* fast mapping. How can young children learn new words so rapidly? Many distinct factors contribute (Hollich, Hirsh-Pasek, & Golinkoff, 2000).

iStock.com/Patrick Heagney

One of the challenges for theories of language learning is to explain how children figure out that the parent's words refer to the object, not to its color or texture.

fast mapping
A child's connections between words and referents that are made so quickly that he or she cannot consider all possible meanings of the word.

Joint Attention. Parents encourage word learning by carefully watching what interests their children. When toddlers touch or look at an object, parents often label it for them. When a youngster points to a banana, a parent may say, "Banana. That's a banana." Such labeling in the context of joint attention promotes word learning, particularly when infants and toddlers participate actively, directing their parents' attention (Beuker et al., 2013).

Of course, to take advantage of this help, infants must be able to tell when parents are labeling instead of just conversing. In fact, when adults label an unfamiliar object, 18- to 20-month-olds assume that the label is the object's name *only* when adults show signs that they are referring to the object (Liebal et al., 2009; Nurmsoo & Bloom, 2008). Young children also consider an adult's credibility as a source: Preschoolers are less likely to learn words from adults who seem uncertain, have given incorrect names for words in the past, or speak with a foreign accent (Corriveau, Kinzler, & Harris, 2013; Jaswal & Konrad, 2016). Thus, beginning in the toddler years, parents and children work together to create conditions that foster word learning: Parents label objects, and youngsters rely on adults' behavior to interpret the words they hear.

Constraints on Word Names. Joint attention simplifies word learning for children, but the problem still remains: How does a toddler know that banana refers to the object that she's touching as opposed to her activity (touching) or to the object's color? Young children follow several simple rules that constrain their inferences about a word's meaning. One simple rule is that if an unfamiliar word is heard in the presence of objects that already have names and objects that don't, the word refers to one of the objects that doesn't have a name. Suppose a shelf includes a book, an apple, and a camera, and that a child knows the names of the first two. If an adult says, "Look at the camera," preschoolers will infer that "camera" refers to the third, unnamed object (Au & Glasman, 1990).

Another simple but useful rule is that a name refers to a whole object, not its parts or its relation to other objects, and refers not just to this particular object, but to all objects of the same type (Hollich, Golinkoff, & Hirsh-Pasek, 2007). For example, when a grandparent points to a stuffed animal on a shelf and says "dinosaur," children conclude that *dinosaur* refers to the entire dinosaur, not just its ears or nose, not to the fact that the dinosaur is on a shelf, and not to this specific dinosaur, but to all dinosaurlike objects.

Rules such as these make it possible for children like Nabina, the child in the vignette, to learn words rapidly because they reduce the number of possible referents. The child being shown a flower follows these rules to decide that *flower* refers to the entire object, not its parts or the action of pointing to it.

Sentence Cues. Children hear many unfamiliar words embedded in sentences containing words they already know. The other words and the overall sentence structure can be helpful clues to a word's meaning (Yuan & Fisher, 2009). For example, when a parent describes an event using familiar words but an unfamiliar verb, children often infer that the verb refers to the action performed by the subject of the sentence (Arunachalam et al., 2013). When youngsters hear "The man is juggling the bats," they will infer that juggling refers to the man's actions because they already know the actor (man) and the object of the action (bats). Similarly, toddlers know that *a* and *the* often precede nouns and that *he, she,* and *they* precede verbs. Thus, they will conclude that "a boz" refers to an object but "she boz" refers to an action (Cauvet et al., 2014).

Cognitive Factors. The naming explosion coincides with a time of rapid cognitive growth, and children's increased cognitive skill helps them learn new words. As children's thinking becomes more sophisticated and, in particular, as they start to have goals and intentions, language becomes a means to express those goals and to achieve them. Thus, intention provides children with an important motive to learn language—to help achieve their goals (Bloom & Tinker, 2001).

In addition, young children's improving attentional and perceptual skills also promote word learning. Infants and young children learn that objects that have the same shape have the same name, and they learn that paying attention to shape is an easy way to learn names (Smith, 2000, 2009). And their improving memory skills forge stronger links between objects and newly discovered names (Samuelson & McMurray, 2016).

Developmental Change in Word Learning. Some of the word-learning tools described in the past few pages are particularly important at different ages (Hirsh-Pasek & Golinkoff, 2008). Before 18 months, infants learn words relatively slowly—often just one new word each day. At this age, children rely heavily on simple attentional processes (e.g., shape) to learn new words. But by 24 months, most children are learning many new words daily. This faster learning reflects children's greater use of language cues (e.g., constraints on names) and a speaker's social cues. At any age, infants and toddlers rely on a mixture of word-learning tools, but with age, they gradually move away from attentional cues to language and social cues.

Naming Errors. Of course, the mechanisms for learning new words are not perfect; initial mappings of words onto meanings are often only partially correct (Hoff & Naigles, 2002). *A common mistake is* underextension, *defining a word too narrowly.* Using *car* to refer only to the family car and *ball* to a favorite toy ball are examples of underextension. *Between 1 and 3 years, children sometimes make the opposite error,* overextension, *defining a word too broadly.* Children may use *car* also to refer to buses and trucks or use *doggie* to refer to all four-legged animals.

Overextension errors occur more frequently when children are producing words than when they are comprehending words. Two-year-old Jason may say "doggie" to refer to a goat but nevertheless correctly point to a picture of a goat when asked. Because overextension is more common in word production, it may reflect another fast-mapping rule that children follow: "If you can't remember the name for an object, say the name of a related object" (Naigles & Gelman, 1995). Both underextension and overextension disappear gradually as youngsters refine meanings for words after increased exposure to language.

underextension

When children define words more narrowly than adults do.

overextension

When children define words more broadly than adults do.

Individual Differences in Word Learning

The naming explosion typically occurs at about 18 months, but like many developmental milestones, the timing of this event varies widely for individual children. Some youngsters have a naming explosion as early as 14 months, but for others, it may be as late as 22 months (Goldfield & Reznick, 1990). Another way to make this point is to look at variation in the size of children's vocabulary at a specific age. At 18 months, for example, an average child knows about 75 words, but a child in the 90th percentile would know nearly 250 words and a child in the 10th percentile fewer than 25 words (Fenson et al., 1994).

This range in vocabulary size for typical 18-month-olds is huge—from 25 to 250 words. What can account for this difference? Two factors contribute. *One is phonological memory, the ability to remember speech sounds briefly.* This is often measured by saying a nonsense word to children—"ballop" or "glistering"—and asking them to repeat it immediately. Children who remember such words accurately tend to have larger vocabularies (Newbury et al., 2016). Children who cannot remember speech sounds accurately find word learning particularly challenging, an outcome that's not surprising because word learning involves associating meaning with an unfamiliar sequence of speech sounds.

However, the single most important factor in growth of vocabulary is the child's language environment. Children have larger vocabularies when they are exposed to much high-quality language. That is, children learn more words when their parents' speech is rich in different words and is grammatically sophisticated (Huttenlocher et al., 2010; Rowe, 2012) and when parents respond promptly and appropriately to their children's talk (Tamis-LeMonda, Kuchirko, & Song, 2014).

Bilingualism. Millions of American children grow up in bilingual households; these youngsters usually speak English and another language. When children are exposed simultaneously to two (or more) languages from birth, they pass through the same milestones in each language as monolingual children, but somewhat more slowly. For example, in each language, their vocabulary is often slightly smaller and their grammar somewhat less complex. But their total vocabulary (i.e., words known in both languages and words known in either language but not both) is greater than that of monolingual children (Hoff et al., 2012).

These patterns depend critically on the circumstances in which children experience multiple languages. Children's language skills progress more rapidly in the language they hear the most (Hoff et al., 2012). If a child hears English from mom and at day care but hears Croatian only from dad, the child's skills in English will probably surpass her skills in Croatian. And children's language develops more rapidly when their language exposure comes from a native speaker (Place & Hoff, 2011). Language acquisition in bilingual children can also be affected by the relative prestige of the two languages as well as the cultures associated with the two languages (Hoff, 2014).

Being bilingual also has some important language and cognitive advantages. Bilingual children better understand that words are simply arbitrary symbols. Bilingual youngsters, for instance, are more likely than monolingual children to understand that as long as all English speakers agreed, *dog* could refer to cats and *cat* could refer to dogs (Bialystok, 1988; Campbell & Sais, 1995). And they are more skilled at switching back and forth between tasks and often are better able to inhibit inappropriate responses (Barac & Bialystok, 2012; Bialystok, 2010), perhaps reflecting their experience of switching between languages and inhibiting relevant words from the "other" language (e.g., when shown a photo of a dog and asked "What's this?" preschoolers bilingual in French and English must respond "dog" while suppressing "chien").

Word Learning Styles. As vocabularies grow, some youngsters adopt a distinctive style of learning language (Bates, Bretherton, & Snyder, 1988; Nelson, 1973). *Some children have a referential style; their vocabularies mainly consist of words that name objects, persons, or actions.* For example, Rachel, a referential child, has 41 name words in her 50-word vocabulary, but only two words for social interaction or questions. *Other children have an expressive style; their vocabularies include some names but also many social phrases that are used like a single word, such as "go away," "what'd you want?" and "I want it."* Elizabeth, an expressive child, has a more balanced vocabulary, with 14 words for social interactions and questions and 24 name words.

Referential and expressive styles represent end points on a continuum; most children are somewhere in between. For children with referential emphasis, language is primarily an intellectual tool: a means of learning and talking about objects (Masur, 1995). In contrast, for children with expressive emphasis, language is more of a social tool: a way of enhancing interactions with others. Of course, both of these functions—intellectual and social—are important functions of language, which explains why most children blend the referential and expressive styles of learning language.

phonological memory

Ability to remember speech sounds briefly; an important skill in acquiring vocabulary.

Think About It

Gavin and Heath are both 16-month-olds. Gavin's vocabulary includes about 14 words, but Heath's has about 150 words, more than 10 times as many as Gavin. What factors contribute to this difference?

referential style

Language-learning style of children whose vocabularies are dominated by names of objects, persons, or actions.

expressive style

Language-learning style of children whose vocabularies include many social phrases that are used like one word.

Encouraging Language Growth

For children to expand their vocabularies, they need to hear others speak. Not surprisingly, children have a larger vocabulary when parents' speech includes more words and more varied words (Newman et al., 2016). Parents can foster word learning by naming objects that are the focus of a child's attention, such as the products in a grocery or objects seen on a walk (Dunham, Dunham, & Curwin, 1993). Reading books with children also helps, particularly when parents describe pictures carefully, ask children questions while reading, talk about the meanings of words that appear, or reread stories (Reese & Cox, 1999; Wasik, Hindman, & Snell, 2016).

Of course, video is an essential part of the lives of young children. Does it help them to learn new words? Sometimes. On the one hand, watching *Sesame Street* regularly promotes word learning (Wright et al., 2001) as do programs that tell a story (e.g., *Thomas the Tank Engine*) and those that ask questions of the viewer (e.g., *Blue's Clues* and *Dora the Explorer*). On the other hand, most cartoons have no benefit for language learning (Linebarger & Vaala, 2010). And videos claiming to promote word learning in infants (e.g., *Baby Einstein, Brainy Baby*) typically are not effective, often because 12- to 18-month-olds have difficulty relating what they see in the video to their own experiences (DeLoache et al., 2010; Linebarger & Vaala, 2010).

Of course, today video is available on demand via touchscreen tablets and smartphones. Many infants and toddlers have daily access to these devices, whether in a car en route to day care, waiting in a dentist's office, or sitting in a shopping cart at Walmart (Barr & Linebarger, 2017). Because this technology is relatively new, scientists are still studying its impact on young children's word learning. However, the emerging evidence suggests that apps for new technology are most likely to be effective when they require children to actively engage with meaningful content and when they use apps with parents who can support children's learning (Zosh et al., 2017).

The research we've described in this section points to a simple but powerful conclusion: Children are most likely to learn new words when they participate in activities that force them to understand the meanings of new words and use those new words.

Parents are more effective than videos in teaching new words to their children.

Courtesy of Robert V. Kail

Speaking in Sentences: Grammatical Development

Within months after saying the first words, children begin to form simple two-word sentences. In their two-word speech, children follow rules to express different meanings. For example, the sentences *truck go* and *Daddy eat* both follow the rule is "agent + action." In contrast, *my truck* follows the rule "possessor + possession." Regardless of the language they learn, children's two-word sentences follow a common set of rules that are useful to describe people and objects, their actions, and their properties (Tager-Flusberg, 1993).

From Two Words to Complex Sentences

Children rapidly move beyond two-word sentences, first by linking two-word statements together: "Rachel kick" and "Kick ball" become "Rachel kick ball." Even longer sentences soon follow; sentences with 10 or more words are common in 3-year-olds' speech. For example, at 1½ years, Laura Kail would say "Gimme juice" or "Bye-bye Ben." As a

2½-year-old, she had progressed to "When I finish my ice cream, I'll take a shower, okay?" and "Don't turn the light out—I can't see better!"

Children's two- and three-word sentences often fall short of adults' standards of grammar. Youngsters will say "He eating" rather than "He is eating" or "two cat" rather than "two cats." *This sort of speech is called* telegraphic *because, like telegrams of days gone by, children's speech includes only words directly relevant to meaning and nothing more.* Before texts and tweets, people sent urgent messages by telegraph, and the cost was based on the number of words. Consequently, telegrams were brief and to the point, containing only important nouns, verbs, adjectives, and adverbs—much like children's two-word speech. *The missing elements,* grammatical morphemes, *are words or endings of words (such as* -ing, -ed, *and* -s) *that make a sentence grammatical.* During the preschool years, children gradually acquire the grammatical morphemes, first mastering those that express simple relations, such as *-ing*, which is used to denote that the action expressed by the verb is ongoing. More complex forms, such as appropriate use of the various forms of the verb *to be*, are mastered later (Peters, 1995).

Children's use of grammatical morphemes is based on their growing knowledge of grammatical rules, not simply memory for individual words. This was first demonstrated in a landmark study by Berko (1958) in which preschoolers were shown pictures of nonsense objects like the one in ▶ Figure 4.6. The experimenter labeled it, saying, "This is a wug." Then youngsters were shown pictures of two of the objects, and the experimenter said, "These are two." Most children spontaneously said, "wugs." Because both the singular and plural forms of this word were novel for these youngsters, they could have generated the correct plural form only by applying the familiar rule of adding *-s*.

Children growing up in homes where English is spoken face the problem that their native language is irregular, with many exceptions to the rules. *Sometimes children apply rules to words that are exceptions to the rule, errors called* overregularizations. With plurals, for example, youngsters may incorrectly add *-s* instead of using an irregular plural— two "mans" instead of two "men." With the past tense, children may add *-ed* instead of using an irregular past tense: "I goed home" instead of "I went home" (Marcus et al., 1992; Mervis & Johnson, 1991).

These examples give some insight into the complexities of mastering the grammatical rules of one's language. Children not only must learn an extensive set of specific rules they also must absorb—on a case-by-case basis—all the exceptions. Despite the enormity of this task, most children have mastered the basics of their native tongue by the time they enter school. How do they do it? Biological, psychological, and sociocultural forces all contribute.

How Do Children Acquire Grammar?

Most youngsters can neither read nor do arithmetic when they enter kindergarten, but virtually all have mastered the fundamentals of grammar of their native tongue. How do they do it? Theorists have proposed several different answers to this question.

The Behaviorist Answer. B. F. Skinner (1957) and other learning theorists once claimed that all aspects of language—sounds, words, grammar, and communication— are learned through imitation and reinforcement (Moerk, 2000; Whitehurst & Vasta, 1975). But critics were quick to point to flaws in this explanation. One problem is that most of children's sentences are novel, an outcome difficult to explain in terms of simple imitation of adults' speech. For example, when young children create questions by inserting a *wh* word at the beginning of a sentence ("What she doing?"), who are they imitating? Also troublesome is that even when children imitate adult sentences, they do not imitate adult grammar. In simply trying to repeat "I am drawing a picture," young children say "I draw picture."

The Linguistic Answer. Many scientists believe that children are born with mechanisms that simplify the task of learning grammar (Slobin, 1985). According to this view, children are born with neural circuits in the brain that allow them to infer the grammar

telegraphic speech

Speech used by young children that contains only the words necessary to convey a message.

grammatical morphemes

Words or endings of words that make a sentence grammatical.

overregularization

Grammatical usage that results from applying rules to words that are exceptions to the rule.

▶ **Figure 4.6**

When shown the two birds, young children usually refer to them as two "wugs," spontaneously adding an *s* to "wug" to make it plural.

This is a wug.

Now there is another one.
There are two of them.
There are two _____.

Berko, 1958.

© 2019 Cengage

of the language that they hear. That is, grammar itself is not built into the child's nervous system, but processes that guide the learning of grammar are. Many findings indirectly support this view.

1. If children are born with a "grammar-learning processor," then specific regions of the brain should be involved in learning grammar. As we discussed on page 92, the left hemisphere of the brain plays a critical role in understanding language and language-specific areas in the left hemisphere are evident in infancy (Dehaene-Lambertz & Spelke, 2015).

2. If learning grammar depends on specialized neural mechanisms that are unique to humans, then efforts to teach grammar to nonhumans should fail. This prediction has been tested by trying to teach grammar to chimpanzees, the species closest to humans on the evolutionary ladder. The result: Chimps master a handful of grammatical rules governing two-word speech, but only with massive effort that is completely unlike the preschool child's learning of grammar (Hoff, 2014).

3. The period from birth through adolescence is a critical period for acquiring language generally and mastering grammar particularly. If children do not acquire language in this period, they never truly master language later (DeKeyser, Alfi-Shabtay, & Ravid, 2010).

Although these findings are consistent with the idea that children have innate grammar-learning mechanisms, they do not prove the existence of such mechanisms. Consequently, scientists have looked for other explanations.

The Cognitive Answer. Some theorists believe that children learn grammar through powerful cognitive skills that help them rapidly detect regularities in their environment, including patterns in the speech they hear. According to this approach, it's as if children establish a huge spreadsheet that has the speech they've heard in one column and the context in which they heard it in a second column; periodically infants scan the columns looking for recurring patterns (Maratsos, 1998). For example, children might be confused the first time they hear -s added to the end of a familiar noun. However, as the database expands to include many instances of familiar nouns with an added -s, children discover that -s is always added to a noun when there are multiple instances of an object. Thus, they create the rule: plural = noun + -s. With this view, children learn language by using powerful analytical tools to detect regularities across many examples that are stored in memory, not through an inborn grammar-learning device (Bannard & Matthews, 2008). Scientists who subscribe to this view argue that infants' impressive ability to extract regularities in the speech sounds that they hear (described on page 140) would work just as effectively to extract regularities in sentence structure (Kidd, 2012).

The Social-Interaction Answer. This approach is eclectic, drawing on each of the views we've considered. From the behaviorist approach, that an environment filled with language is essential; from the linguistic approach, that language learning is distinct; and from the cognitive view, that children have powerful cognitive skills they can use to master language. The unique contribution of this perspective is emphasizing that much language learning takes place in the context of interactions between children and adults, with both parties eager for better communication (Bloom & Tinker, 2001). Children have an ever-expanding repertoire of ideas and intentions that they want to convey to others, and caring adults want to understand their children; so both parties work to improve language skills as a means toward better communication. Thus, improved communication provides an incentive for children to master language and for adults to help them.

None of these accounts provides a comprehensive explanation of how grammar is mastered. But many scientists believe the final explanation will include contributions from the linguistic, cognitive, and social-interaction accounts. That is, children's learning of grammar will be explained in terms of some mechanisms specific to learning grammar, children actively seeking to identify regularities in their environment, and linguistically rich interactions taking place between children and adults (MacWhinney, 1998).

Communicating with Others

When preschoolers argue, they often talk at the same time, their remarks are rambling and incoherent, and neither bothers to listen to the other. For effective oral communication children need to follow a few simple guidelines:

- People should take turns, alternating as speaker and listener.
- A speaker's remarks should be clear from the listener's perspective.
- A listener should pay attention and let speakers know when their remarks don't make sense.

Complete mastery of these elements is a lifelong pursuit. After all, even adults often miscommunicate with one another, violating each of these prescriptions in the process. However, youngsters grasp many of the basics of communication early in life.

Arguments can often be traced to people's failure to follow the fundamental conversational rules of taking turns, speaking clearly, and listening carefully.

Taking Turns

Many parents begin to encourage turn-taking long before infants have said their first words (Field & Widmayer, 1982):

> PARENT: Can you see the bird?
>
> INFANT: (cooing) ooooh.
>
> PARENT: It *is* a pretty bird.
>
> INFANT: ooooh.
>
> PARENT: You're right. It's a cardinal.

Soon after 1-year-olds begin to speak, parents encourage their youngsters to participate in conversational turn-taking. To help their children along, parents often carry both sides of the conversation to show how the roles of speaker and listener are alternated (Hoff, 2014):

> PARENT: (initiating conversation) What's Kendra eating?
>
> PARENT: (illustrating reply for child) She's eating a cookie.

Help of this sort is needed less often by age 2, when spontaneous turn-taking is common in conversations between youngsters and adults (Barton & Tomasello, 1991). By 3 years of age, children have progressed to the point that they can anticipate when speakers are about to finish their turn (Keitel & Daum, 2015) and if a listener fails to reply promptly, the child often repeats his or her remarks to elicit a response and keep the conversation moving (Garvey & Berninger, 1981).

In early parent–child "conversations," parents usually carry both sides of the conversation, alternating as speaker and listener.

Speaking Effectively

When do children first try to initiate communications with others? In fact, what appear to be the first deliberate attempts to communicate typically emerge at 10 months (Golinkoff, 1993). Infants at this age may touch or point to an object while simultaneously looking at another person. They continue this behavior until the person acknowledges them. It's as if the child is saying, "This is a neat toy! I want you to see it, too."

Beginning at 10 months, an infant may point, touch, or make noises to get an adult to do something. An infant in a playpen who wants a toy that is out of reach may make noises while pointing to the toy. The noises capture an adult's attention, and the pointing indicates what the baby wants (Tomasello, Carpenter, & Liszkowski, 2007). The

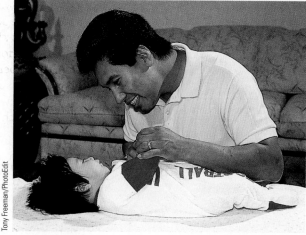

communication may be primitive by adult standards, but it works for babies! And mothers typically translate their baby's pointing into words so that gesture paves the wave for learning words (Goldin-Meadow, Mylander, & Franklin, 2007).

After the first birthday, children begin to use speech to communicate and often initiate conversations with adults (Bloom et al., 1996). Toddlers' first conversations are about themselves, but their conversational scope expands rapidly to include objects in the environment (e.g., toys, food). Later, conversations begin to include more abstract notions, such as hypothetical objects and past or future events (Foster, 1986).

Of course, young children are not always skilled conversational partners. At times, their communications are confusing, leaving a listener to wonder "What was that all about?" Every message—whether an informal conversation or a formal lecture—should have a clear meaning. But saying something clearly is often difficult because clarity can only be judged by considering the listener's age, experience, and knowledge of the topic, along with the context of the conversation. For example, think about the simple request, "Please hand me the Phillips screwdriver." This message may be clear to older listeners who are familiar with variants of screwdrivers, but it is vague to younger listeners, to whom all screwdrivers are alike. Of course, if the toolbox is filled with Phillips screwdrivers of assorted sizes, the message is ambiguous even to a knowledgeable listener.

Consistently constructing clear messages is a fine art, which we would hardly expect young children to have mastered. However, by the preschool years youngsters attempt to calibrate messages, adjusting them to match the listener and the context. For example, preschool children give more elaborate messages to listeners who lack access to critical information than to listeners who have this information (Nadig & Sedivy, 2002; O'Neill, 1996). A child describing where to find a toy will give more detailed directions to a listener whose eyes were covered when the toy was hidden. And if a listener wants to complete a task without help, 5-year-olds sometimes provide helpful information but conceal their intent to help so that the listener thinks she has completed the task without assistance (Grosse, Scott-Phillips, & Tomasello, 2013).

Listening Well

To listen well, a person must continuously decide whether a speaker's remarks make sense. If they do, then a listener needs to reply appropriately, typically by extending the conversation with another remark that's on the topic. Otherwise, the listener needs to provide feedback that the speaker was confusing (e.g., "I don't get what you mean").

Few toddlers master these fundamental conversation skills. Their replies are more likely to be unrelated to the topic than related to it (Bloom, Rocissano, & Hood, 1976). Asked "Where's the sock?" a 1½-year-old may say something like "I'm hungry!" By 3 years, children are more adept at continuing conversations by making remarks that relate to the topic being discussed.

By 4 years of age, children sometimes realize that a message is vague or confusing (Nilsen & Graham, 2012), but they often don't ask speakers to clarify their intent. Instead, young listeners often assume that they know which toy the speaker had in mind (Beal & Belgrad, 1990). Because young children's remarks are often ambiguous and because, as listeners, they often do not detect ambiguities, young children often miscommunicate. Throughout the elementary school years, youngsters gradually master the many skills involved in determining whether a message is consistent and clear (Ackerman, 1993).

Improvement in communication skill is yet another astonishing accomplishment in language during the first five years of life; changes are summarized in ▶ Table 4.2. By the time children are ready to enter kindergarten, they use language with remarkable proficiency and are able to communicate with growing skill.

Think About It

Compare Piaget's theory, Vygotsky's theory, and the information-processing approach in their emphasis on the role of language in cognitive development.

Table 4.2

Major Milestones of Language Development

AGE	MILESTONES
Birth to 1 year	Babies hear language sounds from birth. They begin to coo between 2 and 4 mo[...] at about 6 months.
About the first birthday	Babies begin to talk and to gesture, showing they have begun to use symbols.
1–3 years	Vocabulary expands rapidly (due to fast mapping), particularly at about 18 months. Two-word s[...] emerge in telegraphic speech at about 18 months, and more complex sentences are evident by 3 yea[...] Turn-taking is evident in communication by 2 years.
3–5 years	Vocabulary continues to expand; grammatical morphemes are added; and children begin to adjust their speech to listeners, but as listeners, they often ignore problems in messages they receive.

TEST YOURSELF 4.4

Recall

1. Infants' mastery of language sounds is fostered by _____, in which adults speak slowly and exaggerate changes in pitch and loudness.

2. Older infants' babbling often includes _____, a pattern of rising and falling pitch that distinguishes statements from questions.

3. Youngsters with a(n) _____ style have early vocabularies dominated by words that are names and use language primarily as an intellectual tool.

4. In _____, a young child's meaning of a word is broader than an adult's meaning.

5. Answers to the question "How do children acquire grammar?" include linguistic, cognitive, and _____ influences.

6. When talking to listeners who lack critical information, preschoolers _____.

Interpret

• How do the various explanations of grammatical development differ in their view of the child's role in mastering grammar?

Apply

• According to Piaget's theory, preschoolers are egocentric. How should this egocentrism influence their ability to communicate? Are the findings we have described on children's communication skills consistent with Piaget's view?

Check your answers to the Recall Questions at the end of the chapter.

SUMMARY

4.1 The Onset of Thinking: Piaget's Account

According to Piaget, how do schemes, assimilation, and accommodation provide the foundation for cognitive development throughout the life span?

• In Piaget's view, children construct their own understanding of the world by creating schemes, categories of related events, objects, and knowledge. Infants' schemes are based on actions, but older children's and adolescents' schemes are based on functional, conceptual, and abstract properties.

• Schemes change constantly. In assimilation, experiences are readily incorporated into existing schemes. In accommodation, experiences cause schemes to be modified.

• When accommodation becomes much more common than assimilation, this signals that schemes are inadequate; so

children reorganize them. This reorganization produces four different phases of mental development from infancy through adulthood.

How does thinking become more advanced as infants progress through the sensorimotor stage?

• The first two years of life constitute Piaget's sensorimotor period. Over these two years, infants begin to adapt to and explore their environment, understand objects, and learn to use symbols.

What are the distinguishing characteristics of thinking during the preoperational stage?

• From 2 to 7 years of age, children are in Piaget's preoperational period. Although now capable of using symbols, their

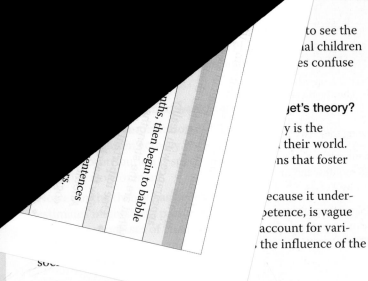

... to see the
... al children
... es confuse

...get's theory?

... y is the
... their world.
... ns that foster

... ecause it under-
... petence, is vague
... account for vari-
... the influence of the

How have contemporary ... ... tended Piaget's theory?

- In contrast to Piaget's idea that children create a comprehensive theory that integrates all their knowledge, the modern view is that children are specialists who generate naïve theories in particular domains, including physics and biology. Infants understand many properties of objects; they know how objects move, what happens when objects collide, and that objects fall when not supported.

- Infants understand the difference between animate and inanimate objects. As preschoolers, children know that, unlike inanimate objects, animate objects move themselves, grow, become ill, and repair through healing. Children's thinking of living things includes teleological explanations (living things exist for a purpose) and essentialism (living things have unseen properties that give them their identities).

4.2 Information Processing During Infancy and Early Childhood

What is the basis of the information-processing approach?

- According to the information-processing view, cognitive development involves changes in mental hardware and in mental software.

How well do young children pay attention?

- Infants use habituation to filter unimportant stimuli. Compared with older children, preschoolers are less able to pay attention to task-relevant information. Their attention can be improved by, for example, encouraging their pretend play.

What kinds of learning take place during infancy?

- Infants are capable of many forms of learning, including classical conditioning, operant conditioning, and imitation.

Do infants and preschool children remember?

- Infants can remember and can be reminded of events they seem to have forgotten. Memory improves during infancy, reflecting growth of the brain. Autobiographical memory

emerges in the preschool years, reflecting children's growing language skills and their sense of self.

- Preschoolers sometimes testify in cases of child abuse. When questioned repeatedly, they often have difficulty distinguishing what they experienced from what others may suggest they experienced. Inaccuracies of this sort can be minimized by following guidelines when interviewing children, such as interviewing them as soon as possible after the event.

What do infants know about numbers?

- Infants are able to distinguish small quantities, such as "twoness" from "threeness." By 3 years of age, children can count small sets of objects and in so doing adhere to the one-to-one, stable-order, and cardinality principles.

4.3 Mind and Culture: Vygotsky's Theory

What is the zone of proximal development? How does it help explain how children accomplish more when they collaborate with others?

- Vygotsky believed that cognition develops first in a social setting and only gradually comes under the child's independent control. The difference between what children can do with assistance and what they can do alone constitutes the zone of proximal development.

Why is scaffolding a particularly effective way of teaching youngsters new concepts and skills?

- Control of cognitive skills is most readily transferred to the child through scaffolding, a teaching style in which teachers let children take on more and more of a task as they master its different components. Scaffolding is common worldwide, but the specific techniques for scaffolding children's learning vary from one culture to the next.

When and why do children talk to themselves as they solve problems?

- Children often talk to themselves, particularly when the task is difficult or when they have made a mistake. Such private speech helps children regulate their behavior, and it represents an intermediate step in the transfer of control of thinking from others to the self.

4.4 Language

When do infants first hear and make speech sounds?

- Infants can hear language sounds soon after birth. They can even hear language sounds that are not used in their native language, but this ability diminishes as infants near the first birthday.

- Infant-directed speech is adults' speech to infants that is slower and has greater variation in pitch and loudness. Infants prefer infant-directed speech, perhaps because it gives them additional language clues.

- Newborns' communication is limited to crying, but babies coo at about 3 months of age. Babbling soon follows, consisting of a single syllable; over several months, infants' babbling comes to include more syllables as well as intonation.

When do children start to talk? How do they learn word meanings?

- After a brief period in which children appear to understand others' speech but do not speak themselves, most infants begin to speak around the first birthday. The first use of words is triggered by the realization that words are symbols. Soon after, the child's vocabulary expands rapidly.

- Most children learn the meanings of words much too rapidly for them to consider all plausible meanings systematically. Instead, children use certain rules to determine the probable meanings of new words. The rules do not always yield the correct meaning. An underextension is a child's meaning that is narrower than an adult's meaning; an overextension is a child's meaning that is broader.

- Individual children differ in vocabulary size, differences that are due to phonological memory and the quality of the child's language environment. Bilingual children learn language readily and better understand the arbitrary nature of words. Some youngsters use a referential word-learning style that emphasizes words as names and that views language as an intellectual tool. Other children use an expressive style that emphasizes phrases and views language as a social tool.

- Children's vocabulary is stimulated by experience. Parents can foster the growth of vocabulary by speaking with children and reading to them. Video helps preschoolers learn new words but is ineffective with infants.

How do young children learn grammar?

- Soon after children begin to speak, they create two-word sentences that are derived from their own experiences. Moving from two-word to more complex sentences involves adding grammatical morphemes. Children first master grammatical morphemes that express simple relations and later those that denote complex relations. Mastery of grammatical morphemes involves learning not only rules but also exceptions to the rules.

- Behaviorists proposed that children acquire grammar through imitation, but that explanation is incorrect. Today's explanations come from three perspectives: The linguistic perspective emphasizes inborn mechanisms that allow children to infer the grammatical rules of their native language, the cognitive perspective emphasizes cognitive processes that allow children to find recurring patterns in the speech they hear, and the social-interaction perspective emphasizes social interactions with adults in which both parties want improved communication.

How well do young children communicate?

- Parents encourage turn-taking even before infants begin to talk, and later, they demonstrate both the speaker and listener roles for their children. By 3 years of age, children spontaneously take turns and prompt one another to take their turn.

- Preschool children adjust their speech in a rudimentary fashion to fit the listener's needs. However, preschoolers are unlikely to identify ambiguities in another person's speech; instead, they are likely to assume that they know what the speaker meant.

Test Yourself: Recall Answers

4.1 1. accommodation **2.** schemes **3.** "out of sight, out of mind" **4.** to use symbols **5.** egocentric **6.** animism **7.** infants and young children **8.** grow **4.2 1.** pretend **2.** let her view a moving mobile **3.** monitoring the sources of their memories **4.** cardinality **4.3 1.** zone of proximal development **2.** scaffolding **3.** private speech **4.4 1.** infant-directed speech **2.** intonation **3.** referential **4.** overextension **5.** social-interaction **6.** provide more elaborate messages

Key Terms

schemes (118)
assimilation (119)
accommodation (119)
equilibration (119)
sensorimotor period (120)
object permanence (121)
egocentrism (122)
animism (123)
centration (123)
core knowledge hypothesis (126)
teleological explanations (128)
essentialism (128)
mental hardware (130)
mental software (130)

attention (131)
orienting response (131)
habituation (131)
classical conditioning (131)
operant conditioning (132)
autobiographical memory (133)
one-to-one principle (135)
stable-order principle (135)
cardinality principle (135)
intersubjectivity (136)
guided participation (136)
zone of proximal development (137)
scaffolding (137)
private speech (138)

infant-directed speech (141)
cooing (141)
babbling (141)
fast mapping (143)
underextension (144)
overextension (144)
phonological memory (145)
referential style (145)
expressive style (145)
telegraphic speech (147)
grammatical morphemes (147)
overregularization (147)

Entering the Social World

Socioemotional Development in Infancy and Early Childhood

5

Humans enjoy one another's company. Social relationships of all sorts—friends, lovers, spouses, parents and children, coworkers, and teammates—make our lives both interesting and satisfying.

In this chapter, we trace the origins of these social relationships. We begin with the first social relationship—between an infant and a parent. You will see how this relationship emerges over the first year and how it is affected by the separation that comes when parents work full-time. Interactions with parents and others are often full of emotions—happiness, satisfaction, anger, and guilt, to name just a few. In the second section, you'll see how children express different emotions and how they recognize others' emotions.

In the third section, you'll learn how children's social horizons expand beyond parents to include peers. Then you'll discover how children play and how they help others in distress.

As children's interactions with others become more wide-ranging, they begin to learn about the social roles they are expected to play. Among the first social roles children learn are those associated with gender—how society expects boys and girls to behave. We'll explore children's awareness of gender roles in the last section of the chapter.

5.1 Beginnings: Trust and Attachment

LEARNING OBJECTIVES

- What are Erikson's first three stages of psychosocial development?

- How do infants become emotionally attached to mother, father, and other significant people in their lives?

- What are the different kinds of attachment relationships, how do they arise, and what are their consequences?

- Is attachment jeopardized when parents of infants and young children are employed outside the home?

Kendra's son Roosevelt is a happy, affectionate 18-month-old. Kendra so enjoys spending time with him that she is avoiding an important decision. She wants to return to her job as a loan officer at the local bank. Kendra knows a woman in the neighborhood who has cared for some of her friends' children, and they all think she is a fantastic babysitter. But Kendra still has a nagging feeling that going back to work isn't a "motherly" thing to do—that being away during the day may hamper Roosevelt's development.

The socioemotional relationship that develops between an infant and a parent (usually, but not necessarily, the mother) is special. This is a baby's first relationship, and scientists and parents believe that it should be satisfying and trouble-free to set the stage for later relationships. In this section, we'll look at the steps involved in creating the baby's first emotional relationship. Along the way, you'll see how this relationship is affected by the separation that sometimes comes when a parent like Kendra works full-time.

Erikson's Stages of Early Psychosocial Development

Some of our keenest insights into psychosocial development come from a theory proposed by Erik Erikson (1982). We first encountered Erikson's theory in Chapter 1; he describes development as a series of eight stages, each with a unique crisis for psychosocial growth. When a crisis is resolved successfully, an area of psychosocial strength is established. When the crisis is not resolved, that aspect of psychosocial development is stunted, often limiting the individual's ability to resolve future crises.

In Erikson's theory, infancy and the preschool years are represented by three stages, shown in ❱ Table 5.1. Let's take a closer look at each stage.

Basic Trust Versus Mistrust

Erikson argues that trust in oneself and others is the foundation of human development. Newborns leave the warmth and security of the uterus for an unfamiliar world. When parents respond to their infant's needs consistently, the infant comes to trust and feel secure in the world. Of course, the world is not always pleasant and is sometimes dangerous. Parents may not always reach a falling baby in time, or they may accidentally feed an infant food that is too hot. Erikson sees value in these experiences because infants learn mistrust. *With a proper balance of trust and mistrust, infants can acquire* hope, *an openness to new experience tempered by wariness that discomfort or danger may arise.*

hope
According to Erikson, openness to new experience tempered by wariness that occurs when trust and mistrust are in balance.

Table 5.1

Erikson's First Three Stages

AGE	CRISIS	STRENGTH
Infancy	Basic trust vs. mistrust	Hope
1–3 years	Autonomy vs. shame and doubt	Will
3–5 years	Initiative vs. guilt	Purpose

Autonomy Versus Shame and Doubt

Between 1 and 3 years of age, children gradually learn that they can control their own actions. With this understanding, children strive for autonomy, for independence from others. However, autonomy is counteracted by doubt that the child can handle demanding situations and by shame that may result from failure. *A blend of autonomy, shame, and doubt gives rise to* will, *the knowledge that within limits, youngsters can act on their world intentionally.*

will
According to Erikson, a young child's understanding that he or she can act on the world intentionally; this occurs when autonomy, shame, and doubt are in balance.

Initiative Versus Guilt

Most 3- and 4-year-olds take some responsibility for themselves (e.g., by dressing themselves). Youngsters also begin to identify with adults and their parents; they begin to understand the opportunities that are available in their culture. Play begins to have purpose as children explore adult roles such as mother, father, teacher, athlete, or writer. Youngsters start to explore the environment on their own, ask numerous questions about the world, and imagine possibilities for themselves.

This initiative is moderated by guilt as children realize that their initiative may place them in conflict with others; they cannot pursue their ambitions with abandon. *Purpose is achieved with a balance between individual initiative and a willingness to cooperate with others.*

purpose
According to Erikson, balance between individual initiative and the willingness to cooperate with others.

Erikson's theory is valuable in tying together psychosocial developments across the entire life span. We will return to the remaining stages in later chapters. For now, let's concentrate on the first of Erikson's crises—the establishment of trust in the world—and see how infants form an emotional bond with their parents.

The Growth of Attachment

In explaining the essential ingredients of these early social relationships, most modern accounts take an evolutionary perspective. *According to* evolutionary psychology, *many human behaviors represent successful adaptation to the environment.* That is, over human history, some behaviors have made it more likely that people will pass on their genes to following generations. For example, we take it for granted that most people enjoy being with other people. But evolutionary psychologists argue that our "social nature" is a product of evolution: For early humans, being part of a group offered protection from predators and made it easier to locate food. Thus, early humans who were social were more likely than their asocial peers to live long enough to reproduce, passing on their social orientation to their offspring (Kurzban, Burton-Chellew, & West, 2015). Over many, many generations, "being social" had such a survival advantage that nearly all people are socially oriented (although in various amounts, as we know from the research on temperament discussed in Chapter 3).

evolutionary psychology
Theoretical view that many human behaviors represent successful adaptations to the environment.

Applied to child development, evolutionary psychology highlights the adaptive value of children's behavior at different points in development (Bjorklund & Jordan, 2013). For example, think about the time and energy parents invest in child rearing. Without such effort, infants and young children would die before they were sexually mature, which means that a parent's genes could not be passed along to grandchildren (Geary, 2002). Here, too, parenting just seems "natural," but it really represents an adaptation to the problem of guaranteeing that one's helpless offspring can survive until they're sexually mature.

Steps Toward Attachment

An evolutionary perspective of early human relationships comes from John Bowlby (1969, 1991). According to Bowlby, *children who form an* attachment *to an adult—that is, an enduring socioemotional relationship—are more likely to survive.* This person is usually the mother but need not be; the key is a strong emotional relationship with a responsive,

attachment
Enduring socioemotional relationship between infants and their caregivers.

Evolutionary psychology emphasizes the adaptive value of parents nurturing their offspring.

Think About It

Based on Piaget's description of infancy (pages 120–122), what cognitive skills might be important prerequisites for the formation of an attachment relationship?

caring person. Attachments can form with fathers, grandparents, or someone else. Bowlby described four phases in the growth of attachment:

- *Preattachment* (birth to 6–8 weeks). During prenatal development and soon after birth, infants rapidly learn to recognize their mothers by smell and sound, which sets the stage for forging an attachment relationship (Hofer, 2006). What's more, evolution has endowed infants with many behaviors that elicit caregiving from adults. When babies cry, smile, or gaze intently at a parent, the parent usually smiles back or holds the baby. The infant's behaviors and the responses they evoke in adults create an interactive system that is the first step in forming attachment relationships.

- *Attachment in the making* (6–8 weeks to 6–8 months). During these months, babies begin to behave differently in the presence of familiar caregivers and unfamiliar adults. Babies smile and laugh more often with the primary caregiver. And when babies are upset, they're more easily consoled by the primary caregiver. Babies are gradually identifying the primary caregiver as the person they can depend on when they're anxious or distressed.

- *True attachment* (6–8 months to 18 months). By approximately 7 or 8 months, most infants have singled out the attachment figure—usually the mother—as a special individual. The attachment figure is now the infant's stable socioemotional base. For example, a 7-month-old will explore a novel environment but periodically look toward his mother, as if asking her to reassure that all is well. The behavior suggests that the infant trusts his mother and indicates that the attachment relationship is established. In addition, this behavior reflects important cognitive growth: It means that the infant has a mental representation of the mother, an understanding that she will be there to meet the infant's needs (Lewis, 1997).

- *Reciprocal relationships* (18 months on). Infants' growing cognitive and language skills and their accumulated experience with their primary caregivers make infants better able to act as partners in the attachment relationship. They often initiate interactions and negotiate with parents ("Please read me another story!"). They begin to understand parents' feelings and goals and sometimes use this knowledge to guide their own behavior (e.g., social referencing, which we describe on page 167). In addition, they cope with separation more effectively because they can anticipate that parents will return.

Forms of Attachment

Thanks to biology, virtually all infants behave in ways that elicit caregiving from adults, and because of this behavior, attachment usually develops between infant and caregiver by 8 or 9 months of age. However, attachment takes different forms, and environmental factors help determine the quality of attachment between infants and caregivers. Mary Ainsworth (1978, 1993) pioneered the study of attachment relationships using a procedure known as the Strange Situation. You can see in ❱ Table 5.2 that the Strange Situation involves a series of brief episodes. The mother and infant enter an unfamiliar room filled with interesting toys. The mother leaves briefly, then mother and baby are reunited. Meanwhile, the experimenter observes the baby and records his or her response to both separation and reunion.

Based on how the infant reacts to separation from—and reunion with—the mother, Ainsworth and other researchers have discovered four primary types of attachment relationships (Ainsworth, 1993; Thompson, 2006). One is a secure attachment, and three are different types of insecure attachment (avoidant, resistant, and disorganized).

secure attachment

Relationship in which infants have come to trust and depend on their mothers.

- Secure attachment: *The baby may or may not cry when the mother leaves, but when she returns, the baby wants to be with her, and if the baby is crying, he or she stops.* Babies in this group seem to be saying, "I missed you terribly; I'm delighted to see you; but now that everything is okay, I'll get back to what I was doing." Approximately 60% to 65% of American babies have secure attachment relationships.

- **Avoidant attachment**: *The baby is not upset when the mother leaves and, when she returns, may ignore her by looking or turning away.* Infants with an avoidant attachment look as if they're saying, "You left me *again*. I always have to take care of myself!" About 20% of American infants have avoidant attachment *relationships, which is one of the three forms of insecure attachment.*
- **Resistant attachment**: *The baby is upset when the mother leaves, and the baby remains upset or even angry when she returns and is difficult to console.* These babies seem to be telling the mother, "Why do you do this? I need you desperately, and yet you just leave me without warning. I get so angry when you're like this." About 10% to 15% of American babies have this resistant attachment relationship, which is another form of insecure attachment.
- **Disorganized (disoriented) attachment**: *The baby seems confused when the mother leaves and when she returns, seems not to understand what's happening.* The baby often behaves in contradictory ways, such as nearing the mother when she returns but not looking at her, as if wondering, "What's happening? I want you to be here, but you left and now you're back. I don't get what's going on!" About 5% to 10% of American babies have this disorganized attachment relationship, the last of the three kinds of insecure attachment.

Quality of attachment during infancy predicts parent–child relations during childhood, adolescence, and young adulthood. Infants with secure attachment relationships tend to report, as adolescents and young adults, that they depend on their parents for care and support. In contrast, infants with insecure attachment relationships often report, as adolescents and young adults, being angry with their parents or deny being close to them (Bretherton, 2010). However, consistency is far from perfect. Stressful life events—the death of a parent, divorce, a life-threatening illness, poverty—help to determine stability and change in attachment. Stressful life events are associated with insecure attachments during adolescence and young adulthood. Consequently, when infants with insecure attachments experience stressful life events, their attachment tends to remain insecure; when infants with secure attachment experience these same events, their attachment often becomes insecure, perhaps because stress makes parents less available and less responsive to their children (Lamb, 2012).

Men and women are equally capable of parenting and babies typically become attached to mothers and fathers at about the same time (Lamb, 2012). And the quality of attachment is often the same; for example, the most common outcome is for infants to have secure attachment relationships with mothers and fathers (Bretherton, 2010). However, because mothers spend more time in caregiving, they often become more

Dorothy Littell Greco/The Image Works

Fathers and mothers differ in how they play with children. Fathers are more likely to engage in vigorous physical play.

avoidant attachment

Relationship in which infants turn away from their mothers when they are reunited following a brief separation.

resistant attachment

Relationship in which, after a brief separation, infants want to be held but are difficult to console.

disorganized (disoriented) attachment

Relationship in which infants don't seem to understand what's happening when they are separated and later reunited with their mothers.

Table 5.2

Sequence of Events in the Strange Situation
1. An observer shows the experimental room to the mother and infant, then leaves the room.
2. The infant is allowed to explore the playroom for 3 minutes; the mother watches but does not participate.
3. A stranger enters the room and remains silent for one minute, talks to the baby for a minute, and then approaches the baby. The mother leaves unobtrusively.
4. The stranger does not play with the baby, but attempts to comfort the baby if necessary.
5. After 3 minutes, the mother returns, greets the baby, and consoles the baby.
6. When the baby has returned to play, the mother leaves again, this time saying "bye-bye" as she leaves.
7. The stranger attempts to calm and play with the baby.
8. After 3 minutes, the mother returns and the stranger leaves.

When infants have an attachment relationship with the mother, they use her as a secure base from which to explore the environment.

skillful at parenting than fathers (Lamb, 2012). Fathers spend more time playing with their babies than taking care of them and they prefer physical play whereas mothers spend more time reading and talking to babies, showing them toys, and playing games such as patty-cake. These differences between mothers' and fathers' behaviors have become smaller as men and women have come to share responsibilities for child care and breadwinning (Lamb & Lewis, 2010).

Consequences of Attachment

Erikson and other theorists (e.g., Waters & Cummings, 2000) believe that infant–parent attachment, the first social relationship, lays the foundation for all of the infant's later social relationships. In this view, infants who experience the trust and compassion of a secure attachment should develop into preschool children who interact confidently and successfully with their peers. In contrast, infants who do not experience a successful, satisfying first relationship should be more prone to problems in their social interactions as preschoolers. In fact, meta-analyses reveal that children with secure attachment relationships are more competent socially, are less prone to externalizing disorders such as bullying and fighting and less prone to internalizing disorders such as depression (Groh et al., 2017.)

Two factors contribute to the benefits for children of a secure attachment relationship. First, secure attachment evidently leads infants to see the world positively and to trust other humans, characteristics that lead to more skilled social interactions later in childhood, adolescence, and adulthood (Dykas & Cassidy, 2011). Second, parents who establish secure attachments with infants tend to provide warm, supportive, and skilled parenting throughout their child's development (McElwain, Booth-LaForce, & Wu, 2011; Thompson, 2006). Thus, continuous exposure to high-quality parenting promotes secure attachment in infancy and positive social relationships in childhood and adolescence. These accounts *are not* mutually exclusive: A successful first relationship and continued warm parenting likely work together to foster children's development.

Of course, attachment is only the first of many steps along the long road of social development. Infants with insecure attachments are not doomed, but this initial misstep *can* interfere with their social development. Consequently, we need to look at the conditions that determine the quality of attachment.

internal working model

Infant's understanding of how responsive and dependable the mother is; thought to influence close relationships throughout the child's life.

When infants who have a resistant attachment relationship are reunited with the mother, they're typically tearful, angry, and difficult to console.

What Determines Quality of Attachment?

Because secure attachment is so important to a child's later development, researchers have tried to identify the factors involved. The most important is the interaction between parents and their babies. A secure attachment is most likely when parents respond to infants predictably and appropriately (Boldt et al., 2016; De Wolff & van IJzendoorn, 1997). For example, when a mother responds promptly to her baby's crying and reassures the baby, the mother's behavior evidently conveys that social interactions are predictable and satisfying. This behavior seems to instill in infants the trust and confidence that are the hallmarks of secure attachment.

Why does predictable and responsive parenting promote secure attachment relationships? To answer this question, think about your own friendships and romantic relationships. These are usually most satisfying when we believe we can trust the other people and depend on them in times of need. The same formula seems to hold for infants. *Infants develop an* internal working model, *a set of expectations about parents' availability and responsiveness, generally and in times of stress.* When parents are dependable and caring, babies come to trust them, knowing they can be relied on for comfort. In other words, babies develop an internal working model in which they believe their parents are concerned about their needs and will try to meet them

(Huth-Bocks et al., 2004; Thompson, 2000). In contrast, when parents respond slowly, intermittently, or angrily, infants come to see social relationships as inconsistent and often frustrating

In a clever demonstration of infants' working models of attachment (Johnson et al., 2010), infants were shown animated videos depicting a large ellipse (mother) paired with a small ellipse (child). The video began with the mother and child ellipses together; then the mother moved away from the child, who began to cry. On some trials, the mother ellipse returned to the child ellipse; on other trials, she continued to move away. Securely attached infants looked longer at the trials depicting an unresponsive mother, but insecurely attached infants looked longer at the trials when the mother returned. Evidently, each group had a working model of how parents respond—securely attached infants expect parents to respond, but insecurely attached infants do not—and they looked longer at the trials that violate their expectations of maternal behavior.

Fortunately, training can help mothers respond more effectively to their baby's needs (Dozier, Zeanah, & Bernard, 2013; Mountain, Cahill, & Thorpe, 2017). Mothers can be taught how to interact more sensitively, affectionately, and responsively, paving the way for secure attachment and the lifelong benefits associated with a positive internal working model of interpersonal relationships.

The formation of attachment illustrates well the combined influence of the different components of the biopsychosocial framework. Many infant behaviors that elicit caregiving in adults—smiling and crying, for example—are biological in origin. When the caregiver is responsive to the infant (a sociocultural force), a secure attachment forms in which the infant trusts caregivers and knows that they can be relied on in stressful situations (a psychological force).

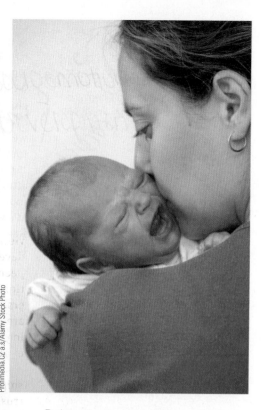

Perhaps the most important ingredient in fostering a secure attachment relationship is responding predictably and appropriately to the infant's needs.

Millions of American infants and preschoolers attend day care or nursery school programs.

Attachment, Work, and Alternative Caregiving

Since the 1970s, more women in the workforce and more single-parent households have made arranging for child care a reality of parenting for many American families. Today, millions of infants and toddlers are cared for by someone other than their mother. Some are cared for in their home by their father, a grandparent, or another relative. Others receive care in the provider's home; the provider is often but not always a relative. Still others attend day care or preschool programs.

Parents and policy makers alike have been concerned about the impact of such care on children generally and, specifically, its impact on attachment. In fact, research shows that, overall, child care experiences are not linked to mother–infant attachment: a secure mother–infant attachment is just as likely regardless of the quality of child care, the time the child spent in care, the age when the child began care, how frequently the parents changed child care arrangements, or the type of child care (e.g., at a child care center or in the home with a nonrelative). However, insecure attachments are more common when infants and toddlers of less sensitive mothers experience low-quality or large amounts of child care (NICHD Early Child Care Research Network, 2001; Sagi et al., 2002).

One other reasonably consistent finding from research on child care is that children who experience many hours of nonparental child care are more often overly aggressive, have more conflicts with teachers, and have less self-control. Part of the problem here is that children who spend long hours in child care are more likely to experience low-quality care, which is typically associated with children being less skilled socially. On a reassuring note, few children in extensive child care experience problem behaviors that would be

Think About It

Imagine that your best friend is the mother of a 3-month-old. Your friend is about to return to her job as a social worker, but she's afraid she'll harm her baby by going back to work. What can you say to reassure her?

clinically significant and most of the effects disappear after first grade (Huston, Bobbitt, & Bentley, 2015).

These results provide clear guidelines for parents like Kendra, the mother in the vignette. They can enroll their infants and toddlers in high-quality day care programs with little fear of lifelong harmful consequences. In trying to find high-quality care for children, parents should look for programs that have a relatively small number of children per caregiver (e.g., three infants or toddlers per caregiver) and the caregivers are well-trained, are responsive, provide age-appropriate stimulating activities, and communicate well with parents (American Academy of Pediatrics, 2011).

Fortunately, today many employers know that convenient, high-quality child care helps attract and retain talented employees. With effort, organization, and help from the community and business, full-time employment and high-quality caregiving can be compatible. We will return to this issue in Chapter 12 from the perspective of the parents. For now, the Real People feature provides one example of a father who stays home to care for his daughter while her mother works full-time.

Responding to the needs of working families, many employers now provide child care on site.

Mark Richards/PhotoEdit

Real People | Applying Human Development

Lois, Bill, and Sarah

Lois, 46, and Bill, 61, had been married nearly four years when Lois gave birth to Sarah. Lois, a kindergarten teacher, returned to work full-time four months after Sarah was born. Bill, who had been halfheartedly pursuing a PhD in education, became a full-time househusband. Bill does the cooking and takes care of Sarah during the day. Lois comes home from school at noon so that the family can eat lunch together, and she is

home from work by 4 in the afternoon. Once a week, Bill takes Sarah to a parent–infant play program. The other parents, all mothers in their twenties and thirties, first assumed that Bill was Sarah's grandfather and had trouble relating to him as an older father. However, he quickly became an accepted member of the group. On weekends, Lois's and Bill's grown children from previous marriages often visit and enjoy caring for and playing with Sarah.

By all accounts, Sarah looks to be a healthy, happy, outgoing 9-month-old. Is this arrangement nontraditional? Clearly. Is it effective for Sarah, Lois, and Bill? Definitely. Sarah receives the nurturing care she needs, Lois goes to work assured that Sarah is in Bill's knowing and caring hands, and Bill relishes being the primary caregiver.

Recall

1. _____ proposed that maturational and social factors come together to pose eight unique challenges for psychosocial growth during the life span.

2. Infants must balance trust and mistrust to achieve _____, an openness to new experience that is coupled with awareness of possible danger.

3. By approximately _____ months of age, most infants have identified a special individual—usually but not always the mother—as the attachment figure.

4. Joan, a 12-month-old, was separated from her mother for about 15 minutes. When they were reunited, Joan would not let her mother pick her up. When her mother approached, Joan would look the other way or toddle to another part of the room. This behavior suggests that Joan has a(n) _____ attachment relationship.

5. The single most important factor in fostering a secure attachment relationship is _____.

6. Children who have a _____ attachment relationship with their parents tend to be more competent socially and are less prone to externalizing disorders.

7. An insecure attachment relationship is likely when an infant receives poor-quality child care and _____.

Interpret

- Compare the infant's contributions to the formation of mother–infant attachment with the mother's contributions.

Apply

- Based on what you know about the normal developmental timetable for the formation of mother–infant attachment, what would seem to be the optimal age range for children to be adopted?

Check your answers to the Recall Questions at the end of the chapter.

5.2 Emerging Emotions

LEARNING OBJECTIVES

- At what ages do children begin to express basic emotions?

- What are complex emotions, and when do they develop?

- When do children begin to understand other people's emotions? How do they use this information to guide their own behavior?

Nicole is ecstatic that she is finally going to see her 7-month-old nephew, Claude. She rushes into the house, sees Claude playing on the floor with blocks, and sweeps him up in a big hug. After a brief, puzzled look, Claude bursts into angry tears and begins thrashing his arms and legs, as if saying to Nicole, "Who are you? What do you want? Put me down! Now!" Nicole quickly hands Claude to his mother, who is surprised by her baby's outburst and even more surprised that he continues to sob while she rocks him.

This vignette illustrates three common emotions. Nicole's initial joy, Claude's anger, and his mother's surprise are familiar to all of us. In this section, we look at when children first express emotions, how children come to understand emotions in others, and how children regulate their emotions. As we do, we'll learn why Claude reacted to Nicole as he did and how Nicole could have prevented Claude's outburst.

The Function of Emotions

Why do people feel emotions? According to the functional approach, emotions are useful because they help people adapt to their environment (Boiger & Mesquita, 2012; Shariff & Tracy, 2011). Consider fear as an example. Most of us would rather not be afraid, but sometimes feeling fearful is adaptive. Imagine you are walking alone late at night in a poorly lit section of campus. You become frightened and, as a consequence, are particularly attentive to sounds that might signal threat and you walk quickly to a safer location. Thus, fear is adaptive because it organizes your behavior around an important goal—avoiding danger (Tooby & Cosmides, 2008).

Similarly, other emotions are adaptive. For example, happiness is adaptive in contributing to stronger interpersonal relationships: When people are happy with another person, they smile, which often causes the other person to feel happy, too, strengthening their relationship (Conway et al., 2013). Disgust is adaptive in keeping people away from substances that might make them ill: When we discover that the milk in a glass is sour, we experience disgust and push the glass away (Oaten, Stevenson, & Case, 2009). Thus, according to the functional approach to human emotion, most emotions developed over the course of human history to meet unique life challenges and help humans to survive.

Experiencing and Expressing Emotions

The three emotions from the vignette—joy, anger, and fear—are considered "basic emotions," as are interest, disgust, and sadness (Lewis, 2016). Basic emotions *are experienced by people worldwide, and each consists of three elements: a subjective feeling, a physiological change, and an overt behavior* (Izard, 2007). For example, suppose you wake to the sound of a thunderstorm and then discover your roommate has left for class with your umbrella. Subjectively, you might feel ready to explode with anger; physiologically, your heart would beat faster; and behaviorally, you would probably be scowling.

Development of Basic Emotions

Using facial expressions and other behaviors, scientists have traced the growth of basic emotions in infants. Many scientists believe that young babies experience just broad positive and broad negative emotional states. These broad emotional categories differentiate rapidly, and by approximately 8 to 9 months of age, infants are thought to experience all basic emotions (Lewis, 2016). For example, the onset of happiness is evident in a baby's smiles. In the first month, infants smile while asleep or when touched softly. The meaning of these smiles isn't clear; they may just represent a reflexive response to bodily states. However, an important change occurs at about 2 to 3 months of age. *At this age, social smiles first appear; infants smile when they see another human face.* Sometimes social smiling is accompanied by cooing, the early form of vocalization described in Chapter 4 (Lavelli & Fogel, 2013). Smiling and cooing seem to be an infant's way of expressing pleasure at interacting with another person.

Anger is one of the first negative emotions to emerge from generalized distress, typically between 4 and 6 months. Infants will become angry, for example, if a favorite food or toy is taken away (Sullivan & Lewis, 2003). Reflecting their growing understanding of goal-directed behavior (see Section 4.1), older infants become increasingly angry when their attempts to achieve a goal are frustrated (Braungart-Rieker, Hill-Soderlund, & Karrass, 2010). For example, when a parent restrains an infant trying to pick up a toy, the guaranteed result is an angry baby.

Like anger, fear emerges later in the first year. *At about 6 months, infants become wary in the presence of an unfamiliar adult, a reaction known as* stranger wariness. When a stranger approaches, a 6-month-old typically looks away and begins to fuss (Stevenson-Hinde & Shouldice, 2009). If a grandmother picks up her grandchild without giving the infant a chance to warm up to her, the outcome is as predictable as it was with Claude, the baby boy in the vignette who was frightened by his aunt: He cries, looks frightened, and reaches with arms outstretched in the direction of someone familiar.

How wary an infant feels around strangers depends on several factors (Brooker et al., 2013; Thompson & Limber, 1991). First, infants tend to be less fearful of strangers when the environment is familiar and more fearful when it is not. Many parents know this firsthand from traveling with their

---

basic emotions

Emotions experienced by humankind that consist of three elements: a subjective feeling, a physiological change, and an overt behavior.

social smiles

Smile that infants produce when they see a human face.

stranger wariness

First distinct signs of fear that emerge around 6 months of age when infants become wary in the presence of unfamiliar adults.

Social smiles emerge at about 2 to 3 months, when infants smile in response to a human face.

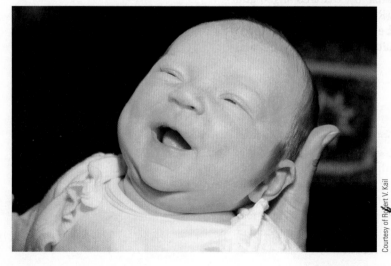
Courtesy of Robert V. Kail

infants: When they enter a friend's house for the first time, their baby clings tightly to his or her mother. Second, a baby's anxiety depends on the stranger's behavior. Instead of rushing to greet or pick up the baby, as Nicole did in the vignette, a stranger should talk with other adults and, in a while, perhaps offer the baby a toy (Mangelsdorf, 1992). Handled this way, many infants will soon be curious about the stranger instead of afraid.

Wariness of strangers is adaptive because it emerges at the same time children begin to master creeping and crawling (described on pages 96–97). Like Curious George, the monkey in a famous series of children's books, babies are inquisitive and want to use their new locomotor skills to explore their world. Being wary of strangers provides a natural restraint against the tendency to wander away from familiar caregivers. However, as youngsters learn to interpret facial expressions and recognize when a person is friendly, their wariness of strangers declines.

Of the negative emotions, we know the least about disgust. Preschool children may respond with disgust at the odor of feces or at being asked to touch a maggot or being asked to eat a piece of candy that's resting on the bottom of a brand-new potty seat (Widen & Russell, 2013). Parents likely play an important role in helping children to identify disgusting stimuli: Mothers respond quite vigorously to disgust-eliciting stimuli when in the presence of their children. They might say "That's revolting!" while moving away from the stimulus (Stevenson et al., 2010). A child's early sensitivity to disgust is useful because many of the cues that elicit disgust are also signals of potential illness: Disgusting stimuli such as feces, vomit, and maggots can all transmit disease.

Emergence of Complex Emotions

In addition to basic emotions such as joy and anger, people feel complex emotions such as pride, guilt, and embarrassment. Most scientists (e.g., Lewis, 2016) believe that complex emotions don't surface until 18 to 24 months of age because they depend on the child having some understanding of the self, which typically occurs between 15 and 18 months. For example, children feel guilty or embarrassed when they've done something they know they shouldn't have done (Kochanska et al., 2002): A child who breaks a toy is thinking, You told me to be careful. But I wasn't! Similarly, children feel pride when they accomplish a challenging task for the first time. Thus, children's growing understanding of themselves enables them to experience complex emotions like pride and guilt (Lewis, 2016).

The features of basic and self-conscious emotions are summarized in ▶ Table 5.3.

Later Developments

As children grow, their catalog of emotions continues to expand. For example, some 5- and 6-year-olds experience regret and relief, and by 9 years of age, most children experience both emotions appropriately (Van Duijvenvoorde, Huizenga, & Jansen, 2014). In addition, cognitive growth means that elementary school children experience shame and guilt in situations they would not have when they were younger (Reimer, 1996). For example, unlike preschool children, many school-age children would be ashamed if they neglected to defend a classmate who had been wrongly accused of a theft.

Think About It
How might an infant's ability to express emotions relate to the formation of attachment? To the temperamental characteristics described on pages 85–86?

Young babies are often wary of strangers; consequently, they're unhappy when strangers hold them before giving them a chance to "warm up."

Courtesy of Robert V. Kail

Think About It
Explain how the different forces in the biopsychosocial framework contribute to the development of basic and complex emotions.

Table 5.3			
Infants' Expression of Emotions			
	DEFINED	**EMERGE**	**EXAMPLES**
Basic	Experienced by people worldwide and include a subjective feeling, a physiological response, and an overt behavior	Birth to 9 months	Happiness, anger, fear
Self-conscious	Responses to meeting or failing to meet expectations or standards	18 to 24 months	Pride, guilt, embarrassment

American children are often quite proud of personal achievement, but Asian children would be embarrassed by such a public display of individual accomplishments.

Fear is another emotion that can be elicited in different ways depending on a child's age. Many preschool children are afraid of the dark and of imaginary creatures. These fears typically diminish during the elementary school years as children grow cognitively and better understand the difference between appearance and reality. Replacing these fears are concerns about school, health, and personal harm (Silverman, La Greca, & Wasserstein, 1995). Such worries are common and not a cause for concern in most children. In some youngsters, however, they become so extreme that they overwhelm the child. For example, some children worry so much about school that they refuse to go (Kearney & Spear, 2013).

Cultural Differences in Emotional Expression

Children worldwide express many of the same basic and complex emotions. However, cultures differ in the extent to which emotional expression is encouraged Outward displays of emotion are encouraged and common in countries like those in North America and Europe that see people as independent; in contrast, emotional restraint is encouraged and common in countries like those in Asia that see people as interdependent with other group members (Camras & Shuster, 2013). Consistent with this view, U.S. children are typically more expressive emotionally than are Chinese children, both in overall expressivity and in terms of specific expressions (e.g., smiling more at funny pictures, more often expressing disgust when smelling vinegar).

Cultures also differ in the events that trigger emotions, particularly complex emotions. Situations that evoke pride in one culture may evoke embarrassment or shame in another. For example, American elementary school children often show pride at personal achievement, such as getting the highest grade on a test or coming in first place in a county fair. In contrast, Asian elementary school children are embarrassed by a public display of individual achievement but show great pride when their entire class is honored for an achievement (Furukawa, Tangney, & Higashibara, 2012; Lewis et al., 2010).

Expression of anger also varies around the world. Suppose a child has just completed a detailed drawing when a classmate spills a drink, ruining the drawing. Most American children would respond with anger. In contrast, children growing up in East Asian countries that practice Buddhism (e.g., Mongolia, Thailand, Nepal) rarely respond with anger because this goes against the Buddhist tenet to be kind to all people, even those whose actions hurt others. Instead, they would probably remain quiet and experience shame that they had left the drawing in a vulnerable position (Cole, Tamang, & Shrestha, 2006).

Thus, culture can influence when and how much children express emotion. Of course, expressing emotion is only part of the developmental story. Children must also learn to recognize others' emotions, which is our next topic.

Recognizing and Using Others' Emotions

Imagine you are short of cash and hope to borrow $20 from your roommate when she returns from class. But when she storms into your apartment, slams the door, and throws her backpack on the floor, you change your mind, realizing that now is a bad time to ask for a loan. This example reminds us that we often need to recognize others' emotions and sometimes change our behavior as a consequence.

When can infants first identify emotions in others? Between 4 and 6 months, infants begin to distinguish facial expressions associated with different emotions. For example, they can distinguish a happy, smiling face from a sad, frowning face (Bornstein & Arterberry, 2003; Montague & Walker-Andrews, 2001), and when they hear happy-sounding voices, they tend to look at happy faces, not ones that appear angry (Bhatt et al., 2016). What's more, like adults, infants are biased toward negative emotions (Vaish, Woodward, & Grossmann, 2008). They attend more rapidly to faces depicting negative emotions (e.g., anger, fear) and pay attention to them longer than they do to emotionless or happy faces (Heck et al., 2016; LoBue & DeLoache, 2010).

Also like adults, infants use others' emotions to direct their behavio. *Infants in an unfamiliar or ambiguous environment often look at a parent as if searching for cues to help them*

Tooga/Stone/Getty Images

interpret the situation, a phenomenon known as social referencing. If a parent looks afraid when shown a novel object, 12-month-olds are less likely to play with the toy than if a parent looks happy (Repacholi, 1998). Infants' use of parents' cues is precise (see ❱ Figure 5.1). If two unfamiliar toys are shown to a parent who expresses disgust at one toy but not the other, 12-month-olds will avoid the toy that elicited the disgust but not the other toy (Moses et al., 2001). And if 12-month-olds encounter an unfamiliar toy in a laboratory setting where one adult seems familiar with the toy but another adult does not, infants will look at the knowledgeable adult's expression to decide whether to play with the toy (Stenberg, 2013).

By 18 months, they're more sophisticated: If one adult demonstrates an unfamiliar toy and a second adult comments in an angry tone, "That's really annoying! That's so irritating!" then 18-month-olds play less with the toy than if the second adult makes neutral remarks in a mild manner. Toddlers apparently decide that they shouldn't play with the toy if it will upset the second adult again (Repacholi & Meltzoff, 2007; Repacholi, Meltzoff, & Olsen, 2008). Thus, social referencing shows that infants are remarkably skilled in using the emotions of adults to help them direct their own behavior.

Although infants and toddlers are remarkably adept at recognizing others' emotions, these skills continue to develop. For example, older children and adolescents are more skilled in recognizing the subtle signals of an emotion (Booker & Dunsmore, 2017). Similarly, compared with younger children, older children more accurately recognize emotions by sound alone (Chronaki et al., 2015). Thus, expressions of emotion are recognized with steadily increasing skill throughout childhood and into adolescence.

What experiences contribute to children's understanding of emotions? Parents and children frequently talk about past emotions and why people felt as they did, particularly for negative emotions such as fear and anger (Lagattuta & Wellman, 2002). Not surprisingly, children learn about emotions when parents talk about feelings, explaining how they differ and the situations that elicit them (Brown & Dunn, 1992; Hughes, White, & Ensor, 2014). Also, a positive and rewarding relationship with parents and siblings is related to children's understanding of emotions (Thompson, Laible, & Ontai, 2003). The nature of this connection is still a mystery. One possibility is that within positive parent–child and sibling relationships, people express a fuller range of emotions (and do so more often) and are more willing to talk about why they feel as they do, providing children with more opportunities to learn about emotions.

social referencing

Behavior in which infants in unfamiliar or ambiguous environments look at an adult for cues to help them interpret the situation.

Regulating Emotions

People often regulate emotions; for example, we routinely try to suppress fear (because we know there's no real need to be afraid of the dark), anger (because we don't want to let a friend know how upset we are), and joy (because we don't want to seem like we're gloating over our good fortune). Sometimes people regulate their emotions behaviorally: we close our eyes to shut out a disturbing scene in a movie, move closer to a loved one when we're frightened, or bite our inner cheeks to avoid laughing.

These behavioral strategies are used throughout the lifespan (Levine, Kaplan, & Davis, 2013). By 4 to 6 months, infants use simple strategies to regulate their emotions (Buss & Goldsmith, 1998; Rothbart & Rueda, 2005). When something frightens or confuses an

❱ **Figure 5.1**

If parents seem frightened by an unfamiliar object, then babies are also wary or even afraid of it.

infant—for example, a menacing stranger—babies often look away. Frightened infants also move closer to a parent, another effective way of helping to control their fear (Parritz, 1996). And by 24 months, a distressed toddler's face typically expresses sadness instead of fear or anger; apparently by this age, toddlers have learned that a sad facial expression is the best way to get a mother's attention and support (Buss & Kiel, 2004).

People also regulate emotions cognitively, often by reappraising the meaning of an event (or of feelings or thoughts) so that it provokes less emotion (John & Gross, 2007). For example, a soccer player nervous about taking a penalty kick can reinterpret her state of physiological arousal as being "pumped up" instead of being "scared to death." Because such strategies depend on cognitive growth, they are more common in school-age children and adolescents (Levine et al., 2013; Silvers, Buhle, & Ochsner, 2014). For example, a child might reduce his disappointment at not receiving a much-anticipated and hoped-for gift by telling himself that he didn't really want the gift in the first place. Or a child nervous about seeing a dentist to have a cavity filled may try to think of the benefits of the visit (Zimmer-Gembeck & Skinner, 2011).

Unfortunately, not all children regulate their emotions well, and those who don't tend to have problems adjusting and interacting with peers (Olson et al., 2011; Zalewski et al., 2011). When children can't control their anger, worry, or sadness, they often have difficulty resolving the conflicts that inevitably surface in peer relationships (Fabes et al., 1999). For example, when children are faced with a dispute over who gets to play with a toy, their unregulated anger can interfere with finding a mutually satisfying solution. Thus, ineffective regulation of emotions leads to more frequent conflicts with peers and, as a result, less satisfying peer relationships and less adaptive adjustment to school (Levine et al., 2013; Olson et al., 2005).

TEST YOURSELF 5.2

Recall

1. Basic emotions include a subjective feeling, a physiological change, and _____.

2. The first detectable form of fear is _____, which emerges at about 6 months.

3. Wariness of strangers is adaptive because it emerges at about the same time _____.

4. Complex emotions such as guilt and shame emerge later than basic emotions because _____.

5. In social referencing, infants use a parent's facial expression _____.

6. Infants often control fear by looking away from a frightening event or by _____.

Interpret

- Distinguish basic emotions from complex emotions.

Apply

- Cite similarities between developmental change in infants' expression and regulation of emotion and developmental change in infants' comprehension and expression of speech (described on pages 139–142 of Chapter 4).

Check your answers to the Recall Questions at the end of the chapter.

5.3 Interacting with Others

LEARNING OBJECTIVES

- When do youngsters first begin to play with each other? How does play change during infancy and the preschool years?

- What determines whether children help one another?

Six-year-old Santiago and his two siblings had been told not to touch their mother's iPad. Consequently, when Santiago dropped the tablet and the screen shattered, he cried and cried. His 3-year-old brother, Alejandro, and his 2-year-old sister, Isabella, watched but did not help. Later, when their mother had soothed Santiago and assured him that the iPad was old and needed to be replaced anyway, she wondered about her younger children's reactions. In the face of their brother's obvious distress, why did Alejandro and Isabella do nothing?

Infants' initial interactions are with parents, but soon they begin to interact with other people, notably their peers. In this section, we'll trace the development of these interactions and learn why children like Santiago and Isabella don't always help others.

The Joys of Play

Peer interactions begin surprisingly early in infancy. By 6 months, babies look, smile, vocalize, and point at each other. These behaviors become more common over the rest of the first year and babies become more likely to respond in kind to these behaviors—smiling or vocalizing in return (Rubin et al., 2015).

Soon after the first birthday, children begin parallel play, *in which each youngster plays alone but maintains a keen interest in what another child is doing.* Two toddlers may each have his or her own toys, but each will watch the other's play, too. Exchanges between youngsters also become more common. Parallel play represents a transition from playing alone to playing with others (Howes, Unger, & Seidner, 1990).

Beginning at roughly 15 to 18 months, toddlers no longer simply watch one another at play. *Instead, they engage in similar activities and talk or smile at one another, illustrating* simple social play. Play has now become interactive (Howes & Matheson, 1992). An example of simple social play is two 20-month-olds pushing toy cars along the floor, making "car sounds" and periodically trading cars.

Toward the second birthday, cooperative play emerges: Now a distinct theme organizes children's play, and they take on special roles based on the theme. They may play hide-and-seek and alternate the roles of hider and seeker, or they may have a tea party and take turns being the host and the guest (Parten, 1932). By the time children are 3½ to 4 years old, parallel play is much less common and cooperative play is the norm (Howes & Matheson, 1992).

Make-Believe

During the preschool years, cooperative play often takes the form of make-believe. Preschoolers have telephone conversations with imaginary partners or pretend to drink imaginary juice. In the early phases of make-believe, children rely on realistic props to support their play. While pretending to drink, younger preschoolers use a real cup; while pretending to drive a car, they use a toy steering wheel. In the later phases of make-believe, children no longer need realistic props; instead, they can imagine that a block is the cup or that a paper plate is the steering wheel.

This gradual movement toward more complex make-believe reflects growth of language and cognitive skills as well as interactions with parents (Karniol, 2016). Parents initiate pretend play with their infants and toddlers. A mother feeding her 15-month-old with a spoon may laugh and say, "Here's the plane flying into Hassan's mouth!" By 24 months, parents often initiate make-believe by saying "Let's pretend," and by age 3, children often engage in pretend play with peers. They usually tell play partners that they want to pretend ("Let's pretend"), then describe those aspects of reality that are being changed ("I'll be the pilot, and this is my plane," referring to the couch). It's as if children mutually agree to enter a parallel universe that's governed by its own set of rules (Wyman, 2014).

As you might suspect, culture influences the development of make-believe. In many cultures (e.g., India, Peru), parents do not routinely engage in pretend play with their children. Without such parental support, children don't begin pretend play until they're older (Callaghan et al., 2011). In addition, the contents of pretend play reflect the values important in a child's culture (Gosso, Morais, & Otta, 2007). For example, adventure and fantasy are favorite themes for European American youngsters, but family roles and everyday activities are favorites of Korean American children. Thus, cultural values influence both the emergence and the content of make-believe (Farver & Shin, 1997).

Vanessa Davies/Dorling Kindersley/Getty Images

In parallel play, children play independently but actively watch what other children are doing.

parallel play

When children play alone but are aware of and interested in what another child is doing.

simple social play

Play that begins at about 15 to 18 months; toddlers engage in similar activities as well as talk and smile at each other.

cooperative play

Play that is organized around a theme, with each child taking on a different role; begins at about 2 years of age.

Think About It

How might Jean Piaget have explained the emergence of make-believe during the preschool years? How would Erik Erikson have explained it?

Make-believe becomes more sophisticated as children develop.

Many teachers and parents believe that make-believe play not only is entertaining for children but also promotes their development. However, the proposed benefits of pretend play are not supported by research. In fact, most of the evidence indicates that pretend play does not enhance (or, for that matter, harm) children's creativity, their cognitive development, or their emotion regulation; pretend play may enhance children's social skills but the findings are inconsistent (Lillard et al., 2013). In short, the main argument for pretend play is that children enjoy it, not that they benefit from it.

For many preschool children, make-believe play involves imaginary companions. Imaginary companions were once thought to be fairly rare, but many preschoolers, particularly girls as well as firstborn and only children, report imaginary companions (Taylor et al., 2004, 2013). Children can usually describe what their imaginary playmates look and sound like (Tahiroglu, Mannering, & Taylor, 2011). Having an imaginary companion is associated with many positive social characteristics (Davis, Meins, & Fernyhough, 2011; Giménez-Dasi, Pons, & Bender, 2016; Roby & Kidd, 2008). Compared with preschool children who lack imaginary friends, preschoolers with imaginary friends tend to be more sociable, have more real friends, and have a more advanced theory of mind. And among older children who are at risk for developing behavior problems, an imaginary companion promotes better adjustment during adolescence (Taylor, Hulette, & Dishion, 2010).

Many children also play with nonhuman animals, particularly family pets. Most families in the United States and Europe have pets, and some children become strongly attached to their pets (Endenburg, van Lith, & Kirpensteijn, 2014). Children without younger siblings are particularly likely to play with pets. Such play sometimes resembles cooperative play, particularly when dogs are involved. For example, "fetch" has the roles of "thrower" and "retriever" that are understood by child and dog. In other common forms of child-animal play, children sometimes pretend to be an animal like the pet (e.g., barking at the pet) or they pretend that the pet is human and hold conversations in which they speak for it and themselves (Melson, 2003, 2010).

Solitary Play

At times throughout the preschool years, many children prefer to play alone. Should parents be worried? Not necessarily. Some children are simply not particularly sociable—they enjoy solitary activities (e.g., coloring, solving puzzles, or assembling Legos), although they are capable of interacting effectively with peers and often do so. However, other children are socially avoidant—they play alone not because they particularly like solitary play but because they're uncomfortable interacting with peers. These children are often anxious and lonely, and are more likely to be excluded by peers. In other words, solitary play is no cause for concern when children enjoy playing alone but is worrisome when children play alone to escape interacting with peers. It's best for these youngsters to see a professional who can help them overcome their reticence in these situations (Coplan, Ooi, & Nocita, 2015).

Gender Differences in Play

Between 2 and 3 years of age, children begin to prefer playing with same-sex peers (Halim et al., 2013). Little boys play together with cars, and little girls play together with dolls. Segregation of playmates by sex occurs spontaneously, and children often resist playing with members of the other sex, even in gender-neutral activities such as playing tag or coloring (Maccoby, 1990, 1998).

This preference increases during childhood, reaching a peak in preadolescence. By age 10 or 11, the vast majority of peer activity is with same-sex children, and most of this involves sex-typed play: Boys are playing sports or playing with cars or action figures; girls are doing artwork or playing with pets or dolls (McHale et al., 2004). Then the tide begins to turn, but even in adulthood, time spent at work and at leisure is commonly segregated by gender (Hartup, 1983).

Why do boys and girls seem so attracted to same-sex play partners? The first reason is self-selection by sex. Boys and girls want to play with others like themselves, and after they know their sex, they pick others on that basis (Martin et al., 2013). Second, boys and girls differ in their styles of play. Boys prefer rough-and-tumble play and generally are more competitive and dominating in their interactions; in contrast, girls' play is more cooperative, prosocial, and conversation-oriented. Generally, boys don't enjoy the way girls play and girls are averse to boys' style of play (Leaper, 2015; Maccoby, 1990, 1998).

Third, when girls and boys play together, girls do not readily influence boys. *Girls' interactions with one another are typically* enabling—*their actions and remarks tend to support others and sustain the interaction.* When drawing together, one girl might say to another, "Cool picture" or "What do you want to do now?" *In contrast, boy's interactions are often* constricting—*one partner tries to emerge as the victor by threatening or contradicting the other, by exaggerating, and so on.* In the same drawing task, one boy might say to another, "My picture's better" or "Drawing is stupid—let's watch TV." When these styles are brought together, girls find that their enabling style is ineffective with boys. The same subtle overtures that work with other girls have no impact on boys. Boys ignore girls' polite suggestions about what to do and ignore girls' efforts to resolve conflicts with discussion (Rose & Rudolph, 2006).

Early segregation of playmates by style of play means that boys learn primarily from boys and girls from girls. Over time, such social segregation by sex reinforces gender differences in play. When young boys spend most of their time playing with other boys, their play becomes more active and more aggressive. In contrast, when young girls spend most of their time playing with other girls, their play becomes less active and less aggressive (Leaper, 2015).

enabling actions

Individuals' actions and remarks that tend to support others and sustain the interaction.

constricting actions

Interaction in which one partner tries to emerge as the victor by threatening or contradicting the other.

At about 2 or 3 years of age, boys and girls start to prefer playing with members of their own sex.

Parental Influence

Parents become involved in their preschool children's play in several ways (Parke & O'Neill, 2000):

Parents influence their children's play in many ways, perhaps none more important than by mediating the disputes that arise when preschoolers play.

- *Playmate.* Many parents enjoy the role of playmate (and many parents deserve an Oscar for their performances). They use the opportunity to scaffold their children's play (see Chapter 4, page 137), often raising it to more sophisticated levels (Tamis-LeMonda & Bornstein, 1996). For example, if a toddler is stacking toy plates, a parent might help the child stack the plates (play at the same level) or might pretend to wash each plate (play at a more advanced level). When parents demonstrate the reciprocal, cooperative nature of play, their children's play with peers is more successful (Lindsey, Cremeens, & Caldera, 2010).

- *Social director.* It takes two to interact, and young children rely on parents to create opportunities for social interactions. Many parents of young children arrange visits with peers, enroll children in activities (e.g., preschool programs), and take children to settings that attract young children (e.g., parks, swimming pools). All this effort is worth it: Children whose parents provide them with frequent opportunities for peer interaction tend to get along better with their peers (Ladd & Pettit, 2002).

- *Coach.* Successful interactions require a host of skills, including how to initiate an interaction, make joint decisions, and resolve conflicts. When parents help their children acquire these skills, children tend to be more competent socially and more accepted by their peers (Grusec, 2011; Mounts, 2011). For example, when mothers emphasize how targets of relational aggression feel, their children are less likely to resort to relational aggression (Werner et al., 2014). But there's a catch: The coaching must be constructive for children to benefit. Parent coaches sometimes make suggestions that are misguided. Bad coaching is worse than none at all, as it harms children's peer relations (Russell & Finnie, 1990).

- *Mediator.* When young children play, they often disagree, argue, and sometimes fight. However, children play more cooperatively and longer when parents are present to help iron out conflicts (Mize, Pettit, & Brown, 1995). When young children can't agree on what to play, a parent can negotiate a mutually acceptable activity. When both youngsters want to play with the same toy, a parent can arrange for them to share. Here, too, parents scaffold their preschoolers' play, smoothing the interaction by providing some of the social skills that preschoolers lack.

Think About It

Suppose friends ask you how their preschool daughter could get along well with peers. What advice would you give them?

In addition to these direct influences on children's play, parents influence children's play indirectly via the quality of the parent–child attachment relationship. Recall that peer relationships in childhood and adolescence are most successful when, as infants, children had a secure attachment relationship with their mother (Groh et al., 2017). A child's relationship with his or her parents is the internal working model for all future social relationships. When the parent–child relationship is of high quality and is emotionally satisfying, children are encouraged to form relationships with other people. Another possibility is that an infant's secure attachment relationship with his or her mother makes the infant feel more confident about exploring the environment, which in turn provides more opportunities to interact with peers. These two views are not mutually exclusive; both may contribute to the relative ease with which securely attached children interact with their peers (Hartup, 1992).

Helping Others

prosocial behavior
Any behavior that benefits another person.

Prosocial behavior *is any behavior that benefits another person.* Cooperation—that is, working together toward a common goal—is one form of prosocial behavior. Of course, cooperation often "works" because individuals gain more than they would by not cooperating. *In contrast,* altruism *is behavior that is driven by feelings of responsibility toward other people, such as helping and sharing, in which individuals do not benefit directly from their actions.* If two youngsters pool their funds to buy a candy bar to share, this is cooperative behavior. If one youngster gives half of her lunch to a peer who forgot his own, this is altruism.

Many scientists believe that humans are biologically predisposed to be helpful, to share, to cooperate, and to be concerned for others (Davidov et al., 2016). Why has prosocial behavior evolved over time? The best explanation has nothing to do with lofty moral principles; it's more pragmatic: People who frequently help others are more likely to receive help themselves, which increases the odds that they'll pass along their genes to future generations. In fact, basic acts of altruism can be seen by 18 months of age. When toddlers and preschoolers see other people who are obviously hurt or upset, they appear concerned, like the child in the photo at the bottom of the page. They try to comfort the person by hugging him or patting him (Zahn-Waxler et al., 1992). And if an adult obviously needs help, most 18-month-olds help spontaneously. For example, when a teacher accidentally drops markers on a floor, most 18-month-olds help the teacher pick them up (Eisenberg, Spinrad, & Knafo-Noam, 2015).

Prosocial behavior typically increases with development: adolescents are more likely to help than children, who are more likely to help than preschoolers. These changes reflect children's growing understanding of others' needs and of appropriate altruistic responses (Eisenberg et al., 2016). Let's look at some specific skills that set the stage for altruistic behaviors.

By 18 months of age, toddlers try to comfort others who are hurt or upset.

Skills Underlying Altruistic Behavior

Remember from Chapter 4 that preschool children are often egocentric, so they may not see the need for altruistic behavior. For example, young children might not share candy with a younger sibling because they cannot imagine how unhappy the sibling is without the candy. In contrast, school-age children, who can more easily take another person's perspective, would perceive the unhappiness and be more inclined to share. In fact, research consistently indicates that altruistic behavior is related to perspective-taking skill. Youngsters who understand others' thoughts and feelings share better with others and help them more often (Imuta et al., 2016; Vaish, Carpenter, & Tomasello, 2009).

Related to perspective taking is empathy, *which is the actual experiencing of another's feelings.* Children who deeply feel another individual's fear, disappointment, sorrow, or loneliness are more inclined to help that person than are children who do not feel those emotions (Eisenberg et al., 2015). In other words, youngsters who are obviously distressed by what they are seeing are most likely to help if they can.

Of course, perspective taking and empathy do not guarantee that children always act altruistically. Even though children have the skills needed to act altruistically, they may not because of the particular situation, as we'll see next.

altruism

Prosocial behavior such as helping and sharing in which the individual does not benefit directly from his or her behavior.

empathy

Act of experiencing another person's feelings.

When children can empathize with others who are sad or upset, they're more likely to offer to help.

Situational Influences

Kind children occasionally disappoint us by being cruel, and children who are usually stingy sometimes surprise us by their generosity. Why? The setting helps determine whether children act altruistically.

- *Feelings of responsibility.* Children act altruistically when they feel responsible for the person in need. For example, children may help siblings and friends more often than strangers simply because they feel a direct responsibility for people they know well (Costin & Jones, 1992). And they're more likely to help when prompted with photos showing two people who look to be friends (Over & Carpenter, 2009). In other words, a simple reminder of the importance of friendship (or affiliation with others) can be enough to elicit helping.

- *Feelings of competence.* Children act altruistically when they believe that they have the skills to help the person in need. Suppose, for example, that a preschooler is growing more and more upset because she can't figure out how to work a computer game; a peer who knows little about computer games is not likely to come to the young girl's aid because the peer doesn't know what to do to help. If the peer tries to help, he or she can end up looking foolish (Peterson, 1983).
- *Mood.* Children act altruistically when they are happy or when they are feeling successful but not when they are feeling sad or feeling as if they have failed (Wentzel, Filisetti, & Looney, 2007). A preschool child who just spent an exciting morning as the "leader" in nursery school is more inclined to share treats with siblings than is a preschooler who was punished by the teacher (Eisenberg, 2000).
- *Costs of altruism.* Children act altruistically when such actions entail few or modest sacrifices. A preschool child who was given a snack that she doesn't like is more inclined to share it with others than a child who was given her favorite food (Eisenberg & Shell, 1986).

So when are children most likely to help? They help when they feel responsible for the person in need, have the needed skills, are happy, and believe they will give up little by helping. When are children least likely to help? They are least likely to help when they feel neither responsible nor capable of helping, are in a bad mood, and believe that helping will entail a large personal sacrifice.

With these guidelines in mind, can you explain why Alejandro and Isabella, the children in the opening vignette, watched idly as their older brother cried? The last two factors—mood and costs—are not likely relevant. However, the first two factors may explain the failure of Alejandro and Isabella to help their older brother. Our explanation appears on page 175, just before Test Yourself.

So far, we've seen that altruistic behavior is determined by children's skills (such as perspective taking) and by characteristics of situations (such as whether children feel competent to help in a particular situation). As we'll see in the next few pages, whether children are altruistic is also determined by genetics and by socialization.

Think About It

Suppose some kindergarten children want to raise money for a gift for one of their classmates who is ill. Based on the information presented here, what advice can you give the children as they plan their fundraising?

The Contribution of Heredity

As mentioned on page 173, many scientists believe that prosocial behavior represents an evolutionary adaptation: People who help others are more likely to be helped themselves and thus are more likely to survive and have offspring. According to this argument, we should expect to find evidence for heritability of prosocial behavior, and in fact, that's the case: Twin studies consistently find that identical twins are more similar in their prosocial behavior than are fraternal twins (Knafo-Noam et al., 2015).

One likely path of genetic influence involves oxytocin, a hormone that influences many social behaviors (e.g., nurturance, empathy, affiliation, and cooperation) and that's been linked to a few specific genes. In this account, some children may inherit oxytocin-promoting genes that facilitate their prosocial behavior (Carter, 2014). For example, oxytocin may enhance perspective-taking and empathy, leading to greater prosocial behavior (Christ, Carlo, & Stoltenberg, 2016).

Genes probably also affect prosocial behavior indirectly by their influence on temperament. For example, children who are temperamentally less able to regulate their emotions (in part due to heredity) may help less often because they're so upset by another's distress that taking action is impossible (Eisenberg et al., 2007). Another temperamental influence may be via inhibition (shyness). Children who are temperamentally shy are often reluctant to help others, particularly people they don't know well (Young, Fox, & Zahn-Waxler, 1999). Even though shy children realize that others need help and are upset by another person's apparent distress, their reticence prevents them from translating these feelings into action. Thus, in both cases, children are aware that others need help. But in the first instance, they're too upset themselves to figure out how to help, and in the second instance, they know how to help but are too inhibited to follow through.

Socialization of Altruism

Dr. Martin Luther King, Jr., said that his pursuit of civil rights for African Americans was particularly influenced by three people: Henry David Thoreau (a 19th-century American philosopher); Mohandas Gandhi (leader of the Indian movement for independence from England); and his father, Dr. Martin Luther King, Sr. As is true of many humanitarians, Dr. King's prosocial behavior started in childhood at home. But how do parents foster altruism in their children? Several factors contribute.

- *Modeling.* When children see adults helping and caring for others, they often imitate such prosocial behavior (Eisenberg et al., 2015). Of course, parents are the models to whom children are most continuously exposed, so they exert a powerful influence. When parents are helpful and responsive, their children often imitate them by being cooperative, helpful, sharing, and less critical of others. And when parents do volunteer work for charitable organizations, their adolescent children are more likely to volunteer, too (McGinley et al., 2010).

- *Disciplinary practices.* Children behave prosocially more often when their parents are warm and supportive, set guidelines, and provide feedback; in contrast, prosocial behavior is less common when parenting is harsh, is threatening, and includes frequent physical punishment (Newton, Thompson, & Goodman, 2016). Particularly important is parents' use of reasoning as a disciplinary tactic with the goal of helping children see how their actions affect others (Farrant et al., 2012). For example, after 4-year-old Rashan grabbed some crayons from a playmate, his mother told Rashan, "You shouldn't grab things from people. It makes them angry and unhappy. Ask first, and if they say 'no,' then you mustn't take them."

- *Opportunities to behave prosocially.* You need to practice to improve skills, and prosocial behaviors are no exception—children and adolescents are more likely to act prosocially when they're routinely given the opportunity to help and cooperate with others. At home, children can help with household tasks such as cleaning and setting the table. Adolescents can be encouraged to participate in community service, such as working at a food bank or tutoring younger children. Experiences like these help sensitize children and adolescents to the needs of others and allow them to enjoy the satisfaction of helping (Carlo et al., 2007). Such experiences help to explain why Mexican American youth are often more prosocial than are their European American peers: Many Mexican American mothers emphasize the importance of families and expect their children to help with household chores such as caring for siblings, experiences that lead children to be attentive to others' needs (Knight & Carlo, 2012).

Thus, parents can foster altruism in their youngsters by behaving altruistically themselves, using reasoning to discipline their children, and encouraging their children to help at home and elsewhere. Situational factors also play a role, and altruism requires perspective taking and empathy. Combining these ingredients, we can give a general account of children's altruistic behavior. As children get older, their perspective-taking and empathic skills develop, which enables them to see and feel another's needs. Nonetheless, children are never invariably altruistic (or, fortunately, invariably nonaltruistic) because particular contexts affect altruistic behavior, too. These factors are summarized in ❱ Table 5.4.

Think About It

Paula worries that her son Elliot is too selfish and wishes that he were more caring and compassionate. As a parent, what can Paula do to encourage Elliot to be more concerned about the welfare of others?

Postscript: Why Didn't Alejandro and Isabella Help?

Here are our explanations. First, neither Alejandro nor Isabella may have felt sufficiently responsible to help because (a) with two children who could help, each child's feeling of individual responsibility is reduced and (b) younger children are less likely to feel responsible for an older sibling. Second, neither was allowed to play with the iPad, so they wouldn't feel competent to help: In other words, they had no idea how to fix the damaged the iPad.

Table 5.4

Factors Contributing to Children's Prosocial Behavior		
GENERAL CATEGORY	**TYPES OF INFLUENCE**	**CHILDREN ARE MORE LIKELY TO HELP WHEN . . .**
Skills	Perspective taking	they can take another person's point of view.
	Empathy	they feel another person's emotions.
Situational influences	Feelings of responsibility	they feel responsible to the person in need.
	Feelings of competence	they feel competent to help.
	Mood	they're in a good mood.
	Cost of altruism	the cost of prosocial behavior is small.
Heredity	Temperament	they're not shy and can control their emotions.
Parents' influence	Modeling	parents behave prosocially themselves.
	Discipline	parents reason with them.
	Opportunities	they practice at home and elsewhere.

TEST YOURSELF 5.3

Recall

1. Toddlers who are 12 to 15 months old often engage in _____ play, in which they play separately but look at one another and sometimes communicate verbally.

2. Children with imaginary companions often are more sociable, have more real friends, and have more advanced _____.

3. When girls interact, conflicts are typically resolved through _____; boys more often resort to intimidation.

4. _____ is the ability to understand and feel another person's emotions.

5. Contextual influences on prosocial behavior include feelings of responsibility, feelings of competence, _____, and the costs associated with behaving prosocially.

6. Parents can foster altruism in their youngsters by behaving altruistically themselves, using reasoning to discipline their children, and _____.

Interpret

- Why must a full account of children's prosocial behavior include an emphasis on skills (e.g., empathy) as well as situations (e.g., whether a child feels responsible)?

Apply

- How might children's temperament, which we discussed in Chapter 3, influence the development of their play with peers?

Check your answers to the Recall Questions at the end of the chapter.

5.4 Gender Roles and Gender Identity

LEARNING OBJECTIVES

- What are our stereotypes about males and females? How well do they correspond to actual differences between boys and girls?

- How do young children learn gender roles?

- How are gender roles changing? What further changes might the future hold?

Meda and Perry want their 6-year-old daughter, Hope, to pick activities, friends, and ultimately a career based on her interests and abilities rather than on her gender. They have done their best to encourage gender-neutral values and behavior. Therefore, both are astonished that Hope seems to be indistinguishable from other 6-year-olds reared by conventional parents. Hope's close friends are all girls. When Hope is with her friends, they play house or play with dolls. What seems to be going wrong with Meda and Perry's plans for a gender-neutral girl?

Family and well-wishers are always eager to know the sex of a newborn. Why are people so interested in a baby's sex? The answer is that being a "boy" or a "girl" is not simply a biological distinction. Instead, these terms are associated with distinct social roles. *Like a role in a play, a* social role *is a set of cultural guidelines as to how a person should behave, particularly with other people.* The roles associated with gender are among the first that children learn, starting in infancy (Shutts, 2015). Youngsters rapidly learn about the behaviors assigned to males and females in their culture. At the same time, they begin to identify with one of these groups. As they do, they take on an identity as a boy or a girl.

In this section, you'll learn about the "female role" and the "male role" in North America today, and you'll also discover why Meda and Perry are having so much trouble rearing a gender-neutral girl.

Somwaya/Fotolia

Assuming that the child is a girl leads to a host of other inferences about her personality and behavior.

Images of Men and Women: Facts and Fantasy

All cultures have gender stereotypes—*beliefs and images about males and females that may or may not be true.* For example, many men and women believe that males are rational, active, independent, competitive, and aggressive. At the same time, many men and women claim that females are emotional, passive, dependent, sensitive, and gentle (Ruble, Martin, & Berenbaum, 2006).

Based on gender stereotypes, we expect males and females to act and feel in particular ways, and we respond to their behavior differently depending on their gender (Smith, Mackie, & Claypool, 2015). For example, if you saw a toddler playing with a doll, you would probably assume that she is a girl, based on her taste in toys. What's more, your assumption would lead you to believe that she plays more quietly and is more readily frightened than a boy (Karraker, Vogel, & Lake, 1995). Once we assume that the child is a girl, our gender stereotypes lead to a host of inferences about behavior and personality.

social role

Set of cultural guidelines about how one should behave, especially with other people.

gender stereotypes

Beliefs and images about males and females that are not necessarily true.

Learning Gender Stereotypes

Children don't live in a gender-neutral world for long. Although 12-month-old boys and girls look equally at gender-stereotyped toys, 18-month-olds do not: Girls look longer at pictures of dolls than at pictures of trucks, but boys look longer at pictures of trucks (Leaper, 2015). By 4 years of age, children know much about gender-stereotyped activities: They believe that girls play hopscotch but boys play football; girls help bake cookies but boys take out the trash; and women feed babies but men chop wood (Gelman, Taylor, & Nguyen, 2004). They've also begun to learn about behaviors and traits that are stereotypically masculine or feminine. Preschoolers believe that boys are more often aggressive physically but that girls tend to be aggressive verbally (Giles & Heyman, 2005).

During the elementary school years, children expand their knowledge of gender-stereotyped traits and behaviors. They learn stereotypes about personality traits—boys are tough and girls are gentle—and about academic subjects—math is for boys and reading is for girls (Cvencek, Meltzoff, & Greenwald, 2011; Kurtz-Costes et al., 2014). By the time they enter middle school, their ideas of gender stereotypes are virtually as well formed as those of adults (Heyman & Legare, 2004).

Beyond the preschool years, children learn that occupations associated with males tend to earn more money and have greater power than those associated with females (Weisgram, Bigler, & Liben, 2010). At some point, children apparently internalize a general belief about male versus female occupations—something like "Jobs for men are more prestigious than jobs for women."

As children develop, they also begin to understand that gender stereotypes do not always apply; older children are more willing than younger children to ignore stereotypes when judging other children. For example, told about a boy who likes to play with girls and pretend to iron, preschoolers think he would still want to play with masculine toys. However, by the middle elementary school years, children realize that this boy's interests are not stereotypic, and he would rather play with stereotypically feminine toys (Blakemore, 2003). In other words, older children see gender stereotypes as general guidelines for behavior that are not necessarily binding for all boys and girls (Conry-Murray & Turiel, 2012). This developmental trend toward greater flexibility is evident in the study described in the Spotlight on Research feature.

Spotlight On Research

Reasoning About Gender-Related Properties

Who were the investigators, and what was the aim of the study? Do children believe that physical and behavioral properties of boys and girls are inherent and stable? Do they believe, for example, that boys necessarily like to build things and grow up to have a beard? Do they believe that girls necessarily like to play with dolls and grow up to have breasts? Marianne Taylor, Marjorie Rhodes, and Susan Gelman (2009) conducted a study to answer these questions.

How did the investigators measure the topic of interest? Taylor and colleagues told participants about a baby girl who, immediately after birth, went to live on an island inhabited only by men, including her uncle. She had no contact with females. Participants were then shown a photo of the baby as a "big kid" and were asked several questions about her physical properties (e.g., "Will she grow up to be a mommy or a daddy?") and some questions about her behavioral properties (e.g., "Will she like to play with a tea set or with trucks?"). They were also told about a baby boy who lives on an island with his aunt and other women and then were asked the same questions.

Who were the participants in the study? The study included 68 5-year-olds, 64 10-year-olds, and 32 college students. At each age, half the children were girls.

What was the design of the study? This study was experimental because Taylor and colleagues were interested in the impact of the domain—physical versus behavioral—on participants' judgments. The study was cross-sectional because it included 5-year-olds, 10-year-olds, and college students, each tested once.

Were there ethical concerns with the study? No, the children enjoyed hearing stories about babies growing up on the island.

What were the results? The investigators recorded the percentage of responses that were consistent with the baby's biological sex (e.g., predicting that the baby girl would like a tea set and want to be a nurse and that she'll grow up to be a mom and have breasts). The

results are shown in ❱ Figure 5.2, separately for physical and behavioral properties.

Let's start with the physical properties. There's little developmental change in these judgments: At all ages, participants expected the baby to acquire physical properties associated with its biological sex. However, the pattern is quite different for behavioral properties, where there is a steady downward developmental trend. Five-year-olds tend to believe that boys and girls will engage in gender-stereotypic behaviors, although they see these as slightly more flexible than physical properties. In contrast, adults believe that a boy brought up by women will behave in a feminine stereotypic manner and that a girl brought up by men will behave in a masculine stereotypic manner. A final result to note is that participants at all ages claimed greater flexibility in behavioral properties for girls than for boys; they thought that girls were more likely to be influenced in a masculine direction than boys were to be influenced in a feminine direction.

What did the investigators conclude? Taylor and colleagues concluded that "young children treat the concepts of 'boy' and 'girl' as equivalent to species, in the extent to which features are inborn, inflexible, and intrinsically linked to category membership.... [By] adulthood, participants viewed both male and female behavior as more open to the environment and flexible ..." (2009, p. 475).

What converging evidence would strengthen these conclusions? Most of the children in this sample were European American, from university towns in the U.S. Midwest. It would be important to see whether children from different backgrounds responded in a similar fashion. In addition, it would be valuable to extend the list of properties to, for example, psychological properties (e.g., personality) to determine whether they're considered more like physical properties or more like behavioral properties in terms of flexibility.

❱ **Figure 5.2**

As children develop, they gradually see behavior and traits as more open to the influence of the environment.

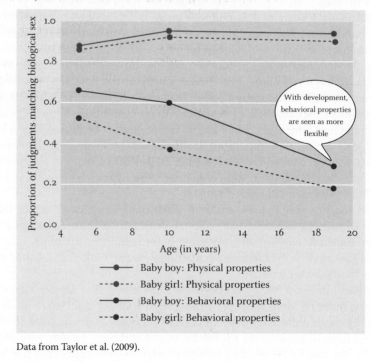

Data from Taylor et al. (2009).

Gender-Related Differences

So far, we've only considered people's *beliefs* about differences between males and females, and many of them are false. Research reveals that males and females often do not differ in the ways specified by cultural stereotypes. What are the bona fide differences between males and females? Of course, in addition to the obvious anatomical differences, males are typically larger and stronger than females throughout most of the life span. As infants, boys are more active than girls, and this difference increases during childhood (Alexander & Wilcox, 2012; Saudino, 2009). In contrast, girls are less susceptible to stress and disease and have a lower death rate (Zaslow & Hayes, 1986).

With regard to social roles, activities for males tend to be more strenuous, involve more cooperation with others, and often require travel. Activities for females are usually less demanding physically, are more solitary, and take place closer to home. This division of roles is much the same worldwide (Whiting & Edwards, 1988).

The extent of gender differences in the intellectual and psychosocial arenas remains uncertain. Research suggests differences between males and females in the following areas:

- *Verbal ability.* Girls have larger vocabularies than boys and are more talkative (Feldman et al., 2000; Leaper & Smith, 2004). During elementary school and high school, girls read better than boys, and this difference is found in virtually all industrialized countries (Miller & Halpern, 2014). Finally, more boys are diagnosed with language-related problems such as reading disability (Halpern, 2012).

- *Mathematics.* During the elementary school years, girls are usually more advanced than boys in arithmetic and mastery of basic math concepts, a difference that may be a by-product of girls' greater language skill (Wei et al., 2012). During high school and college, boys used to get higher scores than girls on standardized math tests, but that difference has diminished substantially over the past 25 years; now boys have a negligible advantage (Lindberg et al., 2010). This change apparently reflects efforts to encourage girls to pursue mathematics generally and to take more math courses specifically. Around the world, gender differences in math are negligible in countries where, compared with males, females have similar access to education, occupations, and political power, but gender differences remain where females are limited to traditionally feminine-stereotyped occupations that do not require math skills (Else-Quest, Hyde, & Linn, 2010).

- *Spatial ability.* On problems like those in ❱ Figure 5.3, which measure the ability to manipulate visual information mentally, you must decide which figures are rotated variants of the standard shown at the left. Beginning in infancy, boys tend to have better mental-rotation skill than girls (Levine et al., 2016). However, on other spatial tasks, sex differences are smaller or nonexistent (Miller & Halperin, 2014).

- *Memory.* Compared with boys and men, girls and women often remember the identity of objects as well as their location more accurately (Miller & Halpern, 2014; Voyer et al., 2007). For example, if shown photos of faces, girls remember those faces more accurately than boys do (Herlitz & Lovén, 2013). In addition, when describing past events (e.g., a trip to a museum, a special visitor at school), girls tend to provide more elaborate and more emotion-filled descriptions (Grysman & Hudson, 2013).

- *Social influence.* Girls are more likely than boys to comply with the directions of adults (Maccoby & Jacklin, 1974). Girls and women are also more readily influenced by others in a variety of situations, particularly when they are under group pressure (Becker, 1986; Eagly, Karau, & Makhijani, 1995). However, these gender differences may simply reflect that females value group harmony more than males do and thus seem to give in to others (Miller, Danaher, & Forbes, 1986; Strough & Berg, 2000). For instance, at a meeting to plan a school function, girls are just as likely as boys to recognize the flaws in a bad idea, but girls are more willing to go along simply because they don't want the group to start arguing.

- *Aggression.* In virtually all cultures that have been studied, boys are more physically aggressive than girls, and this is true by 2 years of age (Hay, 2017). This difference continues throughout the life span (Sanson et al., 1993). In contrast, *girls are more likely to resort to* relational aggression *in which they try to hurt others by damaging their relationships with peers.* They may call children names, make fun of them, spread rumors about them, or pointedly ignore them (Ostrov & Godleski, 2010).

relational aggression

Aggression used to hurt others by undermining their social relationships.

On spatial ability tasks, which involve visualizing information in different orientations, males tend to respond more rapidly and more accurately than females.

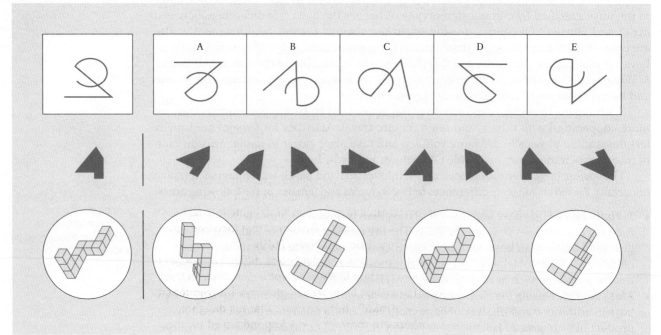

From "Process Analysis of Spatial Aptitude," by J. W. Pellegrino and R. V. Kail, (1982) in R. J. Sternberg (Ed.), *Advances in the Psychology of Human Intelligence*, Vol. 1, p. 316.

- *Emotional sensitivity and expression.* Throughout infancy, childhood, and adolescence, girls identify facial expressions (e.g., happy face versus a sad face) more accurately than boys do (Alexander & Wilcox, 2012; Thompson & Voyer, 2014). In addition, girls are more likely to express happiness and sadness, but boys are more likely to express anger (Chaplin & Aldao, 2013). Finally, for the complex (self-conscious) emotions described on page 165, adolescent girls report experiencing shame and guilt more often than boys do (Else-Quest et al., 2012).

- *Effortful control.* During story time in a preschool classroom, many children sit quietly, listening to the teacher read. But if a child is fidgeting or pestering a nearby child, it's probably a boy. Consistent with this example, girls are more skilled at effortful control: Compared with boys, they are better able to regulate their behavior, to inhibit inappropriate responding, and to focus their attention (Else-Quest et al., 2006; Gagne, Miller, & Goldsmith, 2013). In addition, boys are far more likely to be diagnosed with attentional disorders such as ADHD (Hyde, 2014).

In most other intellectual and social domains, boys and girls are similar. When thinking about areas in which sex differences have been found, keep in mind that gender differences often depend on a person's experiences (Levine et al., 2016). Also, gender differences may fluctuate over time, reflecting historical change in the contexts of childhood for boys and girls. Finally, each result just described refers to a difference in the *average* performance of boys and girls. These differences tend to be small, which means that they do not apply to all boys and girls (Hyde, 2014). For example, many girls have greater spatial ability than some boys, and many boys are more susceptible to social influence than are some girls.

Gender Typing

Folklore holds that parents and other adults—teachers and television characters, for example—directly shape children's behavior toward the roles associated with their sex. Boys are rewarded for boyish behavior and punished for girlish behavior. The folklore even has a theoretical basis. According to social cognitive theorists Albert Bandura (1977, 1986; Bandura & Bussey, 2004) and Walter Mischel (1970), children learn gender roles in much the same way they learn other social behaviors: by watching the world around them and learning the outcomes of different actions. Thus, parents and others shape appropriate gender roles in children, and children learn what their culture considers appropriate behavior for males and females by simply watching how adults and peers act.

How well does research support social learning theory? Overall, parents often treat sons and daughters similarly. Parents interact equally with sons and daughters, are equally warm to both, encourage both sons and daughters to be independent, and discipline sons and daughters similarly (Hallers-Haalboom et al., 2016; Lytton & Romney, 1991). And, although mothers are more engaged than fathers in their children's education, mothers' and fathers' involvement has comparable impact on boys' and girls' success in school (Kim & Hill, 2015). However, in behavior related to gender roles, parents respond differently to sons and daughters (Lytton & Romney, 1991). Activities such as playing with dolls, dressing up, or helping an adult are encouraged more often in daughters than in sons; rough-and-tumble play and playing with blocks are encouraged more in sons than in daughters. Parents tolerate mild aggression in sons to a greater degree than in daughters (Martin & Ross, 2005), and following the birth of a child, especially a firstborn, they become more traditional in gender-related attitudes (Katz-Wise, Priess, & Hyde, 2010).

Fathers are more likely than mothers to treat sons and daughters differently. Fathers often encourage gender-related play and they are more likely to accept dependence in their daughters (Snow, Jacklin, & Maccoby, 1983). A father, for example, may urge his frightened young son to jump off the diving board ("Be a man!") but not insist that his daughter do so ("That's okay, honey"). Apparently mothers are more likely to respond based on their knowledge of the needs of individual children, but fathers respond based on gender stereotypes. A mother responds to her son, knowing that he's smart but unsure of himself; a father may respond based on what he thinks boys generally should be like.

Of course, adults differ in their views on the relative rights and roles of males and females. Some have very traditional views and believe that men should be hired preferentially for some jobs and that it's more important for sons than daughters to attend college; others have more gender-neutral views and believe that women should have the same business and professional opportunities as men and that daughters should have the same educational opportunities as sons. Not surprisingly, parents convey these attitudes to their children (Crouter et al., 2007). Meta-analyses show that children's gender-related interests, attitudes, and self-concepts are more traditional when their parents have traditional views and are more gender-neutral when their parents have nontraditional views (Degner & Dalege, 2013; Tenenbaum & Leaper, 2002).

Peers are also influential. By 3 years, most children's play shows the impact of gender stereotypes—boys prefer blocks and trucks, whereas girls prefer tea sets and dolls—and youngsters are critical of peers who engage in gender-inappropriate play (Hines, 2015). This is particularly true of boys who like feminine toys or who choose feminine activities. Boys who play with dolls and girls (like the one in the photo on page 182) who play with trucks will be ignored, teased, or ridiculed by their peers, but a boy will receive harsher treatment than a girl (Levy, Taylor, & Gelman, 1995). Once children learn rules about gender-typical play, they often harshly punish peers who violate those rules.

Peers influence gender roles in another way, too. We've seen that by 2 or 3 years of age, children most often play with same-sex peers (Leaper, 2015). This early segregation of playmates based on a child's sex means that boys learn primarily from

Think About It
The women's liberation movement became a powerful social force in North America during the 1960s. Describe how you might do research to determine whether the movement has changed the gender roles that children learn.

Fathers are more likely than mothers to encourage their children's gender-related play.

Preschoolers discourage peers from cross-gender play.

gender identity
Sense of oneself as male or a female.

gender-schema theory
Theory that states that children want to learn more about an activity only after first deciding whether it is masculine or feminine.

boys and girls from girls. This helps solidify a youngster's emerging sense of membership in a particular gender group and sharpens the contrast between their own gender and the other gender. Thus, through encouraging words, critical looks, and other forms of praise and punishment, other people influence boys and girls to behave differently.

Gender Identity

If you were to listen to a typical conversation between two preschoolers, you might hear something like this:

MARIA: When I grow up, I'm going to be a singer.

JUANITA: When I grow up, I'm going to be a papa.

MARIA: No, you can't be a papa—you'll be a mama.

JUANITA: No, I wanna be a papa.

MARIA: You can't be a papa. Only boys can be papas, and you're a girl!

Obviously, Maria's understanding of gender is more developed than Juanita's. How can we explain these differences? According to Lawrence Kohlberg (1966; Kohlberg & Ullian, 1974), full understanding of gender is said to develop gradually in three steps. Toddlers know that they are either boys or girls and label themselves accordingly. During the preschool years, children begin to understand that gender is stable—boys become men, and girls become women. Yet at this age, they believe that a girl who wears her hair like a boy will become a boy and that a boy who plays with dolls will become a girl. Not until about 5 or 6 years do children come to understand that maleness and femaleness do not change over situations or according to personal wishes. They understand that a child's sex is unaffected by the clothing that a child wears or the toys that a child likes. *At this point, children begin to identify with one group and to develop a* gender identity—*a sense of the self as a male or a female.*

As soon as children identify themselves as a boy or girl, they begin learning about gender-typical behavior. Explaining how this learning takes places is the aim of a theory proposed by Carol Martin (Martin et al., 1999; Martin & Ruble, 2004) (see ◗ Figure 5.4). *In* gender-schema theory, *children first decide if an object, an activity, or a behavior is associated with females or males; then they use this information to decide whether they should learn more about the object, activity, or behavior.* That is, once children know their gender, they pay attention primarily to experiences and events that are gender-appropriate (Martin & Halverson, 1987). According to gender-schema theory, a preschool boy watching a group of girls playing in sand will decide that playing in sand is for girls and that because he is a boy, playing in sand is not for him. Seeing a group of older boys playing

◗ **Figure 5.4**
According to gender-schema theory, children first decide if an object, an activity, or a behavior is for females or males and then learn more about the objects, activities, or behaviors that are appropriate for their own gender.

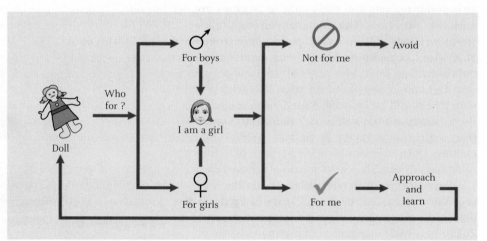

football, he will decide that football is for boys and that because he is a boy, football is acceptable and he should learn more about it.

According to gender-schema theory, after children acquire a gender identity, they seem to view the world through special glasses that allow only gender-typical activities to be in focus (Liben & Bigler, 2002). For example, children who have acquired a gender identity much prefer toys that are liked by others of their sex (Shutts, Banaji, & Spelke, 2010). As Martin and Ruble (2004) put it: "Children are gender detectives who search for cues about gender—who should or should not engage in a particular activity, who can play with whom, and why girls and boys are different" (p. 67).

This account also helps to explain why many 3- to 5-year-old girls adore wearing exceedingly feminine clothing such as pink frilly dresses, yet by the elementary school years they become tomboys, wearing pants, playing sports, and avoiding feminine-stereotyped toys and activities (Bailey, Bechtold, & Berenbaum, 2002; Halim, 2016). A young girl's love of frilly dresses likely reflects the pursuit of salient symbols that match her newly acquired gender identity. However, by school age, children know that gender roles are flexible (e.g., wearing pants doesn't make a girl into boy, wearing nail polish doesn't make a boy into a girl) and that masculine roles often have more status. Consequently, elementary school girls realize that by being a tomboy, they can have some of the status associated with being a boy without jeopardizing their identity as a girl (Halim, 2016).

This selective viewing of the world explains a great deal about children's learning of gender roles, but one final important element needs to be considered: biology.

Biological Influences

Most child development researchers agree that biology contributes to gender roles and gender identity. Evolutionary developmental psychology, for example, reminds us that men and women performed vastly different roles for much of human history. Women were more invested in child rearing, and men were more invested in providing important resources (e.g., food and protection) for their offspring (Geary, 2002). In adapting to these roles, different traits and behaviors evolved for men and women. For example, men became more aggressive because that was adaptive in helping them ward off predators.

If gender roles are based in part on our evolutionary heritage, then behavior genetic research should show the impact of heredity on gender-role learning. Indeed, twin studies show a substantial hereditary impact on gender-role learning (Iervolino et al., 2005). For identical twins, if one strongly prefers sex-typical toys and activities, the other one usually does, too. Fraternal twins are also similar in their preference for sex-typical toys and activities, but not to the extent of identical twins.

Twin studies point to a biological basis for gender-role learning, but the studies don't tell us what factors are responsible. Some scientists believe that the sex hormones are key players; consistent with this idea, for both boys and girls, exposure to testosterone during prenatal development leads to greater interest in masculine sex-typed activities during the elementary school years (Hines, 2015). This link is particularly vivid in studies of children with congenital adrenal hyperplasia (CAH), a genetic disorder in which, beginning in prenatal development, the adrenal glands secrete large amounts of androgen. During childhood and adolescence, girls with CAH prefer masculine activities (such as playing with cars instead of dolls) and male playmates to a much greater extent than girls not exposed to these amounts of androgen, despite strong encouragement from parents to play with feminine toys (Hines, 2015). Apparently the androgen affects the prenatal development of brain regions critical for masculine and feminine gender-role behavior.

Perhaps the most accurate conclusion to draw is that biology, the socializing influence of people, and the child's own efforts to understand gender-typical behavior all contribute to gender roles and differences. Recognizing the interactive nature of these influences on gender learning also enables us to better understand how gender roles are changing today, which we consider next.

Evolving Gender Roles

Gender roles are not etched in stone; they change with the times. In the United States, the range of acceptable roles for girls and boys and women and men has never been greater than today (Liben, 2016). For example, some fathers stay home to be primary caregivers for children, and some mothers work full-time as sole support for the family. What is the impact of these changes on gender roles? Some insights come from the results of the Family Lifestyles Project (Weisner, Garnier, & Loucky, 1994; Weisner & Wilson-Mitchell, 1990). This research has examined families in which the adults were members of the counterculture of the 1960s and 1970s. Some of the families are deeply committed to living their own lives and to rearing their children without traditional gender stereotypes. In these families, men and women share the household, financial, and child care tasks.

Gender roles continue to evolve, and the range of acceptable roles for men and women continues to expand.

David R. Frazier Photolibrary, Inc/Alamy Stock Photo

The results of this project show that parents like Meda and Perry from the opening vignette can influence some aspects of gender stereotyping more readily than others. On the one hand, children in these families tend to have same-sex friends and to like sex-typed activities: The boys enjoy physical play, and the girls enjoy drawing and reading. On the other hand, the children have few stereotypes concerning occupations: They agree that girls can be president of the United States and drive trucks and that boys can be nurses and secretaries. They also have fewer sex-typed attitudes about the use of objects. They claim that boys and girls are equally likely to use an iron, a shovel, a hammer and nails, and a needle and thread.

Apparently some features of gender roles and identities are more readily influenced by experience than others. This is as it should be. For most of our history as a species, Homo sapiens have existed in small groups of families, hunting animals and gathering vegetation. Women have given birth to the children and cared for them. Over the course of human history, it has been adaptive for women to be caring and nurturing because this increases the odds of a secure attachment and, ultimately, the survival of the infant. Men's responsibilities have included protecting the family unit from predators and hunting with other males, roles for which physical strength and aggressiveness are crucial.

Circumstances of life in the 21st century are, of course, substantially different: Often both men and women are employed outside the home and both men and women care for children (Eagly & Wood, 2013). Nevertheless, the cultural changes of the past few decades cannot erase hundreds of thousands of years of evolutionary history. We should not be surprised that boys and girls play differently, that girls tend to be more supportive in their interactions with others, and that boys are usually more aggressive physically.

TEST YOURSELF 5.4

Recall

1. _____ are beliefs and images about males and females that may or may not be true.

2. Research on intellectual functioning and social behavior has revealed sex differences in verbal ability, _____, memory, social influence, aggression, emotional sensitivity and effortful control.

3. _____ may be particularly influential in teaching gender roles because they more often treat sons and daughters differently.

4. According to Martin's theory, children focus on gender-typical activities after they _____.

5. Children studied in the Family Lifestyles Project, whose parents were members of the counterculture of the 1960s and 1970s, had traditional gender-related views toward friends and _____.

Interpret

● How do the different forces in the biopsychosocial framework contribute to the development of gender roles?

Apply

● What advice would you give to a mother who wants her daughter to grow to be gender-free in her attitudes, beliefs, and aspirations?

Check your answers to the Recall Questions at the end of the chapter.

5.1 Beginnings: Trust and Attachment

What are Erikson's first three stages of psychosocial development?

- In Erikson's theory of psychosocial development, individuals face certain psychosocial crises at different phases in development. The crisis of infancy is to establish a balance between trust and mistrust of the world, producing hope; between 1 and 3 years of age, youngsters must blend autonomy and shame to produce will; and between 3 and 5 years, initiative and guilt must be balanced to achieve purpose.

How do infants become emotionally attached to mother, father, and other significant people in their lives?

- Attachment is an enduring socioemotional relationship between infant and parent. For both adults and infants, many of the behaviors that contribute to the formation of attachment are biologically programmed. Bowlby's theory of attachment is rooted in evolutionary psychology and describes four stages in the development of attachment: preattachment, attachment in the making, true attachment, and reciprocal relationships.

What are the different varieties of attachment relationships, how do they arise, and what are their consequences?

- Research with the Strange Situation, in which infant and mother are separated briefly, reveals four primary forms of attachment. Most common is a secure attachment in which infants have complete trust in the mother. Less common are three types of attachment relationships in which this trust is lacking. In avoidant relationships, infants deal with the lack of trust by ignoring their mother; in resistant relationships, infants often seem angry with her; in disorganized relationships, infants do not appear to understand their mother's absence.

- Children who have had secure attachment relationships during infancy tend to be more skilled socially and are at less risk for externalizing disorders. Secure attachment is most likely to occur when mothers respond sensitively and consistently to their infants' needs.

- Responsive caregiving results in infants developing an internal working model in which they expect parents will try to meet their needs.

Is attachment jeopardized when parents of young children are employed outside the home?

- Many U.S. children are cared for at home by a father or another relative, in a day care provider's home, or in a day care center. Infants and young children are not harmed by such care as long as it is of high quality and parents remain responsive to their children.

5.2 Emerging Emotions

At what age do children begin to express basic emotions?

- Basic emotions—which include joy, anger, and fear—emerge in the first year. Fear first appears in infancy as stranger wariness.

What are complex emotions, and when do they develop?

- Complex emotions have an evaluative component and include guilt, embarrassment, and pride. They appear between 18 and 24 months and require more sophisticated cognitive skills than basic emotions. Cultures differ in the rules for expressing emotions and in the situations that elicit particular emotions.

When do children begin to understand other people's emotions? How do they use this information to guide their own behavior?

- By 6 months, infants have begun to recognize the emotions associated with different facial expressions. They use this information to help them evaluate unfamiliar situations. Beyond infancy, children learn more about the causes of different emotions.

- Infants use simple strategies to regulate emotions such as fear. As children grow, they become better skilled at regulating their emotions. Children who do not regulate emotions well tend to have problems interacting with others.

5.3 Interacting with Others

When do youngsters first begin to play with each other? How does play change during infancy and the preschool years?

- Even infants notice and respond to one another, but the first real interactions (at about 12 to 15 months) take the form of parallel play in which toddlers play alone while watching each other. A few months later, simple social play emerges in which toddlers engage in similar activities and interact with one another. At about 2 years of age, cooperative play organized around a theme becomes common. Make-believe play is also common and becomes more sophisticated as children develop. Most forms of solitary play are harmless.

What determines whether children help one another?

- Prosocial behaviors such as helping and sharing are more common in children who understand (by perspective taking) and experience (by empathy) another's feelings.

- Prosocial behavior is more likely when children feel responsible for the person in distress. Also, children help more often when they believe that they have the skills needed, when they are feeling happy or successful, and when they perceive that the costs of helping are small.
- Twin studies show that prosocial behavior is influenced by heredity, probably through its impact on oxytocin, behavioral control (inhibition), and emotion regulation.
- Parents can foster altruism in their youngsters by behaving altruistically themselves, using reasoning to discipline their children, and encouraging their children to help at home and elsewhere.

5.4 Gender Roles and Gender Identity

What are stereotypes about males and females? How well do they correspond to actual differences between boys and girls?

- Gender stereotypes are beliefs about males and females that are often used to make inferences about a person that are based solely on his or her gender; by 4 years of age, children know these stereotypes well.
- Studies of gender differences reveal that girls have greater verbal skill and memory but that boys have greater spatial skill. Differences in math are negligible when females have access to education and occupations where math is valuable. Girls are better able to interpret emotions, are more prone to social influence, and have better effortful control,

but boys are more aggressive. These differences vary based on a number of factors, including the historical period.

How do young children learn gender roles?

- Parents treat sons and daughters similarly, except in sex-typed activities. Fathers may be particularly important in sex typing because they are more likely to treat sons and daughters differently.
- Children gradually learn that gender is stable over time and cannot be changed according to personal wishes. After children understand gender, they begin to learn gender-typical behavior. According to gender-schema theory, children learn about gender by paying attention to behaviors of members of their own sex and ignoring behaviors of members of the other sex.
- Evolutionary developmental psychology reminds us that different roles for males and females caused different traits and behaviors to evolve for men and women. The idea that biology influences some aspects of gender roles is also supported by research on females exposed to male hormones during prenatal development.

How are gender roles changing?

- Gender roles have changed considerably in the past 50 years. However, studies of nontraditional families indicate that some components of gender stereotypes are more readily changed than others.

Test Yourself: Recall Answers

5.1 1. Erik Erikson **2.** hope **3.** 6 or 7 **4.** avoidant insecure **5.** responding consistently and appropriately **6.** secure **7.** insensitive, unresponsive mothering **5.2 1.** an overt behavior **2.** wariness of strangers **3.** infants master creeping and crawling **4.** complex emotions require more advanced cognitive skills **5.** to direct their own behavior (e.g., deciding if an unfamiliar situation is safe or frightening) **6.** moving closer to a parent **5.3 1.** parallel **2.** theory of mind **3.** discussion and compromise **4.** Empathy **5.** mood **6.** providing children with opportunities to practice being altruistic **5.4 1.** Gender stereotypes **2.** spatial ability **3.** Fathers **4.** understand gender **5.** preferred activities

Key Terms

hope (156)
will (157)
purpose (157)
evolutionary psychology (157)
attachment (157)
secure attachment (158)
avoidant attachment (159)
resistant attachment (159)
disorganized (disoriented) attachment (159)

internal working model (160)
basic emotions (164)
social smiles (164)
stranger wariness (164)
social referencing (167)
parallel play (169)
simple social play (169)
cooperative play (169)
enabling actions (171)
constricting actions (171)

prosocial behavior (172)
altruism (173)
empathy (173)
social role (177)
gender stereotypes (177)
relational aggression (179)
gender identity (182)
gender-schema theory (182)

Off to School

Cognitive and Physical Development in Middle Childhood

Every fall, American 5- and 6-year-olds trot off to kindergarten, starting an educational journey that lasts 13 or more years. As the journey begins, many children can read only a few words and know little math; by the end, most can read complete books and many have learned algebra and geometry. This mastery of complex academic skills is possible because of profound changes in children's thinking, changes described in the first section of this chapter.

For most American school children, intelligence and aptitude tests are a common part of their educational travels. In the second section of this chapter, you'll see what tests measure and why some children get lower scores on tests. In the third section, you'll discover how tests are often used to identify school children with atypical or special needs.

Next, we look at the way students learn to read, write, and do math. In this section, you'll discover some of the educational practices that seem to foster students' learning.

Finally, children's growing cognitive skills, when coupled with improved motor coordination, enable them to participate in sports. In the last section, we'll look at such participation and the physical changes that make it possible.

Cognitive Development

LEARNING OBJECTIVES

- What are the distinguishing characteristics of thought during Piaget's concrete-operational and formal-operational stages?

- How do children use strategies and monitoring to improve learning and remembering?

Adrian, a sixth grader in middle school, just took his first social studies test—and failed. He is shocked because he'd always received As and Bs in elementary school. Adrian realizes that glancing through the textbook chapter once before a test is probably not going to work in middle school, but he's not sure what else he should be doing.

Adrian's cognitive skills far surpass those of the infants and toddlers we examined in Chapter 4. Yet the vignette shows that his skills aren't flawless. In this section, we'll learn more about cognitive growth in childhood, first by considering the perspective of Piaget's theory and then by considering the information-processing account.

More Sophisticated Thinking: Piaget's Version

You probably remember Piaget's stages of thinking that we described in Chapters 1 and 4. The first two stages, sensorimotor and preoperational thinking, characterize infancy and the preschool years. In the next few pages, we describe the remaining two stages, the concrete-operational and formal-operational stages, which apply to school-age children and adolescents.

The Concrete-Operational Period

Let's start by reviewing three important limits of preoperational thinking described in Chapter 4.

- Preschoolers are egocentric, believing that others see the world as they do.
- Preschoolers sometimes confuse appearances with reality.
- Preschoolers are unable to reverse their thinking.

None of these limits applies to children in the concrete-operational stage, which extends from approximately 7 to 11 years. Egocentrism wanes gradually as youngsters have more experiences with other people who assert their own perspectives on the world. Understanding that events can be interpreted in different ways leads to the realization that appearances can be deceiving. *Also, thought can be reversed because school-age children have acquired* mental operations, *actions that can be performed on objects or ideas and that consistently yield a result.* Recall from Chapter 4 that on the conservation task, concrete-operational children realize that the amount of liquid is the same after it has been poured into a different beaker—pointing out that the pouring can always be reversed.

As the name implies, concrete-operational thinking is limited to the tangible and real, to the here and now. The concrete-operational youngster takes "an earthbound, concrete, practical-minded sort of problem-solving approach" (Flavell, 1985, p. 98). Thinking abstractly and hypothetically is beyond the ability of concrete-operational children; these skills are acquired in the formal-operational period, as you'll see in the next section.

The Formal-Operational Period

With the onset of the formal-operational period, which extends from roughly age 11 into adulthood, children and adolescents apply psychological operations to abstract entities, too; they are able to think hypothetically and reason abstractly (Siegler & Alibali, 2005).

mental operations

Cognitive actions that can be performed on objects or ideas.

Think About It

Piaget and Erikson propose unique stages for ages 7 to 11 years. How similar are the stages they propose? How do they differ?

To illustrate these differences, let's look at problem-solving, where formal-operational adolescents often take a very different approach from concrete-operational children. In one of Piaget's experiments (Inhelder & Piaget, 1958), children and adolescents were presented with several flasks, each containing what appeared to be the same clear liquid. They were told that one combination of the clear liquids would produce a blue liquid, and they were asked to determine the necessary combination. A typical concrete-operational youngster plunged right in, mixing different liquids haphazardly. In contrast, formal-operational adolescents understood that setting up the problem in abstract terms is the key. The problem is not really about pouring liquids, but about testing all possible combinations. So, formal-operational teens mixed liquid from the first flask with liquids from each of the other flasks. When these combinations failed to produce a blue liquid, the teenagers concluded that the liquid in the first flask is not essential and mixed the liquid in the second flask with each of the remaining liquids. Formal-operational thinkers continued in this manner until they found the critical pair that produces the blue liquid. For adolescents, the problem does not involve the concrete acts of pouring and mixing. Instead, they understand that it involves identifying possible combinations and then evaluating each one. This sort of adolescent combinatorial reasoning is illustrated in the Real People feature.

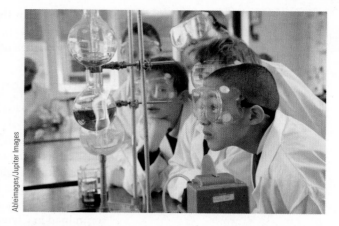

Concrete-operational thinkers often solve problems haphazardly, but formal-operational thinkers more often set up problems in abstract terms.

Adolescents' more sophisticated thinking is also shown in their ability to make appropriate conclusions from facts, which is known as deductive reasoning. Suppose we tell a person the following:

deductive reasoning
Drawing conclusions from facts; characteristic of formal-operational thought.

If you hit a glass with a hammer, the glass will break.

If you then tell the person "You hit the glass with a hammer," he or she would conclude, of course, that "the glass will break," a conclusion that formal-operational adolescents do reach.

Concrete-operational youngsters sometimes reach this conclusion too—but based on their experience, not because the conclusion is logically necessary. To see the difference, imagine that the statement now is:

If you hit a glass with a feather, the glass will break.

Told "You hit the glass with a feather," the conclusion "the glass will break" follows just as logically as it did in the first example. In this instance, however, the conclusion goes against what experience tells us is true. Concrete-operational 10-year-olds resist reaching conclusions that are contrary to known facts, whereas formal-operational 15-year-olds often reach such conclusions (De Neys & Everaerts, 2008). Formal-operational teenagers

Real People | Applying Human Development

Combinatorial Reasoning Goes to the Races

As a 15-year-old, Robert Kail delivered the *Indianapolis Star*. In the spring of 1965, the newspaper announced a contest for all newspaper carriers. The carrier who created the most words from the letters contained in the words *SAFE RACE* would win two tickets to the Indianapolis 500 auto race.

Kail realized that this was a problem in combinatorial reasoning. He needed to create all possible combinations of letters, then look them up in a dictionary. Following this procedure, he had to win (or, at worst, tie). So, he created exhaustive lists of possible words, beginning with each of the letters individually, then all possible combinations of two letters, and working his way up to all possible combinations of all eight letters (e.g., SCAREEFA, SCAREEAF). This was monotonous enough, but no more so than the next step: looking up all those possible words in a dictionary. (Remember, this was in the days before computerized spell-checkers.) Weeks later, he had generated 126 words. As predicted, a few months later, he learned that he had won the contest. Combinatorial reasoning has its payoffs!

understand that these problems are about abstractions that need not correspond to real-world relations. In contrast, concrete-operational youngsters reach conclusions based on their knowledge of the world.

Comments on Piaget's View

We mentioned in Chapter 4 that although Piaget's theory provides our single most comprehensive theory of cognitive development, it has some shortcomings. Specifically, it overestimates adolescents' cognitive competence, is vague concerning processes of change, does not account for variability in children's performance, and undervalues the influence of the sociocultural environment. Because of these limits to Piaget's theory, we need to look at other approaches to understand mental development during childhood and adolescence. In the next few pages, we'll focus on the information-processing approach that we first examined in Chapter 4.

Information-Processing Strategies for Learning and Remembering

You'll remember from Chapter 4 that information-processing psychologists believe that cognitive development proceeds by increases in the efficiency with which children process information. In other words, just as personal computers have become progressively more sophisticated in their hardware and software, information-processing psychologists believe that cognitive development reflects change in mental computing power, including mental hardware and mental software.

One of the key issues in this approach concerns the means by which children store information in permanent memory and retrieve it when needed later. *According to information-processing psychologists, most human thought takes place in* working memory, *where a relatively small number of thoughts and ideas can be stored briefly.* As you read these sentences, for example, the information is stored in working memory. However, as you read additional sentences, they displace the contents of sentences you read earlier. *For you to learn this information, it must be transferred to* long-term memory, *a permanent storehouse of knowledge that has unlimited capacity.* If information you read is not transferred to long-term memory, it is lost.

working memory

Type of memory in which a small number of items can be stored briefly.

long-term memory

Permanent storehouse for memories that has unlimited capacity.

organization

As applied to children's memory, a strategy in which information to be remembered is structured so that related information is placed together.

elaboration

Memory strategy in which information is embellished to make it more memorable.

Memory Strategies

How do you try to learn the information in this book or your other textbooks? If you're like many college students, you probably use some combination of highlighting key sentences, outlining chapters, taking notes, writing summaries, and testing yourself. These are all effective learning strategies that make it easier for you to store text information in long-term memory.

Children begin to use simple strategies fairly early. For example, 7- or 8-year-olds use rehearsal, a strategy of repetitively naming information that is to be remembered. As children grow older, they learn other memory strategies. *One memory strategy is* organization—*structuring information to be remembered so that related information is placed together.* For example, a sixth grader trying to remember major battles of the American Civil War could organize them geographically (e.g., Shiloh and Fort Donelson in Tennessee, Antietam and Monocacy in Maryland).

Another memory strategy is elaboration—*embellishing information to be remembered to make it more memorable.* To see elaboration in action, imagine a child who can never remember if the second syllable of *rehearsal* is spelled *her* (as it sounds) or *hear*. The child could remember the correct spelling by reminding herself that *rehearsal* is like *re-hear-ing*. Thus, thinking about the derivation of *rehearsal* makes it easier to remember how to spell it. Finally, as children grow, they're also more likely to use external aids to memory, such as making notes and writing down information on calendars so they won't forget future events (Eskritt & McLeod, 2008).

As children grow, they make more use of memory aids, such as taking notes.

JPC-PROD/Shutterstock.com

Metacognition

Just as a well-stocked toolbox isn't valuable if you don't know how to use the tools, memory strategies aren't much good unless children know when to use them. For example, rehearsal is a great strategy for remembering phone numbers but lousy for remembering amendments to the U.S. Constitution or the plot of *Hamlet*. During the elementary school years and adolescence, children gradually learn to identify different kinds of memory problems and the memory strategies most appropriate to each. For example, when reading a textbook or watching a television newscast, outlining or writing a summary are good strategies because they identify the main points and organize them. Children gradually become more skilled at selecting appropriate strategies, but even high school students do not always use effective learning strategies when they should (Grammer et al., 2011; Schneider, 2015).

After children choose a memory strategy, they need to monitor its effectiveness. That is, they need to decide if the strategy is working. If it's not, they need to begin anew, reanalyzing the memory task to select a better approach. If the strategy is working, they should determine the portion of the material they have not yet mastered and concentrate their efforts there. Monitoring improves gradually with age. Even preschool children can distinguish what they know from what they don't (Ghetti, Hembacher, & Coughlin, 2013), but older children and adolescents do so more accurately (Bjorklund, 2005).

Diagnosing memory problems accurately and monitoring the effectiveness of memory strategies are two important elements of metamemory, *which refers to a child's intuitive understanding of memory.* That is, as children develop, they learn more about how memory operates and devise naïve theories of memory that represent an extension of the theory of mind described on pages 111–112 (Schneider, 2015). For example, children learn that memory is fallible (i.e., they sometimes forget!) and that some types of memory tasks are easier than others (e.g., remembering the main idea of the Gettysburg address is simpler than remembering it word for word). This growing knowledge of memory helps children use memory strategies more effectively, just as an experienced carpenter's accumulated knowledge of wood tells her when to use nails, screws, or glue to join two boards (Ghetti & Lee, 2011).

Of course, children's growing understanding of memory is paralleled by their increased understanding of all cognitive processes. *Such knowledge and awareness of cognitive processes is called* metacognitive knowledge. Metacognitive knowledge grows rapidly during the elementary school years: Children come to know much about perception, attention, intentions, knowledge, and thinking (Flavell, 2000; McCormick, 2003). For example, school-age children know that sometimes they deliberately direct their attention—as in searching for a parent's face in a crowd—but that sometimes events capture attention—as with an unexpected clap of thunder (Parault & Schwanenflugel, 2000).

One of the most important features of children's metacognitive knowledge is their understanding of the connections among goals, strategies, monitoring, and outcomes, shown in ▶ Figure 6.1. Children come to realize that for a broad spectrum of tasks—ranging from learning words in a spelling list to learning to spike a volleyball to learning to get along with an overly talkative classmate seated nearby—they need to regulate their learning by understanding the goal and selecting a means to achieve that goal. Then they determine whether the chosen method is working. *Effective* cognitive self-regulation—*that is, skill at identifying goals, selecting effective strategies, and monitoring accurately—is a characteristic of successful students* (Usher & Pajares, 2009; Zimmerman, 2001). A student may decide that writing each spelling word twice before the test is a good way to get all the words right. When the student gets only 70% correct on the first test, he or she switches to a new strategy (e.g., writing each word four times and writing its definition), showing the adaptive nature of cognitive processes in self-regulated learners.

Some students do not master these learning strategies spontaneously, but they may acquire them when teachers emphasize them in class (Grammer, Coffman, & Ornstein, 2013; Ornstein et al., 2010). In addition, several programs teach students strategies for studying more effectively (Pressley, 2002). For example, teachers demonstrate several strategies that promote greater reading comprehension, including selecting a goal for reading, making a mental picture of what's going on in the text, periodically predicting what will happen next, and summarizing aloud what's happened so far. Children practice

metamemory
Person's informal understanding of memory; includes the ability to diagnose memory problems accurately and to monitor the effectiveness of memory strategies.

metacognitive knowledge
A person's knowledge and awareness of cognitive processes.

cognitive self-regulation
Skill at identifying goals, selecting effective strategies, and monitoring accurately; a characteristic of successful students.

Think About It
Which elements of the biopsychosocial framework are emphasized in the information-processing approach to cognitive development?

▶ **Figure 6.1**

Effective learning involves understanding the goals of the task, selecting an appropriate strategy, and monitoring the effectiveness of the chosen strategy.

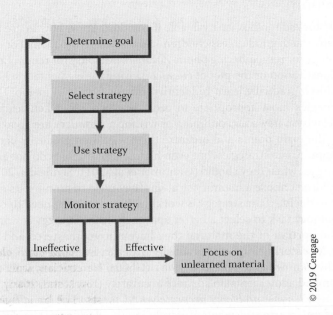

© 2019 Cengage

these strategies separately and as part of a reading "tool kit." Empowered with reading strategies such as these, students' understanding of text is deeper and they typically obtain greater scores on standardized tests of reading comprehension (Pressley & Hilden, 2006).

TEST YOURSELF 6.1

Recall

1. During Piaget's _____ stage, children are first able to represent objects mentally in different ways and to perform mental operations.

2. Hypothetical and deductive reasoning are characteristic of children in Piaget's _____ stage.

3. Children and adolescents often select a memory strategy after they have _____.

4. The term _____ refers to periodic evaluation of a strategy to determine whether it is working.

Interpret

- Do developmental improvements in memory strategies and metacognition emphasize nature, nurture, or both? How?

Apply

- Formal-operational adolescents are able to reason abstractly. How might this ability help them use the study skills shown in Figure 6.1 more effectively?

Check your answers to the Recall Questions at the end of the chapter.

6.2 Aptitudes for School

LEARNING OBJECTIVES

- What is the nature of intelligence?
- Why were intelligence tests first developed? What are their features?
- How well do intelligence tests work?
- How do heredity and environment influence intelligence?
- How and why do test scores vary for different racial and ethnic groups?

Diana is an eager fourth-grade teacher who loves history. Consequently, every year she's frustrated when she teaches a unit on the American Civil War. Although she's passionate about the subject, her enthusiasm is *not* contagious. Instead, her students' eyes glaze over and she can see young minds drifting off. And, of course, they never seem to grasp the war's historical significance. Diana wishes she could teach this unit differently, in a way that would engage her students more effectively.

Before you read further, how would you define intelligence? If you're typical of most Americans, you would mention reasoning logically, connecting ideas, and solving real problems. You might mention verbal ability, meaning the ability to speak clearly and articulately. You might also include social competence: for example, an interest in the world at large and an ability to admit when you make a mistake (Sternberg & Kaufman, 1998).

As you'll see in this section, many of these ideas about intelligence are included in psychological theories of intelligence. We'll begin by considering the theories of intelligence, where we'll get some insight into ways that Diana could make the Civil War come alive for her class. Next, you'll see how intelligence tests were devised initially to assess individual differences in intellectual ability. Then we'll look at a simple question: How well do modern tests work? Finally, we'll examine how race, ethnicity, social class, gender, environment, and heredity influence intelligence.

Theories of Intelligence

Psychometricians *are psychologists who specialize in measuring psychological characteristics such as intelligence and personality.* When psychometricians want to research a particular question, they usually begin by administering many tests to many individuals. Then they look for patterns in performance across the tests. The basic logic underlying this technique resembles the logic a jungle hunter uses to decide whether some dark blobs in a river are three separate rotting logs or a single alligator (Cattell, 1965). If the blobs move together, the hunter decides they are part of the same structure, an alligator. If they do not move together, they are three different structures—three logs. Similarly, if changes in performance on one test are accompanied by changes in performance on a second test—that is, if they move together—then the tests are measuring the same attribute or factor.

psychometricians

Psychologists who specialize in measuring psychological traits such as intelligence and personality.

The Hierarchical View of Intelligence

Research analyzing performance on tests led psychometricians to propose hierarchical theories in which intelligence includes both general and specific components. John Carroll (1993, 1996), for example, proposed the hierarchical theory with three levels shown in ▶ Figure 6.2. At the top of the hierarchy is general intelligence (often referred to as *g*). Underneath general intelligence are eight broad categories of intellectual skill, ranging

▶ **Figure 6.2**

Hierarchical theories of intelligence have different levels that range from general intelligence (*g*) to very specific skills.

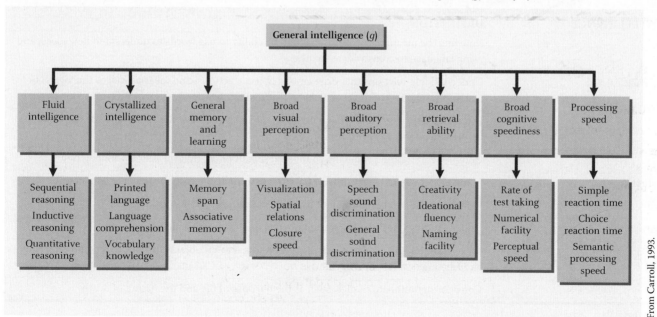

From Carroll, 1993.

from fluid intelligence to processing speed. Each of the abilities in the second level is further divided into the skills listed in the third and most specific level. Crystallized intelligence, for example, includes understanding printed language, comprehending language, and knowing vocabulary.

Hierarchical models of intelligence are valuable because they integrate findings from decades' of research. Nevertheless, some critics find them unsatisfactory because they ignore research and theory on cognitive development. The critics believe we need to look beyond the psychometric approach to understand intelligence. In the remainder of this section then, we'll look at two theories that have done this.

Gardner's Theory of Multiple Intelligences

Other psychologists have viewed intelligence from the perspective of Piaget's theory and information-processing psychology. Among the most ambitious is Howard Gardner's (2011) theory of multiple intelligences. Rather than using test scores as the basis for his theory, Gardner draws on research in child development, studies of brain-damaged persons, and studies of exceptionally talented people. Using these criteria, Gardner identified seven distinct intelligences when he first proposed the theory in 1983. In subsequent work, Gardner (1999, 2002) identified two additional intelligences; the complete list is shown in ❱ Table 6.1.

The first three intelligences in the list—linguistic intelligence, logical-mathematical intelligence, and spatial intelligence—are included in traditional theories of intelligence. The last six intelligences are not: Musical, bodily-kinesthetic, interpersonal, intrapersonal, naturalistic, and existential intelligences are unique to Gardner's theory. According to Gardner, Ariana Grande's beautiful singing, Simone Biles's remarkable routines on the vault, and Oprah Winfrey's grace and charm in dealing with people are all features of intelligence that are ignored in traditional theories.

How did Gardner arrive at these nine distinct intelligences? First, each has a unique developmental history. Linguistic intelligence, for example, develops much earlier than the others. Second, each intelligence is regulated by distinct regions of the brain. For example, spatial intelligence is regulated by particular regions in the right hemisphere of the brain. Third, each intelligence has special cases of talented individuals. There are well-known instances of musically intelligent people, for example, who exhibit incredible talent at an

Table 6.1

Nine Intelligences in Gardner's Theory of Multiple Intelligences	
TYPE OF INTELLIGENCE	**DEFINITION**
Linguistic	Knowing the meanings of words, having the ability to use words to understand new ideas, and using language to convey ideas to others
Logical-mathematical	Understanding relations that exist among objects, actions, and ideas as well as the logical or mathematical operations that can be performed on them
Spatial	Perceiving objects accurately and imagining in the mind's eye the appearance of an object before and after it has been transformed
Musical	Comprehending and producing sounds varying in pitch, rhythm, and emotional tone
Bodily-kinesthetic	Using one's body in highly differentiated ways as dancers, craftspeople, and athletes do
Interpersonal	Identifying different feelings, moods, motivations, and intentions in others
Intrapersonal	Understanding one's emotions and knowing one's strengths and weaknesses
Naturalistic	Understanding the natural world, distinguishing natural objects from artifacts, and grouping and labeling natural phenomena
Existential	Considering "ultimate" issues, such as the purpose of life and the nature of death

SOURCE: Gardner, 1983, 1999, 2002.

early age. Claudio Arrau, one of the 20th-century's greatest pianists, read musical notes before he read words. And Yo-Yo Ma, the famed cellist, performed in concert at 7 years of age for President John F. Kennedy.

Prompted by Gardner's theory, researchers have begun to look at other nontraditional aspects of intelligence. *Probably the best known is* emotional intelligence, *which is the ability to use one's own and others' emotions effectively for solving problems and living happily.* Emotional intelligence includes several distinct facets: perceiving emotions accurately (e.g., recognizing a happy face), understanding emotions (e.g., distinguishing happiness from ecstasy), and regulating one's emotions (e.g., hiding one's disappointment). People who are emotionally intelligent tend to have more satisfying interpersonal relationships, have greater subjective well-being, and to be more effective in the workplace (Joseph & Newman, 2010; Sánchez-Álvarez, Extremera, & Fernández-Berrocal, 2016).

emotional intelligence
Ability to use one's own and others' emotions effectively for solving problems and living happily.

The theory of multiple intelligences has important implications for education. Gardner (1993, 1995) believes that schools should foster all intelligences, not just the traditional linguistic and logical-mathematical intelligences. Teachers should capitalize on the strongest intelligences of individual children. That is, teachers need to know a child's profile of intelligence—the child's strengths and weaknesses—and gear instruction to the strengths (Chen & Gardner, 2005). For example, Diana, the fourth-grade teacher in the opening vignette, could help some of her students understand the Civil War by studying music of that period (musical intelligence). Other students might benefit by emphasizing maps that show the movement of armies in battle (spatial intelligence). Still others might profit from focusing on the experiences of African Americans living in the North and the South (interpersonal intelligence).

These guidelines do not mean that teachers should gear instruction solely to a child's strongest intelligence, pigeonholing youngsters as "numerical learners" or "spatial learners." Instead, whether the topic is the signing of the Declaration of Independence or Shakespeare's *Hamlet*, instruction should try to engage as many different intelligences as possible (Gardner, 1999, 2002). The typical result is a much richer understanding of the topic by all students.

Some American schools have enthusiastically embraced Gardner's ideas (Gardner, 1993). Are these schools better than those that have not? Educators in schools using the theory think so; they cite evidence that their students benefit in many ways (Kornhaber, Fierros, & Veenema, 2004), although some critics are not yet convinced (Waterhouse, 2006). In fact, a general criticism is that the theory has relatively little empirical support (Kaufman, Kaufman, & Plucker, 2013). Nevertheless, Gardner's work has helped liberate researchers from psychometric-based views of intelligence.

Sternberg's Theory of Successful Intelligence

In Robert Sternberg's theory, intelligence is defined as using one's abilities skillfully to achieve one's personal goals (Sternberg, 2015). Goals can be short-term—such as getting an A on a test, making a snack in the microwave, or winning the 100-meter hurdles—or longer-term, such as having a successful career and a happy family life. Achieving these goals by using one's skills defines successful intelligence.

In achieving personal goals, people use three different kinds of abilities. Analytic ability *involves analyzing problems and generating different solutions.* Suppose a teenager wants to download songs to her iPhone, but something isn't working. Analytic intelligence is shown when she considers different causes of the problem—maybe the iPhone is broken or maybe the software to download songs wasn't installed correctly.

Creative ability *involves dealing adaptively with novel situations and problems.* Suppose our 12-year-old discovers that her iPhone is broken just as she's ready to leave with her family on a daylong car trip. Lacking the time (and money) to buy a new phone, creative intelligence is shown in dealing successfully with a novel goal: finding an enjoyable activity to pass the time on a long drive.

Finally, practical ability *involves knowing what solution or plan will actually work.* Problems can be solved in different ways in principle, but in reality, only one solution may

analytic ability
In Sternberg's theory of intelligence, the ability to analyze problems and generate different solutions.

creative ability
In Sternberg's theory of intelligence, the ability to deal adaptively with novel situations and problems.

practical ability
In Sternberg's theory of intelligence, the ability to know which problem solutions are likely to work.

For street vendors in Brazil, successful intelligence involves sophisticated arithmetic operations for buying products, making change, and keeping track of sales.

be practical. Our teenager may realize that surfing the Net for a way to fix the phone's software is the only real choice because her parents wouldn't approve of many of the songs and she doesn't want her sibling to know that she's downloading them anyway.

Like Gardner, Sternberg (1999) argues that instruction is most effective when it is geared to a child's strength. A child with strong analytic ability, for example, may find algebra simpler when the course emphasizes analysis and evaluation; a child with strong practical ability may be at his or her best when the material is organized around practical applications. Thus, the theory of successful intelligence shows how instruction can be matched to students' strongest abilities, enhancing students' prospects for mastering the material (Grigorenko, Jarvin, & Sternberg, 2002).

Sternberg emphasizes that successful intelligence is revealed in people's pursuit of goals. Of course, these goals vary from one person to the next and, just as important, often vary even more in different cultural or ethnic groups. That is, intelligence is partly defined by the demands of an environment or cultural context. What is intelligent for children growing up in cities in North America may not be intelligent for children growing up in the Sahara desert, in the Australian outback, or on a remote island in the Pacific Ocean. For example, in Brazil, many school-age boys sell candy and fruit to bus passengers and pedestrians. These children often cannot identify the numbers on paper money, yet they know how to purchase their goods from wholesale stores, make change for customers, and keep track of their sales (Saxe, 1988).

If the Brazilian vendors were given the tests that measure intelligence in American students, they would fare poorly. Does this mean they are less intelligent than American children? Of course not. The skills important to American conceptions of intelligence and that are assessed on our intelligence tests are less valued in these other cultures and so are not cultivated in the young. Each culture defines what it means to be intelligent, and the vendors with their specialized computing skills are just as intelligent in their cultural settings as Americans with their verbal skills are in their culture (Sternberg & Kaufman, 1998).

As with Gardner's theory, researchers are still evaluating Sternberg's theory and are still debating the question of what intelligence is. However it is defined, the facts are that individuals differ substantially in intellectual ability and that numerous tests have been devised to measure these differences. We'll examine the construction, properties, and limits of these tests in the next section.

Binet and the Development of Intelligence Testing

In the United States, school enrollment nearly doubled between 1890 and 1915 because of an influx of immigrants and because reforms restricted child labor and emphasized education (Giordano, 2005). With the increased enrollment, teachers were confronted with increasing numbers of students who did not learn as readily as the "select few" who had populated their classes previously. How to deal with "feebleminded" children was one of the pressing issues of the day for U.S. educators.

These problems were not unique to the United States. In 1904, the Minister of Public Instruction in France asked two noted psychologists of the day, Alfred Binet and Theophile Simon, to formulate a way of recognizing children who would be unable to learn in school without special instruction. Binet and Simon's approach was to select simple tasks that French children of different ages ought to be able to do, such as naming colors, counting backward, and remembering numbers in order. Based on preliminary testing, Binet and Simon identified problems that typical 3-year-olds could solve, that typical 4-year-olds could solve, and so on. *Children's* mental age (MA) *referred to the difficulty of the problems they could solve correctly.* For example, a child who solved problems that the average 7-year-old could solve would have an MA of 7.

mental age (MA)

In intelligence testing, a measure of children's performance corresponding to the chronological age of those whose performance equals the child's.

Binet and Simon used mental age to distinguish "bright" from "dull" children. A bright child would have the MA of an older child—for example, a 6-year-old with an MA of 9. A dull child would have the MA of a younger child—for example, a 6-year-old with an MA of 4. Binet and Simon confirmed that bright children identified using their test did better in school than did dull children. Voilà—the first objective measure of intelligence!

Think About It
If Jean Piaget were to create an intelligence test, how would it differ from the type of test Binet created?

The Stanford-Binet

Lewis Terman, of Stanford University, revised Binet and Simon's test substantially and published a version known as the Stanford-Binet in 1916. *Terman described performance as an* intelligence quotient (IQ), *which was the ratio of mental age to chronological age (CA) multiplied by 100*:

$$IQ = MA / CA \times 100$$

intelligence quotient (IQ)
Mathematical representation of how a person scores on an intelligence test in relation to how other people of the same age score.

At any age, children who are perfectly average have an IQ of 100 because their mental age equals their chronological age. Furthermore, roughly two-thirds of children taking a test will have IQ scores between 85 and 115. The IQ score can also be used to compare intelligence in children of different ages. A 4-year-old girl with an MA of 5 has an IQ of 125 ($5/4 \times 100$), just like that of an 8-year-old boy with an MA of 10 ($10/8 \times 100$).

IQ scores are no longer computed as the ratio of MA to CA. Instead, children's IQ scores are determined by comparing their test performance to the average IQ score of others their age. When children perform at the average for their age, their IQ is 100. Children who perform above the average have IQs greater than 100; children who perform below the average have IQs less than 100. Nevertheless, the concept of IQ as the ratio of MA to CA helped to popularize the Stanford-Binet test.

By the 1920s, the Stanford-Binet had been joined by many other intelligence tests. Educators greeted these new devices enthusiastically because they seemed to offer an efficient and objective way to assess a student's chances of succeeding in school (Chapman, 1988). Today, nearly 100 years later, the Stanford-Binet remains a popular test; the latest version was revised in 2003. Like the earlier versions, the modern Stanford-Binet consists of various cognitive and motor tasks ranging from the extremely easy to the extremely difficult. The Stanford-Binet, the Wechsler Intelligence Scale for Children-V (WISC-V), and the Kaufman Assessment Battery for Children-II are the primary individualized tests of intelligence in use today.

Do Tests Work?

If tests work, they should predict important outcomes in children's lives: Children who receive higher IQ scores should be more successful in school and after they leave school. In fact, IQ scores are remarkably powerful predictors of developmental outcomes. One expert argued that "IQ is the most important predictor of an individual's ultimate position within American society" (Brody, 1992). Of course, because IQ tests were devised to predict school success, it's not surprising that they do this quite well. IQ scores predict school grades, scores on achievement tests, and number of years of education with correlations that are usually between 0.5 and 0.7 (Brody, 1992; Geary, 2005).

These correlations are far from perfect, which reminds us that some youngsters with high test scores do not excel in school and others with low test scores manage to get good grades. In fact, some researchers find that self-discipline predicts grades in school even better than IQ scores do (Duckworth & Seligman, 2005). In general, however, tests predict school success.

Intelligence scores not only predict success in school but also predict occupational success (Deary, 2012). Individuals with higher IQ scores are more likely to hold high-paying, high-prestige positions in medicine, law, and engineering (Oswald & Hough, 2012). Some of the link between IQ and occupational success occurs because these professions require more education, and IQ scores predict educational success. But even within a profession—where all individuals have the same amount of education—IQ scores predict job performance and earnings, particularly for more complex jobs (Henderson, 2010; Schmidt & Hunter, 2004). And among scientists with equal education, those with higher IQ scores have more patents and more articles published in scientific journals (Park, Lubinski, & Benbow, 2008).

Finally, IQ scores predict outcomes that don't have obvious connections to school success. For example, people with higher IQ scores are more likely to be chosen as leaders of groups, and once chosen, their groups tend to be more productive and they tend to be rated as better leaders and are more popular with group members (Strenze, 2015). Intelligence scores even predict longevity: Individuals with greater IQ scores tend to live longer, in part because they are less likely to smoke, they drink less alcohol, they stay active physically, and they eat more healthfully (Deary, 2012).

Hereditary and Environmental Factors

In a typical elementary school, some first graders will have IQs greater than 120 and others will have IQ scores in the low 80s. Some of this 40-point difference reflects heredity (Bouchard, 2009). For example, identical twins' IQs are more similar than fraternal twins' IQs (Plomin & Deary, 2015). And adopted children's IQ is usually more similar to their biological parents' IQ than to their adoptive parents' IQ (Rhea et al., 2013). What's more, the impact of heredity on intelligence increases across childhood and adolescence. For example, identical twins' IQs become more alike across childhood and adolescence (Plomin & Deary, 2015).

Do these results mean that heredity is the sole determiner of intelligence? No. Three areas of research show the importance of environment on intelligence. The first is research on characteristics of families and homes. If intelligence were solely due to heredity, environment should have little or no impact on children's intelligence. In fact, children have greater IQ scores when the family environment is intellectually stimulating—when parents talk more frequently to the children; when they provide their children with cognitive challenging materials such as puzzles and books; and when they expose children to stimulating experiences outside the home, such as visits to museums (Nisbett et al., 2012).

The impact of the environment on intelligence is also implicated by a dramatic rise in IQ test scores during the 20th century (Flynn & Weiss, 2007; Weber, Dekhtyar, & Herlitz, 2017). For example, scores on the WISC increased by nearly 10 points over a 25-year period (Flynn, 1999). The change may reflect industrialization, which requires a more intelligent workforce and brings about better schools, smaller families, improved health (including better nutrition and hygiene) and more stimulating leisure-time activities (Nisbett et al., 2012). Regardless of the exact causes of greater IQ scores, the increase shows the impact of changing environmental conditions on intelligence.

The importance of a stimulating environment for intelligence is also demonstrated by intervention programs that prepare economically disadvantaged children for school. Children who grow up in poverty often struggle in school because they lack the skills needed for success. However, when such children participate in intervention programs that teach school readiness skills and social skills, they're more successful in school, more likely to work full time, and tend to be healthier. These programs more than pay for themselves in the form of greater earnings (and tax revenues) for participating children and reduced costs associated with the criminal justice system (Englund et al., 2014). And in the process, they show that intelligence is fostered by a stimulating and responsive environment.

Following adoption, children's scores on intelligence tests tend to resemble the scores of their biological parents, not their adoptive parents, which shows the impact of heredity on intelligence.

Denise Hager, Catchlight Visual Services/Alamy Stock Photo

High-quality preschool programs provide stimulating environments that can increase children's scores on intelligence tests and improve their school performance.

The Impact of Ethnicity and Socioeconomic Status

On many intelligence tests, ethnic groups differ in their average scores: Asian Americans tend to have the highest scores, followed by European Americans, Latino Americans, and African Americans (Hunt & Carlson, 2007). The gaps have become smaller since the 1960s and reflect, in part, group differences in socioeconomic status (Nisbett et al., 2012; Rindermann & Thompson, 2013). Children from economically advantaged homes tend to have higher test scores than children from economically disadvantaged homes, and European American and Asian American families are more likely to be economically advantaged, whereas Latino American and African American families are more likely to be economically disadvantaged. Nevertheless, when children from comparable socioeconomic status are compared, group differences in IQ test scores are reduced but not eliminated (Magnuson & Duncan, 2006). Let's look at four explanations for these differences.

A Role for Genetics?

On page 200, you learned that heredity helps determine a child's intelligence: Smart parents tend to beget smart children. Does this also mean that group differences in IQ scores reflect genetic differences between groups? No. Most researchers agree that there is no evidence that some ethnic groups have more "smart genes" than others. Instead, they believe that the environment is largely responsible for these differences (Nisbett et al., 2012).

A popular analogy (Lewontin, 1976) demonstrates the thinking here. Imagine two kinds of corn: Each kind produces both short and tall plants, and height is known to be due to heredity. If one kind of corn grows in a good soil—plenty of water and nutrients—the mature plants will reach their genetically determined heights—some short, some tall. If the other kind of corn grows in poor soil, few plants will reach their full height and overall the plants of this kind will be much shorter. Even though height is heritable for each type of corn, the difference in height between the two groups is due solely to the quality of the environment. Similarly, although IQ scores may be heritable for different groups, less exposure to stimulating environments may mean that one group ends up with lower IQ scores overall (just as the group of plants growing in poor soil do not reach their full height). In other words, differences *within* ethnic groups are partly due to heredity, but differences *between* groups apparently reflect environmental influences.

Experience with Test Contents

Some critics contend that differences in test scores reflect bias in the tests themselves. They argue that test items reflect the cultural heritage of the test creators—typically economically advantaged European Americans—so tests are biased against children from other groups (Champion, 2003). Such critics point to test items such as this one:

A conductor is to an orchestra as a teacher is to what?

book   school   class   eraser

Children whose background includes exposure to orchestras are more likely to answer this question correctly than children who lack this exposure.

The problem of bias led to the development of culture-fair intelligence tests, *which include test items based on experiences common to many cultures.* An example is Raven's Progressive Matrices, which consists items such as the one shown in ▶ Figure 6.3. Examinees are asked to select the piece that would complete the design correctly (piece 6, in this case). Although items such as this are thought to reduce the impact of specific experience on test performance, ethnic group differences remain on so-called culture-fair intelligence tests (Herrnstein & Murray, 1994). Apparently, familiarity with test-related items is not the key factor responsible for group differences.

culture-fair intelligence tests

Intelligence tests devised using items common to many cultures.

Test-Taking Skills

The impact of experience and cultural values can extend beyond particular items to a child's familiarity with the entire testing situation. Tests underestimate a child's intelligence if a child's culture encourages children to solve problems by collaborating with others and discourages them from excelling as individuals. Moreover, because they are wary of questions posed by unfamiliar adults, many economically disadvantaged children often answer test questions by saying, "I don't know." Obviously, this strategy guarantees an artificially low test score. When these children are given extra time to feel at ease with the examiner, they respond less often with "I don't know" and their test scores improve considerably (Zigler & Finn-Stevenson, 1992).

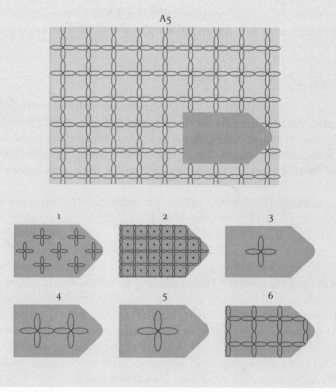

▶ **Figure 6.3**

Culture-fair intelligence tests are designed to minimize the impact of experiences that are unique to some cultures or to some children within a culture.

Based on Raven's Progressive Matrices.

Stereotype Threat

When people know that they belong to a group that is said to lack skill in a domain, they become anxious when performing in that domain for fear of confirming the stereotype; as a result, they often do poorly. *This self-fulfilling prophecy, in which knowledge of stereotypes leads to anxiety and reduced performance consistent with the original stereotype, is called stereotype threat.* Applied to intelligence, the argument is that African American children experience stereotype threat when they take intelligence tests, and this contributes to their lower scores (Steele, 1997; Steele & Aronson, 1995). For example, imagine two 10-year-olds taking an intelligence test for admission to a special program for gifted children. The European American child worries that if he fails the test, he won't be admitted to the program. The African American child has the same fears but also worries that if she does poorly, it will confirm the stereotype that African American children don't get good scores on IQ tests (Suzuki & Aronson, 2005). Consistent with this idea, stereotype threat is reduced (and performance improves) when African American students experience self-affirmation—they remind themselves of values that are important to them and why (Sherman et al., 2013).

stereotype threat
An evoked fear of being judged in accordance with a negative stereotype about a group to which you belong.

Interpreting Test Scores

If all tests reflect cultural influences to at least some degree, how should we interpret test scores? Remember that tests assess successful adaptation to a particular cultural context. Most intelligence tests predict success in a school environment, which usually espouses middle-class values. Regardless of ethnic group, a child with a high test score has the intellectual skills needed for academic work based on middle-class values (Hunt & Carlson, 2007). A child with a low test score apparently lacks those skills. Does a low score mean that a child is destined to fail in school? No. It simply means that based on the child's current skills, he or she is unlikely to do well. We know from intervention projects that improving children's skills improves their school performance.

By focusing on groups of people, it's easy to overlook the fact that individuals within these groups differ in intelligence. The average difference in IQ scores between various ethnic groups is relatively small compared with the entire range of scores for these groups (Sternberg, Grigorenko, & Kidd, 2005). You can easily find youngsters with high IQ scores from all ethnic groups, just as you can find youngsters with low IQ scores from all groups. In the next section, we'll look at children at the extremes of ability.

TEST YOURSELF 6.2

Recall

1. According to _____ theories, intelligence includes both general intelligence and more specific abilities, such as verbal and spatial skill.

2. Gardner's theory of multiple intelligences includes linguistic, logical-mathematical, and spatial intelligences, which are included in psychometric theories, as well as musical, _____, interpersonal, and intrapersonal intelligences, which are ignored in psychometric theories.

3. Based on Gardner's view of intelligence, teachers should _____.

4. According to Sternberg, successful intelligence depends on _____, creative, and practical abilities.

5. As adopted children get older, their IQ scores increasingly resemble the IQ scores of their _____ parents.

6. Evidence for the impact of environment on children's intelligence comes from studies of children's homes, from historical change in IQ scores, and from _____.

7. The problem of cultural bias on intelligence tests led to the development of _____.

Interpret

- Compare and contrast the major perspectives on intelligence in terms of the extent to which they make connections between different aspects of development. That is, to what extent does each perspective emphasize cognitive processes versus integrating physical, cognitive, social, and emotional development?

Apply

- Suppose that a local government official proposes to end all funding for preschool programs for disadvantaged children. Write a letter to this official in which you describe the value of these programs.

Check your answers to the Recall Questions at the end of the chapter.

6.3 Special Children, Special Needs

LEARNING OBJECTIVES

- What are the characteristics of gifted children?
- What are different forms of disability?
- What are the distinguishing features of attention-deficit hyperactivity disorder?

Sanjit, a second grader, has taken two intelligence tests, and both times he had above-average scores. His parents took him to an ophthalmologist, who determined that his vision is 20/30—nothing wrong with his eyes. Nevertheless, Sanjit cannot read. Letters and words are as mysterious to him as Lady Gaga's music would be to Mozart. What is wrong?

Throughout history, societies have recognized children with unusual abilities and talents. Today, we know much about the extremes of human skill. Let's begin with a glimpse at gifted children.

Gifted Children

Traditionally, giftedness was defined by scores on intelligence tests: A score of 130 or greater was the criterion for being gifted. But modern definitions of giftedness are broader and include exceptional talent in an assortment of areas, including art, music, creative writing, dance, and sports (Olszewski-Kubilius, Subotnik, & Worrell, 2017; Winner, 2000).

Whether the field is music or math, though, exceptionally talented children have several characteristics in common (Subotnik, Olszewski-Kubilius, & Worrell, 2011). First, their ability is substantially above average; being smart is necessary but not sufficient for being gifted. Second, gifted children are passionate about their subject and have a powerful desire to master it. Third, gifted children are creative in their thinking, coming up with novel thoughts and actions. *Creativity is associated with* divergent thinking, *where the aim is not a single correct answer (often there isn't one), but fresh and unusual lines of thought* (Callahan, 2000). For example, creativity is shown when children respond in different innovative ways to a common stimulus, as shown in ❱ Figure 6.4.

Fourth, exceptional talent must be nurtured. Without encouragement and support from parents and stimulating and challenging mentors, a youngster's talents will wither. Talented children need a curriculum that is challenging and complex, they need teachers who know how to foster talent, and they need like-minded peers who stimulate their interests (Subotnik et al., 2011). With this support, gifted children's achievement can be remarkable. In a 25-year longitudinal study, gifted teens were, as adults, extraordinarily successful in school and in their careers. For example, about 10% had been awarded patents before they turned 40; many were leaders in the corporate sector, law, and medicine (Makel et al., 2016).

Finally, the stereotype is that gifted children are often troubled emotionally and unable to get along with their peers. In reality, gifted children and adults tend to be more mature than their peers and have fewer emotional problems (Simonton & Song, 2009; Subotnik et al., 2011), and as adults, they report being highly satisfied with their careers, relationships with others, and life in general (Lubinski et al., 2006).

Gifted children represent one extreme of human ability. At the other extreme are youngsters with disability, the topic of the next section.

divergent thinking
Thinking in novel and unusual directions.

❱ **Figure 6.4**
One way to measure creativity is to determine how many original responses children can make to a specific stimulus.

© 2019 Cengage

Children with Disability

"Little David," so named because his father was also named David, was the oldest of four children. He learned to sit only days before his first birthday, he began to walk at 2, and he said his first words as a 3-year-old. By age 5, David was far behind his age-mates developmentally. David had Down syndrome, a disorder described in Section 2.1 that is caused by an extra 21st chromosome.

Children with Intellectual Disability

Down syndrome is an example of a condition that leads to intellectual disability, *which refers to substantial limitations in intellectual ability as well as problems adapting to an environment, with both emerging before 18 years of age.* Limited intellectual skill is often defined as a score of 70 or less on an intelligence test such as the Stanford-Binet. Adaptive behavior includes conceptual skills important for successful adjustment (e.g., literacy, an understanding of money and time), social skills (e.g., interpersonal skill), and practical skills (e.g., personal grooming, occupational skills). It is usually evaluated from interviews with a parent or another caregiver. Only individuals who are under 18, have problems adapting in these areas, *and* have IQ scores of 70 or less are considered to have an intellectual disability (AAIDD Ad Hoc Committee on Terminology and Classification, 2010).[1]

Modern explanations pinpoint four factors that place individuals at risk for intellectual disability:

- Biomedical factors, including chromosomal disorders, malnutrition, traumatic brain injury
- Social factors, such as poverty and impaired parent–child interactions
- Behavioral factors, such as child neglect or domestic violence
- Educational factors, including impaired parenting and inadequate special education services

No individual factor in this list necessarily leads to intellectual disability. Instead, the risk for intellectual disability grows as more of these factors are present (AAIDD Ad Hoc Committee on Terminology and Classification, 2010). For example, the risk is great for a child with Down syndrome whose parents live in poverty and cannot take advantage of special education services.

As you can imagine, the many factors that can lead to intellectual disability means that the term encompasses an enormous variety of individuals. Some people with severe intellectual disability need constant support for activities of daily living, such skills as dressing, feeding, and toileting. At the other extreme are individuals who go to school and master many academic skills, but not as quickly as a typical child. They often work and many marry. In short, although people with intellectual disability face unique challenges, with support and resources from families and communities, their lives can be active, fulfilling, and productive (Iarocci et al., 2008).

Children with Learning Disability

In contrast to people with intellectual disability, children with learning disability have normal intelligence. That is, *children with learning disability (1) have difficulty mastering an academic subject, (2) have normal intelligence, and (3) are not suffering from other conditions that could explain poor performance, such as sensory impairment or inadequate instruction.*

In the United States, about 5% of school-age children are classified as learning disabled, which translates into nearly 2.5 million youngsters (Cortiella & Horowitz, 2014). Three kinds of learning disability are particularly common: difficulties in reading individual words, sometimes known as developmental dyslexia; difficulties understanding words that have been read successfully, which is called impaired reading comprehension; and, finally, difficulties in mathematics, which is termed mathematical learning disability or developmental dyscalculia (Snowling & Hulme, 2015).

Understanding learning disabilities is complicated because each type has its own causes and thus requires its own treatment. For example, developmental dyslexia is the most common type of learning disability. (It's so common that sometimes it's just referred

intellectual disability
Substantially below-average intelligence and problems adapting to an environment that emerge before the age of 18.

Think About It
How might our definitions of giftedness and intellectual disability differ if they were based on Gardner's theory of multiple intelligences?

learning disability
When a child with normal intelligence has difficulty mastering at least one academic subject.

---

[1] What we now call intellectual disability was long known as mental retardation, and much federal and state law in the United States still uses the latter term. However, intellectual disability is the preferred term because it better reflects the condition not as a deficit in the person, but as a poor "fit between the person's capacities and the context in which the person is to function" (AAIDD Ad Hoc Committee on Terminology and Classification, 2010, p. 13).

Children with reading disabilities often have trouble associating sounds with letters.

to as reading disability.) Many children with this disorder have problems in distinguishing sounds in written and oral language. For children with developmental dyslexia—like Sanjit (in the opening vignette) or the boy in the photograph—distinguishing *bis* from *bep* or *bis* from *dis* is very difficult; apparently the words all sound very similar (Hulme & Snowling, 2016).

Children with developmental dyslexia typically benefit from two kinds of instruction: training in phonological awareness—experiences that help them to identify subtle but important differences in language sounds—along with explicit instruction on the connections between letters and their sounds. With intensive instruction of this sort, youngsters with developmental dyslexia can read more effectively (Hulme & Snowling, 2016).

Children with impaired reading comprehension, another common learning disability, have no trouble reading individual words. But they understand far less of what they read. Asked to read sentences such as *The man rode the bus to go to work* or *The dog chased the cat through the woods*, they do so easily but find it difficult to answer questions about what they've read (e.g., *What did the man ride? Where did the man go?*). These problems seem to reflect a limited spoken vocabulary (they simply know fewer words) as well as problems linking words in a sentence to create coherent meaning (Clarke et al., 2014; Hulme & Snowling, 2011). Told to select the picture showing children sitting on a table, they may point to a picture of children sitting on a rug or to a picture of children playing a game on a table, but not sitting on it (Nation et al., 2004). In other words, for these youngsters, impaired reading comprehension seems to be a by-product of impaired oral (spoken) language.

If impaired oral language drives impaired reading comprehension, then extensive instruction in vocabulary and language skills should reduce impaired comprehension. It does (Melby-Lervåg & Lervåg, 2014), as shown in the study that's the focus of the Spotlight on Research feature.

Spotlight   On Research

Improving Children's Knowledge of the Structure of Words Enhances Their Reading Comprehension

Who were the investigators, and what was the aim of the study? One effective way to help children learn new words is to teach them about the structure of words and how words are formed. For example, understanding prefixes helps children master new words. When students who know that *un* means *not* or *the opposite of* first read *unpack* and *unclean*, they immediately grasp the meaning of these words. And since a larger vocabulary promotes better reading comprehension, Solveig-Alma Halaas Lyster and her colleagues, Arne Lervåg and Charles Hulme (2016), wondered whether teaching children about word structure would improve their reading comprehension.

How did the investigators measure the topic of interest? As preschoolers, some children were taught how to recognize prefixes (*un*happy), suffixes (walk*ed*), and compound words (*tooth-brush*). Training included 30-minute sessions over 17 weeks. Children in the control group received no training. As sixth graders, children's reading comprehension was measured with three tasks: one involved reading a long text (about four pages). Two others involved shorter text, one with an accompanying table and one with an accompanying map. After reading, children answered multiple-choice questions about the text.

Who were the participants in the study? The study included 163 Norwegian preschool children; 93 were tested again as sixth graders.

What was the design of the study? This study was experimental. The independent variable was the presence or absence of training in word structure; the dependent variable was the number of questions answered correctly on the three tests. The study was longitudinal because children were tested as preschoolers and sixth graders.

Were there ethical concerns with the study? No. Parents provided consent for their children to participate. The training was valuable for preschoolers and the tasks administered in sixth grade were similar to those used to assess students' reading achievement.

What were the results? ▶ Figure 6.5 shows the percentage of questions that were answered correctly on the three reading tasks. On each task, children who had received training on word structure as preschoolers answered more accurately as sixth graders.

What did the investigators conclude? Lyster and her colleagues concluded that "By giving preschoolers and young schoolchildren knowledge of the . . . structure of words and helping them to integrate meaning with the spoken and (when they begin to read and write) written forms of words, we may . . . enhance their oral and written language development" (Lyster et al., 2016, pp. 1285–1286). They also concluded that enhanced language leads to enhanced reading comprehension.

What converging evidence would strengthen these conclusions? This study was conducted with children learning to read Norwegian, in which words are pronounced more consistently than in English. It would be valuable to see if the results would also hold for students learning to read in English. (Training might be more complicated because English words are more variable in their pronunciation, but the benefits might be greater.) Also, the researchers inferred that training in word structure increased children's reading comprehension skills by increasing children's vocabulary; it would be valuable to measure children's vocabulary and then link changes in vocabulary directly to training and to comprehension.

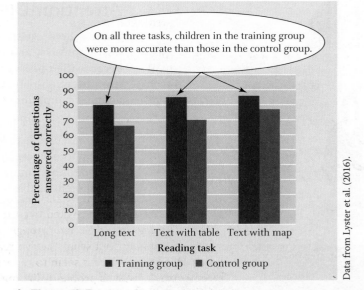

Data from Lyster et al. (2016).

▶ **Figure 6.5**

Children who had, as preschoolers, been taught about the structure of words were more likely, as sixth graders, to comprehend what they read.

A third common form of learning disability is mathematical disability. Roughly 5% to 10% of young children struggle with arithmetic instruction from the very beginning. These youngsters progress slowly in their efforts to learn to count, to add, and to subtract; many are also diagnosed with reading disability. As they move into second and third grade (and beyond), these children often use inefficient methods for computing solutions—for example, still using their fingers as third graders to solve problems such as 9 + 7 (Hulme & Snowling, 2015).

We know far less about mathematical learning disability, largely because mathematics engages a broader set of skills than reading does. Scientists have proposed several factors that may contribute to mathematical learning disability (Hulme & Snowling, 2016. One idea is that the approximate number system (described on page 134) provides less precise estimates of quantities for children with mathematical learning disability. Another possibility is that youngsters with mathematical disability are impaired in counting and retrieving arithmetic facts from memory. Yet another idea is that mathematical disability reflects problems in the basic cognitive processes that are used in doing arithmetic, such as working memory and executive function.

Because mathematical disability is not well understood, effective interventions have just begun. For example, children at risk for mathematical learning disability benefit from intensive practice designed to increase their understanding of numbers as well as their counting and calculation skills (Hulme & Melby-Lervåg, 2015). As we learn more about the core problems that define mathematical disability, researchers and educators should be able to fine-tune instruction for these children. When that happens, children with mathematical disability, like children with developmental dyslexia and impaired reading comprehension, will be able to develop their full intellectual potential.

Attention-Deficit Hyperactivity Disorder

Many school classrooms include children who are chronically restless, impulsive, and distractible; often these children are unpopular because their peers find them annoying. Many of these children suffer from attention-deficit hyperactivity disorder (ADHD), which has three defining symptoms (American Psychiatric Association, 2004):

- *Hyperactivity.* Children with ADHD are unusually energetic, fidgety, and unable to keep still—especially in situations like the one in the photo where they need to limit their activity.

- *Inattention.* Youngsters with ADHD do not pay attention in class and seem unable to concentrate on schoolwork; instead, they skip from one task to another.

- *Impulsivity.* Children with ADHD often act before thinking; they may run into a street before looking for traffic or interrupt others who are already speaking.

Children with ADHD are typically hyperactive as well as inattentive and impulsive.

In the United States, about 6% of all school-age children are diagnosed with ADHD; boys outnumber girls by a 3:1 ratio. The diagnosis is most often made in middle childhood when it becomes obvious that a child can't work alone in a classroom, struggles to make friends, and is disruptive at home. But markers of ADHD can be found in the preschool years: children are more likely to be diagnosed with ADHD if, as preschoolers, they were extremely overactive or had bursts of temper. During adolescence, hyperactivity often fades but inattention and impulsivity remain (Sonuga-Barke & Taylor, 2015). As young adults, few individuals with ADHD complete college and many have work-related problems (Hechtman et al., 2016).

Scientists believe that genes put some children at risk for ADHD by affecting the alerting and executive networks of attention and the brain structures that support those networks (Gizer & Waldman, 2012). But environmental factors also contribute. For example, prenatal exposure to alcohol and other drugs can place children at risk for ADHD as can inadequate diet or exposure to lead (Sonuga-Barke & Taylor, 2015).

ADHD is typically treated in two ways. First, stimulant drugs such as Ritalin (methylphenidate) are effective. It may seem odd that stimulants are given to children who are already overactive, but these drugs stimulate the parts of the brain that normally inhibit hyperactive and impulsive behavior. Thus, stimulants may calm many youngsters with ADHD, allowing them to focus their attention (Barkley, 2004). Second, behavioral treatments, typically involving parents, are beneficial. These are designed to improve children's self-regulation, their organizational skills, and their social relationships (Sonuga-Barke & Taylor, 2015).

Unfortunately, we still know little about the best ways to implement drug and behavioral treatments, individually and in combination. In one study, the most effective way to reduce the number of times that children with ADHD broke classroom rules was to begin with behavioral treatment (for parents and children) and add medication if necessary (Pelham et al., 2016). But the ideal dosages of both kinds of treatments remain unclear. Finally, long-term follow-up studies show that the impact of treatment often vanishes over time (Molina et al., 2009). This result suggests that ADHD is a chronic condition, like diabetes or asthma, one that requires ongoing monitoring and treatment (Hazell, 2009).

Tragically, many children who need these treatments do not receive them. African American and Hispanic American children are far less likely than European American youngsters to be diagnosed with and treated for ADHD, even when they have the same symptoms (Miller, Nigg, & Miller, 2009; Morgan et al., 2013). Why? Income plays a role. African American and Hispanic American families are more often economically disadvantaged and consequently are less able to pay for diagnosis and treatment. Racial bias also contributes: Parents and professionals often attribute the symptoms of ADHD in European American children to a biological problem that can be treated medically, but they more often attribute these symptoms in African American or Hispanic American children to poor parenting, life stresses, or other sources that can't be treated (Kendall & Hatton, 2002).

Obviously, all children with ADHD deserve appropriate treatment. Teachers and other professionals dealing with children need to be sure that poverty and racial bias do not prevent children from receiving the care they need.

TEST YOURSELF 6.3

Recall

1. Giftedness was once defined solely in terms of IQ score but modern definitions are _____.

2. Creativity is associated with _____ thinking, in which the goal is to think in novel and unusual directions.

3. Intellectual disability involves substantial limits in intellectual ability and _____ that emerge before 18 years of age.

4. Biomedical, social, _____, and educational factors place some children at risk for intellectual disability.

5. In developmental dyslexia, children have difficulty with _____.

6. Key symptoms of attention-deficit hyperactivity disorder are overactivity, _____, and impulsivity.

7. ADHD is typically treated with stimulant drugs and _____.

Interpret

- Compare and contrast traditional and modern definitions of giftedness.

Apply

- How might Jean Piaget have explained differences in intellectual functioning between children with intellectual disability and children without intellectual disability? How might an information-processing psychologist explain these differences?

Check your answers to the Recall Questions at the end of the chapter.

6.4 Academic Skills

LEARNING OBJECTIVES

- What are the components of skilled reading?
- As children develop, how does their writing improve?
- How do arithmetic skills change during the elementary school years? How do U.S. students compare with students from other countries?
- What are the hallmarks of effective schools and effective teachers?

Angelique is a fifth grader who loves to read. As a preschooler, Angelique's parents read Dr. Seuss stories to her, and now she has progressed to the point where she can read (and understand!) 400-page novels intended for teens. Her parents marvel at this accomplishment and wish they better understood the skills that were involved so they could help Angelique's younger brother learn to read as well as his sister does.

Reading is complex and reading well is a wonderful accomplishment. Much the same can be said for writing and math. We'll examine each of these academic skills in this section. As we do, you'll learn about the skills that underlie Angelique's mastery of reading. We'll end the section by looking at characteristics that make some schools and some teachers better than others.

Reading

Try reading the following sentence:

Sumisu-san wa nawa o naifu de kirimashita.

Unless you know Japanese, you probably didn't make much headway, did you? Now try this one:

Snore secretary green plastic sleep trucks.

These are English words, and you probably read them quite easily, but did you get anything more out of this sentence than the one in Japanese?

These examples show two important processes involved in skilled reading. **Word recognition** *is the process of identifying a unique pattern of letters.* Unless you know Japanese, your word recognition was unsuccessful in the first sentence. You did not know that *nawa* means *rope* or that *kirimashita* is the past tense of the English verb *cut*. What's more, because you could not recognize individual words, you had no idea of the meaning of the sentence.

Comprehension *is the process of extracting meaning from a sequence of words.* In the second sentence, your word recognition was perfect, but comprehension was impossible because the words were presented randomly. These examples remind us just how difficult learning to read can be.

In the next few pages, we'll look at some of the skills children must acquire if they are to learn to read and to read well. We'll start with the skills that children must have if they are to <u>learn to read</u>, then move to word recognition and comprehension.

Foundations of Reading Skill

English words are made up of individual letters, so children need to know their letters before they can learn to read. Children learn more about letters and word forms when they're frequently involved in literacy-related activities such as reading with an adult, playing with magnetic letters, or trying to print simple words (Robins, Treiman, & Rosales, 2014). And not surprisingly, children who know more about letters and word forms learn to read more easily compared with peers who know less (Levy et al., 2006; Treiman & Kessler, 2003).

A second essential skill is sensitivity to language sounds. *The ability to distinguish the sounds in spoken words is known as* **phonological awareness**. English words consist of syllables, and a syllable is made up of a vowel that's usually but not always accompanied by consonants. For example, *dust* is a one-syllable word that includes the initial consonant *d*, the vowel *u*, and the final consonant cluster *st*. Phonological awareness is shown when children can decompose words in this manner by, for example, correctly answering "What's the first sound in *dust*?" or "*Dust* without the *d* sounds like what?" Phonological awareness is strongly related to success in learning to read: Children who can readily identify different sounds in spoken words learn to read more readily than children who do not (Melby-Lervåg, Lyster, & Hulme, 2012).

Learning to read in English is particularly challenging because letters in English are not pronounced consistently (e.g., compare the sound of "a" in *bat, far, rake*, and *was*) and sounds are not spelled consistently (e.g., the long "e" sound is the same in each of these spellings: *team, feet, piece, lady, receive, magazine*). In contrast, many other languages—Greek, Finnish, German, Italian, Spanish, and Dutch—are far more consistent, which simplifies mapping sounds to letters. For example, in Italian most letters are pronounced the same way; reading a word such as *domani* (tomorrow) is simple because beginning readers just move from left to right converting each letter to sound and using simple rules: *d*, *m*, and *n* are pronounced as in English, *o* as in *cold*, *a* as in *car*, and *i* as in *see* (Barca, Ellis, & Burani, 2007). In fact, children learn to read more rapidly in languages where letter-sound rules are more consistent, but phonological awareness remains the single best predictor of reading success in many languages (Caravolas et al., 2012; Song et al., 2016).

If phonological skills are so essential, how can we help children master them? Reading to children is one approach that's fun for children and parents alike. When parents read stories, their children learn many language-related skills that prepare them for reading (Justice, Pullen & Pence, 2008; Raikes et al., 2006). And the benefits are not limited to the first steps in learning to read, but persist into the middle elementary school years and are just as useful for children learning to read other languages, such as Chinese (Chow et al., 2008; Sénéchal, 2012).

---

word recognition
The process of identifying a unique pattern of letters.

comprehension
The process of extracting meaning from a sequence of words.

phonological awareness
The ability to hear the distinctive sounds of letters.

Recognizing Words

At the very beginning of reading, children sometimes learn to read a few words "by sight," but they have no understanding of the links between printed letters and the word's sound. However, the first step in true reading is learning to decode printed words by sounding out the letters in them: Beginning readers like the boy in the photo often say the sounds associated with each letter and then blend the sounds to produce a recognizable word. After a word has been sounded out a few times, it becomes a known word that can be read by retrieving it directly from long-term memory. That is, children decode words by recognizing familiar patterns of letters and syllables (Nunes, Bryant, & Barros, 2012).

Thus, from their very first efforts to read, most children use retrieval for some words. From that point on, the general strategy is to try retrieval first and, if that fails, to sound out the word or ask a more skilled reader for help. With more experience, the child sounds out fewer words and retrieves more (Siegler, 1986). That is, by sounding out novel words, children increase their store of information about words in long-term memory that is required for direct retrieval (Cunningham et al., 2002; Share, 2008).

Beginning readers usually rely heavily on "sounding out" a word.

Comprehension

As we saw on page 206, decoding words accurately does not guarantee that children will understand what they've read. This phenomenon is captured in the Simple View of Reading model in which reading comprehension is viewed as the product of two general processes: word decoding and language comprehension (Gough & Tunmer, 1986). Children can't comprehend what they read when either a word can't be decoded or it's decoded but not recognized as a familiar word. Thus, skilled reading depends on decoding accurately coupled with understanding the meaning of the decoded word.

As children gain more reading experience, they better comprehend what they read. Several factors contribute to this improved comprehension (Siegler & Alibali, 2005).

- *Children's language skills improve, which allows them to understand words they've decoded.* As children's vocabulary expands, they are more likely to recognize words they've decoded. For example, a first grader with good decoding skills might be able to decode *prosper* but not understand it; by fifth or sixth grade, children's larger vocabulary means that they could decode and understand *prosper*. In addition, older children know more about grammatical structure of sentences, knowledge that helps them comprehend the meaning of an entire sentence (Muter et al., 2004; Oakhill & Cain, 2012).
- *Children become more skilled at recognizing words, allowing more working memory capacity to be devoted to comprehension* (Zinar, 2000). When children struggle to recognize individual words, they often cannot link them to derive the meaning of a passage. In contrast, when children recognize words effortlessly, they can focus their efforts on deriving meaning from the whole sentence.
- *Working memory capacity increases.* Older and better readers can store more of a sentence in memory as they try to identify the propositions it contains (De Beni & Palladino, 2000; Nation et al., 1999). This extra capacity is handy when readers move from sentences such as "Kevin hit the ball" to "In the bottom of the ninth, with the bases loaded and the Cardinals down 7–4, Kevin put a line drive into the left-field bleachers, his fourth home run of the series."
- *Children acquire more knowledge of their physical, social, and psychological worlds.* This allows them to understand more of what they read (Ferreol-Barbey, Piolat, & Roussey, 2000). For example, even if a 6-year-old could recognize all of the words in the longer sentence about Kevin's home run, the child would not fully comprehend the meaning of the passage because he or she lacks the necessary knowledge of baseball.
- *With experience, children use more appropriate reading strategies.* The goal of reading and the nature of the text dictate how you read. For example, when reading a novel,

do you often skip sentences or paragraphs to get to "the good parts"? This approach makes sense for pleasure reading but not for reading textbooks or recipes or how-to manuals. Reading a textbook requires attention to both the overall organization and the relation of details to that organization. Children who know more about effective strategies for reading tend to understand more of what they read (Cain, 1999).

With experience, children better monitor their comprehension. When readers don't grasp the meaning of a passage because it is difficult or confusing, they read it again (Baker, 1994). Try this sentence (adapted from Carpenter & Daneman, 1981): "The Midwest State Fishing Contest would draw fishermen from all around the region, including some of the best bass guitarists in Michigan." When you first encountered *bass guitarists*," you probably interpreted *bass* as a fish. This didn't make much sense, so you reread the phrase to determine that *bass* refers to a type of guitar. Older readers are better able to realize that their understanding is not complete and take corrective action (Oakhill & Cain, 2012).

Thus, several factors contribute to improved comprehension as children get older.

Think About It

Reading and speaking are both important elements of literacy. How is learning to read like learning to speak? How do they differ?

Writing

Although few of us end up being a Maya Angelou, a Sandra Cisneros, or a J. K. Rowling, most adults do write, both at home and at work. The basics of good writing are remarkably straightforward, but writing skill develops only gradually during childhood, adolescence, and young adulthood.

Skills Contributing to Improved Writing

Several factors contribute to improved writing as children develop (Adams Treiman, & Pressley, 1998; Siegler & Alibali, 2005).

Knowledge About Topics. Writing is about telling "something" to others. With age, children have more to tell as they gain more knowledge about the world and incorporate this knowledge into their writing (Benton et al., 1995; Olinghouse, Graham, & Gillespie, 2015). For example, asked to write about a mayoral election, 8-year-olds are apt to describe it as a popularity contest but 12-year-olds more often describe it in terms of complex political issues. Of course, students are sometimes asked to write about topics that are unfamiliar to them. In this case, older children's and adolescents' writing is usually better because they are more adept at finding useful reference material and incorporating it into their writing.

Organizing Writing. One difficult aspect of writing is arranging all the information in a manner that readers find clear and interesting. In fact, children and young adolescents organize their writing differently than do older adolescents and adults (Bereiter & Scardamalia, 1987). *Young writers often use a* knowledge-telling strategy, *writing down information on the topic as they retrieve it from memory.* For example, asked to write about the day's events at school, a second grader wrote:

> It is a rainy day. We hope the sun will shine. We got new spelling books. We had our pictures taken. We sang Happy Birthday to Barbara. (Waters, 1980, p. 155)

The story has no obvious structure. The first two sentences are about the weather, but the last three deal with completely independent topics. Apparently the writer simply described each event as it came to mind.

During the elementary school years, children begin to use a knowledge-transforming strategy, *deciding what information to include and how best to organize it for the point they want to convey to the reader.* This approach involves considering the purpose of writing (e.g., to inform, to persuade, to entertain) and the information needed to achieve that purpose. It also involves considering the needs, interests, and knowledge of the anticipated audience. For example, an adolescent's essay written to entertain peers about humorous events at school would differ from one written to convince parents about problems in schoolwork (Midgette, Haria, & MacArthur, 2008).

knowledge-telling strategy
Writing down information as it is retrieved from memory, a common practice for young writers.

knowledge-transforming strategy
Deciding what information to include and how best to organize it to convey a point.

The Mechanical Requirements of Writing. Compared with speaking, writing is more difficult because it involves spelling, punctuation, and actually forming the letters. These many mechanical aspects of writing can be a burden for all writers, but particularly for young writers. For example, when youngsters such as the child in the photo are absorbed by the task of printing letters correctly, the quality of their writing usually suffers (Medwell & Wray, 2014; Olinghouse, 2008). As children master printed and cursive letters, they can pay more attention to other aspects of writing. Similarly, correct spelling and good sentence structure are particularly hard for younger writers; as they learn to spell and to generate clear sentences, they write more easily and more effectively (Graham et al., 1997; McCutchen et al., 1994).

Skill in Revising. Skilled writers revise and revise, then revise some more. Unfortunately, young writers often don't revise at all—the first draft is usually the final draft. To make matters worse, when young writers revise, the changes do not necessarily improve their writing (Fitzgerald, 1987). As children develop, they're better able to find problems with their writing and to know how to correct them, (MacArthur, 2015).

Teaching Children to Write More Effectively

Writing well is challenging because many complex skills are involved. Word processing software makes writing easier by handling some of these skills (e.g., checking spelling, simplifying revising), and research indicates that writing improves when people use word processing software (Clements, 1995; Rogers & Graham, 2008).

Fortunately, students *can* be taught to write better. When instruction focuses on the building blocks of effective writing—strategies for planning, drafting, and revising text—students' writing improves substantially (Graham & Perin, 2007; Tracy, Reid, & Graham, 2009). For example, one successful program for teaching writing—the Self-Regulated Strategy Development in Writing program—tells students that POW + TREE is a trick that good writers use. As you can see in ▶Figure 6.6, POW provides young writers with a general plan for writing; TREE tells them how to organize their writing in a nicely structured paragraph (Harris & Graham, 2017).

Of course, mastering writing skill often spans all of childhood, adolescence, and adulthood. Much the same can be said for mastering math skills, as we'll see in the next section.

Math Skills

By kindergarten, children have mastered counting and use this skill as the starting point for learning to add. For instance, suppose you ask a child to solve the following problem: "John had four oranges. Then Mary gave him two more oranges. How many oranges does John have now?" Many 6-year-old children count to solve the problem. They first count out four fingers on one hand, then count out two more on the other. Finally, they count all six fingers on both hands. To subtract, they do the same procedure in reverse (Siegler & Jenkins, 1989; Siegler & Shrager, 1984). After children begin to receive formal arithmetic instruction in first grade, addition problems are less often solved by counting aloud or by counting fingers (Jordan et al., 2008). Instead, children add and subtract by counting mentally. That is, children act as if they are counting silently, beginning with the larger number and then adding on. By age 8 or 9, children

Writing can be particularly hard for young children who are still learning how to print or write cursive letters.

▶ **Figure 6.6**

The POW + TREE strategy for good writing provides young writers with a general plan for writing (POW) and a structure for a paragraph (TREE).

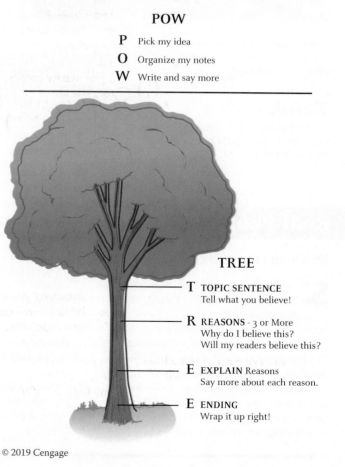

POW

P Pick my idea

O Organize my notes

W Write and say more

TREE

T TOPIC SENTENCE
Tell what you believe!

R REASONS - 3 or More
Why do I believe this?
Will my readers believe this?

E EXPLAIN Reasons
Say more about each reason.

E ENDING
Wrap it up right!

© 2019 Cengage

Young children often solve addition problems by counting, either on their fingers or in their head.

■
Think About It

What information-processing skills may contribute to growth in children's arithmetic skills?

have learned the addition tables so well that sums of the single-digit integers (from 0 to 9) are facts that can be simply retrieved from memory (Ashcraft, 1982).

As children learn arithmetic and math in school, they master mathematical concepts—abstract, general principles—as well as mathematical procedures—actions that solve problems. For example, children learn the concept that fractions can be ordered from smallest to largest (e.g., ¼ < ½ < ¾) and they learn a procedure for adding fractions that have different denominators. Understanding concepts helps children to master procedures, and mastering procedures helps children to understand concepts (Rittle-Johnson, 2017).

Several techniques help children master math concepts and math procedures. One is asking students to show students two solutions to a problem and ask students to compare them. Another is to ask students to explain new information, such as a solution to a problem. Both of these methods increase children's knowledge of math concepts and procedures, apparently by requiring students to pay attention to the underlying mathematical principles, not just the surface features of a problem (Rittle-Johnson & Schneider, 2015). These methods are valuable in helping elementary school students master arithmetic and in helping high school students master algebra, geometry, trigonometry, and calculus.

Comparing U.S. Students with Students in Other Countries

When compared with students worldwide in terms of math skills, U.S. students don't fare well. For example, ❱Figure 6.7 shows the math results from a major international comparison (Organisation for Economic Co-operation and Development, 2016). U.S. high school students have substantially lower scores than do high school students in several nations. Phrased another way, the very best U.S. students only perform at the level of average students in many Asian countries. What's more, these differences in math achievement have been found for at least 25 years and for achievement in elementary school, middle school, and high school (Stevenson & Lee, 1990).

Why do American students rate so poorly? The Real People feature has some answers.

Real People   Applying Human Development

Shin-Ying Loves School

Shin-ying is an 11-year-old attending school in Taipei, the largest city in Taiwan. Like most fifth graders, Shin-ying is in school from 8 a.m. until 4 p.m. daily. Most evenings, she spends two to three hours doing homework. This academic routine is grueling by U.S. standards, where fifth graders typically spend six to seven hours in school each day and less than an hour doing homework. We asked Shin-ying what she thought of school and schoolwork. Her answers surprised us.

US: Why do you go to school?
SHIN-YING: I like what we study.
US: Any other reasons?
SHIN-YING: The things that I learn in school are useful.
US: What about homework? Why do you do it?
SHIN-YING: My teacher and my parents think it's important. And I like doing it.
US: Do you think you would do nearly as well in school if you didn't work so hard?

SHIN-YING: Oh no. The best students are always the ones who work the hardest.

Schoolwork is the focal point of Shin-ying's life. Although many American school children are unhappy when schoolwork intrudes on time for play and television, Shin-ying is enthusiastic about school and school-related activities.

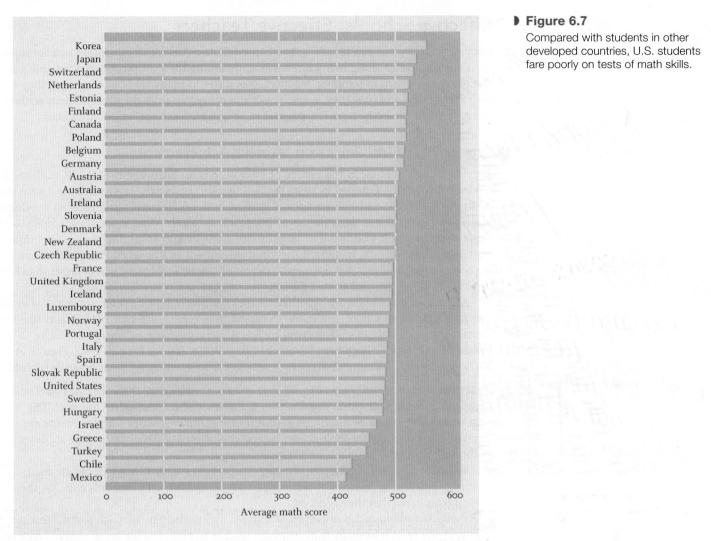

Data from Kelly et al. (2013).

Many of Shin-ying's comments are typical of elementary school students in Asia. Compared with students in the United States, students in Asian countries often spend more time on homework and are more enthusiastic about homework. Asian parents often set higher standards for their students than American parents do; and Asian parents often focus on their children's mistakes, while American parents point to their children's successes. Finally, students in Asia often spend more time in school and more of this time is devoted to activities than in the United States (Ni, Chiu, & Cheng, 2010; Pomerantz et al., 2014; Stevenson & Lee, 1990).

What can Americans learn from Japanese and Taiwanese educational systems? Experts (Stevenson & Stigler, 1992; Tucker, 2011) suggest several ways American schools could be improved:

- Improve teachers' training by allowing them to work closely with older, more experienced teachers and give them more free time to prepare lessons and correct students' work.
- Organize instruction around sound principles of learning, such as providing multiple examples of concepts and giving students adequate opportunities to practice newly acquired skills.
- Create curricula that emphasize problem-solving and critical thinking.
- Set higher standards for children who need to spend more time and effort in school-related activities in order to achieve those standards.

Changing teaching practices and attitudes toward achievement would begin to reduce the gap between American students and students in other industrialized countries, particularly Asian countries. Ignoring the problem will mean an increasingly undereducated workforce and citizenry in a complex world.

Effective Schools, Effective Teachers

Because education is run locally in the United States, American education is a smorgasbord. Schools differ along many dimensions, including their emphasis on academic goals and the involvement of parents. Teachers, too, differ in many ways, such as how they run their classrooms and how they teach. These and other variables do affect student achievement, as you'll see in the next few pages. Let's begin with school-based influences.

School-Based Influences on Student Achievement

Roosevelt High School, in the center of Detroit, has an enrollment of 3,500 students in grades 9 through 12. Opened in 1936, the building shows its age. The rooms are drafty, the desks are decorated with generations of graffiti, and new technology means an overhead projector. Nevertheless, attendance at Roosevelt is good. Most students graduate, and many continue their education at community colleges and state universities. Southport High School, in Newark, has about the same enrollment as Roosevelt High, and the building is about the same age. Yet truancy is commonplace at Southport, where fewer than half the students graduate and almost none go to college.

Although these schools are hypothetical, they accurately depict a common outcome in the United States. Some schools are more successful than others, whether success is defined in terms of the percentage of students who are literate, who graduate, or who go to college. Why? Researchers (El Nokali, Bachman, & Votruba-Drzal, 2010; Good & Brophy, 2008; Preston et al., 2017) have identified a number of characteristics of schools where students typically succeed.

- *Staff and students alike understand that academic excellence is the primary goal and schools provide high-quality instruction to allow students to achieve that goal.* The school day emphasizes instruction—not nonacademic activities—and students are recognized publicly for their academic accomplishments. Teachers engage students through dialogue, feedback, and responsiveness.
- *The school climate is safe and nurturing.* Students know that they can devote their energy to learning (instead of worrying about being harmed in school) and that the staff truly cares that they succeed.
- *Parents and communities are involved.* Parents may participate through parent–teacher organizations or informally (e.g., helping a teacher to prepare a lesson or to grade papers). Social agencies may provide mentors who guide students at risk for dropping out; businesses partner with schools to provide internships or vocational training. Such involvement signals that a network of concerned adults is committed to students' success.
- *Progress of students, teachers, and programs is monitored.* The only way to know whether schools are succeeding is by measuring performance. Students, teachers, and programs are evaluated regularly, using objective measures that reflect academic goals.

In schools where these guidelines are followed regularly, students usually succeed. In schools where the guidelines are ignored, students more often fail.

Of course, on a daily basis, individual teachers have the most potential for impact. Let's see how teachers can influence their students' achievement.

In successful schools, the child's parents are involved—often as tutors.

Michael J. Doolittle/The Image Works

Teacher-Based Influences on Student Achievement

In most schools, some teachers are highly sought after because their classes are very successful: Students learn and the classroom climate is usually positive. What are the keys to the success of these master teachers? Research reveals that several factors are critical for students' achievement (Allen et al., 2013; Good & Brophy, 2008; Walberg, 1995). Students tend to learn the most when teachers:

- *Manage the classroom effectively so that they can devote most of their time to instruction.* When teachers spend much time disciplining students or when students do not move smoothly from one class activity to the next, instructional time is wasted and students are apt to learn less.

- *Believe that they are responsible for their students' learning and that their students will learn when taught well.* When students don't understand a new topic, these teachers may repeat the original instruction (in case the student missed something) or create new instruction (in case the student heard everything but just didn't "get it"). These teachers keep plugging away because they feel at fault if students don't learn.
- *Emphasize mastery of topics.* Teachers introduce a topic, then give students many opportunities to understand, practice, and apply the topic. Just as you'd find it hard to go directly from driver's education to race car driving, students more often achieve when they grasp a new topic thoroughly, then gradually move to other more advanced topics.
- *Teach actively.* Effective teachers don't just talk or give students an endless stream of worksheets. Instead, they demonstrate topics concretely or provide hands-on demonstrations for students. They also have students participate in class activities and encourage students to interact, generating ideas and solving problems together.
- *Pay careful attention to pacing.* Teachers present material slowly enough so that students can understand a new concept but not so slowly that students get bored.
- *Value tutoring.* Teachers work with students individually or in small groups so they can gear their instruction to each student's level and check each student's understanding. They also encourage peer tutoring, in which more capable students tutor less capable students. Children who are tutored by peers *do* learn, and so do the tutors because teaching helps tutors organize their knowledge.
- *Teach students techniques for monitoring and managing their own learning.* Students are more likely to achieve when they are taught how to recognize the aims of school tasks as well as effective strategies for achieving those aims.

Peer tutoring can be very effective; both the tutored student and the tutor usually learn.

Thus, what makes for effective schools and teachers? No single element is crucial. Instead, many factors contribute to making some schools and teachers remarkably effective. Some of the essential ingredients include parents who are involved; teachers who care deeply about their students' learning and manage classrooms well; and a school that is safe, is nurturing, and emphasizes achievement.

TEST YOURSELF 6.4

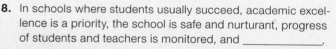

Recall

1. Important prereading skills include knowing letters and _____.

2. Beginning readers typically recognize words by sounding them out; with greater experience, readers often _____.

3. Older and more experienced readers understand more of what they read because the capacity of working memory increases, they have more general knowledge of the world, _____, and they are more likely to use appropriate reading strategies.

4. Children typically use a(n) _____ to organize their writing.

5. Children write best when _____.

6. The simplest way to solve addition problems is to _____; the most advanced way is to retrieve sums from long-term memory.

7. Compared with students in U.S. elementary schools, students in Asia spend more time in school, and a greater proportion of that time is _____.

8. In schools where students usually succeed, academic excellence is a priority, the school is safe and nurturant, progress of students and teachers is monitored, and _____.

9. Effective teachers manage classrooms well, believe they are responsible for their students' learning, _____, teach actively, pay attention to pacing, value tutoring, and show children how to monitor their own learning.

Interpret

- Review the research on pages 211–212 regarding factors associated with skilled reading comprehension. Which of these factors—if any—might also contribute to skilled writing?

Apply

- Imagine two children, both entering first grade. One has mastered prereading skills, can sound out many words, and recognizes a rapidly growing set of words. The second child knows most of the letters of the alphabet but knows only a handful of letter–sound correspondences. How are these differences in reading skills likely to lead to different experiences in first grade?

Check your answers to the Recall Questions at the end of the chapter.

LEARNING OBJECTIVES

- How much do school-age children grow?
- How do motor skills improve during the elementary school years?
- Are American children physically fit?
- What are the consequences of participating in sports?

Miguel and Dan are 9-year-olds playing organized baseball for the first time. Miguel's coach is always upbeat. He constantly emphasizes the positive. When Miguel's team lost a game 12 to 2, the coach complimented all the players on their play in the field and at bat. In contrast, Dan's coach was livid when the team lost, and he was extremely critical of three players who made errors that contributed to the loss. Miguel thinks that baseball is great, but Dan can hardly wait for the season to be over.

During the elementary school years, children grow steadily and their motor skills continue to improve. We'll trace these changes in the first two parts of this section. Then we'll see whether U.S. children are physically fit. We'll end the section by examining children's participation in sports and see how coaches like those in the vignette influence children in organized sports.

Growth

Physical growth during the elementary school years continues at the steady pace established during the preschool years. From ▶ Figure 6.8, you can see that a typical 6-year-old weighs about 45 pounds and is 45 inches tall, but grows to about 90 pounds and 60 inches by age 12. In other words, most children gain about 8 pounds and 2 to 3 inches per year. Many parents notice that their elementary school children outgrow shoes and pants more rapidly than they outgrow sweaters, shirts, or jackets; this is because most of the increase in height comes from the legs, not the trunk.

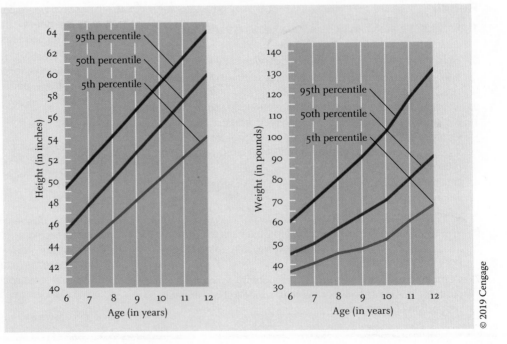

▶ **Figure 6.8**

Height and weight increase steadily during the elementary school years.

Boys and girls are about the same size for most of these years (which is why they are combined in the figure), but girls are more likely than boys to enter puberty toward the end of the elementary school years. Once girls enter puberty, they grow rapidly and become much bigger than the boys their age. (We have more to say about this in Chapter 8.) Thus, at ages 11 and 12, the average girl is about half an inch taller than the average boy.

To support this growth and to provide energy for their busy lives, school-age children need to eat more. Although preschool children need only consume about 1,500 to 1,700 calories per day, the average 7- to 10-year-old needs about 2,400 calories each day. Of course, the exact figure depends on the child's age and size and can range anywhere from roughly 1,700 to 3,300 calories daily.

As was true for preschool children, elementary school children need a well-balanced diet. They should eat regularly from each of the major food groups: grains, vegetables, fruits, milk, meat, and beans. Too often children consume "empty" calories from sweets that have very little nutritional value.

It's also important that school-age children eat breakfast. At this age, many children skip breakfast—often because they're too rushed in the morning. In fact, breakfast should provide about one-fourth of a child's daily calories. When children are well fed, they're better able to pay attention in class and this translates into better grades and higher scores on achievement tests—for children who are well nourished overall as well as for children who are undernourished (Adolphus, Lawton, & Dye, 2013; Littlecott et al., 2016). Therefore, parents should plan mornings so children have enough time for breakfast.

Development of Motor Skills

Elementary school children's greater size and strength contribute to improved motor skills. During these years, children steadily run faster and jump farther. For example, ❱ Figure 6.9 shows how far a typical boy and girl can throw a ball and how far they can jump (in the standing long jump). By the time children are 11 years old, they can throw a ball three times farther than they could at age 6 and can jump nearly twice as far.

❱ **Figure 6.9**

Between 6 and 11 years, children's motor skills improve considerably.

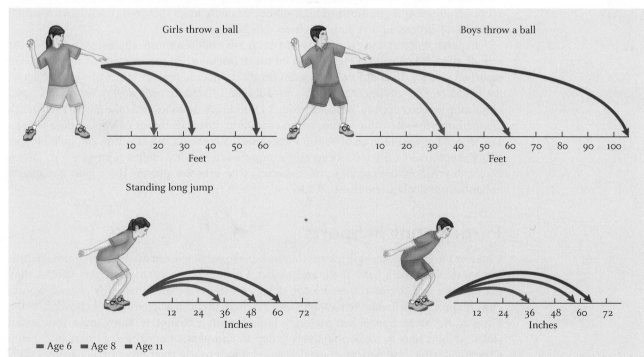

Fine motor skills also improve as children move through the elementary school years. Children's greater dexterity is evident in a host of activities ranging from typing, writing, and drawing to working on puzzles, playing the piano, and building model cars. Children gain much greater control over their fingers and hands, making them more nimble. This greater fine motor coordination is obvious in children's handwriting.

Gender Differences in Motor Skills

In both gross and fine motor skills, there are gender differences in performance levels. For example, girls tend to excel in fine motor skills; their handwriting tends to be better than that of boys. Girls also excel in gross motor skills that require flexibility and balance, such as tumbling. On gross motor skills that emphasize strength, boys usually have the advantage. Figure 6.9 shows that boys throw and jump farther than girls.

Some of the gender differences in gross motor skills that require strength reflect the fact that as children approach and enter puberty, girls' bodies have proportionately more fat and less muscle than do boys' bodies. This difference explains why, for example, boys can hang by their hands or arms from a bar much longer than girls can. However, for other gross motor skills such as running, throwing, and catching, body composition is less important (Duff, Ericsson, & Baluch, 2007; Smoll & Schutz, 1990). In these cases, children's experience is crucial. During recess, elementary school girls are more often found playing on a swing set, jumping rope, or perhaps talking quietly in a group; in contrast, boys are playing football or shooting baskets. Many girls and their parents believe that sports and physical fitness are less valuable for girls than boys. Consequently, girls spend less time in these sports and fitness-related activities than boys, depriving them of the opportunities to practice that are essential for developing motor skills (Fredricks & Eccles, 2005).

Physical Fitness

Exercise has many benefits: Children who are active physically are healthier, have better self-esteem, and greater achievement in school (Booth et al., 2014; Lubans et al., 2016; Rangul et al., 2012). Because of these benefits, the President's Council on Physical Fitness, Sports and Nutrition has long recommended that children and adolescents spend 60 minutes daily in physical activity. Unfortunately, few youth—about half of elementary school children and one-third of high school students meet this goal (President's Council on Physical Fitness, Sports and Nutrition, 2012).

Experts recommend many ways to increase children's and adolescent's fitness. At school, physical education classes can be more frequent, longer, and spend more time in vigorous activity; in addition, classroom time can include regular stints of physical activity. Children and adolescents can be encouraged to walk or ride a bicycle to work, and communities can support these activities by building sidewalks and bike lanes (President's Council on Physical Fitness, Sports and Nutrition, 2012). Families can encourage fitness, too. Instead of spending an afternoon watching TV, parents and children can go biking or play Pokémon Go. Or families can play exergames, which are digital games such as Dance Dance Revolution that combine video gaming with exercise; playing these games regularly enhances physical fitness (Best, 2013).

Participating in Sports

Children's greater motor skill means they are able to participate in many team sports, including baseball, softball, basketball, and soccer. Obviously, when children play sports, they get exercise and improve their motor skills. But there are other benefits as well. Sports can enhance participants' self-esteem and can help them to learn initiative (Bowker, 2006; Eime at al., 2013). Sports can provide children with a chance to learn important social skills, such as how to work effectively (often in complementary roles) as part of a group (Brenner, 2016). And playing sports allows children to use their emerging cognitive skills as they devise new playing strategies or modify the rules of a game.

These benefits of participating in sports are balanced by potential hazards. Specializing in one sport early—before early or mid-adolescence—can lead to injuries because of overuse and can limit children's peer relationships to others participating in the same sport (Brenner, 2016). Also, several studies have linked adolescents' participation in sports to delinquent and antisocial behavior (e.g., Gardner, Roth, & Brooks-Gunn, 2009). However, outcomes are usually positive when sports participation is combined with participation in activities that involve adults, such as school, religious, or youth groups (Linver, Roth, & Brooks-Gunn, 2009; Zarrett et al., 2009). But these potential benefits hinge on the adults who are involved. When adult coaches like the one in the opening vignette encourage their players and emphasize skill development, children usually enjoy playing, often improve their skills, and increase their self-esteem. In contrast, when coaches emphasize winning over skill development and criticize or punish players for bad plays, children lose interest and stop playing (Curran et al., 2015). And when adolescents find sports too stressful, they often get "burned out"—they lose interest and quit (Lu et al., 2016).

To encourage youth to participate, adults (and parents) need to have realistic expectations for children and coach positively, praising children instead of criticizing them. And they need to remember that children play games for recreation, which means they should have fun!

Think About It

What skills of concrete-operational thinking make it possible for children to participate in organized sports?

When adult coaches encourage their team instead of criticizing mistakes, children are likely to enjoy playing sports.

iStock.com/kali9

TEST YOURSELF **6.5**

Recall

1. Boys and girls grow at about the same rate during elementary school years, but at the end of this period, girls _____.

2. When children skip breakfast, _____.

3. Boys typically have the advantage of gross motor skills that emphasize strength, but girls tend to have the advantage of _____.

4. Children may lose interest in sports and quit playing if coaches _____, and criticize or punish players for mistakes.

Interpret

- What are the pros and cons of children and adolescents participating in organized sports?

Apply

- Describe how participation in sports illustrates connections between motor, cognitive, and social development.

Check your answers to the Recall Questions at the end of the chapter.

SUMMARY

6.1 Cognitive Development

What are the distinguishing characteristics of thought during Piaget's concrete-operational and formal-operational stages?

- In progressing to Piaget's stage of concrete operations, children become less egocentric, rarely confuse appearances with reality, and are able to reverse their thinking. They now solve perspective-taking and conservation problems correctly. Thinking at this stage is limited to the concrete and the real.

- With the onset of formal-operational thinking, adolescents can think hypothetically and reason abstractly. In deductive reasoning, they understand that conclusions are based on logic, not on experience.

How do children use strategies and monitoring to improve learning and remembering?

- Rehearsal and other memory strategies are used to transfer information from working memory, a temporary store of information, to long-term memory, a permanent store of knowledge. Children begin to rehearse at about age 7 or 8 and take up other strategies as they grow older.

- Effective use of strategies for learning and remembering begins with an analysis of the goals of a learning task. It also includes monitoring one's performance to determine whether the strategy is working. Teachers can help students master these skills.

6.2 Aptitudes for School

What is the nature of intelligence?

- Traditional approaches to intelligence led to hierarchical theories that include both general intelligence and specific skills, such as verbal and spatial ability.

- Gardner's theory of multiple intelligences proposes nine distinct intelligences. Three are found in psychometric theories (linguistic, logical-mathematical, and spatial intelligence), but six are new (musical, bodily-kinesthetic, interpersonal, intrapersonal, naturalistic, and existential intelligence). Gardner's theory has stimulated research on nontraditional forms of intelligence, such as emotional intelligence. The theory also has implications for education—suggesting, for example, that schools should adjust teaching to each child's unique intellectual strengths.

- According to Robert Sternberg, intelligence is defined as using abilities to achieve short- and long-term goals and

depends on three abilities: analytic ability to analyze a problem and generate a solution, creative ability to deal adaptively with novel situations, and practical ability to know what solutions will work.

Why were intelligence tests first developed? What are their features?

- Binet created the first intelligence test to identify students who would have difficulty in school. Using this work, Terman created the Stanford-Binet in 1916; it remains an important intelligence test. The Stanford-Binet introduced the concept of the intelligence quotient (IQ): MA/CA × 100.

How well do intelligence tests work?

- Intelligence tests are reasonably valid measures of achievement in school. They also predict people's performance in the workplace and their longevity.

How do heredity and environment influence intelligence?

- Evidence for the impact of heredity on IQ comes from the findings that (1) siblings' IQ scores become more alike as siblings become more similar genetically and (2) adopted children's IQ scores are more like their biological parents' test scores than their adoptive parents' scores. Evidence for the influence of the environment comes from the impact on IQ scores of home environments, historical change, and intervention programs.

How and why do test scores vary for different racial and ethnic groups?

- There are substantial differences between ethnic groups in their average scores on IQ tests. This difference is attributed to the greater likelihood of Latino American and African American youth being economically disadvantaged as well as stereotype threat and test-taking skills. IQ scores remain valid predictors of school success because middle-class experience is often a prerequisite for school success.

6.3 Special Children, Special Needs

What are the characteristics of gifted children?

- Traditionally, gifted children have high scores on IQ tests. Modern definitions of giftedness have been broadened to include exceptional talent in the arts. However defined, giftedness must be nurtured by parents and teachers alike. Contrary to folklore, gifted children usually are socially mature and emotionally stable.

What are the different forms of disability?

- Individuals with intellectual disability have IQ scores of 70 or lower and deficits in adaptive behavior. Biomedical, social, behavioral, and educational factors place children at risk for intellectual disability. Children with learning disability have normal intelligence but have difficulty mastering specific academic subjects. The most common is developmental dyslexia, which involves difficulty reading individual words because children haven't mastered language sounds.

What are the distinguishing features of attention-deficit hyperactivity disorder?

- Children with ADHD are distinguished by being hyperactive, inattentive, and impulsive. Treating ADHD with medication and psychosocial treatment is effective in the short run but does not "cure" children of the disorder.

6.4 Academic Skills

What are the components of skilled reading?

- Reading includes a number of component skills. Prereading skills include knowing letters and the sounds associated with them. Word recognition is the process of identifying a word. Beginning readers more often accomplish this by sounding out words; advanced readers more often retrieve a word from long-term memory. Comprehension, the act of extracting meaning from text, improves with age as a result of several factors: Vocabulary and working memory capacity increase, readers gain more world knowledge, and readers are better able to monitor what they read and to match their reading strategies to the goals of the reading task.

As children develop, how does their writing improve?

- As children develop, their writing improves, which reflects several factors: They know more about the world and so have more to say; they use more effective ways of organizing their writing; they master the mechanics of writing (e.g., handwriting, spelling); and they become more skilled at revising their writing.

How do arithmetic skills change during the elementary school years? How do U.S. students compare with students in other countries?

- Children first add and subtract by counting, but soon they use more effective strategies such as retrieving addition facts directly from memory. In mathematics, U.S. students lag behind students in most other industrialized countries, chiefly because of cultural differences in time spent on schoolwork and homework and in parents' attitudes toward school, effort, and ability.

What are the hallmarks of effective schools and effective teachers?

- Schools influence students' achievement in many ways. Students are most likely to achieve when their school emphasizes academic excellence, has a safe and nurturing environment, monitors pupils' and teachers' progress, and encourages parents to be involved.

- Students achieve at higher levels when their teachers manage classrooms effectively, take responsibility for their students' learning, teach mastery of material, pace material well, value tutoring, and show children how to monitor their own learning.

6.5 Physical Development

How much do school-age children grow?

- Elementary school children grow at a steady pace, but more so in their legs than in the trunk. Boys and girls tend to be about the same size for most of these years.

- School-age children need approximately 2,400 calories daily, preferably drawn from each of the basic food groups. Children need to eat breakfast, a meal that should provide approximately one-fourth of their calories. Without breakfast, children often have trouble concentrating in school.

How do motor skills develop during the elementary school years?

- Fine and gross motor skills improve substantially over the elementary school years, reflecting children's greater size and strength. Girls tend to excel in fine motor skills that emphasize dexterity as well as in gross motor skills that require flexibility and balance; boys tend to excel in gross motor skills that emphasize strength. Although some of these differences reflect differences in body makeup, they also reflect different cultural expectations regarding motor skills for boys and girls.

Are American children physically fit?

- Many American school children don't meet today's standards for being physically fit, and childhood obesity is a growing concern.

What are the consequences of participating in sports?

- Many school-age children participate in team sports. Benefits of participation include exercise, enhanced self-esteem, and improved social skills. But participation sometimes leads to antisocial behavior, and when adults are involved, they sometimes overemphasize competition, which can turn "play" into "work."

Test Yourself Recall Answers

6.1 1. concrete-operational **2.** formal-operational **3.** determined the goal of the memory task **4.** monitoring **6.2 1.** hierarchical **2.** bodily-kinesthetic **3.** teach in a manner that engages as many different intelligences as possible **4.** analytic **5.** biological **6.** intervention studies **7.** culture-fair intelligence tests **6.3 1.** are broader and include exceptional talent in many areas **2.** divergent **3.** problems adapting to the environment **4.** behavioral **5.** phonological awareness (distinguishing language sounds) **6.** inattentiveness **7.** psychosocial treatment that improves children's cognitive and social skills **6.4 1.** sounds associated with each letter **2.** retrieve words from long-term memory **3.** they monitor their comprehension more effectively **4.** knowledge-telling strategy **5.** the topic is familiar to them **6.** count on one's fingers **7.** devoted to academic activities **8.** parents are involved **9.** emphasize mastery of topics **6.5 1.** are more likely to enter puberty and grow rapidly **2.** they often have difficulty paying attention and remembering in school **3.** fine motor skills that emphasize dexterity **4.** emphasize winning over skill development

Key Terms

mental operations (190)
deductive reasoning (191)
working memory (192)
long-term memory (192)
organization (192)
elaboration (192)
metamemory (193)
metacognitive knowledge (193)
cognitive self-regulation (193)

psychometricians (195)
emotional intelligence (197)
analytic ability (197)
creative ability (197)
practical ability (197)
mental age (MA) (198)
intelligence quotient (IQ) (199)
culture-fair intelligence tests (202)
stereotype threat (203)

divergent thinking (204)
intellectual disability (205)
learning disability (205)
word recognition (210)
comprehension (210)
phonological awareness (210)
knowledge-telling strategy (212)
knowledge-transforming strategy (212)

Expanding Social Horizons
Socioemotional Development in Middle Childhood

7

Although you've never had a course called "Culture 101," your knowledge of your culture is deep. Like all human beings, you have been learning since birth to live in your culture. *Teaching children the values, roles, and behaviors of their culture—* socialization—*is a major goal of all people.* In most cultures, the task of socialization falls first to parents. In the first section of this chapter, we see how parents set and try to enforce standards of behavior for their children.

Soon other powerful forces contribute to socialization. In the second section, you'll discover how peers become influential through both individual friendships and social groups. Next, you'll learn how the media— particularly television—contribute to socialization as well.

As children become socialized, they begin to understand more about other people. We'll examine this growing understanding in the last section of the chapter.

7.1 Family Relationships

LEARNING OBJECTIVES

- What is a systems approach to parenting?
- What are the primary dimensions of parenting? How do they affect children's development?
- What determines how siblings get along? How do first-born, later-born, and only children differ?

- How do divorce and remarriage affect children?
- What factors lead children to be maltreated?

socialization

Teaching children the values, roles, and behaviors of their culture.

Tanya and Sheila, both sixth graders, wanted to go to a Selena Gomez concert with two boys from their school. When Tanya asked if she could go, her mom said, "No way!" Tanya replied defiantly, "Why not?" Her mother blew up: "Because I say so. That's why. Stop bugging me." Sheila wasn't allowed to go either. When she asked why, her mom said, "I think that you're still too young to be dating. I don't mind your going to the concert. If you want to go just with Tanya, that would be fine. What do you think of that?"

The vignette illustrates what we all know from personal experience—parents go about child rearing in many ways. We study these different approaches in this chapter and learn how Tanya and Sheila are likely to be affected by their mothers' styles of parenting. But we'll start by considering parents as key components of a broader family system.

The Family as a System

Families are rare in the animal kingdom. Only human beings and a handful of other species form family-like units. Why? Compared with the young in other species, children develop slowly. And because children are unable to care for themselves for many years, the family structure evolved as a way to protect and nurture young children during their development (Bjorklund, Yunger, & Pellegrini, 2002). Of course, modern families serve many other functions as well—they're economic units, and they provide emotional support—but child rearing is probably the most important family function.

Today, most theorists view families from a contextual perspective (described in Chapter 1) in which families form a system of interacting elements: Parents and children influence one another (Bronfenbrenner & Morris, 2006; Schermerhorn & Cummings, 2008), and families are part of a much larger system that includes extended family, friends, and teachers as well as institutions that influence development (e.g., schools).

In the systems view, parents influence their children both directly (e.g., by encouraging them to study hard) and indirectly (e.g., by being generous and kind to others). And children influence their parents. By their behaviors, attitudes, and interests, children affect how their parents behave toward them. For example, when children resist discipline, parents may become less willing to reason and more inclined to use force (Ritchie, 1999).

The systems view reveals other, more subtle influences. For example, fathers' behaviors can affect mother–child relationships; a demanding husband may leave his wife with little time, energy, or interest in helping her daughter with her homework. Or when siblings argue constantly, parents may become preoccupied with avoiding problems rather than encouraging their children's development.

The family itself is embedded in other social systems, such as neighborhoods and religious institutions (Parke & Buriel, 1998). These other institutions can affect family dynamics. Sometimes they simplify child rearing, as when neighbors are trusted friends and can help care for each others' children. However, sometimes they complicate child rearing, as when nearby relatives create friction within the family. At times, the impact of the larger systems is indirect, as when work schedules cause a parent to be away from home or when schools eliminate programs that benefit children.

▶ Figure 7.1 summarizes the many interactive influences that exist in a systems view of families. In the remainder of this section, we'll describe parents' influences on children and then discuss how children affect their parents' behavior.

Dimensions and Styles of Parenting

Parenting can be described in terms of general dimensions that are like personality traits in representing stable aspects of parental behavior that hold across different situations (Holden & Miller, 1999). When viewed this way, two general dimensions of parental behavior emerge. One is the degree of warmth and responsiveness that parents show their children. Some parents are openly warm and affectionate with their children. They are involved with them, respond to their emotional needs, and spend much time with them. Other parents are relatively uninvolved with their children and sometimes even hostile toward them. These parents often seem more focused on their own needs and interests than those of their children. Warm parents enjoy hearing their children describe the day's activities; uninvolved or hostile parents aren't interested, considering it a waste of their time. Warm parents see when their children are upset and try to comfort them; uninvolved or hostile parents pay little attention to their children's emotional states and invest little effort in comforting them when they're upset. As you might expect, children benefit from warm and responsive parenting (Pettit, Bates, & Dodge, 1997; Zhou et al., 2002).

A second general dimension of parental behavior involves control, which comes in two forms (Grusec, 2011). Psychological control refers to parents' efforts to manipulate their children's emotional states by, for example, withdrawing their love or making children feel guilty. Behavioral control refers to parents' efforts to set rules for their children and to impose limits on what children can and cannot do. Some parents are dictatorial: They try to regulate every facet of their children's lives, like a puppeteer controlling a marionette. At the other extreme are parents who exert little or no control over their children: These children do whatever they want without asking their parents first or worrying about their parents' response.

What's best for children is minimal psychological control combined with an intermediate amount of behavioral control. Children typically fare best when parents set reasonable standards for children's behavior, expect their children to meet those standards, and know where their children are, what they're doing, and with whom (Racz & McMahon, 2011).

Parenting Styles

Combining the dimensions of warmth and control produces four prototypic styles of parenting, as shown in ▶ Figure 7.2 (Baumrind, 1975, 1991).

- **Authoritarian parenting** *combines high control with little warmth.* These parents lay down the rules and expect them to be followed without discussion. These parents emphasize respect and obedience. There is little give-and-take between parent and child because authoritarian parents do not consider children's needs or wishes. This style is illustrated by Tanya's mother in the opening vignette. She feels no obligation to explain her decision.
- **Authoritative parenting** *combines a fair degree of parental control with being warm and responsive to children.* Authoritative parents explain rules and encourage discussion. This style is exemplified by Sheila's mother in the opening vignette. She explained why she did not want the girls going to the concert with the boys and encouraged her daughter to discuss the issue with her.

▶ **Figure 7.1**

In a systems view of families, parents and children influence each other; this interacting family unit is also influenced by other forces outside the family.

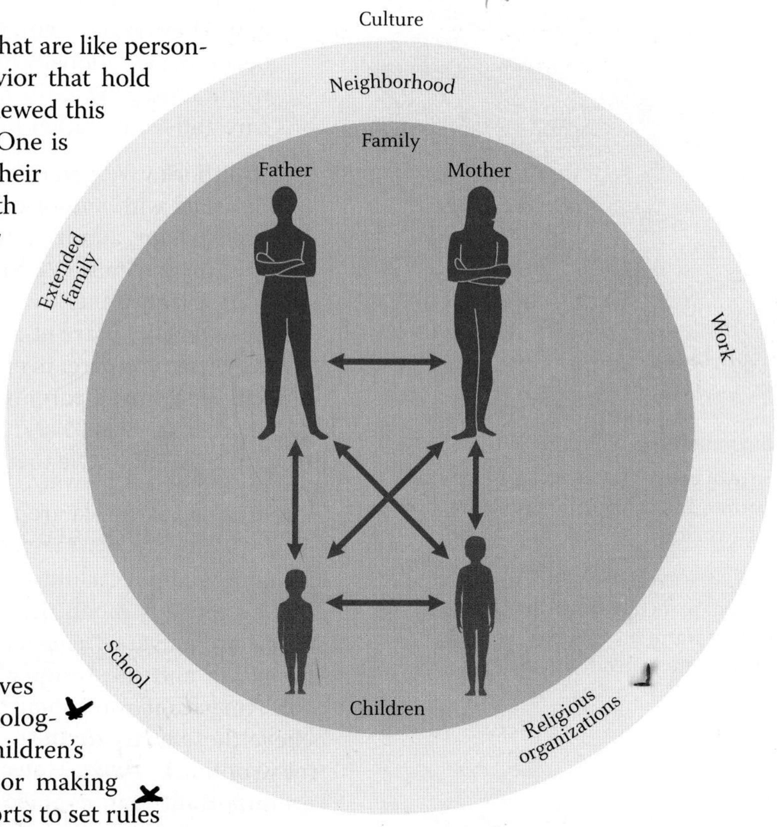

© 2019 Cengage

authoritarian parenting

Style of parenting in which parents show high levels of control and low levels of warmth toward their children.

authoritative parenting

Style of parenting in which parents use a moderate amount of control and are warm and responsive to their children.

Figure 7.2

Combining the two dimensions of parental behavior (warmth and control) creates four prototypic styles of parenting.

	Parental control	
	High	**Low**
High Parental involvement	Authoritative	Permissive
Low	Authoritarian	Uninvolved

© 2019 Cengage

permissive parenting

Style of parenting in which parents offer warmth and caring but little control over their children.

uninvolved parenting

Style of parenting in which parents provide neither warmth nor control and minimize the time they spend with their children.

Authoritative parents are warm and responsive with children and encourage discussion.

Rob Marmion/Shutterstock.com

3. Permissive parenting *offers warmth and caring but little parental control.* These parents generally accept their children's behavior and punish them infrequently. An indulgent-permissive parent would readily agree to Tanya's or Sheila's request to go to the concert simply because it is something the child wants to do.

4. Uninvolved parenting *provides neither warmth nor control.* Indifferent-uninvolved parents provide for their children's basic physical and emotional needs but little else. They try to minimize the time they spend with their children and avoid becoming emotionally involved with them. If Tanya had parents with this style, she might have gone to the concert without asking, knowing that her parents wouldn't care and would rather not be bothered.

Authoritative parenting is best for most children most of the time. Children and adolescents with authoritative parents tend to have higher grades, they are responsible, self-reliant, and friendly, and they're less likely to drink alcohol (Amato & Fowler, 2002; Aunola, Stattin, & Nurmi, 2000; Merianos et al., 2015). In contrast, children with authoritarian parents are often unhappy, have low self-esteem, and frequently are overly aggressive (e.g., Braza et al., 2015; Silk et al., 2003; Zhou et al., 2008). Finally, children with permissive parents are often impulsive and have little self-control, whereas children with uninvolved parents often do poorly in school and are aggressive (Aunola et al., 2000; Barber & Olsen, 1997; Driscoll, Russell, & Crockett, 2008). Thus, children typically thrive on a parental style that combines control, warmth, and affection.

Variations Associated with Culture and Socioeconomic Status

The general aim of child rearing—helping children become contributing members of their culture—is much the same worldwide (Lansford et al., 2016), and warmth and control are universal aspects of parents' behavior. But views about the "proper" amount of warmth and the "proper" amount of control vary with particular cultures. European Americans want their children to be happy and self-reliant individuals, and they believe these goals are best achieved when parents are warm and exert moderate control (Goodnow, 1992). However, in many countries around the world, individualism is less important than cooperation and collaboration. In China, for example, emotional restraint and obedience are seen as the keys to family harmony (Chao, 2001). Consequently, parents in China often rely on an authoritarian style in which they are less often affectionate and expect their children to obey them without question (Lin & Fu, 1990; Zhou et al., 2008).

Another common pattern worldwide is for parents to be warm and controlling (Deater-Deckard et al., 2011). For example, Latino culture typically places greater emphasis on having strong family ties and respecting the roles of all family members, particularly adults; these values lead parents to be more protective of their children and to set more rules for them (Halgunseth, Ispa, & Rudy, 2006). Thus, cultural values help specify appropriate ways for parents to interact with their offspring.

Parental styles vary not only across cultures but also within cultures, depending on parents' socioeconomic status. Within the United States, parents of lower socioeconomic status tend to be more controlling and more punitive—characteristics associated with the authoritarian parenting style—than are parents of higher socioeconomic status (Pace et al., 2017). This difference may reflect educational differences that help to define socioeconomic status. Parents of higher socioeconomic status are, by definition, more educated and consequently often see development as a more complex process requiring the more nuanced and child-friendly approach that marks authoritative parenting (Skinner, 1985). Parents who are relatively uneducated often find themselves employed in positions where they're used to taking orders from others; when they're at home, these parents reverse roles and order their children around (Greenberger, O'Neil, & Nagel, 1994).

Another contributing factor derives from another variable that defines socioeconomic status: income (Melby et al., 2008). Because of their limited financial resources, parents of lower socioeconomic status often lead more stressful lives (e.g., they wonder whether they'll have enough money at the end of the month for groceries) and are far more likely to live in neighborhoods where violence, drugs, and crime are commonplace. Thus, parents of lower socioeconomic status may be too stressed to invest the energy needed for the warmth and moderate control that define authoritative parenting (Simons et al., 2016).

Genetic Influences on Parenting

Families and parenting are adaptations that evolved to provide for children until they mature. In other words, genes linked to behaviors that make for effective parenting (e.g., being nurturing) were more likely to be passed on because they helped children to reach maturity. Consistent with this view, research on twins as parents shows the impact of genetics on parental style. For example, as parents, identical twins are more similar than fraternal twins in the amount of warmth that they express to their children (McAdams et al., 2017); apparently heredity makes it easier for some people to be warm parents. Behavior genetic studies also reveal several environmental influences on parental style, including the quality of the parents' marital relationship and the children themselves (Klahr & Burt, 2014); we'll examine these later in this module.

Parental Behavior

Dimensions and styles are useful as general characterizations of parents, but they tell us little about how parents behave in specific situations and how these parental behaviors influence children's development. Researchers have identified three specific parental behaviors that influence children: direct instruction, modeling, and feedback.

Direct Instruction and Coaching. Parents often tell their children what to do. But ordering children around—"Clean your room!" "Turn off the TV!"—is not very effective. *A better approach is* direct instruction, *which involves telling a child what to do, when, and why.* Instead of just shouting, "Share your candy with your brother!" a parent should explain when and why it's important to share with a sibling.

In addition, just as coaches help athletes master sports skills, parents can help their youngsters master social and emotional skills. Parents can explain links between emotions and behavior: "Catlin is sad because you broke her crayon" (Gottman, Katz, & Hooven, 1996). They can also teach children how to deal with difficult social situations: "When you ask Lindsey if she can sleep over, do it privately so you don't hurt Ali's or Hannah's feelings" (Mize & Pettit, 1997). In general, children who get this sort of parental "coaching" tend to be more socially skilled and, not surprisingly, get along better with their peers.

Modeling. Children learn a great deal from parents simply by watching them. The parents' modeling and the youngsters' observational learning leads to imitation, so children's behavior resembles the behavior they observe. *Observational learning can also produce* counterimitation, *learning what should not be done.* If an older sibling kicks a friend and parents punish the older sibling, the younger child may learn not to kick others.

Observational learning likely contributes to intergenerational continuity of parenting behavior. Parental behavior is often consistent from one generation to the next. When, for example, parents often use harsh physical punishment to discipline their children, these children will, when they are parents, follow suit (Bailey et al., 2009).

Feedback. By giving feedback to their children, parents indicate whether a behavior is appropriate and should continue or is inappropriate and should stop. Feedback comes in two general forms. Reinforcement *is any action that increases the likelihood of the response that it follows.* Parents may use praise to reinforce a child's studying or give a reward for completing household chores. Punishment *is any action that discourages the recurrence of the response that it follows.* Parents may forbid children to watch television when they get poor grades in school or make children go to bed early for neglecting household chores.

direct instruction
Telling a child what to do, when, and why.

counterimitation
Learning what should not be done by observing the behavior.

reinforcement
Consequence that increases the likelihood that a behavior will be repeated in the future.

punishment
Application of an aversive stimulus (e.g., a spanking) or removal of an attractive stimulus (e.g., TV viewing).

Parents can use reinforcement to encourage their children to complete tasks they don't enjoy, such as household chores.

negative reinforcement trap
Unwittingly reinforcing a behavior you want to discourage.

Think About It

When 10-year-old Dylan's family got a puppy, he agreed to walk it every day after school. But when his mom reminds him to do this, he gets angry because he'd rather watch TV. After they argue for about 15 minutes, Dylan's mom gives up and walks the dog herself. And Dylan goes back to watching TV. Analyze this situation. What could Dylan's mom do to prevent these regular arguments?

time-out
Punishment that involves removing children who are misbehaving from a situation to a quiet, unstimulating environment.

Of course, parents have been rewarding and punishing their children for centuries, so what do psychologists know that parents don't know already? In fact, researchers have made some surprising discoveries concerning the nature of reward and punishment. *Parents often unwittingly reinforce the very behaviors they want to discourage, a situation called the* negative reinforcement trap (Patterson, 1980). The negative reinforcement trap occurs in three steps, most often between a mother and her son. In the first step, the mother tells her son to do something he doesn't want to do. She might tell him to clean up his room, to come inside when he's outdoors playing with friends, or to study instead of watching television. In the next step, the son responds with some behavior that most parents find intolerable: He argues, complains, or whines for an extended period of time. In the last step, the mother gives in—saying that the son needn't do as she told him initially—simply to get the son to stop the behavior that is so intolerable. The feedback to the son is that arguing (or complaining or whining) works; the mother rewards that behavior by withdrawing the request that the son did not like.

As for punishment, research shows that it works best when

- administered directly after the undesired behavior occurs, not hours later.
- an undesired behavior *consistently* leads to punishment.
- accompanied by an explanation of why the child was punished and how punishment can be avoided in the future.
- the child has a warm, affectionate relationship with the person administering the punishment.

At the same time, research reveals some serious drawbacks to punishment. One is that punishment is primarily suppressive: Punished responses are stopped, but only temporarily if children do not learn new behaviors to replace those that were punished. For example, denying TV to brothers who are fighting stops the undesirable behavior, but fighting is likely to recur unless the boys learn new ways of solving their disputes.

A second drawback is that punishment can have undesirable side effects. Children become upset when they are being punished, which means they often miss the feedback that punishment is meant to convey. A child denied TV for misbehaving may become angry over the punishment itself and ignore why he's being punished.

Spanking illustrates the problems with punishment. Although used by many parents in the United States and around the world, it is ineffective in getting children to comply with parents and often leads children to aggressive behavior (Altschul, Lee, & Gershoff, 2016). And harsher forms of physical punishment are associated with a range of negative outcomes, including mental health problems, impaired parent–child relationships, and delayed cognitive development (Gershoff, 2013). Because physical punishment is so harmful to children, many countries around the world (e.g., Costa Rica, the Netherlands, New Zealand, Spain) have banned it altogether (Global Initiative to End All Corporal Punishment of Children, 2011).

One method combines the best features of punishment while avoiding its shortcomings. *In* time-out, *a child who misbehaves must briefly sit alone in a quiet, unstimulating location.* Some parents have children sit alone in a bathroom; other parents have children sit in a corner of a room. Time-out is punishing because it interrupts the child's ongoing activity and isolates the child from other family members, toys, books, and generally all forms of rewarding stimulation.

A time-out period usually lasts just a few minutes, which helps parents use the method consistently. During time-out, both parent and child typically calm down. When time-out is over, a parent explains to the child why the punished behavior is objectionable and what the child should do instead. "Reasoning" like this—even with preschool children—is effective

Simon Winnall/Taxi/Getty Images

because it emphasizes why a parent punished initially and how punishment can be avoided in the future.

These techniques can be taught to parents. Many meta-analyses document the effectiveness of programs that teach parenting skills (e.g., using positive reinforcement and using nonphysical punishment consistently), that promote good communication within families, and that make parents feel confident in their ability to be good parents. These kinds of intervention programs make parents feel more satisfied with their parenting, lead them to parent more effectively, and reduce children's behavior problems (Sanders, 2014; Sandler et al., 2015). Thus, although research on genetics shows that the path to good parenting may be easier for some people, most adults can master the skills that foster children's development.

An effective form of punishment is time-out, in which children sit alone briefly.

Influences of the Marital System

When Derek returned from 7-Eleven with a six-pack of beer and chips instead of diapers and baby food, Anita exploded. "How could you! I used the last diaper an hour ago!" Huddled in the corner of the kitchen, their son Randy watched yet another episode in the daily soap opera that featured Derek and Anita.

Although Derek and Anita aren't arguing about Randy—in fact, they're so wrapped up in their conflict that they forget he's in the room—it's easy to imagine that such chronic parental conflict is harmful for children. When parents are constantly in conflict, children and adolescents often become anxious, withdrawn, and aggressive and are more prone to chronic diseases and to be abusive in their own romantic relationships (Miller & Chen, 2010; Narayan, Englund, & Egeland, 2013; Rhoades, 2008).

Parental conflict affects children's development through three distinct mechanisms. First, seeing parents fight jeopardizes a child's feeling that the family is stable and secure, making a child feel anxious, frightened, and sad (Cummings et al., 2012; Davies et al., 2016). Second, chronic conflict between parents often spills over into the parent–child relationship. When a wife is unhappy with her husband, this often leads her to be unhappy with her children as well (Kouros et al., 2014). Third, when parents invest time and energy fighting with each other, they're often too tired or too preoccupied to invest themselves in high-quality parenting (Katz & Woodin, 2002).

Of course, all long-term relationships experience conflict at some point. Does this mean that all children bear at least some scars? Not necessarily. Many parents resolve conflicts in a manner that's constructive instead of destructive. For example, suppose one parent believes that his child should attend a summer camp but the other parent believes it's too expensive and not worthwhile because the child attended the previous summer. Instead of shouting and name calling (e.g., "You're always so cheap!"), some parents seek mutually acceptable solutions: The child could attend the camp if she earns money to cover part of the cost, or the child could attend a different, less expensive camp. When disagreements are routinely resolved this way, children respond positively to conflict, apparently because they believe their family is cohesive and can withstand problems (Bergman, Cummings, & Warmuth, 2016). And youth exposed to this sort of constructive approach rely on it when solving conflicts in their peer and romantic relationships (Miga, Gdula, & Allen, 2012).

The extent and resolution of conflict is an obvious way in which the parental system affects children, but it's not the only way. Another influence concerns parents' effectiveness as a parenting team. Parenting is far less effective when each parent tries to "go it alone" instead of working with the other to achieve shared goals using methods they both accept. When parents don't work together, when they compete, or when they limit each other's access to their children, problems can result; for example, children can become withdrawn (McHale et al., 2002; Scrimgeour et al., 2013).

So far, we've seen that to understand parents' impact on children's development, we need to consider the nature of the marital relationship as well as parenting style and specific parenting behaviors (e.g., use of feedback). In addition, Figure 7.1 reminds us that forces outside the family can influence parenting and children's development. To illustrate, let's consider work-related influences. One such influence is a parent's job security: When children believe that their parents may lose their jobs, children's well-being suffers—they're more likely to be sad or anxious and they're less likely to believe they can succeed—and their grades in school often go down. Children and adolescents lose self-esteem and find it difficult to concentrate in school when their parents become unemployed or, for that matter, when they worry that their parents may become unemployed (Mauno, Cheng, & Lim, 2017).

Another well-known factor is work-related stress. Not surprisingly, when men and women lead stressful lives at work, they parent less effectively. Some frazzled parents withdraw from family interactions; they seem detached and uninterested, which makes children anxious and upset. Others are less warm and less consistent in their parenting (Cooklin, et al., 2016; Crouter & Bumpus, 2001).

Thus, a person's work life can profoundly affect children and adolescents by changing the parenting they experience. For now, another way to view family systems in action is by switching perspectives to see how children affect parenting behavior.

Children's Contributions: Reciprocal Influence

At the beginning of this chapter, we emphasized that the family is a dynamic, interactive system with parents and children influencing each other. In fact, children begin at birth to influence the way their parents treat them. Let's look at two characteristics of children that contribute to this influence.

Age. Parenting changes as children grow. The same parenting that works well with infants and toddlers is inappropriate for adolescents. These age-related changes in parenting are evident in the two basic dimensions of parental behavior: warmth and control. Warmth is beneficial throughout development because toddlers and teens alike enjoy knowing that others care about them. But the manifestation of parental affection changes, becoming more reserved as children develop. The enthusiastic hugging and kissing that delights toddlers embarrasses adolescents.

Parental control also changes as children develop. As children develop cognitively and are better able to make their own decisions, parents gradually relinquish control and expect children to be responsible for themselves. As children enter adolescence, they believe that parents have less authority to make decisions for them, especially in the personal domain (Darling, Cumsille, & Martínez, 2008). Parents do relinquish control—although sometimes not as rapidly as adolescents want them to—and increases in decision-making autonomy are associated with greater adolescent well-being (Eagleton, Williams, & Merten, 2016; Wray-Lake, Crouter, & McHale, 2010).

Temperament and Behavior. A child's temperament can have a powerful effect on parental behavior. To illustrate the reciprocal influence of parents and children, imagine two children with different temperaments as they respond to a parent's authoritative style. The first child has an "easy" temperament; she readily complies with parental requests and responds well to family discussions about parental expectations. But suppose the second child has a "difficult" temperament and complies reluctantly or sometimes not at all. Over time, the parent becomes more controlling and less affectionate. The child in turn complies even less in the future, leading the parent to adopt an authoritarian parenting style (Brody et al., 2017).

As this example illustrates, parenting behaviors and styles often evolve as a consequence of the child's behavior. With a moderately active young child who is eager to please adults, a parent may discover that a modest amount of control is adequate. But for a very active child who is not as eager to please, a parent may need to be more controlling and directive. Influence is reciprocal: Children's behavior helps determine how parents treat them, and the resulting parental behavior influences children's behavior, which in turn causes parents to change their behavior again (Choe, Olson, & Sameroff, 2013; Schermerhorn, Chow, & Cummings, 2010).

As time goes by, these reciprocal influences lead many families to adopt routine ways of interacting with each other. Some families end up functioning smoothly: Parents and children cooperate, anticipate each other's needs, and are generally happy. Unfortunately, other families end up troubled: Disagreements are common, parents spend much time trying unsuccessfully to control their defiant children, and everyone is often angry and upset. Still others are characterized by disengagement: Parents withdraw from each other and are not available to their children (Sturge-Apple, Davies, & Cummings, 2010). These troubled families do not fare well in the long, but they can be helped with therapy that improves a family's communication and problem-solving skills (Liddle, 2016).

When children respond defiantly to discipline, parents often resort to harsher discipline in the future.

Although parent–child relationships are central to human development, other relationships within the family are also influential. For many children, relationships with siblings are very important, as we'll see in the next few pages.

Siblings

Most children—about 85% in the United States—grow up with brothers and sisters. Sibling relationships are complicated from the beginning. Expectant parents typically are excited by the prospect of another child, and their enthusiasm is contagious: Their children, too, eagerly await the arrival of the newest family member. However, the baby's arrival prompts varied responses: Some children are distressed, sad, and less responsive to parents, responses that are more common with younger children (Volling, 2012). Parents can minimize their older children's distress by remaining attentive to their needs (Howe & Ross, 1990).

Many older siblings enjoy helping their parents take care of newborns. Older children play with, console, or feed the baby or change the baby's diapers. In middle-class Western families, such caregiving often occurs in the context of play, with parents nearby. But in many developing nations, children—particularly girls—play an important role in providing care for their younger siblings (Zukow-Goldring, 2002). As the infant grows, interactions between siblings become more frequent and more complicated. For example, toddlers tend to talk more to parents than to older siblings. But by the time the younger sibling is 4 years old, the situation is reversed: Now young siblings talk more to older siblings than to their mother (Brown & Dunn, 1996). Older siblings become a source of care and comfort for younger siblings when they are distressed or upset (Gass, Jenkins, & Dunn, 2007; Kim et al., 2007).

In many cultures, older siblings regularly provide care for younger siblings.

Older siblings also serve as teachers for their younger siblings, teaching them to play games or to cook simple foods (Maynard, 2002). Finally, when older children do well in school and are popular with peers, younger siblings often follow suit (Brody et al., 2003).

As time goes by, some siblings grow close, becoming best friends in ways that nonsiblings can never be. Other siblings constantly argue, compete, and, overall, do not get along with each other. The basic pattern of sibling interaction seems to be established early in development and remains fairly stable (Kramer, 2010). In general, siblings who get along as preschoolers continue to get along as young adolescents, and siblings who quarrel as preschoolers often quarrel as young adolescents (Dunn, Slomkowski, & Beardsall, 1994).

Getting along with siblings makes growing up easier, for children and parents alike. But there are also longer-term effects of the quality of sibling relationship on children's development (McHale, Updegraff, & Whiteman, 2012). When siblings have high-quality relationships, they have better relationships with peers and better well-being overall. Unfortunately, the converse is also true: when siblings have low-quality relationships, they often behave aggressively, bully their peers, and are prone to anxiety and depression (Dirks et al., 2015). Apparently children take the social-interaction skills developed with siblings and apply them with peers, a strategy that's productive with the effective social skills learned in high-quality sibling relationships but not with the antagonistic, coercive skills learned in low-quality relationships.

Why are some sibling relationships so filled with love and respect while others are dominated by jealousy and resentment? First, children's sex and temperament matter. Sibling relations are more likely to be warm and harmonious when siblings are the same sex (Dunn & Kendrick, 1981) and when neither sibling is too emotional (Brody, Stoneman, & McCoy, 1994). Age is also important: Sibling relationships generally improve as the younger child approaches adolescence because siblings begin to perceive one another as equals (Kim et al., 2006; McHale et al., 2013).

Parents contribute to the quality of sibling relationships, both directly and indirectly (Brody, 1998). The direct influence stems from parents' treatment. Siblings more often get along when they believe that parents have no "favorites," but treat all siblings fairly (McGuire & Shanahan, 2010). When parents lavishly praise one child's accomplishments while ignoring another's, children notice the difference, and their sibling relationship suffers (Updegraff, Thayer, et al., 2005).

This doesn't mean that parents must treat all their children the same. Children understand that parents should treat their kids differently—based on their age or personal needs. Only when differential treatment is not justified do sibling relationships deteriorate (Kowal & Kramer, 1997). In fact, during adolescence, siblings get along better when each has a unique, well-defined relationship with parents (Feinberg et al., 2003).

The indirect influence of parents on sibling relationships stems from the quality of the parents' relationship with each other: A warm, harmonious relationship between parents fosters positive sibling relationships. Conflict between parents is associated with conflict between siblings, although intense marital conflict sometimes leads siblings to become closer, as they support each other emotionally (McHale, Updegraff, & Whiteman, 2013).

Many of the features associated with high-quality sibling relationships, such as the sex of the siblings, are common across different ethnic groups. But some unique features also emerge. For example, in a study of African American families, sibling relations were more positive when children had a stronger ethnic identity (McHale et al., 2007). And a study of Mexican American families found that siblings feel closer and spend more time together when siblings have a strong commitment to their family—that is, they felt obligated to their family and viewed it as an important source of support (Updegraff, McHale, et al., 2005).

In the pursuit of family harmony (what many parents call "peace and quiet"), parents can influence some of the factors affecting sibling relationships but not others. Parents *can* help reduce friction between siblings by being equally affectionate, responsive, and caring to all of their children and by caring for one another. At the same time, parents must realize that some dissension is natural in families, especially those with young boys and girls. Children's different interests lead to conflicts that youngsters cannot resolve because their social skills are limited.

Adopted Children

The U.S. government doesn't keep official statistics on the number of adopted children, but the best estimate is that 2% to 4% of U.S. children are adopted. The most common form of adoption is for a foster parent or relative to adopt children who are in foster care because their birth families mistreated them. About 50,000 children are adopted annually in this manner, typically at about 6 or 7 years of age. Also common is for children to be adopted through private agencies, most often because young parents believe they cannot provide adequately for the child. Roughly 14,000 children are adopted annually in this way, usually as infants. Finally, about 10,000 children are adopted annually from other countries, such as China and Ethiopia. These adoptions involve infants and preschool children (Grotevant & McDermott, 2014).

Adopted children often experience adversity before being adopted. For example, children adopted from foster care have often experienced maltreatment that led them to be placed in foster care; many children adopted internationally were abandoned and lived in institutions prior to adoption. These circumstances aren't optimal for children's development, so

Think About It

Calvin, age 8, and his younger sister, Hope, argue over just about everything and constantly compete for their parents' attention. Teenage sisters Melissa and Caroline love doing everything together and enjoy sharing clothes and secrets about their teen romances. Why might Calvin and Hope get along so poorly while Melissa and Caroline get along so well?

it's not surprising that adopted children are at risk for many problems, including antisocial and aggressive behavior, depression and anxiety, and learning problems (Grotevant & McDermott, 2014). However, outcomes are varied. Most adopted children develop within the typical range. Problems are most likely when children are adopted after infancy and when their care before adoption was poor (e.g., they were institutionalized or lived in a series of foster homes). For example, the fall of the Ceaușescu regime in Romania in 1989 revealed hundreds of thousands of children living in orphanages under incredibly primitive conditions. Beginning in the 1990s, many of these children were adopted internationally. Some have shown remarkable catch-up growth, but many show multiple impairments, such as delayed cognitive development and disordered attachment (Kreppner et al., 2007).

Thus, although adoption per se is not a fundamental developmental challenge for most children, quality of life before adoption certainly places some adopted children at risk. And these children often fare well when they receive excellent care after adoption (Grotevant & McDermott, 2014).

In recent years, adopted children (and their adoptive families) are more likely to communicate with the children's birth family, an arrangement known as an open adoption. Open adoptions come in any forms. Contact can be face-to-face or via social media and can be occasional or frequent. Research on the impact of open adoption suggests that adoptees who are satisfied with the amount of contact with their birth families are at less risk for externalizing disorders. In addition, contact with birth families can lead adoptees and their adoptive families to discuss adoption, and these discussions help adopted teens to construct an identity as an adoptee (Grotevant et al., 2013).

open adoption
An adoption in which adopted children (and their adoptive families) communicate with the children's birth family.

Impact of Birth Order

First-born children are often "guinea pigs" for most parents, who have much enthusiasm but little practical experience rearing children. Parents typically have high expectations for their first-borns and are both more affectionate and more punitive toward them. As more children arrive, most parents become more adept at their roles, having learned "the tricks of the trade" from earlier children. With later-born children, parents are more relaxed in their discipline and less likely to punish children for not doing well in school (Hotz & Pantano, 2013).

The different approaches that parents use with their first- and later-born children help explain differences that are commonly observed between these children. First-born children generally have higher scores on intelligence tests, are more likely to go to college,

Contrary to folklore, only children are often smarter and more mature than children with siblings.

and are more conscientious. They are also more willing to conform to parents' and adults' requests. In contrast, perhaps because later-born children are less concerned about pleasing parents and adults, they are more outgoing, more popular with their peers, more innovative, and more likely to task risks (Beck, Burnet, & Vosper, 2006; Bjerkedal et al., 2007; Sulloway & Zweigenhaft, 2010).

What about only children? According to conventional wisdom, parents dote on "onlies," who therefore become selfish and egotistical. Is the folklore correct? No. Only children are more likely to succeed in school than are other children and to have higher levels of intelligence and self-esteem but don't differ in popularity, adjustment, and personality (Falbo, 2012; Falbo & Polit, 1986).

The possibility that only children are selfish has been a concern in China, where only children are common because of governmental efforts to limit population growth. However, many studies have compared only and non-only children in China and most find no differences. One of the few differences is that Chinese only children, like Western only children, are more successful in school (Falbo, 2012; Liu, Lin, & Chen, 2010). Thus, contrary to the popular stereotype, only children are much like children who grow up with siblings.

Whether U.S. children grow up with siblings or as "onlies," they are more likely than children in other countries to have their family relationships disrupted by divorce. What is the impact of divorce on children and adolescents?

Divorce and Remarriage

Today, many North American children experience their parents' divorce. These children often fare poorly in school achievement, conduct, adjustment, self-concept, and parent–child relations when compared with children from intact families. As adults, children of divorce are more likely to experience conflict in their own marriages, to become divorced themselves, and to become depressed (Lansford, 2009). These findings don't mean that children of divorce are destined to be unhappy and unsuccessful during childhood and to have unhappy, conflict-ridden marriages that inevitably lead to divorce, but children of divorce are at greater risk for these outcomes.

joint custody
Custody agreement in which both parents retain legal custody of their children following divorce.

The first year following a divorce is often rocky for parents and children alike. But beginning in the second year, most children begin to adjust to their new circumstances, especially when their parents get along (Sweeper, 2012). In joint custody, *both parents retain legal custody of the children*. Children benefit from joint custody—they adjust better behaviorally and socially, especially when they spend approximately equal time with both parents (Baude, Pearson, & Drapeau, 2016). When joint custody is not an option, mothers have traditionally been awarded custody; when this happens, children benefit when fathers remain involved in parenting, particularly when they get along with their ex-wives (Modecki et al., 2015).

Which Children Are Most Affected by Divorce?

One striking finding of research on the impact of divorce is that although many children suffer in the short term, only a few children suffer serious harm in the longer term. Researchers have identified several features that predict how well children adjust in the longer term. Many features concern parents. Children fare best when custodial and noncustodial parents don't experience psychological problems themselves, when they get along with each other, and when they stay involved with their children and parent effectively (Amato, 2010; Tabor, 2016). In addition, children are less likely to suffer harm from divorce when they are temperamentally easy, are smart, don't consistently interpret life events negatively, and actively cope with problems brought on by divorce (Lansford, 2009; Weaver & Schofield, 2015).

Parents can reduce divorce-related stress and help children adjust to their new life circumstances. Together, parents should explain to their children what divorce means and what their children can expect to happen. They should reassure children that they will always love them and always be their parents; parents must back up these words with actions by remaining involved in their children's lives. Finally, parents must expect that their children will sometimes be angry or sad about the divorce, and they should encourage children to discuss these feelings with them.

To help children deal with divorce, parents should *not* compete with each other for their children's love and attention. Parents should neither take out their anger with each other on their children nor criticize their ex-spouse in front of them. Finally, parents should not ask children to mediate disputes; parents should work out problems without putting children in the middle.

Following all these rules consistently is difficult. After all, divorce is stressful and painful for adults, too. Fortunately, effective programs are available to help parents and children adjust to life following divorce (Vélez, Wolchik, & Sandler, 2014). These programs aim to improve children's behavioral and social skills and allow children to express feelings related to divorce; parents learn how to improve relationships with their children and how to discipline them.

Blended Families

Following divorce, most children live in a single-parent household for about five years. However, most men and women eventually remarry (Sweeney, 2010). *The resulting unit, consisting of a biological parent, a stepparent, and children, is known as a* blended family. (Other terms for this family configuration are "remarried family" and "reconstituted family.") The most common form of blended family is a mother, her children, and a stepfather. Children can thrive in a blended family: Those who report being close to their mother and their stepfather are well-adjusted (Amato, King, & Thorsen, 2016).

blended family
Family consisting of a biological parent, a stepparent, and children.

Adjusting to life in a blended family is more difficult when a stepfather brings his own biological children to the mix. In such families, parents sometimes favor their biological children over their stepchildren—they're more involved with and warmer toward their biological children. Such preferential treatment usually leads to conflict and unhappiness (Dunn & Davies, 2001; Sweeney, 2010).

The best strategy for stepfathers is to be interested in their new stepchildren but to avoid encroaching on established relationships. Newly remarried mothers must be careful that their enthusiasm for their new spouse does not come at the expense of spending time with and showing affection for their children. Both parents and children need to have realistic expectations. The blended family can be successful, but it takes effort because of the complicated relationships, conflicting loyalties, and jealousies that usually exist (Sweeney, 2010; White & Gilbreth, 2001).

Unfortunately, second marriages are slightly more likely than first marriages to end in divorce, particularly when stepchildren are involved (Teachman, 2008). This means that many children relive the trauma of divorce. Fortunately, programs are available to help members of blended families adjust to their new roles (Bullard et al., 2010). Such programs emphasize effective parenting (described on page 231) and, in particular, ways of dealing with behavior problems that children often display with stepparents. These programs result in fewer behavior problems and greater marital satisfaction.

Parent–Child Relationships Gone Awry: Child Maltreatment

The first time that 7-year-old Max came to school with bruises on his face, he explained to his teacher that he had fallen down the basement steps. When Max had similar bruises a few weeks later, his teacher spoke with the school principal, who contacted local authorities. It turned out that Max's mother thrashed him with a paddle for even minor misconduct; for serious transgressions, she beat Max and made him sleep alone in a dark, unheated basement.

Unfortunately, cases like Max's occur far too often in modern America. Maltreatment comes in many forms. The two that often come to mind first are physical abuse involving assault that leads to injuries and sexual abuse involving fondling, intercourse, or other sexual behaviors. Another form of maltreatment is neglect—not

Following divorce, most men and women remarry, creating a blended family.

giving children adequate food, clothing, or medical care. And children can also be harmed by psychological abuse—ridicule, rejection, and humiliation (Wicks-Nelson & Israel, 2015).

The frequency of these various forms of child maltreatment is difficult to estimate because so many cases go unreported. According to the U.S. Department of Health and Human Services (2016), nearly 700,000 children annually suffer maltreatment or neglect. About 75% are neglected, about 17% are abused physically, about 8% are abused sexually, and 6% are maltreated psychologically. (The percentages sum to more than 100 because some children experience more than one form of abuse.)

Who Are the Abusing Parents?

Why would a parent abuse a child? Most abusing parents do not suffer from any specific mental or psychological disorder. Instead, a host of factors put some children at risk for abuse and protect others; the number and combination of factors determine whether the child is a likely target for abuse (Cicchetti & Toth, 2006). Let's look at three of the most important factors: those associated with the cultural context, those associated with parents, and those associated with children themselves.

The most general category of contributing factors is that dealing with cultural values and the social conditions in which parents rear their children. Many countries in Europe and Asia have strong cultural prohibitions against physical punishment. In many countries, including Austria, Croatia, Germany, Israel, and Sweden, spanking is against the law and would be viewed in much the same way we would view American parents who punished their children by not feeding them for a few days. Nevertheless, in the United States, physical punishment is common. Condoning physical punishment in this manner opens the door for child maltreatment.

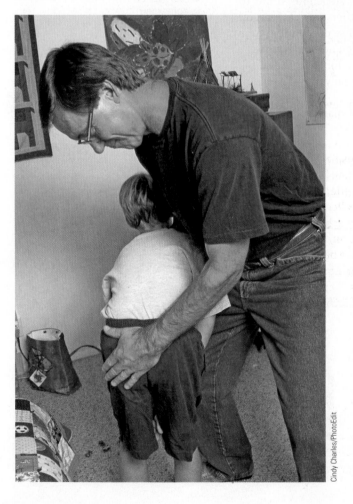

Child abuse is more common in societies that condone physical punishment such as spanking.

What social conditions seem to foster maltreatment? Poverty is one. Maltreatment is more common among children living in poverty, in part because lack of money increases the stress of daily life, and this means that parents are more likely to punish their children physically instead of making the extra effort to reason with them (Bywaters et al., 2016). Social isolation is a second force. Abuse is more likely when families are socially isolated from other relatives or neighbors because living in isolation deprives children of adults who could protect them and deprives parents of social support that would help them better deal with life's stresses (Coulton et al., 2007).

Cultural factors clearly contribute to child abuse, but they are only part of the puzzle. Although maltreatment is more common among families living in poverty, it does not occur in a majority of these families and it occurs in middle- and upper-class families, too. Consequently, we need to look for additional factors to explain why abuse occurs in some families but not in others.

Child development researchers have identified several characteristics of parents that lead them to abuse their children. First, parents who maltreat their children often were maltreated themselves, which may lead them to believe that abuse is a normal part of childhood. This does not mean that abused children inevitably become abusing parents—only about one-third do. But a history of child abuse places adults at risk for mistreating their own children (Widom, Czaja, & DuMont, 2015). Second, parents who mistreat their children often use ineffective parenting techniques (e.g., inconsistent discipline), have such unrealistic expectations that their children can never meet them, and often believe they are powerless to control their children. For example, when abusive parents do not get along with their children, they often chalk this up to factors out of their control, such as children having a difficult temperament or being tired that day; they're less likely to think their own behavior contributed to unpleasant interactions. Third, in families where abuse occurs, the couple's interactions are often unpredictable, unsupportive, and unsatisfying for both husbands and wives. This marital discord makes life more stressful and makes it more difficult for parents to invest effort in child rearing.

To place the last few pieces in the puzzle, we must look at the abused children themselves. Children may inadvertently, through their behavior, contribute to their own abuse. In fact, infants and preschoolers are more often abused than older children are, probably because they are less able to regulate aversive behaviors that may elicit abuse (Sidebotham, Heron, & the ALSPAC Study Team, 2003). You've probably heard stories about a parent who shakes a baby to death because the baby wouldn't stop crying. Because younger children are more likely to cry or whine excessively—behaviors that irritate all parents sooner or later—they are more likely to be the targets of abuse.

For much the same reason, children who are frequently ill or who are disabled are more often abused (Jones et al., 2012). When children are sick or disabled, they often need extra attention and special care (which means additional expense), conditions that increase stress in a family and put children at risk for maltreatment. And, just as Cinderella's stepmother doted on her biological children but abused Cinderella, stepchildren are more prone to abuse and neglect than biological children (Archer, 2013). Adults are less invested emotionally in their stepchildren, and this lack of emotional investment leaves stepchildren more vulnerable.

Thus, cultural, parental, and child factors all contribute to child maltreatment. Any single factor usually will not result in abuse. Maltreatment becomes more likely when cultures condone physical punishment, parents lack effective skills for dealing with children, and a child's behavior is frequently aversive.

Effects of Abuse on Children

The prognosis for youngsters like Max is not very good. Some, of course, suffer permanent physical damage. Even when there is no lasting physical damage, children's social and emotional development is often disrupted. They tend to have poor relationships with peers, either because they withdraw from interactions or because they are too aggressive (Cicchetti, 2016). Their cognitive development and academic performance are also disturbed. Abused youngsters often don't do well in school, they don't regulate their emotions well, they don't recognize others' emotions accurately, and they are at risk for depression (Cyr & Alink, 2017). As adults, children who were abused are at risk for psychiatric disorders (Rehan et al., 2017). In short, when children are maltreated, the effects are usually widespread and long-lasting.

Resilience

Although the overall picture is bleak, some children are remarkably resilient to the impact of abuse. One factor that protects children is their ego resilience, *which denotes children's ability to respond adaptively and resourcefully to new situations.* The effects of abuse tend to be smaller when children are flexible in responding to novel and challenging social situations (Cicchetti, 2013). Another protective factor is being engaged in school: When maltreated children are cognitively engaged in school—they pay attention, complete tasks, and are well organized—they are less prone to antisocial and aggressive behavior (Pears et al., 2013). A final protective factor is a positive mother–child relationship: When children have a positive representation of their mother—they describe her as "kind" and "loving," for example—they suffer relatively few symptoms of maltreatment (Cicchetti, 2013).

Preventing Abuse and Maltreatment

The complexity of child abuse dashes any hopes for a simple solution (Kelly, 2011). Because maltreatment is more apt to occur when several contributing factors are present, eradicating child maltreatment requires many different approaches.

American attitudes toward "acceptable" levels of punishment and poverty would have to change. American children will be abused as long as physical punishment is considered acceptable and effective and as long as poverty-stricken families live in chronic stress from trying to provide food and shelter. Parents also need counseling and training in parenting skills. Abuse will continue as long as parents remain ignorant of effective methods of parenting and discipline.

Think About It

Kevin has never physically abused his 10-year-old son, Alex, but he constantly torments Alex emotionally. For example, when Alex got an F on a spelling test, Kevin screamed, "I skipped Monday Night Football just to help you, but you still flunked. You're such a dummy." When Alex began to cry, Kevin taunted, "Look at Alex, crying like a baby." These interactions occur nearly every day. What are the likely effects of such repeated episodes of emotional abuse?

ego resilience

Person's ability to respond adaptively and resourcefully to new situations.

It would be naïve to expect all these changes to occur overnight. However, by focusing on some of the more manageable factors, the risk of maltreatment can be reduced. Social supports help. When parents know that they can turn to other helpful adults for advice and reassurance, they better manage the stresses of child rearing that might otherwise lead to abuse. Families can also be taught more effective ways of coping with situations that might otherwise trigger abuse (Wicks-Nelson & Israel, 2015). Through role-playing sessions, parents can learn the benefits of authoritative parenting and effective ways of using feedback and modeling to regulate children's behavior.

Providing social supports and teaching effective parenting skills are typically done when maltreatment and abuse have already occurred. Of course, preventing maltreatment in the first place is more desirable and more cost-effective. For prevention, one useful tool is familiar: early childhood intervention programs. Maltreatment and abuse can be reduced when children participate in preschool programs like Head Start (Zhai, Waldfogel, & Brooks-Gunn, 2013). When children attend these programs, their parents become more committed to their children's education. This leads their children to be more successful in school, reducing a source of stress and enhancing parents' confidence in their child-rearing skills, thereby reducing the risks of maltreatment.

Another successful approach focuses specifically on parenting skills in families where children are at risk for maltreatment. In this approach, parents learn how to build warm and positive relationships with their children, to have reasonable expectations for their children, and to use more effective disciplinary practices. When parents of at-risk children participate in programs such as these, they report less stress, their behavior with their children becomes more positive (more praise and fewer commands), and, critically, suspected abuse is reduced (Thomas & Zimmer-Gembeck, 2011).

Finally, we need to remember that most parents who have mistreated their children need our help. Although we must not tolerate child maltreatment, most of these parents and children are attached to each other; maltreatment is typically a consequence of ignorance and burden, not malice.

TEST YOURSELF 7.1

Recall

1. According to the systems approach, the family consists of interacting elements that influence each other, and the family itself is _____.

2. A(n) _____.parental style combines high control with low involvement.

3. Most children seem to benefit when parents rely on a(n) _____ style.

4. Parental behaviors that influence children include direct instruction, modeling (learning through observation), and _____.

5. Some parents do not make a good team: they don't work together, they compete with each other for their children's attention, and _____.

6. Compared with first-born children, later-born children are more outgoing, popular, innovative, and are more likely _____.

7. Following divorce, children often adjust better behaviorally and socially when they spend _____.

8. Children are harmed less from divorce when they are temperamentally easy, are smart, don't interpret life events negatively, and _____.

9. Children are more likely to be abused when they are younger, when they are stepchildren, and when they are _____.

Interpret

- How can child abuse be explained in terms of the biological, psychological, and sociocultural forces in the biopsychosocial framework?

Apply

- Imagine a family in which Mom and Dad both work full-time outside the home. Mom's employer wants her to take a new position in a distant small town. Mom is tempted because the position represents a promotion with more responsibility and higher pay. However, because the town is so small, Dad wouldn't be able to get a job comparable to the one he has now, which he likes. Based on the family systems theory shown in Figure 7.1, how might the move affect the couple's 10-year-old daughter and 4-year-old son?

Check your answers to the Recall Questions at the end of the chapter.

7.2 Peers

LEARNING OBJECTIVES

- What are the benefits of friendship?
- What are the important features of groups of children and adolescents? How do these groups influence individuals?
- Why are some children more popular than others? What are the causes and consequences of being rejected?

- What are some effects of childhood aggression? Why are some children chronic victims of aggression?

Only 36 hours had passed since the campers arrived at Crab Orchard Summer Camp. Nevertheless, groups had already formed spontaneously based on the campers' main interests: arts and crafts, hiking, and swimming. Within each group, leaders and followers had already emerged. This happens every year, but the staff is always astonished at how quickly a "social network" emerges at camp.

The groups that form at summer camps—as well as in schools and neighborhoods—represent one of the more complex forms of peer relationships: Many children are involved, and there are multiple relationships. We'll examine these kinds of interactions later in this section. Let's start by looking at a simpler social relationship, friendship.

Friendships

Over time, children develop special relationships with some peers. Friendship *is a voluntary relationship between two people involving mutual liking.* By age 4 or 5, most children claim to have a "best friend." If you ask them how they can tell a child is their best friend, their response will probably resemble 5-year-old Katelyn's:

Interviewer:	Why is Heidi your best friend?
Katelyn:	Because she plays with me. And she's nice to me.
Interviewer:	Are there any other reasons?
Katelyn:	Yeah, Heidi lets me play with her dolls.

friendship
Voluntary relationship between two people involving mutual liking.

Thus, the key elements of friendship for younger children are that children like each other and enjoy playing together.

As children develop, their friendships become more complex. For older elementary school children (ages 8 to 11), mutual liking and shared activities are joined by features that are more psychological in nature: trust and assistance. At this age, children expect that they can depend on their friends—their friends will be nice to them, will keep their promises, and won't say mean things about them to others. Children also expect friends to step forward in times of need: A friend should willingly help with homework or willingly share a snack.

Adolescence adds another layer of complexity to friendships. Mutual liking, common interests, and trust remain. New to adolescence is intimacy—friends now confide in one another, sharing personal thoughts and feelings. Teenagers reveal their excitement over a new romance or disappointment at not being cast in a school musical. Intimacy is more common in friendships among girls, who are more likely than boys to have one exclusive "best friend" (Markovits, Benenson, & Dolenszky, 2001). Because intimacy is at the core of their friendships, girls are also more likely to be concerned about the faithfulness of their friends and worry about being rejected (Rose & Asher, 2017).

The emergence of intimacy in adolescent friendships means that friends also come to be seen as sources of social and emotional support. Elementary school children generally rely on close family members—parents, siblings, and grandparents—when they need help or are upset. Adolescents sometimes rely on adults, but they also turn to friends for support (van Rijsweijk et al., 2016).

Friends tend to be alike in age, race, and sex.

Hand in hand with the emphasis on intimacy is loyalty. Having confided in friends, adolescents expect friends to stick with them through good and bad times. If a friend is disloyal, adolescents are afraid that they may be humiliated because their intimate thoughts and feelings will become known to a much broader circle of people (Berndt & Perry, 1990).

Who Are Friends?

Most friends are alike in age, gender, and race (Hamm, 2000; Mehta & Strough, 2009). Because friends are supposed to treat each other as equals, friendships are rare between an older, more experienced child and a younger, less experienced child. Because children typically play with same-sex peers, boys and girls rarely become friends.

Friendships are more common between children and adolescents from the same race or ethnic group than between those from different groups, reflecting segregation in American society. Friendships among children of different groups are more common in schools when a child's school is ethnically diverse. Such friendships are valuable: Children from majority groups typically form more positive attitudes toward a minority group following a friendship with a youth from that group (Turner & Cameron, 2016). And children in cross-group friendships are less often targets of relational aggression (Kawabata & Crick, 2011).

Besides being alike in age, sex, and race, friends also tend to be alike in popularity: Highly popular youth befriend popular peers and avoid friendships with less popular peers (Dijkstra, Cillessen, & Borch, 2013). In addition, friends have similar attitudes toward school, recreation, and problem behaviors like breaking rules and using drugs. Children and adolescents befriend others who are similar to them and, as time passes, friends become more similar in their attitudes and values (Franken et al., 2016; Shin & Ryan, 2014). Nevertheless, friends are not photocopies of each other; friends are less similar, for example, than spouses or dizygotic twins (Rushton & Bons, 2005).

Although children's friendships are overwhelmingly with members of their own sex, some children have friendships with opposite-sex children. Children with same- *and* opposite-sex friendships tend to be very well-adjusted, whereas children with only opposite-sex friendships tend to be unpopular, to be less competent academically and socially, and to have lower self-esteem. Children with both same- and opposite-sex friends are so popular that both boys and girls are eager to be their friends. In contrast, children with only opposite-sex friendships are socially unskilled, unpopular youngsters who are rejected by their same-sex peers and form friendships with opposite-sex children as a last resort (Bukowski, Sippola, & Hoza, 1999).

Quality and Consequences of Friendships

You probably remember some childhood friendships that were long-lasting and satisfying as well as others that rapidly wore thin and soon dissolved. What accounts for these differences in the quality and longevity of friendships? Sometimes friendships are brief because children have the skills to create friendships—they know funny stories, they kid around, they know good gossip—but lack the skills to sustain those friendships—they can't keep secrets, are too bossy, or are too emotional (Blair et al., 2014; Jiao, 1999; Parker & Seal, 1996). Sometimes friendships end because when conflicts arise, children are more concerned about their own interests and are unwilling to compromise or negotiate (Glick & Rose, 2011; Rose & Asher, 1999). And sometimes friendships end when children discover that their needs and interests aren't as similar as they initially thought (Gavin & Furman, 1996).

Long-lasting friendships are to be treasured. In fact, children benefit from having good friends (Berndt & Murphy, 2002). Compared with children who lack friends, children with good friends have higher self-esteem, are less likely to be lonely and depressed, and more often share and cooperate (Burk & Laursen, 2005; Hartup & Stevens, 1999).

Children with good friends cope better with stressful experiences, such as doing poorly on an exam or being rejected by peers (Adams, Santo, & Bukowski, 2011; McDonald et al., 2010). And they're less likely to be victimized by peers (Schwartz et al., 2000). The benefits of friendship are long-lasting as well: Children who have friends are, as adults, at less risk for depression, anxiety, and aggressive behavior (Sakyi et al., 2015).

Although children and adolescents benefit from their friends' support, there can be costs as well. *Sometimes friends spend much of their time together discussing each other's personal problems, which is known as* co-rumination. Girls do this more than boys (consistent with the fact that intimacy is more important to girls' friendships). Such co-rumination strengthens girls' friendships but also puts them at greater risk for depression and anxiety. In other words, when Avanti and Fahima spend day after day talking about their problems with parents and schoolwork, they grow closer but also more troubled (Brendgen et al., 2010; Schwartz-Mette & Rose, 2012).

There are other ways in which friendships can be hazardous. For example, when aggressive children are friends, they often encourage each other's aggressive behavior (Dishion, Poulin, & Burraston, 2001; Piehler & Dishion, 2007). Similarly, when teens engage in risky behavior (e.g., when they drink, smoke, or have sex), they often reinforce each other's risky behavior (Huang et al., 2014).

Thus, friends are one important way in which peers influence children's development. Peers also influence development through groups, the topic of the next section.

Image Source/Alamy Stock Photo

When youth have good friends, they're better able to cope with life's stresses.

co-rumination

Conversations about one's personal problems, common among adolescent girls.

Groups

At the summer camp in the vignette, new campers form groups based on common interests. Groups are just as prevalent in American schools. "Jocks," "preps," "burnouts," "druggies," "nerds," and "brains"—you may remember these or similar terms referring to groups of older children and adolescents. During late childhood and early adolescence, the peer group becomes the focal point of social relationships for youth. *The starting point is often a* clique—*a small group of children or adolescents who are friends and tend to be similar in age, sex, race, and attitudes.* Members of a clique spend time together and often dress, talk, and act alike. *A* crowd *is a larger mixed-sex group of older children or adolescents who have similar values and attitudes and are known by a common label such as "jocks" or "nerds"* (Rubin, Bukowski, & Bowker, 2015).

Crowds emerge in the transition from middle school to high school. Crowds have stereotyped identities—brains are smart kids who enjoy school—and younger adolescents gravitate to crowds that match their person identity. Initially, some crowds have more status than others. For example, jocks are often the most prestigious crowd, while burnouts are the least. However, later in high school, the status of crowds becomes less significant and the boundaries between crowds become fuzzy (Brown, 2014)

clique

Small group of friends who are similar in age, sex, and race.

crowd

Large group including many cliques that have similar attitudes and values.

Group Structure

Groups—be they in school, at a summer camp as in the vignette, or elsewhere—typically have a well-defined structure. *Often groups have a* dominance hierarchy, *which is headed by a leader to whom all other members of the group defer.* Other members know their position in the hierarchy. They yield to members who are above them in the hierarchy and assert themselves over members who are below them. A dominance hierarchy is useful in reducing conflict within groups because every member knows his or her place (Rubin et al., 2015).

dominance hierarchy

Ordering of individuals within a group in which group members with lower status defer to those with greater status.

Group leaders tend to be those who have skills that are valuable to the group: Girl Scout patrol leaders, for example, tend to be goal-oriented and to have good ideas.

What determines where members stand in the hierarchy? In children, especially boys, physical power is often the basis for the dominance hierarchy. The leader is usually the member who is the most intimidating physically (Hawley, 2016). Among girls and older boys, hierarchies are often based on individual traits that relate to the group's main function. For example, girls chosen to be patrol leaders in Girl Scouts tend to be bright and goal-oriented and to have new ideas (Edwards, 1994). These characteristics are appropriate because the primary function of patrol leaders is to help plan activities for the entire troop. Similarly, in classroom discussion groups, the leaders are often children who are outgoing and have good ideas (Li et al., 2007). Thus, leadership based on key skills is effective because it gives the greatest influence to those with the skills most important to group functioning.

Peer Influence

Groups establish norms—standards of behavior that apply to all group members—and may urge members to conform to these norms. The stereotype is that teenagers exert enormous, irresistible pressure on each other to behave antisocially. In reality, peer pressure is neither always powerful nor always evil. For example, most junior and senior high students *resist* peer pressure to behave in ways that are clearly antisocial, such as stealing (Cook, Buehler, & Henson, 2009), and such resistance increases from mid- to late adolescence (Steinberg & Monahan, 2007). And peer pressure can be positive, too. Peers often urge one another to work hard in school, to participate in school activities, and to get along with their family (Brown, 2014).

Peer pressure is *not* all-powerful. Instead, peer influence is stronger when youth are younger and more socially anxious, peers have high status or are friends; and standards for appropriate behavior are not clear-cut, as in the case of tastes in music or clothing or standards for smoking and drinking (Allen et al., 2012; Brechwald & Prinstein, 2011). Thus, when 14-year-old Aya's best friend (who's one of the most popular kids in school) gets her hair cut like Taylor Swift, Aya may go along because she's young, the peer is popular and is her friend, and standards for hairstyles are vague. But when an unpopular kid that 18-year-old Kelly barely knows suggests to her that they go to the mall and shoplift some earrings, Kelly will resist because she's older, the peer is unpopular and not a friend, and norms for shoplifting are clear.

Peers can influence behavior through other means beyond pressure. For example, a crowd provides models for how its members should look and act; members go along willingly because they want to identify with the group (Brown et al., 2008). And the mere presence of peers can prime the adolescent brain's reward system, making it particularly sensitive to rewards associated with risky behavior like driving fast or experimenting with drugs (Albert, Chein, & Steinberg, 2013).

Popularity and Rejection

Eileen is the most popular child in her fifth-grade class. Most of the other students like to play with her and to sit near her at lunch or on the school bus. Whenever the class must vote to pick a child for something special—to be class representative to the student council or to recite the class poem on Martin Luther King Day—Eileen invariably wins. In contrast, Jay is the least popular child in the class. When he sits down at the lunch table, other kids move away. When he tries to join a game of four square, others quit. Students in the class detest Jay as much as they like Eileen.

Think About It

Chapter 5 described important differences in the ways that boys and girls interact with same-sex peers. How might these differences help explain why boys' and girls' dominance hierarchies differ?

Popular and rejected children like Eileen and Jay are common. In fact, studies of popularity (Rubin et al., 2015) reveal that most children in elementary school classrooms can be placed, fairly consistently, in one of these five categories:

- **Popular children** *are liked by many classmates.*
- **Rejected children** *are disliked by many classmates.*
- **Controversial children** *are both liked and disliked by classmates.*
- **Average children** *are liked and disliked by some classmates, but without the intensity found for popular, rejected, or controversial children.*
- **Neglected children** *are ignored by classmates.*

Of these categories, we know the most about popular and rejected children. Each of these categories includes two subtypes. Most popular children are skilled academically and socially. They are good students who are usually friendly, cooperative, helpful, and funny. They are more skillful at communicating and better at integrating themselves into an ongoing conversation or play session—they "fit in" instead of "barging in." A smaller group of popular children includes physically aggressive boys who pick fights with peers and relationally aggressive girls who, like the "Plastics" in the film *Mean Girls*, thrive on manipulating social relationships. Although these youth are not particularly friendly, their antisocial behavior nevertheless garners respect from peers (Rubin et al., 2015).

Being well-liked seems straightforward: Be pleasant, friendly, and socially skilled, not obnoxious. These results hold for children in many areas of the world, including Canada, Europe, Israel, and China. However sometimes popular children have other characteristics unique to their cultural setting. For example, in Israel popular children are more likely to be assertive and direct than children in other countries (Krispin, Sternberg, & Lamb, 1992). In China, historically shy children were often popular because their restrained behavior was taken as a sign of social maturity. However, economic reforms in China in the past 25 years have resulted in greater emphasis on taking initiative and being assertive. Consequently, shy children living in urban areas that have experienced economic reform are now rejected by peers, but they remain popular in more traditional rural areas (Chen, Wang, & Cao, 2011). Evidently, good social skills are at the core of popularity in most countries, but other features are important, reflecting culturally specific values.

As for rejected children, many are overly aggressive, hyperactive, socially unskilled, and unable to regulate their emotions. These children are usually more hostile than popular aggressive children and seem to be aggressive for the sheer fun of it, which peers dislike, instead of using aggression as a means toward other ends, which peers may not like but grudgingly respect. Other rejected children are shy, withdrawn, timid, and, not surprisingly, lonely (Rubin et al., 2015).

Causes and Consequences of Rejection

No one enjoys being rejected. Not surprisingly, peer rejection is a major obstacle in children's development. Over time, rejected youngsters become less involved in classroom activities; they end up feeling lonely and disliking school. Repeated peer rejection in childhood can lead youth to drop out of school, commit juvenile offenses, and suffer from psychopathology (Rubin et al., 2015).

Peer rejection can be traced, at least in part, to direct and indirect influences of parents. The direct influence is via disciplinary practices. Harsh discipline and inconsistent discipline are associated with antisocial, aggressive behavior, paving the way for rejection (Kawabata & Crick, 2016). The indirect influence is via modeling: When parents typically respond to interpersonal conflict

popular children
Children who are liked by many classmates.

rejected children
As applied to children's popularity, children who are disliked by many classmates.

controversial children
As applied to children's popularity, children who are intensely liked or disliked by classmates.

average children
As applied to children's popularity, children who are liked and disliked by different classmates, but with relatively little intensity.

neglected children
As applied to children's popularity, children who are ignored—neither liked nor disliked—by their classmates.

Think About It

Effective parents and popular children have many characteristics in common. What are they?

Most popular children are good students and are socially skilled: they tend to be friendly and helpful with peers.

Stockbroker/MBI/Alamy Stock Photo

with intimidation or aggression, their children may imitate them, hampering the development of their social skills and making them less popular (Cummings, Goeke-Morey, & Papp, 2016).

Thus, the origins of rejection are clear: Socially awkward, aggressive children are often rejected because they rely on an aggressive interpersonal style, which can be traced to parenting. The implication is that by teaching youngsters (and their parents) more effective ways of interacting with others, we can make rejection less likely. With improved social skills, rejected children would not need to resort to antisocial behaviors that peers deplore. Training of this sort does work. Rejected children can learn skills that lead to peer acceptance and thereby avoid the long-term harm associated with being rejected (Lochman et al., 2014).

Aggressive Children and Their Victims

instrumental aggression

Aggression used to achieve an explicit goal.

hostile aggression

Unprovoked aggression that seems to have the sole goal of intimidating, harassing, or humiliating another child.

By the time toddlers are old enough to play with one another, they show aggression. For example, 1- and 2-year-olds sometimes use physical aggression to resolve their conflicts (Hay, 2017). In *instrumental aggression*, *a child uses aggression to achieve an explicit goal.* By the start of the elementary school years, another form of aggression emerges (Coie et al., 1991). *Hostile aggression is unprovoked and seems to have as its sole goal to intimidate, harass, or humiliate another child.* Hostile aggression is illustrated by a child who spontaneously says, "You're stupid!" and then kicks a classmate. A third form of aggression is relational aggression, in which children try to hurt others by undermining their social relationships (see Chapter 5). Examples include telling friends to avoid a particular classmate or spreading malicious gossip (Kawabata & Crick, 2016).

Children's tendencies to behave aggressively are stable over time, particularly among children who are highly aggressive at a young age. For example, infants who often bite or strike other people are, as preschoolers, more likely to kick or hit peers to obtain toys (Hay, 2017). And preschool children judged by their teachers to be very aggressive are, as young adults, much more likely to commit crimes (Asendorpf, Denissen, & van Aken, 2008). Finally, aggression during childhood often leads to failure in high school (e.g., dropping out, failing a grade), which leaves few options for employment (Alatupa et al., 2013). Clearly, aggression is not simply a case of playful pushing and shoving that children eventually outgrow. To the contrary, children who are highly aggressive can develop into young adults who wreak havoc.

Most school children are the targets of an occasional aggressive act—a shove or kick to gain a desired toy or a stinging insult by someone trying to save face. However, a small percentage of children are chronic targets of bullying. In both Europe and the United States, 10% to 25% of elementary school children and adolescents are chronic victims of physical attacks, name-calling, backstabbing, and similar aggressive acts (Juvonen & Graham, 2014). In recent years, some youth have been victims of electronic bullying in which they are harassed via cell phones or the Internet (Kowalski et al., 2014).

Children are likely to become chronic victims of aggression if they refuse to defend themselves.

As you can imagine, being tormented daily by peers is hard on children. When children are chronic victims of aggression, they're often lonely, anxious, and depressed; they dislike school and have low self-esteem (Rubin et al., 2015). As adults, they're prone to poor health and unsatisfying social relationships (Wolke et al., 2013). Why do some children suffer the sad fate of being victims? Some victims are aggressive themselves. These youngsters often overreact, are restless, and are easily irritated. Their peers soon learn to insult or ridicule these children, knowing that they will probably start a fight. Other victims tend to be withdrawn and submissive. Because they are unwilling or unable to defend themselves from their peers' aggression, they are usually referred to as passive victims. When attacked, they show obvious signs of distress and usually give in to their attackers, thereby rewarding the aggressive behavior. Thus, both aggressive and withdrawn submissive children end up as victims (Rubin et al., 2015).

Other factors contribute to make children victims of bullying. Children are more likely to be bullied when they are obese, depressed, disabled, or immigrants. In essence, any feature that makes children different from their peers puts them in the sights of bullies (Juvonen & Graham, 2014; Strohmeier, Kärnä, & Salmivalli, 2011). Also, bullying is more likely in classrooms that have a strong status hierarchy—everyone in the class knows which children are high status and which are low status—and when the norm is that bullying is acceptable (Saarento & Salmivalli, 2015).

Researchers have developed effective programs to combat bullying in schools. These programs work at many levels: schools build a school climate in which bullying is not condoned and victims are supported by their peers; teachers learn how to recognize bullying and how to respond when they see it; children who have been victimized learn social skills for dealing with peers and strategies for regulating their emotions; and parents of victimized children learn how to help their children and how to work with school personnel. Programs that include these elements can reduce bullying and the harmful outcomes associated with it (Bradshaw, 2015).

TEST YOURSELF 7.2

Recall

1. Friends are usually similar in age, sex, race, popularity, and _____.

2. Children with friends have higher self-esteem, are less likely to be lonely, and _____than children without friends.

3. As a group forms, a _____typically emerges, with the leader at the top.

4. Peer pressure is most powerful when _____.

5. Popular children are socially skilled; they communicate more effectively and_____.

6. Rejected youngsters are more likely to drop out of school, to commit juvenile offenses, and _____.

7. Some children who are chronic victims of aggression overreact and are easily irritated; other chronic victims are _____.

Interpret

- How could developmental change in the nature of friendship be explained in terms of Piaget's stages of intellectual development, discussed in Chapters 4 and 6?

Apply

- On page 246, you met Jay, who is the least popular child in his class. Jay's mom is worried about her son's lack of popularity and wants to know what she can do to help him. Jay's dad thinks that Jay's mom is upset over nothing—he argues that, like fame, popularity is fleeting and that Jay will turn out okay in the end. What advice would you give to Jay's parents?

Check your answers to the Recall Questions at the end of the chapter.

7.3 Electronic Media

LEARNING OBJECTIVES

- What is the impact of watching television on children's attitudes, behavior, and cognitive development?
- How does playing video games affect youth?
- How does use of social media affect development?

Every day, 7-year-old Roberto follows the same routine when he gets home from school: He watches one action-adventure cartoon after another until it's time for dinner. Roberto's mother is disturbed by her son's constant TV viewing, particularly because of the amount of violence in the shows he likes. Her husband tells her to stop worrying: "Let him watch what he wants. It won't hurt him, and besides, it keeps him out of your hair."

In generations past, children learned their culture's values from parents, teachers, religious leaders, and print media. These sources of cultural knowledge were joined by television in the 1950s, by the Internet in the 1990s, and by social media in the 2000s. In this section, we examine three ways in which technology can influence children and adolescents: by watching television programs, by playing video games, and by communicating via social media. As we look at their influence, we'll see if Roberto's mother should be worried.

Television Programs

"MRS. HORTON, COULD YOU STOP BY SCHOOL TODAY?"

1995 Martha F. Campbell. Reprinted with permission.

The cartoon exaggerates TV's impact on North American children, but only somewhat. Typical U.S. children and adolescents spent about 1½ hours watching programs on TV and another hour watching DVDs or videos (Rideout, 2016). If 30-second TV ads are designed to influence children's preferences in toys, cereals, and hamburgers, the programs themselves ought to have even more impact. And a half-century of research consistently shows that they do. For example, Roberto's mother should be concerned: Children become more aggressive after viewing violence on television. In addition, from watching TV, children learn stereotypes about gender and race and they're more likely to engage in risky behaviors (e.g., use drugs, have unprotected sex) after seeing such behaviors glorified in TV ads or movies (Prot et al., 2014).

Watching television can also help children learn to be more generous and cooperative and have greater self-control. Youngsters who watch TV shows that emphasize prosocial behavior, such as *Mister Rogers' Neighborhood*, are more likely to behave prosocially (Calvert, 2015). However, because prosocial behaviors are portrayed on TV far less frequently than aggressive behaviors, opportunities to learn the former from television are limited; we are far from harnessing the power of television for prosocial uses.

The biggest positive influence of TV on children worldwide has been *Sesame Street*. Big Bird, Bert, Ernie, and their friends have been helping to educate preschool children for nearly 50 years. Youngsters who watch regularly improve their knowledge of numbers, letters, shapes, and colors; they learn more about the physical and social world; and they develop positive attitudes toward social outgroups (Mares & Pan, 2013). Other programs designed to teach young children about language and reading skills (*Martha Speaks, Super Why!, WordGirl*) and about basic science and math concepts (*Cyberchase, Curious George, Dinosaur Train, Sid the Science Kid*) show that TV can be harnessed to help children learn important academic skills (Prot et al., 2014).

For decades, critics have argued that the medium itself—independent of the content of programs—harms viewers, particularly children (Huston & Wright, 1998). One common criticism is that because TV programs consist of many brief segments presented in rapid succession, children who watch a lot of TV develop short attention spans and have difficulty concentrating in school. Another concern heard frequently is that because TV provides ready-made, simple-to-interpret images, children who watch a lot of TV become passive, lazy thinkers and become less creative.

In fact, as stated, neither of these criticisms is consistently supported by research (Huston & Wright, 1998). The first criticism—TV watching reduces attention—is easiest to dismiss. Research repeatedly shows that increased TV viewing does not lead to reduced attention, greater impulsivity, reduced task persistence, or increased activity levels (Foster & Watkins, 2010). The content of TV programs can influence these dimensions of children's behavior—children who watch impulsive models behave more impulsively themselves—but TV per se does not harm children's ability to pay attention.

As for the criticism that TV viewing fosters lazy thinking and stifles creativity, the evidence is mixed. On the one hand, some educational programs depict people being creative and encourage children to pretend; when children watch these programs frequently, they're often more creative. On the other hand, when children often watch programs that are action-oriented, they may be less creative. The content and pacing of these shows often do not provide viewers with the time to reflect that is essential for creativity (Calvert & Valkenburg, 2013).

In general, then, the sheer amount of TV that children watch is not a powerful influence on development. Most of the impact of TV—for good or bad—comes through the content of TV programs that children watch.

Video Games

Adolescent boys spend nearly an hour every day playing video games but girls average less than 10 minutes daily; about 40% of boys play every day compared with less than 10% of girls (Rideout, 2016). The impact of such game playing on youth depends on a game's contents. Many games, including *Tetris* and *Star Fox*, emphasize perceptual–spatial skills, such as estimating the trajectory of a moving object, responding rapidly, and shifting efficiently from one task goal to another. When children play such games frequently, they improve their spatial skills, processing speed, and executive functioning (Cardoso-Leite, & Bavelier, 2014). The Spotlight on Research feature shows the benefits of game-playing on visual-spatial skills.

Spotlight | On Research

Playing a Video Game Improves Children's Visual-Spatial Skill

Who were the investigators, and what was the aim of the study? Visual spatial skills are part of intelligence (pages 193–194) and involve several specific sub-skills, such as the ability to imagine an object's appearance after it has been rotated in space. Many video games require players to rotate two-dimensional objects quickly. Richard De Lisi and Jennifer Wolford (2002) wondered whether playing such games would improve children's spatial skills.

How did the investigators measure the topic of interest? Before training, De Lisi and Wolford assessed children's spatial skills by having children judge whether pairs of figures like those shown in the left panel of ▶ Figure 7-3 would be identical if they appeared in the same orientation. Then, for eleven 30-minute sessions, children played one of two video games: *Tetris*, in which a player moves and rotates rapidly falling tiles to fit into a line, or *Carmen Sandiego*, in which a player is a detective chasing a thief who's trying to steal famous landmarks. After the final video-game session, children again judged pairs of figures like those shown in Figure 7-3.

Who were the participants in the study? The study included 47 8- and 9-year-olds who were in third grade: 23 played *Tetris* and 24 played *Carmen Sandiego*.

What was the design of the study? This study was experimental. The independent variable was the type of video game that children played (*Tetris* or *Carmen Sandiego*); the dependent variable was the number of pairs judged correctly before and after playing the video games. The study was not developmental because the researchers tested only 8- and 9-year-olds.

Were there ethical concerns with the study? No. Parents provided consent for their children to participate and the children enjoyed playing the video games.

What were the results? The right panel of ▶ Figure 7.3 shows the percentage of pairs that children answered correctly before and after playing the video games. Before playing, the groups answered the same percentage of questions accurately. After playing, children who had played *Carmen Sandiego* answered the same percentage of questions correctly as before playing, but children who had played *Tetris* answered significantly more questions correctly. In other words, playing *Tetris* improved performance but playing *Carmen Sandiego* did not.

What did the investigators conclude? De Lisi and Wolford (2002) concluded that "This study provides evidence of a successful training method that led to improved performance on a [visual-spatial] task in third graders" (p. 280). That is, the 5½ hours that children spent playing *Tetris* improved their ability to rotate objects mentally and this generalized to their performance on the mental rotation task administered at the end of the study.

What converging evidence would strengthen these conclusions? The study was conducted with 8- and 9-year-olds and assessed visual-spatial skills immediately after playing video games. It would be valuable to see if the results would hold for younger children as well as for adolescents and to see how long children's improved visual-spatial skills persist.

▶ **Figure 7.3**

Children improved their spatial skill when they played a video game that required them to rapidly rotate stimuli.

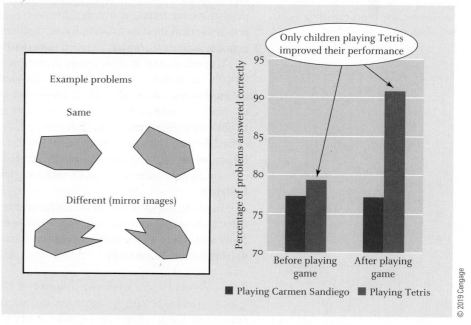

When children play violent video games, they often become more aggressive.

In contrast, many popular games such *Manhunt* and *Grand Theft Auto* are violent, with players killing game characters in extraordinarily gruesome ways. Just as exposure to televised violence can make children behave more aggressively, playing violent video games can make children more aggressive, less empathic, and desensitize them to violence (Calvert et al., 2017).

Finally, a minority—roughly 10%—of youth get "hooked" on video games (Gentile, 2009). They show many of the same symptoms associated with pathological gambling: Playing video games comes to dominate their lives, it provides a "high," and it leads to conflict with others. Not surprisingly, extreme video-game playing is associated with less success in school, apparently because youth spend time playing games instead of studying (Weis & Cerankosky, 2010).

Social Media

Children don't spend much time on social media—less than 20 minutes daily—but adolescents spend nearly 1½ hours daily using social media or video chatting (Rideout, 2016). Teens use social media to stay in touch with friends. Teenage girls send and receive about 40 texts a day, boys about 20 texts a day (Lenhart, 2015). Such communication leads most to feel more connected with their friends. One explanation of this result is that adolescents are more likely to reveal intimate thoughts and feelings to friends over social media. Such self-disclosure promotes high-quality friendships—revealing something personal creates a bond with the other person and encourages that person to reveal in turn (Valkenburg & Peter, 2011).

Using social media helps adolescents form new friends face-to-face. In one study (Koutamanis et al., 2013), teens who messaged often were, a year later, more confident in their friendship skills. One idea is that social media provide a forum where adolescents can practice these friendship-related social skills, a forum where the costs of failure—someone rejects your invitations—are less painful.

There's also a dark side to social media: cyberbullying, *which refers to the use of social media to harm other people, by repeatedly insulting them, excluding them or spreading rumors about them*. You may have received a nasty text—or even sent one—but that doesn't really count as cyberbullying. Instead, cyberbullying refers to repeated, deliberate actions, actions for which a victim is basically defenseless.

Cyberbullying is a relatively common feature of modern adolescence—about 10% to 40% of adolescents report being the victim of cyberbullying, depending on how it's defined (Kowalski et al., 2014). The consequences of cyberbullying are much the same as those for offline bullying: victims are, at the least, embarrassed, and, at the worst, frightened, angry, lonely, and depressed. Another parallel: Perpetrators and victims of cyberbullying tend to be the teens who are perpetrators and victims of offline bullying (Hong et al., 2016; Kowalski et al., 2014). This is "good" news because it means that cyberbullying can be addressed with the same preventive measures that work for offline bullying.

In many respects, social media have changed the *how* of adolescence but not the *what*. As with previous generations, youth still are particularly concerned about their peer relations and some youth pick on others. Social media simply provide different means for accomplishing these tasks.

cyberbullying

Using social media to hurt other people by repeatedly insulting them, excluding them, or spreading rumors about them.

Recall

1. When children watch a lot of TV violence, they often become _____.

2. Contrary to popular criticisms, frequent TV viewing is not consistently related to reduced attention or to a lack of _____.

3. A minority of youth become addicted to video games; playing games dominates their lives, it provides a "high," and it _____.

4. Social media can improve adolescents' friendships by promoting self-disclosure and by _____.

Interpret

- Compare and contrast the ways in which TV viewing and web surfing might affect children's development.

Apply

- Assume that you had the authority to write new regulations for children's TV programs. What shows would you encourage? What shows would you want to limit?

Check your answers to the Recall Questions at the end of the chapter.

7.4 Understanding Others

LEARNING OBJECTIVES

- As children develop, how do their descriptions of others change?

- How does understanding of others' thinking change as children develop?

- When and why do children develop prejudice toward others?

When 12-year-old Ian agreed to babysit Kyle, his 5-year-old brother, their mother reminded Ian to keep Kyle out of the basement because Kyle's birthday presents were there, unwrapped. But as soon as their mother left, Kyle wanted to go to the basement to ride his tricycle. When Ian told him no, Kyle burst into angry tears and shouted, "I'm gonna tell Mom that you were mean to me!" Ian wanted to explain to Kyle, but he knew that would just cause more trouble!

As children spend more time with other people, they begin to understand other people better. In this vignette, for example, Ian realizes why Kyle is angry, and he knows that if he gives in to Kyle now, his mother will be angry when she returns. Children's growing understanding of others is the focus of this section. We begin by looking at how children describe others and then examine their understanding of how others think. Finally, we'll see how children's recognition of different social groups can lead to prejudices.

Describing Others

As children develop, their descriptions of themselves become richer, more abstract, and more psychological. These same changes also occur in children's descriptions of others. Children begin by describing other people in terms of concrete features, such as behavior, and progress to describing them in terms of abstract traits (Barenboim, 1981; Livesley & Bromley, 1973). The Real People feature shows this progression in one child.

Research confirms that Tamsen—the girl in the Real People feature on page 254—describes friends like most children her age do: Descriptions referring to appearances or possessions become less common as children grow older, as do descriptions giving general information such as the person's age, gender, religion, or school. In contrast, descriptions of personality traits (e.g., "friendly" or "conceited") increase between 8 and 14 years of age (Livesley & Bromley, 1973). Thus, children's descriptions of others begin with the concrete and later become more conceptual.

Tell Me About a Girl You Like a Lot

Every few years Tamsen was asked to describe a girl she liked a lot. Her descriptions changed, focusing less on behavior and emphasizing psychological properties. Let's start with the description she gave as a 7-year-old:

> Vanessa is short. She has black hair and brown eyes. She uses a wheelchair because she can't walk. She's in my class. She has dolls just like mine. She likes to sing and read.

Tamsen's description of Vanessa is probably not too different from the way she would have described herself: The emphasis is on concrete characteristics such as Vanessa's appearance, possessions, and preferences. Contrast this with the following description, which Tamsen gave as a 10-year-old:

Kate lives in my apartment building. She is a very good reader and is good at math and science. She's nice to everyone in our class. And she's very funny. Sometimes her jokes make me laugh so-o-o hard! She takes piano lessons and likes to play soccer.

Tamsen's account still includes concrete features, such as where Kate lives and what she likes to do. However, psychological traits are also evident: Tamsen describes Kate as nice and funny. By age 10, children move beyond the purely concrete and observable in describing others. During adolescence, descriptions become even more complex, as you can see in the following, from Tamsen as a 16-year-old:

> Jeannie is very understanding. Whenever anyone at school is upset, she's there to

give a helping hand. Yet in private, Jeannie can be so sarcastic. She can say some really nasty things about people. But I know she'd never say that stuff if she thought people would hear it because she wouldn't want to hurt their feelings.

This description is more abstract: Tamsen now focuses on psychological traits like understanding and concern for others' feelings. It's also more integrated: Tamsen tries to explain how Jeannie can be both understanding and sarcastic.

Each of Tamsen's three descriptions is typical. As a 7-year-old, she emphasized concrete characteristics; as a 10-year-old, she began to include psychological traits; and as a 16-year-old, she tried to integrate traits to form a cohesive account.

More recent research also supports the trend to more abstract and richer psychological descriptions of others but indicates that young children's understanding of other people is more sophisticated than is suggested by their verbal descriptions of people they know (Heyman, 2009). Indeed, 4- and 5-year-olds have begun to think about other people in terms of psychological traits such as being smart, friendly, helpful, and shy. They can use behavioral examples to infer an underlying trait: Told about a child who won't share cookies or won't allow another child to play with a toy, 4- and 5-year-olds accurately describe the child as selfish. In addition, given information about a trait, they correctly predict future behavior: Told about a child who is shy, they believe that the child will not volunteer to help a puppeteer and will be quiet at a meal with many relatives (Liu, Gelman, & Wellman, 2007).

One idiosyncrasy of young children's descriptions of others is that they see others "through rose-colored glasses"—that is, until about 10 years of age, children have a bias to look for positive, not negative, traits in others. Young children are willing to believe that someone is smart (or friendly or helpful) based on relatively little evidence (and based on inconsistent evidence), but they require more evidence (and more consistent evidence) to decide that someone is mean or stupid (Boseovski, 2010).

Understanding What Others Think

One trademark of the preschooler's thinking is difficulty in seeing the world from another person's view. Piaget's term for this is *egocentrism*, and it is a defining characteristic of his preoperational stage of development. As children move beyond the preschool years, they realize that others see the world differently, both literally and figuratively. For example, in the vignette, Ian knows why his little brother, Kyle, is angry: Kyle thinks that Ian is being bossy and mean. Ian understands that Kyle doesn't know that there is a good reason he can't go to the basement.

Sophisticated understanding of how others think is achieved gradually throughout childhood and adolescence. According to a theory proposed by Robert Selman (1980, 1981), understanding other people begins with the egocentric thinking characteristic of preoperational children—they think that others think as they do. As children develop, they are able to take the perspective of other people. In Selman's theory, this perspective-taking skill progresses through five stages, which are shown in ▶ Table 7.1.

Table 7.1

Selman's Stages of Perspective Taking		
STAGE	**APPROXIMATE AGES**	**DESCRIPTION**
Undifferentiated	3–6 years	Children know that self and others can have different thoughts and feelings but often confuse the two.
Social-informational	4–9 years	Children know that perspectives differ because people have access to different information.
Self-reflective	7–12 years	Children can step into another person's shoes and view themselves as others do; they know that others can do the same.
Third-person	10–15 years	Children can step outside the immediate situation to see how they and another person are viewed by a third person.
Societal	14 years to adult	Adolescents realize that a third-person perspective is influenced by broader personal, social, and cultural contexts.

To see the progression from stage to stage, imagine two boys arguing about what to do after school. One wants to go to a playground, and the other wants to watch TV. If the boys were 5-year-olds (undifferentiated stage), neither would understand why the other wants to do something different. Their reasoning is stone simple: "If I want to go to the playground, you should, too!"

During the early elementary school years (social-informational stage), each child understands that the other wants to do something different and they explain their differing views in terms of the other person lacking essential information. Their thinking is along the lines, "I know that you want to watch TV, but if you knew what I knew, you'd want to go to the playground." By the late elementary school years (self-reflective stage), the boys would understand that each wants to do something different and they could "step into the other's shoes" to understand why: "I know you want to go to the playground because you haven't been there all week."

In early adolescence (third-person stage), the boys could step even farther apart and imagine how another person (e.g., a parent or teacher) could view the disagreement. Finally, in late adolescence (societal stage), the boys (now young men, really) can remove themselves even further and appreciate, for example, that many people would think it's silly to watch TV on a beautiful sunny day.

As predicted by Selman's theory, children's reasoning moves through each stage in sequence as they grow older. In addition, children at more advanced cognitive levels tend to be at more advanced stages in perspective taking (Gurucharri & Selman, 1982; Krebs & Gillmore, 1982). However, many scientists are not convinced that more sophisticated perspective taking occurs in such a stagelike fashion; they believe that it improves steadily throughout childhood and adolescence (just as cognitive development is now seen to be more continuous than Piaget's theory predicted).

Some investigators have linked improved perspective taking to the developing theory of mind, described in Chapter 3 (Chandler & Carpendale, 1998). The traditional false-belief task, for example, reveals children's understanding that another person's actions are often based on their beliefs even when those beliefs are wrong. As an illustration, suppose children hear the following story:

> Lindsay and Angela are in the park and see some kids playing softball. Lindsay wants to play, so she runs home for her glove. Angela waits at the park for her, but while Lindsay's away, the kids decide it's too hot for softball and leave to get ice cream.

Children understand false belief if they say that Lindsay will return to the ball field (acting on her false belief that the kids are still playing ball). But we can add a new wrinkle to the story.

Think About It

How do Selman's stages of perspective taking correspond to Piaget's and Erikson's stages?

As the kids are leaving the park, one of them thinks that Lindsay might like to join them for ice cream. So she phones Lindsay and tells her the plan.

Now children are asked: "Where does Angela think Lindsay thinks the kids are?" Children understand second-order belief if they say that Angela thinks that Lindsay will go to the ball field. *This sort of "he thinks that she thinks . . ." reasoning is known as* **recursive thinking**. It emerges at about 5 or 6 years of age and improves steadily during the elementary school years due to the combined effects of increased language skill and greater executive functioning (Miller, 2009).

recursive thinking
Thoughts that focus on what another person is thinking.

One of the benefits of a developing appreciation of others' thoughts and viewpoints is that it allows children to get along better with their peers. That is, children who can readily take another person's perspective and better understand other people's thinking are typically well-liked by their peers (Slaughter et al., 2015). For example, perspective-taking skill allows children to realize that a peer wants to join in their fun and so they invite the peer.

Of course, mere understanding does not guarantee good social behavior; sometimes children who understand what another child is thinking take advantage of that child. In general, however, greater understanding of others seems to promote positive interactions.

Prejudice

Around the world, many adults are prejudiced against individuals based solely on their membership in a social group (e.g., a racial, ethnic, or religious group). Preferring one's group over others is first observed in 2- to 4-year-olds, becomes stronger in 5- to 7-year-olds, and remains strong thereafter (Raabe & Beelmann, 2011). But there's more to the story. By the preschool years, most children can distinguish males from females and can identify people from different racial groups (Nesdale, 2001). After children learn their membership in a specific group, they typically have an enhanced view of that group. That is, preschool and kindergarten children attribute many positive traits, such as being friendly and smart, and few negative traits, such as being mean, to their own group (Bigler, Jones, & Lobliner, 1997; Patterson & Bigler, 2006).

Negative views of other groups form more slowly, beginning in the elementary school years (Buttelmann & Böhm, 2014). During the elementary school years, many children come to see race as a "natural kind"—determined by birth, stable, and referring to people who are similar to each other physically and behaviorally (Rhodes, 2013). At the same time, overt prejudice declines some, in part because children learn norms that discourage openly favoring their own group over others (Apfelbaum et al., 2008). But implicit bias remains—many children automatically associate their group with positive features and associate other groups with bad features (Baron, 2015).

One effective way to reduce prejudice is for children from different races to work together toward a common goal, such as completing a class project.

As children move into the elementary school years, their knowledge of racial stereotypes and prejudices increases steadily; by 10 or 11 years of age, most children are aware of broadly held racial stereotypes (Pauker, Ambady, & Apfelbaum, 2010).

Some scientists believe that bias and prejudice emerge naturally out of children's efforts to understand their social world (Bigler & Liben, 2007). Young children actively categorize animate and inanimate objects as they try to understand the world around them. As children's social horizons expand beyond their parents to include peers, they continue to categorize and try to decide how different groups of people "go together." They use perceptually salient features (e.g., race, gender, age) as well as verbal labels that adults may apply to different groups (e.g., "The girls go to lunch first, then the boys"). After children have identified the salient features that define peers in their environment, they begin to classify people they encounter along these dimensions. Jacob is now seen as a white boy; Kalika is now seen as a black girl (Patterson & Bigler, 2006).

What can parents, teachers, and other adults do to rid children of prejudice? One way is to encourage friendly and constructive contacts between children from different groups. However, contact alone usually accomplishes little. Intergroup contact is most likely to reduce when the participating groups of children are equal in status, when the contact between groups involves pursuing common goals (not competing), when parents and teachers support the goal of reducing prejudice, and when children are ready for contact—they're not anxious about interacting with children from the other group and have a positive attitude toward the interactions (Cameron et al., 2006; Turner & Cameron, 2016). For example, adults might have children from different groups work together toward common goals. In school, this might be a class project. In sports, it might be mastering a new skill. By working together, Gary starts to realize that Farès acts, thinks, and feels as he does simply because he's Farès, not because he's a Lebanese American.

Another useful approach is to ask children to play different roles (Davidson & Davidson, 1994; Tynes, 2007). They can be asked to imagine that—because of their race, ethnic background, or gender—they have been insulted verbally or not allowed to participate in special activities. A child might be asked to imagine that she can't go to a private swimming club because she's African American or that she wasn't invited to a party because she's Hispanic American. Afterward, children reflect on how they felt when prejudice and discrimination was directed at them. They're also asked to think about what would be fair: What should be done in situations like these?

A final strategy against prejudice involves education. In one study (Hughes, Bigler, & Levy, 2007), European American elementary school children learned about the racism that famous African Americans experienced. For example, they learned that Jackie Robinson played for a team in the old Negro Leagues because the white people in charge of Major League Baseball wouldn't allow African Americans to play. The study also included a control group in which the biographies omitted the experiences of racism. When children learned about racism directed at African Americans, they had more positive attitudes toward African Americans.

From experiences like these, children and adolescents discover for themselves that a person's membership in a social group tells very little about that person. They learn, instead, that all children are different and that each person is a unique mix of experiences, skills, and values.

TEST YOURSELF 7.4

Recall

1. When adolescents describe others, they usually _____.

2. In the most advanced stage of Selman's theory, adolescents _____.

3. One view is that bias and prejudice emerge naturally out of _____.

Interpret

- How might an information-processing theorist describe the stages of Selman's perspective-taking theory?

Apply

- Based on what you've learned in this section, what can parents and teachers do to discourage prejudice in children?

Check your answers to the Recall Questions at the end of the chapter.

7.1 Family Relationships

What is a systems approach to parenting?

- According to the systems approach, the family consists of interacting elements; that is, parents and children influence each other. The family itself is influenced by other social systems, such as neighborhoods and religious organizations.

What are the primary dimensions of parenting? How do they affect children's development?

- One key factor in parent–child relationships is the degree of warmth that parents express: Children clearly benefit from warm, caring parents. A second factor is control, which is complicated because neither too much nor too little control is desirable. Effective parental control involves setting appropriate standards, enforcing them, and trying to anticipate conflicts.

- Taking into account both warmth and control, four prototypic parental styles emerge: Authoritarian parents are controlling but uninvolved; authoritative parents are fairly controlling but are also responsive to their children; permissive parents are loving but exert little control; and uninvolved parents are neither warm nor controlling. Authoritative parenting seems best for children in terms of both cognitive and social development, but important exceptions are associated with culture and socioeconomic status.

- Parents influence development by direct instruction and coaching. In addition, parents serve as models for their children, who sometimes imitate parents' behavior directly. Sometimes children behave in ways that are similar to what they have seen and sometimes in ways that are the opposite of what they've seen (counterimitation).

- Parents also use feedback to influence children's behavior. Sometimes parents fall into the negative reinforcement trap, inadvertently reinforcing behaviors that they want to discourage.

- Punishment is effective when it is prompt, consistent, accompanied by an explanation, and delivered by a person with whom the child has a warm relationship. Punishment has limited value because it suppresses behaviors but does not eliminate them, and it often has side effects. Time-out is one useful form of punishment.

- Chronic conflict is harmful to children, but children benefit when their parents solve problems constructively. Parenting is a team sport, but not all parents play well together because they may disagree in child-rearing goals or parenting methods.

- Parenting is influenced by characteristics of children themselves. A child's age and temperament will influence how a parent tries to exert control over the child.

What determines how siblings get along? How do first-born, later-born, and only children differ?

- The birth of a sibling can be stressful for children, particularly when they are still young and parents ignore their needs. Siblings get along better when they are of the same sex, believe that parents treat them similarly, enter adolescence, and have parents who get along well.

- Although most adopted children develop within the typical range, experiencing adversity before being adopted puts some adopted children at risk for problems such as disordered attachment and delayed cognitive development. Problems are most likely when children are adopted after infancy and when their care before adoption was inadequate.

- Parents have higher expectations for first-born children, which explains why such children are more intelligent and more likely to go to college. Later-born children are more popular and more innovative. Contradicting the folklore, only children are rarely worse off than children with siblings; in some respects (such as intelligence and self-esteem), they are often better off.

How do divorce and remarriage affect children?

- Divorce can harm children in a number of areas, ranging from school achievement to adjustment. Many children suffer from divorce in the short-term; in the longer-term children fare better when parents get along and stay involved and when the children are easy, smart, and actively cope with problems.

- Children can thrive in a blended family but this is more difficult when a stepfather brings his own children to the family.

What factors lead children to be maltreated?

- Factors that contribute to child abuse include poverty, social isolation, and a culture's views on violence. Parents who abuse their children were often neglected or abused themselves and tend to be unhappy, socially unskilled individuals. Younger or unhealthy children are more likely to be targets of abuse. Children who are abused often lag behind in cognitive and social development.

7.2 Peers

What are the benefits of friendship?

- Friendships among preschoolers are based on mutual liking. As children grow, loyalty, trust, and intimacy become more important features in their friendships. Friends are usually similar in age, sex, race, and attitudes. Children with friends are more skilled socially and are better adjusted.

What are the important features of groups of children and adolescents? How do these groups influence individuals?

- Older children and adolescents often form cliques—small groups of like-minded individuals—that become part of a crowd. Some crowds have higher status than others.

- Common to most groups is a dominance hierarchy, a well-defined structure with a leader at the top. Physical power often determines the dominance hierarchy, particularly among boys. However, with older children and adolescents, dominance hierarchies are more often based on skills that are important to the group.

- Peer pressure is neither totally powerful nor totally evil. In fact, groups influence individuals primarily in areas where standards of behavior are unclear, as in tastes in music or clothing or with regard to drinking, drug use, and sex.

Why are some children more popular than others? What are the causes and consequences of being rejected?

- Most popular children are skilled academically and socially. A far smaller number of popular children use aggression to achieve their social goals.

- Some children are rejected by their peers because they are too aggressive. Other children are rejected for being too timid or withdrawn. Repeated peer rejection often leads to school failure and behavioral problems.

What are some effects of childhood aggression? Why are some children chronic victims of aggression?

- Many highly aggressive children end up being violent as adults. Children who are chronic victims of aggression typically overreact or refuse to defend themselves.

7.3 Electronic Media

What is the impact of watching television on children's attitudes, behavior, and cognitive development?

- TV programs can cause children to become more aggressive, to adopt gender stereotypes, and to act prosocially.

Programs designed to foster children's cognitive skills, such as *Sesame Street*, are effective. Many criticisms about TV as a medium (e.g., it shortens children's attention span) are not supported by research.

How does playing video games affect youth?

- The content of playing video games affects children and adolescents. Playing some games improves youth's cognitive skills (e.g., visual-spatial skill); playing other games makes youth more aggressive.

How does use of social media affect development?

- Children use social media infrequently, but adolescents use it often, primarily to communicate with friends. Such communication strengthens friendships and allows teens to develop social skills. Cyberbullying parallels offline bullying: the consequences, perpetrators, and victims are similar.

7.4 Understanding Others

As children develop, how do their descriptions of others change?

- Children's descriptions of others change in much the same way children's descriptions of themselves change. During the early elementary school years, descriptions emphasize concrete characteristics. In the late elementary school years, they emphasize personality traits. In adolescence, they emphasize providing an integrated picture of others.

How does understanding of others' thinking change as children develop?

- According to Selman's theory, children's understanding of how others think progresses through five stages. In the first (undifferentiated) stage, children often confuse their own and another person's view. In the last (societal) stage, adolescents can take a third-person perspective and know that this perspective is influenced by context.

When and why do children develop prejudice toward others?

- Prejudice, which emerges in the preschool years and becomes stronger in the elementary school years, is a common byproduct of children's efforts to categorize social groups. Ways to reduce prejudice include exposure to individuals from other social groups and by educating children about the ills of prejudice.

Test Yourself Recall Answers

7.1 1. embedded in other social systems, such as neighborhoods **2.** authoritarian **3.** authoritative **4.** feedback (reward and punishment) **5.** they limit each other's access to the child **6.** to take risks **7.** approximately equal time with both parents **8.** actively cope with problems brought on by divorce **9.** often ill **7.2 1.** attitudes **2.** more often act prosocially (sharing and cooperating) **3.** dominance hierarchy **4.** standards for appropriate behavior are vague **5.** better integrate themselves into ongoing conversations **6.** to suffer from psychopathology **7.** unwilling or unable to defend themselves **7.3 1.** more aggressive **2.** creativity **3.** leads to conflict with others **4.** allowing them to practice friendship skills **7.4 1.** try to provide a cohesive, integrated account **2.** provide a third-person perspective on situations and recognize the influence of context on this perspective **3.** children's efforts to understand their social world

Key Terms

socialization (228)
authoritarian parenting (229)
authoritative parenting (229)
permissive parenting (230)
uninvolved parenting (230)
direct instruction (231)
counterimitation (231)
reinforcement (231)
punishment (231)
negative reinforcement trap (232)

time-out (232)
open adoption (237)
joint custody (238)
blended family (239)
ego resilience (241)
friendship (243)
co-rumination (245)
clique (245)
crowd (245)
dominance hierarchy (245)

popular children (247)
rejected children (247)
controversial children (247)
average children (247)
neglected children (247)
instrumental aggression (248)
hostile aggression (248)
cyberbullying (252)
recursive thinking (256)

Rites of Passage

Physical and Cognitive Development in Adolescence

8

At age 13, Miley Cyrus premiered in the title role of *Hannah Montana*, which quickly became a top-rated TV series; at age 15, she was included in *Time* magazine's list of the 100 most influential people in the world; and a few weeks before she turned 21, her recording of "Wrecking Ball" became her first number-one single in the United States. Miley's steady march to the top of her profession over her adolescent years is a remarkable feat. Yet in a less dramatic and less public way, these years are times of profound changes for all adolescents. In this chapter, we'll examine physical and cognitive developments in adolescence. We'll begin by describing the important features of physical growth in the teenage years. Then we'll consider some of the necessary ingredients for healthy growth in adolescence. Next, we'll examine the nature of information processing during adolescence. Finally, we'll end the chapter by examining how adolescents reason about moral issues.

LEARNING OBJECTIVES

- What physical changes during adolescence mark the transition to a mature young adult?

- What factors cause the physical changes associated with puberty?

- How do physical changes affect adolescents' psychological development?

Pete just celebrated his 15th birthday, but as far as he is concerned, there is no reason to celebrate. Although most of his friends have grown about 6 inches in the past year or so, have a much larger penis and larger testicles, and have mounds of pubic hair, Pete looks just as he did when he was 10 years old. He is embarrassed by his appearance, particularly in the locker room, where he looks like a little boy among men. "Won't I ever change?" he wonders.

The appearance of body hair, the emergence of breasts, and the enlargement of the penis and testicles are all signs that the child is gone and the adolescent has arrived. Many adolescents take great satisfaction in these signs of maturity. Others, like Pete, worry through their teenage years as they wait for the physical signs of adolescence.

In this section, we'll begin by describing the normal pattern of physical changes that take place in adolescence and look at the mechanisms responsible for them. Then we'll discover the impact of these physical changes on adolescents' psychological functioning. As we do, we'll learn about the possible effects of Pete's maturing later than his peers.

puberty

Collection of physical changes that marks the onset of adolescence, including a growth spurt and the growth of breasts or testes.

During the growth spurt, girls are often much taller than boys of the same age.

Justin Pumfrey/Getty Images

Signs of Physical Maturation

Puberty denotes two general types of physical changes that mark the transition from childhood to young adulthood. The first are bodily changes, including a large increase in height and weight, as well as changes in the body's fat and muscle content. The second concern sexual maturation, including change in the reproductive organs and the appearance of secondary sexual characteristics such as facial and body hair and growth of the breasts.

Physical Growth

For physical growth, the elementary school years are the calm before the adolescent storm. ▶ Figure 8.1 shows that in an average year, a typical 6- to 10-year-old gains about 5 to 7 pounds and grows 2 to 3 inches. In contrast, during the peak of the adolescent growth spurt, a girl may gain as many as 14 to 15 pounds in a year and a boy 16 to 17 pounds (Tanner, 1970).

Figure 8.1 also shows that girls typically begin their growth spurt about two years before boys. Girls typically start the growth spurt at about age 11, reach their peak rate of growth at about 12, and achieve their mature stature at about 15. In contrast, boys start the growth spurt at age 13, hit peak growth at 14, and reach mature stature at 17. This two-year difference in the growth spurt can lead to awkward social interactions between 11- and 12-year-old boys and girls because the girls are often taller and look more mature than the boys.

Body parts don't mature at the same rate. Instead, the head, hands, and feet usually begin to grow first, followed by growth in the arms and legs. The trunk and shoulders are the last to

Children grow steadily taller and heavier until puberty, when they experience a rapid increase known as the adolescent growth spurt.

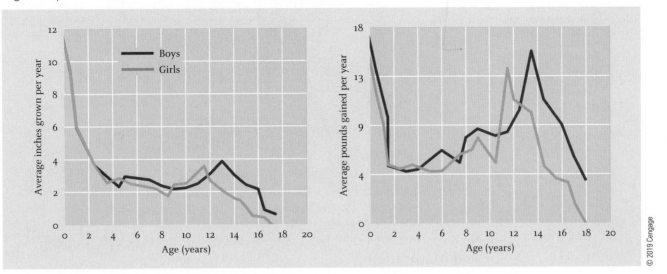

© 2019 Cengage

grow (Tanner, 1990). The result of these differing growth rates is that an adolescent's body sometimes seems out of proportion—teens have a head and hands that are too big for the rest of their body. Fortunately, these imbalances don't last long as the later developing parts catch up.

During the growth spurt, bones become longer (which, of course, is why adolescents grow taller) and denser. Bone growth is accompanied by several other changes that differ for boys and girls. Muscle fibers become thicker and denser during adolescence, producing substantial increases in strength, particularly for boys (Smoll & Schutz, 1990). Body fat also increases during adolescence, but more rapidly in girls than in boys. Finally, heart and lung capacity increases more in adolescent boys than in adolescent girls. Together, these changes help to explain why the typical adolescent boy is stronger, is quicker, and has greater endurance than the typical adolescent girl.

Think About It

Compare and contrast the events of puberty for boys and girls.

Brain Growth in Adolescence

At the beginning of adolescence, the brain is nearly full size—it's about 95% of the size and weight of an adult's brain. Nevertheless, adolescence is important for fine-tuning the brain's functioning. Two features of brain development that begin early in life (and that we discussed in Chapter 3) are nearly complete in adolescence: myelination, which is the acquisition of fatty insulation that allows neurons to transmit information faster, and synaptic pruning, which is the weeding out of unnecessary connections between neurons (Jernigan & Stiles, 2017). These changes mean that different regions in the adolescent brain are well connected and that information is rapidly conveyed between them, which means that adolescents can process information more efficiently than the child, a theme that we will explore more on pages 274–275.

Another distinguishing feature of the adolescent brain is that some, but not all, brain regions reach maturity. Some brain systems that are sensitive to reward (especially to rewards from peers) may reach maturity in adolescence but the systems responsible for self-control aren't fully specialized until adulthood (Casey, 2015). As shown in ▶ Figure 8.2, this makes adolescents vulnerable: The reward- and pleasure-seeking systems are more mature than the systems for controlling behavior. Consequently, even though adolescents may know that behaviors involve risk, the anticipated rewards and pleasure of risky behavior sometimes swamp the adolescent's ability to suppress the desire to engage in such activities (Sturman & Moghaddam, 2012). As we'll see on page 275, this makes adolescents vulnerable to high-risk activities (e.g., drinking, unprotected sex).

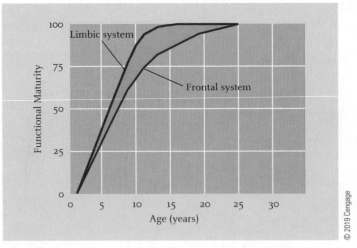

▶ Figure 8.2

Adolescence is a vulnerable time because the reward- and pleasure-seeking centers of the brain (limbic system) mature more rapidly than the behavioral control systems (frontal system); the gap between the two systems is particularly great in adolescence.

© 2019 Cengage

From Casey et al., 2008, "The Adolescent Brain," *Annals of the New York Academy of Sciences*, 1124, Fig. 3, p. 116.

Sexual Maturation

Not only do adolescents become taller and heavier, they also become mature sexually. *Sexual maturation includes change in* primary sex characteristics, *which refer to organs that are directly involved in reproduction.* These include the ovaries, uterus, and vagina in girls and the scrotum, testes, and penis in boys. *Sexual maturation also includes changes in* secondary sex characteristics, *which are physical signs of maturity not directly linked to the reproductive organs.* These include the growth of breasts and the widening of the pelvis in girls, the appearance of facial hair and the broadening of shoulders in boys, and the appearance of body hair and changes in voice and skin in both boys and girls.

Changes in primary and secondary sexual characteristics occur in a predictable sequence for boys and for girls. For girls, puberty begins with growth of the breasts and the growth spurt, followed by the appearance of pubic hair. Menarche, *the onset of menstruation, typically occurs at about age 13.* Early menstrual cycles are usually irregular and without ovulation.

For boys, puberty usually commences with the growth of the testes and scrotum, followed by the appearance of pubic hair, the start of the growth spurt, and growth of the penis. *At about age 13, most boys reach* spermarche, *the first spontaneous ejaculation of sperm-laden fluid.* Initial ejaculations often contain relatively few sperm; only months or sometimes years later are there sufficient sperm to fertilize an egg (Dorn et al., 2006).

Mechanisms of Maturation

What causes the many physical changes that occur during puberty? The pituitary gland is key: It helps to regulate physical development by releasing growth hormone. In addition, the pituitary regulates pubertal changes by signaling other glands to secrete hormones. During the early elementary school years—long before there are any outward signs of puberty—the pituitary signals the adrenal glands to release androgens, initiating the biochemical changes that will produce body hair. A few years later, in girls, the pituitary signals the ovaries to release estrogen, which causes the breasts to enlarge, the female genitals to mature, and fat to accumulate. In boys, the pituitary signals the testes to release the androgen hormone testosterone, which causes the male genitals to mature and muscle mass to increase.

Although estrogen is often described as a "female hormone" and androgen as a "male hormone," estrogen and androgen are present in both boys and girls. As we've seen, in girls, the adrenal glands secrete androgens. The amount is tiny compared with that secreted by boys' testes, but it is enough to influence the emergence of body hair. In boys, the testes secrete very small amounts of estrogen, which explains why some boys' breasts temporarily enlarge early in adolescence.

primary sex characteristics

Physical signs of maturity that are directly linked to the reproductive organs.

secondary sex characteristics

Physical signs of maturity that are not directly linked to reproductive organs.

menarche

Onset of menstruation.

spermarche

First spontaneous ejaculation of sperm.

The timing of pubertal events is regulated, in part, by genetics (Cousminer et al., 2013). This is shown by the closer synchrony of pubertal events in identical twins than in fraternal twins: If one identical twin has body hair, the odds are that the other twin will too (Mustanski et al., 2004). Genetic influence is also shown by the fact that a mother's age at menarche is related to her daughter's age at menarche (Belsky, Bakermans-Kranenburg, & van IJzendoorn, 2007). However, these genetic forces are strongly influenced by the environment, particularly an adolescent's nutrition and health. In general, puberty occurs earlier in adolescents who are well nourished and healthy than in adolescents who are not (St. George, Williams, & Silva, 1994).

The social environment also influences the onset of puberty, at least for girls. Menarche occurs at younger ages in girls who experience chronic stress or harsh punishment, or who are depressed (James et al., 2012). When young girls experience chronic socioemotional stress, this may release hormones that activate the hormones that trigger menarche.

This mechanism has an evolutionary advantage: If events of a girl's life suggest that her future reproductive success is uncertain—as indicated by chronic socioemotional stress—then it may be adaptive to reproduce as soon as possible instead of waiting until later when she would be more mature and better able to care for her offspring. That is, the evolutionary gamble in this case might favor "lower-quality" offspring early over "higher-quality" offspring later (Cabeza de Baca & Ellis, 2017).

Iakov Filimonov/Alamy Stock Photo

Young adolescents are often quite concerned about their appearance.

Psychological Impact of Puberty

Of course, teenagers are well aware of the changes taking places in their bodies. Not surprisingly, some of these changes affect adolescents' psychological development.

Body Image

Compared with children and adults, adolescents are more concerned about their overall appearance. Many teenagers look in the mirror regularly, checking for signs of additional physical change. Generally, girls worry more than boys about appearance and are more likely to be dissatisfied with their appearance (Vander Wal & Thelen, 2000). Girls are particularly likely to be unhappy with their looks when appearance is a frequent topic of conversation with friends, leading girls to spend more time comparing their own appearance with that of their peers. Peers have relatively little influence on boys' satisfaction with their looks; instead, boys are unhappy with their appearance when they expect to have an idealized strong, muscular body but do not (Carlson Jones, 2004).

Response to Menarche and Spermarche

Carrie was horror writer Stephen King's first novel (and later a movie starring Sissy Spacek); it opens with a riveting scene in which the title character has her first menstrual period in the shower at school and, not knowing what is happening, fears that she will bleed to death. Fortunately, most adolescent girls today know about menstruation beforehand—usually from discussions with their mothers. Being prepared, their responses are usually fairly mild. Most girls are moderately pleased at this new sign of maturity but moderately irritated by the inconvenience and messiness of menstruation (Brooks-Gunn & Ruble, 1982). Girls usually tell their moms about menarche right away, and after two or three menstrual periods, they tell their friends, too (Brooks-Gunn & Ruble, 1982).

Menarche is usually a private occasion for adolescents living in industrialized countries, but in traditional cultures, it is often celebrated. For example, the Western Apache, who live in the southwest portion of the United States, traditionally have a spectacular ceremony to celebrate a girl's menarche (Basso, 1970). After a girl's first menstrual period, a group of older adults decide when the ceremony will be held and select a sponsor—a

Think About It
The Apache have an elaborate celebration for menarche. Can you think of other similar ceremonies—perhaps not as elaborate—that take place to celebrate other milestones of adolescent development?

Anders Ryman/Alamy Stock Photo

woman of good character and wealth (she helps to pay for the ceremony) who is unrelated to the initiate. On the day before the ceremony, the sponsor serves a large feast for the girl and her family; at the end of the ceremony, the family reciprocates, symbolizing that the sponsor is now a member of their family.

The ceremony itself begins at sunrise and lasts a few hours; it includes eight distinct phases in which the initiate, dressed in ceremonial attire, dances or chants, sometimes accompanied by her sponsor or a medicine man. The intent of these actions is to transform the girl into "Changing Woman," a heroic figure in Apache myth. With this transformation comes longevity and perpetual strength. The ceremony is a signal to all in the community that the initiate is now an adult, and it tells the initiate that her community now has adult-like expectations for her.

In contrast to menarche, much less is known about boys' reactions to spermarche. Most boys know about spontaneous ejaculations beforehand, and they get their information by reading, not by asking parents (Gaddis & Brooks-Gunn, 1985). When boys are prepared for spermarche, they feel more positively about it. Nevertheless, boys rarely tell parents or friends about this new development (Stein & Reiser, 1994).

Moodiness

Adolescents are often thought to be extraordinarily moody—quickly moving from joy to sadness to—reflecting the influx of hormones associated with puberty. In fact, adolescents are moodier than children or adults, but this is not due primarily to hormones (Steinberg, 1999). Scientists often find that rapid increases in hormone levels are associated with greater irritability and greater impulsivity, but the correlations tend to be small and are found primarily in early adolescence (Buchanan, Eccles, & Becker, 1992).

Instead of reflecting hormones, teenagers' moodiness reflects frequent changes in their activities and social settings. Teens are more likely to report being in a good mood when hanging out with friends or when recreating; they tend to report being in a bad mood when in adult-regulated settings such as school classrooms or at a part-time job. Because adolescents often change activities and social settings many times in a single day, they appear to be moodier than adults (Larson, Csikszentmihalyi, & Graef, 2014).

Rate of Maturation

Although puberty begins at age 10 in the average girl and age 12 in the average boy, for many children, puberty begins months or even years before or after these norms. An early-maturing boy might begin puberty at age 11, whereas a late-maturing boy might start at 15 or 16. An early-maturing girl might start puberty at age 9; a late-maturing girl, at 14 or 15.

Maturing early can be harmful for girls. Girls who mature early often lack self-confidence, are less popular, are more likely to be depressed and have behavior problems, and are more likely to smoke and drink. Early maturation often leads girls to relationships with older boys, and these girls are ill-prepared to cope with the demands of these relationships (Skoog & Stattin, 2014). In turn, this can result in life-changing effects on early-maturing girls who are pressured into sex and become mothers while still teenagers: as adults, they typically have less prestigious and lower-paying jobs (Mendle, Turkheimer, & Emery, 2007). These harmful outcomes are more likely when early-maturing girls live in poverty or experience harsh punishment from parents (Skoog & Stattin, 2014). Fortunately, when early-maturing girls have warm, supportive parents, they are less likely to suffer the harmful consequences of early maturation (Ge et al., 2002).

Maturing early can be harmful for boys, too. Early-maturing boys are at risk for psychological disorders such as depression; they are also more prone to substance abuse and to sexual activity (Mendle & Ferrero, 2012). Being physically advanced for their age may cause early-maturing boys to have problems with their peers who have not yet matured (leading to depression) and cause them to spend more time with older boys (exposing them to risky behavior). However, the effects of early maturation are weaker for boys than they are for girls (Graber, 2013).

For boys and girls, maturing late poses few risks. Late-maturing girls fare well; late-maturing boys are at somewhat greater risk for depression (Mendle & Ferrero, 2012). But otherwise, Pete, the late-maturing boy in the opening vignette, has nothing to worry about. When he finally matures, others will treat him like an adult, and the few extra years of being treated like a child will not be harmful (Weichold & Silbereisen, 2005).

Peter Hvizdak/The Image Works

Because children enter puberty at different ages, early-maturing teens tower over their later-maturing age-mates.

TEST YOURSELF 8.1

Recall

1. Puberty refers to changes in height and weight, to changes in the body's fat and muscle content, and to _____.

2. Girls tend to have their growth spurts about _____ earlier than boys.

3. During adolescent physical growth, boys have greater muscle growth than girls, acquire less _____, and have greater increases in heart and lung capacity.

4. Primary sex characteristics are organs directly related to reproduction, whereas secondary sex characteristics are _____.

5. During puberty in girls, the ovaries secrete estrogen, which causes the breasts to enlarge, the genitals to mature, and _____.

6. Influence of the social environment on the onset of puberty is illustrated by the findings that menarche occurs earlier for girls who experience chronic stress or _____ or who are depressed.

7. Adolescents are moodier than children and adults primarily because _____.

8. Early maturation tends to be harmful to girls because _____.

Interpret

- Compare and contrast the impact of rate of maturation—that is, maturing early versus late—on boys and girls.

Apply

- At first blush, the onset of puberty would seem to be due entirely to biology. In fact, the child's environment influences the onset of puberty. Summarize the ways in which biology and experience interact to trigger the onset of puberty.

Check your answers to the Recall Questions at the end of the chapter.

LEARNING OBJECTIVES

- What are the elements of a healthy diet for adolescents? Why do some adolescents suffer from eating disorders?

- Do adolescents get enough exercise? What are the pros and cons of participating in sports in high school?

- What are common obstacles to healthy growth in adolescence?

Dana had just started the seventh grade and was overjoyed that he could try out for the middle school football team. He'd always excelled in sports and was usually the star football player on the playground or in gym class. But this was Dana's first opportunity to play on an actual team—with a real helmet, jersey, and pads—and he was jazzed! Dana's dad played football in high school and thought Dana could benefit from the experience. His mom wasn't so sure—she was afraid that he would get hurt and have to deal with the injury for the rest of his life.

Adolescence is a time of transition with regard to health. On the one hand, teens are less affected by the minor illnesses that would have kept them home in bed as children. On the other hand, teens are at greater risk for harm because of their unhealthy and risky behaviors. In this section, we'll look at some of the factors essential to adolescent health and see whether Dana's mother should be worried about sports-related injuries. We'll start with nutrition.

Nutrition

The physical growth associated with puberty means that the body has special nutritional needs. A typical teenage girl should consume about 2,200 calories per day; a typical boy should consume about 2,700 calories. (The exact levels depend on a number of factors, including body composition, growth rate, and activity level.) Teenagers also need calcium for bone growth and iron to make extra hemoglobin, the matter in

Many American teenagers eat far too many fast-food meals, which are notoriously high in calories.

red blood cells that carries oxygen. Boys need additional hemoglobin because of their increased muscle mass; girls need hemoglobin to replace that lost during menstruation.

Unfortunately, although many U.S. teenagers consume enough calories each day, too much of their intake consists of fast food rather than well-balanced meals. The result of too many meals of burgers, french fries, and a shake is that teens may get inadequate iron or calcium and far too much sodium and fat. With inadequate iron, teens are often listless and moody; with inadequate calcium, bones may not develop fully, placing the person at risk later in life for osteoporosis.

Obesity

In part because of a diet high in fast foods, many American children and adolescents are overweight. *The technical definition of "overweight" is based on the* body mass index (BMI), *which is an adjusted ratio of weight to height.* Children and adolescents who are in the upper 5% (very heavy for their height) are defined as being overweight. Childhood obesity in the United States has reached epidemic proportions. In the past 25 to 30 years, the number of overweight children has doubled and the number of overweight adolescents has tripled so that today, roughly one adolescent out of five is overweight (Ogden et al., 2015). This trend is not unique to the United States: it is evident in many developed nations and in developing nations as they adopt diets and lifestyles like those in Western countries (World Health Organization, 2010).

Overweight youngsters are often unpopular and at risk for depression and anxiety (Pryor et al., 2016). They are also at risk for many medical problems throughout life, including high blood pressure and diabetes, because the vast majority of overweight children and adolescents become overweight adults (U.S. Department of Health and Human Services, 2010).

No single factor causes children to become obese. Instead, several factors contribute, including the following:

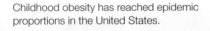

body mass index (BMI)
Adjusted ratio of weight to height; used to define "overweight".

- **Heredity** Obesity runs in families, showing that genes contribute perhaps by causing some people to overeat, to be sedentary, or to be less able to convert fat to fuel (Cheung & Mao, 2012).
- **Parents** Some parents urge children to "clean their plates" even when the children are not hungry. Other parents use food to comfort children who are upset. Both practices cause children to rely on external cues to eat instead of eating only when they're hungry (Coelho et al., 2009; Wansink & Sobal, 2007). In contrast, authoritative parenting seems to protect youth from obesity, apparently because authoritative parents are more likely to eat healthily themselves as well as monitor their children's eating (Harrist et al., 2017; Sleddens et al., 2011).
- **Sedentary lifestyle** Youth are more prone to obesity when they are physically inactive, such as watching television instead of playing outdoors (de Rezende et al., 2014).
- **Too little sleep** Adolescents who do not sleep enough tend to gain weight, perhaps because they have more opportunities to eat because they are awake longer, they experience increasing feelings of hunger, or they are too tired to exercise (Magee & Hale, 2012).

Childhood obesity has reached epidemic proportions in the United States.

PNC/Getty Images

Individually these factors may not lead to obesity. But collectively they may put children and adolescents on the path to obesity: A youth is at greater risk if she is genetically prone to overeat, is sedentary, and is chronically sleepy. To understand obesity during childhood and adolescence, we need to consider all of these risk factors, as well as the amount and quality of food that's available to children and adolescents (Harrison et al., 2011).

Obese youth can lose weight. The most effective weight-loss programs focus on changing children's eating habits and encouraging them to become more active. Children and adolescents set goals for eating and exercise; parents help them set realistic goals, reward them for progress, and monitor their own eating and exercising. When programs incorporate these features, obese youth do lose weight (Mitchell, Amaro, & Steele, 2016). However, even after losing weight, many youth participating in these programs remain overweight. Consequently, it is best to avoid overweight and obesity in the first place by encouraging children and adolescents to eat healthfully and to be active physically.

Yet another food-related problem common in adolescence are two similar eating disorders, anorexia and bulimia.

anorexia nervosa

Persistent refusal to eat accompanied by an irrational fear of being overweight.

bulimia nervosa

Disease in which people alternate between binge eating—periods when they eat uncontrollably—and purging with self-induced vomiting, laxatives, fasting, or excessive exercise.

Adolescent girls with anorexia nervosa believe that they are overweight, and they refuse to eat.

Bubbles Photolibrary/Alamy Stock Photo

Anorexia and Bulimia

In 2010, French model and actress Isabelle Caro died of respiratory disease just months after turning 26. Near her death, she weighed less than 75 pounds. *Caro suffered from* anorexia nervosa, *a disorder marked by a persistent refusal to eat and an irrational fear of being overweight.* Individuals with anorexia nervosa have a grossly distorted image of their body and claim to be overweight despite being painfully thin. Anorexia is a serious disorder that, left untreated, can result in death (Attia, 2017).

A related eating disorder is bulimia nervosa. *Individuals with* bulimia nervosa *alternate between binge eating periods, when they eat uncontrollably, and purging through self-induced vomiting, laxatives, fasting, or excessive exercise.* During binge eating, adolescents with bulimia consume two days' worth of calories in two hours or less, then purge once or twice daily (Keel, 2017).

Anorexia and bulimia are alike in many respects. Both disorders primarily affect females and emerge in adolescence and many of the same factors put teenage girls at risk for both eating disorders. Heredity puts some girls at risk as do psychosocial factors, such as adverse life experiences (e.g., stressful or traumatic events) and low self-esteem. However, the most important risk factor for adolescents is being overly concerned about one's body and internalizing the thin body that is often thought to be ideal in Western cultures. Teenage girls are at risk when they frequently watch TV shows that emphasize attractive, thin characters and when their friends frequently talk about weight and diet constantly to stay thin (von Ranson & Wallace, 2014).

Although eating disorders are far more common in girls, boys make up about 10% of diagnosed cases of eating disorders. Boys with eating disorders have a distorted body image but, instead of worrying that they're not sufficiently thin, they worry that they're not sufficiently muscular. In trying to achieve a muscular ideal, boys with eating disorders reduce their intake of calories and they exercise excessively (Weltzin, 2017).

Fortunately, there are programs that can help protect teens from eating disorders (Becker et al., in press). These programs work to change attitudes toward being thin and provide ways to resist social pressure to be thin. One such program is described in the Spotlight on Research feature.

Evaluating a Program for Preventing Eating Disorders

Who were the investigators, and what was the aim of the study? One way to prevent teenage girls from developing eating disorders is to help them see faults in the thin female body that is often idealized in the media. Teens who participate in activities critiquing this ideal are less prone to eating disorders; for example, they no longer find the thin ideal as attractive, they're less likely to diet, and they report fewer symptoms of eating disorders. However, research demonstrating the effectiveness of this prevention has been conducted under highly controlled conditions (e.g., in a research center, with facilitators who are highly trained and closely monitored); Eric Stice and colleagues (2009) wanted to confirm that the prevention would work when administered in a more realistic setting—in this case, by school personnel (e.g., nurses, counselors) in a high school.

How did the investigators measure the topic of interest? Stice and colleagues recruited high school girls who had concerns about their body image. Half of the girls were assigned to a control condition in which they were given a brochure describing eating disorders and suggesting ways to improve one's body image. The other half were assigned to an intervention condition in which they attended four 1-hour sessions that included a variety of exercises designed to show girls the costs of the thin ideal. For example, they engaged in role play in which they tried to convince group leaders why girls shouldn't pursue the thin ideal and they completed homework in which they listed pressures they experienced to be thin and ways to resist those pressures. Before the intervention started and at 1, 6, and 12 months after it ended, girls in both groups completed questionnaires measuring their adherence to the thin ideal, their body

dissatisfaction, their dieting behavior, and their symptoms of eating disorders.

Who were the participants in the study? The researchers tested 306 adolescent girls; 139 were in the intervention condition, and 167 were in the control condition.

What was the design of the study? This study was experimental because Stice and colleagues were interested in comparing the impact of the prevention program, relative to the control condition, on adolescent girls' attitudes and behaviors related to eating disorders. The researchers did not investigate age differences, so the study was neither cross-sectional nor longitudinal.

Were there ethical concerns with the study? No. The researchers obtained informed consent from the adolescents and their parents. The measures and the prevention program posed no obvious risks to participants. Any girls in either condition who showed symptoms of eating disorders were referred to treatment.

What were the results? The results were similar for the different outcome measures. For simplicity, we focus on dieting behavior, which was measured with a questionnaire that included items such as "Do you try to eat less at meal times than you would like to eat?" and "Do you deliberately eat foods that are slimming?" Scores on the scale ranged from 1 (never) to 5 (always). The results, shown in ▶ Figure 8.3, indicate that at the pretest, girls in both groups occasionally endorsed dieting-related behaviors. What's noteworthy is that these responses were reasonably stable for girls in the control condition but declined for girls in the prevention group. In other words, the prevention condition caused girls to be less likely to report dieting-related behaviors.

What did the investigators conclude? These findings, like the prior work, illustrate that girls change their body- and eating-related attitudes and behaviors after participating in a prevention emphasizing the costs and

shortcomings of an ideal thin body. As Stice and colleagues put it, "the findings from the present trial suggest that positive intervention effects still emerge when real-world providers deliver the prevention program in ecologically valid settings with a heterogeneous population" (p. 831).

What converging evidence would strengthen these conclusions? All four outcome measures were obtained from questionnaires completed by the adolescents. An obvious way to provide converging evidence would be to measure some of these outcomes differently, such as by asking parents to describe their daughter's dieting-related behaviors, by using experimental tasks to estimate body dissatisfaction, or by obtaining physiological measures that reflect eating disorders.

▶ **Figure 8.3**

When teenage girls participate in programs that emphasize the costs and shortcomings of an ideal thin body, they change their body- and eating-related attitudes and behaviors.

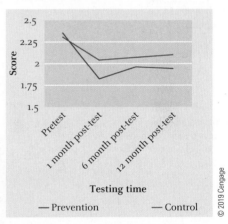

SOURCE: Stice, E., Rohde, P., Gau, J., & Shaw, H. (2009). An effectiveness trial of dissonance-based eating disorder prevention program for high-risk adolescent girls. *Journal of Consulting and Clinical Psychology*, 77, 825–834.

Programs such as the one described in the Spotlight on Research feature are effective: At-risk adolescents who participate in these programs are more satisfied with their appearance and are less likely to diet or overeat (Stice, South, & Shaw, 2012). For those teens affected by eating disorders, treatment is available: Like prevention programs, treatment typically focuses on modifying key attitudes and behaviors (Puhl & Brownell, 2005).

Think About It

Describe how obesity, anorexia, and bulimia represent the different forces in the biopsychosocial network.

Think About It

Many teenagers do not eat well-balanced meals, and many do not get enough exercise. What would you do to improve teenagers' dietary and exercise habits?

Physical Fitness

Being physically active promotes mental and physical health during adolescence and throughout adulthood. Individuals who regularly engage in physical activity reduce their risk for obesity, cancer, heart disease, diabetes, and psychological disorders, including depression and anxiety. "Regular activity" typically means exercising for 30 minutes at least three times a week at a pace that keeps an adolescent's heart rate at about 140 beats per minute (President's Council on Physical Fitness and Sports, 2004). Running, vigorous walking, swimming, aerobic dancing, biking, and cross-country skiing are all examples of activities that can provide this level of intensity.

Unfortunately, all the evidence indicates that most adolescents rarely get enough exercise. Part of the problem is that physical education classes provide the only regular opportunity for many high school students to exercise, yet a minority of high school students are enrolled in physical education and most who are enrolled do not attend daily.

Many teenagers get exercise by participating in organized sports. Today, approximately 4.5 million boys and 3.3 million girls participate in sports (National Federation of State High School Associations, 2017). Participating in sports has many benefits for youth. Sports can enhance participants' self-esteem and can help them to learn initiative (Bowker, 2006; Eime et al., 2013). Sports can also provide adolescents a chance to learn important social skills, such as how to work effectively as part of a group, often in complementary roles.

These benefits of participating in sports are balanced by potential hazards. About 15% of high school athletes will be injured, requiring some medical treatment. Fortunately, most of these injuries are not serious (Nelson, 1996). Dana's mom can rest easy; the odds are that he won't be injured, and if he is, it won't be serious. Another concern is that several studies have linked youth participation in sports to delinquent and antisocial behavior (e.g., Gardner, Roth, & Brooks-Gunn, 2009). However, outcomes are usually positive when sports participation is combined with participation in activities that involve adults, such as school, religious, or youth groups (Linver, Roth, & Brooks-Gunn, 2009; Zarrett et al., 2009).

A more serious problem is the use of illegal drugs to improve performance. Some athletes use anabolic steroids—drugs that are chemically similar to the male hormone testosterone—to increase muscle size and strength and to promote more rapid recovery from injury. Approximately 3% of high school students report having used anabolic steroids, with boys more likely than girls to use steroids (LaBotz & Griesemer, 2016). This is worrisome because steroid use has been linked to cardiovascular disease, cancer, and mental health problems (Bird et al., 2015).

From participating in sports, youth can improve their self-esteem and learn skills about how to work effectively as part of a group.

ZUMA Press, Inc./Alamy Stock Photo

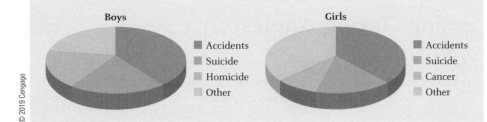

From Federal Interagency Forum on Child and Family Statistics, 2005.

Figure 8.4
Adolescent boys and girls are more likely to die from accidents involving cars or firearms than any other single cause.

Parents, coaches, and health professionals need to make sure that high school athletes are aware of the dangers of steroids and should encourage youth to meet their athletic goals through methods that do not involve drug use (LaBotz & Griesemer, 2016).

Threats to Adolescent Well-Being

Every year approximately 1 U.S. adolescent out of 2,000 dies, with boys more than twice as likely as girls to die. ❱ Figure 8.4 shows that for boys and girls, most deaths are due to accidents involving motor vehicles (for boys and girls) or firearms for boys). The next most common cause of death for boys and girls is suicide, followed by homicide for boys and cancer for girls (Heron, 2016).

Sadly, many of these deaths are preventable. Far too many adolescents are killed because they drive too fast, drive while drunk or texting, or drive without wearing a seat belt (Centers for Disease Control and Prevention, 2012). And deaths due to guns are often linked to "all-too-easy" access to firearms in the home: In far too many homes, firearms are stored loaded, unlocked, or both (Johnson et al., 2006).

Adolescent deaths from accidents can be explained in part because adolescents take risks that adults often find unacceptable (Nell, 2002). Teens drive cars recklessly, engage in unprotected sex, and sometimes use illegal and dangerous drugs (we'll discuss the latter behaviors more in Chapter 9). Why? Many adolescents believe they are invulnerable—only others experience the harmful consequences of risky behaviors (Hill, Duggan, & Lapsley, 2012).

In addition, adolescents find the rewards associated with risky behavior far more appealing than adults do—so much so that they're willing to ignore the risks. For many adolescents, the pleasure, excitement, and intimacy of sex far outweigh the risks of disease and pregnancy, just as the relaxation associated with smoking outweighs the threat of lung cancer (Albert & Steinberg, 2011). And as we saw earlier in this chapter (pages 263–264), the appeal of high-risk behaviors reflects the maturity of the pleasure-seeking brain regions relative to those regions that control behavior (Casey, 2015).

Adolescents are far more accident-prone than children or adults, in part because they believe the rewards of risky behavior far outweigh the potential harm.

TEST YOURSELF 8.2

Recall

1. An adolescent's diet should contain adequate calories, _____, and iron.
2. Individuals with _____ alternate between binge eating and purging.
3. During adolescence, the most important risk factor for anorexia and bulimia is _____.
4. Regular physical activity helps to promote _____ and physical health.
5. Some teenage athletes use anabolic steroids to increase muscular strength and to _____.
6. More teenager die from _____ than from any other single cause.

7. Because they place greater emphasis on the _____ actions, adolescents make what adults think are risky decisions.

Interpret

- Distinguish the biological factors that contribute to obesity from the environmental factors.

Apply

- How does adolescent risk taking illustrate the idea that individuals help to shape their own development?

Check your answers to the Recall Questions at the end of the chapter.

LEARNING OBJECTIVES

- How do working memory and processing speed change in adolescence?

- How do increases in content knowledge, strategies, and metacognitive skill influence adolescent cognition?

- What changes in problem-solving and reasoning take place in adolescence?

Amir, a 14-year-old boy, was an enigma to his mother, Faiza. On one hand, Amir's growing reasoning skills impressed and sometimes surprised her: He not only readily grasped technical discussions of her medical work but also was becoming adept at finding loopholes in her explanations of why he wasn't allowed to do some activities with his friends. On the other hand, sometimes Amir was a real teenage "space cadet." Simple problem-solving stumped him, or he made silly mistakes and got the wrong answer. Amir didn't correspond to Faiza's image of the formal-operational thinker that she remembered from her college human development class.

For information-processing theorists, adolescence does not represent a distinct, qualitatively different stage of cognitive development. Instead, adolescence represents a transition from the rapidly changing cognitive processes of childhood to the mature cognitive processes of young adulthood. Cognitive changes take place during adolescence, but they are small compared with those seen in childhood. Adolescence is a time when cognitive processes are tweaked to adult levels. We'll describe these changes in this section, and as we do, we'll see why adolescents such as Faiza's son don't always think as effectively as they might.

Working Memory and Processing Speed

Working memory is the site of ongoing cognitive processing, and processing speed is the speed with which people complete basic cognitive processes. Both of these capacities achieve adultlike levels during adolescence. Adolescents' working memory has about the same capacity as adults' working memory, which means that teenagers are better able than children to store information needed for ongoing cognitive processes. In addition, processing speed becomes faster, as illustrated in ❱ Figure 8.5 and exemplified by

❱ **Figure 8.5**

Response time declines steadily during childhood and reaches adultlike levels during middle adolescence.

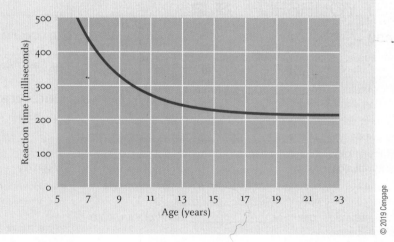

Data from Kail (2004).

performance on a simple response-time task in which individuals press a button as rapidly as possible in response to a visual stimulus. The time needed to respond drops steadily during childhood—from about one-third of a second at age 8 to one-quarter of a second at age 12—but changes little thereafter. This pattern of change is not specific to simple response time; instead, it is found for a wide range of cognitive tasks: Adolescents generally process information just about as quickly as young adults (Kail, 2004). Change in working memory and processing speed means that compared with children, adolescents process information very efficiently.

These changes in efficiency reflect changes to the brain described earlier in this chapter (page 263). Increases in myelination during adolescence allow nerve impulses to travel more rapidly, which contributes to more rapid and more efficient information processing during this period (Scantlebury et al., 2014).

Content Knowledge, Strategies, and Metacognitive Skill

As children move into adolescence, they acquire adultlike levels of knowledge and understanding in many domains. For example, many parents turn to their teens for help in learning how to use fancy features on their smartphone. This increased knowledge is useful for its own sake, but it also has the indirect effect of enabling adolescents to learn, understand, and remember more of new experiences (Schneider, 2015). Imagine two middle school students—one a baseball expert, the other not—watching a baseball game. Compared with the novice, the adolescent expert would understand many of the nuances of the game and, later, remember more features of the game.

As their content knowledge increases, adolescents also become better skilled at identifying strategies appropriate for a specific task, then monitoring the chosen strategy to verify that it is working (Schneider, 2015). For example, adolescents are more likely to outline and highlight information in a text. They are more likely to make lists of material they don't know well and should study more, and they more often embed these activities in a master study plan (e.g., a list of assignments, quizzes, and tests for a two-week period). All these activities help adolescents learn more effectively and remember more accurately (Schneider, 2015).

Problem-Solving and Reasoning

When solving problems, two approaches are common (Evans & Stanovich, 2013). One is to rely on heuristics, rules of thumb that do not guarantee a solution but are useful in solving a range of problems. Heuristics tend to be fast and require little effort. Another approach is to determine an answer mathematically or logically. Compared with heuristics, analytic solutions are slower and require more effort.

To see the difference between heuristic and analytic solutions, think about the following problem (based on Kail, 2013):

> Gabriela wants a new smartphone. A well-known tech website reports that consumers rate the Stratosphere as the best model, but Gabriela's aunt has a Superba that she likes a lot. Which phone should Gabriela get, the Stratosphere or the Superba?

The heuristic solution relies on personal testimony from familiar people. In this case, that means relying on the aunt's experience. In contrast, the analytic solution relies on the statistical information from consumers' ratings.

Courtesy of Robert V. Kail

Adolescents often have adultlike skills in some domains, such as using an iPad, which allows them to teach adults.

Think About It

Students typically are introduced to the study of complex topics such as philosophy and experimental science during adolescence. Explain how their maturing cognitive skills contribute to the study of these and other subject areas.

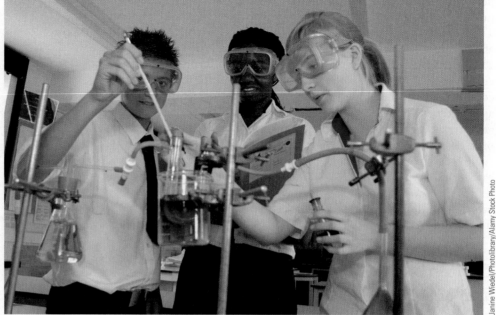

When children reach adolescence, they are more likely to use reasoning skills and solve problems analytically.

Janine Wiedel/Photolibrary/Alamy Stock Photo

Heuristics are used throughout childhood, adolescence, and adulthood, but analytic solutions become more common in adolescence (Klaczynski, 2013). In other words, teens are more likely than children to rely on logic or math and would be more likely to suggest that Gabriela pick the phone with the higher ratings from consumers. This developmental change reflects adolescents' mastery of formal operational thinking (described on pages 188–190). But it also reflects adolescents' greater working-memory capacity (needed because analytic solutions require effort) and their greater self-regulation (needed to suppress fast-acting heuristics).

Adolescents also are better skilled at finding weaknesses in arguments. In logical reasoning, they can pinpoint flaws in arguments (Weinstock, Neuman, & Glassner, 2006). In scientific reasoning, adolescents recognize the hazards in making generalizations from extremely small samples. They would be wary of concluding that people from another country are particularly friendly based on meeting just two people from that country (Klaczynski & Lavallee, 2005).

Of course, adolescents may not always use their skills effectively. Sometimes they resort to heuristics because they take less effort and are "good enough" for the problem. Also, sometimes adolescents' beliefs interfere with effective thinking: When evidence is inconsistent with adolescents' beliefs, they may dismiss the evidence as being irrelevant or try to reinterpret the evidence to make it consistent with their beliefs. For example, an American teenager may be quick to find flaws in a study showing that Americans are self-centered but overlook similar flaws in a study showing that Americans are better leaders than people in other countries (Byrnes & Dunbar, 2014). Thus, adolescents use their reasoning skills selectively, raising their standards to dismiss findings that threaten their beliefs and lowering them to admit findings compatible with their beliefs.

Findings such as these tell us that Faiza, the mother in the opening vignette, should not be so perplexed by her son's seemingly erratic thinking: Adolescents (and adults, for that matter) do not always use the most powerful levels of thinking that they possess. The information-processing account of intellectual functioning in adolescence is a description of how children and adolescents *can* think, not how they always or even usually think.

These changing features of information processing are summarized in ▶ Table 8.1. Change in each of these elements of information processing occurs gradually. When combined, they contribute to the steady progress to mature thinking that is the destination of adolescent cognitive development.

Table 8.1

FEATURE	STATE IN ADOLESCENCE
Working memory and processing speed	Adolescents have adultlike working memory capacity and processing speed, enabling them to process information efficiently.
Content knowledge	Adolescents' greater knowledge of the world facilitates understanding and memory of new experiences.
Strategies and metacognition	Adolescents are better able to identify task-appropriate strategies and to monitor the effectiveness of those strategies.
Problem-solving and reasoning	Adolescents often solve problems analytically by relying on mathematics or logic, and they can detect weaknesses in scientific evidence and logical arguments.

© 2019 Cengage

TEST YOURSELF 8.3

Recall

1. According to information-processing theorists, adolescence is a time of important changes in working memory, processing speed, _____, strategies, and metacognition.

2. Information-processing theorists view adolescence as a time of _____.

3. When solving problems, adolescents are more likely than children to solve problems _____.

4. When evidence is inconsistent with their beliefs, adolescents often _____.

Interpret

- The information-processing account of cognitive change in adolescence emphasizes working memory, knowledge, and strategies. How might each of these factors be influenced by nature? By nurture?

Apply

- How can the information-processing skills described here—and, in particular, the limits in adolescent thinking—help to explain adolescent risk taking described on page 275.

Check your answers to the Recall Questions at the end of the chapter.

8.4 Reasoning About Moral Issues

LEARNING OBJECTIVES

- How do adolescents reason about moral issues?
- What other factors influence moral reasoning?
- What factors help promote more sophisticated reasoning about moral issues?

Howard, the least popular boy in the eighth grade, had been wrongly accused of stealing a sixth grader's iPod. Min-shen, another eighth grader, knew that Howard was innocent but said nothing to the school principal for fear of what his friends would say about siding with Howard. A few days later when Min-shen's father heard about the incident, he was upset that his son apparently had so little "moral fiber." Why hadn't Min-shen acted in the face of an injustice?

One day the local paper had two articles about youth from the area. One article was about a 15-year-old girl who was badly burned while saving her younger brothers from a fire in their apartment. Her mother said she wasn't surprised by her daughter's actions because she had always been an extraordinarily caring person. The other article was about two 17-year-old boys who had beaten an elderly man to death. They had only planned to steal his wallet, but when he insulted them and tried to punch them, they became enraged.

Reading articles like these, you can't help but question why some teenagers (and adults) act in ways that earn our deepest respect and admiration, whereas others earn our utter contempt as well as our pity. And at a more mundane level, we wonder why Min-shen didn't tell the principal the truth about the stolen iPod. In this section, we'll start our exploration of moral reasoning with an influential theory proposed by Lawrence Kohlberg.

Kohlberg's Theory

Some of the world's great novels are based on moral dilemmas. For example, Victor Hugo's *Les Misérables* begins with the protagonist, Jean Valjean, stealing a loaf of bread to feed his sister's starving child. You can probably give many reasons for Valjean to have stolen the bread as well as argue why he shouldn't have stolen the bread. Lawrence Kohlberg created stories like this one in which decisions were difficult because every alternative involved some undesirable consequences. In fact, there is no "correct" answer—that's why the stories are referred to as moral "dilemmas." Kohlberg was more interested in the reasoning used to justify a decision—Why should Jean Valjean steal the bread? Why should he not steal the bread?—than in the decision itself.

Kohlberg's (1969) best-known moral dilemma is this story about Heinz, whose wife is dying:

> In Europe, a woman was near death from cancer. One drug might save her, a form of radium that a druggist in the same town had recently discovered. The druggist was charging $2,000, ten times what the drug cost him to make. The sick woman's husband, Heinz, went to everyone he knew to borrow the money, but he could only get together about half of what it cost. He told the druggist that his wife was dying and asked him to sell it cheaper or let him pay later. But the druggist said, "No." The husband got desperate and broke into the man's store to steal the drug for his wife. (p. 379)

Thus, Heinz and Jean Valjean both face moral dilemmas in which the various alternative courses of action have desirable and undesirable features.

Kohlberg analyzed children's, adolescents', and adults' responses to a large number of dilemmas and identified three levels of moral reasoning, each divided into two stages. Across the six stages, the basis for moral reasoning shifts. In the earliest stages, moral reasoning is based on external forces, such as the promise of reward or the threat of punishment. At the most advanced levels, moral reasoning is based on a personal, internal moral code and is unaffected by others' views or society's expectations.

Kohlberg identified three levels of moral reasoning: preconventional, conventional, and postconventional. Each level is subdivided into two substages. *At the preconventional level, moral reasoning is based on external forces.* For most children, many adolescents, and some adults, moral reasoning is controlled almost exclusively by rewards and punishments. *Individuals in stage 1 moral reasoning assume an* obedience orientation, *which means believing that authority figures know what is right and wrong.* Consequently, stage 1 individuals do what authorities say is right to avoid being punished. At this stage, one might argue that Heinz shouldn't steal the drug because an authority figure (e.g., parent or police officer) said he shouldn't do it. Alternatively, one might argue that Heinz should steal the drug because he would get into trouble if he let his wife die.

In stage 2 of the preconventional level, people adopt an instrumental orientation, *in which they look out for their own needs.* Stage 2 individuals are nice to others because they

preconventional level

First level of reasoning in Kohlberg's theory, where moral reasoning is based on external forces.

obedience orientation

Characteristic of Kohlberg's stage 1, in which moral reasoning is based on the belief that adults know what is right and wrong.

instrumental orientation

Characteristic of Kohlberg's stage 2, in which moral reasoning is based on the aim of looking out for one's own needs.

expect the favor to be returned in the future. Someone at this stage could justify stealing the drug because Heinz's wife might do something nice for Heinz in return. Or someone might argue that Heinz shouldn't steal the drug because it will create more problems for him.

At the conventional level, *adolescents and adults look to society's norms for moral guidance.* In other words, people's moral reasoning is largely determined by others' expectations of them. *In stage 3, adolescents' and adults' moral reasoning is based on* interpersonal norms. The aim is to win the approval of other people by behaving as "good boys" and "good girls" would. Stage 3 individuals might argue that Heinz shouldn't steal the drug because he must keep his reputation as an honest man or that he should steal the drug because no one would think negatively of him for trying to save his wife's life.

Stage 4 of the conventional level focuses on social system morality. Here, adolescents and adults believe that social roles, expectations, and laws exist to maintain order within society and to promote the good of all people. Stage 4 individuals might reason that Heinz shouldn't steal the drug, even though his wife might die, because it is illegal and no one is above the law. Alternatively, they might claim that he should steal it to live up to his marriage vow of protecting his wife even though he will face negative consequences for his theft.

At the postconventional level, *moral reasoning is based on a personal moral code.* The emphasis is no longer on external forces such as punishment, reward, or social roles. *In stage 5, people base their moral reasoning on a* social contract. Adults agree that members of social groups adhere to a social contract because a common set of expectations and laws benefits all group members. However, if these expectations and laws no longer promote the welfare of individuals, they become invalid. Consequently, stage 5 individuals might reason that Heinz should steal the drug because social rules about property rights no longer benefit individuals' welfare. Alternatively, they could argue that he shouldn't steal the drug because it would create social anarchy.

Finally, in stage 6 of the postconventional level, universal ethical principles *dominate moral reasoning.* Abstract principles such as justice, compassion, and equality form the basis of a personal code that may conflict with society's expectations and laws. Stage 6 individuals might argue that Heinz should steal the drug because saving a life takes precedence over everything else, including the law. Or they might claim that Heinz's wife has a right to die and that he should not force his views on her by stealing and administering the drug.

Putting the stages together, the entire sequence of moral development looks like this:

Preconventional Level: Punishment and Reward
    Stage 1: Obedience to authority
    Stage 2: Nice behavior in exchange for future favors

Conventional Level: Social Norms
    Stage 3: Live up to others' expectations
    Stage 4: Follow rules to maintain social order

Postconventional Level: Moral Codes
    Stage 5: Adhere to a social contract when it is valid
    Stage 6: Personal moral system based on abstract principles

This developmental sequence usually unfolds over many years, but sometimes it happens more dramatically, such as when individuals undergo a major transformation in their moral motivation. One noteworthy example of such a transformation was depicted in Steven Spielberg's Oscar-winning movie *Schindler's List,* as described in the Real People feature.

conventional level

Second level of reasoning in Kohlberg's theory, where moral reasoning is based on society's norms.

interpersonal norms

Characteristic of Kohlberg's stage 3, in which moral reasoning is based on winning the approval of others.

social system morality

Characteristic of Kohlberg's stage 4, in which moral reasoning is based on maintenance of order in society.

postconventional level

Third level of reasoning in Kohlberg's theory, in which morality is based on a personal moral code.

social contract

Characteristic of Kohlberg's stage 5, in which moral reasoning is based on the belief that laws are for the good of all members of society.

universal ethical principles

Characteristic of Kohlberg's stage 6, in which moral reasoning is based on moral principles that apply to all.

Schindler's List

In 1939, Oskar Schindler was an entrepreneur who made a great deal of money working for the Germans after they conquered Poland. Motivated at first strictly by the potential for personal profit, he opened—with few qualms—a factory in which he employed Jews as slave labor.

Schindler's company was quite successful. But as the war continued, Jewish citizens in Poland were rounded up and shipped to concentration camps or summarily executed. This deeply disturbed Schindler, and his attitudes began to change. His employees suggested that he give the Germans a list of workers essential to the factory's continued operation. The list protected employees because the plant's products were used in the war effort. No longer driven by profit,

Schindler went to great lengths to preserve life: He created cover stories to support his claims that certain employees were essential and went to Auschwitz to rescue employees who were sent there despite being included on his list.

Schindler's list saved many lives. Profits were made (and helped provide the perfect cover), but he employed Jews in his factory primarily to save them from the gas chamber. Schindler may have begun the war at Kohlberg's preconventional level—where he was motivated solely by personal profit—but he ultimately moved to the postconventional level—where he was motivated by the higher principle of saving lives. It is at the postconventional level that heroes are made.

During World War II, Oskar Schindler saved the lives of many Jews by adding their names to lists of employees who were essential for his factory's operation.

Evaluating Kohlberg's Theory

Research supports many features of Kohlberg's theory. For example, Kohlberg proposed that individuals move through the six stages only in the order listed and longitudinal studies confirm this prediction: individuals progress through each stage in sequence, rarely skipping stages (Colby et al., 1983). In addition, because less advanced moral reasoning reflects the influence of external forces (e.g., rewards) but more advanced reasoning is based on a personal moral code, only individuals with advanced reasoning should be compelled to moral action when external forces may not favor it. Consistent with this claim, adolescents who defend their principles in difficult situations tend to be more advanced in Kohlberg's stages (Gibbs et al., 1986). In contrast, Min-shen, the boy in the vignette, said nothing because speaking out on behalf of the unpopular student is unlikely to lead to being rewarded by his peers.

On some other features, the theory does not fare as well. For example, Kohlberg claimed that the sequence of stages is universal: However, except for the earliest stages, moral reasoning in other cultures is often not described well by Kohlberg's theory, mainly because not all cultures and religions share the theory's emphasis on individual rights and justice. For example, the Hindu religion emphasizes duty and responsibility to others. Consistent with this emphasis, when Hindu children and adults respond to moral dilemmas, they favor solutions that provide care for others even when individual rights or justice may suffer (Miller & Bersoff, 1992). Thus, the bases of moral reasoning are not universal as Kohlberg claimed; instead, they reflect cultural values.

Even for people living in Western cultures, research does not consistently support the theory's emphasis on justice. Many children, adolescents, and adults think about moral issues in terms of justice and caring, depending on the nature of the moral dilemma and the context (Turiel, 2006). To illustrate, suppose a child forgot to bring her lunch to school. One classmate might refuse to share her lunch with the child and justify it in justice terms by saying, first, that the lunch is the child's property and she has the right to eat all of it, and, second, that the lunch room rules prohibit sharing. Another classmate might be eager to share her lunch and justifying it in caring terms by saying that helping others is paramount and requires that she share.

Think About It

Research shows that people sometimes do not reason at the most advanced levels of which they are capable; instead, they revert to simpler, less mature levels. Might this happen in the realm of moral reasoning too? What factors might cause a person's moral reasoning to revert to a less sophisticated level?

Teenagers who engage in moral behavior, such as participating in protest marches, often reason at high levels in Kohlberg's theory.

Also inconsistent with Kohlberg's theory is work on the impact on membership in social groups on moral reasoning. The peer group is particularly salient during adolescence and teens' judgments of what's fair reflect their ideas about what's best for their group. For example, adolescents are more likely to exclude peers if they believe that those peers will hurt a group's identity or functioning. If a school band decides to enter a competition, adolescents are more likely than children to say that only the best players should be in the competitive band (Mulvey, 2016). Similarly, adolescents are more likely to favor peers whose views benefit a group, even if they believe those views are unfair. If a group traditionally shares resources equally with other groups but one group member suggests keeping more resources for the group, adolescents view the group member more favorably than children do (Rutland & Killen, 2017). Thus, adolescents are more likely than children to balance being fair to others with being loyal to one's group, a phenomenon that's not well integrated into Kohlberg's theory.

Promoting Moral Reasoning

Whether it is based on justice or care, most cultures and most parents want to encourage adolescents to think carefully about moral issues. What can be done to help adolescents develop more mature forms of moral reasoning? Sometimes simply being exposed to more advanced moral reasoning is sufficient to promote developmental change (Walker, 1980). Adolescents may notice, for example, that older friends do not wait to be rewarded to help others. Or a teenager may notice that respected peers take courageous positions regardless of the social consequences. Such experiences apparently cause adolescents to reevaluate their reasoning on moral issues and propel them toward more sophisticated thinking.

Discussion can be particularly effective in revealing shortcomings in moral reasoning (Berkowitz et al., 2006). When people reason about moral issues with others whose reasoning is at a higher level, the usual result is that individuals reasoning at lower levels improve. This is particularly true when the conversational partner with the more sophisticated reasoning tries to understand the other's view by asking the other child to clarify or paraphrase his or her thinking (Walker, Hennig, & Krettenauer, 2000).

Adolescents' moral reasoning (and moral behavior) is also influenced by their involvement in religion. Adolescents who are more involved in religion have greater concern for others and place more emphasis on helping them (Saroglou et al., 2005). An obvious explanation for this link is that religion provides moral beliefs and guidelines for adolescents.

When adolescents discuss moral issues together, the thinking of those at lower stages in Kohlberg's theory is often influenced by those whose thinking is at the higher stages; that is, individuals who reason at the lower levels typically move their thinking to a more sophisticated stage.

Paul Conklin/PhotoEdit

But participation in religion can promote moral reasoning in a second, less direct way. Involvement in a religious community—typically through youth groups associated with a church, synagogue, or mosque—connects teens to an extended network of caring peers and adults. From interacting with individuals in this network, earning their trust, and sharing their values, adolescents gain a sense of responsibility to and concern for others (King & Furrow, 2008).

Research findings such as these send an important message to parents: The best way for them to promote their children's moral reasoning is through discussion (Walker & Taylor, 1991). Research consistently shows that mature moral reasoning comes about when adolescents are free to express their opinions on moral issues to their parents, who in turn express their own opinions and thus expose their adolescent children to more mature moral reasoning (Hoffman, 1988, 1994).

TEST YOURSELF 8.4

Recall

1. Kohlberg's theory includes the preconventional, conventional, and _____ levels.

2. For children and adolescents in the preconventional level, moral reasoning is strongly influenced by _____.

3. Supporting Kohlberg's theory are findings that people progress through the stages in the predicted sequence, and that_____.

4. Although Kohlberg's theory emphasizes the role of justice in moral reasoning, research shows that _____ also influences moral reasoning.

5. In adolescents' moral reasoning, they often balance fairness with _____.

6. If parents want to foster their children's moral development, they should _____ with them.

Interpret

- How similar is Piaget's stage of formal operational thought to Kohlberg's stage of conventional moral reasoning?

Apply

- Imagine that you were the father of Min-shen, the boy in the vignette who did not stand up for the boy who was wrongly accused of stealing the iPod. Based on the research described in this section, what might you do to try to advance Min-shen's level of moral reasoning?

Check your answers to the Recall Questions at the end of the chapter.

SUMMARY

8.1 Pubertal Changes

What physical changes during adolescence mark the transition to a mature young adult?

- Puberty includes bodily changes in height and weight as well as sexual maturation. Girls typically begin the growth spurt earlier than boys, who acquire more muscle, less fat, and greater heart and lung capacity. The brain communicates more effectively, and the frontal cortex continues to mature. Sexual maturation, which includes primary and secondary sex characteristics, occurs in predictable sequences for boys and girls.

What factors cause the physical changes associated with puberty?

- Pubertal changes take place when the pituitary gland signals the adrenal gland, ovaries, and testes to secrete hormones that initiate physical changes. The timing of puberty is influenced strongly by health and nutrition. Its timing is also influenced by the social environment; for example, puberty occurs earlier for girls who experience stress, harsh punishment, or depression.

How do physical changes affect adolescents' psychological development?

- Pubertal changes affect adolescents' psychological functioning. Teens, particularly girls, become concerned about their appearance. When forewarned, adolescents respond positively to menarche and spermarche. Adolescents are moodier than children or adults primarily because their moods shift in response to frequent changes in activities and social setting. Early maturation tends to be harmful, especially for girls.

8.2 Health

What are the elements of a healthy diet for adolescents? Why do some adolescents suffer from eating disorders?

- For proper growth, teenagers need to consume adequate calories, calcium, and iron. Unfortunately, many teenagers do not eat properly and do not receive adequate nutrition.

- Anorexia and bulimia, eating disorders that typically affect adolescent girls, are characterized by an irrational fear of being overweight. Adolescents are at greatest risk for eating disorders when they're overly concerned with their bodies and have internalized the thin-body ideal. Treatment and prevention programs emphasize changing adolescents' views toward thinness and their eating-related behaviors.

Do adolescents get enough exercise? What are the pros and cons of participating in sports in high school?

- Individuals who work out at least three times weekly often have improved physical and mental health. Unfortunately, many high school students do not get enough exercise.

- Millions of American boys and girls participate in sports. The benefits of participating in sports include improved physical fitness, enhanced self-esteem, and an understanding about teamwork. The potential costs include injury and abuse of performance-enhancing drugs.

What are common obstacles to healthy growth in adolescence?

- Accidents involving automobiles or firearms are the most common cause of death in American teenagers. Many of these deaths could be prevented if, for example, adolescents did not drive recklessly (e.g., too fast and without wearing seat belts). Adolescents often seem themselves as invulnerable to risk and often place greater value on the rewards associated with risky behavior.

8.3 Information Processing During Adolescence

How do working memory and processing speed change in adolescence?

- Working memory increases in capacity, and processing speed becomes faster. Both achieve adultlike levels during adolescence.

How do increases in content knowledge, strategies, and metacognitive skill influence adolescent cognition?

- Content knowledge increases to expertlike levels in some domains, and strategies and metacognitive skills become more sophisticated.

What changes in problem-solving and reasoning take place in adolescence?

- Adolescents often solve problems analytically, using mathematics or logic. They also acquire skill in detecting weaknesses in scientific evidence and in logical arguments. But they don't consistently use these skills, sometimes resorting to simpler heuristics and sometimes allowing beliefs to interfere with reasoning.

8.4 Reasoning About Moral Issues

How do adolescents reason about moral issues?

- Kohlberg proposed that moral reasoning includes preconventional, conventional, and postconventional levels. Moral reasoning is first based on rewards and punishments and much later on personal moral codes.

What other factors influence moral reasoning?

- As predicted by Kohlberg's theory, people progress through the stages in sequence and morally advanced reasoning is associated with more frequent moral behavior. However, Kohlberg's theory ignores the impact of caring, which often influences moral reasoning. And adolescents often balance fairness with group loyalty.

What factors help promote more sophisticated reasoning about moral issues?

- Many factors can promote more sophisticated moral reasoning, including (1) observing others reasoning at more advanced levels; (2) discussing moral issues with peers, teachers, and parents; and (3) being involved in a religious community that connects adolescents to a network of caring peers and adults.

Test Yourself: Recall Answers

8.1 1. sexual maturation **2.** two years **3.** fat **4.** physical signs of maturity that are not linked directly to reproductive organs, such as the appearance of body hair **5.** fat to accumulate **6.** harsh punishment **7.** they change activities and social settings frequently and their moods track these changes **8.** it leads them to associate with older adolescents, which means they may become involved in activities for which they are ill-prepared, such as drinking and sex **8.2 1.** calcium **2.** bulimia nervosa **3.** internalizing the "thin ideal" and being overly concerned about one's body **4.** mental health **5.** promote more rapid recovery from injury **6.** accidents **7.** rewards associated with their **8.3 1.** content knowledge **2.** gradual cognitive change **3.** analytically, using mathematics or logic **4.** ignore or dismiss the evidence **8.4 1.** postconventional **2.** reward or punishment **3.** more advanced moral reasoning is associated with moral action **4.** caring for others **5.** loyalty to their group **6.** discuss moral issues

Key Terms

puberty (264)
primary sex characteristics (266)
secondary sex characteristics (266)
menarche (266)
spermarche (266)
body mass index (BMI) (271)

anorexia nervosa (272)
bulimia nervosa (272)
preconventional level (280)
obedience orientation (280)
instrumental orientation (280)
conventional level (281)

interpersonal norms (281)
social system morality (281)
postconventional level (281)
social contract (281)
universal ethical principles (281)

Moving into the Adult Social World

Socioemotional Development in Adolescence

You probably have vivid memories of your teenage years. Remember the exhilarating moments—high school graduation, your first paycheck from a part-time job, and your first feelings of love and sexuality? Of course, there were also painful times—not being able to do anything right on your first day on the job, not knowing what to say on a date with a person you desperately wanted to impress, and arguing repeatedly with your parents. Feelings of pride and accomplishment accompanied by feelings of embarrassment and bewilderment are common to individuals who are on the threshold of adulthood.

Adolescence represents the transition from childhood to adulthood and is a time when individuals grapple with their identity; many have their first experiences with love and sex, and some enter the world of work. In the first three sections of this chapter, we investigate these challenging developmental issues. Then we look at the special obstacles that sometimes make adolescence difficult to handle.

LEARNING OBJECTIVES

- How do adolescents achieve an identity?
- What are the stages and results of acquiring an ethnic identity?
- How does self-esteem change in adolescence?

Dea was born in Seoul of Korean parents but was adopted by a Dutch couple in Michigan when she was 3 months old. Growing up, she considered herself a red-blooded American. In college, however, Dea realized that others saw her as an Asian American, an identity about which she had never given much thought. She began to wonder, "Who am I really? American? Dutch American? Asian American?"

Like Dea, do you sometimes wonder who you are? Self-concept refers to the attitudes, behaviors, and values that make a person unique. In adolescence, self-concept takes on special significance as individuals struggle to achieve an identity that will allow them to participate in the adult world. Youth search for an identity to integrate the many different and sometimes conflicting elements of the self. In this section, we'll learn more about the adolescent search for an identity. Along the way, we'll learn more about Dea's struggle to figure out who she is.

The Search for Identity

Erik Erikson's (1968) account of identity formation has been particularly influential in our understanding of adolescence. Erikson argued that adolescents face a crisis between identity and role confusion. This crisis involves balancing the desire to try out many possible selves and the need to select a single self. Adolescents who achieve a sense of identity are well prepared to face the next developmental challenge: establishing intimate, sharing relationships with others. However, Erikson believed that teenagers who are confused about their identity do not experience intimacy in human relationships but remain isolated and respond to others stereotypically.

How do adolescents achieve an identity? They use the hypothetical reasoning skills of the formal-operational stage to experiment with different selves to learn more about possible identities. Adolescents' advanced cognitive skills enable them to imagine themselves in different roles.

As part of their search for an identity, adolescents often try on different roles (e.g., imagining what life might be like as a rock star).

Juice Images/Alamy Stock Photo

Table 9.1

Four Identity Statuses		
STATUS	**DEFINITION**	**EXAMPLE**
Diffusion	The individual is overwhelmed by the task of achieving an identity and does little to accomplish the task.	Larry hates the idea of deciding what to do with his future, so he spends most of his free time playing video games.
Foreclosure	The individual has a status determined by adults rather than by personal exploration.	For as long as she can remember, Sakura's parents have told her that she should be an attorney and join the family law firm. She plans to study prelaw in college, although she's never given the matter much thought.
Moratorium	The individual is examining different alternatives but has yet to find one that's satisfactory.	Brad enjoys most of his high school classes. Some days he thinks it would be fun to be a chemist, some days he wants to be a novelist, and some days he'd like to be an elementary school teacher. He thinks it's a little weird to change his mind so often, but he also enjoys thinking about different jobs.
Achievement	The individual has explored alternatives and has deliberately chosen a specific identity.	Throughout middle school, Efrat wanted to play in the WNBA. During 9th and 10th grades, she thought it would be cool to be a physician. In 11th grade, she took a computing course and everything finally "clicked"—she'd found her niche. She knew that she wanted to study computer science in college.

© 2019 Cengage

Marcia (1980).

Much of the testing and experimentation is career-oriented. Some adolescents may envision themselves as rock stars; others may imagine being professional athletes, Peace Corps workers, or best-selling novelists. Other testing is romantically oriented. Teens may fall in love and imagine living with the loved one. Still other exploration involves religious and political beliefs (Lopez, Huynh, & Fuligni, 2011). Teens give different identities a trial run just as you might test-drive different cars before buying one. By fantasizing about the future, adolescents begin to discover who they will be.

As adolescents strive to achieve an identity, they often progress through different phases or statuses as shown in ▶ Table 9.1. Unlike Piaget's stages, these four phases do not necessarily occur in sequence. Most young adolescents are in a state of diffusion or foreclosure. The common element in these phases is that teens are not exploring alternative identities. They are avoiding the crisis altogether or have resolved it by taking on an identity suggested by parents or other adults. As individuals move beyond adolescence into young adulthood and have more opportunity to explore alternative identities, diffusion and foreclosure become less common and achievement and moratorium become more common (Meeus et al., 2010).

However, identity is not set in stone in adolescence. Periodically, adolescents and adults evaluate different features of their identity. Sometimes these evaluations reassure people of their chosen identity: When a college student who has long wanted to be an elementary-school teacher enjoys tutoring a first grader, this reaffirms the student's choice to be a teacher. But sometimes evaluations cause people to reconsider their identity: When a teenager who has long identified as a member of a religious group discovers that her values are not shared by most of the other members of the group, she may question this aspect of her identity. Reevaluations like these cause adolescents and young adults to shift between moratorium and achievement (Crocetti, 2017).

During the search for identity, adolescents reveal a number of characteristic ways of thinking. They are often very self-oriented. *The self-absorption that marks the teenage search for identity is referred to as* adolescent egocentrism (Elkind, 1978). Unlike preschoolers, adolescents know that others have different perspectives on the world. Adolescents are simply *much* more interested in their own feelings and experiences than in

adolescent egocentrism
Self-absorption that is characteristic of teenagers as they search for identity.

Adolescents often believe that others are constantly watching them, a phenomenon known as the imaginary audience; as a result, they're often upset or embarrassed when they make obvious mistakes or blunders, such as spilling food or drink.

imaginary audience

Adolescents' feeling that their behavior is constantly being watched by their peers.

personal fable

Belief of many adolescents that their feelings and experiences are unique and have never been experienced by anyone else.

illusion of invulnerability

Adolescents' belief that misfortunes cannot happen to them.

anyone else's experiences. In addition, as they search for an identity, many adolescents wrongly believe that they are the focus of others' thinking. A teen who spills food on herself may imagine that all her friends are thinking only about the stain on her blouse and how sloppy she is. *Many adolescents believe that they are, in effect, actors whose performance is watched constantly by their peers, a phenomenon known as the* imaginary audience.

Adolescent self-absorption is also demonstrated by the personal fable, *teenagers' belief that their experiences and feelings are unique and that no one has ever felt or thought as they do.* Whether it is the excitement of first love, the despair of a broken relationship, or the confusion of planning for the future, adolescents often believe they are the first to experience these feelings and that no one else could possibly understand the power of their emotions (Elkind & Bowen, 1979). *Adolescents' belief in their uniqueness also contributes to an* illusion of invulnerability: *the belief that misfortune happens only to others.* They think that they can have sex without becoming pregnant or that they can drive recklessly without being in an auto accident. These characteristics of adolescents' thinking are summarized in ▶ Table 9.2.

As adolescents progress toward achieving an identity, adolescent egocentrism, imaginary audiences, personal fables, and the illusion of invulnerability become less common. What circumstances help adolescents achieve identity? Parents are influential. When parents encourage discussion and recognize children's autonomy, their children are more likely to reach the achievement status. Apparently these youth feel encouraged to undertake the personal experimentation that leads to identity. In contrast, when parents set rules with little justification and enforce them without explanation, children are more likely to remain in the foreclosure status. These teens are discouraged from experimenting personally; instead, their parents simply tell them what identity to adopt. Overall, adolescents are most likely to establish a well-defined identity in a family atmosphere where parents encourage children to explore alternatives on their own but do not pressure or provide explicit direction (Crocetti, 2017; Koepke & Denissen, 2012).

Sean Murphy/The Image Bank/Getty Images

Table 9.2

Characteristics of Adolescents' Thinking

FEATURE	DEFINITION	EXAMPLE
Adolescent egocentrism	Adolescents are overly concerned with their own thoughts and feelings.	When Levi's grandmother died unexpectedly, Levi was preoccupied with how the funeral would affect his weekend plans and ignored how upset his mother was by her own mother's death.
Imaginary audience	Adolescents believe that others are watching them constantly.	Tom had to ride his bike to football practice because his dad wouldn't let him have the car; he was sure that all his car-driving friends would see and make fun of him.
Personal fable	Adolescents believe that their experiences and feelings are unique.	When Rosa's boyfriend decided to date another girl, Rosa cried and cried. She couldn't believe how sad she was, and she was sure that her mom had never felt this way.
Illusion of invulnerability	Adolescents think that misfortune happens only to others.	Kumares and his girlfriend had been having sex for about six months. Although she thought it would be a good idea to use birth control, he thought it was unnecessary: There was no way his girlfriend would get pregnant.

Beyond parents, peers are also influential. When adolescents have close friends whom they trust, they feel more secure exploring alternatives (Doumen et al., 2012). The broader social context also contributes (Bosma & Kunnen, 2001). Exploration takes time and access to resources; neither may be readily available to adolescents living in poverty (e.g., they can't explore because they drop out of school to support themselves and their family). Finally, through their personality, adolescents themselves may affect the ease with which they achieve an identity. Individuals who are more open to experience and are more agreeable (friendly, generous, helpful) are more likely to achieve an identity (Crocetti et al., 2008; Klimstra et al., 2013).

Think About It

Although Piaget's theory of cognitive development was not concerned with identity formation, how might his theory explain why identity is a central issue in adolescence?

Ethnic Identity

Roughly one-third of the adolescents and young adults living in the United States are members of ethnic minority groups, including African Americans, Asian Americans, Latino Americans, and Native Americans. *These individuals typically develop an ethnic identity: They feel a part of their ethnic group and learn the special customs and traditions of their group's culture and heritage* (Phinney, 2005).

ethnic identity
Feeling that one belongs to a specific ethnic group.

Achieving an ethnic identity seems to occur in three phases. Initially, adolescents have not examined their ethnic roots. A teenage Vietnamese American girl in this phase remarked, "Why should I learn about the Boat People? I'm not interested in what happened in Vietnam before I was born. Besides, I'm an American." For this girl, ethnic identity is not yet an important personal issue.

In the second phase, adolescents begin to explore the personal impact of their ethnic heritage. The curiosity and questioning that is characteristic of this stage is captured in the comments of a teenage African American girl who said, "I want to learn more about our history—back in Africa, in slavery, and during the Civil Rights movement. Going to the Black Cultural Center is one way I can find out about myself." Part of this phase involves learning cultural traditions; for example, many adolescents learn to prepare ethnic food.

In the third phase, individuals achieve a distinct ethnic self-concept. One Latino American adolescent explained his ethnic identification this way: "I was born in LA, but my parents grew up in Mexico and came here when they were teenagers like me. I love hearing them talk about their lives there, and I'm proud that I can speak Spanish with my cousins who live in Mexico. But I'm also proud to be an American and I like to learn about my country's heritage."

To see if you understand the differences between these stages of ethnic identity, reread the vignette on page 290 about Dea, the Dutch Asian American college student. Then decide which stage applies to her. Our answer appears on page 296, just before Test Yourself.

Older adolescents are more likely than younger ones to have achieved an ethnic identity because they are more likely to have had opportunities to explore their cultural heritage (French et al., 2006). As adolescents explore their ethnic identity, they often change the way they refer to themselves. For example, a U.S. teen whose parents were born in Vietnam might refer to herself at different times as Vietnamese, Vietnamese American, or Asian American, in no particular order (Fuligni et al., 2008).

Do adolescents benefit from a strong ethnic identity? Yes. Adolescents who have achieved an ethnic identity tend to have greater self-esteem and find their interactions with family and friends more satisfying (Mandara et al., 2009; Rivas-Drake et al., 2014). They're also happier and worry less (Kiang et al., 2006). In addition, adolescents with a strong ethnic identity are less affected by discrimination—they maintain their self-worth after experiencing racial or ethnic discrimination (Neblett, Rivas-Drake, & Umaña-Taylor, 2012; Tynes et al., 2012).

Part of the search for an ethnic identity involves learning cultural traditions, such as how to prepare foods associated with one's ethnic group.

Purestock/Alamy Stock Photo

However, we need to remember that racial and ethnic groups living in the United States are diverse. African American, Asian American, Hispanic American, and Native American cultures and heritages differ; thus, we should expect that the nature and consequences of a strong ethnic self-concept may differ across these and other ethnic groups (Phinney, 2005).

Even within a particular group, the nature and consequences of ethnic identity may change over successive generations. As successive generations become more assimilated into mainstream culture, they may identify less strongly with ethnic culture (Marks, Patton, & García Coll, 2011). When parents maintain strong feelings of ethnic identity that their children don't share, problems sometimes develop, as immigrant parents cling to the "old ways" but their children embrace the new culture. For example, in one study of Korean American families (Choi et al., 2017), adolescents who identified strongly with the United States were more prone to depression and antisocial behavior. Thus, children's failure to identify with their parent's cultural roots can lead to difficulties.

Finally, let's think about adolescents for whom an ethnic identity is a particular challenge—those whose parents come from different racial or ethnic groups. For these adolescents, identity can be quite fluid (Doyle & Kao, 2007). Some biracial adolescents first identify themselves as monoracial and then embrace a biracial identity; others shift in the opposite direction, converging on a single racial identity; and still others shift from one racial identity to another. Collectively, youth with shifting racial identities tend to have lower self-esteem than those with a consistent biracial identity (Csizmadia, Brunsma, & Cooney, 2012). And U.S. biracial adolescents who identify themselves as white have less self-esteem and are less successful in school (Burke & Kao, 2013; Csizmadia & Ispa, 2014).

Self-Esteem in Adolescence

Self-esteem is normally very high in preschool children but declines gradually during the early elementary school years as children compare themselves to others. By the beginning of adolescence, self-esteem has usually stabilized—it neither increases nor decreases in these years (Harter, Whitesell, & Kowalski, 1992). Evidently, children learn their place in the "pecking order" of different domains and adjust their self-esteem accordingly. However, self-esteem sometimes drops when children move from elementary school to middle school or junior high (Harris et al., 2017). Apparently when students from different elementary schools enter the same middle school or junior high, they know where they stand compared with their old elementary school classmates but not compared with students from other elementary schools. Thus, peer comparisons begin anew, and self-esteem often suffers temporarily. As a new school becomes familiar and students gradually adjust to the new pecking order, self-esteem again increases.

These changes in overall level of self-esteem are accompanied by another important change: Self-esteem becomes more differentiated as children enter adolescence (Boivin, Vitaro, & Gagnon, 1992). Youth are able to evaluate themselves in more domains as they develop, and their evaluations in each domain are increasingly independent. That is, children's ratings of self-esteem are often consistent across different dimensions of self-esteem, but adolescents' ratings more often vary from one domain to another. For example, a 9-year-old may have high self-esteem in the academic, social, and physical domains, but a 15-year-old might have high self-esteem in the academic domain, moderate self-esteem in the social domain, and low self-esteem in the physical domain.

As children progress through elementary school and enter junior high or middle school, their academic self-concepts become particularly well defined (Marsh & Martin, 2011). As students accumulate successes and failures in school, they form beliefs about their ability in different content areas (e.g., English, math, science), and these beliefs contribute to their overall academic self-concept. A teen who believes she is skilled at English and math but not so skilled in science will probably have a positive academic self-concept overall. But a teen who believes he is untalented in most academic areas will have a negative academic self-concept.

***Think* About It**
What factors in the biopsychosocial framework are shown by adolescents who develop an ethnic identity?

During adolescence, the social component of self-esteem becomes particularly well differentiated. Adolescents distinguish self-worth in many different social relationships. A teenager may, for example, feel very positive about her relationships with her parents but believe that she's a loser in romantic relationships. Another teen may feel loved and valued by his parents but believe that the coworkers at his part-time job can't stand him (Harter, Waters, & Whitesell, 1998).

Growth of self-worth among U.S. children and adolescents also varies depending on their ethnicity. Compared with European American children, African Americans and Hispanic Americans have lower self-esteem during most of the elementary school years. However, in adolescence, the gap narrows for Hispanic Americans and actually reverses for African American adolescents, who have greater self-esteem than their European American peers (Gray-Little & Hafdahl, 2000; Herman, 2004; Twenge & Crocker, 2002). One explanation of this change is that as African American and Hispanic American teens take pride in belonging to a distinct social and cultural group, their self-worth increases (Gray-Little & Hafdahl, 2000; Umaña-Taylor, Diversi, & Fine, 2002).

Thus, between the late preschool years and adolescence, self-esteem becomes more complex as older children and adolescents identify distinct domains of self-worth. This growing complexity is not surprising; it reflects the older child's and adolescent's greater cognitive skill and the more extensive social world of older children and adolescents.

Influences on Adolescents' Self-Esteem

What factors contribute to adolescents' self-esteem? Heredity contributes indirectly. Genes help to make some youth smarter, more sociable, more attractive, and more skilled athletically. Consequently, such youth are more likely to have greater self-worth because they are competent in so many domains. In other words, genes lead to greater competence, which fosters greater self-worth (Harter, 2012; Neiss, Sedikides, & Stevenson, 2006).

Children's and adolescents' self-worth is also affected by how others view them, particularly other people who are important to them. Parents matter, of course—even to adolescents. Children are more likely to view themselves positively when their parents are affectionate toward them and are involved with them (Behnke et al., 2011; Ojanen & Perry, 2007). Around the world, children have greater self-esteem when families live in harmony and parents nurture their children (Scott, Scott, & McCabe, 1991). A father who routinely hugs his daughter and gladly takes her to piano lessons is saying to her, "You are important to me." When children hear this regularly from parents, they evidently internalize the message and come to see themselves positively. That said, when adults use inflated praise—for example, saying to their children "You played that song amazingly well!" when the playing was mediocre—children with low self-esteem tend to shy away from challenges because they're afraid they won't succeed (Brummelman et al., 2014).

Parents' discipline also is related to self-esteem. Children with high self-esteem generally have parents who have reasonable expectations for their children and are willing to discuss rules and discipline with their children (Awong, Grusec, & Sorenson, 2008; Laible & Carlo, 2004). Parents who fail to set rules are implicitly telling their children they don't care—they don't value their children enough to go to the trouble of creating rules and enforcing them. In much the same way, parents who refuse to discuss discipline with their children are saying, "Your opinions don't matter to me." Not surprisingly, when children internalize these messages, the result is lower overall self-worth.

Peers' views are important, too. Children's and particularly adolescents' self-worth is greater when they believe that their peers think highly of them (Harter, 2012). Lauren's self-worth increases, for example, when she hears that Pedro, Matt, and Michael think that she's the smartest girl in the eighth grade. Conversely, self-esteem drops when peers provide negative feedback, especially when those peers are popular themselves (Thomas et al., 2010).

The Myth of Storm and Stress

According to novelists and filmmakers, the search for identity that we just described is inherently a struggle, a time of storm and stress for adolescents. Although this view may make for best-selling novels and hit movies, in reality, the rebellious teen is vastly overstated. Adolescents generally enjoy happy and satisfying relationships with their parents (Steinberg, 2001). Most teens love their parents and feel loved by them. And they embrace many of their parents' values and look to them for advice.

Evidence from around the world documents that adolescence is not necessarily a time of turmoil and conflict. Teens in the U.S. Midwest reported that their parents support them—they listen, give good advice, and help make good decisions (Rueger et al., 2014). Adolescents in Turkey and Belgium rated their mothers as being very supportive, endorsing items such as "My mother supports me in dealing with problems" and "My mother talks to me in a comforting way" (Güngör & Bornstein, 2010). Finally, Palestinian teens who were refugees in Jordan described their families as being very close (Ahmad, Smetana, & Klimstra, 2015). These findings undercut the myth of adolescence as necessarily being a time when adolescent storms rain on parent–child relationships.

Of course, parent–child relations *do* change during adolescence. As teens become more independent, their relationships with their parents become more egalitarian. Parents must adjust to their children's growing sense of autonomy by treating them more like equals (Laursen & Collins, 1994). This growing independence means that teens spend less time with their parents; are less affectionate toward them; and argue more often with them about matters of style, taste, and freedom (Shanahan et al., 2007; Stanik, Riina, & McHale, 2013). Although adolescents do have more disagreements with parents, these disputes are usually relatively mild—bickering, not all-out shouting matches—and usually concern an adolescent's personal choices (e.g., hairstyle, clothing), autonomy, and responsibilities (Chen-Gaddini, 2012; Ehrlich, Dykas, & Cassidy, 2012). These changes are natural by-products of an evolving parent–child relationship in which the "child" is nearly a fully independent young adult (Steinberg & Silk, 2002).

Before you think that this portrait of parent–child relationships in adolescence is too good to be true, we want to add two cautionary notes. First, conflicts between parents and their adolescent children are often very distressing for *parents*, who may read far more into these conflicts than their teenagers do (Steinberg, 2001). Parents sometimes fear that arguments over attire or household chores may reflect more fundamental disagreements about values: A mother may interpret her son's refusal to clean his room as a rejection of values concerning the need for order and cleanliness, when the son simply doesn't want to waste time cleaning a room that he knows will soon become a mess again. Second, for a minority of families (roughly 25%), parent–child conflicts in adolescence are more serious and are associated with behavior problems in adolescents (Ehrlich et al., 2012). These more harmful conflicts are more common among adolescents who don't regulate their emotions well (Eisenberg et al., 2008), and they often predate adolescence—as children, these adolescents were prone to conflict with their parents (Steeger & Gondoli, 2013; Steinberg, 2001).

Response to question on page 293 about Dea's ethnic identity. Dea, the Dutch Asian American college student, doesn't know how to integrate the Korean heritage of her biological parents with the Dutch American culture in which she was reared. This would put her in the second phase of acquiring an ethnic identity. On the one hand, she is examining her ethnic roots, which means she's progressed beyond the initial stages. On the other hand, she has not yet integrated her Asian and European roots and so has not reached the third and final phase.

Recall

1. According to Erikson, adolescents face a crisis between identity and _____.

2. The _____ status would describe an adolescent who has attained an identity based almost entirely on her parents' advice and urging.

3. A person who has simply put off searching for an identity because it seems too confusing and too overwhelming is in the _____ status.

4. _____ refers to the fact that adolescents sometimes believe their lives are a performance with their peers watching them constantly.

5. Adolescents are most likely to achieve an identity when parents encourage them _____.

6. In the second phase of achieving an ethnic identity, adolescents _____.

7. Self-esteem often drops when students enter middle school or junior high school because young adolescents _____.

Interpret

- How do parent–child relationships change in adolescence? Do these changes indicate a period of storm and stress?

Apply

- The Tran family has just immigrated to the United States from Vietnam. The mother and father want their two children to grow up appreciating their Vietnamese heritage but worry that a strong ethnic identity may not be good for their kids. What advice would you give Mr. and Mrs. Tran about the impact of ethnic identity on children's development?

Check your answers to the Recall Questions at the end of the chapter.

9.2 Romantic Relationships and Sexuality

LEARNING OBJECTIVES

- Why do teenagers date?
- Why are some adolescents sexually active? Why do so few use contraceptives?
- Who are sexual-minority youth?
- What circumstances make date violence especially likely?

For six months, 15-year-old Gretchen has been dating Jeff, a 17-year-old. She thinks she is truly in love for the first time, and she often imagines being married to Jeff. They have had sex a few times, each time without contraception. It sometimes crosses Gretchen's mind that if she gets pregnant, she could move into her own apartment and begin a family.

The fires of romantic relationships have long warmed the hearts of American adolescents. Often, as with Jeff and Gretchen, romance leads to sex. In this section, we'll explore adolescent dating and sexual behavior. As we do, you'll better understand Gretchen's reasons for having unprotected sex with Jeff.

Romantic Relationships

The social landscape adds a distinctive landmark in adolescence—romantic relationships. These are uncommon during elementary school, but by high school, roughly two-thirds of U.S. adolescents have had a romantic relationship within the previous one-and-a-half years and most have been involved in a romance lasting nearly a year (Carver, Joyner, & Udry, 2003). However, cultural factors influence the timing of romantic relationships for teenagers in America. Traditional Latino American and Asian American parents emphasize family ties and loyalty to parents. Because romantic relationships are a sign of independence and usually result in less time spent with family, it's not surprising that Latino American and Asian American adolescents often begin to date at an older age and date less frequently (Collins, Welsh, & Furman, 2009).

Think About It

According to the "storm and stress" view of adolescence, sexual behavior is one way for adolescents to rebel against their parents. Does research on adolescent sexuality support this prediction?

Adolescent romantic relationships build on friendships and offer companionship as well as an outlet for sexual exploration.

Romantic relationships build on friendships. Like friends, romantic partners tend to be similar in popularity and physical attractiveness. And a best friendship serves as both a prototype for and a source of support during ups and downs of close relationships (Collins et al., 2009). What's more, romantic relationships change over time in ways that resemble changes in friendship: For younger adolescents, romantic relationships offer companionship (like that provided by a best friend) and an outlet for sexual exploration. For older adolescents like those in the photo, intimacy, trust, and support become important features of romantic relationships (Shulman & Kipnis, 2001). Finally, like friendships, when children have high-quality parenting, they more readily invest in romantic relationships as adults (Oriña et al., 2011).

It's tempting to dismiss teen romances as nothing more than puppy love, but they are often developmentally significant (Collins et al., 2009). On the one hand, adolescents involved in a romantic relationship are often more self-confident and have greater self-esteem. And high-quality adolescent romances are associated with positive relationships during adulthood. On the other hand, adolescents in romantic relationships report more emotional upheaval and conflict. In addition, early dating with many different partners is associated with a host of problems in adolescence (e.g., drug use, lower grades) and is associated with less satisfying romantic relationships in adulthood (Furman & Rose, 2015).

Sexual Behavior

We've already seen that sexual exploration is an important feature of romantic relationships for younger adolescents. In fact, by the end of high school, about two-thirds of American adolescents will have had intercourse at least once (Eaton et al., 2008). No single factor predicts adolescent sexual behavior. Instead, adolescents are more likely to be sexually active when they acquire (from parents, peers, and media) permissive attitudes toward sex, when their parents don't monitor their behavior, when they are more physically mature, and when they drink alcohol regularly (Belsky et al., 2010; Collins et al., 2011; Hipwell et al., 2010; Zimmer-Gembeck & Helfand, 2008). What's more, adolescents exposed to harsh environments (e.g., living in poverty) start having sex at younger ages, but adolescents with better executive functioning start at older ages (Carlson, Mendle, & Harden, 2014; Khurana et al., 2012).

Although a majority of boys and girls have sex at some point during adolescence, sexual activity has very different meanings for boys and girls (Brooks-Gunn & Paikoff, 1993). Girls tend to describe their first sexual partner as "someone they love," but boys describe their first partner as a "casual date." Girls report stronger feelings of love for their first sexual partner than for a later partner, but boys don't. Girls have mixed feelings after their first sexual experience—fear and guilt mixed with happiness and excitement—whereas boys' feelings are more uniformly positive. Finally, when describing their sexual experiences to peers, girls' peers typically express some disapproval but boys' peers typically do not. In short, for boys, sexual behavior is viewed as recreational and self-oriented; for girls, sexual behavior is viewed as romantic and is interpreted through their capacity to form intimate interpersonal relationships (Steinberg, 1999).

Sexually Transmitted Diseases

Adolescent sexual activity is cause for concern because a number of diseases are transmitted from one person to another through sexual intercourse. ❱ Table 9.3 lists several of the most common types of sexually transmitted infections (STIs). Most STIs are readily cured with antibiotics. In contrast, the prognosis is bleak for individuals who contract the human immunodeficiency virus (HIV), which typically leads to acquired immunodeficiency syndrome (AIDS). In persons with AIDS, the immune system is no longer able to protect the body from infections, and they often die from one of these infections.

Table 9.3

Features of Sexually Transmitted Infections			
DISEASE	**U.S. FREQUENCY**	**SYMPTOMS**	**COMPLICATIONS**
Caused by Bacteria			
Chlamydia	3.3% of adolescent females and 0.7% of adolescent males	75% of women and 50% of men have no symptoms; sometimes abnormal discharge of pus from the vagina or penis or pain while urinating	Infections of the cervix and Fallopian tubes that can lead to infertility; rare in men
Gonorrhea	0.6% of adolescent females and 0.3% of adolescent males	Often no symptoms at all; pus discharged from the penis or vagina, pain associated with urination; for women, pain during intercourse; for men, swollen testicles	Pelvic inflammatory disease, a serious infection of the female reproductive tract that can lead to infertility; in men, epididymitis, an infection of the testicles that can lead to infertility
Syphilis	About 4,000 cases annually among 15- to 24-year-olds	A sore, called a chancre, at the site of the infection—usually the penis, vulva, or vagina	Left untreated, can damage internal organs such as the brain, nerves, eyes, heart, bones, and joints
Caused by Virus			
Genital herpes	At least 45 million of age 12 and older (roughly 1 in 5 adolescents and adults)	Itching, burning, or pain in the genital or anal area; sores on the mouth, penis, or vagina	Recurrent sores; pregnant women can pass the virus (which can be fatal to the newborn) to the baby during birth
Genital human papilloma virus (HPV)	20 million	Usually no symptoms; sometimes genital warts or discharge from the penis or vagina	Usually goes away; in rare cases leads to cervical cancer
Hepatitis B	About 75,000 annually	Jaundice, fatigue, loss of appetite, abdominal pain	Death from chronic liver disease
HIV	About 40,000 diagnosed annually	Initially a flulike illness; later, enlarged lymph nodes, lack of energy, weight loss, frequent fevers	Loss of immune cells (AIDS), cancer, death

© 2019 Cengage

SOURCE: Centers for Disease Control and Prevention, 2007, 2010.

Young adults—those in their 20s—account for roughly one-third of all new cases of AIDS in the United States and many contracted the disease during adolescence (Centers for Disease Control and Prevention, 2016). Many factors make adolescents especially susceptible to AIDS. Teenagers and young adults are more likely than older adults to engage in unprotected sex and to use intravenous drugs, which are common pathways for the transmission of AIDS.

Teenage Pregnancy and Contraception

Adolescents' sexual behavior is also troubling because among American adolescent girls who have had intercourse, approximately one in eight becomes pregnant. The result is that nearly a quarter million babies are born to American teenagers annually. African American and Latino American adolescents are most likely to become pregnant (Kost & Maddow-Zimet, 2016).

Teen pregnancy is common because many sexually active teens do not use birth control consistently or correctly (Guttmacher Institute, 2013). Some adolescents see no need because they believe they are invulnerable—that only others become pregnant. Others don't know how to use contraception or where to obtain it (Ralph & Brindis, 2010). And some adolescent girls, like Gretchen from the opening vignette, avoid contraception because they see becoming pregnant as a way to break away from parents and gain status as an independent-living adult (Phipps et al., 2008).

How can we reduce adolescent sexual behavior and teen pregnancy? Parents matter: when they discuss sex with their teenage children, those children are more likely to use contraception (Widman et al., 2016). However, more effective are comprehensive sex education programs that teach the biological aspects of sex and emphasize sexual behavior that is responsible and safe. Teens who participate in such programs know more about the risks of unprotected sex and better understand contraception as well as have safer sexual practices, such as using contraceptives and limiting sexual partners (Denford et al., 2017).

Think About It

Suppose you had to convince a group of 15-year-olds about the hazards of adolescent sex and teenage pregnancy. What would you say?

Sexual Minority Youth

For most adolescents, dating and romance involve members of the opposite sex. However, in early and mid-adolescence, some identify as gay, lesbian, bisexual, queer, intersex, or transgender; collectively, these adolescents are often described as sexual-minority youth (Martin-Storey, 2016). The paths that lead to youth to identify with a sexual minority are poorly understood. For boys who identify as gay, one idea is that genes and hormones may lead some boys to feel "different" during early adolescence; these feelings lead to an interest in gender-atypical activities and, later, attraction to other males (Diamond, 2007). For females, the path to a sexual-minority identity is more variable. During adolescence, some girls are attracted to girls and consistently identify as lesbians thereafter. For some women, attraction to other females does not emerge until later in life, often growing out of deep feelings for a particular woman. And still other women have repeated transitions in their sexual orientation and identity (Farr, Diamond, & Boker, 2014).

Scientists know even less about transgender youth—those whose gender identity does not match their biological sex. This identity often emerges early. For example, some preschool boys insist that they are girls and resist parental efforts to become more masculine but are happy when allowed to wear their hair long and wear girl's clothing. These children were once thought to be confused about their gender identity and they received treatment designed to align their gender identity with their biological sex. An alternative, more recent view is a transgender identity is simply an uncommon but normal gender identity, one that's most likely in children who insist they *are* members of the other sex, not just that they wish they were members of the other sex (Olson, 2016).

Although the origins of gender identity in sexual-minority youth are not yet well understood, it is clear that they face many challenges. Their behavior and appearance often differ from what's considered appropriate for their gender, leading them to be harassed and attacked by others; in turn, this may lead sexual-minority youth to experience mental health problems, including depression and anxiety (Martin-Storey, 2016). However, in recent years, more (and more visible) role models and more centers for sexual-minority youth are making it easier for these youth to cope; most end up as well-adjusted as heterosexual youth (Olson et al., 2016; Saewyc, 2011).

About 5% of adolescents identify themselves as gay or lesbian.

Greg Ceo/The Image Bank/Getty Images

Dating Violence

As adolescents begin to explore romantic relationships and sex, many teens experience violence in dating, which can include physical violence (e.g., being hit or kicked), emotional violence (e.g., experiencing threats or bullying designed to harm self-worth), sexual violence (being forced to engage in sexual activity against one's will), or stalking (being harassed or threatened in a way designed to frighten). Roughly 20% of adolescent girls and 10% of adolescent boys report these experiences, and, as you can imagine, these youth often don't do well in school and suffer from mental health and behavioral problems (Centers for Disease Control, 2016).

Several factors make teenage boys and girls more likely to perpetrate dating violence. Parents contribute: Teens are more likely to be violent during dating when they're exposed to violence at home—either through maltreatment from their parents or from observing violence between their parents (Calvete et al., 2017). But dating violence is less likely when teens have caring parents who communicate well with them (Kast, Eisenberg, & Sieving, 2016). Peers matter as well: Dating violence is more common when teens believe that their peers condone dating violence, when they know peers who are in abusive relationships, and when their school's climate condones dating violence (Garthe, Sullivan, & McDaniel, 2017; Giordano et al., 2015). Finally, teens are more likely to commit dating violence when they're antisocial, aggressive, not successful in school, and use drugs (Foshee & Reyes, 2012; Johnson et al., 2017).

Because dating violence leads to many harmful consequences for victims, including depression, antisocial behavior, and substance abuse, scientists have devised programs to prevent dating violence. For example, in a program called "Families for Safe Dates," teens and parents completed activities designed to reduce the risk of dating abuse (e.g., how to recognize data abuse). For example, one booklet used dating scenarios to teach teens and caregivers how to recognize dating abuse. Compared with teens in the control condition, teens in the treatment condition were much less accepting of dating abuse and they experienced less physical abuse (Foshee et al., 2012, 2015).

Most colleges and universities offer workshops on dating abuse. The first generation of programs focused on individuals, aiming to change attitudes and behaviors that put individuals at risk. However, newer programs take a community-based approach, one that emphasizes that all members of a community (e.g., a college campus) have a stake in preventing dating violence. Accordingly, bystanders learn to recognize situations conducive to sexual violence and learn strategies for intervening effectively and safely. For example, One Act is a program developed at the University of North Carolina–Chapel Hill that includes four hours of instruction—typically given to student organizations (e.g., fraternities)—in which students use role play to learn to recognize warning signs, to learn effective strategies (e.g., create a distraction), and to learn how to follow up to be sure the situation is resolved. Programs like these make students less tolerant of dating violence as well as more willing and better able to intervene (Alegría-Flores et al., 2017).

TEST YOURSELF 9.2

Recall

1. For younger adolescents, romantic relationships offer companionship and _____.

2. Adolescents are more likely to have sex when they acquire permissive attitudes toward sex and when they're exposed to _____ environments.

3. Adolescents and young adults are at particular risk for contracting AIDS when they _____ and use intravenous drugs.

4. Adolescents often fail to use contraception because they believe they are invulnerable, don't know how to use contraception or where to obtain it, and _____.

5. For some boys, the first step toward a gay sexual orientation occurs in early development when they _____.

6. Teens are more likely to perpetrate dating violence when their parents' discipline is harsh, when they believe that their peers _____ and when they are antisocial, aggressive, not successful in school, and use drugs.

Interpret

- Some sexually active teenagers do not use contraceptives. How do the reasons for this failure show connections between cognitive, social, and emotional development?

Apply

- Prepare a brief fact sheet for incoming college freshmen that summarizes the factors that put women at risk for dating violence.

Check your answers to the Recall Questions at the end of the chapter.

- How do adolescents select an occupation?
- What is the impact of part-time employment on adolescents?

When 15-year-old Aaron announced that he wanted an after-school job at the local supermarket, his mother was delighted, believing that he would learn much from the experience. Five months later, she has her doubts. Aaron has lost interest in school, and they argue constantly about how he spends his money.

"What do you want to be when you grow up?" Children are often asked this question in fun. However, it takes on special significance in adolescence because work is such an important element of the adult life that looms on the horizon. A job—be it as a bricklayer, reporter, or child care worker—helps define who we are. In this section, we'll see how adolescents begin to think about possible occupations. We'll also look at adolescents' first exposure to the world of work, which usually occurs in the form of part-time jobs after school or on weekends. As we do, we'll see whether Aaron's changed behavior is typical of teens who work part-time.

Career Development

In most developed nations, adolescence is a time when youth face the challenge of selecting a career. According to a theory proposed by Donald Super (1976, 1980), identity is a primary force in an adolescent's choice of a career. *At about age 13 or 14, adolescents use their emerging identity as a source of ideas about careers, a process called* crystallization. Teenagers use their ideas about their own talents and interests to limit potential career prospects. A teenager who is extroverted and sociable may decide that working with people is the career for him. Decisions are provisional, and adolescents experiment with hypothetical careers, trying to envision what each is like. Discussions with parents help adolescents refine their emerging ideas; schools also help by providing job fairs and assessing students' job-related interests (Diemer, 2007).

crystallization

First phase in Super's theory of career development, in which adolescents use their emerging identities to form ideas about careers.

In the specification stage of career development, adolescents try to learn more about different careers, sometimes by serving an apprenticeship.

Mark Richard/PhotoEdit

At about age 18, adolescents extend the activities associated with crystallization and enter a new phase. *During* specification, *individuals further limit their career possibilities by learning more about specific lines of work and starting to obtain the training required for a specific job.* The extroverted teenager who wants to work with people may decide that a career in sales is a good match for his abilities and interests. The teen who likes math may have learned more about careers and decided that she'd like to be an accountant. Some teens may begin an apprenticeship as a way to learn a trade.

The end of the teenage years or the early 20s marks the beginning of the third phase. *During* implementation, *individuals enter the workforce and learn firsthand about jobs.* This is a time of learning about responsibility and productivity, of learning to get along with coworkers, and of altering lifestyle to accommodate work. This period is often unstable; individuals may change jobs frequently as they adjust to the reality of life in the workplace.

In the Real People feature, you can see these three phases in one young woman's career development.

specification

Second phase in Super's theory of career development, in which adolescents learn more about specific lines of work and begin training.

implementation

Third phase in Super's theory of career development, in which individuals enter the workforce.

Real People   Applying Human Development

"The Life of Lynne": A Drama in Three Acts

Act 1: Crystallization. Throughout high school, Lynne was active in a number of organizations. She often served as the treasurer and found it satisfying to keep the financial records in order. By the end of her junior year, Lynne decided that she wanted to study business in college, a decision that fit with her good grades in English and math.

Act 2: Specification. Lynne was accepted into the business school of a large state university. She decided that accounting fit her

skills and temperament, so this became her major. During the summers, she worked as a cashier at Target. This helped pay for college and gave her experience in the world of retail sales.

Act 3: Implementation. A few months after graduation, Lynne was offered a junior accounting position with Walmart. Her job required that she work Tuesday through Friday, auditing Walmart stores in several nearby cities. Lynne liked the pay, the company car,

the pay, the feeling of independence, and the pay. However, having to hit the road every morning by 7:30 was a jolt to someone used to rising at 10. Also, Lynne often found it awkward to deal with store managers, many of whom were twice her age and often intimidating. She was coming to the conclusion that there was more to a successful career as an accountant than simply having the numbers add up correctly.

"The Life of Lynne" illustrates the progressive refinement that takes place in a person's career development. An initial interest in math and finance led to a degree in business, which led to a job as an accountant. However, one other aspect of Lynne's life sheds more light on Super's theory. After 18 months on the job, Lynne's accounting group was merged with another. The merger would have required Lynne to move to another state; she quit instead. After six months looking for another accounting job, Lynne gave up and began studying to become a real estate agent. The moral? Economic conditions and opportunities also shape career development. Changing times can force individuals to take new, often unexpected career paths.

Personality-Type Theory

Super's (1976, 1980) work helps to explain how self-concept and career aspirations develop hand in hand, but his theory does not explain why particular individuals are attracted to one line of work rather than another. Explaining the match between people and occupations has been the aim of a theory devised by John Holland (1985, 1987, 1996). *According to Holland's* personality-type theory, *people find work fulfilling when the important features of a job or profession fit their personality.* Holland identified six prototypic personalities that are relevant to the world of work. Each one is best suited to a specific set of occupations, as indicated in the right-hand column of ▶ Table 9.4. Remember, these are merely prototypes. Most people do not match any one personality type exactly. Instead, their work-related personalities are a blend of the six.

personality-type theory

View proposed by Holland that people find their work fulfilling when the important features of a job or profession fit their personality.

Table 9.4

Personality Types in Holland's Theory

PERSONALITY TYPE	DESCRIPTION	CAREERS
Realistic	Individuals enjoy doing physical labor and working with their hands; they like to solve concrete problems.	Mechanic, truck driver, construction worker
Investigative	Individuals are task-oriented and enjoy thinking about abstract relations.	Scientist, technical writer
Social	Individuals are skilled verbally and interpersonally; they enjoy solving problems using these skills.	Teacher, counselor, social worker
Conventional	Individuals have verbal and quantitative skills that they like to apply to structured, well-defined tasks assigned to them by others.	Bank teller, payroll clerk, traffic manager
Enterprising	Individuals enjoy using their verbal skills in positions of power, status, and leadership.	Business executive, television producer, real estate agent
Artistic	Individuals enjoy expressing themselves through unstructured tasks.	Poet, musician, actor

© 2019 Cengage

When people have jobs that match their personality type, they are more productive employees in the short run and they have more stable career paths in the long run (Holland, 1996; Nye et al., 2012). For example, an enterprising youth is likely to be successful in business because he enjoys positions of power in which he can use his verbal skills. This model is useful in describing the career preferences of African, Asian, European, Native, and Latino American adolescents (Gupta, Tracey, & Gore, 2008).

Social Cognitive Career Theory

Another approach to career choice combines elements of Super's focus on development and Holland's focus on the match between interests and careers. According to social cognitive career theory (Brown & Lent, 2016; Lent, 2005) progress toward a vocation rests on self-efficacy, which refers to youths' beliefs about their ability to succeed in specific domains and their outcome expectations, which refers to youths' beliefs about the likely outcome of their behavior. These beliefs are based on youths' history of success and failures. As children and adolescents experience success and failure on different activities and tasks, they develop beliefs about themselves and beliefs about usual outcomes. These beliefs lead to interests—youth enjoy activities in which they're skilled and likely to succeed. And interests lead to goals—youth decide that they should pursue activities in which they're interested. Pursuing these activities often leads to additional success, strengthening youths' beliefs about themselves and the outcomes they're likely to experience.

According to Holland's personality-type theory, people are satisfied with a job when it matches their personality; for example, adolescents with an enterprising personality type enjoy working in business because this allows them to use verbal skills in positions of leadership.

Dmitry Kalinovsky/Shutterstock.com

We've summarized these connections in ▶Figure 9.1 and you can see them in an example. Imagine a fourth grader who is often successful on math tests. Over time, she comes to believe that she's good at math and that she's usually successful on math-related activities. These beliefs forge an interest in math and promote math-related goals (e.g., joining a math club), and participating in these activities would typically reinforce her beliefs about her strengths in math. As she starts to think about work, she naturally thinks about occupations that would allow her to pursue her math-related interests and goals. Similarly, success in art, sports, or literature could forge beliefs, interests, and goals in those domains. Thus, social cognitive career theory helps to explain why adolescents

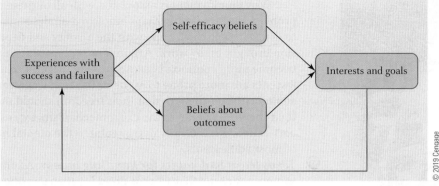

Based on Lent (2005), Figure 7.2.

▶ **Figure 9.1**

In social cognitive career theory, experiences lead to beliefs, which are linked to interests and goals.

develop interests in some domains but not in others and it explains how, over time, experiences, beliefs, and interests gradually lead adolescents to target occupations that are well suited to them.

Of course, whether a person pursues a specific job (and is successful in it) depends on more than the match between interests, skills, and the important features of a job. Even when people are potentially well suited for a job, they may not be able to obtain the education or experience that's necessary (e.g., the fourth grader who's a math star may be unable to afford to go to college). Or they may get a job for which they're well suited but not enjoy it because of stress in the workplace or frequent conflicts between work and family obligations (Hammer et al., 2005). We'll discuss these issues in more detail in Chapter 12. Nevertheless, the theories we've described here describe the first steps in moving toward a vocation.

Part-Time Employment

About 20% of American high-school students hold part-time jobs, typically in retail (Child Trends, 2016). Most adults praise teens for working, believing that early exposure to the workplace teaches adolescents self-discipline, self-confidence, and important job skills (Stevens, 2016). For most adolescents, however, the reality is quite different. Part-time work can actually be harmful, for several reasons.

(1.) *School performance suffers.* When students work more than approximately 15 to 20 hours per week, they become less engaged in school and are less likely to be successful in college, particularly if they are European Americans (Bachman et al., 2013; Hwang & Domina, 2017). Many high school students apparently do not have the foresight and discipline necessary to consistently meet the combined demands of work and school.

(2.) *Mental health and behavioral problems.* Adolescents who work long hours—more than 15 or 20 hours a week—are more likely to experience anxiety and depression; in addition, their self-esteem and quality of life often suffer. Many adolescents find themselves in jobs that are repetitive and boring but stressful, and such conditions undermine self-esteem and breed anxiety. Extensive part-time work frequently leads to substance abuse and frequent problem behavior (e.g., antisocial behavior, including theft), especially for younger teens who attend school sporadically (Graves et al., 20117; Monahan, Steinberg, & Cauffman, 2013).

Think About It

How do the different personality types in Holland's theory relate to the different types of intelligence proposed by Howard Gardner, described in Chapter 6?

Many American adolescents hold part-time jobs; these can be beneficial but not when adolescents work more than 15 to 20 hours a week.

When adolescents work long hours in a part-time job, they often have trouble juggling the demands of work, school, and sleep.

Think About It

Think back to your own high school years and those of your friends. Think of students (including yourself) who showed harmful effects from part-time work. Think of people who benefited from part-time work.

Why employment is associated with all of these problems is not clear. Perhaps employed adolescents turn to drugs to help them cope with the anxiety and depression brought on by work. Arguments with parents may become more common because anxious, depressed adolescents are more prone to argue or because wage-earning adolescents may believe that their freedom should match their income. Whatever the exact mechanism, extensive part-time work is clearly detrimental to the mental health of most adolescents.

3. *Teens learn bad habits for handling money.* Adults sometimes argue that work is good for teenagers because it teaches them "the value of a dollar," but in reality, the typical teenage pattern is to "earn and spend." Working adolescents spend most of their earnings on themselves: to buy clothing, snack food, or cosmetics and to pay for entertainment. Few working teens set aside much of their income for future goals, such as a college education, or use it to contribute to their family's expenses (Bachman et al., 2014). Because parents customarily pay for many of the essential expenses associated with independent living—rent, utilities, and groceries, for example—working adolescents often have a much higher percentage of their income available for discretionary spending than do working adults. Thus, for many teens, the part-time work experience provides unrealistic expectations about how income can be allocated.

The message that emerges repeatedly from research on part-time employment is hardly encouraging. Like Aaron, the teenage boy in the vignette, adolescents who work long hours at part-time jobs do not benefit from the experience. To the contrary, they do worse in school, are more likely to have behavioral problems, and learn how to spend rather than manage money. Ironically, though, there is a long-term benefit: Young adults who had a stressful part-time job as an adolescent are better able to cope with stressful adult jobs (Mortimer & Staff, 2004).

Does this mean that teenagers who are still in school should never work part-time? Not necessarily. Part-time employment can be a good experience, depending on the circumstances. One key is the number of hours of work. Although the exact number of hours varies from one student to the next, most students could easily work five hours a week without harm, and many could work ten hours a week. Another key is the type of job. When adolescents have jobs that allow them to use their skills (e.g., bookkeeping, computing, or typing) and acquire new ones, self-esteem is enhanced and they learn from their work experience (Staff, Mont'Alvao, & Mortimer, 2015). Yet another factor is the link between work and school: Teens often benefit from apprenticeships or internships that are explicitly linked to school so that work experiences complement classroom experiences (Symonds, Schwartz, & Ferguson, 2011). A final factor is how teens spend their earnings. When they save their money or use it to pay for clothes and school expenses, the relationship with their parents often improves (Shanahan et al., 1996).

By these criteria, who is likely to show the harmful effects of part-time work? A teen who spends 30 hours a week bagging groceries and spends most of it on food, clothes, and video games. Who is likely to benefit from part-time work? A teen who likes to create apps for smartphones and spends Saturdays working at an Apple store, setting aside some of his earnings for college.

Finally, summer jobs typically do not involve conflict between work and school. Consequently, many of the harmful effects associated with part-time employment during the school year do not hold for summer employment. In fact, such employment has benefits. Following a summer of full-time employment, many high school students do better in school and are less likely to be involved in criminal activity (Heller, 2014; Schwartz, Leos-Urbel, & Wiswall, 2015).

Recall

1. During the _____ phase of vocational choice, adolescents learn more about specific lines of work and begin training.

2. Individuals with a(n) _____ personality type are best suited for a career as a teacher or counselor.

3. Adolescents who work extensively at part-time jobs during the school year often get lower grades, have behavior problems, and _____.

4. Part-time employment during the school year can be beneficial if adolescents limit the number of hours they work and _____.

Interpret

- Based on the description of Lynne's career, how would you describe continuity of vocational development during adolescence and young adulthood?

Apply

- Suppose that you are a high school guidance counselor and have been asked to prepare a set of guidelines for students who want to work part-time. What would you recommend?

Check your answers to the Recall Questions at the end of the chapter.

9.4 The Dark Side

LEARNING OBJECTIVES

- Why do teenagers drink and use drugs?

- What leads some adolescents to become depressed? How can depression be treated?

- What are the causes of juvenile delinquency?

Jaylen was an excellent student and a starter on his high school basketball team. He was looking forward to going to the senior prom with Makayla, his long-time girlfriend, and then going to the state college with her in the fall. Then, without a hint that anything was wrong in their relationship, Makayla dropped Jaylen and moved in with the singer in a hip hop band. Jaylen was stunned and miserable. Without Makayla, life meant so little. Basketball and college seemed pointless. Some days Jaylen wondered if he should just kill himself to make the pain go away.

Some young people do not adapt well to the new demands and responsibilities of adolescence and respond in ways that are unhealthy. In this last section of Chapter 9, we look at three problems, often interrelated, that create the "three Ds" of adolescent development: drugs, depression, and delinquency. As we look at these problems, you'll understand why Jaylen feels so miserable without Makayla.

Drug Use

Teenage Drinking

Teen use of illicit drugs such as cocaine and methamphetamine often makes headlines, but in reality, most adolescents avoid drugs, with one glaring exception—alcohol. About half of U.S. high school seniors have drunk alcohol within the past year, and about one-third report that they've been drunk (Johnston et al., 2017).

Teens are more likely to drink when their parents drink, when their parents do not monitor their teen's behavior, and when parents are not warm toward them (Donaldson, Handren, & Crano, 2016). Also, they're more likely to drink when peers do (Leung, Toumbourou, & Hemphill, 2014). Finally, teens who report frequent life stresses—problems with parents or peers and, for minority teens, racial discrimination—more often drink (Goldbach et al., 2015).

Adolescents often drink because their peers encourage them.

depression

Disorder characterized by pervasive feelings of sadness, irritability, and low self-esteem.

Adolescents sometimes become depressed when they feel as if they've lost control of their lives.

Because teenage drinking has so many causes, no single approach is likely to eliminate alcohol abuse. Adolescents who drink to reduce their tension can profit from therapy designed to teach them more effective means of coping with stress. School-based programs that are interactive—featuring student-led discussion—can be effective in teaching the facts about drinking and strategies for resisting peer pressure to drink (Agabio et al., 2017). Stopping teens from drinking before it becomes habitual is essential because adolescents who drink are at risk for becoming alcohol-dependent, depressed, or anxious as adults (Cable & Sacker, 2008; Trim et al., 2007).

Teenage Smoking

Approximately 30% of American teens experiment with cigarette smoking at some point in their teenage years (Johnston et al., 2017). American teenagers who smoke typically begin sometime between sixth and ninth grade. As was true for teenage drinking, parents and peers are influential in determining whether youth smoke. When parents smoke, their teenage children are more likely to smoke, too. But the parent–child relationship also contributes: Teens are less likely to smoke when they experience the supportive parenting associated with authoritative parenting (Foster et al., 2007). Like parents, peer influences can be direct and indirect. Teenagers more often smoke when peers do (Fujimoto, Unger, & Valente, 2012). However, a more subtle influence of peers on teen smoking comes from informal school norms. When most students in a school think that it's okay to smoke—even though many of them do not themselves smoke—teens are more likely to start smoking (Su & Supple, 2016).

The dangers of cigarette smoking for adults are well known. Many teenage smokers believe that cigarette smoking is harmless. But they're wrong: Smoking can interfere with the growth of the lungs, and teens who smoke often have a variety of health problems such as respiratory illnesses. What's more, smoking is often the fateful first step on the path to abuse of more powerful substances, including alcohol, marijuana, and cocaine (Strong, Juon, & Ensminger, 2016).

Faced with these many harmful consequences of teenage smoking, health care professionals and human development researchers have worked hard to create effective programs to discourage adolescents from smoking. In fact, just as comprehensive school-based programs can reduce teenage sex, such programs are effective in reducing teenage smoking. These programs typically provide information about short- and long-term health and social consequences of smoking and provide students with effective ways to respond to peer pressure to smoke. In addition, programs are most effective when they are implemented alongside community initiatives, such as banning smoking in public places popular with youth (Dobbins et al., 2008).

Depression

The challenges of adolescence can lead some youth to become depressed (Fried, 2005). *When suffering from* depression, *adolescents have pervasive feelings of sadness, are irritable, have low self-esteem, sleep poorly, and are unable to concentrate.* About 5% to 15% of adolescents are depressed; adolescent girls are more often affected than boys, probably because social challenges in adolescence are greater for girls than boys (Garber & Rao, 2014). Depressed adolescents are often unhappy, angry, and annoyed. They believe that family and peers are not friendly to them (Cole & Jordan, 1995), and they are often extremely lonely (Mahon et al., 2006). Rather than being satisfying and rewarding, life is empty and joyless for depressed adolescents.

Depression is often triggered when adolescents experience a serious loss, disappointment, or failure, such as when a loved one dies or when a much-anticipated date turns out to be a fiasco (Schneiders et al., 2006). Think back to Jaylen, the adolescent in the vignette at the beginning of this section. His girlfriend had been the center of his life. When she left him unexpectedly, he felt helpless to control his own destiny. Similarly, an athlete may play poorly in the championship game because of illness, or a high school senior may get a lower score on the SAT exam because of a family crisis the night before the test. In each case, the adolescent could do nothing to avoid an undesirable result.

Of course, many adolescents experience negative events like these, but don't become depressed. Why? Heredity plays a role, putting some adolescents at greater risk for depression. Another contributing factor is temperament: Children who are less able to regulate their emotions are, as adolescents, more prone to depression. A third factor is a belief system in which adolescents see themselves in an extremely negative light. Depression-prone adolescents are, for example, more likely to blame themselves for failure (Gregory et al., 2007). Thus, after the disappointing date, a depression-prone teen is likely to think "I acted like a fool," instead of placing blame elsewhere by thinking "Gee—he was a real jerk!" (Garber & Rao, 2014).

Parents and families can also put an adolescent at risk for depression. Not surprisingly, adolescents more often become depressed when their parents are critical of them, don't respect their opinions and choices, and seem unwilling to accept them as they are. In addition, adolescents are at risk when parents are inconsistent in their discipline and when they're frequently in conflict with one another (Yap et al., 2014).

Another potential trigger for depression—racial discrimination—is the focus of the Spotlight on Research feature.

> **Think** About It
>
> How does depression illustrate the interaction of biological, psychological, and sociocultural forces on development?

Spotlight On Research

Does Racial Discrimination Lead to Depression?

Who were the investigators, and what was the aim of the study? Many African American adolescents are subject to racial discrimination, an experience that is extremely stressful. Because other stress-producing events (e.g., parental conflict) have been linked to depression, Devin English, Sharon Lambert, and Nicholas Ialongo (2014) wondered whether experiencing racial discrimination would make African American youth more prone to depression.

How did the investigators measure the topic of interest? The investigators had African American youth complete two questionnaires. One assessed their perception of racial discrimination. For example, they were asked how often they believed they had been left out of a group activity because of discrimination. The second questionnaire assessed frequency of symptoms of depression, such as feeling sad and lonely and sleeping poorly.

Who were the participants in the study? The study included 504 African American teenagers living in Baltimore, Maryland. They were tested annually in grades 7 to 10.

What was the design of the study? The study was correlational because researchers examined links between perceived racial discrimination and symptoms of depression. The study was longitudinal because adolescents were tested in four successive years.

Were there ethical concerns with the study? No. The questionnaires were ones used often by other researchers. The teens agreed to participate and their parents provided consent.

What were the results? The left panel of ▶ Figure 9.2 shows correlations between racial discrimination and symptoms of depression two years later (racial discrimination at grade 7 and depression at grade 9; racial discrimination at grade 8 and depression at grade 10). The correlations—positive and statistically significant—indicate that greater perceived racial discrimination was associated with more symptoms of depression. The right panel shows the complementary correlations—predicting racial discrimination

[Continued on next page]

from depressive symptoms. In both cases, these correlations are not significant.

What did the investigators conclude? Racial discrimination, a well-established stressor, can put African American youth at risk for depression. English and his colleagues note "for African American adolescents, experienced racial discrimination predicted depressive symptoms … the persistence of this predictive association across adolescence suggests that experiencing racial discrimination is a phenomenon that is chronic and detrimental across the life span for African Americans" (p. 1194).

What converging evidence would strengthen these conclusions? One limitation of the study is that racial discrimination and depression were both estimated by responses from the adolescents themselves. The findings would be more compelling if one of the constructs were measured independently; for example, parents could be asked to judge adolescents' depressive symptoms. In addition, stress is the assumed link between racial discrimination and depression; it would be valuable to assess stress and to assess those links (racial discrimination→stress and stress→depression) directly.

▶ **Figure 9.2**

African American adolescents who perceive that they are victims of racial discrimination are more likely to become depressed.

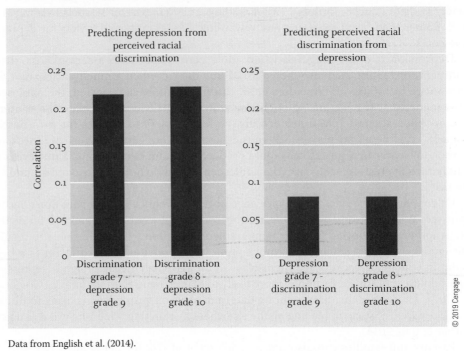

Data from English et al. (2014).

Treating Depression

Drugs and psychotherapy are successful in helping adolescents who are depressed. Drugs operate by allowing the brain regions that regulate mood to communicate more effectively. Although drug treatment reduces the symptoms of depression, many adolescents dislike this kind of treatment and often don't take drugs that are prescribed. Consequently, psychotherapy is often the preferred approach. For example, in cognitive behavioral therapy, adolescents learn to replace negative thoughts (e.g., blaming themselves) with more positive thoughts and they learn how to become involved in activities that are pleasurable and rewarding. These methods work, but we still don't know the conditions under which they are most effective (Asarnow & Miranda, 2014).

Preventing Teen Suicides

Suicide is the third most frequent cause of death (after accidents and homicide) among U.S. adolescents: Nearly 10% of adolescents report having attempted suicide. Girls are nearly twice as likely as boys to attempt suicide; Native American and Latino teens are more likely to attempt suicide than other groups (Centers for Disease Control and Prevention, 2015).

Many features are linked to suicide, including substance abuse and a family history of suicide, but the strongest predictor is depression. Between 40 and 80% of teens who attempt suicide are depressed (Cash & Bridge, 2009). Few suicides are truly spontaneous, and in most cases, there are warning signs, such as talking about death or looking for ways to kill one's self. If someone you know shows these signs, *don't ignore them* and don't leave him or her alone. Seek help immediately: call 911 or contact a mental health professional (Rudd et al., 2006).

Delinquency

Adolescents are responsible for much of the criminal activity committed in the United States. For example, they account for about 15% of all arrests for violent crimes (Federal Bureau of Investigation, 2016). To understand such delinquent behavior, we need to distinguish two forms of antisocial behavior (Piquero & Moffitt, 2014). The most common form is relatively mild: **Adolescent-limited antisocial behavior** *refers to relatively minor criminal acts by adolescents who aren't consistently antisocial.* These youth may become involved in petty crimes such as shoplifting or using drugs but may be careful to follow all school rules. As the name implies, their antisocial behavior is short-lived, usually vanishing in late adolescence or early adulthood.

A second form of delinquent behavior is far more serious but, fortunately, much less common. **Life-course persistent antisocial behavior** *refers to antisocial behavior that emerges at an early age and continues throughout life.* These individuals may start hitting at 3 years of age and progress to shoplifting at age 12 and then to stealing cars at age 16. Fewer than 5% of youth fit this pattern of antisocial behavior, but they account for most adolescent criminal activity.

Researchers have identified several forces that contribute to this type of antisocial and delinquent behavior.

1. **Biological contributions.** *Born to Be Bad* is the title of at least two movies, two songs, and three books. Implicit in this popular title is the idea that from birth, some individuals follow a developmental track that leads to destructive, violent, or criminal behavior. In other words, the claim is that biology pushes people to be aggressive long before experience can affect development.

   Is there any truth to this idea? In fact, biology and heredity *do* contribute to aggressive and violent behavior, but not in the manner suggested by the epithet "born to be bad." Twin studies make it clear that heredity contributes: Identical twins are usually more alike in their levels of physical aggression than are fraternal twins (Brendgen et al., 2006; Lacourse et al., 2014). But these studies do not tell us that aggression per se is inherited; instead, they indicate that some children inherit factors that place them at risk for aggressive or violent behavior. Temperament is one such factor: Youngsters who temperamentally have trouble regulating and processing emotions (especially negative ones like anger) are more likely to be aggressive. What's more these children seem to be prone to sensation seeking and find that aggressive behavior is rewarding (van Goozen, 2015). Hormones represent another factor: Higher levels of the hormone testosterone are often associated, weakly, with greater aggression and stronger responses to provocation (Carré, McCormick, & Hariri, 2011; Tremblay et al., 1998).

   These factors don't *cause* a child to be aggressive. But they do make aggressive behavior more likely: For instance, children who are emotional and easily irritated may be disliked by their peers and be in frequent conflict with them, opening the door for aggressive responses. Thus, biological factors place children at risk for aggression; to understand which youth actually become aggressive, we need to look at interactions between inherited factors and youth's experiences (van Goozen, 2015).

2. **Cognitive processes.** The cognitive skills described in Chapters 6 and 8 also play a role in antisocial behavior. One general factor is executive functioning. Children who are less skilled in inhibiting, shifting, and updating behaviors and thoughts are prone to aggressive behavior (McQuade, 2017).

   Cognitive processes contribute to antisocial behavior in another way, too: Aggressive youth often respond aggressively because they are not skilled at interpreting other people's intentions. Without a clear interpretation in mind, they respond aggressively by default. That is, aggressive boys far too often think, "I don't know what you're up to, and when in doubt, attack" (Crick & Dodge, 1994; Galán et al., 2017). When others inadvertently get in their way, delinquent adolescents often respond without regard to the nature of the other person's acts or intentions.

3. **Family processes.** Antisocial behavior has roots in parenting. Adolescents are more likely to become involved in delinquent acts when their parents use harsh discipline or don't monitor effectively (Gershoff, 2013; Lee, Altschul, & Gershoff,

adolescent-limited antisocial behavior

Behavior of youth who engage in relatively minor criminal acts but aren't consistently antisocial.

life-course persistent antisocial behavior

Antisocial behavior that emerges at an early age and continues throughout life.

Think About It

A letter to the editor of your local paper claims that "juvenile delinquents should be thrown in jail because they're born as 'bad apples' and will always be that way." Write a reply that states the facts correctly.

Aggressive teens see the world as a hostile place and typically respond aggressively by default.

2013; Vieno et al., 2009). Parents may also contribute to delinquent behavior if their marital relationship is marked by constant conflict. When parents constantly argue and fight, their children are more likely to be antisocial (Cummings et al., 2006; Narayan, Englund, & Englund, 2013). Of course, children have ringside seats for many of these confrontations; thus, they can see firsthand how parents use verbal and physical aggression against each other. And, sadly, children come to believe that these patterns of interacting represent "natural" ways of solving problems (Graham-Bermann & Brescoll, 2000).

4. *Poverty.* Aggressive and antisocial behavior is more common among children living in poverty than among children who are economically advantaged (Williams, Conger, & Blozis, 2007). As we've seen, living in poverty is extremely stressful for parents and often leads to the very parental behaviors that promote aggression—harsh discipline and lax monitoring (Shaw & Shelleby, 2014). In addition, violent crime is far more common in poverty-stricken neighborhoods. Older children and adolescents exposed to such violence are more likely to be aggressive and violent themselves as they get older (Bingenheimer, Brennan, & Earls, 2005).

Obviously, many factors contribute to making some adolescents prone to violent behavior. As you can imagine, when risk factors mount up in children's lives, they are at ever-greater risk for aggressive behavior (Greenberg et al., 1999). What's more, many of the factors operate in a cascading fashion, such that later risk factors build on prior factors (Vaillancourt et al., 2013): Poverty or maternal depression can lead to harsh, ineffective parenting. In turn, this leads children to be unprepared for school (both academically and socially), which leads to school failure and conduct problems. These difficulties cause some parents to become less active and less invested in parenting, which means that they monitor their adolescents less often, allowing them to associate with deviant, aggressive peers (Dodge, Greenberg, & Malone, 2008).

Thus, the developmental journey that leads to a violent, aggressive, antisocial adolescent starts in early childhood but gains momentum along the way. Consequently, efforts to prevent children from taking this path must begin early, be maintained over childhood, and target children and their parents. An example of a successful intervention program is Fast Track (Conduct Problems Prevention Research Group, 2015), which is designed to teach academic and social skills to elementary school children and life and vocational skills to adolescents. In addition, parents are taught skills for effective child rearing and, later, ways to stay involved with their children and to monitor their behavior. As young adults—seven years after the program had ended—antisocial behavior, criminal activity, and substance abuse were reduced among those who had participated in Fast Track.

Of course, this sort of successful program comes with an expensive price tag. But costs of prevention programs are a fraction of the costs associated with the by-products of aggressive behavior: One analysis suggests that each dollar invested in such programs saves more than $15 in crime-related costs, including payments to victims, court costs, and costs of incarceration (Farrington & Koegl, 2015). Thus, programs such as Fast Track not only improve children's lives (and the lives of people around them) but also are cost-effective.

In the What Do *You* Think? feature, we describe a very different approach to dealing with adolescent crime.

What Do *YOU* Think?

When Juveniles Commit Serious Crimes, Should They Be Tried as Adults?

Traditionally, when adolescents under 18 commit crimes, the case is handled in the juvenile justice system. Although procedures vary from state to state, most adolescents who are arrested do not go to court; instead, law enforcement and legal authorities have considerable discretionary power. They may, for example, release arrested adolescents into the custody of their parents. However, when adolescents commit serious or violent crimes, there will be a hearing with a judge. This hearing is closed to the press and public; no jury is involved. Instead, the judge receives reports from police, probation officers, school officials, medical authorities, and other interested parties. Adolescents judged guilty can be placed on probation at home, in foster care outside the home, or in a facility for youth offenders.

Because juveniles are committing more serious crimes, many law enforcement and legal authorities believe that juveniles should be tried as adults. Advocates of this position argue for lowering the minimum age for mandatory transfer of a case to adult courts, increasing the range of offenses that must be tried in adult court, and giving prosecutors more authority to file cases with juveniles in adult criminal court. Critics argue that treating juvenile offenders as adults ignores the fact that juveniles are less able than adults to understand the nature and consequences of committing a crime. Also, they argue, punishments appropriate for adults are inappropriate for juveniles (Monahan, Steinberg, & Piquero, 2015).

What do you think? Should we lower the age at which juveniles are tried as adults? Based on the theories of development we discussed, what guidelines would you propose in deciding when a juvenile should be tried as an adult?

TEST YOURSELF 9.4

Recall

1. The main factors that determine whether teenagers drink include parents, peers, and _____.

2. Peers influence teenage smoking indirectly by _____.

3. The factors that put adolescents at risk for depression include heredity, temperament, a belief system in which adolescents blame themselves, parents, and, for adolescents who are members of minority groups, _____.

4. Treatments for depression include drugs and psychotherapy that emphasizes _____.

5. _____ refers to antisocial behavior that begins at an early age and continues throughout life.

6. The factors that contribute to juvenile delinquency include biology, cognitive processes, _____, and poverty.

Interpret

- Describe potential biological and environmental contributions to delinquency.

Apply

- Prepare a fact sheet that middle schools could use to educate antisocial adolescents about ways to resolve conflicts and achieve goals without relying on aggression.

Check your answers to the Recall Questions at the end of the chapter.

SUMMARY

9.1 Identity and Self-Esteem

How do adolescents achieve an identity?

- The task for adolescents is to find an identity, a search that typically involves four statuses: Diffusion and foreclosure are more common in early adolescence; moratorium and achievement are more common in late adolescence and young adulthood. As they seek identity, adolescents often believe that others are constantly watching them and that no one else has felt as they do.

- Adolescents are more likely to achieve an identity when parents encourage discussion and recognize their autonomy; they are least likely to achieve an identity when parents set rules and enforce them without explanation.

What are the stages and results of acquiring an ethnic identity?

- Adolescents from ethnic groups often progress through three phases in acquiring an ethnic identity: initial disinterest, exploration, and identity achievement. Achieving an ethnic identity usually results in higher self-esteem.

How does self-esteem change in adolescence?

- Social comparisons begin anew when children move from elementary school to middle or junior high school; consequently, self-esteem usually declines somewhat during this transition. In middle and late adolescence, self-esteem becomes differentiated, especially in the academic and social domains. Self-esteem is linked to adolescents' actual competence in domains that matter to them and is linked to how parents and peers view them.

- The parent–child relationship becomes more egalitarian during the adolescent years, reflecting adolescents' growing independence. Contrary to myth, adolescence is not usually a period of storm and stress. Most adolescents love their parents, feel loved by them, rely on them for advice, and adopt their values.

9.2 Romantic Relationships and Sexuality

Why do teenagers date?

- Romantic relationships emerge in mid-adolescence. For younger adolescents, dating is for both companionship and sexual exploration; for older adolescents, it is a source of trust and support. Adolescents in romantic relationships are more self-confident but also report more emotional upheaval.

Why are some adolescents sexually active? Why do so few use contraceptives?

- By the end of adolescence, most American boys and girls have had sexual intercourse, which boys view as recreational but girls see as romantic. Adolescents are more likely to be sexually active if they believe that their parents and peers approve of sex. Adolescents do not use birth control consistently because they do not see the need for contraception, don't know where to obtain contraceptives, and sometimes find pregnancy appealing. Because they use contraception infrequently, they are at risk for contracting sexually transmitted diseases and becoming pregnant.

Who are sexual-minority youth?

- Sexual-minority youth identify as gay, lesbian, bisexual, queer, intersex, or transgender. For boys who identify as gay, the first step involves feeling different from other boys and becoming interested in gender-atypical activities. For females, the path to a sexual-minority identity is more variable. Sexual-minority youth face special challenges, and some suffer from mental health problems.

What circumstances make dating violence likely?

- Many adolescents experience dating violence, particularly if they've experience harsh parenting, their peers are familiar with and accept dating violence, and they're aggressive and antisocial. Programs to prevent dating violence provide greater awareness of dating abuse and emphasize that all community members have a stake in preventing dating violence.

9.3 The World of Work

How do adolescents select an occupation?

- In his theory of vocational choice, Super proposes three phases of vocational development during adolescence and young adulthood: crystallization, in which basic interests are identified; specification, in which jobs associated with interests are identified; and implementation, which marks entry into the workforce.

- Holland proposes six different work-related personalities: realistic, investigative, social, conventional, enterprising, and artistic. Each is uniquely suited to certain jobs. People are more productive when their personality fits their job and less productive when it does not.

- According to social cognitive career theory, vocational choice reflects beliefs about their abilities and beliefs about the outcome of their behavior.

What is the impact of part-time employment on adolescents?

- Most adolescents in the United States have part-time jobs. Adolescents who are employed more than 15 to 20 hours per week during the school year typically do poorly in school, often have lowered self-esteem and increased anxiety, and have problems interacting with others. Most employed adolescents save little of their income. Instead, they spend it on clothing, food, and entertainment, which can yield misleading expectations about how to allocate income.

- Part-time employment can be beneficial if adolescents work relatively few hours, if the work allows them to use existing skills or acquire new ones, and if teens save some of their earnings. Summer employment, which does not conflict with the demands of school, can also be beneficial.

9.4 The Dark Side

Why do teenagers drink and use drugs?

- Many adolescents drink alcohol regularly. The primary factors that influence whether adolescents drink are encouragement from others (parents and peers) and stress. Similarly, teenage smoking is influenced by parents and peers.

What leads some adolescents to become depressed? How can depression be treated?

- Depressed adolescents have little enthusiasm for life, believe that others are unfriendly, and want to be left alone. Depression can be triggered by a negative event; those adolescents who are most likely to be affected can't control their emotions and see themselves in a negative light. Treating depression relies on medications and on therapy designed to improve social skills and restructure adolescents' interpretation of life events.

What are the causes of juvenile delinquency?

- Many young people engage in antisocial behavior briefly during adolescence. In contrast, the small percentage of adolescents who engage in life-course persistent antisocial behavior are involved in many of the serious crimes committed in the United States. Life-course persistent antisocial behavior has been linked to biology, cognitive processes, family processes, and poverty. Efforts to reduce adolescent criminal activity must address all of these variables.

Test Yourself: Recall Answers

9.1 1. role confusion **2.** foreclosure **3.** diffusion **4.** Imaginary audience **5.** to explore alternative identities but do not pressure them or provide direction **6.** start to explore the personal impact of their ethnic roots **7.** no longer know where they stand among their peers, which means they must establish a new pecking order **9.2 1.** an outlet for sexual exploration **2.** harsh **3.** engage in unprotected sex **4.** see becoming pregnant as a way to become an adult **5.** feel different and are interested in gender-atypical activities; **6.** condone dating violence **9.3 1.** specification **2.** social **3.** learn bad habits for handling money **4.** hold jobs that allow them to use their skills and develop new ones **9.4 1.** stress **2.** establishing an informal school norm in which smoking is approved **3.** racial discrimination **4.** improving cognitive and social skills **5.** Life-course persistent antisocial behavior **6.** family processes

Key Terms

adolescent egocentrism (291)
imaginary audience (292)
personal fable (292)
illusion of invulnerability (292)
ethnic identity (293)

crystallization (302)
specification (303)
implementation (303)
personality-type theory (303)
depression (308)

adolescent-limited antisocial behavior (311)
life-course persistent antisocial behavior (311)

Becoming an Adult

Physical, Cognitive, and Personality Development in Young Adulthood

10

There comes a time in life when we feel the urge to move beyond adolescence and aspire to be an adult. In some societies, the transition to adulthood is abrupt and dramatic, marked by clear rites of passage. In Western society, it is fuzzier; the only apparent marker may be a birthday ritual. We may even ask "real" adults what it's like to be one. Adulthood is marked in numerous ways, some of which we explore in the first section.

Without question, young adulthood is the peak of physical processes and health. It is also a time when people who acquired unhealthy habits earlier in life may decide to adopt a healthier lifestyle. Young adulthood also marks the peak of some cognitive abilities and the next step in the continued development of others.

On a more personal level, young adulthood is a time when we make plans and dream of what lies ahead. It is a time when we think about what life as an adult will be like. But above all, it is a time when we lay the foundation for the developmental changes that we will experience during the rest of our lives. We will consider these issues as we examine young adulthood in this chapter.

LEARNING OBJECTIVES

- What role transitions mark entry into adulthood?
- What evidence from neuroscience helps us understand behavioral development in young adulthood?
- How do going to college, obtaining career training, and entering the workforce reflect the transition to adulthood?
- When do people achieve adulthood inn contemporary American society?

Marcus woke up with the worst headache he could ever remember having. "If this is adulthood, they can keep it," he muttered to himself. Like many young adults in the United States, Marcus spent his 21st birthday celebrating at a bar with his friends. But the phone call from his mother that woke him in the first place reminds him that he isn't an adult in every way; she called to see if he needs money.

Think for a minute about the first time you felt like an adult. When was it? What was the context? Who were you with? How did you feel?

Even though becoming an adult is one of the most important life transitions, it is difficult to pin down exactly when this occurs in Western societies. In the United States, for example, the age needed to achieve "adult" status includes 12 or so for purchasing movie theater tickets, 16 for driving a car (in many states), 18 for voting and joining the military, 21 for consuming alcoholic beverages, and 26 for losing medical insurance coverage on the policy of one's parents under the 2010 Affordable Care Act. Clearly, in the United States, there is no age that signals a clean break with adolescence and full achievement of adulthood. Certainly Marcus may feel like an adult because he can purchase alcohol legally, but he may not feel that way in other respects, such as financially.

emerging adulthood

Period between late teens and mid- to late 20s when individuals are not adolescents but are not yet fully adults.

Some human developmentalists view the period from the late teens to the mid- to late 20s as distinctive. *They refer to it as* emerging adulthood, *a period when individuals are not adolescents but are not yet fully adults* (Arnett, 2013, 2016). Emerging adulthood is a time to explore careers, self-identity, and commitments. It is also a time when certain biological and physiological developmental trends peak and brain development continues in different ways.

In this section, we examine some of the ways societies mark the transition to adulthood, and we'll see that the criteria vary widely from culture to culture.

Milestone birthdays such as turning 21 are often marked with celebrations.

Role Transitions Marking Adulthood

When people become adults in different cultures depends on how you define adulthood and the kind of role transitions cultures create. Consider the following three women. Ganika looked older than her 20 years; her son was playing quietly on the floor. She and her husband live in a small house in a village in rural India. Sheree graduated from high school a few years ago. She works full time at the Old Navy store and rents a small apartment nearby. Claudia recently graduated from college in Germany. She just started a job at a tech firm, so until she saves enough money for her own apartment she is living with her mother.

Are these women adults? Yes and no. As we will see, it all depends on how you define adulthood and the kind of role transitions cultures create. A role transition is movement into the next stage of development marked by assumption of new responsibilities and duties.

Cross-Cultural Evidence of Role Transitions

Cultures in the developing world tend to be clear about when a person becomes an adult (Mazur & Li, 2016; Nelson, Badger, & Wu, 2004). *Rituals marking initiation into adulthood, often among the most important ones in a culture, are termed* rites of passage. Rites of passage may involve highly elaborate steps that take days or weeks, or they may be compressed into a few minutes. Initiates are usually dressed in apparel reserved for the ritual to denote their special position. We still have traces of these rites in Western culture; consider, for example, the ritual attire for graduations and weddings.

In many cultures, rites of passage to adulthood are connected with religious rituals (Levete, 2010). For example, Christian traditions use a ritual called confirmation to mark the transition from being a child spiritually to being an adult. Judaism celebrates bar and bat mitzvahs. In many Latin American countries, a girl's 15th birthday is celebrated as the transition between childhood and young womanhood. In some countries, this ceremony, called the quinceañera, is preceded by a Mass if the girl's family is Catholic.

Marriage is the most important rite of passage to adulthood in many cultures because it is a prelude to childbearing, which in turn provides clear evidence of achieving adulthood (Hall & Willoughby, 2016; Mensch, Singh, & Casterline, 2006). In this sense, Ganika is an adult in her culture. In many cultures in developed economies, establishing a career is the most likely alternative pathway to adulthood (Hall & Willoughby, 2016).

Some tribal cultures mark the transition to adulthood in public ways so that the whole community witnesses it. In a few cultures, it may involve pain or mutilation, such as the controversial practice of female circumcision (Castro, 2010), or may involve being given a specific tattoo (Irish, 2009). Because rites in such cultures change little over time, they provide continuity across generations (Keith, 1990); older adults lead young people through the same rites they themselves experienced years earlier. American counterparts not tied directly to specific ethnic groups are less formalized and are hard to identify; indeed, you may be hard-pressed to think of any. A father buying his son his first razor or a mother helping her daughter with her first menstrual period may be as close as we get in American society.

Role Transitions in Western Cultures

In Western cultures, the most widely used criteria for deciding whether a person has reached adulthood are role transitions, *which involve assuming new responsibilities and duties.* Certain role transitions are key markers for attaining adulthood: voting, completing one's education, beginning full-time employment, leaving home and establishing financial independence, getting married, and becoming a parent. However, many people in their 20s in industrialized countries spread these achievements over several years (Arnett, 2013, 2016).

The point in the life span when these marker events for role transitions happen, though, has changed over the years. Such changes are examples of cohort effects, described in Chapter 1. For example, in the United States, the average age for completing all of one's formal schooling

rites of passage
Rituals marking initiation into adulthood.

role transitions
Movement into the next stage of development marked by assumption of new responsibilities and duties.

This couple from India reflects a culture in which the passage to adulthood for many occurs with marriage.

Robert Harding Images/Masterfile

rose steadily during the 20th century as the proportion of people going to college at some point in adulthood increased from roughly 10% in the early part of the century to roughly two-thirds today. Likewise, the age at first marriage has increased in the United States to about 29 for men and 27 for women (Census Bureau, 2016), a remarkable change of over 7 years since the 1970s. Similarly, the number of adult children living with their parents increased significantly during and after the Great Recession (Davis, Kim, & Fingerman, in press).

What does this mean for the transition from adolescence to adulthood? It means that Western society has no clear age-constant rituals that clearly mark the transition to adulthood (Ivory, 2004). As a result, young people create their own, such as being initiated into student organizations (e.g., fraternities and sororities) and drinking alcohol (a topic we explore later in this chapter). The lack of clearly defined rituals makes it difficult to use any one event as the marker for becoming an adult. Although the trend is that living independently from one's parents, financial independence, and romantic involvement are associated with increased assumption of adult roles, individual patterns are diverse. So depending on how you look at it, Sheree and Claudia may—or may not—be considered adults.

We will consider some of the components of the role transitions in Western culture and how they help shape role transitions. First, let's consider new evidence from neuroscience about important changes during emerging adulthood.

Neuroscience, Behavior, and Emerging Adulthood

Emerging adulthood is a time of very important developments in the brain, especially in terms of strengthening interconnections across different brain structures that help integrate different modes of thinking and feeling. This neuroscience research has raised intriguing questions: Could continuing brain development during early adulthood explain shifts in thinking and behavior, and possibly provide a physiological marker for adulthood?

There is considerable evidence that the prefrontal cortex, a part of the brain involved in high-level thinking, is not fully developed until a person reaches his or her mid-20s (Cohen et al., 2016). Additionally, important connections between the prefrontal cortex and the parietal lobe involved in the processing of emotional information also matures in adulthood. The key point is that the brain structures and connections that govern much of the higher level reasoning we associate with adulthood is not possible prior to early adulthood. We will come back to these aspects of brain development later in this chapter.

From a psychological perspective, the neurological developments are observed through changes in behavior. Cognitively, young adults think in different ways than do adolescents, especially in their ability to take different points of view (King & Kitchener, 2015). We will consider this developmental change later in this chapter.

Emerging adults engage in more risky behaviors than do any other age group of adults (Arnett, 2013, 2015). *The desire to live life more on the edge through physically and emotionally threatening situations on the boundary between life and death is termed* edgework (Brymer & Mackenzie, 2017; Lyng, 2012; PetersonLund, 2013). Edgework is seen through such sports as base jumping, waterfall kayaking, free solo climbing, and other extreme sports in which the slightest mistake likely results in death.

There is an important distinction between edgework, which involves high levels of risk but a great deal of expertise and planning, and reckless behavior, which involves high levels of risk but tends to be more spontaneous (Zinn, 2016). People who engage in edgework activities tend to share their experiences with other like-minded individuals across the spectrum of socioeconomic dimensions and as a mode of escape from the modern everyday world (Lyng, 2012).

Managing to deal with intense emotions when faced with real danger is a delicate balance, and how men and women accomplish this differs. For example, in thinking about or planning future dangerous activities, men tend to be highly confident in their ability to extricate themselves from tough positions

edgework

The desire to live life more on the edge through physically and emotionally threatening situations on the boundary between life and death.

Risky behavior such as this tends to decrease over the course of young adulthood.

PeopleImages/E+/Getty Images

and do not feel a need to rehearse just in case. Women, though, are more likely to have qualms, which they ease by rehearsing.

On the psychosocial front, young adulthood marks the transition from concern with identity (see Chapter 9) to concern with behaviors related to autonomy and intimacy, which we explore later in this chapter and in Chapter 11 (Erikson, 1982). Becoming independent from one's parents entails being able to fend for oneself, but it does not imply a complete severing of the relationship. On the contrary, adult children usually establish a rewarding relationship with their parents, as we will see in Chapter 13.

Achieving Milestones: Education, Workforce, and Erikson's Intimacy

As we noted earlier, a key marker of the transition to adulthood is achieving certain milestones, such as the launching of one's career and reaching developmental markers such as Erikson's stage of intimacy. Let's take a look at how they are accomplished.

Education and Workforce Attainment

For nearly 70% of all high school graduates in the United States, a marker of the transition to adulthood is going straight to college—although the rates vary significantly across income groups. As shown in ❱ Figure 10.1, enrollment of high school graduates from high-income families was 26 points higher (84%) than from low-income families (58%) (National Center for Educational Statistics, 2016). Racial and ethnic differences are also found, but these gaps are closing. For example, Asian Americans had the highest overall participation rate immediately after high school at 91%, followed by African Americans at 70%, whites at 68%, and Latinos at 65% (National Center for Education Statistics, 2016).

Considerable research has documented how students develop while they are in college (King & Kitchener, 2015; Patton et al., 2016; Perry, 1970). This work provides a theoretical and practical frame for understanding how adult students learn specific content (Nickerson & Thurkettle, 2013; Sargent & Borthick, 2013). Students start acting and thinking like adults because of advances in intellectual development and personal and social identity. It is thought that much of this developmental change in college occurs through social interaction, especially when it is supported within an active learning process. Indeed there is a belief that the college social experience can either facilitate or frustrate the development of one's sense of identity, including ethnic/racial identity (Guiffrida, 2009). Campus discussions and activities around such movements as Black Lives Matter and safe spaces are examples of these processes.

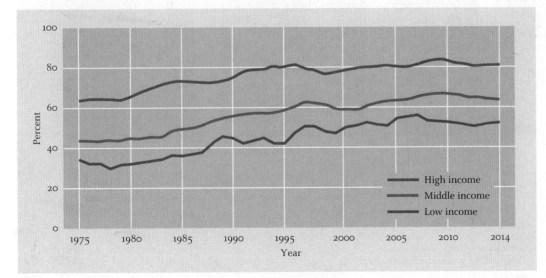

SOURCE: National Center for Education Statistics. Retrieved from nces.ed.gov/programs/digest/d15/tables/dt15_302.30.asp and nces.ed.gov/programs/digest/d15/tables/dt15_302.20.asp.

❱ **Figure 10.1**
Percentage of high school completers who were enrolled in 2- or 4-year colleges by the October immediately following high school completion, by family income: 1975–2014.

Those changes may well describe the experience of people who go directly from high school to college. But take a look around, literally, at your classmates. In addition to the ethnic and racial diversity you see, the age diversity you also likely experience is a reflection of the changing nature of college and university campuses.

Large numbers of students are in at least their mid-20s or older. For them, going to college isn't the marker of adulthood. *Colleges usually refer to students over age 25 as* returning adult students, *which implies that these individuals have already reached adulthood.*

Overall, returning adult students tend to be problem solvers, self-directed, and pragmatic; may have increased stress due to work-family-school conflict; may prefer having clearer understanding of the pathways from courses to careers; and have relevant life experiences they can integrate with their course work (Cleary et al., 2017; Patton et al., 2016; Swingle, 2013). Balancing employment and families along with their college courses often causes stress, especially early in returning adult students' academic studies. However, support from family and employers, as well as the positive effects of continuing one's education, are stress reducers. But many returning adult students, especially middle-aged women, express a sense of self-discovery they had not experienced before (Miles, 2009). The main conclusion here is that going to college impacts students of all ages; for traditional-aged students (ages 18 to 25), it helps foster the transition to adulthood.

As we noted earlier, a key indicator of becoming an adult for many people is establishing financial independence by joining the workforce. For some of the 30% of high school graduates who do not go on to college and for some of those who do not finish high school, an intermediary step may include learning a trade such as plumbing, welding, auto mechanics, and so forth. In any case, there are many pathways to financial independence: working a series of part-time jobs, finding full-time employment, or starting one's own business.

The ease with which one can launch one's career is related to educational attainment. As shown in ❱ Figure 10.2, for each increased educational level beyond high school, the odds of being employed increase. Estimates are that as of 2016, people with some college

❱ **Figure 10.2**

Percent of 20- to 24-year-olds employed, by sex and educational attainment: 2015.

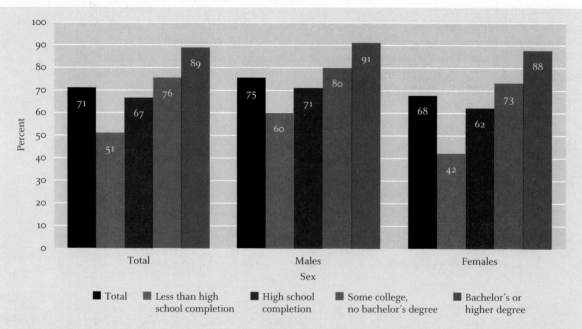

NOTE: For each group presented, the employment to population ratio, or employment rate, is the number of persons in that group who are employed as a percentage of the civilian population in that group. Data exculde persons enrolled in school. "Some college, no bachelor's degree" inculdes persons with an associate's degree. "High school completion" inculdes equivalency credentials, such as the GED credential.

SOURCE: National Center for Education Statistics. (2016). *Employment rates of college graduates*. Retrieved from nces.ed.gov/fastfacts/display.asp?id=561.

education obtained 11.5 of the 11.6 million jobs created in the recovery from the Great Recession (Carnevale, Jayasundera, & Gulish, 2016). Clearly, educational attainment is increasingly the pathway to financial independence.

Regardless of when and how it occurs, reaching financial independence is a major achievement and serves as a marker of becoming an adult. There are barriers, though. College graduates who have significant student loan debt may experience delays in achieving financial independence and turn to living with parents to make quicker progress.

Establishing Intimacy

According to Erikson, the major task for young adults is dealing with the psychosocial conflict of intimacy versus isolation. This is the sixth step in Erikson's theory of psychosocial development (see Chapter 1). Once a person's identity is established, Erikson (1982) believed that he or she is ready to create a shared identity with another—intimacy. Without a clear sense of identity, Erikson argued, young adults would be afraid of committing to a long-term relationship with another person or might become overly dependent on the partner for his or her identity.

But is this explanation, developed in the mid-20th century, applicable to contemporary emerging adults? Research evidence for Erikson's view is conflicting. For example, a meta-analytic study (see Chapter 1) of the connection between identity and intimacy showed that men and women resolve identity and intimacy issues differently under certain circumstances (Årseth et al., 2009). For example, some women resolve intimacy issues before identity issues by marrying and rearing children, and only later do they deal with the question of their own identity. Middle-aged women who go to college for the first time is an example of this form of identity development (Miles, 2009).

The challenges adults face in their 20s in modern society can be difficult and present challenges for Erikson's model. Robbins and Wilner (2001) coined the term *quarter-life crisis* to describe how life in one's 20s is far from easy as individuals struggle to find their way. Adjusting to the "real world" is increasingly difficult for college graduates who face significant debt from educational loans, and for all early adults who face challenges from workplace politics, networking, time management, and other daily hassles. Indeed, Byock (2010) and Robinson, Wright, and Smith (2013) argue that a crisis in emerging or early adulthood represents a period of self-exploration and search for meaning. Jung described a similar search for meaning in his original theory of the midlife crisis (a topic we will explore more in Chapter 13). It may be that adults reflect on their life from time to time and seek clarity on its direction.

Robinson (2015) lays out an expanded approach based on both Erikson and modern theory and research about emergent adulthood. Robinson argues that early adulthood should be separated into two distinct stages: emerging adulthood, which pertains to the flux and instability of the 18 to 25 age range, and early adulthood, which is a more settled phase. At the beginning of early adulthood is a normative period of turmoil, referred to as the "quarter-life crisis" (Robinson, 2015; Robinson & Smith, 2010; Robinson & Wright, 2013; Robinson et al., 2013), which was not accounted for in Erikson's model.

Robinson proposes that the quarter-life crisis can take two forms; the *locked-out form* (feeling unable to enter adult roles) or the *locked-in form* (feeling trapped in adult roles). Further, Robinson suggests that the issues in early adulthood be reframed away from Erikson's intimacy–isolation toward commitment–independence. This extension of Erikson's theory reflects the longer time it takes more recent generations to traverse the challenges of early adulthood compared to earlier generations. As noted earlier and will be repeated in subsequent chapters, this is reflected in later ages at first marriage and other key life indicators, such as lower home ownership rates.

So When Do People Become Adults?

Evidence is clear that the years between late adolescence and the late twenties to early thirties may reflect a distinct life stage researchers call *emerging adulthood* (Arnett, 2013, 2015). Additional evidence is mounting that social and demographic trends are perhaps

intimacy versus isolation
Sixth stage in Erikson's theory and the major psychosocial task for young adults.

Think About It
Why do you think it mattered to Erikson whether identity issues are resolved before intimacy issues?

creating two developmental periods between adolescence and middle age, much as similar changing circumstances created the period of adolescence in the early 20th century. All of the evidence points to the conclusion that achieving adulthood takes much longer now than in generations past, and that the psychosocial issues people face are more complex.

As society continues to shed formal rites of passage, especially those connected to religious ceremonies, the exact moment a person becomes an adult will become less and less certain. The perspectives considered in this section do not provide any definitive answers to the question of when people become adults. All we can say is that the transition depends on numerous cultural and psychological factors. In cultures without clearly defined rites of passage, defining oneself as an adult rests on one's perception of whether personally relevant key criteria have been met. In Western society, this can be very complicated—for example, when success comes at a young age, as discussed in the Real People feature. Read the story of Lorde to see how.

Real People | Applying Human Development

Does Being Rich and Famous Mean You're an Adult?

Ella Maria Lani Yelich-O'Connor, better known as Lorde, is a world-famous singer-songwriter from New Zealand. Born November 7, 1996, Lorde's talent was recognized early—she received a contract to work with songwriters at Universal when she was barely in her teens.

Lorde's leap to world stardom came with the release of her first single, "Royals," which hit number one in the Billboard Hot 100 in 2013. Her first album, *Pure Heroine*, was an international best-seller. She had a hit single, "Yellow Flicker Beat" from *The Hunger Games: Mockingjay—Part 1* soundtrack. Music critics have already noted her talent by bestowing numerous awards and having her perform at major ceremonies. Her recording and publishing contracts are worth millions of dollars, so she is already wealthy at a young age.

Lorde has also risen to prominence in other ways, too. She has become a sought-after spokesperson on a number of major issues, and her endorsement of other entertainers carries significant weight. Her loyal following has a great deal of purchasing power, so she has developed important financial influence. There is no question that Lorde is famous and wealthy. The question is whether that is enough to make her an adult. What do *you* think about that? Is fame and wealth enough?

Kevin Winter/Getty Images Entertainment/Getty Images

TEST YOURSELF 10.1

Recall

1. The most widely used criteria for deciding whether a person has reached adulthood are _____.

2. Rituals marking initiation into adulthood are called _____.

3. Students over 25 are referred to as _____.

4. Behaviorally, a major difference between adolescence and adulthood is a significant drop in the frequency of _____.

5. According to Erikson, young adults must resolve the psychosocial conflict of _____.

Interpret

- Why are formal rites of passage important? What has Western society lost by eliminating them? What has it gained?

- Why is understanding how rites of passage occur in different cultures important?

Apply

- When do you think people become adults? Why?

- How do legal definitions of adulthood matter in professions such as law enforcement and health care?

Check your answers to the Recall Questions at the end of the chapter.

LEARNING OBJECTIVES

- In what respects are young adults at their physical peak?
- How healthy are young adults in general?
- How do smoking, alcohol, and nutrition affect young adults' health?

- How does the health of young adults differ as a function of socioeconomic status, ethnicity, and education?

Juan is a 25-year-old who started smoking cigarettes in high school to be popular. Juan wants to quit, but he knows it will be difficult. He also heard that it doesn't really matter if he quits because his health will never recover. Juan wonders whether it is worthwhile to try.

Juan is at the peak of his physical functioning. Most young adults are in the best physical shape of their lives. Indeed, the early 20s are the best years for strenuous work, trouble-free reproduction, and peak athletic performance. But people's physical functioning is affected by several health-related behaviors, including smoking.

Growth, Strength, and Physical Functioning

Physical functioning generally peaks during young adulthood (Aldwin & Gilmer, 2013). You're as tall as you will ever be. Physical strength, coordination, and dexterity in both sexes peaks during the late 20s and early 30s, declining slowly throughout the rest of life even when you maintain an active lifestyle. Because of these trends, few professional athletes remain at the top of their sport in their mid-30s. Indeed, individuals such as Brett Favre, who played quarterback in the National Football League into his early 40s, Jaromír Jágr, who played in his mid-40s in the National Hockey League, Diana Nyad, who swam roughly 90 miles from Cuba to Key West at age 64, and Dara Torres, who set the record for the oldest swimmer to win Olympic medals by winning three in Beijing in 2008 at age 41, are famous partly because they are exceptions.

Sensory acuity is also at its peak in the early 20s (Fozard & Gordon-Salant, 2001). Visual acuity remains high until middle age, when people tend to become farsighted and require glasses for reading. Hearing begins to decline somewhat by the late 20s, especially for high-pitched tones.

Dara Torres, shown on the right, won three medals at the Beijing Olympics in 2008 at age 41.

Lifestyle Factors in Health

Because they are so healthy overall, American young adults rarely die from disease (Heron, 2016). So what is the leading cause of death among young adults in the United States? Between the ages of 25 and 44, it's accidents.

There are important gender and ethnic differences in these statistics. Young adult men aged 25 to 34 are nearly 2.5 times as likely to die as women of the same age. African American and Latino young adult males are 2 to 2.5 times as likely to die as their European American male counterparts, but Asian and Pacific Islander young adult males are likely to die at only about half the rate of their European American male counterparts (Heron, 2016).

AP Images/Mark Baker

In emerging and young adulthood, three behaviors set the stage for health across the rest of adulthood: smoking, alcohol use, and nutrition. Let's see how people can lay a good foundation for health.

Smoking

Smoking is the single biggest contributor to health problems. In the United States alone, roughly 480,000 people die each year from tobacco use and exposure to secondhand smoke (American Lung Association, 2016), and medical treatment of smoking-related ailments alone costs over $170 billion annually (Centers for Disease Control and Prevention, 2016a).

The risks of smoking are many. ▶ Figure 10.3 shows the various forms of cancer and other chronic diseases that are caused by smoking. And smoking during one's lifetime has a significant negative impact on cognitive functioning in adults over age 50 (Dregan, Stewart, & Gulliford, 2013).

Juan, the young man in the vignette, is typical of people who want to stop smoking. Most people begin the process in young adulthood. More than 90% of those who stop do so on their own. But as Juan suspects, quitting is not easy; most people who try to quit smoking relapse within six months. For most people, success is attained only after a long period of stopping and relapsing.

Regardless of how it happens, quitting smoking has enormous health benefits (American Cancer Society, 2016a). For example, in less than a year after quitting, the lungs regain their normal ability to move mucus out. The risks of stroke and coronary heart disease return to normal after a period of roughly 15 years. Even people who do not quit until late life show marked improvements in health. Check out the American Cancer Society's *Guide to Quitting Smoking* for key information about how to quit and a quiz about whether you need help to quit.

Drinking Alcohol

About 60% of women and 70% of men in the United States drink alcohol at least occasionally (Centers for Disease Control and Prevention, 2016b). Rates of at least occasional drinking increase with income for both men and women; for instance, for those below the official poverty line, only 56% of men and 43% of women drink at last occasionally.

For the majority of people, drinking alcohol poses no serious health problems as long as they do not drink and drive. Evidence suggests that moderate drinkers (one or two

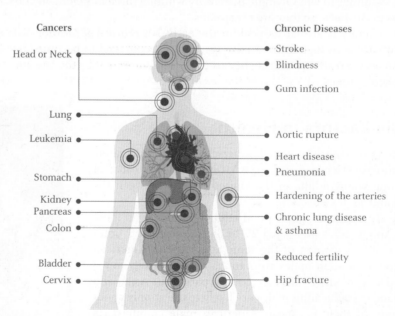

▶ **Figure 10.3**

Smoking can damage every part of the body.

SOURCE: Centers for Disease Control. Retrieved from www.cdc.gov/tobacco/basic_information/health_effects/cancer/index.htm.

glasses of beer or wine per day for men, one per day for women) have a 25% to 40% reduction in risk of cardiovascular disease and stroke than either abstainers or heavy drinkers, even after controlling for hypertension, prior heart attack, and other medical conditions (Harvard School of Public Health, 2010). However, moderate drinking also increases the risk for certain types of cancer, so whether moderate drinking is an appropriate health behavior depends on the balance between lowering cardiovascular risk and increasing cancer risk (LeWine, 2013).

For many students, college parties and drinking alcohol are virtually synonymous. Unfortunately, drinking among college students often goes beyond moderate intake to become binge drinking. Binge drinking *is defined for men as consuming five or more drinks in a row and for women as consuming four or more drinks in a row within the past two weeks.* Binge drinking has been identified as a major health problem in the United States since the 1990s (National Institute on Alcohol Abuse and Alcoholism [NIAAA], 2007; Wechsler et al., 1994). Surveys of drinking behavior among young adults aged 18 to 24 show that the rate of binge drinking at about 34% among men and 26% among women (Centers for Disease Control and Prevention, 2016c). Being a college student does not appreciably affect the likelihood of binge drinking overall, but college students tend to drink more at parties and are especially at risk during the first six weeks of freshman year (NIAAA, 2015).

Research indicates that average binge drinking among college students is an international problem (Crawford-Williams, Roberts, & Watts, 2016; Karam, Kypri, & Salamoun, 2007; Kypri et al., 2009), with rates in many countries roughly on par with those in the United States.

Students between the ages of 18 and 24 are more likely than older students to binge drink. They are significantly more likely to binge drink if alcohol is readily available, if they are a member of a social fraternity or sorority, or if they feel positively about what they are doing, which tends to make some people behave rashly (NIAAA, 2015). Women college students are more likely to exceed guidelines of weekly alcohol intake than are college men (Hoeppner et al., 2013). In addition, college men tend to mature out of weekly binge drinking more quickly than do college women. Because women metabolize alcohol differently than men do, it takes less alcohol for women to experience deterioration of judgment and behavior.

Studies of binge drinking, differential metabolism of alcohol in men and women, and the cognitive and behavioral effects of alcohol intoxication set off a firestorm of debate regarding whether college women should be educated about the dangers of binge drinking. On one thing, all sides agree: alcohol is a factor in most sexual assaults, especially incapacitated sexual assault, on college campuses (Bird et al., 2016). From there, people take sides. On the one hand, some (e.g., Marcus, 2013; Yoffe, 2013) argue that educating women about potential unwanted and dangerous outcomes from binge drinking is simply a prudent practice. Others (e.g., Adelman, 2013; Ryan, 2013) argue that such approaches constitute "blaming the victim" and that women have every right to engage in binge drinking should they choose to do so and that unwanted outcomes such as sexual assault were the perpetrators' fault. As we will see, binge drinking has consequences for both the drinker and the people around the drinker, and education programs take these outcomes into account.

Nearly 100,000 college students annually are victims of alcohol-related date rape, about 700,000 are assaulted by a student who has been drinking, and over 1,800 young adult college students aged 18 to 24 die every year in the United States from drinking too much (NIAAA, 2015). Estimates of sexual assault rates are likely to be low due to the tendency of victims not to report incidents. Indeed, this is a major reason why the Obama administration launched a series of major efforts to raise awareness and enforcement of sexual assault prevention on college campuses beginning in 2014. ❱ Figure 10.4 shows the rate of a variety of problems related to binge drinking.

Numerous programs aim to reduce the number of college students who binge. These efforts include establishing low tolerance levels for the antisocial behaviors associated with binge drinking; working with athletes, fraternities, and sororities; changing the expectations of

binge drinking
Type of drinking defined for men as consuming five or more drinks in a row and for women as consuming four or more drinks in a row within the past two weeks.

Binge drinking is viewed by many as a rite of passage in college, but it is an especially troublesome behavior for young adults that can cause academic and social problems.

DisobeyArt/Shutterstock.com

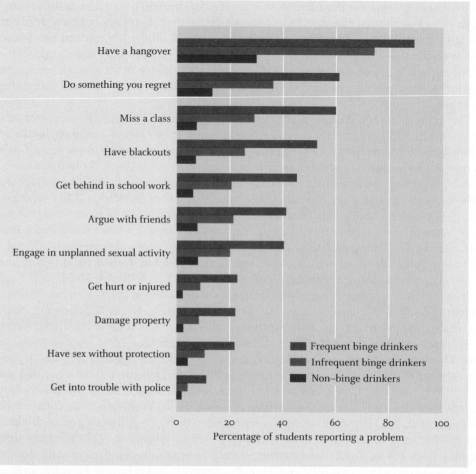

Figure 10.4

Troublesome behaviors increase with binge drinking. Note that all binge drinkers report more problems than non–binge drinkers.

SOURCE: Adapted from a table in Wechsler et al. (2002). Wechsler, H., Lee, J. E., Kuo, M., Seibrung, M., Nelson, T. F., & Lee, H. (2002). Trends in college binge drinking during a period of increased prevention efforts. *Journal of American College Health, 2002*, 203–217).

incoming freshmen; increasing the number of nonalcoholic activities available to students; and working to enforce underage drinking laws (New York Times, 2016; NIAAA, 2015). Education programs about the hazards of binge drinking can be effectively delivered online (O'Rourke, Humphris, & Baldacchino, 2016; Weaver et al., 2014).

The National Institute on Alcohol Abuse and Alcoholism (2002, 2007, 2015) has offered several strategies that focus on all these issues. Evidence is growing that programs based on social norms and the involvement of students themselves are key and underlie the most effective strategies to reduce risky behavior both in the United States (Miller & Prentice, 2016) and around the world (McAlaney, Bewick, & Hughes, 2011). The social norms approach focuses on changing the culture of drinking in college from one that strongly supports binge drinking to one in which binge drinking is something that popular people do not do. This approach is based on the idea that many college students think that their peers' attitudes toward drinking are more permissive than they really are (McAlaney et al., 2011; Miller & Prentice, 2016; NIAAA, 2007).

For most young adults, binge drinking declines across one's 20s. However, in the United States, nearly 8% of adults 18 to 24 years old and 5% of those aged 25 to 44 are considered heavy drinkers and likely candidates to develop alcohol use disorder (Centers for Disease Control and Prevention, 2016c). Significantly more men than women are at risk. Rates are also higher for European Americans and Native Americans than for other ethnic groups.

What constitutes alcohol use disorder? Alcohol use disorder *is a drinking pattern that results in significant and recurrent consequences that reflect loss of reliable control over alcohol use.* Alcohol use disorder is diagnosed whenever anyone meets any two of the 11 criteria listed in ▶ Table 10.1 during a 12-month period.

alcohol use disorder

Drinking pattern that results in significant and recurrent consequences that reflect loss of reliable control over alcohol use.

Table 10.1

Diagnosis of alcohol use disorder (AUD) based on DSM-5

SYMPTOMS

In the past year, have you:

- Had times when you ended up drinking more, or longer, than you intended?
- More than once wanted to cut down or stop drinking, or tried to, but couldn't?
- Spent a lot of time drinking? Or being sick or getting over other aftereffects?
- Wanted a drink so badly you couldn't think of anything else?
- Found that drinking—or being sick from drinking—often interfered with taking care of your home or family? Or caused job troubles? Or school problems?
- Continued to drink even though it was causing trouble with your family or friends?
- Given up or cut back on activities that were important or interesting to you, or gave you pleasure, in order to drink?
- More than once gotten into situations while or after drinking that increased your chances of getting hurt (such as driving, swimming, using machinery, walking in a dangerous area, or having unsafe sex)?
- Continued to drink even though it was making you feel depressed or anxious or adding to another health problem? Or after having had a memory blackout?
- Had to drink much more than you once did to get the effect you want? Or found that your usual number of drinks had much less effect than before?
- Found that when the effects of alcohol were wearing off, you had withdrawal symptoms, such as trouble sleeping, shakiness, restlessness, nausea, sweating, a racing heart, or a seizure? Or sensed things that were not there?

SEVERITY

The severity of the **AUD** is defined as:

- **Mild** The presence of 2 to 3 symptoms
- **Moderate** The presence of 4 to 5 symptoms
- **Severe** The presence of 6 or more symptoms

Source: Based on NIH Publication 13-7999. (2016). Alcohol Use Disorder: A Comparison Between DSM-IV and DSM-5. National Institutes of Health (NIH), National Institute on Alcohol Abuse and Alcoholism. Available at pubs.niaaa.nih.gov/publications/dsmfactsheet/dsmfact.pdf.

Neuroscience research has discovered that alcohol "does a number" on our brain, especially in disrupting the balance in neurotransmitters (Bjork & Gilman, 2014; Lovinger & Roberto, 2013) and impairing neuroplasticity (Loheswaran et al., 2016). These neurotransmitters include gamma-aminobutyric acid (GABA), which inhibits impulsiveness; glutamate, which excites the nervous system; norepinephrine, which is released in response to stress; and dopamine, serotonin, and opioid peptides, which are responsible for pleasurable feelings. Excessive long-term drinking can cause the body to crave alcohol to restore good feelings or to avoid negative feelings. In addition, other factors come into play: genetics; high stress, anxiety, or emotional pain; close friends or partners who drink excessively; and sociocultural factors that glorify alcohol.

Treatment for alcohol use disorder focuses on three goals (NIAAA, 2014): stabilization and reduction of substance consumption, treatment of coexisting problems, and arrangement of appropriate social interventions. Three main options for treatment are available: mutual-support groups, behavioral treatments, and medications.

Mutual-support groups are the most widely known and include Alcoholics Anonymous (AA) and other 12-step groups. These groups provide peer support to help people stop abusing various drugs and alcohol. Behavioral treatments rely on individual or group counseling to stop or reduce drinking or drugging.

The U.S. Food and Drug Administration has approved three types of medications for use in treating alcohol use disorder (NIAAA, 2014):

- Disulfiram (Antabuse) is used to block alcohol metabolism, and causes very unpleasant symptoms such as nausea to help people stop drinking. Disulfiram has been used for nearly a century, but some people stop taking it to stop the unpleasant effects.

- Naltrexone reduces the pleasure received from drinking and reduces the cravings that compel chronic drinking by blocking the endorphin receptors in the brain. Research evidence is mostly positive on the effectiveness of naltrexone, especially when combined with other treatments.
- Acamprosate (Campral) reduces the unpleasant symptoms experienced from alcohol withdrawal by stabilizing the neurotransmitters in the brain. Research results on the effectiveness of acamprosate is mixed.

Perhaps the most important thing with people who have alcohol use disorder is to encourage them to get treatment. Unfortunately, only a minority of people who need such treatment actually get it.

Nutrition

Once on a vacation trip, one of us (John Cavanaugh) took this photo outside a restaurant in Megalochori, Greece. It captures the essence of how you should approach diet as part of healthy living.

The photo may remind you of disagreements with parents (or now with your own children) about food. As an adult yourself, you may now realize those lima beans and other despised foods your parents urged you to eat really are healthy.

Experts agree nutrition directly affects one's mental, emotional, and physical functioning (Hammar & Östgren, 2013; McKee & Schüz, 2015). Diet has been linked to cancer, cardiovascular disease, diabetes, anemia, and digestive disorders. To stay maximally healthy, though, we must recognize that nutritional requirements and eating habits change across the life span. *This change is due mainly to differences in* metabolism, *or how much energy the body needs.* Body metabolism and the digestive process slow down with age (Janssen, 2005).

The U.S. Department of Agriculture publishes dietary guidelines based on current research. In its *Dietary Guidelines for Americans 2015–2020* (Health.gov, 2015), the USDA recommends we eat a variety of nutrient-dense foods and beverages across the basic food groups. The general guidelines for adults can be seen in ❱ Figure 10.5.

As you can see, the USDA approaches nutrition from the perspective of ensuring people eat a healthy plate of food at each meal, and the contents of that plate be appropriately balanced. Most important, we should choose foods that limit the intake of added sugar, saturated fats, sodium, and alcohol. And we need to keep our target calorie intake in mind. The full report contains much more detail about the specific foods that are best for you.

Of course, most people do not eat perfectly all the time. From time to time, each of us craves something—whether a triple-dip cone of premium ice cream or really high-end chocolate. If you feel even a tiny bit guilty after you enjoy that splurge, you are among the people who have taken to heart (literally) the link between diet and cardiovascular disease. The American Heart Association (2016a) makes it clear foods high in saturated fat (such as our beloved ice cream) should be replaced with foods low in fat (such as fat-free frozen yogurt). Check out their website for the latest in advice on eating a heart-healthy diet.

Healthy aging and eating is also the focus of minority communities. For example, the American Heart Association has partnered with Native American tribes to create the *Seeds of Native Health* campaign for indigenous nutrition as a way to connect traditional native foods to healthy eating and healthy aging (American Heart Association, 2016b).

Much of the focus of the American Heart Association's various guidelines and initiatives is to lower the risk of cardiovascular disease. To achieve this goal, it is important to understand an important difference between two different types of lipoproteins reflected in different types of cholesterol. Lipoproteins are fatty chemicals attached to proteins carried in the blood. Low-density lipoproteins (LDLs) *cause fatty deposits to accumulate in arteries, impeding blood flow, whereas* high-density lipoproteins (HDLs) *help keep arteries clear and break down LDLs.* It is not so much the overall cholesterol number but the ratio

John C. Cavanaugh

Eating a healthy diet is an important part of preventing disease.

metabolism
How much energy the body needs.

low-density lipoproteins (LDLs)
Chemicals that cause fatty deposits to accumulate in arteries, impeding blood flow.

high-density lipoproteins (HDLs)
Chemicals that help keep arteries clear and break down LDLs.

Key Recommendations:

Consume a healthy eating pattern that accounts for all foods and beverages within an appropriate calorie level.

A healthy eating pattern includes:[1]

- A variety of vegetables from all of the subgroups—dark green, red and orange, legumes (beans and peas), starchy, and other
- Fruits, especially whole fruits
- Grains, at least half of which are whole grains
- Fat-free or low-fat dairy, including milk, yogurt, cheese, and/or fortified soy beverages
- A variety of protein foods, including seafood, lean meats and poultry, eggs, legumes (beans and peas), and nuts, seeds, and soy products
- Oils

A healthy eating pattern limits:

- Saturated fats and *trans* fats, added sugars, and sodium

Key Recommendations that are quantitative are provided for several components of the diet that should be limited. These components are of particular public health concern in the United States, and the specified limits can help individuals achieve healthy eating patterns within calorie limits:

- Consume less than 10 percent of calories per day from added sugars[2]
- Consume less than 10 percent of calories per day from saturated fats[3]
- Consume less than 2,300 milligrams (mg) per day of sodium[4]
- If alcohol is consumed, it should be consumed in moderation—up to one drink per day for women and up to two drinks per day for men—and only by adults of legal drinking age.[5]

In tandem with the recommendations above, Americans of all ages—children, adolescents, adults, and older adults—should meet the *Physical Activity Guidelines for Americans* to help promote health and reduce the risk of chronic disease. Americans should aim to achieve and maintain a healthy body weight. The relationship between diet and physical activity contributes to calorie balance and managing body weight. As such, the *Dietary Guidelines* includes a Key Recommendation to

- Meet the *Physical Activity Guidelines for Americans*.[6]

[1] Definitions for each food group and subgroup are provided throughout Chapter 1: Key Elements of Healthy Eating Patterns and are compiled in Appendix 3. USDA Food Patterns: Healthy U.S.-Style Eating Pattern.

[2] The recommendation to limit intake of calories from added sugars to less than 10 percent per day is a target based on food pattern modeling and national data on intakes of calories from added sugars that demonstrate the public health need to limit calories from added sugars to meet food group and nutrient needs within calorie limits. The limit on calories from added sugars is not a Tolerable Upper Intake Level (UL) set by the Institute of Medicine (IOM). For most calorie levels, there are not enough calories available after meeting food group needs to consume 10 percent of calories from added sugars and 10 percent of calories from saturated fats and still stay within calorie limits.

[3] The recommendation to limit intake of calories from saturated fats to less than 10 percent per day is a target based on evidence that replacing saturated fats with unsaturated fats is associated with reduced risk of cardiovascular disease. The limit on calories from saturated fats is not a UL set by the IOM. For most calorie levels, there are not enough calories available after meeting food group needs to consume 10 percent of calories from added sugars and 10 percent of calories from saturated fats and still stay within calorie limits.

[4] The recommendation to limit intake of sodium to less than 2,300 mg per day is the UL for individuals ages 14 years and older set by the IOM. The recommendations for children younger than 14 years of age are the IOM age- and sex-appropriate ULs (see Appendix 7. Nutritional Goals for Age-Sex Groups Based on Dietary Reference Intakes and Dietary Guidelines Recommendations).

[5] It is not recommended that individuals begin drinking or drink more for any reason. The amount of alcohol and calories in beverages varies and should be accounted for within the limits of healthy eating patterns. Alcohol should be consumed only by adults of legal drinking age. There are many circumstances in which individuals should not drink, such as during pregnancy. See Appendix 9. Alcohol for additional information.

[6] U.S. Department of Health and Human Services. *2008 Physical Activity Guidelines for Americans*. Washington (DC): U.S. Department of Health and Human Services; 2008. ODPHP Publication No. U0036. Available at: http://www.health.gov/paguidelines. Accessed August 6, 2015.

SOURCE: health.gov/dietaryguidelines/2015/resources/2015-2020_Dietary_Guidelines.pdf.

of LDLs to HDLs that matters most in cholesterol screening. High levels of LDLs are a risk factor in cardiovascular disease, and high levels of HDLs are considered a protective factor. Reducing LDL levels is effective in diminishing the risk of cardiovascular disease in adults of all ages; in healthy adults, a high level of LDL (over 160 mg/dL) is associated with higher risk for cardiovascular disease (Mayo Clinic, 2016). In contrast, higher levels of HDL are good (in healthy adults, levels at least above 40 mg/dL for men and 50 mg/dL for women). LDL levels can be lowered and HDL levels can be raised through various interventions such as exercise and a high-fiber diet. Weight control is also an important component.

If diet and exercise are not effective in lowering cholesterol, numerous medications exist for treating cholesterol problems. The most popular of these drugs are from a family of medications called *statins* (e.g., Lipitor, Crestor). These medications lower LDL and moderately increase HDL. Before prescribing statins, healthcare professionals also assess a person's risk of

Classification of overweight and obesity by BMI, waist circumference, and associated disease risks.

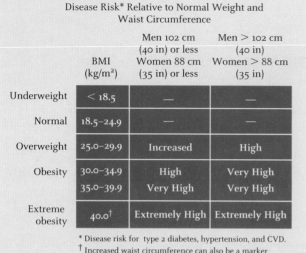

		Disease Risk* Relative to Normal Weight and Waist Circumference	
	BMI (kg/m²)	Men 102 cm (40 in) or less Women 88 cm (35 in) or less	Men > 102 cm (40 in) Women > 88 cm (35 in)
Underweight	< 18.5	—	—
Normal	18.5–24.9	—	—
Overweight	25.0–29.9	Increased	High
Obesity	30.0–34.9	High	Very High
	35.0–39.9	Very High	Very High
Extreme obesity	40.0†	Extremely High	Extremely High

* Disease risk for type 2 diabetes, hypertension, and CVD.
† Increased waist circumference can also be a marker for increased risk even in persons of normal weight.

SOURCE: www.nhlbi.nih.gov/health/public/heart/obesity/lose_wt/bmi_dis.htm.

body mass index (BMI)

Ratio of body weight and height related to total body fat.

cardiovascular disease from family history and lifestyle, among other factors. If statins are prescribed, their potential side effects on liver functioning should be monitored, and patients should consult with their physicians on a regular basis.

Obesity is a serious and growing health problem related to diet. One good way to assess your own status is to compute your body mass index. Body mass index (BMI) *is a ratio of body weight and height and is related to total body fat.* You can compute BMI as follows:

$$BMI = w/h^2$$

where w = weight in kilograms (or weight in pounds divided by 2.2), and h = height in meters (or inches divided by 39.37).

The Centers for Disease Control and Prevention (2016c) defines healthy weight as having a BMI of less than 25. However, this calculation may overestimate body fat in muscular athletic people (e.g., professional athletes) and underestimate body fat in those who appear of normal weight but have little muscle mass.

Obesity is related to the risk of serious medical conditions and mortality: the higher one's BMI, the higher one's risk (Centers for Disease Control and Prevention, 2016d). ▶ Figure 10.6 shows the increased risk for several diseases and mortality associated with increased BMI (and obesity).

In the United States, obesity rates have increased very significantly since the 1970s. Today, nearly half of African Americans and over 40% of Latinos are obese (Centers for Disease Control and Prevention, 2016d). Across all racial and ethnic groups, over one-third of older adults are obese. Reductions in these statistics is a primary focus of the federal government's nutrition and exercise guidelines.

Based on these data, you may want to lower your BMI if it's above 25. But be careful—lowering your BMI too much (below 18.5) may not be healthy either. Very low BMIs may indicate malnutrition, which is also related to increased mortality.

Socioeconomic, Ethnic, and Education Issues in Health

The three most important social influences on health are socioeconomic status (which is a strong predictor having access to insurance and good health care), ethnicity, and education (a good predictor of being able to access a wider array of healthy living options and avoid certain diseases). In the United States, being poor in any setting is a major predictor of health challenges.

Disparities in access to quality health care and to healthy lifestyle choices (e.g., fresh food) in the United States as related to ethnicity has been documented for decades, and the National Institute on Minority Health and Health Disparities is charged with conducting programs and research to address these differences (National Institute on Minority Health and Health Disparities, 2016). Even when poor minorities in the United States have access to health care, they are less likely than European Americans to receive treatment for chronic disease (Agency for Healthcare Research and Quality, 2016). Such socioeconomic differences also hold internationally (Huisman et al., 2013).

Educational level also matters. The risk of dying increases as educational level decreases (Centers for Disease Control and Prevention, 2016e; Huisman et al., 2013). Quantity and

Many inner-city residents must rely on overcrowded clinics for their primary health care.

Tom Carter/PhotoEdit

quality of care as well as outcomes are also poorer with lower educational levels when looking at specific conditions such as rheumatoid arthritis (McCollum & Pincus, 2009).

Does socioeconomic status, ethnicity, or education *cause* good (or poor) health? Not exactly. As we discussed in Chapter 1, correlation research does not address cause and effect. In this case, higher educational level is also associated with higher income and with more awareness of dietary and lifestyle influences on health. Thus, more highly educated people are in a better position to afford health care and to know about the kinds of foods and lifestyle that affect health. The discussion of these issues continues in the What Do *You* Think? feature.

What Do *You* Think?   Healthcare Disparities in the United States

As noted in the text, access to quality health care in the United States depends a great deal on socioeconomic status, ethnicity, and education. As a researcher, an important question to ask is whether access to quality health care is improving, thereby reducing healthcare disparities in the United States. The answer, sadly, is no.

As described in the annual *National Healthcare Disparities Report* (Agency for Healthcare Research and Quality, 2016) and in the annual report on the overall health in the U.S. (Centers for Disease Control and Prevention, 2016e), many Americans,

especially Americans of color, do not get the care they need, and the care they do get may actually cause them harm. Despite some improvements in the quality of care overall and the access to quality care for certain groups who were formerly uninsured, many aspects of health disparities across demographic groups are not improving. In particular, the most troubling disparities apply to care for diabetes, maternal and pediatric care, and cancer care.

The most important factor in these disparities is financial status. As shown in ▶ Figure 10.7, those in poor income groups received care that was worse than people

in high income groups on 60% of the quality indicators studied.

These disparities in health care mean that millions of Americans do not get the care they need despite the United States having the best health care in the world. This and other similar disparities reflect the fact that these individuals are usually much sicker by the time they get care, meaning that it is more difficult and expensive to treat them. Although its implementation was problematic, a goal of the Affordable Care Act was to provide more people with access to quality health care that is affordable. Whether that goal can be reached fully, however, remains to be seen.

▶ **Figure 10.7**

Number and percentage of quality measures for which members of selected groups experienced better, same, or worse quality of care compared with reference group.

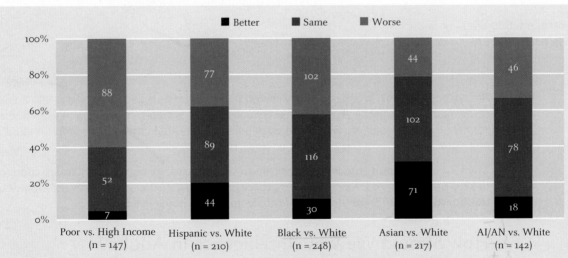

KEY: AI/AN = American Indian or Alaska Native; n = number of measures.

NOTE: Numbers of measures differ across groups because of sample size limitations. The relative difference between a selected group and its reference group is used to assess disparities. For income, the reference group is High income. For race and ethnicity, the reference group is White.

- **Better** = Population received better quality of care than reference group. Differences are statistically significant, are equal to or larger than 10%, and favor the selected group.
- **Same** = Population and reference group received about the same quality of care. Differences are not statistically significant or are smaller than 10%.
- **Worse** = Population received worse quality of care than reference group. Differences are statistically significant, equal to or larger than 10%, and favor the reference group.

SOURCE: Figure on p. 11 from www.ahrq.gov/sites/default/files/wysiwyg/research/findings/nhqrdr/nhqdr15/2015nhqdr.pdf.

Recall

1. In young adulthood, most people reach their maximum _____.

2. Sensory acuity peaks during a person's _____.

3. During the early 20s, death from disease is _____.

4. Young adults are most likely to die from _____.

5. _____ is the biggest contributor to health problems.

6. In terms of alcohol drinking patterns, _____ peaks in emerging adulthood.

7. The two most important social influences on health are education and _____.

Interpret

- How would you design a healthcare system that provides strong incentives for young adults leading healthy lifestyles?

Apply

- In your job as a nutritionist, you have been asked to design a comprehensive educational campaign to promote healthy lifestyles. What information would you include?

- As a nurse, what information besides basic health status would you want to know from a new patient?

Check your answers to the Recall Questions at the end of the chapter.

10.3 Cognitive Development

LEARNING OBJECTIVES

- What is intelligence in adulthood?

- What are primary and secondary mental abilities? How do they change?

- What are fluid and crystallized intelligence? How do they change?

- How has neuroscience research furthered our understanding of intelligence in adulthood?

- What is postformal thought? How does it differ from formal operations?

- How do emotion and logic become integrated in adulthood? How do emotional intelligence and impression formation demonstrate this integration?

Susan, a 33-year-old woman recently laid off from her job as a secretary, slides into a seat on her first day of classes at the community college. She is clearly nervous. "I'm worried that I won't be able to compete with these younger students—that I may not be smart enough," she sighs. "Guess we'll find out soon enough, huh?"

Many returning adult students such as Susan worry that they may not be "smart enough" to keep up with 18- or 19-year-olds. Are these fears realistic? We will see how the answer to this question depends on the types of intellectual skills being used.

How Should We View Intelligence in Adults?

multidimensional

Characteristic of theories of intelligence that identify several types of intellectual abilities.

multidirectionality

Developmental pattern in which some aspects of intelligence improve and other aspects decline during adulthood.

interindividual variability

Patterns of change that vary from one person to another.

Take a sheet of paper and write down all the abilities that you think reflect intelligence in adults. It's a safe bet that you listed more than one ability. You are not alone. *Most theories of intelligence are* multidimensional—*that is, they identify several types of intellectual abilities.*

Sternberg (1985, 2008; Sternberg, Jarvin, & Grigorenko, 2009) emphasized multidimensionality in his theory of successful intelligence (also discussed in Chapter 6). Based on the life-span perspective (described in Chapter 1), Baltes and colleagues (Baltes et al., 2006) introduced three other concepts as being vital to intellectual development in adults: multidirectionality, interindividual variability, and plasticity.

Over time, the various abilities underlying adults' intelligence show multidirectionality: *Some aspects of intelligence improve and other aspects decline during adulthood. Closely related to this is* interindividual variability: *These patterns of change also vary from one* person to another. Finally, people's abilities reflect plasticity: *They are not fixed, but can be modified under the right conditions at just about any point in adulthood.* Because most research on plasticity has focused on older adults, we return to this topic in Chapter 14. In general, Baltes and colleagues emphasize that intelligence has many components and that these components show varying development in different abilities and different people.

Given that intelligence in adults is complex and multifaceted, how might we study it? Two common ways are formal testing and assessing practical problem-solving skills. Formal testing assesses a wide range of abilities and involves tests from which we can compute overall IQ scores such as those discussed in Chapter 6. Tests of practical problem solving assess people's ability to apply intellectual skills to everyday situations. Let's see how each approach describes intellectual development.

The psychometric approach focuses on the interrelationships among intellectual abilities, so a major goal has long been to describe the ways these relationships are organized (Sternberg, 1985). *This organization of interrelated intellectual abilities is termed the structure of intelligence.* The most common way to describe the structure of intelligence is to think of it as a five-level hierarchy, depicted in ▶ Figure 10.8 (Cunningham, 1987).

Each higher level of this hierarchy represents a higher level of organizing the components of the level below. The lowest level consists of individual test questions—the specific items people answer on an intelligence test. These items or questions can be organized into intelligence tests, which constitute the second level.

The third level reflects interrelationships among scores on intelligence tests that assess similar abilities; these clusters of abilities are called primary mental abilities. Continuing to move up the hierarchy, the interrelationships existing among the primary mental abilities produce the secondary mental abilities at the fourth level. Finally, general intelligence at the top refers to the interrelationships among the secondary mental abilities.

Keep in mind that each time we move up the hierarchy we move away from people's actual performance. Each level above the first represents a theoretical description of how things fit together. Thus, there are no tests of primary abilities per se; primary abilities represent theoretical relationships among tests, that in turn represent theoretical relationships among actual performances.

So exactly how do researchers construct this theoretical hierarchy? The structure of intelligence is uncovered through sophisticated statistical detective work using a technique called *factor analysis.* First, researchers obtain people's performances on many types of problems. Second, the results are examined to determine whether performance on one type of problem, such as filling in missing letters in a word, predicts performance on another type of problem, like unscrambling letters to form a word. *If the performance on one test is highly related to the performance on another, the abilities measured by the two tests are interrelated and are called a* <u>factor</u>.

Most psychometric theorists believe intelligence consists of several factors. However, we should note although factor analysis is a sophisticated statistical technique, it is not an exact technique. Thus, estimates of the exact number of factors vary from a few to over 100. Most researchers and theorists believe the number to be relatively small. We examine two factors: primary and secondary mental abilities.

Primary and Secondary Mental Abilities

Since the 1930s, researchers agreed intellectual abilities can be studied as groups of related skills (such as memory or spatial ability) organized into hypothetical constructs called primary mental abilities. *In turn, related groups of primary mental abilities can be clustered into a half dozen or so broader skills termed* secondary mental abilities.

plasticity
Concept that intellectual abilities are not fixed but can be modified under the right conditions at just about any point in adulthood.

structure of intelligence
The organization of interrelated intellectual abilities.

factor
The interrelated abilities measured by two tests if the performance on one test is highly related to the performance on another.

primary mental abilities
Groups of related intellectual skills (such as memory or spatial ability).

secondary mental abilities
Broader intellectual skills that subsume and organize the primary abilities.

▶ **Figure 10.8**
Secondary mental abilities reflect several primary mental abilities and their respective measurements. This figure shows those relations regarding crystallized intelligence.

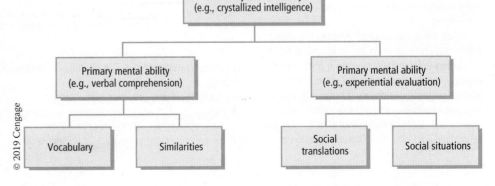

© 2019 Cengage

Roughly 25 primary mental abilities have been identified (Horn, 1982). Because it is difficult to study all of them, researchers focused on five representative ones:

- *Number*: the basic skills underlying our mathematical reasoning
- *Word fluency*: how easily we produce verbal descriptions of things
- *Verbal meaning*: our vocabulary ability
- *Inductive reasoning*: our ability to extrapolate from particular facts to general concepts
- *Spatial orientation*: our ability to reason in the three-dimensional world

Even with a relatively small number of primary mental abilities, it is still hard to discuss intelligence by focusing on separate abilities. As a result, theories of intelligence emphasize clusters of related primary mental abilities as a framework for describing the structure of intelligence. Because they are one step removed from primary mental abilities, secondary mental abilities are not measured directly.

The Spotlight on Research feature describes the definitive developmental study of primary mental abilities.

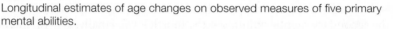

Spotlight On Research

The Seattle Longitudinal Study

Who was the investigator, and what was the aim of the study? To provide a more thorough picture of intellectual change, K. Warner Schaie began the Seattle Longitudinal Study in 1956.

How did the investigator measure the topic of interest? Schaie used standardized tests of primary mental abilities to assess a wide range of abilities such as logical reasoning and spatial ability.

Who were the participants in the study? Over the course of the study, more than 5,000 individuals were tested at eight different times (1956, 1963, 1970, 1977, 1984, 1991, 1998, and 2005). The participants were representative of the upper 75% of the socioeconomic spectrum and were recruited through a large health maintenance organization in Seattle.

What was the design of the study? Schaie invented a new type of research design—the sequential design (see Chapter 1). Participants were tested every seven years.

Were there ethical concerns with the study? Because people's names must be retained for future contact, the researchers were careful about keeping personal information secure.

What were the results? Among the many important findings from the study are differential changes in abilities over time and cohort effects. As you can see in ▶ Figure 10.9, scores on tests of primary mental abilities improve gradually until the late 30s or early 40s. Small declines begin in the 50s, increase as people age into their 60s, and become

▶ **Figure 10.9**

Longitudinal estimates of age changes on observed measures of five primary mental abilities.

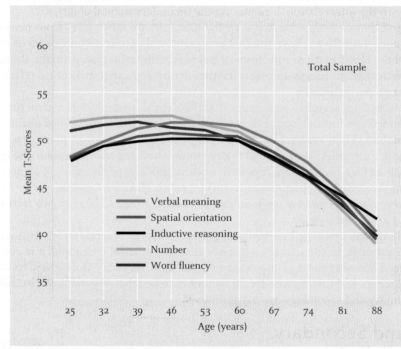

SOURCE: Based on Intellectual development across adulthood by Warner Schaie, K., and Zanjani, Faika A. K., in *Handbook of Adult Development and Learning*, ed. by Hoare, C., p. 102.

increasingly large in the 70s (Schaie & Zanjani, 2006).

Cohort differences were also found. ▶ Figure 10.10 shows that on some skills (e.g., inductive reasoning ability) but not others, more recently born younger and middle-aged

cohorts performed better than cohorts born earlier. These cohort effects probably reflect differences in educational experiences.

Schaie uncovered many individual differences as well; some people showed developmental patterns closely approximating the

[Continued on next page]

overall trends, but others showed unusual patterns. For example, some individuals showed steady declines in most abilities beginning in their 40s and 50s, others showed declines in some abilities but not others, and some people showed little change in most abilities over a 14-year period.

What did the investigator conclude? Three points are clear. First, intellectual development during adulthood is marked by a gradual leveling off of gains between young adulthood and middle age followed by a period of relative stability and then a time of gradual decline in most abilities. Second, these trends vary from one cohort to another. Third, individual patterns of change vary considerably from person to person.

What converging evidence would strengthen these conclusions? Although Schaie's study is one of the most comprehensive ever conducted, it is limited. Studying people who live in different locations around the world would provide evidence as to whether the results are limited geographically. Additional cross-cultural evidence comparing people with different economic backgrounds and different access to health care would also provide insight into the effects of these variables on intellectual development.

▶ **Figure 10.10**

Cohort gradients showing cumulative cohort difference on five primary mental abilities for cohorts born in 1889 to 1973.

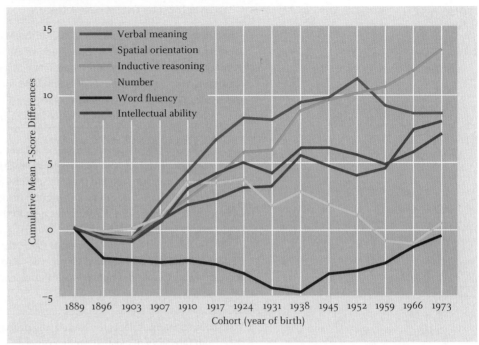

SOURCE: Based on Intellectual development across adulthood by Warner Schaie, K., and Zanjani, Faika A. K., in *Handbook of Adult Development and Learning*, ed. by Hoare, C., p. 102.

Fluid and Crystallized Intelligence

As noted earlier, primary abilities are themselves organized into clusters of secondary mental abilities. A summary of the major secondary mental abilities is presented in ▶ Table 10.2. Two secondary mental abilities have received a great deal of attention in adult developmental research: fluid intelligence and crystallized intelligence (Horn, 1982).

Fluid intelligence *consists of the abilities that make you a flexible and adaptive thinker, allow you to make inferences, and enable you to understand the relations among concepts.* It includes the abilities you need to understand and respond to any situation, but especially new ones: inductive reasoning, integration, abstract thinking, and the like (Horn, 1982). An example of a question that taps fluid abilities is the following: What letter comes next in the series *d f i m r x e?*[1]

Crystallized intelligence *is the knowledge you have acquired through life experience and education in a particular culture.* Crystallized intelligence includes your breadth of knowledge, comprehension of communication, judgment, and sophistication with information (Horn, 1982). Many popular television game shows (such as *Jeopardy* and *Wheel of Fortune*) are based on contestants' accumulated crystallized intelligence.

Developmentally, fluid and crystallized intelligence follow two different paths, as you can see in ▶ Figure 10.11. Notice that fluid intelligence declines throughout adulthood, whereas crystallized intelligence improves. Although we do not yet fully understand why fluid intelligence declines, it likely is related to underlying changes in the brain (see Chapter 2). In contrast, the increase in crystallized intelligence (at least until late life) indicates people continue adding knowledge every day.

fluid intelligence
Abilities that make you a flexible and adaptive thinker, allow you to make inferences, and enable you to understand the relations among concepts.

crystallized intelligence
The knowledge you have acquired through life experience and education in a particular culture.

[1]The next letter is *m*. The rule is to increase the difference between adjacent letters in the series by one each time and use a continuous circle of the alphabet for counting. Thus, *f* is two letters from *d*, *i* is three letters from *f*, and *e* is seven letters from *x*.

Table 10.2
Descriptions of Major Secondary Mental Abilities
CRYSTALLIZED INTELLIGENCE (Gc)
Crystallized intelligence reflects the breadth of knowledge and experience, understanding communications and social conventions, judgment, and reason. The components of Gc include the primary abilities of verbal comprehension, concept formation, logical reasoning, and general reasoning, among others. Tests of Gc include vocabulary (What does *timid* mean?) and analogies (Plato is to Kant as Shakespeare is to _____), among others. Gc is a rough estimate of the knowledge and sophistication that underlies the intelligence of a culture.
FLUID INTELLIGENCE (Gf)
Fluid intelligence reflects the abilities to see relationships among patterns, draw inferences from relationships, and comprehend the implications of relationships. The primary abilities underlying Gf include inductive reasoning, figural flexibility, and integration, among others. Tests of Gf include letter series (What comes next in the series *d f i m r x e*?), matrices (Identify the relationships among elements in a 2×2 matrix.), and shapes (From among a set of overlapping circles, squares, and triangles, choose a figure that enables you to place a dot inside a circle and triangle but outside of a square.) Gf provides a rough estimate of a person's problem solving and abstracting ability. It does not reflect cultural learning.
VISUAL ORGANIZATION (Gv)
Visual organization reflects the underlying primary abilities: visualization, spatial orientation, speed and flexibility of closure, among others. Gv is tested through holistic closure (Identify a figure that has missing parts.), form board (Put cutout parts together to create and match a specific figure.), and embedded figures (Find the duck in a complex visual image.). Gv differs from Gf in that Gv reflects relationships among visual patterns that are obvious, and not inferred (which would reflect Gf).
AUDITORY ORGANIZATION (Ga)
Auditory organization reflects underlying primary abilities such as time tracking, auditory cognition of relations, and speech perception when the speech is degraded or distorted, among others. Tests of Ga include repeated tones (Identify the first occurrence of a tone that is played several times.), tonal series (Indicate which tone comes next in a specific series of tones.), and word identification in noise (Identify a specific word when it is embedded in a noisy background environment.), among others.
SHORT-TERM ACQUISITION AND RETRIEVAL
This ability reflects the ability to be aware of and retain information long enough to do something with it. The underlying primary abilities all reflect aspects of short-term memory. Tests of Gstar include span memory (repeat increasingly long lists of numbers or words.), associative memory (remember word pairs of related words), among others.
LONG-TERM STORAGE AND RETRIEVAL
This type of intelligence reflects the ability to store information and retrieve information that was acquired in the distant past.

Source: Horn, J. L. (1982). The aging of human abilities. In B. B. Wolman (Ed.), *Handbook of Developmental Psychology* (pp. 847–870). Englewood Cliffs, NJ: Prentice Hall. Reprinted with permission.

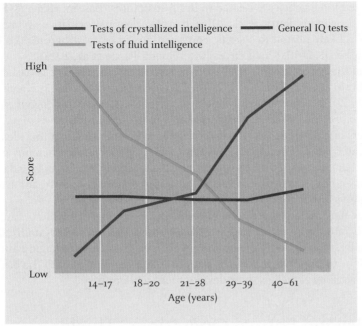

SOURCE: Based on Organization of data on life-span development of human abilities by Horn, J. L. in Goulet, L. R. and Baltes, P. B. (Eds.), *Life-Span Developmental Psychology: Research and Theory*, p. 463.

▶ **Figure 10.11**

Note the opposite developmental patterns for fluid and crystallized intelligence.

What do these different developmental trends imply? First, they indicate that—although it continues through adulthood—performance or learning that depends on basic underlying skills becomes more difficult with age, whereas performance or learning that is based on what we already know continues to improve, at least until very late in life.

Second, intellectual development varies a great deal from one set of skills to another. Whereas individual differences in fluid intelligence remain relatively uniform over time, individual differences in crystallized intelligence increase with age, mainly because maintaining crystallized intelligence depends on being in situations that require its use (Horn, 1982; Horn & Hofer, 1992). For example, few adults get much practice in solving complex letter series tasks like the one on page 23, so individual differences tend to be minimal. But because people improve their vocabulary skills by reading and they vary considerably in how much they read, individual differences are likely to increase.

Neuroscience Research and Intelligence

Considerable research shows specific areas in the brain are associated with intellectual abilities, and developmental changes in these areas are related to changes in performance.

Research now shows that the <u>prefrontal cortex</u>, along with the <u>parietal lobe</u> (an area of the brain at the top of the head), plays an important role in general intellectual abilities. Based on 37 studies using various types of neuroimaging techniques, Jung and Haier (2007) proposed the parieto-frontal integration theory. *The parieto-frontal integration theory (P-FIT) proposes that intelligence comes from a distributed and integrated network of neurons in the parietal and frontal areas of the brain.* ▶ Figure 10.12. Shows these key brain areas. In general, P-FIT accounts for individual differences in intelligence as having their origins in individual differences in brain structure and function. For example, research indicates that the P-FIT predicts fluid intelligence (Nikolaidis et al., in press; Pineda-Pardo et al., 2016).

In general, P-FIT accounts for individual differences in intelligence as having their origins in individual differences in brain structure and function. The P-FIT model has been tested in several studies. Results indicate support for the theory when measures of fluid

parieto-frontal integration theory (P-FIT)

Theory that proposes that intelligence comes from a distributed and integrated network of neurons in the parietal and frontal lobes of the brain.

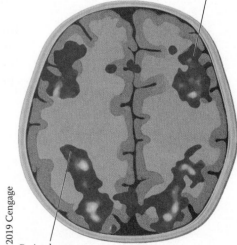

© 2019 Cengage

▶ **Figure 10.12**

Brain imaging research indicates that active connections between the parietal and frontal lobes, shown in the colored areas here, are key to understanding intelligence.

and crystallized intelligence are related to brain structures (Basten, Hilger, & Fiebach, 2015; Brancucci, 2012; Pineda-Pardo et al., 2016). It is also clear performance on measures of specific abilities is likely related to specific combinations of brain structures (Di Domenico et al., 2015; Haier et al., 2010; Kievit et al., 2016; Pineda-Pardo et al., 2016).

A second theory of intelligence based on neuroscience evidence is based on how efficiently the brain works (Brancucci, 2012; Di Domenico et al., 2015; Kievit et al., 2016; Langer et al., 2012). *The neural efficiency hypothesis states intelligent people process information more efficiently, showing weaker neural activations in a smaller number of areas than less intelligent people.* Research evidence is mounting that this idea holds merit, and with greater intelligence does come demonstrably increased efficiency in neural processing (e.g., Kievit et al., 2016; Langer et al., 2012; Lipp et al., 2012; Pineda-Pardo et al., 2016). However, how this neural efficiency develops is not yet known, nor are its developmental pathways understood.

It is clear neuroscience and related research on intelligence will continue to provide many insights into the bases for both the development of fluid and crystallized intelligence as well as understanding individual differences in each. As neuroimaging and other techniques continue to improve, it is likely that our understanding of both the brain structure-intelligence relations as well as their development will improve.

Going Beyond Formal Operations: Thinking in Adulthood

Suppose you are faced with the following dilemma:

> You are a member of your college's or university's student judicial board and are currently hearing a case involving plagiarism. The student handbook states plagiarism is a serious offense resulting in expulsion. The student accused of plagiarizing a paper admits copying from Wikipedia but says she has never been told she needed to use a formal citation and quotation marks. Do you vote to expel the student?

When this and similar problems are presented to older adolescents and young adults, interesting differences emerge. Adolescents tend to approach the problem in formal-operational terms and point out the student handbook is clear and the student ignored it, concluding the student should be expelled. Formal-operational thinkers are certain such solutions are right because they are based on their own experience and are logically driven.

But many adults are reluctant to draw conclusions based on the limited information in the problem, especially when the problem can be interpreted in different ways (Commons, 2016). They point out there is much about the student we don't know: Has she ever been taught the proper procedure for using sources? Was the faculty member clear about what plagiarism is? For adults, the problem is more ambiguous. Adults may eventually decide

neural efficiency hypothesis
States intelligent people process information more efficiently, showing weaker neural activations in a smaller number of areas than less intelligent people.

Because people using the initial stages of reflective judgment perceive commentators such as Megyn Kelly as authority figures, they believe that what the commentators say must be true.

the student is (or is not) expelled, but they do so only after considering aspects of the situation that go well beyond the information given in the problem.

Based on numerous investigations, researchers concluded this different type of thinking represents a qualitative change beyond formal operations (King & Kitchener, 2015; Lemieux, 2012; Sinnott, 2014). *Postformal thought* *is characterized by recognition that truth (the correct answer) may vary from situation to situation, solutions must be realistic to be reasonable, ambiguity and contradiction are the rule rather than the exception, and emotion and subjective factors usually play a role in thinking.* In general, the research evidence indicates post formal thinking has its origins in young adulthood (King & Kitchener, 2015; Sinnott, 2014).

Several research-based descriptions of the development of thinking in adulthood have been offered. *One of the best is the description of the development of* reflective judgment, *a way adults reason through dilemmas involving current affairs, religion, science, personal relationships, and the like.* Based on decades of longitudinal and cross-sectional research, King and Kitchener (2002; 2015) refined descriptions and identified a systematic progression of reflective judgment in young adulthood. A summary of these stages is shown in ▶ Table 10.3.

The first three stages in the model represent prereflective thought. People in these stages typically do not acknowledge and may not even perceive that knowledge is uncertain. Consequently, they do not understand some problems exist when there is not a clear and absolutely correct answer. A student pressuring her instructor for the "right" theory to explain human development reflects this stage. She is also likely to hold firm positions on controversial issues and does so without acknowledging other people's ability to reach a different (but nevertheless equally logical) position.

About halfway through the developmental progression, students think differently. In Stages 4 and 5, students are likely to say nothing can be known for certain and to change their conclusions based on the situation and the evidence. At this point, students argue knowledge is quite subjective. They are also less persuasive with their positions on controversial issues: "Each person is entitled to his or her own view; I cannot force my opinions on anyone else." King and Kitchener refer to thinking in these stages as "quasi-reflective" thinking.

As they continue their development into Stages 6 and 7, individuals begin to show true reflective judgment, understanding that people construct knowledge using evidence and argument after careful analysis of the problem or situation. They once again hold firm

postformal thought
Thinking characterized by recognizing that the correct answer varies from one situation to another, that solutions should be realistic, that ambiguity and contradiction are typical, and that subjective factors play a role in thinking.

reflective judgment
Way in which adults reason through real-life dilemmas.

Table 10.3
Description of the Stages of Reflective Judgment
PREREFLECTIVE REASONING (STAGES 1–3)
Belief that "knowledge is gained through the word of an authority figure or through firsthand observation, rather than, for example, through the evaluation of evidence. [People who hold these assumptions] believe that what they know is absolutely correct, and that they know with complete certainty. People who hold these assumptions treat all problems as though they were well-structured" (King & Kitchener, 2004, p. 39). Example statements typical of Stages 1–3: "I know it because I see it." "If it's on Fox News, it must be true."
QUASI-REFLECTIVE REASONING (STAGES 4 AND 5)
Recognition "that knowledge—or more accurately, knowledge claims—contain elements of uncertainty, which [people who hold these assumptions] attribute to missing information or to methods of obtaining the evidence. Although they use evidence, they do not understand how evidence entails a conclusion (especially in light of the acknowledged uncertainty), and thus tend to view judgments as highly idiosyncratic" (King & Kitchener, 2004, p. 40). Example statement typical of stages 4 and 5: "I would believe in climate change if I could see the proof. How can you be sure the scientists aren't just making up the data?"
REFLECTIVE REASONING (STAGES 6 AND 7)
People who hold these assumptions accept "that knowledge claims cannot be made with certainty, but [they] are not immobilized by it; rather, [they] make judgments that are 'most reasonable' and about which they are 'relatively certain,' based on their evaluation of available data. They believe they must actively construct their decisions, and that knowledge claims must be evaluated in relationship to the context in which they were generated to determine their validity. They also readily admit their willingness to reevaluate the adequacy of their judgments as new data or new methodologies become available" (King & Kitchener, 2004, p. 40). Example statement typical of stages 6 and 7: "It is difficult to be certain about things in life, but you can draw your own conclusions about them based on how well an argument is put together based on the data used to support it."

convictions but reach them only after careful consideration of several points of view. They also realize they must continually reevaluate their beliefs in view of new evidence.

Even though people are able to think at complex levels, do they? Not usually (King & Kitchener, 2004, 2015). Why? Mostly because the environment does not provide the supports necessary for using one's highest-level thinking, especially for issues concerning knowledge and experience you already have. People may not always purchase the product with the least impact on the environment, such as a fully electric car, even though philosophically they are strong environmentalists, because recharging stations are currently not widely available. However, if pushed and if given the necessary supports (e.g., easily available charging stations), people demonstrate a level of thinking and performance far higher than they typically show on a daily basis.

Integrating Emotion and Logic in Emerging and Young Adulthood

You may have noticed that a hallmark of postformal thinking is the movement from thinking "I'm right because I've experienced it" to thinking "I'm not sure who's right because your experience is different from mine." Problem situations that seemed fairly straightforward in adolescence appear more complicated to young adults; the "right thing to do" is much tougher to figure out.

In addition to an increased understanding there is more than one "right" answer, adult thinking is characterized by the integration of emotion with logic (Labouvie-Vief, 2015). Labouvie-Vief (2015; Labouvie-Vief, Grühn, and Mouras, 2009) describes this emotional development as paralleling intellectual development, demonstrating both gains and losses with increasing age. These parallel processes create tension, resulting in the cognitive-emotional integration and interplay that middle-aged and older adults use when confronted with real-life problems.

As they mature, adults tend to make decisions and analyze problems not so much on logical grounds as on pragmatic and emotional grounds. Rules and norms are viewed as relative, not absolute. Mature thinkers realize thinking is an inherently social enterprise that demands making compromises with other people and tolerating contradiction and ambiguity. Such shifts mean one's sense of self also undergoes a fundamental change.

A good example of this developmental shift is the difference between how late adolescents or emerging adults view an emotionally charged issue—such as unethical behavior at work—compared to the views of middle-aged adults. Emerging adults may view such behavior as completely inexcusable, with firing of the employee an inescapable outcome. Middle-aged adults may take contextual factors into account and consider what factors may have forced the person to engage in the behavior. Some might argue this is because the topic is too emotionally charged for adolescents to deal with intellectually whereas young adults are better able to incorporate emotion into their thinking.

As people grow older, two things happen in terms of the integration of emotion and thought (Labouvie-Vief, 2015). First, the rich emotional experience people have accumulated can be brought to bear on tasks that are not too difficult in terms of cognitive demands, meaning that in these situations older adults have an easier time than younger adults at integrating emotions and thought. In contrast, when the demands of the task are great, the arousal that is created narrows their ability to bring emotions to bear.

Neuroimaging Evidence

We noted earlier that important changes occur in the brain beginning in emerging adulthood. Evidence from neuroimaging research indicates emotion and

Blogging has become a common way of documenting the integration of thought and emotion.

Westend61/Getty Images

logic processing is indeed integrated in adults (Gu et al., 2013). This integration occurs in the prefrontal cortex and the anterior insula (an area of the brain deep inside the cortex). Additional research indicates the amygdala is also involved in processing emotion, and this information is also integrated with thought.

Evidence of certain neural pathways in the brain associated with cognition-emotion integration can be used as a baseline for understanding what happens when the neural connections are altered or absent. Evidence is now clear that these interconnections are different in some forms of mental disorders (Anticevic, Repovs, & Barch, 2012; Hamilton, Hiatt Racer, & Newman, 2015). This means intellectual and emotion processing share common brain pathways in healthy adults, but various other pathways in adults who experience mental disorders.

The integration of emotion with logic that happens in adulthood provides the basis for decision making in the personal and sometimes difficult arenas of love and work that we examine in detail in Chapters 11 and 12, respectively. It also provides the basis for broader perspectives about life and the ability to see points of view different from one's own.

Think About It
Why are formal operations inadequate for integrating emotion and thought?

Emotional Intelligence

The increased integration of emotion and thought across emerging and young adulthood provides a way of examining how cognitive abilities operate in social situations. The basic goal of the social cognition approach is to understand how people make sense of themselves, others, and events in everyday life (Fiske & Taylor, 2013; Frith & Frith, 2012; Kornadt et al., in press; Weiss, in press).

A key ability in social contexts is *emotional intelligence* (Goleman, 1995; Salovey & Mayer, 1990). Emotional intelligence (EI) *refers to people's ability to recognize their own and others' emotions, to correctly identify and appropriately tell the difference between emotions, and use this information to guide their thinking and behavior.* Emotional intelligence consists of two aspects. First, EI can be viewed as a trait that reflects a person's self-perceived dispositions and abilities. Second, EI can be viewed as an ability that reflects the person's success at processing emotional information and using it appropriately in social contexts. EI has been applied to a wide variety of situations, from everyday social cognition and problem solving to bullying to business to leadership. Although still controversial (Hunt & Fitzgerald, 2013, 2014), EI has been mapped onto brain structures (Barbey et al., 2014; Operskalski et al., 2015).

Research indicates that emotional intelligence increases with age (Chen, Peng, & Fang, 2016; Mankus, Boden, & Thompson, 2016), though there is some evidence that the specific ability to perceive others' emotions in the work context declines late in life (Doerwald et al., 2016). An important finding is that older adults' increased emotional intelligence may be a source of their higher subjective well-being (Chen et al., 2016).

EI may well be an underlying factor in the social cognitive situations, one of which, impression formation, we will now consider. Keep in mind that variations in a person's ability to sort out the emotional information available in any given social situation may play an important role in how he or she behaves.

emotional intelligence (EI)
The ability to recognize their own and others' emotions, to correctly identify and appropriately tell the difference between emotions, and use this information to guide their thinking and behavior.

Impression Formation

When people meet each other, they tend to immediately come to conclusions about them on many dimensions. Researchers (e.g., Adams et al., 2012; Kotter-Grühn, 2016; Leshikar, Cassidy, & Gutchess, 2016) examine age differences in social judgments by examining impression formation. Impression formation *is the way we form and revise first impressions about others.* Researchers examine how people use diagnostic trait information (aspects about people that appear critical or unique) in making initial impressions of an individual, and how this process varies with age.

A common way of studying impression formation is to have two groups of adults presented with information about a person, either through descriptions or inferences. One group gets positive information first, such as evidence of honesty. The other group is presented with negative information first, such as incidents of dishonest behavior. Each group then subsequently gets the opposite information about the person (e.g., the group that got positive information first then gets negative information).

impression formation
The way we form and revise first impressions about others.

What happens to people's first impressions as a function of age is a well-established finding. As you can see from ❯ Figure 10.13, in a study that helped create this area of research focus, Hess and Pullen (1994) found all study participants modified their impressions. When new negative information was presented after the initial positive portrayal of the target person, older adults modified their impression of the target from positive to negative. Interestingly, however, they modified their first impression *less* when the negative portrayal was followed by positive information.

In contrast, younger adults did not show this pattern. Instead, they were more concerned with making sure the new information was consistent with their initial impression. To do so, they modified their impressions to correspond with the new information regardless of whether it was positive or negative. Younger adults, then, make their impression based on the most recent information they have. ❯

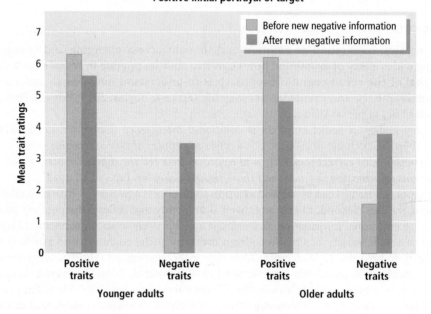

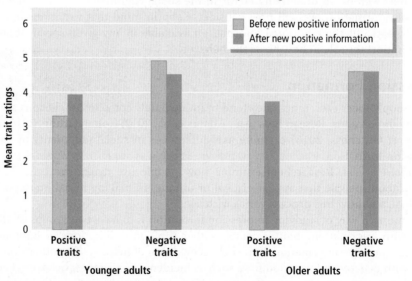

❯ **Figure 10.13**

Mean trait ratings before and after presentation of new negative or positive information.

SOURCE: A modified graph of the Hess, T. M., & Pullen, S. M. (1994). Adult age differences in impression change processes. *Psychology and Aging, 9*, p. 239.

Why do younger and older adults differ? Hess and Pullen suggest older adults may rely more on life experiences and social rules of behavior when making their interpretations, whereas younger adults may be more concerned with situational consistency of the new information presented.

Given the consistency of these patterns over many studies, knowing how to create positive (or negative) impressions about people, such as in political campaigns, job interviews, or dating, requires understanding of the order in which certain personal characteristics should be presented.

TEST YOURSELF 10.3

Recall

1. Most modern theories of intelligence are _____ in that they identify many domains of intellectual abilities.

2. Number, verbal fluency, and spatial orientation are some of the _____ mental abilities.

3. _____ reflects knowledge that you have acquired through life experience and education in a particular culture.

4. Kitchener and King describe a kind of postformal thinking called _____.

5. Life problems provide a context for understanding the integration of _____ and _____.

Interpret

- Many young adult college students seemingly get more confused about what field they want to major in and less certain about what they know as they progress through college. From a cognitive-developmental approach, why does this happen?

- Political movements often are led by a combination of late adolescents/young adults and older adults. From a cognitive development perspective, why would this tend to be the case?

Apply

- Two of LuSharon's friends explained their decision to support different candidates during the 2016 U.S. presidential campaign. One friend said that she had an intuition that her candidate's campaign statements were based on facts and were absolutely trustworthy; the other friend said that her candidate's statements always had to be put into a specific context in order to be analyzed. Based on the reflective judgment model, what levels of thinking do LuSharon's friends demonstrate?

- How does experience on the job relate to the stages of reflective judgment?

Check your answers to the Recall Questions at the end of the chapter.

10.4 Who Do You Want to Be? Personality in Young Adulthood

LEARNING OBJECTIVES

- How do adults create scenarios and life stories?

- What are possible selves? Do they show differences during adulthood?

- What are personal control beliefs?

Felicia is a 19-year-old sophomore at a community college. She expects her study of early childhood education to be difficult but rewarding. She figures that along the way, she will meet a great guy and marry him soon after graduation. They will have two children before she turns 30. Felicia sees herself getting a good job teaching preschool children and someday owning her own day-care center.

Maya Angelou (1969) perhaps said it best: "There is no agony like bearing an untold story inside of you." True to her conviction, she spent a lifetime writing her story in numerous books, poems, and other literary works. She described an incredible developmental path of oppression, hatred, and hurt that ultimately resulted in self-awareness, understanding, and compassion.

In Chapter 9, we saw how children and adolescents begin creating their stories by answering the question, What do you want to be when you grow up? As a young adult, Felicia has arrived at the "grown-up" part and is experimenting with some idealistic answers to the question. Are Felicia's answers typical of most emerging adults?

In this section, we examine how the search for identity gets transformed through the cognitive, social, and personal reality of adulthood. As a result, people create life scenarios and life stories, possible selves, self-concept, and personal control beliefs. Let's begin by considering how Felicia and the rest of us construct images of our adult lives.

Creating Life Stories

Figuring out what (and whom) you want to be as an adult takes a great deal of thought, hard work, and time. *Based on personal experience and input from other people, young adults create a* life-span construct *that represents a unified sense of the past, present, and future.* Several factors influence the development of a life-span construct; identity, values, and society are only a few. Together they not only shape the creation of the life-span construct but also influence how it is played out and whether it remains stable (Fraley & Roberts, 2005). The life-span construct represents a link between Erikson's notion of identity, which is a major focus during adolescence, and our adult view of ourselves.

The first way the life-span construct is manifested is through the scenario, *which consists of expectations about the future.* The scenario takes aspects of a person's identity that are particularly important now and projects them into a plan for the future. For example, you may find yourself thinking about the day you will graduate and will be able to apply all of the knowledge and skills you have learned. In short, a scenario is a game plan for how your life will play out in the future.

Felicia, the sophomore human development student, has a fairly typical scenario. She plans on completing a degree in early childhood education, marrying after graduation, and having two children by age 30. *Tagging future events with a particular time or age by which they are to be completed creates a* social clock. This personal timetable gives people a way to track progress through adulthood, and it may use biological markers of time (such as menopause), social aspects of time (such as marriage), and historical time (such as the turn of the century) (Hagestad & Neugarten, 1985).

Felicia will use her scenario to evaluate progress toward her personal goals. With each new event, she will check where she is against where her scenario says she should be. If she is ahead of her plan, she may be proud of having made it. If she is lagging behind, she may chastise herself for being slow. But if she criticizes herself too much, she may change her scenario altogether. For example, if she does not go to college, she may decide to change her career goals entirely: Instead of owning her own day care center, she may aim to be a manager in a department store.

How Felicia and the rest of us actually create the stories about ourselves is a fascinating process of integrating thought and emotion, along with the lived experiences we have. Let's see in more detail how this happens by examining the best known explanation of the process.

McAdams's Life-Story Model

McAdams (2001, 2015) argues a person's sense of identity cannot be understood using the language of dispositional traits or personal concerns. Identity is not just a collection of traits, nor is it a collection of plans, strategies, or goals. Instead, it is based on a story of how the person came into being, where the person has been, where he or she is going, and who he or she will become, much like Felicia's story. *McAdams argues that people create a* life story *that is an internalized narrative with a beginning, middle, and an anticipated ending.* The life story is created and revised throughout adulthood as people change and the changing environment places different demands on them.

McAdams's research indicates people in Western societies begin forming their life story during late adolescence and emerging adulthood, but its roots lie in one's earliest attachments in infancy. As in Erikson's theory, adolescence marks the full initiation into forming an identity, and thus, a coherent life story begins. In emerging adulthood it is continued and refined through intimacy, and from midlife and beyond it is refashioned in the wake of major and minor life changes.

---

life-span construct

Unified sense of the past, present, and future based on personal experience and input from other people.

scenario

Manifestation of the life-span construct through expectations about the future.

social clock

Tagging future events with a particular time or age by which they are to be completed.

life story

An internalized narrative with a beginning, middle, and an anticipated ending.

Paramount in these life stories is the changing personal identity reflected in the emotions conveyed in the story (from tragedy to optimism or through comic and romantic descriptions). In addition, motivations change and are reflected in the person repeatedly trying to attain his or her goals over time. The two most common goal themes are *agency* (reflecting power, achievement, and autonomy) and *communion* (reflecting love, intimacy, and a sense of belonging). Finally, life stories indicate one's beliefs and values, or the ideology a person uses to set the context for his or her actions.

Every life story contains episodes that provide insight into perceived change and continuity in life. People prove to themselves and others they have either changed or remained the same by pointing to specific events supporting the appropriate claim. The main characters, representing the roles we play, in our lives represent idealizations of the self, such as "the dutiful mother" or "the reliable worker." Integrating these various aspects of the self into a coherent whole begins in emerging adulthood, and continues to be a major challenge of midlife and later adulthood. Finally, all life stories need an ending so the self can leave a legacy that creates new beginnings. As we will see in Chapters 13 and 15, life stories in middle-aged and older adults have a clear quality of "giving birth to" a new generation.

One of the more popular methods for examining the development of life stories is through autobiographical memory (Dunlop, Guo, & McAdams, 2016; Lilgendahl & McAdams, 2011; McLean, 2016; McLean & Pasupathi, 2012). When people tell their life stories to others, the stories are a joint product of the speaker and the audience, which includes other key people in a person's life, such as family (Pasupathi, 2013; McLean, 2016). This co-construction of identity is a good example of conversational remembering, much like collaborative cognition discussed in Chapter 8.

Overall, McAdams (2001, 2015) believes the model for change in identity over time is a process of fashioning and refashioning one's life story. This process appears to be strongly influenced by culture. At times, the reformulation may be at a conscious level, such as when people make explicit decisions about changing careers. At other times, the revision process is unconscious and implicit, growing out of everyday activities. The goal is to create a life story that is coherent, credible, open to new possibilities, richly differentiated, reconciling of opposite aspects of oneself, and integrated within one's sociocultural context.

Possible Selves

When we are asked questions like, "What do you think you'll be like a few years from now?" it requires us to imagine ourselves in the future. When we speculate like this, we create a *possible self* (Markus & Nurius, 1986). Possible selves *represent what we could become, what we would like to become, and what we are afraid of becoming.* What we could or would like to become often reflects personal goals; we may see ourselves as leaders, as rich and famous, or in great physical shape. What we are afraid of becoming may show up in our fear of being alone, or overweight, or unsuccessful. Our possible selves are powerful motivators (Ko, Mejia, & Hooker, 2014); indeed, how we behave is largely an effort to achieve or avoid these various possible selves and protect the current view of self (Baumeister, 2010).

In a rare set of similar studies conducted across time and research teams by Cross and Markus (1991) and Hooker and colleagues (Frazier et al., 2000; Frazier et al., 2002; Hooker, 1999; Hooker et al., 1996; Morfei et al., 2001), people across the adult life span were asked to describe their hoped-for and feared possible selves. The responses were grouped into categories (e.g., family, personal, material, relationships, and occupation).

Several interesting age differences emerged. In terms of hoped-for selves, young adults listed family concerns—for instance, marrying the right person—as most important. In contrast, adults in their 30s listed family concerns last; their main issues involved personal concerns, such as being a more loving and caring person. By ages 40 to 59, family issues again became most common—such as being a parent who can "let go" of the children. Reaching and maintaining satisfactory performance in one's occupational career as

possible selves
Representations of what we could become, what we would like to become, and what we are afraid of becoming.

well as accepting and adjusting to the physiological changes of middle age were important to this age group.

For adults over 60, researchers find personal issues are most prominent—like being active and healthy for at least another decade. The greatest amount of change occurred in the health domain, which predominated the hoped-for and feared-for selves. The health domain is the most sensitive and central to the self in the context of aging and people's possible self with regard to health is quite resilient in the face of health challenges in later life.

Overall, young adults have multiple possible selves and believe they can actually become the hoped-for self and successfully avoid the feared self. Their outlook tends to be quite positive (Remedios, Chasteen, & Packer, 2010). Life experience may dampen this outlook. By old age, both the number of possible selves and the strength of belief have decreased. Older adults are more likely to believe neither the hoped-for nor the feared-for self is under their personal control. These findings may reflect differences with age in personal motivation, beliefs in personal control, and the need to explore new options.

The emergence of online social media has created new opportunities for young adults to create possible selves (Lefkowitz, Vukman, & Loken, 2012). Such media present different ways for them to speculate about themselves to others.

The connection between possible selves and how we construct meaning in our lives is important. The link is through the process of setting personal goals that derive from the possible selves we envision.

Think About It

How might the development of possible selves be related to cognitive development?

personal control beliefs

The degree to which you believe your performance in a situation depends on something you do.

Larry Page, cofounder of Google, is likely to have a high sense of personal control.

Emmanuel Dunand/AFP/Getty Images

Personal Control Beliefs

Do you feel you have control over your life? Personal control beliefs *reflect the degree to which you believe your performance in a situation depends on something you do.* For example, suppose you are not offered a job when you think you should have been. Was it your fault? Or was it because the company was too shortsighted to recognize your true talent? The option you select provides insight into a general tendency. Do you generally believe that outcomes depend on the things you do? Or are they due to factors outside yourself, such as luck or the power of others?

Answering these questions requires the integration of several different sources of information, along with one's emotions. The result of this integration are various conclusions about how much control one has in any specific situation. A high sense of personal control implies a belief that performance is up to you, whereas a low sense of personal control implies that your performance is under the influence of forces other than your own.

Personal control is an extremely important idea in a variety of settings and cultures because of the way it guides behavior (Brandtstädter, 1997, 1999; Fung & Siu, 2010). Successful people such as Stefani Joanne Angelina Germanotta (better known as Lady Gaga) need to exude a high sense of personal control to demonstrate that they are in charge.

Personal control is an important concept that can be applied broadly to several domains, including social networks, health, and careers (Fung & Siu, 2010). It is related to the nearly universal desire to make a difference in the world through one's life (Dowd, 2012).

Personal control beliefs are important not only in personality development but also (as we will see in Chapter 14) in memory performance in late life. Research indicates that people experience four types of personal control (Tiffany & Tiffany, 1996): control from within oneself, control over oneself, control over the environment, and control from the environment.

Despite its importance, we do not have a clear picture of the developmental course of personal control beliefs. Evidence from both cross-sectional and longitudinal studies (Lang & Heckhausen, 2006) is contradictory. Some data indicate that younger adults are less likely to hold internal control beliefs (i.e., believe they are in control of outcomes) than are older adults. Other research finds the opposite.

The contradiction may derive from the complex nature of personal control beliefs in the context of the situation (Vazire & Doris, 2009). These beliefs vary depending on which domain, such as intelligence or health, is being assessed. Indeed, other research shows that perceived control over one's development declines with age, whereas perceived control over marital happiness increases (Brandtstädter, 1989). In addition, younger adults are more satisfied when attributing success in attaining a goal to their own efforts, whereas older adults are more satisfied when they attribute such success to their ability (Lang & Heckhausen, 2001, 2006). Clearly, people of all ages and cultures try to influence their environment regardless of whether they believe they will be successful.

Heckhausen and Wrosch (Haase, Heckhausen, & Wrosch, 2013; Heckhausen, Wrosch, & Schulz, 2010) pulled together the various perspectives on control beliefs and proposed a motivational theory of life-span development to describe how people optimize primary and secondary control. *Primary control is behavior aimed at affecting the individual's external world; working a second job to increase one's earnings is an example.* One's ability to influence the environment is heavily influenced by biological factors (e.g., stamina to work two jobs); so it changes over time—from very low influence during early childhood to high influence during middle age and then to very low again in late life. *Secondary control is behavior or cognition aimed at affecting the individual's internal world; an example is believing that one is capable of success even when faced with challenges.*

primary control
Behavior aimed at affecting the individual's external world.

secondary control
Behavior or cognition aimed at affecting the individual's internal world.

The developmental patterns of both types of control are shown in ▶ Figure 10.14. The figure also shows that people of all ages strive to control their environment, but how they do this changes over time. Note that for the first half of life, primary and secondary control operate in parallel. During midlife, primary control begins to decline but secondary control does not. Thus, the desire for control does not change; what differs with age is whether we can affect our environment or whether we need to think about things differently. We will return to these ideas in Chapter 15 when we see how our interaction with the environment changes in late life.

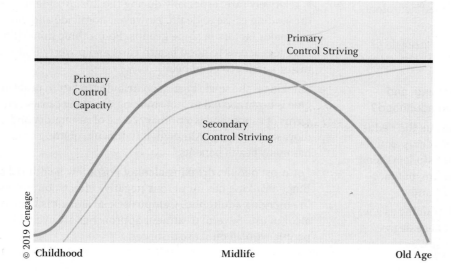

▶ **Figure 10.14**
Hypothetical life-span trajectories for primary control potential and primary and secondary control striving.

Recall

1. A(n) _____ is a unified sense of a person's past, present, and future.

2. A personal narrative that organizes past events into a coherent sequence is a(n) _____.

3. Representations of what we could become, what we would like to be, and what we are afraid of becoming are our _____.

4. _____ reflect the degree to which a person's performance in a situation is believed to be under his or her control.

Interpret

● How might people's scenarios, life stories, and other aspects of personality vary as a function of cognitive developmental level and self-definition as an adult?

● How do possible selves reflect people's life experiences?

Apply

● In the context of a bad economy, how could you determine whether your performance on job interviews is under your control?

● How has your view of your possible selves influenced your choice of career?

Check your answers to the Recall Questions at the end of the chapter.

SUMMARY

10.1 Emerging Adulthood

What role transitions mark entry into adulthood?

● The most widely used criteria for deciding whether a person has reached adulthood are role transitions, which involve assuming new responsibilities and duties.

● Some societies use rituals, called rites of passage, to mark this transition clearly. However, such rituals are largely absent in Western culture.

What evidence from neuroscience helps us understand behavioral development in young adulthood?

● The prefrontal cortex fully develops during young adulthood and forms key connections with other areas of the brain.

● Edgework may reflect aspects of this continued neurological development.

● Young adults make the transition to Erikson's struggle of intimacy and isolation.

How do going to college, obtaining career training, and entering the workforce reflect the transition to adulthood?

● Roughly 70% of high school graduates continue their education at the postsecondary level. College students experience transitions in thinking. Returning adult students tend to be more focused on their academic program, but face challenges balancing education, career, and family.

● Many emerging adults obtain career or job training as a way to further education without obtaining a college degree.

● Joining the workforce is a major step toward financial independence, which in turn is a major marker of achieving adulthood.

10.2 Physical Development and Health

In what respects are young adults at their physical peak?

● Young adulthood is the time when certain physical abilities peak: strength, muscle development, coordination, dexterity, and sensory acuity. Most of these abilities begin to decline in middle age.

How do smoking, alcohol, and nutrition affect young adults' health?

● Young adults are at the peak of health. Death from disease is relatively rare, especially during the 20s. Accidents are the leading cause of death. However, homicide and violence are major factors in some groups. Poor ethnic minorities have less access to good health care, and poverty is also a major barrier to good health.

● Smoking is the single biggest contributor to health problems. One is never too old to quit smoking. Smoking causes several forms of cancer and is a primary cause of respiratory and cardiovascular disease. Although it is difficult, quitting smoking has many health benefits.

● For most people, drinking alcohol poses few health risks. Binge drinking has numerous negative effects, but peaks in emerging adulthood. Campus sexual assault is related to alcohol use. Several treatment approaches are available for people with alcohol use disorder.

- Nutritional needs change somewhat during adulthood, mostly due to changes in metabolism. Some nutrient needs, such as carbohydrates, change. The ratio of LDLs to HDLs in serum cholesterol, which can be controlled through diet or medication in most people, is an important risk factor in cardiovascular disease.

How does young adults' health differ as a function of socioeconomic status, ethnicity, and education?

- The three most important social factors in health are socioeconomic status, ethnicity, and education. Poverty is the most important factor in limiting access to quality health care.

- Even with other variables held equal, people of color have poorer access to quality health care than European Americans.

- Higher education is associated with better health via better access to health care and more knowledge about proper diet and lifestyle.

10.3 Cognitive Development

What is intelligence in adulthood?

- Most modern theories of intelligence are multidimensional. Research reveals interindividual variability and plasticity.

- Intellectual abilities are organized into factors of interrelated abilities that form the structure of intelligence.

What are primary and secondary mental abilities? How do they change?

- Intellectual abilities can be studied as groups of related skills known as primary mental abilities.

- Clusters of related primary abilities are called secondary mental abilities. Secondary mental abilities are not measured directly.

- These abilities develop differently and change in succeeding cohorts. More recent cohorts perform better on some skills, such as inductive reasoning, but older cohorts perform better on number skills.

What are fluid and crystallized intelligence? How do they change?

- Fluid intelligence consists of abilities that make people flexible and adaptive thinkers. Fluid abilities generally decline during adulthood.

- Crystallized intelligence reflects knowledge that people acquire through life experience and education in a particular culture. Crystallized abilities improve until late life.

How has neuroscience research furthered our understanding of intelligence in adulthood?

- Neuroscience research has begun mapping specific areas in the brain that relate to intelligence. One prominent theory based on this work is the parieto-frontal integration theory (P-FIT).

What is postformal thought? How does it differ from formal operations?

- Postformal thought is characterized by a recognition that truth may vary from one situation to another, that solutions must be realistic, that ambiguity and contradiction are the rule, and that emotion and subjectivity play a role in thinking. One example of postformal thought is reflective judgment.

How do emotion and logic become integrated in adulthood? How do emotional intelligence and impression formation demonstrate this integration?

- Cognition (logic) and emotion become integrated during young adulthood and middle age. This means that the way people approach and solve practical problems in life differs from adolescence through middle age.

- Emotional intelligence refers to the ability to recognize and correctly identify one's own and other's emotion, and to use this information to guide thinking and behavior. Emotional intelligence increases with age and likely underlies many social cognitive situations.

- Impression formation is the way we form and revise first impressions. How this process influences judgments about people differs with age.

10.4 Who Do You Want to Be? Personality in Young Adulthood

What is the life-span construct? How do adults create scenarios and life stories?

- Young adults create a life-span construct that represents a unified sense of the past, present, and future. This is manifested in two ways: through a scenario that maps the future based on a social clock and in the life story, which creates an autobiography.

What are possible selves? Do they show differences during adulthood?

- People create possible selves by projecting themselves into the future and thinking about what they would like to become, what they could become, and what they are afraid of becoming.

- Age differences in these projections depend on the dimension examined. In hoped-for selves, 18- to 24-year-olds and 40- to 59-year-olds report family issues as most important, whereas 25- to 39-year-olds and older adults consider personal issues to be most important. However, all groups include physical aspects as part of their most feared selves.

What are personal control beliefs?

- Personal control is an important concept with broad applicability. However, the developmental trends are complex because personal control beliefs vary considerably from one domain to another.

Test Yourself Recall Answers

10.1 1. role transitions **2.** rites of passage **3.** returning adult students **4.** reckless behavior **5.** intimacy versus isolation **10.2 1.** height **2.** 20s **3.** rare **4.** accidents **5.** Smoking **6.** binge drinking **7.** socioeconomic status **10.3 1.** multidimensional **2.** primary **3.** Crystallized intelligence **4.** reflective judgment **5.** emotion, logic **10.4 1.** life-span construct **2.** life story **3.** possible selves **4.** Personal control beliefs

Key Terms

emerging adulthood (318)
rites of passage (319)
role transitions (319)
edgework (320)
returning adult students (322)
intimacy versus isolation (323)
binge drinking (327)
alcohol use disorder (328)
metabolism (330)
low-density lipoproteins (LDLs) (330)
high-density lipoproteins (HDLs) (330)

body mass index (BMI) (332)
multidimensional (334)
multidirectionality (334)
interindividual variability (334)
plasticity (335)
structure of intelligence (335)
factor (335)
primary mental abilities (335)
secondary mental abilities (335)
fluid intelligence (337)
crystallized intelligence (337)
parieto-frontal integration theory (P-FIT) (339)

neural efficiency hypothesis (340)
postformal thought (341)
reflective judgment (341)
emotional intelligence (EI) (343)
impression formation (343)
life-span construct (346)
scenario (346)
social clock (346)
life story (346)
possible selves (347)
personal control beliefs (348)
primary control (349)
secondary control (349)

Being with Others: Relationships in Young and Middle Adulthood

Imagine yourself years from now. Your children are grown and have children and grandchildren of their own. In honor of your 80th birthday, they have all come together, along with your friends, to celebrate. Their present to you is a video made from hundreds of photographs and dozens of videos created over the decades of your life. As you watch it, you realize how lucky you've been to have so many wonderful people in your life. Your relationships have made your adult life fun and worthwhile. As you watch, you wonder what it must be like to go through life alone—no family, no friends (even on Facebook), no followers of your Twitter postings. You think of all the wonderful experiences you would have missed in early and middle adulthood—never knowing what friendship is all about, never being in love, never dreaming about children and becoming a parent.

That is what we'll explore in this chapter—the ways in which we share our lives with others. First, we consider what makes good friendships and love relationships. Because these relationships form the basis of our lifestyle, we examine these lifestyle influences next. In the third section, we consider what it is like to be a parent. Finally, we see what happens when marriages or partnerships end. Throughout this chapter, the emphasis is on aspects of relationships that nearly everyone experiences during young adulthood and middle age. In Chapter 13, we examine aspects of relationships specific to middle-aged adults; in Chapter 14, we do the same for relationships in later life.

LEARNING OBJECTIVES

- What role do friends play across adulthood? How do they develop?

- What characterizes love relationships? How do they vary across cultures?

- What is the nature of violence in some relationships?

Jamal and Kahlid have known each other all their lives. They grew up together in New York, attended the same schools, and even married sisters. Their business careers took them in different directions, but they and their families always got together on major holidays. Now as older men, they feel a special bond; many of their other friends have died.

Having other people in our lives we can count on is essential to our well-being. Just imagine how difficult life would be if you were totally alone, without even a Facebook "friend" to communicate with. In this section, we consider the different types of relationships we have with other people, and learn how these relationships help—and sometimes hurt us.

Friendships

Jamal and Kahlid remind us some of the most important people in our lives are our friends. They are often the people to whom we are closest, and are there when we need someone to lean on.

What is an adult friend? Someone who is there when you need to share? Someone that's not afraid to tell you the truth? Someone you have fun with? Friends, of course, are all of these and more. Researchers define friendship as a mutual relationship in which those involved influence one another's behaviors and beliefs, and define friendship quality as the satisfaction derived from the relationship (Blieszner, 2014; Blieszner & Roberto, 2012; Hall, 2016).

The role and influence of friends for young adults is extremely important from the late teens through the 20s, and friends continue to be a source of support across adulthood (Arnett, 2013; Nehamas, 2016). Friendships are predominantly based on feelings and grounded in reciprocity and choice. Friendships are different from love relationships mainly because friendships are less emotionally intense and usually do not involve sex (Nehamas, 2016). Having good friendships boosts self-esteem, especially early in emerging adulthood (Miething et al., 2016), and happiness across adulthood (Adams & Taylor, 2015; Demir et al., 2015; Fiori & Denckla, 2015). Friendships also help us become socialized into new roles throughout adulthood.

Friendship in Adulthood

From a developmental perspective, adult friendships can be viewed as having identifiable stages (Levinger, 1980, 1983): Acquaintanceship, Buildup, Continuation, Deterioration, and Ending. This ABCDE model describes the stages of friendships and how they change. Whether a friendship develops from Acquaintanceship to Buildup depends on where the individuals fall on several dimensions, such as the basis of the attraction, what each person knows about the other, how good the communication is between the partners, the perceived importance of the friendship, and so on. Although many friendships reach the Deterioration stage, whether a friendship ultimately ends depends heavily on the availability of alternative relationships. If potential friends appear, old friendships may end; if not, they may continue even though they are no longer considered important by either person.

Longitudinal research shows how friendships change across adulthood, some in ways that are predictable and others not. As you probably have experienced, life transitions (e.g., going away to college, getting married) usually result in fewer friends and less contact with the friends you keep (Blieszner, 2014; Blieszner & Roberto, 2012). People tend to have more friends and acquaintances during young adulthood than at any subsequent period (Demir et al., 2015). Friendships are important throughout adulthood, in part because a person's life satisfaction is strongly related to the quantity and quality of contacts with friend. College students with strong friendship networks adjust better to stressful life events whether those networks are face-to-face (e.g., Brissette, Scheier, & Carver, 2002) or through online social networks (Antheunis, 2016; DeAndrea et al., 2012).

The importance of maintaining contacts with friends cuts across ethnic lines as well. People who have friendships that cross ethnic groups have more positive attitudes toward people with different backgrounds (Aberson, Shoemaker, & Tomolillo, 2004), including Facebook networks (Schwab & Greitemeyer, 2015). Thus, regardless of one's background, friendships play a major role in determining how much we enjoy life.

Why does friendship have such positive benefits for us? Although scientists do not know for certain, they are gaining insights through neuroscience research. Coan and colleagues (Beckes & Coan, 2013; Beckes, Coan, & Hasselmo, 2013; Coan, 2008; Coan & Sbarra, 2015) propose Social Baseline Theory, a perspective that integrates the study of social relationships with principles of attachment, behavioral ecology, cognitive neuroscience, and perception science. Social Baseline Theory suggests the human brain expects access to social relationships that mitigate risk and diminish the level of effort needed to meet a variety of goals by incorporating relational partners into neural representations of the self.

When people are faced with threatening situations, their brains process the situation differently when faced alone compared to with a close friend. Specifically, neuroimaging definitively shows the parts of the brain that respond to threat operate when facing threat alone but do not operate when facing the same threat with a close friend. A close friendship literally changes the way the brain functions, resulting in our perception of feeling safer and the trials we face are more manageable with friends than without them.

Three broad themes characterize both traditional (e.g., face-to-face) and new forms (e.g., online) of adult friendships (de Vries, 1996; Ridings & Gefen, 2004):

- The *affective or emotional basis* of friendship refers to self-disclosure and expressions of intimacy, appreciation, affection, and support, and all are based on trust, loyalty, and commitment.
- The *shared, or communal nature*, of friendship reflects how friends participate in or support activities of mutual interest.
- The *sociability and compatibility* dimension represents how our friends keep us entertained and are sources of amusement, fun, and recreation.

In the case of online friendships (e.g., through social media), trust develops on the basis of four sources: (1) reputation; (2) performance, or what users do online; (3) precommitment, through personal self-disclosure; and (4) situational factors, especially the premium placed on intimacy and the relationship (Håkansson & Witmer, 2015; Henderson & Gilding, 2004). Online social network friendships develop much like face-to-face ones in that the more time people spend online with friends the more likely they are to self-disclose (Chang & Hsiao, 2014). Online environments are more conducive to people who are lonely (Blachnio et al., 2016). A study of Facebook users in Australia showed that they were extremely positive about their online friendship activity (Young, 2013). However, they mentioned that the risk of "de-friending" is a real phenomenon, so that the psychological consequences can be both positive (gaining new friends and a social network) and negative (dealing with the hurt of being de-friended).

A special type of friendship exists with one's siblings, who are the friends people typically have the longest and that share the closest bonds; the importance of these relationships varies with age (Carr & Moorman, 2011;

Despite concerns, social networking websites such as Facebook have not reduced the quality of friendships.

iStock.com/Dem10

Merz & De Jong Gierveld, 2016; Moorman & Greenfield, 2010). The centrality of siblings depends on several things, such as proximity, health, prior relationship, and degree of relatedness (full, step-, or half-siblings). No clear pattern of emotional closeness emerges when viewing sibling relationships on the basis of gender.

Men's, Women's, and Cross-Sex Friendships

Men's and women's friendships tend to differ in adulthood, reflecting continuity in the learned behaviors from childhood (Blieszner & Roberto, 2012; Levine, 2009). Four characteristics of same-sex friends do not appear to differ between men and women and are similar across cultures and age groups: geographic proximity, similarity of interests and values, inclusion, and symmetrical reciprocity (Hall, 2016). Three characteristics that distinguish female same-sex friendships from males' same-sex friendships are: communion and self-disclosure, greater effort and expectations from friends in general, and a greater risk of corumination (extensively discussing and re-visiting problems, and focusing on negative feelings) (Hall, 2016). In contrast, men tend to base friendships on shared activities or interests.

What about friendships between men and women? These friendships are mainly a product of the 20th century (Hart, Adams, & Tullett, 2016), and have a beneficial effect, especially for men (Piquet, 2007). Cross-sex friendships help men have lower levels of dating anxiety and higher capacity for intimacy. These patterns hold across ethnic groups, too. Cross-sex friendships can also prove troublesome because of misperceptions. Misperception about one's own or one's partner's sexual attractiveness to others is common and can be the basis for relationship difficulties (Hart et al., 2016; Haselton & Galperin, 2013). Some research shows men overestimate and women underestimate their friends' sexual interest in them (Koenig, Kirkpatrick, & Ketelaar, 2007). Maintaining cross-sex friendships once individuals enter into exclusive dating relationships, marriage, or committed relationships is difficult, and often results in one partner feeling jealous (Hart et al., 2016; Haselton & Galperin, 2013).

Physical attraction tends to be high early in a relationship.

Caroline Schiff/Blend Images/Getty Images

Love Relationships

Love is one of those things we feel but cannot fully describe. (Test yourself: Can you explain fully what you mean when you look at someone special and say, "I love you"?) One way researchers try to understand love is to think about what components are essential. In an interesting series of studies, Sternberg (2006) found love has three basic components: (1) *passion*, an intense physiological desire for someone; (2) *intimacy*, the feeling that you can share all your thoughts and actions with another; and (3) *commitment*, the willingness to stay with a person through good and bad times. Ideally, a true love relationship has all three components; when couples have equivalent amounts and types of love, they tend to be happier, even as the balance among these components shifts over time.

Love Through Adulthood

The different combinations of love help us understand how relationships develop (Sternberg, 2006). Research shows the development of romantic relationships in emerging adulthood is a complex process influenced by relationships in childhood and adolescence (Collins & van Dulmen, 2006; Oudekerk et al., 2015). Early in a romantic relationship, passion is usually high whereas intimacy and commitment tend to be low. This is infatuation: an intense, physically based relationship when the two people have a high risk of misunderstanding and jealousy. Indeed, it is sometimes difficult to establish the boundaries between casual sex and hook-ups and dating in young adulthood (Giordano et al., 2012).

Infatuation is short-lived. As passion fades, either a relationship acquires emotional intimacy or it is likely to end. Trust, honesty, openness, and acceptance must be a part of any strong relationship; when they are present, romantic love develops.

Although it may not be the basis for best-selling romance novels or movies, this pattern is a good thing. Research shows people who select a partner for a more permanent relationship (e.g., marriage) during the height of infatuation are likely to support the notion of "love at first sight" and are more likely to divorce (Hansen, 2006). If the couple spends more time and works at their relationship, they may become committed to each other. By spending much of their time together, making decisions together, caring for each other, sharing possessions, and developing ways to settle conflicts, they increase the chances that their relationship will last. Such couples usually show outward signs of commitment, such as wearing a lover's ring, having children together, or simply sharing the mundane details of daily life, from making toast at breakfast to following before-bed rituals.

Campbell and Kaufman (2015) surveyed 1,529 people across the United States in order to better understand the connections among love, personality, and creativity. They found that as time goes on, physical intimacy and passion decrease but emotional intimacy and commitment increase. This and related research indicate that good relationships tend to deepen as time goes on, even if intense physical passion decreases.

Falling in Love

In his book *The Prophet*, Kahlil Gibran (1923) points out love is two-sided: Just as it can give you great ecstasy, so can it cause you great pain. Yet most of us are willing to take the risk.

As you may have experienced, taking the risk is fun (at times) and difficult (at other times). Making a connection can be ritualized, as when people use pickup lines in a bar, or it can happen almost by accident, as when two people literally run into each other in a crowded corridor. The question that confronts us is "How do people fall in love?" Do birds of a feather flock together? Or do opposites attract?

The best explanation of the process is the theory of assortative mating, *that states people find partners based on their similarity to each other.* Assortative mating occurs along many dimensions, including education, religious beliefs, physical traits, age, socioeconomic status, intelligence, and political ideology, among others (Horwitz et al., 2016). Such nonrandom mating occurs most often in Western societies that allow people to have more control over their own dating and pairing behaviors. Common activities are one basis for identifying potential mates, except, that is, in speed dating situations. In that case, it comes down to physical attractiveness (Luo & Zhang, 2009).

People meet people in all sorts of places, both face-to-face and virtually. Does how people meet influence the likelihood they will "click" on particular dimensions and form a couple? Kalmijn and Flap (2001) found that it does. Using data from more than 1,500 couples, they found meeting at school, for example, was most likely to result in *homogamy*—the degree to which people are similar. Not surprisingly, the pool of available people to meet is strongly shaped by the opportunities available, that in turn constrain the type of people one is likely to meet.

Speed dating provides a way to meet several people in a short period of time. Speed dating is practiced most by young adults (Fein & Schneider, 2013; Whitty & Buchanan, 2009). The rules governing partner selection during a speed dating session seem quite similar to traditional dating: physically attractive people, outgoing and self-assured people, and moderately self-focused people are selected more often and their dates are rated as smoother (Herrenbrueck et al., 2016).

The popularity of online dating means an increasing number of people meet this way (Fein & Schneider, 2013; Lomanowska & Guitton, 2016; Whitty & Buchanan, 2009). Surveys indicate nearly 1 in every 5 couples in the United States meet online (compared with 1 in 10 in Australia, and 1 in 20 in Spain and the United Kingdom; Dutton et al., 2009). Emerging research indicates virtual dating sites offer both problems and possibilities, especially in terms of the accuracy of personal descriptions. As in the offline world, physical

assortative mating
Theory stating that people find partners based on their similarity to each other.

These Egyptian women, performing traditional cultural tasks, are more likely to be desired as mates.

attractiveness strongly influences initial selections online (Sritharan et al., 2010), especially on sites such as Tinder and Grindr (Sumter, Vandenbosch, & Ligtenberg, 2017). Over a third of couples who marry first met online, often via online dating sites (Johnson, 2016).

One increasing trend among emerging adults is the hookup culture of casual sex, often without even knowing the name of one's sexual partner (Garcia et al., 2013; Kratzer & Stevens Aubrey, 2016). Research indicates both men and women are interested in having hookup sex but also prefer a more romantic relationship over the long run. However, the perception there are no strings attached to hookup sex appear wrong, as nearly three-fourths of both men and women eventually expressed some level of regret at having hookup sex.

How do couple-forming behaviors compare cross-culturally? A few studies have examined the factors that attract people to each other in different cultures. In one now classic study, Buss and a large team of researchers (1990) identified the effects of culture and gender on heterosexual mate preferences in 37 cultures worldwide. Men and women in each culture displayed unique orderings of their preferences concerning the ideal characteristics of a mate. When all of the orderings and preferences were compared, two main dimensions emerged.

In the first main dimension, the characteristics of a desirable mate changed because of cultural values—that is, whether the respondents' country has more traditional values or Western-industrial values. In traditional cultures, men place a high value on a woman's chastity, desire for home and children, and ability to be a good cook and housekeeper; women place a high value on a man being ambitious and industrious, being a good financial prospect, and holding favorable social status. China, India, Iran, and Nigeria represent the traditional end of this dimension. In contrast, people in Western-industrial cultures value these qualities to a much lesser extent. The Netherlands, Great Britain, Finland, and Sweden represent this end of the dimension; people in these countries place more value on Western ideals.

The second main dimension reflects the relative importance of education, intelligence, and social refinement—as opposed to a pleasing disposition—in choosing a mate. For example, people in Spain, Colombia, and Greece highly value education, intelligence, and social refinement; in contrast, people in Indonesia place a greater emphasis on having a pleasing disposition. Note that this dimension emphasizes the same traits for both men and women.

Chastity proved to be the characteristic showing the most variability across cultures, being highly desired in some cultures but mattering little in others. It is interesting that in their respective search for mates, men around the world value physical attractiveness in women, whereas women around the world look for men capable of being good providers. But men and women around the world agree that love and mutual attraction are most important, and nearly all cultures rate dependability, emotional stability, kindness, and understanding as important factors. Attraction, it seems, has some characteristics that transcend culture.

Overall, Buss and his colleagues concluded that mate selection is a complex process no matter where you live. However, each culture has a describable set of high-priority traits that men and women look for in the perfect mate. The study also shows that socialization within a culture plays a key role in being attractive to the opposite sex; characteristics that are highly desirable in one culture may not be so desirable in another.

As described in the Spotlight on Research feature, Schmitt and his team of colleagues (2004) studied 62 cultural regions. They showed secure romantic attachment was the norm in nearly 80% of cultures and "preoccupied" romantic attachment was particularly common in East Asian cultures. In general, multicultural studies show there are global patterns in mate selection and romantic relationships. The romantic attachment profiles of individual nations were correlated with sociocultural indicators in ways that supported evolutionary theories of romantic attachment and basic human mating strategies.

Patterns and Universals of Romantic Attachment Around the World

Who were the investigators and what was the aim of the study? One's attachment style may have a major influence on how one forms romantic relationships. In order to test this hypothesis, David Schmitt (2004) assembled a large international team of researchers.

How did the investigators measure the topic of interest? Great care was taken to ensure equivalent translation of the survey across the 62 cultural regions included. The survey was a two-dimension four-category measure of adult romantic attachment (the Relationship Questionnaire) that measured models of self and others relative to each other: secure romantic attachment (high scores indicate positive models of self and others), dismissing romantic attachment (high scores indicate a positive model of self and a negative model of others), preoccupied romantic attachment (high scores indicate a negative model of self and a positive model of others), and fearful romantic attachment (high scores indicate negative models of self and others). An overall score of model of self is computed by adding together the secure and dismissing scores and subtracting the combination of preoccupied and fearful scores. The overall model of others score is computed by adding together the secure and preoccupied scores and subtracting the combination of dismissing and fearful scores.

Additionally, there were measures of self-esteem, personality traits, and sociocultural correlates of romantic attachment (e.g., fertility rate, national profiles of individualism versus collectivism).

Who were the participants in the study? A total of 17,804 people (7,432 men and 10,372 women) from 62 cultural regions around the world took part in the study. Such large and diverse samples are unusual in developmental research.

What was the design of the study? Data for this cross-sectional, nonexperimental study were gathered by research teams in each country. The principal researchers asked the research collaborators to administer a nine-page survey to the participants that took 20 minutes to complete.

Were there ethical concerns with the study? Because the study involved volunteers, there were no ethical concerns. However, ensuring all participants' rights were protected was a challenge because of the number of countries and cultures involved.

What were the results? The researchers first demonstrated the model of self and others measures were valid across cultural regions, that provided general support for the independence of measures (i.e., they measure different things). Specific analyses showed 79% of the cultural groups studied demonstrated secure romantic attachments, but North American cultures tended to be dismissive and East Asian cultures tended to be high on preoccupied romantic attachment. These patterns are shown in ❱ Figure 11.1. Note all the cultural regions except East Asia showed the pattern of model of self-scores higher than model of others scores.

What did the investigators conclude? Overall, Schmitt and colleagues concluded although the same attachment pattern holds across most cultures, no one pattern holds across all of them. East Asian cultures in particular tend to fit a pattern in which people report others do not get as emotionally close as the respondent would like, and respondents find it difficult to trust others or to depend on them.

❱ **Figure 11.1**

In research across 10 global regions, note that only in East Asian cultures were the "model of others" scores higher than the "model of self" scores.

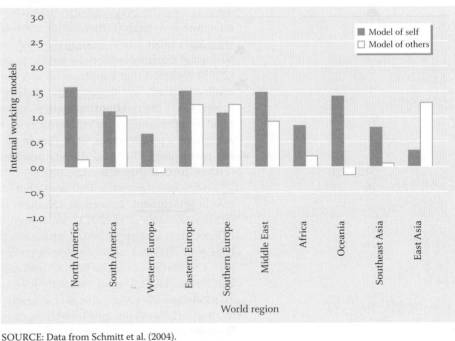

SOURCE: Data from Schmitt et al. (2004).

Culture and evolution are powerful forces shaping mate selection choices (Buss, 2016). Specifically, Buss (2016) argues that mate selection serves many deeply held, and deeply programmed, human needs. The kinds of partners we choose are driven by certain hardwired biological and psychological needs and desires that play out in many ways.

Love styles within European cultures also predict relationship satisfaction (Rohmann, Führer, & Bierhoff, 2016). Cultural norms are sometimes highly resistant to change. Loyalty of the individual to the family is an important value in India, so despite many changes in mate selection, about 95% of marriages in India are carefully arranged to ensure an appropriate mate is selected (Dommaraju, 2010).

Similarly, Islamic societies use matchmaking as a way to preserve family consistency and continuity and ensure couples follow the prohibition on premarital relationships between men and women (Adler, 2001). Matchmaking in these societies occurs both through family connections and personal advertisements in newspapers. To keep up with the Internet age, Muslim matchmaking has gone online too (Lo & Aziz, 2009), increasing the pressure for the individuals in the couple to make their own decisions (Ahmad, 2012). As urbanization and globalization effects continue, pressures to move toward individual selection and commitment and away from traditional matchmaking continues to increase in many societies (Abela & Walker, 2014).

Think About It

What are the effects of increasing interactions among cultures on mate selection?

Developmental Forces, Neuroscience, and Love Relationships

As you no doubt know from your own experience, finding a suitable relationship, especially a love relationship, is tough. Many things must work just right: timing, meeting the right person, luck, and effort are but a few of the factors that shape the course of a relationship. Centuries of romance stories describe this magical process and portray it as one of life's great mysteries.

From our discussion here, you know that who chooses whom (and whether the feelings will be mutual) results from the interaction of developmental forces described in the biopsychosocial model presented in Chapter 1. Neuroscience research is revealing how.

Love is one of three discrete, interrelated emotion systems (the sex drive and attachment are the other two; Fisher, 2016; Pfaff & Fisher, 2012; see also Helen Fisher's series of TED Talks). The brain circuitry involved in romantic love, maternal love, and long-term attachment overlap (Fisher, 2016; Stein & Vythilingum, 2009). In terms of love, neurochemicals related to the amphetamines come into play early in the process, providing a biological explanation for the exhilaration of falling madly in love. Aron and colleagues (2005) reported that couples who were in the early stages of romantic love showed high levels of activity in the dopamine system, which is involved in all of the basic biological drives. Once the relationship settles into what some people might call long-term commitment and tranquility, the brain processes switch neurochemically to substances related to morphine, a powerful narcotic. People with a predilection to fall in love also tend to show left hemisphere chemical dominance and several changes in neurochemical processing (Fisher, 2016; Kurup & Kurup, 2003).

Additional research indicates that the hormone oxytocin may play an important role in attachment. In men, it enhances their partner's attractiveness compared to other females (Scheele et al., 2013); in women, it enhances their orgasms, among other things (Cacioppo & Cacioppo, 2013), which has earned it the nickname of the "cuddle hormone" (Lee et al., 2009). Love really does a number on your brain!

And that's not all. The interactions among psychological aspects, neurological aspects, and hormonal aspects of romantic love help explain why couples tend to have exclusive relationships with each other. For women (but not men), blood levels of serotonin increase during periods of romantic love (Langeslag, van der Veen, & Fekkes, 2012). In addition, the stronger the romantic bond with their boyfriend, the less likely they are to be able to identify the body odor of a different male friend (Lundström & Jones-Gotman, 2009). That means that women's attention is deflected from other potential male partners the more they are romantically involved with one specific male.

Psychologically, as we saw in Chapter 10, an important developmental issue is intimacy; according to Erikson, mature relationships are impossible without it. In addition, the kinds of relationships you saw and experienced as a child (and whether they involved violence) affect how you define and act in relationships you develop as an adult. Sociocultural forces shape the characteristics you find desirable in a mate and determine whether you are likely to encounter resistance from your family when you have made your choice. Life-cycle forces matter, too; different aspects of love are more or less important depending on your stage in life. For example, romantic love tends to be most prominent in young adulthood, whereas the aspect of companionship becomes more important later in life.

In short, to understand adult relationships, we must take the forces of the biopsychosocial model into account. Relying too heavily on one or two of the forces provides an incomplete description of why people are or are not successful in finding a partner or a friend. Unfortunately, the developmental forces do not influence only good relationships. As we will see next, sometimes relationships turn violent.

Violence in Relationships

Up to this point, we have been considering relationships that are healthy and positive. Sadly, this is not always the case. *Sometimes relationships become violent; one person becomes aggressive toward the partner, creating an* abusive relationship. Such relationships have received increasing attention since the early 1980s, when the U.S. criminal justice system ruled that, under some circumstances, abusive relationships can be used as an explanation for one's behavior (Walker, 1984). *For example,* battered woman syndrome *occurs when a woman believes she cannot leave the abusive situation and may even go so far as to kill her abuser.*

Being female, Latina, African American, having an atypical family structure (something other than two biological parents), having more romantic partners, early onset of sexual activity, and being a victim of child abuse predicts a higher likelihood of being a survivor of relationship violence. Although overall national rates of sexual assault have declined more than 60% since the early 1990s, acquaintance rape or date rape is still a major problem. College women are more likely to be survivors of sexual assault than are women in other age groups (Rape, Abuse, and Incest National Network, 2016). The Obama administration made campus sexual assault a major policy focus, creating the *Not Alone* campaign (NotAlone.gov, 2016).

What range of aggressive behaviors occurs in abusive relationships? What causes such abuse? Based on considerable research on abusive partners, O'Leary (1993) proposed a continuum of aggressive behaviors toward a partner, and progresses as follows: verbally aggressive behaviors, physically aggressive behaviors, severe physically aggressive behaviors, and murder (see ▶ Table 11.1). The causes of the abuse also vary with the type of abusive behavior being expressed.

Two points about the continuum should be noted. First, there may be fundamental differences in the types of aggression independent of level of severity. Overall, each year about 5 million women and 3 million men experience partner-related physical assaults and rape in the United States (Rape, Abuse, and Incest National Network, 2016); worldwide, between 10% and 69% of women report being physically assaulted or raped, making it one of the priority areas for the World Health Organization (World Health Organization, 2013).

The second point, depicted in the table, is the suspected underlying causes of aggressive behaviors differ as the type of aggressive behaviors change (O'Leary, 1993; Sugimoto-Matsuda & Guerrero, 2016). Although anger and hostility in the perpetrator are associated with various forms of physical abuse, especially in young adulthood, the exact nature of this relationship remains elusive (Giordano et al., 2016).

Heterosexual men and members of the LGBTQ community are also the victims of violence from intimate partners, though at a reporting rate lower that of women (Rape, Abuse and Incest National Network, 2016). All victims need to be supported and provided avenues that provide safe ways for them to report assaults.

Culture is also an important contextual factor in understanding partner abuse. In particular, violence against women worldwide reflects cultural traditions, beliefs, and values of patriarchal societies;

abusive relationship
Relationships in which one person becomes aggressive toward the partner.

battered woman syndrome
Situation occurring when a woman believes that she cannot leave the abusive situation and may even go so far as to kill her abuser.

Many communities have established shelters for women who have experienced abuse in relationships.

John Birdsall/The Image Works

Table 11.1

Continuum of progressive behaviors in abusive relationships

VERBAL AGGRESSION →	PHYSICAL AGGRESSION →	SEVERE AGGRESSION →	MURDER
Insults	Pushing	Beating	
Yelling	Slapping	Punching	
Name-calling	Shoving	Hitting with object	
CAUSES			
Need to control* ———————————————————————→			
Misuse of power* ———————————————————————→			
Jealousy* ———————————————————————→			
Marital discord ———————————————————————→			
	Accept violence as a means of control ————————→		
	Modeling of physical aggression ————————→		
	Abused as a child ————————→		
	Aggressive personality styles ————————→		
	Alcohol abuse ————————→		
		Personality disorders ————→	
		Emotional lability ————→	
		Poor self-esteem ————→	
CONTRIBUTING FACTORS			
Job stresses			
unemployment			

NOTE: Need to control and other variables on the left are associated with all forms of aggression; acceptance of violence and other variables in the middle are associated with physical aggression, severe aggression, and murder. Personality disorders and the variables on the right are associated with severe aggression and murder.

*More relevant for males than for females.

SOURCE: O'Leary, K.D. (1993). Through a psychological lens: Personality traits, personality disorders, and levels of violence. In R. J. Gelles & D. R. Loseke (Eds.), *Current Controversies on Family Violence* (pp. 7–30). Copyright © 1993 by Sage Publications. Reprinted by permission of the publisher.

this can be seen in the commonplace violent practices against women that include sexual slavery, female genital cutting, intimate partner violence, and "honor" killing (Ghanim, 2015; World Health Organization, 2013).

Additionally, international data indicate rates of abuse are higher in cultures that emphasize female purity, virginity, male status, and family honor. A common cause of women's murders in Arab countries is brothers or other male relatives performing so-called honor killings, murdering the victim because she violated the family's honor (Ghanim, 2015). Intimate partner violence is prevalent in China (43% lifetime risk in one study) and has strong associations with male patriarchal values, male unemployment, and conflict resolutions (Xu et al., 2005; Yang et al., 2016).

Alarmed by the seriousness of abuse, many communities established shelters for people who experience abuse. However, the legal system in many localities is still not set up to deal with domestic violence; for example, women in some locations cannot sue their husbands for assault, and restraining orders all too often offer little real protection from additional violence. Much remains to be done to protect people from the fear and the reality of abuse.

Recall

1. Friendships based on intimacy and emotional sharing are more characteristic of _____.

2. Competition is a major part of most friendships among _____.

3. Love relationships in which intimacy and passion are present but commitment is not are termed _____.

4. Chastity is an important quality that men look for in a potential female mate in _____ cultures.

5. Aggressive behavior that is based on abuse of power, jealousy, or the need to control is more likely to be displayed by _____.

Interpret

- Why, according to Erikson, is intimacy (discussed in Chapter 9) a necessary prerequisite for adult relationships? What aspects of relationships discussed here support (or refute) this view?

Apply

- Based on Schmitt and colleagues' (2004) research, what attachment pattern would Korean women likely have regarding romantic attachment?

Check your answers to the Recall Questions at the end of the chapter.

11.2 Lifestyles and Relationships

LEARNING OBJECTIVES

- What are the challenges and advantages of being single?
- Why do people cohabit?
- What are LGBTQ relationships like?
- What is marriage like across adulthood?

Kevin and Beth are on cloud nine. They got married one month ago and have recently returned from their honeymoon. Everyone who sees them can tell that they love each other a great deal. They are highly compatible and have much in common, sharing most of their leisure activities. Kevin and Beth wonder what lies ahead in their marriage.

Developing relationships is only part of the picture in understanding how adults live their lives with other people. Putting relationships such as Kevin and Beth's in context is important for us to understand how relationships come into existence and how they change over time. In the following sections, we explore relationship lifestyles: singlehood, cohabitation, same-sex couples, and marriage.

Singlehood

Adult men and women are single—defined as not living with an intimate partner—at multiple points in their lives: before marriage or other long-term commitment, following divorce, and in widowhood are common examples. In this section, we focus most on young adult singles; elsewhere we return to singlehood in the context of divorce or the death of a spouse/partner.

What's it like to be a single young adult in the United States? It's tougher than you might think. Several researchers (e.g., Budgeon, 2016; Casper et al., 2016; DePaulo, 2006) point out numerous stereotypes and biases against single people, especially women. For example, married people are perceived as kinder and more giving, and public policy also tends to favor married individuals. Additionally, research indicates that rental agents and certain housing programs prefer married couples over singles (Goodsell, 2013; Morris, Sinclair, & DePaulo, 2007).

Many women and men remain single as young adults to focus on establishing their careers rather than marriage or relationships that most do later. Others report they simply did not meet "the right person" or prefer singlehood, a factor especially important among strongly religious groups (Engelberg, 2016; Ibrahim & Hassan, 2009). However, the pressure to marry is especially strong for women (Budgeon, 2016).

Men remain single a bit longer in young adulthood because they marry about two years later on average than women (Census Bureau, 2016). Fewer men than women remain unmarried throughout adulthood, though, mainly because men find partners more easily as they select from a larger age range of unmarried women.

Ethnic differences in singlehood reflect differences in age at marriage as well as social factors. Nearly twice as many African Americans are single during young adulthood as European Americans, and more are choosing to remain so. Singlehood is also increasing among Latinos, in part because the average age of Latinos in the United States is lower than other ethnic groups (e.g., 28 for Latinos versus 42 for white non-Hispanic) and in part because of poor economic opportunities for many Latinos (Pew Research Center, 2015).

The millennial generation is also changing the assumptions about singlehood. The Urban Institute (Martin, Astone, & Peters, 2014) projects that the percentage of millennials who will remain single until at least age 40 may be as high as 30%, higher than any previous generation. However, also likely are millennials who decide to live with a partner and forego the legality of marriage.

Globally, the meanings and implications of remaining single are often tied to strongly held cultural and religious beliefs. Muslim women who remain single in Malaysia speak in terms of *jodoh* (the soul mate one finds through fate at a time appointed by God) as a reason; they believe God simply has not decided to have them meet their mate at this time (Ibrahim & Hassan, 2009). But because the role of Malaysian women is to marry, they also understand their marginalized position in society through their singlehood. In Southeast Asia, the number of single adults has increased steadily as education levels have risen over the past several decades (Hull, 2009). However, family systems in these cultures have not yet adapted to these changing lifestyle patterns (Jones, 2010).

An important distinction is between adults who are temporarily single (i.e., those who are single only until they find a suitable marriage partner) and those who choose to remain single. For most singles, the decision to never marry is a gradual one. This transition is represented by a change in self-attributed status that occurs over time and is associated with a cultural timetable for marriage. It marks the experience of "becoming single" that occurs when an individual identifies more with singlehood than with marriage (Davies, 2003). Choosing to remain single can also reflect an economic-based decision, especially for millennials, who are less likely to think they are better off than their parents than their own parents and grandparents thought at the same age (Kalish, 2016).

Cohabitation

Being unmarried does not necessarily mean living alone. *People in committed, intimate, sexual relationships but who are not married may decide living together, or* cohabitation, *provides a way to share daily life.* Cohabitation is becoming an increasingly popular lifestyle choice in the United States as well as in Canada, Europe, Australia, and elsewhere, especially among millennials and older adults (Luxenberg, 2014; Martin et al., 2014).

In the United States, evidence clearly indicates that cohabitation is common, and has increased over the past several decades (Copen et al., 2013). For example, roughly half of all women cohabit with, rather than marry, a partner as a first committed relationship. Such cohabitation patterns range from about 70% for women with less than a high school diploma to about half of women with a baccalaureate degree or higher, and are longest for Latina women (33 months on average) and shortest for European American women (19 months on average). Cohabitation rates for adults 50 years of age and older have more than doubled since 2000.

The global picture differs by culture (Popenoe, 2009; Therborn, 2010). In most European, South American, and Caribbean countries, cohabitation is a common alternative to marriage for young adults. Cohabitation is extremely common in the Netherlands, Norway, and Sweden, where this lifestyle is part of the culture; 99% of married couples in Sweden lived together before they married and nearly one in four couples are not legally married. Decisions to marry in these countries are typically made to legalize the relationship after

cohabitation
People in committed, intimate, sexual relationships who live together but are not married.

children are born—in contrast to Americans, who marry to confirm their love and commitment to each other.

Interestingly, having cohabitated does not seem to make marriages any better; in fact, under certain circumstances it may do more harm than good, resulting in lower quality marriages (Johnson, 2016). These findings reflect two underlying issues that can cause problems (Johnson, 2016): couples who have children while cohabiting, especially for European American women (as compared with African American and Latina women; Tach & Halpern-Meekin, 2009), and couples who are using cohabitation to test their relationship and keep separate finances (Addo, 2017).

Essentially, the happiest cohabiting couples are those who look very much like happily married couples: they share financial responsibilities and child care. Longitudinal studies find few differences in couples' behavior after living together for many years regardless of whether they married without cohabiting, cohabited then married, or simply cohabited (Stafford, Kline, & Rankin, 2004). Additionally, many countries extend the same rights and benefits to cohabiting couples as they do to married couples, and have done so for many years. Argentina provides pension rights to cohabiting partners, Canada extends insurance benefits, and Australia has laws governing the disposition of property when cohabiting couples sever their relationship (Neft & Levine, 1997).

Think About It
Why might there be large differences in cohabitation rates among countries?

LGBTQ Relationships

The current generation of adults in the LGBTQ community have largely experienced various forms of oppression and discrimination throughout their adult lives (Robinson-Wood & Weber, 2016). This is especially true for those who also have low income and for people of color. However, social attitudes toward the LGBTQ community have changed and continue to change rapidly, especially in view of the legal support for same-sex marriage (King, 2016).

For the most part, the relationships of gay and lesbian couples have many similarities to those of heterosexual couples (Kurdek, 2004). Most gay and lesbian couples are in dual-earner relationships, much like the majority of married heterosexual couples, and are likely to share household chores. However, gay and lesbian couples differ from heterosexual couples in the degree to which both partners are similar on demographic characteristics such as race, age, and education; gay and lesbian couples tend to be more dissimilar, except regarding education (Ciscato, Galichon, & Gousse, 2015).

King (2016) argues that the experiences of older lesbian, gay, and bisexual adults cannot be put into need categories, even generational ones. Rather, King emphasizes that the LGB community is at least as diverse as the heterosexual community, and needs to be understood as such.

With the advent of legalized same-sex marriage, numerous issues that heterosexual married couples have long taken for granted are being confronted in the LGBTQ community, including end-of-life issues and legal matters regarding caregiving (Godfrey, 2016; Orel & Coon, 2016). Changes to state laws will continue as reforms and revisions continue to keep pace with change.

When compared to LGB individuals living with partners, LGB individuals living alone or with others (but not in a relationship with them) reported higher degrees of loneliness (Kim & Fredriksen-Goldsen, 2016). This finding parallels that in heterosexual individuals in similar living arrangements, and highlights the fact that there are many similarities in personal outcomes across various gender identity groups.

Little research has been conducted examining the development of transgender and gender nonconforming (TGNC) individuals across adulthood (Witten, 2016). One detailed examination of experiences of TGNC adults found that many barriers to accessing key services such as health care and social services exist, largely due to anti-TGNC prejudice, discrimination, and lack of appropriate and adequate training of professionals (Porter et al., 2016). Additionally, research indicates that transgender older adults experience social isolation more than most other groups (Harley, Gassaway, & Dunkley, 2016). However, relationship stress patterns and outcomes parallel that seen in other types of couple relationships (Randall & Bodenmann, 2017).

As we explore marriage in the next section, keep in mind that although most of the research has been conducted with heterosexual couples, key findings regarding what matters most in relationship satisfaction, decisions about parenting, and caring for a spouse/partner hold for LGBTQ individuals who are married or in long-term committed relationships.

Marriage

Most adults want their love relationships to result in marriage. However, U.S. residents are in less of a hurry to achieve this goal; the median age at first marriage for adults in the United States has been rising for several decades. As shown in ❱ Figure 11.2, between 1970 and 2015, the median age for first marriage rose almost 7 years for both men and women (Census Bureau, 2016).

An important fact to keep in mind is that these statistics reflect heterosexual marriage. Until the 2015 *Obergefell v. Hodges* decision in the U.S. Supreme Court, same-sex marriage was still illegal in 14 states. This case is highlighted in the Real People feature.

What Is a Successful Marriage and What Predicts It?

marital success ❯

Umbrella term referring to any marital outcome.

marital quality ❯

Subjective evaluation of the couple's relationship on a number of different dimensions.

marital adjustment ❯

Degree to which a husband and wife accommodate to each other over a certain period of time.

marital satisfaction ❯

Global assessment of one's marriage.

You undoubtedly know couples who appear to have a successful marriage. But what does that mean, really? *Minnotte (2010) differentiates* marital success, *an umbrella term referring to any marital outcome (such as divorce rate),* marital quality, *a subjective evaluation of the couple's relationship on a number of different dimensions,* marital adjustment, *the degree spouses accommodate each other over a certain period of time, and* marital satisfaction, *a global assessment of one's marriage.* Each of these provides a unique insight into the workings of a marriage.

Marriages, like other relationships, differ from one another, but some important predictors of future success can be identified. One key factor is age. In general, the younger the partners are, the lower the odds the marriage will last—especially when the people are in their teens or early 20s (Census Bureau, 2013). Other reasons that increase or decrease the likelihood a marriage will last include financial security and pregnancy at the time of the marriage.

❱ **Figure 11.2**

Note the median age at first marriage has been increasing for many years during the 20th and early 21st centuries.

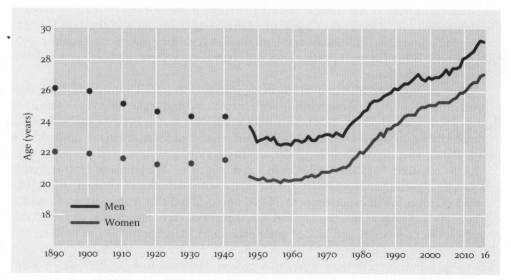

SOURCE: U.S Census Bureau, Current Population Survey, Annual Social and Economic Supplements, 1947–2012. Data for years prior to 1947 are from decennial censuses. www.census.gov/hhes/families/data/marital.html.

James Obergefell and John Arthur Make History

When James (Jim) Obergefell met John Arthur in Cincinnati in 1992, there was no way they thought that their love relationship would make history. Neither one of them had ever been an activist, and it took tragedy and loss to set them on their mission.

After they fell in love, they lived and worked together as consultants. They were avid art collectors and had a large social network of friends and family. Nearly 20 years into their relationship, though, everything changed. Arthur, who had been experiencing severe mobility problems, was diagnosed with amyotrophic lateral sclerosis (ALS), also known as Lou Gehrig's disease. As the disease progressed, Jim became Arthur's primary caregiver. By 2013, Arthur's condition had progressed very significantly.

What both of them wanted was to be married so that Jim could be recognized as Arthur's surviving spouse on Arthur's death certificate. Unfortunately for them, Ohio voters had passed a constitutional amendment banning same-sex marriage. However, such marriages were legal in Maryland. With support from friends, Jim hired a medical plane to fly them to Maryland, where Arthur's aunt officiated at their wedding on the tarmac at Baltimore-Washington International Thurgood

Marshall Airport on July 11, 2013. Arthur died three months later.

Shortly before Arthur's death, they sued the state of Ohio in order for Jim to be listed as the surviving spouse on Arthur's death certificate. They lost the case but were granted a hearing by the U.S. Supreme Court. Their case was combined with several others for the hearing. By a 5 to 4 decision, the Court ruled that the U.S. Constitution supports same-sex marriage, thereby making these marriages legal in the entire country.

Together with the *Loving v. Virginia* (1967) decision (depicted in the movie *Loving*) that banned anti-miscegenation laws, the *Obergefell v. Hodges* decision opened marriage to all couples who had, in one way or another, been refused that right in U.S. history.

Andrew Harrer/Bloomberg/Getty Images

James (Jim) Obergefell

A second important predictor of successful marriage is homogamy, *or the similarity of values and interests a couple shares.* As we saw in relation to choosing a mate, the extent the partners share similar age, values, goals, attitudes (especially the desire for children), socioeconomic status, certain behaviors (such as drinking alcohol), and ethnic background increases the likelihood their relationship will succeed (Kippen, Chapman, & Yu, 2009).

- **homogamy**
  Similarity of values and interests.

A third factor in predicting marital success is a feeling the relationship is equal. *According to* exchange theory, *marriage is based on each partner contributing something to the relationship the other would be hard-pressed to provide.* Satisfying and happy marriages result when both partners perceive there is a fair exchange, or equity, in all the dimensions of the relationship. Problems achieving equity arise because of the competing demands of work and family, an issue we take up again in Chapter 12.

- **exchange theory**
  Relationship, such as marriage, based on each partner contributing something to the relationship that the other would be hard-pressed to provide.

Cross-cultural research supports these factors. Couples in the United States and Iran (Asoodeh et al., 2010; Hall, 2006) say trust, consulting each other, honesty, making joint decisions, and commitment make the difference between a successful marriage and an unsuccessful marriage. Couples for whom religion is important also point to commonly held faith as a key factor.

So what really matters in predicting whether a relationship is likely to be successful? Dey and Ghosh (2016)'s findings point to several key predictors: respect for emotion, attitude toward marriage, expression of love, regard for views and importance to the likings of the spouse, ignoring weaknesses of the spouse, sexual adjustment, temperament, value, taste, and interest. We will see in the next few sections how these, and other factors, play out at specific times during the course of marriage across adulthood.

Do Married Couples Stay Happy?

Few sights are happier than a couple on their wedding day. Newlyweds, like Kevin and Beth in the vignette, are at the peak of marital bliss. The beliefs people bring into a marriage influence how satisfied they will be as the marriage develops. But as you may have experienced, feelings change over time, sometimes getting better and stronger, sometimes not.

Research shows for most couples, overall marital satisfaction is highest at the beginning of the marriage, falls until the children begin leaving home, and stabilizes or continues to decline in later life; this pattern holds for both married and never-married cohabiting couples with children (Kulik, 2016). However, there is considerable variability across couples. For some couples, satisfaction declines only slightly, while for others it rebounds in late life, while for still others it declines more precipitously and the couple becomes, in essence, emotionally divorced (Proulx, 2016).

The pattern of a particular marriage over the years is determined by the nature of the dependence of each spouse on the other. When dependence is mutual and about equal and both people hold similar values that form the basis for their commitment to each other, the marriage is strong and close (Givertz, Segrin, & Hanzal, 2009). When the dependence of one partner is much higher than that of the other, however, the marriage is likely to be characterized by stress and conflict. Learning how to deal with these changes is the secret to long and happy marriages.

The fact that marital satisfaction has a general downward trend but varies widely across couples led Karney and Bradbury (1995) to propose a vulnerability–stress–adaptation model of marriage, depicted in ❯ Figure 11.3. *The* vulnerability–stress–adaptation model *sees marital quality as a dynamic process resulting from the couple's ability to handle stressful events in the context of their particular vulnerabilities and resources.* As a couple's ability to adapt to stressful situations gets better over time, the quality of the marriage will probably improve. How well couples adapt to various stresses on the relationship determines whether the marriage continues or they get divorced. Let's see how this works over time.

vulnerability–stress–adaptation model
Model that proposes that marital quality is a dynamic process resulting from the couple's ability to handle stressful events in the context of their particular vulnerabilities and resources.

Setting the Stage: The Early Years of Marriage

Marriages are most intense in their early days. Early on, husbands and wives share many activities and are open to new experiences together, so bliss results (Olson & McCubbin, 1983). But bliss doesn't come from avoiding tough issues. Discussing financial matters honestly is key since many newly married couples experience their first serious marital stresses around money issues (Parkman, 2007). How tough issues early in the marriage are handled sets the stage for the years ahead.

Early in a marriage, couples tend to have global adoration for their spouse regarding the spouse's qualities (Karney, 2010; Seychell, 2016). For wives, but not for husbands, more accurate specific perceptions of what their spouses are really like were associated

❯ **Figure 11.3**
The vulnerability-stress-adaptation model shows how adapting to vulnerabilities and stress can result in either adaptation or dissolution of the marriage.

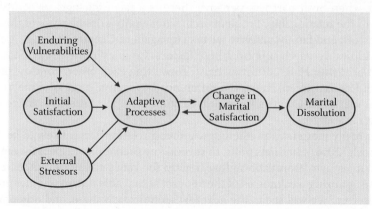

SOURCE: From "Keeping marriages healthy, and why it's so difficult," by B. R. Karney.

with more supportive behaviors, feelings of control in the marriage, and a decreased risk of divorce. Couples who are happiest in the early stage of their marriage focus on the good aspects, not the annoyances; nit-picking and nagging do not bode well for long-term wedded bliss (Seychell, 2016).

As time goes on and stresses increase, marital satisfaction declines (Kulik, 2016). For many couples, the primary reason for this drop is having children. It's not just a matter of having a child. The temperament of the child matters, with fussier babies creating more marital problems (Greving, 2007; Meijer & van den Wittenboer, 2007). Parenthood also means having substantially less time to devote to the marriage.

However, using the birth of a child as the explanation for the drop in marital satisfaction is much too simplistic, because child-free couples also experience a decline in marital satisfaction (Kulik, 2016). Longitudinal research indicates disillusionment—as demonstrated by a decline in feeling in love, in demonstrations of affection, and in the feeling that one's spouse is responsive, as well as an increase in feelings of ambivalence—and other personality characteristics such as narcissism are key predictors of marital dissatisfaction (Lavner et al., 2016).

Young married military couples face special types of stress on their relationship.

During the early years of their marriage, many couples may spend significant amounts of time apart, especially those who are in the military (Fincham & Beach, 2010). Spouses who serve in combat areas on active duty assignment and who suffer from post-traumatic stress disorder (PTSD) are particularly vulnerable, as they are at greater risk for other spouse-directed aggression.

What the nondeployed spouse believes turns out to be important. If the nondeployed spouse believes the deployment will have negative effects on the marriage, then problems are much more likely. In contrast, if the nondeployed spouse believes such challenges make the relationship stronger, then they typically can do so (Lewis, Lamson, & White, 2016; Renshaw, Rodrigues, & Jones, 2008). Research indicates the effects of deployment may be greater on wives than on husbands; divorce rates for women service members who are deployed is higher than for their male counterparts (Karney & Crown, 2007).

Keeping Marriages Happy

Although no two marriages are exactly the same, couples must be flexible and adaptable. Couples who have been happily married for many years show an ability to "roll with the punches" and to adapt to changing circumstances in the relationship. For example, a serious problem of one spouse may not be detrimental to the relationship and may even make the bond stronger if the couple use good stress- and conflict-reduction strategies. Successful couples also find a way to keep the romance in the relationship, a very important determinant of marital satisfaction over the long run. Being motivated to meet a partner's sexual needs seems to be a key factor (Birnbaum et al., 2016; Muise et al., 2013).

Sharing religious beliefs and spirituality with one's spouse is another good way to ensure higher quality marriages, and that's especially the case among couples in lower socioeconomic groups (Lichter & Carmalt, 2009). It appears that this effect goes beyond merely doing an activity together, as religion and spirituality may provide a framework for conflict resolution and a way to put one's marriage in a bigger, more significant context.

But when you get down to basics, it's how well couples communicate their thoughts, actions, and feelings to each other and show intimacy and support each other that largely determines the level of conflict couples experience and, by extension, how happy they are likely to be over the long term (Patrick et al., 2007). This is especially important with regard to high-stress areas such as children and work and after long separations such as military deployments (Wadsworth, Hughes-Kirchubel, & Riggs, 2014).

Think About It

What types of interventions would help keep married couples happier?

So what are the best ways to "stack the deck" in favor of a long, happy marriage? Based on research, here are the best:

- Make time for your relationship.
- Express your love to your spouse.
- Be there in times of need.
- Communicate constructively and positively about problems in the relationship.
- Be interested in your spouse's life.
- Confide in your spouse.
- Forgive minor offenses and try to understand major ones.

TEST YOURSELF 11.2

Recall

1. A difficulty for many single people is that other people may expect them to _____.
2. Young adults view cohabitation as a(n) _____ marriage.
3. Same-sex relationships are similar to _____.
4. According to _____, marriage is based on each partner contributing something to the relationship that the other would be hard-pressed to provide.
5. For most couples, marital satisfaction _____ after the birth of the first child.

Interpret

- What sociocultural forces affect decisions to marry rather than to cohabit indefinitely?

Apply

- Ricardo and Maria are engaged to be married. Ricardo works long hours as a store manager at a local coffee shop, while Maria works regular hours as an administrative assistant for a large communications company. Based on your understanding of the factors that affect marital success, what other characteristics would you want to know about Ricardo and Maria before evaluating the likely success of their marriage?

Check your answers to the Recall Questions at the end of the chapter.

11.3 Family Dynamics and the Life Course

LEARNING OBJECTIVES

- What is it like to be a parent?
- What diverse forms of parenting are there?

Bob, 32, and Denise, 33, just had their first child, Matthew, after several years of trying. They've heard that having children in their thirties can have advantages, but Bob and Denise wonder whether people are just saying that to be nice to them. They are also concerned about the financial obligations they are likely to face.

Bob and Denise are increasingly typical of first-time parents, as more people than ever delay having children. As all parents discover, having a child changes everything. New parents are often overwhelmed with the responsibility.

In this section, we consider the dynamics of families, from deciding whether to have children through caring for aging parents and grandparenthood. As we do so, we must recognize the concept of "family" is undergoing change.

nuclear family
Most common form of family in Western societies, consisting only of parent(s) and child(ren).

extended family
Most common form of family around the world; one in which grandparents and other relatives live with parents and children.

The Parental Role

The birth of a child transforms a couple (or a single parent) into a family. *The most common form of family in most Western societies is the* nuclear family, *consisting only of parent(s) and child(ren). However, the most common family form globally is the* extended family, *in which grandparents and other relatives live with parents and children.* Let's see how adding children to either family form matters.

Deciding Whether to Have Children

One of the biggest decisions couples (and many singles) make is whether to have children. You would think that potential parents must weigh the many benefits of child rearing—such as feeling personal satisfaction, fulfilling personal needs, continuing the family line, and enjoying companionship—with the many drawbacks, including expense and lifestyle changes, especially the balance between work and family. But you would be wrong—this is not what most people actually do.

Rijken (2009; Rijken & Knijn, 2009) reports potential parents actually don't think deliberately or deeply about when to have a child, and those who are career-oriented or like their freedom do not often deliberately postpone parenthood because of those factors. Rather, thoughts about having children are implicit and do not cross their minds until they are ready to begin thinking about having children.

Whether the pregnancy is planned or not (and more than half of all U.S. pregnancies are unplanned), a couple's first pregnancy is a milestone event in a relationship, with both benefits and stresses (Lavner & Bradbury, 2017; Meijer & van den Wittenboer, 2007). Parents largely agree children add affection, improve family ties, and give parents a feeling of immortality and sense of accomplishment. Most parents willingly sacrifice a great deal for their children and hope they grow up to be happy and successful. In this way, children bring happiness to their parents' relationship.

Nevertheless, finances are of great concern to most parents because children are expensive. How expensive? According to the U.S. Department of Agriculture (2017), a typical family who had a child born in 2015 would spend about $ 233,610 for food, housing, and other necessities by the time the child turns 18 years old. College expenses would be additional. These costs do not differ significantly between two-parent and single-parent households but clearly are a bigger financial burden for single parents. Costs vary substantially across levels of household income. Take a look at ▶Figure 11.4 and see where the money goes.

For many reasons that include personal choice, financial instability, and infertility, an increasing number of couples are child-free. Social attitudes in many countries (Austria, Germany, Great Britain, Ireland, Netherlands, and United States) are improving toward child-free couples (Blackstone & Stewart, 2016; Gubernskaya, 2010).

Couples without children have some advantages: higher marital satisfaction, more freedom, and higher standards of living on average. Yet, they also must deal with societal expectations regarding having children and may feel defensive about their decision not to be a parent. A major international study of older adult couples without children in Australia, Finland, Germany, Japan, the Netherlands, the United Kingdom, and the United States revealed highly similar patterns across all countries except Japan (Koropeckyj-Cox & Call, 2007). In Japan, the cultural norm of children caring for older parents created difficulties for childless older couples.

The factors that influence the decision to be child-free appear to differ for women and men (Waren & Pals, 2013). For women, higher levels of education and economic factors increase the likelihood of remaining child-free, whereas holding traditional sex role beliefs decrease the chances of that decision. For men, though, neither education nor economic factors predict deciding to remain child-free, but traditional sex role beliefs lower the odds of that decision.

Today, parents in the United States typically have fewer children and have their first child later than in the past. The average age at the time of the birth of a woman's first child is nearly 26.3 (National Center for Health Statistics, 2016c).

▶ **Figure 11.4**

The Cost of Raising a Child from Birth to 18.

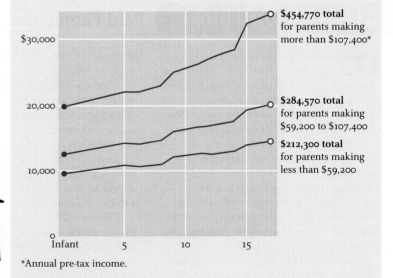

A new USDA report found that parents in each income bracket will spend vastly different sums of money each year as their children grow from infancy to age 17. This chart shows the estimated annual cost of raising a child born in 2015 for married parents in each income group.

$454,770 total for parents making more than $107,400*

$284,570 total for parents making $59,200 to $107,400

$212,300 total for parents making less than $59,200

*Annual pre-tax income.

SOURCE: USDA Expenditures on Children by Families, 2013, United States Department of Agriculture, Center for Nutrition Policy and Promotion, Miscellaneous Publication Number 1528–2013. Retrieved from www.cnpp.usda.gov/sites/default/files/expenditures_on_children_by_families/crc2013.pdf.

Having a child later in adulthood has many benefits.

This average age has been increasing steadily since 1970 as a result of many women postponing having children because they marry later, they want to establish careers first, or they make a deliberate choice to delay childbearing.

Being older at the birth of one's first child is advantageous. Older mothers, like Denise in the vignette, are more at ease being parents, spend more time with their babies, and are more affectionate, sensitive, and supportive to them. In addition, there is a higher maternal investment in middle childhood and less child-perceived conflict in adolescence (Camberis et al., 2016; Schlomer & Belsky, 2012). The age of the father also makes a difference in how he interacts with children (Palkovitz & Palm, 2009). Compared to men who become fathers in their 20s, men such as Bob who become fathers in their 30s are generally more invested in their paternal role and spend up to three times as much time caring for their preschool children as younger fathers do. Father involvement has increased significantly, due in part to social attitudes that support it (Fogarty & Evans, 2010). Research clearly shows that being a father is an important aspect of men's lives across adulthood (Marsiglio & Roy, 2013).

Parenting skills do not come naturally; they must be acquired. Having a child changes all aspects of couples' lives. As we have seen, children place a great deal of stress on a relationship. Both motherhood and fatherhood require major commitment and cooperation. Parenting is full of rewards, but it also takes a great deal of work. Caring for young children is demanding. It may create disagreements over division of labor, especially if both parents are employed outside the home (see Chapters 4 and 12). Even when mothers are employed outside the home (and roughly 70% of women with children under age 18 in the United States are), they still perform most of the child-rearing tasks. Even when men take employment leave, although more likely to share tasks, they still do not spend more time with children than fathers who do not take leave (Seward & Stanley-Stevens, 2014).

The United States is the only major industrialized country not to provide mandatory paid leave for new parents. Although some states and cities have passed laws requiring paid parental leave, most have not. The What Do *You* Think? feature explores the issue of paid parental leave in more detail.

What Do *You* Think? Paid Family Leave

Does your employer provide paid time off if you have a new child? In order to care for an ill child or older parent? If you have a serious illness or need to recover after surgery? If so, you are fortunate. One of the biggest needs for most employees is access to these types of benefits, especially employees in smaller organizations or employers that do not provide paid time off. In fact, the United States is the only industrialized country that does not either have a national government program or an employer mandate to provide such benefits (A Better Balance, 2016).

Currently, the federal Family and Medical Leave Act of 1993 (FMLA) is the only national program in the U.S. It requires employers to provide *unpaid* leave for up to 12 weeks for employees to care for a new child or seriously ill family member, to recover from one's own serious health condition, or to deal with certain obligations (including child care and related activities) arising from a spouse, parent or child being on, or called to, active duty in the military. The FMLA also provides up to 26 weeks of unpaid leave per year for workers whose spouse, child, parent or next of kin is a seriously ill or injured member of the armed services (A Better Balance, 2016).

However, due to the specific provisions that create coverage gaps in the law, roughly 40% of employees are not covered. And, the unpaid nature of the law means that only those who can afford to lose their income take it. To address these gaps and provide some income coverage, the Family Act was introduced in Congress in 2015. It would provide 12 weeks of paid leave for the situations covered in FMLA. It has yet to be enacted.

Fortunately, a few states have taken the lead to create *paid* family leave programs. For example, California, New Jersey, New York, Rhode Island, and Washington, DC have different types of paid leave. Several other states are working to enact other versions. (Find out what the policy is in your home state.) Many advocates and employees agree that paid leave for family reasons is important. Many businesses do as well. As we have seen, the evidence is strong that being able to care for one's family or oneself improves well-being, and helps the employee be more productive. What do you think should be done?

In general, parents manage to deal with the many challenges of child rearing reasonably well. They learn how to compromise when necessary and when to apply firm but fair discipline. Given the choice, most parents do not regret their decision to have children.

Ethnic Diversity and Parenting

Ethnic background matters a great deal in terms of family structure and the parent–child relationship. African American husbands are more likely than their European American counterparts to help with household chores, regardless of their wives' employment status (Dixon, 2009). Overall, most African American parents provide a cohesive, loving environment that often exists within a context of strong religious beliefs (Smith-Bynum, 2013; Teachman, Tedrow, & Kim, 2013), pride in cultural heritage, self-respect, and cooperation with the family (Coles, 2016).

As a result of several generations of oppression, many Native American parents have lost the cultural parenting skills that were traditionally part of their culture: children were valued, women were considered sacred and honored, and men cared for and provided for their families (Davis, Dionne, & Fortin, 2014). Thus, restoring and retaining a strong sense of tribalism is an important consideration for Native American families. Indeed, research shows that American Indian families receive more support from relatives in child rearing than do European Americans (Limb & Shafer, 2014). This support helps with the transmission of cultural values.

Nearly 25% of all children under 18 in the United States are Latino, and most are at least second generation (ChildStats.gov, 2016). Among two-parent families, Mexican American mothers and fathers both tend to adopt similar authoritative behaviors toward their preschool children (Gamble, Ramakumar, & Diaz, 2007).

Latino families demonstrate two key values: familism and the extended family. *Familism refers to the idea the well-being of the family takes precedence over the concerns of individual family members.* This value is a defining characteristic of Latino families; Brazilian and Mexican families consider familism a cultural strength (Carlo et al., 2007; Lucero-Liu, 2007). Indeed, familism accounts for the significantly higher trend for Latino college students to live at home (Desmond & López Turley, 2009). The extended family is also strong among Latino families and serves as the venue for a wide range of exchanges of goods and services, such as child care and financial support (Almeida et al., 2009).

familism
Idea that the family's well-being takes precedence over the concerns of individual family members.

Asian American adolescents report very high feelings of obligation to their families compared with European American adolescents, although in fact, most caregiving is done by daughters or daughters-in-law, not sons (Rodriguez-Galán, 2014). Contrary to commonly portrayed stereotypes, Asian American families do not represent the "Model Minority," but experience the same challenges with parenting as all other groups (Xia, Do, & Xie, 2013). In general, males enjoy higher status in traditional Asian families (Tsuno & Homma, 2009). Among recent immigrants, though, women are expanding their role by working outside the home. Research shows that Chinese American parents experience less marital stress during the transition to parenthood than European American couples do, perhaps because of the clearer traditional cultural division of tasks between husbands and wives (Burns, 2005).

Multiethnic families in the U.S. are increasing in number.

Raising multiethnic children presents challenges not experienced by parents of same-race children. For example, parents of biracial children report feeling discrimination and being targets of prejudicial behavior from others (Hubbard, 2010; Kilson & Ladd, 2009). These parents also worry that their children may be rejected by members of both racial communities. Perhaps that is why parents of multiracial children tend to provide more economic and cultural resources to their children than do parents of single-race children (Cheng & Powell, 2007).

In multiethnic families, you might think that the parent from a minority group takes primary responsibility for guiding that aspect

FatCamera/E+/Getty Images

of the child's ethnic identity. However, it is the mothers who are key in most respects (Schlabach, 2013). A study of children of European mothers and Maori fathers in New Zealand showed that the mothers played a major role in establishing the child's Maori identity (Kukutai, 2007). Similarly, European American mothers of biracial children whose fathers were African American tended to raise them as African American in terms of public ethnic identity (O'Donoghue, 2005). In general, multiracial adolescents experience more negative outcomes socially and emotionally if their mothers, rather than fathers, are a minority (Schlabach, 2013).

It is clear that ethnic groups vary a great deal in how they approach the issue of parenting and what values are most important. Considered together, there is no one parenting standard that applies equally to all groups.

Diverse Family Forms

The traditional family form of two married parents with their biological parents does not reflect the wide diversity of family forms in American society. You likely are in or know people who live in one of these forms. Let's take a closer look.

Single Parents

About 40% of births in the U.S. are to mothers who are not married, a rate that has declined 14% since peaking in 2008 (National Center for Health Statistics, 2016d). As can be seen in ▶ Figure 11.5, the percentage of births to nonmarried mothers differs considerably across race and ethnicity, from 72% among African Americans to 29.2% among European Americans. Among African American mothers, two-thirds of these mothers have no high school diploma, and evidence suggests that the education disadvantage significantly affects the child's future development (McLanahan & Jencks, 2015).

Single parents, regardless of gender, face considerable obstacles. Financially, they are usually much less well-off than their married counterparts. Integrating the roles of work and parenthood are more difficult. Single mothers are hardest hit, mainly because women typically are paid less than men.

Many divorced single parents report complex feelings toward their children, such as frustration, failure, guilt, and a need to be overindulgent (Amato & Boyd, 2014). Loneliness when children grow up and leave or are visiting the noncustodial parent can be especially difficult to deal with (Langlais, Anderson, & Greene, 2016).

▶ **Figure 11.5**

Percentage of All Births that Were to Unmarried Women, by Race and Hispanic Origin: Selected Years, 1960–2014

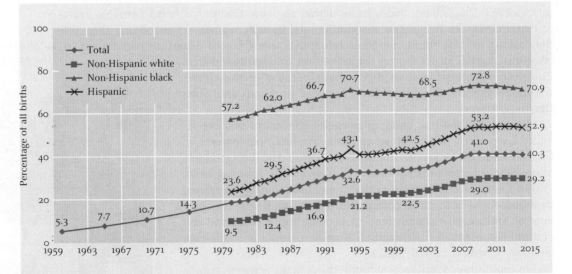

SOURCE: www.childtrends.org/wp-content/uploads/2015/03/75_Births_to_Unmarried_Women.pdf.

Single parents, regardless of gender, face considerable obstacles. Financially, they are usually less well-off than their married counterparts, especially single mothers. Having only one source of income puts additional pressure on single parents to provide all of the necessities. Integrating the roles of work and parenthood are difficult enough for two people; for the single parent, the hardships are compounded. Financially, single mothers are hardest hit, mainly because women typically are paid less than men and because single mothers may not be able to afford enough child care to provide the work schedule flexibility needed for higher-paying jobs.

Being a single parent presents many challenges, but also satisfaction.

One particular concern for many divorced single parents is dating. Several common questions asked by single parents involve dating: "How do I become available again?" "How will my children react?" "How do I cope with my own sexual needs?" They have reason to be concerned. Research indicates that single parents tend to report that children may interfere with dating and romance (Sommer et al., 2013). They report feeling insecure about sexuality and wondering how they should behave around their children in terms of having partners stay overnight (Langlais et al., 2016; Lampkin-Hunter, 2010).

Military families experience unique aspects of single parenting. When one parent in a two-parent household deploys, the remaining parent becomes a single parent. Separation anxiety is common among deployed parents, and the cycling of experience as a single parent and partner in a two-parent household with both parents present can create stress (Wadsworth, Hughes-Kirchubel, & Riggs, 2014).

Step-, Foster-, Adoptive, and Same-Sex Couple Parenting

Roughly one-third of North American couples become stepparents or foster or adoptive parents at some time during their lives. In general, there are few differences among parents who have their own biological children or who become parents in some other way, but there are some unique challenges (Doss & Rhoades, 2017; Ganong & Coleman, 2017).

A big issue for foster parents, adoptive parents, and stepparents is how strongly the child will bond with them. Although infants less than 1 year old will probably bond well, children who are old enough to have formed attachments with their biological parents may have competing loyalties. For example, some stepchildren remain strongly attached to the noncustodial parent and actively resist attempts to integrate them into the new family ("My real mother wouldn't make me do that"), or they may exhibit behavioral problems. As a result, the dynamics in blended families can best be understood as a complex system (Dupuis, 2010). Stepparents must often deal with continued visitation by the noncustodial parent, which may exacerbate any difficulties. These problems are a major reason that second marriages are at high risk for dissolution, as discussed later in this chapter. They are also a major reason why behavioral and emotional problems are more common among stepchildren (Ganong & Coleman, 2017).

Still, many stepparents and stepchildren ultimately develop good relationships with each other (Coleman, Ganong, & Russell, 2013). Stepparents must be sensitive to the relationship between the stepchild and his or her biological, noncustodial parent. Allowing stepchildren to develop a relationship with the stepparent at their own pace also helps. What style of stepparenting ultimately develops is influenced by the expectations of the stepparent, stepchild, spouse, and nonresidential parent (Ganong & Coleman, 2017).

Adoptive parents also contend with attachment to birth parents, but in different ways. Adopted children may wish to locate and meet their birth parents. Such searches can strain the relationships between these children and their adoptive parents who may interpret these actions as a form of rejection (Curtis & Pearson, 2010).

Families with children adopted from another culture pose challenges of how to establish and maintain connection with the child's culture of origin (Yngvesson, 2010). For mothers of transracially adopted Chinese and Korean children, becoming connected to the appropriate Asian American community is a way to accomplish this (Johnston et al., 2007).

Research in the Netherlands found children adopted from Columbia, Sri Lanka, and Korea into Dutch homes struggled with looking different, and many expressed desires to be white (Juffer, 2006). Canadian parents who adopted children from China took several different approaches to introducing their children to Chinese culture, from not at all ("my child is simply Canadian" to deliberately blending both cultures to leaving is up to the child (Bian, Blachford, & Durst, 2015).

Foster parents have the most tenuous relationship with their children because the bond can be broken for any of a number of reasons having nothing to do with the quality of the care being provided. Dealing with attachment is difficult; foster parents want to provide secure homes, but they may not have the children long enough to establish continuity. Furthermore, because many children in foster care have been unable to form attachments at all, they are less likely to form ones will inevitably be broken. Despite the challenges, placement in good foster care results in the development of attachment between foster parents and children who were placed out of institutional settings (Alper & Howe, 2015; Smyke et al., 2010).

Finally, many gay men and lesbian women also want to be parents. Although changes in laws regarding same-sex couples and parenting have changed in important ways, barriers remain (Frank, 2016). Some have biological children themselves, whereas others choose adoption or foster parenting.

Research indicates that children reared by gay or lesbian parents do not experience any more problems than children reared by heterosexual parents and are as psychologically healthy as children of heterosexual parents (Bos et al., 2016; Frank, 2016). Substantial evidence exists that children raised by gay or lesbian parents do not develop sexual identity problems or any other problems any more than children raised by heterosexual parents (Goldberg, 2009). Children of gay and lesbian parents were no more likely than children of heterosexual parents to identify as gay, lesbian, bisexual, transgendered, or questioning.

The evidence is clear that children raised by gay or lesbian parents suffer no adverse consequences compared with children raised by heterosexual parents. Children of lesbian couples and heterosexual couples are equally adjusted behaviorally, show equivalent cognitive development, have similar behaviors in school, and do not show different rates of use of illegal drugs or delinquent behavior (Biblarz & Savci, 2010; Patterson, 2013).

Children of gay or lesbian parents might be better adjusted than adult children of heterosexual parents in that the adult children of gay and lesbian parents exhibit lower levels of homophobia and less fear of negative evaluation than do the adult children of heterosexual parents. Gay men are often especially concerned about being good and nurturing fathers, and they try hard to raise their children with nonsexist, egalitarian attitudes (Goldberg, 2009; Patterson, 2013). Evidence shows that gay parents have more egalitarian sharing of child rearing than do fathers in heterosexual households (Biblarz & Savci, 2010).

These data will not eliminate the controversy, much of which is based on long-held beliefs (often religion-based) and prejudices. In the United States, the topic of lesbian and gay couples' right to be parents is likely to continue to play out in political agendas for years to come.

TEST YOURSELF 11.3

Recall

1. The series of relatively predictable changes that families experience is called _____.

2. Major influences on the decision to have children are marital factors, career factors, lifestyle factors, and

   _____.

3. A new father who is invested in his parental role, but who may feel ambivalent about time lost to his career, is probably over age _____.

4. A major issue for foster parents, adoptive parents, and step-parents is _____.

Interpret

- What difference would it make to view children as a financial asset (i.e., a source of income) as opposed to a financial burden (i.e., mainly an expense)? Which of these attitudes characterizes most Western societies? Give an example of the other type.

Apply

- Would northern European cultures be likely to demonstrate familism? Why or why not?

Check your answers to the Recall Questions at the end of the chapter.

11.4 Divorce and Remarriage

LEARNING OBJECTIVES

- Who gets divorced? How does divorce affect parental relationships with children?

- What are remarriages like? How are they similar to and different from first marriages?

Frank and Marilyn, both in their late 40s, thought that their marriage would last forever. However, they weren't so lucky and have just been divorced. Although two of their children are married, their youngest daughter is still in college. The financial pressures Marilyn feels now that she's on her own are beginning to take their toll. She wonders whether her financial situation is similar to that of other recently divorced women.

Despite what Frank and Marilyn pledged on their wedding day, their marriage did not last until death parted them; they dissolved their marriage through divorce. Even though divorce is stressful and difficult, thousands of people each year choose to try again. Most enter their second (or third or fourth) marriage with renewed expectations of success. Are these new dreams realistic? As we'll see, it depends on many things; among the most important is whether children are involved.

Divorce

Most couples enter marriage with the idea their relationship will be permanent. Rather than growing together, though, many couples grow apart.

Who Gets Divorced and Why?

You or someone you know has experienced divorce. No wonder. Divorce in the United States is common, and the divorce rate is substantially higher than in many other countries around the world. As you can see in ▶ Figure 11.6, American couples have roughly a 50–50 chance of remaining married for life. In contrast, the ratio of divorces to marriages in Japan, Israel, and Greece are substantially lower as are rates in Africa and Asia. Divorce rates in nearly every developed country increased over the past several decades, and tend to vary as a function of religion.

Of those marriages in the U.S. ending in divorce within 20 years, Asian American couples have the lowest risk and African Americans the highest. College educated women have much lower divorce rates than women who have a high school or lower education (Wang, 2015).

Research indicates that men and women tend to agree on the reasons for divorce (Braver & Lamb, 2013). Infidelity is the most commonly reported cause, followed by incompatibility, drinking or drug use, and growing apart. An individual couple's specific reasons for divorcing vary with gender, social class, and life-course variables. Former husbands and wives are more likely to blame their ex-spouses than themselves for the problems that led to the divorce. Former husbands and wives agree, however, that the women were more likely to have initiated the divorce.

Why people divorce has been the focus of much research. Divorce touches every aspect of relationships: emotional, psychological, social, economic, and more (Coates, 2017). Still, we can gain insight into who is most likely to divorce, and why they do.

A great deal of attention has been devoted to the notion that success or failure depends critically on how couples handle conflict. Although conflict management is important, it has become clear from research in couples therapy that the reasons couples split are complex (Kayser, 2010).

Gottman and Levenson (2000; Gottman & Silver, 2015) developed two models that predicted divorce early (within the first 7 years of marriage) and later (when the first child

▶ Figure 11.6

The United States has one of the highest divorce rates in the world.

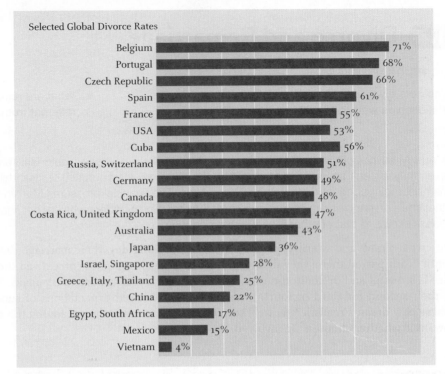

Selected Global Divorce Rates

Belgium	71%
Portugal	68%
Czech Republic	66%
Spain	61%
France	55%
USA	53%
Cuba	56%
Russia, Switzerland	51%
Germany	49%
Canada	48%
Costa Rica, United Kingdom	47%
Australia	43%
Japan	36%
Israel, Singapore	28%
Greece, Italy, Thailand	25%
China	22%
Egypt, South Africa	17%
Mexico	15%
Vietnam	4%

SOURCE: U.S. Bureau of Labor Statistics, updated and revised from "Families and Work in Transition in 12 Countries, 1980–2001," *Monthly Labor Review*, September 2003, with unpublished data. www.bls.gov/opub/mlr/2003/09/art1full.pdf.

reaches age 14) with 93% accuracy over the 14-year period of their study. Negative emotions displayed during conflict between the couple predicted early divorce, but not later divorce. In general, this reflects a destructive interaction pattern of demand-withdraw (Baucom et al., 2015; Christensen, 1990) in which, during conflict, one partner places a demand on the other, who then withdraws either emotionally or physically. In contrast, the lack of positive emotions in a discussion of events-of-the-day and during conflict predicted later divorce, but not early divorce. An example would be a wife talking excitedly about a project she had just been given at work and her husband showing disinterest. Such "unrequited" interest and excitement in discussions likely carries over to the rest of the relationship.

Gottman's and other similar (e.g., Baucom et al., 2015) research is important because it clearly shows how couples show emotion is critical to marital success. Couples who divorce earlier typically do so because of high levels of negative feelings such as contempt, criticism, defensiveness, and stonewalling experienced as a result of intense marital conflict. But for many couples, such intense conflict is generally absent. But the mere absence of conflict does not mean the marriage is full of positive feelings. Although the absence of intense conflict makes it easier to stay in a marriage longer, the lack of positive emotions eventually takes its toll and results in later divorce. For a marriage to last, people need to be told regularly they are loved and that what they do and feel really matters to their partner.

We must be cautious about applying Gottman's model to all married couples. Kim, Capaldi, and Crosby (2007) reported in lower-income high-risk couples, the variables Gottman says predict early divorce did not hold for that sample. The priority given to couples' communication as the source of marital satisfaction is not always apparent (Lavner, Karney, & Bradbury, 2016). For older, long-term married couples, the perception of the spouse's support is the most important predictor of remaining married (Landis et al., 2013).

The high divorce rate in the United States has led to many approaches to increase the likelihood that marriages will last. One approach to keeping couples together, termed *covenant marriage*, makes divorce much harder to obtain. Covenant marriage *expands the marriage contract to a lifelong commitment between the partners within a supportive community*. This approach is a religious-centered view founded on the idea that if getting

covenant marriage

Expands the marriage contract to a lifelong commitment between the partners within a supportive community.

married and getting divorced were grounded in religious and cultural values and divorce was made more difficult, couples would be more likely to stay together (Felkey, in press). The couple wanting to celebrate a covenant marriage agrees to participate in mandatory premarital counseling and, should problems arise later, the grounds for divorce become very limited (White, 2010).

Other approaches to decreasing the likelihood of divorce focus on teaching couples the skills necessary for maintaining strong relationships, such as good communication skills and joint problem-solving strategies. Research related to these initiatives has focused on the positive aspects of marriage and on the need to do a better job with marriage education (Fincham & Beach, 2010). Will they succeed in helping couples stay married longer? That remains to be seen.

Effects of Divorce on the Couple

Divorce takes a high toll on the couple. Unlike the situation when one's spouse dies, divorce often means the person's ex-spouse is present to provide a reminder of the failure. As a result, divorced people are typically unhappy in general, at least for a while.

Research in the United States and Spain shows great similarity in how both partners in a failed marriage feel: deeply disappointed, misunderstood, and rejected (Doohan, Carrère, & Riggs, 2010; Yárnoz-Yaben, 2010). Unlike the situation of a spouse dying, divorce often means that one's ex-spouse is present to provide a reminder of the unpleasant aspects of the relationship and, in some cases, feelings of personal failure. Divorced people suffer negative health consequences as well (Lamela, Figueiredo, & Bastos, 2014). Especially because of the financial effects of divorce, the effects can even be traced to future generations due to long-term negative consequences on education and on quality of parenting (Amato & Cheadle, 2005; Friesen et al., 2017). Divorced people suffer negative health consequences as well (Lamela et al., 2016).

Divorced people sometimes find the transition difficult; researchers refer to these problems as "divorce hangover" (Walther, 1991). Divorce hangover reflects divorced partners' inability to let go, develop new friendships, or reorient themselves as single parents. Forgiving the ex-spouse is also important for eventual adjustment postdivorce (Rye et al., 2004; Sbarra, 2015). Both low preoccupation and forgiveness may be indicators ex-spouses are able to move on with their lives.

Divorce in middle age has some special characteristics. If women initiate the divorce, they report self-focused growth and optimism; if they did not initiate the divorce, they tend to ruminate and feel vulnerable. Many middle-aged women who divorce also face significant financial challenges if their primary source of income was the ex-husband's earnings (Sakraida, 2005).

We must not overlook the financial problems that many divorced women face (Braver & Lamb, 2013). These problems are especially keen for the middle-aged divorcee who may have spent years as a homemaker and has few marketable job skills. For her, divorce presents an especially difficult financial hardship, which is intensified if she has children in college and the father provides little support.

Relationships with Young Children

When it involves children, divorce becomes a complicated matter, especially when viewed from a global perspective (Amato & Boyd, 2014). In most countries, mothers tend to obtain custody but often do not obtain sufficient financial resources to support the children. This puts an extreme financial burden on divorced mothers, whose standard of living is typically reduced.

In contrast, divorced fathers often pay a higher psychological price. Although many would like to remain active in their children's lives, few actually do. Child support laws in some states also may limit fathers' contact with their children (Wadlington, 2005). When mothers who have custody remarry, visits from noncustodial fathers usually decline (Anderson & Greene, 2013).

collaborative divorce
Voluntary, contractually based alternative dispute resolution process for couples who want to negotiate a resolution of their situation rather than have a ruling imposed on them by a court or an arbitrator.

Think About It

Given the serious impact of divorce, what changes in mate selection might lower the divorce rate?

One hopeful direction that addresses the usually difficult custody situations following divorce is the Collaborative Divorce Project, based on collaborative law (Mosten, 2009; Pruett, Insabella, & Gustafson, 2005). Collaborative divorce *is a voluntary, contractually based alternative dispute resolution process for couples who want to negotiate a resolution of their situation rather than have a ruling imposed on them by a court or an arbitrator* (Ballard et al., 2014). Collaborative divorce is an intervention designed to assist the parents of children 6 years and younger as they begin the separation/divorce process.

Results from this approach are positive (DeLucia-Waack, 2010). In addition to positive evaluations from both parents, couples benefited in terms of less conflict, greater father involvement, and better outcomes for children than in the control group. Attorneys and court records indicate that intervention families were more cooperative and were less likely to need custody evaluations and other costly services. The Collaborative Divorce Project is evidence that programs can be designed and implemented to benefit all members of the family.

Divorce and Relationships with Adult Children

We saw in Chapter 5 that young children can be seriously affected by their parents' divorce. But what happens when the parents of adult children divorce? Are adult children affected, too? It certainly looks that way. Young adults whose parents divorce experience a great deal of emotional vulnerability and stress (Cooney & Uhlenberg, 1990). One young man put it this way:

> The difficult thing was that it was a time where, you know, [you're] making the transition from high school to college . . . your high school friends are dispersed . . . they're all over the place. . . . It's normally a very difficult transition [college], new atmosphere, new workload, meeting new people. You've got to start deciding what you want to do, you've got to sort of start getting more independent, and so forth. And then at the same time you find out about a divorce. You know, it's just that much more adjustment you have to make. (Cooney et al., 1986)

The effects of experiencing the divorce of one's parents while growing up can be quite long-lasting. College-age students report poorer relations with their parents if their parents are divorced (Yu et al., 2010). Parental divorce also affects young adults' views on intimate relationships and marriage, often having negative effects on them (Ottaway, 2010). Wallerstein and Lewis (2004) report the findings from a 25-year follow-up study of individuals whose parents divorced when they were between 3 and 18 years old. Results show an unexpected gulf between growing up in intact versus divorced families as well as the difficulties that children of divorce encounter in achieving love, sexual intimacy, and commitment to marriage and parenthood. Even when the length of time spent in the intact two-parent family was taken into account, negative effects of divorce on adult children were still found in a large Dutch study (Kalmijn, 2013). The "marriage protection" factor outweighed biological relatedness, especially for fathers. There is no doubt that divorce has significant effects regardless of when it occurs in a child's life.

Remarriage

The trauma of divorce does not always deter people from beginning new relationships that often lead to another marriage. As you can see in ▶ Figure 11.7, though, rates of remarriage differ dramatically by age (Livingston, 2014). Additionally, the likelihood of ever remarrying has dropped in nearly all age groups since the mid-20th century. For example, for those under age 35, remarriage declined from 72% in 1960 to 42% in 2013, from 76% to 57% in those 35 to 44, and from 69% to 63% in those 45 to 54. Interestingly, for those in older age groups, the trend is reversed: for those 55 to 64, remarriage increased from 55% to 67% and for those over 65, it increased from 34% to 50%.

Overall, women are less likely to remarry than are men, but this gender gap is closing, mainly because men are less likely in general to remarry now than in the past (Livingston, 2014). European Americans are the most likely group to remarry (60% of those couples do),

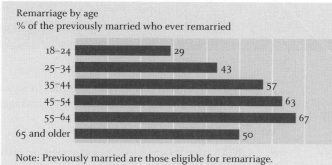

Remarriage by age
% of the previously married who ever remarried

Age	%
18–24	29
25–34	43
35–44	57
45–54	63
55–64	67
65 and older	50

Note: Previously married are those eligible for remarriage.

SOURCE: Pew Research Center (2014). Retrieved from www.pewsocialtrends.org/2014/11/14/four-in-ten-couples-are-saying-i-do-again/st_2014-11-14_remarriage-06/.

and African Americans (48%) and Asian Americans (46%) least likely. Finally, the age difference between spouses is likely to be greater in remarriage; whereas among wives in a first marriage only 14% are at least 6 years younger than their spouse, for remarried women that increases to 31%.

Cultural differences are apparent in the ability of women, in particular, to remarry; in Namibia widows are constrained in their options and typically must depend on others (Thomas, 2008). Among older adults, adult children may voice strong opposition to their parent remarrying that can put sufficient pressure on the parent that they remain single.

Adapting to new relationships in remarriage is stressful. Partners may have unresolved issues from the previous marriage that may interfere with satisfaction with the new marriage (Faber, 2004; Gold, 2016; Martin-Uzzi & Duval-Tsioles, 2013). The challenges can include antagonism toward ex-spouses that interferes with child custody, differing loyalties among stepchildren, and financial difficulties. The effects of remarriage on children is complicated, at least for emerging adults (Collardeau & Ehrenberg, 2016; Gold, 2016). Parental divorce can have long-term consequences on children's attitudes toward marriage and divorce. The extent to which parental conflict was openly present and the religious affiliation of emerging adults influences their attitudes. For instance, those who were exposed to high levels of parental conflict have more positive views of divorce.

Remarriages tend to be less stable than first marriages, and have become less so since the 1990s (Council on Contemporary Families, 2015). The typical first marriage lasts 13 years, whereas the typical remarriage lasts 10. These differences do not reflect relationship quality, which is equivalent; rather, pressures from complex family relationships, lower commitment, and financial pressures take a higher toll on remarriages. Nevertheless, couples who are very committed to and work diligently at making the remarriage strong are usually successful.

TEST YOURSELF 11.4

Recall

1. Following divorce, most women suffer disproportionately in the _____ domain compared with most men.

2. On average, within two years after a divorce, _____ fathers remain central in their children's lives.

3. Even many years later, divorced _____ may not experience positive relationships with their adult children.

4. Remarriages tend to be _____ than first marriages.

Interpret

• Despite greatly increased divorce rates over the past few decades, the rate of marriage has not changed very much. Why?

Apply

• Ricardo and Maria are engaged to be married. Ricardo works long hours as the manager of a local coffee shop, while Maria works regular hours as an administrative assistant at a large communications company. Based on what you know about why couples get divorced, what factors may increase the likelihood that Ricardo and Maria's marriage will fail?

Check your answers to the Recall Questions at the end of the chapter.

11.1 Relationship Types and Issues

What role do friends play across adulthood? How do they develop?

- People tend to have more friendships during young adulthood than during any other period. Face-to-face and virtual friendships are based on the same principles: affective or emotional self-disclosure, sharing activities of mutual interest, and as sources of fun.

- Men have fewer close friends and base them on shared activities. Women have more close friends and base them on emotional sharing. Cross-gender friendships may create challenges due to misperceptions.

What characterizes love relationships? How do they vary across cultures?

- Passion, intimacy, and commitment are the key components of love.

- The theory of assortative mating does the best job explaining the process of forming love relationships.

- Selecting a mate works best when there are shared values, goals, and interests. There are cross-cultural differences in which specific aspects of these are most important.

- Neuroscience research shows a great deal of brain activity and related neurochemical activity when people are in love.

What is the nature of violence in some relationships?

- Levels of aggressive behavior range from verbal aggression to physical aggression to murdering one's partner. People remain in abusive relationships for many reasons, including cultural factors, low self-esteem, and the belief they cannot leave.

11.2 Lifestyles and Relationships

What are the challenges and advantages of being single?

- Most adults in their 20s are single. People remain single for many reasons; gender differences exist. Ethnic differences in rates of singlehood reflect differences in age at marriage and social factors.

- Singles recognize the pluses and minuses in the lifestyle. There are health and longevity consequences from remaining single for men but not for women.

Why do people cohabit?

- Cohabitation is on the increase globally.

- Three primary reasons for cohabiting are convenience (e.g., to share expenses), trial marriage, or substitute

marriage. Cultural differences abound; in some cultures, cohabitation is a viable alternative to marriage.

What are LGBTQ relationships like?

- LGBTQ couples are similar to married heterosexual couples in terms of relationship issues. Lesbian couples tend to be more egalitarian. The option to marry is changing the nature of LGBTQ relationships.

What is marriage like across adulthood?

- The most important factors in creating stable marriages are maturity, similarity (called homogamy), and conflict resolution skills. Exchange theory is an important explanation of how people contribute to their relationships.

- Exchange theory argues that happy marriages result when both partners perceive they contribute roughly equally.

- For couples with children, marital satisfaction tends to decline until the children leave home, although individual differences are apparent, especially in long-term marriages.

- Marriages are most intense during the early years. Most long-term marriages tend to be happy, and partners in them express fewer negative emotions. Sharing values and beliefs helps sustain marriages.

11.3 Family Dynamics and the Life Course

What is it like to be a parent? What are the key issues across ethnic groups?

- Most couples choose to have children, although for many different reasons. The timing of parenthood determines in part how involved parents are in their families as opposed to their careers. Couples without children can be happier.

- Being older at the birth of one's first child is an advantage. Instilling cultural values in children is important for parents. In some cultures, familism changes the unit of analysis from the individual to the family.

What diverse forms of parenting are there?

- Single parents face many problems, especially if they are women and are divorced. The main problem is reduced financial resources.

- A major issue for adoptive parents, foster parents, and stepparents is how strongly the child will bond with them. Each of these relationships has special characteristics. Same-sex couple parents still face discrimination, and are good parents.

11.4 Divorce and Remarriage

Why do couples divorce?

- Currently, half of all new marriages end in divorce. Reasons for divorce include a lack of the qualities that make a strong marriage. Also, societal attitudes against divorce have eased and expectations about marriage have increased.

- Recovery from divorce is different for men and women. Men tend to have a tougher time in the short run. Women clearly have a harder time in the long run, often for financial reasons. Difficulties between divorced partners usually involve visitation and child support.

Why do people remarry?

- Most divorced couples remarry. Second marriages are especially vulnerable to stress if stepchildren are involved. Remarriage in later life tends to be happy, but may be resisted by adult children.

Test Yourself: Recall Answers

11.1 1. women **2.** men **3.** romantic love **4.** traditional **5.** men   **11.2 1.** marry **2.** step toward **3.** heterosexual marriages **4.** exchange theory **5.** decreases   **11.3 1.** the family life cycle **2.** psychological factors **3.** 30 **4.** how strongly the child will bond with them   **11.4 1.** financial **2.** few **3.** fathers **4.** less stable

Key Terms

assortative mating (359)
abusive relationship (363)
battered woman syndrome (363)
cohabitation (366)
marital success (368)
marital quality (368)

marital adjustment (368)
marital satisfaction (368)
homogamy (369)
exchange theory (369)
vulnerability-stress-adaptation
  model (370)

nuclear family (372)
extended family (372)
familism (375)
covenant marriage (380)
collaborative divorce (382)

Working and Relaxing

12

When you were young, you were undoubtedly asked, "What do you want to be when you grow up?" Now that we are "grown up," the question has changed to "What do you do?"

Work is a central aspect of life and a defining characteristic of who we are. For some, work *is* life; for all, our work is a prime source of identity in adulthood.

The world of work has changed dramatically over the past few decades in large part to the continuing replacement of jobs with technology (witness the new use of robots and iPads in restaurants instead of human servers, and the advent of driverless cars that could eliminate taxi and share-service drivers). The so-called gig economy, based on short-term contracts rather than on long-term employment, is the fastest growing sector of the labor force (Intuit, 2016; Irwin, 2016). Employment as a series of short-term jobs largely eliminates the traditional employer–employee relationship, and mostly eliminates the availability of key benefits such as employer-paid health care, paid family leave, and retirement savings plans to workers. Intuit (2016) predicts that by 2020, 40% of all American workers will be in the gig economy and not employed in a traditional long-term way.

Aging baby boomers are also redefining work and retirement. The Great Recession of the late 2000s and early 2010s affected the workplace by forcing boomers who lost a significant part of their retirement savings to continue working, making it more difficult for younger adults to enter or advance in the workforce.

As a result, our understanding of what work is, what it means, and how people engage in it is undergoing fundamental change. We consider the complexities of the world of work throughout this chapter as we confront the reality of rapidly changing occupational conditions and opportunities, and how those are shaping adult development and aging, and raising issues about basic assumptions people have about retirement.

12.1 Occupational Selection and Development

LEARNING OBJECTIVES

- How do people view work?
- How do people choose their occupations?

- What factors influence occupational development?
- What is the relationship between job satisfaction and age?

Fatima, a 28-year-old senior communications major, wonders about careers. Should she enter the broadcast field as a behind-the-scenes producer, or would she be better suited as a public relations spokesperson? She thinks her outgoing personality is a factor she should consider in making this decision.

Choosing one's work is serious business. Like Fatima, we try to select a field in which we are trained and maximizes the odds that we can meet our goal of doing meaningful work. You may be taking this course as part of your preparation for a career in human development, social services, psychology, nursing, allied, health, or other field, so in that sense it is career preparation. But work is more than that. Work is a source for friends and often for spouses or partners. People arrange personal activities around work schedules. Parents often choose child care centers on the basis of proximity to where they work. People often choose where they live in terms of where they work.

The Meaning of Work

Studs Terkel, author of the fascinating classic book *Working* (1974), writes work is "a search for daily meaning as well as daily bread, for recognition as well as cash, for astonishment rather than torpor; in short, for a sort of life rather than a Monday through Friday sort of dying" (xiii). Kahlil Gibran (1923), in his mystical book *The Prophet*, put it this way: "Work is love made visible."

The meaning most of us derive from working includes both the money that can be exchanged for life's necessities (and perhaps a few luxuries) and the possibility of personal growth (Lips-Wiersma, Wright, & Dik, 2016; Rosso, Dekas, & Wrzesniewski, 2010). Schwartz (2015) says the belief that people only work for a paycheck is wrong; most people want to do something meaningful with people who they respect and who respect them. To achieve that true goal, Schwartz says most people would even be willing to make less money.

The upshot is that the specific occupation a person holds appears to have no effect on his or her need to derive meaning from work. Finding meaning in one's work can mean the difference between feeling work is the source of one's life problems or a source of fulfillment and contentment (Grawitch, Barber, & Justice, 2010). Blue- and pink-collar workers tend to derive meaning most from finding unity with others and developing the inner self, whereas white-collar workers place more emphasis on expressing full potential.

Contemporary business theory supports the idea that meaning matters. *The concept called* meaning-mission fit *explains how corporate executives with a better alignment between their personal intentions and their firm's mission care more about their employees' happiness, job satisfaction, and emotional well-being* (Abbott, Gilbert, & Rosinski, 2013; Salomaa, 2014). Ensuring such fit is a major focus of talent management efforts in organizations.

Given the various meanings that people derive from work, occupation is clearly a key element of a person's sense of identity and self-efficacy (Lang & Lee, 2005). This can be readily observed when adults introduce themselves socially. You've probably noticed that when people are asked to tell something about themselves, they usually provide information about what they do for a living. Occupation affects your life in a host of ways and often influences where you live, what friends you make, and even what clothes you wear. In short, the impact of work cuts across all aspects of life. Work, then, is a major social role and influence on adult life. Occupation is an important anchor that complements the other major role of adulthood—love relationships.

As we will see, occupation is part of human development. Young children, in their pretend play, are in the midst of the social preparation for work. Adults are always asking them, "What do you want to be when you grow up?" School curricula, especially in high school and college, are geared toward preparing people for particular occupations. Young adult college students as well as older returning students have formulated perspectives on the meanings they believe they will get from work. Hance (2000) organized these beliefs into three main categories: working to achieve social influence; working to achieve personal fulfillment; and working because of economic reality. These categories reflect fairly well the actual meanings that working adults report.

Because work plays such a key role in providing meaning for people, an important question is how people select an occupation. Let's turn our attention to two theories explaining how and why people choose the occupations they do.

Hassling with our commute makes us think about why we work.

meaning-mission fit
Alignment between people's personal intentions and their company's mission.

Occupational Choice Revisited

Decisions about what people want to do in the world of work do not initially happen in adulthood. Even by adolescence, there is evidence occupational preferences are related to their personalities. But what are people preparing for? Certainly, much has been written about the rapidly changing nature of work and how people cannot prepare for a stable career where a person works for the same organization throughout his or her working life (Fouad et al., 2016; Savickas, 2013).

Currently, it is more appropriate to consider careers as something people construct themselves rather than enter (Di Fabio, 2016; Hartung & Santilli, 2017; Savickas, 2013). Career construction theory *posits people build careers through their own actions that result from the interface of their own personal characteristics and the social context.* What people "do" in the world of work, then, results from how they adapt to their environment, that in turn is a result of bio-psychosocial processes grounded in the collection of experiences they have during their life.

career construction theory
Posits that people build careers through their own actions that result from the interface of their own personal characteristics and the social context.

social cognitive career theory (SCCT)

Proposes career choice is a result of the application of Bandura's social cognitive theory, especially the concept of self-efficacy.

In this regard, two specific theories about how people adapt themselves to their environment have influenced research. First, Holland's (1997) personality-type theory proposes people choose occupations to optimize the fit between their individual traits (such as personality, intelligence, skills, and abilities) and their occupational interests. Second, *social cognitive career theory (SCCT) proposes career choice is a result of the application of Bandura's social cognitive theory, especially the concept of self-efficacy.*

Holland categorizes occupations by the interpersonal settings that people must function and their associated lifestyles. He identifies six personality types that combine these factors: investigative, social, realistic, artistic, conventional, and enterprising, that he believes are optimally related to occupations.

How does Holland's theory help us understand the continued development of occupational interests in adulthood? Fatima, the college senior in the vignette, found a good match between her outgoing nature and her major, communications. Indeed, college students of all ages prefer courses and majors that fit well with their own personalities. You are likely to be one of them. Later on, that translates into the tendency of people to choose occupations and careers they like.

Complementarily, social cognitive career theory proposes people's career choices are heavily influenced by their interests (Brown & Lent, 2016; Lent, 2013; Sheu et al., 2010). As depicted in ▶ Figure 12.1, SCCT has two versions. The simplest includes four main factors: Self-Efficacy (your belief in your ability), Outcome Expectations (what you think will happen in a specific situation), Interests (what you like), and Choice Goals (what you want to achieve). The more complex version also includes Supports (environmental things that help you) and Barriers (environmental things that block or frustrate you). Several studies show support for the six-variable version of the model (Brown & Lent, 2016; Sheu et al., 2010).

Over four decades, Donald Super (1957, 1976, 1980; Super, Savickas, & Super, 1996) developed a theory of occupational development based on self-concept, first introduced in Chapter 9. He proposed a progression through five distinct stages during adulthood as a result of changes in individuals' self-concept and adaptation to an occupational role: implementation, establishment, maintenance, deceleration, and retirement (see ▶ Figure 12.2). *People are located along a continuum of vocational maturity through their working years; the more congruent their occupational behaviors are with what is expected of them at different ages, the more vocationally mature they are.*

vocational maturity

Degree of congruence between people's occupational behavior and what is expected of them at different ages.

Super proposed five developmental tasks, the first two (crystallization and specification) occurring primarily in adolescence. The remaining three (implementation, stabilization, and consolidation) occur over the course of adulthood. Each of the tasks in adulthood has distinctive characteristics, as follows.

▶ **Figure 12.1**

The four-variable (paths 1–6) and six-variable (paths 1–13) versions of the Social Cognitive Career Theory interest and choice models.

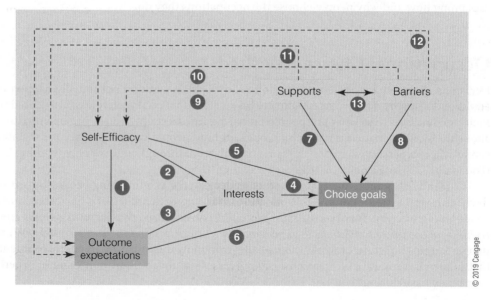

© 2019 Cengage

Figure 12.2 Super's occupational stages during adulthood.

- The *implementation* task begins in the early 20s, when people take a series of temporary jobs to learn firsthand about work roles and to try out possible career choices. Summer internships that many students use to gain experience are one example.
- The *stabilization* task begins in the mid-20s with selecting a specific occupation during young adulthood. It continues until the mid-30s as the person confirms the occupational choice that was made.
- The *consolidation* task begins in the mid-30s and continues throughout the rest of the person's working life as he or she advances up the career ladder. Taking a position in a law firm and working one's way up to partner or beginning as a salesclerk in a store at a mall and moving up to store manager are two examples.

These adult tasks overlap a sequence of developmental stages, beginning at birth, that continues during adulthood: exploratory (age 15 to 24), establishment (age 24 to 44), maintenance (age 45 to 64), and decline (age 65 and beyond). These stages reflect the overall occupational cycle from choosing what one wants to do through achieving the maximum possible in a career to the reduction in work in late adulthood.

Super's theory applies to people who enter and stay in a particular career their entire adult lives and to those who change occupations. Because it is now typical for Americans to have a series of careers, Super's notion is that we cycle and recycle through the tasks and stages as we adapt to changes in ourselves and the workplace (Super et al., 1996).

Super may be right. A longitudinal study of 7,649 individuals born in the United Kingdom showed that occupational aspirations at age 16 in science and health fields predicted actual occupational attainments in science, health professions, or engineering at age 33 (Schoon, 2001). Adult occupational attainment was also related to belief in one's ability, mathematical test performance, several personality characteristics, sociocultural background, and gender. These results point to the importance of viewing occupational development as a true developmental process, as Super claimed, as well as the importance of personal characteristics, as proposed in occupational selection theories.

Perspectives on Theories of Career Development

How well do these theories work in actual practice, particularly in the rapidly changing world in which we live and where people's careers are no longer stable? Certainly, the relations among occupation, personality, and demographic variables are complex (Brown & Lent, 2016; Hartung & Santilli, 2017). However, even given the lack of stable careers and the real need to change jobs frequently, there is still a strong tendency on people's part to find occupations in which they feel comfortable and they like (Brown & Lent, 2016; Hartung & Santilli, 2017). As we will see later, loss of self-efficacy through job loss and long-term unemployment provides support for the role the self-statements underling self-efficacy and SCCT are key.

SCCT has also been used as a framework for career counselors and coaches to help people identify and select both initial occupations and navigate later occupational changes. The goal is to have people understand the work world changes rapidly and they need to develop coping and compensatory strategies to deal with that fact.

Although people may have underlying tendencies relating to certain types of occupations, unless they believe they could be successful in those occupations and careers they are unlikely to choose them. These beliefs can be influenced by external factors. Occupational prestige and gender-related factors need to be taken into account (Deng, Armstrong, & Rounds, 2007).

Occupational Development

It is said that advancing through one's career is not just a function of being smart and doing all of the written requirements of a job. It also depends on the socialization that occurs through learning the unwritten rules of an organization, in combination with one's own expectations of what the career should entail.

Certainly, the relations among occupation, personality, and demographic variables are complex (e.g., Barrick, Mount, & Li, 2013). However, even given the lack of stable careers and the real need to change jobs frequently, there is still a strong tendency on people's part to find occupations in which they feel comfortable and that they like (Lent, 2013). As we will see later, loss of self-efficacy through job loss and long-term unemployment supports the fact that the self-statements that underlie self-efficacy and SCCT are key.

SCCT has also been used as a framework for career counselors and coaches to help people identify and select initial occupations and navigate later occupational changes. The goal is for people to understand that the work world changes rapidly and that they need to develop coping and compensatory strategies to deal with that fact.

Although people may have underlying tendencies that relate to certain types of occupations, unless they believe they could be successful in those occupations and careers, they are unlikely to choose them. These beliefs can be influenced by external factors. For example, occupational prestige and gender-related factors need to be taken into account (Deng, Armstrong, & Rounds, 2007).

Occupational Expectations

Think About It

How does one's level of cognitive development relate to one's choice of occupation?

Especially in adolescence, people begin to form opinions about what work in a particular occupation will be like, based on what they learn in school and from their parents, peers, other adults, and the media. These expectations influence what they want to become and when they hope to get there.

In adulthood, personal experiences affect people's opinions of themselves as they continue to refine and update their occupational expectations and development (Fouad, 2007; Fouad et al., 2016). This usually involves trying to achieve an occupational goal, monitoring progress toward it, and changing or even abandoning it as necessary. Modifying the goal happens for many reasons, such as realizing interests have changed, the occupation was not a good fit for them, they never got the chance to pursue the level of education necessary to achieve the goal, or because they lack certain essential skills and cannot acquire them. Still other people modify their goals because of age, race, or sex discrimination, a point we consider later in this chapter.

Research shows most people who know they have both the talent and the opportunity to achieve their occupational and career goals often attain them. When high school students identified as academically talented were asked about their career expectations and outcomes, it turned out that 10 and even 20 years later they had been surprisingly accurate (Perrone et al., 2010).

Reality shock typically hits younger workers soon after they begin an occupation.

Marc Romanelli/The Image Bank/Getty Images

In general, research shows young adults modify their expectations at least once, usually on the basis of new information, especially about their academic ability. The connection between adolescent expectations and adult reality reinforces the developmental aspects of occupations and careers.

Many writers believe occupational expectations also vary by generation. Nowhere has this belief been stronger than in the supposed differences between the baby boom generation (born between 1946 and 1964) and the current millennial generation (born since 1983). What people in these generations, on average, expect in occupations appears to be different (Stewart et al., 2017). Millennials are more likely to change jobs more often than the older generations did, and are likely to view traditional organizations with more distrust and cynicism. Experts recommend that metrics used to evaluate job performance need to reflect these generational differences.

Contrary to most stereotypes, millennials are no more egotistical, and are just as happy and satisfied as young adults in every generation since the 1970s (Trzesniewski & Donnellan, 2010). However, millennials tend to have an inherent mistrust in organizations, prefer a culture focused on employee development, create information through interactive social media, are more globally aware and comfortable working with people from diverse socio-ethnic backgrounds, and do best in situations that value innovation through team-work (Dannar, 2013; Stewart et al., in press).

The importance of occupational expectations can be seen clearly in the transition from school to the workplace (Moen, 2016a, 2016b; Moen & Roehling, 2005). The 21st-century workplace is not one where hard work and long hours necessarily lead to a stable career. *It can also be a place where you experience reality shock, a situation that what you learn in the classroom does not always transfer directly into the "real world" and does not represent all you need to know.* When reality shock sets in, things never seem to happen the way we expect. Reality shock befalls everyone. You can imagine how a new teacher feels when her long hours preparing a lesson result in students who act bored and unap-preciative of her efforts.

reality shock

Situation in which what you learn in the classroom does not always transfer directly into the "real world" and does not represent all you need to know.

Many professions, such as nursing and teaching, have gone to great lengths to allevi-ate reality shock (Hinton & Chirgwin, 2010; Shayshon & Popper-Giveon, in press). This problem is one best addressed through internship and practicum experiences for students under the careful guidance of experienced people in the field.

The Role of Mentors and Coaches

Entering an occupation involves more than the relatively short formal training a person receives. Instead, most people are oriented by a more experienced person who makes a specific effort to do this, taking on the role of a *mentor* or *coach*.

A mentor is part teacher, sponsor, model, and counselor who facilitates on-the job learning to help the new hire do the work required in his or her present role and to prepare for future career roles (Volpe et al., 2016). *A developmental coach is an individual who helps a person focus on their goals, motivations, and aspirations to help them achieve focus and apply them appropriately* (Hunt & Weintraub, 2016). Mentoring and coaching are viewed as primary ways that organizations invest in developing their talent and future leadership (Smits & Bowden, 2013). Although mentors and coaches work with people at all career stages, mentoring is found most often with people new to a position, whereas coaching tends to focus on those with more experience.

mentor

A person who is part teacher, sponsor, model, and counselor who facilitates on-the-job learning to help a new hire do the work required in his or her present role and to prepare for future roles.

developmental coach

Individual who helps a person focus on their goals, motivations, and aspirations to help them achieve focus and apply them appropriately.

The mentor helps a young worker avoid trouble and also provides invaluable informa-tion about the unwritten rules governing day-to-day activities in the workplace, and being sensitive to the employment situation (Smith, Howard, & Harrington, 2005). Good men-tors makes sure their protégés are noticed and receives credit from supervisors for good work. Thus, occupational success often depends on the quality of the mentor–protégé relationship and the protégé's perceptions of its importance (Eddleston, Baldridge, & Veiga, 2004).

What do mentors get from the relationship? Helping a younger employee learn the job is one way to achieve Erikson's phase of gen-erativity (see Chapter 9; Marcia & Josselson, 2013).

Developmental coaching is a process that helps people make fundamental changes in their lives by focusing on general skill devel-opment and performance improvement (Volpe et al., 2016). It tends not to focus on specific aspects of a job; rather, the intent is more general improvement of one's overall career success. Thus, coach-ing complements mentoring and helps people develop all of the key aspects of themselves.

Women and minorities have an especially important need for both mentors and coaches (Hunt & Weintraub, 2016; Ortiz-Walters & Gilson, 2013; Pratt, 2010; Williams, Phillips, & Hall, 2014). When paired with mentors and coaches, women benefit by

Women employees typically prefer and may achieve more from a female mentor.

having higher expectations; mentored women also have better perceived career development (Schulz & Enslin, 2014). Latina nurses in the U.S. Army benefitted from mentors in terms of staying in the military and getting better assignments (Aponte, 2007). It is also critical to adopt a culturally conscious model of mentoring and coaching in order to enhance the advantages of developing minority mentees (Campinha-Bacote, 2010). Culturally conscious mentoring and coaching involves understanding how an organization's and employee's cultures mutually affect employees, and explicitly building those assumptions, interrelationships, and behaviors into the mentoring or coaching situation.

Despite the evidence that having a mentor or coach has many positive effects on one's occupational development, there is an important caveat; the quality of the mentor or coach really matters (Tong & Kram, 2013; Volpe et al., 2016). Having a poor mentor or coach is worse than having no mentor at all. Consequently, people must be carefully matched. It is in the best interest of the organization to get the match correct. How can prospective matches happen more effectively? Some organizations have taken a page from dating and created speed mentoring as a way to create better matches (Berk, 2010; Cook, Bahn, & Menaker, 2010).

Job Satisfaction

job satisfaction

Positive feeling that results from an appraisal of one's work.

psychological capital theory

Notion that having a positive outlook improves processes and outcomes.

What does it mean to be satisfied with one's job or occupation? Job satisfaction *is the positive feeling that results from an appraisal of one's work.* Research indicates that job satisfaction is a multifaceted concept but that certain characteristics—including hope, resilience, optimism, and self-efficacy—predict both job performance and job satisfaction. *This research has resulted in the creation of* psychological capital theory, *the notion that having a positive outlook improves processes and outcomes* (Luthans et al., 2007; Youssef-Morgan & Luthans, 2013).

Satisfaction with some aspects of one's job increases gradually with age, and successful aging includes a workplace component (Robson et al., 2006). Why is this? Is it because people sort themselves out and end up in occupations they like? Is it they simply learn to like the occupation they are in? What other factors matter?

So how does job satisfaction evolve over young and middle adulthood? You may be pleased to learn research shows, given sufficient time, most people eventually find a job where they are reasonably happy (Hom & Kinicki, 2001). Optimistically, this indicates there is a job out there, somewhere, where you will be happy. That's good, because research grounded in positive psychology theory indicates happiness fuels success (Achor, 2010).

It's also true job satisfaction does not increase in all areas and job types with age. White-collar professionals show an increase in job satisfaction with age, whereas those in blue-collar positions generally do not, and these findings hold with both men and women (Aasland, Rosta, & Nylenna, 2010). This is also true across cultures. A study of Filipino and Taiwanese workers in the long-term healthcare industry in Taiwan showed workers with 4 or 5 years' experience had lower job satisfaction than workers with less experience, but job satisfaction among older physicians in Norway increases over time (Aasland et al., 2010; Tu, 2006).

However, the changes in the labor market in terms of lower prospects of having a long career with one organization have begun to change the notion of job satisfaction (Bidwell, 2013; Böckerman et al., 2013). Specifically, the fact that companies may eliminate jobs and workers not based on performance, but on stereotypes about older workers, for instance, makes it more difficult for employees to develop a sense of organizational commitment, thereby making the relationship between worker age and job satisfaction more complicated (Abrams, Swift, & Drury, 2016; Bayl-Smith & Griffin, 2014).

Also complicating traditional relations between job satisfaction and age is the fact that the type of job one has and the kinds of family responsibilities one has at different career stages—as well as the flexibility of work options such as telecommuting and family leave benefits to accommodate those responsibilities—influence the relationship between age and job satisfaction (Marsh & Musson, 2008). For instance, family caregiving responsibilities may collide with work demands, resulting in lower job satisfaction, especially if the employer has no flexible work options to accommodate the employee's needs (Paulson et al., 2016).

This suggests the accumulation of experience, changing context, and the stage of one's career development all influence job satisfaction over time. The general increase in job satisfaction, then, may reflect the reality of workers figuring out how to manage their lives, understanding the limited alternative options they have, or taking advantage of alternative work assignments, such as telecommuting.

Alienation and Burnout

All jobs create a certain level of stress. For most workers, such negatives are merely annoyances. But for others, extremely stressful situations on the job may result in alienation and burnout.

When workers feel what they are doing is meaningless and their efforts are devalued, or when they do not see the connection between what they do and the final product, a sense of alienation *is likely to result.* Terkel (1974) reported employees are most likely to feel alienated when they perform routine, repetitive actions. Alienation can also result from employees feeling abandoned by their employer, such as experiencing long periods without pay increases.

It is essential for companies to provide positive work environments to ensure the workforce remains stable and committed (Griffin et al., 2010). How can employers avoid alienating workers and improve organizational commitment? Research indicates that leaders who show trust and ethics are key (Bachman, 2017; Bligh, 2017), as is a perception among employees the employer deals with people fairly and impartially (Howard & Cordes, 2010). It is also helpful to involve employees in the decision-making process, create flexible work schedules, and institute employee development and enhancement programs.

Sometimes the pace and pressure of the occupation becomes more than a person can bear, resulting in burnout, *a depletion of a person's energy and motivation, the loss of occupational idealism, and the feeling that one is being exploited.* Burnout is a state of physical, emotional, and mental exhaustion that negatively affects self-esteem as a result of job stress (Shoji et al., 2016). Burnout is most common among people in the helping professions—such as police (McCarty & Skogan, 2013), teaching, social work, health care (Bermejo-Toro, Prieto-Ursúa, & Hernández, 2016; Shanafelt et al., 2016), and for those in the military (Simons et al., 2016). The tendency of organizations to keep employee numbers smaller during times of economic uncertainty adds to the workload for people on the job, increasing the risk of burnout (Bosco, di Masi, & Manuti, 2013).

First responders and people in helping professions must constantly deal with other people's complex problems, usually under time constraints. Dealing with these pressures every day, along with bureaucratic paperwork, may become too much for the worker to bear. Frustration builds, and disillusionment and exhaustion set in—burnout. Importantly, burnout negatively affects the quality of the services people are supposed to receive from the burned-out employee (Rowe & Sherlock, 2005).

Burnout has several bad effects on the brain (Michel, 2016). For instance, highly stressed workers are much less able to regulate negative emotions, resulting from weakened connections between the amygdala, anterior cingulate cortex, and prefrontal cortex (Golkar et al., 2014). Such structural changes probably underlie episodes of poorer judgment and emotional outbursts seen in highly stressed people.

We know burnout does not affect everyone in a particular profession. Why? Vallerand (2015) proposes the difference relates to people feeling different types of passion (obsessive and harmonious) toward their jobs. *A* passion *is a strong inclination toward an activity individuals like (or even love), they value (and thus find important), and where they invest time and energy* (Vallerand, 2015). Vallerand's (2015) Passion Model proposes people develop a passion toward enjoyable activities that are incorporated into identity.

High-stress jobs such as intensive care nursing often result in burnout.

alienation

Situation in which workers feel they are doing is meaningless and their efforts are devalued, or when they do not see the connection between what they do and the final product.

burnout

The depletion of a person's energy and motivation, the loss of occupational idealism, and the feeling of being exploited.

passion

A strong inclination toward an activity that individuals like (or even love), that they value (and thus find important), and in which they invest time and energy.

Vallerand's model differentiates between two kinds of passion: obsessive and harmonious. A critical aspect of obsessive passion is the internal urge to engage in the passionate activity, which makes it difficult for the person to fully disengage from thoughts about the activity, leading to conflict with other activities in the person's life (Vallerand, 2015).

In contrast, harmonious passion results when individuals do not feel compelled to engage in the enjoyable activity; rather, they freely choose to do so, and it is in harmony with other aspects of the person's life (Vallerand, 2015).

Research in France and Canada indicates the Passion Model accurately predicts employees' feelings of burnout (Vallerand, 2008; Vallerand et al., 2010). As shown in ▶ Figure 12.3, obsessive passion predicts higher levels of conflict that in turn predicts higher levels of burnout. In contrast, harmonious passion predicts higher levels of satisfaction at work, and predicts lower levels of burnout.

The best ways to lower burnout are intervention programs that focus on both the organization and the employee (Awa, Plaumann, & Walter, 2010; Bagnall et al., 2016) and foster passion (Vallerand, 2015). At the organizational level, job restructuring and employee-provided programs are important. For employees, stress-reduction techniques, lowering other people's expectations, cognitive restructuring of the work situation, and finding alternative ways to enhance personal growth and identity are most effective (e.g., Allexandre et al., 2016).

▶ **Figure 12.3**

Model of the relations among passion, satisfaction at work, conflict, and burnout. Harmonious passion predicts higher levels of satisfaction at work that predict lower levels of burnout. In contrast, obsessive passion predicts higher levels of conflict, predicting higher levels of burnout.

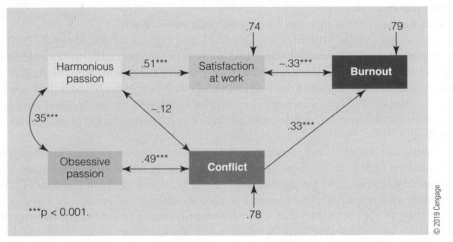

SOURCE: From "On the role of passion for work in burnout: A process model," by R. J. Vallerand, Y. Paquet, F. L. Philippe, and J. Charest, in *Journal of Personality*, vol. 78.

TEST YOURSELF 12.1

Recall

1. For most people, the main reason to work is _____.

2. Holland's theory deals with the relationship between occupation and _____.

3. _____ says that occupational selection is based in part on a person's self-efficacy regarding his or her occupation.

4. The role of a mentor is part teacher, part sponsor, part model, and part _____.

5. For many workers, job satisfaction tends to _____ in midlife.

6. Two salient aspects of job dissatisfaction are alienation and _____.

Interpret

• What is the relation between occupational development and job satisfaction? Would these relations be different in the case of a person with a good match between personality and occupation versus a person with a poor match?

• How could interventions that help people avoid alienation be made culturally sensitive?

Apply

• If you were the director of the campus career services office, what would you do to provide students with realistic and accurate information about potential careers?

• If you were a company's director of human resources, how would you design a new employee orientation program?

Check your answers to the Recall Questions at the end of the chapter.

LEARNING OBJECTIVES

- How do women's and men's occupational selection differ? How are people viewed when they enter occupations not traditional for their gender?

- What factors are related to women's occupational development?

- What factors affect ethnic minority workers' occupational experiences and occupational development?

- What types of bias and discrimination hinder the occupational development, especially of women and ethnic minority workers?

Janice, a 35-year-old African American manager at a business consulting firm, is concerned because her career is not progressing as rapidly as she hoped. Janice works hard and receives excellent performance ratings every year. She noticed there are few women in upper management positions in her company. Janice wonders whether she will ever be promoted.

Occupational choice and development are not equally available to all, as Janice is experiencing. Gender, ethnicity, and age may create barriers to achieving one's occupational goals. Men and women in similar occupations may nonetheless have different life experiences and probably received different socialization as children and adolescents that made it easier or difficult for them to set their sights on a career. Bias and discrimination also create barriers to occupational success.

Gender Differences in Occupational Selection

About 58% of all women over age 16 in the United States participate in the labor force (down from its peak of 60% in 1999), and they represent roughly 47% of the total workforce (U.S. Department of Labor Women's Bureau, 2016a). Across ethnic groups, African American women participate the most (about 59%) and Latina women the least (about 56%). Compared to other countries, women in the United States tend to be employed at a higher rate (see ▸ Figure 12.4). Still, structural barriers remain for women in the United States. Let's take a look at both traditional and nontraditional occupations for women.

What work people do has changed in many ways, not the least in terms of the gender breakdown of workers in specific jobs. A growing number of women work in occupations that have been traditionally male-dominated, such as construction and engineering. The U.S. Department of Labor (2016a) categorizes women's nontraditional occupations as those in which women constitute 25% or less of the total number of people employed; the skilled trades (electricians, plumbers, carpenters) still have among the lowest participation rates of women. Data for several occupations can be seen in ▸ Figure 12.5. Note the pay differentials between women and men; we will consider that a bit later.

Despite the efforts to counteract gender stereotyping of occupations, male-dominated occupations tend to pay more than women-dominated occupations (Price, 2016). Although the definition of *nontraditional* varies across cultures, women who choose nontraditional occupations and are successful in them are viewed negatively as compared with similarly successful men.

In patriarchal societies, both women and men gave higher "respectability" ratings to males than females in the same occupation (Sharma & Sharma, 2012). In the United States, research shows men prefer to date women who are in traditional occupations (Kapoor et al., 2010). Additionally, sexual objectification in the workplace, especially in nontraditional occupations, results in higher sexual harassment and worse work performance (Gervais et al., 2016).

Figure 12.4
Labor force participation rate by sex, race, and Hispanic ethnicity: 2015 annual averages and 2024 projections.

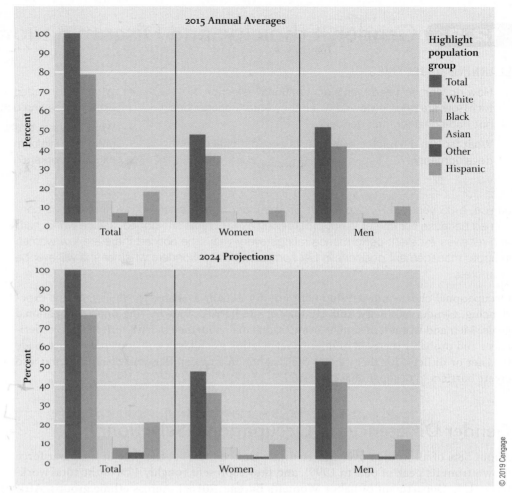

SOURCE: U.S. Department of Labor. (2016). *Latest annual data: Women of working age.* Retrieved from www.dol.gov/wb/stats/latest_annual_data.htm.

Women and Occupational Development

The characteristics and aspirations of women who entered the workforce in the 1950s and those from the baby boomers (born between 1946 and 1964), generation X (born between 1965 and 1982), and the millennials (born since 1983) are significantly different (Wegman et al., in press). The biggest difference across generations is the progressive increase in opportunities for employment choice.

In the 21st century, women entrepreneurs are starting small businesses but are disadvantaged in gaining access to capital (McLymont, 2016). As the millennial generation heads into the workforce, it will be interesting to see whether their high degree of technological sophistication and broader experience and background in entrepreneurship will provide more occupational and career options (Wegman et al., in press).

In the corporate world, unsupportive or insensitive work environments, organizational politics, and the lack of occupational development opportunities are most important for women working full-time. Greater empowerment of women is an essential element in ensuring occupational development and remaining in their jobs (Cornwall, 2016). Female professionals leave their jobs for two main reasons. First, the organizations where women work are felt to idealize and reward masculine values of working—individuality, self-sufficiency, and individual contributions—while emphasizing tangible outputs, competitiveness, and rationality. Most women prefer organizations that highly value relationships, interdependence, and collaboration.

▶ Figure 12.5

Women's nontraditional occupations and median weekly earnings, 2014 annual averages.

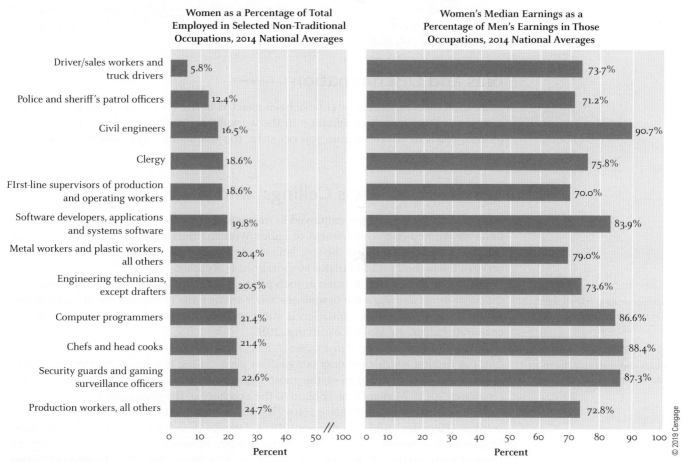

Notes:

• Nontraditional or male-dominated occupations are those in which women represent 25 percent or less of total employed. Occupations include those with a sample size of at least 50,000 people employed.

• Median weekly earnings are 2014 annual averages based on full-time wage and salary workers only. http://www.bls.gov/cps/cpsaat39.ht

SOURCE: www.dol.gov/wb/stats/Nontraditional%20Occupations.pdf.

— Second, women may feel disconnected from the workplace. By midcareer, women may conclude they must leave these unsupportive organizations in order to achieve satisfaction, growth, and development at work and rewarded for the relational skills they consider essential for success. As we see a bit later, whether women leave their careers or plateau before reaching their maximum potential level in the organization because of lack of support, discrimination, or personal choice is controversial.

Ethnicity and Occupational Development

Unfortunately, little research has been conducted from a developmental perspective related to occupational selection and development for people from ethnic minorities. Rather, most researchers focused on the limited opportunities ethnic minorities have and on the structural barriers, such as discrimination, they face.

Women do not differ significantly in terms of participation in nontraditional occupations across ethnic groups (Hegewisch & Hartman, 2014). However, African American women who choose nontraditional occupations tend to plan for more formal education than necessary to achieve their goal. This may actually make them overqualified for the jobs they get; a woman with a college degree may be working in a job that does not require that level of education.

Whether an organization is responsive to the needs of ethnic minorities makes a big difference for employees. Ethnic minority employees of a diverse organization in the several countries report more positive feelings about their workplace when they perceived their organizations as responsive and communicative in supportive and transparent ways (Boehm et al., 2014; Hofhuis, van der Rijt, & Vlug, 2016).

Bias and Discrimination

Since the 1960s, numerous laws have been enacted in the United States to prohibit various types of bias and discrimination in the workplace. Despite anti-discrimination laws, though, bias and discrimination still occur far too frequently. Let's consider some of the most common forms.

Gender Bias, Glass Ceilings, and Glass Cliffs

More than half of all people employed in management, professional, and related occupations are women (U.S. Department of Labor Women's Bureau, 2016a). However, women are still underrepresented at the top. Janice's observation in the vignette that few women serve in the highest ranks of major corporations is accurate.

gender discrimination

Denying a job to someone solely on the basis of whether the person is a man or a woman.

Why are there so few women in such positions? *The most important reason is* gender discrimination: *denying a job to someone solely on the basis of whether the person is a man or a woman.* Gender discrimination is still pervasive, and gets worse the higher up the corporate ladder one looks (LeanIn.org, 2016).

glass ceiling

The level to which a woman may rise in an organization but beyond which they may not go.

Women themselves refer to a glass ceiling, *the level they may rise within an organization but beyond which they may not go.* The glass ceiling is a major barrier for women (LeanIn.org, 2016), and one of the most important sources of loss of women leaders (Heppner, 2013). Men are largely blind to the existence of the glass ceiling.

The glass ceiling is pervasive across higher management and professional workplace settings (Heppner, 2013; LeanIn.org, 2016). Despite decades of attention to the issue, little overall progress is being made in the number of women who lead major corporations or serve on their boards of directors (Cundiff & Stockdale, 2013; LeanIn.org, 2016). The glass ceiling has also been used to account for African American men's and Asian American men's lack of advancement in their careers as opposed to European American men (Cundiff & Stockdale, 2013; Hwang, 2007). It also provides a framework for understanding limitations to women's careers in many countries around the world such as South Africa (Kiaye & Singh, 2013).

glass cliff

A situation in which a woman's leadership position in an organization is precarious.

Interestingly, a different trend emerges if one examines who is appointed to critical positions in organizations in times of crisis. Research shows that women are more likely put in leadership positions when a company is in crisis. *Consequently, women often confront a* glass cliff *where their leadership position is precarious.* Evidence shows companies are more likely to appoint a woman to their board of directors if their financial performance had been poor in the recent past; and women are more likely to be political candidates if the seat is a highly contested one (Ryan, Haslam, & Kulich, 2010; Ryan et al., 2016).

What can be done to eliminate the glass ceiling and the glass cliff? Kolb, Williams, and Frohlinger (2010) argue women can and must be assertive in getting their rightful place at the table by focusing on five key things: drilling deep into the organization so you can make informed decisions, getting critical support, getting the necessary resources, getting buy-in, and making a difference.

Much debate has erupted over the issue of women rising to the top. There is no doubt the glass ceiling and glass cliff exist. The controversy surrounds the extent women decide not to pursue or reluctance to pursue the top positions. As discussed in the Current Controversies feature, this debate is likely to rage for years.

STAN HONDA/AFP/Getty Images

Women CEOs of major corporations, such as Mary Barra at General Motors, are still few in number.

Sheryl Sandberg is unquestionably successful. She has held the most important, powerful positions in the most recognizable technology companies in the world. When she published her book *Lean In: Women, Work, and the Will to Lead* in 2013, she set off a fierce debate. Sandberg claimed there is discrimination against women in the corporate world. She also argued an important reason women do not rise to the top more often is because of their own unintentional behavior that holds them back. She claimed women do not speak up enough, need to abandon the myth of "having it all," set boundaries, get a mentor, and not to "check out of work" when thinking about starting a family.

The national debate around these issues raised many issues: Sandberg's ability to afford to pay for support may make her points irrelevant for women who do not have those resources; she was "blaming the victim"; no one ever puts men in these situations of having to choose; and so on. When her husband died unexpectedly in 2015, she reassessed some of her arguments and acknowledged her privileged position. Still, she pushed hard on the issue of gender discrimination in the workplace, and founded LeanIn.org, an organization dedicated to helping women advance in their careers and to educate all in the overt and subtle ways gender discrimination operates.

Through LeanIn.org, Sheryl has also focused on documenting the problems and highlighting best practices in stopping gender discrimination. The report *Women in the Workplace 2016* provided rich data on numerous aspects of the problem.

Sheryl Sandberg has made gender discrimination an important focus of her life. She, and many others, are convinced that limits on women's careers will never be eliminated without a focused effort on everyone's part. Can gender discrimination be eliminated? Will women eventually be welcomed into every occupation? What do *you* think?

Equal Pay for Equal Work

In addition to discrimination in hiring and promotion, women are also subject to salary discrimination. According to the National Women's Law Center (2016), 98% of all occupations show a gender-based wage gap. Overall, the U.S. Department of Labor Women's Bureau (2016b) notes that women who work full-time earn about 79% of men's median annual earnings. As you can see in ❱ Figure 12.6, the wage gap depends on ethnicity and has been narrowing in some groups since the 1980s.

Many people have argued that there are legitimate reasons for the wage gap, such as women stepping out of their careers to raise children, or their taking lower paying jobs in the first place. However, evidence of discrimination is apparent; for instance, research indicates that average earnings for individuals who undergo gender reassignment from male to female fall by about one-third (National Women's Law Center, 2016).

In the United States, the first law regarding pay equity was passed by Congress in 1963. Forty-six years later in 2009, President Obama signed the Lilly Ledbetter Fair Pay Act, showing clearly that gender-based pay inequity still exists. Nearly a decade after this law was enacted, inequity remains (Lips, 2016).

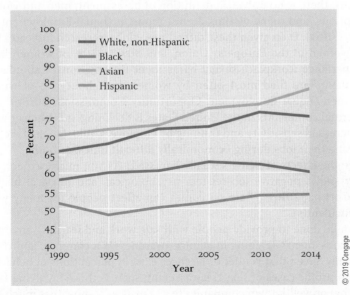

SOURCE: www.dol.gov/wb/stats/earnings_race_ethnic_percent_white_nonhisp
_mens_earn_87_14_txt.htm.

❱ **Figure 12.6**

Women's earnings by race and ethnicity as a percentage of white, non-Hispanic men's earnings, March 1987–2014.

© 2019 Cengage

Why? Consider this: Only one year out of college, a woman earns on average about $0.80 for every $1.00 a male college graduate earns. Over time, the difference gets bigger, not smaller. This is even after controlling for such important variables as occupation, hours worked, parenthood, and other factors associated with pay (Maatz & Hedgepath, 2013).

What if women choose a college major associated with high-paying jobs, such as those in science, technology, engineering, mathematics, and medicine (STEMM)? Will that help reduce the pay differential? No. Even after controlling for differences in academic field, women earn on average 11% less than men in first-year earnings after receiving their doc-toral degree (Shen, 2016). Does choosing to enter a traditionally male-dominated major will solve the problem? No. Women software developers, for example, earn only 81% of their male counterparts earn.

A woman is also significantly disadvantaged when it comes to the division of labor at home if she is married to or living with a man (Shen, 2016). Despite decades of effort in getting men to do more of the housework and child care tasks, little has changed in terms of the amount of time men actually spend on these tasks. In effect, this means women have two careers, one in the workplace and the other at home. If a college-educated woman stays at home to care for a child or parent, then her return to the workforce will be at a lower salary than it would have been otherwise.

Only through a concerted effort on the part of employers and policymakers can the gender-based pay gap be addressed. But more will be needed. Besides fairer pay rules and policies, we will also need a change in attitudes in the men who are the women's spouses and partners. They will need to step up and do an equal share of the work around the house and in child care. Because unless both aspects are addressed, the pay gap will never be closed.

Sexual Harassment

Suppose you have been working hard on a paper for a course and think you've done a good job. When you receive an "A" for the paper, you are elated. When you discuss your paper (and your excitement) with your instructor, you receive a big hug. How do you feel? What if this situation involved a major project at work and the hug came from your boss? Your coworker? What if it were a kiss on your lips instead of a hug?

Whether such behavior is acceptable, or whether it constitutes sexual harassment, depends on many situational factors, including the setting, people involved, and the relationship between them.

How many people have been sexually harassed? That's a hard question to answer for several reasons: there is no universal definition of harassment, men and women have different perceptions, and many victims do not report it (Equal Employment Opportunity Commission, 2016a). Even given these difficulties, global research indicates between 40% and 50% of women in the European Union, and 30% to 40% of women in Asia-Pacific countries experience workplace sexual harassment (International Labour Organization, 2013). Complaints are filed most often by women, but about 17% of workplace cases are filed by men (Equal Employment Opportunity Commission, 2016b). Although the number of formal complaints in the United States is declining, it is unclear whether this is because of increased sensitivity and training by employers, reluctance of victims to report for fear of losing their jobs during economically difficult times, or both.

What are the effects of being sexually harassed? As you might expect, research evidence clearly shows negative job-related, psychological, and physical health outcomes (Holland & Cortina, 2016). These outcomes can affect people for many years after the harassment incident(s).

What can be done to provide people with safe work and learning environments, free from sexual harassment? Training in gender awareness is a common approach that often works, especially given that gender differences exist in perceptions of behavior. However, even very high profile cases of sexual harassment, such as those involving famous people (e.g., Bill Cosby) or well-known companies (e.g., Fox News) show that much remains to be done to eradicate sexual harassment.

Age Discrimination

Another structural barrier to occupational development is age discrimination, *that involves denying a job or promotion to someone solely on the basis of age.* The U.S. Age Discrimination in Employment Act of 1986 protects workers over age 40. A law that brought together all of the anti-discrimination legislation in the United Kingdom, the Equality Act of 2010, includes a prohibition against age discrimination, and more European countries are protecting middle-aged and older workers (Equality and Human Rights Commission, 2016; Lahey, 2010). These laws stipulate people must be hired based on their ability, not their age and that employers cannot segregate or classify workers or otherwise denote their status on the basis of age.

Age discrimination is difficult to document, because employers can use such things as earnings history or other variable appear to be a deciding factor. Or they can attempt to get rid of older workers by using retirement incentives. Or supervisors can let their stereotypes about aging interfere with their assessment of the quality of older workers' performance. As noted by the Equal Employment Opportunity Commission (2016c), treating an older worker less favorably because of her or his age is illegal.

Employment prospects for middle-aged people around the world are lower than for their younger counterparts (Lahey, 2010; Vansteenkiste, Deschacht, & Sels, 2015). For example, age discrimination toward those over age 45 is common in Hong Kong (Cheung, Kam, & Ngan, 2011), resulting in longer periods of unemployment. Such practices may save companies money in the short run, but the loss of expertise and knowledge comes at a high price. *Indeed, an emerging model of employment is* boomerang employees, *individuals who terminate employment at one point in time but return to work in the same organization at a future time.* Boomerang employees sometimes return as employees on the company's payroll but increasingly are returning as contract workers who are not eligible for benefits, thereby meeting the company's needs for both expertise and lower costs (Shipp et al., 2014).

Age discrimination usually happens before or after interaction with professional human resources staff by other employees making the hiring decisions, and it can be covert (Lahey, 2010; Pillay, Kelly, & Tones, 2006). For example, employers can make certain types of physical or mental performance a job requirement and argue that older workers cannot meet the standard prior to an interview. Or they can attempt to get rid of older workers by using retirement incentives. Supervisors' stereotyped beliefs sometimes factor in performance evaluations for raises or promotions or in decisions about which employees are eligible for additional training (Sterns & Spokus, 2013).

Employers cannot make a decision not to hire this woman solely on the basis of her age.

age discrimination

Denying a job or a promotion to a person solely on the basis of age.

boomerang employees

Individuals who terminate employment at one point in time but return to work in the same organization at a future time.

TEST YOURSELF 12.2

Recall

1. Women who choose nontraditional occupations are viewed _____ by their peers.

2. Among the reasons women in well-paid occupations leave, _____ are most important for part-time workers.

3. Ethnic minority workers are more satisfied with and committed to organizations that are responsive and provide _____.

4. Three barriers to women's occupational development are sex discrimination, the glass ceiling, and _____.

Interpret

- What steps need to be taken to eliminate gender, ethnic, and age bias in the workplace?

Apply

- Suppose you are the CEO of a large organization and you need to make personnel reductions through layoffs. Many of your most expensive employees are over age 40. How can you accomplish this without being accused of age discrimination?

Check your answers to the Recall Questions at the end of the chapter.

LEARNING OBJECTIVES

- Why do people change occupations?
- Is worrying about potential job loss a major source of stress?
- How does job loss affect the amount of stress experienced?

Fred has 32 years of service for an automobile manufacturer making pickup trucks. Over the years, more and more assembly-line jobs have been eliminated by new technology (including robots) and the export of manufacturing jobs to other countries. Although Fred has been assured his job is safe, he isn't so sure. He worries he could be laid off at any time.

In the past, people like Fred commonly chose an occupation during young adulthood and stayed in it throughout their working years. Today, however, not many people have that option. Corporations have restructured so often employees now assume occupational changes are part of the career process. Such corporate actions mean people's conceptions of work and career are in flux and losing one's job no longer has only negative meanings (Biggs et al., in press; Haworth & Lewis, 2005).

Several factors have been identified as important in determining who will remain in an occupation and who will change. Some factors—such as whether the person likes the occupation—lead to self-initiated occupation changes.

However, other factors—such as obsolete skills and larger economic trends—may cause forced occupational changes. Continued improvement of robots has caused some auto industry workers to lose their jobs; corporations send jobs overseas to increase profits; and economic recessions usually result in large-scale layoffs and high levels of unemployment.

Retraining Workers

When you are hired into a specific job, you are selected because your employer believes you offer the best fit between the abilities you already have and those needed to perform the job. As most people can attest, though, the skills needed to perform a job usually change over time. Such changes may be based in the introduction of new technology, additional responsibilities, or promotion.

career plateauing
Situation occurring when there is a lack of challenge in the job or promotional opportunity in the organization or when a person decides not to seek advancement.

Unless a person's skills are kept up-to-date, the outcome is likely to be either job loss or a career plateau (da Costa & Oliveira, 2016; Jiang, 2016). Career plateauing *occurs when there is a lack of challenge in one's job or promotional opportunity in the organization or when a person decides not to seek advancement.* Research in Canada (Foster, Lonial, & Shastri, 2011), Asia (Lee, 2003), and Australia (Rose & Gordon, 2010) shows feeling one's career has plateaued usually results in less organizational commitment, lower job satisfaction, and a greater tendency to leave. But attitudes can remain positive if it is only the lack of challenge and not a lack of promotion opportunity responsible for the plateauing (da Costa & Oliveira, 2016; Jiang, 2016).

In cases of job loss or a career plateau, retraining may be an appropriate response. Around the world, large numbers of employees participate each year in programs and courses offered by their employer or by a college or university and aimed at improving existing skills or adding new job skills. For midcareer employees, retraining might focus on how to advance in one's occupation or how to find new career opportunities—for example, through résumé preparation and career counseling. Increasingly, such programs are offered online in order to make them easier and more convenient for people to access. For people who were involuntarily separated from their employer, severance packages may provide a way to pay for these courses.

Alternatively, mid-career individuals may choose to change fields altogether. In this case, people may head back to college and earn a credential in a completely different field. Increasingly, middle-aged adults are seeking coaches to help them navigate through the decision to change careers (Stoltz, 2016).

The retraining of midcareer and older workers highlights the need for lifelong learning as a way to stay employable (Froehlich, Beausaert, & Segers, 2016). If corporations are to meet the challenges of a global economy, it is imperative they include retraining in their employee development programs. Such programs will improve people's chances of advancement in their chosen occupations and also assist people in making successful transitions from one occupation to another.

Occupational Insecurity

Over the past few decades, changing economic realities (e.g., increased competition in a global economy), changing demographics, continued advancements in technology, and a global recession forced many people out of their jobs. Heavy manufacturing and support businesses (such as the steel, oil, and automotive industries) and farming were the hardest-hit sectors during the 1970s and 1980s. The service sector (e.g., financial services) were hard hit during the Great Recession. No one is immune any more from layoff. The Great Recession that began in 2008 put many middle- and upper-level corporate executives out of work worldwide; previously, recession-driven layoffs hit lower-level employees harder.

As a result, many people feel insecure about their jobs much of the time. Economic downturns create significant levels of stress, especially when such downturns create massive job loss (Sinclair et al., 2010). Continued shifts from in-person retail to online retail result in nearly constant retrenchment in retail jobs. The advent of driverless cars even threatens the jobs of taxi, Uber, and Lyft drivers.

Like Fred, the autoworker in the vignette, many worried workers have numerous years of dedicated service to a company. Unfortunately, people who worry about their jobs tend to have poorer physical and psychological well-being (Gonza & Burger, in press; McKee-Ryan et al., 2005). Anxiety about one's job may result in negative attitudes about one's employer or even about work in general, and in turn may result in diminished desire to be successful. Whether there is an actual basis for people's feelings of job insecurity may not matter; sometimes what people *think* is true about their work situation is more important than what is actually the case. Just the possibility of losing one's job can negatively affect physical and psychological health.

So how does the possibility of losing one's job affect employees? Mantler and colleagues (2005) examined coping strategies for comparable samples of laid-off and employed high-technology workers. They found although unemployed participants reported higher levels of stress compared with employed participants, employment uncertainty mediated the association between employment status and perceived stress. That is, people who believe their job is in jeopardy—even if it is not—show levels of stress similar to unemployed participants.

This result is due to differences in coping strategies. There are several ways people deal with stress, and two of the more common are emotion-focused coping and problem-focused coping. Some people focus on how the stressful situation makes them feel, so they cope by making themselves feel better about it. Others focus on the problem itself and do something to solve it. People who used emotional avoidance as a strategy reported higher levels of stress, particularly when they were fairly certain of the outcome. Thus, even people whose jobs aren't really in jeopardy can report high levels of stress if they tend to use emotion-focused coping strategies.

Coping with Unemployment

Losing one's job can have enormous personal impact that can last a long time (Gregor-Gonza & Burger, in press; McKee-Ryan et al., 2005; Norris, 2016). When the overall U.S. unemployment rates hit 10.6% in January 2010, millions of people could relate. Years later, the psychological impact remained (Gregor-Gonza & Burger, in press), even for people who found other jobs. When unemployment lasts and re-employment does not occur soon, unemployed people commonly experience a wide variety of negative effects (Norris, 2016) that range from a decline in immune system functioning (Cohen et al., 2007) to decreases in well-being (Gregor-Gonza & Burger, in press).

Coping with unemployment involves both financial and personal issues. As noted in the Discovering Development feature, the financial support people receive varies across states and situations. Unemployment compensation is typically much lower than one's original salary, often resulting in severe financial hardship and difficult choices for individuals. People risk losing their homes to foreclosure, for instance, as well as encountering difficulties with other everyday expenses.

In a comprehensive study of the effects of unemployment, McKee-Ryan and colleagues (2005) found several specific results from losing one's job. Unemployed workers had significantly lower mental health, life satisfaction, marital or family satisfaction, and subjective physical health (how they perceive their health to be) than their employed counterparts. With reemployment, these negative effects disappear. ▶ Figure 12.7 shows physical and psychological health following job displacement is influenced by several factors (McKee-Ryan et al., 2005).

The effects of job loss vary with age, gender, and education (Norris, 2016). In the United States, middle-aged men are more vulnerable to negative effects than older or younger men—largely because they have greater financial responsibilities than the other two groups and they derive more of their identity from work—but women report more negative effects over time (Bambra, 2010; Norris, 2016). Research in Spain indicates gender differences in responding to job loss are complexly related to family responsibilities and social class (Artazcoz et al., 2004). Specifically, to the extent work is viewed as your

Real People   The Politics of Unemployment

Millions of workers in the U.S. struggle daily with the cold reality of employment uncertainty, either because they have already lost their jobs or are worried that they are about to lose them. Perhaps you, or someone you know, is in this situation. As noted in the text, there are many reasons for this, with the most important ones being education (e.g., the need for increased technical skills) and technology (e.g., human jobs replaced by robots).

Acknowledgment of the anxiety and other emotions felt by these workers as well as how to bring them back into the labor force was a central issue in the presidential election of 2016. Hillary Clinton emphasized the need for better access to education and the need to shift jobs from traditional manufacturing and extraction industries (e.g., coal mining) to more technology-focused opportunities. Donald Trump argued that he could and would restore the traditional opportunities for these displaced workers.

In the aftermath of Donald Trump's victory, analysts (e.g., Kolko, 2016) pointed out that Trump did best in those areas of the country where the economy was in the worst shape and jobs were most in jeopardy in the future. Many union members, who traditionally had voted for Democratic candidates including Barack Obama, backed Trump because of his message. First-person accounts, such as in J. D. Vance's *Hillbilly Elegy* (2016), provide pictures of people whose understanding of the American Dream has been completely disrupted.

In areas of the United States with high unemployment and underemployment, one of the most visible and deadly problems has been a rapid increase in opioid and heroin addiction and overdoses. This, along with other health, personal, and mental effects of the actual or feared loss of one's job has brought issues once associated with urban areas into the suburbs and rural parts of the country.

Displaced workers can feel forgotten and can become a potent political force.

What to do about the human cost of continuing economic modernization will be one of the most important issues facing the United States and other countries the rest of the 21st century. The solutions are neither obvious nor easy. Without them, though, the human cost will continue to mount.

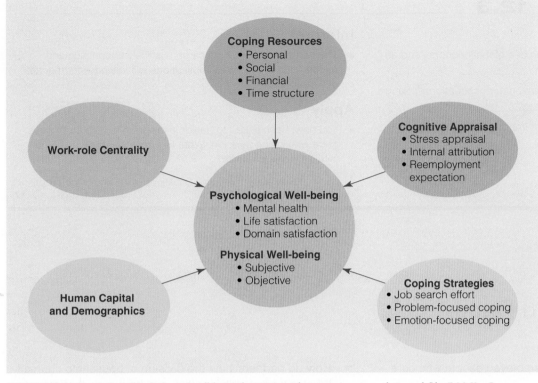

▶ **Figure 12.7**
Psychological and physical well-being after losing one's job are affected by many variables.

SOURCE: From "Psychological and physical well-being during unemployment: A meta-analytic study," by F. McKee-Ryan, Z. Song, C. R. Wanberg, and A. J. Kinicki, in *Journal of Applied Psychology*, vol. 90.

expected contribution to the family, losing one's job has a more substantial negative effect. Because this tends to be more the case for men than for women, it helps explain the gender differences. The higher one's education levels, the less stress one typically feels immediately after losing a job, probably because higher education level usually result in faster re-employment (Mandemakers & Monden, 2013).

Because unemployment rates are substantially higher for African Americans and Latinos than for European Americans (Bureau of Labor Statistics, 2016a), the effects of unemployment are experienced by a greater proportion of people in these groups. Economic consequences of unemployment are often especially difficult. Compared to European Americans, it usually takes minority workers significantly longer to find another job.

How long you are unemployed also affects how people react. People who are unemployed for at least a year perceive their mental health significantly more negatively than either employed people or those who have removed themselves from the labor force (e.g., have stopped looking for work). For example, suicide risk increases the longer unemployment lasts (Gunnell & Chang, 2016) Those who lost their jobs involuntarily feel a loss of control over their "work" environment and feel less demand placed on them. Importantly, a reasonable amount of "demand" is critical to maintaining good health, whereas too little demand lowers health.

Research also offers some advice for adults who are trying to manage occupational transitions (Ebberwein, 2001):

- Approach job loss with a healthy sense of urgency.
- Consider your next career move and what you must do to achieve it, even if there are no prospects for it in sight.
- Acknowledge and react to change as soon as it is evident.
- Be cautious of stopgap employment.
- Identify a realistic goal and then list the steps you must take to achieve it.

Additionally, the U.S. Department of Labor offers tips for job seekers, as do online services such as LinkedIn that also provides networking groups. These steps may not guarantee you will find a new job quickly, but they will help create a better sense that you are in control.

Recall

1. One response to the pressures of a global economy and an aging workforce is to provide _____.

2. Two factors that may cause involuntary occupational change are economic trends and _____.

3. Fear of job loss is often a more important determinant of stress than is _____.

4. The age group that is most at risk for negative effects of job loss is _____.

Interpret

- The trend toward multiple careers is likely to continue and become the norm. What implications will this have for theories of career development?

Apply

- You have been asked to design a program to help employees cope with losing their job. What key components would you include in this program?

Check your answers to the Recall Questions at the end of the chapter.

LEARNING OBJECTIVES

- What are the issues faced by employed people who care for dependents?

- How do partners view the division of household chores? What is work–family conflict, and how does it affect couples' lives?

Jennifer, a 38-year-old sales clerk at a department store, feels her husband, Mustafa, doesn't do his share of the housework or child care. Mustafa says men don't do housework and he's really tired when he comes home from work. Jennifer thinks this isn't fair, especially because she works as many hours as her husband.

One of the most difficult challenges facing adults like Jennifer is trying to balance the demands of occupation with the demands of family. Over the past few decades, the rapid increase in the number of families where both parents are employed has fundamentally changed how we view the relationship between work and family. This can even mean taking a young child to work as a way to deal with the pushes and pulls of being an employed parent. In roughly half of married-couple families, both spouses are employed (Bureau of Labor Statistics, 2016b). Why? Families need the dual income to pay their bills and maintain a moderate standard of living, especially given the relatively flat incomes since the Great Recession.

We will see dual-earner couples with children experience both benefits and disadvantages. The stresses of living in this arrangement are substantial, and gender differences are clear—especially in the division of household chores.

The Dependent Care Dilemma

Many employed adults must also provide care for dependent children or parents. Deciding how to divide the chores is a major source of stress, as we will see.

Employed Caregivers

Many mothers have no option but to return to work after the birth of a child. In fact, about 64% of mothers with children under the age of 6 years, and roughly 75% of those with children between 6 and 17-years old are in the labor force (Bureau of Labor Statistics, 2016c).

Despite high participation rates, mothers grapple with the decision of whether they want to return to work. Surveys of mothers with preschool children reveal the motivation for returning to work tends to be related to financial need and how attached mothers are to their work. The amount of leave time a woman has matters; the passage of the Family and Medical Leave Act (FMLA) in 1993 entitled workers to take unpaid time off to care for their dependents with the right to return to their jobs. (It should be noted that the United States is the only developed country in the world that does not have a national mandatory paid family leave benefit.)

FMLA resulted in an increase in the number of women who returned to work at least part-time (Schott, 2010). Evidence from the few states with paid family leave show similar trends; for instance, mothers in California who take paid leave extend their time off roughly five weeks longer, and show more work hours during the second year of the child's life (Baum & Ruhm, 2016).

A concern for many women is whether stepping out of their occupations following childbirth will negatively affect their career paths. Indeed, evidence clearly indicates it does (Evertsson, Grunow, & Aisenbrey 2016; LeanIn.org, 2016). Women in the United States are punished, even for short leaves. In women-friendly countries such as Sweden, long leaves typically result in a negative effect on upward career movement, but with shorter leaves in Sweden and Germany no negative effects are observed. These universally negative impacts in the U.S. need to be taken into account as more states consider implementing paid family leave programs.

Often overlooked is the increasing number of workers who must also care for an aging parent or partner. As we saw in Chapter 11, providing this type of care takes a high toll through stress and has a generally negative impact on one's career.

Whether assistance is needed for one's children or parents, key factors in selecting an appropriate care site are quality of care, price, and hours of availability (Helpguide.org, 2016; National Association for the Education of Young Children, 2016). Depending on one's economic situation, it may not be possible to find affordable and quality care available when needed. In such cases, there may be no option but to drop out of the workforce or enlist the help of friends and family.

Dependent Care and Effects on Workers

Being responsible for dependent care has significant negative effects on caregivers. Whether responsible for the care of an older parent or a child, women and men report negative effects on their work, higher levels of stress, and problems with coping (Neal & Hammer, 2007). Roxburgh (2002) introduced the notion that parents of families dealing with time pressures feel much more stress; indeed, subsequent research clearly shows not only are stress levels higher, but "fast-forward families" also often deal with negative impacts on career advancement and physical and mental health consequences of this life style (Ochs & Kremer-Sadlik, 2013). Unsurprisingly, women's careers are usually affected more negatively than men's.

How can these negative effects be lessened? When women's partners provide good support and women have average or high control over their jobs, employed mothers are significantly less distressed than employed nonmothers or mothers without support (Cram, Alkadry, & Tower, 2016). One of the most important factors in this outcome is the realization that it is impossible to "have it all" for either mothers or fathers (Cram et al., 2016; LeanIn.org, 2016).

Dependent Care and Employer Responses

Employed parents with small children or dependent spouses/partners or parents are confronted with the difficult prospect of leaving them in the care of others. This is especially problematic when the usual care arrangement is unavailable, such as due to weather-related closures of the care facility. *A growing need in the workplace is for* backup care, *that provides emergency care for dependent children or adults so*

backup care

Emergency care for dependent children or adults so the employee does not need to lose a day of work.

Employers who provide day care and after-school centers on-site have more satisfied employees.

the employee does not need to lose a day of work. Does providing a workplace care center or backup care make a difference in terms of an employee's feelings about work, absenteeism, and productivity?

There is no simple answer. Making a child care center available to employees does tend to reduce employee stress, but does not necessarily reduce parents' work–family conflict or their absenteeism (Hipp, Morrissey, & Warner, 2017). A "family-friendly" company must also pay attention to the attitudes of their employees and make sure the company provides broad-based support (Aryee et al., 2013; Hill et al., 2016). The keys are how supervisors act and the number and type of benefits the company provides. Cross-cultural research in Korea confirms having a family-friendly supervisor matters (Aryee et al., 2013). The most important single thing a company can do is allow the employee to leave work without penalty to tend to family needs (Lawton & Tulkin, 2010).

Research also indicates there may not be differences for either mothers or their infants between work-based and nonwork-based child-care centers in terms of the mothers' ease in transitioning back to work or the infants' ability to settle into day care (Hill et al., 2016; Hipp et al., 2016; Skouteris et al., 2007).

It will be interesting to watch how these issues— especially flexible schedules—play out in the United States, where such practices are not yet common. A global study of parental leave showed the more generous parental leave policies are, the lower the infant mortality rates, clearly indicating parental leave policies are a good thing (Ferrarini & Norström, 2010).

Juggling Multiple Roles

When both members of a heterosexual couple with dependents are employed, who cleans the house, cooks the meals, and takes care of the children when they are ill? This question goes to the heart of the core dilemma of modern, dual-earner couples: How are household chores divided? How are work and family role conflicts handled?

Dividing Household Chores

Despite much media attention and claims of increased sharing in the duties, women still perform the lion's share of housework, regardless of employment status. As shown in ❱ Figure 12.8, this is true globally (OECD, 2016). This unequal division of labor causes the most arguments and the most unhappiness for dual-earner couples. This is the case with Jennifer and Mustafa, the couple in the vignette; Jennifer does most of the housework.

The additional burden women carry with respect to household chores, including child rearing, is still reflected in millennials, despite their endorsement of more gender-equal views on the matter. It appears that deeply held cultural beliefs about gender-based divisions of labor are difficult to change. There are indications, though, that change may be happening, slowly. The gap between women's and men's time spent on household chores and child rearing is narrowing.

Ethnic differences in the division of household labor are also apparent. In Mexican American families with husbands born in Mexico, men help more when family income is lower and their wives contribute a proportionately higher share of the household income (Pinto & Coltrane, 2009). Comparisons of Latino, African American, and European American men consistently show European American men help with the chores less than Latino or African American men (Omori & Smith, 2009).

Work–Family Conflict

work–family conflict
The feeling of being pulled in multiple directions by incompatible demands from job and family.

When people have both occupations and children, they must figure out how to balance the demands of each. *These competing demands cause* work–family conflict, *the feeling of being pulled in multiple directions by incompatible demands from one's job and one's family.*

Time spent in unpaid work and leisure (minutes per day).

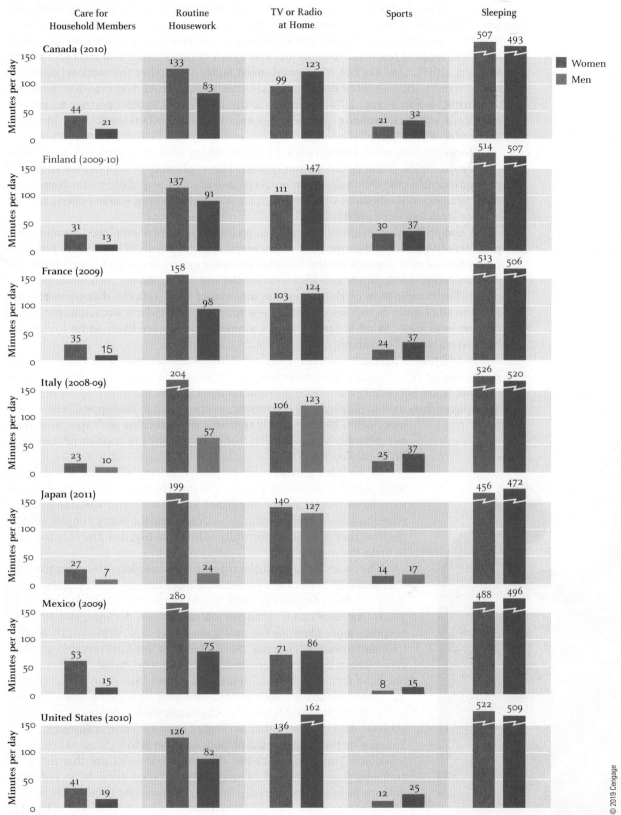

SOURCE: OECD. (2016). Balancing paid work, unpaid work and leisure. Retrieved from www.oecd.org/gender/data/balancingpaidworkunpaidworkandleisure.htm.

© 2019 Cengage

Dual-earner couples must find a balance between their occupational and family roles. Many people believe work and family roles influence each other: When things go badly at work, the family suffers, and when there are troubles at home, work suffers. That's true, but the influence is not the same in each direction (Andreassi, 2011). Whether work influences family or vice versa is a complex function of personality, coping skills, support resources, type of job, and a host of other issues that interact (Repetti & Wang, 2017). One key but often overlooked factor is whether the work schedules of both partners allow them to coordinate activities such as child care (van Klaveren, van den Brink, & van Praag, 2013). Another is the ability of a spouse/partner to provide emotional and social support for the other spouse/partner when work stress increases (Repetti & Wang, 2017).

Understanding work–family conflict requires taking a life-stage approach to the issue (Blanchard-Fields, Baldi, & Constantin, 2004). The availability of support for employed parents that takes the child's developmental age into account (e.g., day care for young children, flexible work schedules when children are older) goes a long way to helping parents balance work and family obligations.

A comprehensive review of the research on the experience of employed mothers supports this conclusion (Edwards, 2012). How juggling the demands of housework and child care affect women depends on the complex interplay among the age of the children, the point in career development and advancement the woman is, and her own developmental phase. The combination of challenges that any one of these reflects changes over time. Because all of these factors are dynamic, how they help or hinder a woman in her career changes over time. What is certain is that women's careers are likely to be irreparably harmed without it (LeanIn.org, 2016).

In addition to having impacts on each individual, dual-earner couples often have difficulty finding time for each other, especially if both work long hours. The amount of time together is not necessarily the most important issue; as long as the time is spent in shared activities such as eating, playing, and conversing, couples tend to be happy (Ochs & Kremer-Sadlik, 2013). Actively soliciting support from one's spouse or partner generally brings results, that in turn results in happier relationships (Wang & Repetti, 2016)

When both partners are employed, getting all of the schedules to work together smoothly can be a major challenge. However, ensuring joint family activities are important for creating and sustaining strong relations among family members. Unfortunately, many couples find by the time they have an opportunity to be alone together, they are too tired to make the most of it.

The issues faced by dual-earner couples are global: burnout from the dual demands of work and parenting is more likely to affect women across many cultures (Aryee et al, 2013; van Klaveren et al., 2013; Spector et al., 2005). Japanese career women's job satisfaction declines, and turnover becomes more likely, to the extent they have high work–family conflict (Honda-Howard & Homma, 2001). Research in China revealed a significant relation between overcommitment and work-family conflict on the one hand with symptoms of depression on the other (Kan & Yu, 2016).

The work-family conflicts described here are arguably worse for couples in the United States because Americans work more hours with fewer vacation days than any other developed country (Frase & Gornick, 2013). You may be thinking that the obvious solution is to legislate shorter work schedules. Surprisingly, it's not that simple. It turns out that in the 32 countries Ruppanner and Maume (2016) studied, there is no reduction in work-to-family interference. In fact, the opposite occurs—there is an *increase* in such interference when work hours are reduced. Why? The most likely answer is that reduced work hours results in higher expectations of better work-family balance, so people get more sensitive to even little disruptions, thereby increasing feelings of unhappiness.

Dual-earner couples must learn how to grapple with work–family conflict in balancing job and family demands.

Purestock/Getty Images

So what is a couple to do? For one thing, they can work together to help mitigate the stress. Most important, they can negotiate schedules around work commitments throughout their careers, taking other factors such as child care and additional time demands into account (van Wanrooy, 2013). These negotiations should include discussion of such joint activities as meals and other family activities, too (Ochs and Kremer-Sadlik, 2013). In short, communicate about all of the demands and come to an understanding and compromise that provides an optimal solution for all concerned.

TEST YOURSELF 12.4

Recall

1. Parents report lower work–family conflict and have lower absenteeism when supervisors are sympathetic and supportive regarding _____.
2. Men are satisfied with an equitable division of labor based on _____, whereas women are satisfied _____.

Interpret

- What can organizations do to help ease work–family conflict?

Apply

- Suppose you are the vice president for human resources and you are thinking about creating a way to help employees who face dependent care issues. What factors will you need to consider before implanting a plan?

Check your answers to the Recall Questions at the end of the chapter.

12.5 Taking Time to Relax: Leisure Activities

LEARNING OBJECTIVES

- What activities are leisure activities? How do people choose among them?
- What changes in leisure activities occur with age?
- What do people derive from leisure activities?

Claude is a 55-year-old electrician who has enjoyed outdoor activities his whole life. From the time he was a boy he fished the trout rivers and snow-skied in the mountains of Montana. Although he doesn't ski double black diamond runs any more, Claude still enjoys both sports every chance he gets.

Adults do not work every waking moment of their lives. As each of us knows, we need to disconnect from our smartphones, relax, and engage in leisure activities. Intuitively, leisure consists of activities not associated with work. Leisure *is discretionary activity that includes simple relaxation, activities for enjoyment, and creative pursuits.* Simply finding the time to fit leisure into an already busy schedule can be challenging. For too many people, leisure just becomes another scheduled component in our overall time management problem (Corbett & Hilty, 2006).

leisure

A discretionary activity that includes simple relaxation, activities for enjoyment, and creative pursuits.

Types of Leisure Activities

Leisure can include virtually any activity. To organize the options, researchers classified leisure activities into several categories. Jopp and Hertzog (2010) developed an empirically based set of categories that includes a wide variety of activities: physical (e.g., lifting weights, backpacking, jogging), crafts (e.g., woodworking, household repairs), games (e.g., board/online games, puzzles, card games), watching TV, social-private (e.g., going out with a friend, visiting relatives, going out to dinner), social-public (e.g., attending a club meeting, volunteering), religious (e.g., attending a religious service, praying), travel (e.g., travel

Participating in leisure activities improves one's well-being.

abroad, travel out of town), experiential (e.g., collect stamps, read for leisure, gardening, knitting), developmental (e.g., read as part of a job, study a foreign language, attend public lecture), and technology use (e.g., photography, use computer software, play an instrument).

More complete measures of leisure activities not only provide better understanding of how adults spend their time, but can help in clinical settings. Declines in the frequency of leisure activities is associated with depression (Schwerdtfeger & Friedrich-Mei, 2009), with lower well-being (Paggi, Jopp, & Hertzog, 2016), and with a later diagnosis of dementia (Hertzog et al., 2009). Monitoring changes in leisure activity levels during and after intervention programs can provide better outcomes assessments.

Given the wide range of options, how do people pick their leisure activities? Apparently, each of us has a leisure repertoire, a personal library of intrinsically motivated activities we do regularly and we take with us into retirement (Nimrod, 2007a, b). The activities in our repertoire are determined by two things: perceived competence (how good we think we are at the activity compared to other people our age) and psychological comfort (how well we meet our personal goals for performance). As you might expect, men and women differ in their views of leisure, as do people in different ethnic and age groups (van der Pas & Koopman-Boyden, 2010).

Personality factors are related to one's choice of leisure activities (Gaudron & Vautier, 2007), and it is possible to construct interest profiles that map individuals to specific types of leisure activities, and to each other (Leuty, Hansen, & Speaks, 2016). Other factors are important as well: income, health, abilities, transportation, education, and social characteristics. Some leisure activities, such as downhill skiing, are relatively expensive and require transportation and reasonably good health and physical coordination for maximum enjoyment. In contrast, reading requires minimal finances (if one uses a public library or other free sources) and is far less physically demanding.

The use of computer technology in leisure activities has increased dramatically. Most usage involves e-mail, Facebook, Twitter, or other social networking tools for such activities as keeping in touch with family and friends, pursuing hobbies, and lifelong learning. Multi-participant video streaming and multiplayer interactive computer gaming have also increased among adult players. All of these online activities provide opportunities to create virtual friendship networks that provide the same types of support as traditional face-to-face networks.

Developmental Changes in Leisure

Cross-sectional studies report age differences in leisure activities. Emerging adults participate in a greater range of activities than middle-aged adults. Furthermore, emerging adults prefer intense leisure activities that provide a "rush," such as rock climbing, whitewater kayaking, and hang gliding. In contrast, middle-aged adults focus more on home-based and family-oriented activities. In later middle age, they spend less of their leisure time in strenuous physical activities and more in sedentary activities such as reading and watching television and in moderately strenuous activities such as tennis and hiking (van der Pas & Koopman-Boyden, 2010).

Longitudinal studies of changes in individuals' leisure activities over time show considerable stability in leisure interests over reasonably long periods. Specifically, studies in the United States, Finland, Great Britain, and Japan show that level of activity in young adulthood predicts activity level later in life, and leisure physical activity in emerging adulthood bodes well for health later in life (Hillsdon et al., 2005; Lahti et al., 2016).

Claude, the 55-year-old in the vignette who likes to fish and ski, is a good example of this overall trend. As Claude demonstrates, frequent participation in particular leisure activities earlier in life tends to continue into adulthood. Similar findings hold for the pre- and postretirement years. Apparently, one's preferences for certain types of leisure activities are established early in life; they tend to change over the life span primarily in terms of how physically intense they are. Explore these findings in more detail in the Spotlight On Research feature.

Spotlight   On Research

Long-Term Effects of Leisure Activities

Who were the investigators and what was the aim of the study? It is well established that physical activity is related to better health at all ages in adulthood. However, much of the existing research has focused on more formal exercise programs, with much less attention paid to leisure forms of activity, and whether leisure time physical activity during emerging adulthood is related to subsequent health and well-being in midlife. To answer these questions, Jouni Lahti and colleagues (2016) followed adults in Finland, Great Britain, and Japan.

How did the investigators measure the topic of interest? The investigators used the Short Form-36 health questionnaire to assess physical and mental health. The eight subscales of the SF-36 include: physical functioning, role limitations due to physical problems, bodily pain, general health perceptions, mental health, role limitations due to

emotional problems, social functioning and vitality. Scores can range from 0 to 100. Low scores imply poor health functioning, whereas high scores imply good health functioning. The SF-36 has very good reliability and validity.

Who were the participants in the study? Participants in the study were prospective employee cohorts originally recruited for the Finnish HHS study (2000–2002 and 2007, N = 5958), British WHII I study (1997–1999 and 2003–2004, N = 4142) and Japanese Civil Servants Study (JACS) (1998–1999 and 2003, N = 1768). Across the three study samples, participants ranged in age from 20 to 60.

What was the design of the study? The research used a longitudinal design. As noted in Chapter 1, the strength of longitudinal designs is being able to measure a behavior over time in the same individual; the confound is the age of the person at the time of measurement.

Were there ethical concerns with the study? All participants were informed of the

nature of the larger study and had given their consent to participate.

What were the results? Leisure physical activity was associated with better subsequent physical health functioning in all three cohorts. However, results varied somewhat across country and gender. Differences were the clearest among Finnish women (inactive: 46.0, active vigorous: 49.5) and men (inactive: 47.8, active vigorous: 51.1) and British women (inactive: 47.3, active vigorous: 50.4). For mental health functioning, the differences were generally smaller and not clearly related to the intensity of physical activity.

What did the investigators conclude? Lahti and colleagues concluded that vigorous physical activity was associated with better subsequent physical health functioning in all three cohorts, although with some differences in magnitude across countries. For mental health functioning, the intensity of physical activity was less important. Promoting leisure time physical activity may prove useful for the maintenance of health functioning among midlife employees.

Consequences of Leisure Activities

What do people gain from participating in leisure activities? Researchers have long known involvement in leisure activities is related to well-being (Paggi et al., 2016; Warr, Butcher, & Robertson, 2004). This relation holds in other countries, such as China, as well (Dai, Zhang, & Li, 2013). Research shows participating in leisure activities helps promote better mental health (e.g., Lahti et al., 2016). This is especially true for spouses who use family-based leisure as a means to cope during their spouse/partner's military deployment (Werner & Shannon, 2013), and buffers the effects of stress and negative life events. It even helps lower the risk of mortality (Talbot et al., 2007).

Studies show leisure activities provide an excellent forum for the interaction of the biopsychosocial forces discussed in Chapter 1 (Cheng & Pegg, 2016; Kleiber, 2013). Leisure activities are a good way to deal with stress, which—as we have seen in Chapter 4—has significant biological effects. This is especially true for unforeseen negative events, such as cancer (Chun et al., 2016). Psychologically, leisure activities have been well documented as one of the primary coping mechanisms people use, such as providing a sense of purpose in life (Chun et al., 2016; Patry, Blanchard, & Mask, 2007).

How people cope by using leisure varies across cultures depending on the various types of activities that are permissible and available. Likewise, leisure activities vary across social class; basketball is one activity that cuts across class because it is inexpensive, whereas downhill scuba diving is more associated with people who can afford to travel to diving resorts and pay the fees.

How do leisure activities provide protection against stress? Kleiber and colleagues (2002; Kleiber, 2013) offer four ways leisure activities serve as a buffer against negative life events:

- Leisure activities distract us from negative life events.
- Leisure activities generate optimism about the future because they are pleasant.
- Leisure activities connect us to our personal past by allowing us to participate in the same activities over much of our lives.
- Leisure activities can be used as vehicles for personal transformation.

Whether the negative life events we experience are personal, such as the loss of a loved one, or societal, such as a terrorist attack, leisure activities are a common and effective way to deal with them. They truly represent the confluence of biopsychosocial forces and are effective at any point in the life cycle.

Participating with others in leisure activities may also strengthen feelings of attachment to one's partner, friends, and family (Carnelley & Ruscher, 2000). Adults use leisure as a way to explore interpersonal relationships or to seek social approval. In fact, research indicates marital satisfaction is linked with leisure time; marital satisfaction is even helped when couples spend some leisure time with others in addition to spending it just as a couple (Zabriskie & Kay, 2013). But there's no doubt couples who play together are happier (Johnson, Zabriskie, & Hill, 2006).

There is a second sense of attachment that can develop as a result of leisure activities: place attachment. Place attachment occurs when people derive a deep sense of personal satisfaction and identity from a particular place (Di Masso, Dixon, & Hernández, 2017). Place attachment is an active process, bringing the individual a sense of belonging that might not be experienced elsewhere. As a result, place attachment generally drives people to return to the location over and over, and the meaning of being there continues to deepen over time.

What if leisure activities are pursued seriously? In some cases, people create leisure–family conflict by engaging in leisure activities to extremes (Heo et al., 2010). When things get serious, problems may occur. Only when there is support from others for such extreme involvement are problems avoided. For instance, professional quilters felt much more valued when family members were supportive (Stalp & Conti, 2011). As in most things, moderation in leisure activities is probably best, unless you know you have excellent support.

You have probably heard the saying "no vacation goes unpunished." It appears to be true, and the trouble is not just afterward. Research shows pre-vacation workload is associated with lower health and well-being for both men and women, and pre-vacation homeload (extra work that needs to be done at home) has the same negative effect for women (Nawijn, de Bloom, & Geurts, 2013).

Once on vacation, it matters what you do. If you detach from work, enjoy the activities during vacation, and engage in conversation with your partner, then the vacation can improve health and well-being, even after you return home (de Bloom, Geurts, & Kompier, 2012). Indeed, some have suggested that vacations and tourism be prescribed like a medication due to its positive benefits. However, workers report high post-vacation workloads eliminate most of the positive effects of a vacation within about a week (de Bloom et al., 2010).

★ One frequently overlooked outcome of leisure activity is social acceptance. For persons with disabilities, this is a particularly important consideration (Choi, Johnson, & Kriewitz, 2013). There is a positive connection between frequency of leisure activities and positive identity, social acceptance, friendship development, and acceptance of differences. These findings highlight the importance of designing inclusive leisure activity programs.

Recall

1. Activities in which people engage for relaxation or, enjoyment or as creative pursuits are considered _____ activities.

2. Compared with younger adults, middle-aged adults prefer leisure activities that are more family- and home-centered and _____.

3. Being involved in leisure activities is related to _____.

Interpret

- How are choices of leisure activities related to physical, cognitive, and social development?

Apply

- Workers in the United States tend to take fewer vacation days compared with workers in European countries. What might the consequences of this be for U.S. workers?

Check your answers to the Recall Questions at the end of the chapter.

SUMMARY

12.1 Occupational Selection and Development

How do people view work?.

- Although most people work for money, other reasons are highly variable.

- Meaning-mission fit can set the tone for an organization and help people derive meaning.

How do people choose their occupations?

- Holland's theory is based on the idea people choose occupations to optimize the fit between their individual traits and their occupational interests. Six personality types, representing different combinations of these, have been identified. Support for these types has been found in several studies.

- Social cognitive career theory emphasizes how people choose careers is also influenced by what they think they can do and how well they can do it, as well as how motivated they are to pursue a career.

- Super's developmental view of occupations is based on self-concept and adaptation to an occupational role. Super describes five stages in adulthood: implementation, establishment, maintenance, deceleration, and retirement.

What factors influence occupational development?

- Reality shock is the realization one's expectations about an occupation are different from what one actually experiences. Reality shock is common among young workers.

- Few differences exist across generations in terms of their occupational expectations.

- A mentor or developmental coach is a co-worker who teaches a new employee the unwritten rules and fosters occupational development. Mentor–protégé relationships, like other relationships, develop through stages over time.

What is the relationship between job satisfaction and age?

- Older workers report higher job satisfaction than younger workers, but this may be partly due to self-selection; unhappy workers may quit. Other reasons include intrinsic satisfaction, good fit, lower importance of work, finding nonwork diversions, and life-cycle factors.

- Alienation and burnout are important considerations in understanding job satisfaction. Both involve significant stress for workers.

- Vallerand's Passion Model proposes people develop a passion toward enjoyable activities that are incorporated into identity. Obsessive passion happens when people experience an uncontrollable urge to engage in the activity; harmonious passion results when individuals freely accept the activity as important for them without any contingencies attached to it.

12.2 Gender, Ethnicity, and Discrimination Issues

How do women's and men's occupational selection differ? How are people viewed when they enter occupations that are not traditional for their gender?

- Boys and girls are socialized differently for work, and their occupational choices are affected as a result. Women choose nontraditional occupations for many reasons, including expectations and personal feelings. Women in such occupations are still viewed more negatively than men in the same occupations.

What factors are related to women's occupational development?

- Women leave well-paid occupations for many reasons, including family obligations and workplace environment. Women who continue to work full-time have adequate child care and look for ways to further their occupational development.

- The glass ceiling, that limits women's occupational attainment, and the glass cliff, that puts women leaders in a precarious position, affect how often women achieve top executive positions and how successful women leaders are.

What factors affect ethnic minority workers' occupational experiences and occupational development?

- Vocational identity and vocational goals vary in different ethnic groups. Whether an organization is sensitive to ethnicity issues is a strong predictor of satisfaction among ethnic minority employees.

What types of bias and discrimination hinder the occupational development, especially of women and ethnic minority workers?

- Gender bias remains the chief barrier to women's occupational development. In many cases, this operates as a glass ceiling. Pay inequity is also a problem; women are often paid less than what men earn in similar jobs.

- Sexual harassment is a problem in the workplace. Current criteria for judging harassment are based on the "reasonable person" standard.

- Denying employment to anyone over 40 because of age is age discrimination and is illegal.

12.3 Occupational Transitions

Why do people change occupations?

- Important reasons people change occupations include personality, obsolescence, and economic trends. Occupational change can be voluntary or involuntary.

- To adapt to the effects of a global economy and an aging workforce, many corporations are providing retraining opportunities for workers. Retraining is especially important in cases of outdated skills and career plateauing.

Is worrying about potential job loss a major source of stress?

- Occupational insecurity is a growing problem. Fear that one may lose one's job is a better predictor of anxiety than the actual likelihood of job loss.

How does job loss affect the amount of stress experienced?

- Job loss is a traumatic event that can affect every aspect of a person's life. The degree of financial distress and the extent of attachment to the job are the best predictors of distress. Job loss and job insecurity an influence political outcomes through people's anxieties about their future.

12.4 Work and Family

What are the issues faced by employed people who care for dependents?

- Caring for children or aging parents creates dilemmas for workers. Whether a woman returns to work after having a child depends largely on how attached she is to her work. Simply providing child care on-site does not always result in higher job satisfaction. A more important factor is the degree that supervisors are sympathetic.

How do partners view the division of household chores? What is work–family conflict? How does it affect couples' lives?

- Although women have reduced the amount of time they spend on household tasks over the past two decades, they still do most of the work. European American men are less likely than either African American or Latino American men to help with traditionally female household tasks.

- Flexible work schedules and the number of children are important factors in role conflict. Recent evidence shows work stress has a much greater impact on family life than family stress has on work performance. Some women pay a high personal price for having careers.

12.5 Taking Time to Relax: Leisure Activities

What activities are leisure activities?

- Leisure activities can be simple relaxation, activities for enjoyment, or creative pursuits. Views of leisure activities varies by gender, ethnicity, and age.

What changes in leisure activities occur with age?

- As people grow older, they tend to engage in leisure activities that are less strenuous and more family-oriented. Leisure preferences in adulthood reflect those earlier in life.

What do people derive from leisure activities?

- Leisure activities enhance well-being and can benefit all aspects of people's lives.

Test Yourself: Recall Answers

12.1 1. to earn a living **2.** personality **3.** Social Cognitive Career Theory or SCCT **4.** counselor **5.** increase **6.** burnout **12.2 1.** negatively **2.** family obligations **3.** positive work environments **4.** pay discrimination **12.3 1.** worker retraining **2.** obsolete skills **3.** actual likelihood of job loss **4.** middle-aged adults **12.4 1.** family issues and child care **2.** the number of hours spent; when men perform traditionally female chores **12.5 1.** leisure **2.** less physically intense **3.** well-being

Key Terms

meaning-mission fit (389)

career construction theory (389)

social cognitive career theory (SCCT) (390)

vocational maturity (390)

reality shock (393)

mentor (393)

developmental coach (393)

job satisfaction (394)

psychological capital theory (394)

alienation (395)

burnout (395)

passion (395)

gender discrimination (400)

glass ceiling (400)

glass cliff (400)

age discrimination (403)

boomerang employee (403)

career plateauing (404)

backup care (409)

work–family conflict (410)

leisure (413)

Making It in Midlife

The Biopsychosocial Challenges of Middle Adulthood

13

There's an old saying that life begins at 40. Perhaps that was society's way of saying that the changes that occur around this time of life—wrinkles, gray hair, and a bulging waistline—were OK.

But times—and attitudes—have changed. Increasingly, middle age is being viewed as a time when adults achieve new heights in cognitive development, reevaluate their personal goals and change their behavior if they choose, develop adult relationships with their children, and ease into grandparenthood. Along the way, they must deal with stress, changes in the way they learn, and the challenges of helping their aging parents. People's health is generally good, and their earnings are at their peak.

These days, people think that it's much harder to define middle age and put much less emphasis on chronological age than on perceived age. Eight in ten Brits believe that the line between young and old is much fuzzier than it used to be (benenden health, 2013). Let's take a closer look at the issues confronting people during midlife.

LEARNING OBJECTIVES

- How does appearance change in middle age?
- What changes occur in bones and joints?
- What reproductive changes occur in men and women in middle age?

- What is stress? How does it affect physical and psychological health?
- What benefits are there to exercise?

By all accounts, LuTimothy is extremely successful. Among other things, he became the head of a moderate-sized manufacturing firm by the time he was 43. LuTimothy has always considered himself to be a rising young star in the company. Then one day he found more than the usual number of hairs in his brush. "Oh no!" he exclaimed. "I can't be going bald! What will people say?" What does LuTimothy think about these changes?

One morning when you least expect it, you'll be staring into the bathroom mirror when the reality of middle age strikes. Standing there, peering through half-awake eyes, you see *it*. One solitary gray hair or one tiny wrinkle at the corner of your eye—or, like LuTimothy, some excess hairs falling out—and you worry that your youth is gone, your life is over, and you will soon be acting the way your parents did when they embarrassed you in your younger days. Middle-aged people become concerned that they are over-the-hill, sometimes going to great lengths to prove that they are still vibrant.

Crossing the boundary to middle age in the United States is typically associated with turning 40 (or "the big four-oh," as many people term it). This event is frequently marked with a special party, and the party often has an over-the-hill motif. Such events are society's attempt to create a rite of passage between youth and maturity.

As people move into middle age, they begin experiencing some of the physical changes associated with aging. In this section, we focus on the changes most obvious in middle-aged adults: appearance, reproductive capacity, and stress and coping. In Chapter 14, we will consider changes that may begin in middle age but are usually not apparent until later in life, such as slower reaction time and sensory changes. A critical factor in setting the stage for healthy aging is living a healthy lifestyle in young adulthood and middle age. Eating a healthy diet and exercising regularly across adulthood can help reduce the chances of chronic disease later in life (Aldwin & Gilmer, 2013).

Changes in Appearance

On that fateful day when the hard truth stares back at you in the bathroom mirror, it probably doesn't matter to you that getting wrinkles and gray hair is universal and inevitable. Wrinkles are caused by changes in the structure of the skin and its connective and supporting tissues as well as by the cumulative effects of damage from exposure to sunlight and cigarette smoke (Blume-Peytavi et al., 2016; Tobin, 2017). You have control over how quickly your face wrinkles, mainly by limiting your exposure to the sun.

It may not make you feel better to know that gray hair is perfectly natural and caused by a normal cessation of pigment production in hair follicles. Male pattern baldness, a genetic trait in which hair is lost progressively beginning at the top of the head, often begins to appear in middle age. No, the scientific evidence that gradual thinning and graying of hair with age is nearly universal isn't what matters most (Adhikari et al., 2016). What matters is that these changes are affecting *you*.

To make matters worse, you also may have noticed that your clothes aren't fitting properly even though you carefully watch what you eat. You remember a time not very long ago when you could eat whatever you wanted; now it seems that as soon as you look at food you put on weight. Your perceptions are correct; most people gain weight between their early 30s and mid-50s, producing the infamous "middle-aged bulge" as metabolism slows down (Aldwin & Gilmer, 2013).

People's reactions to these changes in appearance vary. LuTimothy wonders how people will react to him now that he's balding. Some people rush out to purchase hair coloring and wrinkle cream, or investigate hair plug procedures. Others just take it as another stage in life. You've probably experienced several different reactions yourself. There is a wide range of individual differences, especially those between men and women and across cultures. For example, certain changes on men in Western society are viewed as positive, but the same changes in women are not.

Changes in Bones and Joints

The bones and the joints change with age, sometimes in potentially preventable ways and sometimes because of genetic predisposition or disease. Let's take a closer look.

Osteoporosis

One physical change that can be potentially serious is loss of bone mass. Skeletal maturity, *the point at which bone mass is greatest and the skeleton is at peak development, occurs at around 18 for women and 20 in men* (Gilsanz & Ratib, 2012; National Institute of Arthritis and Musculoskeletal and Skin Diseases, 2015a). Bone mass stays about the same until women experience menopause and men reach late life. For women, there is a rapid loss of bone mass in the first few years after menopause, which greatly increases the risk of problems with disease and broken bones.

Loss of bone mass makes bones weaker and more brittle, thereby making them easier to break. Because there is less bone mass, bones also take longer to heal in middle-aged and older adults. *Severe loss of bone mass results in* osteoporosis, *a disease in which bones become porous and extremely easy to break* (see ❭ Figure 13.1). In severe cases, osteoporosis can cause spinal vertebrae to collapse, causing the person to stoop and to become shorter (Bartl, Bartl, & Frisch, 2015; National Osteoporosis Foundation, 2016a; see ❭ Figure 13.2). About 40 million Americans either have osteoporosis or are at high risk due to low bone density. Non-Latina white women and Asian women are at highest risk, and osteoporosis is the leading cause of broken bones in older women. Although the severe effects of osteoporosis typically are not observed until later life, this disease can occur in people in their 50s.

Osteoporosis is caused in part by having low bone mass at skeletal maturity (the point at which your bones reach peak development), deficiencies in calcium and vitamin D, estrogen depletion, and lack of weight-bearing exercise that builds up bone mass. Other risk factors include smoking; high-protein diets; and excessive intake of alcohol, caffeine, and sodium. Women who are being treated for asthma, cancer, rheumatoid arthritis, thyroid problems, or epilepsy are also at increased risk because the medications used can lead to the loss of bone mass.

skeletal maturity
The point at which bone mass is greatest and the skeleton is at peak development, occurs at around 18 for women and 20 in men.

osteoporosis
Disease in which bones become porous and extremely easy to break.

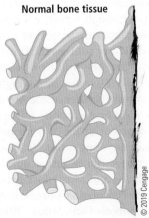

Osteoporotic bone tissue   Normal bone tissue

© 2019 Cengage

❭ **Figure 13.1**
The difference between normal bone (on the right) and osteoporosis (on the left) is easy to see.

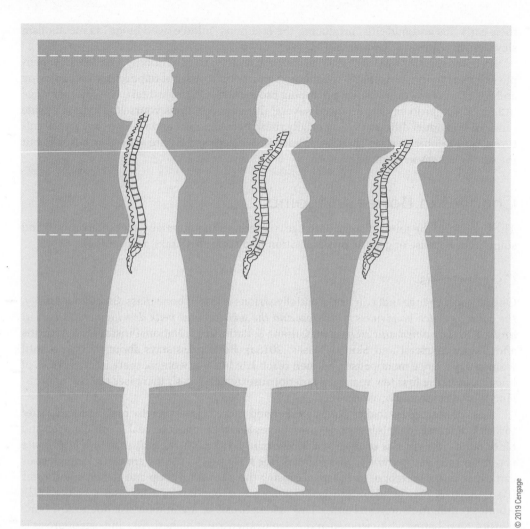

▶ **Figure 13.2**
Notice how osteoporosis eventually causes a person to stoop and to lose height, owing to compression of the vertebrae.

Based on Ebersole, P., & Hess, P. (1998). *Toward healthy aging* (5th ed., p. 395).

dual-energy X-ray absorptiometry (DXA) test

Test of bone mineral density (BMD) at the hip and spine.

The National Osteoporosis Foundation (2016b) recommends getting enough vitamin D and dietary calcium as ways to prevent osteoporosis. There is evidence that calcium supplements after menopause may slow the rate of bone loss and delay the onset of osteoporosis, but benefits appear to be greater when the supplements are provided before menopause. People should consume foods (such as milk, sardines, collard greens, broccoli, or kale) that are high in calcium and should also take calcium supplements if necessary. Recommended calcium intake for men and women of various ages is shown in ▶ Table 13.1. Although sunlight is a good source for vitamin D, due to the risk of skin cancer from overexposure to the sun, most people get their recommended amounts of vitamin D from dietary sources (National Osteoporosis Foundation, 2016c).

Women who are late middle-aged or over age 65 are encouraged to have their bone mineral density (BMD) tested by having a dual-energy X-ray absorptiometry (DXA) test, *which measures bone density at the hip and spine.* The DXA test results are usually compared with the ideal or peak bone mineral density of a healthy 30-year-old adult, and you are given a T-score. A score of 0 means that your bone mineral density is equal to the norm for a healthy young adult. A T-score between +1 and -1 is considered normal or healthy. The greater the negative number, the more severe the osteoporosis (National Institute of Arthritis and Musculoskeletal and Skin Diseases, 2015b).

Lowering the risk of osteoporosis involves dietary, medication, and activity approaches (National Osteoporosis Foundation, 2016a, b). Some evidence also supports the view that taking supplemental magnesium, zinc, vitamin K, and special forms of fluoride may be effective. Estrogen replacement is effective in preventing women's bone loss after menopause but is controversial because of potential side effects (as discussed later). There is also evidence that regular weight-bearing exercise (e.g., weight lifting, jogging, or other exercise that forces you to work against gravity) is beneficial.

In terms of medication interventions, bisphosphonates are the most commonly used and are highly effective, but can have serious side effects if used over a long time (Adler et al., 2016). Bisphosphonates slow the bone breakdown process by helping to maintain bone density during menopause. Research indicates that using bisphosphonates for up to five years appears relatively safe if followed by stopping the medication (called a "drug holiday"); there is evidence for protective effects lasting up to five years more. Periodic reevaluation of people taking medications to assess whether continued medication treatment is needed is crucial to appropriate and effective use of these drugs (Adler et al., 2016).

Raloxifene (e.g., Evista) is also approved for the treatment and prevention of osteoporosis. It is one of a relatively new group of drugs known as selective estrogen receptor modulators. Selective estrogen receptor modulators (SERMs) *are not estrogens, but are compounds that have estrogen-like effects on some tissues and estrogen-blocking effects on other tissues.*

The newest classes of medications for osteoporosis are the RANK ligand inhibitors, such as denosumab (Lipton et al., 2014). Related research indicates that romosozumab is effective in stimulating bone growth in postmenopausal women (McClung et al., 2014). Although these medications are very promising, additional research will be needed to ensure that they are effective over the long run and that side effects are minimal.

selective estrogen receptor modulators (SERMs)

Compounds that are not estrogens, but have estrogen-like effects on some tissues and estrogen-blocking effects on other tissues.

Table 13.1

Recommended Calcium and Vitamin D Intakes

AGE	CALCIUM (MILLIGRAMS)	VITAMIN D (INTERNATIONAL UNITS)
INFANTS		
Birth–6 months	200	400
6 months–1 year	260	400
CHILDREN/YOUNG ADULTS		
1–3 years	700	600
4–8 years	1,000	600
9–13 years	1,300	600
14–18 years	1,300	600
ADULT WOMEN AND MEN		
19–30 years	1,000	600
31–50 years	1,000	600
51- to 70-year-old males	1,000	600
51- to 70-year-old females	1,200	600
Over 70 years	1,200	800
PREGNANT OR LACTATING WOMEN		
18 years or younger	1,300	600
19–50 years	1,000	600

SOURCE: Food and Nutrition Board, Institute of Medicine, National Academy of Sciences, 2010, www.niams.nih.gov/Health_Info/Bone/Osteoporosis/osteoporosis_hoh.asp#calcium.

Figure 13.3

Rheumatoid arthritis versus osteoarthritis. Osteoarthritis, the most common form of arthritis, involves the wearing away of the cartilage that caps the bones in your joints. With rheumatoid arthritis, the synovial membrane that protects and lubricates joints becomes inflamed, causing pain and swelling. Joint erosion may follow.

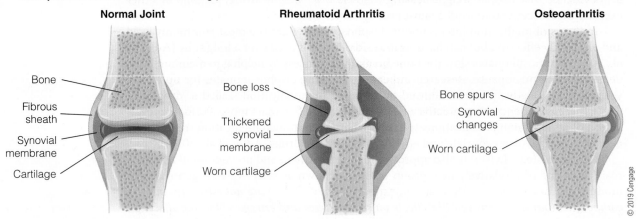

Normal Joint

Bone

Fibrous sheath

Synovial membrane

Cartilage

Rheumatoid Arthritis

Bone loss

Thickened synovial membrane

Worn cartilage

Osteoarthritis

Bone spurs

Synovial changes

Worn cartilage

© 2019 Cengage

SOURCE: MayoClinic.com. 2016. Arthritis. www.mayoclinic.org/diseases-conditions/arthritis/home/ovc-20168903

Arthritis

Many middle-aged and older adults have good reason to complain of aching joints. Beginning in the 20s, the protective cartilage in joints shows signs of deterioration, such as thinning and becoming cracked and frayed. Two types of arthritis can result: osteoarthritis and rheumatoid arthritis. These diseases are illustrated in ❫ Figure 13.3.

Over time and repeated use, the bones underneath the cartilage become damaged, which can result in osteoarthritis, *a disease marked by gradual onset and progression of pain and disability, with minor signs of inflammation* (National Institute of Arthritis and Musculoskeletal and Skin Diseases, 2014a). The disease usually becomes noticeable in late middle age or early old age, and it is especially common in people whose joints are subjected to routine overuse and abuse, such as athletes and manual laborers. Because it is caused by overuse and abuse of joints, osteoarthritis is considered a wear-and-tear disease. Pain from osteoarthritis typically is worse when the joint is used, but skin redness, heat, and swelling are minimal or absent. Osteoarthritis usually affects the hands, spine, hips, and knees, sparing the wrists, elbows, shoulders, and ankles. Effective management consists mainly of certain steroids and anti-inflammatory drugs, rest, nonstressful exercises that focus on range of motion, diet, and a variety of homeopathic remedies.

A second form of arthritis is rheumatoid arthritis, *a more destructive disease of the joints that also develops slowly and typically affects different joints and causes other types of pain and more inflammation than osteoarthritis* (National Institute of Arthritis and Musculoskeletal and Skin Diseases., 2014b). Most often, a pattern of morning stiffness and aching develops in the fingers, wrists, and ankles on both sides of the body. Joints appear swollen.

The American College of Rheumatology (Singh et al., 2016) has adopted guidelines for treating rheumatoid arthritis. The typical low-level therapy consists of aspirin or other nonsteroidal anti-inflammatory drugs, such as Advil or Aleve. Newer treatments include disease-modifying anti-rheumatic drugs (DMARDs) (such as hydroxycholorquine and methotrexate) that limit the damage occurring in the joints, glucocorticoids, and TNF-alpha inhibitors that act as an anti-inflammatory agent and have been shown to stop the disease's progression in some patients. Rest and passive range-of-motion exercises are also helpful.

Both osteoarthritis (Warner & Valdes, 2016) and rheumatoid arthritis (Yarwood, Huizinga, & Worthington, 2016) have genetic components. Although the exact nature of these inheritance factors are unknown, several potential locations have been identified as possible markers. Further advances in our knowledge of these genetic links could result in more effective and more individualized treatments.

osteoarthritis

Most common form of arthritis, a disease marked by gradual onset of bone damage with progression of pain and disability together with minor signs of inflammation from wear and tear.

rheumatoid arthritis

More destructive disease of the joints that develops slowly; it typically affects different joints and causes different types of pain than osteoarthritis does.

Surgical interventions may be an option if medications do not provide relief. For example, *arthroplasty*, or the total replacement of joints damaged by arthritis, continues to improve as new materials help artificial joints last longer. Hip and knee replacement surgery is becoming both more common and more effective as less invasive surgical techniques are developed that dramatically reduce recovery time. When joints become inflamed, surgeons may be able to remove enough affected tissue to provide relief. In some cases, cartilage may be transplanted into a damaged joint. These latter two approaches help patients avoid full joint replacement, generally viewed as the method of last resort.

Osteoporosis, osteoarthritis, and rheumatoid arthritis can appear similar and cause similar symptoms., As we have seen, though, they are different diseases requiring different treatment approaches. Comparisons among osteoporosis, osteoarthritis, and rheumatoid arthritis can be seen in ▶ Table 3.2.

Reproductive Changes

If you watched any television recently, you undoubtedly saw programs and advertisements showing middle-aged and older couples who clearly have active sex lives. Belsky (2007) reports that couples can and often do have sexual relationships that are very much alive and may be based on a newfound or re-found respect and love for each other. A major

Table 13.2

Similarities and Differences Among Osteoporosis, Osteoarthritis, and Rheumatoid Arthritis

	OSTEOPOROSIS	OSTEOAR-THRITIS	RHEUMATOID ARTHRITIS
RISK FACTORS	X	X	
Age-related	X	X	
Menopause	X		
Family history	X	X	X
Use of certain medications such as glucocorticoids or seizure medications	X		
Calcium deficiency or inadequate	X		
vitamin D			
Inactivity	X		
Overuse of joints		X	
Smoking	X		
Excessive alcohol	X		
Anorexia nervosa	X		
Excessive weight		X	
PHYSICAL EFFECTS			
Affects entire skeleton	X		
Affects joints		X	X
Is an autoimmune disease			X
Bony spurs		X	X
Enlarged or malformed joints	X	X	
Height loss	X		

SOURCES: National Institute of Arthritis and Musculoskeletal and Skin Diseases (2010), www.niams.nih.gov/Health_Info/Bone/Osteoporosis/Conditions_Behaviors/osteoporosis_arthritis.asp.

national survey by AARP (Fisher, 2010) found that middle-aged adults not only tend to continue to enjoy active sex lives but also enjoy romantic weekends, and about six of every ten middle-aged men and women report that a satisfying sex life is important for their quality of life.

Still, middle age brings changes to the reproductive systems of men and women. These changes are more significant for women, but men also experience certain changes. Let's see what they are and how people learn to cope with them.

Reproductive Changes in Women

As women enter midlife, they experience a major biological process called the climacteric, *during which they pass from their reproductive to nonreproductive years.* Menopause *is the point at which menstruation stops.* Men do not endure such sweeping biological changes but experience several gradual changes. These changes have important psychological implications because midlife is thought by many to be a key time for people to redefine themselves, an issue we will examine later in this chapter. For example, some women view climacteric as the loss of the ability to have children, whereas others view it as a liberating change because they no longer need to worry about getting pregnant.

The major reproductive change in women during adulthood is the loss of the natural ability to bear children. (Pregnancy and childbirth are still possible, though, through medical intervention.) This change begins in the 40s as menstrual cycles become irregular, and by age 50 to 55 it is usually complete (MedlinePlus, 2014). *This time of transition from regular menstruation to menopause is called* perimenopause, *and how long it lasts varies considerably.* The gradual loss and eventual end of monthly periods is accompanied by decreases in estrogen and progesterone levels, changes in the reproductive organs, and changes in sexual functioning.

A variety of physical and psychological symptoms may accompany perimenopause and menopause with decreases in hormonal levels (WomensHealth.gov, 2010): hot flashes, night sweats, headaches, sleep problems, mood changes, more urinary infections, pain during sex, difficulty concentrating, vaginal dryness, less interest in sex, and an increase in body fat around the waist. Many women report no symptoms at all, but most women experience at least some, and there are large differences across social, ethnic, and cultural groups in how they are expressed (Nosek, Kennedy, & Gudmundsdottir, 2012). For example, women in the Mayan culture of Mexico and Central America welcome menopause and its changes as a natural phenomenon and do not attach any stigma to aging (Mahady et al., 2008). In the United States, Latinas and African Americans, especially working-class women, tend to view menopause more positively, whereas European American women describe it more negatively (Dillaway et al., 2008). Women in South American countries report a variety of symptoms that impair quality of life, many of which persisted five years beyond menopause (Blümel et al., 2012).

The decline in estrogen that women experience after menopause is a very big deal. Estrogen loss is related to numerous health conditions, including increased risk of osteoporosis, cardiovascular disease, stress urinary incontinence (involuntary loss of urine during physical stress, as when exercising, sneezing, or laughing), weight gain, and memory loss, in short, almost every major body system (Women's Health Research Institute, 2016). Consider just one negative effect: cardiovascular disease. At age 50 (prior to menopause) women have three times less risk of heart attacks than men on average. Ten years after menopause, when women are about 60, their risk equals that of men. Clearly, estrogen depletion has a negative effect on health.

In response to these increased risks and to the estrogen-related symptoms that women experience, one approach is the use of menopausal hormone therapy (MHT): *women take low doses of estrogen, which is often combined with progestin (synthetic form of progesterone).* Hormone therapy is controversial and has been the focus of many research studies with conflicting results (North American Menopause Society, 2016). There appear to be both benefits and risks with MHT, as discussed in the What Do *You* Think? feature.

climacteric

Biological process during which women pass from their reproductive to nonreproductive years.

menopause

Point at which menstruation stops.

perimenopause

Individually varying time of transition from regular menstruation to menopause.

menopausal hormone therapy (MHT)

Therapy in which women take low doses of estrogen, which is often combined with progestin (a synthetic form of progesterone).

Despite physical changes associated with middle age, women and men continue to enjoy sexual activity.

Big Cheese Special/Big Cheese Photo LLC/Alamy Stock Photo

For many years, women have had the choice of taking medications to replace the female hormones that are no longer produced naturally by the body after menopause. Hormone therapy may involve taking estrogen alone or in combination with progesterone (or progestin in its synthetic form). Research on the effects of menopause hormone therapy have helped clarify the appropriate use of such medications.

Until about 2003, it was thought that menopausal hormone therapy was beneficial for most women, and results from several studies were positive. But results from the Women's Health Initiative research in the United States and from the Million Women Study in the United Kingdom indicated that, for some types of MHT, there were several potentially serious side effects. As a result, physicians are now far more cautious in recommending MHT.

The Women's Health Initiative (WHI), begun in the United States in 1991, was a very large study (National Heart, Lung, and Blood Institute, 2010). The estrogen plus progestin trial used 0.625 milligram of estrogen taken daily plus 2.5 milligrams of medroxyprogesterone acetate (Prempro) taken daily. This combination was chosen because it is the mostly commonly prescribed form of the combined hormone therapy in the United States and, in several observational studies, had appeared to benefit women's health. The women in the WHI estrogen plus progestin study were aged 50 to 79 when they enrolled in the study between 1993 and 1998. The health

of study participants was carefully monitored by an independent panel called the Data and Safety Monitoring Board (DSMB). The study was stopped in July 2002 because investigators discovered a significant increased risk for breast cancer and that overall the risks outnumbered the benefits. However, in addition to the increased risk of breast cancer, heart attack, stroke, and blood clots, MHT resulted in fewer hip fractures and lower rates of colorectal cancer.

The Million Women Study began in 1996 and includes one in four women over age 50 in the United Kingdom, the largest study of its kind ever conducted. Like the Women's Health Initiative, the study examines how MHT (both estrogen/progestin combinations and estrogen alone) affects breast cancer, cardiovascular disease, and other aspects of women's health. Results from this study confirmed the Women's Health Initiative outcome of increased risk for breast cancer associated with MHT.

A third important study is the Kronos Early Estrogen Prevention Study (KEEPS). In the primary study, 727 women were randomly assigned to three groups. One group received a dose of Premarin that was lower than in the WHI study, another group received a patch, and the third group received a placebo. Both treatment groups experienced a drop in menopausal symptoms. Most important, all three groups showed similar changes in cardiovascular function and no significant changes in biomarkers, no significant differences in breast cancer rates, or in rate of blood clots.

The combined results from the WHI, the Million Women Study, and the KEEPS led physicians to modify their recommendations regarding MHT (Moyer, Miller, & Faubion, 2016; North American Menopause Society, 2016; Women's Health Research Institute, 2016). Specifically, the joint recommendation of the American Society for Reproductive Medicine, the Endocrine Society, and the North American Menopause Society is that MHT is reasonably safe for healthy women under age 60 who have moderate to severe menopausal symptoms. Advances in genomics is likely to make MHT more precise because of the increasing ability to tailor the hormone therapy to each woman's own genetics (Moyer et al., 2016; Panay, 2016).

MHT is not recommend for women over age 60 or for those who have significant risk factors for side effects (e.g., blood clots). Additionally, women over age 60 who begin MHT are at increased risk for certain cancers.

In sum, women face difficult choices when deciding whether to use MHT as a means of combatting certain menopausal symptoms and protecting themselves against other diseases. For example, MHT can help reduce hot flashes and night sweats, help reduce vaginal dryness and discomfort during sexual intercourse, slow bone loss, and perhaps ease mood swings. On the other hand, MHT can increase a woman's risk of blood clots, heart attack, stroke, breast cancer, and gallbladder disease.

Women's genital organs undergo progressive change after menopause. The vaginal walls shrink and become thinner, the size of the vagina decreases, vaginal lubrication is reduced and delayed, and the external genitalia shrink somewhat. These changes have important effects on sexual activity, such as an increased possibility of painful intercourse and a longer time and more stimulation needed to reach orgasm. Failure to achieve orgasm is more common in midlife and beyond than in a woman's younger years. However, maintaining an active sex life throughout adulthood lowers the degree to which problems are encountered. Despite these changes, there is no physiological reason not to continue having an active and enjoyable sex life from middle age through late life. The vaginal dryness that occurs, for example, can be countered by using personal lubricants, such as K-Y or Astroglide.

Whether women continue to have an active sex life has a lot more to do with the availability of a suitable partner than a woman's desire for sexual relations. This is especially true for older women. The AARP *Modern Maturity* sexuality study (AARP, 1999), the *Sex in America* study (AARP, 2005), and the *Sex, Romance,* and *Relationships* (AARP, 2010) studies all found that older married women were far more likely to have an active sex life than unmarried women. The primary reason for the decline in women's sexual activity with age is the lack of a willing or appropriate partner, not a lack of physical ability or desire (AARP, 1999, 2005, 2010).

Reproductive Changes in Men

Unlike women, men do not have a physiological (and cultural) event to mark reproductive changes, although there is a gradual decline in testosterone levels (Gunes et al., 2016) that can occur to a greater extent in men who are obese or have diabetes (Nigro & Christ-Crain, 2012). Men do not experience a complete loss of the ability to father children, as this varies widely from individual to individual, but men do experience a normative decline in the quantity of sperm (Gunes et al., 2016). However, even at age 80 a man is still half as fertile as he was at age 25 and is quite capable of fathering a child.

With increasing age the prostate gland enlarges, becomes stiffer, and may obstruct the urinary tract. Prostate cancer becomes a real threat during middle age; annual screenings are often recommended for men over age 50 (American Cancer Society, 2012).

Men experience some physiological changes in sexual performance. By old age, men report less perceived demand to ejaculate, a need for longer time and more stimulation to achieve erection and orgasm, and a much longer resolution phase during which erection is impossible (Gunes et al., 2016). Older men also report more frequent failures to achieve orgasm and loss of erection during intercourse (AARP, 1999, 2005, 2010). However, the advent of Viagra, Cialis, and other medications to treat erectile dysfunction has provided older men with easy-to-use medical treatments and the possibility of an active sex life well into later life.

As with women, as long as men enjoy sex and have a willing partner, sexual activity is a lifelong option. Also as with women, the most important ingredient of sexual intimacy for men is a strong relationship with a partner (AARP, 1999, 2005, 2010). For example, married men in early middle age tend to have intercourse four to eight times per month, but this rate drops about 20% per decade. The loss of an available partner is a significant reason frequency of intercourse decreases with age. Still, late middle-aged and older people continue to enjoy themselves. Nearly three-quarters of people 57 to 64 had sex during the past year, as did over half of those 65 to 74 and over 25% of those 75 to 85 (Watson, 2013). Practicing safe sex is equally important for older adults, as sexually transmitted disease remains a major concern.

As with women, if men enjoy sex and have a willing partner, sexual activity is a lifelong option. Like women, the most important ingredient of sexual intimacy for men is a strong relationship with a partner (Fisher, 2010).

Stress and Health

You know what it feels like to be stressed. Whether it's from the upcoming exam in this course, the traffic jam you sat in on your way home yesterday, or the demands your children or your job place on you, stress seems to be everywhere.

There is plenty of scientific evidence that over the long term, stress is very bad for your health. But despite thousands of scientific studies that result in our certainty about what stress does to us, scientists still cannot agree on a formal definition of what stress is. What is clear is that stress involves both physiological and psychological aspects (Levy & Bavishi, in press).

The most widely applied approaches to stress involve: (a) focusing on the physiological responses the body makes through the nervous and endocrine systems; and (b) the idea that stress is what people define as stressful. Let's consider each in more detail.

Stress as a Physiological Response

There is widespread agreement across many research studies that people differ in their physiological responses to stress (Campbell & Ehlert, 2012; Laurent et al., 2016). Prolonged exposure to stress results in damaging influences from the sympathetic nervous system (which controls such things as heart rate, respiration, perspiration, blood

Work-related stress is a major problem around the world and can have serious negative effects on physical and psychological health.

Susan Vogel/UpperCut Images/Getty Images

flow, muscle strength, and mental activity) and a weakening of the immune system. As Cohen and colleagues (2012) discussed in their model of these effects, prolonged stress has a direct causative effect on susceptibility to a wide range of diseases, from the common cold to cardiovascular disease to cancer. At the cellular level, stress may play a role in shortening telomeres (see Chapter 3; Mathur et al., 2016).

Gender differences in physiological stress responses have also been documented. For example, there is some evidence that the hormone oxytocin plays a different role in women than in men. Oxytocin is the hormone important in women's reproductive activities and for establishing strong bonds with one's children (Kim, Strathearn, & Swain, 2016). Researchers speculate that when stressed, men opt for a "flight or fight" approach whereas women opt for a "tend and befriend" approach (Taylor, 2006). Fischer-Shofty, Levkovitz, and Shamay-Tsoory (2013) showed that oxytocin improves accurate perception of social interactions, but in different ways in men and women. In men, performance improved only for competition recognition, whereas in women it improved for kinship recognition.

The Stress and Coping Paradigm

Suppose you are stuck in a traffic jam. Depending on whether you are late for an important appointment or have plenty of time on your hands, you will probably feel very different about your situation. *The* stress and coping paradigm *views stress not as an environmental stimulus or as a response but as the interaction of a thinking person and an event* (Lazarus, 1984; Lazarus et al., 1985; Lazarus & Folkman, 1984). How we interpret an event such as being stuck in traffic is what matters, not the event itself or what we do in response to it. Put more formally, stress is "a particular relationship between the person and the environment that is appraised by the person as taxing or exceeding his or her resources and endangering his or her well-being" (Lazarus & Folkman, 1984, p. 19). Note that this definition states that stress is a transactional process between a person and the environment, that it takes into account personal resources, that the person's appraisal of the situation is key, and that unless the situation is considered to be threatening, challenging, or harmful, stress does not result. A diagram of the transactional model is shown in ❱ Figure 13.4.

stress and coping paradigm

Framework that views stress not as an environmental stimulus or as a response, but as the interaction of a thinking person and an event.

❱ **Figure 13.4**

An example of a transactional model of stress.

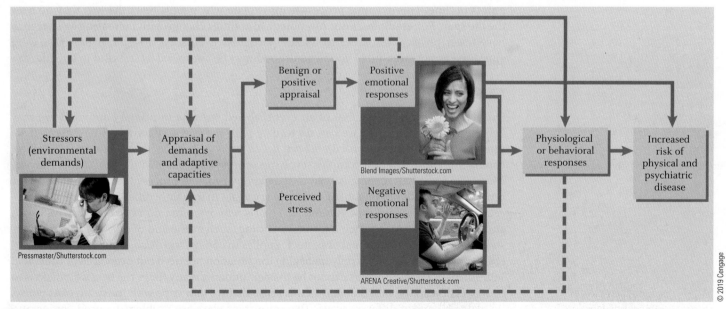

Pressmaster/Shutterstock.com

Blend Images/Shutterstock.com

ARENA Creative/Shutterstock.com

© 2019 Cengage

SOURCE: From Cohen, S., Kessler, R. C., & Gordon, L. U. (eds.). *Measuring Stress: A Guide for Health and Social Scientists,* Copyright © 1995 by Oxford University Press. Used with permission from Oxford University Press.

Appraisal

primary appraisal

Process that categorizes events into three groups based on the significance they have for one's well-being: irrelevant, benign or positive, and stressful.

Lazarus and Folkman (1984) describe three types of appraisals of stress. Primary appraisal *categorizes events into three groups based on the significance they have for our well-being: irrelevant, benign or positive, and stressful.* Primary appraisals filter the events we experience. Specifically, any event that is appraised as either irrelevant (things that do not affect us) or as benign or positive (things that are good or at least neutral) is not stressful. So, we literally decide which events are potentially stressful and which ones are not. This is an important point for two reasons. First, it means we can effectively sort out the events that may be problems and those that are not, allowing us to concentrate on dealing with life's difficulties more effectively. Second, it means that we could be wrong about our reading of an event. A situation that may appear at first blush to be irrelevant, for example, may actually be very important, or a situation deemed stressful initially may turn out not to be. Such mistakes in primary appraisal could set the stage for real (or imagined) crises later on.

secondary appraisal

Process that evaluates one's perceived ability to cope with harm, threat, or challenge.

If a person believes that an event is stressful, a second set of decisions, called secondary appraisal, is made. Secondary appraisal *evaluates our perceived ability to cope with harm, threat, or challenge.* Secondary appraisal is the equivalent of asking three questions: "What can I do?" "How likely is it that I can use one of my options successfully?" and "Will this option reduce my stress?" How we answer these questions sets the stage for addressing them effectively. For example, if you believe there is something you can do in a situation that will make a difference, then your perceived stress may be reduced, and you may be able to deal with the event successfully. In contrast, if you believe there is little that you can do to address the situation successfully or reduce your feelings of stress, then you may feel powerless and ineffective, even if others around you believe there are steps you could take.

reappraisal

Process of making a new primary or secondary appraisal resulting from changes in the situation.

Sometimes, you learn additional information or experience another situation that indicates you should reappraise the original event. Reappraisal *involves making a new primary or secondary appraisal resulting from changes in the situation.* For example, you may initially dismiss an accusation that your partner is cheating on you (i.e., make a primary appraisal that the event is irrelevant), but after being shown pictures of your partner in a romantic situation with another person, you reappraise the event as stressful. Reappraisal can either increase stress (if your partner had initially denied the encounter) or lower stress (if you discovered that the photographs were fakes).

The three types of appraisals demonstrate that determining whether an event is stressful is a dynamic process. Initial decisions about events may be upheld over time, or they may change in light of new information or personal experience. Different events may be appraised in the same way, and the same event may be appraised differently at any two points in time. This dynamic process helps explain why people react the way they do over the life span. For example, as our physiological abilities change with increasing age, we may have fewer physical resources to handle particular events. As a result, events that were appraised as not stressful in young adulthood may be appraised as stressful in late life.

Coping

coping

Attempt to deal with stressful events.

During the secondary appraisal of an event labeled stressful in primary appraisal, we may believe there is something we can do to deal with the event effectively. *Collectively, these attempts to deal with stressful events are called* coping. Lazarus and Folkman (1984) view coping more formally as a complex, evolving process of dealing with stress that is learned. Much like appraisals, coping is seen as a dynamic, evolving process that is fine-tuned over time. Our first attempt might fail, but if we try again in a slightly different way we may succeed. Coping is learned, not automatic. That is why we often do not cope very well with stressful situations we are facing for the first time (such as the end of our first love relationship). The saying "practice makes perfect" applies to coping, too. Also, coping takes time and effort. Finally, coping entails only managing the situation; we need not overcome or control it. Indeed, many stressful events cannot be fixed or undone; many times the best we can do is to learn to live with the situation. It is in this sense that we may cope with the death of a spouse.

problem-focused coping

Attempts to tackle a problem head-on.

People cope in different ways. Two important ways are problem-focused coping and emotion-focused coping. Problem-focused coping *involves attempts to tackle the problem head-on*. Taking medication to treat a disease and spending more time studying for an examination are examples of problem-focused coping with the stress of illness or failing a prior test. In general, problem-focused coping entails doing something directly about the problem at hand. Emotion-focused coping *involves dealing with one's feelings about the stressful event.* Allowing oneself to express anger or frustration over becoming ill or failing an exam is an example of this approach. The goal here is not necessarily to eliminate the problem, although this may happen. Rather, the purpose may be to help oneself deal with situations that are difficult or impossible to tackle head-on.

Several other behaviors can also be viewed in the context of coping. Many people use their relationship with God as the basis for their coping (Bade, 2012; Kinney et al., 2003). For believers, using religious coping strategies usually results in positives outcomes when faced with negative events.

How well we cope depends on several factors. For example, healthy, energetic people are better able to cope with an infection than frail, sick people. Psychologically, a positive attitude about oneself and one's abilities is also important. Good problem-solving skills put people at an advantage by creating several options with which to manage the stress. Social skills and social support are important in helping people solicit suggestions and assistance from others. Finally, financial resources are important; having the money to pay a mechanic to fix your car allows you to avoid the frustration of trying to do it yourself.

The most effective ways to deal with stress are through various relaxation techniques. Whether you prefer yoga, visualization, progressive muscle relaxation, meditation or contemplative prayer, massage, or just chilling does not really matter. All good relaxation methods have similar effects: slowing the pulse, lowering blood pressure, slowing down breathing, reducing tension, focusing concentration, lowering anger and fatigue, and boosting confidence.

Keep in mind that the number of stressful events, per se, is less important than one's appraisal of them and whether the person has effective skills to deal with them. Of course, should the number of stressful issues exceed one's ability to cope, then the number of issues being confronted would be a key issue.

Effects of Stress on Physical Health

How does stress affect us? If the stress is short, such as being stuck in a traffic jam for an hour when we're already late in an otherwise relaxed day, the answer is that it probably will have little effect other than on our temper. But if the stress is continuous, or chronic, then the picture changes dramatically.

There is ample evidence that perceived stress is related to brain structures; for instance, the size of the hippocampus, a brain structure intimately involved in cognition is smaller in people who report moderate to high levels of chronic stress (Lindgren, Bergdahl, & Nyberg, 2016). Likewise, chronic stress has been clearly shown to have very significant negative effects on health, including pervasive negative effects on the immune system that cause increased susceptibility to viral infections, increased risk of atherosclerosis and hypertension, and impaired memory and cognition, as well as psychopathology (Frank et al., 2016; Webster-Marketon & Glaser, 2008). Effects can last for decades; severe stress experienced in childhood has effects that last well into adulthood (Shonkoff et al., 2012).

Research indicates that different types of appraisals that are interpreted as stressful create different physiological outcomes (Frank et al., 2016; Webster-Marketon & Glaser, 2008). This may mean that how the body reacts to stress depends on the appraisal process; the reaction to different types of stress is not the same. In turn, this implies that changing people's appraisal may also be a way to lower the impact of stress on the body.

Research indicates that one of the most serious consequences of chronic stress is that it increases the level of LDL cholesterol, which has significant negative consequences (see Chapter 3; McKay, 2016). LDL cholesterol levels rise as a result of chronic stress for several reasons: people stop exercising, eat more unhealthy foods, and have higher levels of cortisol and adrenaline (which stimulate the production of triglycerides and free fatty acids, which in turn increase LDL cholesterol levels over time). High levels of LDL cholesterol are associated with cardiovascular disease and stroke (see Chapter 3).

emotion-focused coping
Dealing with one's feelings about a stressful event.

Think About It
How might life experience and cognitive developmental level influence one's ability to appraise and cope with stress?

Effects of Stress on Psychological Health

Experiencing stress can trigger psychological processes and reactions. Although stress does not directly cause psychopathology, it does influence how people react and behave. For example, the stress many people experienced after the terrorist attacks of September 11, 2001, resulted in higher levels of anxiety experienced through nightmares, flashbacks, insomnia, traumatic grief, emotional numbing, and avoidance (LeDoux & Gorman, 2001).

post-traumatic stress disorder (PTSD)

An anxiety disorder that can develop after exposure to a terrifying event or ordeal in which grave physical harm occurred or was threatened.

One very important effect of stress on psychological health is post-traumatic stress disorder (PTSD). *The National Institute of Mental Health (2016f) defines* post-traumatic stress disorder (PTSD) *as an anxiety disorder that can develop after exposure to a terrifying event or ordeal in which grave physical harm occurred or was threatened.* The kinds of traumatic events that may trigger PTSD include violent personal assaults, natural or human-caused disasters, accidents, or military combat.

PTSD affects nearly 8 million Americans and can be a debilitating condition. Because not everyone who is exposed to very stressful situations develops PTSD, our understanding of what causes it is limited. Treatment is typically done through psychotherapy, with the addition of certain antidepressant medications in limited circumstances.

mindfulness-based stress reduction

Being aware and nonjudgmental of whatever is happening at that moment.

Because stress is such a ubiquitous aspect of life, much effort (and consumer spending) goes into stress reduction techniques. *For example, one popular approach is* mindfulness-based stress reduction, *being aware and nonjudgmental of whatever is happening at that moment* (University of Massachusetts Medical School Center for Mindfulness, 2017). Common approaches using mindfulness-based stress reduction include yoga and meditation. Research indicates that using mindfulness-based techniques has many positive effects on physical and psychological health (Sharma, 2014). In addition, mindfulness techniques result in functional and structural changes in the brain, especially in areas related to control of stress and emotion as well as attention, memory, and sensory processing (Esch, 2014).

Exercise

Since the ancient Greeks, physicians and researchers have known that exercise significantly slows the aging process. Indeed, evidence suggests a program of regular exercise, in conjunction with a healthy lifestyle, can slow the physiological aging process and improve the immune system (Bartlett & Huffman, 2017; Parrella & Vormittag, 2017). Being sedentary is absolutely hazardous to your health.

Engaging in a mindfulness-based stress reduction program such as yoga throughout middle age is a great way to counter a stressful lifestyle.

Markus Gann/Shutterstock.com

Adults benefit from aerobic exercise, *exercise that places moderate stress on the heart by maintaining a pulse rate between 60% and 90% of the person's maximum heart rate.* You can calculate your maximum heart rate by subtracting your age from 220. Thus, if you are 40 years old, your target range would be 108 to 162 beats per minute. The minimum time necessary for aerobic exercise to be of benefit depends on its intensity; at low heart rates, sessions may need to last an hour, whereas at high heart rates, 15 minutes may suffice. Examples of aerobic exercise include jogging, step aerobics, Zumba®, swimming, and cross-country skiing.

What happens when a person exercises aerobically (besides becoming tired and sweaty)? Physiologically, adults of all ages show improved cardiovascular functioning and maximum oxygen consumption; lower blood pressure; and better strength, endurance, flexibility, and coordination (Mayo Clinic, 2015). Psychologically, people who exercise aerobically report lower levels of stress, better moods, and better cognitive functioning.

The best way to gain the benefits of aerobic exercise is to maintain physical fitness throughout the life span, beginning at least in middle age. The benefits of various forms of exercise are numerous, and include lowering the risk of cardiovascular disease, osteoporosis (if the exercise is weight bearing), and a host of other conditions. The Mayo Clinic's *Healthy Lifestyle Fitness* websites provide an excellent place to start. In planning an exercise program, three points should be remembered. First, check with a physician before beginning an aerobic exercise program. Second, bear in mind that moderation is important. Third, just because you intend to exercise doesn't mean you will; you must take the necessary steps to turn your intention into action (Paech, Luszczynska, & Lippke, 2016; Schwarzer, 2008). If you do, and stick with it, you may feel much younger (Joyner & Barnes, 2013).

Without question, regular exercise is one of the two most important behaviors you can do to promote healthy living and good aging (not smoking is the other). In addition to the wide variety of positive effects on health (e.g., lower risk of cardiovascular disease, diabetes, hypertension), there is also substantial evidence exercise is also connected to less cortical atrophy, better brain function, and enhanced cognitive performance (Erickson, Gildengers, & Butters, 2013; Suo et al., 2016). Specifically, exercise has a positive effect on the prefrontal and hippocampal areas of the brain, increased gray matter, and reversed the progression of white matter hypersensitivities (a biomarker of cerebrovascular disease) and is closely associated with memory and other cognitive functions.

Whether exercise can delay or prevent diseases associated with these brain structures, such as Alzheimer's disease, remains to be seen. But the evidence to date points in that direction (e.g., Suo et al., 2016), so researchers and clinicians are promoting exercise as a way to a healthy, better functioning brain in later life. A better functioning brain may well be related to the mood improvements seen as another positive benefit of exercise, as shown in ▶ Figure 13.5.

aerobic exercise

Exercise that places moderate stress on the heart by maintaining a pulse rate between 60% and 90% of a person's maximum heart rate.

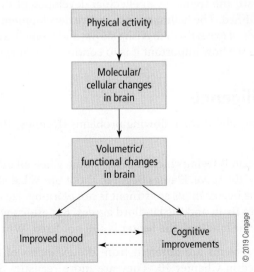

▶ Figure 13.5

A schematic representation of the general path by which cognitive function and mood are improved by physical activity. It could be hypothesized that improvements in cognitive function mediate the improvements in mood or that improvements in mood mediate some of the improvements in cognitive function. The dotted lines represent these hypothesized paths.

SOURCE: Erickson, K. I., Gildengers, A. G., & Butters, M. A. (2013). Physical activity and brain plasticity in late adulthood. *Dialogues in Clinical Neuroscience, 15,* 99–108. Retrieved from www.ncbi.nlm.nih.gov/pmc/articles/PMC3622473/. Image retrieved from www.ncbi.nlm.nih.gov/pmc/articles/PMC3622473/figure/DialoguesClinNeurosci-15-99-g001/.

In summary, if you want to maximize the odds of healthy aging, exercise. Guidelines state about 150 minutes of moderate aerobic exercise weekly with additional whole-body strength training and balance work is sufficient to produce positive effects (Batt, Tanji, & Börjesson, 2013).

TEST YOURSELF   13.1

Recall

1. Severe bone loss may result in the disease _____.
2. The cessation of menstruation is termed _____.
3. Reduction of fertility in men usually occurs _____.
4. The stress and _____ paradigm defines stress on the basis of the person's appraisal of a situation as taxing his or her well-being.
5. Research indicates that _____ is an effective approach for lowering stress.

Interpret

- The media are full of advertisements for anti-aging creams, diets, and exercise plans. Based on what you have read in this section, how would you evaluate these ads?

Apply

- What would be an ideal stress reduction exercise program for middle-aged adults?

Check your answers to the Recall Questions at the end of the chapter.

13.2 Cognitive Development

LEARNING OBJECTIVES

- How does practical intelligence develop in adulthood?
- How does a person become an expert?
- What is meant by lifelong learning? What differences are there between adults and young people in how they learn?

A'isha a 54-year-old social worker, is widely regarded as the resident expert when it comes to working the system of human services. Her coworkers admire her ability to get several agencies to cooperate, which they do not do normally, and to keep clients coming in for routine matters and follow-up visits. A'isha claims that there is nothing magical about it—it's just her experience that makes the difference.

Compared with the rapid cognitive growth of childhood or the controversies about post-formal cognition in young adulthood, cognitive development in middle age is relatively quiet. For the most part, the trends in intellectual development discussed in Chapter 10 are continued and solidified. The hallmark of cognitive development in middle age involves developing higher levels of expertise like A'isha shows and being flexible in solving practical problems. We will also see how important it is to continue learning throughout adulthood.

Practical Intelligence

Take a moment to think about the following problems (Denney, 1984; Denney, Pearce, & Palmer, 1982):

- A middle-aged woman is frying chicken in her home when all of a sudden a grease fire breaks out on top of the stove. Flames begin to shoot up. What should she do?
- A man finds that the heater in his apartment is not working. He asks his landlord to send someone out to fix it, and the landlord agrees. But after a week of cold weather and several calls to the landlord, the heater is still not fixed. What should the man do?

These practical problems are different from the examples of measures of fluid and crystallized intelligence in Chapter 10. They are more realistic; they reflect real-world situations that people routinely face. Many researchers argue that using such problems to assess cognition provides a better assessment of the kinds of skills adults actually use in everyday life (Gamaldo & Allaire, 2016; Margrett et al., 2010; Mayer, 2014). Most people spend more time at tasks such as managing their personal finances, dealing with uncooperative people, and juggling busy schedules than they do solving esoteric mazes.

The shortcomings of traditional tests of adults' intelligence led to different ways of viewing intelligence that differentiate academic (or traditional) intelligence from other skills (Diehl et al, 2005; Margrett et al., 2010). *The broad range of skills related to how individuals shape, select, or adapt to their physical and social environments is termed practical intelligence*. The examples at the beginning of this section illustrate how practical intelligence is measured. Such real-life problems differ in three main ways from traditional tests (Diehl et al., 2005): People are more motivated to solve them; personal experience is more relevant; and they have more than one correct answer. Research evidence shows that performance on these kinds of tests, while related to basic cognitive abilities such as fluid intelligence, are also strongly related to lived experience, age, and crystallized intelligence (Frank et al., 2016; Gamaldo & Allaire, 2016; Margrett et al., 2010).

practical intelligence
Broad range of skills related to how individuals shape, select, or adapt to their physical and social environments.

Applications of Practical Intelligence

Practical intelligence and postformal thinking (see Chapter 10) across adulthood have been linked. Specifically, the extent to which a practical problem evokes an emotional reaction, in conjunction with experience and one's preferred mode of thinking, determines whether one will use a cognitive analysis (thinking one's way through the problem), a problem-focused action (tackling the problem head-on by doing something about it), passive-dependent behavior (withdrawing from the situation), or avoidant thinking and denial (rationalizing to redefine the problem and so minimize its seriousness).

Research indicates that adults tend to blend emotion with cognition in their approach to practical problems, whereas adolescents tend not to because they get hung up in the logic. Summarizing over a decade of her research, Blanchard-Fields (2007) notes that for late middle-aged adults, highly emotional problems (issues with high levels of feelings, such as dealing with unexpected deaths) are associated most with passive-dependent and avoidant-denial approaches. In contrast, problems concerned more with instrumental issues (issues related to daily living such as grocery shopping, getting from place to place, etc.) and home management (issues related to living in one's household) are dealt with differently. Middle-aged adults use problem-focused strategies more frequently in dealing with instrumental problems than do adolescents or young adults. Clearly, middle-aged adults put considerable weight on the context in which the problem is set, and take situational factors into account more than do younger adults. Thus, we cannot characterize problem-solving in middle age in any one way.

Mechanics and Pragmatics of Intelligence

When we combine the research on practical intelligence with the research on the components or mechanics of intelligence discussed in Chapter 10, we have a more complete description of cognition in adulthood. The two-component model of life-span intelligence (Baltes et al., 2006) is grounded in the dynamic interplay among the biopsychosocial forces (see Chapter 1). *The mechanics of intelligence reflects those aspects of intelligence comprising fluid intelligence* (see Chapter 10). The pragmatics of intelligence *refers to those aspects of intelligence reflecting crystallized intelligence* (see Chapter 10). However, as Baltes and colleagues point out, the biopsychosocial forces differentially influence the mechanics and pragmatics of intelligence. Whereas the mechanics of intelligence is more directly an expression of the neurophysiological architecture of the mind, the pragmatics of intelligence is associated more with the bodies of knowledge that are available from and mediated through one's culture (Baltes et al., 2006).

mechanics of intelligence
Those aspects of intelligence comprising fluid intelligence.

pragmatics of intelligence
Refers to those aspects of intelligence reflecting crystallized intelligence.

These concepts are illustrated in the left side of ❱ Figure 13.6. The mechanics of intelligence in later life is more associated with the fundamental organization of the central nervous system (i.e., biological forces). Thus, it is more closely linked with a gradual loss of brain efficiency with age (Horn & Hofer, 1992), a finding supported by brain imaging studies (Sugiura, 2016).

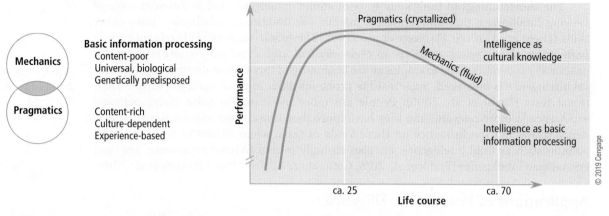

> **Figure 13.6**
> Conceptualization of the mechanics and pragmatics of intelligence across the life span. As described later, the mechanics of intelligence correspond to fluid intelligence and the pragmatics to crystallized intelligence.

Based on Baltes, P. B. (1993). The aging mind: Potential and limits. *The Gerontologist, 33,* 580–594.

On the other hand, the pragmatics of intelligence is more closely associated with psychological and sociocultural forces. At the psychological level, knowledge structures change as a function of the accumulated acquisition of knowledge over time. For example, the more you learn about the American Revolution, the more differentiated your knowledge system becomes, going, for example, from a basic knowledge that the Americans declared their independence from Great Britain and won the war to a more elaborate knowledge about the various battles, how the Americans nearly lost the war, and that many people in America sided with the British. At the sociocultural level, knowledge structures are also influenced by how we are socialized given the particular historical period in which we are raised. For example, during the Vietnam War era, the U.S. government viewed the Hanoi government as the enemy. Today, trade and other interactions occur routinely between the two, implying that on certain issues they are allies. As a result, how people view and consider dilemmas and problems that are influenced by historical context may result in very different solutions. Such differences reflect the sociocultural and historical contexts of particular points in time. Overall, these knowledge structures influence the way we implement our professional skills, solve everyday problems, and conduct the business of life (Baltes et al., 2006).

Finally, as the right portion of Figure 13.6 shows, the developmental pathways the mechanics and pragmatics of intelligence take across the course of adult life differ. Given that biological and genetic forces govern the mechanics more, there is a downward trajectory with age beginning by middle age. However, given that the pragmatics of intelligence is governed more by environmental and cultural factors, there is an upward trajectory that is maintained across the adult life span.

Becoming an Expert

One day John Cavanaugh was driving along when his car suddenly began coughing and sputtering. As deftly as possible, he pulled over to the side of the road, turned off the engine, opened the hood, and proceeded to look inside. It was hopeless; to him, it looked like a jumble of unknown parts. After the car was towed to a garage, a middle-aged mechanic set about fixing it. Within a few minutes, the car was running like new. How?

We saw earlier in this chapter aspects of intelligence grounded in experience (crystallized intelligence) tend to improve throughout most of adulthood. In a real-world experiential perspective, each of us becomes an expert at something important to us, such as our work, interpersonal relationships, cooking, sports, or auto repair. In this sense, an expert is someone who is much better at a task than people who have not put much effort into it. We tend to become selective experts in some areas while remaining amateurs or novices at others.

What makes experts better than novices? It's how experts handle the problem (Ericsson & Towne, 2010; Hambrick et al., 2016). For novices, the goal for accomplishing the activity is to reach as rapidly as possible a satisfactory performance level that is stable and "autonomous." In contrast, experts build up a wealth of knowledge about alternative ways of solving problems or making decisions. These well-developed knowledge structures are the major difference between experts and novices, and they enable experts to bypass steps needed by novices (Chi, 2006).

Experts don't always follow the rules as novices do; they are more flexible, creative, and curious; and they have superior strategies grounded on superior knowledge for accomplishing a task (Ericsson & Towne, 2010). Even though experts may be slower in terms of raw speed because they spend more time planning, their ability to skip steps puts them at a decided advantage. In a way, this represents "the triumph of knowledge over reasoning" (Charness & Bosman, 1990).

What happens to expertise over the adult life span? Research evidence indicates expert performance tends to peak by middle age and drops off slightly after that (Masunaga & Horn, 2001). However, the declines in expert performance are not nearly as great as they are for the abilities of information processing, memory, and fluid intelligence that underlie expertise, and expertise may sometimes compensate for declines in underlying cognitive abilities (Masunaga & Horn, 2001; Taylor et al., 2005).

Such compensation is seen in expert judgments about such things as how long certain figure skating maneuvers will take. Older people who were experts were as good as younger adults who were still skating at predicting the amount of time skating moves take (Diersch et al., 2012). Thus, it appears knowledge based on experience is an important component of expertise. Indeed, researchers argue that people become "experts by experience" (Tolkko, 2016). But how do people keep acquiring knowledge? That's achieved through lifelong learning.

Think About It

Can expertise be taught? Why or why not?

Lifelong Learning

Many people work in occupations where information and technology change rapidly. To keep up with these changes, many organizations and professions now emphasize the importance of learning how to learn, rather than learning specific content that may become outdated in a couple of years. For most people, a college education will probably not be the last educational experience they have in their careers. Workers in many professions— such as medicine, nursing, social work, psychology, auto mechanics, and teaching— are now required to obtain continuing education credits to stay current in their fields. Online learning has made lifelong learning more accessible to professionals and interested adults alike (Council for Adult and Experiential Learning, 2016).

Lifelong learning is gaining acceptance as the best way to approach the need for keeping active cognitively and is viewed as a critical part of aging globally (Formosa, 2014; Swindell, 2012), but should lifelong learning be approached as merely an extension of earlier educational experiences? Knowles, Holton, and Swanson (2015) argue teaching aimed at children and youth differs from teaching aimed at adults. Adult learners differ from their younger counterparts in several ways:

- Adults have a higher need to know why they should learn something before undertaking it.
- Adults enter a learning situation with more and different experience on which to build.
- Adults are most willing to learn those things they believe are necessary to deal with real-world problems rather than abstract, hypothetical situations.
- Most adults are more motivated to learn by internal factors (such as self-esteem or personal satisfaction) than by external factors (such as a job promotion or pay raise).

Lifelong learning is becoming increasingly important, but educators need to keep in mind learning styles change as people age. Effective lifelong learning requires smart decisions about how to keep knowledge updated and what approach works best among the many different learning options available (Knowles et al., 2015).

As described in the Spotlight on Research feature, software companies would do well to take into account differences in expertise and in learning when designing updated versions of familiar programs and apps.

Spotlight On Research

Designing Software for Middle-Aged and Older Nonexperts

Who were the investigators, and what was the aim of the study? Ali Darejeh and Dalbir Singh (2014) observed that software companies such as Microsoft periodically make significant changes to their core products. Such changes are often well-founded and greatly enhance the functionality of the program or app. However, the changes may be difficult for some people to adapt to, thereby impairing their ability to use the program or app effectively and efficiently.

Darejeh and Singh were especially interested in how well middle-aged adults could learn how to use the Ribbon interface in Microsoft (MS) Office Outlook, as the introduction of the Ribbon was a major design change.

How did the investigators measure the topic of interest? Darejeh and Singh observed participants' actions while they were using MS Outlook. Participants also completed several evaluation forms, and they were interviewed.

Who were the participants in the study? The participants were four men and six women staff or students of Apple English Institute in Kuala Lumpur, Malaysia, between the ages of 52 and 66. None of the participants had significant background knowledge about computers, worked on computers daily, were very familiar with programming languages, or were proficient with Microsoft Outlook.

What was the design of the study? The design was a longitudinal design that lasted 62 days during which tasks to be completed on MS Office were assigned (e.g., create a new e-mail and attach a file to it; create a new meeting). Sessions lasted 45 minutes each.

Were there ethical concerns with the study? There were no ethical concerns as participants were appropriately informed about the study.

What were the results? Darejeh and Singh found that only two of the nine tasks could be completed by more than half the participants using MS Outlook as designed by Microsoft. However, based on interviews and other assessments, Darejeh and Singh redesigned the MS Outlook interface to include such changes as using more meaningful icons, showing only those tools that were useful for the tasks at hand, and providing more complete descriptions of how tools are used. When this redesigned interface was provided, all but one of the tasks was completed by at least 80% of the participants.

What did the investigators conclude? Darejeh and Singh concluded that users who are not experts learn better when provided more appropriately designed interfaces with embedded help. The redesigned interface greatly improved self-learning as measured by a decrease in the time and in the number of steps needed as well as much improved performance. In sum, upgrades to software need to take learner differences into account.

What converging evidence would strengthen their conclusions? Future research should include people at different levels of expertise with the target software or app, and participants should be of a wider age range.

TEST YOURSELF 13.2

Recall

1. The skills and knowledge necessary for people to function in everyday life make up _____.
2. The two components of a life-span model of intelligence are _____ and _____.
3. The triumph of knowledge over reasoning is one way to describe _____.
4. Due to rapidly changing technology and information, many educators now support the concept of _____.

Interpret

Based on the cognitive-developmental changes described in this section, what types of jobs would be done best by middle-aged adults?

Apply

- If you were asked to design a cognitive training program for middle-aged adults, what strategies would you include?

Check your answers to the Recall Questions at the end of the chapter.

LEARNING OBJECTIVES

- What is the five-factor model? What evidence is there for stability in personality traits?

- What changes occur in people's priorities and personal concerns? How does a person achieve generativity? How is midlife best described?

Abby was attending her 25th high school reunion. She hadn't seen her friend Michelle since they graduated. Abby remembered that in high school Michelle was always surrounded by a group of people. She always walked up to people and initiated conversations, was at ease with strangers, pleasant, and often described as the "life of the party." Abby wondered if Michelle would be the same outgoing person she was in high school.

Many of us eventually attend a high school reunion. It is amusing, so it is said, to see how our classmates changed over the years. In addition to noticing gray or missing hair and a few wrinkles, we should pay attention to personality characteristics. The questions that surfaced for Abby are similar to the ones we generate ourselves. For example, will Katy be the same outgoing person she was as captain of the cheerleaders? Will Ted still be as concerned about social issues at 43 as he was at 18?

To learn as much about our friends as possible we could make careful observations of our classmates' personalities over the course of several reunions. Then, at the gathering marking 25 years since graduation, we could examine the trends we observed. Did our classmates' personalities change substantially or did they remain essentially the same as they were 60 years earlier?

How we think these questions will be answered provides clues to our personal biases concerning personality stability or change across adulthood. As we will see, biases about continuity and discontinuity are more obvious in personality research than in any other area of adult development.

The Five-Factor Trait Model

In the past few decades, one of the most important advances in research on adult development and aging has been the emergence of a personality theory aimed specifically at describing adults. Due mostly to the efforts of Robert McCrae and Paul Costa, Jr. (Costa & McCrae, 2011; McCrae, 2016; McCrae & Costa, 2003), we are now able to describe adults' personality traits using five dimensions: neuroticism, extraversion, openness to experience, agreeableness, and conscientiousness. These dimensions (the five-factor model or the so-called Big Five traits) are strongly grounded in cross-sectional, longitudinal, and sequential research. First, though, let's take a closer look at each dimension.

- *People who are high on the* neuroticism *dimension tend to be anxious, hostile, self-conscious, depressed, impulsive, and vulnerable.* They may show violent or negative emotions that interfere with their ability to get along with others or to handle problems in everyday life. People who are low on this dimension tend to be calm, even-tempered, self-content, comfortable, unemotional, and hardy.
- *Individuals who are high on the* extraversion *dimension thrive on social interaction, like to talk, take charge easily, readily express their opinions and feelings, like to keep busy, have boundless energy, and prefer stimulating and challenging environments.* Such people tend to enjoy people-oriented jobs such as social work and sales, and they often have humanitarian goals. People who are low on this dimension tend to be reserved, quiet, passive, serious, and emotionally unreactive.

neuroticism

Personality trait dimension associated with the tendency to be anxious, hostile, self-conscious, depressed, impulsive, and vulnerable.

extraversion

Personality trait dimension associated with the tendency to thrive on social interaction, to like to talk, to take charge easily, to readily express their opinions and feelings, to keep busy, to have boundless energy, and to prefer stimulating and challenging environments.

openness to experience

Personality dimension that reflects a tendency to have a vivid imagination and dream life, an appreciation of art, and a strong desire to try anything once.

agreeableness

Dimension of personality associated with being accepting, willing to work with others, and caring.

conscientiousness

Dimension of personality in which people tend to be hard-working, ambitious, energetic, scrupulous, and persevering.

- *Being high on the* openness to experience *dimension tends to have a vivid imagination and dream life, an appreciation of art, and a strong desire to try anything once.* These individuals tend to be naturally curious about things and to make decisions based on situational factors rather than absolute rules. People who are readily open to new experiences place a relatively low emphasis on personal economic gain. They tend to choose jobs such as the ministry or counseling, which offer diversity of experience rather than high pay. People who are low on this dimension tend to be down-to-earth, uncreative, conventional, uncurious, and conservative.

- *Scoring high on the* agreeableness *dimension is associated with being accepting, willing to work with others, and caring.* People who score low on this dimension (i.e., demonstrate high levels of antagonism) tend to be ruthless, suspicious, stingy, antagonistic, critical, and irritable.

- *People who show high levels of* conscientiousness *tend to be hard-working, ambitious, energetic, scrupulous, and persevering.* Such people have a strong desire to make something of themselves. People at the opposite end of this scale tend to be negligent, lazy, disorganized, late, aimless, and nonpersistent.

The five-factor model has been examined cross-culturally (Church, 2016; McCrae, 2016). Research evidence generally shows that the same five factors appear across at least 50 cultures, including rarely studied Arabic and Black African groups (McCrae & Terracciano, 2005). Heine and Buchtel (2009) point out, though, that much of this research has been conducted by Westerners; so it remains to be seen whether similar studies conducted by local researchers will have the same outcomes. Additionally, Church (2016) points out that it is difficult to validate the five-factor model in preliterate cultures.

What Happens to Traits Across Adulthood?

Costa and McCrae have investigated whether the general traits that make up their model remain stable across adulthood (e.g., Costa & McCrae, 2011; McCrae, 2016; McCrae & Costa, 2003). They suggest personality traits stop changing by age 30, after which they appear to be "set in plaster" (Costa & McCrae, 1994, p. 21). The data from the Costa, McCrae, and colleagues' studies came from the Baltimore Longitudinal Study of Aging for the 114 men who took the Guilford-Zimmerman Temperament Survey (GZTS) on three occasions, with each of the two follow-up tests about six years apart.

What Costa and colleagues found was surprising. Even over a 12-year period, the 10 traits measured by the GZTS remained highly stable; the correlations ranged from .68 to .85. In much of personality research we might expect to find this degree of stability over a week or two, but to see it over 12 years is noteworthy.

We would normally be skeptical of such consistency over a long period. But similar findings were obtained in other studies. In a longitudinal study of 60-, 80-, and 100-year-olds, Martin, Long, and Poon (2002) found stability higher for those in their 70s and 80s than for centenarians. However, some interesting changes did occur in the very old. There was an increase in suspiciousness and sensitivity that could be explained by increased wariness of victimization in older adulthood.

Most occupations require the acquisition of new information over time through lifelong learning so that workers can do their jobs well and stay up-to-date on the latest information.

Stability was also observed in longitudinal data conducted over various lengths of time, from a 7-year period (Mõttus, Johnson, & Deary, 2012; Roberts & DelVecchio, 2000) to as long as a 30-year span (Leon et al., 1979). According to this evidence, it appears individuals change little in self-reported personality traits over periods of up to 30 years long and over the age range of 20 to 90 years of age.

However, there is evidence both stability and change can be detected in personality trait development across the adult life span (Allemand, Zimprich, & Hendriks, 2008; Caspi, Roberts, & Shiner, 2005; Debast et al., 2014; Mõttus et al., 2012; Schultz & Schultz, 2017). These findings came about because of advances in statistical techniques in teasing apart longitudinal and cross-sectional data (see Chapter 1). Researchers find the way people differ in

Photographee.eu/Shutterstock.com

their personality becomes more pronounced with older age. For example, researchers find extraversion and openness decrease with age whereas agreeableness increases with age. Conscientious appears to peak in middle age. Most interestingly, neuroticism often disappears or is much less apparent in late life. Such changes are found in studies that examine larger populations across a larger age range (e.g., 16 to mid-80s) and greater geographical regions (e.g., United States and Great Britain).

Ursula Staudinger and colleagues have a perspective that reconciles both stability and change in personality traits (Mühlig-Versen, Bowen, & Staudinger, 2012; Staudinger, 2015). They suggest personality takes on two forms: adjustment and growth. Personality adjustment *involves developmental changes in terms of their adaptive value and functionality, such as functioning effectively within society, and how personality contributes to everyday life running smoothly.* Personality growth *refers to ideal end states such as increased self-transcendence, wisdom, and integrity.* Examples of this will be discussed later and includes Erikson's theory.

Both of these personality dimensions interact because growth cannot occur without adjustment. However, Staudinger (2015) argues while growth in terms of ideal end states does not necessarily occur in everyone, since it is less easily acquired, strategies for adjustment develops across the latter half of the life span. This framework can be used to interpret stability and change in the Big Five personality factors.

First, the consensus regarding change in the Big Five with increasing age is the absence of neuroticism and the presence of agreeableness and conscientiousness. These three traits are associated with personality adjustment, especially in terms of becoming emotionally less volatile and more attuned to social demands and social roles (Mühlig-Versen et al., 2012; Staudinger, 2015). These characteristics allow older adults to maintain and regain levels of well-being in the face of loss, threats, and challenges; common occurrences in late life.

Studies also show a decrease in openness to new experiences with increasing age (e.g., Graham & Lachman, 2012; Helson et al., 2002; Roberts et al., 2006; Srivastava et al., 2003). Staudinger argues openness to experience is related to personal maturity because it is highly correlated with ego development, wisdom, and emotional complexity. Evidence suggests these three aspects of personality (ego level, wisdom, and emotional complexity) do not increase with age and may show decline (Grühn et al., 2013; Mühlig-Versen et al., 2012; Staudinger, Dörner, & Mickler, 2005; Staudinger, 2015). Staudinger concludes personal growth in adulthood appears to be rare rather than normative.

To summarize, there appears to be increases in adjustment aspects of personality with increasing age, and it could be normative. At the same time, however, the basic indicators of personality growth tend to show stability or decline. You might ask, what's going on?

The most likely answer is personality growth or change across adulthood does not normally occur unless there are special circumstances and with an environmental push for it to occur. Thus, the personality-related adjustment that grows in adulthood does so in response to ever-changing developmental challenges and tasks, such as establishing a career, marriage, and family.

Based upon a detailed analysis of individual patterns of personality stability and change, Wrzus and Roberts (2017) propose a model that accounts for both developmental patterns. The **T**riggering situations, **E**xpectancy, **S**tates/**S**tate Expressions, and Reactions (TESSERA) model, shown in ❱ Figure 13.7, describes a process by which long-term personality development is the product of repeated short-term, situational processes. These short-term processes repeat and create a feedback loop. These processes in turn can result in changes in personality characteristics and behavior over time, showing up eventually as changes in personality. That these short-term processes differ across people is why some people show changes in personality traits and others do not. It can also explain why the life narratives of people also differ, a topic we will explore next.

Changing Priorities in Midlife

Joyce, a 52-year-old preschool teacher, thought carefully about what she believes is important in life. "I definitely feel differently about what I want to accomplish. When I was younger, I wanted to advance and be a great teacher. Now, although I still want to be good,

personality adjustment
Developmental changes in terms of their adaptive value and functionality such as whether one can function effectively within society and how personality contributes to everyday life running smoothly.

personality growth
Form of personality that refers to ideal end states such as increased self-transcendence, wisdom, and integrity.

Think About It
Does evidence of stability in traits support the idea that some aspects of personality are genetic? Why or why not?

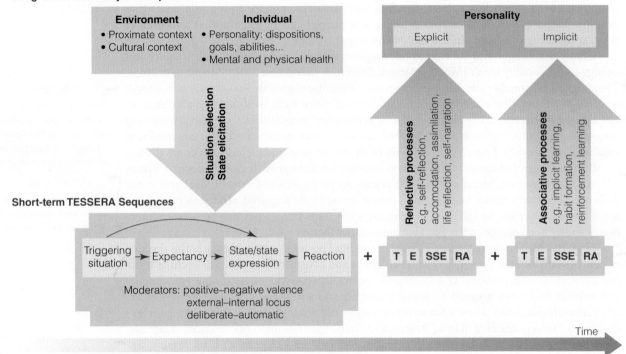

▶ **Figure 13.7**

TESSERA framework of adult personality development

Long-term Personality Development

SOURCE: Wrzus, C., & Roberts, B. W. (2017). Processes of personality development in adulthood: The TESSERA framework. *Personality and Social Psychology Review*, doi:10.1177/1088868316652279

I'm more concerned with providing help to the new teachers around here. I've got a lot of on-the-job experience that I can pass along."

Joyce is not alone. Despite the evidence that personality traits remain stable during adulthood, many middle-aged people report that their personal priorities change during middle age. In general, they report that they are increasingly concerned with helping younger people achieve rather than with getting ahead themselves. *In his psychosocial theory, Erikson argued that this shift in priorities reflects generativity, or being productive by helping others to ensure the continuation of society by guiding the next generation.*

Achieving generativity can be enriching. It is grounded in the successful resolution of the previous six phases of Erikson's theory (see Chapter 1). There are numerous avenues for generativity (Kotre, 2005; McAdams, 2001, 2015; McAdams & Guo, 2015), such as parenting, mentoring, and creating one's legacy by doing something of lasting importance. Sources of generativity do not vary across ethnic groups (Bates, 2009).

Some adults do not achieve generativity. Instead, they become bored, self-indulgent, and unable to contribute to the continuation of society. *Erikson referred to this state as* stagnation, *in which people are unable to deal with the needs of their children or to provide mentoring to younger adults.*

What Are Generative People Like?

Research shows that generativity is different from traits; for example, generativity is more related to societal engagement than are traits (Wilt, Cox, & McAdams, 2010). One of the best approaches to generativity is McAdams's model (McAdams, 2015), shown in ▶ Figure 13.8.

This multidimensional model shows how generativity results from the complex interconnections among societal and inner forces. The tension between creating a product or an outcome that outlives oneself and selflessly bestowing one's efforts as a gift to the next generation (reflecting a concern for what is good for society) results in a concern for the

generativity

In Erikson's theory, being productive by helping others to ensure the continuation of society by guiding the next generation.

stagnation

In Erikson's theory, the state in which people are unable to deal with the needs of their children or to provide mentoring to younger adults.

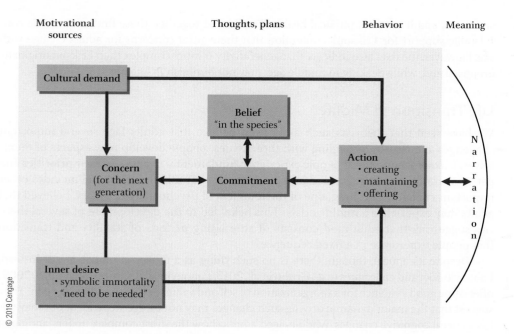

| Motivational sources | | Thoughts, plans | | Behavior | Meaning |

next generation and a belief in the goodness of the human enterprise. The positive resolution of this conflict finds middle-aged adults developing a generative commitment, which produces generative actions. *A person derives personal meaning from being generative by constructing a life story or* narrative, *which helps create the person's identity.*

The components of McAdams's model relate differently to personality traits. For example, generative *concern* is a general personality tendency of interest in caring for younger individuals, and generative action is the actual behaviors that promote the well-being of the next generation. Generative concern relates to life satisfaction and overall happiness, whereas generative *action* does not. For example, new grandparents may derive much satisfaction from their grandchildren and are greatly concerned with their well-being, but have little desire to engage in the daily hassles of caring for them on a regular basis.

Although they can be expressed by adults of all ages, certain types of generativity are more common at some ages than others. For example, middle-aged and older adults show a greater preoccupation with generativity themes than do younger adults in their accounts of personally meaningful life experiences (McAdams, 2015; McAdams & Guo, 2015). Middle-aged adults make more generative commitments (e.g., "save enough money for my daughter to go to medical school"), reflecting a major difference in the inner and outer worlds of middle-aged and older adults as opposed to younger adults. An important aspect of generativity is leaving a personal legacy (Newton & Jones, 2016).

Similar research focusing specifically on middle-aged women yields comparable results. Hills (2013) argues that leaving a legacy, a major example of generativity in practice, is a core concern in midlife, more so than at any other age. Schoklitsch & Bauman (2012) point out that the capacity of generativity peaks during midlife but that people continue to accomplish generative tasks into late life (e.g., great-grandparenthood).

How well do these ideas generalize across ethnic groups and cultures? A study of second-generation Chinese American women found similar trends in generativity with European American women (Grant, 2007). In one of the few studies to examine generativity across cultures, Hofer et al. (2008) examined it in Cameroon, Costa Rica, and Germany. They found that McAdams's model could be successfully applied across the three cultures.

These data demonstrate that the personal concerns of middle-aged adults are fundamentally different from those of younger adults. In fact, generativity may be a stronger predictor of emotional and physical well-being in midlife and old age (Gruenewald, Liao, & Seeman, 2012; McAdams, 2015; McAdams & Guo, 2015; Wilt et al., 2010). For example, among both women and men, generativity is associated with positive emotion and satisfaction with life

narrative

Way in which a person derives personal meaning from being generative by constructing a life story, which helps create the person's identity.

and work, and it predicts physical health. Considered together, these findings provide considerable support for Erikson's contention that the central concerns for adults change with age. However, the data also indicate that generativity is more complex than Erikson originally proposed and, while peaking in middle age, may not diminish in late life.

Life Transition in Midlife

We have seen that theorists such as Erikson believe that adults face several important challenges and that by struggling with these issues, people develop new aspects of themselves. Erikson's notion that people experience fundamental changes in their priorities and personal concerns was grounded in the possibility that middle adulthood includes other important changes. Carl Jung, one of the founders of psychoanalytic theory, believed that adults may experience a midlife crisis. This belief led to the development of several theories suggesting that adulthood consists of alternating periods of stability and transition that people experience in a fixed sequence.

Despite its appeal, though, there is no such thing as a universal midlife crisis. Instead, Labouvie-Vief and colleagues (e.g., Grühn et al., 2013; Labouvie-Vief, Grühn, & Mouras, 2009) offer some good evidence for a reorganization of self and values across the adult life span. They suggest that the major dynamic driving such changes may not be age-dependent but may follow general cognitive changes. Middle-aged adults show the most complex understanding of self, emotions, and motivations. Cognitive complexity also is shown to be the strongest predictor of higher levels of complexity in general. From this approach, a midlife "crisis" may be the result of general gains in cognitive complexity from early to middle adulthood.

This increase in cognitive complexity may help people make what could be called midlife corrections. Abigail Stewart (Newton & Stewart, 2012; Torges, Stewart, & Duncan, 2008) found that well-educated women who reported regrets for adopting a traditional feminine role in life (i.e., they wished they had pursued an education or a career) and subsequently made adjustments in midlife were better off than those who did not make adjustments or had no role regrets at all. *Stewart suggests that rather than a midlife crisis, such an adjustment may be more appropriately considered a* midlife correction, *reevaluating one's roles and dreams and making the necessary corrections.*

Perhaps the best way to view midlife is as a time of both gains and losses (Lachman, 2004). That is, the changes people perceive in midlife can be viewed as representing both gains and losses. Competence, ability to handle stress, sense of personal control, purpose in life, and social responsibility are all at their peak, whereas physical abilities, women's ability to bear children, and physical appearance are examples of changes that many view as negative. This gain–loss view emphasizes two things. First, the exact timing of change is not fixed but occurs over an extended period of time. Second, change can be both positive and negative at the same time. Thus, rather than seeing midlife as a time of crisis, one may want to view it as a period during which several aspects of one's life acquire new meanings.

midlife correction
Reevaluating one's roles and dreams and making the necessary correction.

TEST YOURSELF 13.3

Recall

1. The dimensions in the five-factor theory of personality include neuroticism, extraversion, openness to experience, agreeableness, and _____.

2. According to Erikson, an increasing concern with helping younger people achieve is termed _____.

3. According to McAdams, the meaning one derives from being generative happens through the process of _____.

4. Reevaluating one's roles and dreams and making the necessary corrections in middle age is called _____.

Interpret

- How can you reconcile the data from trait research, which indicates little change, with the data from other research, which shows substantial change in personality during adulthood?

Apply

- If psychotherapy assumes that a person can change behavior over time, what is the relation between personality and behavior from this perspective?

Check your answers to the Recall Questions at the end of the chapter.

LEARNING OBJECTIVES

- Who are the kinkeepers in families?
- How does the relationship between middle-aged parents and their young adult children change?
- How do middle-aged adults deal with their aging parents?
- How do grandchildren and grandparents interact? How is grandparenthood meaningful? What issues matter for grandparents caring for grandchildren?

Lily is facing a major milestone: Her youngest child, Megan, is about to head off to college. But instead of feeling depressed, as she thought she would, Lily feels almost elated at the prospect. She and Huang are finally free of the day-to-day parenting duties of the past 30 years. Lily is looking forward to getting to know her husband again. She wonders whether there is something wrong with her for being excited that her daughter is leaving.

People such as Lily connect generations. Family ties across the generations provide the context for socialization and for continuity in the family's identity. At the center agewise are members of the middle-aged generation, such as Lily, who serve as the links between their aging parents and their own maturing children (Deane et al., 2016; Fingerman et al., 2012; Hareven, 2001). *Middle-aged mothers (more than fathers) tend to take on this role of* kinkeeper, *the person who gathers family members together for celebrations and keeps them in touch with each other.*

Think about the major issues confronting a typical middle-aged couple: maintaining a good marriage, parenting responsibilities, dealing with children who are becoming adults themselves, handling job pressures, and worrying about aging parents, just to name a few. Middle-aged adults truly have a lot to deal with every day in balancing their responsibilities to their children and their aging parents (Boyczuk & Fletcher, 2016). *Indeed, middle-aged adults are sometimes referred to as the* sandwich generation ← *because they are caught between the competing demands of two generations: their parents and their children.*

kinkeeper

Person who gathers family members together for celebrations and keeps them in touch with each other, usually a middle-aged mother.

sandwich generation

Middle-aged adults who are caught between the competing demands of two generations: their parents and their children.

Adult children's relationships with their parents often include a friendship dimension.

Letting Go: Middle-Aged Adults and Their Children

Sometime during middle age, most parents experience two positive developments with regard to their children (Buhl, 2008). Suddenly their children see them in a new light, and the children leave home.

The extent parents support and approve of their children's attempts at being independent matters. Most parents manage the transition successfully (Owen, 2005). That's not to say parents are heartless. As depicted in the cartoon, when children leave home, emotional bonds are disrupted. Mothers in all ethnic groups report feeling sad at the time children leave, but have more positive feelings about the potential for growth in their relationships with their children (Feldman, 2010). Still, parents provide considerable emotional support (by staying in touch) and financial help (such as paying college tuition, providing a free place to live until the child finds employment) when possible (Farris, 2016).

A positive experience with launching children is strongly influenced by the extent the parents perceive a job well done and their children have turned out well (Farris, 2016; Mitchell, 2010).

John Lund/Sam Diephuis/Blend Images/Alamy Stock Photo

Children are regarded as successes when they meet parents' culturally based developmental expectations, and they are seen as "good kids" when there is agreement between parents and children in basic values.

Parents' satisfaction with the empty nest is sometimes short-lived. Roughly half of young adults in the United States return to their parents' home at least once after moving out (Farris, 2016). There is evidence these young adults, called "boomerang kids" (Farris, 2016; Mitchell, 2006), reflect a less permanent, more mobile contemporary society.

Why do children move back? A major impetus is the increased costs of living on their own when saddled with college debt, especially if the societal economic situation is bad and jobs are not available. This was especially true during the Great Recession of the late 2000s and early 2010s. It also reflects the different kind of relationship millennial adults have with their parents and a different attitude about living back at home (Farris, 2016).

Giving Back: Middle-Aged Adults and Their Aging Parents

Most middle-aged adults have parents who are in reasonably good health. But for nearly a quarter of adults like Joan in the Real People feature, being a child of aging parents involves providing some level of care (Hyer, Mullen & Jackson, 2017). How adult children become care providers varies a great deal from person to person, but the job of caring for older parents usually falls to a daughter or a daughter-in-law (Barnett, 2013), and daughters also tend to coordinate care provided by multiple siblings (Friedman & Seltzer, 2010). In Japan, even though the oldest son is responsible for parental care, it is his wife who actually does the day-to-day caregiving for her own parents and her in-laws (Lee, 2010).

filial obligation

Sense of obligation to care for one's parents if necessary.

Most adult children feel a sense of responsibility, termed filial obligation, *to care for their parents if necessary.* Adult child care providers sometimes express the feeling they "owe it to Mom or Dad" to care for them; after all, their parents provided for them for many years, and now the shoe is on the other foot (Gans, 2007). Adult children often provide the majority of care when needed to their parents in all Western and non-Western cultures studied, but the same is true especially in Asian cultures (Barnett, 2013; Haley, 2013; Lai, 2010).

Real People   Applying Human Development

Taking Care of Mom

Everything seemed to be going well for Joan. Her career was taking off, her youngest daughter Kelly had just entered high school, and her marriage to Bill was better than ever. So when her phone rang one June afternoon, she was taken by surprise.

The voice on the other end was matter-of-fact. Joan's mother had suffered a major stroke and would need someone to care for her. Because her mother did not have sufficient medical and long-term care insurance to afford a nursing home, Joan made the only decision she could— her mom would move

in with her, Bill, and Kelly. Joan firmly believed that because her mom had provided for her, Joan owed it to her mom to do the same now that she was in need.

What Joan didn't count on was that taking care of her mom was the most difficult yet most rewarding thing she had ever done. Joan quickly realized that her days of lengthy business trips and seminars were over, as was her quick rise up the company leadership ladder. Other employees now brought back the great new ideas and could respond to out-of-town crises quickly. As hard as it was, Joan knew that

her career trajectory had taken a different turn. And she and Bill had more disagreements than she could ever remember, usually about the decreased amount of time they had to spend with each other. Kelly's demands to be driven here and there also added to Joan's stress.

But Joan and her mom were able to develop the kind of relationship they could not have otherwise and to talk about issues they had long suppressed. Although caring for a physically disabled mother was extremely taxing, Joan and her mother's ability to connect on a different level made it worthwhile.

Roughly 50 million Americans provide unpaid care for older parents, in-laws, grand-parents, and other older loved ones (National Alliance for Caregiving & AARP, 2015). The typical care provider is a middle-aged woman who is employed outside the home, has an average household income of under $46,000, and provides more than 20 hours per week of unpaid care. They expect to care for their loved one for about 10 years.

Stresses and Rewards of Providing Care

Providing care is a major source of both stress and reward. On the stress side, adult children and other family caregivers are especially vulnerable from two main sources (Pearlin et al., 1990):

- Adult children may have trouble coping with declines in their parents' functioning, especially those involving cognitive abilities and problematic behavior, and with work overload, burnout, and loss of the previous relationship with a parent.
- If the care situation is perceived as confining or seriously infringes on the adult child's other responsibilities (spouse, parent, employee, etc.), then the situation is likely to be perceived negatively, and that may lead to family or job conflicts, economic problems, loss of self-identity, and decreased competence.

When caring for an aging parent, even the most devoted adult child caregiver will at times feel depressed, resentful, angry, or guilty (Cavanaugh, 1999; Haley, 2013; Hyer et al., 2017). Many middle-aged care providers are hard pressed financially: They may still be paying child care or college tuition expenses, perhaps trying to save adequately for their own retirement, and having to work more than one job to do it. Financial pressures are especially serious for those caring for parents with chronic conditions, such as Alzheimer's disease, that require services, such as adult day care, not adequately covered by medical insurance even if the older parent has supplemental coverage. In some cases, adult children may need to quit their jobs to provide care if adequate alternatives, such as adult day care, are unavailable or unaffordable, usually creating even more financial stress.

The stresses of caring for a parent mean the caregiver needs to carefully monitor his or her own health. Indeed, many professionals point out caring for the care provider is an important consideration to avoid care provider burnout (Ghosh, Capistrant, & Friedemann-Sánchez, 2017; Tamayo et al., 2010).

On the plus side, caring for an aging parent also has rewards. Caring for aging parents can bring parents and their adult children closer together and provide a way for adult children to feel they are giving back to their parents (Miller et al., 2008). Cross-cultural research examining Taiwanese (Lee, 2007) and Chinese (Zhan, 2006) participants confirms adults caring for aging parents can find the experience rewarding.

Cultural values enter into the care providing relationship in an indirect way (Mendez-Luck et al., 2016). Care providers in all cultures studied to date show a common set of outcomes: Care providers' stressors are appraised as burdensome, that creates negative health consequences for the care provider. However, cultural values influence the kinds of social support available to the care provider.

Things aren't always rosy from the parents' perspective, either. Independence and autonomy are important traditional values in some ethnic groups, and their loss is not taken lightly. Older adults in these groups are more likely to express the desire to pay a professional for assistance rather than ask a family member for help; they may find it demeaning to live with their children and express strong feelings about "not wanting to burden them" (Cahill et al., 2009). Most move in only as a last resort. Many adults who receive help with daily activities feel negatively about the situation, although cultural norms supporting the acceptance of help, such as in Japanese culture, significantly lessen those feelings (Park et al., 2013).

Caring for an older parent creates both stresses and rewards.

Jed Share/Taxi/Getty Images

Determining whether older parents are satisfied with the help their children provide is a complex issue (Cahill et al., 2009; Park et al., 2013). Based on a critical review of the research, Newsom (1999) proposes a model of how certain aspects of care can produce negative perceptions of care directly or by affecting the interactions between care provider and care recipient (see ▶ Figure 13.9). The important thing to conclude from the model is even under the best circumstances, there is no guarantee the help adult children provide their parents will be well received. Misunderstandings can occur, and the frustration caregivers feel may be translated directly into negative interactions.

Grandparenthood

Becoming a grandparent takes some help. Being a parent yourself, of course, is a prerequisite. But it is your children's decisions and actions that determine whether you experience the transition to grandparenthood, making this role different from most others we experience throughout life.

Most people become grandparents in their 40s and 50s, though some are older, or perhaps as young as their late 20s or early 30s. For many middle-aged adults, becoming a grandparent is a peak experience (Gonyea, 2013; Hoffman, Kaneshiro, & Compton, 2012). Although most research on grandparenting has been conducted with respect to heterosexual grandparents, attention to lesbian, gay, and transgender grandparents is increasing as these family forms increase in society (Allen & Roberto, 2016; Orel & Fruhauf, 2013).

How Do Grandparents Interact with Grandchildren?

Grandparents have many different ways of interacting with their grandchildren. Categorizing these styles has been attempted over many decades (e.g., Neugarten & Weinstein, 1964), but none of these attempts has been particularly successful because grandparents use different styles with different grandchildren and styles change as grandparents and grandchildren age (Gonyea, 2013; Hoffman et al., 2012).

Think About It

Why does parental caregiving fall mainly to women?

▶ **Figure 13.9**

Whether a care recipient perceives care to be good depends on interactions with the care provider and whether those interactions are perceived negatively.

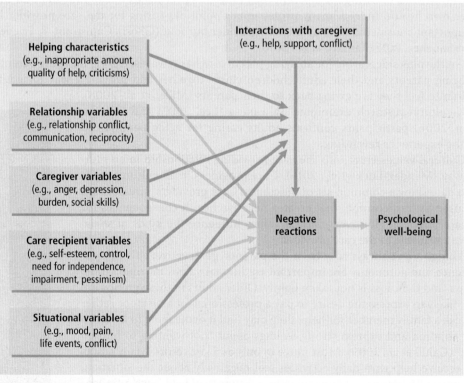

SOURCE: Newsom, J. T. (1999). Another side to caregiving: Negative reactions to being helped. *Current Directions in Psychological Science, 8*, 185.

An alternative approach involves considering the many functions grandparents serve and the changing nature of families (Hills, 2010). The social dimension includes societal needs and expectations of what grandparents are to do, such as passing on family history to grandchildren. The personal dimension includes the personal satisfaction and individual needs fulfilled by being a grandparent. Many grandparents pass on skills—as well as religious, social, and vocational values (social dimension)—through storytelling and advice, and they may feel great pride and satisfaction (personal dimension) from working with grandchildren on joint projects.

Grandchildren give grandparents a great deal in return. Grandchildren keep grandparents in touch with youth and the latest trends. Sharing the excitement of surfing the web in school may be one way grandchildren keep grandparents on the technological forefront.

Being a Grandparent Is Meaningful

Being a grandparent really matters. Most grandparents derive multiple meanings, and they are linked with generativity (Gonyea, 2013; Hayslip & Blumenthal, 2016). For some, grandparenting is the most important thing in their lives. For others, meaning comes from being seen as wise, from spoiling grandchildren, from recalling the relationship they had with their own grandparents, or from taking pride in the fact they will be followed by not one but two generations.

Grandchildren also highly value their relationships with grandparents, even when they are young adults (Alley, 2004; Hayslip & Blumenthal, 2016). Grandparents are valued as role models as well as for their personalities, the activities they share, and the attention they show to grandchildren. Emerging adult grandchildren (ages 21–29) derive both stress and rewards from caring for grandparents, much the same way middle-aged adults do when they care for their aging parents (Fruhauf, 2007).

Ethnic Differences

How grandparents and grandchildren interact varies in different ethnic groups. Intergenerational relationships are especially important and historically have been a source of strength in African American families (Waites, 2009) and Latino families (Hayslip & Blumenthal, 2016). African American grandparents play an important role in many aspects of their grandchildren's lives, such as family storytelling (Fabius, 2016) and religious education (King et al., 2006; Lewis, Seponski, & Camp, 2011). African American grandfathers, in particular, tend to perceive grandparenthood as a central role to a greater degree than do European American grandfathers (Kivett, 1991).

Latino American grandparents are more likely to participate in child rearing owing to a cultural core value of family (Burnette, 1999).

Native American grandparents are important in their grandchildren's lives, especially when the grandchildren live in urban settings and are reasonably close by (Limb, Shafer, & Sandoval, 2014). These grandparents provide grandchildren with a way to connect with their cultural heritage, and they are also likely to provide a great deal of care for their grandchildren (Mutchler, Baker, & Lee, 2007). Research indicates Native American grandparents also use their own experiences of cultural disruption to reinvest in their grandchildren to ensure the continuity of culture (Thompson, Cameron, & Fuller-Thompson, 2013). In general, Native American grandmothers take a more active role than do grandfathers, and are more likely to pass on traditional rituals (Woodbridge, 2008).

How grandparents and grandchildren interact varies across ethnic groups.

Brian Skyum/Alamy Stock Photo

Asian American grandparents, particularly if they are immigrants, serve as a primary source of traditional culture for their grandchildren (Yoon, 2005). When these grandparents become heavily involved in caring for their grandchildren, they especially want and need services that are culturally and linguistically appropriate.

When Grandparents Care for Grandchildren

Grandparenthood today is tougher than it used to be. Families are more mobile, which means grandparents are more often separated from their grandchildren by geographical distance. Grandparents also are more likely to have independent lives apart from their children and grandchildren. What being a grandparent entails in the 21st century is more ambiguous than it once was (Hayslip & Blumenthal, 2016; Hyer et al., 2017).

Perhaps the biggest change worldwide for grandparents is the increasing number serving as custodial parents or primary caregivers for their grandchildren (Choi, Sprang, & Eslinger, 2016). Estimates are that over 2.5 million grandparents provide basic needs (food, shelter, clothing) for one or more of their grandchildren (AARP, 2016). These situations are due to several factors (Choi et al., 2016): the most frequent is due to both parents being employed outside the home; when the parents are deceased, addicted, incarcerated, or unable to raise their children for some other reason; or when discipline or behavior problems have been exhibited by the grandchild.

Because most grandparents in this situation do not have legal custody of their grandchild, problems and challenges such as dealing with schools and obtaining school or health records are frequent. Typically, social service workers must assist grandparents in navigating the many unresponsive policies and systems they encounter when trying to provide the best possible assistance to their grandchildren (Cox, 2007). Clearly, public policy changes are needed to address these issues, especially regarding grandparents' rights regarding schools and health care for their grandchildren (Ellis, 2010).

Raising grandchildren is not easy. Financial stress, cramped living space, and social isolation are only some of the issues facing custodial grandparents (Choi et al, 2016; Hayslip & Blumenthal, 2016). All of these stresses are also reported cross-culturally; full-time custodial grandmothers in Kenya reported higher levels of stress than part-time caregivers (Oburu & Palmérus, 2005).

Even custodial grandparents raising grandchildren without these problems report more stress and role disruption than noncustodial grandparents, though most grandparents are resilient and manage to cope (Hayslip & Blumenthal, 2016; Hayslip et al., 2013). Most custodial grandparents consider their situation better for their grandchild than any other alternative and report surprisingly few negative effects on their marriages.

TEST YOURSELF 13.4

Recall

1. The term _____ refers to middle-aged adults who have both living parents and children of their own.

2. The people who gather the family together for celebrations and keep family members in touch are called_____.

3. Most caregiving for aging parents is provided by

   _____.

4. The sense of personal responsibility to care for one's parents is called _____.

5. An increasing number of children are being raised by their

   _____.

Interpret

- If you were to create a guide to families for middle-aged adults, what would be your most important pieces of advice? Why did you select these?

Apply

- What are the connections between the first part of this chapter, on health, and this section, on caregiving?

Check your answers to the Recall Questions at the end of the chapter.

SUMMARY

13.1 Physical Changes and Health

How does appearance change in middle adulthood?

- Some of the signs of aging appearing in middle age include wrinkles, gray hair, and weight gain.

What changes occur in bones and joints?

- An important change— especially in women— is loss of bone mass, which in severe form may result in the disease osteoporosis. This disease can be very serious and result in broken bones and loss of height.

- Osteoarthritis, a disease marked by gradual onset and progressive pain and disability, generally becomes noticeable in late middle or early old age. Rheumatoid arthritis, a more destructive disease, is a more common form affecting fingers, wrists, and ankles.

What reproductive changes occur in men and women in middle age?

- The climacteric (loss of the ability to bear children by natural means) and menopause (cessation of menstruation) occur in the 40s and 50s and constitute a major change in reproductive ability in women.

- The decline of estrogen has been correlated with certain physical changes. Menopausal hormone therapy is a controversial approach to treatment of menopausal symptoms.

- Reproductive changes in men are much less dramatic; even older men usually are still fertile. Physical changes do affect sexual response.

What is stress? How does it affect physical and psychological health?

- In the stress and coping paradigm, stress results from a person's primary and secondary appraisal of an event as taxing his or her resources. Daily hassles are viewed as the primary source of stress.

- Coping is the response to deal with stress. Problem-focused coping and emotion-focused coping are two examples.

- Long-term stress has potentially serious negative health effects, such as on the immune and cardiovascular systems. It is also related to mental health problems, such as post-traumatic stress disorder.

What are the benefits of exercise?

- Aerobic exercise has numerous benefits, especially with regard to cardiovascular health and cognitive fitness. The best results are obtained with a moderate exercise program maintained throughout adulthood.

13.2 Cognitive Development

How does practical intelligence develop in adulthood?

- Intelligence in middle age shows more clearly the mechanics (the underlying skills) and pragmatics (practical applications of crystallized intelligence). Research on practical intelligence reveals connections to postformal thinking. Emotion is more strongly blended with cognition in midlife than in younger adulthood.

How does a person become an expert?

- People tend to become experts in some areas and not in others. Experts tend to think in more flexible ways compared with novices and can skip steps in solving problems. Expert performance tends to peak in middle age.

What is meant by lifelong learning? What differences are there between adults and young people in how they learn?

- Adults learn differently than children and youth. Older students need practical connections and a rationale for learning, and they are more motivated by internal factors.

13.3 Personality

What is the five-factor model? What evidence is there for stability in personality traits?

- The five-factor model postulates five dimensions of personality: neuroticism, extraversion, openness to experience, agreeableness, and conscientiousness. Several longitudinal studies indicate that personality traits show long-term stability in general, but certain traits can change across adulthood. The Triggering situations, Expectancy, States/State Expressions, and Reactions (TESSERA) model accounts for both stability and change.

What changes occur in people's priorities and personal concerns? How does a person achieve generativity? How is midlife best described?

- Erikson believed that middle-aged adults become more concerned with doing for others and passing social values and skills to the next generation— a set of behaviors and beliefs he labeled *generativity*. Those who do not achieve generativity are thought to experience stagnation. People derive personal meaning from constructing a life story or narrative.

- Priorities and personal concerns change with age, shown in the experience of a midlife correction.

13.4 Family Dynamics and Middle Age

Who are the kinkeepers in families?

- Middle-aged mothers tend to adopt the role of kinkeepers to keep family traditions alive as a way of linking generations.

- Middle age is sometimes referred to as the sandwich generation because middle-aged adults are caring for both their aging parents and their own children.

How does the relationship between middle-aged parents and their young adult children change?

- Parent–child relations improve dramatically when children grow out of adolescence. Most parents look forward to having an empty nest. Difficulties emerge to the extent that raising children has been a primary source of personal identity for parents. However, once children leave home, parents still provide considerable support.

- Young adult children move back home primarily for financial reasons. In general, neither parents nor children prefer this arrangement.

How do middle-aged adults deal with their aging parents?

- Caring for aging parents usually falls to a daughter or daughter-in-law. Caregiving creates a stressful situation due to conflicting feelings and roles. The potential for conflict is high, as is financial pressure.

- Caregiving stress is usually greater in women, who must deal with multiple roles. Older parents are often dissatisfied with the situation as well.

What styles of grandparenthood do middle-aged adults experience? How do grandchildren and grandparents interact?

- Becoming a grandparent means assuming new roles. Styles of interaction vary among grandchildren and with the age of the grandchild. Also relevant are the social and personal dimensions of grandparenting.

- Grandparents derive several types of meaning regardless of style. Most children and young adults report positive relationships with grandparents, and young adults feel a responsibility to care for them if necessary.

- Ethnic differences are found in the extent to which grandparents take an active role in their grandchildren's lives.

- In an increasingly mobile society, grandparents are more frequently assuming a distant relationship with their grandchildren. An increasing number of grandparents serve as the custodial parent. These arrangements are typically stressful.

Test Yourself: Recall Answers

13.1 1. osteoporosis **2.** menopause **3.** gradually **4.** coping **5.** mind fulness-based stress reduction **13.2 1.** practical intelligence **2.** mechanics and pragmatics **3.** expertise **4.** life long learning **13.3 1.** conscientiousness **2.** generativity **3.** narrative **4.** midlife correction **13.4 1.** sandwich generation **2.** kinkeepers **3.** daughters and daughters-in-law **4.** filial obligation **5.** grandparents

Key Terms

skeletal maturity (423)

osteoporosis (423)

dual-energy X-ray absorptiometry (DXA) test (424)

selective estrogen receptor modulators (SERMs) (425)

osteoarthritis (426)

rheumatoid arthritis (426)

climacteric (428)

menopause (428)

perimenopause (428)

menopausal hormone therapy (MHT) (428)

stress and coping paradigm (431)

primary appraisal (432)

secondary appraisal (432)

reappraisal (432)

coping (432)

problem-focused coping (432)

emotion-focused coping (433)

post-traumatic stress disorder (PTSD) (434)

mindfulness-based stress reduction (434)

aerobic exercise (435)

practical intelligence (437)

mechanics of intelligence (437)

pragmatics of intelligence (437)

neuroticism (441)

extraversion (441)

openness to experience (442)

agreeableness (442)

conscientiousness (442)

personality adjustment (443)

personality growth (443)

generativity (444)

stagnation (444)

narrative (445)

midlife correction (446)

kinkeeper (447)

sandwich generation (447)

filial obligation (448)

The Personal Context of Later Life

Physical, Cognitive, and Mental Health Issues

Think about all the descriptions of older adults you have heard or used yourself, and write down as many as you can think of. Odds are, at least several of them are not positive. Later life is a time of life that provides much fodder for stereotypes that often paint a not-so-pretty picture of growing older. A quick look at birthday cards verifies that negative stereotypes of aging are common.

How accurate are these images? In this chapter and in Chapter 15, we check the facts. We will sort through the common beliefs people have about aging and find out that some of them, such as slowing down, are based in fact, and others, such as a general decline in all aspects of memory, are not. Most important, we will learn that lifestyle factors under our control can heavily influence what our experience of later life will be.

LEARNING OBJECTIVES

- What are the characteristics of older adults in the population?

- How long will most people live? What factors influence this?
- What is the distinction between the third and fourth age?

Sarah is an 87-year-old African American woman who comes from a family of long-lived individuals. She has never been to a physician, and she has never been seriously ill. Sarah figures it's just as well that she has never needed a physician because for most of her life, she had no health insurance. Because she feels healthy and has more living that she wants to do, Sarah believes that she'll live for several more years.

What is it like to be old? Do you want your own late life to be described by the words and phrases you wrote at the beginning of the chapter? Do you look forward to becoming old, or are you afraid of what may lie ahead? Most of us probably want to be like Sarah and enjoy a long, healthy life. Growing old is not something we think about very much until we have to. Most of us experience the coming of old age as a surprise. It's as if we go to bed one night middle-aged and wake up the next day feeling old. But we can take comfort in knowing that when the day comes, we will have plenty of company.

The Demographics of Aging

Did you ever stop to think about how many older adults you see in your day-to-day life? Did you ever wonder whether your great-grandparents had the same experience? Actually, you are privileged—there have never been as many older adults alive as there are now, so you see many more older people than your great-grandparents (or even your parents) did when they were your age. The proportion of older adults in the population of developed countries has increased tremendously, mainly due to better health care over the past century (e.g., the elimination or prevention of previously fatal acute diseases, especially during childhood, better treatment for chronic diseases) and to lowering women's mortality rate during childbirth.

demographers

People who study population trends.

population pyramid

Graphic technique for illustrating population trends.

People who study population trends, called demographers, *use a graphic* technique *called* a population pyramid *to illustrate these changes.* ▶ Figure 14.1 shows average population pyramids for the most developed and least developed countries around the world. Let's consider developed countries first (they're down the left side of the figure). Notice the shape of the population pyramid in 1950, shown in the top panel of the figure. In the middle of the 20th century, there were fewer people over age 60 than under age 60; so the figure tapers toward the top. Compare this to projections for 2050; you can see that a dramatic change will occur in the number of people over 65.

These changes also occur in developing countries, shown in the lighter color. The figures for both 1950 and 2015 look more like pyramids when you look at both the male and female halves together because there are substantially fewer older adults than younger people. But by 2050, the number of older adults even in developing countries will have increased dramatically, substantially changing the shape of the figure.

Because the growth of the child population in the United States slowed in the 20th century and essentially stops by the middle of this century, the average age of Americans will continue to rise (Pew Research Center, 2015). By 2030, all of the baby boomers will have reached at least age 65, meaning that one in five Americans will be 65 or older (Census Bureau, 2015).

The sheer number of older Americans will place enormous pressure on pension systems (especially Social Security), health care (especially Medicare, Medicaid, and long-term care), and other human services. The costs will be borne by smaller numbers of taxpaying workers behind them, meaning that each worker will have a higher tax burden in the future in order to keep benefits at their current levels.

Figure 14.1

Population pyramids for developed and developing countries 1950–2050. Note the changing shapes of the distributions in terms of the proportion of the population that is young versus old over time and as a function of whether countries are considered developed or developing.

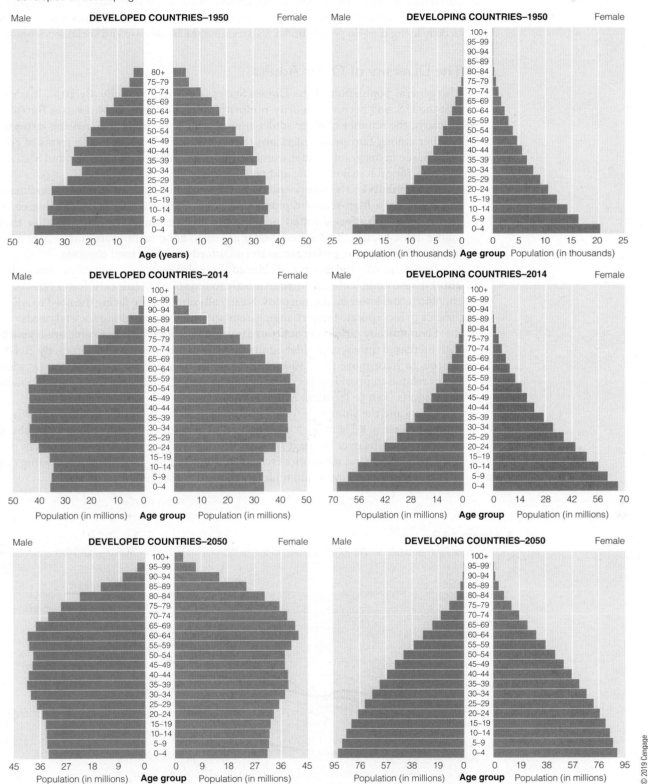

From International programs: International database, by U.S. Census Bureau. Copyright © U.S. Census Bureau. Retrieved from www.census.gov/population/international/data/idb/ (1950 developed countries). Remaining data extracted from census data tables. See Kail and Cavanaugh, *Essentials of Human Development*, 2nd ed., p. 369.

The growing strain on social service systems will intensify because the most rapidly growing segment of the U.S. population is the group of people over age 85, as you can see in the graphs. The number of such people will increase nearly 500% between 2000 and 2050, compared with about a 50% increase in the number of 20- to 29-year-olds during the same period. Individuals over age 85 generally need more assistance with the tasks they have to accomplish in daily living than do people under 85, straining the healthcare and social service systems.

The Diversity of Older Adults

The general population of the United States is changing rapidly. By 2044, it is expected that the U.S. will become majority-minority, up from 38% in 2014 (Census Bureau, 2015). Similarly, the number of older adults among minority groups is increasing faster than the number among European Americans (Pew Research Center, 2015). In terms of gender, as you can see in the graphs, older women outnumber older men in the United States. This is true also for each major ethnic and racial group.

Older adults in the future will be better educated, too. By 2030, it is estimated that 85% will have a high-school diploma and about 75% will have a college degree (Census Bureau, 2014). Better-educated people tend to live longer—mostly because they have higher incomes, which give them better access to good health care and a chance to follow healthier lifestyles (e.g., have access to and afford healthier food choices).

Internationally, the number of older adults is also growing rapidly (Pew Research Center, 2015). These rapid increases are due mostly to improved health care, lower rates of death in childbirth, and lower infant mortality. Nearly all countries are facing the need to adapt social policies to incorporate these changing demographics and resulting societal needs.

Economically powerful countries around the world, such as China, are trying to cope with increased numbers of older adults that strain the country's resources. By 2040, China expects to have more than 300 million people over age 60. So it is already addressing issues related to providing services and living arrangements for the increasing number of older adults (Ren & Treiman, 2014).

China and the United States are not alone in facing increased numbers of older adults. As you can see in ❭ Figure 14.2, the population of many countries will include substantially more older adults over the next few decades. All of these countries will need to deal with an increased demand for services to older adults and, in some cases, competing demands with children and younger and middle-aged adults for limited resources.

❭ **Figure 14.2**

The proportion of older adults (65 years and older) is increasing in many countries and will continue to do so.

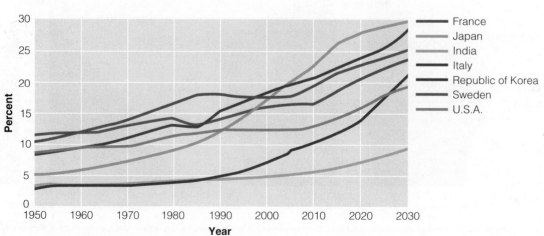

From United Nations, Statistics Bureau, Ministry of Public Management, Home Affairs, Post and Telecommunications, Ministry of Health, Labour, and Welfare. See Kail and Cavanaugh, *Essentials of Human Development*, 2nd ed., p. 370.

The general aging of the population is a global phenomenon. It is due mainly to two factors: a declining birth rate in many countries, often tied to increases in opportunities for women (such as education and careers) and especially to more people living longer. Let's take a closer look at longer life spans, and how they affect societies.

Think About It

How will the demographic changes in the first 30 years of the 21st century affect social policy?

Longevity

The length of life has an enormous impact on everything from decisions about government healthcare programs (e.g., how much money should Congress allocate to Medicare) to retirement policy (e.g., the age at which people may collect maximum retirement benefits) to life insurance premiums (e.g., longer lives on average mean cheaper rates for young adults).

How long we live depends on complex interactions among biological, psychological, socioeconomic, and life-cycle forces. Let's begin by exploring the concept of longevity for yourself. To get started, complete the exercise at www.livingto100.com, based on research from the New England Centenarian Study. How long will you live? Only time will tell!

Average and Maximum Longevity

How long you live, called longevity, is jointly determined by genetic and environmental factors. Researchers distinguish between two different types of longevity: average longevity and maximum longevity. Average longevity *is commonly called average life expectancy and refers to the age at which half of the individuals who are born in a particular year will have died.* Average longevity is affected by both genetic and environmental factors.

average longevity
Age at which half of the people born in a particular year will have died.

Average longevity can be computed for people at any age. The most common method is to compute average longevity at birth, which is the projected age at which half of the people born in a certain year will have died. The current average longevity is about 79 years at birth for people in the United States (National Center for Health Statistics, 2016a). This means that of the people born in 2016, for example, half of them will still be alive when the group reaches age 79.

When average longevity is computed at other points in the life span, the calculation is based on all the people who are alive at that age; people who died earlier are not included. For example, computing the average longevity for people currently 65 years old would provide a predicted age at which half of those people will have died. In the United States, females currently aged 65 can expect to live on average about 20 more years; men about 18 more years (National Center for Health Statistics, 2016b).

For people in the United States, average longevity has been increasing steadily since 1900; recent estimates for longevity at birth, at age 65, and at age 75 are presented in ▶ Figure 14.3. Pay attention to some important aspects of the data. First, data were only collected and reported for certain racial/ethnic groups. Second, whereas data on life expectancy at birth has been collected for over a century, data on life expectancy at ages 65 and 75 have only been collected and reported more recently. These differences reflect changes in both research design and in an understanding that data need to be reported separately for various racial/ethnic groups.

Note in the figure that the most rapid increases in average longevity at birth occurred in the first half of the 20th century. These increases in average longevity were caused mostly by better health care. The decrease in the number of women who died during childbirth was especially important in raising average life expectancies for women. Advances in medical technology and improvements in health care mean that more people survive to old age, thereby increasing average longevity in the general population.

Maximum longevity *is the oldest age to which any individual of a species lives.* Even if we were able to eliminate all diseases and other environmental influences, most researchers estimate the limit to be somewhere around 120 years because key body systems such as the cardiovascular system have limits on how long they can last (Hayflick, 1996).

maximum longevity (life expectancy)
Oldest age to which any person lives.

▶ **Figure 14.3**

Average longevity for men and women in the United States 1900–2014.

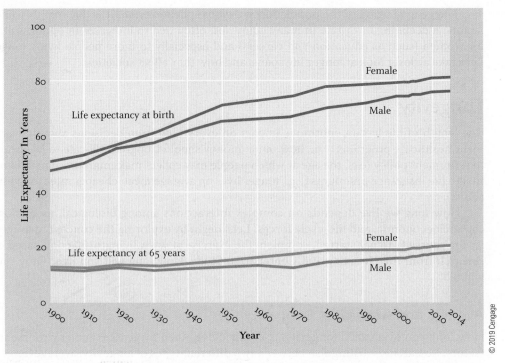

Adapted from National Center for Health Statistics. (2016a). Health, United States, 2015. Retrieved from www.cdc.gov/nchs/data/hus/hus15.pdf.

active life expectancy ▬

Number of years that a person is free from debilitating chronic disease and impairment.

dependent life expectancy ▬

Number of years a person lives with a debilitating chronic disease in which the person depends on others for care.

Increasingly, researchers are differentiating between active life expectancy and dependent life expectancy; *the difference is between living to a healthy old age (active life expectancy) and the length of time one lives with a debilitating condition in which the person depends on others for care (dependent life expectancy)*. Said another way, it is the difference between adding years to life and adding life to years. One's active life expectancy ends at the point when one loses independence or must rely on others for most activities of daily living (e.g., cooking meals, bathing). The remaining years of one's life constitute living in a dependent state. How many active and dependent years one has in late life depends a great deal on the interaction of genetic and environmental factors, to which we now turn.

Genetic and Environmental Factors in Average Longevity

Our average longevity is influenced most by genetic, environmental, ethnic, and gender factors. Clearly, these factors interact. But it is important to examine each of these factors and see how they influence our longevity. Let's begin with genetic and environmental factors.

We have known for a long time that a good way to have a greater chance of a long life is to come from a family with a history of long-lived individuals. Research indicates that about 25% of the variation in human longevity is due to a person's genetics (Passarino, De Rango, & Montesanto, 2016).

Although genes are a major determinant of longevity, environmental factors also affect the life span, often in combination with genes (Passarino et al., 2016). Diseases, such as cardiovascular disease and Alzheimer's disease, and lifestyle issues, such as smoking and exercise, receive a great deal of attention from researchers. Environmental toxins, encountered mainly as air and water pollution, are a continuing problem.

Living in poverty shortens longevity. The impact of socioeconomic status on longevity results from reduced access to medical care and healthy food, that characterizes certain ethnic minority groups, the poor, and many older adults, as clearly demonstrated in a very large study (566,402 participants) of premature mortality in community dwelling adults (Doubeni et al., 2012). Most of these people have restricted access to good health care and cannot afford healthy food. For many living in urban areas, air pollution, poor drinking water, and lead poisoning from old water pipes are serious problems, but they simply cannot afford to move.

Coming from a family of long-lived individuals shows the role of genetics in longevity.

The sad part about most environmental factors is that human activity is responsible for most of them. Denying adequate health care to everyone, continuing to pollute our environment, and failing to address the underlying causes of poverty have undeniable consequences: These causes needlessly shorten lives and dramatically increase the cost of health care.

Ethnic and Gender Differences in Average Longevity

People in different ethnic groups do not have the same average longevity at birth. For example, although African Americans' average life expectancy at birth is about 4 years less for men and about 3 years less for women than it is for European Americans, by age 65 this gap has narrowed to about 2 and 1 years, respectively, for men and women. By age 85, African Americans tend to outlive European Americans. Why the shift over time?

Lower access to good-quality health care in general means that those African Americans who live to age 85 may be in better health on average than their European American counterparts. But this is just a guess, because Latinos have higher average life expectancies than European Americans and African Americans at all ages despite having, on average, less access to health care (National Center for Health Statistics, 2016a). The full explanation for these ethnic group differences remains to be discovered.

Women live longer, on average, than do men. Women's average longevity is about 5 years more than men's at birth, narrowing to roughly 1 year by age 85 (National Center for Health Statistics, 2016a). Despite these patterns, no one really knows for certain why women tend to live longer.

International Differences in Average Longevity

Countries around the world differ dramatically in how long their populations live on average. As you can see for countries in the Organisation for Economic Co-operation and Development (OECD) in ◗ Figure 14.4, the current range extends from 71.7 years in Mexico to over 82 years in Japan. In contrast, some developing countries, such as Sierra Leone in Africa, have an average longevity at birth of less than 40 years. Such a wide divergence in life expectancy reflects vast discrepancies in genetic, sociocultural and economic conditions, health care, disease, and the like across industrialized and developing nations. The differences also mean that populations in countries such as Sierra Leone are very much younger, on average, than they are in countries such as Japan or the United States.

Think About It

How do ethnic and gender differences in life expectancy relate to biological, psychological, sociocultural, and life-cycle factors?

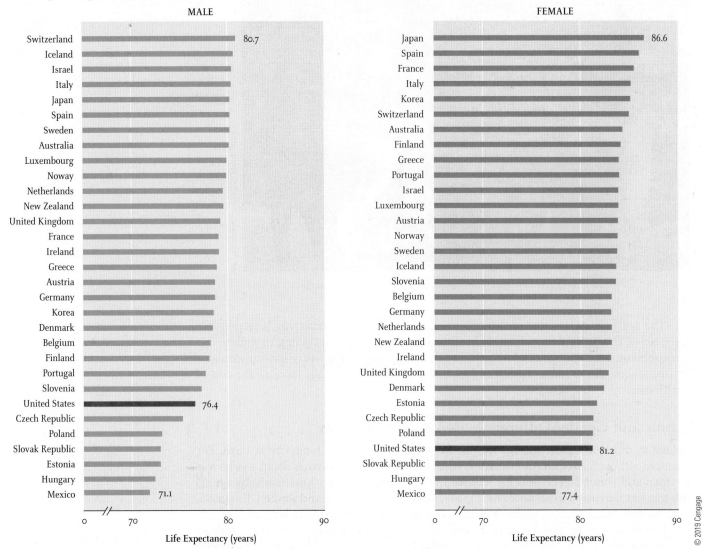

Based on CDC/NCHS, Health, United States, 2015, Figure 1 and Tables 14 and 15. Data from the National Vital Statistics System (NVSS) and the Organisation for Economic Co-operation and Development (OECD).

The Third–Fourth Age Distinction

The development of the science of gerontology, the study of older adults, in the latter part of the 20th century led to cultural, medical, and economic advances for older adults (e.g., longer average longevity, increased quality of life) that in turn resulted in fundamental positive changes in how older people are viewed in society. Gerontologists and policy makers became optimistic that old age was a time of potential growth rather than of decline. This combination of factors is termed the Third Age (Baltes & Smith, 2003). As we will see in this chapter and in Chapter 15, much research has documented that the young-old (ages 60 to 80) do have much to look forward to.

However, recent research shows conclusively that the oldest-old (over age 80) typically have a much different experience, which is referred to as the Fourth Age (Baltes & Smith, 2003; Gilleard & Higgs, 2010; Lamb, 2014). The oldest-old are at the limits of their functional capacity, and few interventions to reverse the effects of aging have been successful to date. A major focus is the choice of housing, whether to age in place or to move to alternative placements (Koss & Ekerdt, in press). We will see that the rates of diseases such as cancer and dementia increase dramatically in the oldest-old and that other aspects of psychological functioning (e.g., memory) also undergo significant and fairly rapid decline.

Baltes and Smith (2003) view the differences between the Third Age and the Fourth Age as important for research and social policy. They characterize the Third Age as the "good news" about aging and the Fourth Age as the "bad news."

The "Good News": The Third Age (Young-Old) ↩

- Increased life expectancy, with more older people living longer and aging successfully
- Substantial potential for physical and mental fitness, with improvement in each generation
- Evidence of cognitive and emotional reserves in the aging mind
- High levels of emotional and personal well-being
- Effective strategies to master the gains and losses of later life

The "Bad News": The Fourth Age (Oldest-Old) ↩

- Sizeable losses in cognitive potential and ability to learn
- Increases in the negative effects of chronic stress
- High prevalence of dementia (50% in people over age 90), frailty, and multiple chronic conditions
- Problems with quality of life and dying with dignity

The Third and Fourth Ages approach is grounded in the "selective optimization with compensation" model described in Chapter 1. The description of gains and losses in the Third and Fourth Ages flows naturally from this life-span perspective. As you proceed through this chapter and the next, keep in mind the distinction between the Third and the Fourth Ages. Note the different developmental patterns shown by the young-old and oldest-old. In Chapter 15, we will consider some of the social policy implications of this distinction.

TEST YOURSELF 14.1

Recall

1. The fastest-growing segment of the population in the United States is people over age _____ .
2. The age at which half of the people born in a particular year will have died is called _____ .
3. The Fourth Age refers to the _____ old.

Interpret

- Think back to the lifestyle influences on health discussed in Chapter 12. If most people actually exhibited a healthy lifestyle, what would happen to average life expectancy?

Apply

- If you were to design an intervention program to maximize the odds that people will live to maximum longevity, what would you emphasize?

Check your answers to the Recall Questions at the end of the chapter.

14.2 Physical Changes and Health

LEARNING OBJECTIVES

- What are the major biological theories of aging?
- What physiological changes normally occur in later life?
- What are the principal health issues for older adults?

Frank is an 80-year-old man who has been physically active his whole life. He still enjoys sailing, long-distance biking, and cross-country skiing. Although he considers himself to be in excellent shape, he has noticed that his endurance has decreased and that his hearing isn't quite as sharp as it used to be. Frank wonders whether he can do something to stop these declines or whether they are an inevitable part of growing older.

If your family has kept photograph albums for many years, you are able to see how your grandparents and/or great-grandparents changed over the years. Some of the more visible differences are changes in the color and amount of hair and the addition of wrinkles, but many other physical changes are harder to see. In this section, we consider some of these changes, as well as a few things that adults can do to improve their health. As noted in Chapter 13, many aging changes begin during middle age. However, most of these changes typically do not affect people's daily lives until later in life, as Frank is discovering. But first, we will ask a basic question: Why do people grow old in the first place?

Biological Theories of Aging

Much research on aging has focused on answering the question of why people and other living organisms grow old and die. With regard to human aging, three groups of theories have provided the most insights.

Metabolic Theories

One theory of aging that makes apparent common sense postulates that organisms have only so much energy to expend in a lifetime. (Couch potatoes might like this theory, and may use it as a reason why they are not physically active.) The basic idea is that the rate of a creature's metabolism is related to how long it lives (Barzilai et al., 2012).

Although some research indicates that significantly reducing the number of calories animals and people eat may increase longevity, research focusing on nonhuman primates shows that longer lives do not always result from restricting calories alone (Chaudhari et al., 2016).

Cellular Theories

A second family of ideas points to causes of aging at the cellular level. One notion focuses on the number of times cells can divide, which presumably limits the life span of a complex organism. Cells grown in laboratory culture dishes undergo only a fixed number of divisions before dying, with the number of possible divisions dropping depending on the age of the donor organism; this phenomenon is called the Hayflick limit, after its discoverer, Leonard Hayflick (Bernadotte, Mikhelson, & Spivak, 2016; Hayflick, 1996).

What causes cells to limit their number of divisions? *Evidence suggests that the tips of the chromosomes, called* telomeres, *play a major role in aging by adjusting the cell's response to stress and growth stimulation based on cell divisions and DNA damage, and by typically shortening with each cell replication* (Bernadotte et al., 2016). Healthy, normal telomeres help regulate the cell division and reproduction process.

An enzyme called telomerase *is needed in DNA replication to fully reproduce the telomeres when cells divide.* But telomerase normally is not present in somatic cells, so with each replication the telomeres become shorter. Eventually, the chromosomes become unstable and cannot replicate because the telomeres become too short. This process is depicted in ▶ Figure 14.5.

Chronic stress may accelerate the changes that occur in telomeres and thereby shorten one's life span (Oliveira et al., 2016; Spivak, Mikhelson, & Spivak, 2016). Research also shows that moderate levels of exercise may maintain telomere length or at least slow the rate at which telomeres shorten, which may help slow the aging process itself (Savela et al., 2013; Silva et al., 2016). However, the precise mechanisms for this process are not understood (Denham, O'Brien, & Charchar, 2016).

A second type of cellular theory proposes that aging is caused by unstable molecules called free radicals, *which are highly reactive chemicals produced randomly in normal metabolism* (Dutta et al., 2012). When these free radicals interact with nearby molecules,

telomeres

Tips of chromosomes that play a major role in aging by adjusting the cell's response to stress and growth stimulation based on cell divisions and DNA damage.

telomerase

Enzyme needed in DNA replication to fully reproduce the telomeres when cells divide.

free radicals

Highly reactive chemicals produced randomly in normal metabolism.

The process by which telomeres shorten as we age.

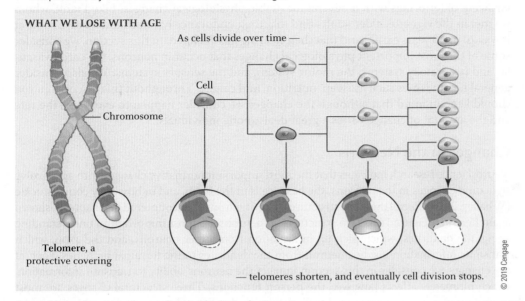

Adapted from telomeres-aging.com/images/shorteningdna.jpg

problems may result. For example, free radicals may cause cell damage to the heart by changing the oxygen levels in cells. There is also evidence that free radicals may have a role in the development of Alzheimer's disease (Wojtunik-Kulesza et al., 2016).

The most important evidence that free radicals may be involved in aging comes from research with substances that prevent the development of free radicals in the first place. These substances, called antioxidants, prevent oxygen from combining with susceptible molecules to form free radicals. Common antioxidants include vitamins A, C, and E, and coenzyme Q. A growing body of evidence shows that ingesting antioxidants postpones the appearance of age-related diseases such as cancer, cardiovascular disease, and immune system dysfunction (Suja et al., 2016), but there is no direct evidence yet that eating a diet high in antioxidants actually increases the life span (Berger et al., 2012).

Genetic Programming Theories

What if aging were programmed into our genetic code? This possibility seems much more likely as the extremely rapid growth of knowledge about human genetics continues to unlock the secrets of our genetic code (Mitteldorf, 2016). Even when cell death appears random, researchers believe that such losses may be part of a master genetic program that underlies the aging process (Freitas & de Magalhães, 2011; Mackenzie, 2012).

Programmed cell death appears to be a function of physiological processes, the innate ability of cells to self-destruct, and the ability of dying cells to trigger key processes in other cells, all of which are also thought to be influenced by external environmental factors (Arbeev, Ukraintseva, & Yashin, 2016; Ukraintseva et al., 2016). At present, we do not know how this genetic self-destruct program is activated, nor do we understand how it works. Nevertheless, there is increasing evidence that many diseases associated with aging (such as Alzheimer's disease) have genetic aspects.

It is quite possible that the other explanations we have considered in this section and the changes we examine throughout this text are the result of a genetic program. We will consider many diseases throughout the text that have known genetic bases, such as Alzheimer's disease. As genetics research continues, it is likely that we will have some exciting answers to the question, Why do we age?

Physiological Changes

Growing older brings with it several inevitable physiological changes. Like Frank, whom we met in the vignette, older adults find that their endurance has declined relative to what it was 20 or 30 years earlier and that their hearing has declined. In this section, we consider some of the most important physiological changes that occur in neurons, the cardiovascular and respiratory systems, the motor system, and the sensory systems. We also consider general health issues such as sleep, nutrition, and cancer. Throughout this discussion, you should keep in mind that although the changes we consider happen to everyone, the rate and the amount of change varies a great deal among individuals.

Changes in the Neurons

Neuroscience research indicates that the most important normative changes with age involve structural changes in the neurons, the basic cells in the brain, and in how they communicate (Whalley, 2015). Recall the basic structures of the neuron we encountered in Chapter 3, shown again here in ❱ Figure 14.6. Two structures in neurons are most important in understanding aging: the dendrites, which pick up information from other neurons, and the axon, which transmits information inside a neuron from the dendrites to the terminal branches. Each of the changes we consider in this section impairs the neurons' ability to transmit information, which ultimately affects how well the person functions. Three structural changes are most important in normal aging: neurofibrillary tangles, dendritic changes, and neuritic plaques.

For reasons that are not understood, fibers that compose the axon sometimes become twisted together to form spiral-shaped masses called neurofibrillary tangles. These tangles interfere with the neuron's ability to transmit information down the axon. Some degree of tangling occurs normally with age, but large numbers of neurofibrillary tangles are associated with Alzheimer's disease and other forms of dementia (Sala Frigerio & De Strooper, 2016). ❱ Figure 14.7 shows how this process works.

Changes in the dendrites are more complicated. Some dendrites shrivel up and die, making it more difficult for neurons to communicate with each other and transmit information (Voss et al., 2013). However, research indicates that dendrites continue to grow in some areas of the brain, and embryonic stem cell research indicates that inducing growth may be a future way to treat brain disease and injury (West, 2010). This may help explain why older adults continue to improve in some areas, as we will discover later in this chapter. Why some dendrites degenerate and others do not is poorly understood; it may reflect the existence of two different families of neurons.

Neuritic or amyloid plaques are spherical structures consisting of a core of beta-amyloid, *a protein, surrounded by degenerated fragments of dying or dead neurons.* The plaques are found in various parts of the brain, with the amount of beta-amyloid moderately related to the severity of the disease (National Institute on Aging, 2015b). A depiction of beta-amyloid plaques is also shown in ❱ Figure 14.7.

neurofibrillary tangles

Spiral-shaped masses formed when fibers that compose the axon become twisted together.

beta-amyloid

A protein that is the basis for neuritic plaques and is thought to be a basis for dementia.

❱ **Figure 14.6**

Basic structure of the neuron.

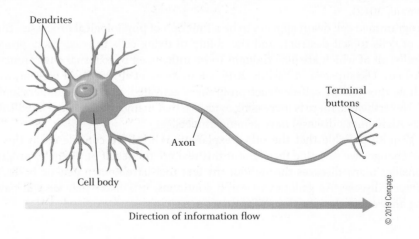

Dendrites

Terminal buttons

Axon

Cell body

Direction of information flow

© 2019 Cengage

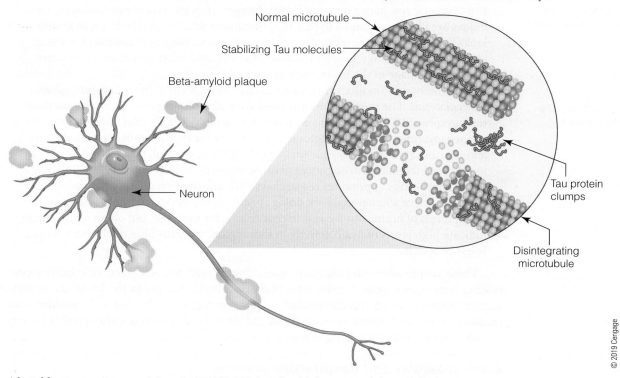

▶ Figure 14.7

Action of beta-amyloid and tau proteins in relation to neurons. Each disrupts neurons, but in different ways.

Normal microtubule

Stabilizing Tau molecules

Beta-amyloid plaque

Neuron

Tau protein clumps

Disintegrating microtubule

© 2019 Cengage

Adapted from www.nytimes.com/interactive/2012/02/02/science/in-alzheimers-a-tangled-protein.html

Considerable recent research has focused on beta-amyloid as a major factor in Alzheimer's disease, both in terms of the cause and possible avenues for treatment. The role of beta-amyloid is controversial, though. Some researchers view concentration of beta-amyloid as a biomarker of Alzheimer's disease (Sala Frigerio & De Strooper, 2016). Others consider it an early warning of potential cognitive decline, even in the absence of any behavioral symptoms (Gandy & DeKosky, 2013; Singh et al., 2016). We will consider the controversy surrounding diagnostic categories related to Alzheimer's disease a bit later.

Because neurons do not physically touch each other, they must communicate via chemicals called neurotransmitters. With age, the levels of these neurotransmitters decline (Behl & Ziegler, 2014). An especially important neurotransmitter in this respect is dopamine, involved in several key cognitive processes (Mather, 2016; Park & Festini, 2017). These declines in dopamine as well as other neurotransmitters, are believed to be responsible for numerous age-related behavioral changes, including those in memory and sleep, and for diseases such as Parkinson's disease (Parkinson's Disease Foundation, 2016a).

Because all of these changes in neurons are a normal part of aging, it is difficult to say precisely how they may also cause cognitive and other diseases late in life. May researchers believe that disease occurs when these changes occur at a much greater rate, but they cannot specify the exact point at which this happens. This point is important because it means that serious behavioral changes (e.g., severe memory impairment) are not a result of normative age changes in the brain; rather, they are indicators of disease.

Through technological advances in noninvasive imaging and in assessing psychological functioning, we are learning a great deal about the relations between changes in the brain and changes in behavior (Linden, 2016; Sugiura, 2016). Neuroimaging is an important tool for understanding both normal and abnormal cognitive aging. Two neuroimaging techniques are used most often:

neurotransmitters

Chemicals released by neurons in order for them to communicate with each other.

structural neuroimaging

Neuroimaging technique such as CT and MRI scans that provides highly detailed images of anatomical features in the brain.

- **Structural neuroimaging** *provides highly detailed images of anatomical features in the brain.* The most commonly used are X-rays, computerized tomography (CT) scans, and magnetic resonance imaging (MRI). Images from structural neuroimaging techniques are like photographs in that they document what a specific brain structure looks like at a specific point in time. Structural neuroimaging is usually effective at identifying such things as bone fractures, tumors, and other conditions that cause structural damage in the brain, such as strokes.

functional neuroimaging

Neuroimaging technique that provides an indication of brain activity but not high anatomical detail.

- **Functional neuroimaging** *provides an indication of brain activity but not high anatomical detail.* The most commonly used are single photon emission computerized tomography (SPECT), positron emission tomography (PET), functional magnetic resonance imaging (fMRI), magnetoencephalograpy (or multichannel encephalography), and near infrared spectroscopic imaging (NIRSI). In general, fMRI is the most commonly used technique in cognitive neuroscience research (Poldrack, 2012). Functional neuroimaging provides researchers with information about what parts of the brain are active when people are doing specific tasks. A typical image will show different levels of brain activity as different colors; for example, red on an image might indicate high levels of brain activity in that region, whereas blue might indicate low levels of activity.

These noninvasive imaging techniques coupled with sensitive tests of cognitive processing have shown quite convincingly that age-related changes in the brain are, at least in part, responsible for the age-related declines in cognition that we will consider later (Sugiura, 2016). Why these declines occur has yet to be discovered, although fMRI offers considerable promise in helping researchers unlock this mystery.

Cardiovascular and Respiratory Systems

Having a healthy heart and circulatory system, as well as healthy lungs are two key factors for people to enjoy a high quality of life as they grow older. Let's take a closer look at the changes that occur to us all, as well as problems that can develop.

Cardiovascular System Changes. You may already know that cardiovascular disease is the most common cause of death in the United States. The incidence of cardiovascular diseases such as heart attack, irregular heartbeat, stroke, and hypertension (high blood pressure) increases dramatically with age and is much higher among African Americans, American Indians, and Native Hawaiians (Mozaffarian et al., 2016). However, the overall death rates from these diseases have been declining over recent decades, mainly because fewer adults smoke cigarettes and many people have reduced the amount of fat in their diets.

Two important age-related structural changes in the heart are the accumulation of fat deposits and the stiffening of the heart muscle caused by tissue changes. By the late 40s and early 50s, the fat deposits in the lining around the heart may form a continuous sheet. Meanwhile, healthy muscle tissue is being replaced by connective tissue, which causes a thickening and stiffening of the heart muscle and valves that forces the remaining muscle to work harder (National Institute on Aging, 2015a).

Two important age-related changes occur in the circulatory system. First, the walls of the arteries stiffen due to calcification of the arterial walls and by replacement of elastic fibers with less elastic ones. Second, fat deposits in the arteries can create blockages that restrict blood flow and may result in a myocardial infarction (heart attack). *Calcification and blockages in the arteries cause the disease* atherosclerosis.

atherosclerosis

A disease caused by calcification and blockages in the arteries.

As people grow older, their chances of having a stroke increase. Strokes, or cerebral vascular accidents (CVAs), *are caused by interruptions in the blood flow in the brain due to blockage or a hemorrhage in a cerebral artery.* Blockages of arteries may be caused by clots or by atherosclerosis. Hemorrhages are caused by ruptures of the artery. CVAs are the leading cause of disability (and fourth leading cause of death) in the United States.

strokes, or cerebral vascular accidents (CVAs)

Interruption of the blood flow in the brain due to blockage or a hemorrhage in a cerebral artery.

Treatment of CVA has advanced significantly. The most important advance is use of the clot-dissolving drug tissue plasminogen activator (tPA) to treat CVAs (American Stroke Association, 2016). Currently, tPA is the only approved treatment for CVAs caused by blood clots, which constitute 80% of all CVAs. Not every patient should receive tPA treatment, and tPA is effective only if given promptly, which is vitally important. So if you or a person you know thinks they are experiencing a CVA, get medical attention immediately because to be most effective, tPA therapy must be started within three hours after the onset of a stroke. Recovery from CVA depends on the severity of the stroke, area and extent of the brain affected, and patient age.

Older adults often experience transient ischemic attacks (TIAs), *which involve an interruption of blood flow to the brain and are often early warning signs of stroke.* A single, large cerebral vascular accident may produce serious cognitive impairment, such as the loss of the ability to speak, or physical problems, such as the inability to move one's arm. The nature and severity of the impairment in functioning that a person experiences are usually determined by which specific area of the brain is affected. Recovery from a single stroke depends on many factors, including the extent and type of the loss, the ability of other areas in the brain to assume the functions that were lost, and personal motivation.

Numerous small cerebral vascular accidents can result in a disease termed vascular dementia. Unlike Alzheimer's disease, another form of dementia discussed later in this chapter, vascular dementia can have a sudden onset and may progress slowly (Leys, Murao, & Pasquier, 2014). Typical symptoms include hypertension, specific and extensive alterations on an MRI, and differential impairment on neuropsychological tests, although we still have a great deal to learn about precise diagnosis (Shim, 2014). The differential impairment refers to a pattern of scores showing some functions intact and others significantly below average. Individuals' specific symptom patterns may vary a great deal depending on which specific areas of the brain are damaged. In some cases, vascular dementia has a much faster course than Alzheimer's disease, resulting in death an average of two to three years after onset; in other cases, the disease may progress more slowly with idiosyncratic symptom patterns.

Single cerebral vascular accidents and vascular dementia are diagnosed similarly. Evidence of damage may be obtained from diagnostic structural imaging (e.g., CT scan or MRI), which provides pictures such as the one shown in ▶ Figure 14.8, that is then

transient ischemic attacks (TIAs)
Interruption of blood flow to the brain; often an early warning sign of stroke.

vascular dementia
Disease caused by numerous small cerebral vascular accidents.

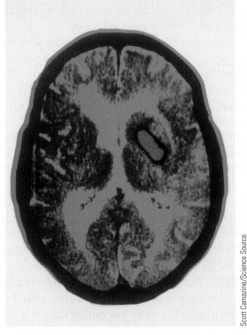

▶ **Figure 14.8**
Neuroimaging is especially helpful in diagnosing a cerebrovascular accident (shown in red).

Scott Camazine/Science Source

confirmed by neuropsychological tests. Known risk factors for both conditions include hypertension and a family history of the disorders.

Respiratory System Changes. Although the size of the lungs does not change with age, the maximum amount of air in one breath drops 40% from age 25 to age 85, due mostly to stiffening of the rib cage and air passages with age and to destruction of the air sacs in the lungs by pollution and smoking (Copley, 2016). This decline is the main cause of shortness of breath after physical exertion in later life.

Because of the cumulative effects of breathing polluted air over a lifetime, it is hard to say how many of these changes are strictly age-related. *The most common form of incapacitating respiratory disease among older adults is* chronic obstructive pulmonary disease (COPD). COPD can be a debilitating condition and may result in depression, anxiety, and the need to be continually connected to oxygen (American Lung Association, 2016). Emphysema is the most common form of COPD; although most cases of emphysema are due to smoking, some forms are genetic. Chronic bronchitis and asthma are other common types of COPD. COPD can severely restrict a person's ability to function, interact with others, and enjoy good quality of life.

Sensory Changes

Growing older brings with it several normative changes in sensory abilities. These changes can affect people's ability to enjoy life but in most cases can be adequately compensated for through various types of interventions.

Vision. Age-related changes in vision are fairly obvious—just watch as middle-aged and older adults' arms become too short for them to see things clearly close up. This change is due to age-related changes in the lens's ability to adjust, and focus declines as the muscles around it stiffen (Alavi, 2016). *This is what causes difficulty in seeing close objects clearly (called* presbyopia), *necessitating either longer arms or corrective lenses.* To complicate matters further, the time our eyes need to change focus from near to far (or vice versa) increases. This also poses a major problem in driving. Because drivers are constantly changing their focus from the instrument panel to other autos and signs on the highway, older drivers may miss important information because of their slower refocusing time. In addition, as we grow older, the lens becomes more yellow, causing poorer color discrimination in the green–blue–violet end of the spectrum.

Other changes also occur that affect how well we see in later life. One is a decrease in the amount of light that passes through the eye, resulting in the need for more light to do tasks such as reading. As you might suspect, this change is one reason older adults do not see as well in the dark, which may account in part for their reluctance to go places at night. One logical response to the need for more light would be to increase illumination levels in general. However, this solution does not work in all situations because we also become increasingly sensitive to glare (Sanford, 2014).

Another major change is that our ability to adjust to changes in illumination, called *adaptation*, declines. Going from outside into a darkened movie theater involves dark adaptation; going back outside involves light adaptation. Research indicates that the time it takes for both types of adaptation increases with age (Andersen, 2012). These changes are especially important for older drivers, who have more difficulty seeing after being confronted with the headlights of an oncoming car.

chronic obstructive pulmonary disease (COPD)
Most common form of incapacitating respiratory disease among older adults.

presbyopia
Difficulty seeing close objects clearly.

Older adults must adjust to several changes in vision, including the need for reading glasses.

Jack.Q/Shutterstock.com

A third structural change affects the ability to see detail and to discriminate different visual patterns, called *acuity*. Acuity declines steadily between ages 20 and 60, with a more rapid decline thereafter. Loss of acuity is especially noticeable at low light levels (Andersen, 2012).

Besides these normative structural changes, some people experience diseases caused by abnormal structural changes. *First, opaque spots called* cataracts *may develop on the lens, which limits the amount of light transmitted.* Cataracts often are treated by surgical removal and replacement of the lenses. *Second, the fluid in the eye may not drain properly, causing very high internal pressure; this condition, called* glaucoma, *can cause internal damage and loss of vision.* Glaucoma is a fairly common disease in middle and late adulthood and is usually treated with eye drops.

The second major family of changes in vision results from changes in the retina. The retina lines approximately two-thirds of the interior of the eye. The specialized receptor cells for vision, the rods and cones, are contained in the retina. They are most densely packed toward the rear, especially at the focal point of vision, a region called the *macula*. At the center of the macula is the *fovea*, where incoming light is focused for maximum acuity, as when one is reading. With increasing age, the probability of degeneration of the macula increases (Lighthouse International, 2014). Age-related macular degeneration *involves the progressive and irreversible destruction of receptors from any of a number of causes.* This disease results in the loss of the ability to see details; for example, reading becomes extremely difficult and television is often reduced to a blur. Roughly one in five people over age 75, especially smokers and European American women, have macular degeneration, making it the leading cause of functional blindness in older adults.

A second age-related retinal disease is a by-product of diabetes. Diabetes is accompanied by accelerated aging of the arteries, with blindness being one of the more serious side effects. Diabetic retinopathy, *as this condition is called, can involve fluid retention in the macula, detachment of the retina, hemorrhage, and aneurysms* (National Eye Institute, 2015). Because it takes many years to develop, diabetic retinopathy is more common among people who developed diabetes early in life.

Hearing. The age-related changes in vision we have considered can significantly affect people's ability to function in their environment. Similarly, age-related changes in hearing can also have this effect and interfere with people's ability to communicate with others. Hearing loss is one of the well-known normative changes associated with aging (Davis et al., 2016). A visit to any housing complex for older adults will easily verify this point; you will quickly notice that television sets and radios are turned up fairly loud in most of the apartments. But you don't have to be old to experience significant hearing problems.

Loud noise is the enemy of hearing at any age. You probably have seen people who work in noisy environments (such as factories and airports) wearing protective gear on their ears so that they are not exposed to loud noise over extended periods of time.

However, you can do serious damage to your hearing with short exposure, too. But you don't need to be at a loud rock concert or next to a jet engine to damage your hearing either. Using headphones or earbuds, especially at high volume, can cause the same serious damage and should be avoided (Jiang et al., 2016). It is especially easy to cause hearing loss with headphones or earbuds if you wear them while exercising; the increased blood flow to the ear during exercise makes hearing receptors more vulnerable to damage. Because young adults do not see their music listening behavior as a risk (Gilliver et al., 2012), hearing loss from this and other sources of loud noise is on the rise. The worst news is that hearing loss is likely to increase among older adults in the future (Davis et al., 2016).

The cumulative effects of noise and normative age-related changes create the most common age-related hearing problem: reduced sensitivity to high-pitched tones or presbycusis, *which occurs earlier and more severely than the loss of sensitivity to low-pitched tones.*

cataracts
Opaque spots on the lens that limit the amount of light transmitted.

glaucoma
Disease in which the fluid in the eye does not drain properly, causing very high internal pressure that can damage the eye and cause loss of vision.

age-related macular degeneration
Progressive and irreversible destruction of receptors from any of a number of causes.

diabetic retinopathy
Eye disease that is a result of diabetes and can involve fluid retention in the macula, detachment of the retina, hemorrhage, and aneurysms.

presbycusis
Reduced sensitivity to high-pitched tones.

Research indicates that by their late 70s, roughly half of older adults have presbycusis. Men typically have greater loss than women, but this may be due to differential exposure to noisy environments. Hearing loss usually is gradual at first, but accelerates during the 40s, a pattern seen clearly in ▶ Figure 14.9.

Presbycusis results from four types of changes in the inner ear (Nagaratnam, Nagaratnam & Cheuk, 2016): sensory, consisting of atrophy and degeneration of receptor cells; neural, consisting of a loss of neurons in the auditory pathway in the brain; metabolic, consisting of a diminished supply of nutrients to the cells in the receptor area; and mechanical, consisting of atrophy and stiffening of the vibrating structures in the receptor area. Knowing the cause of a person's presbycusis is important because the different causes have different implications for other aspects of hearing. Sensory presbycusis has little effect on other hearing abilities. Neural presbycusis seriously affects the ability to understand speech. Metabolic presbycusis produces severe loss of sensitivity to all pitches. Finally, mechanical presbycusis also produces loss across all pitches, but the loss is greatest for high pitches.

▶ **Figure 14.9**

Hearing loss occurs in all adults but is greatest for high-pitched tones and greater for men than for women. As a reference, the highest note on a piano is 4,186 Hz; normal human hearing ranges from 27 Hz to 20,000 Hz.

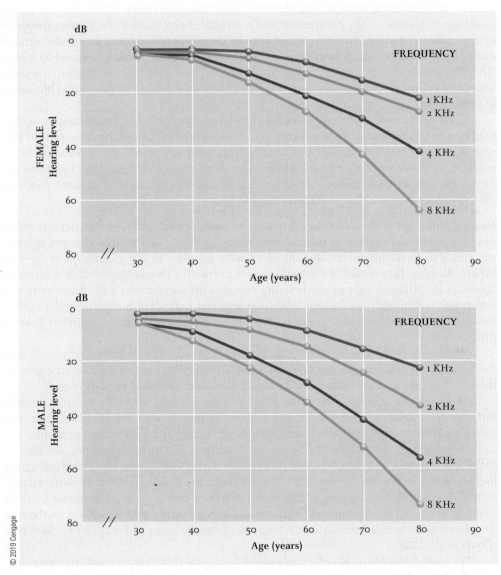

© 2019 Cengage

Based on Ordy, J. M., Brizzee, K. R., Beavers, T., and Medart, P. (1979). Age differences in the functional and structural organization of the auditory system in man. In J. M. Ordy and K. R. Brizzee (Eds.), *Sensory systems and communication in the elderly*, San Diego, CA: Raven Press.

Loss of hearing in later life can also cause numerous adverse emotional reactions, such as loss of independence, social isolation, irritation, paranoia, and depression (Cherko, Hickson, & Bhutta, 2016). Much research indicates hearing loss per se does not cause social maladjustment or emotional disturbance. However, friends and relatives of an older person with undiagnosed or untreated hearing loss often attribute emotional changes to hearing loss, which strains the quality of interpersonal relationships (Li-Korotky, 2012). Thus, hearing loss may not directly affect older adults' self-concept or emotions, but it may negatively affect how they feel about interpersonal communication, especially between couples. Moreover, over 11% of adults with hearing loss report having experienced moderate to severe depression, double the rate of adults without hearing loss (Li et al., 2014). By understanding hearing loss problems and ways to overcome them, people who have no hearing loss can play a large part in minimizing the effects of hearing loss on the older people in their lives.

Fortunately, many people with hearing loss can be helped through two types of amplification systems and cochlear implants. Analog hearing aids are the most common and least expensive, but they provide the lowest-quality sound. Digital hearing aids include microchips that can be programmed for different hearing situations. Cochlear implants do not amplify sound; rather, a microphone transmits sound to a receiver, which stimulates auditory nerve fibers directly. Although technology continues to improve, none of these devices can duplicate our original equipment; so be kind to your ears.

Think About It

How might changes in hearing affect people's cognitive performance?

Chronic Disease and Lifestyle Health Issues

Older adults face numerous health challenges that are influenced by both lifestyle and genetics and their interaction.

Chronic Disease

Nearly half of adults in the United States have a chronic health condition (National Center for Health Statistics, 2016a). Some of the most common are diabetes mellitus and cancer, discussed here, and arthritis, discussed in Chapter 13.

Diabetes Mellitus. *The disease* diabetes mellitus *occurs when the pancreas produces insufficient insulin.* The primary characteristic of diabetes mellitus is above-normal sugar (glucose) in the blood and urine caused by problems in metabolizing carbohydrates. People with diabetes mellitus can go into a coma if the level of sugar gets too high, and they may lapse into unconsciousness if it gets too low.

There are two general types of diabetes (American Diabetes Association, 2016a). Type 1 diabetes *usually develops earlier in life and requires the use of insulin; hence, it is sometimes called insulin-dependent diabetes.* Type 2 diabetes *typically develops in adulthood and is often effectively managed through diet.* There are three groups of older adults with diabetes: those who develop diabetes as children, adolescents, or young adults; those who develop diabetes in late middle age and typically develop cardiovascular problems; and those who develop diabetes in late life and usually show mild problems. This last group includes the majority of older adults with diabetes mellitus. In adults, diabetes mellitus often is associated with obesity and is usually diagnosed during other medical procedures, such as eye examinations or hospitalizations for other conditions.

Diabetes is more common among older adults and members of minority groups (American Diabetes Association, 2016a). The chronic effects of increased glucose levels may result in serious complications, including nerve damage, diabetic retinopathy (discussed earlier), kidney disorders, stroke, cognitive dysfunction, damage to the coronary arteries, skin problems, and poor circulation in the arms and legs, which may lead to gangrene.

diabetes mellitus
Disease that occurs when the pancreas produces insufficient insulin.

Type 1 diabetes
Type of diabetes that usually develops earlier in life and requires the use of insulin; sometimes called insulin-dependent diabetes.

Type 2 diabetes
Type of diabetes that typically develops in adulthood and is often effectively managed through diet.

Although it cannot be cured, diabetes can be managed effectively through a low-carbohydrate and low-calorie diet; exercise; proper care of skin, gums, teeth, and feet; and medication (insulin) (American Diabetes Association, 2016b). Taking the appropriate steps to avoid diabetes in the first place is the best strategy, of course, so monitoring diet and weight are important aspects of an overall wellness-based lifestyle.

Cancer. Cancer is the second leading cause of death in the United States, behind cardiovascular disease (National Center for Health Statistics, 2016a). The risk of dying from cancer is slightly less than one in four for men and one in five for women (American Cancer Society, 2016b). The risk of getting cancer increases markedly with age. Many current deaths caused by cancer are preventable: Stopping smoking, limiting exposure to the sun's ultraviolet rays, and eating a healthy diet can prevent many cancers.

Why older people have a much higher incidence of cancer is not understood fully American Cancer Society, 2016a, b, c). Certainly, genetic predisposition is a major factor. Another key reason is the cumulative effect of poor health habits over a long period of time, such as cigarette smoking and poor diet. In addition, the cumulative effects of exposure to pollutants and cancer-causing chemicals are partly to blame. Some researchers believe that normative age-related changes in the immune system, resulting in a decreased ability to inhibit the growth of tumors, may also be responsible.

Research in molecular biology and microbiology is increasingly pointing to genetic links, likely in combination with environmental factors (Battista et al., 2012). For example, three breast cancer susceptibility genes that have been identified are *BRCA1* on chromosome 17, *BRCA2* on chromosome 13, and *PALB2* which works in conjunction with *BRCA2*. When a woman carries a mutation in either *BRCA1* or *BRCA2*, she is at a greater risk of being diagnosed with breast or ovarian cancer. Similarly, a potential susceptibility locus for prostate cancer has been identified on chromosome 1, called *HPC1*, which may account for about 1 in 500 cases of prostate cancer. An additional rare mutation of *HOXB13*, on chromosome 17, has also been identified.

Screening for cancer remains controversial in some areas, such as for breast cancer and prostate cancer. For example, a 25-year study of nearly 90,000 Canadian women showed that annual mammography did not reduce deaths from breast cancer (Miller et al., 2014). Other research finds similar results for regular screening for breast and prostate cancer. Despite evidence that routine screening for everyone does not reduce deaths from these cancers—and can even result in unnecessary medical procedures—some physicians still encourage routine screening.

Occasionally, a famous person's handling of a personal health issue impacts general public behavior. That was certainly the case when Angelina Jolie went public with her genetic predisposition to breast cancer, as discussed in the ❯ Real People feature.

Lifestyle Health Issues

Two key factors in staying healthy are getting enough good sleep and eating a healthy diet. Let's see how these are accomplished later in life.

Sleep. Nearly every aspect of sleep undergoes age-related changes (Mattis & Sehgal, 2016). It takes older adults longer to fall asleep, they are awake more at night, and they are more easily awakened. *Older adults experience major shifts in their sleep–wake cycles, called* circadian rhythms. Across adulthood, circadian rhythms move from a two-phase pattern of sleep (awake during the day and asleep at night for most people) to a multiphase rhythm reminiscent of that of infants (daytime napping and shorter sleep cycles at night).

These changes are related to the changes in regulating core body temperature. Other major causes of sleep disturbance include sleep apnea (stopping breathing for 5 to 10 seconds), periodic leg jerks, heartburn, frequent need to urinate, poor physical health, and

circadian rhythms
Sleep–wake cycle.

Angelina Jolie is one of the most famous actresses in the world. Because of her fame, many people watch her behavior carefully, and base their own actions on what she does. In 2013, Angelina learned that she carried the BRCA1 gene, which, considered in the context of the rest of her family health history and other tests that detected protein abnormalities, gave her an estimated 87% risk of breast cancer and 50% change of ovarian cancer. What she did next created both a media sensation and greatly increased awareness of the challenges and decisions that confront thousands of women each year.

Angelina decided to have a double mastectomy and reconstructive surgery, and subsequently had her ovaries and Fallopian tubes removed. After her mastectomies, she had reconstructive surgery using her own tissue. She decided to be public about her situation to raise awareness of breast cancer and ovarian cancer risks and the options women have. She wrote two op-eds in the *New York Times* (Jolie, 2013, 2015) to explain her decision making. Her decision, and her fame, made a very big difference.

It became clear that an "Angelina Jolie effect" resulted. Research in the United Kingdom indicates that following her announcement of her breast cancer risk and surgery in May 2013, referrals for genetic screening for breast cancer more than doubled (Evans et al., 2014). Such increases were found globally (Lebo et al., 2015). In general,

women expressed increased knowledge of breast cancer screening, techniques of reconstructive surgery, and genetic testing and risk.

Angelina Jolie's public discussion of her learning of her cancer risk, how and why she made the decisions she did, and her recovery process caused some controversy. Some argued that she should have monitored her health and not undergone surgery. Others

argued that she provided additional support for the stereotype of female beauty. Still others thought her decision was a brave one. What is indisputable is that her fame raised the issues much higher in the public's mind, resulting in many more women consulting their physicians about potential genetic risk and health screening. And that is a very good and important outcome.

Angelina Jolie

---

depression. Among the most effective treatments of sleep problems are increasing physical exercise, reducing caffeine intake, avoiding daytime naps, and making sure that the sleeping environment is as quiet and dark as possible (Boswell, Thai, & Brown, 2015).

Nutrition. Experts agree nutrition directly affects one's mental, emotional, and physical functioning (Hammar & Östgren, 2013; McKee & Schüz, 2015). Diet has been linked to cancer, cardiovascular disease, diabetes, anemia, and digestive disorders. To stay maximally healthy, though, we must recognize that nutritional requirements and eating habits change across the life span. *This change is due mainly to differences in, or how much energy the body needs, termed* metabolism. Body metabolism and the digestive process slow down with age (Janssen, 2005).

metabolism
The rate at which energy is needed and used in the body.

The U.S. Department of Agriculture publishes dietary guidelines based on current research. In its *Dietary Guidelines for Americans 2015–2020* (Health.gov, 2015), the USDA recommends we eat a variety of nutrient-dense foods and beverages across the basic food groups. The general guidelines for adults can be seen in ❱ Figure 14.10.

Key Recommendations:

A healthy eating pattern accounts for all foods and beverages within an appropriate calorie level.

A healthy eating pattern includes:

- A variety of vegetables from all of the subgroups—dark green, red and orange, legumes (beans and peas), starchy, and other
- Fruits, especially whole fruits
- Grains, at least half of which are whole grains
- Fat-free or low-fat dairy, including milk, yogurt, cheese, and/or fortified soy beverages
- A variety of protein foods, including seafood, lean meats and poultry, eggs, legumes (beans and peas), and nuts, seeds, and soy products
- Oils

A healthy eating pattern limits:

- Saturated fats and *trans* fats, added sugars, and sodium

Calorie limits can help individuals achieve healthy eating patterns:

- Consume less than 10 percent of calories per day from added sugars[1]
- Consume less than 10 percent of calories per day from saturated fats[2]
- Consume less than 2,300 milligrams (mg) per day of sodium[3]
- If alcohol is consumed, it should be consumed in moderation—up to one drink per day for women and up to two drinks per day for men—and only by adults of legal drinking age.[4]

The importance of exercise:

The relationship between diet and physical activity contributes to calorie balance and managing body weight. As such, the *Dietary Guidelines* includes a Key Recommendation to:

- Meet the *Physical Activity Guidelines for Americans.*[5]

© 2019 Cengage

[1] The recommendation to limit intake of calories from added sugars to less than 10 percent per day is a target based on food pattern modeling and national data on intakes of calories from added sugars that demonstrate the public health need to limit calories from added sugars to meet food group and nutrient needs within calorie limits. The limit on calories from added sugars is not a Tolerable Upper Intake Level (UL) set by the Institute of Medicine (IOM). For most calorie levels, there are not enough calories available after meeting food group needs to consume 10 percent of calories from added sugars and 10 percent of calories from saturated fats and still stay within calorie limits.

[2] The recommendation to limit intake of calories from saturated fats to less than 10 percent per day is a target based on evidence that replacing saturated fats with unsaturated fats is associated with reduced risk of cardiovascular disease. The limit on calories from saturated fats is not a UL set by the IOM. For most calorie levels, there are not enough calories available after meeting food group needs to consume 10 percent of calories from added sugars and 10 percent of calories from saturated fats and still stay within calorie limits.

[3] The recommendation to limit intake of sodium to less than 2,300 mg per day is the UL for individuals ages 14 years and older set by the IOM. The recommendations for children younger than 14 years of age are the IOM age- and sex-appropriate ULs (see Appendix 7. Nutritional Goals for Age-Sex Groups Based on Dietary Reference Intakes and Dietary Guidelines Recommendations).

[4] It is not recommended that individuals begin drinking or drink more for any reason. The amount of alcohol and calories in beverages varies and should be accounted for within the limits of healthy eating patterns. Alcohol should be consumed only by adults of legal drinking age. There are many circumstances in which individuals should not drink, such as during pregnancy. See Appendix 9. Alcohol for additional information.

[5] U.S. Department of Health and Human Services. *2008 Physical Activity Guidelines for Americans.* Washington (DC): U.S. Department of Health and Human Services; 2008. ODPHP Publication No. U0036. Available at: http://www.health.gov/paguidelines. Accessed August 6, 2015.

From health.gov/dietaryguidelines/2015/resources/2015-2020_Dietary_Guidelines.pdf, p. xiii.

Recall

1. The tips of the chromosomes, called _____, play a major role in aging.

2. A protein that is the basis for neuritic plaques and that plays a role in Alzheimer's disease is _____.

3. The risk of getting cancer _____ markedly with age.

Interpret

- In this section, we have concentrated on the biological forces in development. Think about the other forces (psychological, social, and life cycle) and list some reasons why scientists have yet to propose a purely biological theory that accounts for all aspects of aging.

Apply

- How do the sensory changes that occur with age affect an older adult's everyday life?

Check your answers to the Recall Questions at the end of the chapter.

14.3 Cognitive Processes

LEARNING OBJECTIVES

- What changes occur in information processing as people age? How do these changes relate to everyday life?

- What changes occur in memory with age? What can be done to remediate these changes?

- What are creativity and wisdom, and how do they relate to age?

Rocio is a 75-year-old widow who believes that she does not remember recent events—such as whether she took her medicine—as well as she used to, but she has no trouble remembering things that happened in her 20s. Rocio wonders if this is normal or whether she should be worried.

Rocio, like many older people, takes medications for arthritis, allergies, and high blood pressure. However, each drug has its own pattern; some are taken only with meals, others are taken every eight hours, and still others are taken twice daily. Keeping these regimens straight is important to avoid potentially dangerous interactions and side effects, and older people face the problem of remembering to take each medication at the proper time.

Such situations place a heavy demand on cognitive resources such as attention and memory. In this section, we examine age-related changes in these and other cognitive processes, including reaction time, intelligence, and wisdom.

Information Processing

In Chapter 1, we saw that one theoretical framework for studying cognition is information-processing theory. This framework provides a way to identify and study the basic mechanisms by which people take in, store, and remember information. Innovations and discoveries in neuroscience have resulted in major advances in our understanding of how people process information across the life span. Neuroscience has guided investigators as they examine age-related differences in basic processes such as attention and reaction time, particularly through the use of neuroimaging (Linden, 2016; Sugiura, 2016). Earlier in this chapter, we considered ways of investigating brain processes through neuroimaging; such research is essential for understanding age-related changes in cognition.

Speed of Processing

You are driving home from a friend's house when all of a sudden a car pulls out of a driveway directly into your path. If you don't hit the brakes as fast as possible, you will have an accident. How quickly can you move your foot from the accelerator to the brake?

This real-life situation is an example of speed of processing, *how quickly and efficiently the early steps in information processing are completed.* Speed of processing is one of the most investigated phenomena of aging, and hundreds of studies point to the same conclusion: People slow down as they get older. In fact, the slowing-with-age finding is so well documented that many researchers accept it as the only universal behavioral change in aging discovered so far (Salthouse, 2014a, b). However, data show that the rate at which cognitive processes slow down from young adulthood to late life varies a great deal depending on the task (Salthouse, 2014a, b).

The most important reason speed of processing slows down is that older adults take longer to decide that they need to respond, especially when the situation involves ambiguous information (Salthouse, 2014a, b). Even when the information presented indicates that a response will be needed, there is an orderly slowing of responding with age. As the uncertainty of whether a response is needed increases, older adults become differentially slower; the difference in reaction time between older adults and middle-aged adults increases as the uncertainty level increases.

Because the decrease in processing speed is a universal phenomenon, researchers have argued that it may explain a great deal of the age differences in cognition (e.g., Salthouse, 2014a, b). Indeed, processing speed is a very good predictor of cognitive performance, but research has shown that there's a catch. The prediction is best when the task requires little effort. If the task requires more effort and is more difficult, then working memory (which we consider later) is a better predictor of performance. Also, exercise can mediate the effects of normative aging and improve several aspects of cognition (Dulac & Aubertin-Leheudre, 2016).

speed of processing
How quickly and efficiently the early steps in information processing are completed.

Due to sensory and attention changes, older adults are more challenged when driving.

Jose Luis Pelaez Inc./Blend Images/Getty Images

Dividing Attention Among Multiple Tasks

Adults spend much of their time doing more than one task simultaneously, such as walking and talking on a phone, cooking multiple items for a meal, and driving a car. Such multitasking requires us to spread our attention across all the tasks. Divided attention *concerns how well people perform multiple tasks simultaneously*. Driving a car is a classic divided attention task—you pay attention to other cars, the gauges in your car, pedestrians along the side of the street, and perhaps your passengers as you have a conversation with them.

divided attention
The ability of people to perform more than one task simultaneously.

Although it is widely believed older adults have more trouble than younger adults at dividing attention, it turns out the age differences observed are due to older adults' difficulties with the individual tasks and not to spreading their attention across them per se (Horwood & Beanland, 2016; Rizzuto, Cherry, & LeDoux, 2012). Observations in the workplace show older workers are just as able to multitask, but they perform each task a bit more slowly than younger workers. However, when the tasks become complex, older adults encounter difficulties dividing their attention and their performance suffers as a result.

Age differences on divided-attention tasks can be minimized if older adults are given training, thereby reducing the demands on attention. Such training can even be through online computer games (Toril et al., 2016; van Muijden, Band, & Hommel, 2012). These results imply that older adults may be able to learn through experience how to divide their attention effectively between tasks.

So, you may ask, when do older adults have difficulty performing multiple tasks simultaneously? You may have observed older adults having difficulty trying to remember something as they are walking down a staircase, or trying to simply walk and talk at the same time. Li and colleagues (Li et al., 2001) found older adults prioritize walking and maintaining balance at the expense of memory. In other words, older adults focused on the task most important to them; walking and balancing to prevent falls. This finding is supported by neurological research (Holtzer et al., 2016). Younger adults, on the other hand, optimized their memory performance and ignored walking and balancing.

Memory

Memory is the most important cognitive ability we have. It gives us our identity through the recordings of our past. It gets us through our lives by enabling us to find our way home, to our job, our school, and to so many other places. It enables us to recognize ourselves and loved ones and friends (and to know who we have never met). It provides our vast repertoire of information about everything under the sun. Memory really is the core of our being.

Perhaps that is why we put so much value on maintaining a good memory in old age. In fact, the ability to remember is a common measure of how well we are doing in late life, because older adults are stereotyped as people whose memory is on the decline, people for whom forgetting is not to be taken lightly. Like Rocio in the opening vignette, many people think forgetting to buy a loaf of bread when they are 25 is annoying but otherwise all right, but forgetting it when they are 70 is cause for concern ("Do I have Alzheimer's disease?"). We will see that forgetting is part of daily life, and the belief it only happens in late life or the fact that it happens in later life automatically means something is seriously awry is wrong. In fact, older adults are quite adept at using strategies in their everyday life contexts to remember what they need to know.

Working Memory

One day at work, you suddenly remember that your significant other's birthday is a week from tomorrow. You decide that a romantic dinner would be a great way to celebrate; so you go online, find a restaurant that is perfect for a romantic dinner, see that you must call to make a reservation, look at the phone number, pick up your phone, and call.

working memory

Processes and structures involved in holding information in mind and simultaneously using it for other functions.

Remembering the number long enough to dial it successfully requires good working memory. Working memory *involves the processes and structures involved in holding information in mind and simultaneously using it to solve a problem, make a decision, perform some function, or learn new information.*

Researchers typically consider working memory an umbrella term for many similar short-term holding and computational processes relating to a wide range of cognitive skills and knowledge domains (Sternberg & Sternberg, 2017). This places working memory right in the thick of things—it plays an active, critical, and central role in encoding, storage, and retrieval of information.

Working memory has a relatively small capacity. Because working memory deals with information that is being used at the moment, it acts as a kind of mental scratch pad or buffer. Unless we take some action to keep the information active (perhaps by rehearsal) or pass it along to long-term storage, the "page" we are using will be filled up quickly; to handle more information, some of the old information must be discarded.

Most evidence indicates there is significant age-related decline in working memory (Heathcote, 2016), although the extent of the decline is still in doubt. Neuroimaging studies reveal why these age differences occur. It turns out that both younger and older adults activate the prefrontal area of their brains (an area behind the forehead) during working memory tasks. But older adults activate more of it on easier tasks; they also exhaust their resources sooner (Cappell, Gmeindl, & Reuter-Lorenz, 2010; Heinzel et al., 2014). In a sense, older adults must devote more "brain power" to working memory compared with younger adults on average; so older adults run out of resources sooner, resulting in poorer performance. However, research shows that older adults can be trained to increase their working memory, which is reflected in more efficient brain processing (Heinzel et al., 2014).

Implicit and Explicit Memory

implicit memory

Unconscious remembering of information learned at some earlier time.

explicit memory

Deliberate and conscious remembering of information that is learned and remembered at a specific time.

episodic memory

General class of memory having to do with the conscious recollection of information from a specific time or event.

semantic memory

General class of memory concerning the remembering of meanings of words or concepts not tied to a specific time or event.

In addition to working memory, we can further divide memory into two other types: implicit memory, *the unconscious remembering of information learned at some earlier time, and* explicit memory, *the deliberate and conscious remembering of information that is learned and remembered at a specific time. Explicit memory is further divided into* episodic memory, *the general class of memory having to do with the conscious recollection of information from a specific time or event, and* semantic memory, *the general class of memory concerning the remembering of meanings of words or concepts not tied to a specific time or event.*

Implicit memory is much like getting into a routine—we do things from memory, but we do not have to think about them. For example, the way we brush our teeth tends not to be something we consciously think about at the time. We just remember how to do it. Whether age differences in implicit memory are observed depends on the specific kind of implicit memory task in question (Howard & Howard, 2012, 2013, 2016). For example, learning sequences tend to show age differences, whereas learning spatial context does not.

Much more research has focused on explicit memory, and it is here where consistent age-related differences are observed, although even here there are exceptions (Light, 2012). When we probe a bit deeper, we find that on tests of memory for recall of explicit bits of information, older adults omit more information, remember information that was not actually presented, and repeat more previously recalled items. These age differences have been well documented, are large, and are not reliably lowered by a slower presentation or by cues or reminders given during recall. On recognition tests, age differences are smaller but still present. Older adults also tend to be less efficient at spontaneously using memory strategies to help themselves remember, but they can learn to use such strategies effectively (Berry et al., 2010; Brehmer et al., 2016). In contrast, age differences on semantic memory tasks are typically absent in normative aging but are found in persons with dementia, making this difference one way to diagnose probable cases of abnormal cognitive aging (Grady, 2012).

A final area of memory research concerns autobiographical memory, *memory for* autobiographical memory *events that occur during one's life.* Autobiographical memories tend to be organized according to the periods in one's life when they occurred such that remembering some events from a particular time period can trigger others (Mace & Clevinger, 2013). When simply asked to remember whatever events they choose, older adults tend to report fewer details than do younger adults (Addis, Wong, & Schacter, 2008) and tend to remember more positive than negative events and even put a more positive spin on events once remembered more negatively (Boals, Hayslip, & Banks, 2014).

◄ autobiographical memory
Memory for events that occur during one's life.

Neuroimaging studies indicate that when older adults take in and encode information, their prefrontal cortex shows overactivity, indicating that they are attempting to compensate for age-related brain changes (Meunier, Stamatakis, & Tyler, 2014). When older adults retrieve information, neuroimaging studies show age-related differences in how the prefrontal cortex and hippocampus work together (Wang & Giovanello, 2016). This research also indicates age-related compensatory brain activity in older adults for retrieval, similar to that seen in other cognitive processing (Oedekoven et al., 2013). Specifically, younger adults have more extensive neural network connections in the parietal and frontal regions involved in retrieval than do older adults. However, older adults show higher levels of brain activity more generally in these regions, indicating a likely compensatory strategy for less extensive networks.

Overall, these data support the view that older adults process information in their brains differently than younger adults. These differences in part represent attempts at working around, or compensating for, the normal age-related changes that occur in information processing. In the area of memory, though, these compensation attempts are insufficient on their own, but with training they can mitigate some of the losses in performance.

When Is Memory Change Abnormal?

As we noted earlier, older adults are sensitive to the stereotype that their forgetfulness is indicative of something much worse. Because people are concerned that memory failures may reflect disease, identifying true cases of memory-impairing disease is extremely important. Differentiating normal and abnormal memory changes is usually accomplished through a wide array of tests that are grounded in the research findings that document the various developmental patterns discussed previously (American Psychiatric Association, 2013). Such testing focuses on measuring performance and identifying declines in aspects of memory that typically do not change, such as tertiary memory (which is essentially long-term memory) (Stoner, O'Riley, & Edelstein, 2010).

Even if a decline is identified in an aspect of memory that is cause for concern, it does not automatically follow that there is a serious problem. A first step is to find out whether the memory problem is interfering with everyday functioning. When the memory problem does interfere with functioning, such as not remembering your spouse's name or how to get home, it is appropriate to suspect a serious, abnormal underlying reason.

Once a serious problem is suspected, the next step is to obtain a thorough examination (Stoner et al., 2010). This should include a complete physical and neurological examination and a complete battery of neuropsychological tests. These may help identify the nature and extent of the underlying problem and provide information about what steps, if any, can be taken to alleviate the difficulties. Neuroimaging can help sort out the specific type of problem or disease the individual may be experiencing.

The most important point to keep in mind is that there is no magic number of times a person must forget something before it becomes a matter for concern. Indeed, many memory-impairing diseases progress slowly, and poor memory performance may only be noticed gradually over an extended period of time. The best course is to have the person examined; only with complete and thorough testing can these concerns be checked appropriately.

External memory aids such as pill organizers help people remember when certain medications need to be taken.

external memory aids

Memory aids that rely on environmental resources, such as notebooks and calendars.

internal memory aids

Memory aids that rely on mental processes, such as imagery.

Remediating Memory Problems

Remember Rocio, the person in the vignette who had to remember when to take several different medications? In the face of normal age-related declines, how can her problem be addressed?

Support programs can be designed to help people to remember. Sometimes people such as Rocio who are experiencing normal age-related memory changes need extra help because of the high memory demands they face. At other times, people need help because the memory changes they are experiencing are greater than normal.

Camp and colleagues (1993; Camp, 2005; Malone & Camp, 2007) developed the E-I-E-I-O framework to handle both situations. The E-I-E-I-O framework combines two types of memory: explicit and implicit. The framework also includes two types of memory aids. *External memory aids* *are memory aids that rely on environmental resources, such as notebooks and calendars.* *Internal memory aids* *are memory aids that rely on mental processes, such as imagery.* The "aha" experience that comes with suddenly remembering something (as in, "Oh, now I remember!") is the O that follows these Es and Is. As you can see in ▶ Figure 14.11, the E-I-E-I-O framework allows different types of memory to be combined with different types of memory aids to provide a broad range of intervention options to help people remember.

You are probably most familiar with the explicit-external and explicit-internal types of memory aids. Explicit-internal aids such as rehearsal help people remember phone numbers. Explicit-external aids are used when information needs to be better organized and remembered, such as using a smartphone to remember appointments. Implicit-internal aids represent nearly effortless learning, such as the association between the color of the particular wing of the apartment building one lives in and the fact that one's residence is there. Implicit-external aids such as icons representing time of day and the number of pills to take help older adults remember their medication.

In general, explicit-external interventions are most frequently used to remediate the kinds of memory problems that older adults face, probably because such methods are easy to use and widely available (Berry et al., 2010; Mercer, 2016). For example, virtually everyone owns a smartphone or an address book in which they store addresses and phone numbers.

Explicit-external interventions have other important applications, too. Ensuring that older adults take the proper medication at the proper time is a problem best solved by an explicit-external intervention: a pillbox that is divided into compartments corresponding to days of the week and different times of the day, which research shows to be the easiest to load and results in the fewest medication errors (Ownby, Hertzog, & Czaja, 2012). Nursing homes also use explicit-external interventions, such as bulletin boards with the date and weather conditions and activities charts, to help residents keep in touch with current events.

▶ **Figure 14.11**

The E-I-E-I-O model of memory helps categorize different types of memory aids.

Type of memory	Type of memory aid	
	External	Internal
Explicit	Appointment book	Mental imagery
	Grocery list	Rote rehearsal
Implicit	Color-coded maps	Spaced retrieval
	Sandpaper letters	Conditioning

© 2019 Cengage

Creativity and Wisdom

Two aspects of cognition that have been examined for age-related differences are creativity and wisdom. Each has been the focus of stereotypes: Creativity is assumed to be a function of young people, whereas wisdom is assumed to be the province of older adults. Let's see whether these views are accurate.

Creativity

Researchers define creativity in adults as the ability to produce work that is novel, high in demand, and task appropriate (Kaufman, 2016; Simonton, in press). Creative output, in terms of the number of creative ideas a person has or the major contributions a person makes, varies across the adult life span and disciplines (Franses, 2016; Jones, 2010; Kaufman, 2016; Kozbelt & Durmysheva, 2007; Simonton, in press). When considered as a function of age, the overall number of creative contributions a person makes tends to increase through one's 30s, peak in the late 30s to early 40s, and decline thereafter. A typical life-span trend is shown for painters and composers in ▶ Figure 14.12.

The age-related decline from midlife on does *not* mean people stop being creative altogether, just that they produce fewer creative ideas than when they were younger (Damian & Simonton, 2015). For example, the age when people made major creative contributions, such as research that resulted in winning the Nobel Prize, increased throughout the 20th century (Jones, 2010). And because creativity results from the interaction of cognitive abilities, personality, and developmental forces, all of these continue to operate throughout people's lives.

Exciting neuroimaging research is supporting previous research that one's most innovative contribution tends to happen most often during the 30s or 40s, as well as showing that creative people's brains are different. This research shows white matter brain structures that connect brain regions in very different locations, and coordinate the cognitive control of information among them, are related to creativity and are more apparent in creative people (Heilman, 2016; Zhu et al., 2016). Such research has also linked certain brain pathways to actual everyday creative behavior.

As an example of such focused research, additional neuroimaging studies show different areas of the prefrontal and parietal areas are responsible for different aspects of creative thinking (Abraham et al., 2012). This research supports the belief creativity

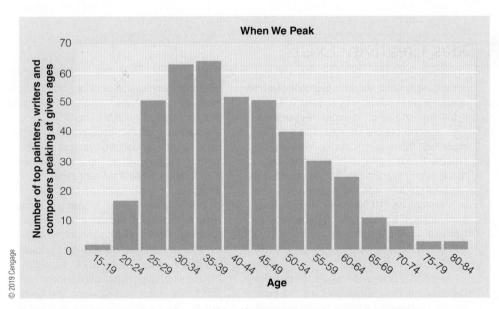

Based on img.washingtonpost.com/blogs/wonkblog/files/2016/06/creative_age.png&w=1484.

▶ **Figure 14.12**

Age at which peak creative output was reached for painters, writers, and composers.

involves connecting disparate ideas in new ways, as different areas of the brain are responsible for processing different kinds of information. Because white matter tends to change with age, this finding also suggests there are underlying brain maturation reasons why innovative thinking tends to occur most often during late young adulthood and early middle age.

Building upon neuroimaging research, Jung, Flores, and Hunter (2016) developed the Hunter Imagination Questionnaire (HIQ) designed to assess imagination over time in a naturalistic way. Scores on the HIQ have been shown to be related to a wide array of brain volume in areas such as the hippocampus, areas of the frontal lobe, and other brain regions. It will likely be the case that such measures will continue to be refined, and may eventually show utility in helping to identify both high levels of creativity and potential early signs of brain disorders.

Even with this evidence, though, a nagging question remains for many researchers and theorists (e.g., Ericsson, 2014; Gladwell, 2008): Is what the typical person calls *creativity* nothing more than a high level of expertise that is honed after years of practice? To find out why that question is not yet settled, consider the arguments in the What Do *You* Think? feature.

Wisdom

For thousands of years, cultures around the world greatly admired people who were wise. Based on years of research using in-depth think-aloud interviews with young, middle-aged, and older adults about normal and unusual problems people face, Baltes and colleagues (Ardelt, 2010; Baltes & Staudinger, 2000; Scheibe, Kunzmann, & Baltes, 2007) describe four characteristics of wisdom:

- Wisdom deals with important or difficult matters of life and the human condition.
- Wisdom is truly "superior" knowledge, judgment, and advice.
- Wisdom is knowledge with extraordinary scope, depth, and balance that is applicable to specific situations.
- Wisdom, when used, is well intended and combines mind and virtue (character).

Researchers used this framework to discover that people who are wise are experts in the basic issues in life (Ardelt, 2010; Baltes & Staudinger, 2000). Wise people know a great deal about how to conduct life, how to interpret life events, and what life means. Kunz

What Do *You* Think? Does Creativity Exist?

Lin-Manuel Miranda's *Hamilton*, a painting by Diego Rivera, Stephanie Kwolek's invention of Kevlar—these and many thousands more items in our world are generally described as creative works. For thousands of years, creativity was viewed as the purview of a few people who received inspiration from some special source (Simonton, in press). Creative people were, and still are by many, seen as different—they thought differently, they felt things differently, they did things differently.

By the 20th century, an alternative view became more prominent. That view, expressed clearly through authors and researchers such as Ericsson (2014) and Gladwell (2008), sees creativity as not

something special, but as a trainable skill that is essentially achievable by anyone who puts in the time and practice. From this perspective, what people call creative output is little more than the next logical step in an ongoing process that is the result of expertise, and that is largely predictable. In his book *Outliers*, Gladwell (2008) made this quite prescriptive with his famous "10,000-Hour Rule," derived from research by Ericsson, which set the typical amount of practice time it takes to become sufficiently expert to produce "creative" things.

As popular and optimistic as the practice notion of creativity is, however, it is not that simple. Macnamara, Hambrick, and Oswald (2014) conducted a meta-analysis of studies

examining the relation between practice and creativity or expert performance. They found that although practice is certainly an important factor in such performance in a wide range of fields, such as music, sports, and games, it is far from the only factor. Thus, they concluded that practice, while important, does not explain creative or highly expert output.

Does creativity exist? It seems to come down to this. Until we have a fuller understanding of what happens cognitively when a person puts many, often disparate ideas together in a novel way, we are left without a good alternative explanation. Something about that outcome is different. You cannot simply practice and make it happen. What do *you* think?

(2007) refers to this as the strengths, knowledge, and understanding learned only by living through the earlier stages of life.

Research studies indicate that, contrary to what many people expect, there is no association between age and wisdom (Ardelt, 2010; Baltes & Staudinger, 2000). In fact, the framework on wisdom discussed above has been applied to emerging adults (Booker & Dunsmore, 2016). As envisioned by Baltes and colleagues, whether a person is wise depends on whether he or she has extensive life experience with the type of problem given and has the requisite cognitive abilities and personality. Thus, wisdom could be related to crystallized intelligence, knowledge that builds over time and through experience (Ardelt, 2010).

Culture matters, though, in understanding wisdom. For instance, younger and middle-aged Japanese adults use more wisdom-related reasoning strategies (e.g., recognition of multiple perspectives, the limits of personal knowledge, and the importance of compromise) in resolving social conflicts than younger or middle-aged Americans (Grossman et al., 2012). However, older adults in both cultures used similar wisdom-related strategies.

So what specific factors help one become wise? Baltes (1993) identified three factors: (1) *general personal conditions* such as mental ability; (2) *specific expertise conditions* such as mentoring or practice; and (3) *facilitative life contexts* such as education or leadership experience. Personal growth during adulthood, reflecting Erikson's concepts of generativity and integrity also fosters the process, as do facing and dealing with life crises (Ardelt, 2010). All of these factors take time. Thus, although growing old is no guarantee of wisdom, it does provide the time, if used well, creates a supportive context for developing wisdom.

Becoming wise is one thing; having one's wisdom recognized is another. Interestingly, peer ratings of wisdom are better indicators of wisdom than self-ratings (Redzanowski & Glück, 2013). It appears people draw from a wide array of examples of wisdom (Westrate, Ferrari, & Ardelt, 2016) and are better at recognizing wisdom in others than they are in themselves. Perhaps it is better that way.

Interestingly, there is a debate over whether with wisdom comes happiness. There is research evidence that wise people are happier, have better mental health, are humble, and better quality of life (Bergsma & Ardelt, 2012; Etezadi & Pushkar, 2013; Krause, 2016; Thomas et al., 2017). Wise people tend to have higher levels of perceived control over their lives and use problem-focused and positive reappraisal coping strategies more often than people who are not wise. On the other hand, some evidence indicates the attainment of wisdom brings increased distress (Staudinger & Glück, 2011). Perhaps because with the experience that brings wisdom comes an understanding that life does not always work out the way one would like.

TEST YOURSELF **14.3**

Recall

1. _____ refers to how quickly and efficiently the early steps of information processing are completed.

2. The two types of explicit memory are and _____.

3. Three factors that help a person become wise are general personal conditions, special expertise conditions, and _____.

Interpret

• How would the view that wisdom involves life experience fit into the discussion of expertise in Chapter 13?

Apply

• If you were to design a training program for older drivers, what elements would you include?

Check your answers to the Recall Questions at the end of the chapter.

LEARNING OBJECTIVES

- How does depression in older adults differ from depression in younger adults? How is it diagnosed and treated?

- How are anxiety disorders treated in older adults?

- What is Alzheimer's disease? How is it diagnosed and managed? What causes it?

Mary lived by herself for 30 years after her husband died. For all but the last five years or so, she managed very well. Little by little, family members and friends began noticing that Mary wasn't behaving quite right. For example, her memory slipped, she sounded confused sometimes, and her moods changed without warning. Her appearance deteriorated. Some of her friends attribute these changes to the fact that Mary is in her 80s. But others wonder whether it is something more than normal aging.

Suppose Mary is a relative of yours. How would you deal with the situation? How would you decide whether her behavior is normal? What would you do to try to improve Mary's life? We'll consider interventions later in this section that might help Mary if she has a serious disease such as Alzheimer's.

Every day, families turn to mental health professionals for help in dealing with the psychological problems of their aging relatives. Unfortunately, myths interfere with appropriate mental health diagnoses and interventions for older adults. For example, many people mistakenly believe that nearly all older adults are depressed, demented, or both. When they observe older adults behaving in these ways, they take no action because they believe that nothing can be done.

In this section, we will see that such beliefs are wrong. Only a minority of older adults have mental health problems, and most of these problems respond to therapy. Sometimes these problems manifest themselves differently in younger and older adults, so we need to know what to look for. Accurate diagnosis is essential. Let's examine some of the most commonly occurring and widely known disorders: depression, anxiety disorders, and Alzheimer's disease.

Depression

Most people feel down or sad from time to time, perhaps in reaction to a problem at work or in one's relationships. But does this mean that most people are depressed? How is depression diagnosed? Are there age-related differences in the symptoms examined in diagnosis? How is depression treated?

First of all, let's dispense with a myth. Contrary to the popular belief that most older adults are depressed, for healthy people, the rate of severe depression *declines* from young adulthood to old age as shown in ❱ Figure 14.13; the average age of onset is 32 (National Institute of Mental Health, 2016a). However, this downward age trend does not hold in all cultures; for example, depressive symptoms among Chinese older adults rose over a 24-year period (1987–2010, inclusive) (Shao et al., 2013). For those people who do experience depression, let's examine its diagnosis and treatment.

How Is Depression Diagnosed in Older Adults?

Depression in later life is usually diagnosed on the basis of two clusters of symptoms that must be present for at least two weeks: feelings and physical changes. *As with younger people, the most prominent symptom of depression in older adults is feeling sad or down, termed* dysphoria. But whereas younger people are likely to label these feelings directly as "feeling depressed," older adults may refer to them as "feeling helpless" or in terms of physical health such as "feeling tired" (NIHSeniorHealth, 2016; Segal, Qualls, & Smyer, 2011). Older adults are also more likely than younger people to appear apathetic and expressionless, to

dysphoria
Feeling sad or down.

Twelve-month prevalence of major depressive episode among U.S. adults (2014).

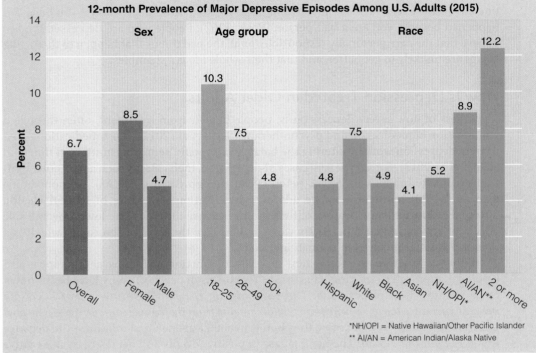

Adapted from National Institute of Mental Health (2013). 12-Month Prevalence of Major Depressive Episode Among U.S. Adults. Retrieved from www.nimh.nih.gov/health/statistics/prevalence/major-depression-among-adults.shtml.

confine themselves to bed, to neglect themselves, and to make derogatory statements about themselves.

The second cluster of symptoms includes physical changes such as loss of appetite, insomnia, and trouble breathing (NIHSeniorHealth, 2016; Segal et al., 2011). In young people, these symptoms usually indicate an underlying psychological problem, but in older adults, they may simply reflect normal, age-related changes. Thus, older adults' physical symptoms of depression must be evaluated very carefully (Chew-Graham & Ray, 2016).

An important step in diagnosis is ruling out other possible causes of the symptoms. For example, underlying health problems that appear as depression include vitamin deficiencies (e.g., B12), diabetes, cardiovascular disease, chronic pain, hypothyroidism, cancer, Cushing's syndrome, certain viruses, dementia, Parkinson's disease, rheumatoid arthritis, and medication interactions and side effects (Chew-Graham & Ray, 2016).

Finally, it is important to establish whether the symptoms interfere with daily life. Can the person carry out normal responsibilities at home? How well does he or she interact with others? There must be clear evidence that daily life is affected.

What Causes Depression?

There are two main schools of thought about the causes of depression. One focuses on biological and physiological processes, particularly on imbalances of specific neurotransmitters, genetic predisposition, and changes in certain types of brain cells (Ménard, Hodes, & Russo, 2016). Research evidence indicates that the most likely cause of severe depression in later life is an imbalance in neurotransmitters such as low levels of serotonin and the action of brain-derived neurotrophic factor (BDNF; Hashimoto, 2013). The general view that severe depression has a biochemical basis underlies current approaches to drug therapies, discussed a little later.

The second view focuses on psychosocial factors, such as loss and internal belief systems. Although several types of loss or negative events have been associated with depression—including loss of a spouse, a job, or one's health—it is how a person interprets a loss, rather than the event itself, that causes depression (Segal et al., 2011). *In this approach,* internal belief systems, *or what one tells oneself about why certain things are happening, are emphasized as the cause of depression.* For example, experiencing an unpredictable and uncontrollable event such as the death of a spouse may cause depression if you believe it happened because you are a bad person (Beck, 1967). People who are depressed tend to believe that they are personally responsible for all the bad things that happen to them, that things are unlikely to get better, and that their whole life is a shambles.

How Is Depression Treated in Older Adults?

Regardless of how severe depression is, people benefit from treatment, often through a combination of medication and psychotherapy (Segal et al., 2011). Most medications used to treat depression work by altering the balance of specific neurotransmitters in the brain (Jainer et al. 2013). For very severe cases of depression, medications such as selective serotonin reuptake inhibitors (SSRIs), heterocyclic antidepressants (HCAs), or monoamine oxidase (MAO) inhibitors can be administered (National Institute of Mental Health, 2016b). SSRIs are the medication of first choice because they have the lowest overall side effects of any antidepressant. SSRIs work by boosting the level of serotonin, which is a neurotransmitter involved in regulating moods.

Either as an alternative to medication or in conjunction with it, psychotherapy is also a popular approach to treating depression. Two forms of psychotherapy have been shown to be effective with older adults. *The basic idea in* behavior therapy *is that depressed people experience too few rewards or reinforcements from their environment.* Thus, the goal of behavior therapy is to increase the good things that happen and minimize the negative things (Lewinsohn, 1975). The net increase in positive events and net decrease in negative events comes about through practice and homework assignments during the course of therapy, such as going out more or joining a club to meet new people.

A second effective approach is cognitive therapy, *which is based on the idea that maladaptive beliefs or cognitions about oneself are responsible for depression.* From this perspective, those who are depressed view themselves as unworthy and inadequate, the world as insensitive and ungratifying, and the future as bleak and unpromising (Beck et al., 1979). In a cognitive therapy session, a person is taught how to recognize these thoughts and to reevaluate the self, the world, and the future more positively, resulting in a change in the underlying beliefs. Cognitive behavior therapy is especially effective for older adults (Carr & McNulty, 2016; Jeste & Palmer, 2013). This is good news, because medications may not be as effective or as tolerated by older adults because of age-related changes in metabolism.

The most important fact to keep in mind about depression is that it is treatable. Thus, if an older person behaves in ways that indicate depression, it is a good idea to have him or her examined by a mental health professional. Even if the malady turns out not to be depression, another underlying and possibly treatable condition may be uncovered. A major healthcare problem in the United States is that less than 40% of adults of all ages receive minimally adequate treatment for depression (National Institute of Mental Health, 2016a).

Anxiety Disorders

Imagine you are about to give a speech to an audience of several hundred people. During the last few minutes before you begin, you start to feel nervous, your heart begins to pound, your mouth gets dry, and your palms get sweaty. These feelings, common even to veteran speakers, are similar to those experienced more frequently and intensely by people with anxiety disorders.

Anxiety disorders *involve excessive, irrational dread in everyday situations and include problems such as feelings of severe anxiety for no apparent reason, phobias with regard to specific things or places, and obsessions or compulsions in which thoughts or actions are performed repeatedly* (National Institute of Mental Health, 2016c, d).

---

internal belief systems
View of a cause of depression of what one tells oneself about why certain things are happening.

behavior therapy
Type of therapy based on the notion that depressed people experience too few rewards or reinforcements from their environment.

cognitive therapy
Type of therapy based on the idea that maladaptive beliefs or cognitions about oneself are responsible for depression.

anxiety disorders
Problems such as feelings of severe anxiety, phobias, and obsessive-compulsive behaviors.

The prevalence of anxiety disorders in adults of all ages is about 18%, but the lifetime prevalence is about twice as high in young and middle-aged adults as it is in older adults. Overall, women are 60% more likely than men to experience an anxiety disorder over their lifetime (National Institute of Mental Health, 2016e). The reasons for this gender difference are unknown.

Common to all the anxiety disorders are physical changes that interfere with social functioning, personal relationships, or work. These physical changes include dry mouth, sweating, dizziness, upset stomach, diarrhea, insomnia, hyperventilation, chest pain, choking, frequent urination, headaches, and a sensation of a lump in the throat (Segal et al., 2011). These symptoms occur in adults of all ages, but they are particularly common in older adults because of loss of health, relocation stress, isolation, fear of losing control over their lives, or guilt resulting from feelings of hostility toward family and friends.

An important issue concerning anxiety disorders in older adults is that anxiety may be an appropriate response to the situation. For example, helplessness anxiety is generated by a potential or actual loss of control or mastery (Varkal et al., 2013). For example, a study in Turkey showed that older adults are anxious about their memory, reflecting at least in part a realistic assessment of normative, age-related decline.

In addition, a series of severe negative life experiences may result in a person's reaching the breaking point and appearing highly anxious. Many older adults who show symptoms of anxiety disorder have underlying health problems that may be responsible for the symptoms. In all cases, the anxious behavior should be investigated first as an appropriate response that may not warrant medical intervention. The important point is to evaluate the older adult's behavior in context.

These issues make it difficult to diagnose anxiety disorders, especially in older adults (Carr & McNulty, 2016; Segal et al., 2011). The problem is that there usually is nothing specific that a person can point to as the specific trigger or cause. In addition, anxiety in older adults often accompanies an underlying physical disorder or illness.

Anxiety disorders can be treated with medication and psychotherapy (Carr & McNulty, 2016; Chew-Graham & Ray, 2016). The most commonly used medications are benzodiazepine (e.g., Valium® and Librium®), SSRIs (Paxil®, among others), buspirone, and beta-blockers. Although moderately effective, these drugs must be monitored carefully in older adults because the amount needed to treat the disorder is very low and the potential for harmful side effects is great. For older adults, the clear treatment of choice is psychotherapy, specifically cognitive behavioral or relaxation therapy, especially when anxiety disorders first occur in later life (Carr & McNulty, 2016; Hendriks et al., 2012). Relaxation therapy is exceptionally effective, easily learned, and presents a technique that is useful in many situations (e.g., falling asleep at night; Segal et al., 2011). The advantage of these psychotherapeutic techniques is they usually involve only a few sessions, have high rates of success, and offer clients procedures they can take with them.

Dementia

Probably no other condition associated with aging is more feared than the family of disorders known as dementia. In dementia individuals can literally lose their personal identity through the loss of autobiographical memory and the ability even to recognize one's spouse and children. Dementias serious enough to impair independent functioning affect nearly 48 million people globally (World Health Organization, 2015). The Alzheimer's Association (2016a) reports that dementia costs the United States roughly $236 billion annually, and 15 million caregivers provide well over 18 billion hours of unpaid care each year.

Alzheimer's disease involves memory loss to an extent that may include forgetting the names of family members.

dementia

Family of diseases involving serious impairment of behavioral and cognitive functioning and some form of permanent damage to the brain.

Dementia is not a specific disease but rather a family of diseases characterized by cognitive and behavioral deficits involving some form of permanent damage to the brain. The most common and widely known of these is Alzheimer's disease, but others are important as well: vascular dementia, Parkinson's disease, Huntington's disease, alcoholic dementia, Lewy body, and AIDS dementia complex.

Alzheimer's Disease

Alzheimer's disease

Disease marked by gradual declines in memory, attention, and judgment; confusion as to time and place; difficulties in communicating; decline in self-care skills; inappropriate behavior; and personality changes.

Alzheimer's disease is the most common form of progressive, degenerative, and fatal dementia, accounting for between 60% and 80% of all cases of dementia (Alzheimer's Association, 2016c). The prevalence increases with age, rising from extremely low rates in the 50s to about half of all people aged 85 and older. As the number of older adults increases rapidly over the next several decades, the number of cases is expected to roughly triple.

What Are the Symptoms of Alzheimer's Disease? The key symptoms of Alzheimer's disease are gradual declines in memory, learning, attention, and judgment; confusion as to time and place; difficulties in communicating and finding the right words; decline in personal hygiene and self-care skills; inappropriate social behavior; and changes in personality. These classic symptoms may be vague and may occur only occasionally in the beginning with little behavioral impact, but as the disease progresses, the symptoms become more pronounced and are exhibited more regularly (Alzheimer's Association, 2016b, d). Wandering away from home and not being able to remember how to return increases. Delusions, hallucinations, and other related behaviors develop and get worse over time. Spouses become strangers. Patients may not even recognize themselves in a mirror; they wonder who is looking back at them. In its advanced stages, Alzheimer's disease often causes

incontinence

Loss of bladder or bowel control.

incontinence, *the loss of control of bladder or bowels.* It may also result in a total loss of mobility.

People with Alzheimer's disease may become completely dependent on others for care. At this point, many caregivers seek facilities such as adult day-care centers and other sources of help, such as family and friends, to provide a safe environment for the Alzheimer's patient while the primary caregiver is at work or needs to run basic errands.

The rate of deterioration in Alzheimer's disease varies widely from one person to the next (Gandy & DeKosky, 2013). Alzheimer's disease has an average duration of 9 years (but can range anywhere from 1 to over 20 years) from the onset of noticeable symptoms through death (Alzheimer's Association, 2016e). The early stage is marked especially by memory loss, disorientation to time and space, poor judgment, and personality changes. The middle stage is characterized by increased memory problems, increased difficulties with speech, restlessness, irritability, and loss of impulse control. People in the late stage of Alzheimer's disease experience incontinence of urine and feces, lose motor skills, have decreased appetite, have great difficulty with speech and language, may not recognize family members or oneself in a mirror, lose most if not all self-care abilities, and decreased ability to fight off infections. These stages are depicted in ❱ Figure 14.14.

How Is Alzheimer's Disease Diagnosed? Given that the behavioral symptoms of Alzheimer's disease eventually become quite obvious, one would assume that diagnosis would be straightforward. Quite the contrary. Accurate early diagnosis of Alzheimer's disease depends on a thorough assessment of the number and severity of neurological and behavioral changes (Ismail et al., 2016).

For an early diagnosis to be accurate, however, it must be comprehensive and broad. ❱ Figure 14.15 provides an overview of the process used to differentiate Alzheimer's disease from other conditions. Note a great deal of the diagnostic effort goes into ruling out other possible causes for the observed cognitive deficits: All possible treatable causes for the symptoms must be eliminated before a diagnosis of Alzheimer's disease can be made.

A great deal of attention has been given to the development of more definitive tests for Alzheimer's disease while the person is still alive. Much of this work has focused on beta-amyloid, a protein that is produced in abnormally high levels in persons with Alzheimer's

---

■ **Think** About It

How do the memory problems in Alzheimer's disease differ from those in normal aging?

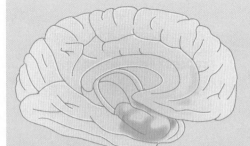

▶ **Figure 14.14**
Progression of Alzheimer's disease
through the brain.

Earliest Alzheimer's
Changes may begin 20 years
or more before diagnosis.

**Mild to moderate
Alzheimer's stages**
Generally last from 2 to 10 years

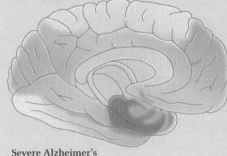

Severe Alzheimer's
May last from 1 to 5 years.

**Progression of Alzheimer's
Through the Brain**

Plaques and tangles (shown in the blue-
shaded areas) tend to spread through the
cortex in a predictable pattern as Alzheimer's
disease progresses.
The rate of progression varies greatly. People
with Alzheimer's live an average of eight
years, but some people may survive up to 20
years. The course of the disease depends in
part on age at diagnosis and whether a
person has other health conditions.

© 2019 Cengage

From Alzheimer's Association. (2016). Progression through the brain. Retrieved from www.alz.org/braintour/early_
stage.asp (Slide 13).

disease, perhaps causing the neurofibrillary tangles and neuritic plaques described earlier.
Considerable recent research has focused on beta-amyloid as a major factor in Alzheimer's disease in terms of potential diagnosis as well as a possible cause and avenue for treatment. The role of beta-amyloid is controversial, though (Molin & Rockwood, 2016). As we will see in the next section, some researchers view concentration of beta-amyloid as a biomarker of Alzheimer's disease, whereas others caution that many people with increased levels of beta amyloid do not develop Alzheimer's disease.

What Causes Alzheimer's Disease? We do not know for sure what causes Alzheimer's disease (Scheff, Neltner, & Nelson, 2014). What we do know is that early-onset (before age 65) forms of Alzheimer's disease are mostly caused by single-gene mutations related to beta-amyloid protein production (Nicolas et al., 2016). Single-gene mutation forms of Alzheimer's disease usually involve mutations in the presenillin-1 (PSEN1), presenillin-2 (PSEN2) and amyloid (A4) precursor protein (APP) genes. The genetic inheritance aspect of early-onset Alzheimer's disease is a major concern of families.

Other genetic links to later-onset (after age 65) Alzheimer's disease involve the complex interaction of several genes, processes that are not yet well documented or understood. Several sites on various chromosomes have been tentatively identified as being potentially involved in the transmission of Alzheimer's disease, including chromosomes 1, 12, 14, 19, and 21. The most promising work noted links between the genetic markers and the production of beta-amyloid protein, the major component of neuritic plaques (as noted earlier). Much of this research focuses on apolipoprotein ε4 (APOE-ε4), associated with chromosome 19, that may play a central role in creating neuritic plaques. People with the APOE-ε4 trait are more likely to get Alzheimer's disease than those with the more common APOE-ε3 trait (Di Battista, Heinsinger, & Rebeck, 2016). Additionally, a related mutation (TREM2) may be involved with APOE-ε4 as well by interfering with the brain's ability to contain inflammation (Jonsson et al., 2013; Sala Frigerio & De Strooper, 2016).

Think About It

If an accurate diagnostic test for Alzheimer's disease is developed and there is no treatment for the disease, should the test be made available?

▶ Figure 14.15

Differential diagnosis in Alzheimer's disease algorithm.

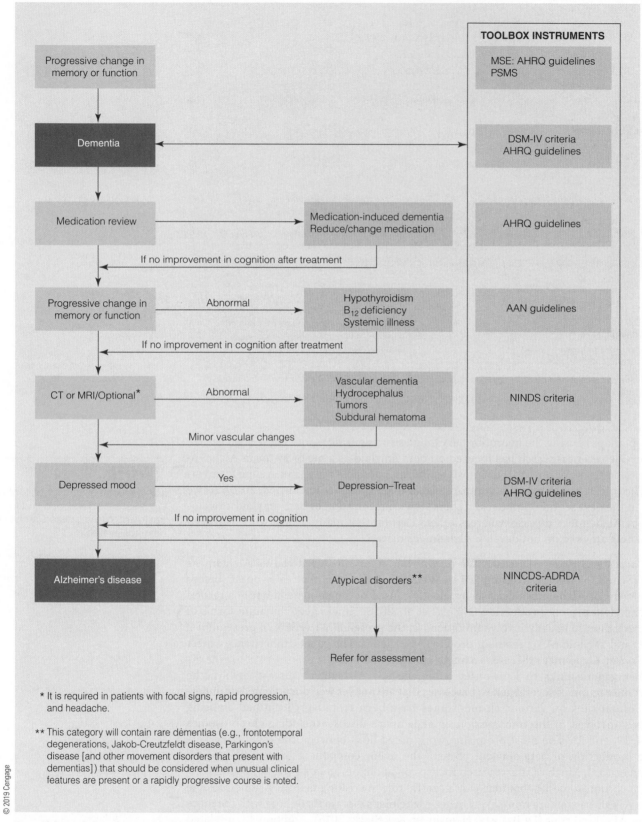

* It is required in patients with focal signs, rapid progression, and headache.

** This category will contain rare dementias (e.g., frontotemporal degenerations, Jakob-Creutzfeldt disease, Parkingon's disease [and other movement disorders that present with dementias]) that should be considered when unusual clinical features are present or a rapidly progressive course is noted.

© 2019 Cengage

From Alzheimer's Association online document. www.alz.org/medical/rtalgrthm.htm. Developed and endorsed by the TriAD Advisory Board. Copyright 1996 Pfizer Inc. and Esai Inc. with special thanks to J. L. Cummings. Algorithm reprinted from TriAD, Three for the Management of Alzheimer's Disease, with permission.

Interestingly, another version, APOE-ε2, seems to have the reverse effect from APOE-ε4: It decreases the risk of Alzheimer's disease (Liu et al., 2013). Despite the relation between APOE-ε4 and neuritic plaques, and between APOE-ε4 and beta-amyloid buildup, researchers have yet to establish strong relations directly between apolipoprotein ε and general cognitive functioning (Wu & Zhao, 2016).

A mutation on the ABCA7 gene has been identified that roughly doubles the chances for African Americans to get late-onset Alzheimer's disease (Cukier et al., 2016). This mutation creates overproduction of cholesterol and lipids, which in turn are known to be risks for cardiovascular disease and strokes, both of which have higher rates in African Americans.

Much of the genetics and related biomarker research focuses on beta-amyloid and its proposed relation to Alzheimer's disease reviewed earlier. When viewed as a cause of Alzheimer's disease, researchers refer to the beta-amyloid cascade hypothesis as the process by which this occurs (Selkoe, 2016). *The* beta-amyloid cascade hypothesis *refers to the process by which beta-amyloid deposits create neuritic plaques, that in turn lead to neurofibrillary tangles, that cause neuronal death and, when this occurs severely enough, Alzheimer's disease.* As noted earlier, there is considerable evidence beta-amyloid is involved in Alzheimer's disease. Although there is insufficient evidence at this point to conclude it is the main cause, data are quite clear that it is at least an initiating factor (Selkoe, 2016).

What Can Be Done for Victims of Alzheimer's Disease? Currently there is no effective treatment for Alzheimer's disease and no way to prevent it. The best we can do today is alleviate some of the symptoms. Most of the research is focused on drugs aimed at improving cognitive functioning. Unfortunately, the medications approved by the Food and Drug Administration to date provide little relief over the long run, and few medications in development show promising results.

To date, the most effective interventions for Alzheimer's disease are behavioral strategies; these approaches are recommended over medications because they give better and more effective outcomes (Barton et al., 2016). These strategies can be used from the time of initial diagnosis throughout the duration of the disease. Behavioral strategies range from simple interventions, such as large calendars to help with orientation to time, to the more complex, such as more elaborate memory interventions based on the E-I-E-I-O approach discussed earlier in the section on memory.

In designing interventions for those with Alzheimer's disease, the guiding principle should be optimizing the person's functioning. Regardless of the level of impairment, attempts should be made to help the person cope as well as possible with the symptoms. The key is helping all individuals maintain their dignity as human beings. This can be achieved in some very creative ways, such as adapting the principles of Montessori methods of education to bring older adults with Alzheimer's disease together with preschool children so that they can perform tasks together (Malone & Camp, 2007; Materne, Luszcz, & Goodwin-Smith, 2014). One example of this approach is discussed in the Spotlight on Research feature.

Parkinson's Disease

Parkinson's disease *is known primarily for its characteristic motor symptoms: very slow walking, difficulty getting into and out of chairs, and a slow hand tremor, but it can develop into a form of dementia.* These problems are caused by a deterioration of neurons in the midbrain that produce the neurotransmitter dopamine. Former boxing champion Muhammad Ali (who died in 2016) and actor Michael J. Fox are some of the more famous individuals who have Parkinson's disease. Over 1 million people in the United States (over 4 million globally) have Parkinson's disease (Parkinson's Disease Foundation, 2016a).

Symptoms are treated effectively with several medications (Parkinson's Disease Foundation, 2016b); the most popular are levodopa, which raises the functional level of dopamine in the brain; Sinemet® (a combination of levodopa and carbidopa), that gets more levodopa to the brain; and Stalevo® (a combination of Sinemet® and entacapone), that

beta-amyloid cascade hypothesis
Theory of Alzheimer's disease in which beta-amyloid deposits create neuritic plaques, that in turn lead to neurofibrillary tangles, that cause neuronal death and Alzheimer's disease.

Parkinson's disease
Brain disease known primarily for its characteristic motor symptoms: very slow walking, difficulty getting into and out of chairs, and a slow hand tremor, but it can develop into a form of dementia.

Training Persons with Dementia to Be Group Activity Leaders

Who were the investigators, and what was the aim of the study? Dementia is marked by progressive and severe cognitive decline. But despite these losses, can people with dementia be trained to be group leaders? Most people might think the answer is no, but Cameron Camp, Michael Skrajner, and Marty Kelly (2005) decided to find out by using a training technique based on the Montessori method.

How did the investigators measure the topic of interest? The Montessori method is based on self-paced learning and developmentally appropriate activities. As Camp and Skrajner point out, many techniques used in rehabilitation (e.g., task breakdown, guided repetition, moving from simple to complex and concrete to abstract) and in intervention programs for people with dementia (e.g., use of external cues and implicit memory) are consistent with the Montessori method.

For this study, a program was developed to train group leaders for memory bingo (see Camp, 1999a and 1999b, for details about this game). Group leaders had to learn which cards to pick for the game, where the answers were located on the card, where

to "discard" the used (but not the winning) cards, and where to put the winning cards. Success in the program was measured by research staff raters, who made ratings of the type and quality of engagement in the task shown by the group leader.

Who were the participants in the study? Camp and colleagues tested four people who had been diagnosed as probably having dementia who were also residents of a special care unit of a nursing home.

What was the design of the study? The study used a longitudinal design so that Camp and Skrajner could track participants' performance over several weeks.

Were there ethical concerns with the study? Having persons with dementia as research participants raises important issues regarding informed consent. Because of their serious cognitive impairments, these individuals may not fully understand the procedures. Thus, family members such as a spouse or adult child caregiver are also asked to give informed consent. Additionally, researchers must pay careful attention to participants' emotions; if participants become agitated or frustrated, the training or testing session must be stopped. Camp and Skrajner took all these precautions.

What were the results? Results showed that at least partial adherence to the

established game protocols was achieved at a very high rate. Indeed, staff assistance was not required at all for most of the game sessions for any leader. All of the leaders said that they enjoyed their role, and one recruited another resident to become a leader in the next phase of the project.

What did the investigators conclude? It appears that persons with dementia can be taught to be group activity leaders through a procedure based on the Montessori method. This is important because it provides a way for such individuals to become more engaged in an activity and to be more productive.

Although more work is needed to continue refining the technique, applications of the Montessori method offer a promising intervention approach for people with cognitive impairments.

What converging evidence would strengthen these conclusions? Camp and Skrajner studied only four residents; more evidence that the approach works with different types of people would bolster their conclusions. Although the Montessori method is effective for training persons with dementia, the approach has not yet been demonstrated to be effective with other diseases that cause serious memory loss.

---

extends the effective dosage time of Sinemet®. Research indicates a device called a neurostimulator, that acts like a brain pacemaker by regulating brain activity when implanted deep inside the brain, may prove effective in significantly reducing the tremors, shaking, rigidity, stiffness, and walking problems when medications.

For reasons we do not yet understand, some people with Parkinson's disease also develop severe cognitive impairment and eventually dementia (Zheng et al., 2014). Lewy bodies characterize dementia in Parkinson's disease; the key factor in the latter case is that the dementia component occurs later.

Chronic Traumatic Encephalopathy

An issue of growing concern is the long-term effects of experiencing brain concussions, or traumatic brain injury (TBI; White & Venkatesh, 2016). Two situations brought TBI to the forefront: war veterans and sports injuries (Finkbeiner et al., 2016; Schulz-Helk et al., 2016). Estimates are about 350,000 U.S. veterans have been diagnosed with TBI since 2000 (Defense and Veterans Brain Injury Center, 2016). Regarding sports, a significant number of athletes who received numerous concussions during their playing careers have evidence of chronic traumatic encephalopathy.

chronic traumatic encephalopathy (CTE)

Form of dementia caused by repeated head trauma such as concussions.

Chronic traumatic encephalopathy (CTE) *is a form of dementia caused by repeated head trauma such as concussions.* CTE can occur as the result of repeated brain trauma (Sorg et al., 2014). Emerging evidence shows that irrespective of the cause, there is structural damage to various parts of the brain that have to do with executive functions and memory.

Because of the concern over CTE, the National Institute of Neurological Disease and Stroke (NINDS) and the National Institute of Biomedical and Bioengineering established specific neuropathological criteria for the diagnosis of CTE (McKee et al., 2016). These criteria, established following the death of the individual, can now be used to definitively diagnose cases of CTE.

Clearly, there is more awareness of the problems associated with repeated TBI. Whether sports, or at least certain sports involving physical contact, should now be considered dangerous remains to be seen. What is certain, though, is the effects of repeated TBI last well into adulthood, and can cause serious cognitive impairment, and perhaps death, even at a relatively early age.

TEST YOURSELF   14.4

Recall

1. Compared with younger adults, older adults are less likely to label their feelings of sadness as_____

2. A form of psychotherapy that focuses on people's beliefs about the self, the world, and the future is called_____

3. Relaxation techniques are an effective therapy for_____

4. Early onset Alzheimer's disease is caused by_____

5. _____is characterized by several characteristic motor symptoms.

Interpret

- After reading about the symptoms of Alzheimer's disease, what would be the most stressful aspects of caring for a parent who has the disease? (You may want to refer to the section on caring for aging parents in Chapter 13.)

Apply

- If a friend asked you the difference between dementia and the normative increases in forgetting that occur with age, what would you tell him or her?

Check your answers to the Recall Questions at the end of the chapter.

SUMMARY

14.1 What Are Older Adults Like?

What are the characteristics of older adults in the population?

- The number of older adults is growing rapidly, especially the number of people over age 85. In the future, older adults will be more ethnically diverse and better educated than they are now.

How long will most people live? What factors influence this?

- Average longevity or life expectancy has increased dramatically over the past century, due mainly to improvements in health care. Maximum longevity or life expectancy is the longest time any human can live. Active life expectancy refers to the number of years that a person is free from debilitating disease; dependent life expectancy also considers the length of time a person experiences debilitating chronic disease.

- Genetic factors that can influence longevity include familial longevity and a family history of certain diseases. Environmental factors include acquired diseases, toxins, pollutants, and lifestyle.

- Women have a longer average life expectancy at birth than men. Ethnic group differences are complex; depending on how old people are, the patterns of differences change.

What is the distinction between the Third Age and the Fourth Age?

- The Third Age refers to changes in research that led to cultural, medical, and economic advances for older adults (e.g., longer average longevity, increased quality of life). In contrast, the Fourth Age reflects that the oldest-old are at the limits of their functional capacity, the rates of diseases such as cancer and dementia increase dramatically, and other aspects of psychological functioning (e.g., memory) undergo significant and fairly rapid decline.

14.2 Physical Changes and Health

What are the major biological theories of aging?

- There are several theories of biological aging. Metabolic theories focus on the rate of metabolism. Cellular theories focus on limits on cell division and the role played by telomeres, the tips of chromosomes that play a role in aging by adjusting the cell's response to stress and growth stimulation and by shortening with each cell replication, and on free radicals, unstable highly reactive chemicals produced in metabolism. Genetic programming theories are based on ideas that propose aging as programmed into the genetic code.

What physiological changes normally occur in later life?

- Three important structural changes in the neurons are neurofibrillary tangles, dendritic changes, and neuritic plaques caused by beta-amyloid. These have important consequences for functioning because they reduce the effectiveness with which neurons transmit information.

- Neuroimaging provides significant insights into aging. Techniques include structural neuroimaging (e.g., X-ray, CT, and MRI scans) and functional neuroimaging (e.g., PET, SPECT, and fMRI).

- The risk of cardiovascular disease increases with age. Normal changes in the cardiovascular system include buildup of fat deposits in the heart and arteries (atherosclerosis), a decrease in the amount of blood the heart can pump, a decline in heart muscle tissue, and stiffening of the arteries. Transient ischemic attacks and vascular dementia are possible results. Most of these changes are affected by lifestyle. Stroke causes significant cognitive impairment depending on the location of the brain damage.

- Strictly age-related changes in the respiratory system are hard to identify because of the lifetime effects of pollution. However, older adults may suffer shortness of breath and face an increased risk of chronic obstructive pulmonary disorder (COPD).

- Age-related declines in vision and hearing are well documented, and include presbyopia, glaucoma, diabetic retinopathy, and age-related macular degeneration. The main changes in vision concern the structure of the eye and the retina. Changes in hearing mainly involve presbycusis, reduced sensitivity to high-pitched tones.

What are the principal health issues for older adults?

- Older adults experience higher rates of chronic diseases. Diabetes (Type 1 and Type 2) pose several risks. The risk of cancer is much higher in older adults. Several risk genes have been identified, especially for breast and prostate cancers.

- Older adults have more sleep disturbances than do younger adults. Nutritionally, most older adults do not need vitamin or mineral supplements. Diabetes mellitus is a significant problem for many older adults. Cancer risk increases sharply with age.

14.3 Cognitive Processes

What changes occur in information processing as people age? How do these changes relate to everyday life?

- Older adults' speed of processing is slower than younger adults'. However, the amount of slowing is lessened if older adults have practice or expertise in the task.

- Older adults are generally less able to perform divided attention tasks. Sensory and information-processing changes create problems for older drivers.

What changes occur in memory with age? What can be done to remediate these changes?

- Working memory declines with age. Older adults typically do worse on tests of episodic recall; age differences are less on recognition tasks. Semantic and implicit memory are both largely unaffected by aging.

- Distinguishing memory changes associated with aging from memory changes due to disease should be accomplished through comprehensive evaluations. Neuroimaging and careful and thorough diagnosis can help make this distinction.

- Memory training can be achieved in many ways. A useful framework is to combine explicit-implicit memory distinctions with external-internal types of memory aids.

What are creativity and wisdom, and how do they relate to age?

- Research indicates that creative output peaks in late young adulthood or early middle age and declines thereafter, but the point of peak activity varies across disciplines and occupations.

- Wisdom has more to do with being an expert in living than with age per se. Three factors that help people become wise are personal attributes, specific expertise, and facilitative life contexts.

14.4 Mental Health and Intervention

How does depression in older adults differ from depression in younger adults? How is it diagnosed and treated?

- The key symptom of depression is persistent sadness. Other psychological and physical symptoms also occur, but the importance of these depends on the age of the person reporting them. Older and younger adults differ significantly in how they describe their symptoms and experiences.

- Major causes of depression include imbalances in neurotransmitters and psychosocial forces such as loss and internal belief systems.

- Depression can be treated with medications and through psychotherapy such as behavioral or cognitive therapy.

How are anxiety disorders treated in older adults?

- Many older adults are afflicted with a variety of anxiety disorders. All of them can be effectively treated with either medications or psychotherapy, especially relaxation techniques.

What is Alzheimer's disease? How is it diagnosed and managed? What causes it?

- Dementia is a family of diseases that causes severe cognitive impairment. Alzheimer's disease is the most common form of irreversible dementia.

- Symptoms of Alzheimer's disease include memory impairment, personality changes, and behavioral changes. These symptoms usually worsen gradually, with rates varying considerably among individuals.

- Definitive diagnosis of Alzheimer's disease can only be made only after very careful and thorough testing, including biomarker and genetic marker screening. The diagnostic categories of Alzheimer's disease remain controversial.

- Most researchers are focusing on a probable genetic cause of Alzheimer's disease. Early-onset Alzheimer's disease is caused by single-gene mutations; later onset is likely related to various marker or risk genes.

- Although Alzheimer's disease is incurable, various behavioral interventions may improve the quality of the patient's life.

- Parkinson's disease is usually marked by tremors and difficulty walking, but in many cases, it also develops into a form of dementia.

- Chronic traumatic encephalopathy (CTE) is of growing concern for individuals who experience repeated head trauma.

Test Yourself Recall Answers

14.1 1. 85 **2.** average life expectancy **3.** oldest **14.2 1.** telomeres **2.** beta-amyloid **3.** increases **14.3 1.** Speed of processing **2.** episodic and semantic **3.** facilitative life contexts **14.4 1.** depression **2.** cognitive therapy **3.** anxiety disorders **4.** single-gene mutations **5.** Parkinson's disease

Key Terms

demographers (458)
population pyramid (458)
average longevity (life expectancy) (461)
maximum longevity (life expectancy) (461)
active life expectancy (462)
dependent life expectancy (462)
telomeres (466)
telomerase (466)
free radicals (466)
neurofibrillary tangles (468)
beta-amyloid (468)
neurotransmitters (469)
structural neuroimaging (470)
functional neuroimaging (470)
atherosclerosis (470)
strokes, or cerebral vascular accidents (CVAs) (470)
transient ischemic attacks (TIAs) (471)

vascular dementia (471)
chronic obstructive pulmonary disease (COPD) (472)
presbyopia (472)
cataracts (473)
glaucoma (473)
age-related macular degeneration (473)
diabetic retinopathy (473)
presbycusis (473)
diabetes mellitus (475)
type 1 diabetes (475)
type 2 diabetes (475)
circadian rhythm (476)
metabolism (477)
speed of processing (480)
divided attention (481)
working memory (482)
implicit memory (482)

explicit memory (482)
episodic memory (482)
semantic memory (482)
autobiographical memory (483)
external memory aids (484)
internal memory aids (484)
dysphoria (488)
internal belief systems (490)
behavior therapy (490)
cognitive therapy (490)
anxiety disorders (490)
dementia (492)
Alzheimer's disease (492)
incontinence (492)
beta-amyloid cascade hypothesis (495)
Parkinson's disease (495)
chronic traumatic encephalopathy (CTE) (496)

Social Aspects of Later Life

Psychosocial, Retirement, Relationship, and Societal Issues

15

What's it really like to be an older adult? As we saw in Chapter 14, aging brings with it both physical limits (such as declines in vision and hearing) and psychological gains (such as increased expertise). Old age also brings social challenges. Older adults are sometimes stereotyped as being marginal and powerless in society, much like children. Psychosocial issues confront older adults as well. How do people think about their lives and bring meaning and closure to them as they approach death? What constitutes well-being for older people? How do they use their time once they are no longer working full-time? Do they like being retired? What roles do relationships with friends and family play in their lives? How do older people cope when their partner is ill and requires care? What if their partner dies? When older people need assistance, where do they live?

These are a few of the issues we will examine in this chapter. As in Chapter 14, our main focus will be on the majority of older adults who are healthy and live in the community. The distinction made in Chapter 1 between young-old adults (60- to 80-year-olds) and old-old adults (80-year-olds and up) is important. We know the most about young-old people, even though the old-old reflect the majority of frail elderly and those who live in nursing homes.

Like other times in life, getting along in the environment is a complicated issue. We begin by considering a few ideas about how to optimize our fit with the environment. Next, we examine how we bring the story of our lives to a culmination. After that, we consider how interpersonal relationships and retirement provide contexts for life satisfaction. We conclude with an examination of the social contexts of aging.

15.1 Theories of Psychosocial Aging

LEARNING OBJECTIVES

- What is social involvement and successful aging?
- What is the competence–environmental press model, and how do docility and proactivity relate to the model?
- What is the preventive and corrective proactivity model?

Since Sandy retired from her job as secretary at the local African Methodist Episcopal Church, she has hardly slowed down. She sings in the gospel choir, is involved in the Black Women's Community Action Committee, and volunteers one day a week at a local Head Start school. Sandy's friends say that she has to stay involved because that's the way she's always been. They claim you'd never know that Sandy is 81 years old.

Understanding how people grow old is not as simple as asking someone how old he or she is, as Sandy shows. As we saw in Chapter 14, aging is an individual process involving many variations in physical changes, cognitive functioning, and mental health. Psychosocial approaches to aging recognize these individual differences. Consider Sandy—her life reflects several key points. Her level of activity has remained constant across her adult life. This consistency fits well in continuity theory, the first framework considered in this section. Her ability to maintain this level of commitment indicates that the match between her abilities and her environment is just about right, as discussed in the competence–environmental press theory later in this section.

More older adults are experiencing healthy aging by avoiding disease and engaging in life.

kali9/E+/Getty Images

The Goal of Healthy Aging

One of the most important aspects of research on older adults has been a rethinking of late life as one of mostly inevitable decline to one that is a more multidimensional view that also has positive aspects, such as productive engagement with life and social involvement (Johnson & Mutchler, 2014). The coming demographic changes in the United States and the rest of the world present a challenge for improving the kind of lives older adults live. For this reason, promoting wellness and healthy lifestyles in all living settings (community, long-term care, etc.) is seen as one of the top healthcare priorities of the 21st century (Parrella & Vormittag, 2017). Remaining healthy is important for decelerating the rate of aging (Aldwin & Gilmer, 2013).

As researchers and theorists have approached healthy aging, they have focused on optimizing the individual outcome of the interplay of biopsychosocial forces and the individual over a lifetime (Aldwin & Gilmer, 2013; Centers for Disease Control and Prevention, 2016e; Hostetler & Paterson, 2017; Samanta, 2017). Healthy aging *in this sense involves avoiding disease, being engaged with life, and maintaining high cognitive and physical functioning*. Healthy aging is both measurable (e.g., in terms of specific health metrics, cognitive performance, other specific behaviors) and subjective (e.g., well-being). It is reached when a person achieves his or her desired goals with dignity and as independently as possible.

The life-span perspective can be used to create a formal model for healthy aging. Heckhausen, Wrosch, & Schulz (2010; Barlow et al., 2017) developed a theory of life-span development based on motivation and control by applying core assumptions that recognize aging as a complex process that involves increasing specialization and is influenced by factors unrelated to age. The basic premises of healthy aging include keeping a balance between the various gains and losses that occur over time and minimizing the influence of factors unrelated to aging. In short, these premises involve paying attention to both internal and external factors impinging on the person. The antecedents include all the changes that happen to a person. The mechanisms in the model are the selection, optimization, and compensation (SOC) processes that shape the course of development, as we discussed in Chapter 1. Finally, the outcomes of the model denote that enhanced competence, quality of life, and future adaptation are the visible signs of healthy aging.

Using the SOC model, enhanced by Heckhausen and colleague's (2010; Barlow et al., 2017) notions of control and motivation, various types of interventions can be created to help people achieve healthy aging. In general, such interventions focus on the individual or on aspects of tasks and the physical and social environment that emphasize competence (Aldwin & Gilmer, 2013; Lindbergh, Dishman, & Miller, 2016; Thornton, Paterson, & Yeung, 2013). When designing interventions aimed primarily at the person, it is important to understand the target person's goals (rather than the goals of the researcher). For example, in teaching older adults how to use technology, it is essential to understand the kinds of concerns and fears older adults have and ensure the training program addresses them (Lesnoff-Caravaglia, 2010).

Performance on tests of everyday competence predicts longer term outcomes, as we saw in Chapter 14 (Allaire & Willis, 2006; Lindbergh et al., 2016). Careful monitoring of competence can be an early indicator of problems, and appropriate interventions should be undertaken as soon as possible. Because maintaining competence is an important element in determining quality of life, we now turn to a more focused consideration of what competence means in everyday contexts.

Competence and Environmental Press

Understanding psychosocial aging requires attention to individuals' needs rather than treating all older adults alike. One method focuses on the relation between the person and the environment (Aldwin, 2015; Aldwin & Igarashi, 2012). The competence–environmental press approach is a good example of a theory incorporating elements of the biopsychosocial model into the person–environment relation (Lawton & Nahemow, 1973; Nahemow, 2000; Pynoos, Caraviello, & Cicero, 2010).

Competence *is defined as the upper limit of a person's ability to function in five domains: physical health, sensory-perceptual skills, motor skills, cognitive skills, and ego strength*. These domains are viewed as underlying all other abilities and reflect the biological and psychological forces. Environmental press *refers to the physical, interpersonal, or social demands that environments put on people*. Physical demands might include having to walk up three flights of stairs to your apartment. Interpersonal demands may require adjusting your behavior patterns to different types of people. Social demands involve dealing with laws or customs that place certain expectations on people. These aspects of the theory reflect biological, psychological, and social forces. Both competence and environmental press change as people move through the life span; what you are capable of doing

healthy aging

Growing old by avoiding disease, being engaged with life, and maintaining high cognitive and physical functioning.

competence

Upper limit of a person's ability to function in five domains: physical health, sensory-perceptual skills, motor skills, cognitive skills, and ego strength.

environmental press

Physical, interpersonal, or social demands that environments put on people.

as a 5-year-old differs from what you are capable of doing as a 25-, 45-, 65-, or 85-year-old. Similarly, the demands put on you by the environment change as you age. Thus, the competence–environmental press framework also reflects life-cycle factors.

The competence and environmental press model depicted in ▶ Figure 15.1 shows how the two are related. Low to high competence is represented on the vertical axis, and weak to strong environmental press is displayed on the horizontal axis. Points in the figure represent various combinations of the two. Most important, the shaded areas show adaptive behavior and positive affect can result from many different combinations of competence and environmental press levels. Adaptation level *is the area where press level is average for a particular level of competence; this is where behavior and affect are normal. Slight increases in press tend to improve performance; this area on the figure is labeled the* zone of maximum performance potential. *Slight decreases in press create the* zone of maximum comfort, *in which people are able to live happily without worrying about environmental demands.* Combinations of competence and environmental press that fall within either of these two zones result in adaptive behavior and positive emotion that translate into a high quality of life.

As a person moves away from these areas, behavior becomes increasingly maladaptive and affect becomes negative. Notice that these outcomes can result from several different combinations and for different reasons. For example, too many environmental demands on a person with low competence and too few demands on a person with high competence both result in maladaptive behaviors and negative emotion.

What does this mean with regard to late life? Is aging merely an equation relating certain variables? The important thing to realize about the competence–environmental press model is that each person has the potential of being happily adapted to some living situations, but not to all. Whether people function well depends on if what they are able to do fits what the environment forces them to do. When their abilities match the demands, people adapt; when there is a mismatch, they don't. In this view, aging is more than an equation, because the best fit must be determined on an individual basis.

How do people deal with changes in their particular combinations of environmental press (such as adjusting to a new living situation) and competence (perhaps reduced abilities due to illness)? People respond in two basic ways (Lawton, 1989; Nahemow, 2000).

adaptation level

When press level is average for a particular level of competence.

zone of maximum performance potential

When press level is slightly higher, tending to improve performance.

zone of maximum comfort

When press level is slightly lower, facilitating a high quality of life.

▶ **Figure 15.1**

The competence–environmental press model.

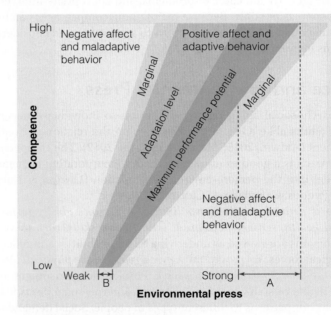

From Lawton, M. P. & Nahemow, L. (1973). Ecology and the aging process. In C. Eisdorfer and M. P. Lawton (Eds.), *The psychology of adult development and aging* (pp. 619-674). Copyright © 1973 American Psychological Association.

When people choose new behaviors to meet new desires or needs, they exhibit proactivity and exert control over their lives. In contrast, when people allow the situation to dictate the options they have, they demonstrate docility and have little control. Lawton (1989) argues that proactivity is more likely to occur in people with relatively high competence, and docility in people with relatively low competence.

The model has considerable research support. For example, the model accounts for why people choose the activities they do (Lawton, 1982), how well people adhere to medication regimens (LeRoux & Fisher, 2006), and how they adapt to changing housing needs over time (Iwarsson, Slaug, & Fänge, 2012; Granbom et al., 2016). This model helps us understand how well people adapt to various care settings (Golant, 2012; Scharlach & Lehning, 2016). In short, there is considerable merit to the view that aging is a complex interaction between a person's competence level and environmental press, mediated by choice. This model can be applied in many different settings.

Before leaving Lawton and Nahemow's model, we need to note an important implication for aging. To the extent people experience declines in competence (such as resulting from declines in health, sensory processes, motor skills, cognitive skills, or ego strength), they are less able to cope with environmental demands. That is why the home modifications discussed later in the chapter, such as grab bars, and smartphones, are important—they functionally increase competence. Interventions based on artificial intelligence, such as robots and self-driving cars, will do even more to increase functional competence and enable people to live in the community. City planners now incorporate aspects of the competence–environmental press model in designing housing and neighborhoods (Lewis & Groh, 2016).

Additionally, the competence and environmental press model has been the basis for evaluating and optimizing living situations with people who have severe cognitive impairments, such as those of Alzheimer's disease (Dalton, 2014). To manage severe cognitive impairment effectively, caregivers must identify the right level of environmental support based on the patient's level of competence. For example, people with mild cognitive impairment may be able to live independently, but as the impairment increases additional levels of support are needed. The model has provided the basis for designing special care units for people with Alzheimer's disease. In these units, environmental supports such as color-coded room doors, help people with dementia identify where they belong.

Preventive and Corrective Proactivity Model

Maintaining a high quality of life is a key goal for adults of all ages. From the competence–environmental press approach we saw proactivity, exerting control over one's life, is central to achieving that goal. Because proactivity is so important, Kahana and Kahana (2003; Midlarsky, Kahana, & Belser, 2015) built a model of successful aging on the core concept of proactivity. The model is shown in ▶ Figure 15.2.

The Preventive and Corrective Proactivity (PCP) model explains how life stressors (such as life events, chronic illnesses) and lack of good congruence in person–environment interactions (Component B), especially when the person has nothing to help buffer or protect against these things, result in poor life outcomes (Component F). The helpful buffers include external resources (Component E) such as friends or home modifications, internal resources or dispositions (Component C) such as a positive outlook on life, and specific proactive behaviors (Component D), such as physical exercise, work to lower the negative impact of the stressors and prepare people to cope better in the future. In brief, the PCP model proposes proactive adaptations and helpful external resources reduce the effect of life stressors on quality-of-life outcomes.

What kinds of actions reflect proactive adaptations? Kahana, Kahana, and Zhang (2005) described two types of proactive adaptations: preventive and corrective. Preventive adaptations *are actions that avoid stressors and increase or build social resources.* An example of a preventive adaptation would be increasing one's social network by adding friends. Corrective adaptations *are actions taken in response to stressors and can be facilitated by internal and external resources.* An example of a corrective adaptation is changing one's diet after having a heart attack.

proactivity
When people choose new behaviors to meet new desires or needs and exert control over their lives.

docility
When people allow their situation to dictate the options they have.

preventive adaptations
Actions that avoid stressors and increase or build social resources.

corrective adaptations
Actions taken in response to stressors that can be facilitated by internal and external resources.

Figure 15.2

Model of emerging proactive options for successful aging.

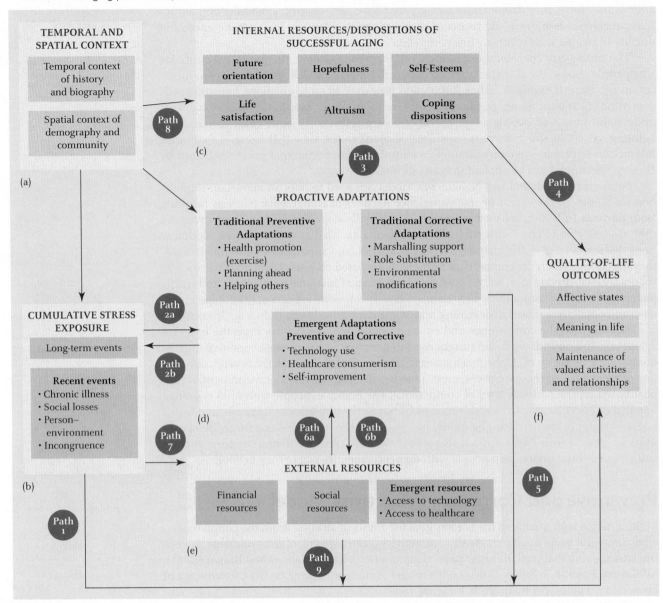

From Kahana, E., Kahana, B., & Zhang, J. (2006). Motivational antecedents of preventive proactivity in late life: Linking future orientation and exercise. *Motivation and Emotion*, 29, 438–459 (Figure 1). doi: 10.1007/s11031-006-9012-2

Older adults tend to engage in more corrective adaptations than preventive adaptations, at least initially. However, many actions that start as corrective adaptations turn into preventive adaptations. A great example of this is exercise. Many people begin an exercise program only after they are told to, perhaps as part of a recovery regimen after a health crisis. However, continued exercise becomes preventive by helping the person avoid future recurrences of the original health problem and avoid other problems altogether.

Research supports the importance of proactivity as described in the PCP model. Kahana, Kelley-Moore, & Kahana (2012) showed life stressors can still have a negative effect on quality-of-life outcomes four years after they occur, but proactive adaptations (such as exercise, planning ahead, and gathering support) significantly reduce this negative impact. Longitudinal research in China also showed the importance of proactivity and other external and internal resources in improving quality-of-life outcomes in the oldest-old residents in the community and in long-term care facilities (Liu et al., 2012).

Katherine Johnson, Human Computer for NASA

Imagine being an African American born in 1918 and growing up in segregated West Virginia in the early part of the 20th century. Imagine also being a brilliant young woman who graduated high school at age 14. Imagine being that African American woman as a graduate of West Virginia State College, *summa cum laude*, at age 18, then being one of the first three African Americans (and only woman) to attend graduate school at West Virginia University. To top it off, her specialties were physics and math.

This was reality for Katherine Coleman Goble Johnson who, in 1953, began a career at the National Advisory Committee for Aeronautics (later, the National Aeronautics and Space Administration—NASA) as one of the so-called colored computers at the Guidance and Control Division of Langley's Flight Research Division in Hampton, Virginia. Because of the Jim Crow laws in the segregated South, Katherine and her other African American women colleagues faced workplace discrimination, including separate working, eating, and bathroom facilities (located across the compound) apart from their European American counterparts. She also faced significant gender discrimination in the otherwise all-male environment.

Despite the obstacles and discrimination, Katherine was a true trailblazing star. Her job entailed, among other things, precisely calculating rocket launch and orbital trajectories by hand at a time when digital computers were in their early stages of development. She was so good, in fact, that John Glenn refused to fly his mission in 1962 unless Katherine personally verified the digital computer's calculations. In 1969 she calculated the trajectory for the Apollo 11 mission to the moon, and in 1970 her work on backup procedures helped return the Apollo 13 crew safely after an explosion onboard forced the mission to be aborted. Katherine retired from NASA in 1986 after subsequently working on the Space Shuttle program, the Earth Resources Satellite, and on plans for a Mars mission. She was consulted for the book *Hidden Figures* and was depicted in the 2016 film adaptation.

Katherine Johnson is a great example of the interplay between competence and environmental press. Her science and math skills competencies are unquestionably stellar. Equally strong was her competence regarding her ability to succeed despite the legal and other discriminatory barriers (environmental press) put in her way throughout her early life and career. Even in her late 90s, as various ailments slowed her physically, her mental competence was still clearly apparent. Katherine Johnson managed to maximize her adaptation level throughout her long life.

Science History Images/Alamy Stock Photo

Katherine Johnson

Understanding how people age usually entails taking a broader perspective than any single theory can offer. The Real People feature about Katherine Coleman Goble Johnson, a trailblazing African American physicist and mathematician who helped make NASA's human space flight programs successful, shows that both successful aging and competence–environmental press theory are important.

> *Think* About It
>
> How does the competence–environmental press approach help explain which coping strategies might work best in a particular situation?

TEST YOURSELF 15.1

Recall

1. _____ involves avoiding disease, being engaged with life, and maintaining high cognitive and physical functioning.

2. A person's ability to function in several key domains is termed _____, whereas demands put on a person from external sources are termed _____.

Interpret

- How does continuity theory incorporate aspects of the biopsychosocial model?

Apply

- How would a new state law requiring older adults to pass a vision test before they could renew their driver's license be an example of changes in environmental press?

Check your answers to the Recall Questions at the end of the chapter.

LEARNING OBJECTIVES

- What is integrity in late life? How do people achieve it?

- How is well-being defined in adulthood? How do people view themselves differently as they age?

- What role does spirituality play in late life?

Fatima is a spry 88-year-old who spends more time thinking and reflecting about her past than she used to. She also tends to be less critical of decisions she made years ago. Fatima remembers her visions of the woman she wanted to become and concludes that she has come pretty close. Fatima wonders if this process of reflection is something that most older adults go through.

Think for a minute about the older adults you know. What are they like? How do they see themselves today? How do they visualize their lives a few years from now? Do they see themselves the same as or different from the way they were in the past? These questions have intrigued authors since the early days of psychology. In the late 19th century, William James (1890), one of the early pioneers in psychology, wrote that a person's personality traits are set by young adulthood. Some researchers agree; as we saw in Chapter 13, some aspects of personality remain relatively stable throughout adulthood. But people also change in important ways, as Carl Jung (1960/1933) argued, by integrating such opposite tendencies as masculine and feminine traits. As we saw in Chapter 1, Erik Erikson (1982) was convinced that personality development takes a lifetime, unfolding over a series of eight stages from infancy through late life.

In this section, we explore how people such as Fatima assemble the final pieces in the personality puzzle, and we see how important aspects of personality continue to evolve in later life. We begin with Erikson's issue of integrity, the process by which people try to make sense of their lives. Next, we see how well-being is achieved and how personal aspirations play out. Finally, we examine how spirituality is an important aspect of many older adults' lives.

Integrity Versus Despair

integrity versus despair

According to Erikson, the process in late life by which people try to make sense of their lives.

As people enter late life, they begin the struggle of integrity versus despair, *which involves the process by which people try to make sense of their lives.* According to Erikson (1982), this struggle comes about as older adults such as Fatima try to understand their lives in terms of the future of their family and community. Thoughts of a person's own death are balanced by the realization that they will live on through children, grandchildren, great-grandchildren, and the community as a whole. This realization produces what Erikson calls a "life-affirming involvement" in the present.

life review

Process by which people reflect on the events and experiences of their lifetimes.

The struggle of integrity versus despair requires people to engage in a life review, *the process by which people reflect on the events and experiences of their lifetimes.* To achieve integrity, a person must come to terms with the choices and events that made his or her life unique. There must also be an acceptance of the fact that one's life is drawing to a close. Looking back on one's life may resolve some of the second-guessing of decisions made earlier in adulthood (Erikson, Erikson, & Kivnick, 1986). People who were unsure whether they made the right choices concerning their children, for example, now feel satisfied that things worked out well. In contrast, others feel bitter about their choices, blame themselves or others for their misfortunes, see their lives as meaningless, and greatly fear death. These people end up in despair rather than living with integrity.

Research shows a connection between engaging in a life review and achieving integrity; so life review forms the basis for effective mental health interventions (Villar & Serrat, 2017; Westerhof, Bohlmeijer, & Webster, 2010), especially for older individuals with depression (Hallford & Mellor, 2013). A therapeutic technique called "structured life review" (Haight & Haight, 2007, 2013) has been shown to be effective in helping people deal with stressful life events.

Who reaches integrity? Erikson (1982) emphasizes that people who demonstrate integrity come from various backgrounds and cultures and arrive there having taken different paths. Such people have made many different choices and follow many different lifestyles; the point is that everyone has this opportunity to achieve integrity if they strive for it. Those who reach integrity become self-affirming and self-accepting; they judge their lives to have been worthwhile and good. They are glad to have lived the lives they did.

Well-Being and Emotion

How is your life going? Are you reasonably content, or do you think you could be doing better? Answers to these questions provide insight into your subjective well-being, *an evaluation of one's life that is associated with positive feelings.* In life-span developmental psychology, subjective well-being is usually assessed by measures of life satisfaction, happiness, and self-esteem (Oswald & Wu, 2010).

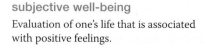

subjective well-being
Evaluation of one's life that is associated with positive feelings.

Overall, well-being across adulthood looks like a U-shaped function, like that shown in ❯ Figure 15.3 (Cheng, Powdthaveea, & Oswald, 2014). Young-older adults are characterized by improved subjective well-being compared with middle-aged adults, although the extent of the difference depends on several factors, such as hardiness, chronic illness, marital status, the quality of one's social network, and stress (Charles & Carstensen, 2010).

These happiness-related factors and the overall shape of the function hold across cultures as well; for example, studies of Australian, German, Taiwanese, and Tanzanian older adults showed similar predictors of successful aging (Cheng et al., 2014; Hsu, 2005; Mwanyangala et al., 2010). Although gender differences in subjective well-being have been found to increase with age, they are most likely due to older women being particularly disadvantaged compared with older men with regard to chronic illness and its effect on ability to care for oneself, everyday competence, quality of social network, socioeconomic status, and widowhood (Charles & Carstensen, 2010). Such gender differences are smaller in more recent cohorts, indicating that societal changes over the past few decades have led to improvements in the way older women view themselves.

Given the findings about higher level of well-being in older adults, researchers began wondering how well-being was related to emotions. People's feelings are clearly important, as they get expressed in daily moods and underlie mental health problems such as depression, and show a tendency to focus on more positive feelings (Cacioppo et al., 2011; Isaacowitz, 2014; Zhou et al., 2017). So how emotions are regulated in later life may provide insights into people's subjective well-being.

Emotion-focused research in neuroscience is providing answers to the question of why subjective well-being tends to increase with age (Cacioppo et al., 2011; Mather, 2016). A brain structure called the amygdala, an almond-shaped set of nuclei deep in the brain, helps regulate emotion. Evidence is growing that age-related changes in how the amygdala functions may play a key role in understanding emotional regulation in older adults. Here's how. In young adults, arousal of the amygdala is associated with negative emotional arousal. When negative emotional arousal occurs, for example, memory for events associated with the emotion is stronger. But the situation is different for older adults—both amygdala activation and emotional arousal are lower. That may be one reason older adults experience less negative emotion, lower rates of depression, and better well-being (Mather, 2016). But that's not the whole story. In Chapter 13, we discovered that brain activity in the prefrontal cortex, which is associated with cognition, changes with age. Neuroimaging research shows that changes in cognitive processing in the prefrontal cortex also are associated with changes in emotional regulation in older adults. For example, research shows that the connection between certain parts of the prefrontal cortex

❯ **Figure 15.3**
The pattern of a typical person's happiness through life.

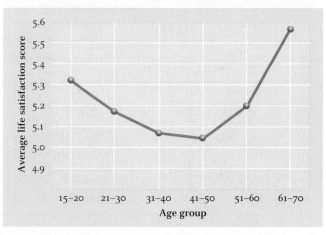

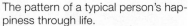

From A. Oswald "Happiness, health, and economics," Warwick University, imechanica.org/files/andrew_oswald_presentation_071129.pdf.

(the medial prefrontal cortex) and the amygdala are more connected and active while older adults are at rest than it is in younger adults, and such connectivity is likely the reason older adults remember more positive emotional content (Mather, 2016; Sakaki, Nga, & Mather, 2013). A good example of the kind of neuroimaging research that has led to these conclusions is described in the Spotlight on Research feature.

Spotlight | On Research

The Aging Emotional Brain

Who were the investigators, and what was the aim of the study? Although much research has examined the behavioral side of emotions, very little has examined the specific underlying neural mechanisms in the brain. Winecoff and colleagues (2011) decided to examine these mechanisms and discover whether they differed with age.

How did the investigators measure the topic of interest? Winecoff and colleagues used a battery of tests to measure cognitive performance and emotional behavior. They tested participants' immediate recall, delayed recall, and recognition for 16 target words as measures of memory. They also administered

a response-time test to measure psychomotor speed (see Chapter 14), and a digit-span test to measure working memory (see Chapter 14). The researchers also had participants complete three questionnaires to measure various types of emotions.

After these measures were obtained, participants were given the cognitive reappraisal task depicted in ❯ Figure 15.4. In brief, participants learned a reappraisal strategy that involved thinking of themselves as an emotionally detached and objective third party. During the training session, they told the experimenter what they were thinking about the image to ensure task compliance, but they were instructed not to speak during the scanning session. During the functional

magnetic resonance imaging (fMRI) session, participants completed 60 positive image trials (30 "Experience" and 30 "Reappraise"), 60 negative image trials (30 "Experience" and 30 "Reappraise"), and 30 neutral image trials (all "Experience"). Within each condition, half of the images contained people and the other half did not. The fMRI session provided images of ongoing brain activity.

Who were the participants in the study? The sample consisted of 22 younger adults (average age = 23; range = 19 to 33 years) and 20 older adults (average age = 69; range = 59 to 73 years). Participants were matched on demographic variables, including education. Participants received the cognitive/memory/emotion tests on one day and the reappraisal

❯ **Figure 15.4**

Cognitive reappraisal task. Participants were trained in the use of a reappraisal strategy for emotion regulation. (A) On "Experience" trials, participants viewed an image and then received an instruction to experience naturally the emotions evoked by that image. The image then disappeared, but participants continued to experience their emotions throughout a 6-second delay period. At the end of the trial, the participants rated the perceived emotional valence of that image using an eight-item rating scale. (B) "Reappraise" trials had similar timing, except that the cue instructed participants to decrease their emotional response to the image by reappraising the image (e.g., distancing oneself from the scene). Shown are examples of the negative (A) and positive (B) images used in the study.

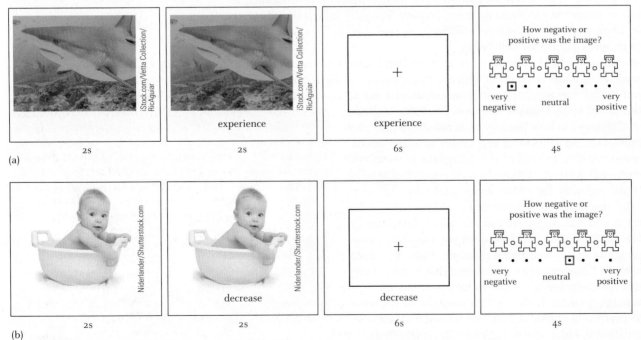

From Winecoff, A., et al. (2011). Cognitive and neural contributions to emotion regulation in aging. *Social Cognitive and Affective Neuroscience, 6,* 165–176.

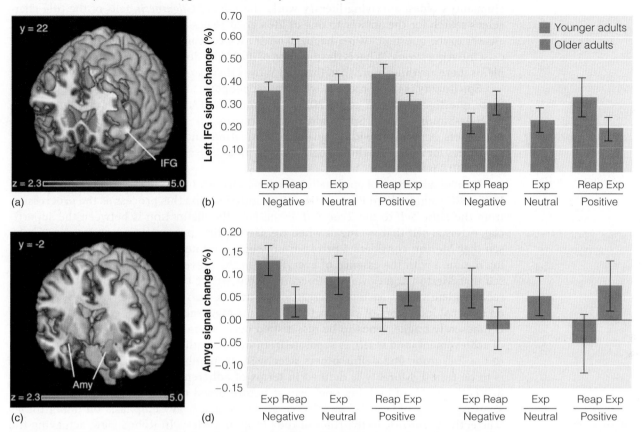

▶ **Figure 15.5**

Modulation of prefrontal and amygdalar activation by emotion regulation.

From Winecoff, A., LaBar, K. S. Madden, D. J., Cabeza, R., & Huettel, S. A. (2011). Cognitive and neural contributions to emotion regulation in aging. *Social Cognitive and Affective Neuroscience, 6,* 165–176. By permission of Oxford University Press. doi:10.1093/scan/nsq030

task in the fMRI session on a second day. Participants were paid $55.

What was the design of the study? The study used a cross-sectional design, with testing of two age groups over two sessions.

Were there ethical concerns with the study? All participants provided written consent under a protocol approved by the Institutional Review Board of Duke University Medical Center.

What were the results? Younger and older adults performed the reappraisal tasks similarly; that is, in the reappraisal condition, positive images were reported as less positive and negative images were reported as less negative. However, older adults' reports of negative emotion were higher than those of younger adults in the negative reappraisal situation.

Examination of the fMRI results showed that reappraisals involved significant activation of specific areas in the prefrontal cortex for both positive and negative emotions. For both age groups, activity in the prefrontal area increased and activity in the amygdala decreased during the reappraisal phase. These patterns are shown in ▶ Figure 15.5. As

you can see in the top figure, certain areas in the prefrontal cortex showed a pattern of activation that followed participants' self-reports of emotion regulation. Shown here are voxels activated in the contrast between "Reappraise-Negative" and "Experience-Negative" conditions. The top graphs show that for both positive and negative stimuli and for both younger and older adults, prefrontal activation increased in "Reappraise" trials compared with "Experience" trials. In contrast, the lower graphs show that in the amygdala (Amy), there was a systematic decrease in activation during emotion regulation between "Experience-Negative" and "Reappraise-Negative" conditions.

Additional analyses of the fMRI data showed that emotion regulation modulates the functional interaction between the prefrontal cortex and the amygdala. Compared with older adults, younger adults showed more activity in the prefrontal cortex during "Reappraise" trials for negative pictures. No age difference in brain activation for positive pictures was found. Cognitive abilities were related to the degree of decrease in amygdala activation, independent of age.

What did the investigators conclude? Winecoff and colleagues concluded that the prefrontal cortex plays a major role in emotional regulation, especially for older adults. In essence, the prefrontal cortex may help suppress (regulate) emotions in the same way that area of the brain is involved in inhibiting other behaviors. Importantly, the degree of emotional regulation was predicted by cognitive ability, with higher cognitive ability associated with higher emotional regulation. This may mean that as cognitive abilities decline, people are less able to regulate their emotions, a pattern typical in diseases such as dementia. Thus, besides evidence of underlying brain structures playing critical roles in emotion regulation, there may be a neurological explanation for the kinds of emotional outbursts that occur in dementia and related disorders.

What converging evidence would strengthen these conclusions? Winecoff and colleagues studied only two age groups of healthy adults and did not include either old-old participants or adults with demonstrable cognitive impairment. It will be important to study those groups to map brain function changes and behavior more completely.

Spirituality in Later Life

Humanity's oldest surviving literary work, the *Epic of Gilgamesh*, tells of the title character's search for the answer to one of life's great issues: the search for eternal life as an answer to the question "What happens next?" We continue to seek answers to life's great existential questions: What is the meaning of life? Why do bad things happen to good people? Is there anything more than this life? Why is there so much suffering? Why am I here?

Spirituality is the context in which most people search for meaning and answers to these questions (Aldwin et al., 2014; Pargament, 2013; Park, 2013; Park, Edmondson, & Hale-Smith, 2013). Spirituality "can inform all aspects of meaning, informing beliefs . . . and providing ultimate motivation and primary goals for living and guidelines for achieving those goals, along with a deep sense of purpose and mattering" (Park, 2013 p. 42).

Individuals' sense of spirituality develops across adulthood. Thomas Merton (1949, 1955, 1962) and Richard Rohr (2011, 2013) both describe this process as the progression from the *False Self* to the *True Self*. Essentially the distinction is between the superficial, external self that we mean when we use the first person singular pronoun "I," the self that Merton considers a prison from which we must escape, and the joy of dwelling in union with the essence of everything in the universe in the core of our soul, the self that Merton argues we must become. Rohr writes that the False Self is rooted in a relative identity that each of us creates for ourselves, an identity that depends critically on external indicators of success (e.g., title, prestige, salary, status, etc.). The False Self is inherently fragile, tends to be dissatisfied because it depends on external definitions of achievement, and is felt as separate from others in the sense that we want to belong to the "in" group and define others selectively as members of the "out" group. Change is to be feared. Morality is defined in terms of adherence to rules. In short, the False Self is the result of building one's ego structure based on incorporating external messages regarding of "values" and "success." There is a heavy emphasis on doing things "correctly" according to the rules of the group or society. In Rohr's view, achieving the True Self involves (re)discovering the universality and wholeness, an "authentic inner knowing," that has always been within, but has gone unrecognized or unacknowledged. The True Self does not see anything with absolute certainty. The True Self is the fulfillment of the search for answers to the core existential questions. It entails a letting go and an acceptance of what is.

As you probably surmised, the developmental transition from False Self to True Self is a reflection of underlying cognitive (described in Chapters 10, 13, and 14) and personality development (described in this chapter and in Chapters 10 and 13). Cavanaugh (in press) argues that it is these underlying processes that permit the shift in perspective reflected in the transition from False Self to True Self.

This change in perspective is also a key factor in how many older adults cope with life stresses. According to research, older adults in many countries and from many different backgrounds use their religious faith and spirituality as the basis for coping, often more than they use family or friends (Ai et al., 2013, 2017; Ai, Wink, & Ardelt, 2010; Ardelt et al., 2013). For some older adults, especially African Americans, a strong attachment to God is what they believe helps them deal with the challenges of life (Dilworth-Anderson, Boswell, & Cohen, 2007; Harvey, Johnson, & Heath, 2013).

There is considerable evidence linking spirituality, religious-based coping, and health (Ai et al., 2010, 2017; Harvey et al., 2013; Krause, 2012; Park, 2007). In general, older adults who are more involved with and committed to their faith have better physical and mental health

The spirituality of these Buddhist monks can serve as an important coping strategy.

KIM-JAE-HWAN/AFP/Getty Images

than older adults who are not religious. For example, older Mexican Americans who pray to the saints and the Virgin Mary on a regular basis tend to have greater optimism and better health (Krause & Bastida, 2011). Spirituality also helps improve psychological well-being (George, Palmore, & Cohen, 2014; Hayward et al., 2016) and helps patients following cardiac surgery (Ai et al., 2010).

Researchers have increasingly focused on spiritual support—*which includes seeking pastoral care, participating in organized and nonorganized religious activities, and expressing faith in a God who cares for people—as a key factor in understanding how older adults cope.* Even when under high levels of stress, such as during critical illness or other major life trauma, people who rely on spiritual support report greater personal well-being (Ai et al., 2010, 2017; Hayward et al., 2016). Lucette and colleagues (2016; Krause, 2006) report that maintaining a sense of spirituality helps people cope with chronic health conditions.

Neuroscience research has shown a connection between certain spiritual mindfulness practices and brain activity (Dobkin & Hassed, 2016; Tang & Posner, 2012). For example, there is evidence that people who have practiced meditation show positive structural changes in areas of the brain related to attention and memory (Esch, 2014; Luders, 2014; Newberg et al., 2014). Thus, neurological evidence indicates that there may be changes in brain activity and in brain structure associated with spiritual practices that help people cope. An example of the changes that occur in brain activity between a normal resting state and a meditative state is shown in ▶Figure 15.6. Notice the significant increase in activity during meditation.

This kind of positive structural change has led some researchers (Luders, 2014; Luders & Cherbuin, 2016; Newberg et al., 2014) to argue that meditation might offer promise as a way to help slow down, and perhaps even prevent, the brain changes that underlie brain diseases such as dementia. While it is still too early to tell for certain, the possibility that a practice done for centuries among all of the major world religions in one form or another, mindful meditation or contemplation, could prevent or reverse negative changes in the brain will undoubtedly be the focus of a great deal of research.

▶ **Figure 15.6**

SPECT scans of a subject at rest and during peak meditation showing increased cerebral blood flow (arrows) during meditation.

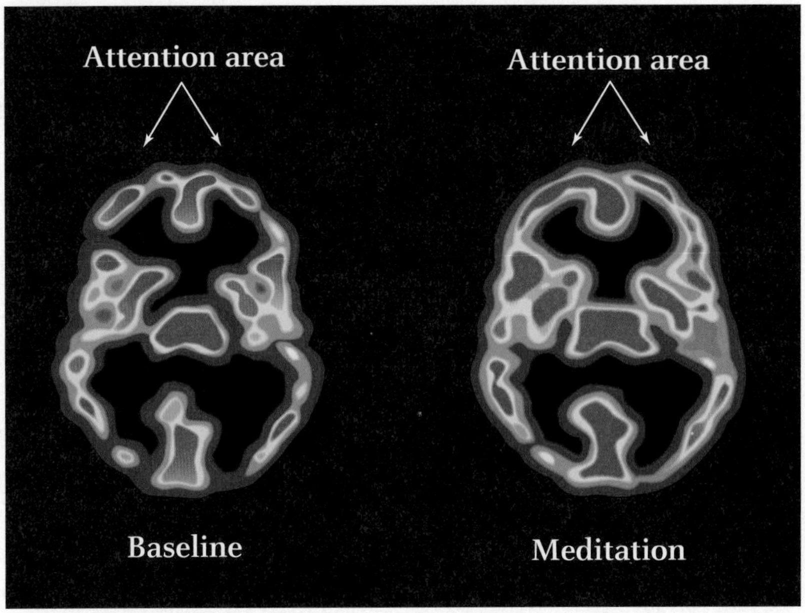

© 2019 Cengage

spiritual support

Type of coping strategy that includes seeking pastoral care, participating in organized and nonorganized religious activities, and expressing faith in a God who cares for people.

Think About It

How might the transition from the False Self to the True Self reflect postformal cognitive development?

TEST YOURSELF 15.2

Recall

1. The Eriksonian struggle that older adults face is termed _____.

2. An evaluation of one's life that is associated with positive feelings is termed _____.

3. The transition from False Self to True self is one aspect of the development of _____.

Interpret

- How might different spiritual traditions influence personal well-being?

Apply

- Given that the prefrontal cortex is activated for both positive and negative emotions for younger and older adults, what might account for older adults' increased reaction to negative emotions?

Check your answers to the Recall Questions at the end of the chapter.

LEARNING OBJECTIVES

- What does being retired mean?
- Why do people retire?
- How do people adjust to retirement?
- What employment and volunteer opportunities are available for older adults?

Marcus is a 77-year-old retired construction worker who labored hard all of his life. He managed to save a little money, but he and his wife rely primarily on his monthly Social Security checks. Although not rich, they have enough to pay the bills. For the most part, Marcus is happy with retirement, and he stays in touch with his friends. He thinks that maybe he's a little strange, though, because he has heard that retirees are supposed to be isolated and lonely.

Did you know that until 1934, when a railroad union sponsored a bill promoting mandatory retirement, and 1935, when Social Security was inaugurated, retirement was not even considered a possibility by most Americans like Marcus (McClinton, 2010; Sargent et al., 2013)? Only since World War II has there been a substantial number of retired people in the United States (McClinton, 2010).

Although we take retirement for granted, economic downturns have a major disruptive effect on people's retirement decisions and plans. New view of aging and increased health for the typical older adult has also had an effect on people's notions about retirement. These realities have, in turn, affected social policy. As more people retire and take advantage of longer lives, a significant social challenge is created regarding how to fund retiree benefits and how to support older adults who are still active (Monahan, 2017; Quinn & Cahill, 2016; Wise, 2017).

After having one or several careers across adulthood, many older adults find themselves questioning whether they want to continue in that line of work anymore, or find themselves being forced to go through that questioning because they lost their jobs. This period of questioning and potential exploration enables people to think about their options: retiring, looking for work in the same of a different field, volunteering, or some combination of all of these.

With the movement of the baby-boom generation into old age, increasing numbers of these adults are redefining what "retirement" and "work" mean in late life. Realizing these generational shifts reflect important changes in how people view the latter part of one's working life, AARP created the *Life Reimagined*® tool that assists people in finding their path, including reawakening long-dormant interests.

As we consider retirement and other options in late life, keep in mind the world is changing, resulting in increased options and the likelihood more older adults will continue in the labor force by choice and necessity.

Retirement provides many people with the opportunity to do things they want to do rather than things they must do.

iStock.com/Xavier Arnau

What Does Being Retired Mean?

Retirement means different things to men and women, and to people in different ethnic groups and careers (James, Matz-Costa, & Smyer, 2016; Loretto & Vickerstaff, 2013; Silver, 2016). It has also taken on new and different meanings since the beginning of the Great Recession in 2008 because of the abrupt change in people's planning and expectations as a result of the loss of savings or pensions (Quinn & Cahill, 2016; Sargent et al., 2013).

Part of the reason it is difficult to define retirement precisely is that the decision to retire involves the loss of occupational identity with no obvious replacement for that loss. Not having a specific job any more means we either put that aspect of our lives in the past tense—"I used to work as a manager at the Hilton"—or say nothing at all. Loss of this aspect of ourselves can be difficult to face, so some look for a label other than "retired" to describe themselves.

That's why researchers view retirement as another one of many transitions people experience in life (Kojola & Moen, 2016; Moen, 2016a; Sargent et al., 2013). This view makes retirement a complex process where people withdraw from full-time participation in an occupation (Moen, 2016a; Sargent et al., 2013), recognizing there are many pathways to this end (Kojola & Moen, 2016; Moen, 2016a, b; Sargent et al., 2013).

Think About It

In the absence of mandatory retirement, is there such a concept as "early retirement?"

Why Do People Retire?

Provided they have good health, more workers retire by choice than for any other reason (Cohen-Mansfield & Regev, in press; Kojola & Moen, 2016), as long they feel financially secure after considering projected income from Social Security, pensions and other structured retirement programs, and personal savings (Quinn & Cahill, 2016). Of course, some people are forced to retire because of health problems or because they lose their jobs. As corporations downsize during economic downturns or after corporate mergers, some older workers accept buyout packages involving supplemental payments if they retire. Others are permanently furloughed, laid off, or dismissed.

The decision to retire is influenced by one's occupational history and goal expectations (Moen, 2016a; Sargent et al., 2013). Whether people perceive they will achieve their personal goals through work or retirement influences the decision to retire and its connection with health and disability.

The rude awakening many people received during the Great Recession was that the best made plans are only as good as external factors allow them to be, especially when it comes to financial savings and pensions. Many people lost much of their investment savings and home equity as the value of stocks plummeted, companies eliminated pension plans, and the housing market collapsed. Consequently, many people were forced to delay their retirement until they had the financial resources to do so, or to continue working part time when they had not planned to do so to supplement their income.

Income security is now at the forefront in retirement decisions (Monahan, 2017; Quinn & Cahill, 2016). Although 42% of respondents in one poll thought the ideal retirement age is between 60 and 65, only 29% thought they would actually be able to achieve that goal (Boschma, 2015). Indeed, 30% of respondents thought that they would be unable to retire before age 70, if ever, mainly due to pessimism regarding financial security.

How much do you need to have in savings to be comfortable in retirement? A decent rule of thumb is to save enough to generate between 70% and 80% of your current income, and to plan for about 25 years in retirement. This figure takes into account typical living and medical expenses. The bottom line is longer life expectancies have added to the amount of money you will need in retirement—and that amount is usually much greater than people think.

Gender and Ethnic Differences

Women's experience of retiring can be quite different from men's (Loretto & Vickerstaff, 2013; Silver, 2016). Women's employment career may have developed differently, such as having starts and stops related to dependent care responsibilities, or may reflect later entry into the workforce. Because of the pay gap and possible interruptions in work history, many women have fewer financial resources for retirement.

For women who were never employed outside the home, the process of retirement is especially unclear (Loretto & Vickerstaff, 2013), even when such spouses are eligible for Social Security benefits. Because they were not paid for all of their work raising children and caring for the home, it is rare for them to have their own pensions or other sources of income in retirement beyond spousal survivor benefits. Additionally, the work they have always done in caring for the home continues, often nearly uninterrupted (Ciani, 2016).

We know less about the experiences of older women and adults of color in retirement than we do about male European Americans.

kali9/E+/Getty Images

There has not been much research examining the process of retirement as a function of ethnicity. African American and Latino older adults are likely to continue working beyond age 65, mainly due to greater financial vulnerability on average (Angel & Angel, 2015; Sullivan & Meschede, 2016; Troutman, Nies, & Mavellia, 2011).

Adjustment to Retirement

How do people who go through the process of retirement adjust to it? Researchers agree on one point: New patterns of personal involvement must be developed in the context of changing roles and lifestyles in retirement (Ajrouch, Antonucci, & Webster, 2014; Potočnik, Tordera, & Peiró, 2013). People's adjustment to retirement evolves over time as a result of complex interrelations involving physical health, financial status, to the degree their retirement was voluntary, and feelings of personal control (Moen, 2016a; Ng et al., 2016).

How do most people fare? As long as people have financial security, health, a supportive network of relatives and friends, and an internally driven sense of motivation, they report feeling good about being retired (Hershey & Henkens, 2014; Moen, 2016a; Ng et al., 2016; Potočnik et al., 2013). What motivates most people, though, is finding a sense of fulfillment in ways previously unavailable to them (James et al., 2016).

Many people think being retired has negative effects on health. Research findings show the relation between health and retirement is complex. On the one hand, there is no evidence voluntary retirement has immediate negative effects on health (Hershey & Henkens, 2014). In contrast, there is ample evidence being forced to retire is correlated with significantly poorer physical and mental health (Hershey & Henkens, 2014).

Employment and Volunteering

Retirement is an important life transition, one best understood through a life-course perspective that takes other aspects of one's life, such as one's marital relationship, into account (Moen, 2016a; Wickrama, O'Neal, & Lorenz, 2013). This life change means retirees must look for ways to adapt to new routines and patterns, while maintaining social integration and being active in various ways (e.g., friendship networks, community engagement).

Employment in Late Life

For an increasing number of people, especially for those whose retirement savings is insufficient, "retirement" involves working at least part-time. Employment for them is a financial necessity to make ends meet, especially for those whose entire income would consist only of Social Security benefits.

For others, the need to stay employed at least part-time represents a way to stay involved beyond an income supplement, and a way for employers to continue benefiting from employees' experience. For example, even in the rapidly changing knowledge industry, employment of workers over age 65 has been shown to benefit both older adults and companies (Bartkowiak, 2017).

As you can see in ❯ Figure 15.7, the percentage of adults age 65 and over who are in the workforce increased dramatically between 2000 and 2016, even as the overall percentage of Americans who were employed declined (DeSilver, 2016). Note also the trend has been consistently upward, indicating the forces keeping older adults in the labor force have been acting for many years.

Overall, labor force participation of older adults in the United States and other developed countries has been increasing most rapidly among women (DeSilver, 2016; Sterns & Chang, 2010). This is due mostly to more women being in the labor force across adulthood than in decades past, more older women being single, and greater financial need. The Great Recession exacerbated the need for older adults to work at least part-time to ensure greater financial security (Quinn & Cahill, 2016).

Older workers face many challenges, not the least of which are ageism and discrimination (Jackson, 2013). Employers may believe older workers are less capable, and there

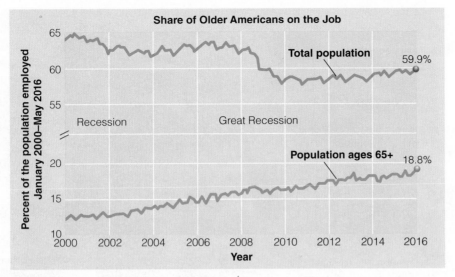

From DeSilver, D. (2016). *More older Americans are working, and working more, than they used to.* Retrieved from www.pewresearch.org/fact-tank/2016/06/20/more-older-americans-are-working-and-working-more-than-they-used-to/.

is evidence this translates into lower likelihood of getting a job interview compared to younger or middle-aged workers, all other things being equal (Abrams, Swift, & Drury, 2016). As we noted earlier in this chapter, despite the fact age discrimination laws in the United States protect people over age 40, such barriers are still widespread.

The relationship between age and job performance is extremely complex (Sterns & Chang, 2010). This is because it depends a great deal on the kind of job one is considering, such as one that requires a great deal of physical exertion or one that involves a great deal of expertise and experience. In general, older workers show more reliability (e.g., showing up on time for work), organizational loyalty, and safety-related behavior.

How have companies adapted to having more older workers? One example is BMW, a company that changed a number of things in its automobile assembly plants to better meet the needs of older workers (de Pommereau, 2012). BMW provides physical trainers on the factory floor, has new, softer floors, offers chairs that rise up and down to make tasks easier, uses larger print fonts on computer screens, and provides special shoes.

The trend for companies to employ older workers, especially on a part-time basis, is likely to continue because it is a good option for companies (Beck, 2013; Coleman, 2015). Some companies find they need the expertise older workers bring, as well as the flexibility of older workers in terms of hours and the type of benefits they need (or do not need) often make it less expensive. Consequently, "retirement" is likely to continue to evolve as a concept, and is likely to include some aspect of employment well into late life.

Coleman (2015) argues that the benefits of hiring and retaining older workers could make companies stronger and more successful. However, a change in approach will require overcoming stereotypes of aging, as well as balancing the need to provide opportunities for younger workers with the need to retain the experience and knowledge of older workers.

Volunteering

Healthy, active retired adults often find meaning and explore things they always wished they had had a chance to do by volunteering (Ajrouch et al., 2014; Kleiber, 2013). Older adults report they volunteer for many reasons that benefit their well-being (Ajrouch et al., 2015; Greenfield & Marks, 2005), such as to provide service to others, to maintain social interactions and improve their communities, and to keep active.

Why do so many people volunteer? Several factors are responsible (Ajrouch et al., 2015; Tang, Morrow-Howell, & Choi, 2010): changing characteristics of social networks, developing a new aspect of the self, finding a personal sense of purpose, desiring to share one's skills and expertise, redefining the nature and merits of volunteer work, and having a

Some retired adults volunteer as a way to stay active.

Mike Greenlar/The Image Works

more highly educated and healthy population of older adults along with greatly expanded opportunities for people to become involved in volunteer work they enjoy. Research in New Zealand documents older adults who find volunteering enables them to give back to their local communities (Wiles & Jayasinha, 2013). Brown and colleagues (2011) argue volunteerism offers a way for society to tap into the vast resources older adults offer.

There is also evidence the expectations of people who volunteer in retirement are changing. Seaman (2012) notes women in the leading edge of the baby-boom generation are interested in volunteering for personal, rather than purely altruistic reasons and do so on their own terms. They are not as willing as volunteers were in previous generations to serve on time-consuming boards and to engage in fundraising. As a result, organizations that rely on volunteers need to be in touch with the concerns and motivations of their pool of volunteers.

The U.S. government has been tapping into this pool of talented volunteers since President John F. Kennedy's presidency, when the Senior Corps was created. As part of the Corporation for National and Community Service, the Senior Corps consists of three major programs: Foster grandparents, Retired Senior Volunteer Program (RSVP), and Senior Companions (Corporation for National and Community Service, 2016). These national programs have chapters across the country, and interested people aged 55 and over are encouraged to explore local opportunities. These and other programs provide organized ways to get and stay active and to find meaningful forms of engagement.

Think About It

With regard to politics, what might the opportunity for more older adults to volunteer for organizations mean?

TEST YOURSELF 15.3

Recall

1. One useful way to view retirement is as a(n) _____.
2. The most common reason people retire is _____.
3. Overall, most retirees are _____ with retirement.
4. Many retirees maintain contacts in their communities by _____.

Interpret

Why does forced retirement have a negative effect on health?

Apply

- Using the information from Chapter 12 on occupational development, create a developmental description of occupations that incorporates retirement.

Check your answers to the Recall Questions at the end of the chapter.

LEARNING OBJECTIVES

- What roles do friends and family play in late life? What is socioemotional selectivity?

- What are older adults' marriages and same-sex partnerships like?

- What is it like to provide basic care for one's partner?

- How do people cope with widowhood? How do men and women differ?

- What special issues are involved in being a great-grandparent?

Alma was married to Charles for 46 years. Even though he died 20 years ago, Alma still speaks about him as if he only recently passed away. Alma still gets sad on special dates—their wedding anniversary, Charles's birthday, and the date on which he died. Alma tells everyone that she and Chuck, as she called him, had a wonderful marriage and that she still misses him terribly even after all these years.

To older adults such as Alma, the most important thing in life is relationships. In this section, we consider many of the relationships that older adults have. Whether it is friendship or family ties, having relationships with others is what keeps people connected. Thus, when one's partner is in need of care, it is not surprising to find wives and husbands devoting themselves to caregiving. Widows such as Alma also feel close to their departed partners. For a growing number of older adults, becoming a great-grandparent is an exciting time.

We have seen throughout this text how our lives are shaped by others and how we share the company of others. *The term* social convoy *is used to suggest how a group of people journeys with us throughout our lives, providing support in good and bad times.* People form the convoy, and under ideal conditions, that convoy provides a protective, secure cushion that permits people to explore and learn about the world (English & Carstensen, 2014; Luong, Charles, & Fingerman, 2011). Especially for older adults, the social convoy also provides a source of affirmation of who they are and what they mean to others, which leads to better mental health and well-being.

social convoy

Group of people who journey with us throughout our lives, providing support in good times and bad.

Several studies have shown that the size of one's social convoy and the amount of support it provides do not differ across generations. This finding strongly supports the conclusion that friends and family are essential aspects of all adults' lives. Social support is especially important in the African American community, as these networks provide all sorts of informal assistance for health-related and other issues (Warren-Findlow & Issel, 2010). Social networks also play a critical role in helping immigrants; for example, when settling in their new country, older Mexican American and Filipino immigrants are assisted by family members in their network (Miller-Martinez & Wallace, 2007; Molina, 2012).

Friends, Siblings, and Socioemotional Selectivity

By late life, a person may have been friends with members of his or her social network for several decades. Research consistently finds that older adults have the same need for friends as do people in younger generations; it also shows that their life satisfaction is poorly correlated with the number or quality of relationships with younger family members yet is strongly correlated with the number and quality of their friendships (Blieszner & Roberto, 2012). Why? As will become clear, friends serve as confidants and sources of support in ways that relatives (e.g., children or nieces and nephews) typically do not.

Friendships

In Chapter 11, we explored the meanings and qualities of friendships across young adulthood and middle age. Patterns of friendship among older adults tend to mirror those in young adulthood (Rawlins, 2004). That is, older women have more numerous and more intimate friendships than older men do (Blieszner & Roberto, 2012).

There are some important differences in later life, though. The quality and purpose of late-life friendships are particularly important (Bromell & Cagney, 2014; Schulz & Morycz, 2013). Friends are sometimes even more important to older adults in part because older adults do not want to become burdens to their families (Blieszner & Roberto, 2012; Moorman & Greenfield, 2010). As a result, friends help each other foster independence. Having friends also provides a buffer against the loss of roles and status that accompany old age, such as retirement or the death of a loved one, and can increase people's happiness and self-esteem (Schulz & Morycz, 2013). People who live alone especially benefit from friends in the neighborhood (Bromell & Cagney, 2014). And people who have ambivalent feelings about their social networks have shorter telomeres than people who have strong feelings about theirs (Uchino et al., 2012).

In the case of online friendships (e.g., through social media), trust develops on the basis of four sources: (1) reputation; (2) performance, or what users do online; (3) precommitment (through personal self-disclosure); and (4) situational factors, especially the premium placed on intimacy and the relationship (Henderson & Gilding, 2004). Not surprisingly, online social network friendships develop much like face-to-face friendships in that the more time people spend online with friends, the more likely they are to self-disclose (Chang & Hsiao, 2014). Online environments are more conducive to people who are lonely (e.g., live alone), which make them potentially important for older adults (Cotton, Anderson, & McCullough, 2013).

Siblings

A special type of friendship exists with one's siblings; they are the friends who people typically have the longest and with whom people share the closest bonds. The importance of these relationships varies with age (Carr & Moorman, 2011; Moorman & Greenfield, 2010). The centrality of siblings in later life depends on several things: proximity, health, and degree of relatedness (full, step-, or half-siblings), for example. No clear pattern of emotional closeness emerges when viewing sibling relationships on the basis of gender.

When sibling relationships are close and one sibling dies, the surviving sibling often reports reflecting, about or talking to the deceased sibling for advice (Vacha-Haase, Donaldson, & Foster, 2014). What is also clear is that sibling relationships in later life are affected by events in the lives of the siblings that may have occurred decades earlier (Knipscheer & van Tilburg, 2013). If there was no contact between the siblings over an extended period of time, it is unlikely that these relational rifts will be repaired. An important source for such tension is hard feelings stemming from perceived parental favoritism among siblings. This tension subsequently plays out when aging parents need care, and it may continue into the siblings' own late life (Gilligan et al., 2013). In such situations, jealousies that have their roots in childhood fester for decades, only to resurface when siblings need to coordinate parental care.

More research into sibling relationships in late life is needed to provide a better understanding of how siblings (and step-siblings) get along and how they come to rely on each other for assistance in certain situations.

Socioemotional Selectivity

Why are friends important to older adults? Some researchers believe one reason may be older adults' not wanting to become burdens to their families (Adams & Taylor, 2015; Blieszner & Roberto, 2012; Moorman & Greenfield, 2010). As a result, friends help each other remain independent by providing transportation, checking on neighbors, and doing errands.

Older adults tend to have fewer relationships with people in general and develop fewer new relationships than people do in midlife and particularly in young adulthood (Adams & Taylor,

Think About It

What role might siblings play in an older adult's autobiographical memory (see Chapter 14)?

Siblings play an important role in the lives of older adults.

Brownie Harris/Corbis/Getty Images

2015; Carr & Moorman, 2011). Carstensen and colleagues (Carstensen, 2006; Charles & Carstensen, 2010; English & Carstensen, 2016; Reed & Carstensen, 2012) have shown the changes in social behavior seen in late life reflect a more complicated and important process. *They propose a life-span theory of* socioemotional selectivity, *that argues social contact is motivated by a variety of goals, including information seeking, self-concept, and emotional regulation.*

Each of these goals is differentially salient at different points of the adult life span and results in different social behaviors. When information seeking is the goal, such as when a person is exploring the world trying to figure out how he or she fits in, what others are like, and so forth, meeting many new people is an essential part of the process. However, when emotional regulation is the goal, people become highly selective in their choice of social partners and nearly always prefer people who are familiar to them.

Carstensen and colleagues believe information seeking is the predominant goal for young adults, emotional regulation is the major goal for older people, and both goals are in balance in midlife. Their research supports this view; people become increasingly selective in whom they choose to have contact with. Additionally, evidence suggests there is an increase with age in emotional competency (e.g., Doerwald et al., 2016; Magai, 2008). Older adults appear to orient more toward emotional aspects of life and personal relationships as they grow older, and emotional expression and experience become more complex and nuanced. Carstensen's theory provides a complete explanation of why older adults tend not to replace, to any great extent, the relationships they lose: Older adults are more selective and have fewer opportunities to make new friends, especially in view of the emotional bonds involved in friendships.

Marriage and Same-Sex Partnerships

"It's great to be 72 and still married," said Lucia. "Yeah, it's great to have Juan around to share old times with and to have him know how I feel even before I tell him." Lucia and Juan are typical of most older married couples.

Marital satisfaction in long-term marriages—that is, marriages of 40 years or more—is a complex issue. In general, marital satisfaction among older couples increases shortly after retirement but then decreases with health problems and advancing age, and is directly related to the level of perceived support each partner receives (Landis et al., 2013; Proulx, 2016). The level of satisfaction in these marriages appears to be unrelated to the amount of past or present sexual interest or sexual activity, but it is positively related to the degree of social engagement such as interaction with friends (Bennett, 2005). In keeping with the married-singles concept, many older couples have simply developed detached, contented styles (Connidis, 2001; Lamanna, Riedmann, & Stewart, 2015; Proulx, 2016).

Older married couples show several specific characteristics (O'Rourke & Cappeliez, 2005). Many older couples show a selective memory regarding the occurrence of negative events and perceptions of their partner. Older couples have a reduced potential for marital conflict and greater potential for pleasure, are more likely to be similar in terms of mental and physical health, and show fewer gender differences in sources of pleasure. This is especially true if the couple have developed strong dyadic coping strategies, that is, coping strategies that rely on the interconnectedness of the couple (Berg et al., 2016). In short, older married couples developed adaptive ways to avoid conflict and grew more alike. In general, marital satisfaction among older couples remains high until health problems begin to interfere with the relationship (Connidis, 2001).

Being married in late life has several benefits. A study of 9,333 European Americans, African Americans, and Latino Americans showed marriage helps people deal better with chronic illness, functional problems, and disabilities (Pienta, Hayward, & Jenkins, 2000). Although the division of

socioemotional selectivity
Theory that argues that social contact is motivated by a variety of goals, including information seeking, self-concept, and emotional regulation.

Older, long-term married couples tend to emphasize their partner's positive attributes.

Lisa F. Young/Shutterstock.com

household chores becomes more egalitarian after the husband retires than it was when the husband was employed, irrespective of whether the wife was working outside the home, women still do more than half of the work (Kulik, 2011).

King (2016) argues that the experiences of older lesbian, gay, and bisexual adults cannot be put into need categories, even generational ones. Rather, King emphasizes that the LGB community is at least as diverse as the heterosexual community, and needs to be understood as such.

With the advent of legalized same-sex marriage, numerous issues that heterosexual married couples have long taken for granted are being confronted in the LGBTQ community, including end-of-life issues and legal matters regarding caregiving (Godfrey, 2016; Orel & Coon, 2016). Changes to state laws will continue as reforms and revisions continue to keep pace with change.

When compared to LGB individuals living with partners, LGB individuals living alone or with others (but not in a relationship with them) reported higher degrees of loneliness (Kim & Fredriksen-Goldsen, 2016). This finding parallels that of heterosexual individuals in similar living arrangements, and highlights the fact that there are many similarities in personal outcomes across various gender identity groups.

Little research has been conducted examining the development of transgender and gender nonconforming (TGNC) individuals across adulthood (Witten, 2016). One detailed examination of experiences of TGNC adults over age 50 found that many barriers to accessing key services such as health care and social services exist, largely due to anti-TGNC prejudice, discrimination, and lack of appropriate and adequate training of professionals (Porter et al., 2016). Additionally, research indicates that transgender older adults experience social isolation more than most other groups (Harley, Gassaway, & Dunkley, 2016).

So how do long-term relationships change and develop from midlife through late life? Wickrama et al. (2013) developed a model that takes into account the influences of genetic markers, personal characteristics, cumulative life experiences, and stressful events during the period from late midlife through later life. The model, shown in ❱ Figure 15.8, shows how all of these influences interact.

The key point in the model is that people bring their past with them when they enter late life, and those experiences, including their genetic makeup, work together to create the relationships that people experience as older adults. Although Wickrama et al. (2013) initially created the model to describe baby boomers' marriages as they experience retirement, the researchers point out that the model is likely applicable to other forms of long-term relationships, such as same-sex relationships and cohabitation.

❱ **Figure 15.8**

Marital functioning from middle to later years: A life course–stress process framework.

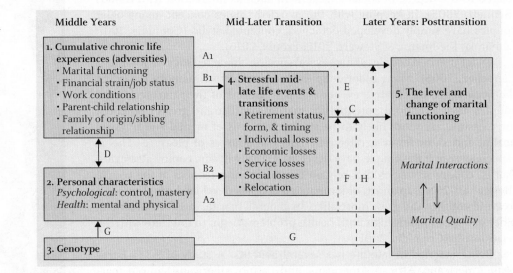

From Wickrama, K. A. S., O'Neal, C. W., & Lorenz, F. O. (2013). Marital functioning from middle to later years: A life course–stress process framework. *Journal of Family Theory & Review*, 5, 15–34. doi: 10.1111/jftr.12000. Retrieved from onlinelibrary.wiley.com/doi/10.1111/jftr.12000/full.

Caring for a Partner

When couples pledge their love to each other "in sickness and in health," most of them envision the sickness part to be no worse than an illness lasting a few weeks. That may be the case for many couples, but for others, the illness they experience severely tests their pledge.

Francine and Ron are one such couple. After 51 years of mostly good times together, Ron was diagnosed with Alzheimer's disease. When she was first contacted by researchers, Francine had been caring for Ron for six years. "At times, it's very hard, especially when he looks at me and doesn't have any idea who I am. Imagine after all these years not to recognize me. But I love him, and I know that he would do the same for me. But to be perfectly honest, we're not the same couple we once were. We're not as close; I guess we really can't be."

Francine and Ron are typical of couples in which one partner cares for the other. Caring for a chronically ill partner presents different challenges from caring for a chronically ill parent. The partner caregiver assumes the new role after decades of shared responsibilities. Often without warning, the division of labor that had worked for years must be readjusted. Such change inevitably puts stress on the relationship (Haley, 2013). This is especially true when one's spouse/partner has a debilitating chronic disease.

Studies of partner caregivers of persons with Alzheimer's disease show that satisfaction with the relationship is much lower than for healthy couples (Cavanaugh & Kinney, 1994; Haley, 2013; Kulik, 2016; Proulx, 2016). Spousal and same-sex partner caregivers report a loss of companionship and intimacy over the course of caregiving, but also receive more rewards compared with adult child caregivers (Croghan, Moone, & Olson, 2014; Kimmel, 2014; Raschick & Ingersoll-Dayton, 2004; Revenson et al., 2016). Marital satisfaction is also an important predictor of spousal caregivers' reports of depressive symptoms; the better the perceived quality of the marriage, the fewer symptoms caregivers report (Kinney & Cavanaugh, 1993), a finding that holds across European American and minority spousal caregivers (Chiao, Wu, & Hsiao, 2015; Parker, 2008).

Most partner caregivers adopt the caregiver role out of necessity. Although evidence about the mediating role of caregivers' appraisal of stressors is unclear, interventions that help improve the functional level of the ill partner generally improve the caregiving partner's situation (Revenson et al., 2016; van den Wijngaart, Vernooij-Dassen, & Felling, 2007).

The importance of feeling competent as a partner caregiver fits with the docility component of the competence–environmental press model presented earlier in this chapter. Caregivers attempt to balance their perceived competence with the environmental demands of caregiving. Perceived competence allows them to be proactive rather than merely reactive (and docile), which gives them a better chance to optimize their situation.

Even in the best of committed relationships, providing full-time care for a partner is both stressful and rewarding in terms of the relationship (Haley, 2013; Kimmel, 2014; Revenson et al., 2016). For example, coping with a wife who may not remember her husband's name, who may act strangely, and who has a chronic and fatal disease presents serious challenges even to the happiest of couples. Yet even in that situation, the caregiving husband may experience no change in marital happiness despite the changes in his wife due to the disease.

Widowhood

Alma, the woman in our vignette, still feels the loss of her husband, Chuck. "There are many times when I feel him around. When you're together for so long, you take it for granted that your husband will always be there. And there are times when I just don't want to go on without him. But I suppose I'll get through it."

Like Alma and Chuck, virtually all older married couples see their marriages end legally when one partner dies. For most people, the death of a partner is one of the most traumatic events they experience, causing an increased risk of death among older European Americans (but not African Americans), an effect that lasts several years (Moorman & Greenfield, 2010). An extensive study of widowed adults in Scotland showed the increased

Widowers are less likely than widows to form new friendships, continuing a trend throughout adulthood that men have fewer close friends than do women.

Colin Young-Wolff/PhotoEdit

likelihood of dying lasted for at least 10 years (Boyle, Feng, & Raab, 2011). Despite the stress of losing one's partner, most widowed older adults manage to cope reasonably well (Moorman & Greenfield, 2010).

The effects are broader than just mortality, though. Lucy Kalanithi (2016) described how her marriage vows to love, to honor, and to be loyal to her husband did not end with his death at age 37 from cancer. For her, marriage did not end with her transition to being a widow.

Women are much more likely to be widowed than are men. More than half of all women over age 65 are widows, but only 15% of men the same age are widowers. Women have longer life expectancies and typically marry men older than themselves. Consequently, the average married woman can expect to live at least 10 years as a widow.

The impact of widowhood goes well beyond the ending of a long-term partnership (Boyle et al., 2011; Brenn & Ytterstad, 2016; McCoyd & Walter, 2016). For example, there is evidence of increased mortality, especially within the first week of widowhood (Brenn & Ytterstad, 2016).

Loneliness is a major problem. Widowed people may be left alone by family and friends who do not know how to deal with a bereaved person. As a result, widows and widowers may lose not only a partner, but also those friends and family who feel uncomfortable with including a single person rather than a couple in social functions (McCoyd & Walter, 2016).

Feelings of loss do not dissipate quickly, as the case of Alma shows clearly. Men and women react differently to widowhood. In general, those who were most dependent on their partners during the marriage report the highest increase in self-esteem in widowhood when they learn to do the tasks formerly done by their partners (Carr, 2004). Widowers may recover more slowly unless they have strong social support systems (Bennett, 2010). Widows often suffer more financially because survivor's benefits are usually only half of their husband's pensions (Weaver, 2010). For many women, widowhood results in difficult financial circumstances, particularly regarding medical expenses (McGarry & Schoeni, 2005).

For many reasons, including the need for companionship and financial security, some widowed people cohabit or remarry. A newer variation on repartnering is "living alone together," an arrangement where two older adults form a romantic relationship but maintain separate living arrangements (Moorman & Greenfield, 2010). Repartnering in widowhood can be difficult because of family objections (e.g., resistance from children), objective limitations (decreased mobility, poorer health, poorer finances), absence of incentives common to younger ages (desire for children), and social pressures to protect one's estate (Moorman & Greenfield, 2010).

Great-Grandparenthood

As discussed in Chapter 13, grandparenting is an important and enjoyable role for many adults. With increasing numbers of people—especially women—living to very old age, more people are experiencing great-grandparenthood. Age at first marriage and age at parenthood also play a critical role; people who reach these milestones at relatively young ages are more likely to become great-grandparents.

Although surprisingly little research has been conducted on great-grandparents, their investment in their roles as parents, grandparents, and great-grandparents forms a single family identity (Drew & Silverstein, 2004; Even-Zohar & Garby, 2016; Moorman & Greenfield, 2010). That is, great-grandparents see a true continuity of the family through the passing on of genes. However, their sources of satisfaction and meaning apparently differ from those of grandparents (Doka & Mertz, 1988; Even-Zohar & Garby, 2016; Wentkowski, 1985). Compared with grandparents, great-grandparents are more similar as a group in what they derive from the role, largely because they are less involved with the children than the grandparents are.

Three aspects of great-grandparenthood appear to be most important (Doka & Mertz, 1988). First, being a great-grandparent provides a sense of personal and family renewal—important components for achieving integrity. Their grandchildren have produced new life, renewing their own excitement for life and reaffirming the continuance of their lineage. Seeing their families stretch across four generations may also provide psychological support, through feelings of symbolic immortality, to help them face death. They take pride and comfort in knowing that their families will live many years beyond their own lifetime. Keeping the family together is a major source of meaning (Even-Zohar & Garby, 2016).

Second, great-grandchildren provide new diversions in great-grandparents' lives. There are now new people with whom they can share their experiences. Young children can learn from a person they perceive as "really old" (Mietkiewicz & Venditti, 2004).

Third, becoming a great-grandparent is a major milestone, a mark of longevity that most people never achieve. The sense that one has lived long enough to see the fourth generation is perceived very positively.

As you might expect, people with at least one living grandparent and great-grandparent interact more with their grandparent, who is also perceived as more influential (Roberto & Skoglund, 1996). Unfortunately, some great-grandparents must assume the role of primary caregiver to their great-grandchildren, a role for which few great-grandparents are prepared (Bengtson, Mills, & Parrott, 1995; Burton, 1992). As more people live longer, it will be interesting to see whether the role of great-grandparents changes and becomes more prominent.

TEST YOURSELF 15.4

Recall

1. The longest relationship most people have is with their _____.

2. In general, older couples have reduced likelihood of _____.

3. Compared to noncaregiver spouses, marital satisfaction in spousal caregivers is _____.

4. _____ are at special risk of experiencing a drop in living standard following the death of their spouse.

5. Three aspects of being a great-grandparent that are especially important are personal and family renewal, diversion, and _____.

Interpret

- Why would widows and widowers want to establish a new cohabitation relationship?

Apply

- How do the descriptions of marital satisfaction and spousal caregiving presented here fit with the descriptions of marital satisfaction in Chapter 11 and caring for aging parents in Chapter 13? What similarities and differences are there?

Check your answers to the Recall Questions at the end of the chapter.

15.5 Social Issues and Aging

LEARNING OBJECTIVES

- Who are frail older adults? How common is frailty?
- What housing options are available for older adults?
- How do you know whether an older adult is abused, neglected, or exploited?
- What are the key social policy issues affecting older adults?

Sakhra is an 82-year-old woman who still lives in the same neighborhood where she grew up. She has been in relatively good health for most of her life, but in the last year, she has needed help with tasks such as preparing meals and shopping for personal items. Sakhra very much wants to continue living in her own home. She doesn't want to be placed in a nursing home, but her family wonders whether that might be the best option.

frail older adults

Older adults who have physical disabilities, are very ill, may have cognitive or psychological disorders, and need assistance with everyday tasks.

activities of daily living (ADLs)

Basic self-care tasks such as eating, bathing, toileting, walking, and dressing.

instrumental activities of daily living (IADLs)

Actions that require some intellectual competence and planning.

physical limitations (PLIMs)

Activities that reflect functional limitations such as walking a block or sitting for about two hours.

Older adults over age 85 are more likely to be frail and to need help with basic daily tasks.

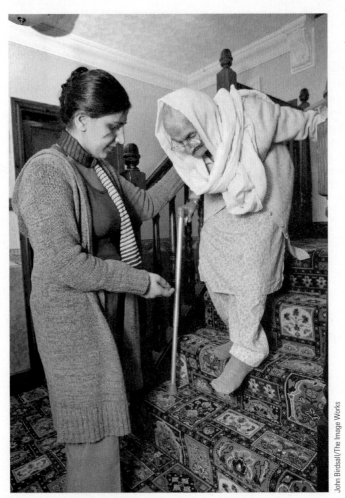

John Birdsall/The Image Works

Our consideration of late life thus far has focused on the experiences of the typical older adult. In this final section, we consider people such as Sakhra, who represent a substantial number but still a minority of all older adults. Like Sakhra, some older adults experience problems completing common tasks such as taking care of themselves. We will consider the prevalence and kinds of problems such people face. Although most older adults live in the community, some reside in other settings; we will consider the housing options that older adults have. Unfortunately, some older adults are the victims of abuse or neglect; we will examine some of the key issues relating to how elder abuse happens. Finally, we will conclude with an overview of the most important emerging social policy issues.

All of these issues are critical when viewed from Baltes and Smith's (2003) Fourth Age perspective, as described in Chapter 14. We will see that it is the oldest-old who make up most of the frail older adults living in both the community and long-term care facilities such as nursing homes. With the rapid increase in the number of oldest-old on the horizon (the baby-boom generation), finding ways to deal with these issues is essential.

Frail Older Adults

In our discussion about aging to this point, we focused on the majority of older adults who are healthy, are cognitively competent, are reasonably financially secure, and have good family relationships. Some older adults are not as fortunate. *They are the* frail older adults *who have physical disabilities, are very ill, may have cognitive or psychological disorders, and need assistance with everyday tasks.* These frail older adults constitute a minority of the population over age 65, but the size of this group increases considerably with age.

Frail older adults are people whose competence (in terms of the competence–environmental press model presented earlier) is declining. They do not have one specific problem that differentiates them from their active, healthy counterparts; instead, they tend to have multiple problems (Wilhelm-Leen et al., 2014). Some researchers zero in on the age-related loss of muscle mass and strength, called *sarcopenia* (Afilalo, 2016). Other researchers argue that frailty is the result of accumulated deficits in several functional areas (Rockwood, 2016). In either case, to identify the areas in which people experience limited functioning, researchers have developed observational and self-report techniques to measure how well people can accomplish daily tasks.

Everyday competence assessment consists of examining how well people can complete activities of daily living and instrumental activities of daily living, and whether they have other physical limitations (Verbrugge, Brown, & Zajacova, 2017). Activities of daily living (ADLs) *include basic self-care tasks such as eating, bathing, toileting, walking, or dressing.* A person can be considered frail if he or she needs help with one or more of these tasks. Instrumental activities of daily living (IADLs) *are actions that entail some intellectual competence and planning.* Which activities constitute IADLs varies widely across cultures. For example, for most adults in Western culture, IADLs would include shopping for personal items, paying bills, making telephone calls, taking medications appropriately, and keeping appointments. In other cultures, IADLs might include caring for animal herds, making bread, threshing grain, and tending crops. *A third way of assessing competence is to focus on* physical limitations (PLIMs), *activities that reflect functional limitations such as walking a block or sitting for about two hours.*

▶ Figure 15.9

Mean disability of the AHEAD living cohort by gender, 1993–2010. Mean disability of the AHEAD living cohort by gender, 1993–2010. Waves 1–9 are years 1993, 1995, 1998, 2000, 2002, 2004, 2006, 2008, 2010.

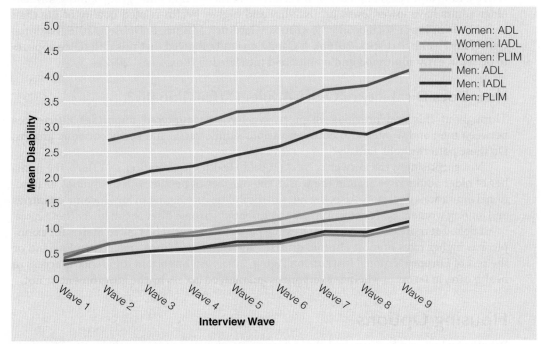

From Verbrugge, L. M., Brown, D. C., & Zajacova, A. (in press). Disability rises gradually for a cohort of older Americans, *Journals of Gerontology: Psychological Sciences*. doi:10.1093/geronb/gbw002

As you can see in ▶ Figure 15.9, the number of difficulties with ADLs, IADLs, and PLIMs increases as men and women age (Verbrugge et al., 2017). Such limitations increase rapidly when the person nears death. People who live longer show both fewer disabilities on average as well as slower increases in disability over time. By paying close attention to the number and extent of disabilities, healthcare professionals and family members may get advance warning of serious underlying problems.

What Causes Functional Limitations and Disability in Older Adults?

If you and your classmates created a list of all the conditions you believe cause functional limitations and disabilities in older adults, the list undoubtedly would be long. (Try it and see for yourself.) But by strategically combining a large representative sample of conditions with sophisticated statistical analyses, this list can be shortened greatly. If these steps are taken, what conditions best predict future problems in functioning?

In a classic longitudinal study conducted over three decades, Strawbridge and colleagues (1998) found that smoking, heavy drinking, physical inactivity, depression, social isolation, and fair or poor perceived health predicted who would become disabled in some way. As predicted by Verbrugge and Jette (1994), lack of physical activity is a powerful predictor of later disability and with higher rates of cancer, cardiovascular disease, diabetes, and obesity, all of which result in higher rates of disability and premature death (Afilalo, 2016; Gretebeck et al., 2012; Rockwood, 2016).

How Important Are Socioeconomic Factors?

Once we have identified the specific conditions that are highly predictive of future functional limitations, an important question is whether the appropriate intervention and prevention programs should be targeted at particular groups of people. That is, would people who are well educated and have high incomes have the same rate of key chronic conditions as people in lower socioeconomic groups? If not, then people with different socioeconomic backgrounds have different needs.

Research indicates a fairly strong and consistent relationship between socioeconomic status and health-related quality of life. Across all racial and ethnic groups, more affluent older adults have lower levels of disability and higher health-related quality of life than individuals in lower socioeconomic groups (Gardiner, Mishra, & Dobson, 2016; National Center for Health Statistics, 2016a). A Canadian study showed that this difference appears to be set in early adulthood and maintained into late life (Ross et al., 2012).

How Does Disability in Older Adults Differ Globally?

Throughout this and previous chapters, we have encountered important differences between men and women and between various ethnic/racial and socioeconomic groups. Do these patterns hold globally?

Not surprisingly, the answer is "yes" (World Health Organization, 2012). As the number of older adults rises around the world, the number of people with disabilities or functional limitations does, too. Also, the rates of disabilities are higher in low-income countries and among women. Early detection and treatment of chronic disease can lower these rates.

Looked at more closely, some interesting patterns emerge. The United States, for example, has higher rates of most chronic diseases and functional impairment than England or the rest of Europe (National Institute on Aging, 2012). An important difference is access to health care, in terms of whether everyone is guaranteed access by the government or not.

Housing Options

Where you live, and how you feel about it, is a critical aspect of personal identity. We experience this every time someone asks us, "Where do you live?" For most people, it is the sense of place that makes the difference. A sense of place refers to the cognitive and emotional attachments that a person puts on his or her place of residence, by which a "house" is made into a "home."

Throughout adulthood, people adapt to changes in the places where they live, sometimes severing connections with past settings (Rowles & Watkins, 2003; Wahl, 2015). Making a change in where people live, and having to psychologically disconnect with a place where they may have lived for many decades, can be difficult and traumatic. There is no question people develop attachments to place, develop a sense of place, and derive a major portion of their identity from it.

Rowles (2006) discusses the process of how a place becomes a home. Because of the psychological connections, the sense that one is "at home" becomes a major concern in relocation, especially if the relocation involves giving up one's home. This attachment to place appears to be cross-cultural phenomenon (Felix et al., 2015).

Aging in Place

Feeling one is "at home" is a major aspect of aging in place. Providing older adults a place to call their own that supports the development of the psychological attachments necessary to convert the place to a home is key for successful aging in place (Scheidt & Schwarz, 2010; Wahl, 2015). Aging in place provides a way for older adults to continue finding aspects of self-identity in where they live, and to take advantage of support systems that are established and familiar by balancing environmental press and competence through selection and compensation. Being able to maintain one's independence in the community is often important for people, especially in terms of their self-esteem and ability to continue engaging in meaningful ways with friends, family, and others.

Whether a person can age in place usually depends on their functional health. Functional health *refers to the ability to perform the activities of daily living (ADLs), instrumental activities of daily living (IADLs), and physical limitations (PLIMs) discussed earlier in this section.* As a person's functional health diminishes, the level of support needed from the environment increases and the optimal housing situation changes.

---

sense of place

Cognitive and emotional attachments that a person puts on his or her place of residence, by which a "house" is made into a "home."

functional health

Ability to perform the activities of daily living (ADLs), instrumental activities of daily living (IADLs), and physical limitations (PLIMs).

The competence–environmental press model provides two options for people who experience difficulties dealing with the tasks of daily life. On one hand, people can increase their competency and develop better or new skills for handling. To better remember where you put your car keys, you can learn a new memory strategy. On the other hand, people can lower the environmental press by modifying the environment to make the task easier; putting a hook for the car keys next to the door you exit so you see them on your way out.

These two options represent applications of theory to real-world settings that also apply to helping people deal with the challenges they face in handling tasks of daily living in their homes. When it comes to these kinds of issues, the most frequent solution involves modifying one's home (i.e., changing the environment) in order to create a new optimal balance or better "fit" between competence and environmental press (Scharlach & Lehning, 2016; Scheidt & Schwarz, 2010).

Many strategies are available for modifying a home to help a person accommodate changing competencies. Minor structural changes, such as installing assistive devices (e.g., hand rails in bathrooms and door handles that are easier to grip), are common strategies. In other cases, more extensive modifications may be needed to make a home fully accessible, such as widening doorways, lowering countertops, adding power stairlifts, and constructing ramps.

Although minor alterations can often be done at low cost, more extensive modifications needed by people with greater limitations may be unaffordable for low-income individuals. Even though the cost of such interventions is significantly lower than placement in long-term care facilities or assisted living, many people simply cannot afford them. As a result, many older adults with functional impairments experience a mismatch between their competency and their environment (Granbom et al., 2016; Iwarsson et al., 2012; Wahl, 2015).

Research indicates home modifications done to address difficulties with accomplishing activities of daily living (ADLs) typically reduce disability-related outcomes (Iwarsson et al., 2012; Wahl, 2015; Yuen & Vogtle, 2016). Although home modification can help reduce falls in older adults (Ripp, Jones, & Zhang, 2016), understanding the role of self-efficacy beliefs in falling is also an important factor to address in successful interventions to reduce falling (Dadgari et al., 2015).

One way that older adults can age in place is to renovate their home

Assisted Living

Bessie lived in the same home for 57 years. Her familiar surroundings enabled her to compensate for and manage the challenges of failing eyesight and worsening arthritis that made it hard to walk. Eventually, though, her health problems interfered with her ability to live alone. Finally, her children convinced her that she needed to relocate to an assisted living facility that would provide the necessary support for her to continue to have her own space.

Bessie is fairly typical of people who move to assisted living facilities. Assisted living facilities *provide a supportive living arrangement for people who need assistance with ADLs or IADLs but who are not so impaired physically or cognitively that they need 24-hour care.* Estimates are that nearly two-thirds of residents of assisted living facilities over age 65 have an ADL or IADL limitation (AgingStats.gov, 2016) and that about half have some degree of memory impairment (Pynoos et al., 2010). Assisted living facilities usually provide support for activities of daily living (e.g., assistance with bathing) as well as meals and other services. Healthcare personnel are available to assist with medications and certain other procedures.

Assisted living facilities provide a range of services and care, but they are not designed to provide intensive, around-the-clock medical care. As residents become frailer, their needs may go beyond those the facility can provide. Policies governing discharge for this reason, usually to a long-term care facility, may result in competing interests between providing

assisted living facilities
Supportive living arrangement for people who need assistance with ADLs or IADLs but who are not so impaired physically or cognitively that they need 24-hour care.

for the residents' increasing medical needs and providing a familiar environment. To help families choose the best option, the National Center for Assisted Living (2016) provides a *Consumer's Guide* that leads families through a series of issues such as the level of care needs, now and in the future, location, and various key metrics regarding staffing. Unfortunately, some older adults eventually need a higher level of care that is available at assisted living facilities, so they must turn to long-term care facilities such as nursing homes.

Nursing Homes

The last place Sadie thought she would end up was in a bed in a nursing home. "That's a place where old people go to die," she would tell her friends. "It's not gonna be for me." But here she is. Sadie fell a few weeks ago and broke her hip. Because she lives alone, she needs to stay in the facility for rehabilitation until she recovers. She detests the food; "tasteless," she calls it. Doris, who is 87 and has dementia, lives a few doors down. Doris is likely to live there for the remainder of her life.

Sadie and Doris are representative of the people who live in nursing homes—some temporarily, some permanently. If given the choice, the vast majority of older adults do not want to live there; they and their families would prefer that they age in place. Sometimes, though, placement in a nursing home is necessary because of the older person's needs or the family's circumstances.

A nursing home *is a type of long-term care facility that provides medical care 24 hours a day, 7 days a week using a team of healthcare professionals that includes physicians (who must be on call at all times), nurses, therapists (e.g., physical, occupational), and others.* Misconceptions about nursing homes are common. Contrary to what some people believe, only about 5% of older adults live in nursing homes on any given day. As you can see in ▶ Figure 15.10, the percentage of older adults enrolled in Medicare who live in a long-term care facility at any given point in time increases from 1% in those aged 65 to74 to 15% of

nursing home

Type of long-term care facility that provide medical care 24 hours a day, 7 days a week using a team of healthcare professionals that includes physicians (who must be on call at all times), nurses, therapists (e.g., physical, occupational), and others.

▶ **Figure 15-10**

Percentage distribution of Medicare beneficiaries age 65 and over residing in selected residential settings, by age group, 2013.

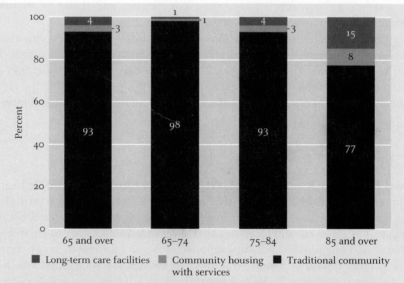

NOTE: Community housing with services applies to respondents who reported they lived in retirement communities or apartments, senior citizen housing, continuing care retirement facilities, assisted living facilities, staged living communities, board and care facilities/homes, and similar situations and who reported they had access to one or more of the following services through their place of residence: meal preparation, cleaning or housekeeping services, laundry services, or help with medications. Respondents were asked about access to these services, but not whether they actually used the services. A residence (or unit) is considered a long-term care facility if it is certified by Medicare or Medicaid; or has 3 or more beds, is licensed as a nursing home or other long-term care facility, and provides at least one personal care service; or provides 24-hour, 7-day-a-week supervision by a non-family, paid caregiver. Reference population: These data refer to Medicare beneficiaries.

From Centers for Medicare and Medicaid Services. (2016). 2013 *Medicare current beneficiary access to care PUF.* Retrieved from www.cms.gov/Research-Statistics-Data-and-Systems/Downloadable-Public-Use-Files/MCBS-Public-Use-File/index.html.

adults over age 85 (AgingStats.gov, 2016). Someone who turns 65 today has a nearly 70% chance of spending some time in a long-term care facility, with women requiring longer care (3.7 years on average) than men (2.2 years on average) (LongTermCare.gov, 2016). The gender difference is due to the fact that older women take care of their husbands at home, but then they, in turn, need to relocate to long-term care facilities for their own care because their husbands are, on average, deceased.

The decision to place a family member in a nursing home is a difficult one (Caron, Ducharme, & Griffith, 2006; Krull, 2013). Placement decisions can occur in reaction to a crisis, such as a person's impending discharge from a hospital or another health emergency, or can be the outcome of many months or even years of conversation among family members. Because the level of impairment of nursing home residents is typically severe (with an average of four out of a possible five areas of impairment with ADLs and 60% with moderate to severe cognitive impairment; Centers for Medicare and Medicaid Services, 2016b), the placement decision tends to be made by partners or adult children, often in consultation with medical and spiritual advisers, a finding that generalizes across ethnic groups (Koss & Ekerdt, in press; Krull, 2013; Lord et al., 2016; Ruiz et al., 2016).

Selecting a nursing home should be done carefully. The Centers for Medicare and Medicaid Services (2016a) provides a detailed *Nursing Home Quality Initiative* website that is a guide for choosing a nursing home based on several key quality factors. Among the most important things to consider are quality of life for residents (e.g., whether residents are well groomed, the food is tasty, and rooms contain comfortable furniture); quality of care (whether staff members respond quickly to calls, whether staff and family are involved in care decisions); safety (whether there are enough staff members, whether hallways are free of clutter); and other issues (whether outdoor areas are available for residents to use). These aspects of nursing homes reflect the dimensions that states consider in their inspections and licensing process.

Emerging Housing Arrangements

In response to the need to provide support for older adults who require assistance with ADLs and IADLs and their desire to age in place, new approaches to housing options have emerged that provide both. These movements include programs that infuse a different culture into nursing homes as well as those approaches that create small-scale living (usually six to ten residents) in a community-based setting with an emphasis on living well rather than on receiving care (Pynoos et al., 2010).

The Eden Alternative (Eden Alternative, 2017) seeks to eliminate loneliness, helplessness, and boredom from the lives of those living in long-term care facilities and to create a community in which life is worth living. This can be achieved by rethinking how care is provided in the older person's own home or in long-term care facilities through training.

The Green House Project (Jenkins, 2016) creates small neighborhood-integrated homes for six to ten residents in which older adults receive a high level of personal and professional care. The Green House Project takes the principles of the Eden Alternative and creates a different culture of care in the community.

The Pioneer Network (Pioneer Network, 2017) focuses on changing the culture of aging in America irrespective of where older adults live. Like the Eden Alternative, this approach focuses on respecting older adults and providing maximally supportive environments for them. The Pioneer Network, as part of the larger cultural change in caring for older adults, advocates for a major emphasis on making nursing homes more like a home.

Various cohousing and cluster housing options provide additional alternative approaches. Cohousing is a planned community that is modest in size and is built around an open, walkable space designed to foster social interaction among neighbors (Klimczuk, 2017; Pynoos et al., 2010). Neighbors provide care for each other when it is needed as a way to foster personal autonomy. Cluster housing combines the aging-in-place philosophy with supportive services (de Jong et al., 2012). A key feature is that services are provided to the residents by staff hired by the owner or by a service provider under contract. The aging-in-place philosophy in these settings emphasizes individual choice on the part of residents in terms of what services to use. This approach is also being adopted in other countries, such as the Netherlands and Spain (de Jong et al., 2012; Fernández-Carro, 2016).

These alternatives to traditional housing options for older adults indicate that the choices for how one spends late life are becoming more varied and that appropriate support systems are in place. Such alternatives will be important as the baby-boom generation enters the years in which support services will be needed even more. Researchers need to focus their attention on documenting the types of advantages these alternatives offer and exploring their relative effectiveness.

Elder Abuse and Neglect

Arletta, an 82-year-old woman in relatively poor health, has been living with her 60-year-old daughter, Sally, for the past two years. Recently, neighbors became concerned because they had not seen Arletta very often for the last several months. When they did, she looked rather worn, thin, and unkempt. Finally, the neighbors decided that they should do something; so they called the local office of the Department of Human Services. Upon hearing the details of the situation, a caseworker immediately investigated. The caseworker found that Arletta was severely malnourished, had not bathed in weeks, and appeared disoriented. Based on these findings, the agency concluded that Arletta was a victim of neglect. She was moved temporarily to a county nursing home.

Although elder abuse, neglect, and exploitation are difficult to define precisely, the following categories are commonly used (National Center for State Courts, 2016):

- *Physical abuse:* use of physical force that may result in bodily injury, physical pain, or impairment
- *Sexual abuse:* nonconsensual sexual contact of any kind
- *Emotional or psychological abuse:* infliction of anguish, pain, or distress
- *Financial or material exploitation:* illegal or improper use of an older adult's funds, property, or assets
- *Abandonment:* desertion of an older adult by an individual who had physical custody or otherwise had assumed responsibility for providing care for the older adult
- *Neglect:* refusal or failure to fulfill any part of a person's obligation or duties to an older adult
- *Self-neglect:* behaviors of an older person that threaten his or her health or safety, excluding those conscious and voluntary decisions made by a mentally competent and healthy adult

Researchers estimate that perhaps one in four vulnerable older adults are at risk for some type of abuse, neglect, or exploitation (Nerenberg, 2010; Roberto, 2016; Wong & Rothenhaus, 2014). Unfortunately, only a small proportion of these cases are reported to authorities; of those that are, neglect is the most common type. Elder abuse is often noted by physicians first, either through routine examinations or in emergency departments in hospitals (Linden & Olshaker, 2014). Financial exploitation, particularly through electronic means, costs older adults billions of dollars annually (DeLiema, Yon, & Wilber, 2016). Researchers and policy makers argue that prevention of financial exploitation can be greatly assisted by banks and other financial institutions, who can monitor account activity and question unusual withdrawals (Lichtenberg, 2016).

Current approaches to elder abuse, especially by adult children, conceptualize it not as an outcome of a caregiving situation, but as a development from the longer ongoing relationship between parent and child (Pickering & Phillips, 2014). Similarly, abuse by intimate partners may also be tied to former existing relationship issues even if abuse had not been present previously (Bows, in press; Roberto, McPherson, & Brossoie, 2013). Understanding, detecting, and addressing elder abuse requires culturally sensitive approaches that reflect the values of older adults in different societies (Teaster, Harley, & Kettaneh,

Think About It

How are housing options related to cognitive ability and to the competence–environmental press model?

2014). Although certain characteristics, such as a correlation with disability, occur across cultures, how those characteristics are manifest differ. Likewise, prevention and intervention strategies must take cultural differences into account.

As with abuse at other points in the life span, identifying and reporting it is everyone's concern. If you suspect that an older adult is a victim of elder abuse, neglect, or exploitation, the best thing you can do is contact your local adult protective services office and report it.

Social Security and Medicare

Without doubt, the most important societal changes in the United States regarding older adults during the 20th century were the creation of retirement income plans such as Social Security and other pension plans as well as universal basic healthcare plans such as Medicare (Polivka, 2010). Similar programs also were initiated in other developed countries. Even though the costs of such programs continue to rise dramatically, Social Security and Medicare are so strongly supported that elected officials are often afraid to discuss and implement much-needed reforms.

Such programs have reduced the number of older adults who live below the poverty line (AgingStats.gov, 2016). However, projections indicate that baby boomers and Generation X members will have lower incomes in old age due to fundamental changes in pension availability and lower savings rates.

In analyzing the financial well-being of older adults, economists argue that older adults should be evaluated by different standards compared with younger or middle-aged adults (AgingStats.gov, 2016). Economists often argue that older adults need 200% of the federal poverty limit to make ends meet, especially with respect to healthcare costs. By this measure, women and minorities are especially at risk financially.

To capture these issues, the Wider Opportunities for Women and the Gerontology Institute at the University of Massachusetts Boston developed the Elder Economic Security Standard™ Index. The Elder Index is a measure of the income that older adults need to meet their basic housing, health care, transportation, food, and other essential costs and to age in place. Separate indices are available for cities and counties in the United States.

The aging of the baby boomers presents difficult and expensive problems. In fiscal year 2017, federal spending on the various parts of Social Security and Medicare alone was expected to be over $1.5 trillion in a total budget of roughly $4 trillion (Congressional Budget Office, 2017). Note that this expenditure for just these two programs is more than 37% of the federal budget. Without major reforms in these programs, such growth will force extremely difficult choices in how to pay for them.

Social Security

Social Security began in 1935 as an initiative by President Franklin D. Roosevelt to "frame a law which will give some measure of protection to the average citizen and to his family against the loss of a job and against poverty-ridden old age" (Roosevelt, 1935). Thus, Social Security was originally intended to provide a *supplement* to savings and other means of financial support.

Two key things have changed since then. First, the proportion of people who reach age 65 has increased significantly. In 1940, only about 54% of men and 61% of women reached age 65. Today, that's increased to about 75% of men and 85% of women. Since 1940, men collect payments about 3 years longer, and women collect about 5 years longer. Both trends increase the cost of the program.

Second, revisions to the original law have changed Social Security so it now represents the primary source of financial support after retirement for most U.S. citizens, and the only source for many (Polivka, 2010). Since the 1970s, more workers have been included in employer-sponsored defined contribution plans such as 401(k), 403(b), 457 plans, and mutual funds, as well as various types of individual retirement accounts (IRAs), but fewer defined benefit traditional pension plans (Polivka, 2010; Polivka & Luo, 2015). A key difference in these plans is defined contribution plans rely a great deal on employee participation (i.e., workers saving money for retirement) whereas traditional pension programs did not require employee participation as they provided a monthly income for life paid completely by the company.

The primary challenge facing Social Security is the aging of the baby boomers and the much smaller Generation X that immediately follows (National Academy of Social Insurance, 2016). Because Social Security is funded by payroll taxes, the amount of money each worker must pay depends to a large extent on the ratio of the number of people paying Social Security taxes to the number of people collecting benefits. By 2030, this ratio will drop nearly in half; that is, by the time baby boomers have largely retired, there will only be two workers paying into Social Security to support every person collecting benefits, down from 3-to-1 today.

One point that confuses many people is the benefits received do not come from an "account" that reflects what you actually contributed over your employed career. Because Social Security is a revenue-in/payments-out model, people do not build up Social Security "savings." Rather, the money they pay in taxes today goes out as payments to those who are collecting benefits today. So the payments current workers receive in the future will actually be from the taxes paid by workers in the labor force at that future time. That's why the payee/recipient ratio matters—Social Security tax rates must inevitably go up or the benefits received must go down if there are fewer people paying to support an increasing number of recipients.

Over most of the history of Social Security, revenues were greater than payments because of the large number of people paying in compared to the lower number of people collecting benefits. Excess revenue was saved for the future. But that changed in 2010, when benefit payments first exceeded revenues, a situation that remains true today. The interest from those previous saved revenues in the Social Security Trust Fund is now being spent to make up the difference, and will keep the gap closed until around 2020. After that, the Trust Fund itself gets spent. By 2034, all of the Trust Fund assets will be gone. At that point, revenue from Social Security taxes would only cover about 75% of the benefits promised (Social Security and Medicare Boards of Trustees, 2016).

Despite knowing the fiscal realities for decades, Congress has not yet taken the actions necessary to ensure the long-term financial stability of Social Security.

Medicare

Over 55 million U.S. citizens depend on Medicare for their medical insurance (Kaiser Family Foundation, 2016). To be eligible, a person must meet one of the following criteria: be over age 65, be disabled, or have permanent kidney failure. Medicare consists of three parts (Centers for Medicare and Medicaid Services, 2016d): Part A, that covers inpatient hospital services, skilled nursing facilities, home health services, and hospice care; Part B, covers the cost of physician services, outpatient hospital services, medical equipment and supplies, and other health services and supplies; and Part D, that provides some coverage for prescription medications. Expenses relating to most long-term care needs are funded by Medicaid, another major healthcare program funded by the U.S. government and aimed at people who are poor. Out-of-pocket expenses associated with copayments and other charges are often paid by supplemental insurance policies, sometimes referred to as "Medigap" policies (Medicare.gov, 2016).

Like Social Security, Medicare is funded by a payroll tax. However, whereas the Social Security payroll tax has an upper limit on the salary used to compute how much people pay (the upper limit of salary increases each year), the Medicare payroll tax is applied to one's entire salary. Still, the funding problems facing Medicare are similar to those facing Social Security and are greatly exacerbated by the aging of the baby boomers. In addition, Medicare costs have increased dramatically as a result of the rapidly increasing costs of health care (Social Security and Medicare Boards of Trustees, 2016).

Cost containment of health care remains a major political concern, and the issue has been caught in the overall debate about healthcare reform in the United States. Also, because Medicare is a government-run healthcare program, it continues to be controversial among those who oppose such approaches to health care. But unlike Social Security, Medicare has already been subjected to significant cuts in expenditures, typically through reduced payouts to healthcare providers. President Obama included reductions to the Medicare Advantage (Part C) program in his Affordable Care Act as part of his overall strategy to control increase in healthcare costs.

Taken together, the challenges facing society concerning older adults' financial security and health insurance coverage will continue to be major political and economic issues throughout the first half of the 21st century at least. There are no easy answers and many political challenges, but open discussion of the various arguments and the stark budget realities will be essential for creating the optimal solution. Public misperceptions of how the programs actually work, and the tough choices that must be faced are discussed in more detail in the What Do *You* Think? feature.

What Do *You* Think? What to Do About Social Security and Medicare?

As pointed out earlier in the chapter, the amount of benefits people collect in Social Security and Medicare is not directly connected to the amount they paid in taxes over their working careers. That's a point many people misunderstand—they think they get out what they have put in their personal account. As explained in the text, this misperception makes it very difficult to make changes in the benefits structure (the cost) of these programs.

The fact is, the average person collects substantially more in lifetime Medicare benefits than he or she paid in total taxes during his or her working career (Steuerle & Quakenbush, 2015). This imbalance (and misperception) is a major reason why restructuring the benefits or raising copayments to control costs is so difficult to do, and why the current benefit structure is unsustainable.

There's another aspect to the problem. To keep Medicare Part B and Part D premiums affordable, the typical older American only pays about 25% of the actual cost through premiums, deductibles, and co-insurance (higher income people pay a larger share, up to 80%). Where does the rest of the money come from? General revenue in the national budget pays for the rest, and is why there is increasing pressure to cut reimbursements to healthcare providers under Medicare.

Similar analyses can be done for Social Security, but with a different outcome. Whereas nearly all Medicare recipients get much more out of the program than they paid in taxes, that's not true for many people regarding Social Security. Most people will pay more in taxes to support current beneficiaries (Steuerle & Quakenbush, 2015).

The biggest challenge is controlling the costs of Medicare given the arrival of the baby boomers as beneficiaries. But explaining to those who are already receiving or are about to receive the benefit is a daunting task. That's why most proposals under discussion target individuals who are about 10 years away from receiving Medicare benefits.

The political debates around Social Security and Medicare will not end soon. What is clear, though, is the current financial model is unsustainable over the long run, and action, especially with respect to Medicare, is needed now.

TEST YOURSELF 15.5

Recall

1. Activities of daily living (ADLs) include functioning in the areas of bathing, toileting, walking, dressing, and _____.

2. A type of long-term care facility that provides medical care 24 hours per day, 7 days per week using a variety of health-care professionals is a _____.

3. Refusal or failure to fulfill any part of a person's obligation or duties to an older adult is officially termed _____.

4. The two most important public policy issues in the United States that are being affected by the aging baby-boom generation are Social Security and _____.

Interpret

- How might the large generation now graduating from high school affect Social Security in the future?

Apply

- How would the competence–environmental press framework, presented earlier in this chapter, apply specifically to the various types of housing and nursing homes discussed in this section?

Check your answers to the Recall Questions at the end of the chapter.

15.1 Theories of Psychosocial Aging

What is social involvement and healthy aging?

- Healthy aging involves avoiding disease, being engaged with life, and maintaining high cognitive and physical functioning. The basic premises of healthy aging include keeping a balance between the various gains and losses that occur over time and minimizing the influence of factors unrelated to aging.

What is the competence–environmental press model, and how do docility and proactivity relate to the model?

- According to the competence–environmental press theory, people's optimal adaptation occurs when there is a balance between their ability to cope and the level of environmental demands placed on them. When balance is not achieved, behavior becomes maladaptive. The model has wide applicability in aging.

- People exhibit proactivity when they choose new behaviors to meet new desires and exert control over their lives. In contrast, people demonstrate docility when they allow the situation to dictate the options they have.

What is the proactivity and corrective proactivity model?

- The preventive and corrective proactivity model explains how life stressors and lack of good congruence in person-environment interactions result in poor life outcomes. Key buffers (external and internal resources) and proactive behaviors lower the negative impact of stressors and help people cope.

- Preventive adaptations are actions that avoid stressors and increase or build social resources. Corrective adaptations are actions taken in response to stressors and can be facilitated by internal and external resources.

15.2 Personality, Social Cognition, and Spirituality

What is integrity in late life? How can people achieve it?

- Older adults face the Eriksonian struggle of integrity versus despair primarily through a life review. Integrity involves accepting one's life for what it is; despair involves bitterness about one's past. People who reach integrity become self-affirming and self-accepting, and they judge their lives to have been worthwhile and good.

How is well-being defined in adulthood? How do people view themselves differently as they age?

- Subjective well-being is an evaluation of one's life that is associated with positive feelings. In life-span developmental psychology, subjective well-being is usually assessed by measures of life satisfaction, happiness, and self-esteem.

- Neuroscience research shows a developmental connection with brain activity in the prefrontal cortex and the amygdala.

What role does spirituality play in late life?

- By later life, most people have made the transition from False Self (the superficial, external self) to True Self (the experience of dwelling in union with the essence of everything in the universe, a sense of "inner knowing" that does not see anything with absolute certainty).

- Spiritual support is a key factor in older adults' coping. People who are more involved and committed to their faith have better physical and mental health.

15.3 I Used to Work at . . . : Living in Retirement

What does being retired mean?

- Retirement is a complex process by which people withdraw from full-time employment. No single definition is adequate for all ethnic groups; self-definition involves several factors, including eligibility for certain social programs.

Why do people retire?

- People generally retire because they choose to, although some people are forced to retire or do so because of serious health problems, such as cardiovascular disease or cancer. However, there are important gender and ethnic differences in why people retire and how they label themselves after retirement.

How do people adjust to retirement?

- Retirement is an important life transition. Most people are satisfied with retirement. Most retired people maintain their health, friendship networks, and activity levels—at least in the years immediately following retirement. For men, personal life priorities are all-important; little is known about women's retirement satisfaction.

What employment and volunteer opportunities are available for older adults?

- Increasingly, people continue some level of participation in the labor force during retirement, usually for financial reasons. Labor force participation among older adults continues to increase. Volunteer work is another way of achieving personal fulfillment and staying active in retirement.

15.4 Friends and Family in Late Life

What role do friends and family play in late life?

- A person's social convoy is an important source of satisfaction in late life. Patterns of friendships among older adults are similar to those among young adults, but older adults are more selective. Sibling relationships are especially important in old age. Because people cannot choose their siblings as they do their friends, compared with friendships, these relationships often take more work. Although they tend to have smaller social networks, older adults' social contact is motivated by a variety of goals, including information seeking, self-concept, and emotional regulation, explained in the theory of socioemotional selectivity.

What are older adults' marriages and same-sex partnerships like?

- Long-term marriages tend to be happy until one partner develops serious health problems. Older married couples show a lower potential for marital conflict and greater potential for pleasure. Long-term gay and lesbian relationships tend to be similar in characteristics to long-term heterosexual marriages; issues pertaining to legal rights continue to present challenges.

What is it like to provide basic care for one's partner?

- Caring for a partner puts considerable strain on the relationship. The degree of marital satisfaction strongly affects how spousal caregivers perceive stress. Although caught off guard initially, most spousal caregivers are able to provide adequate care. Perceptions of competence among spousal caregivers at the outset of caregiving may be especially important.

How do people cope with widowhood? How do men and women differ?

- Widowhood is a difficult transition for most people. Feelings of loneliness are hard to cope with. Men generally have problems in social relationships and in household tasks; women tend to have more severe financial problems. Some widowed people remarry, partly to solve loneliness and financial problems.

What special issues are involved in being a great-grandparent?

- Becoming a great-grandparent is an important source of personal satisfaction for many older adults. Great-grandparents as a group are more similar to each other than grandparents are. Three aspects of great-grandparenthood are important: It offers a sense of personal and family renewal, provides new diversions in life, and is a major life milestone.

15.5 Social Issues and Aging

Who are frail older adults? How common is frailty?

- The number of frail older adults is growing. Frailty is defined in terms of impairment in activities of daily living (basic self-care skills) and instrumental activities of daily living (actions that require intellectual competence or planning). As many as half of those over age 85 may need assistance with ADLs, IADLs, or PLIMs. Supportive environments are useful in optimizing the balance between competence and environmental press.

What housing options are available for older adults?

- Most older adults prefer to age in place; home modification offers one option to achieve that. Assisted living facilities offer support for ADLs and IADLs while providing a significant degree of independence. Nursing homes provide 24/7 medical care for those who need continual assistance. Newer alternatives include the Eden Alternative, the Green House Project, and cohousing options that focus on providing greater support for people to remain in the community.

How do you know whether an older adult is abused, neglected, or exploited?

- Abuse and neglect of older adults is an increasing problem. However, abuse and neglect are difficult to define precisely. Several categories are used, including physical abuse, sexual abuse, emotional or psychological abuse, financial or material exploitation, abandonment, neglect, and self-neglect. Most perpetrators are family members, usually partners or adult children of the victims. Research indicates that abuse results from a complex interaction of characteristics of the caregiver and care recipient.

What are the key social policy issues affecting older adults?

- Although initially designed as an income supplement, Social Security has become the primary source of retirement income for most U.S. citizens. The aging of the baby-boom generation will place considerable stress on the system's financing.

- Medicare is the principal health insurance program for adults in the United States over age 65. Cost containment is a major concern, and there are no easy answers for ensuring the system's future viability.

Test Yourself Recall Answers

15.1 1. Healthy aging **2.** competence, environmental press **15.2 1.** integrity versus despair **2.** subjective well-being **3.** spirituality **15.3 1.** complex process by which people gradually withdraw from employment **2.** because they choose to do so **3.** satisfied **4.** volunteering **15.4 1.** siblings **2.** marital conflict **3.** lower **4.** Widows **5.** the fact that it is a milestone **15.5 1.** eating **2.** nursing home **3.** neglect **4.** Medicare

Key Terms

healthy aging (503)

competence (503)

environmental press (503)

adaptation level (504)

zone of maximum performance potential (504)

zone of maximum comfort (504)

proactivity (505)

docility (505)

preventive adaptations (505)

corrective adaptations (505)

integrity versus despair (508)

life review (508)

subjective well-being (509)

spiritual support (513)

social convoy (519)

socioemotional selectivity (521)

frail older adults (526)

activities of daily living (ADLs) (526)

instrumental activities of daily living (IADLs) (526)

physical limitations (PLIMs) (526)

sense of place (528)

functional health (528)

assisted living facilities (529)

nursing home (530)

Dying and Bereavement

When famous people such as Prince or Amy Winehouse die unexpectedly, people are confronted with the reality that death happens to everyone. Many of us die from the same conditions; the most likely ways people die across the life span are shown in ▶ Figure 16.1. But the plain truth is that each of us makes the transition from life to death.

We have a paradoxical relationship with death. Sometimes we are fascinated by it. As tourists, we visit places where famous people died or are buried. We watch as television newscasts show scenes of devastation in natural disasters and war. But when it comes to pondering our own death or that of people close to us, we experience difficulty. As French writer and reformer La Rochefoucauld wrote over 300 years

Amy Winehouse

Prince

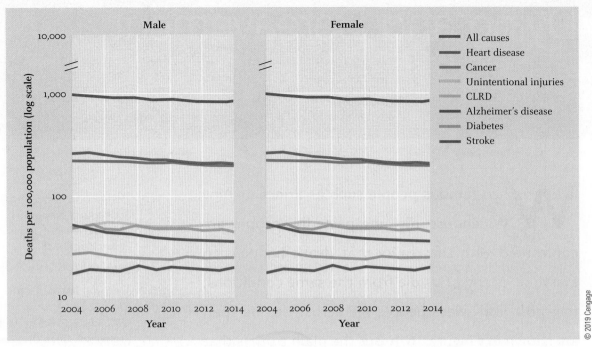

Figure 16.1

Age-adjusted death rates for selected causes of death for all ages, by sex: 2004–2014.

From National Center for Health Statistics. (2016). Health, United States, 2015. Figure 2. Retrieved from www.cdc.gov/nchs/data/hus/hus15.pdf.

© 2019 Cengage

ago, "looking into the sun is easier than contemplating our death." When death is personal, we become uneasy. Looking at the sun is hard indeed.

In this chapter we delve into thanatology. **Thanatology** *is the study of death, dying, grief, bereavement, and social attitudes toward these issues*. We first consider definitional and ethical issues surrounding death. Next, we look specifically at the process of dying. Dealing with grief is important for survivors, so we consider this topic in the third section. Finally, we examine how people view death at different points in the life span.

thanatology

Study of death, dying, grief, bereavement, and social attitudes toward these issues.

16.1 Definitions and Ethical Issues

LEARNING OBJECTIVES

- How is death defined?
- What legal and medical criteria are used to determine when death occurs?
- What are the ethical dilemmas surrounding euthanasia?
- What issues surround the costs of life-sustaining care?

Ernesto and Paulina had been married 48 years when Ernesto developed terminal pancreatic cancer. Ernesto was suffering terrible pain and begged Paulina to make it stop. He said she would not let their pet suffer this way, so why let him? Paulina heard about "mercy killing" that involved administering high dosages of certain medications, but she believed this was the same as murder. Yet, she could hardly bear to watch her beloved husband suffer. Paulina wondered what she should do.

When one first thinks about it, death seems a simple concept to define: It is the point when a person is no longer alive. Similarly, dying appears to be simply the process of making the transition from being alive to being dead. It all seems clear enough, doesn't it? But death and dying are actually far more complicated concepts.

As we will see, there are many cultural and religious differences in the definition of death and the customs surrounding it. The meaning of death depends on the observer's perspective as well as the specific medical and biological criteria one uses.

Sociocultural Definitions of Death

Although death is one of the few truly universal experiences, each culture has its own ways of thinking about, defining, and ritualizing it (Bustos, 2007; Gire, 2014; Penson, 2004). All cultures have their own views. Some cultures ritually pull their hair as a sign of grief (Lewis, 2013). Melanesians have a term, *mate*, that includes the extremely sick, the very old, and the dead; the term *toa* refers to all other living people (Counts & Counts, 1985). Other cultures believe the life force leaves the body during sleep or illness, or involves reaching a certain age (Gire, 2014). Still other cultures view death as a transition to a different type of existence that still allows interaction with the living, and some believe there is a circular pattern of multiple deaths and rebirths (Gire, 2014). In Ghana people are said to have a "peaceful" or "good" death if the dying person finished all business and made peace with others before death, and implies being at peace with his or her own death (van der Geest, 2004).

The symbols we use when people die, such as these elaborate caskets from Ghana, provide insights into how cultures think about death.

Mourning rituals, expressions of grief, and states of bereavement also vary in different cultures (Lee, 2010; Norton & Gino, 2014). In the United States and many other countries, the death of a dignitary is marked by lowering flags to half-staff and declaring a formal period of mourning. Some cultures have formalized periods of time during which certain prayers or rituals are performed. After the death of a close relative, Orthodox Jews recite ritual prayers and cover all the mirrors in the house. The men slash their ties as a symbol of loss. In Papua New Guinea, there are accepted time periods for phases of grief (Hemer, 2010). The Muscogee Creek tribe's rituals include digging the grave by hand and giving a "farewell handshake" by throwing a handful of dirt into the grave before covering it (Walker & Balk, 2007). Ancestor worship, a deep respectful feeling toward individuals from whom a family is descended or who are important to them, is an important part of customs of death in many Asian cultures (Roszko, 2010). We must keep in mind the experiences of our culture or particular group may not generalize to other cultures or groups.

Death can be a truly cross-cultural experience. The international outpouring of grief over the death of world leaders such Nelson Mandela in 2013, the thousands killed in various terrorist attacks against the United States and other countries, and the hundreds of thousands killed in such natural disasters as the earthquake in Haiti in 2010 drew much attention to the ways the deaths of people we do not know personally can still affect us. It is at these times we realize death happens to us all and death can simultaneously be personal and public.

The many ways of viewing death can be seen in various funeral customs. You may have experienced a range of different types of funeral customs, from small, private services to elaborate rituals. Variations in the customs surrounding death are reflected in some of the most iconic structures on earth, such as the pyramids in Egypt, and some of the most beautiful, such as the Taj Mahal in India.

Legal and Medical Definitions

Sociocultural approaches help us understand the different ways people conceptualize and understand death, but they do not address a fundamental question: How do we determine someone has died? The medical and legal communities grappled with this question for centuries and continue to do so today. Let's see what the current answers are.

Determining when death occurs has always been subjective. *For hundreds of years, people accepted and applied the criteria that now define* clinical death: *lack of heartbeat and respiration. Today, however, the definition used in most countries is* whole-brain death. In 2010, the American Academy of Neurology proposed new guidelines for determining brain death (Wijdicks et al., 2010). The goal in this revision of the criteria was to provide guidelines that were based on research. According to the guidelines, there are three signs that a person's brain has permanently stopped functioning. First, the person is in a coma, and the cause of the coma is known. Second, all brainstem reflexes have permanently stopped working. Third, breathing has permanently stopped, so that a ventilator, or breathing machine, must be used to keep the body functioning.

The guidelines describe several complex steps physicians must follow to diagnose brain death. In some cases, this involves more than 25 specific tests. For example, the guidelines describe the best way to demonstrate absence of breathing. In contrast to previous guidelines, the current revision states that laboratory tests such as EEG or cerebral flow studies are not needed to determine brain death. The guidelines also make clear that this complex determination of brain death must be completed by a physician who has been trained in diagnosing brain death.

Although these criteria marked a significant advance over earlier definitions, they have still not been adopted at all hospitals in the United States (Greer et al., 2016). This means that somewhat different criteria for determining brain death are applied at different hospitals. This can result in misdiagnosis, delays in organ transplants, and emotionally wrenching decisions for families (Kaplan, 2015).

Brain death is also controversial from some religious perspectives. For example, there is no general consensus whether brain death is accepted as true death under Islamic law (Al-Bar & Chamsi-Pasha, 2015; Miller, 2016). Roman Catholics focus on what they term "natural death" (Kassim & Alias, 2016). When these perspectives are considered, the determination of death can be difficult.

It is possible for a person's cortical functioning to cease while brainstem activity continues; this is a persistent vegetative state, *from which the person does not recover.* This condition can occur following disruption of the blood flow to the brain, a severe head injury, or a drug overdose. Persistent vegetative state allows for spontaneous heartbeat and respiration but not for consciousness. The whole-brain standard does not permit a declaration of death for someone who is in a persistent vegetative state. Because of conditions like persistent vegetative state, family members sometimes face difficult ethical decisions concerning care for the individual. These issues are the focus of the next section.

Ethical Issues

An ambulance screeches to a halt and emergency personnel rush a woman into the emergency room. As a result of an accident at a swimming pool, she has no pulse and no respiration. Working rapidly, the trauma team reestablishes a heartbeat through electric shock. A respirator is connected. An EEG and other tests reveal extensive and irreversible brain damage—she is in a persistent vegetative state. What should be done?

clinical death

Lack of heartbeat and respiration.

whole-brain death

Declared only when the deceased meets eight criteria, which were established in 1981.

persistent vegetative state

Situation in which a person's cortical functioning ceases while brainstem activity continues.

This is an example of the kinds of problems faced in the field of bioethics, *the study of the interface between human values and technological advances in health and life sciences.* Bioethics grew from two bases: respect for individual freedom and the impossibility of establishing any single version of morality by rational argument or common sense. Both of these factors are increasingly based on empirical evidence and cultural contexts (Priaulx, 2013; Sherwin, 2011). In practice, bioethics emphasizes the importance of individual choice and the minimization of harm over the maximization of good. That is, bioethics requires people to weigh how much the patient will benefit from a treatment relative to the amount of suffering he or she will endure as a result of the treatment. Examples of the tough choices required are those facing cancer patients about aggressive treatment for cancer that is quite likely to be fatal in any case and those facing family members about whether to turn off a life-support machine attached to their loved one.

In the arena of death and dying, the most important bioethical issue is euthanasia—*the practice of ending life for reasons of mercy.* The moral dilemma posed by euthanasia becomes apparent when trying to decide the circumstances a person's life should be ended, that implicitly forces one to place a value on the life of another (Bedir & Aksoy, 2011; Kassim & Alias, 2016; Munoz & Fox, 2013). It also makes us think about the difference between "killing" and "letting die" at the end of life (Dickens, Boyle, & Ganzini, 2008). In our society, this dilemma occurs most often when a person is being kept alive by machines or when someone is suffering from a terminal illness. This is the situation confronting Ernesto and Paulina in the opening vignette.

Euthanasia

Euthanasia can be carried out in two different ways: actively and passively (Moeller, Lewis, & Werth, 2010). Active euthanasia *involves the deliberate ending of someone's life, that may be based on a clear statement of the person's wishes or be a decision made by someone else who has the legal authority to do so.* Usually, this involves situations when people are in a persistent vegetative state or suffer from the end stages of a terminal disease. Examples of active euthanasia would be administering a drug overdose or ending a person's life through so-called mercy killing.

A second form of euthanasia, passive euthanasia, *involves allowing a person to die by withholding available treatment.* A ventilator might be disconnected, chemotherapy might be withheld from a patient with terminal cancer, a surgical procedure might not be performed, or food could be withdrawn.

There is debate regarding the need to differentiate active and passive euthanasia (e.g., European Association of Palliative Care, 2011; Garrard & Wilkinson, 2005; Strinic, 2015). Some argue the single label "euthanasia" suffices; others prefer to distinguish between the traditional labels. The main point is that a decision to continue or terminate a person's life is made.

Most Americans favor such actions as disconnecting life support in situations involving patients in a persistent vegetative state, withholding treatment if the person agrees or is in the later stages of a terminal illness, and the concept of assisted death. But feelings also run strongly against such actions for religious or other reasons (Meilaender, 2013; Strinic, 2015). Even political debates incorporate the issue, as demonstrated in the summer of 2009 in the United States when opponents of President Obama's healthcare reform falsely claimed "death panels" would make decisions about terminating life support if the reform measure passed.

Globally, opinions about euthanasia vary (Bosshard & Materstvedt, 2011; Strinic, 2015). Western Europeans tend to view active euthanasia more positively based on less influence of religion and more social welfare services than residents of Eastern European and Islamic countries, who are more influenced by religious beliefs arguing against such practices (Baumann et al., 2011; Hains & Hulbert-Williams, 2013; Miller, 2016; Nayernouri, 2011).

Disconnecting a life-support system is one thing; withholding nourishment from a terminally ill person is quite another issue for many people. Indeed, such cases often end up in court. The first high-profile legal case involving passive euthanasia in the United

bioethics
Study of the interface between human values and technological advances in health and life sciences.

euthanasia
Practice of ending life for reasons of mercy.

active euthanasia
Deliberate ending of someone's life.

passive euthanasia
Practice of allowing a person to die by withholding available treatment.

Think About It
How do sociocultural forces shape attitudes about euthanasia?

States was brought to the courts in 1990; the U.S. Supreme Court took up the case of Nancy Cruzan, whose family wanted to end her forced feeding. The court ruled that unless clear and incontrovertible evidence is presented to indicate that an individual desires to have nourishment stopped, such as through a healthcare power of attorney or living will, a third party (such as a parent or partner) cannot decide to terminate nourishment. We will consider later in this chapter how to ensure that one's wishes about these matters are expressed clearly.

Physician-Assisted Suicide

Taking one's own life through suicide has never been popular in the United States because of religious and other prohibitions. In other cultures, such as Japan, suicide is viewed as an honorable way to die under certain circumstances (Joiner, 2010).

physician-assisted suicide
Process in which physicians provide dying patients with a fatal dose of medication that the patient self-administers.

Attitudes regarding suicide in certain situations are changing. *Much of this change concerns the topic of* physician-assisted suicide, *in which physicians provide dying patients with a fatal dose of medication that the patient self-administers.* Most Americans, as do people in other countries, favor having a choice regarding assisted suicide if they should ever be diagnosed with a terminal disease. However, many oppose it on moral or religious grounds, irrespective of the wishes of the dying person.

In some cases this option has been put into law. Several countries—including Switzerland, Belgium, the Netherlands, and Colombia—have legalized physician-assisted suicide. Each of these laws sets clear guidelines for when this option is permitted. For example, in the Netherlands, five criteria must be met before a terminally ill person can request physician-assisted suicide as an option:

1. The patient's condition is intolerable with no hope for improvement.
2. No relief is available.
3. The patient is competent.
4. The patient makes a request repeatedly over time.
5. Two physicians review the case and agree with the patient's request.

In the United States, voters in Oregon passed the Death with Dignity Act in 1994, the first physician-assisted suicide law in the country. Although the U.S. Supreme Court ruled in two cases in 1997 (*Vacco v. Quill* and *Washington v. Glucksberg*) there is no right to assisted suicide, the Court decided in 1998 not to overturn the Oregon law. As of 2016, physician-assisted suicide was also legal by state law in California, Colorado, District of Columbia, Vermont, and Washington, and by court decision in Montana. Several other states are considering legislation or have cases under court review.

In general, all of these laws permit people to obtain and use prescriptions for self-administered lethal doses of medication. The laws often require a physician to inform the person he or she is terminally ill and describe alternative options (e.g., hospice care, pain control). The person must be mentally competent and make multiple requests. Such provisions are included to ensure people making the request fully understand the issues and the request is not made hastily.

Available data indicate laws such as Oregon's have psychological benefits for patients, who value having autonomy in death as in life, especially in situations involving unbearable suffering (Hendry et al., 2013). Still, the idea of physicians helping people end their lives is a difficult topic for many.

A controversial case of assisted suicide involved Brittany Maynard, a 29-year-old woman who had terminal brain cancer and committed suicide in 2014. As discussed in the What Do *You* Think? feature, such cases reveal the difficult legal, medical, and ethical issues as well as the high degree of emotion surrounding the topic of euthanasia and death with dignity.

There is no question the debate over physician-assisted suicide will continue. As the technology to keep people alive continues to improve, the ethical issues about active euthanasia in general and physician-assisted suicide in particular will continue to become more complex and will likely focus increasingly on quality of life and death with dignity (Gostin & Roberts, 2016).

On November 2, 2014, Brittany Maynard took a lethal dose of medication prescribed by her physician and ended her life. She was 29 years old, and had been suffering from terminal brain cancer, a diagnosis she received on New Year's Day 2014. She died in her bedroom, surrounded by loved ones (Bever, 2014a, b, c).

Those are the bare facts of Brittany's case. The broader context and debate that her case created is more complicated. Rather than keep her situation private, Brittany went public, conducting several interviews with media and making her thoughts widely known. From there, debate raged.

Brittany's disease progressed rapidly. Nine days after her diagnosis, surgeons removed part of her brain and performed a partial resection of her temporal lobe to stop the tumor from growing. By April 2014, it was clear that this procedure did not work—the tumor was back, and it was more aggressive. Brittany was given about 6 months to live.

Because of her diagnosis, Brittany qualified for physician-assisted suicide under the Death with Dignity Act discussed earlier in the chapter. At the time, Brittany and her husband, Dan Diaz, lived in San Francisco. After carefully considering the various treatment options, which would not cure her, as well as hospice options, she made her decision. Because California does not have a death with dignity law, Brittany and her family moved to Portland, Oregon.

Brittany spent much of her remaining life working on behalf of the death with dignity movement, volunteering for Compassion & Choices. Because she was public and open about her dying process, her case has been a focal point for the right-to-die debate. Critics of death-with-dignity laws, such as National Right to Life, argue that terminal illness does not carry with it the "right" to be "assisted" in dying.

The Brittany Maynard case raises many serious personal, ethical, and moral issues. It also forces us to confront our anxieties about death, how we confront death as a society, and what we truly believe. Each of us must take the time to think through these issues and make our desires known. What do *you* think about what Brittany chose?

Brittany Maynard

AP Images/PR NEWSWIRE/Compassion & Choices

The Price of Life-Sustaining Care

A growing debate in the United States, particularly in the aftermath of the Affordable Care Act passed in 2010, concerns the financial, personal, and moral costs of keeping people alive on life-support machines and continuing aggressive care when people have terminal conditions. Debate continues on whether secondary health conditions in terminally ill people should be treated. The argument is such care is expensive, these people will die soon anyway, and needlessly prolonging life is a burden on society.

However, many others argue all means possible should be used, whether for a premature infant or an older adult, to keep them alive despite the high cost and possible risk of negative side effects of the treatment or intervention. They argue life is precious, and humans should not "play God" and decide when it should end.

There is no question extraordinary interventions are expensive. Healthcare costs can soar during the last year of a person's life. Data indicate less than 7% of people who receive hospital care die each year, but account for nearly 25% of all Medicare expenditures (Adamy & McGinty, 2012). One example involves the continued use of chemotherapy for end-stage cancer patients; the higher costs of care given the evidence of limited benefit and potential harm of continued treatment are coming under increased scrutiny (Garrido et al., 2016). Expenditures for end-of-life care are typically less for those having advance directives (discussed later in this chapter) who receive palliative care.

Think About It

How should the biopsychosocial model influence political debates about dying and death?

The biggest challenge in confronting these differences in approach and cost is the difficulty in deciding when to treat or not treat a disease a person has. There are no easy answers. Witness the loud criticism when research evidence indicated various types of cancer screening (e.g., breast, prostate) should not be provided to everyone as early or as often as initially thought. Despite the lack of evidence to support and the cost of continuing traditional approaches, many patients and physicians do so anyway. Failure to base care on evidence has a price. Whether that is affordable in the long run seems unlikely.

TEST YOURSELF 16.1

Recall

1. Flying a flag at half-staff is an example of a(n) _____ definition of death.

2. The difference between brain death and a persistent vegetative state is _____.

3. Withholding an antibiotic from a person who dies as a result is an example of _____.

Interpret

- What is the difference between the Oregon Death with Dignity Act and active euthanasia?

Apply

- Describe how people at each level of Kohlberg's theory of moral reasoning (described in Chapter 8) would deal with the issue of euthanasia.

Check your answers to the Recall Questions at the end of the chapter.

16.2 Thinking About Death: Personal Aspects

LEARNING OBJECTIVES

- How do feelings about death change over adulthood?
- How do people deal with their own death?
- What is death anxiety, and how do people show it?

Jean is a 49-year-old woman whose parents have both died in the past three years. She now realizes she is the oldest living member of her family (she has two younger siblings). She started thinking about the fact that someday she too will die. Jean gets anxious when she thinks about her death and tries to block it out of her mind.

Like Jean, most people are uncomfortable thinking about their own death, especially if they think it will be unpleasant. As one research participant put it, "You are nuts if you aren't afraid of death" (Kalish & Reynolds, 1976). Still, death is a paradox, as we noted at the beginning of the chapter. That is, we are afraid of or anxious about death but we are drawn to it, sometimes in public ways. We examine this paradox at the personal level in this section. Specifically, we focus on two questions: How do people's feelings about death differ with age? What is it about death we fear or that makes us anxious?

Before we begin, let's take a moment and reflect on how people are remembered after death. One common way to remember people immediately after they die is through an obituary, an experience we may have with hundreds of people we know but never our own. Here's a chance to think about one's own death from that perspective. Take a few minutes and do the following exercise:

- In 200 words or less, write your own obituary. Be sure to include your age and cause of death. List your lifetime accomplishments. Don't forget to list your survivors.

- Think about all the things you will have done that are not listed in your obituary. List some of them.
- Think of all the friends you will have made and how you will have affected them.
- Would you make any changes in your obituary now?

A Life-Course Approach to Dying

Suppose you learned today you had only a few months to live. How would you feel about dying? That's what Randy Pausch, a professor at Carnegie Mellon University, faced when he was told he had 3 to 6 months to live after his pancreatic cancer came back. What happened next, describe in the Real People feature, touched millions of people around the world.

It probably doesn't surprise you to learn feelings about dying vary with age and cultures (Gire, 2014). Each person comes to terms with death in an individual and a family-based way, and together they cocreate ways the patient meets his or her goals (Bergdahl et al., 2013; Carlander et al., 2011; Milligan et al., 2016).

Although not specifically addressed in research, the shift from formal operational thinking to post-formal thinking (see Chapter 7) could be important in young adults' contemplation of death. Presumably, this shift in cognitive development is accompanied by a lessening of the feeling of immortality in adolescence to one that integrates personal feelings and emotions with their thinking.

Midlife is the time when most people in developed countries confront the death of their parents. Until that point, people tend not to think much about their own death; the fact their parents are still alive buffers them from reality. After all, in the normal course of events, our parents are supposed to die before we do.

Once their parents die, people realize they are now the oldest generation of their family—the next in line to die. Reading the obituary pages, they are reminded of this, as the ages of many of the people who died get closer and closer to their own.

Real People   Randy Pausch's Last Lecture

Randy Pausch was a famous computer scientist on the faculty at Carnegie Mellon University. He cofounded the Entertainment Technology Center there and invented a highly innovative way to teach computer programming, called Alice. But that's not what made him world famous. He was a pioneer of virtual reality.

At the age of 46, Randy was told that his pancreatic cancer had recurred and he had between 3 and 6 months to live. So instead of just getting depressed about it, he decided to give a lecture a month later about achieving one's childhood dreams. His lecture is both moving and funny. Rather than talking about dying, Randy focused on overcoming obstacles and seizing every moment of one's life because, as he put it, "Time is all you have . . . and you may find one day that you have less than you think." He spoke of his love for his wife and three children. He had a birthday cake brought onto the stage for his wife. Randy lived several more months after his lecture, dying in July 2008 at age 47.

Randy Pausch

Pittsburgh Post-Gazette/ZUMA Press/Newscom

You can see Randy's lecture by searching YouTube. It was also published as a book. In a strange twist, the coauthor of the book, Jeff Zaslow, was himself killed in an automobile accident at age 53.

One never knows when one's life will end; it is said that the end comes like a thief in the night. But people such as Randy Pausch help us put our own death into perspective by reminding us what is important.

Probably as a result of this growing realization of their own mortality, middle-aged adults' sense of time undergoes a subtle yet profound change. It changes from an emphasis on how long they have already lived to how long they have left to live, a shift that increases into late life (Cicirelli, 2006; Maxfield et al., 2010). This may lead to occupational change or other redirection such as improving relationships that deteriorated over the years. It is also the case that certain strategies are used to deflect attention from or buffer the reality of death anxiety. For example, Yaakobi (2015) found that the desire to work serves as a death anxiety buffer for adults.

In general, older adults are less anxious about death and more accepting of it than any other age group. Still, because the discrepancy between desired and expected number of years left to live is greater for young-old than for mid-old adults, anxiety is higher for young-old adults (Cicirelli, 2006). In part, the greater overall acceptance of death results from the achievement of ego integrity, as described in Chapter 15. For other older adults, the joy of living is diminishing. More than any other group, they experienced loss of family and friends and have come to terms with their own mortality. Older adults have more chronic diseases that are not likely to go away. They may feel their most important life tasks have been completed (Kastenbaum, 1999).

Understanding how adults deal with death, end-of-life issues, and grief can be approached from the perspective of attachment theory (Hales, 2016; Stroebe, Schut, & Stroebe, 2005). In this view, a person's reactions are a natural consequence of forming attachments and then losing them. We consider adult grief a bit later in the chapter.

Dealing with One's Own Death

Many authors have tried to describe the dying process, often using the metaphor of a trajectory that captures the duration of time between the onset of dying (e.g., from the diagnosis of a fatal disease) as well as death and the course of the dying process (D'Angelo et al., 2015; Field & Cassel, 2010). These dying trajectories vary a great deal across diseases, as illustrated in ❱ Figure 16.2. Some diseases, such as lung cancer, have a clear and rapid period of decline; this "terminal phase" is often used to determine eligibility for certain services (e.g., hospice, discussed later). Other diseases, such as congestive heart failure, have no clear terminal phase. The two approaches of describing the dying process we consider will try to account for both types of trajectories.

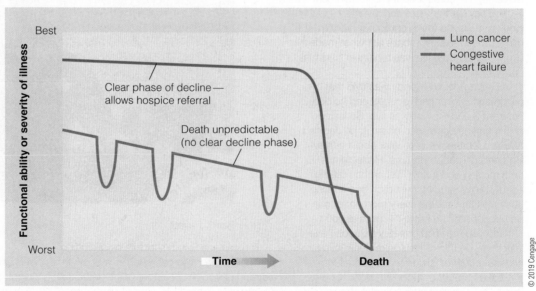

❱ **Figure 16.2**

Some fatal diseases, such as lung cancer, have a clear decline phase, whereas others, such as congestive heart failure, do not.

© 2019 Cengage

From Skolnick, A. A. (1998). MediCaring project to demonstrate and evaluate innovative end-of-life program for chronically ill. *Journal of the American Medical Association, 279,* 1511–1512. Reprinted with permission of the American Medical Association.

Kübler-Ross's Work

Elisabeth Kübler-Ross changed the way we approach dying. When she began her investigations into the dying process in the 1960s, such research was controversial; her physician colleagues initially were outraged and some even denied their patients were terminally ill. Still, she persisted. More than 200 interviews with terminally ill people convinced her most people experienced several emotional reactions. Using her experiences, she described five reactions that represented the ways people dealt with death: denial, anger, bargaining, depression, and acceptance (Kübler-Ross, 1969). Although they were first presented as a sequence, it was subsequently realized the emotions can overlap and be experienced in different order.

Although she believed these five stages represent the typical range of emotional development in the dying, Kübler-Ross (1974) cautioned not everyone experiences all of them or progresses through them at the same rate or in the same order. Research supports the view her "stages" should not be viewed as a sequence (Charlton & Verghese, 2010; Parkes, 2013). In fact, we could actually harm dying people by considering these stages as fixed and universal. Individual differences are great. Emotional responses may vary in intensity throughout the dying process. Thus, the goal in applying Kübler-Ross's ideas to real-world settings would be to help people achieve an appropriate death: one that meets the needs of the dying person, allowing him or her to work out each problem as it comes.

A Contextual Theory of Dying

Describing the process of dying is difficult. One reason for these problems is the realization there is no one right way to die, although there may be better or worse ways of coping (Corr, 2010a,b; Corr & Corr, 2013; Corr, Corr, & Nabe, 2008; Pope, 2017). Corr identified four dimensions of the issues or tasks a dying person faces from their perspective: bodily needs, psychological security, interpersonal attachments, and spiritual energy and hope. This holistic approach acknowledges individual differences and rejects broad generalizations. Corr's task work approach also recognizes the importance of the coping efforts of family members, friends, and caregivers as well as those of the dying person.

Kastenbaum and Thuell (1995) argue what is needed is an even broader contextual approach that takes a more inclusive view of the dying process. They point out theories must be able to handle people who have a wide variety of terminal illnesses and be sensitive to dying people's own perspectives and values related to death. The socio-environmental context where dying occurs often changes over time and must be recognized. A person may begin the dying process living independently but end up in a long-term care facility. Such moves may have profound implications for how the person copes with dying. A contextual approach provides guidance for healthcare professionals and families for discussing how to protect the quality of life, provide better care, and prepare caregivers for dealing with the end of life. Such an approach would also provide research questions such as how does one's acceptance of dying change across various stages?

Although we do not yet have a comprehensive theory of dying, we examine people's experiences as a narrative that can be written from many points of view (e.g., the patient, family members, caregivers). What emerges would be a rich description of a dynamically changing, individual process.

Death Anxiety

We have seen how people view death varies with age. In the process, we encountered the notion of feeling anxious about death. Death anxiety *refers to people's anxiety or even fear of death and dying.* Death anxiety is tough to pin down; indeed, it is the ethereal, unknown nature of death, rather than something about it in particular, that makes us feel so uncomfortable. Because of this, we must look for indirect behavioral evidence to document death anxiety. Research findings suggest death anxiety is a complex, multidimensional construct.

death anxiety
Feeling of anxiety or even fear of death and dying.

Think About It

Why does death anxiety have so many components?

For nearly three decades, researchers have applied terror management theory as a framework to study death anxiety (Burke, Martens, & Faucher, 2010; Park & Pyszczynski, 2016). Terror management theory *addresses the issue of why people engage in certain behaviors to achieve particular psychological states based on their deeply rooted concerns about mortality.* The theory proposes that ensuring the continuation of one's life is the primary motive underlying behavior and that all other motives can be traced to this basic one. An overview of the theory is shown in ❱ Figure 16.3 (Arndt & Goldenberg, 2017).

Essentially, terror management theory explains how health conditions affect how we think about death. Basically, when mortality concerns are in our conscious thought, our health-related decisions are determined by our short-term goal of reducing our perceived vulnerability to the health threat and its related concerns about mortality.

Additionally, some suggest older adults present an existential threat for the younger and middle-aged adults because they remind us all that death is inescapable, the body is fallible, and the bases that we may secure self-esteem (and manage death anxiety) are transitory (Martens, Goldenberg, & Greenberg, 2005). That may be why some people seek cosmetic surgery as a way to deal with their death anxiety (Tam, 2013). Thus, death anxiety is a reflection of one's concern over dying, an outcome that would violate the prime motive.

Neuroimaging research shows terror management theory provides a useful framework for studying brain activity related to death anxiety. Quirin and colleagues (2012) found brain activity in the right amygdala, left rostral anterior cingulate cortex, and right caudate nucleus was greater when male participants were answering questions about fear of death and dying than when they were answering questions about dental pain. Similarly, electrical

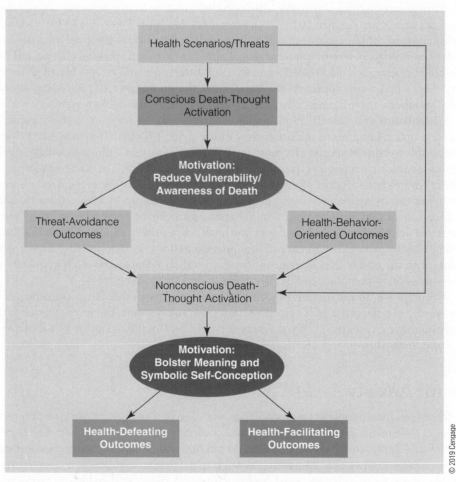

❱ **Figure 16.3**
The Terror Management Health Model

© 2019 Cengage

From Arndt, J., & Goldenberg, J. L. (2017). Where health and death intersect: Insights from a Terror Management Health Model. *Current Directions in Psychological Science, 26,* 126–131. Figure 1, p. 127. doi:10.1177/0963721416689563

activity in the brain indicates people defend themselves against emotions related to death (Klackl, Jonas, & Kronbichler, 2013). And younger adults show greater brain responses to death-related terms than do older adults, indicating a fundamental shift in how adults process death-related concepts with age (Bluntschli et al., in press). There is neurophysiological evidence that shows Jean's attempts to block thoughts of her own death in the opening vignette are common across people.

On the basis of several diverse studies using many different measures, researchers now conclude death anxiety consists of several components. Each of these components is most easily described with terms that reflect areas of great concern (anxiety) but that cannot be tied to any one specific focus. These components of death anxiety include pain, body malfunction, humiliation, rejection, nonbeing, punishment, interruption of goals, being destroyed, and negative impact on survivors (Power & Smith, 2008). To complicate matters further, each of these components can be assessed at any of three levels: public, private, and nonconscious. What we admit feeling about death in public may differ greatly from what we feel when we are alone with our own thoughts from what we may be unaware of that still influences our behavior. In short, the measurement of death anxiety is complex, and researchers need to specify what aspects they are assessing.

Much research has been conducted to learn what demographic and personality variables are related to death anxiety. Although the results often are ambiguous, some patterns have emerged. Older adults tend to have lower death anxiety than younger adults, perhaps because of their tendency to engage in life review, have a different perspective about time, and their higher level of religious motivation (Henrie, 2010). Men show greater fear of the unknown than women, but women report more specific fear of the dying process (Cicirelli, 2001). Death anxiety varies across cultures in how it is (or is not) expressed (Park & Pyszczynski, 2016). In Taiwan, higher death anxiety among patients with cancer is associated with not having a purpose in life and level of fear of disease relapse (Tang et al., 2011).

Strange as it may seem, death anxiety may have a beneficial side. For one thing, being afraid to die means we often go to great lengths to make sure we stay alive, as argued by terror management theory (Burke et al., 2010; Park & Pyszczynski, 2016). Because staying alive ensures the continuation and socialization of the species, fear of death serves as a motivation to have children and raise them properly.

Learning to Deal with Death Anxiety

Although some degree of death anxiety may be appropriate, we must guard against letting it become powerful enough to interfere with normal daily routines. Several ways exist to help us in this endeavor. Perhaps the one most often used is to live life to the fullest. Kalish (1984, 1987) argues people who do this enjoy what they have; although they may still fear death and feel cheated, they have few regrets.

Koestenbaum (1976) proposes several exercises and questions to increase one's death awareness. Some of these are to write your own obituary (like you did earlier in this chapter) and to plan your own death and funeral services. You can also ask yourself: "What circumstances would help make my death acceptable?" "Is death the sort of thing that could happen to me right now?"

These questions serve as a basis for an increasingly popular way to reduce anxiety: death education. Most death education programs combine factual information about death with issues aimed at reducing anxiety and fear to increase sensitivity to others' feelings. These programs vary widely in orientation; they

Facing death on a regular basis often forces people to confront their death anxiety.

kaninstudio/123RF

include such topics as philosophy, ethics, psychology, drama, religion, medicine, art, and many others. Additionally, they focus on death, the process of dying, grief and bereavement, or any combination of those. In general, death education programs help primarily by increasing our awareness of the complex emotions felt and expressed by dying people and their families. It is important to make education programs reflect the diverse backgrounds of the participants (Fowler, 2008).

Research shows participating in experiential workshops about death significantly lowers death anxiety in younger, middle-aged, and older adults and raises awareness about the importance of advance directives (Moeller et al., 2010).

Think About It

How might different approaches to lowering death anxiety be useful to you as a healthcare worker?

TEST YOURSELF 16.2

Recall

1. _____ are most likely to face the death of their parents.

2. The _____ acknowledges individual differences and rejects broad generalizations.

3. The primary framework for studying death anxiety is _____.

Interpret

- Why is it important to confront the issue of death as a part of human development?

Apply

- Using Erikson's theory as a framework, explain how death anxiety changes from adolescence to late life.

Check your answers to the Recall Questions at the end of the chapter.

16.3 End-of-Life Issues

LEARNING OBJECTIVES

- What are end-of-life issues? What is a final scenario?
- What is hospice? How does hospice relate to end-of-life issues?
- How does one make end-of-life desires and decisions known?

Jean is a 72-year-old woman recently diagnosed with advanced colon cancer. She has vivid memories of her father dying a long, protracted death in great pain. Jean is afraid she will suffer the same fate. She heard the hospice in town emphasizes pain management and provides a lot of support for families. Jean wonders whether that is something she should explore in the time she has left.

When people think about how they would like to die, no one chooses a slow, painful process where medical intervention continues well beyond the point of increasing quality of life over quantity of life. However, medical intervention such as life support or cardiopulmonary resuscitation (CPR), are common, often required by law, even in situations in which people would prefer them not to be used. How can people make their wishes known about how they want to experience the end of their life?

Creating a Final Scenario

end-of-life issues

Issues pertaining to management of the final phase of life, after-death disposition of the body and memorial services, and distribution of assets.

When given the chance, many adults would like to discuss a variety of issues, collectively called end-of-life issues: *management of the final phase of life, after-death disposition of their body, memorial services, and distribution of assets* (Moeller et al., 2010). We are experiencing a major shift in how people handle end-of-life issues. Prior to the current generation of older adults, people rarely planned ahead for or made their wishes known about medical care they did or did not want. Now, people want to manage the final part of their lives by thinking through the choices between traditional care (e.g., provided by hospitals and nursing homes) and alternatives (such as hospices, that we discuss in the next section), completing advance directives (e.g., healthcare power of attorney, living will), resolving key personal relationships, and perhaps choosing the alternative of ending one's life prematurely through euthanasia.

Consider the issue of rituals surrounding the time immediately following death. What happens to one's body and how one is memorialized matters to most people. But decisions about these have to be made. Is a traditional burial preferred over cremation? A traditional funeral over a memorial service? Such choices often are based in people's religious beliefs and their desire for privacy for their families after they have died.

Making sure one's estate and personal effects are passed on appropriately often is overlooked. Making a will is especially important to ensure one's wishes are carried out. Providing for the informal distribution of personal effects also helps prevent disputes between family members.

Whether people choose to address these issues formally or informally, it is important they be given the opportunity to do so. In many cases, family members are reluctant to discuss these matters with the dying relative because of their own anxiety about death. *Making such choices known about how they do and do not want their lives to end constitutes a* final scenario.

One of the most difficult and important parts of a final scenario for most people is the process of separation from family and friends (Corr & Corr, 2013; Wanzer & Glenmullen, 2007). The final days, weeks, and months of life provide opportunities to affirm love, resolve conflicts, and provide peace to dying people. The failure to complete this process often leaves survivors feeling they did not achieve closure in the relationship, and can result in bitterness toward the deceased.

Healthcare workers realize the importance of giving dying patients the chance to create a final scenario and recognize the uniqueness of each person's final passage. A key part of their role is to ease this process through good communication with the family (Curtis et al., 2016; Wanzer & Glenmullen, 2007). Any given final scenario reflects the individual's personal past, that is the unique combination of the development forces the person experienced. Primary attention is paid to how people's total life experiences prepared them to face end-of-life issues (Curtis et al., 2016).

One's final scenario helps family and friends interpret one's death, especially when the scenario is constructed jointly, such as between spouses, and when communication is open and honest. The different perspectives of everyone involved are unlikely to converge without clear communication and discussion. Respecting each person's perspective is basic and greatly helps in creating a good final scenario.

Encouraging people to decide for themselves how the end of their lives should be handled helps people take control of their dying (Hains & Hulbert-Williams, 2013) and think through issues such as euthanasia are processed at the individual level (Feltz, 2015). Taking personal control over one's dying process is a trend occurring even in cultures such as Japan that traditionally defer to physician's opinions (Alden, Merz, & Akashi, 2012). The emergence of final scenarios as an important consideration fits well with the emphasis on addressing pain through palliative care, an approach underlying hospice.

final scenario
Way for people to make their choices known about how they do and do not want their lives to end.

Deciding whether to have a traditional funeral is part of the creation of one's final scenario.

Emipress/Shutterstock.com

The Hospice Option

As we have seen, most people would like to die at home among family and friends. An important barrier to this choice is the availability of support systems when the person has a terminal disease. Most people believe they have no choice but to go to a hospital or nursing home. However, another alternative exists. Hospice *is an approach to assist dying people emphasizing pain management, or palliative care, and death with dignity* (Knee, 2010; Winslow & Meldrum, 2013). The emphasis in a hospice is on the dying person's quality of life. This approach grows out of an important distinction between the prolongation of life and the prolongation of death, a distinction important to Jean, the woman we met in the vignette. In a hospice the concern is to make the person as peaceful and as comfortable as possible, not to delay an inevitable death. *An approach to care based on an ethic of controlling and relieving pain or other symptoms and not on attempting to cure disease is called palliative care* (Prince-Paul & Daly, 2016). Hospice is the leading provider of such care, but palliative care is also adopted in other settings.

Modern hospices are modeled after St. Christopher's Hospice in England, founded in 1967 by Dr. Cicely Saunders. Hospice services are requested only after the person or physician believes no treatment or cure is possible, making the hospice program markedly different from hospital or home care. The differences are evident in the principles that underlie hospice care (Knee, 2010):

- Clients and their families are viewed as a unit, clients should be kept free of pain, emotional and social impoverishment must be minimal;
- Clients must be encouraged to maintain competencies, conflict resolution and fulfillment of realistic desires must be assisted; and
- Clients must be free to begin or end relationships, an interdisciplinary team approach is used, and staff members must seek to alleviate pain and fear.

Two types of hospices exist: inpatient and outpatient. Inpatient hospices provide all care for clients; outpatient hospices provide services to clients who remain in their own homes. The outpatient variation, when a hospice nurse visits clients in their home, is becoming increasingly popular, largely because more clients can be served at a lower cost. Having hospice services available to people at home is a viable option for many people, especially in helping home-based caregivers cope with loss, but should be provided by specially trained professionals (Newman, Thompson, & Chandler, 2013).

Hospices do not follow a hospital model of care. The role of the staff in a hospice is not so much to treat the client as it is just to be with the client. A client's dignity is always maintained; often more attention is paid to appearance and personal grooming than to medical tests. Hospice staff members also provide a great deal of support to the client's family.

Increasingly, this support includes different ways of being present to and with the person who is dying. Many hospices have the option for *death doulas* who help ease the passage through death. For some dying individuals, the doula may simply hold their hand; for others it may be through playing special music and sitting or meditating with them. The main role is to ensure that dying people are not alone, and that families, if present, have personal support.

Hospice and hospital patients differ in important ways (Knee, 2010). Hospice clients are more mobile, less anxious, and less depressed; spouses visit hospice clients more often and participate more in their care; and hospice staff members are perceived as more accessible. Research consistently shows significant improvements in clients' quality of life occur after hospice placement or beginning palliative care (Blackhall et al., 2016; Rocque & Cleary, 2013).

Although the hospice is a valuable alternative for many people, it may not be appropriate for everyone. Those who trust their physician regarding medical care options are more likely to select hospice than those who do not trust their physician, especially among African Americans, who as a group prefer more aggressive treatment options (Ludke & Smucker, 2007; Smith-Howell et al., 2016). Most people who select hospice suffer from

Hospice outpatient healthcare workers provide help for people with terminal diseases who choose to die at home.

cancer, AIDS, cardiovascular disease, pulmonary disease, or a progressive neurological condition such as dementia; two-thirds are over age 65; and most are in the last six months of life (Hospice Foundation of America, 2016a).

Needs expressed by staff, family, and clients differ (Hiatt et al., 2007). Staff and family members tend to emphasize pain management, whereas many clients want more attention paid to personal issues, such as spirituality and the process of dying. This difference means the staff and family members may need to ask clients more often what they need instead of making assumptions about what they need.

How do people decide among various care options, such as hospice, home health, or skilled care? Families should ask several key questions (Hospice Foundation of America, 2016b; Karp & Wood, 2012; Knee, 2010):

- *Is the person completely informed about the nature and prognosis of his or her condition?* Full knowledge and the ability to communicate with healthcare personnel are essential to understanding what hospice has to offer.
- *What options are available at this point in the progress of the person's disease?* Knowing about all available treatment options is critical. Exploring treatment options also requires healthcare professionals to be aware of the latest approaches and be willing to disclose them.
- *What are the person's expectations, fears, and hopes?* Some older adults, like Jean, remember or have heard stories about people who suffered greatly at the end of their lives. This can produce anxiety about one's own death. Similarly, fears of becoming dependent play an important role in a person's decision making. Discovering and discussing these anxieties help clarify options.
- *How well do people in the person's social network communicate with each other?* Talking about death is taboo in many families. In others, intergenerational communication is difficult or impossible. Even in families with good communication, the pending death of a loved relative is difficult. As a result, the dying person may have difficulty expressing his or her wishes. The decision to explore the hospice option is best made when it is discussed openly.
- *Are family members available to participate actively in terminal care?* Hospice relies on family members to provide much of the care that is supplemented by professionals and volunteers. We saw in Chapters 11 and 13 being a primary caregiver can be highly stressful. Having a family member who is willing to accept this responsibility is essential for the hospice option to work.

- *Is a high-quality hospice care program available?* Hospice programs are not uniformly good. As with any healthcare provider, patients and family members must investigate the quality of local hospice programs before making a choice. The Hospice Foundation of America provides excellent material for evaluating a hospice.
- *Is hospice covered by insurance?* Hospice services are reimbursable under Medicare in most cases, but any additional expenses may or may not be covered under other forms of insurance.

Hospice provides an important end-of-life option for many terminally ill people and their families. Moreover, the supportive follow-up services they provide are often used by surviving family and friends. Most important, the success of the hospice option has had important influences on traditional health care. For example, the American Academy of Pain Medicine (2016) publishes official position papers regarding the appropriate use of medical and behavioral interventions to provide pain management. The Centers for Disease Control and Prevention (2016c) also published guidelines for the appropriate use of opioids for pain management due to the risk of addiction from these medications.

Despite the importance of the hospice option for end-of-life decisions, terminally ill persons face the barriers of family reluctance to face the reality of terminal illness and participate in the decision-making process, and healthcare providers who hinder access to hospice care (Knee, 2010; Moon, 2017; Torres et al., 2016).

As the end of life approaches, the most important thing to keep in mind is that the dying person has the right to state-of-the-art approaches to treatment and pain management. Irrespective of the choice of traditional health care or hospice, the wishes of the dying person should be honored, and family members and primary care providers must participate.

Making Your End-of-Life Intentions Known

End-of-life realities raise complex legal, political, and ethical issues. In most jurisdictions, ending life through such means as euthanasia or assisted suicide is legal only when a person has made known his or her wishes concerning medical or other intervention. Unfortunately, many people fail to explicitly state their wishes, perhaps because it is difficult to think about such situations or because they do not know the options available to them. Without clear directions, though, medical personnel may be unable to take a patient's preferences into account. For instance, many states have laws requiring CPR or other attempts at resuscitation be used in the absence of clear evidence that the person does not want them used.

There are two ways to make one's intentions known. *In a living will, a person simply states his or her wishes about life support and other treatments. In a* healthcare power of attorney, *an individual appoints someone to act as his or her agent for healthcare decisions* (see ▶ Figure 16.4). A major purpose of both is to make one's wishes known about the use of life-support interventions in the event the person is unconscious or otherwise incapable of expressing them, along with other related end-of-life issues such as organ transplantation and other healthcare options. Without them, the ethical considerations of life-sustaining intervention for terminally ill patients is fraught with ethical dilemmas (Awadi & Mrayyan, 2016; Portnoy et al., 2015). A durable power of attorney for health care has an additional advantage: It names an individual who has the legal authority to speak and make decisions for the person if necessary.

A living will or a durable power of attorney for health care can be the basis for a "do not resuscitate" medical order. *A* do not resuscitate (DNR) order *means cardiopulmonary resuscitation (CPR) is not started should one's heart and breathing stop.* In the normal course of events, a medical team will immediately try to restore normal heartbeat and respiration. With a DNR order, this treatment is not done. As with living wills and healthcare power of attorney, it is extremely important to let all appropriate medical personnel know a DNR order is in effect.

Although there is considerable support for both living wills and healthcare power of attorney, there are several challenges as well (Alspach, 2016; Izumi & Son, 2016). States vary in their laws relating to advance directives. Many people fail to inform their relatives and physicians about their healthcare decisions. Others do not tell the person named in a durable

living will

Document in which a person states his or her wishes about life support and other treatments.

healthcare power of attorney

Document in which an individual appoints someone to act as his or her agent for healthcare decisions.

do not resuscitate (DNR) order

Medical order that means that cardiopulmonary resuscitation (CPR) is not started should one's heart and breathing stop.

3. General statement of authority granted.

Except as indicated in section 4 below, I hereby grant to my health care agent named above full power and authority to make health care decisions on my behalf, including, but not limited to, the following:

A. To request, review, and receive any information, verbal or written, regarding my physical or mental health, including, but not limited to, medical and hospital records, and to consent to the disclosure of this information;

B. To employ or discharge my health care providers;

C. To consent to and authorize my admission to and discharge from a hospital, nursing or convalescent home, or other institution;

D. To give consent for, to withdraw consent for, or to withhold consent for, X ray, anesthesia, medication, surgery, and all other diagnostic and treatment procedures ordered by or under the authorization of a licensed physician, dentist, or podiatrist. This authorization specifically includes the power to consent to measures for relief of pain.

E. To authorize the withholding or withdrawal of life-sustaining procedures when and if my physician determines that I am terminally ill, permanently in a coma, suffer severe dementia, or am in a persistent vegetative state. Lifesustaining procedures are those forms of medical care that only serve to artificially prolong the dying process and may include mechanical ventilation, dialysis, antibiotics, artificial nutrition and hydration, and other forms of medical treatment which sustain, restore or supplant vital bodily functions. Life-sustaining procedures do not include care necessary to provide comfort or alleviate pain.

　　　I DESIRE THAT MY LIFE NOT BE PROLONGED BY LIFE-SUSTAINING PROCEDURES IF I AM TERMINALLY ILL, PERMANENTLY IN A COMA, SUFFER SEVERE DEMENTIA, OR AM IN A PERSISTENT VEGETATIVE STATE.

F. To exercise any right I may have to make a disposition of any part or all of my body for medical purposes, to donate my organs, to authorize an autopsy, and to direct the disposition of my remains.

G. To take any lawful actions that may be necessary to carry out these decisions, including the granting of releases of liability to medical providers.

4. Special provisions and limitations.

(Notice: The above grant of power is intended to be as broad as possible so that your health care agent will have authority to make any decisions you could make to obtain or terminate any type of health care. If you wish to limit the scope of your health care agent's powers, you may do so in this section.)

In exercising the authority to make health care decisions on my behalf, the authority of my health care agent is subject to the following special provisions and limitations *(Here you may include any specific limitations you deem appropriate such as: your own definition of when life-sustaining treatment should be withheld or discontinued, or instructions to refuse any specific types of treatment that are inconsistent with your religious beliefs, or unacceptable to you for any other reason.):*

_____

_____

_____

_____

5. Guardianship provision.

If it becomes necessary for a court to appoint a guardian of my person, I nominate my health care agent acting under this document to be the guardian of my person, to serve without bond or security.

6. Reliance of third parties on health care agent.

A. No person who relies in good faith upon the authority of or any representations by my health care agent shall be liable to me, my estate, my heirs, successors, assigns, or personal representatives, for actions or omissions by my health care agent.

© 2019 Cengage

From North Carolina State University, A&T State University Cooperative Extension.

power of attorney where the document is kept. Obviously, this puts relatives at a serious disadvantage if decisions concerning the use of life-support systems need to be made.

Fortunately, since 2016 Medicare covers advance care planning as a separate service provided by physicians and other healthcare professionals such as nurse practitioners (Henry J. Kaiser Family Foundation, 2016). This makes it easier for patients to discuss their wishes with a healthcare professional and to learn about options. Ideally, these discussions result in the actual documentation of a person's specific wishes.

Think About It

Have you made your end-of-life intentions known?

Patient Self-Determination and Competency Evaluation

Making your decisions about health care known presumes that you are competent and able to make those decisions for yourself. To aid healthcare providers in this process, the Patient Self-Determination Act, passed in 1990, requires most healthcare facilities to provide information to patients in writing that they have the right to:

- Make their own healthcare decisions.
- Accept or refuse medical treatment.
- Make an advance healthcare directive.

Patients must be asked if they have an advance directive, and, if so, it must be included in the medical record. Staff at the healthcare facility must receive training about advance directives, and cannot make admissions or treatment decisions based on whether those directives exist.

One major concern regarding the appropriate implementation of the Patient Self-Determination Act is whether the person is cognitively or legally able to make the decisions about end-of-life care (Moye, Sabatino, & Brendel, 2013). There are two types of determination: the *capacity* to make decisions, that is a clinical determination, and a *competency* decision, made legally by the court (Wettstein, 2013). With capacity determinations, the issue is whether the individual is able to make a decision about specific tasks, and the abilities necessary are subject to measurement. With competency determinations, the individual is being judged either with respect to a specific task or in general, and the determination can be made subjectively by the court.

At this point, the case law is limited regarding whether a person who lacks the capacity to make healthcare decisions can still designate a surrogate to make them on their behalf. This situation is rather common, though, given the tendency for families to not discuss these issues, individual's reluctance to face the potential need, and the politicization of the conversation in the healthcare arena. Guidelines for professionals regarding the assessment of competence are available, and they provide insight into both the psychological and legal issues surrounding such evaluations (Moye et al., 2013; Wettstein, 2013).

Research indicates family members and other surrogate decision-makers are often wrong about what loved ones, even spouses or partners, really want (Moorman & Inoue, 2013). This further emphasizes the critical need, especially for couples, to discuss end-of-life issues ahead of time and ensure the appropriate advance directives are in place and key individuals are aware of them (Queen, Berg, & Lowrance, 2015).

Think About It

What steps are necessary to ensure that your advance directives about health care are followed?

TEST YOURSELF **16.3**

Recall

1. Making choices known about what people do and do not want their lives to end constitutes a(n) _____.

2. _____ is an approach to assisting dying people that emphasizes pain management, or palliative care, and death with dignity.

3. In a(n) _____, a person states his or her wishes about life support and other treatments.

Interpret

• Why is there a difference in treatment approach between hospitals and hospices?

Apply

• How does creating a final scenario incorporate the biopsychosocial forces of development?

Check your answers to the Recall Questions at the end of the chapter.

16.4 Surviving the Loss: The Grieving Process

LEARNING OBJECTIVES

• How do people experience the grief process?

• What feelings do grieving people have?

• How do people cope with grief?

• What are the types of ambiguous loss?

• What is the difference between normal and complicated grief?

• What is disenfranchised grief?

After 67 years of marriage, Bertha recently lost her husband. At 90, Bertha knew neither she nor her husband was likely to live much longer, but the death was a shock just the same. Bertha thinks about him much of the time and often finds herself making decisions on the basis of "what John would have done" in the same situation.

Each of us suffers many losses over a lifetime. Whenever we lose someone close to us through death or other separation, like Bertha we experience bereavement, grief, and mourning. Bereavement *is the state or condition caused by loss through death.* Grief *is the sorrow, hurt, anger, guilt, confusion, and other feelings that arise after suffering a loss.* Mourning *concerns the ways we express our grief.* You can tell people in some cultures are bereaved and in mourning because of the clothing they wear. Mourning is highly influenced by culture. For some, mourning may involve wearing black, attending funerals, and observing an official period of grief; for others, it means drinking, wearing white, and marrying the deceased spouse's sibling. Grief corresponds to the emotional reactions following loss, whereas mourning is the culturally approved behavioral manifestations of those feelings. Even though mourning rituals may be fairly standard within a culture, how people grieve varies, as we see next. We will also see how Bertha's reactions are fairly typical of most people.

bereavement

State or condition caused by loss through death.

grief

Sorrow, hurt, anger, guilt, confusion, and other feelings that arise after suffering a loss.

mourning

Ways in which people express their grief.

The Grief Process

How do people grieve? What do they experience? Perhaps you already have a good idea about the answers to these questions from your own experience. If so, you already know the process of grieving is a complicated and personal one. Just as there is no right way to die, there is no right way to grieve. Recognizing there are plenty of individual differences, we consider these patterns in this section.

The grieving process is often described as reflecting many themes and issues people confront that may be expressed through rituals, both in-person and digital (Gamba, 2015; Norton & Gino, 2014). Like the process of dying, grieving does not have clearly demarcated stages through which we pass in a neat sequence, although there are certain issues people must face similar to those faced by dying people. When someone close to us dies, we must reorganize our lives, establish new patterns of behavior, and redefine relationships with family and friends. Indeed, Attig (1996) provided one of the best descriptions of grief when he wrote grief is the process by which we relearn the world.

Unlike bereavement, over which we have no control, grief is a process that involves choices in coping, from confronting the reality and emotions to using religion to ease one's pain (Cummings, 2015; Norton & Gino, 2014). From this perspective, grief is an active process when a person must do several things (Worden, 1991):

- *Acknowledge the reality of the loss.* We must overcome the temptation to deny the reality of our loss; we must fully and openly acknowledge it and realize it affects every aspect of our life.
- *Work through the emotional turmoil.* We must find effective ways to confront and express the complete range of emotions we feel after the loss and must not avoid or repress them.
- *Adjust to the environment where the deceased is absent.* We must define new patterns of living that adjust appropriately and meaningfully to the fact the deceased is not present.
- *Loosen ties to the deceased.* We must free ourselves from the bonds of the deceased in order to reengage with our social network. This means finding effective ways to say good-bye.

Grief is an active coping process (Bagbey Darian, 2014). In processing grief, survivors must come to terms with and integrate the

Dealing with the death of friends is often especially difficult for young adults.

DreamPictures/Blend Images/Getty Images

physical world of things, places, and events as well as their spiritual place in the world; the interpersonal world of interactions with family and friends, the dead, and, in some cases, God; and aspects of our inner selves and our personal experiences. Bertha, the woman in the vignette, is in the middle of this process. Even the matter of deciding what to do with the deceased's personal effects can be part of this active coping process (Attig, 1996).

To make sense of grief, we need to keep several things in mind. First, grieving is a highly individual experience (Bagbey Darian, 2014; Cummings, 2015; Steck & Steck, 2016). A process that works well for one person may not be the best for someone else. Second, we must not underestimate the amount of time people need to deal with the various issues. To a casual observer, it may appear a survivor is "back to normal" after a few weeks (Harris, 2016). Actually, what may look like a return to normal activities may reflect bereaved people feeling social pressure to "get on with things." It takes most people much longer to resolve the complex emotional issues faced during bereavement. Researchers and therapists alike agree a person needs at least a year following the loss to begin recovery, and two years is not uncommon.

Finally, "recovery" may be a misleading term. It is probably more accurate to say we learn to live with our loss rather than we recover from it (Attig, 1996). The impact of the loss of a loved one lasts a long time, perhaps for the rest of one's life. Still, most people reach a point of moving on with their lives (Bagbey Darian, 2014; Bonanno, 2009; Harris, 2016).

Recognizing these aspects of grief makes it easier to know what to say and do for bereaved people. Among the most useful things are simply to let the person know you are sorry for his or her loss, you are there for support, and mean what you say.

Risk Factors in Grief

Bereavement is a life experience most people have many times, and most people eventually handle it, often better than we might suspect (Bagbey Darian, 2014; Bonanno, 2009; Bonanno, Westphal, & Mancini, 2011; Cummings, 2015; Steck & Steck, 2016). However, there are some risk factors that make bereavement more difficult. Several of the more important are the mode of death, personal factors (e.g., personality, religiosity, age, gender, income), and interpersonal context (social support, kinship relationship).

Most people believe the circumstances of death affects the grief process. A person whose family member was killed in an automobile accident has a different situation to deal with than a person whose family member died after a long period of suffering with Alzheimer's disease. *It is believed when death is anticipated, people go through a period of anticipatory grief before the death that supposedly serves to buffer the impact of the loss when it does come and to facilitate recovery* (Shore et al., 2016). Indicators of anticipatory grief may appear as pre-loss grief, and as depression, anxiety, or pain.

The research evidence for whether anticipatory grief helps people cope with loss better is mixed. Anticipating the loss of a loved one from cancer or other terminal disease can provide a framework for understanding family members' reactions (Coombs, 2010; Shore et al., 2016). However, anticipatory grief does not appear to alleviate the outcome of the bereavement; in fact, it may even make it more difficult to reach a positive outcome (Nielsen et al., 2016).

The strength of attachment to the deceased person does make a difference in dealing with a sudden as opposed to an expected death. Attachment theory provides a framework for understanding different reactions (Hales, 2016; Stroebe & Archer, 2013). When the deceased person was one for whom the survivor had a strong and close attachment and the loss was sudden, the grief is greater. However, such secure attachment styles tend to result in less depression after the loss because of less guilt over unresolved issues (because there are fewer of them), things not provided (because more were likely provided), and so on.

Few studies of personal risk factors have been done, and few firm conclusions can be drawn. To date there are no consistent findings regarding personality traits that either help buffer people from the effects of bereavement or exacerbate them (Haley, 2013;

anticipatory grief

Grief that is experienced during the period before an expected death occurs that supposedly serves to buffer the impact of the loss when it does come and to facilitate recovery.

Stroebe & Archer, 2013). Some evidence suggests church attendance or spirituality in general helps people to deal with bereavement and subsequent grief through the post-grief period (Gordon, 2013). There are, however, consistent findings regarding gender. Men and women differ in the ways they express emotions related to grief (Kersting & Nagl, 2016). Men have higher mortality rates following bereavement than women, who have higher rates of depression and complicated grief (discussed later in this section) than men, but the reasons for these differences are unclear (Kersting et al., 2011). Research also consistently shows older adults suffer the least health consequences following bereavement, with the impact perhaps being strongest for middle-aged adults, but strong social support networks, including virtual ones, lessen these effects to varying degrees (Chang et al., 2016; Papa & Litz, 2011).

Think About It

How is grief influenced by sociocultural factors?

Typical Grief Reactions

The feelings experienced during grieving are intense; these feelings not only make it difficult to cope but can also make a person question her or his own reactions. The feelings involved usually include sadness, denial, anger, loneliness, and guilt.

Many authors refer to the psychological side of coming to terms with bereavement as grief work. Whether the loss is ambiguous and lacking closure (e.g., waiting to learn the fate of a missing loved one) or certain (e.g., verification of death through a dead body), people need space and time to grieve (Berns, 2011; Harris, 2016). However, a major challenge in American society is that, as noted earlier, people feel pressured to "move on" quickly after a loss, especially if that loss is not of a spouse or child. That is not how people really feel or want to deal with their grief; they want the opportunity to work through their feelings on their own terms and timeline.

grief work

Psychological side of coming to terms with bereavement.

Muller and Thompson (2003) examined people's experience of grief in a detailed interview study and found five themes. *Coping* concerns what people do to deal with their loss in terms of what helps them. *Affect* refers to people's emotional reactions to the death of their loved one, such as certain topics that serve as emotional triggers for memories of their loved one. *Change* involves the ways survivors' lives change as a result of the loss; personal growth (e.g., "I didn't think I could deal with something that painful, but I did") is a common experience. *Narrative* relates to the stories survivors tell about their deceased loved one, that sometimes includes details about the process of the death. Finally, *relationship* reflects who the deceased person was and the nature of the ties between that person and the survivor. Collectively, these themes indicate the experience of grief is complex and involves dealing with one's feelings as a survivor as well as memories of the deceased person.

How openly grief is expressed varies considerably across cultures.

How people show their feelings of grief varies across ethnic and cultural groups (Bordere, 2016; Gire, 2014). For example, families in KwaZulu-Natal, South Africa, have a strong desire for closure and need for dealing with the "loneliness of grief" (Brysiewicz, 2008). In many cultures the bereaved construct a relationship with the person who died, but how this happens differs widely, from "ghosts" to appearances in dreams to connection through prayer and ancestor worship (Cacciatore & DeFrain, 2015). Differences in dealing with grief and bereavement can also be observed across different subgroups within ethnic groups. For instance, various Hispanic groups (e.g., Mexican, Puerto Rican, Central American) differ somewhat from each other in ritual practices (Schoulte, 2011).

In addition to psychological grief reactions, there are also physiological ones (McCoyd &

Kursat Bayhan/Getty Images News/Getty Images

Walter, 2016). Physical health may decline, illness may result, and use of healthcare services may increase. Some people report sleep disturbances as well as neurological and circulatory problems (Kowalski & Bondmass, 2008; Naef et al., 2013). Widowers in general report major disruptions in their daily routines (Naef et al., 2013).

In the time following the death of a loved one, dates having personal significance may reintroduce feelings of grief. Holidays such as Thanksgiving or birthdays that were spent with the deceased person may be difficult times. The actual anniversary of the death can be especially troublesome. *The term* anniversary reaction *refers to changes in behavior related to feelings of sadness on this date.* Personal experience and research show recurring feelings of sadness or other examples of the anniversary reaction are common in normal grief (DiBello, 2015; Holland & Neimeyer, 2010; Rostila et al., 2015). Such feelings also accompany remembrances of major catastrophes across cultures, such as Thais remembering the victims of a tsunami and major flood (Assanangkornchai et al., 2007).

Most research on how people react to the death of a loved one is cross-sectional. This work shows grief tends to peak within the first six months following the death of a loved one (Maciejewski et al., 2007) but may never fully go away, with effects on cognitive well-being greater than for emotional well-being in general (Luhmann et al., 2012).

Research has been done to examine longitudinal effects of grief. Some widows show no sign of lessening of grief after 5 years (Kowalski & Bondmass, 2008). Rosenblatt (1996) reported people still felt the effects of the deaths of family members 50 years after the event. The depth of the emotions over the loss of loved ones sometimes never totally goes away, as people still cry and feel sad when discussing the loss despite the length of time that had passed. In general, though, people move on with their lives and deal with their feelings reasonably well (Bagbey Darian, 2014; Bonanno, 2009; Bonnano et al., 2011; Cummings, 2015; Steck & Steck, 2016).

Coping With Grief

Thus far, we considered the behaviors people show when they are dealing with grief. We have also seen these behaviors change over time. How does this happen? How can we explain the grieving process?

Numerous theories have been proposed to account for the grieving process, such as general life-event theories, psychodynamic, attachment, and cognitive process theories (Stroebe & Archer, 2013; Stroebe, Schut, & Boerner, 2010). All of these approaches to grief are based on more general theories that result in none of them providing an adequate explanation of the grieving process. Three integrative approaches have been proposed specific to the grief process: the four-component model, the dual-process model of coping with bereavement, and the model of adaptive grieving dynamics.

The Four-Component Model

The four-component model *proposes understanding grief is based on four things: (1) the context of the loss, referring to the risk factors such as whether the death was expected; (2) continuation of subjective meaning associated with loss, ranging from evaluations of everyday concerns to major questions about the meaning of life; (3) changing representations of the lost relationship over time; and (4) the role of coping and emotion regulation processes that cover all coping strategies used to deal with grief* (Bonanno, 2009; Bonanno et al., 2011). The four-component model relies heavily on emotion theory, has much in common with the transactional model of stress, and has empirical support. According to the four-component model, dealing with grief is a complicated process only understood as a complex outcome that unfolds over time.

There are several important implications of this integrative approach. One of the most important in helping a grieving person involves helping her or him make meaning from the loss (Bratkovich, 2010; Wong, 2015). Second, this model implies encouraging people to express their grief may actually not be helpful. *An alternative view, called the* grief work as rumination hypothesis, *not only rejects the necessity of grief processing for recovery from loss*

anniversary reaction
Changes in behavior related to feelings of sadness on the anniversary date of a loss.

four-component model
Model for understanding grief that is based on (1) the context of the loss, (2) continuation of subjective meaning associated with loss, (3) changing representations of the lost relationship over time, and (4) the role of coping and emotion-regulation processes.

grief work as rumination hypothesis
Approach that not only rejects the necessity of grief processing for recovery from loss but also views extensive grief processing as a form of rumination that may increase distress.

but views extensive grief processing as a form of rumination that may actually increase distress (Bonanno, Papa, & O'Neill, 2001). Although it may seem people who think obsessively about their loss or who ruminate about it are confronting the loss, rumination is actually considered a form of avoidance because the person is not dealing with his or her real feelings and moving on (Bui et al., 2015; Eisma et al., 2015; Robinaugh & McNally, 2013).

One prospective study shows, for instance, bereaved individuals who were not depressed prior to their spouse's death but then evidenced chronically elevated depression through the first year and a half of bereavement (i.e., a chronic grief pattern) also tended to report more frequently thinking about and talking about their recent loss at the 6-month point in bereavement (Bonanno, Wortman, & Neese, 2004). Thus, some bereaved individuals engage in minimal grief processing whereas others are predisposed toward more extensive grief processing. Furthermore, the individuals who engage in minimal grief processing will show a relatively favorable grief outcome, whereas those who are predisposed to more extensive grief processing tend toward ruminative preoccupation and, consequently, to a more prolonged grief course (Bonanno, 2009; Bonanno et al., 2011; Bui et al., 2015; Robinaugh & McNally, 2013).

In contrast to the traditional perspective that equates the absence of grief processing with grief avoidance, the grief work as rumination framework assumes resilient individuals are able to minimize processing of a loss through relatively automated processes, such as distraction or shifting attention toward more positive emotional experiences (Bonanno, 2009; Bonanno et al., 2011; Eisma et al., 2015). The grief work as rumination framework argues the deliberate avoidance or suppression of grief actually makes the experience of grief worse (Bonanno, 2009; Bonanno et al., 2011).

The Dual Process Model

The dual process model (DPM) *of coping with bereavement integrates existing ideas regarding stressors* (Stroebe & Archer, 2013; Utz & Pascoe, 2016). As shown in ▶ Figure 16.5, the DPM defines two broad types of stressors. *Loss-oriented stressors* concern the loss itself, such as the grief work that needs to be done. *Restoration-oriented stressors* are those that involve adapting to the survivor's new life situation, such as building new relationships and finding new activities. The DPM proposes dealing with these stressors is a dynamic process, as indicated by the lines connecting them in the figure. This is a distinguishing feature of DPM. It shows how bereaved people cycle back and forth between dealing mostly with grief and trying to move on with life. At times the emphasis will be on grief; at other times on moving forward.

The DPM captures well the process bereaved people themselves report—at times they are nearly overcome with grief, while at other times they handle life well. The DPM also helps us understand how, over time, people come to a balance between the long-term effects of bereavement and the need to live life. Understanding how people handle grief

dual process model (DPM)
View of coping with bereavement that integrates loss-oriented stressors and restoration-oriented stressors.

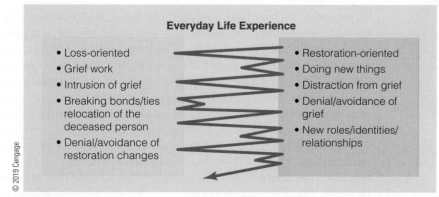

© 2019 Cengage

From Stroebe, M., & Schut, H. (2001). Models of coping with bereavement: A review. In M. S. Stroebe, R. O. Hansson, W. Stroebe, & H. Schut (Eds.), *Handbook of bereavement research: Consequences, coping, and care* (pp. 375–403). Washington, DC: American Psychological Association.

▶ **Figure 16.5**
The dual process model of coping with bereavement shows the relation between dealing with the stresses of the loss itself (loss-oriented) and moving on with one's life (restoration-oriented).

requires understanding the various contexts in which people live and interact with others (Sandler, Wolchik, & Ayers, 2007; Sandler et al., 2013).

The Model of Adaptive Grieving Dynamics

For anyone who has experienced the loss of a loved one, grieving is an intense, personal, complicated process that does not follow a straight path through predictable stages (Bagbey Darian, 2014). Consequently, to understand grief is to understand that multiple responses to loss may each prove adaptive in different ways. Only when they are considered together and in their unique combination for each grieving person is a more complete understanding of grief possible.

The basic structure of the model of adaptive grieving dynamics is shown in ❱ Figure 16.6. As can be seen, the model of adaptive grieving dynamics (MAGD) *is based on two sets of pairs of adaptive grieving dynamics.* One pair consists of *lamenting* and *heartening* responses to grief; the other pair consists of *integrating* and *tempering* responses to grief. These four interrelated dynamics are defined as follows (Bagbey Darian, 2014):

- *Lamenting:* experiencing and/or expressing grieving responses that are distressful, disheartening, and/or painful;
- *Heartening:* experiencing and/or expressing grieving responses that are gratifying, uplifting, and/or pleasurable;
- *Integrating:* assimilating internal and external changes catalyzed by a grief-inducing loss, and reconciling differences in past, present, and future realities in light of these changes; and
- *Tempering:* avoiding chronic attempts to integrate changed realities impacted by a grief-inducing loss that overwhelm a griever's and/or community's resources and capacities to integrate such changes.

Bagbey Darian (2014) argues that although the pairs of dynamics appear to be contradictory, in processing grief they actually work together. For instance, grieving people often experience both joy and sorrow simultaneously when remembering a loved one. This simultaneity of experience is a key difference between MAGD and the dual process model, as the dual process model argues that grieving people oscillate between loss-oriented tasks and restoration-oriented tasks.

According to the MAGD, the outcome of grief is not "working things through," or necessarily finding meaning in the loss. Rather, it aims at understanding how people continually negotiate and renegotiate their personal and interpersonal equilibrium over time. Grieving never really ends; how the person continues finding balance given that reality is the issue.

Ambiguous Loss

To this point we have been considering grief reactions to loss in which there is the possibility of closure. In these situations, there is proof of death, usually a physical dead body, and the likelihood of a funeral or some other ritual for support of the survivors. But this is not always the case. Consider major natural disasters, such as tsunamis, or major explosions, accidents, or repressive governments who kidnap or otherwise make people "disappear." The tsunami in Japan in 2011 left thousands unaccounted for.

Boss (2015) coined the term *ambiguous loss* for these circumstances. Ambiguous loss *refers to situations of loss in which there is no resolution or closure.* Boss (2010, 2015) describes two types of ambiguous loss. The first type refers to a missing person who is physically absent but still very present psychologically to family and friends. Examples of this type include people missing after disasters, victims of kidnapping, and those never recovered from accidents.

---

model of adaptive grieving dynamics (MAGD)

Model of grieving based on two sets of pairs of adaptive grieving dynamics: lamenting and heartening responses to grief; integrating and tempering responses to grief.

ambiguous loss

Situations of loss in which there is no resolution or closure to a loss.

❱ **Figure 16.6**

Model of adaptive grieving dynamics

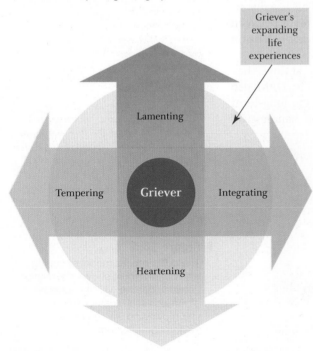

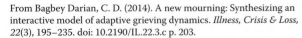

From Bagbey Darian, C. D. (2014). A new mourning: Synthesizing an interactive model of adaptive grieving dynamics. *Illness, Crisis & Loss,* 22(3), 195–235. doi: 10.2190/IL.22.3.c p. 203.

The primary challenge for the families and friends of the missing is the unending pain of not knowing for certain what happened, where their loved one is at present, and their specific fate. It is this pain that terrorists rely on to inflict constant pain and suffering. Typical grief reactions are postponed indefinitely, making it essentially impossible for people to move on with their lives, sometimes for generations (Boss, 2015). What motivates these families and friends is hope for an eventual return of the loved one (Boss, 2015; Wayland et al., 2016).

A second type of ambiguous loss involves a loved one who is psychologically absent but who is still physically present. They are what people term "here but gone," as is the case in certain diseases such as dementia. Families caring for loved ones with Alzheimer's disease, for instance, report going through grieving as their loved one loses more and more of what makes them who they are, ultimately coming to a point at which they think of their loved one as "dead" even though they are physically alive (Boss, 2010).

The common aspect of both types of ambiguous loss is that as long as certainty is not reached, closure is not possible in the usual sense. Families and friends report feeling pressure to stop holding out hope, on one hand, or are accused of being cold on the other. Either way, ambiguous grief is especially difficult to deal with.

Complicated or Prolonged Grief Disorder

Not everyone is able to cope with grief well and begin rebuilding a life. Sometimes the feelings of hurt, loneliness, and guilt are so overwhelming they become the focus of the survivor's life to such an extent there is never any closure and the grief continues to interfere indefinitely with one's ability to function. *When this occurs, individuals are viewed as having* complicated grief, *which is characterized by persistent and intrusive feelings of grief lasting beyond the expected period of adaptation to loss, and is associated with separation distress and traumatic distress* (Arizmendi, Kaszniak, & O'Connor, 2016). *Symptoms of* separation distress *include preoccupation with the deceased to the point it interferes with everyday functioning, upsetting memories of the deceased, longing and searching for the deceased, and isolation following the loss. Symptoms of* traumatic distress *include feeling disbelief about the death, mistrust, anger, and detachment from others as a result of the death, feeling shocked by the death, and the experience of physical presence of the deceased.*

Complicated grief forms a separate set of symptoms from depression (Stroebe, Abakoumkin, & Stroebe, 2010). Individuals experiencing complicated grief report high levels of separation distress (such as yearning, pining, or longing for the deceased person), along with specific cognitive, emotional, or behavioral indicators (such as avoiding reminders of the deceased, diminished sense of self, difficulty in accepting the loss, feeling bitter or angry), as well as increased morbidity, increased smoking and substance abuse, and difficulties with family and other social relationships. Similar distinctions have been made between complicated or prolonged grief disorder and anxiety disorders.

Arizmendi and colleagues (2016) report that people who experience complicated grief process grief emotions differently. Specifically, they do not engage those areas of the brain that are typically involved in regulating emotions, supporting the idea that complicated grief involves avoidance and a disruption of emotion regulation.

The presence of complicated grief transcends culture. For example, Li & Prigerson (2016) validated a measure of complicated grief in a sample of Chinese adults. Likewise, complicated grief was validated in a sample of Spanish adults in terms of how they respond to emotion (Fernández-Alcántara et al., 2016).

Some researchers believe that complicated grief may be more likely with certain types of loss (such as the death of a child). In addition, some also speculate that whether a person has a supportive social network may make a difference. However, too little research has been conducted for clear conclusions to be drawn.

The Spotlight on Research feature explores grief work regarding a common but under-researched topic: the degree to which partners influence each other's grieving process (Stroebe, Finkenauer et al., 2013). As you read it, note how grief, which is typically thought of in an individual context, is experienced in a social context.

complicated grief or prolonged grief disorder

Expression of grief that is distinguished from depression and from normal grief in terms of separation distress and traumatic distress.

separation distress

Expression of complicated or prolonged grief disorder that includes being preoccupied with the deceased to the point that it interferes with everyday functioning, having upsetting memories of the deceased, longing and searching for the deceased, and feeling isolated following the loss.

traumatic distress

Expression of complicated or prolonged grief disorder that includes disbelief about the death; mistrusting others, feeling anger, and being detachment from others as a result of the death; feeling shocked by the death; and experiencing the physical presence of the deceased.

The Costs of Holding in Grief for the Sake of One's Partner

Who were the investigators, and what was the aim of the study? When parents experience the loss of a child, they must cope with two main things: how to deal with the worst thing imaginable with the death of their child and how to deal with each other. Surprisingly, little research has been done to examine how partners work through the grieving process alone and together. Stroebe and colleagues wanted to know how each partner regulates or tries to protect the other from the pain of the loss and from his or her own grief.

How did the investigators measure the topic of interest? The researchers administered the Dutch version of the Inventory of Complicated Grief, items that measured Partner-Oriented Self-Regulation (POSR, such as "I stay strong for my partner") and items that assessed expressions of concern for one's partner.

Who were the participants in the study? Participants were 463 Dutch couples who had lost a child and were invited to participate. Parents who also were grandparents and single parents were excluded. A total of 219 couples agreed to participate. Their age range was 26–68 years, the causes of death of the children were varied, and roughly two-thirds of the children were males.

What was the design of the study? The study used a longitudinal design with three times of measurement (6, 13, and 20 months after the death of the child).

Were there ethical concerns in the study? There were no ethical concerns, as participants were carefully screened, were provided detailed information about the nature of the project, and were given the opportunity to stop their participation at any time.

What were the results? Several findings are noteworthy. First, grief lessened over time for both partners, with a recognition that grief was always greater for women than for men. Higher levels of POSR mattered;

individuals whose partner reported more POSR experienced more grief themselves, as did their partner. These relations held over time. Expressions of concern for the partner showed the opposite—more expressions of concern were related to lower levels of grief in the partner being targeted by those expressions.

What did the investigators conclude? The researchers argued that behaviors intended to show that one is strong for one's partner are actually unhelpful in lowering the experience of grief. On the other hand, one partner who expresses grief and concern about his or her partner can be helpful in the couples' and the individuals' coping with grief.

What converging evidence would strengthen these conclusions? Because the study included only Dutch couples, more diverse samples would be beneficial. Also, more analyses on the cause of death and the age of the child at death may provide additional insightful information.

Disenfranchised Grief

As we have noted repeatedly throughout this chapter, the experience of loss and the subsequent grief we feel is a highly personal matter. *Sometimes, a loss that appears insignificant to others is highly consequential to the person who suffers the loss; such situations give rise to* **disenfranchised grief**. A good example of disenfranchised grief is the loss of a pet. To most of the world, the loss is not a big deal—an animal has died. But to the person whose pet died, the loss may be very traumatic and result in social isolation in grief.

Disenfranchised grief stems from the social expectations we place on people to "move on" after loss (Harris, 2016). However, those expectations can result in failure to understand the personal impact that every loss has on someone and a failure to be empathetic to that person's experience. Such failure may also reflect certain stereotypes or bias regarding the value of various people's lives, such as drug addicts or very old people. In this context, it is good to keep in mind John Donne's passage from his *Devotions upon Emergent Occasions*, written in December 1623 as he recovered from a very serious illness:

> No man is an island,
>
> Entire of itself,
>
> Every man is a piece of the continent,
>
> A part of the main.
>
> If a clod be washed away by the sea,
>
> Europe is the less.
>
> As well as if a promontory were.
>
> As well as if a manor of thy friend's
>
> Or of thine own were:

disenfranchised grief

A loss that appears insignificant to others is highly consequential to the person who suffers the loss.

Any man's death diminishes me,

Because I am involved in mankind,

And therefore never send to know for whom the bell tolls;

It tolls for thee.

Think About It

How would you use the biopsychosocial model to create a support group for bereaved people?

TEST YOURSELF 16.4

Recall

1. Feeling sad on the date when your grandmother died the previous year is an example of a(n) _____.

2. Compared with other age groups,_____ show the most negative effects following bereavement.

3. Separation distress and _____ are two characteristics of complicated or prolonged grief disorder.

Interpret

- What connections might there be between bereavement and stress?

Apply

- If you were to create a brochure listing the five most important things to do and not to do in reacting to someone who just lost a close family member or friend through death, what would you include? Why?

Check your answers to the Recall Questions at the end of the chapter.

16.5 Dying and Bereavement Experiences Across the Life Span

LEARNING OBJECTIVES

- What do children understand about death? How should adults help them deal with it?

- How do adolescents deal with death?

- How do adults deal with death? What special issues do they face concerning the death of a child or parent?

- How do older adults face the loss of a child, grandchild, or partner?

Donna and Carl have a 6-year-old daughter, Jennie, whose grandmother just died. Jennie and her grandmother were very close, as the two saw each other almost every day. Other adults have told her parents not to take Jennie to the funeral. Donna and Carl aren't sure what to do. They wonder whether Jennie will understand what happened to her grandmother, and they worry about how she will react.

Coming to grips with the reality of death may be one of the hardest things we have to do in life. American society does not help much either, as it tends to distance itself from death through euphemisms, such as "passed away" or "dearly departed," and by eliminating many rituals from the home (for example, viewings no longer take place there, no more official mourning visits to the bereaved's house).

These trends make it difficult for people such as Donna, Carl, and Jennie to learn about death in its natural context. Dying itself has been moved from the home to hospitals and other institutions such as nursing homes. The closest most people get to death is a quick glance inside a nicely lined casket at a corpse that has been made to look as if the person were still alive.

What do people, especially children such as Jennie, understand about death? How do Donna and Carl feel? How do the friends of Jennie's grandmother feel? In this section, we consider how our understanding of death changes throughout the life span.

Childhood

Parents often take their children to funerals of relatives and close friends. But many adults, such as Donna and Carl in the vignette, wonder whether young children really know what death means. Children's understanding of death must be understood in terms of their cultural background and the fact that it changes with their development (Rosengren, Gutiérrez, & Schein, 2014a). Preschoolers tend to believe that death is temporary and magical, something dramatic that comes to get you in the middle of the night like a burglar or a ghost. Not until children are 5 to 7 years of age do they realize that death is permanent, that it eventually happens to everyone, and that dead people no longer have any biological functions.

Why does this shift occur? There are three major areas of developmental change in children that affect their understanding of death and grief (Rosengren et al., 2014a; Webb, 2010a): cognitive-language ability, emotional/psychosocial development, and coping skills. In terms of cognitive-language ability, think back to Chapters 4 and 6, especially to the discussion of Piaget's theory of cognitive development. Consider Jennie, the 6-year-old daughter of Donna and Carl in the vignette. Where would she be in Piaget's terms? In this perspective, the ages 5 to 7 include the transition from preoperational to concrete-operational thinking. Concrete-operational thinking permits children to know that death is final and permanent. Therefore, Jennie is likely to understand what happened to her grandmother. With this more mature understanding of death comes a lower fear of death, too (Gutiérrez et al., 2014; Rosengren et al., 2014b).

Children's expressions of grief at the loss of a loved one vary with age, too (Halliwell & Franken, 2016; Webb, 2010b). Several common manifestations of grief among children are shown in ❱ Figure 16.7. Typical reactions in early childhood include regression, guilt for causing the death, denial, displacement, repression, and wishful thinking that the deceased will return. In later childhood, common behaviors include problems at school, anger, and physical ailments. As children mature, they acquire more coping skills that permit a shift to problem-focused coping, which provides a better sense of personal control. Children will often flip between grief and normal activity, a pattern they may learn from adults (Stroebe et al., 2005), and may be more likely to disclose their true feelings online (Halliwell & Franken, 2016). Sensitivity to these feelings and how they get expressed is essential so that the child can understand what happened and that he or she did not cause the death.

Research shows that bereavement per se during childhood typically does not have long-lasting effects such as depression (Miller, Rosengren, & Gutiérrez, 2014; Webb, 2010b). Problems are more likely to occur if the child does not receive adequate care and attention following the death.

Understanding death can be particularly difficult for children when adults are not open and honest with them, especially about the meaning of death (Miller & Rosengren, 2014). Most adults believe that it is best to shield their children, especially younger children, from death. The use of euphemisms such as "Grandma has gone away" and "Mommy is only sleeping" reflects this belief, but is unwise. First, young children do not understand the deeper level of meaning in such statements and are likely to take them literally. Second, and more important, adults cannot fully shield children from the reality of death.

When explaining death to children, it is best to deal with them on their terms. Keep explanations simple, at a level they can understand. Try to allay their fears and reassure them that whatever reaction they have is okay. Providing loving support for the child will maximize the potential for a successful (albeit painful) introduction to one of life's realities. One male college student recalled how, when he was 9, his father helped him deal with his feelings after his grandfather's death:

> The day of my grandfather's death my dad came over to my aunt and uncle's house where my brother and I were staying. He took us into one of the bedrooms and sat us down. He told us Granddaddy Doc had died. He explained to us that it was okay if we needed to cry. He told us that he had cried, and that if we did cry we wouldn't be babies, but would just be men showing our emotions. (Dickinson, 1992, pp. 175–176)

Children show their grief in many ways, including physiological (somatic), emotional (intrapsychic), and behavioral.

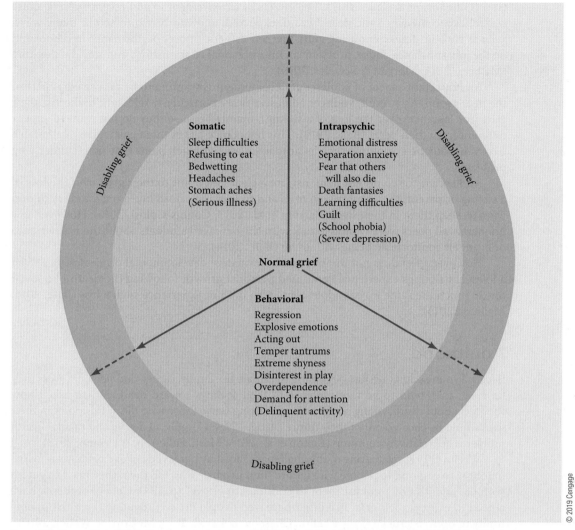

Somatic
- Sleep difficulties
- Refusing to eat
- Bedwetting
- Headaches
- Stomach aches
- (Serious illness)

Intrapsychic
- Emotional distress
- Separation anxiety
- Fear that others will also die
- Death fantasies
- Learning difficulties
- Guilt
- (School phobia)
- (Severe depression)

Normal grief

Behavioral
- Regression
- Explosive emotions
- Acting out
- Temper tantrums
- Extreme shyness
- Disinterest in play
- Overdependence
- Demand for attention
- (Delinquent activity)

Disabling grief

© 2019 Cengage

From Oltjenbruns, K. A. (2001). Developmental context of childhood: Grief and regrief phenomena. In M. S. Stroebe, R. O. Hansson, W. Stroebe, & H. Schut, (Eds.), *Handbook of Bereavement Research: Consequences, Coping, and Care* (Fig. 8-1, p. 177). Washington, DC: American Psychological Association. Copyright © 2001 by the American Psychological Association.

It is important for children to know that it is okay for them to feel sad, to cry, or to show their feelings in whatever way they want. Reassuring children that it's okay to feel this way helps them deal with their confusion at some adults' explanations of death. Young adults remember feeling uncomfortable as children around dead bodies, often fearing that the deceased person would come after them. Still, researchers believe it is very important for children to attend the funeral of a relative or to have a private viewing (Miller & Rosengren, 2014; Webb, 2010b). They will process the experience in age-appropriate ways, especially if they have understanding adults available to answer questions.

Think About It

How could parents use knowledge of child development to help children understand death?

Adolescence

Adolescents have more personal experience with death and grief than many people realize (Balk, 2014). Surveys of college students indicate that between 40 and 70% of traditional-aged college students will experience the death of someone close to them during their college years, such as a parent, sibling, or friend.

Adolescence is a time of personal and physical change, when one is trying to develop a theory of self. When teenagers experience the death of someone close to them, they may have considerable trouble making sense of the event, especially if this is their first experience (Oltjenbruns & Balk, 2007). The effects of bereavement in adolescence can be quite severe, especially when the death was unexpected, and can be expressed in many ways, such as chronic illness, enduring guilt, low self-esteem, poorer performance in school and on the job, substance abuse, problems in interpersonal relationships, and suicidal thinking (Malberg, 2014; Morgan & Roberts, 2010).

An important aspect of adolescent development is wanting to be perceived as part of the peer group. As a result, younger adolescents are particularly reluctant to discuss their grief (for instance, over the loss of a sibling), mainly because they do not want to appear different from their peers (Balk, 2014). This reluctance leaves them particularly vulnerable to psychosomatic symptoms such as headaches and stomach pains that signal underlying problems.

Adolescents often do not demonstrate a clear end point to their grief over the loss of a sibling or parent; they continue to miss and to love their dead loved ones and try to find ways to keep them in their lives (Barrera et al., 2013; Collins-Colosi, 2016). However, few nonbereaved peers were willing to talk with the bereaved students about their experience or even felt comfortable being with them (Balk, 2014).

However, grief does not interfere with normative developmental processes. Bereaved adolescent siblings experience continued personal growth following the death of a loved one in much the same way as adolescents who did not experience such a loss (Balk, 2014; Malberg, 2014).

Adulthood

Because young adults are just beginning to pursue the family, career, and personal goals they have set, they tend to be more intense in their feelings toward death. When asked how they feel about death, young adults report a strong sense those who die at this point in their lives would be cheated out of their future (Attig, 1996). Complicated grief and mental health problems are relatively common (Bolton et al., 2016; Mash, Fullerton, & Ursano, 2013).

Wrenn (1999) relates one of the challenges faced by bereaved college students is learning "how to respond to people who ignore their grief, or who tell them they need to get on with life and it's not good for them to continue to grieve" (p. 134). College students have a need to express their grief like other bereaved people do, so providing them the opportunity to do so is crucial (Fajgenbaum, Chesson, & Lanzl, 2012; McCoyd & Walter, 2016).

Becoming a widow as a young adult can be especially traumatic.

Monashee Frantz/OJO Images/Getty Images

Experiencing the loss of one's partner in young adulthood can be traumatic, not only because of the loss itself but also because such loss is unexpected. As Trish Straine, a 32-year-old widow whose husband was killed in the World Trade Center attack put it: "I suddenly thought, 'I'm a widow.' Then I said to myself, 'A widow? That's an older woman, who's dressed in black. It's certainly not a 32-year-old like me'" (Lieber, 2001). One of the most difficult aspects for young widows and widowers is they must deal with both their own and their young children's grief and provide the support their children need, and that can be extremely difficult. "Every time I look at my children, I'm reminded of Mark," said Stacey, a 35-year-old widow whose husband died of bone cancer. "And people don't want to hear you say you don't feel like moving on, even though there is great pressure from them to do that."

The death of a girlfriend or boyfriend in young adulthood is often unacknowledged as bereavement. Leichtentritt and colleagues (2013) found that girlfriends of soldiers killed in battle felt socially isolated and lonely in dealing with their loss. Clearly, this is a missed opportunity to be sensitive to people's loss and to provide support.

Death of One's Child

The death of one's child, for most parents, brings unimaginable grief (McCoyd & Walter, 2016; Stroebe et al., 2013). Because children are not supposed to die before their parents, it is as if the natural order of things has been violated, shaking parents to their core (Rubin & Malkinson, 2001). Mourning and relationship stress are always intense; some parents never recover or reconcile themselves to the death of their child and may terminate their relationship with each other, while others find solace and strength in each other (Albuquerque, Pereira, & Narciso, 2016). The intensity of feelings is due to the strong parent–child bond that begins before birth and lasts a lifetime (Maple et al., 2010; Rosenbaum, Smith, & Zollfrank, 2011).

Young parents who lose a child unexpectedly report high anxiety, a more negative view of the world, and much guilt, that results in a devastating experience (Seyda & Fitzsimons, 2010). The most overlooked losses of a child are those that happen through stillbirth, miscarriage, abortion, or neonatal death (Earle, Komaromy, & Layne, 2012; McCoyd & Walter, 2016). Attachment to the child begins before birth, especially for mothers, so the loss hurts deeply. For this reason, ritual is extremely important to acknowledge the death and validate parents' feelings of grief (Nuzum et al., 2015).

Yet parents who experience this type of loss are expected to recover quickly. The lived experience of parents tells a different story (Seyda & Fitzsimons, 2010). These parents talk about a life-changing event and report a deep sense of loss and hurt, especially when others do not understand their feelings. Worst of all, if societal expectations for quick recovery are not met, the parents may be subjected to unfeeling comments. As one mother notes, parents often just wish somebody would acknowledge the loss (Okonski, 1996).

The loss of a young adult child for a middle-aged parent is experienced differently but is equally devastating (Maple et al., 2013; Schneider, 2013). Complicated grief is more common among bereaved parents than in other groups, most likely due to the very different nature of the parent–child relationship (Zetumer et al., 2015).

Death of One's Parent

Most parents die after their children are grown. But whenever parental death occurs, it hurts. Losing a parent in adulthood is a rite of passage as one is transformed from being a "son" or "daughter" to being "without parents" (Abrams, 2013; McCoyd & Walter, 2016). We, the children, are now next in line.

The loss of a parent is significant. For young adult women transitioning to motherhood, losing their own mother during adolescence raises many feelings, such as deep loss at not being able to share their pregnancies with their mothers and fear of dying young themselves (Franceschi, 2005). Death of one's parent in adulthood has understandable effects on adult children, largely depending on the quality of the relationship with the deceased parent (Stokes, 2016).

The feelings accompanying the loss of an older parent reflect a sense of letting go, loss of a buffer against death, better acceptance of one's own eventual death, and a sense of relief the parent's suffering is over (Abrams, 2013; Igarashi et al., 2013; McCoyd & Walter, 2016). Yet, if the parent died from a cause such as Alzheimer's disease, which involves the loss of the parent–child relationship along the way, then bodily death can feel like the second time the parent died (Shaw, 2007). Whether the adult child now tries to separate from the deceased parent's expectations or finds comfort in the memories, the impact of the loss is great.

Late Adulthood

In general, older adults are less anxious about death and more accepting of it than any other age group (Kastenbaum, 1999). They may believe that their most important life tasks have been completed. However, that is not to say that older adults are unaffected by loss. Far from it.

Death of One's Child or Grandchild in Late Life

The loss of a child can happen at any point over the adult life span. Older bereaved parents tend to reevaluate their grief as experienced shortly after the loss and years and decades later. Even more than 30 years after the death of a child, older adults still feel a keen sense of loss and have continued difficulty coming to terms with it (Malkinson & Bar-Tur, 2004–2005). The long-lasting effects of the loss of a child are often accompanied by a sense of guilt that the pain affected the parents' relationships with the surviving children. Loss of a child in young adulthood may also result in lower cognitive functioning in late life (Greene et al., 2014).

The loss of a grandchild results in similar feelings: intense emotional upset, survivor guilt, regrets about the relationship with the deceased grandchild, and a need to restructure relationships with the surviving family. However, bereaved grandparents tend to control and hide their grief behavior in an attempt to shield their child (the bereaved parent) from the level of pain being felt. In cases in which older adults were the primary caregivers for grandchildren, feelings can be especially difficult. For example, custodial grandparents in South Africa whose grandchildren in their care died from AIDS go through emotionally difficult times due to the loss and to the social stigma regarding the disease (Boon et al., 2010).

Death of One's Partner

Experiencing the loss of one's partner is the type of loss in late life we know most about. The death of a partner differs from other losses. It clearly represents a deep personal loss, especially when the couple has had a long and close relationship (Lee, 2014). In a very real way, when one's partner dies, a part of oneself dies, too.

There is pressure from society to mourn the loss of one's partner for a period of time and then to "move on" (Jenkins, 2003). Typically, this pressure is manifested if the survivor begins to show interest in finding another partner before an "acceptable" period of mourning has passed. Although Americans no longer specify the length of the mourning period, many believe that about a year is appropriate. The fact that such pressure and negative commentary usually do not accompany other losses is another indication of the seriousness with which most people take the death of a partner.

Older bereaved spouses may grieve a great deal for a long time (Lee, 2014); research has shown that grief can sometimes last for years (Naef et al., 2013). Given that, you might wonder whether having a supportive social network can help people cope. Research findings on this topic are mixed, however. Some studies find that social support plays a significant role in the outcome of the grieving process. For example, some data show that during the first two years after the death of a partner, the quality of the support system—rather than simply the number of friends—is especially important for the grieving partner. Survivors who have confidants are better off than survivors who have many acquaintances (Hansson & Stroebe, 2007). In contrast, other studies find that

The loss of a spouse or partner can be especially traumatic after a long relationship.

PHOVOIR/Alamy Stock Photo

having a supportive social network plays little role in helping people cope (DiGiacomo et al., 2013). Issues may include whether there is a complex relationship involving the bereaved person, whether he or she wants to have contact with others, who in the social network is willing to provide support, and whether that support is of high quality.

When one's partner dies, how he or she felt about the relationship can play a role in coping with bereavement. For instance, widowed older adults who felt worsening regret about unfinished aspects of their marriages over time had the hardest time dealing with grief (Holland et al., 2014).

Several studies of widows document a tendency for some older widows to "sanctify" their husbands (Lopata, 1996). Sanctification involves describing a deceased spouse in idealized terms, and it serves several functions: validating that the widow had a strong marriage, is a good and worthy person, and is capable of rebuilding her life. European American women who view being a wife as above all other roles a woman can perform are somewhat more likely to sanctify their husbands (Lopata, 1996). In fact, the higher the quality of the relationship, the more bereaved spouses yearn for their lost spouse (Stroebe, Abakoumkin, & Stroebe, 2010).

Older bereaved spouses who can talk about their feelings concerning their loss exhibit reduced levels of depression and functional impairment (Pfoff, Zarotney, & Monk, 2014). Cognitive-behavioral therapy is one especially effective intervention to help bereaved people make sense of the loss and deal with their other feelings and thoughts (Lichtenthal & Sweeney, 2014). A key to this process is helping people make meaning from the death (Neimeyer & Wogrin, 2008).

Gay and lesbian couples may experience other feelings and reactions in addition to typical feelings of grief (Clarke et al., 2010). For example, a partner may feel disenfranchised by family members of the deceased at the funeral, making it hard for the partner to bring closure to the relationship (McNutt & Yakushko, 2013). For gay partners who were also caregivers, the loss affects one's sense of identity in much the same way as the death of a spouse, and making sense of the death becomes the primary issue (Cadell & Marshall, 2007). Lesbian widows report similar feelings (Bent & Magilvy, 2006). As same-sex marriage becomes more accepted, it will be important for researchers to document the experience of same-sex widows and widowers.

Think About It
Why do many older adults continue to "talk" with their deceased partners?

Conclusion

Death is not as pleasant a topic as children's play or occupational development. It's not something we can go to college to master. What it represents to many people is the end of their existence, and that is a scary prospect. But because we all share in this fear at some level, each of us is equipped to provide support and comfort for grieving survivors.

Death is the last life-cycle force we encounter, the ultimate triumph of the biological forces that limit the length of life. Yet the same psychological and social forces so influential throughout life help us deal with death, either our own or someone else's. As we come to the end of our life journey, we understand death through an interaction of psychological forces—such as coping skills and intellectual and emotional understanding of death—and the sociocultural forces expressed in a particular society's traditions and rituals.

Learning about and dealing with death is clearly a developmental process across the life span that fits well in the biopsychosocial framework. Most apparent is that biological forces are essential to understanding death. The definition of death is based on whether certain biological functions are present; these same definitions create numerous ethical dilemmas that must be dealt with psychologically and socioculturally. Life-cycle forces also play a key role. We have seen, depending on a person's age, the concept of death has varied meanings beyond the mere cessation of life.

How a person's understanding of death develops is also the result of psychological forces. As the ability to think and reflect undergoes fundamental change, the view of death changes from a mostly magical approach to one that can be transcendent and transforming. As we have seen, people who face their own imminent death experience certain feelings. Having gained experience through the deaths of friends and relatives, a person's level of comfort with his or her own death may increase. Such personal experience may also come about by sharing the rituals defined through sociocultural forces. People observe how others deal with death and how the culture sets the tone and prescribes behavior for survivors. The combined action of forces also determines how they cope with the grief that accompanies the loss of someone close. Psychologically, confronting grief depends on many things, including the quality of the support system we have.

Thus, just as the beginning of life represents a complex interaction of biological, psychological, sociocultural, and life-cycle factors, so does death. What people believe about what follows after death is also an interaction of these factors. So, as we bring our study of human development to a close, we end where we began: What we experience in our lives cannot be understood from only a single perspective.

TEST YOURSELF 16.5

Recall

1. In general, adults should be _____ when discussing death with children.
2. Compared with other age groups, _____ are especially reluctant to talk about their grief experiences.
3. The most devastating type of loss for an adult is the loss of a(n) _____.
4. _____ involves describing a deceased spouse in idealized terms.

Interpret

- What similarities and differences would you expect to find between the survivors in heterosexual marriages and in gay or lesbian relationships when the spouse or partner dies?

Apply

- How do the different ways that adults view death relate to the stages of Erikson's theory discussed in Chapters 10, 13, and 15?

Check your answers to the Recall Questions at the end of the chapter.

SUMMARY

13.1 Definitions and Ethical Issues

How is death defined?

- Death is a difficult concept to define precisely. Different cultures have different meanings and rituals surrounding death.

What legal and medical criteria are used to determine when death occurs?

- For many centuries, a clinical definition of death was used: the absence of a heartbeat and respiration. Currently, whole-brain death is the most widely used definition. It is based on several highly specific criteria that are assessed by trained healthcare professionals. The condition of persistent vegetative state often creates a complicated situation for determination of death.

What are the ethical dilemmas surrounding euthanasia?

- Two types of euthanasia are distinguished. Active euthanasia consists of deliberately ending someone's life, such as turning off a life-support system. Passive euthanasia is ending someone's life by withholding some type of intervention or treatment (e.g., by stopping nutrition). Physician-assisted suicide is a controversial issue and is being addressed in some states through laws. It is essential people make their wishes known through either a healthcare power of attorney or a living will.

- The personal and financial costs of prolonging life when the patient would have preferred another option are significant, as are the ethical issues regarding prolonging life without considering quality of life.

13.2 Thinking About Death: Personal Aspects

How do feelings about death change over adulthood?

- Cognitive developmental level is important for understanding how young adults view death and the lessening of feelings of immortality.

- Middle-aged adults usually experience the death of their parents and begin to confront their own mortality, undergoing a change in their sense of time lived and time until death.

- Older adults are les anxious about and more accepting of death.

How do people deal with their own death?

- Kübler-Ross's approach includes five stages: denial, anger, bargaining, depression, and acceptance. People may be in more than one stage at a time and do not necessarily go through them in order.

- A contextual theory of dying emphasizes the tasks a dying person must face. Four dimensions of these tasks have been identified: bodily needs, psychological security, interpersonal attachments, and spiritual energy and hope. A contextual theory incorporates differences in reasons people die and the places people die.

What is death anxiety, and how do people show it?

- Most people exhibit some degree of anxiety about death, even though it is difficult to define and measure. Terror management theory is a common frame for understanding death anxiety. Young adults show greater brain activity when exposed to death-related concepts than do older adults.

- The main ways death anxiety is shown are by avoiding death (e.g., refusing to go to funerals) and deliberately challenging it (e.g., engaging in dangerous sports). The many components of death anxiety affect many different aspects of behavior.

- Death education has been shown to be extremely effective in helping people deal with death anxiety.

13.3 End-of-Life Issues

How do people deal with end-of-life issues and create a final scenario?

- Managing the final aspects of life, after-death disposition of the body, memorial services, and distribution of assets are important end-of-life issues. Making choices about what people want and do not want done constitute making a final scenario. One of the most difficult parts of a final scenario is separation from family and friends. Jointly creating a final scenario among the dying person, family, and health-care professionals is optimal.

What is hospice?

- The goal of a hospice is to maintain the quality of life and manage the pain of terminally ill patients. Hospice clients typically have cancer, AIDS, or a progressive neurological disorder. Family members tend to stay involved in the care of hospice clients. Pain management can also be achieved in ways other than through hospice.

How does one make one's end-of-life desires and decisions known?

- End-of-life decisions are made known most often through a living will, healthcare power of attorney, and specific medical requests such as a do not resuscitate order. It is important family and healthcare professionals are aware of these decisions. The Patient Self-Determination Act requires healthcare facilities to inform patients of these rights but must take the patient's competence to make decisions into account.

13.4 Surviving the Loss: The Grieving Process

How do people experience the grief process?

- Grief is an active process of coping with loss. Four aspects of grieving must be confronted: the reality of the loss, the emotional turmoil, adjusting to the environment, and loosening the ties with the deceased. When death is expected, survivors go through anticipatory grief; unexpected death is usually more difficult for people to handle.

- "Recovery" may be a misleading term, as the process of adjusting and readjusting to life following a loss never ends.

- The mode of death, personal factors, and extent of social support make a difference in dealing with grief.

- Anticipatory grief does not appear to make the grieving process any easier. However, the degree of attachment to the person who died does.

What feelings do grieving people have?

- Dealing with grief, called *grief work*, usually takes more time than society wants to allot. Grief is equally intense for both expected and unexpected death. Normal grief reactions include sorrow, sadness, denial, disbelief, guilt, and anniversary reactions.

- How people demonstrate grief varies across cultures.

How do people cope with grief?

- Three general approaches help explain how people cope with grief.

- The four-component model is based on the processes of: the context of the loss; continuation of subjective meaning of the loss; changing representations of the lost relationship over time; and the role of coping and emotion regulation processes. However, the grief work as rumination hypothesis rejects the need for grief as a basis for recovering form loss.

- The dual process model integrates existing ideas about stress into the context of loss and restoration. These stressors operate in a dynamic relation.

What are the types of ambiguous loss?

- Ambiguous loss refers to situations of loss in which there is no resolution or closure. There are two types of ambiguous loss. The first type refers to a missing person who is physically absent but still very present psychologically to family and friends. The second type refers to situations in which the loved one is psychologically absent but still physically present.

What is the difference between normal and complicated grief?

- Complicated grief involves symptoms of separation distress and traumatic distress. Separation distress is preoccupation with the deceased to the extent that it interferes with everyday functioning. Excessive guilt and self-blame are common manifestations of traumatic grief.

What is disenfranchised grief?

- Disenfranchised grief, in which a loss is downplayed by others in a bereaved person's social network, is an important consideration in understanding grief.

16.5 Dying and Bereavement Experiences Across the Life Span

What do children understand about death? How should adults help them deal with it?

- The cognitive and psychosocial developmental levels of children determine their understanding of and ability to cope with death. This is especially evident in the behaviors children use to display their grief.

- Research indicates that there are few long-lasting effects of bereavement in childhood.

How do adolescents deal with death?

- Adolescents may have difficulty making sense of death and are often severely affected by bereavement. Adolescents may be reluctant to discuss their feelings of loss, and peers often provide little support.

How do adults deal with death? What special issues do they face concerning the death of a child or parent?

- Young and middle-aged adults usually have intense feelings about death. Attachment theory provides a useful framework for understanding these feelings.

- Midlife is a time when people usually deal with the death of their parents and confront their own mortality.

- The death of one's child is especially difficult to cope with.

- The death of one's parent deprives an adult of many important things, and the feelings accompanying it are often complex.

How do older adults face the loss of a child, grandchild, or partner?

- Older adults are usually less anxious about death and deal with it better than any other age group.

- The death of a grandchild can be traumatic for older adults, and the feelings of loss may never go away.

- The death of one's partner represents a deep personal loss, especially when the couple had a long and close relationship. The history of the relationship influences the grief process.

Test Yourself: Recall Answers

16.1 1. sociocultural **2.** the brainstem still functions in a persistent vegetative state **3.** passive euthanasia   **16.2 1.** Middle-aged adults **2.** contextual theory of dying **3.** terror management theory   **16.3 1.** final scenario **2.** Hospice **3.** living will   **16.4 1.** anniversary reaction **2.** middle-aged adults **3.** traumatic distress   **16.5 1.** honest **2.** adolescents **3.** child **4.** Sanctification

Key Terms

thanatology (542)
clinical death (544)
whole-brain death (544)
persistent vegetative state (544)
bioethics (545)
euthanasia (545)
active euthanasia (545)
passive euthanasia (545)
physician-assisted suicide (546)
death anxiety (551)
terror management theory (552)
end-of-life issues (554)

final scenario (555)
hospice (556)
palliative care (556)
living will (558)
healthcare power of attorney (558)
do not resuscitate (DNR) order (558)
bereavement (561)
grief (561)
mourning (561)
anticipatory grief (562)
grief work (563)
anniversary reaction (564)

four-component model (564)
grief work as rumination hypothesis (564)
dual process model (DPM) (565)
model of adaptive grieving dynamics (MAGD) (566)
ambiguous loss (566)
complicated or prolonged grief disorder (567)
separation distress (567)
traumatic distress (567)
disenfranchised grief (568)

Glossary

Note: Many familiar words have specialized meanings and usage in psychology. Several of these, used in the text, are defined here. When a glossary term is used to define another glossary term, it appears in **bold**.

abusive relationship Relationships in which one person becomes aggressive toward the partner.

accommodation According to Piaget, changing existing knowledge based on new knowledge.

active euthanasia Deliberate ending of someone's life.

active life expectancy Number of years that a person is free from debilitating chronic disease and impairment.

activities of daily living (ADLs) Basic self-care tasks such as eating, bathing, toileting, walking, and dressing.

adaptation level When press level is average for a particular level of **competence**.

adolescent egocentrism Self-absorption that is characteristic of teenagers as they search for identity.

adolescent-limited antisocial behavior Behavior of youth who engage in relatively minor criminal acts but aren't consistently antisocial.

aerobic exercise Exercise that places moderate stress on the heart by maintaining a pulse rate between 60% and 90% of a person's maximum heart rate.

age discrimination Involves denying a job or promotion to someone solely on the basis of age.

age of viability Age at which a fetus can survive outside the womb because most of its bodily systems function adequately; typically at seven months after conception.

age-related macular degeneration Progressive and irreversible destruction of receptors in the retina from any of a number of causes.

agreeableness Dimension of personality associated with being accepting, willing to work with others, and caring.

alcohol use disorder Drinking pattern that results in significant and recurrent consequences that reflect loss of reliable control over alcohol use.

alert inactivity State in which a baby is calm with eyes open and attentive; the baby seems to be deliberately inspecting the environment.

alienation When workers believe that what they are doing is meaningless and that their efforts are devalued or when they do not see the connection between what they do and the final product.

alleles Variations of **genes**.

altruism **Prosocial behavior** such as helping and sharing in which the individual does not benefit directly from his or her behavior.

Alzheimer's disease Disease marked by gradual declines in memory, **attention**, and judgment; confusion as to time and place; difficulties in communicating; decline in self-care skills; inappropriate behavior; and personality changes.

ambiguous loss Situations of loss in which there is no resolution or closure.

amniocentesis Prenatal diagnostic technique that uses a syringe to withdraw a sample of **amniotic fluid** through the mother's abdomen.

amnion Inner sac in which the developing child rests.

amniotic fluid Fluid that surrounds the fetus.

analytic ability In Sternberg's **theory** of intelligence, the ability to analyze problems and generate different solutions.

animism Phenomenon of crediting inanimate objects with life and lifelike properties such as feelings.

anniversary reaction Changes in behavior related to feelings of sadness on the anniversary date of a loss.

anorexia nervosa Persistent refusal to eat accompanied by an irrational fear of being overweight.

anticipatory grief **Grief** that is experienced during the period before an expected death occurs that supposedly serves to buffer the impact of the loss when it does come and to facilitate recovery.

anxiety disorders Problems such as feelings of severe anxiety, phobias, and obsessive-compulsive behaviors.

assimilation According to Piaget, taking in information that is compatible with what one already knows.

assisted living facilities Supportive living arrangement for people who need assistance with **ADLs** or **IADLs** but who are not so impaired physically or cognitively that they need 24-hour care.

assortative mating **Theory** stating that people find partners based on their similarity to each other.

attachment Enduring socioemotional relationship between infants and their caregivers.

attention Processes that determine which information will be processed further by an individual.

authoritarian parenting Style of parenting in which parents show high levels of control and low levels of warmth toward their children.

authoritative parenting Style of parenting in which parents use a moderate amount of control and are warm and responsive to their children.

autobiographical memory Memory for events that occur during one's life.

autosomes First 22 pairs of **chromosomes**.

average children As applied to children's popularity, children who are liked and disliked by different classmates, but with relatively little intensity.

average longevity (life expectancy) Age at which half of the people born in a particular year will have died.

avoidant attachment Relationship in which infants turn away from their mothers when they are reunited following a brief separation.

axon Tubelike structure that emerges from the **cell body** and transmits information to other **neurons**.

babbling Speechlike sounds that consist of vowel–consonant combinations; common at about 6 months.

backup care Emergency care for dependent children or adults so that an employee does not need to lose a day of work.

basic cry Cry that starts softly and gradually becomes more intense; often heard when babies are hungry or tired.

basic emotions Emotions experienced by humankind that consist of three elements: a subjective feeling, a physiological change, and an overt behavior.

battered woman syndrome Situation occurring when a woman believes that she cannot leave the abusive situation and may even go so far as to kill her abuser.

behavior therapy Type of therapy based on the notion that depressed people experience too few rewards or **reinforcements** from their environment.

behavioral genetics The branch of genetics that studies the inheritance of behavioral and psychological traits.

bereavement State or condition caused by loss through death.

beta amyloid Protein that is produced in abnormally high levels in persons with **Alzheimer's disease**.

beta-amyloid cascade hypothesis **Theory** of **Alzheimer's disease** in which **beta-amyloid** deposits create neuritic plaques, that in turn lead to **neurofibrillary tangles**, that cause neuronal death and **Alzheimer's disease**.

binge drinking Type of drinking defined for men as consuming five or more drinks in a row and for women as consuming four or more drinks in a row within the past two weeks.

binocular disparity The condition in which the left and right eyes often see slightly different versions of the same scene.

bioethics Study of the interface between human values and technological advances in health and life sciences.

biological forces All genetic and health-related factors that affect development.

biopsychosocial framework A useful way to organize the biological, psychological, and sociocultural forces on **human development**.

blended family Family consisting of a biological parent, a stepparent, and children.

body mass index (BMI) Ratio of body weight and height related to total body fat.

boomerang employees Individuals who terminate employment at one point in time but return to work in the same organization at a future time.

bulimia nervosa Disease in which people—most often adolescent girls—alternate between binge eating—periods when they eat uncontrollably—and purging with laxatives or self-induced vomiting.

burnout Depletion of a person's energy and motivation, the loss of occupational idealism, and the feeling that one is being exploited.

cardinality principle Counting principle that states that the last number name denotes the number of objects being counted.

career construction theory Theory that posits that people build careers through their own actions that result from the interface of their personal characteristics and the social context.

career plateauing Situation that occurs when there is a lack of challenge in one's job or promotional opportunity in the organization or when a person decides not to seek advancement.

cataracts Opaque spots on the lens of the eye that limit the amount of light transmitted.

cell body Center of the **neuron** that keeps the **neuron** alive.

centration According to Piaget, narrowly focused type of thought characteristic of pre-operational children.

cephalocaudal principle A principle of physical growth that states that structures nearest the head develop first.

cerebral cortex Wrinkled surface of the brain that regulates many functions that are distinctly human.

cesarean section (C-section) Surgical removal of an infant from the uterus through an incision made in the mother's abdomen.

chorionic villus sampling (CVS) Prenatal diagnostic technique that involves taking a sample of tissue from the **placenta**.

chromosomes Threadlike structures in the nuclei of cells that contain genetic material.

chronic obstructive pulmonary disease (COPD) Most common form of incapacitating respiratory disease among older adults.

chronic traumatic encephalopathy (CTE) Form of **dementia** caused by repeated head trauma such as concussions.

circadian rhythm Sleep–wake cycle.

classical conditioning A form of learning that involves pairing a neutral stimulus and a response originally produced by another stimulus.

climacteric Biological process during which women pass from their reproductive to non-reproductive years.

clinical death Lack of heartbeat and respiration.

clique Small group of friends who are similar in age, sex, and race.

co-rumination Conversations about one's personal problems, common among adolescent girls.

cognitive self-regulation Skill at identifying goals, selecting effective strategies, and monitoring accurately; a characteristic of successful students.

cognitive therapy Type of therapy based on the idea that maladaptive beliefs or cognitions about oneself are responsible for **depression**.

cohabitation People in committed, intimate, sexual relationships who live together but are not married.

cohort effects Problem with cross-sectional designs in which differences between age groups (cohorts) may result as much from environmental events as from developmental processes.

collaborative divorce Voluntary, contractually based alternative dispute resolution process for couples who want to negotiate a resolution of their situation rather than have a ruling imposed on them by a court or an arbitrator.

competence Upper limit of a person's ability to function in five domains: physical health, sensory-perceptual skills, **motor skills**, cognitive skills, and ego strength.

complicated or prolonged grief disorder Expression of **grief** that is distinguished from **depression** and from normal **grief** in terms of **separation distress** and **traumatic distress**.

comprehension The process of extracting meaning from a sequence of words.

cones Specialized **neurons** in the back of the eye that sense color.

conscientiousness Dimension of personality in which people tend to be hard-working, ambitious, energetic, scrupulous, and persevering.

constricting actions Interaction in which one partner tries to emerge as the victor by threatening or contradicting the other.

continuity–discontinuity issue Whether a particular developmental phenomenon represents a smooth progression throughout the life span (continuity) or a series of abrupt shifts (discontinuity).

controversial children As applied to children's popularity, children who are intensely liked or disliked by classmates.

conventional level Second level of reasoning in Kohlberg's **theory**, where moral reasoning is based on society's norms.

cooing Early vowel-like sounds that babies produce.

cooperative play Play that is organized around a theme, with each child taking on a different role; begins at about 2 years of age.

coping Attempt to deal with stressful events.

core knowledge hypothesis Infants are born with rudimentary knowledge of the world, which is elaborated based on experiences.

corpus callosum Thick bundle of **neurons** that connects the two **hemispheres**.

corrective adaptations Actions taken in response to stressors that can be facilitated by internal and external resources.

correlation coefficient An expression of the strength and direction of a relation between two variables.

correlational study Investigation looking at relations between variables as they exist naturally in the world.

counterimitation Learning what should not be done by observing the behavior.

covenant marriage Expands the marriage contract to a lifelong commitment between the partners within a supportive community.

creative ability In Sternberg's **theory** of intelligence, the ability to deal adaptively with novel situations and problems.

cross-sectional study Study in which developmental differences are identified by testing people of different ages.

crowd Large group including many **cliques** that have similar attitudes and values.

crowning Appearance of the top of the baby's head during labor.

crying State in which a baby cries vigorously, usually accompanied by agitated but uncoordinated movement.

crystallization First phase in Super's **theory** of career development, in which adolescents use their emerging identities to form ideas about careers.

crystallized intelligence The knowledge you have acquired through life experience and education in a particular culture.

culture-fair intelligence tests Intelligence tests devised using items common to many cultures.

cyberbullying Using social media to hurt other people by repeatedly insulting them, excluding them, or spreading rumors about them.

death anxiety Feeling of anxiety or even fear of death and dying.

deductive reasoning Drawing conclusions from facts; characteristic of formal-operational thought.

dementia Family of diseases involving serious impairment of behavioral and cognitive functioning and some form of permanent damage to the brain.

demographers People who study population trends.

dendrite End of the **neuron** that receives information; it looks like a tree with many branches.

deoxyribonucleic acid (DNA) Molecule composed of four nucleotide bases that is the biochemical basis of heredity.

dependent life expectancy Number of years a person lives with a debilitating chronic disease in which the person depends on others for care.

dependent variable The behavior being observed in an **experiment**.

depression Disorder characterized by pervasive feelings of sadness, irritability, and low self-esteem.

developmental coach Individual who helps a person focus on their goals, motivations, and aspirations to help them achieve focus and apply them appropriately.

diabetes mellitus Disease that occurs when the pancreas produces insufficient insulin.

diabetic retinopathy Eye disease that is a result of diabetes and can involve fluid retention in the macula, detachment of the retina, hemorrhage, and aneurysms.

differentiation Distinguishing and mastering individual motions.

direct instruction Telling a child what to do, when, and why.

disenfranchised grief A loss that appears insignificant to others is highly consequential to the person who suffers the loss.

disorganized (disoriented) attachment Relationship in which infants don't seem to understand what's happening when they are separated and later reunited with their mothers.

divergent thinking Thinking in novel and unusual directions.

divided attention The ability of people to perform more than one task simultaneously.

dizygotic twins The result of two separate eggs fertilized by two sperm; also called fraternal twins.

do not resuscitate (DNR) order Medical order that means that cardiopulmonary resuscitation (CPR) is not started should one's heart and breathing stop.

docility When people allow their situation to dictate the options they have.

dominance hierarchy Ordering of individuals within a group in which group members with lower status defer to those with greater status.

dominant Form of an **allele** whose chemical instructions are followed.

dual process model (DPM) View of **coping** with **bereavement** that integrates loss-oriented stressors and restoration-oriented stressors.

dual-energy X-ray absorptiometry (DXA) test Test of bone mineral density (BMD) at the hip and spine.

dynamic systems theory **Theory** that views motor development as involving many distinct skills that are organized and reorganized over time to meet specific needs.

dysphoria Feeling sad or down.

ecological theory **Theory** based on idea that **human development** is inseparable from the environmental contexts in which a person develops.

ectoderm Outer layer of the **embryo**, which becomes the hair, outer layer of skin, and nervous system.

edgework The desire to live life more on the edge through physically and emotionally threatening situations on the boundary between life and death.

ego resilience Person's ability to respond adaptively and resourcefully to new situations.

egocentrism Difficulty in seeing the world from another's point of view; typical of children in the preoperational period.

elaboration Memory strategy in which information is embellished to make it more memorable.

electroencephalography The study of brain waves recorded from electrodes that are placed on the scalp.

embryo Term given to the **zygote** once it is completely embedded in the uterine wall.

emerging adulthood Period between late teens and mid- to late twenties when individuals are not adolescents but are not yet fully adults.

emotional intelligence (EI) Ability to use one's own and others' emotions effectively for solving problems and living happily.

emotion-focused coping Dealing with one's feelings about a stressful event.

empathy Act of experiencing another person's feelings.

enabling actions Individuals' actions and remarks that tend to support others and sustain the interaction.

end-of-life issues Issues pertaining to management of the final phase of life, after-death disposition of the body and memorial services, and distribution of assets.

endoderm Inner layer of the **embryo**, which becomes the lungs and digestive system.

environmental press Physical, interpersonal, or social demands that environments put on people.

epigenetic principle In Erikson's **theory**, the idea that each psychosocial strength has its own special period of particular importance.

episodic memory General class of memory having to do with the conscious recollection of information from a specific time or event.

equilibration According to Piaget, the process by which children reorganize their **schemes** to return to a state of equilibrium when disequilibrium occurs.

essentialism Children's belief that all living things have an essence that can't be seen but gives a living thing its identity.

ethnic identity Feeling that one belongs to a specific ethnic group.

eugenics Effort to improve the human species by letting only people whose characteristics are valued by a society mate and pass along their **genes**.

euthanasia Practice of ending life for reasons of mercy.

evolutionary psychology Theoretical view that many human behaviors represent successful adaptations to the environment.

exchange theory Relationship, such as marriage, based on each partner contributing something to the relationship that the other would be hard-pressed to provide.

exosystem Social settings that a person may not experience firsthand but that still influence development.

experience-dependent growth Process by which an individual's unique experiences over a lifetime affect brain structures and organization.

experience-expectant growth Process by which the wiring of the brain is organized by experiences that are common to most humans.

experiment A systematic way of manipulating the key factor(s) that the investigator thinks causes a particular behavior.

explicit memory Deliberate and conscious remembering of information that is learned and remembered at a specific time.

expressive style Language-learning style of children whose vocabularies include many social phrases that are used like one word.

extended family Most common form of family around the world; one in which grandparents and other relatives live with parents and children.

external memory aids Memory aids that rely on environmental resources, such as notebooks and calendars.

extraversion Personality trait dimension associated with the tendency to thrive on social interaction, to like to talk, to take charge easily, to readily express their opinions and feelings, to keep busy, to have boundless energy, and to prefer stimulating and challenging environments.

extremely low birth weight Newborns who weigh less than 1,000 grams (2.2 pounds).

factor The interrelated abilities measured by two tests if the performance on one test is highly related to the performance on another.

familism Idea that the family's well-being takes precedence over the concerns of individual family members.

fast mapping A child's connections between words and referents that are made so quickly that he or she cannot consider all possible meanings of the word.

fetal alcohol spectrum disorder (FASD) Disorder affecting babies whose mothers consumed large amounts of alcohol while they were pregnant.

fetal therapy Field of medicine concerned with treating prenatal problems before birth.

filial obligation Sense of obligation to care for one's parents if necessary.

final scenario Way for people to make their choices known about how they do and do not want their lives to end.

fine motor skills **Motor skills** associated with grasping, holding, and manipulating objects.

fluid intelligence Abilities that make you a flexible and adaptive thinker, allow you to make inferences, and enable you to understand the relations among concepts.

four-component model Model for understanding **grief** that is based on (1) the context of the loss, (2) continuation of subjective meaning associated with loss, (3) changing representations of the lost relationship over time, and (4) the role of **coping** and emotion-regulation processes.

frail older adults Older adults who have physical disabilities, are very ill, and may have cognitive or psychological disorders.

free radicals Highly reactive chemicals produced randomly in normal **metabolism**.

friendship Voluntary relationship between two people involving mutual liking.

frontal cortex Brain region that regulates personality and goal-directed behavior.

functional health Ability to perform the **activities of daily living (ADLs)** and **instrumental activities of daily living (IADLs)**.

functional magnetic resonance imaging (fMRI) Method of studying brain activity by using magnetic fields to track blood flow in the brain.

functional neuroimaging Neuroimaging technique that provides an indication of brain activity but not high anatomical detail.

gender discrimination Act of denying a job to someone solely on the basis of whether the person is a man or a woman.

gender identity Sense of oneself as male or a female.

gender stereotypes Beliefs and images about males and females that are not necessarily true.

gender-schema theory **Theory** that states that children want to learn more about an activity only after first deciding whether it is masculine or feminine.

gene Group of nucleotide bases that provides a specific set of biochemical instructions.

generativity In Erikson's **theory**, being productive by helping others to ensure the continuation of society by guiding the next generation.

genotype Person's hereditary makeup.

germ disc Small cluster of cells near the center of the **zygote** that eventually develop into the baby.

glass ceiling Level to which women may rise in an organization but beyond which they may not go.

glass cliff Situation in which a woman's leadership position is precarious.

glaucoma Disease in which the fluid in the eye does not drain properly, causing very high internal pressure that can damage the eye and cause loss of vision.

grammatical morphemes Words or endings of words that make a sentence grammatical.

grief Sorrow, hurt, anger, guilt, confusion, and other feelings that arise after suffering a loss.

grief work as rumination hypothesis Approach that not only rejects the necessity of **grief** processing for recovery from loss but also views extensive **grief** processing as a form of rumination that may increase distress.

grief work Psychological side of coming to terms with **bereavement**.

guided participation Children's involvement in structured activities with others who are more skilled, typically producing cognitive growth.

habituation Act of becoming unresponsive to a stimulus that is presented repeatedly.

healthcare power of attorney Document in which an individual appoints someone to act as his or her agent for health care decisions.

healthy aging Growing old by avoiding disease, being engaged with life, and maintaining high cognitive and physical functioning.

hemispheres Right and left halves of the cortex.

heritability coefficient A measure (derived from a **correlation coefficient**) of the extent to which a trait or characteristic is inherited.

heterozygous When the **alleles** in a pair of **chromosomes** differ from each other.

high-density lipoproteins (HDLs) Chemicals that help keep arteries clear and break down **LDLs**.

homogamy Similarity of values and interests.

homozygous When the **alleles** in a pair of **chromosomes** are the same.

hope According to Erikson, openness to new experience tempered by wariness that occurs when trust and mistrust are in balance.

hospice Approach to assisting dying people that emphasizes pain management, or **palliative care**, and death with dignity.

hostile aggression Unprovoked aggression that seems to have the sole goal of intimidating, harassing, or humiliating another child.

human development The multidisciplinary study of how people change and how they remain the same over time.

Huntington's disease Progressive and fatal type of **dementia** caused by **dominant alleles**.

hypoxia A birth complication in which umbilical blood flow is disrupted and the infant does not receive adequate oxygen.

illusion of invulnerability Adolescents' belief that misfortunes cannot happen to them.

imaginary audience Adolescents' feeling that their behavior is constantly being watched by their peers.

imitation or observational learning Learning that occurs by simply watching how others behave.

implantation Step in which the **zygote** burrows into the uterine wall and establishes connections with the woman's blood vessels.

implementation Third phase in Super's **theory** of career development, in which individuals enter the workforce.

implicit memory Unconscious remembering of information learned at some earlier time.

impression formation The way we form and revise first impressions about others.

in vitro fertilization Process by which sperm and an egg are mixed in a petri dish to create a **zygote**, which is then placed in a woman's uterus.

incomplete dominance Situation in which one **allele** does not dominate another completely.

incontinence Loss of bladder or bowel control.

independent variable The factor being manipulated in an **experiment**.

infant mortality The number of infants out of 1,000 births who die before their first birthday.

infant-directed speech Speech that adults use with infants that is slow and has exaggerated changes in pitch and volume; it helps children master language.

information-processing theory Theory proposing that human cognition consists of **mental hardware** and **mental software**.

instrumental activities of daily living (IADLs) Actions that require some intellectual **competence** and planning.

instrumental aggression Aggression used to achieve an explicit goal.

instrumental orientation Characteristic of Kohlberg's stage 2, in which moral reasoning is based on the aim of looking out for one's own needs.

integration Linking individual motions into a coherent, coordinated whole.

integrity versus despair According to Erikson, the process in late life by which people try to make sense of their lives.

intellectual disability Substantially below-average intelligence and problems adapting to an environment that emerge before the age of 18.

intelligence quotient (IQ) Mathematical representation of how a person scores on an intelligence test in relation to how other people of the same age score.

interindividual variability Patterns of change that vary from one person to another.

internal belief systems View of a cause of **depression** of what one tells oneself about why certain things are happening.

internal memory aids Memory aids that rely on mental processes, such as imagery.

internal working model Infant's understanding of how responsive and dependable the mother is; thought to influence close relationships throughout the child's life.

interpersonal norms Characteristic of Kohlberg's stage 3, in which moral reasoning is based on winning the approval of others.

intersensory redundancy Infants' sensory systems are attuned to information presented simultaneously to different sensory modes.

intersubjectivity Mutual, shared understanding among participants in an activity.

intimacy versus isolation Sixth stage in Erikson's **theory** and the major psychosocial task for young adults.

irregular or rapid-eye-movement (REM) sleep Irregular sleep in which an infant's eyes dart rapidly beneath the eyelids while the body is quite active.

job satisfaction Positive feeling that results from an appraisal of one's work.

joint custody Custody agreement in which both parents retain legal custody of their children following divorce.

kinetic cues Cues to depth perception in which motion is used to estimate depth.

kinkeeper Person who gathers family members together for celebrations and keeps them in touch with each other, usually a middle-aged mother.

knowledge-telling strategy Writing down information as it is retrieved from memory, a common practice for young writers.

knowledge-transforming strategy Deciding what information to include in writing and how best to organize it to convey a point.

learning disability When a child with normal intelligence has difficulty mastering at least one academic subject.

leisure Discretionary activity that includes simple relaxation, activities for enjoyment, and creative pursuits.

life review Process by which people reflect on the events and experiences of their lifetimes.

life story A personal **narrative** that organizes past events into a coherent sequence.

life-course persistent antisocial behavior Antisocial behavior that emerges at an early age and continues throughout life.

life-course perspective Description of how various generations experience the biological, psychological, and sociocultural forces of development in their respective historical contexts.

life-cycle forces Differences in how the same event affects people of different ages.

life-span construct Unified sense of the past, present, and future based on personal experience and input from other people.

life-span perspective View that **human development** is multiply determined and cannot be understood within the scope of a single framework.

linear perspective A cue to depth perception based on the fact that parallel lines come together at a single point in the distance.

living will Document in which a person states his or her wishes about life support and other treatments.

locomote To move around in the world.

longevity Number of years a person can expect to live.

longitudinal study A research design in which the same individuals are observed or tested repeatedly at different points in their lives.

long-term memory Permanent storehouse for memories that has unlimited capacity.

low birth weight Newborns who weigh less than 2,500 grams (5.5 pounds).

low-density lipoproteins (LDLs) Chemicals that cause fatty deposits to accumulate in arteries, impeding blood flow.

macrosystem The cultures and subcultures in which the **microsystem, mesosystem,** and **exosystem** are embedded.

mad cry More intense version of a **basic cry**.

malnourished Being small for one's age because of inadequate nutrition.

marital adjustment Degree to which a husband and wife accommodate to each other over a certain period of time.

marital quality Subjective evaluation of the couple's relationship on a number of different dimensions.

marital satisfaction Global assessment of one's marriage.

marital success Umbrella term referring to any marital outcome.

maximum life expectancy Oldest age to which any person lives.

meaning-mission fit Alignment between an executive's personal intentions and his or her firm's mission.

mechanics of intelligence Those aspects of intelligence comprising **fluid intelligence**.

menarche Onset of menstruation.

menopausal hormone therapy (MHT) Therapy in which women take low doses of estrogen, which is often combined with progestin (a synthetic form of progesterone).

menopause Point at which menstruation stops.

mental age (MA) In intelligence testing, a measure of children's performance corresponding to the chronological age of those whose performance equals the child's.

mental hardware Mental and neural structures that are built in and allow the mind to operate.

mental operations Cognitive actions that can be performed on objects or ideas.

mental software Mental "programs" that are the basis for performing particular tasks.

mentor Person who is part teacher, part sponsor, part model, and part counselor who facilitates on-the-job learning to help a new hire do the work required in his or her present role and to prepare for future roles.

mesoderm Middle layer of the **embryo**, which becomes the muscles, bones, and circulatory system.

mesosystem Provides connections across **microsystems**.

meta-analysis A tool that enables researchers to synthesize the results of many studies to estimate relations between variables.

metabolism How much energy the body needs.

metacognitive knowledge A person's knowledge and awareness of cognitive processes.

metamemory Person's informal understanding of memory; includes the ability to diagnose memory problems accurately and to monitor the effectiveness of memory strategies.

microsystem The people and objects in an individual's immediate environment.

midlife correction Reevaluating one's roles and dreams and making the necessary corrections.

mindfulness-based stress reduction Stress reduction technique based on being aware and nonjudgmental of whatever is happening at that moment.

model of adaptive grieving dynamics (MAGD) Model of grieving based on two sets of pairs of adaptive grieving dynamics: lamenting and heartening responses to **grief**; integrating and tempering responses to **grief**.

monozygotic twins The result of a single fertilized egg splitting to form two new individuals; also called identical twins.

motion parallax Kinetic cue to depth perception based on the fact that nearby moving objects move across our visual field faster than do distant objects.

motor skills Coordinated movements of the muscles and limbs.

mourning Ways in which people express their **grief**.

multidimensional Characteristic of theories of intelligence that identify several types of intellectual abilities.

multidirectionality Developmental pattern in which some aspects of intelligence improve and other aspects decline during adulthood.

myelin Fatty sheath that wraps around **neurons** and enables them to transmit information more rapidly.

narrative Way in which a person derives personal meaning from being generative by constructing a **life story**, which helps create the person's identity.

naturalistic observation Technique in which people are observed as they behave spontaneously in a real-life situation.

nature–nurture issue The degree to which genetic or hereditary influences (nature) and experiential or environmental influences (nurture) determine the kind of person you are.

negative reinforcement trap Unwittingly reinforcing a behavior you want to discourage.

neglected children As applied to children's popularity, children who are ignored—neither liked nor disliked—by their classmates.

neural efficiency hypothesis States intelligent people process information more efficiently, showing weaker neural activations in a smaller number of areas than less intelligent people.

neural plate Flat group of cells present in **prenatal development** that becomes the brain and spinal cord.

neurofibrillary tangles Spiral-shaped masses formed when fibers that compose the **axon** become twisted together.

neuron Basic cellular unit of the brain and nervous system that specializes in receiving and transmitting information.

neuroscience The study of the brain and nervous system, especially in terms of brain–behavior relationships.

neuroticism Personality trait dimension associated with the tendency to be anxious, hostile, self-conscious, depressed, impulsive, and vulnerable.

neurotransmitters Chemicals released by the **terminal buttons** that allow **neurons** to communicate with each other.

niche-picking Process of deliberately seeking environments that are compatible with one's genetic makeup.

non-invasive prenatal testing (NIPT) A prenatal diagnostic technique that analyzes genetic material released from the **placenta** that circulates in a pregnant woman's blood stream.

nonshared environmental influences Forces within a family that make siblings different from one another.

nuclear family Most common form of family in Western societies, consisting only of parent(s) and child(ren).

nursing home Type of long-term care facility that provide medical care 24 hours a day 7 days a week using a team of health care professionals that includes physicians (who must be on call at all times), nurses, therapists (e.g., physical, occupational), and others.

obedience orientation Characteristic of Kohlberg's stage 1, in which moral reasoning is based on the belief that adults know what is right and wrong.

object permanence Understanding, acquired in infancy, that objects exist independently of oneself.

one-to-one principle Counting principle that states that there must be one and only one number name for each object counted.

open adoption An adoption in which adopted children (and their adoptive families) communicate with the children's birth family.

openness to experience Personality dimension that reflects a tendency to have a vivid imagination and dream life, an appreciation of art, and a strong desire to try anything once.

operant conditioning Learning paradigm proposed by B. F. Skinner in which the consequences of a behavior determine whether a behavior is repeated.

organization As applied to children's memory, a strategy in which information to be remembered is structured so that related information is placed together.

orienting response An individual views a strong or unfamiliar stimulus, and changes in heart rate and brain-wave activity occur.

osteoarthritis Most common form of arthritis, a disease marked by gradual onset of bone damage with progression of pain and disability together with minor signs of inflammation from wear and tear.

osteoporosis Disease in which bones become porous and extremely easy to break.

overextension When children define words more broadly than adults do overregularization grammatical usage that results from applying rules to words that are exceptions to the rule.

pain cry Cry that begins with a sudden long burst, followed by a long pause and gasping.

palliative care Care that is focused on providing relief from pain and other symptoms of disease at any point during the disease process.

parallel play When children play alone but are aware of and interested in what another child is doing.

parieto-frontal integration theory (P-FIT) Theory that proposes that intelligence comes from a distributed and integrated network of **neurons** in the parietal and frontal lobes of the brain.

Parkinson's disease Brain disease known primarily for its characteristic motor symptoms: very slow walking, difficulty getting into and out of chairs, and a slow hand tremor, but it can develop into a form of **dementia**.

passion Strong inclination toward an activity that individuals like (or even love), that they value (and thus find important), and in which they invest time and energy.

passive euthanasia Practice of allowing a person to die by withholding available treatment.

perception Processes by which the brain receives, selects, modifies, and organizes incoming nerve impulses that are the result of physical stimulation.

perimenopause Individually varying time of transition from regular menstruation to **menopause**.

period of the fetus Longest period of **prenatal development**, extending from the 9th until the 38th week after conception.

permissive parenting Style of parenting in which parents offer warmth and caring but little control over their children.

persistent vegetative state Situation in which a person's cortical functioning ceases while brainstem activity continues.

personal control beliefs The degree to which you believe your performance in a situation depends on something you do.

personal fable Attitude of many adolescents that their feelings and experiences are unique and have never been experienced by anyone else.

personality adjustment Developmental changes in terms of their adaptive value and functionality such as whether one can function effectively within society and how personality contributes to everyday life running smoothly.

personality growth Form of personality that refers to ideal end states such as increased self-transcendence, wisdom, and integrity.

personality-type theory View proposed by Holland that people find their work fulfilling when the important features of a job or profession fit their personality.

phenotype Physical, behavioral, and psychological features that result from the interaction between one's **genes** and the environment.

phenylketonuria (PKU) Inherited disorder in which the infant lacks a liver enzyme.

phonological awareness The ability to hear the distinctive sounds of letters.

phonological memory Ability to remember speech sounds briefly; an important skill in acquiring vocabulary.

physical limitations (PLIMs) Activities that reflect functional limitations such as walking the equivalent of about a city block or sitting for about two hours.

physician-assisted suicide Process in which physicians provide dying patients with a fatal dose of medication that the patient self-administers.

pictorial cues Cues to depth perception that are used to convey depth in drawings and paintings.

placenta Structure through which nutrients and wastes are exchanged between the mother and the developing child.

plasticity Concept that intellectual abilities are not fixed, but can be modified under the right conditions at just about any point in adulthood.

polygenic inheritance When **phenotypes** are the result of the combined activity of many separate **genes**.

popular children Children who are liked by many classmates.

population pyramid Graphic technique for illustrating population trends.

populations Broad groups of people that are of interest to researchers.

possible selves Representations of what we could become, what we would like to become, and what we are afraid of becoming.

post-traumatic stress disorder (PTSD) Anxiety disorder that can develop after exposure to a terrifying event or ordeal in which grave physical harm occurred or was threatened.

postconventional level Third level of reasoning in Kohlberg's **theory**, in which morality is based on a personal moral code.

postformal thought Thinking characterized by recognizing that the correct answer varies from one situation to another, that solutions should be realistic, that ambiguity and contradiction are typical, and that subjective factors play a role in thinking.

practical ability In Sternberg's **theory** of intelligence, the ability to know which problem solutions are likely to work.

practical intelligence Broad range of skills related to how individuals shape, select, or adapt to their physical and social environments.

pragmatics of intelligence Those aspects of intelligence reflecting **crystallized intelligence**.

preconventional level First level of reasoning in Kohlberg's **theory**, where moral reasoning is based on external forces.

preimplantation genetic screening (PGS) A procedure used to test the heredity of an egg fertilized with assisted reproductive technology, typically to determine the presence of genetic disorders.

prenatal development The many changes that turn a fertilized egg into a newborn human.

presbycusis Reduced sensitivity to high-pitched tones.

presbyopia Difficulty seeing close objects clearly.

preterm or premature Babies born before the 36th week after conception.

preventive adaptations Actions that avoid stressors and increase or build social resources.

primary appraisal Process that categorizes events into three groups based on the significance they have for one's well-being: irrelevant, benign or positive, and stressful.

primary control Behavior aimed at affecting the individual's external world.

primary mental abilities Groups of related intellectual skills (such as memory or spatial ability).

primary sex characteristics Physical signs of maturity that are directly linked to the reproductive organs.

private speech A child's comments that are not intended for others but are designed to help regulate the child's own behavior.

proactivity When people choose new behaviors to meet new desires or needs and exert control over their lives.

problem-focused coping   Attempts to tackle a problem head-on.

prosocial behavior   Any behavior that benefits another person.

proximodistal principle   Principle of physical growth that states that structures nearest the center of the body develop first.

psychodynamic theories   Theories proposing that development is largely determined by how well people resolve conflicts they face at different ages.

psychological capital theory   Notion that having a positive outlook improves processes and outcomes.

psychometricians   Psychologists who specialize in measuring psychological traits such as intelligence and personality.

psychosocial theory   Erikson's proposal that personality development is determined by the interaction of an internal maturational plan and external societal demands.

puberty   Collection of physical changes that marks the onset of adolescence, including a growth spurt and the growth of breasts or testes.

punishment   A consequence that decreases the likelihood of the behavior that it follows.

purpose   According to Erikson, balance between individual initiative and the willingness to cooperate with others.

qualitative research   Method that involves gaining in-depth understanding of human behavior and what governs it.

reality shock   Situation in which what you learn in the classroom does not always transfer directly to the real world and does not represent all that you need to know.

reappraisal   Process of making a new **primary** or **secondary appraisal** resulting from changes in the situation.

recessive   **Allele** whose instructions are ignored in the presence of a **dominant allele**.

recursive thinking   Thoughts that focus on what another person is thinking.

referential style   Language-learning style of children whose vocabularies are dominated by names of objects, persons, or actions.

reflective judgment   Way in which adults reason through real-life dilemmas.

reflexes   Unlearned responses triggered by specific stimulation.

regular or nonREM sleep   Sleep in which heart rate, breathing, and brain activity are steady.

reinforcement   Consequence that increases the likelihood that a behavior will be repeated in the future.

rejected children   As applied to children's popularity, children who are disliked by many classmates.

relational aggression   Aggression used to hurt others by undermining their social relationships.

reliability   Extent to which a measure provides a consistent index of a characteristic.

resistant attachment   Relationship in which, after a brief separation, infants want to be held but are difficult to console.

returning adult students   College students over age 25.

rheumatoid arthritis   More destructive disease of the joints that develops slowly; it typically affects different joints and causes different types of pain than **osteoarthritis** does.

rites of passage   Rituals marking initiation into adulthood.

role transitions   Movement into the next stage of development marked by assumption of new responsibilities and duties.

sample   A subset of the population.

sandwich generation   Middle-aged adults who are caught between the competing demands of two generations: their parents and their children.

scaffolding   A style in which teachers gauge the amount of assistance they offer to match the learner's needs.

scenario   Manifestation of the **life-span construct** through expectations about the future.

schemes   According to Piaget, mental structures that organize information and regulate behavior.

secondary appraisal   Process that evaluates one's perceived ability to cope with harm, threat, or challenge.

secondary control   Behavior or cognition aimed at affecting the individual's internal world.

secondary mental abilities   Broader intellectual skills that subsume and organize the primary abilities.

secondary sex characteristics   Physical signs of maturity that are not directly linked to reproductive organs.

secure attachment   Relationship in which infants have come to trust and depend on their mothers.

selective estrogen receptor modulators (SERMs)   Compounds that are not estrogens, but have estrogen-like effects on some tissues and estrogen-blocking effects on other tissues.

selective optimization with compensation (SOC)   Model in which three processes (selection, optimization, and compensation) form a system of behavioral action that generates and regulates development and aging.

self-efficacy   People's beliefs about their own abilities and talents.

self-reports   People's answers to questions about the topic of interest.

semantic memory   General class of memory concerning the remembering of meanings of words or concepts not tied to a specific time or event.

sense of place   Cognitive and emotional attachments that a person puts on his or her place of residence, by which a "house" is made into a "home".

sensorimotor period   First of Piaget's four stages of cognitive development, which lasts from birth to approximately 2 years.

separation distress   Expression of **complicated or prolonged grief disorder** that includes being preoccupied with the deceased to the point that it interferes with everyday functioning, having upsetting memories of the deceased, longing and searching for the deceased, and feeling isolated following the loss.

sequential design   Developmental research design based on cross-sectional and longitudinal designs.

sex chromosomes   23rd pair of **chromosomes**; these determine the sex of the child.

sickle-cell trait   Disorder in which individuals show signs of mild anemia only when they are seriously deprived of oxygen; occurs in individuals who have one **dominant allele** for normal blood cells and one **recessive** sickle-cell **allele**.

simple social play   Play that begins at about 15 to 18 months; **toddlers** engage in similar activities as well as talk and smile at each other.

skeletal maturity   Point at which bone mass is greatest and the skeleton is at peak development, around 18 for women and 20 in men.

sleeping   State in which a baby alternates between being still and breathing regularly to moving gently and breathing irregularly; the eyes are closed throughout.

social clock   Tagging future events with a particular time or age by which they are to be completed.

social cognitive career theory (SCCT)   Theory that proposes that career choice is a result of the application of Bandura's social cognitive **theory**, especially the concept of **self-efficacy**.

social contract   Characteristic of Kohlberg's Stage 5, in which moral reasoning is based on the belief that laws are for the good of all members of society.

social convoy   Group of people who journey with us throughout our lives, providing support in good times and bad.

social referencing   Behavior in which infants in unfamiliar or ambiguous environments look at an adult for cues to help them interpret the situation.

social role   Set of cultural guidelines about how one should behave, especially with other people.

social smiles   Smile that infants produce when they see a human face.

social system morality   Characteristic of Kohlberg's stage 4, in which moral reasoning is based on maintenance of order in society.

socialization   Teaching children the values, roles, and behaviors of their culture.

socioemotional selectivity   Theory that argues that social contact is motivated by a variety of goals, including information seeking, self-concept, and emotional regulation.

specification   Second phase in Super's **theory** of career development, in which adolescents learn more about specific lines of work and begin training.

speed of processing   How quickly and efficiently the early steps in information processing are completed.

spermarche   First spontaneous ejaculation of sperm.

spina bifida   Disorder in which the **embryo's** neural tube does not close properly.

spiritual support Type of **coping** strategy that includes seeking pastoral care, participating in organized and nonorganized religious activities, and expressing faith in a God who cares for people.

stable-order principle Counting principle that states that number names must always be counted in the same order.

stagnation In Erikson's **theory**, the state in which people are unable to deal with the needs of their children or to provide mentoring to younger adults.

stereotype threat An evoked fear of being judged in accordance with a negative stereotype about a group to which you belong.

stranger wariness First distinct signs of fear that emerge around 6 months of age when infants become wary in the presence of unfamiliar adults.

stress Physical and psychological responses to threatening or challenging conditions.

stress and coping paradigm Framework that views **stress** not as an environmental stimulus or as a response, but as the interaction of a thinking person and an event.

strokes, or cerebral vascular accidents (CVAs) Interruption of the blood flow in the brain due to blockage or a hemorrhage in a cerebral artery.

structural neuroimaging Neuroimaging technique such as CT and MRI scans that provides highly detailed images of anatomical features in the brain.

structure of intelligence The organization of interrelated intellectual abilities.

structured observations Technique in which a researcher creates a setting that is likely to elicit the behavior of interest.

subjective well-being Evaluation of one's life that is associated with positive feelings.

successful aging Pathway through late life that focuses on positive outcomes through health and social engagement to achieve well-being.

sudden infant death syndrome (SIDS) When a healthy baby dies suddenly for no apparent reason.

synaptic pruning Gradual reduction in the number of synapses, beginning in infancy and continuing until early adolescence.

systematic observation Watching people and carefully recording what they do or say.

telegraphic speech Speech used by young children that contains only the words necessary to convey a message.

teleological explanations Children's belief that living things and parts of living things exist for a purpose.

telomerase Enzyme needed in **DNA** replication to fully reproduce the **telomeres** when cells divide.

telomeres Tips of **chromosomes** that play a major role in aging by adjusting the cell's

response to **stress** and growth stimulation based on cell divisions and **DNA** damage.

temperament Consistent style or pattern of behavior.

teratogen An agent that causes abnormal **prenatal development**.

terminal buttons Small knobs at the end of the **axon** that release **neurotransmitters**.

terror management theory Theory that addresses the issue of why people engage in certain behaviors to achieve particular psychological states based on their deeply rooted concerns about mortality.

texture gradient Perceptual cue to depth based on the fact that the texture of objects changes from coarse and distinct for nearby objects to finer and less distinct for distant objects.

thanatology Study of death, dying, **grief**, **bereavement**, and social attitudes toward these issues.

theory An organized set of ideas that is designed to explain development.

theory of mind Ideas about connections between thoughts, beliefs, intentions, and behavior that create an intuitive understanding of the link between mind and behavior.

time-out **Punishment** that involves removing children who are misbehaving from a situation to a quiet, unstimulating environment.

toddler Young children who have just learned to walk.

toddling Early, unsteady form of walking done by infants.

transient ischemic attacks (TIAs) Interruption of blood flow to the brain; often an early warning sign of stroke.

traumatic distress Expression of **complicated or prolonged grief disorder** that includes disbelief about the death; mistrusting others, feeling anger, and being detachment from others as a result of the death; feeling shocked by the death; and experiencing the physical presence of the deceased.

type 1 diabetes Type of diabetes that usually develops earlier in life and requires the use of insulin; sometimes called insulin-dependent diabetes.

type 2 diabetes Type of diabetes that typically develops in adulthood and is often effectively managed through diet.

ultrasound Prenatal diagnostic technique that uses sound waves to generate an image of the fetus.

umbilical cord Structure containing veins and arteries that connects the developing child to the **placenta**.

underextension When children define words more narrowly than adults do.

uninvolved parenting Style of parenting in which parents provide neither warmth nor control and minimize the time they spend with their children.

universal and context-specific development issue Whether there is one path of development or several paths.

universal ethical principles Characteristic of Kohlberg's stage 6, in which moral reasoning is based on moral principles that apply to all.

validity Extent to which a measure actually assesses what researchers think it does.

vascular dementia Disease caused by numerous small cerebral vascular accidents.

vernix Substance that protects the fetus's skin during development.

very low birth weight Newborns who weigh less than 1,500 grams (3.3 pounds).

visual acuity Smallest pattern that one can distinguish reliably.

visual cliff Glass-covered platform that appears to have a "shallow" and a "deep" side; used to study infants' depth perception.

visual expansion Kinetic cue to depth perception that is based on the fact that an object fills an ever-greater proportion of the retina as it moves closer.

vocational maturity Degree of congruence between people's occupational behavior and what is expected of them at different ages.

vulnerability–stress–adaptation model Model that proposes that **marital quality** is a dynamic process resulting from the couple's ability to handle stressful events in the context of their particular vulnerabilities and resources.

waking activity State in which a baby's eyes are open but seem unfocused while the arms or legs move in bursts of uncoordinated motion.

wear-and-tear disease Degenerative disease caused by injury or overuse.

whole-brain death Declared only when the deceased meets eight criteria, which were established in 1981.

will According to Erikson, a young child's understanding that he or she can act on the world intentionally; this occurs when autonomy, shame, and doubt are in balance.

word recognition The process of identifying a unique pattern of letters.

work–family conflict Feeling of being pulled in multiple directions by incompatible demands from one's job and one's family.

working memory Processes and structures involved in holding information in mind and simultaneously using it for other functions.

zone of maximum comfort When press level is slightly lower, facilitating a high quality of life.

zone of maximum performance potential When press level is slightly higher, tending to improve performance.

zone of proximal development Difference between what children can do with assistance and what they can do alone.

zygote Fertilized egg.

References

A Better Balance. (2016). *The need for paid family leave.* Retrieved from www.abetterbalance.org/web/ourissues/familyleave.

AAIDD Ad Hoc Committee on Terminology and Classification. (2010). *Intellectual disability* (11th ed.). Washington, DC: American Association on Intellectual and Developmental Disabilities.

AARP. (1999). *AARP/Modern maturity sexuality survey.* Retrieved from assets.aarp.org/rgcenter/health/mmsexsurvey.pdf.

AARP. (2005). *Sexuality at midlife and beyond: 2004 update of attitudes and behaviors.* Retrieved from assets.aarp.org/rgcenter/general/2004_sexuality.pdf.

AARP. (2010). *Sex, romance, and relationships: AARP survey of midlife and older adults.* Retrieved from assets.aarp.org/rgcenter/general/srr_09.pdf.

AARP. (2016). *About GrandFacts.* Retrieved from www.aarp.org/relationships/friends-family/grandfacts-sheets/.

Aasland, O. G., Rosta, J., & Nylenna, M. (2010). Healthcare reforms and job satisfaction among doctors in Norway. *Scandinavian Journal of Public Health, 38,* 253–258. doi:10.1177/1403494810364559

Abbott, G., Gilbert, K., & Rosinski, P. (2013). Cross-cultural working in coaching and mentoring. In J. Passmore, D. B. Peterson, & T. Freire (Eds.), *The Wiley-Blackwell handbook of coaching and mentoring* (pp. 483–500). Oxford, UK: Wiley-Blackwell.

Abela, A., & Walker, J. (2014). Global changes in marriage, parenting, and family life: An overview. In A. Abela & J. Walker (Eds.), *Contemporary issues in family studies: Global perspectives on partnerships, parenting and support in a changing world* (pp. 5–15). New York: Wiley.

Aberson, C. L., Shoemaker, C., & Tomolillo, C. (2004). Implicit bias and contact: The role of interethnic friendships. *Journal of Social Psychology, 144,* 335–347. doi:10.3200/SOCP.144.3.335–347

Aboud, F. E., & Yousafzai, A. K. (2015). Global health and development in early childhood. *Annual Review of Psychology, 66,* 433–457.

Abraham, A., Beudt, S., Ott, D. V. M., & von Cramon, D. Y. (2012). Creative cognition and the brain: Dissociations between frontal, parietal-temporal and basal ganglia groups. *Brain Research, 1482,* 55–70. doi:10.1016/j.bbr.2011.03.031

Abrams, D., Swift, H. J., & Drury, L. (2016). Old and unemployable? How age-based stereotypes affect willingness to hire job candidates. *Journal of Social Issues, 72,* 105–121. doi:10.1111/josi.12158

Abrams, R. (2013). *When parents die: Learning to live with the loss of a parent* (3rd ed.). New York: Routledge.

Achor, S. (2010). *The happiness advantage: The seven principles of positive psychology that fuel success and performance at work.* New York: Random House.

Ackerman, B. P. (1993). Children's understanding of the speaker's meaning in referential communication. *Journal of Experimental Child Psychology, 55,* 56–86.

Adams, J. (1999). On neurodevelopmental disorders: Perspectives from neurobehavioral teratology. In H. Tager-Flusberg (Ed.), *Neurodevelopmental disorders* (pp. 451–468). Cambridge, MA: MIT Press.

Adams, M. J., Treiman, R., & Pressley, M. (1998). Reading, writing, and literacy. In W. Damon (Ed.), *Handbook of child psychology,* Vol. 4 (pp. 275–356). New York: Wiley.

Adams, R. B., Jr., Nelson, A. J., Soto, J. A., Hess, U., & Kleck, R. E. (2012). Emotion in the neutral face: A mechanism for impression formation? *Cognition and Emotion, 26,* 431–441. doi:10.1080/02699931.2012.666502

Adams, R. E., Santo, J. B., & Bukowski, W. M. (2011). The presence of a best friend buffers the effects of negative experiences. *Developmental Psychology, 47,* 1786–1791.

Adams, R. G., & Taylor, E, M. (2015). Friendship and happiness in the third age. In M. Demir (Ed.), *Friendship and happiness* (pp. 155–169). New York: Springer.

Adamy, J., & McGinty, T. (2012). *The crushing cost of care.* Retrieved from online.wsj.com/article/SB10001424052702304441045774830509767 66184.html.

Addis, D. R., Wong, A. T., & Schacter, D. L. (2008). Age-related changes in the episodic simulation of future events. *Psychological Science, 19,* 33–41. doi:10.1111/j.1467-9280.2008.02043.x

Addo, F. R. (2017). Financial integration and relationship transitions of young adult cohabiters. *Journal of Family and Economic Issues, 38,* 84–99. doi:10.1007/s10834-016-9490-7

Adelman, L. (2013). *"Dear Prudence" columnist publishes rape denial manifesto advising women to "stop getting drunk."* Retrieved from feministing.com/2013/10/16/emily-yoffe-aka-dear-prudence-publishes-rape-denialism-manifesto-tells-women-point-blank-to-stop-getting-drunk-to-avoid-rape/.

Adhikari, K., Fontanil, T., Cal, S., Mendoza-Revilla, J., Fuentes-Guajardo, M., Chacón-Duque, J.-C. et al. (2016). A genome-wide association scan in admixed Latin Americans identifies loci influencing facial and scalp hair features. *Nature Communications, 7(Article 10815).* Retrieved from www.nature.com/ncomms/2016/160301/ncomms10815/full/ncomms10815.html.

Adler, L. L. (2001). Women and gender roles. In L. L. Adler & U. P. Gielen (Eds.), *Cross-cultural topics on psychology* (2nd ed., pp. 103–114). Westport, CT: Praeger/Greenwood.

Adler, R. A., Fuleihan, G. E.-H., Bauer, D. C., Camacho, P. M., Clarke, B. L., Clines, G. A., et al. (2016). Managing osteoporosis in patients on long-term bisphosphonate treatment: Report of a task force of the American Society for Bone and Mineral Research. *Journal of Bone and Mineral Research, 31,* 16–35. doi:10.1002/jbmr.2708

Adolph, K. (2002). Learning to keep balance. In R. V. Kail (Ed.), *Advances in child development and behavior* (Vol. 30, pp. 1–40). Orlando, FL: Academic Press.

Adolph, K. E. (2000). Specificity of learning: Why infants fall over a veritable cliff. *Psychological Science, 11,* 290–295.

Adolph, K. E., & Berger, S. E. (2015). Physical and motor development. In M. H. Bornstein & M. E. Lamb (Eds.), *Developmental science: An advanced textbook* (7th ed., pp. 261–333). New York: Psychology Press/Taylor & Francis.

Adolph, K. E., & Robinson, S. R. (2013). The road to walking: What learning to walk tells us about development. In P. Zelazo (Ed.), *Oxford handbook of developmental psychology* (pp. 403–443). New York: Oxford University Press.

Adolph, K. E., Cole, W. G., Komati, M., Garciaguirre, J. S., Badaly, D., Lingeman, J. M., et al. (2012). How do you learn to walk? Thousands of steps and dozens of falls per day. *Psychological Science, 23,* 1387–1394.

Adolphus, K., Lawton, C. L., & Dye, L. (2013). The effects of breakfast on behavior and academic performance in children and adolescents. *Frontiers of Human Neuroscience, 7,* 425.

Afilalo, J. (2016). Conceptual models of frailty: The sarcopenia phenotype. *Canadian Journal of Cardiology, 32,* 1051–1055. doi:10.1016/j.cjca.2016.05.017

Agabio, R., Trincas, G., Floris, F., Mura, G., Sancassiani, F., & Angermeyer, M. C. (2017). A systematic review of school-based alcohol and other drug prevention programs. *Clinical Practice and Epidemiology, 13,* 102–112.

Agency for Healthcare Research and Quality. (2016). *2015 national healthcare quality and disparities report and 5th anniversary update on the national quality strategy.* Retrieved from www.ahrq.gov/sites/default/files/wysiwyg/research/findings/nhqrdr/nhqdr15/2015nhqdr.pdf.

AgingStats.gov. (2016). *Older Americans 2016: Key indicators of well-being.* Retrieved from agingstats.gov/docs/LatestReport/Older-Americans-2016-Key-Indicators-of-WellBeing.pdf.

Ahmad, F. (2012). Graduating toward marriage? Attitudes towards marriage and relationships among university-educated British Muslim women. *Culture and Religion: An Interdisciplinary Journal, 13*, 193–210. doi:10.1080/14755610.2012.674953

Ahmad, I., Smetana, J. G., & Klimstra, T. (2015). Maternal monitoring, adolescent disclosure, and adolescent adjustment among Palestinian refugee youth in Jordan. *Journal of Research on Adolescence, 25*, 403–411.

Ai, A. L., Richardson, R., Plummer, C., Ellison, C. G., Lemieux, C., Tice, T. N., et al. (2013). Character strength and deep connections following Hurricanes Katrina and Rita: Spiritual and secular pathways to resistance among volunteers. *Journal for the Scientific Study of Religion, 52*, 537–556. doi:10.1111/jssr.12043

Ai, A. L., Wink, P., & Ardelt, M. (2010). Spirituality and aging: A journey for meaning through deep interconnection in humanity. In J. C. Cavanaugh & C. K. Cavanaugh (Eds.), *Aging in America: Vol. 3: Societal issues* (pp. 222–246). Santa Barbara, CA: Praeger Perspectives.

Ai, A. L., Wink, P., Gall, T. L., Dillon, M., & Tice, T. N. (2017). Assessing reverence in contexts: A positive emotion related to psychological functioning. *Journal of Humanistic Psychology, 57*, 64–97. doi:10.1177/0022167815586657

Ainsworth, M. S. (1978). The development of infant–mother attachment. In B. M. Caldwell & H. N. Ricciuti (Eds.), *Review of child development research* (Vol. 3, pp. 1–94). Chicago: University of Chicago Press.

Ainsworth, M. S. (1993). Attachment as related to mother–infant interaction. *Advances in Infancy Research, 8*, 1–50.

Ajrouch, K. J., Antonucci, T. C., & Webster, N. J. (2014). Volunteerism: Social network dynamics and education. *Journal of Gerontology: Social Sciences, 71*, 309–319. doi:10.1093/geronb/gbu166

Al-Bar, M. A., & Chamsi-Pasha, H. (2015). Brain death. In M. A. Al-Bar & H. Chamsi-Pasha (Eds.), *Contemporary bioethics* (pp. 227–242). New York: Springer. doi:10.1007/978-3-319-18428-9_14

Alatupa, S., Pulkki-Råback, L., Hintsanen, M., Elovainio, M., Mullola, S., & Keltikangas-Järvinen, L. (2013). Disruptive behavior in childhood and socioeconomic position in adulthood: A prospective study over 27 years. *International Journal of Public Health, 58*, 247–256.

Alavi, M. V. (2016). Aging and vision. In C. B. Rickman, M. M. LaVail, R. E. Anderson, C. Grimm, J. Hollyfield, & J. Ash (Eds.), *Retinal degenerative diseases* (pp. 393–399). New York: Springer. doi:10.1007/978-3-319-17121-0_52

Albert, D., & Steinberg, L. (2011). Judgment and decision making in adolescence. *Journal of Research on Adolescence, 21*, 211–224.

Albert, D., Chein, J., & Steinberg, L. (2013). Peer influences on adolescent decision making. *Current Directions in Psychological Science, 22*, 114–120.

Alberts, A. E. (2005). Neonatal behavioral assessment scale. In C. B. Fisher & R. M. Lerner (Eds.), *Encyclopedia of applied developmental science* (Vol. 1, pp. 111–115). Thousand Oaks, CA: Sage.

Albuquerque, S., Pereira, M., & Narciso, I. (2016). Couple's relationship after the death of a child: A systematic review. *Journal of Child and Family Studies, 25*, 30–53. doi:10.1007/s10826-015-0219-2

Alden, D. L., Merz, M. Y., & Akashi, J. (2012). Young adult preference for physician decision-making style in Japan and the United States. *Asia-Pacific Journal of Public Health, 24*, 173–184. doi:10.1177/1010539510365098

Aldridge, V., Dovey, T. M., & Halford, J. C. G. (2009). The role of familiarity in dietary development. *Developmental Review, 29*, 32–44.

Aldwin, C. M. (2015). How can developmental systems theories cope with free will? The importance of stress-related growth and mindfulness. *Research in Human Development, 12*, 189–195. doi:10.1080/15427609.2015.1068042

Aldwin, C. M., & Gilmer, D. F. (2013). *Health, illness, and optimal aging: Biological and psychosocial perspectives* (2nd ed.). New York: Springer.

Aldwin, C. M., Park, C. L., Jeong, Y.-J., & Nath, R. (2014). Differing pathways between religiousness, spirituality, and health: A self-regulation perspective. *Psychology of Religion and Spirituality, 6*, 9–21. doi: 10.1037/a0034416

Aldwin, C., & Igarashi, H. (2012). An ecological model of resilience in late life. *Annual Review of Gerontology and Geriatrics, 32*, 115–130. doi:10.1891/0198-8794.32.115

Alegría-Flores, K., Raker, K., Pleasants, R. K., Weaver, M. A., & Weinberger, M. (2017). Preventing interpersonal violence on college campuses: The effect of One Act training on bystander intervention. *Journal of Interpersonal Violence, 32*, 1103–1126.

Alexander, G. M., & Wilcox, T. (2012). Sex differences in early infancy. *Child Development Perspectives, 6*, 400–406.

Allaire, J. C., & Willis, S. L. (2006). Competence in everyday activities as a predictor of cognitive risk and morbidity. *Aging, Neuropsychology, and Cognition, 13*, 207–224. doi:10.1080/13825580490904228

Allemand, M., Zimprich, D., & Hendriks, A. A. J. (2008). Age differences in five personality domains across the life span. *Developmental Psychology, 44*, 758–770. doi:10.1037/0012-1649.44.3.758

Allen, J. P., Chango, J., Szwedo, D., Schad, M., & Marston, E. (2012). Predictors of susceptibility to peer influence regarding substance use in adolescence. *Child Development, 83*, 337–350.

Allen, J., Gregory, A., Mikami, A., Lun, J., Hamre, B., & Pianta, R. (2013). Observations of effective teacher–student interactions in secondary school classrooms: Predicting student achievement with the Classroom Assessment Scoring System—Secondary. *School Psychology Review, 42*, 76–98.

Allen, K. R., & Roberto, K. A. (2016). Family relationships of older LGBT adults. In D. A Harley & P. B. Teaster (Eds.), *Handbook of LGBT elders* (pp. 43–64). New York: Springer.

Allexandre, D., Bernstein, A. M., Walker, E., Hunter, J., Roizen, M. F., & Morledge, T. J. (2016). A web-based mindfulness stress management program in a corporate call center. *Journal of Occupational and Environmental Medicine, 58*, 254–264. doi:10.1097/JOM.0000000000000680

Alley, J. L. (2004). The potential meaning of the grandparent-grandchild relationship as perceived by young adults: An exploratory study. *Dissertation Abstracts International. Section B. Sciences and Engineering, 65(3-B)*, 1536.

Almeida, J., Molnar, B. E., Kawachi, I., & Subramanian, S. V. (2009). Ethnicity and nativity status as determinants of perceived social support: Testing the concept of familism. *Social Science and Medicine, 68*, 1852–1858 doi:10.1016/j.socscimed.2009.02.029

Alspach, J. G. (2016). When it's your time, will it be your way? *Critical Care Nurse, 36*, 10–13. doi:10.4037/ccn2016452

Altschul, I., Lee, S. J., & Gershoff, E. T. (2016). Hugs, not hits: Warmth and spanking as predictors of child social competence. *Journal of Marriage and Family, 78*, 695–714.

Alzheimer's Association. (2016a). *Quick facts.* Retrieved from www.alz.org/facts/overview.asp.

Alzheimer's Association. (2016b). *Alzheimer's and dementia basics.* Retrieved from www.alz.org/alzheimers_disease_what_is_alzheimers.asp.

Alzheimer's Association. (2016c). 2016 Alzheimer's disease facts and figures. *Alzheimer's and Dementia, 12*, 459–509. Retrieved from www.alz.org/documents_custom/2016-facts-and-figures.pdf.

Alzheimer's Association. (2016d). *10 early signs and symptoms of Alzheimer's.* Retrieved from alz.org/10-signs-symptoms-alzheimers-dementia.asp.

Alzheimer's Association. (2016e). *Stages of Alzheimer's.* Retrieved from www.alz.org/alzheimers_disease_stages_of_alzheimers.asp.

Amato, P. R. (2010). Research on divorce: Continuing trends and new developments. *Journal of Marriage and Family, 72*, 650–666.

Amato, P. R., & Boyd, L. M. (2014). Children and divorce in world perspective. In A. Abela & J. Walker (Eds.), *Contemporary issues in family studies: Global perspectives on partnerships, parenting, and support in a changing world* (pp. 227–244). New York: Wiley.

Amato, P. R., & Cheadle, J. (2005). The long reach of divorce: Divorce and child well-being across three generations. *Journal of Marriage & Family, 67*, 191–206. doi:10.1111/j.0022-2445.2005.00014.x

Amato, P. R., & Fowler, F. (2002). Parenting practices, child adjustment, and family diversity. *Journal of Marriage and Family, 64*, 703–716.

Amato, P. R., King, V., & Thorsen, M. L. (2016). Parent-child relationships in stepfather families and adolescent adjustment: A latent class analysis. *Journal of Marriage and Family, 78*, 482–497.

American Academy of Pain Medicine. (2016) *Position statements to support your pain practice.* Retrieved from www.painmed.org/practicemanagement/position-statements/.

American Academy of Pediatrics. (2011). *Caring for our children: National health and safety performance standards; guidelines for early child care and education programs* (3rd ed.). Elk Grove Village, IL: Author.

American Cancer Society. (2012). *Prostate cancer.* Retrieved from www.cancer.org/cancer/prostatecancer/index.

American Cancer Society. (2016). *Benefits of quitting smoking over time.* Retrieved from www.cancer.org/healthy/stayawayfromtobacco/benefits-of-quitting-smoking-over-time.

American Cancer Society. (2016a). *American Cancer Society skin cancer prevention activities.* Retrieved from www.cancer.org/healthy/morewaysacshelpsyoustaywell/acs-skin-cancer-prevention-activities.

American Cancer Society. (2016b). *Lifetime risk of developing or dying from cancer.* Retrieved from www.cancer.org/cancer/cancerbasics/lifetime-probability-of-developing-or-dying-from-cancer.

American Cancer Society. (2016c). *Stay healthy.* Retrieved from www.cancer.org/healthy/index.

American College of Obstetricians and Gynecologists. (2011a). *Frequently asked questions: Cesarean birth.* Washington DC: Author.

American College of Obstetricians and Gynecologists. (2011b). *Frequently asked questions: Pain relief during labor and delivery.* Washington DC: Author.

American College of Obstetricians and Gynecologists. (2015). *Cell-free DNA prenatal screening test.* Washington, DC: Author.

American Diabetes Association. (2016a). *Diabetes basics.* Retrieved from www.diabetes.org/diabetes-basics/?loc=db-slabnav.

American Diabetes Association. (2016b). *Living with diabetes.* Retrieved from www.diabetes.org/living-with-diabetes/?loc=lwd-slabnav.

American Heart Association. (2016a). *The American Heart Association's diet and lifestyle recommendations.* Retrieved from www.heart.org/HEARTORG/HealthyLiving/HealthyEating/Nutrition/The-American-Heart-Associations-Diet-and-Lifestyle-Recommendations_UCM_305855_Article.jsp#.V_jurPkrLIU.

American Heart Association. (2016b). *Seeds of native health: A campaign for indigenous nutrition.* Retrieved from http://seedsofnativehealth.org/fertile-ground-ii/.

American Lung Association. (2016). *COPD.* Retrieved from www.lung.org/lung-health-and-diseases/lung-disease-lookup/copd/.

American Lung Association. (2016). *Smoking facts.* Retrieved from www.lung.org/stop-smoking/smoking-facts/.

American Psychiatric Association. (2004). *Diagnostic and statistical manual of mental disorders* (4th ed.). Washington, DC: Author.

American Psychiatric Association. (2013). *Diagnostic and statistical manual of mental disorders: DSM-5™* (5th ed.). Arlington, VA: American Psychiatric Association.

American Stroke Association. (2016). *Stroke treatments.* Retrieved from www.strokeassociation.org/STROKEORG/AboutStroke/Treatment/Stroke-Treatments_UCM_310892_Article.jsp#.VzEmpWP7048.

Amso, D., & Johnson, S. P. (2006). Learning by selection: Visual search and object perception in young infants. *Developmental Psychology, 42,* 1236–1245.

Andersen, G. J. (2012). Aging and vision: Changes in function and performance from optics to perception. *Wiley Interdisciplinary Reviews: Cognitive Science, 3,* 403–410. doi:10.1002/wcs.1167

Anderson, E. R., & Greene, S. M. (2013). Beyond divorce: Research on children in repartnered and remarried families. *Family Court Review, 51,* 119–130. doi:10.1111/fcre.12013

Anderson, S. W., Damasio, H., Tranel, D., & Damasio, A. R. (2001). Long-term sequelae of prefrontal cortex damage acquired in early childhood. *Developmental Neuropsychology, 18,* 281–296.

Andreassi, J. K. (2011). What the person brings to the table: Personality, coping, and work-family conflict. *Journal of Family Issues, 32,* 1474–1499. doi:10.1177/0192513X11401815

Angel, R. J., & Angel, J. L. (2015). *Latinos in an aging world: Social, psychological, and economic perspectives.* New York: Routledge.

Anisfeld, M. (1996). Only tongue protrusion modeling is matched by neonates. *Developmental Review, 16,* 149–161.

Antheunis, M. L. (2016). Friendships and the internet. In C. R. Berger, M. E. Roloff, S. R. Wilson, J. P. Dillard, J. Caughlin, & D. Solomon (Eds.), *The international encyclopedia of interpersonal communication.* New York: Wiley. doi:10.1002/9781118540190.wbeic261

Anticevic, A., Repovs, G., & Barch, D. M. (2012). Emotion effects on attention, amygdala activation, and functional capacity in schizophrenia. *Schizophrenia Bulletin, 38,* 967–980. doi:10.1093/schbul/sbq168

Anzures, G., Quinn, P. C., Pascalis, O., Slater, A. M., Tanaka, J. W., & Lee, K. (2013). Developmental origins of the other-race effect. *Current Directions in Psychological Science, 22,* 173–178.

Anzures, G., Wheeler, A., Quinn, P. C., Pascalis, O., Slater, A. M., Heron-Delaney, M., et al. (2012). Brief daily exposures to Asian females reverses perceptual narrowing for Asian faces in Caucasian infants. *Journal of Experimental Child Psychology, 112,* 484–495.

Apfelbaum, E. P., Pauker, K., Ambady, N., Sommers, S. R., & Norton, M. I. (2008). Learning (not) to talk about race: When older children underperform in social categorization. *Developmental Psychology, 44,* 1513–1518.

Apgar, V. (1953). A proposal for a new method of evaluation of the newborn infant. *Current Researches in Anesthesia and Analgesia, 32,* 260–267.

Aponte, M. (2007). Mentoring: Career advancement of Hispanic army nurses. *Dissertation Abstracts International. Section A. Humanities and Social Sciences, 68(4-A),* 1609.

Arbeev, K. G., Ukraintseva, S. V., & Yashin, A. I. (2016). Dynamics of biomarkers in relation to aging and mortality. *Mechanisms of Ageing and Development, 156,* 42–54. doi:10.1016/j.mad.2016.04.010

Archer, J. (2013). Can evolutionary principles explain patterns of family violence? *Psychological Bulletin, 139,* 403–440.

Ardelt, M. (2010). Age, experience, and the beginning of wisdom. In D. Dannefer & C. Phillipson (Eds.), *The SAGE handbook of social gerontology* (pp. 306–316). Thousand Oaks, CA: Sage Publications.

Ardelt, M., Landes, S. D., Gerlach, K. R., & Fox, L. P. (2013). Rediscovering internal strengths of the aged: The beneficial impact of wisdom, mastery, purpose in life, and spirituality on aging well. In J. D. Sinnott (Ed.), *Positive psychology* (pp. 97–119). New York: Springer.

Arizmendi, B., Kaszniak, A. W., & O'Connor, M.-F. (2016). Disrupted prefrontal activity during emotion processing in complicated grief: An fMRI investigation. *NeuroImage, 124 (Part A),* 968–976. doi:10.1016/j.neuroimage.2015.09.054

Arndt, J., & Goldenberg, J. L. (2017). Where health and death intersect: Insights from a Terror Management Health Model. *Current Directions in Psychological Science, 26,* 126–131. doi:10.1177/0963721416689563

Arnett, J. J. (2013). *Adolescence and emerging adulthood: A cultural approach* (5th ed.). Upper Saddle River, NJ: Pearson.

Arnett, J. J. (2016). Introduction: Emerging adulthood theory and research: Where we are and where we should go. In J. J. Arnett (Ed.), *The Oxford handbook of emerging adulthood* (pp. 1–7). New York: Oxford University Press.

Aron, A., Fisher, H., Mashek, D. J., Strong, G., Li, H., & Brown, L. L. (2005). Reward, motivation, and emotion systems associated with early-stage intense romantic love. *Journal of Neurophysiology, 94,* 327–337. doi:10.1152/jn.00838.2004

Arseneault, L., Tremblay, R. E., Boulerice, B., & Saucier, J. F. (2002). Obstetrical complications and violent delinquency: Testing two developmental pathways. *Child Development, 73,* 496–508.

Årseth, A. K., Kroger, J., Martinussen, M., & Marcia, J. E. (2009). Meta-analytic studies of identity status and the relational issues of attachment and intimacy. *Identity, 9,* 1–32. doi:10.1080/15283480802579532

Artazcoz, L., Benach, J., Borrell, C., & Cortès, I. (2004). Unemployment and mental health: Understanding the interactions among gender, family roles, and social class. *American Journal of Public Health, 94,* 82–88. doi:10.2105/AJPH.94.1.82

Arunachalam, S., Escovar, E., Hansen, M. A., & Waxman, S. R. (2013). Out of sight, but not out of mind: 21-month-olds use syntactic information to learn verbs even in the absence of a corresponding event. *Language and Cognitive Processes, 28,* 417–425.

Aryee, S., Chu, C. W. L., Kim, T.-Y., & Ryu, S. (2013). Family-supportive work environment and employee work behaviors: An investigation of mediating mechanisms. *Journal of Management, 39,* 792–813. doi:10.1177/0149206311435103

Asarnow, J. R., & Miranda, J. (2014). Improving care for depression and suicide risk in adolescents: Innovative strategies for bringing treatments to community settings. *Annual Review of Clinical Psychology, 10,* 275–303.

Asbridge, M., Brubacher, J. R., & Chan, H. (2013). Cell phone use and traffic crash risk: A culpability analysis. *International Journal of Epidemiology, 42,* 259–267.

Asendorpf, J. B., Denissen, J. J. A., & van Aken, M. A. G. (2008). Inhibited and aggressive preschool children at 23 years of age: Personality and social transitions into adulthood. *Developmental Psychology, 44,* 997–1011.

Ashcraft, M. H. (1982). The development of mental arithmetic: A chronometric approach. *Developmental Review, 2,* 212–236.

Aslin, R. (2017). Statistical learning: a powerful mechanism that operates by mere exposure. *WIREs Cognitive Science, 8,* e1373.

Asoodeh, M. H., Khalili, S., Daneshpour, N., & Lavasani, M. G. (2010). Factors of successful marriage: Accounts from self-described happy couples. *Procedia Social and Behavioral Sciences, 5,* 2042–2046. doi:10.1016/j.sbspro.2010.07.410

Assanangkornchai, S., Tangboonngam, S., Samangsri, N., & Edwards, J. G. (2007). A Thai community's anniversary reaction to a major catastrophe. *Stress and Health, 23,* 43–50. doi:10.1002/smi.1118

Attia, E. Anorexia nervosa. In K. D. Brownell & B. T. Walsh (Eds.), *Eating disorders and obesity* (3rd ed., pp. 176–181). New York: Guilford.

Attig, T. (1996). *How we grieve: Relearning the world.* New York: Oxford University Press.

Au, T. K., & Glusman, M. (1990). The principle of mutual exclusivity in word learning: To honor or not to honor? *Child Development, 61,* 1474–1490.

Aunola, K., Stattin, H., & Nurmi, J.-E. (2000). Parenting styles and adolescents' achievement strategies. *Journal of Adolescence, 23,* 205–222.

Awa, W. L., Plaumann, M., & Walter, U. (2010). Burnout prevention: A review of intervention programs. *Patient Education and Counseling, 78,* 184–190. doi:10.1016/j.pec.2009.04.008

Awadi, M. A., & Mrayyan, M. T. (2016). Opponents and proponents views regarding palliative sedation at end of life. *Journal of Palliative Care & Medicine, 6,* 242. doi:10.4172/2165-7386 .1000242. Retrieved from www.omicsgroup .org/journals/opponents-and-proponents-views-regarding-palliative-sedation-at-end-oflife-2165-7386-1000242.php?aid=66887.

Awong, T., Grusec, J. E., & Sorenson, A. (2008). Respect-based control and anger as determinants of children's socio-emotional development. *Social Development, 17,* 941–959.

Bachman, B. (2017). *Ethical leadership in organizations.* New York: Springer.

Bachman, J. G., Staff, J., O'Malley, P. M., & Freedman-Doan, P. (2013). Adolescent work intensity, school performance, and substance use: Links vary by race/ethnicity and socioeconomic status. *Developmental Psychology, 49,* 2125–2134.

Bachman, J. G., Staff, J., O'Malley, P.M., Freedman-Doan, P. (2014). *What do teenagers do with their earnings, and does it matter for their academic achievement and development?* (Monitoring the Future Occasional Paper No. 78). Ann Arbor, MI: Institute for Social Research, The University of Michigan.

Bade, M. K. (2012). *Personal growth in the midst of negative life experiences: The role of religious coping strategies and appraisals.* Dissertation submitted to Texas Tech University. Retrieved from ttu-ir.tdl.org/ttu-ir/handle/2346/10475/.

Baer, D. M., & Wolf, M. M. (1968). The reinforcement contingency in preschool and remedial education. In R. D. Hess & R. M Baer (Eds.), *Early education: Theory, research and practice* (pp. 119–130). Chicago: Aldine.

Bagbey Darian, C. D. (2014). A new mourning: Synthesizing an interactive model of adaptive grieving dynamics. *Illness, Crisis & Loss, 22,* 195–235. doi:10.2190/IL.22.3.c

Bagnall, A.-M., Jones, R., Akter, H., & Woodall, J. (2016). *Interventions to prevent burnout in high risk individuals: Evidence review.* Retrieved from www.gov.uk/government/uploads/system/uploads/attachment_data/file/506777/25022016_Burnout_Rapid_Review_2015709.pdf.

Bahrick, L. E., & Lickliter, R. (2002). Intersensory redundancy guides early perceptual and cognitive development. In R. V. Kail (Ed.), *Advances in child development and behavior* (Vol. 30, pp. 153–177). Orlando, FL: Academic Press.

Bahrick, L. E., & Lickliter, R. (2012). The role of intersensory redundancy in early perceptual, cognitive, and social development. In A. Bremner, D. J. Lewkowicz, and C. Spence (Eds.), *Multisensory development* (pp. 183–205). Oxford, UK: Oxford University Press.

Bahrick, L. E., Lickliter, R., Castellanos, I., & Todd, J. T. (2015). Intrasensory redundancy facilitates infant detection of tempo: Extending predictions of the intersensory redundancy hypothesis. *Infancy, 20,* 377–404.

Bailey, J. A., Hill, K. G., Oesterle, S., & Hawkins, J. D. (2009). Parenting practices and problem behavior across three generations: Monitoring, harsh discipline, and drug use in the intergenerational transmission of externalizing behavior. *Developmental Psychology, 45,* 1214–1226.

Bailey, J. M., Bechtold, K. T., & Berenbaum, S. A. (2002). Who are tomboys and why should we study them? *Archives of Sexual Behavior, 31,* 333–341.

Baillargeon, R. (1987). Object permanence in 3½- and 4½-month-old infants. *Developmental Psychology, 23,* 655–664.

Baillargeon, R. (1994). How do infants learn about the physical world? *Current Directions in Psychological Science, 3,* 133–140.

Baillargeon, R., Scott, R. M., & Bian, L. (2016). Psychological reasoning in infancy. *Annual Review of Psychology, 67,* 159–186.

Baker, L. (1994). Fostering metacognitive development. In H. W. Reese (Ed.), *Advances in child development and behavior* (Vol. 25, pp. 201–239). San Diego, CA: Academic Press.

Bakolis, I., Kelly, R., Fecht, D., Best, N. Millet, C., Garwood, K., et al. (2016). Protective effects of smoke-free legislation on birth outcomes in England: A regression discontinuity design. *Epidemiology, 27,* 810–818.

Balk, D. E. (2014). *Dealing with dying, death, and grief during adolescence.* New York: Routledge.

Ballard, R. H., Rudd, B. N., Applegate, A. G., & Holtzworth-Munroe, A. (2014). Hearing the voice of the child in divorce. In M. K. Miller, J. Chamberlain, & T. Wingrove (Eds.), *Psychology, law, and the wellbeing of children* (pp. 121–137). New York: Oxford University Press.

Baltes, B. B., & Heydens-Gahir, H. A. (2003). Reduction of work-family conflict through the use of selection, optimization, and compensation behaviors. *Journal of Applied Psychology, 88,* 1005–1018. doi:10.1037/0021-9010.88.6.1005

Baltes, M. M., & Carstensen, L. L. (1999). Social-psychological theories and their applications to aging: From individual to collective. In V. L. Bengtson & K. W. Schaie (Eds.), *Handbook of theories of aging* (pp. 209–226). New York: Springer.

Baltes, P. B. (1993). The aging mind: Potential and limits. *The Gerontologist, 33,* 580–594. doi:10.1093/geront/33.5.580

Baltes, P. B. (1997). On the incomplete architecture of human ontogeny: Selection, optimization, and compensation as foundation of developmental theory. *American Psychologist, 52,* 366–380. doi:10.1037/0003-066X .52.4.366

Baltes, P. B., & Smith, J. (2003). New frontiers in the future of aging: From successful aging of the young old to the dilemmas of the fourth age. *Gerontology, 49,* 123–135. doi:10.1159/000067946

Baltes, P. B., & Staudinger, U. M. (2000). Wisdom: A metaheuristic (pragmatic) to orchestrate mind and virtue toward excellence. *American Psychologist, 55,* 122–136. doi:10.1037/0003-066X.55.1.122

Baltes, P. B., Lindenberger, U., & Staudinger, U. M. (2006). Life-span theory in developmental psychology. In R. M. Lerner & W. Damon (Eds.), *Handbook of child psychology: Vol. 1. Theoretical models of human development* (6th ed., pp. 569–664). Hoboken, NJ: Wiley.

Bambra, C. (2010). Yesterday once more? Unemployment and health in the 21st century. *Journal of Epidemiology and Community Health, 64,* 213–215. doi:10.1136/jech.2009.090621

Bandura, A. (1977). *Social learning theory.* Englewood Cliffs, NJ: Prentice Hall.

Bandura, A. (1986). *Social foundations of thought and action: A social-cognitive theory.* Englewood Cliffs, NJ: Prentice Hall.

Bandura, A., & Bussey, K. (2004). On broadening the cognitive, motivational, and sociostructural scope of theorizing about gender development and functioning: Comment on Martin, Ruble, and Szkrybalo (2002). *Psychological Bulletin, 130,* 691–701.

Banerjee, K., & Bloom, P. (2015). "Everything happens for a reason": Children's beliefs about purpose in life events. *Child Development, 86,* 503–518.

Bannard, C., & Matthews, D. (2008). Stored word sequences in language learning: The effect of familiarity on children's repetition of four-word combinations. *Psychological Science, 19,* 241–248.

Barac, R., & Bialystok, E. (2012). Bilingual effects on cognitive and linguistic development: Role of language, cultural background, and education. *Child Development, 83,* 413–422.

Barber, B. K., & Olsen, J. A. (1997). Socialization in context: Connection, regulation, and autonomy in the family, school, and neighborhood, and with peers. *Journal of Adolescent Research, 12,* 287–315.

Barbey, A. K., Colom, R., & Grafman, J. (2014). Distributed neural system for emotional intelligence revealed by lesion mapping. *Social Cognitive and Affective Neuroscience, 9,* 265–272. doi:10.1093/scan/nss124

Barca, L., Ellis, A. W., & Burani, C. (2007). Context-sensitive rules and word naming in Italian children. *Reading & Writing, 20,* 495–509.

Barenboim, C. (1981). The development of person perception in childhood and adolescence: From behavioral comparisons to psychological constructs to psychological comparisons. *Child Development, 52,* 129–144.

Barker, E. D., Copeland, W., Maughan, B., Jaffee, S. R., & Uher, R. (2012). Relative impact of maternal depression and associated risk factors on offspring psychopathology. *The British Journal of Psychiatry, 200,* 124–129.

Barkley, R. A. (2004). Adolescents with attention deficit/hyperactivity disorder: An overview of empirically based treatments. *Journal of Psychiatric Review, 10,* 39–56.

Barlow, M., Wrosch, C., Heckhausen, J., & Schulz, R. (2017). Control strategies for managing physical health problems in old age: Evidence for the motivational theory of lifespan development. In F. J. Infurna & J. W. Reich (Eds.), *Perceived control: Theory, research, and practice in the first 50 years* (pp.). New York: Oxford University Press.

Barnett, A. E. (2013). Pathways of adult children providing care to older parents. *Journal of Marriage and the Family, 75,* 178–190. doi:10.1111/j.1741-3737.2012.01022.x

Baron-Cohen, S. (2005). The Empathizing System: A revision of the 1994 model of the Mind Reading System. In B. J. Ellis & D. F. Bjorklund (Eds.), *Origins of the social mind: Evolutionary psychology and child development* (pp. 468–492). New York: Guilford.

Baron, A. S. (2015). Constraints on the development of implicit intergroup attitudes. *Child Development Perspectives, 9,* 50–54.

Baron, R., Manniën, J., de Jonge, A., Heymans, M. W., Klomp, T., Hutton, E. K., et al. (2013). Socio-demographic and lifestyle-related characteristics associated with self-reported any, daily and occasional smoking during pregnancy. *PLoS ONE, 8*(9), e74197.

Barr, R., & Hayne, H. (1999). Developmental changes in imitation from television during infancy. *Child Development, 70,* 1067–1081.

Barr, R., & Linebarger, D. N. (2017). The new blooming, buzzing confusion: Introduction to media exposure during infancy and early childhood. In R. Barr & D. N. Linebarger (Eds.), *Media exposure during infancy and early childhood* (pp. xi–xv). Cham, Switzerland: Springer.

Barrera, M., Alam, R., D'Agostino, N. M., Nicholas, D. B., & Schneiderman, G. (2013). Parental perceptions of siblings' grieving after a childhood cancer death: A longitudinal study. *Death Studies, 37,* 25–46. doi:10.1080/07481187.2012.678262

Barrick, M. R., Mount, M. K., & Li, N. (2013). The theory of purposeful work behavior: The role of personality, higher order goals, and job characteristics. *Academy of Management Review, 38,* 132–153. doi:10.5465/amr.2010.0479

Bartkowiak, G. (2017). Best practices in the employment of knowledge workers 65 and over and the benefits of employing them (An empirical approach). In M. H. Bilgin, H. Danis, E. Demir, & U. Can (Eds.), *Financial environment and business development* (pp. 463–471). New York: Springer.

Bartl, R., Bartl, C., & Frisch, B. (2015). *Osteoporosis: Diagnosis, prevention, therapy* (3rd ed.). New York: Springer.

Bartlett, D. B., & Huffman, K. M. (2017). Lifetime interventions to improve immunesenescence. In V. Bueno, J. M. Lord, & T. A. Jackson (Eds.), *The ageing immune system and health* (pp. 161–176). New York: Springer.

Barton, C., Ketelle, R., Merrilees, J., & Miller, B. (2016). Non-pharmacological management of behavioral symptoms in frontotemporal and other dementias. *Current Neurology and Neuroscience Reports, 16,* 14. doi:10.1007/s11910-015-0618-1

Barton, M. E., & Tomasello, M. (1991). Joint attention and conversation in mother-infant-sibling triads. *Child Development, 62,* 517–529.

Barzilai, N., Huffman, D. M., Muzumdar, R. H., & Bartke, A. (2012). The critical role of metabolic pathways in aging. *Diabetes, 61,* 1315–1322. doi:10.2337/db11-1300

Basso, K. H. (1970). *The Cibecue Apache.* New York: Holt, Rinehart, & Winston.

Baste, V., Oftedal, G., Møllerløkken, O. J., Hansson Mild, K., & Moen, B. E. (2015). Prospective study of pregnancy outcomes after parental cell phone exposure: The Norwegian Mother and Child Cohort study. *Epidemiology, 26,* 613–621.

Basten, U., Hilger, K., & Fiebach, C. J. (2015). Where smart brains are different: A quantitative meta-analysis of functional and structural brain imaging studies on intelligence. *Intelligence, 51,* 10–27. doi:10.1016/j.intell.2015.04.009

Bates, E., Bretherton, I., & Snyder, L. (1988). *From first words to grammar: Individual differences and dissociable mechanisms.* New York: Cambridge University Press.

Bates, J. S. (2009). *Generative grandfathering, commitment, and contact: How grandfathers nurture relationships with grandchildren and the relational and mental health benefits for aging men.* Dissertation submitted in partial fulfillment of the doctor of philosophy degree at Syracuse University.

Batt, M. E., Tanji, J., & Börjesson, M. (2013). Exercise at 65 and beyond. *Sports Medicine, 43,* 525–530. doi:10.1007/s40279-013-0033-1

Battista, R. N., Blancquaert, I., Laberge, A.-M., van Schendel, N., & Leduc, N. (2012). Genetics in health care: An overview of current and emerging models. *Public Health Genomics, 15,* 34–45. doi:10.1159/000328846

Baucom, B. R., Dickenson, J. A., Atkins, D. C., Baucom, D. H., Fischer, M. S., Weusthoff, S. et al. (2015). The interpersonal process model of demand/withdraw behavior. *Journal of Family Psychology, 29,* 80–90. doi:10.1037/fam0000044

Baude, A., Pearson, J., & Drapeau, S. (2016). Child adjustment in joint physical custody versus sole custody: A meta-analytic review. *Journal of Divorce & Remarriage, 57,* 338–360.

Bauer, P. J. (2015). Development of episodic and autobiographical memory: The importance of remembering forgetting. *Developmental Review, 38,* 146–166.

Bauer, P. J., & Lukowski, A. F. (2010). The memory is in the details: Relations between memory for the specific features of events and long-term recall during infancy. *Journal of Experimental Child Psychology, 107,* 1–14.

Bauer, P. J., San Souci, P., & Pathman, T. (2010). Infant memory. *WIREs Cognitive Science, 1,* 267–277.

Baum, C. L., II, & Ruhm, C. J. (2016). The effects of paid family leave in California on labor market outcomes. *Journal of Policy Analysis and Management, 35,* 333–356. doi:10.1002/pam.21894

Baumann, A., Claudot, F., Audibert, G., Mertes, P.-M., & Puybasset, M. (2011). The ethical and legal aspects of palliative sedation in severely brain-injured patients: A French perspective. *Philosophy, Ethics, and Humanities in Medicine, 6.* Retrieved from preview.peh-med.com/content/pdf/1747-5341-6-4.pdf.

Baumeister, R. F. (2010). The self. In R. F. Baumeister & E. J. Finkel (Eds.), *Advanced social psychology: The state of the science* (pp. 139–175). New York: Oxford University Press.

Baumrind, D. (1975). *Early socialization and the discipline controversy.* Morristown, NJ: General Learning Press.

Baumrind, D. (1991). Parenting styles and adolescent development. In R. M. Lerner, A. C. Petersen, & J. Brooks-Gunn (Eds.), *Encyclopedia of adolescence* (pp. 746–758). New York: Garland.

Baxter, A. J., Brugha, T. S., Erskine, H. E., Scheurer, R. W., Vos, T., & Scott, J. G. (2015). The epidemiology and global burden of autism spectrum disorders. *Psychological Medicine, 45*, 601–613.

Bayl-Smith, P. H., & Griffin, B. (2014). Age discrimination in the workplace: Identifying as a late career worker and its relationship with engagement and intended retirement age. *Journal of Applied Social Psychology, 44*, 588–599. doi:10.1111/jasp.12251

Bayley, N. (1969). *Bayley scales of infant development: Manual.* New York, New York: The Psychological Corporation.

Beal, C. R., & Belgrad, S. L. (1990). The development of message evaluation skills in young children. *Child Development, 61*, 705–712.

Beauchamp, G. K., & Mennella, J. A. (2011). Flavor perception in human infants: Development and functional significance. *Digestion, 83*, 1–6.

Beck, A. T. (1967). *Depression: Clinical, experimental, and theoretical aspects.* New York: Harper & Row.

Beck, A. T., Rush, J., Shaw, B., & Emery, G. (1979). *Cognitive therapy of depression.* New York: Guilford.

Beck, E., Burnet, K. L., & Vosper, J. (2006). Birth-order effects on facets of extraversion. *Personality and Individual Differences, 40*, 953–959.

Beck, V. (2013). Employers' use of older workers in the recession. *Employee Relations, 35*, 257–271. doi:10.1108/01425451311320468

Becker, B. J. (1986). Influence again: An examination of reviews and studies of gender differences in social influence. In J. S. Hyde & M. C. Linn (Eds.), *The psychology of gender differences. Advances through meta-analysis.* Baltimore, MD: Johns Hopkins University Press.

Becker, C. B., Perez, M., Kilpela, L. S., Diedrichs, P. C., Trujillo, E., & Stice, E. (in press). Engaging stakeholder communities as body image intervention partners: The Body Project as a case example. *Eating Behaviors.*

Beckes, L., & Coan, J. A. (2013). Voodoo versus me-you correlations in relationship neuroscience. *Journal of Social and Personal Relationships, 30*, 189–197. doi:10.1177/0265407512454768

Beckes, L., Coan, J. A., & Hasselmo, K. (2013). Familiarity promotes the blurring of self and other in the neural perception of threat. *Social Cognitive and Affective Neuroscience, 8*, 670–677. doi:10.1093/scan/nss046

Bedir, A., & Aksoy, S. (2011). Brain death revisited: It is not "complete death" according to Islamic sources. *Journal of Medical Ethics, 37*, 290–294. doi:10.1136/jme.2010.040238

Behl, C., & Ziegler, C. (2014). *Cell aging: Molecular mechanisms and implications for disease.* New York: Springer.

Behnke, A. O., Plunkett, S. W., Sands, T., & Bámaca-Colbert, M. Y. (2011). The relationship between Latino adolescents' perceptions of discrimination, neighborhood risk, and parenting on self-esteem and depressive symptoms. *Journal of Cross-Cultural Psychology, 42*, 1179–1197.

Behnke, M., & Eyler, F. D. (1993). The consequences of prenatal substance use for the developing fetus, newborn, and young child. *International Journal of the Addictions, 28*, 1341–1391.

Belsky, G. (2007). *Over the hill and between the sheets: Sex, love and lust in middle age.* New York: Springboard Press.

Belsky, J., Bakermans-Kranenburg, M. J., & van IJzendoorn, M. H. (2007). For better and for worse: Differential susceptibility to environmental influences. *Current Directions in Psychological Science, 16*, 300–304.

Belsky, J., Steinberg, L., Houts, R. M., Halpern-Felsher, B., and the NICHD Early Child Care Research Network. (2010). The development of reproductive strategy in females: Early maternal harshness → earlier menarche → increased sexual risk taking. *Developmental Psychology, 46*, 120–128.

beneden health. (2013). *Study reveals changing attitudes to middle age.* Retrieved from www.benenden.co.uk/newsroom/research/research-archive/study-reveals-changing-attitudes-to-middle-age/.

Bengtson, V. L., Mills, T. L., & Parrott, T. M. (1995). Ageing in the United States at the end of the century. *Korea Journal of Population and Development, 24*, 215–244.

Bennett, K. M. (2005). Psychological wellbeing in later life: The longitudinal effects of marriage, widowhood and marital status change. *International Journal of Geriatric Psychiatry, 20*, 280–284. doi:10.1002/gps.1280

Bennett, K. M. (2010). How to achieve resilience as an older widower: Turning points or gradual change? *Ageing and Society, 30*, 369–382. doi:10.1017/S0144686X09990572

Bent, K. N., & Magilvy, J. K. (2006). When a partner dies: Lesbian widows. *Issues in Mental Health Nursing, 27*, 447–459. doi:10.1080/01612840600599960

Benton, S. L., Corkill, A. J., Sharp, J. M., Downey, R. G., et al. (1995). Knowledge, interest, and narrative writing. *Journal of Educational Psychology, 87*, 66–79.

Bereiter, C., & Scardamalia, M. (1987). *The psychology of written composition.* Hillsdale, NJ: Erlbaum.

Berg, C. A., Sewell, K. K., Hughes Lansing, A. E., Wilson, S. J., & Brewer, C. (2016). A developmental perspective to dyadic coping across adulthood. In J. Bookwala (Ed.), *Couple relationships in the middle and later years: Their nature, complexity, and role in health and illness* (pp. 259–280). Washington, DC: American Psychological Association.

Bergdahl, E., Benzein, E., Ternestedt, B.-M., Elmberger, E., & Andershed, B. (2013). Co-creating possibilities for patients in palliative care to reach vital goals—A multiple case study of home-care nursing encounters. *Nursing Inquiry, 20*, 341–351. doi:10.1111/nin.12022

Berger, R. G., Lunkenbein, S., Ströhle, A., & Hahn, A. (2012). Antioxidants in food: Mere myth or magic medicine? *Critical Reviews in Food Science and Nutrition, 52*, 162–171. doi:10.1080/10408398.2010.499481

Berger, S. E., Adolph, K. E., & Lobo, S. A. (2005). Out of the toolbox: Toddlers differentiate wobbly and wooden handrails. *Child Development, 76*, 1294–1307.

Bergman, K. N., Cummings, E. M., & Warmuth, K. A. (2016). The benefits of marital conflict: constructiveness and resolution as predictors of child positive outcomes. In D. Narvaez et al. (Eds.), *Contexts for young children flourishing: Evolution, family, and society* (pp. 233–244). New York: Oxford University Press.

Bergsma, A., & Ardelt, M. (2012). Self-reported wisdom and happiness: An empirical investigation. *Journal of Happiness Studies, 13*, 481–499. doi:10.1007/s10902-011-9275-5

Berk, L. E. (2003). Vygotsky, Lev. In L. Nadel (Ed.), *Encyclopedia of cognitive science* (Vol. 6). London: Macmillan.

Berk, R. A. (2010). Where's the chemistry in mentor-mentee academic relationships? Try speed mentoring. *The International Journal of Mentoring and Coaching, 8*, 85–92. Retrieved from www.ronberk.com/articles/2010_mentor.pdf.

Berko, J. (1958). The child's learning of English morphology. *Word, 14*, 150–177.

Berkowitz, M. W., Sherblom, S., Bier, M., & Battistich, V. (2006). Educating for positive youth development. In M. Killen & J. G. Smetana (Eds.), *Handbook of moral development* (pp. 683–702). Mahwah, NJ: Erlbaum.

Bermejo-Toro, L., Prieto-Ursúa, M., & Hernández, V. (2016). Towards a model of teacher well-being: Personal and job resources involved in teacher burnout and engagement. *Educational Psychology, 36*, 481–501. doi:10.1080/01443410.2015.1005006

Bernadotte, A., Mikhelson, V. M., & Spivak, I. M. (2016). Markers of cellular senescence. Telomere shortening as a marker of cellular senescence. *Aging, 8*, 3–11. www.ncbi.nlm.nih.gov/pmc/articles/PMC4761709/.

Bernal, S., Dehaene-Lambertz, G., Millotte, S., & Christophe, A. (2010). Two-year-olds compute syntactic structure on-line. *Developmental Science, 13*, 69–76.

Berndt, T. J., & Murphy, L. M. (2002). Influences of friends and friendships: Myths, truths, and research recommendations. *Advances in Child Development and Behavior, 30*, 275–310.

Berndt, T. J., & Perry, T. B. (1990). Distinctive features and effects of adolescent friendships. In R. Montemayer, G. R. Adams, & T. P. Gullotta (Eds.), *From childhood to adolescence: A transition period?* London: Sage.

Bernier, A., Carlson, S. M., & Whipple, N. (2010). From external regulation to self-regulation: Early parenting precursors of young children's executive functioning. *Child Development, 81,* 326–339.

Berns, N. (2011). *Closure: The rush to end grief and what it costs.* Philadelphia: Temple University Press.

Berry, J., Hastings, E., West, R., Lee, C., & Cavanaugh, J. C. (2010). Memory aging: Deficits, beliefs, and interventions. In J. C. Cavanaugh & C. K. Cavanaugh (Eds.), *Aging in America*: Vol. 1: Psychological Aspects (pp. 255–299). Santa Barbara, CA: Praeger.

Bertenthal, B. H., & Clifton, R. K. (1998). Perception and action. In W. Damon (Ed.), *Handbook of child psychology* (Vol. 2). New York: Wiley.

Best, J. R. (2013). Exergaming in youth: Effects on physical and cognitive health. *Zeitschrift für Psychologie, 221,* 72–78.

Beuker, K. T., Rommelse, N. N. J., Donders, R., & Buitelaar, J. K. (2013). Development of early communication skills in the first two years of life. *Infant Behavior and Development, 36,* 71–83.

Bever, L. (2014a). Cancer patient Brittany Maynard, 29, has scheduled her death for Nov. 1. *Washington, Post.* Retrieved from http://wapo.st/10O22rQ.

Bever, L. (2014b). Brittany Maynard, as promised, ends her life at 29. *Washington Post.* Retrieved from http://wapo.st/1yPi6F0.

Bever, L. (2014c). How Brittany Maynard may change the right-do-die debate. *Washington Post.* Retrieved from http://wapo.st/1A3F9QR.

Bhatt, R. S., Hock, A., White, H., Jubran, R., & Galati, A. (2016). The development of body structure knowledge in infancy. *Child Development Perspectives, 10,* 45–52.

Bialystok, E. (1988). Levels of bilingualism and levels of linguistic awareness. *Developmental Psychology, 24,* 560–567.

Bialystok, E. (2010). Global-local and trail-making tasks by monolingual and bilingual children: Beyond inhibition. *Developmental Psychology, 46,* 93–105.

Bian, F., Blachford, D., & Durst, D. (2015). The color purple: Perspectives of Canadian parents of adopted children from China. *Journal of Comparative Social Work, 10*(2). Retrieved from journal.uia.no/index.php/JCSW/article/view/345/289.

Biblarz, T. J., & Savci, E. (2010). Lesbian, gay, bisexual, and transgender families. *Journal of Marriage and Family, 72,* 480–497. doi:10.1111/j.1741-3737.2010.00714.x

Bidwell, M. (2013). What happened to long-term employment? The role of worker power and environmental turbulence in explaining declines in worker tenure. *Organization Science, 24,* 1061–1082. doi:10.1287/orsc.1120.0816

Biggs, S., McGann, M., Bowman, D., & Kimberley, H. (2017). Work, health and the commodification of life's time: Reframing work-life balance and the promise of a long life. *Ageing and Society, 37,* 1458–1483. doi:10.1017/S0144686X16000404

Bigler, R. S., & Liben, L. S. (2007). Developmental intergroup theory: Explaining and reducing children's social stereotyping and prejudice. *Current Directions in Psychological Science, 16,* 162–166.

Bigler, R. S., Jones, L. C., & Lobliner, D. B. (1997). Social categorization and the formation of intergroup attitudes in children. *Child Development, 68,* 530–543.

Bingenheimer, J. B., Brennan, R. T., & Earls, F. J. (2005). Firearm violence exposure and serious violent behavior. *Science, 308,* 1323–1326.

Bird, E. R., Gilmore, A. K., George, W. H., & Lewis, M. A. (2016). The role of social drinking factors in the relationship between incapacitated sexual assault and drinking before sexual activity. *Addictive Behaviors, 52,* 28–33. doi:10.1016/j.addbeh.2015.08.001

Bird, S., Burke, L., Goebel, C., & Greaves, R. (2015). Doping in sport and exercise: Anabolic, ergogenic, health and clinical issues. *Annals of Clinical Biochemistry, 53,* 196–221.

Birnbaum, G. E., Reis, H. T., Mizrahi, M., Kanat-Maymon, Y., Sass, O., Granovski-Milner, C. (2016). Intimately connected: The importance of partner responsiveness for experiencing sexual desire. *Journal of Personality and Social Psychology, 111,* 530–546. doi:10.1037/pspi0000069

Bjerkedal, T., Kristensen, P., Skjeret, G. A., & Brevik, J. I. (2007). Intelligence test scores and birth order among young Norwegian men (conscripts) analyzed within and between families. *Intelligence, 35,* 503–514.

Bjork, J. M., & Gilman, J. M. (2014). The effects of acute alcohol administration on the human brain: Insights from neuroimaging. *Neuropharmacology, 84, 101–110.* doi:10.1016/j.neuropharm.2013.07.039

Bjorklund, D. F. (2005). *Children's thinking: Cognitive development and individual differences* (4th ed.). Belmont, CA: Wadsworth.

Bjorklund, D. F., & Jordan, A. C. (2013). Human parenting from an evolutionary perspective. In W. B. Wilcox & K. K. Kline (Eds.), *Gender and parenthood: Biological and social scientific perspectives* (pp. 61–90). New York: Columbia University Press.

Bjorklund, D. F., Yunger, J. L., & Pellegrini, A. D. (2002). The evolution of parenting and evolutionary approaches to childrearing. In M. H. Bornstein (Ed.), *Handbook of parenting: Vol. 2. Biology and ecology of parenting* (pp. 3–30). Mahwah, NJ: Erlbaum.

Blachnio, A., Przepiorka, A., Balakier, E., & Boruch, W. (2016). Who discloses the most on Facebook? *Computers in Human Behavior, 55 Part B,* 664–667. doi:10.1016/j.chb.2015.10.007

Black, J. E. (2003). Environment and development of the nervous system. In I. B. Weiner, M. Gallagher, & R. J. Nelson (Eds.), *Handbook of psychology, Vol. 3: Biological psychology* (pp. 655–668). Hoboken, NJ: Wiley.

Blackhall, L. J., Read, P., Stukenborg, G., Dillon, P., Barclay, J., Romano, A. et al. (2016). CARE Track for advanced cancer: Impact and timing of an outpatient palliative clinic. *Journal of Palliative Medicine, 19,* 57–63. doi:10.1089/jpm.2015.0272

Blackstone, A., & Stewart, M. D. (2016). "There's more thinking to decide": How the childfree decide not to parent. *The Family Journal, 24,* 296–303. doi:10.1177/1066480716648676

Blair, B. L., Perry, N. B., O'Brien, M., Calkins, S. D., Keane, S. P., & Shanahan, L. (2014). The indirect effects of maternal emotion socialization on friendship quality in middle childhood. *Developmental Psychology, 50,* 566–576.

Blair, C. (2016). Executive function and early childhood education. *Current Opinion in Behavioral Sciences, 10,* 102–107.

Blakemore, J. E. O. (2003). Children's beliefs about violating gender norms: Boys shouldn't look like girls, and girls shouldn't act like boys. *Sex Roles, 48,* 411–419.

Blanchard-Fields, F. (2007). Everyday problem solving and emotion: An adult developmental perspective. *Current Directions in Psychological Science, 16,* 26–31. doi:10.1111/j.1467-8721.2007.00469.x

Blanchard-Fields, F., Baldi, R. A., & Constantin, L. P. (2004). *Interrole conflict across the adult lifespan: The role of parenting stage, career stages and quality of experiences.* Unpublished manuscript, School of Psychology, Georgia Institute of Technology.

Blieszner, R. (2014). The worth of friendship: Can friends keep us happy and healthy? *Generations, 38,* 24–30.

Blieszner, R., & Roberto, K. A. (2012). Partners and friends in adulthood. In S. K. Whitbourne & M. J. Sliwinski (Eds.), *The Wiley-Blackwell handbook of adulthood and aging* (pp. 381–398). Oxford, UK: Wiley-Blackwell.

Bligh, M. C. (2017). Leadership and trust. In J. Marques & S. Dhiman (Eds.), *Leadership today* (pp. 21–42). New York: Springer.

Bloom, L., & Tinker, E. (2001). The intentionality model and language acquisition. *Monographs of the Society for Research in Child Development, 66* (Serial No. 267).

Bloom, L., Margulis, C., Tinker, E., & Fujita, N. (1996). Early conversations and word learning: Contributions from child and adult. *Child Development, 67,* 3154–3175.

Bloom, L., Rocissano, L., & Hood, L. (1976). Adult-child discourse: Developmental interaction between information processing and linguistic knowledge. *Cognitive Psychology, 8,* 521–552.

Bloom, P. (2000). *How children learn the meanings of words.* Cambridge MA: MIT Press.

Blume-Peytavi, U., Kottner, J., Sterry, W., Hodin, M. W., Griffiths, T. W., Watson, R. E. B., et al. (2016). Age-associated skin conditions and diseases: Current perspectives and future options. *The Gerontologist, 56,* S230–S242. doi:10.1093/geront/gnw003

Blümel, J. E., Chedraui, P., Baron, G., Belzares, E., Bencosme, A., Calle, A. et al. (2012). Menopausal symptoms appear before the menopause and persist 5 years beyond: A detailed analysis of a multinational study. *Climacteric, 15,* 542–551. doi:10.3109/13697137.2012.658462

Bluntschli, J. R., Maxfield, M. M., Grasso, R. L., & Kisley, M. A. (in press). The last word: A comparison of younger and older adults' brain responses to reminders of death. *Journals of Gerontology: Psychological Sciences and Social Sciences*. doi:10.1093/geronb/gbv115

Boals, A., Hayslip, B., & Banks, J. B. (2014). Age differences in autobiographical memories of negative events. *International Journal of Aging and Human Development, 78*, 47–65. doi:10.2190/AG.78.1.d

Böckerman, P., Ilmakunnas, P. Jokisaari, M., & Yuori, J. (2013). Who stays unwillingly in a job? A study based on a representative random sample of employees. *Economic and Industrial Democracy, 34*, 25–43. doi:10.1177/0143831X11429374

Boehm, S. A., Dwertmann, D. J. G., Kunze, F., Michaelis, B., Parks, K. M., & McDonald, D. P. (2014). Expanding insights on the diversity climate-performance link: The role of workgroup discrimination and group size. *Human Resource Management, 53*, 379–402. doi:10.1002/hrm.21589ER

Boiger, M., & Mesquita, B. (2012). The construction of emotion in interactions, relationships, and cultures. *Emotion Review, 4*, 221–229.

Boivin, M., Vitaro, F., & Gagnon, C. (1992). A reassessment of the self-perception profile for children: Factor structure, reliability, and convergent validity of a French version among second through sixth grade children. *International Journal of Behavioral Development, 15*, 275–290.

Boldt, L. J., Kochanska, G., Grekin, R., & Brock, R. L. (2016). Attachment in middle childhood: Predictors, correlates, and implications for adaptation. *Attachment and Human Development, 18*, 115–140.

Bolton, J. M., Au, W., Chateau, D., Walld, R., Leslie, W. D., Enns, J. et al. (2016). Bereavement after sibling death: A population-based longitudinal case-control study. *World Psychiatry, 15*, 59–66. doi:10.1002/wps.20293

Bonanno, G. A. (2009). *The other side of sadness: What the new science of bereavement tells us about life after loss.* New York: Basic Books.

Bonanno, G. A., Papa, A., & O'Neill, K. (2001). Loss and human resilience. *Applied and Preventive Psychology, 10*, 193–206. doi:10.1016/S0962-1849(01)80014-7

Bonanno, G. A., Papa, A., Lalande, K., Zhang, N., & Noll, J. G. (2005). Grief processing and deliberate grief avoidance: A prospective comparison of bereaved spouses and parents in the United States and the People's Republic of China. *Journal of Consulting and Clinical Psychology, 73*, 86–98. doi:10.1037/0022-006X.73.1.86

Bonanno, G. A., Westphal, M., & Mancini, A. D. (2011). Resilience to loss and trauma. *Annual Review of Clinical Psychology, 7*, 511–535. doi:10.1146/annurevclinpsy-032210-104526

Bonanno, G. A., Wortman, C. B., & Neese, R. M. (2004). Prospective patterns of resilience and maladjustment during widowhood. *Psychology and Aging, 19*, 260–271. doi:10.1037/0882-7974.19.2.260

Booker, J. A., & Dunsmore, J. C. (2016). Profiles of wisdom among emerging adults: Associations with empathy, gratitude, and forgiveness. *Journal of Positive Psychology, 11*, 315–325. doi:10.1080/17439760.2015.1081970

Booker, J. A., & Dunsmore, J. C. (2017). Affective social competence in adolescence: Current findings and future directions. *Social Development, 26*, 3–20.

Boon, H., Ruiter, R. U. C., James, S., van den Borne, B., Williams, E., & Reddy, P. (2010). Correlates of grief among older adults caring for children and grandchildren as a consequence of HIV and AIDS in South Africa. *Journal of Aging and Health, 22*, 48–67. doi:10.1177/0898264309349165

Booth, J. N., Leary, S. D., Joinson, C., Ness, A. R., Tomporowski, P. D. Boyle, J. M. et al. (2014). Associations between objectively measured physical activity and academic attainment in adolescents from a UK cohort. *British Journal of Sports Medicine, 48*, 265–270.

Bordere, T. C. (2016). Social justice conceptualizations in grief and loss. In D. L. Harris & T. C. Bordere (Eds.), *Handbook of social justice in loss and grief: Exploring diversity, equity, and inclusion* (pp. 9–20). New York: Routledge.

Bornstein, M. H., & Arterberry, M. E. (2003). Recognition, discrimination, and categorization of smiling by 5-month-old infants. *Developmental Science, 6*, 585–599.

Bornstein, M. H., Putnick, D. L., Gartstein, M. A., Hahn, C-S., Auestad, N., & O'Connor, D. L. (2015). Infant temperament: Stability by age, gender, birth order, term status, and SES. *Child Development, 86*, 844–863.

Bornstein, M. H., Putnick, D. L., Suwalsky, J. T., & Gini, M. (2006). Maternal chronological age, prenatal and perinatal history, social support, and parenting of infants. *Child Development, 77*, 875–892.

Bortfeld, H., & Morgan, J. L. (2010). Is early word-form processing stress-full? How natural variability supports recognition. *Cognitive Psychology, 60*, 241–266.

Bos, H. M., Knox, J. R., van Rijn-van Gelderen, L., & Gartrell, N. K. (2016). Same-sex and different-sex parent households and child health outcomes: Findings from the National Survey of Children's Health. *Journal of Developmental & Behavioral Pediatrics, 37*, 179–187. doi:10.1097/DBP.0000000000000288

Boschma, J. (2015, June 23). When do Americans think they'll actually retire? *The Atlantic.* Retrieved from www.theatlantic.com/business/archive/2015/06/ideal-retirement-age-work/396464/.

Bosco, A., di Masi, M. N., & Manuti, A. (2013). Burnout internal factors—self-esteem and negative affectivity in the workplace: The mediation role of organizational identification in times of job uncertainty. In S. Bährer-Kohler (Ed.), *Burnout for experts* (pp. 145–158). New York: Springer.

Boseovski, J. J. (2010). Evidence for "rose-colored glasses": An examination of the positivity bias in young children's personality judgments. *Child Development Perspectives, 4*, 212–218.

Bosma, H. A., & Kunnen, E. S. (2001). Determinants and mechanisms in ego identity development: A review and synthesis. *Developmental Review, 21*, 39–66.

Boss, P. (2010). The trauma and complicated grief of ambiguous loss. *Pastoral Psychology, 59*, 137–145. doi:10.1007/s11089-009-0264-0

Boss, P. (2015). Coping with the suffering of ambiguous loss. In R. E. Anderson (Ed.), *World suffering and quality of life* (pp. 125–134). New York: Springer. doi:10.1007/978-94-017-9670-5_10

Bosshard, G., & Materstvedt, L. J. (2011). Medical and societal issues in euthanasia and assisted suicide. In R. Chadwick, H. Ten Have, & E. M. Meslin (Eds.), *The SAGE handbook of health care ethics* (pp. 202–218). Thousand Oaks, CA: Sage Publications.

Boswell, J., Thai, J., & Brown, C. (2015). Older adults' sleep. In A. Green & C. Brown (Eds.), *An occupational therapist's guide to sleep and sleep problems* (pp. 185–206). Philadelphia: Jessica Kingsley Publishers.

Bouchard, T. J. (2004). Genetic influence on human psychological traits. *Current Directions in Psychological Science, 13*, 148–151.

Bouchard, T. J. (2009). Genetic influence on human intelligence (Spearman's g): How much? *Annals of Human Biology, 36*, 527–544.

Bowker, A. (2006). The relationship between sports participation and self-esteem during early adolescence. *Canadian Journal of Behavioral Science, 38*, 214–229.

Bowlby, J. (1969). *Attachment and loss* (Vol. 1). New York: Basic Books.

Bowlby, J. (1991) Ethological light on psychoanalytical problems. In P. Bateson (Ed.), *The development and integration of behaviour: Essays in honour of Robert Hinde* (pp. 301–313). New York: Cambridge University Press.

Bows, H. (in press). Sexual violence against older people: A review of the empirical literature. *Trauma, Violence, & Abuse.* Retrieved from journals.sagepub.com/doi/full/10.1177/1524838016683455. doi:10.1177/1524838016683455

Boyce, W. T., & Kobor, M. S. (2015). Development and the epigenome: The "synapse" of gene-environment interplay. *Developmental Science, 18*, 1–23.

Boyczuk, A. M., & Fletcher, P. C. (2016). The ebbs and flows: Stresses of sandwich generation caregivers. *Journal of Adult Development, 23*, 51–61. doi:10.1007/s10804-015-9221-6

Boyle, P. J., Feng, Z., & Raab, G. M. (2011). Does widowhood increase mortality risk? Testing for selection effects by comparing causes of spousal death. *Epidemiology, 22*, 1–5. doi:10.1097/EDE.0b013e3181fdcc0b

Bradshaw, C. P. (2015). Translating research to practice in bullying prevention. *American Psychologist, 70*, 322–332.

Brainerd, C. J. (1996). Piaget: A centennial celebration. *Psychological Science, 7*, 191–203.

Brancucci, A. (2012). Neural correlates of cognitive ability. *Journal of Neuroscience Research, 90*, 1299–1309. doi:10.1002/jnr.23045

Brandtstädter, J. (1989). Personal self-regulation of development: Cross-sequential analyses of development-related control beliefs and emotions. *Developmental Psychology, 25,* 96–108. doi:10.1037/0012-1649.25.1.96

Brandtstädter, J. (1997). Action culture and development: Points of convergence. *Culture and Psychology, 3,* 335–352. doi:10.1177/1354067X9733007

Brandtstädter, J. (1999). Sources of resilience in the aging self. In T. M. Hess & F. Blanchard-Fields (Eds.), *Social cognition and aging* (pp. 123–141). San Diego: Academic Press.

Bratkovich, K. L. (2010). *The relationship of attachment and spirituality with posttraumatic growth following a death for college students.* Doctoral dissertation submitted to the Department of Psychology at Oklahoma State University.

Braungart-Rieker, J. M., Hill-Soderlund, A. L., & Karrass, J. (2010). Fear and anger reactivity trajectories from 4 to 16 months: The roles of temperament, regulation, and maternal sensitivity. *Developmental Psychology, 46,* 791–804.

Braungart, J. M., Plomin, R., DeFries, J. C., & Fulker, D. W. (1992). Genetic influence on tester-rated infant temperament as assessed by Bayley's Infant Behavior Record: Nonadoptive and adoptive siblings and twins. *Developmental Psychology, 28,* 40–47.

Braver, S. L., & Lamb, M. E. (2013). Marital dissolution. In G. W. Peterson & K. R. Bush (Eds.), *Handbook of marriage and the family* (3rd ed., pp. 487–516). New York: Springer.

Braza, P., Carreras, R., Muñoz, J. M., Braza, F., Azurmendi, A., Pascual-Sagastizábal, E., et al. (2015). Negative maternal and paternal parenting styles as predictors of children's behavioral problems: Moderating effects of the child's sex. *Journal of Child and Family Studies, 24,* 847–856.

Brazelton, T. B., & Nugent, J. K. (1995). *Neonatal behavioral assessment scale* (3rd ed.). London: Mac Keith.

Brechwald, W. A., & Prinstein, M. J. (2011). Beyond homophily: A decade of advances in understanding peer influence processes. *Journal of Research on Adolescence, 21,* 166–179.

Brehmer, Y., Shing, Y. L., Heekeren, H. R., Lindenberger, U., & Bäckman, L. (2016). Training-induced changes in subsequent-memory effects: No major differences among children, younger adults, and older adults. *NeuroImage, 131,* 214–225. doi:10.1016/j.neuroimage.2015.11.074

Bremner, J. G., Slater, A. M., & Johnson, S. P. (2015). Perception of object persistence: The origins of object permanence in infancy. *Child Development Perspectives, 9,* 7–13.

Bremner, J. G., Slater, A. M., Mason, U. C., Spring, J., & Johnson, S. P. (2013). Trajectory perception and object continuity: Effects of shape and color change on 4-month-olds' perception of trajectory identity. *Developmental Psychology, 49,* 1021–1026.

Brendgen, M., Lamarche, V., Wanner, B., & Vitaro, F. (2010). Links between friendship relations and early adolescents' trajectories of depressed mood. *Developmental Psychology, 46,* 491–501.

Brendgen, M., Vitaro, F., Boivin, M., Dionea, G., & Perusse, D. (2006). Examining genetic and environmental effects on reactive versus proactive aggression. *Developmental Psychology, 42,* 1299–1312.

Brenn, T., & Ytterstad, E. (2016). Increased risk of death immediately after losing a spouse: Cause-specific mortality following widowhood in Norway. *Preventive Medicine, 89,* 251–256. doi:10.1016/j.ypmed.2016.06.019

Brenner, J. S. (2016). Sports specialization and intensive training in young athletes. *Pediatrics, 138,* e20162148.

Bretherton, I. (2010). Fathers in attachment theory and research: a review. *Early Child Development and Care, 180,* 9–23.

Brissette, I., Scheier, M. F., & Carver, C. S. (2002). The role of optimism in social network development, coping, and psychological adjustment during a life transition. *Journal of Personality and Social Psychology, 82,* 102–111. doi:10.1037//0022-3514.82.1.102

Brockington, I. (1996). *Motherhood and mental health.* Oxford, UK: Oxford University Press.

Brody, G. H. (1998). Sibling relationship quality: Its causes and consequences. *Annual Review of Psychology, 49,* 1–24.

Brody, G. H., Kim, S., Murry, V. M., & Brown, A. C. (2003). Longitudinal direct and indirect pathways linking older sibling competence to the development of younger sibling competence. *Developmental Psychology, 39,* 618–628.

Brody, G. H., Stoneman, A., & McCoy, J. K. (1994). Forecasting sibling relationships in early adolescence from child temperament and family processes in middle childhood. *Child Development, 65,* 771–784.

Brody, G. H., Yu, T., Barton, A. W., & Miller, G. E. (2017). Youth temperament, harsh parenting, and variation in the oxytocin receptor gene forecast allostatic load during emerging adulthood. *Development and Psychopathology, 29,* in press.

Brody, N. (1992). *Intelligence* (2nd ed.). San Diego, CA: Academic Press.

Bromell, L., & Cagney, K. A. (2014). Companionship in the neighborhood context: Older adults' living arrangements and perceptions of social cohesion. *Research on Aging, 36,* 228–243. doi:10.1177/0164027512475096

Bronfenbrenner, U., & Morris, P. (2006). The ecology of developmental processes. In W. Damon & R. M. Lerner (Eds.), *Handbook of child psychology* (6th ed., Vol. 1, pp. 793–828). New York: Wiley.

Brooker, R. J., Buss, K. A., Lemery-Chalfant, K., Aksan, N., Davidson, R. J., & Goldsmith, H. H. (2013). The development of stranger fear in infancy and toddlerhood: normative development, individual differences, antecedents, and outcomes. *Developmental Science, 16,* 864–878.

Brooks-Gunn, J., & Paikoff, R. (1993). "Sex is a gamble, kissing is a game": Adolescent sexuality, contraception, and sexuality. In S. P. Millstein, A. C. Petersen, & E. O. Nightingale (Eds.), *Promoting the health behavior of adolescents* (pp. 180–208). New York: Oxford University Press.

Brooks-Gunn, J., & Ruble, D. N. (1982). The development of menstrual-related beliefs and behaviors during early adolescence. *Child Development, 53,* 1567–1577.

Brown, B. B. (2014). An autobiographical journey through adolescents' social world: Peer groups, peer influence, and the effects of electronic media on social adjustment in college. In R. M. Lerner et al. (Eds.), *The developmental science of adolescence: History through biography* (pp. 45–54). New York: Psychology Press.

Brown, B. B., Bakken, J. P., Ameringer, S. W., & Mahon, S. D. (2008). A comprehensive conceptualization of the peer influence process in adolescence. In M. J. Prinstein & K. Dodge (Eds.), *Understanding peer influences in children and adolescents* (pp. 17–44). New York: Guilford Publications.

Brown, D. A., & Lamb, M. E. (2015). Can children be useful witnesses? It depends how they are questioned. *Child Development Perspectives, 9,* 250–255.

Brown, J. R., & Dunn, J. (1996). Continuities in emotion understanding from three to six years. *Child Development, 67,* 789–802.

Brown, J. W., Chen, S-L., Mefford, L., Brown, A., Callen, B., & McArthur, P. (2011). Becoming an older volunteer: A grounded theory study. *Nursing Research and Practice, 2011.* doi:10.1155/2011/361250

Brown, J., & Dunn, J. (1992). Talk with your mother or your sibling? Developmental changes in early family conversations about feelings. *Child Development, 63,* 336–349.

Brown, S. D., & Lent, R. W. (2016). Vocational psychology: Agency, equity, and well-being. *Annual Review of Psychology, 67,* 541–565. doi:10.1146/annurev-psych-122414-033237

Brummelman, E., Thomaes, S., Orobio de Casto, B., Overbeek, G., & Bushman, B. J. (2014). "That's not just beautiful—that's incredibly beautiful!" The adverse impact of inflated praise on children with low self-esteem. *Psychological Science, 25,* 728–735.

Brymer, E., & Mackenzie, S. H. (2017). Psychology and the extreme sport experience. In F. Feletti (Ed.), *Extreme sports medicine* (pp. 3–13). New York: Springer.

Brysiewicz, P. (2008). The lived experience of losing a loved one to a sudden death in KwaZulu-Natal, South Africa. *Journal of Clinical Nursing, 17,* 224–231. doi:10.1111/j.1365-2702.2007.01972.x

Buchanan, C. M., Eccles, J. S., & Becker, J. B. (1992). Are adolescents the victims of raging hormones? Evidence for activational effects of hormones on moods and behavior at adolescence. *Psychological Bulletin, 111,* 62–107.

Buckingham-Howes, S., Berger, S. S., Scaletti, L. A., & Black, M. M. (2013). Systematic review of prenatal cocaine exposure and adolescent development. *Pediatrics, 131*, e1917-d1936.

Budgeon, S. (2016). The "problem" with single women: Choice, accountability and social change. *Journal of Social and Personal Relationships, 33*, 401–418. doi:10.1177/026540 7515607647

Buhl, H. (2008). Development of a model describing individuated adult child-parent relationships. *International Journal of Behavioral Development, 32*, 381–389. doi:10.1177/0165025408093656

Bui, E., Mauro, C., Robinaugh, D. J., Skritskaya, N. A., Wang, Y., Gribbin, C. et al. (2015). The Structured Clinical Interview for Complicated Grief: Reliability, validity, and explanatory factor analysis. *Depression and Anxiety, 32*, 485–492. doi:10.1002/da.22385

Bukowski, W. M., Sippola, L. K., & Hoza, B. (1999). Same and other: Interdependency between participation in same- and other-sex friendships. *Journal of Youth & Adolescence, 28*, 439–459.

Bullard, L., Wachlarowicz, M., DeLeeuw, J., Snyder, J., Low, S., Forgatch, M., et al. (2010). Effects of the Oregon model of Parent Management Training (PMTO) on marital adjustment in new stepfamilies: A randomized trial. *Journal of Family Psychology, 24*, 485–496.

Bullock, M., & Lütkenhaus, P. (1990). Who am I? The development of self-understanding in toddlers. *Merrill-Palmer Quarterly, 36*, 217–238.

Bureau of Labor Statistics. (2016a). *Unemployment rates by age, sex, race, and Hispanic or Latino ethnicity*. Retrieved from www.bls.gov/web/empsit/cpsee_e16.htm.

Bureau of Labor Statistics. (2016b). *Families by presence and relationship of employed members and family type, 2014–2015 annual averages*. Retrieved from www.bls.gov/news.release/ famee.t02.htm.

Bureau of Labor Statistics. (2016c). *Employment characteristics of families—2015*. Retrieved from www.bls.gov/news.release/pdf/famee.pdf.

Burk, W. J., & Laursen, B. (2005). Adolescent perceptions of friendship and their associations with individual adjustment. *International Journal of Behavioral Development, 29*, 156–164.

Burke, B. L., Martens, A., & Faucher, E. H. (2010). Two decades of terror management theory: A meta-analysis of mortality salience research. *Personality and Social Psychology Review, 14*, 155–195. doi:10.1177/1088868309352321

Burke, R., & Kao, G. (2013). Bearing the burden of whiteness: The implications of racial self-identification for multiracial adolescents' school belonging and academic achievement. *Ethnic and Racial Studies, 36*, 747–773.

Burnette, D. (1999). Social relationships of Latino grandparent caregivers: A role theory perspective. *The Gerontologist, 39*, 49–58. doi:10.1093/ geront/39.1.49

Burns, S. T. (2005). The transition to parenthood: The effects of gender role attitudes and level of culture change in Chinese-American couples.

Dissertation Abstracts International. Section B. Sciences and Engineering, 66(6-B), 3461.

Burton, L. M. (1992). Black grandparents rearing children of drug-addicted parents: Stressors, outcomes, and social service needs. *The Gerontologist, 32*, 744–751. doi:10.1093/geront/ 32.6.744

Buss, D. (2016). *Evolutionary psychology: The new science of the mind* (5th ed.). New York: Routledge.

Buss, D. M., Abbott, M., Angleitner, A., Asherian, A., Biaggio, A., Blanco-Villasenor, A., et al. (1990). International preferences in selecting mates: A study of 37 cultures. *Journal of Cross-Cultural Psychology, 21*, 5–47. doi:10.1177/0022022190211001

Buss, K. A., & Goldsmith, H. H. (1998). Fear and anger regulation in infancy: Effects on the temporal dynamics of affective expression. *Child Development, 69*, 359–374.

Buss, K. A., & Kiel, E. J. (2004). Comparison of sadness, anger, and fear facial expressions when toddlers look at their mothers. *Child Development, 75*, 1761–1773.

Bustos, M. L. C. (2007). La muerte en la cultura occidental: Antropología de la muerte [Death in Western culture: Anthropology of death]. *Revista Colombiana de Psiquiatría, 36*, 332–339. Retrieved from www.redalyc.org/ articulo.oa?id=80636212.

Buttelmann, D., & Böhm, R. (2014). The ontogeny of the motivation that underlies in-group bias. *Psychological Science, 25*, 921–927.

Byock, S. D. (2010, August). *The quarterlife crisis and the path to individuation in the first half of life*. Master's thesis completed at the Pacifica Graduate Institute, Carpinteria, CA.

Byrnes, J. P., & Dunbar, K. N. (2014). The nature and development of critical-analytic thinking. *Educational Psychology Review, 26*, 477–493.

Bywaters, P., Bunting, L., Davidson, G., Hanratty, J., Mason, W., McCartan, C., et al. (2016). *The relationship between poverty, child abuse and neglect: An evidence review*. York, UK: Joseph Rowntree Foundation.

Cabeza de Baca, T., & Ellis, B. J. (2017). Early stress, parental motivation, and reproductive decision-making: applications of life history theory to parental behavior. *Current Opinion in Psychology, 15*, 1–6.

Cable, N., & Sacker, A. (2008). Typologies of alcohol consumption in adolescence: Predictors and adult outcomes. *Alcohol and Alcoholism, 43*, 81–90.

Cacciatore, J., & DeFrain, J. (2015). *The world of bereavement*. New York: Springer.

Cacioppo, J. T., Berntson, G. G., Bechara, A., Tranel, D., & Hawkley, H. C. (2011). Could an aging brain contribute to subjective well-being? The value added by a social neuroscience perspective. In A. Todorov, S. Fiske, & D. Prentice (Eds.), *Social neuroscience: toward understanding the underpinnings of the social mind* (pp. 249–262). New York: Oxford University Press.

Cacioppo, S., & Cacioppo, J. T. (2013). Lust for life. *Scientific American Mind, 24*(5), 56–63.

Cadell, S., & Marshall, S. (2007). The (re) construction of self after the death of a partner to HIV/AIDS. *Death Studies, 31*, 537–548. doi:10.1080 /07481180701356886

Cahill, E., Lewis, L. M., Barg, F. K., & Bogner, H. R. (2009). "You don't want to burden them": Older adults' views on family involvement in care. *Journal of Family Nursing, 27*, 295–317. doi:10.1177/1074840709337247

Cain, K. (1999). Ways of reading: How knowledge and use of strategies are related to reading comprehension. *British Journal of Developmental Psychology, 17*, 293–312.

Callaghan, T., Moll, H., Rakoczy, H., Warneken, F., Liszkowski, U., Behne, T. et al. (2011). Early social cognition in three cultural contexts. *Monographs of the Society for Research in Child Development, 76*, Serial No. 299.

Callahan, C. M. (2000). Intelligence and giftedness. In R. J. Sternberg (Ed.), *Handbook of intelligence* (pp. 159–175). Cambridge, UK: Cambridge University Press.

Calvert, S. L. (2015). Children and digital media. In R. M. Lerner (Ed.), *Handbook of child psychology and developmental science* (Vol. 4, pp. 375–415). Hoboken, NJ: Wiley.

Calvert, S. L., & Valkenburg, P. M. (2013). The influence of television, video games, and the Internet on children's creativity. In M. Taylor (Ed.), *The Oxford handbook of the development of imagination* (pp. 438–450). New York: Oxford.

Calvert, S. L., Appelbaum, M., Dodge, K. A., Graham, S. Nagayama Hall, G. C., Hamby, S. et al. (2017). The American Psychological Association Task Force assessment of violent video games: Science in the service of public interest. *American Psychologist, 72*, 126–143.

Calvete, E., Fernández-González, L., Orue, I., & Little, T. D. (2017). Exposure to family violence and dating violence perpetration in adolescents: Potential cognitive and emotional mechanisms. *Psychology of Violence*, in press.

Camberis, A.L., McMahon, C. A., Gibson, F. L., & Bolvin, J. (2016). Maternal age, psychological maturity, parenting cognitions, and mother-infant interaction. *Infancy, 21*, 396–422. doi:10.1111/infa.1211

Cameron, L., Rutland, A., Brown, R., & Douch, R. (2006). Changing children's intergroup attitudes toward refugees: Testing different models of extended contact. *Child Development, 77*, 1208–1219.

Camp, C. J. (1999a). Memory interventions for normal and pathological older adults. In R. Schulz, M. P. Lawton, & G. Maddox (Eds.), *Annual review of gerontology and geriatrics* (Vol. 18, pp. 155–189). New York: Springer.

Camp, C. J. (2005). Spaced retrieval: A model for dissemination of a cognitive intervention for persons with dementia. In D. K. Attix & K. A. Velsh-Bohmer (Eds.). *Geriatric neuropsychology: Assessment and intervention* (pp. 275–292). New York: Guilford Press.

Camp, C. J. (Ed.). (1999b). *Montessori-based activities for persons with dementia* (Vol. 1). Beachwood, OH: Menorah Park Center for Senior Living.

Camp, C. J., Foss, J. W., Stevens, A. B., Reichard, C. C., McKitrick, L. A., & O'Hanlon, A. M. (1993). Memory training in normal and demented elderly populations: The E-I-E-I-O model. *Experimental Aging Research, 19*, 277–290. doi: 10.1080/03610739308253938

Camp, C. J., Skrajner, M. J., & Kelly, M. (2005). Early stage dementia client as group leader. *Clinical Gerontologist, 28*, 81–85. doi:10.1300/J018v28n04_06

Campbell, J., & Ehlert, U. (2012). Acute psychosocial stress: Does the emotional stress response correspond with physiological responses? *Psychoneuroendocrinology, 37*, 1111–1134. doi: 10.1016/j. psyneuen.2011.12.010

Campbell, K., & Kaufman, J. (2015). Do you pursue your heart or your art? Creativity, personality, and love. *Journal of Family Issues, 38*:3, 287-311. doi:10.1177/0192513X15570318

Campbell, R., & Sais, E. (1995). Accelerated metalinguistic (phonological) awareness in bilingual children. *British Journal of Developmental Psychology, 13*, 61–68.

Campinha-Bacote, J. (2010). A culturally conscious model of mentoring. *Nurse Educator, 35*, 130–135. doi:10.1097/NNE.0b013e3181d950bf

Campos, J. J., Anderson, D. I., Barbu-Roth, M. A., Hubbard, E. M., Hertenstein, M. J., & Witherington, D. (2000). Travel broadens the mind. *Infancy, 1*, 149–219.

Campos, J. J., Hiatt, S., Ramsay, D., Henderson, C., & Svedja, M. (1978). The emergence of fear on the visual cliff. In M. Lewis & L. Rosenblum (Eds.), *The origins of affect.* New York: Plenum.

Camras, L. A., & Shuster, M. (2013). Children's expressive behavior in different cultural contexts. In D. Hermans, B. Rimé, & B. Mesquita (Eds.), *Changing emotions* (pp. 24–30). Hove, UK: Psychology Press.

Candel, I., Hayne, H., Strange, D., & Prevoo, E. (2009). The effect of suggestion on children's recognition memory for seen and unseen details. *Psychology, Crime, & Law, 15*, 29–39.

Cappell, K. A., Gmeindl, L., & Reuter-Lorenz, P. A. (2010). Age differences in prefrontal recruitment during verbal working memory maintenance depend on memory load. *Cortex, 46*, 462–473. doi:10.1016/j.cortex .2009.11.009

Caravolas, M., Lervåg, A., Mousikou, P., Efrim, C., Litavský, M., Onochie-Quintanilla, E., et al. (2012). Common patterns of prediction of literacy development in different alphabetic orthographies. *Psychological Science, 23*, 678–686.

Cardoso-Leite, P., & Bavelier, D. (2014). Video game play, attention, and learning: how to shape the development of attention and influence learning? *Current Opinion in Neurology, 27*, 185–191.

Carlander, I., Ternestedt, B.-M., Sahlberg-Blom, E., Hellström, I., & Sandberg, J. (2011). Being me and being us in a family living close to death at home. *Qualitative Health Research, 5*, 683–695. doi: 10.1177/1049732310396102

Carlo, G., Koller, S., Raffaelli, M., & de Guzman, M. R. T. (2007). Culture-related strengths among Latin American families: A case study of Brazil. *Marriage & Family Review, 41*, 335–360. doi:10.1300/ J002v41n03_06

Carlo, G., McGinley, M., Hayes, R., Batenhorst, C., & Wilkinson, J. (2007). Parenting styles or practices? Parenting, sympathy, and prosocial behaviors among adolescents. *Journal of Genetic Psychology, 168*, 147–176.

Carlson Jones, D. (2004). Body image among adolescent girls and boys: A longitudinal study. *Developmental Psychology, 40*, 823–835.

Carlson, M. D., Mendle, J., & Harden, K. P. (2014). Early adverse environments and genetic influences on age at first sex: Evidence for gene × environment interaction. *Developmental Psychology, 50*, 1532–1542.

Carnelley, K., & Ruscher, J. B. (2000). Adult attachment and exploratory behavior in leisure. *Journal of Social Behavior and Personality, 15*, 153–165. Retrieved from crawl.prod. proquest.com.s3.amazonaws.com/fpcache/ cdd5594c53a7864881fb71e54a7422f1.pdf?A WSAccessKeyId=AKIAJF7V7KNV2KKY2NU Q&Expires=1476725696&Signature=EiFM03 6jVPsv4iNCNcf8At5HlAY%3D.

Carnevale, A. P., Jayasundera, T., & Gulish, A. (2016). *America's divided recovery: College haves and have-nots.* Retrieved from cew.georgetown. edu/cew-reports/americas-divided-recovery/.

Caron, C. D., Ducharme, F., & Griffith, J. (2006). Deciding on institutionalization for a relative with dementia: The most difficult decision for caregivers. *Canadian Journal on Aging, 25*, 193–205. doi:10.1353/cja.2006.0033

Carpenter, P. A., & Daneman, M. (1981). Lexical retrieval and error recovery in reading: A model based on eye fixations. *Journal of Verbal Learning and Verbal Behavior, 20*, 137–160.

Carpenter, R., McGarvey, C., Mitchell, E. A., Tappin, D. M., Vennemann, M. M., Smuk, M., et al. (2013). Bedsharing when parents do not smoke: Is there a risk of SIDS? An individual level analysis of five major case-control studies. *British Medical Journal Open, 3*:e002299.

Carr, A., & McNulty, M. (2016). Cognitive behaviour therapy. In A. Carr & M. McNulty (Eds.), *The handbook of adult clinical psychology* (2nd ed.). Abingdon, UK: Routledge.

Carr, D. (2004). Gender, preloss marital dependence, and older adults' adjustment to widowhood. *Journal of Marriage and Family, 66*, 220–235. doi: 10.1111/j.0022-2445.2004.00016.x

Carr, D., & Moorman, S. M. (2011). Social relations and aging. In R. A. Settersten & J. L. Angel (Eds.), *Handbook of sociology of aging* (pp. 145–160). New York: Springer.

Carré, J. M., McCormick, C. M., & Hariri, A. R. (2011). The social neuroendocrinology of human aggression. *Psychoneuroendocrinology, 36*, 935–944.

Carroll, J. B. (1993). *Human cognitive abilities: A survey of factor-analytic studies.* New York: Cambridge University Press.

Carroll, J. B. (1996). A three-stratum theory of intelligence: Spearman's contribution. In I. Dennis & P. Tapsfield (Eds.), *Human abilities: Their nature and measurement* (pp. 1–18). Mahwah, NJ: Erlbaum.

Carroll, J. L., & Loughlin, G. M. (1994). Sudden infant death syndrome. In F. A. Oski, C. D. DeAngelis, R. D. Feigin, J. A. McMillan, & J. B. Warshaw (Eds.), *Principles and practice of pediatrics.* Philadelphia: Lippincott.

Carstensen, L. L. (2006). The influence of a sense of time on human development. *Science, 312*, 1913–1915. doi: 10.1126/science.1127488

Carter, C. S. (2014). Oxytocin pathways and the evolution of human behavior. *Annual Review of Psychology, 65*, 17–39.

Carver, K., Joyner, K., & Udry, J. R. (2003). National estimates of adolescent romantic relationships. In P. Florsheim (Ed.), *Adolescent romantic relations and sexual behavior: Theory, research, and practical implications* (pp. 23–56). Mahwah, NJ: Erlbaum.

Caselli, M. C., Rinaldi, P., Stefanini, S., & Volterra, V. (2012). Early action and gesture "vocabulary" and its relation with word comprehension and production. *Child Development, 83*, 526–542.

Casey, B. J. (2015). Beyond simple models of self-control to circuit-based accounts of adolescent behavior. *Annual Review of Psychology, 66*, 295–319.

Casey, B. J., & Caudle, K. (2013). The teenage brain: Self-control. *Current Directions in Psychological Science, 22*, 82–87.

Casey, B. J., Tottenham, N., Liston, C., & Durston, S. (2005). Imaging the developing brain: What have we learned about cognitive development? *Trends in Cognitive Neuroscience, 9*, 104–110.

Cash, S. J., & Bridge, J. A. (2009). Epidemiology of youth suicide and suicidal behavior. *Current Opinion in Pediatrics, 21*, 613–619.

Casper, W. J., Marquardt, D. J., Roberto, K. J., & Buss, C. (2016). The hidden family lives of single adults without dependent children. In T. D. Allen & L. T. Eby (Eds.), *The Oxford handbook of work and family* (pp. 182–195). New York: Oxford University Press.

Caspi, A., Roberts, B. W., & Shiner, R. (2005). Personality development. *Annual Review of Psychology, 56*, 453–484. doi:10.1146/annurev .psych.55.090902.141913

Castro, A. S. (2010). *The rite to womanhood: An interdisciplinary study of female circumcision among the Gikuyu of Kenya.* Bachelor's degree thesis completed at Wesleyan University. Retrieved from wesscholar.wesleyan.edu/cgi/viewcontent. cgi?article=1516&context=etd_hon_theses.

Cattell, R. B. (1965). *The scientific analysis of personality.* Baltimore, MD: Penguin.

Cauvet, E., Limissuri, R., Millotte, S., Skoruppa, K., Cabrol, D., & Christophe, A. (2014). Function words constrain on-line recognition of verbs and nouns in French 18-month-olds. *Language Learning and Development, 10*, 1–18.

Cavanaugh, J. C. (1999). Caregiving to adults: A life event challenge. In I. H. Nordhus, G. R. VandenBos, S. Berg, & P. Fromholt (Eds.), *Clinical geropsychology* (pp. 131–135). Washington, DC: American Psychological Association.

Cavanaugh, J. C. (in press). Spirituality as a framework for confronting life's existential questions in later adulthood. In J. D. Sinnott

(Ed.), *Identity flexibility during adulthood: Perspectives on adult development*. New York: Springer.

Cavanaugh, J. C., & Kinney, J. M. (1994, July). *Marital satisfaction as an important contextual factor in spousal caregiving*. Paper presented at the 7th International Conference on Personal Relationships, Groningen, The Netherlands.

Ceci, S. J., & Bruck, M. (1998). Children's testimony: Applied and basic issues. In W. Damon (Ed.), *Handbook of child psychology* (Vol. 4). New York: Wiley.

Census Bureau. (2013). *Valentine's Day 2013: Feb. 14*. Retrieved from www.census.gov/newsroom/releases/archives/facts_for_features_special_editions/cb13-ff06.html.

Census Bureau. (2014). *Educational attainment*. Retrieved from www.census.gov/hhes/socdemo/education/index.html.

Census Bureau. (2015). *New Census Bureau report analyzes U.S. population projections*. Retrieved from www.census.gov/newsroom/press-releases/2015/cb15-tps16.html.

Census Bureau. (2016). *Median age at first marriage: 1890 to present*. Retrieved from www.census.gov/hhes/families/files/graphics/MS-2.pdf.

Centers for Disease Control and Prevention. (2012). Youth risk behavior surveillance—United States, 2011. *Morbidity and Mortality Weekly Report, 61*. Atlanta GA: Author.

Centers for Disease Control and Prevention. (2015). *2015 Assisted Reproductive Technology National Summary Report*. Atlanta, GA: US Department of Health and Human Services.

Centers for Disease Control and Prevention. (2015). *Suicide: Facts at a glance, 2015*. Atlanta, GA: Author.

Centers for Disease Control and Prevention. (2016). *Diagnoses of HIV infection in the United States and dependent areas. HIV surveillance report*, Vol. 27. Atlanta, GA: Author.

Centers for Disease Control and Prevention. (2016a). *Economic facts about U.S. tobacco production and use*. Retrieved from www.cdc.gov/tobacco/data_statistics/fact_sheets/economics/econ_facts/.

Centers for Disease Control and Prevention. (2016b). *Health behaviors of adults: United States 2011–2014. Table ALC-2a*. Retrieved from ftp.cdc.gov/pub/Health_Statistics/NCHS/NHIS/SHS/2011-2014_AHB_Table_ALC-2.pdf.

Centers for Disease Control and Prevention. (2016c) *Guideline for prescribing opioids for chronic pain*. Retrieved from www.cdc.gov/drugoverdose/pdf/guidelines_factsheet-a.pdf.

Centers for Disease Control and Prevention. (2016c). *Early release of selected estimates based on data from the National Health Interview Survey, 2015: Data for Figure 9.2*. Retrieved from www.cdc.gov/nchs/data/nhis/earlyrelease/earlyrelease201605.pdf.

Centers for Disease Control and Prevention. (2016d). *About adult BMI*. Retrieved from www.cdc.gov/healthyweight/assessing/bmi/adult_bmi/index.html.

Centers for Disease Control and Prevention. (2016e). *Adult obesity facts*. Retrieved from www.cdc.gov/obesity/data/adult.html.

Centers for Disease Control and Prevention. (2016e). *Health, United States, 2015: With special feature on racial and ethnic health disparities*. Retrieved from www.cdc.gov/nchs/data/hus/hus15.pdf.

Centers for Disease Control. (2016). *Understanding teen dating violence: Fact sheet 2016*. Retrieved from www.cdc.gov/violenceprevention/intimatepartnerviolence/teen_dating_violence.html.

Centers for Medicare and Medicaid Services. (2016a). *Nursing Home Quality Initiative*. Retrieved from www.cms.gov/Medicare/Quality-Initiatives-Patient-Assessment-Instruments/NursingHomeQualityInits/index.html?redirect=/NursinghomeQualityinits/.

Centers for Medicare and Medicaid Services. (2016b). *Nursing home data compendium 2015*. Retrieved from www.cms.gov/Medicare/Provider-Enrollment-and-Certification/CertificationandComplianc/Downloads/nursinghomedatacompendium_508-2015.pdf.

Centers for Medicare and Medicaid Services. (2016c). *Five-Star Quality Rating System*. Retrieved from www.cms.gov/medicare/provider-enrollment-and-certification/certificationandcomplianc/fsqrs.html.

Centers for Medicare and Medicaid Services. (2016d). *Medicare program—General information*. Retrieved from www.cms.gov/Medicare/Medicare-General-Information/MedicareGenInfo/index.html.

Central Intelligence Agency. (2013). *The World Factbook* 2013–14. Washington, DC: Author.

Champion, T. B. (2003). A "matter of vocabulary": Performance of low-income African-American Head Start children on the Peabody Picture Vocabulary Test. *Communication Disorders Quarterly, 24*, 121–127.

Chandler, M. J., & Carpendale, J. I. M. (1998). Inching toward a mature theory of mind. In M. D. Ferrari & R. J. Sternberg (Eds.), *Self-awareness: Its nature and development* (pp. 148–190). New York: Guilford Press.

Chang, J. E. Sequeira, A., McCord, C. E., & Garney, W. R. (2016). Videoconference grief group counseling in rural Texas: Outcomes, challenges, and lessons learned. *Journal for Specialists in Group Work, 41*, 140–160. doi:10.1080/01933922.2016.114376

Chang, T.-S., & Hsiao, W.-H. (2014). Time spent on social networking sites: Understanding user behavior and social capital. *Systems Research and Behavioral Science, 31*, 102–114. doi:10.1002/sres.2169

Chao, R. K. (2001). Extending research on the consequences of parenting style for Chinese Americans and European Americans. *Child Development, 72*, 1832–1843.

Chaplin, T. M., & Aldao, A. (2013). Gender differences in emotion expression in children: A meta-analytic review. *Psychological Bulletin, 139*, 735–765.

Chapman, P. D. (1988). *Schools as sorters: Lewis M. Terman, applied psychology, and the intelligence testing movement, 1890–1930*. New York: NYU Press.

Charles, S. T., & Carstensen, L. L. (2010). Social and emotional aging. *Annual Review of Psychology, 61*, 383–409. doi:10.1146/annurev.psych.093008.100448

Charlton, B., & Verghese, A. (2010). Caring for Ivan Ilyich. *Journal of General Internal Medicine, 25*, 93–95. doi:10.1007/s11606-009-1177-4

Charness, N., & Bosman, E. A. (1990). Expertise and aging: Life in the lab. In T. M. Hess (Ed.), *Aging and cognition: Knowledge organization and utilization* (pp. 343–385). Amsterdam: North-Holland.

Chaudhari, A., Gupta, R., Makwana, K., & Kondratov, R. (2016). Circadian clocks, diets, and aging. *Nutrition and Healthy Aging*. Retrieved from content.iospress.com/articles/nutrition-and-healthy-aging/nha160006.

Chen-Gaddini, M. (2012). Chinese mothers and adolescents' views of authority and autonomy: A study of parent-adolescent conflict in urban and rural China. *Child Development, 83*, 1846–1852.

Chen, J., & Gardner, H. (2005). Assessment based on multiple intelligences theory. In D. P. Flanagan & P. L. Harrison (Eds.), *Contemporary intellectual assessment: Theories, tests, and issues* (pp. 77–102). New York: Guilford Press.

Chen, X., Wang, L., & Cao, R. (2011). Shyness-sensitivity and unsociability in rural Chinese children: Relations with social, school, and psychological adjustment. *Child Development, 82*, 1531–1543.

Chen, Y., Norton, D. J., McBain, R., Gold, J., Frazier, J. A., & Coyle, J. T. (2012). Enhanced local processing of dynamic visual information in autism: Evidence from speed discrimination. *Neuropsychologia, 50*, 733–739.

Chen, Y., Peng, Y., & Fang, P. (2016). Emotional intelligence mediates the relationship between age and subjective well-being. *International Journal of Aging and Human Development, 83*, 91–107. doi:10.1177/0091415016648705

Cheng, E., & Pegg, S. (2016). "If I'm not gardening, I'm not at my happiest": Exploring the positive subjective experiences derived from serious leisure gardening by older adults. *World Leisure Journal, 58*, 285–297. doi:10.1080/16078055.2016.1228219

Cheng, S., & Powell, B. (2007). Under and beyond constraints: Resource allocation to young children from biracial families. *American Journal of Sociology, 112*, 1044–1094. doi:10.1086/508793

Cheng, T. C., Powdthavee, N., & Oswald, A. J. (2014) *Longitudinal evidence for a midlife nadir in human well-being: Results from four data sets*. Working Paper. Coventry, UK: University of Warwick, Department of Economics. Retrieved from www2.warwick.ac.uk/fac/soc/economics/research/workingpapers/2014/twerp_1037_oswald.pdf.

Cherko, M., Hickson, L., & Bhutta, M. (2016). Auditory deprivation and health in the elderly. *Maturitas, 88,* 52–57. doi:10.1016/j.marturitas.2016.03.008

Cheung, C. K., Kam, P. K., & Ngan, R. M. H. (2011). Age discrimination in the labour market from the perspectives of employers and older workers. *International Social Work, 54,* 118–136. doi:10.1177/0020872810372368

Cheung, W. W., & Mao, P. (2012). Recent advances in obesity: Genetics and beyond. *ISRN Endocrinology,* Article ID 536905.

Chew-Graham, C. A., & Ray, M. (Eds.). (2016). *Mental health and older people: A guide for primary care practitioners.* New York: Springer.

Chi, M. T. H. (2006). Laboratory methods for assessing experts' and novices' knowledge. In K. A. Ericsson, N. Charness, P. J. Feltovich, & R. R. Hoffman (Eds.), *The Cambridge handbook of expertise and expert performance* (pp. 167–184). New York: Cambridge University Press.

Chiao, C.-Y., Wu, H.-S., & Hsiao, C.-Y. (2015). Caregiver burden for informal caregivers of patients with dementia: A systematic review. *International Nursing Review, 62,* 340–350. doi:10.1111/inr.12194

Child Trends. (2016). *Youth employment.* Bethesda, MD: Author.

ChildStats.gov. (2016). *America's children in brief: Key national indicators of well-being, 2016.* Retrieved from www.childstats.gov/americaschildren/index.asp

Choe, D. E., Olson, S. L., & Sameroff, A. J. (2013). The interplay of externalizing problems and physical and inductive discipline during childhood. *Developmental Psychology, 49,* 2029–2039.

Choi, H. S., Johnson, B., & Kriewitz, K. (2013). Benefits of inclusion and segregation for individuals with disabilities in leisure. *International Journal on Disability and Human Development, 12,* 15–23. doi:10.1515/ijdhd-2012-0120

Choi, M., Sprang, G., & Eslinger, J. G. (2016). Grandparents raising grandchildren: A synthetic review and theoretical model for interventions. *Family & Community Health, 39,* 120–128. doi:10.1097/0000000000000097

Choi, Y., Kim, T. Y., Pekelnicky, D. D., Kim, K., & Kim, Y. S. (2017). Impact of youth cultural orientation on perception of family process and development among Korean Americans. *Cultural Diversity and Ethnic Minority Psychology, 23,* 244–257.

Chomitz, V. R., Cheung, L. W. Y., & Lieberman, E. (1995). The role of lifestyle in preventing low birth weight. *The Future of Children, 5,* 121–138.

Chow, B. W., McBride-Chang, C., Cheung, H., & Chow, C. S. (2008). Dialogic reading and morphology training in Chinese children: Effects on language and literacy. *Developmental Psychology, 44,* 233–244.

Christ, C. C., Carlo, G., & Stoltenberg, S. F. (2016). Oxytocin receptor (OXTR) single nucleotide polymorphisms indirectly predict prosocial behavior through perspective yaking and empathic concern. *Journal of Personality, 84,* 204–213.

Christensen, A. (1990). Gender and social structure in the demand/ withdrawal pattern of marital conflict. *Journal of Personality and Social Psychology, 59,* 73–81. doi:10.1037/0022-3514.59.1.73

Chronaki, G., Hadwin, J. A., Garner, M., Maurage, P., & Sonuga-Barke, E. J. S. (2015). The development of emotion recognition from facial expressions and non-linguistic vocalizations during childhood. *British Journal of Developmental Psychology, 33,* 218–236.

Chun, S., Heo, J., Lee, S., & Kim, J. (2016). Leisure-related predictors on a sense of purpose in life among older adults with cancer. *Activities, Adaptation & Aging, 40,* 266–280. doi:10.1080/01924788.2016.1199517

Church, A. T. (2016). Personality traits across cultures. *Current Opinion in Psychology, 8,* 22–30. doi:10.1016/j.copsyc.2015.09.014

Ciani, E. (2016). Retirement, pension eligibility and home production. *Labour Economics, 38,* 106–120. doi:10.1016/j.labeco.2016.01.004

Cicchetti, D. (2013). Annual research review: Resilient functioning in maltreated children: Past, present, and future perspectives. *Journal of Child Psychology and Psychiatry, 54,* 402–422.

Cicchetti, D. (2016). Socioemotional, personality, and biological development: Illustrations from a multilevel developmental psychopathology perspective on child maltreatment. *Annual Review of Psychology, 67,* 187–211.

Cicchetti, D., & Toth, S. L. (2006). Developmental psychopathology and preventive intervention. In W. Damon & R. M. Lerner (Eds.), *Handbook of child psychology* (Vol. 4, pp. 497–547). New York: Wiley.

Cicirelli, V. G. (2001). Personal meaning of death in older adults and young adults in relation to their fears of death. *Death Studies, 25,* 663–683. doi:10.1080/713769896

Cicirelli, V. G. (2006). Fear of death in mid-old age. *Journals of Gerontology: Psychological Sciences, 61B,* P75–P81. Retrieved from psychsocgerontology.oxfordjournals.org/content/61/2/P75.full.

Ciscato, E., Galichon, A., & Gousse, M. (2015). *Like attract like?* A structural comparison of monogamy across same-sex and different-sex households. *Social Science Research Network.* doi:10.2139/ssm.2530724 Retrieved from ssrn.com/abstract=2530724.

Clarke, P. J., Truelove, E., Hulme, C., & Snowling, M. J. (2014). *Developing reading comprehension.* Chichester West Sussex, UK: Wiley.

Clarke, V., Ellis, S. J., Peel, E., & Riggs, D. W. (2010). *Lesbian, gay, bisexual, trans and queer psychology: An introduction.* Cambridge, UK: Cambridge University Press.

Cleary, M. N., Wozniak, K., Marienau, C., Wilbur, G., Tolliver, D. E., & Meyer, P. (2017). Learning, adults, and competency-based education. In K. Rasmussen, P. Northrup, & R. Colson (Eds.), *Handbook of research on competency-based education in university settings* (pp. 210–231). Hershey, PA: IGI Global.

Clements, D. H. (1995). Teaching creativity with computers. *Educational Psychology Review, 7,* 141–161.

Cleveland, K. C., Quas, J. A., & Lyon, T. D. (2016). Valence, implicated actor, and children's acquiescence to false suggestions. *Journal of Applied Developmental Psychology, 43,* 1–7.

Coan, J. A. (2008). Toward a neuroscience of attachment. In J. Cassidy & P. R. Shaver (Eds.), *Handbook of attachment: Theory, research, and clinical implications* (2nd ed., pp. 241–265). New York: Guilford.

Coan, J. A., & Sbarra, D. A. (2015). Social baseline theory: The social regulation of risk and effort. *Current Opinion in Psychology, 1,* 87–91. doi:10.1016/j.copsyc.2014.12.021

Coates, B. A. (2017). *Divorce with decency* (5th ed.). Honolulu, HI: Latitude 20.

Coelho, J. S., Jansen, A., Roefs, A., & Nederkoom, C. (2009). Eating behavior in response to food-cue exposure: Examining the cue-reactivity and counteractive-control models. *Psychology of Addictive Behaviors, 23,* 131–139.

Cohen Kadosh, K., Johnson, M. H., Dick, F., Cohen Kadosh, R., & Blakemore, S. J. (2013). Effects of age, task performance, and structural brain development on face processing. *Cerebral Cortex, 23,* 1630–1642.

Cohen-Mansfield, J., & Regev, I. (in press). Retirement preparation programs: An examination of retirement perceptions, self-mastery, and well-being. *Research on Social Work Practice.* doi:10.1177/1049731516645194

Cohen, A. O., Breiner, K., Steinberg, L., Bonnie, R. J., Scott, E. S., Taylor-Thompson, K. A. et al. (2016). When is an adolescent an adult? Assessing cognitive control in emotional and nonemotional contexts. *Psychological Science, 27,* 549–562. doi:10.1177/0956797615627625

Cohen, F., Kemeny, M. E., Zegans, L., Johnson, P., Kearney, K. A., & Sites, D. P. (2007). Immune function declines with unemployment and recovers after stressor termination. *Psychosomatic Medicine, 69,* 225–234. doi:10.1097/PSY.0b013e31803139a6.

Cohen, R. W., Martinez, M. E., & Ward, B. W. (2010). *Health insurance coverage: Early release of estimates from the National Health Interview Survey, 2009.* Hyattsville MD: National Center for Health Statistics.

Cohen, S., & Williamson, G. M. (1991). Stress and infectious disease in humans. *Psychological Bulletin, 109,* 5–24.

Cohen, S., Janicki-Deverts, D., Doyle, W. J., Miller, G. E., Frank, E., Rabin, B. S., et al. (2012). Chronic stress, glucocorticoid receptor resistance, inflammation, and disease risk. *Proceedings of the National Academy of Sciences, 109,* 5995–5999. doi:10.1073/pnas.1118355109

Coie, J. D., Dodge, K. A., Terry, R., & Wright, V. (1991). The role of aggression in peer relations: An analysis of aggression episodes in boys' play groups. *Child Development, 62,* 812–826.

Colby, A., Kohlberg, L., Gibbs, J. C., & Lieberman, M. (1983). A longitudinal study of moral development. *Monographs of the Society for Research in Child Development, 48* (Serial No. 200).

Cole, D. A., & Jordan, A. E. (1995). Competence and memory: Integrating psychosocial and cognitive correlates of child depression. *Child Development, 66,* 459–473.

Cole, M. (2006). Culture and cognitive development in phylogenetic, historical, and ontogenetic perspective. In W. Damon & R. M. Lerner (Eds.), *Handbook of child psychology* (6th ed., Vol. 2). New York: Wiley.

Cole, P. M., Tamang, B. L., & Shrestha, S. (2006). Cultural variations in the socialization of young children's anger and shame. *Child Development, 77,* 1237–1251.

Coleman-Jensen, A., Rabbitt, M. P., Gregory, C. A., & Singh, A. (2016). *Household Food Security in the United States in 2015.* Washington DC: U.S. Department of Agriculture, Economic Research Service.

Coleman, J. (2015). *Unfinished work: The struggle to build an aging American workforce.* New York: Oxford University Press.

Coleman, M., Ganong, L., & Russell, L. T. (2013). Resilience in stepfamilies. In D. S. Becvar (Ed.), *Handbook of family resilience* (pp. 85–103). New York: Springer.

Coles, R. L. (2016). *Race and family: A structural approach* (2nd ed.). Lanham, MD: Rowman & Littlefield.

Collardeau, F., & Ehrenberg, M. (2016). Parental divorce and attitudes and feelings toward marriage and divorce in emerging adulthood: New insights from a multiway-frequency analysis. *Journal of European Psychology Students.* Retrieved from jeps.efpsa.org/articles/10.5334/jeps.341/.

Collins-Colosi, K. (2016). *Young adult narratives of sibling loss and bereavement during adolescence.* Unpublished dissertation, Health Psychology, Walden University.

Collins, R. L., Martino, S. C., Elliot, M. N., & Miu, A. (2011). Relationships between adolescent sexual outcomes and exposure to sex in media: Robustness to propensity-based analysis. *Developmental Psychology, 47,* 585–591.

Collins, W. A., & van Dulmen, M. (2006). "The course of true love(s)...": Origins and pathways in the development of romantic relationships. In A. C. Crouter & A. Booth (Eds.), *Romance and sex in adolescence and emerging adulthood: Risks and opportunities* (pp. 63–86). Mahwah, NJ: Erlbaum.

Collins, W. A., Welsh, D. P., & Furman, W. (2009). Adolescent romantic relationships. *Annual Review of Psychology, 60,* 631–652.

Commons, M. L. (2016). The fundamental issues with behavioral development. *Behavioral Development Bulletin, 21,* 1–12. doi:10.1037/bdb0000022

Conduct Problems Prevention Research Group. (2015). Impact of early intervention on psychopathology, crime, and well-being at age 25. *American Journal of Psychiatry, 172,* 59–70.

Congressional Budget Office. (2017). *Budget.* Retrieved from www.cbo.gov/topics/budget.

Connidis, I. A. (2001). *Family ties and aging.* Thousand Oaks, CA: Sage.

Conradt, E. (2017). Using behavioral epigenetic principles to advance the field of early life stress research. *Child Development Perspectives, 11,* 107–112.

Conry-Murray, C., & Turiel, E. (2012). Jimmy's baby doll and Jenny's truck: Young children's reasoning about gender norms. *Child Development, 83,* 146–158.

Conway, A. M., Tugade, M. M., Catalino, L. I., & Fredrickson, B. L. (2013). The broaden-and-build theory of positive emotions: form, function, and mechanisms. In S. A. David, I. Boniwell, & A. C. Ayers (Eds.), *Oxford handbook of happiness* (pp. 17–34). Oxford UK: Oxford University Press.

Cook, D. A., Bahn, R. S., & Menaker, R. (2010). Speed mentoring: An innovative method to facilitate mentoring relationships. *Medical Teacher, 32,* 692–694. doi:10.3109/01421591003686278

Cook, E. C., Buehler, C., & Henson, R. (2009). Parents and peers as social influences to deter antisocial behavior. *Journal of Youth & Adolescence, 38,* 1204–1252.

Cooke, L. J., Chambers, L. C., Añez, E. V., Croker, H. A. Boniface, D., Yeomans, M. R., et al. (2011). Eating for pleasure or profit: The effects of incentives on children's enjoyment of vegetables. *Psychological Science, 22,* 190–196.

Cooklin, A. R., Westrupp, E. M., Strazdins, L., Giallo, R., Martin, A., & Nicholson, J. M. (2016). Fathers at work: Work-family conflict, work-family enrichment, and parenting in an Australian cohort. *Journal of Family Issues, 37,* 1611–1635.

Coombs, M. A. (2010). The mourning that comes before: Can anticipatory grief theory inform family care in adult intensive care? *International Journal of Palliative Nursing, 16,* 580–584. doi:10.12968/ijpn.2010.16.12.580

Cooney, T. M., & Uhlenberg, P. (1990). The role of divorce in men's relations with their adult children after mid-life. *Journal of Marriage and Family, 52,* 677–688.

Cooney, T. M., Smyer, M. A., Hagestad, G. O., & Klock, R. (1986). Parental divorce in young adulthood: Some preliminary findings. *American Journal of Orthopsychiatry, 56,* 470–477. doi:10.1111/j.1939-0025.1986.tb03478.x

Copen, C. E., Daniels, K., Mosher, W. D., & Division of Vital Statistics. (2013). *First premarital cohabitation in the United States: 2006-2010 National Survey of Family Growth.* Retrieved from www.cdc.gov/nchs/data/nhsr/nhsr064.pdf.

Coplan, R. J., Ooi, L. L., & Nocita, G. (2015). When one is company and two is a crowd: Why some children prefer solitude. *Child Development Perspectives, 9,* 133–137.

Copley, S. J. (2016). Morphology of the aging lung on computed tomography. *Journal of Thoracic Imaging, 31,* 140–150. doi:10.1097/RTI.0000000000000211

Coppus, A. M. W. (2013). People with intellectual disability: What do we know about adulthood and life expectancy. *Developmental Disabilities Research Reviews, 18,* 6–16.

Corbett, B. A., & Hilty, D. M. (2006). Managing your time. In L. W. Roberts & D. M. Hilty (Eds.), *Handbook of career development in academic psychiatry and behavioral sciences* (pp. 83–91). Washington, DC: American Psychiatric Publishing.

Cornelius, M., Taylor, P., Geva, D., & Day, N. (1995). Prenatal tobacco exposure and marijuana use among adolescents: Effects on offspring gestational age, growth, and morphology. *Pediatrics, 95,* 738–743.

Cornwall, A. (2016). Women's empowerment: What works? *Journal of International Development, 28,* 342–359. doi:10.1002/jid.3210

Corporation for National and Community Service. (2016). *Senior Corps.* Retrieved from www.nationalservice.gov/programs/senior-corps.

Corr, C. A. (2010a). Children, development, and encounters with death, bereavement, and coping. In C. A. Corr & D. E. Balk (Eds.), *Children's encounters with death, bereavement, and coping* (pp. 3–19). New York: Springer.

Corr, C. A. (2010b). Children's emerging awareness and understandings of loss and death. In C. A. Corr & D. E. Balk (Eds.), *Children's encounters with death, bereavement, and coping* (pp. 21–37). New York: Springer.

Corr, C. A., & Corr, D. M. (2013). *Death and dying: Life and living* (7th ed.). Belmont, CA: Wadsworth.

Corr, C. A., Corr, D. M., & Nabe, C. M. (2008). *Death and dying: Life and living.* Belmont, CA: Wadsworth.

Corriveau, K. H., Kinzler, K. D., & Harris, P. L. (2013). Accuracy trumps accent in children's endorsement of object labels. *Developmental Psychology, 49,* 470–479.

Cortiella, C., & Horowitz, S. H. (2014). *The state of learning disabilities: Facts, trends and emerging issues.* New York: National Center for Learning Disabilities.

Costa, P. T., Jr., & McCrae, R. R. (1994). Set like plaster? Evidence for the stability of adult personality. In T. F. Heatherton & J. L. Weinberger (Eds.), *Can personality change?* (pp. 21–40). Washington, DC: Academic Psychological Association.

Costa, P. T., Jr., & McCrae, R. R. (2011). Five-factor theory, and interpersonal psychology. In L. M. Horowitz & S. Strack (Eds.), *Handbook of interpersonal psychology: Theory, research, assessment, and therapeutic interventions* (pp. 91–104). Hoboken, NJ: Wiley.

Costin, S. E., & Jones, D. C. (1992). Friendship as a facilitator of emotional responsiveness and prosocial interventions among young children. *Developmental Psychology, 28,* 941–947.

Cotton, S. R., Anderson, W. A., & McCullough, B. M. (2013). Impact of Internet use on loneliness and contact with others among older adults: Cross-sectional analysis. *Journal of Medical Internet Research, 15,* e39. doi:10.2196/jmir.2306

Coulton, C. J., Crampton, D. S., Irwin, M., Spilsbury, J. C., & Korbin, J. E. (2007). How neighborhoods influence child maltreatment: A review of the literature and alternative pathways. *Child Abuse and Neglect, 31,* 1117–1142.

Council for Adult and Experiential Learning. (2016). *Higher education.* Retrieved from www.cael.org/higher-education.

Council on Contemporary Families. (2015). *Remarriage in the United States: If at first they don't succeed, do most Americans "try, try again"?* Retrieved from contemporaryfamilies.org/remarriage-brief-report/.

Counts, D., & Counts, D. (Eds.). (1985). *Aging and its transformations: Moving toward death in Pacific societies.* Lanham, MD: University Press of America.

Cousminer, D. L., Berry, D. J., Timpson, N. J., Ang, W., Thiering, E., Byrne, E.M., et al. (2013). Genome-wide association and longitudinal analyses reveal genetic loci linking pubertal height growth, pubertal timing, and childhood adiposity. *Human Molecular Genetics, 22,* 2735–2747.

Cox, C. B. (2007). Grandparent-headed families: Needs and implications for social work interventions and advocacy. *Families in Society, 88,* 561–566. doi:10.1606/1044-3894.3678

Coyne, C. A., Långström, N., Rickert, M. E., Lichtenstein, P., & D'Onofrio, B. M. (2013). Maternal age at first birth and offspring criminality: Using the children of twins design to test causal hypotheses. *Development and Psychopathology, 25,* 17–35.

Cram, B., Alkadry, M. G., & Tower, L. E. (2016). Social costs: The career-family tradeoff. In M. L. Connerley & J. Wu (Eds.), *Handbook of well-being of working women* (pp. 473–487). New York: Springer.

Crawford-Williams, F. M., Roberts, R. M., & Watts, D. (2016). Alcohol consumption and protective behavioural strategy use among Australian young adults. *International Journal of Adolescence and Youth, 21,* 119–123. doi:10.1080/02673843.2013.831363

Crick, N. R., & Dodge, K. A. (1994). A review and reformulation of social-information processing mechanisms in children's social adjustment. *Psychological Bulletin, 115,* 74–101.

Cristia, A., Seidl, A., Singh, L., & Houston, D. (2016). Test-retest reliability in infant speech perception tasks. *Infancy, 21,* 684–667.

Crocetti, E. (2017). Identity formation in adolescence: The dynamic of forming and consolidating identity commitments. *Child Development Perspectives, 11,* 145-150.

Crocetti, E., Rubini, M., Luyckx, K., & Meeus, W. (2008). Identity formation in early and middle adolescence from various ethnic groups: From three dimensions to five statuses. *Journal of Youth & Adolescence, 37,* 983–996.

Croghan, C. F., Moone, R. P., & Olson, A. M. (2014). Friends, family, and caregiving among midlife and older lesbian, gay, bisexual, and transgender adults. *Journal of Homosexuality, 61,* 79–102. doi:10.1080/00918369.2013.835238

Cross, S., & Markus, H. (1991). Possible selves across the lifespan. *Human Development, 34,* 230–255. doi:10.1159/000277058

Crouter, A. C., & Bumpus, M. F. (2001). Linking parents' work stress to children's and adolescents' psychological adjustment. *Current Directions in Psychological Science, 10,* 156–159.

Crouter, A. C., Whiteman, S. D., McHale, S. M., & Osgood, D. (2007). Development of gender attitude traditionality across middle childhood and adolescence. *Child Development, 78,* 911–926.

Csizmadia, A., & Ispa, J. M. (2014). Black-White biracial children's social development from kindergarten to fifth grade: Links with racial identification, gender, and socioeconomic status. *Social Development, 23,* 157–177.

Csizmadia, A., Brunsma, D. L., & Cooney, T. M. (2012). Racial identification and developmental outcomes among Black-White multiracial youth: A review from a life course perspective. *Advances in Life Course Research, 17,* 34–44.

Cukier, H. N., Kunkle, B. W., Vardarajan, B. N., Rolati, S., Hamilton-Nelson, K. L., Kohli, M. A., et al. (2016). *ABCA7* frameshift deletion associated with Alzheimer disease in African Americans. *Neurology Genetics, 2,* e79. doi:10.1212/NXG.0000000000000079. Retrieved from ng.neurology.org/content/2/3/e79.full.

Cummings, E. M., George, M. R. W., McCoy, K., P., & Davies, P. T. (2012). Interparental conflict in kindergarten and adolescent adjustment: Prospective investigation of emotional security as an explanatory mechanism. *Child Development, 83,* 1703–1715.

Cummings, E. M., Goeke-Morey, M. C., & Papp, L. M. (2016). Couple conflict, children, and families. In A. Booth et al., (Eds.), *Couples in conflict* (pp. 117–147). New York: Routledge.

Cummings, E., Schermerhorn, A. C., Davies, P. T., Goeke-Morey, M. C., & Cummings, J. S. (2006). Interparental discord and child adjustment: Prospective investigations of emotional security as an explanatory mechanism. *Child Development, 77,* 132–152.

Cummings, K. (2015). *Coming to grips with loss: Normalizing the grief process.* Boston: Sense Publishers.

Cundiff, N. L., & Stockdale, M. S. (2013). Social psychological perspectives on discrimination against women leaders. In M. A. Paludi (Ed.), *Women and management: Global issues and promising solutions* (pp. 155–174). Santa Barbara, CA: ABC-CLIO.

Cunningham, A. E., Perry, K. E., Stanovich, K. E., & Share, D. L. (2002). Orthographic learning during reading: Examining the role of self-teaching. *Journal of Experimental Child Psychology, 82,* 185–199.

Cunningham, W. R. (1987). Intellectual abilities and age. In K. W. Schaie (Ed.), *Annual review of gerontology and geriatrics* (Vol. 7, pp. 117–134). New York: Springer.

Curran, T., Hill, A. P., Hall, H. K., & Jowett, G. E. (2015). Relationships between the coach-created motivational climate and athlete engagement in youth sport. *Journal of Sport and Exercise Psychology, 37,* 193–198.

Currie, J. (2013). Pollution and infant health. *Child Development Perspectives, 7,* 237–242.

Currie, J., & Walker, R. (2011). Traffic congestion and infant health: Evidence from EZPass. *American Economic Journals: Applied Economics, 3,* 65–90.

Curtis, J. R., Treece, P. D., Nielsen, E. L., Gold, J., Ciechanowski, P. S., Shannon, S. E. et al. (2016). Randomized trial of communication facilitators to reduce family distress and intensity of end-of-life care. *Respiratory and Critical Care Medicine, 193,* 154–162. doi:10.1164/rccm.201505-0900OC

Curtis, R., & Pearson, F. (2010). Contact with birth parents: Differential psychological adjustment for adults adopted as infants. *Journal of Social Work, 10,* 347–367. doi:10.1177/1468017310369273

Cvencek, D., Meltzoff, A. N., & Greenwald, A. G. (2011). Math-gender stereotypes in elementary school children. *Child Development, 82,* 766–779.

Cyr, C., & Alink, L. R. A. (2017). Child maltreatment: The central roles of parenting capacities and attachment. *Current Opinion in Psychology, 15,* 81–86.

D'Angelo, D., Mastroianni, C., Hammer, J. M., Piredda, M., Vellone, E., Alvaro, R. et al. (2015). Continuity of care during end of life: An evolutionary concept analysis. *International Journal of Nursing Knowledge, 26,* 80–89. doi:10.1111/2047-3095.12041

D'Onofrio, B. M., Class, Q. A., Lahey, B. B., & Larsson, H. (2014). Testing the developmental origins of health and disease hypothesis for psychopathology using family-based quasi-experimental designs. *Child Development Perspectives, 8,* 151–157.

D'Onofrio, B. M., Goodnight, J. A., Van Hulle, C. A., Rodgers, J. L., Rathouz, P. J., Waldman, I. D., & Lahey, B. B. (2009). Maternal age at childbirth and offspring disruptive behaviors: Testing the causal hypothesis. *Journal of Child Psychology & Psychiatry, 50,* 1018–1028.

da Costa, J. F., & Oliveira, T. C. (2016). Managing careers: Anchored, plateaued or drifting? In C. Machado & J. P. Davim (Eds.), *Organizational management* (pp. 31–62). New York: Springer.

Dadgari, A., Hamid, T. A., Hakim, M. N., Mousavi, S. A., Dadvar, L., Mohammadi, M. et al. (2015). The role of self-efficacy on fear of falls and fall among elderly community dwellers in Shahroud, Iran. *Nursing Practice Today, 2,* 112–120. Retrieved from npt.tums.ac.ir/index.php/npt/article/view/54/58.

Dai, B., Zhang, B., & Li, J. (2013). Protective factors for subjective well-being in Chinese older adults: The roles of resources and activity. *Journal of Happiness Studies, 14,* 1225–1239. doi:10.1007/s10902-012-9378-7

Dalton, C. (2014). Including smart architecture in environments for people with dementia. In J. van Hoof, G. Demiris, & E. J. M. Wouters (Eds.), *Handbook for smart homes, health care and well-being* (pp. 1–10). New York: Springer. doi:10.1007/978-3-319-0194-8_57-1

Damian, R. I., & Simonton, D. K. (2015). Four psychological perspectives on creativity. *Emerging Trends in the Social and Behavioral*

Sciences: An Interdisciplinary, Searchable, and Linkable Resource. doi:10.1002/978111 8900772.etrds0134

Daniels, H. (2011). Vygotsky and psychology. In U. Goswami (Ed.), *The Wiley-Blackwell handbook of childhood cognitive development* (2nd ed., pp. 673–696). West Sussex, UK: Wiley-Blackwell.

Dannar, P. R. (2013). Millennials: What they offer our organizations and how leaders can make sure they deliver. *Journal of Values-Based Leadership, 6,* Article 3. Retrieved from scholar.valpo.edu/cgi/viewcontent.cgi?article=1073&context=jvbl.

Dannefer, D., & Miklowski, C. (2006). Developments in the life course. In J. A. Vincent, C. R. Phillipson, & M. Downs (Eds.), *The futures of old age* (pp. 30–39). Thousand Oaks, CA: Sage.

Darejeh, A., & Singh, D. (2014). Increasing Microsoft Office usability for middle-aged and elder users with less computer literacy. *Journal of Industrial and Intelligent Information, 2.* Retrieved from www.jiii.org/uploadfile/2013/1230/20131230041823416.pdf.

Darling, N., Cumsille, P., & Martínez, M. L. (2008). Individual differences in adolescents' beliefs about the legitimacy of parental authority and their own obligation to obey: A longitudinal investigation. *Child Development, 79,* 1103–1118.

Davidov, M., Vaish, A., Knafo-Noam, A., & Hastings, P. D. (2016). The motivational foundations of prosocial behavior from a developmental perspective—evolutionary roots and key psychological mechanisms: Introduction to the special section. *Child Development, 87,* 1655–1667.

Davidson, F. H., & Davidson, M. M. (1994). *Changing childhood prejudice: The caring work of the schools.* Westport, CT: Bergin & Garvey/Greenwood.

Davies, L. (2003). Singlehood: Transitions within a gendered world. *Canadian Journal on Aging, 22,* 343–352. doi:10.1017/S0714980800004219

Davies, P. T., Martin, M. J., Coe, J. L., & Cummings, E. M. (2016). Transactional cascades of destructive interparental conflict, children's emotional insecurity, and psychological problems across childhood and adolescence. *Development and Psychopathology, 28,* 653–671.

Davis, A., McMahon, C. M., Pichora-Fuller, K. M. Russ, S., Lin, F., Olusanya, B. O., et al. (2016). Aging and hearing health: The life-source approach. *The Gerontologist, 56,* S256–S267. doi:10.1093/geront/gnw033

Davis, B., Dionne, R., & Fortin, M. (2014). Parenting in two cultural worlds in the presence of one dominant worldview: The American Indian experience. In H. Selin (Ed.), *Parenting across cultures* (pp. 367–377). New York: Springer.

Davis, E. M., Kim, K., & Fingerman, K. L. (in press). Is an empty nest best?: Coresidence with adult children and parental marital quality before and after the Great Recession. *Journal of Gerontology: Psychological Sciences.* doi:10.1093/geronb/gbw022

Davis, E. P., & Sandman, C. A. (2010). The timing of prenatal exposure to maternal cortisol and psychosocial stress is associated with human cognitive development. *Child Development, 81,* 131–148.

Davis, K. M., Gagnier, K. R., Moore, T. E., & Todorow, M. (2013). Cognitive aspects of fetal alcohol spectrum disorder. *WIREs Cognitive Science, 4,* 81–92.

Davis, P. E., Meins, E., & Fernyhough, C. (2011). Self-knowledge in childhood: Relations with children's imaginary companions and understanding of mind. *British Journal of Developmental Psychology, 29,* 680–686.

De Beni, R., & Palladino, P. (2000). Intrusion errors in working memory tasks: Are they related to reading comprehension ability? *Learning and Individual Differences, 12,* 131–143.

de Bloom, J., Geurts, S. A. E., & Kompier, M. A. J. (2012). Effects of short vacations, vacation activities and experiences on employee health and well-being. *Stress and Health, 28,* 305–318. doi:10.1002/smi.1434

de Bloom, J., Geurts, S. A. E., Taris, T. W., Sonnentag, S., de Weerth, C., & Kompier, M. A. J. (2010). Effects of vacation from work on health and well-being: Lots of fun, quickly gone. *Work and Stress, 24,* 196–216. doi:10.1080/02678373.2010.493385

de Haan, M., Wyatt, J. S., Roth, S., Vargha-Khadem, F., Gadian, D., & Mishkin, M. (2006). Brain and cognitive-behavioral development after asphyxia at term birth. *Developmental Science, 9,* 441–442.

de Jong, P., Rouwendal, J., van Hattum, P., & Brouwer, A. (2012). *Housing preferences of an ageing population: Investigation in the diversity among Dutch older adults.* Retrieved from arno.uvt.nl/show.cgi?fid=123055.

De Lisi, R., & Wolford, J. L. (2002). Improving children's mental rotation accuracy with computer game playing. *Journal of Genetic Psychology 163,* 272–283.

De Neys W., & Everaerts, D. (2008). Developmental trends in everyday conditional reasoning: The retrieval and inhibition interplay. *Journal of Experimental Child Psychology, 100,* 252–263.

de Pommereau, I. (2012). *How BMW reinvents the factory for older workers.* Retrieved from www.csmonitor.com/World/Europe/2012/0902/How-BMW-reinvents-the-factory-for-older-workers.

de Rezende, L. F. M., Lopes, M. R., Rey-López, J. P., Matsudo ,V. K. R., & do Carmo Luiz, O. (2014). Sedentary behavior and health outcomes: An overview of systematic reviews. *PLoS One, 9,* e105620.

de Vries, B. (1996). The understanding of friendship: An adult life course perspective. In C. Magai & S. H. McFadden (Eds.), *Handbook of emotion, adult development, and aging* (pp. 249–268). San Diego: Academic Press.

De Wolff, M. S., & van IJzendoorn, M. H. (1997). Sensitivity and attachment: A meta-analysis on parental antecedents of infant attachment. *Child Development, 68,* 571–591.

DeAndrea, D. C., Ellison, N. B., LaRose, R., Steinfield, C., & Fiore, A. (2012). Serious social media: On the use of social media for improving students' adjustment to college. *The Internet and Higher Education, 15,* 15–23. doi:10.1016/j.iheduc.2011.05.009

Deane, G., Spitze, G. Ward, R. A., & Zhuo, Y. (2016). Close to you? How parent-adult child contact is influenced by family patterns. *Journal of Gerontology: Social Sciences, 71,* 344–357. doi:10.1093/geronb/gbv036

Deary, I. (2012). Intelligence. *Annual Review of Psychology, 63,* 453–482.

Deary, I. J., Pattie, A., & Starr, J. M. (2013). The stability of intelligence from age 11 to age 90 years: The Lothian birth cohort of 1921. *Psychological Science, 24,* 2361–2368. doi:10.1177/095679761348648

Deater-Deckard, K., Lansford, J. E., Malone, P. S., Alampay, L. P., Sorbring, E., Bacchini, D., et al. (2011). The association between parental warmth and control in thirteen cultural groups. *Journal of Family Psychology, 25,* 790–794.

Debast, I., van Alphen, S. P. J., Rossi, G., Tummers, J. H. A., Bolwerk, N., Derksen, J. J. L., et al. (2014). Personality traits and personality disorders in late middle and old age: Do they remain stable? A literature review. *Clinical Gerontologist, 37,* 253–271. doi:10/1080/0731 7115.2014.885917

Declercq, E. (2012). The politics of home birth in the United States. *Birth, 39,* 281–285.

Defense and Veterans Brain Injury Center. (2016). *DoD Worldwide numbers of rTBI.* Retrieved from dvbic.dcoe.mil/dod-worldwide-numbers-tbi.

Degner, J., & Dalege, J. (2013). The apple does not fall far from the tree, or does it? A meta-analysis of parent–child similarity in intergroup attitudes. *Psychological Bulletin, 139,* 1270–1304.

Dehaene-Lambertz, G., & Spelke, E. S. (2015). The infancy of the human brain. *Neuron, 88,* 93–109.

DeKeyser, R., Alfi-Shabtay, I., & Ravid, D. (2010). Cross-linguistic evidence for the nature of age effects in second language acquisition. *Applied Psycholinguistics, 31,* 413–438.

Dekovic, M., & Janssens, J. M. (1992). Parents' child-rearing style and child's sociometric status. *Developmental Psychology, 28,* 925–932.

del Valle, J. F., Bravo, A., & Lopez, M. (2010). Parents and peers as providers of support in adolescents' social network: A developmental perspective. *Journal of Community Psychology, 38,* 16–27.

Delaney, C. (2000). Making babies in a Turkish village. In J. S. DeLoache & A. Gottlieb (Eds.), *A world of babies: Imagined childcare guides for seven societies.* New York: Cambridge University Press.

DeLiema, M., Yon, Y., & Wilber, K. H. (2016). Tricks of the trade: Motivating sales agents to con older adults. *The Gerontologist, 56,* 335–344. doi:10.1093/geront/gnu039

DeLoache, J. S., Chiong, C., Sherman, K., Islam, N., Vanderborght, M., Troseth, G. L., Strouse, G. A., & O'Doherty, K. (2010). Do babies learn from baby media? *Psychological Science, 21,* 1570–1574.

DeLucia-Waack, J. L. (2010). Children of divorce groups. In G. L. Greif & P. H. Ephross (Eds.), *Group work with populations at risk* (3rd ed., pp. 93–114). New York: Oxford University Press.

Demir, A., Levine, S. C., & Goldin-Meadow, S. (2010). Narrative skill in children with unilateral brain injury: A possible limit to functional plasticity. *Developmental Science, 13*, 636–647.

Demir, M., Orthel-Clark, H., Özdemir, M., & Özdemir, S. B. (2015). Friendship and happiness among young adults. In M. Demir (Ed.), *Friendship and happiness* (pp. 117-135). New York: Springer.

Denford, S., Abraham, C., Campbell, R., & Busse, H. (2017). A comprehensive review of reviews of school-based interventions to improve sexual-health. *Health Psychology Review, 11*, 33–52.

Deng, C.-P., Armstrong, P. I., & Rounds, J. (2007). The fit of Holland's RIASEC model to US occupations. *Journal of Vocational Behavior, 71*, 1–22. doi:10.1016/j.jvb.2007.04.002

Denham, J., O'Brien, B. J., & Charchar, F. J. (2016). Telomere length maintenance and cardio-metabolic disease prevention through exercise training. *Sports Medicine, 46*, 1213–1237. doi:10.1007/s40279-016-0482-4

Denney, N. W. (1984). A model of cognitive development across the life span. *Developmental Review, 4*, 171–191. doi:10.1016/0273-2287(84)90006-6

Denney, N. W., Pearce, K. A., & Palmer, A. M. (1982). A developmental study of adults' performance on traditional and practical problem-solving tasks. *Experimental Aging Research, 8*, 115–118. doi:10.1080/03610738208258407

DePaulo, B. M. (2006). *Singled out: How singles are stereotyped, stigmatized, and ignored, and still live happily ever after.* New York: St Martin's Press.

Deprest, J., Ghidini, A., Van Mieghem, T., Bianchi, D. W., Faas, B., & Chitty, L. S. (2016). In case you missed it: The *Prenatal Diagnosis* editors bring you the most significant advances of 2015. *Prenatal Diagnosis, 36*, 3–9.

DeSilver, D. (2016). *More older Americans are working, and working more, than they used to.* Retrieved from www.pewresearch.org/fact-tank/2016/06/20/more-older-americans-are-working-and-working-more-than-they-used-to/.

Desmond, N., & López Turley, R. N. (2009). The role of familism in explaining the Hispanic-white college application gap. *Social Problems, 56*, 311–334. doi:10.1525/sp.2009.56.2.311

Dey, S., & Ghosh, J. (2016). Factors in the distribution of successful marriage. *International Journal of Social Sciences and Management, 3*, 60–64. doi:10.3126/ijssm.v3i1.14315

Di Battista, A. M., Heinsinger, N. M., & William Rebeck, G. (2016). Alzheimer's disease genetic risk factor APOE-ε4 also affects normal brain function. *Current Alzheimer Research, 13*, 1200–1207.

Di Domenico, S., Rodrigo, A. H., Ayaz, H., Fournier, M. A., & Ruocco, A. C. (2015). Decision-making conflict and the neural efficiency hypothesis of intelligence: A functional near-infrared spectroscopy investigation. *NeuroImage, 109*, 307–317. doi:10.1016/j.neuroimage.2015.01.039

Di Fabio, A. (2016). Life design and career counseling innovative outcomes. *The Career Development Quarterly, 64*, 35–48. doi:10.1002/cdq.12039

Di Masso, A., Dixon, J., & Hernández, B. (2017). Place attachment, sense of belonging and the micro-politics of place satisfaction. In G. Fleury-Bahi, E. Pol, & O. Navarro (Eds.), *Handbook of environmental psychology and quality of life research* (pp. 85–104). New York: Springer.

Diamond, A., & Lee, K. (2011). Interventions shown to aid executive function development in children 4 to 12 years old. *Science, 333*, 959–964.

Diamond, A., Prevor, M. B., Callender, G., & Druin, D. P. (1997). Prefontal cortex deficits in children treated early and continuously for PKU. *Monographs of the Society for Research in Child Development, 62*(4, Serial No. 252).

Diamond, L. M. (2007). A dynamical systems approach to the development and expression of female same-sex sexuality. *Perspectives on Psychological Science, 2*, 142–161.

DiBello, K. K. (2015). Grief & depression at the end of life. *Nurse Practitioner, 40*, 22–28. doi:10.1097/01.NPR.0000463781.50345.95

Dick-Read, G. (1959). *Childbirth without fear.* New York: Harper & Brothers.

Dickens, B. M., Boyle, J. M., Jr., & Ganzini, L. (2008). Euthanasia and assisted suicide. In P. A. Singer & A. M. Viens (Eds.), *The Cambridge textbook of bioethics* (pp. 72–77). New York: Cambridge University Press.

Dickinson, G. E. (1992). First childhood death experiences. *Omega: The Journal of Death and Dying, 25*, 169–182. doi:10.2190/M8F0-TN3F-EFCB-H8N3

Diehl, M., Marsiske, M., Horgas, A. L., Rosenberg, A., Saczynski, J. S., & Willis, S. L. (2005). The Revised Observed Tasks of Daily Living: A performance-based assessment of everyday problem solving in older adults. *Journal of Applied Gerontology, 24*, 211–230. doi:10.1177/0733464804273772

Diemer, M. A. (2007). Parental and school influences upon the career development of poor youth of color. *Journal of Vocational Behavior, 70*, 502–524.

Diersch, N., Cross, E. S., Stadler, W., Schütz-Bosbach, S., & Rieger, M. (2012). Representing others' actions: The role of expertise in the aging mind. *Psychological Research, 76*, 525–541. doi:10.1007/s00426-011-0404-x

DiGiacomo, M., Davidson, P. M., Byles, J., & Nolan, M. T. (2013). An integrative and socio-cultural perspective of health, wealth, and adjustment in widowhood. *Health Care for Women International, 34*, 1067–1083. doi:10.1080/07399332.2012.712171

Dijkstra, J. K., Cillessen, A. H. N., & Borch, C. (2013). Popularity and adolescent friendship networks: Selection and influence dynamics. *Developmental Psychology, 49*, 1242–1252.

Dillaway, H., Byrnes, M., Miller, S., & Rehnan, S. (2008). Talking "among *us* ": How women from different racial-ethnic groups define and discuss menopause. *Health Care for Women International, 29*, 766–781. doi:10.1080/07399330802179247

Dilworth-Anderson, P., Boswell, G., & Cohen, M. D. (2007). Spiritual and religious coping values and beliefs among African American caregivers: A qualitative study. *Journal of Applied Gerontology, 26*, 355–369. doi:10.1177/0733464807302669

DiPietro, J. A., Caulfield, L., Costigan, K. A., Merialdi, M., Nguyen, R. H. N., Zavaleta, N., & Gurewitsch, E. D. (2004). Fetal neurobehavioral development: A tale of two cities. *Developmental Psychology, 40*, 445–456.

DiPietro, J. A., Costigan, K. A., & Voegtline, K. M. (2015). Studies in fetal behavior: Revisited, renewed, and reimagined. *Monographs of the Society for Research in Child Development, 80*(3), 1–151.

DiPietro, J. A., Novak, M. F., Costigan, K. A., Atella, L. D., & Reusing, S. P. (2006). Maternal psychological distress during pregnancy in relation to child development at age two. *Child Development, 77*, 573–587.

Dirks, M. A., Persram, R., Recchia, H. E., & Howe, N. (2015). Sibling relationships as sources of risk and resilience in the development and maintenance of internalizing and externalizing problems during childhood and adolescence. *Clinical Psychology Review, 42*, 145–155.

Dishion, T. J., Poulin, F., & Burraston, B. (2001). Peer group dynamics associated with iatrogenic effects in group interventions with high-risk young adolescents. In D. W. Nangle & C. A. Erdley (Eds.), *The role of friendship in psychological adjustment* (pp. 79–92). San Francisco, CA: Jossey-Bass.

Divan, H. A., Kheifets, L., Obel, C., & Olsen, J. (2012). Cell phone use and behavioural problems in young children. *Journal of Epidemiology and Community Health, 66*, 524–529.

Dixon, P. (2009). Marriage among African Americans: What does the research reveal? *Journal of African American Studies, 13*, 29–46. doi:10.1007/s12111-008-9062-5

Dobbins, M., DeCorby, K., Manske, S., & Goldblatt, E. (2008). Effective practices for school-based tobacco use prevention. *Preventive Medicine, 46*, 289–297.

Dobkin, P. L., & Hassed, C. S. (2016). Scientific underpinnings and evidence pertaining to mindfulness. In P. L. Dobkin & C. S. Hassed (Eds.), *Mindful medical practitioners: A guide for clinicians and educators* (pp. 9–31). New York: Springer.

Dodge, K. A., Greenberg, M. T., & Malone, P. S. (2008). Testing an idealized dynamic cascade model of the development of serious violence in adolescence. *Child Development, 79*, 1907–1927.

Doerwald, F., Scheibe, S., Zacher, H., & Van Yperen, N. W. (2016). Emotional competencies across adulthood: State of knowledge and implications for the work context. *Work, Aging and Retirement, 2*, 159–216. doi:10.1093/worker/waw013

Doka, K. J., & Mertz, M. E. (1988). The meaning and significance of great-grandparenthood. *The Gerontologist, 28*, 192–197. doi:10.1093/geront/28.2.192

Dommaraju, P. (2010). *The changing demography of marriage in India.* Podcast retrieved from ari.nus.edu.sg/Publication/Detail/1630.

Donaldson, C. D., Handren, L. M., & Crano, W. D. (2016). The enduring impact of parents' monitoring, warmth, expectancies, and alcohol use on their children's future binge drinking and arrests: A longitudinal analysis. *Prevention Science, 17*, 606–614.

Doohan, E.-A. M., Carrère, S., & Riggs, M. L. (2010). Using relational stories to predict the trajectory toward marital dissolution: The oral history interview and spousal feelings of flooding, loneliness, and depression. *Journal of Family Communication, 10*, 57–77. doi:10.1080/15267430903396401

Dorn, L. D., Dahl, R. E., Woodward, H. R., & Biro, F. (2006). Defining the boundaries of early adolescence: A user's guide to assessing pubertal status and pubertal timing in research with adolescents. *Applied Developmental Science, 10*, 30–56.

Doss, B. D., & Rhoades, G. K. (2017). The transition to parenthood: Impact on couples' romantic relationships. *Current Opinion in Psychology, 13*, 25–28. doi:10.1016/j.copsyc.2016.04.003

Doubeni, C. A., Schootman, M., Major, J. M., Torres Stone, R. A., Laiyemo, A. O., Park, Y., et al. (2012). Health status, neighborhood socioeconomic context, and premature mortality in the United States: The National Institutes of Health—AARP Diet and Health Study. *American Journal of Public Health, 102*, 680–688. doi:10.2105/AJPH.2011.300158

Doumen, S., Smits, I., Luyckx, K., Duriez, B., Vanhalst, J., Verschueren, K., et al. (2012). Identity and perceived peer relationship quality in emerging adulthood: The mediating role of attachment-related emotions. *Journal of Adolescence, 35*, 1417–1425.

Dowd, J. J. (2012). Aging and the course of desire. *Journal of Aging Studies, 26*, 285–295. doi:10.1016/j.aging.2012.01.004

Doyle, J. M., & Kao, G. (2007). Are racial identities of multiracials stable? Change self-identification among single and multiple race individuals. *Social Psychology Quarterly, 70*, 405–423.

Dozier, M., Zeanah, C. H., & Bernard, K. (2013). Infant and toddlers in foster care. *Child Development Perspectives, 7*, 166–171.

Drew, L. M., & Silverstein, M. (2004). Inter-generational role investments of great-grandparents: Consequences for psychological well-being. *Ageing and Society, 24*, 95–111. doi:10.1017/S0144686X03001533

Driscoll, A. K., Russell, S. T., & Crockett, L. J. (2008). Parenting styles and youth well-being

across immigrant generations. *Journal of Family Issues, 29*, 185–209.

Duckworth, A. L., & Seligman, M. E. (2005). Self-discipline outdoes IQ in predicting academic performance of adolescents. *Psychological Science, 16*, 939–944.

Duff, L. J., Ericsson, K. A., & Baluch, B. (2007). In search of the loci for sex differences in throwing: The effects of physical size and differential recruitment rates on high levels of dart performance. *Research Quarterly for Exercise and Sport, 78*, 71–78.

Dulac, M. C., & Auertin-Leheudre, M. (2016). Exercise: An important key to prevent physical and cognitive frailty. *Journal of Frailty and Aging, 5*, 3–5. doi:10.14283/jfa.2015.72

Dunham, P. J., Dunham, F., & Curwin, A. (1993). Joint-attentional states and lexical acquisition at 18 months. *Developmental Psychology, 29*, 827–831.

Dunlop, W. L., Guo, J., & McAdams, D. P. (2016). The autobiographical author through time: Examining the degree of stability and change in redemptive and contaminated personal narratives. *Social Psychological and Personality Science, 7*, 428–436. doi:10.1177/1948550616644654

Dunn, J., & Brophy, M. (2005). Communication, relationships, and individual differences in children's understanding of mind. In J. W. Astington & J. A. Baird (Eds.), *Why language matters for theory of mind* (pp. 50–69). New York: Oxford.

Dunn, J., & Davies, L. (2001). Sibling relationships and interpersonal conflict. In J. Grych & F. D. Fincham (Eds.), *Interparental conflict and child development* (pp. 273–290). New York: Cambridge University Press.

Dunn, J., & Kendrick, C. (1981). Social behavior of young siblings in the family context: Differences between same-sex and different-sex dyads. *Child Development, 52*, 1265–1273.

Dunn, J., Slomkowski, C., & Beardsall, L. (1994). Sibling relationships from the preschool period through middle childhood and early adolescence. *Developmental Psychology, 30*, 315–324.

Dunphy-Lelii, S., LaBounty, J., Lane, J. D., & Wellman, H. M. (2014). The social context of infant intention understanding. *Journal of Cognition and Development, 15*, 60–77.

Dunson, D. B., Colombo, B., & Baird, D. D. (2002). Changes in age in the level and duration of fertility in the menstrual cycle. *Human Reproduction, 17*, 1399–1403.

Dupuis, S. (2010). Examining the blended family: The application of systems theory toward an understanding of the blended family system. *Journal of Couple and Relationship Therapy, 9*, 239–251. doi:10.1080/15332691.2 010.491784

Durik, A. M., Hyde, J. S., & Clark, R. (2000). Sequelae of cesarean and vaginal deliveries: Psychosocial outcomes for mothers and infants. *Developmental Psychology, 36*, 251–260.

Dutta, D., Calvani, R., Bernabei, R., Leeuwenburgh, C., & Marzetti, E. (2012). Contribution of impaired mitochondrial

autophagy to cardiac aging: Mechanisms and therapeutic opportunities. *Circulation Research, 110*, 1125–1138. doi:10.1161/CIRCRESAHA.111.246108

Dutton, W. H., Helsper, E. J., Whitty, M. T., Li, N., Buckwalter, J. G., & Lee, E. (2009). The role of the Internet in reconfiguring marriages: A cross-national study. *Interpersona: An International Journal on Personal Relationships, 3*(Suppl. 2). Retrieved from abpri.files.wordpress.com/2010/12/interpersona-3-suppl-2_1.pdf.

Dykas, M. J., & Cassidy, J. (2011). Attachment and the processing of social information across the life span: Theory and evidence. *Psychological Bulletin, 137*, 19–46.

Eagleton, S. G., Williams, A. L., & Merten, M. J. (2016). Perceived behavioral autonomy and trajectories of depressive symptoms from adolescence to adulthood. *Journal of Child and Family Studies, 25*, 198–211.

Eagly, A. H., & Wood, W. (2013). The nature-nurture debates: 25 years of challenges in understanding the psychology of gender. *Perspectives on Psychological Science, 8*, 340–357.

Eagly, A. H., Karau, S. J., & Makhijani, M. G. (1995). Gender and the effectiveness of leaders: A meta-analysis. *Psychological Bulletin, 117*, 125–145.

Earle, S., Komaromy, C., & Layne, L. (Eds.). (2012). *Understanding reproductive loss: Perspectives on life, death and fertility.* Farnham, UK: Ashgate.

Easterbrook, M. A., Kisilevsky, B. S., Muir, D. W., & Laplante, D. P. (1999). Newborns discriminate schematic faces from scrambled faces. *Canadian Journal of Experimental Psychology, 53*, 231–241.

Eaton, D. K., Kann, L., Kinchen, S., Shanklin, S., Ross, J., Hawkins, J., et al. (2008). Youth risk behavior surveillance—United States, 2007. *Morbidity & Mortality Weekly Report, 57*, 1–131.

Ebberwein, C. A. (2001). Adaptability and the characteristics necessary for managing adult career transition: A qualitative investigation. *Dissertation Abstracts International. Section B. Sciences and Engineering, 62(1-B)*, 545.

Eddleston, K. A., Baldridge, D. C., & Veiga, J. F. (2004). Toward modeling the predictors of managerial career success: Does gender matter? *Journal of Managerial Psychology, 19*, 360–385. doi:10.1108/02683940410537936

Edelson, L. R., Mokdad, C., & Martin. N. (2016). Prompts to eat novel and familiar fruits and vegetables in families with 1–3 year-old children: Relationships with food acceptance and intake. *Appetite, 99*, 138–148.

Eden Alternative. (2017). *Mission, vision, values, principles.* Retrieved from www.edenalt.org/about-the-eden-alternative/mission-vision-values/.

Edwards, C. A. (1994). Leadership in groups of school-age girls. *Developmental Psychology, 30*, 920–927.

Edwards, L. A., Wagner, J. B., Simon, C. E., & Hyde, D. C. (2016). Functional brain organization for number processing in pre-verbal infants. *Developmental Science, 19*, 757–769.

Edwards, M. R. (2012). A temporal multifaceted adaptation approach to the experiences of employed mothers. *Marriage and Family Review, 48,* 732–768. doi:10.1080/01494929.2012.700911

Edwards, R. C., Thullen, M. J., Isarowong, N., Shiu, C-S., Henson, L., & Hans, S. L. (2012). Supportive relationships and the trajectory of depressive symptoms among young, African American mothers. *Journal of Family Psychology, 26,* 585–594.

Ehrlich, K. B., Dykas, M. J., & Cassidy, J. (2012). Tipping points in adolescent adjustment: Predicting social functioning from adolescents' conflict with parents and friends. *Journal of Family Psychology, 26,* 776–783.

Eime, R. M., Young, J. A., Harvey, J. T., Charity, M. J., & Payne, W. R. (2013). A systematic review of the psychological and social benefits of participation in sport for children and adolescents: Informing development of a conceptual model of health through sport. *International Journal of Behavioral Nutrition and Physical Activity, 10,* 98.

Eisenberg, N. (2000). Emotion, regulation, and moral development. *Annual Review of Psychology, 51,* 665–697.

Eisenberg, N., & Shell, R. (1986). Prosocial moral judgment and behavior in children: The mediating role of cost. *Personality and Social Psychology Bulletin, 12,* 426–433.

Eisenberg, N., Hofer, C., Spinrad, T., Gershoff, E., Valiente, C., Losoya, S. L., et al. (2008). Understanding parent-adolescent conflict discussions: Concurrent and across-time prediction from youths' dispositions and parenting. *Monographs of the Society for Research in Child Development, 73,* Serial No. 290.

Eisenberg, N., Michalik, N., Spinrad, T. L., Hofer, C., Kupfer, A., Valiente, C., et al. (2007). The relations of effortful control and impulsivity to children's symptoms: A longitudinal study. *Cognitive Development, 22,* 544–567.

Eisenberg, N., Spinrad, T. L., & Knafo-Noam, A. (2015). Prosocial development. In R M. Lerner (Ed)., *Handbook of child psychology and developmental science* (7th ed., Vol. 3., pp. 610–656). Hoboken, NJ: Wiley.

Eisenberg, N., VanSchyndel, S. K., & Spinrad, T. L. (2016). Prosocial motivation: Inferences from an opaque body of work. *Child Development, 87,* 1668–1678.

Eisma, M. C., Schut, H. A. W., Stroebe, M. S., Voerman, K., van den Bout, J., Stroebe, W. et al. (2015). Psychopathology symptoms, rumination and autobiographical memory specificity: Do associations hold after bereavement? *Applied Cognitive Psychology, 29,* 478–484. doi:10.1002/acp.3120 a

Eizenman, D. R., & Bertenthal, B. I. (1998). Infants' perception of object unity in translating and rotating displays. *Developmental Psychology, 34,* 426–434.

El Nokali, N. E., Bachman, H. J., & Votruba-Drzal, E. (2010). Parent involvement and children's academic and social development in elementary school. *Child Development, 81,* 988–1005.

Elbert, T., Pantev, C., Weinbruch, C., Rockstroh, B., & Taub, E. (1995). Increased cortical representation of the fingers of the left hand in strings players. *Science, 270,* 305–307.

Elkind, D. (1978). *The child's reality: Three developmental themes.* Hillsdale, NJ: Erlbaum.

Elkind, D., & Bowen, R. (1979). Imaginary audience behavior in children and adolescents. *Developmental Psychology, 15,* 38–44.

Ellis, B. J. (2004). Timing of pubertal maturation in girls: An integrated life history approach. *Psychological Bulletin, 130,* 920–958.

Ellis, J. W. (2010). Yours, mine, ours? Why the Texas legislature should simplify caretaker consent capabilities for minor children and the implications of the addition of Chapter 34 to the Texas Family Code. *Texas Tech Law Review, 42,* 987. Retrieved from papers.ssrn.com/sol3/papers.cfm?abstract_id=1811045.

Else-Quest, N. M., Higgins, A., Allison, C., & Morton, L. C. (2012). Gender differences in self-conscious emotional experience: A meta-analysis. *Psychological Bulletin, 138,* 947–981.

Else-Quest, N. M., Hyde, J. S., & Linn, M. C. (2010). Cross-national patterns of gender differences in mathematics: A meta-analysis. *Psychological Bulletin, 136,* 103–127.

Else-Quest, N. M., Hyde, J. S., Goldsmith, H. H., & Van Hulle, C. A. (2006). Gender differences in temperament: A meta-analysis. *Psychological Bulletin, 132,* 33–72.

Emerson, R. W., & Cantlon, J. F. (2015). Continuity and change in children's longitudinal neural response to numbers. *Developmental Science, 18,* 314–326.

Endenburg, N., van Lith, H. A., & Kirpensteijn, J. (2014). Longitudinal study of Dutch children's attachment to companion animals. *Society & Animals, 22,* 390–414.

Engel, S. M., Berkowitz, G. S., Wolff, M. S., & Yehuda, R. (2005). Psychological trauma associated with the World Trade Center attacks and its effect on pregnancy outcome. *Paediatric & Perinatal Epidemiology, 19,* 334–341.

Engelberg, A. (2016). Religious Zionist singles: Caught between "family values" and "young adulthood." *Journal for the Scientific Study of Religion, 55,* 349–364. doi:10.1111/jssr.12259

English, D., Lambert S. F., & Ialongo, N. S. (2014). Longitudinal associations between experienced racial discrimination and depressive symptoms in African American adolescents. *Developmental Psychology, 50,* 1190–1196.

English, T., & Carstensen, L. L. (2014). Selective narrowing of social networks across adulthood is associated with improved emotional experience in daily life. *International Journal of Behavioral Development.* doi:10.1177/0165025413515404

English, T., & Carstensen L. L. (2016). Socioemotional selectivity theory. In N. A Pachana (Ed.), *Encyclopedia of geropsychology.* New York: Springer. doi:10.1007/978-287-080-3_110-1

Englund, M. M., White, B., Reynolds, A. J., Schweinhart, L. J., & Campbell, F. A. (2014). Health outcomes of the Abecedarian, Child-Parent Center, and HighScope Perry preschool programs. In A. J. Reynolds, A. J. Rolnick, & J. A. Temple (Eds.), *Health and education in early childhood: Predictors, interventions, and policies* (pp. 257–285). Cambridge, UK: Cambridge University Press.

Equal Employment Opportunity Commission. (2016a). *Sexual harassment.* Retrieved from www.eeoc.gov/laws/types/sexual_harassment.cfm.

Equal Employment Opportunity Commission. (2016b). *Charges alleging sexual harassment FY2010-FY2015.* Retrieved from www.eeoc.gov/eeoc/statistics/enforcement/sexual_harassment_new.cfm.

Equal Employment Opportunity Commission. (2016c). *Age discrimination.* Retrieved from www.eeoc.gov/laws/types/age.cfm.

Equality and Human Rights Commission. (2016). *What is the Equality Act?* Retrieved from www.equalityhumanrights.com/en/equality-act-2010/what-equality-act.

Erickson, K. I., Gildengers, A. G., & Butters, M. A. (2013). Physical activity and brain plasticity in late adulthood. *Dialogues in Clinical Neuroscience, 15,* 99–108. Retrieved from www.ncbi.nlm.nih.gov/pmc/articles/PMC3622473/.

Ericsson, K. A. (2014). Creative genius: A view from the expert-performance approach. In D. K. Simonton (Ed.), *The Wiley-Blackwell handbook of genius* (pp. 321–349). Oxford, UK: Wiley-Blackwell.

Ericsson, K. A., & Towne, T. J. (2010). Expertise. *Wiley Interdisciplinary Reviews: Cognitive Science, 1,* 404–416. doi:10.1002/wcs.47

Erikson, E. H. (1968). *Identity: Youth and crisis.* New York: Norton.

Erikson, E. H. (1982). *The life cycle completed: Review.* New York: Norton.

Erikson, E. H., Erikson, J. M., & Kivnick, H. Q. (1986). *Vital involvement in old age.* New York: Norton.

Esch, T. (2014). The neurobiology of meditation and mindfulness. In S. Schmidt & H. Walach (Eds.), *Meditation—Neuroscientific approaches and philosophical implication* (pp. 153–173). New York: Springer.

Eskritt, M., & McLeod, K. (2008). Children's note taking as a mnemonic tool. *Journal of Experimental Child Psychology, 101,* 52–74.

Espy, K. A., Fang, H., Johnson, C., Stopp, C., Wiebe, S. A., & Respass, J. (2011). Prenatal tobacco exposure: Developmental outcomes in the neonatal period. *Developmental Psychology, 47,* 153–169.

Etezadi, S., & Pushkar, D. (2013). Why are wise people happier? An explanatory model of wisdom and emotional well-being in older adults. *Journal of Happiness Studies, 14,* 929–950. doi:10.1007/s10902-012-9362-2

Ethics Committee of the American Society for Reproductive Medicine. (2013). Oocyte or embryo donation to women of advanced reproductive age: An Ethics Committee opinion. *Fertility and Sterility, 100,* 337–340.

Ethics Committee of the American Society for Reproductive Medicine. (2015). Sex selection for nonmedical reasons. *Fertility and Sterility, 103*, 1418–1422.

European Association for Palliative Care. (2011). *The EAPC ethics task force on palliative care and euthanasia.* Retrieved from www.eapcnet.eu/Themes/Ethics/PCeuthanasiataskforce/tabid/232/Default.aspx.

Evans, D. G. R., Barwell, J., Eccles, D. M., Collins, A., Izatt, L., Jacobs, C., et al. (2014). The Angelina Jolie effect: How high celebrity profile can have a major impact on provision of cancer-related services. *Breast Cancer Research, 16,* 442. doi:10.1186/s13058-014-0442-6. Retrieved from breast-cancer-research.biomedcentral.com/articles/10.1186/s13058-014-0442-6.

Evans, J. St. B. T., & Stanovich, K. E. (2013). Dual-process theories of higher cognition: Advancing the debate. *Perspectives on Psychological Science, 8,* 223–241.

Even-Zohar, A., & Garby, A. (2016). Great-grandparents' role perception and its contribution to their quality of life. *Journal of Intergenerational Relationships, 14,* 197–219. doi:10.1080/15350770.2016.1195246

Evertsson, M., Grunow, D., & Aisenbrey, S. (2016). Work interruptions and young women's career prospects in Germany, Sweden, and the US. *Work, Employment and Society, 30,* 291–308. doi:10.1177/0950017015598283

Faber, A. J. (2004). Examining remarried couples through a Bowenian family systems lens. *Journal of Divorce & Remarriage, 40,* 121–133. doi:10.1300/J087v40n03_08

Fabes, R. A., Eisenberg, N., Jones, S., Smith, M., Guthrie, I., Poulin, R., et al. (1999). Regulation, emotionality, and preschoolers' socially competent peer interactions. *Child Development, 70,* 432–442.

Fabius, C. D. (2016). Toward an integration of narrative identity, generativity, and storytelling in African American elders. *Journal of Black Studies, 47,* 423–434. doi:10.1177/0021934716638801

Fagard, J. (2013). The nature and nurture of human infant hand preference. *Annals of the New York Academy of Sciences, 1288,* 114–123.

Fajgenbaum, D., Chesson, B., & Lanzl, R. G. (2012). Building a network of grief support on college campuses: A national grassroots initiative. *Journal of College Student Psychotherapy, 26,* 99–120. doi:10.1080/87568225.2012.659159

Falbo, T. (2012). Only children: An updated review. *Journal of Individual Psychology, 68,* 38–49.

Falbo, T., & Polit, E. F. (1986). Quantitative review of the only child literature: Research evidence and theory development. *Psychological Bulletin, 100,* 176–186.

Farr, R. H., Diamond, L. M., & Boker, S. M. (2014). Female same-sex sexuality from a dynamical systems perspective: Sexual desire, motivation, and behavior. *Archives of Sexual Behavior, 43,* 1477–1490.

Farrant, B. M., Devine, T. A. J., Maybery, M. T., & Fletcher, J. (2012). Empathy, perspective taking and prosocial behaviour: The importance of parenting practices. *Infant and Child Development, 21,* 175–188.

Farrant, B. M., Maybery, M. T., & Fletcher, J. (2012). Language, cognitive flexibility, and explicit false belief understanding: Longitudinal analysis in typical development and specific language impairment. *Child Development, 83,* 223–235.

Farrington, D. P., & Koegl, C. J. (2015). Monetary benefits and costs of the Stop Now and Plan Program for boys aged 6–11, based on the prevention of later offending. *Journal of Quantitative Criminology, 31,* 263–287.

Farris, D. N. (2016). *Boomerang kids: The demography of previously launched adults.* New York: Springer.

Farver, J. M., & Shin, Y. L. (1997). Social pretend play in Korean- and Anglo-American preschoolers. *Child Development, 68,* 544–556.

Fasig, L. G. (2000). Toddlers' understanding of ownership: Implications for self-concept development. *Social Development, 9,* 370–382.

Fazel, S., Bakiyeva, L., Cnattingius, S., Grann, M., Hultman, C. M., Litchtenstein, P., et al. (2012). Perinatal risk factors in offenders with severe personality disorder: A population-based investigation. *Journal of Personality Disorders, 26,* 737–750.

Federal Bureau of Investigation. (2016). *Crime in the United States, 2015.* Washington DC: Author.

Fein, E., & Schneider, S. (2013). *Not your mother's rules: The new secrets for dating.* New York: Grand Central Publishing.

Feinberg, M. E., McHale, S. M., Crouter, A. C., & Cumsille, P. (2003). Sibling differentiation: Sibling and parental relationships trajectories in adolescence. *Child Development, 74,* 1261–1274.

Feldman, H. M., Dollaghan, C. A., Campbell, T. F., Kurs-Lasky, M., Janosky, J. E., & Paradise, J. L. (2000). Measurement properties of the MacArthur Communicative Development Inventories at one and two years. *Child Development, 71,* 310–322.

Feldman, K. (2010). *Post parenthood redefined: Race, class, and family structure differences in the experience of launching children.* Doctoral dissertation completed at Case Western Reserve University. Retrieved from etd.ohiolink.edu/pg_10?0::NO:10:P10_ACCESSION_NUM:case1267730564.

Feldman, R. (2015). Mutual influences between child emotion regulation and parent–child reciprocity support development across the first 10 years of life: Implications for developmental psychopathology. *Development and Psychopathology, 27,* 1007–1023.

Felix, E., De Haan, H., Vaandrager, L., & Koelen, M. (2015). Beyond thresholds: The everyday lived experience of the house by older people. *Journal of Housing for the elderly, 29,* 329–347. doi:10.1080/027633893.2015.1055027

Felkey, A. J. (in press). Covenant marriages: Increasing commitment or costs? *Eastern Economic Journal.* doi:10.1057/eej.2016.3

Feltz, A. (2015). Everyday attitudes about euthanasia and the slippery slope argument. In M. Cholbi & J. Varelius (Eds.), *New directions in the ethics of assisted suicide and euthanasia* (pp. 217–237). New York: Springer. doi:10.1007/978-3-319-22050-55_13

Fenson, L., Dale, P. S., Reznick, J. S., Bates, E., et al. (1994). Variability in early communicative development. *Monographs of the Society for Research in Child Development, 59* (Whole No. 173).

Fergusson, D. M., & Woodward, L. J. (2000). Teenage pregnancy and female educational underachievement: A prospective study of a New Zealand birth cohort. *Journal of Marriage & the Family, 62,* 147–161.

Fernández-Alcántara, M., Cruz-Quintana, Pérez-Marfil, M. N., Catena-Martinez, A., Pérez-Garcia, M., & Turnbull, O. H. (2016). Assessment of emotional and emotional recognition in complicated grief. *Frontiers in Psychology, 7.* doi:10.3389/fpsyg.2016.00126. Retrieved from www.ncbi.nlm.nih.gov/pmc/articles/PMC4751347/

Fernández-Carro, C. (2016). Ageing at home, co-residence or institutionalisation? Preferred care and residential arrangements of older adults in Spain. *Ageing and Society, 36,* 586–6132. doi:10.1017/S0144686X1400138X

Fernyhough, C. (2010). Inner speech. In H. Pashler (Ed.), *Encyclopaedia of the mind.* Thousand Oaks, CA: Sage.

Ferrarini, T., & Norström, T. (2010). Family policy, economic development, and infant mortality: A longitudinal comparative analysis. *International Journal of Social Welfare, 19,* S89–S102. doi:10.1111/j.1468-2397.2010.00736.x

Ferreol-Barbey, M., Piolat, A., & Roussey, J. (2000). Text recomposition by eleven-year-old children: Effects of text length, level of reading comprehension, and mastery of prototypical schema. *Archives de Psychologie, 68,* 213–232.

Fidler, E. (2012). Sickle cell trait: A review and recommendations for training. *Strength and Conditioning Journal, 34,* 28–32.

Field, M. J., & Cassel, C. K. (2010). Approaching death: Improving care at the end of life. In D. Meier, S. L. Isaacs, & R. G. Hughes (Eds.), *Palliative care: Transforming the care of serious illness* (pp. 79–91). San Francisco: Jossey-Bass.

Field, T. (2010). Postpartum depression effects on early interactions, parenting, and safety practices: A review. *Infant Behavior & Development, 33,* 1–6.

Field, T. M., & Widmayer, S. M. (1982). Motherhood. In B. J. Wolman (Ed.), *Handbook of developmental psychology.* Englewood Cliffs, NJ: Prentice Hall.

Field, T., Diego, M., & Hernandez-Reif, M. (2010). Preterm infant message therapy research: A review. *Infant Behavior and Development, 33,* 115–124.

Fincham, F. D., & Beach, S. R. H. (2010). Marriage in the new millennium: A decade in review. *Journal of Marriage and Family, 72,* 630–649. doi:10.1111/j.1741-3737.2010.00722.x

Fingerman, K. L., Pillemer, K. A., Silverstein, M., & Suitor, J. J. (2012). The baby boomers' intergenerational relationships. *The Gerontologist, 52,* 199–209. doi:10.1093/geront/gnr139

Finkbeiner, N. W. B., Max, J. E., Longman, S., & Debert, C. (2016). Knowing what we don't know: Long-term psychiatric outcomes following adult concussion in sports. *The Canadian Journal of Psychiatry, 61,* 27–276. doi:10.1177/0706743716644953

Fiori, K. L., & Denckla, C. A. (2015). Friendship and happiness among middle-aged adults. In M. Demir (Ed.), *Friendship and happiness* (pp. 137–154). New York: Springer.

Fischer-Shofty, M., Levkovitz, Y., & Shamay-Tsoory, S. G. (2013). Oxytocin facilitates accurate perception of competition in men and kinship in women. *Social Cognitive and Affective Neuroscience.* doi:10.1093/scan/nsr100

Fisher, H. (2016). *Anatomy of love: A natural history of mating, marriage, and why we stray* (revised and updated). New York: W. W. Norton.

Fisher, L. L. (2010). *Sex, romance, and relationships: AARP survey of midlife and older adults.* Retrieved from assets.aarp.org/rgcenter/general /srr_09.pdf.

Fiske, S. T., & Taylor, S. E. (2013). *Social cognition: From brains to culture* (2nd ed.). Thousand Oaks, CA: Sage.

Fitzgerald, J. (1987). Research on revision in writing. *Review of Educational Research, 57,* 481–506.

Fivush, R. (2014). Maternal reminiscing style: The sociocultural construction of autobiographical memory across childhood and adolescence. In P J. Bauer & R. Fivush (Eds.), *The Wiley handbook on the development of children's memory* (pp. 568–585). Chichester, UK: Wiley.

Flavell, J. H. (1985). *Cognitive development* (2nd ed.). Englewood Cliffs, NJ: Prentice Hall.

Flavell, J. H. (1996). Piaget's legacy. *Psychological Science, 7,* 200–203.

Flavell, J. H. (2000). Development of children's knowledge about the mental world. *International Journal of Behavioral Development, 24,* 15–23.

Fleming, P. J., & Blair, P. S. (2015). Making informed choices on co-sleeping with your baby. *BMJ, 350:*h563.

Flynn, J. R. (1999). Searching for justice: The discovery of IQ gains over time. *American Psychologist, 54,* 5–20.

Flynn, J. R., & Weiss, L. G. (2007). American IQ gains from 1932 to 2002: The WISC subtests and educational progress. *International Journal of Testing, 7,* 209–224.

Fogarty, K., & Evans, G. D. (2010). Being an involved father: What does it mean? Retrieved from edis.ifas.ufl.edu/he141.

Formosa, M. (2014). Four decades of universities of the Third Age: Past, present, future. *Ageing and Society, 34,* 42–66. doi:10.1017/S0144686X12000797

Foshee, V. A., & Reyes, H. L. (2012). Dating abuse: Prevalence, consequences, and predictors. In R J. R. Levesque (Ed.), *Encyclopedia of adolescence* (Vol. 1, pp. 602–615). New York: Springer.

Foshee, V. A., Benefield, T., Dixon, K. S., Chang, L-Y., Senkomago, V., Ennett, S. T. et al. (2015). The effects of *Moms and Teens for Safe Dates*: A dating abuse prevention program for adolescents exposed to domestic violence. *Journal of Youth and Adolescence, 44,* 995–1010.

Foshee, V. A., Reyes, H. L. M., Ennett, S. T., Cance, J. D., Bauman, K. E., & Bowling, J. M. (2012). Assessing the effects of Families for Safe Dates, a family-based teen dating abuse prevention program. *Journal of Adolescent Health, 51,* 349–356.

Foster, B. P., Lonial, S., & Shastri, T. (2011). Mentoring, career plateau tendencies, turnover intentions and implications for narrowing pay and position gaps due to gender—Structural equations modeling. *Journal of Applied Business Research, 27,* 71–84. Retrieved from www.journals.cluteonline.com/index.php/JABR/article/view/6467/6545.

Foster, E. M., & Watkins, S. (2010). The value of reanalysis: TV viewing and attention problems. *Child Development, 81,* 368–375.

Foster, S. E., Jones, D. J., Olson, A. L., Forehand, R., Gaffney, C. A., Zens, M. S., et al. (2007). Family socialization of adolescents' self-reported cigarette use: The role of parents' history of regular smoking and parenting style. *Journal of Pediatric Psychology, 32,* 481–493.

Foster, S. H. (1986). Learning discourse topic management in the preschool years. *Journal of Child Language, 13,* 231–250.

Fouad, N. A. (2007). Work and vocational psychology: Theory, research, and applications. *Annual Review of Psychology, 58,* 543–564. doi:10.1146/annurev.psyc.58.110405.085713

Fouad, N., Ghosh, A., Chang, W-h., Figueiredo, C., & Bachhuber, T. (2016). Career exploration among college students. *Journal of College Student Development, 57,* 460–464. doi:10.1353/csd.2016.0047

Fowler, K. L. (2008). "The wholeness of things": Infusing diversity and social justice into death education. *Omega: Journal of Death and Dying, 57,* 53–91. doi:10.2190/OM.57.1.d

Fox, S. E., Levitt, P., & Nelson, C. A. (2010). How the timing and quality of early experiences influence the development of brain architecture. *Child Development, 81,* 28–40.

Fozard, J. L., & Gordon-Salant, S. (2001). Changes in vision and hearing with aging. In J. E. Birren & K. W. Schaie (Eds.), *Handbook of the psychology of aging* (5th ed., pp. 241–266). San Diego, CA: Academic Press.

Fraley, R. C., & Roberts, B. W. (2005). Patterns of continuity: A dynamic model for conceptualizing the stability of individual differences in psychological constructs across the life course. *Psychological Review, 112,* 60–74. doi:10.1037/0033-295X.112.1.60

Franceschi, K. A. (2005). The experience of the transition to motherhood in women who have suffered maternal loss in adolescence. *Dissertation Abstracts International: Section B: The Sciences and Engineering, 65*(8-B), 4282.

Frank, D. J., Jordano, M. L., Browne, K., & Touron, D. R. (2016). Older adults' use of retrieval strategies in everyday life. *Gerontology, 62,* 624–635. doi:10.1159/000446277

Frank, M. G., Weber, M. D., Watkins, L. R., & Maier, S. F. (2016). Stress-induced neuroinflammatory priming: A liability factor in the etiology of psychiatric disorders. *Neurobiology of Stress, 66,* 82–90. doi:10.1016/j.ynstr.2015.12.004

Frank, N., (2016). Moving beyond anti-LGBT politics: Commentary on "Same-sex and different-sex parent households and child health outcomes: Findings from the National Survey of Children's Health." *Journal of Developmental & Behavioral Pediatrics, 37,* 245–247. doi:10.1097/DBP.0000000000000295

Franken, A., Prinstein, M. J., Dijkstra, J. K., Steglich, C. E. G., Harakeh, Z., & Vollebergh, W. A. M. (2016). Early adolescent friendship selected based on externalizing behavior: the moderating role of pubertal development. *Journal of Abnormal Child Psychology, 44,* 1647–1657.

Franses, P. H. (2016). When did classic composers make their best work? *Creativity Research Journal, 28,* 219–221. doi:10.1080/10400419.2016.1162489

Frase, P., & Gornick, J. C. (2013). The time divide in cross-national perspective: The work week, education and institutions that matter. *Social Forces, 91,* 697–724. doi:10.1093/sf/sos189

Frazier, L. D., Hooker, K., Johnson, P. M., & Kaus, C. R. (2000). Continuity and change in possible selves in later life: A 5-year longitudinal study. *Basic and Applied Social Psychology, 22,* 237–243. doi:10.1207/S15324834BASP2203_10

Frazier, L. D., Johnson, P. M., Gonzalez, G. K., & Kafka, C. L. (2002). Psychosocial influences on possible selves: A comparison of three cohorts of older adults. *International Journal of Behavioral Development, 26,* 308–317. doi:10.1080/01650250143000184

Fredricks, J. A., & Eccles, J. S. (2005). Family socialization, gender, and sport motivation and involvement. *Journal of Sport & Exercise Psychology, 27,* 3–31.

Freitas, A. A., & de Magalhães, J. P. (2011). A review and appraisal of the DNA damage theory of aging. *Mutation Research/Reviews in Mutation Research, 728,* 12–22. doi:10.1016/j.mrrev.2011.06.01

French, S. E., Seidman, E., Allen, L., & Aber, J. (2006). The development of ethnic identity during adolescence. *Developmental Psychology, 42,* 1–10.

Fried, A. (2005). Depression in adolescence. In C. B. Fisher & R. M. Lerner (Eds.), *Encyclopedia of applied developmental science* (Vol. 1, pp. 332–334). Thousand Oaks, CA: Sage.

Friedman, E. M., & Seltzer, J. A. (2010). *Providing for older parents: Is it a family affair?* California Center for Population Research paper #PWP-CCPR-2010-12. Retrieved from papers.ccpr.ucla.edu/papers/PWP-CCPR-2010-012/PWP-CCPR-2010-012.pdf.

Friesen, M. D., Horwood, L. J., Fergusson, D. M., & Woodward, L. J. (2017). Exposure to parental separation in childhood and later parenting quality as an adult: Evidence from a 30-year longitudinal study. *Journal of Child Psychology and Psychiatry, 58*, 30–37. doi:10.1111/jcpp.12610

Frith, C. D., & Frith, U. (2012). Mechanisms of social cognition. *Annual Review of Social Cognition, 63*, 287–313. doi:10.1146/annurevpsych-120710-100449

Froehlich, D. E., Beausaert, S., & Segers, M. (2016). Aging and the motivation to stay employable. *Journal of Managerial Psychology, 31*, 756–770. doi:10.1108/JMP-08-2014-0224

Fruhauf, C. A. (2007). Grandchildren's perceptions of caring for grandparents. *Dissertation Abstracts International. Section A. Humanities and Social Sciences, 68(3-A)*, 1120.

Fujimoto, K., Unger, J. B., & Valente, T. W. (2012). A network method of measuring affiliation-based peer influence: Assessing the influences of teammates' smoking on adolescent smoking. *Child Development 83*, 442–451.

Fuligni, A. J., Kiang, L., Witkow, M. R., & Baldelomar, O. (2008). Stability and change in ethnic labeling among adolescents from Asian and Latin American immigrant families. *Child Development, 79*, 944–956.

Fung, H. H., & Siu, T. M. Y. (2010). Time, culture, and life-cycle changes of social goals. In T. W. Miller (Ed.), *Handbook of stressful transitions across the lifespan* (pp. 441–464). New York: Springer.

Furman, W., & Rose, A. J. (2015). Friendships, romantic relationships, and peer relationships. In R. M. Lerner (Ed.), *Handbook of child psychology and developmental science* (Vol 3., pp. 932–974). Hoboken NJ: Wiley.

Furukawa, E., Tangney, J., & Higashibara, F. (2012). Cross-cultural continuities and discontinuities in shame, guilt, and pride: A study of children residing in Japan, Korea, and the USA. *Self and Identity, 11*, 90–133.

Gaddis, A., & Brooks-Gunn, J. (1985). The male experience of pubertal change. *Journal of Youth and Adolescence, 14*, 61–69.

Gagliardi, A. (2005). Postpartum depression. In C. B. Fisher & R. M. Lerner (Eds.), *Encyclopedia of applied developmental science* (Vol. 2, pp. 867–870). Thousand Oaks, CA: Sage.

Gagne, J. R., Miller, M. M., & Goldsmith, H. H. (2013). Early—but modest—gender differences in focal aspects of childhood temperament. *Personality and Individual Differences, 55*, 95–100.

Galán, C. A., Shaw, D. S., Dishion, T. J., & Wilson, M. N. (2017). Neighborhood deprivation during early childhood and conduct problems in middle childhood: Mediation by aggressive response generation. *Journal of Abnormal Child Psychology,* in press.

Galle, M. E., & McMurray, B. (2014). The development of voicing categories: A quantitative review of over 40 years of infant speech perception research. *Psychonomic Bulletin & Review, 21*, 884–906.

Galván, A. (2013). The teenage brain: Sensitivity to rewards. *Current Directions in Psychological Science, 22*, 88–93.

Gamaldo, A. A., & Allaire, J. C. (2016). Daily fluctuations in everyday cognition: Is it meaningful? *Journal of Aging and Health, 28*, 834–849. doi:10.1177/0898264315611669

Gamba, F. (2015). *The digital age of grieving rituals: Mobility and the hybridization of memory. A project.* Retrieved from http://wp.lancs.ac.uk/futures-of-the-end-of-life/files/2015/11/Fiorenza-Gamba.pdf.

Gamble, W. C., Ramakumar, S., & Diaz, A. (2007). Maternal and paternal similarities and differences in parenting: An examination of Mexican-American parents of young children. *Early Childhood Research Quarterly, 22*, 72–88. doi:10.1016/j. ecresq.2006.11.004

Gandy, S., & DeKosky, S. T. (2013). Toward the treatment and prevention of Alzheimer's disease: Rational strategies and recent progress. *Annual Review of Medicine, 64*, 367–383. doi:10.1146/annurevmed-092611-084441

Ganong, L., & Coleman, M. (2017). *Stepfamily relationships: Development, dynamics, and interventions* (2nd ed.). New York: Springer.

Gans, D. (2007). Normative obligations and parental care in social context. *Dissertation Abstracts International. Section A. Humanities and Social Sciences, 68(5-A)*, 2115.

Garber, J., & Rao, U. (2014). Depression in children and adolescents. In M. Lewis & K. D. Rudolph (Eds.), *Handbook of developmental psychopathology* (pp. 489–520). New York: Springer Science+Business Media.

Garcia, J. R., Reiber, C., Massey, S. G., & Merriwether, A. M. (2013). Sexual hook-up culture. *Monitor on Psychology, 44*, 60–67.

Garciaguirre, J. S., Adolph, K. E., & Shrout, P. E. (2007). Baby carriage: Infants walking with loads. *Child Development, 78*, 664–680.

Gardiner, P. A., Mishra, G. D., & Dobson, A. J. (2016). The effect of socioeconomic status across adulthood on trajectories of frailty in older women. *Journal of the American Medical Directors Association, 17*, 372.e1–372.e3. doi:10.1016/j.jamda.2015.12.090

Gardner, H. (1983). *Frames of mind: The theory of multiple intelligences.* New York: Basic Books.

Gardner, H. (1993). *Multiple intelligences: The theory in practice.* New York: Basic Books.

Gardner, H. (1995). Reflections on multiple intelligences: Myths and messages. *Phi Delta Kappan, 77*, 200–203, 206–209.

Gardner, H. (1999). *Intelligence reframed: Multiple intelligences for the 21st century.* New York: Basic Books.

Gardner, H. (2002). *MI millennium: Multiple intelligences for the new millennium* [Video recording]. Los Angeles, CA: Into the Classroom Media.

Gardner, H. (2011). *Frames of mind: The theory of multiple intelligences.* New York: Basic Books.

Gardner, M., Roth, J., & Brooks-Gunn, J. (2009). Sports participation and juvenile delinquency: The role of the peer context among adolescent boys and girls with varied histories of problem behavior. *Developmental Psychology, 45*, 341–353.

Garrard, E., & Wilkinson, S. (2005). Passive euthanasia. *Journal of Medical Ethics, 31*, 64–68. doi:10.1136/jme.2003.005777

Garrido, M. M., Prigerson, H. G., Bao, Y., & Maciejewski, P. K. (2016). Chemotherapy use in the months before death and estimated costs of care in the last week of life. *Journal of Pain and Symptom Management, 51*, 875–881. doi:10.1016/j.painsymman.2015.12.323

Garthe, R. C., Sullivan, T. N., & McDaniel, M. A. (2017). A meta-analytic review of peer risk factors and dating violence. *Psychology of Violence, 7*, 45–57.

Gartstein, M. A., Bridgett, D. J., Rothbart, M. K., Robertson, C., Iddins, E., Ramsay, K., & Schlect, S. (2010). A latent growth examination of fear development in infancy: Contributions of maternal depression and the risk for toddler anxiety. *Developmental Psychology, 46*, 651–668.

Gartstein, M. A., Knyazev, G. G., & Slobodskaya, H. R. (2005). Cross-cultural differences in the structure of infant temperament: United States of America and Russia. *Infant Behavior and Development, 28*, 54–61.

Garvey, C., & Berninger, G. (1981). Timing and turn taking in children's conversations. *Discourse Processes, 4*, 27–59.

Gass, K., Jenkins, J., & Dunn, J. (2007). Are sibling relationships protective? A longitudinal study. *Journal of Child Psychology and Psychiatry, 48*, 167–175.

Gaudron, J.-P., & Vautier, S. (2007). Analyzing individual differences in vocational, leisure, and family interests: A multitrait-multimethod approach. *Journal of Vocational Behavior, 70*, 561–573. doi:10.1016/j. jvb.2007.01.004

Gavin, L. A., & Furman, W. (1996). Adolescent girls' relationships with mothers and best friends. *Child Development, 67*, 375–386.

Ge, X., Brody, G. H., Conger, R. D., Simons, R. L., & Murphy, V. M. (2002). Contextual amplification of pubertal transition effects on deviant peer affiliation and externalizing behavior among African American children. *Developmental Psychology, 38*, 45–54.

Geary, D. C. (2002). Sexual selection and human life history. In R. V. Kail (Ed.), *Advances in child development and behavior* (Vol. 30, pp. 41–102). San Diego, CA: Academic Press.

Geary, D. C. (2005). *The origin of mind: Evolution of brain, cognition, and general intelligence.* Washington, DC: American Psychological Association.

Geerdts, M. S., Van de Walle, G. A., & LoBue, V. (2015). Daily animal exposure and children's biological concepts. *Journal of Experimental Child Psychology, 130*, 132–146.

Gelman, R., & Meck, E. (1986). The notion of principle: The case of counting. In J. Hiebert (Ed.), *Conceptual and procedural knowledge: The case of mathematics.* Hillsdale, NJ: Erlbaum.

Gelman, S. A. (2003). *The essential child.* New York: Oxford.

Gelman, S. A., Taylor, M. G., & Nguyen, S. P. (2004). Mother-child conversations about gender. *Monographs of the Society for Research in Child Development, 69* (Serial No. 275).

Gentile, D. (2009). Pathological video-game use among youth ages 8 to 18: A national study. *Psychological Science, 20,* 594–602.

George, L. K., Palmore, E., & Cohen, H. J. (2014). The Duke Center for the Study of Aging: One of our earliest roots. *The Gerontologist, 54,* 59–66. doi:10.1093/geront/gnt049

Gerry, D. W., Faux, A. L., & Trainor, L. J. (2010). Effects of Kindermusik training on infants' rhythmic enculturation. *Developmental Science, 13,* 545–551.

Gershoff, E. T. (2013). Spanking and child development: We know enough now to stop hitting our children. *Child Development Perspectives, 7,* 133–137.

Gervais, S. J., Wiener, R. L., Allen, J., Farnum, K. S., & Kimble, K. (2016). Do you see what I see? The consequences of objectification in work settings for experiencers and third-party predictors. *Analyses of Social Issues and Public Policy, 16,* 143–174. doi:10.1111/asap.12118

Ghanim, D. (2015). *The virginity trap in the Middle East.* New York: Springer.

Ghetti, S. (2008). Rejection of false events in childhood: A metamemory account. *Current Directions in Psychological Science, 17,* 16–20.

Ghetti, S., & Lee, J. (2011). Children's episodic memory. *WIREs Cognitive Science, 2,* 365–373.

Ghetti, S., Hembacher, E., & Coughlin, C. A. (2013). Feeling uncertain and acting on it during the preschool years: A metacognitive approach. *Child Development Perspectives, 7,* 160–165.

Ghosh, S., Capistrant, B., & Friedemann-Sánchez, G. (2017). Who will care for the elder caregiver? Outlining theoretical approaches and future research questions. In T. Samanta (Ed.), *Cross-cultural and cross-disciplinary perspectives in social gerontology* (pp. 23–43). New York: Springer.

Gibbs, J. C., Clark, P. M., Joseph, J. A., Green, J. L., Goodrick, T. S., & Makowski, D. (1986). Relations between moral judgment, moral courage, and field independence. *Child Development, 57,* 185–193.

Gibran, K. (1923). *The prophet.* New York: Knopf.

Gibson, E. J., & Walk, R. D. (1960). The "visual cliff." *Scientific American, 202,* 64–71.

Giles, J. W., & Heyman, G. D. (2005). Reconceptualizing children's suggestibility: Bidirectional and temporal properties. *Child Development, 76,* 40–53.

Gilleard, C., & Higgs, P. (2010). Aging without agency: Theorizing the fourth age. *Aging and Mental Health, 14,* 121–128. doi:10.1080/13607860903228762

Gilleard, C., & Higgs, P. (2016). Connecting life span development with the sociology of the life course: A new direction. *Sociology, 50,* 301–315. doi:10.1177/0038038515577906

Gilligan, M., Suitor, J. J., Kim, S., & Pillemer, K. (2013). Differential effects of perceptions of mothers' and fathers' favoritism on sibling tension in adulthood. *Journal of Gerontology: Social Sciences, 68B,* S593–S598. doi:10.1093/geronb/gbt039

Gilliver, M., Carter, L., Macoun, D., Rosen, J., & Williams, W. (2012). Music to whose ears? The effect of social norms on young people's risk perceptions of hearing damage resulting from their music listening behavior. *Noise and Health, 14,* 47–51. Retrieved from www.noiseandhealth.org/article.asp?issn=1463-1741;year=2012;volume=14;issue=57;spage=47;epage=51;aulast=Gilliver.

Gilsanz, V., & Ratib, O. (2012). *Hand bone age* (2nd ed.). New York: Springer.

Giménez-Dasi, M., Pons, F., & Bender, P. K. (2016). Imaginary companions, theory of mind and emotion understanding in young children. *European Early Childhood Education Research Journal, 24,* 186–197.

Giordano, G. (2005). *How testing came to dominate American schools: The history of educational assessment.* New York: Peter Lang.

Giordano, P. C., Copp, J. E., Longmore, M. A., & Manning, W. D. (2016). Anger, control, and intimate partner violence in young adulthood. *Journal of Family Violence, 31,* 1–13. doi:10.1007/s10896-015-9753-3

Giordano, P. C., Kaufman, A., Manning, W. D., & Longmore, M. A. (2015). Teen dating violence: the influence of friendships and school context. *Sociological Focus, 48,* 150–171.

Giordano, P. C., Manning, W. D., Longmore, M. A., & Flanigan, C. M. (2012). Developmental shifts in the character of romantic and sexual relationships from adolescence to young adulthood. In A. Booth, S. L. Brown, N. S. Landale, W. D. Manning, & S. M. McHale (Eds.), *Early adulthood in a family context* (pp. 133–164). New York: Springer.

Gire, J. (2014). How death imitates life: Cultural influences on conceptions of death and dying. *Online Readings in Psychology and Culture, 6*(2). doi:10.9707/2307-0919.1120

Givertz, M., Segrin, C., & Hansal, A. (2009). The association between satisfaction and commitment differs across marital couple types. *Communication Research, 36,* 561–584. doi:10.1177/0093650209333035

Gizer, I. R., & Waldman, I. D. (2012). Double dissociation between lab measures of inattention and impulsivity and the dopamine transporter gene (DAT1) and the dopamine D4 receptor gene (DRD4). *Journal of Abnormal Psychology, 121,* 1011–1023.

Gladwell, M. (2008). *Outliers: The story of success.* New York: Little, Brown.

Glick, G. C., & Rose, A. J. (2011). Prospective associations between friendship adjustment and social strategies: Friendship as a context for building social skills. *Developmental Psychology, 47,* 1117–1132.

Global Initiative to End All Corporal Punishment of Children. (2011). States with full prohibition. Retrieved from www.endcorporalpunishment.org.

Godfrey, D. (2016). End-of-life issues for LGBT elders. In D. A. Harley & P. B. Teaster (Eds.), *Handbook of LGBT elders* (pp. 439–454). New York: Springer.

Golant, S. M. (2012). Out of their residential comfort and mastery zones: Toward a more relevant environmental gerontology. *Journal of Housing for the Elderly, 26,* 26–43. doi:10.1080/027663893.2012.655654

Gold, J. M. (2016). *Stepping in, stepping out: Creating stepfamily rhythm.* Alexandria, VA: American Counseling Association.

Goldbach, J. T., Cardoso, J. D., Cervantes, R. C., & Duan, L. (2015). The relation between stress and alcohol use among Hispanic adolescents. *Psychology of Addictive Behaviors, 29,* 960–968.

Goldberg, A. E. (2009). *Lesbian and gay parents and their children: Research on the family life cycle.* Washington, DC: American Psychological Association.

Goldfield, B. A., & Reznick, J. S. (1990). Early lexical acquisition: Rate, content, and the vocabulary spurt. *Journal of Child Language, 17,* 171–184.

Goldin-Meadow, S., Mylander, C., & Franklin, A. (2007). How children make language out of gesture: Morphological structure in gesture systems developed by American and Chinese deaf children. *Cognitive Psychology, 55,* 87–135.

Goldsmith, H. H., Buss, K. A., & Lemery, K. S. (1997). Toddler and childhood temperament: Expanded content, stronger genetic evidence, new evidence for the importance of environment. *Developmental Psychology, 33,* 891–905.

Goldstein, M. H., & Schwade, J. A. (2008). Social feedback to infants' babbling facilitates rapid phonological learning. *Psychological Science, 19,* 515–523.

Goleman, D. (1995). *Emotional intelligence.* New York: Bantam Books.

Golinkoff, R. M. (1993). When is communication a "meeting of minds"? *Journal of Child Language, 20,* 199–207.

Golinkoff, R. M., Can, D. D., Soderstrom, M., & Hirsh-Pasek, K. (2015). (Baby) talk to me: The social context of infant-directed speech and its effects on early language acquisition. *Current Directions in Psychological Science, 24,* 339–344.

Golkar, A., Johansson, E., Kasahara, M., Osika, W., Perski, A., & Savic, I. (2014). The influence of work-related chronic stress on the regulation of emotion and on functional connectivity in the brain. *PLOS ONE 9*: e104550. doi:10.1371/journal.pone.0104550

Golombok, S. (2013). Families created by reproductive donation: Issues and research. *Child Development Perspectives, 7,* 61–65.

Gonyea, J. G. (2013). Midlife, multigenerational bonds, and caregiving. In R. C. Talley & R. J. V Montgomery (Eds.), *Caregiving across the lifespan* (pp. 105–130). New York: Springer.

Gonza, G., & Burger, A. (in press). Subjective well-being during the 2008 economic crisis: Identification of mediating and moderating factors. *Journal of Happiness Studies.* doi:10.1007/s10902-016-9797-y

Good, T. L., & Brophy, J. E. (2008). *Looking in classrooms.* Boston: Pearson/Allyn & Bacon.

Goodman, S. H., Rouse, M. H., Connell, A. M., Broth, M. R. Hall, C. M., & Heyward, D. (2011). Maternal depression and child psychopathology: A meta-analytic review. *Clinical Child and Family Psychology Review, 14,* 1–27.

Goodnow, J. J. (1992). *Parental belief systems: The psychological consequences for children.* Hillsdale, NJ: Erlbaum.

Goodsell, T. L. (2013). Familification: Family, neighborhood change, and housing policy. *Housing Studies, 28,* 845–868. doi:10.1080/02673037.2013.768334

Goodwyn, S. W., & Acredolo, L. P. (1993). Symbolic gesture versus word: Is there a modality advantage for onset of symbol use? *Child Development, 64,* 688–701.

Gordon, B. N., Baker-Ward, L., & Ornstein, P. A. (2001). Children's testimony: A review of research on memory for past experiences. *Clinical Child & Family Psychology Review, 4,* 157–181.

Gordon, R. A., Chase-Lansdale, P. L., & Brooks-Gunn, J. (2004). Extended households and the life course of young mothers: Understanding the associations using a sample of mothers with premature, low birth weight babies. *Child Development, 75,* 1013–1038.

Gordon, T. A. (2013). Good grief: Exploring the dimensionality of grief experiences and social work support. *Journal of Social Work in End-of-Life and Palliative Care, 9,* 27–42. doi:10.1080/15524256.2012.758607

Gosso, Y., Morais, M. L. S., & Otta, E. (2007). Pretend play of Brazilian children: A window into different cultural worlds. *Journal of Cross-Cultural Psychology, 38,* 539–558.

Gostin, L. O., & Roberts, A. E. (2016). Physician-assisted dying: A turning point? *JAMA, 315*(3), 249–250. doi:10.1001/jama.2015.16586

Gottman, J. M., Katz, L. F., & Hooven, C. (1996). Parental meta-emotion philosophy and the emotional life of families: Theoretical models and preliminary data. *Journal of Family Psychology, 10,* 243–268.

Gottman, J. M., & Levenson, R. W. (2000). The timing of divorce: Predicting when a couple will divorce over a 14-year period. *Journal of Marriage and the Family, 62,* 737–745. doi:10.1111/j.1741-3737.2000.00737.x

Gottman, J. M., & Silver, N. (2015). *The seven principles for making marriage work* (rev. ed.). New York: Harmony Books.

Gough, P. B., & Tunmer, W. E. (1986). Decoding, reading and reading disability. *Remedial and Special Education, 7,* 6–10.

Graber, J. A. (2013). Pubertal timing and the development of psychopathology in adolescence and beyond. *Hormones and Behavior, 64,* 262–269.

Grady, C. (2012). The cognitive neuroscience of ageing. *Nature Reviews Neuroscience, 13,* 491–505. doi:10.1038/nrn3256

Graham-Bermann, S. A., & Brescoll, V. (2000). Gender, power, and violence: Assessing the family stereotypes of the children of batterers. *Journal of Family Psychology, 14,* 600–612.

Graham, E. K., & Lachman, M. E. (2012). Personality and aging. In S. K. Whitbourne &

M. J. Sliwinski (Eds.), *The Wiley-Blackwell handbook of adulthood and aging* (pp. 254–272). Oxford, UK: Wiley-Blackwell.

Graham, S., & Perin, D. (2007). A meta-analysis of writing instruction for adolescent students. *Journal of Educational Psychology, 99,* 445–476.

Graham, S., Berninger, V. W., Abbott, R. D., Abbott, S. P., & Whitaker, D. (1997). Role of mechanics in composing of elementary school students: A new methodological approach. *Journal of Educational Psychology, 89,* 170–182.

Grammer, J. K., Purtell, K. M., Coffman, J. L., & Ornstein, P. A. (2011). Relations between children's metamemory and strategic performance: Time-varying covariates in early elementary school. *Journal of Experimental Child Psychology, 108,* 139–155

Grammer, J., Coffman, J. L., & Ornstein, P. (2013). The effect of teachers' memory-relevant language on children's strategy use and knowledge. *Child Development, 84,* 1989–2002.

Granbom, M., Slaug, B., Löfqvist, C., Oswald, F., & Iwarsson, S. (2016). Community relocation in very old age: Changes in housing accessibility. *American Journal of Occupational Therapy, 70,* 7002270020p1–7002270020p9. doi:10.5014/ajot.2016.016147

Grant, L. M. (2007). Second generation Chinese American women and the midlife transition: A qualitative analysis. *Dissertation Abstracts International. Section B. Sciences and Engineering, 67*(10-B), 6095.

Graves, J. M., Mackelprang, J. L., Barbosa-Leiker, C., Miller, M. E., & Li, A. Y. (2017). Quality of life among working and non-working adolescents. *Quality of Life Research, 26,* 107–120.

Graves, R., & Landis, T. (1990). Asymmetry in mouth opening during different speech tasks. *International Journal of Psychology, 25,* 179–189.

Grawitch, M. J., Barber, L. K., & Justice, L. (2010). Rethinking the work-life interface: It's not about balance, it's about resource allocation. *Health and Well-Being, 2,* 127–159. doi:10.1111/j.1758-0854.2009.01023.x

Gray-Little, B., & Hafdahl, A. R. (2000). Factors influencing racial comparisons of self-esteem: A quantitative review. *Psychological Bulletin, 126,* 26–54.

Greenberg, M. T., & Crnic, K. A. (1988). Longitudinal predictors of developmental status and social interaction in premature and full-term infants at age two. *Child Development, 59,* 554–570.

Greenberg, M. T., Lengua, L. J., Coie, J. D., Pinderhughes, E. E., & the Conduct Problems Prevention Research Group. (1999). Predicting developmental outcomes at school entry using a multiple-risk model: Four American communities. *Developmental Psychology, 35,* 403–417.

Greenberger, E., O'Neil, R., & Nagel, S. K. (1994). Linking workplace and homeplace: Relations between the nature of adults' work and their parenting behaviors. *Developmental Psychology, 30,* 990–1002.

Greene, D., Tschanz, J. T., Smith, K. R., Østbye, T., Corcoran, C., Welsh-Bohmer, K. A., et al. (2014). Impact of offspring death on cognitive health in late life: The Cache County study. *American Journal of Geriatric Psychiatry, 22,* 1307–1315. doi:10.1016/j.jagp.2013.05.002

Greenfield, E. A., & Marks, N. F. (2005). Formal volunteering as a protective factor for older adults' psychological well-being. *Journals of Gerontology: Social Sciences, 59,* S258–S264. doi:10.1093/geronb/59.5.S258

Greenough, W. T., & Black, J. E. (1992). Induction of brain structure by experience: Substrates for cognitive development. In M. Gunnar & C. Nelson (Eds.), *Minnesota symposia on child psychology: Vol. 24: Developmental behavioral neuroscience* (pp. 155–200). Hillsdale, NJ: Erlbaum.

Greer, D. M., Want, H. H., Robinson, J. D., Varelas, P. N., Henderson, G. V., & Wijdicks, E. F. M. (2016). Variability of brain death policies in the United States. *JAMA Neurology, 73,* 213–218. doi:10.1001/jamaneurol.2015.3943

Gregory, A. M., Rijsdijk, F., Lau, J. Y. F., Napolitano, M., McGuffin, P., & Eley, T. C. (2007). Genetic and environmental influences on interpersonal cognitions and associations with depressive symptoms in 8-year-old twins. *Journal of Abnormal Psychology, 116,* 762–775.

Gretebeck, R. J., Ferraro, K. F., Black, D. R., Holland, K., & Gretebeck, K. A. (2012). Longitudinal change in physical activity and disability in adults. *American Journal of Health Behavior, 36,* 385–394. doi:10.5993/AJHB.36.3.9

Greving, K. A. (2007). Examining parents' marital satisfaction trajectories: Relations with children's temperament and family demographics. *Dissertation Abstracts International. Section A. Humanities and Social Sciences, 68*(4-A), 1676.

Griffin, M. L., Hogan, N. L., Lambert, E. G., Tucker-Gail, K. A., & Baker, D. N. (2010). Job involvement, job stress, job satisfaction, and organizational commitment and the burnout of correctional staff. *Criminal Justice and Behavior, 37,* 239–255. doi:10.1177/0093854809351682

Grigorenko, E. L., Jarvin, L., & Sternberg, R. J. (2002). School-based tests of the triarchic theory of intelligence: Three settings, three samples, three syllabi. *Contemporary Educational Psychology, 27,* 167–208.

Gripshover, S. J., & Markman, E. M. (2013). Teaching young children a theory of nutrition: Conceptual change and the potential for increased vegetable consumption. *Psychological Science, 24,* 1541–1553.

Grizenko, N., Fortier, M., Gaudreau-Simard, M., Jolicoeur, C., & Joober, R. (2015). The effect of maternal stress during pregnancy on IQ and ADHD symptomatology. *Journal of the Canadian Academy of Child and Adolescent Psychiatry, 24,* 92–99.

Groh, A. M., Pasco Fearon, R. M., van Ijzendoorn, M. H., Bakermans-Kranenburg, M. J., & Roisman, G. I. (2017). Attachment in the early life course: Meta-analytic evidence for its role in socioemotional development. *Child Development Perspectives, 11,* 70–76.

Grosse, G., Scott-Phillips, T. C., & Tomasello, M. (2013). Three-year-olds hide their communicative intentions in appropriate contexts. *Developmental Psychology, 49,* 2095–2101.

Grossman, I., Karasawa, M., Izumi, S., Na, J., Varnum, M. E. W., Kitayama, S., et al. (2012). Aging and wisdom: Culture matters. *Psychological Science, 23,* 1059–1066. doi:10.1177/0956797612446025

Grotevant, H. D., & McDermott, J. M. (2014). Adoption: Biological and social processes linked to adaptation. *Annual Review of Psychology, 65,* 235–265.

Grotevant, H. D., McRoy, R. G., Wrobel, G. M., & Ayes-Lopez, S. (2013). Contact between adoptive and birth families: Perspectives from the Minnesota/Texas Adoption Research Project. *Child Development Perspectives, 7,* 193–198.

Gruenewald, T. L., Liao, D. H., & Seeman, T. E. (2012). Contributing to others, contributing to oneself: Perceptions of generativity and health in later life. *Journal of Gerontology: Psychological Sciences, 67,* 660–665. doi:10.1093/geronb/gbs034

Grühn, D., Lumley, M. A., Diehl, M., Labouvie-Vief, G. (2013). Time-based indicators of emotional complexity: Interrelations and correlates. *Emotion, 13,* 226–237. doi:10.1037/a0030363

Grusec, J. E. (2011). Socialization processes in the family: Social and emotional development. *Annual Review of Psychology, 62,* 243–269.

Grysman, A., & Hudson, J. A. (2013). Gender differences in autobiographical memory: Developmental and methodological considerations. *Developmental Review, 33,* 239–272.

Gu, X., Liu, X., Van Dam, N. T., Hof, P. R., & Fan, J. (2013). Cognition-emotion integration in the anterior insular cortex. *Cerebral Cortex, 23,* 20–27. doi:10.1093/cercor/bhr367

Gubernskaya, Z. (2010). Changing attitudes toward marriage and children in six countries. *Sociological Perspectives, 53,* 179–200. doi:10.1525/sop.2010.53.2.179

Gudmundson, J. A., & Leerkes, E. M. (2012). Links between mothers' coping styles, toddler reactivity, and sensitivity to toddlers' negative emotions. *Infant Behavior and Development, 35,* 158–166.

Gunderson, E. A., & Levine, S. C. (2011). Some types of parent number talk count more than others: Relations between parents' input and children's cardinal-number knowledge. *Developmental Science, 14,* 1021–1032.

Gunes, S., Hekim, G. N. T., Arslan, M. A., & Asci, R. (2016). Effects of aging on the male reproductive system. *Journal of Assisted Reproduction and Genetics, 33,* 441–454. doi:10.1007/s10815-016-0663-y

Güngör, D., & Bornstein, M. H. (2010). Culture-general and -specific associations of attachment avoidance and anxiety with perceived parental warmth and psychological control among Turk and Belgian adolescents. *Journal of Adolescence, 33,* 593–602.

Gunnell, D., & Chang, S.-S. (2016). Economic recession, unemployment, and suicide. In R. C. O'Connor & J. Pirkis (Eds.), *The international handbook of suicide prevention* (2nd ed., pp. 284–300). Malden, MA: Wiley.

Gupta, S., Tracey, T. J. G., & Gore, P. A. (2008). Structural examination of RIASEC scales in high school students: Variation across ethnicity and method. *Journal of Vocational Behavior, 72,* 1–13.

Gurucharri, C., & Selman, R. L. (1982). The development of interpersonal understanding during childhood, preadolescence, and adolescence: A longitudinal follow-up study. *Child Development, 53,* 924–927.

Gutiérrez, I. T., Miller, P. J., Rosengren, K. S., & Schein, S. S. (2014). Affective dimensions of death: Children's books, questions, and understandings. *Monographs of the Society for Research in Child Development, 79,* 43–61. doi:10.1111/mono.12078

Guttmacher Institute. (2013). *Facts on American teens' sexual and reproductive health.* New York: Author.

Haase, C. M., Heckhausen, J., & Wrosch, C. (2013). Developmental regulation across the life span: Toward a new synthesis. *Developmental Psychology, 49,* 964–972. doi:10.1037/a0029231

Hagestad, G. O., & Dannefer, D. (2001). Concepts and theories of aging: Beyond microfication in social science approaches. In R. H. Binstock & L. K. George (Eds.), *Handbook of aging and the social sciences* (5th ed., pp. 3–21). San Diego, CA: Academic Press.

Hagestad, G. O., & Neugarten, B. L. (1985). Age and the life course. In R. H. Binstock & E. Shanas (Eds.), *Handbook of aging and the social sciences* (2nd ed., pp. 35–61). New York: Van Nostrand Reinhold.

Haier, R. J., Schroeder, D. H., Tang, C., Head, K., & Colom, R. (2010). Gray matter correlates of cognitive ability tests used for vocational guidance. *BMC Research Notes, 3.* Retrieved from www.biomedcentral.com/1756-0500/3/206.

Haight, B. K., & Haight, B. S. (2007). *The handbook of structured life review.* Baltimore, MD: Health Professions Press.

Haight, B. K., & Haight, B. S. (2013). Confidentiality in the structured life review. *International Journal of Reminiscence and Life Review, 1,* 36–38. Retrieved from www.ijrlr.org/ojs/index.php/IJRLR/article /view/21/6.

Hains, C.-A. M., & Hulbert-Williams, N. J. (2013). Attitudes toward euthanasia and physician-assisted suicide: A study of the multivariate effects of healthcare training, patient characteristics, religion and locus of control. *Journal of Medical Ethics, 39,* 713–716. doi:10.1136/medethics-2012-100729

Haist, F., Adamo, M., Han, J., Lee, K., & Stiles, J. (2013). The functional architecture for face-processing expertise: FMRI evidence of the developmental trajectory of the core and extended face systems. *Neuropsychologia, 51,* 2893–2908.

Håkansson, P., & Witmer, H. (2015). Social media and trust: A systematic literature review. *Journal of Business and Economics, 6,* 517–524. doi:10.15341/jbe(2155-7950)/03.06.2015/010

Hakeem, G. F., Oddy, L., Holcroft, C. A., & Abenhaim, H. A. (2015). Incidence and determinants of sudden infant death syndrome: a population-based study on 37 million births. *World Journal of Pediatrics, 11,* 41–47.

Halberda J., & Feigenson L. (2008). Developmental change in the acuity of the "Number Sense": The approximate number system in 3-, 4-, 5-, and 6-year-olds and adults. *Developmental Psychology, 44,* 1457–1465.

Hales, S. (2016). Attachment and the end of life experience. In J. Hunter & R. Maunder (Eds.), *Improving patient treatment with attachment theory* (pp. 93–103). New York: Springer. doi:10.1007/978-3-319-233000-0_7

Haley, W. E. (2013). Family caregiving at the end-of-life: Current status and future directions. In R. C. Talley & R. J. V Montgomery (Eds.), *Caregiving across the lifespan* (pp. 157–175). New York: Springer.

Halgunseth, L. C., Ispa, J. M., & Rudy, D. (2006). Parental control in Latino families: An integrated review of the literature. *Child Development, 77,* 1282–1297.

Halim, M. D. (2016). Princesses and superheroes: Social-cognitive influences on early gender rigidity. *Child Development Perspectives, 10,* 155–160.

Halim, M. L., Ruble, D., Tamis-Lemonda, C., & Shrout, P. E. (2013). Rigidity in gender-typed behaviors in early childhood. *Child Development, 84,* 1269–1284.

Hall, J. A. (2016). Same-sex friendships. In C. R. Berger, M. E. Roloff, S. R. Wilson, J. P. Dillard, J. Caughlin, & D. Solomon (Eds.), *The international encyclopedia of interpersonal communication.* New York: Wiley. doi:10.1002/9781118540190.wbeic138.

Hall, S. S. (2006). Marital meaning: Exploring young adult's belief systems about marriage. *Journal of Family Issues, 27,* 1437–1458. doi:10.1177/0192513X06290036

Hall, S. S., & Willoughby, B. J. (2016). Relative work and family role centralities: Beliefs and behaviors related to the transition to adulthood. *Journal of Family and Economic Issues, 37,* 75–88. doi:10.1007/s10834-014-9436-x

Hallers-Haalboom, E. T., Groeneveld, M. G., van Berkel, S. R., Endendijk, J. J., van der Pol, L. D., Bakermans-Kranenburg, M. J., et al. (2016). Wait until your mother gets home! Mothers' and fathers' discipline strategies. *Social Development, 25,* 82–98.

Hallford, D., & Mellor, D. (2013). Reminiscence-based therapies for depression: Should they be used only with older adults? *Clinical Psychology: Science and Practice, 20,* 452–468. doi:10.1111/cpsp.12043

Halliwell, D., & Franken, N. (2016). "He was supposed to be with me for the rest of my life": Meaning-making in bereaved siblings' online stories. *Journal of Family Communication, 16*, 337–354. doi:10.1080/15267431.2016.1194841

Halpern, D. F. (2012). *Sex differences in cognitive abilities* (4th ed.). New York: Psychology Press.

Halpern, L. F., MacLean, W. E., & Baumeister, A. A. (1995). Infant sleep-wake characteristics: Relation to neurological status and the prediction of developmental outcome. *Developmental Review, 15*, 255–291.

Hambrick, D. Z., Macnamara, B. N., Campitelli, G., Ullén, F., & Mosing, M. A. (2016). Chapter One—Beyond born versus made: A new look at expertise. *Psychology of Learning and Motivation, 64*, 1–55. doi:10.1016/bs.plm.2015.09.001

Hamilton, B. E., Martin, J. A., & Ventura, S. J. (2010). Births: Preliminary data for 2008. *National Vital Statistics Reports*, Vol. 58. Hyattsville, MD: National Center for Health Statistics.

Hamilton, R. K. B., Hiatt Racer, K., & Newman, J. P. (2015). Impaired integration in psychopathology: A unified theory of psychopathic dysfunction. *Psychological Review, 122*, 770–791. doi:10.1037/a0039703

Hamm, J. V. (2000). Do birds of a feather flock together? The variable bases for African American, Asian American, and European American adolescents' selection of similar friends. *Developmental Psychology, 36*, 209–219.

Hammar, M., & Östgren, C. J. (2013). Healthy aging and age-adjusted nutrition and physical fitness. *Best Practices and Research Clinical Obstetrics and Gynaecology, 27*, 741–752. doi:10.1016/j.bpobgyn.2013.01.004

Hammer, L. B., Neal, M. B., Newsom, J. T., Brockwood, K.-J., & Colton, C. L. (2005). A longitudinal study of the effects of dual-earner couples' utilization of family-friendly workplace supports on work and family outcomes. *Journal of Applied Psychology, 90*, 799–810.

Hance, V. M. (2000). An existential perspective describing undergraduate students' ideas about meaning in work: A q-method study. *Dissertation Abstracts International. Section A. Humanities and Social Sciences, 61(3-A)*, 878.

Hannon, E. E., Soley, G., & Levine, R. S. (2011). Constraints on infants' musical rhythm perception: effects of interval ratio complexity and enculturation. *Developmental Science, 14*, 865–872.

Hansen, S. R. (2006). Courtship duration as a correlate of marital satisfaction and stability. *Dissertation Abstracts International: Section B: The Sciences and Engineering, 67(4-B)*, 2279.

Hansson, R. O., & Stroebe, M. S. (2007). *Bereavement in late life: Coping, adaptation, and developmental influences*. Washington, DC: American Psychological Association.

Harden, K. P. (2014). Genetic influences on adolescent sexual behavior: Why genes matter for environmentally oriented researchers. *Psychological Bulletin, 140*, 434–465.

Hareven, T. K. (1995). Introduction: Aging and generational relations over the life course. In T. K. Hareven (Ed.), *Aging and generational relations over the life course: A historical and cross-cultural perspective* (pp. 1–12). Berlin, Germany: de Gruyter.

Hareven, T. K. (2001). Historical perspectives on aging and family relations. In R. H. Binstock & L. K. George (Eds.), *Handbook of aging and the social sciences* (5th ed., pp. 141–159). San Diego, CA: Academic Press.

Harley, D. A., Gassaway, L., & Dunkley, L. (2016). Isolation, socialization, recreation, and inclusion of LGBT elders. In D. A. Harley & P. B. Teaster (Eds.), *Handbook of LGBT elders* (pp. 563–581). New York: Springer.

Harris, D. L. (2016). Social expectations of the bereaved. In D. L. Harris & T. C. Bordere (Eds.), *Handbook of social justice in loss and grief: Exploring diversity, equity, and inclusion* (pp. 165–174). New York: Routledge.

Harris, K. R., & Graham, S. (2017). Self-regulated strategy development: Theoretical bases, critical instructional elements, and future research. In R. Fidalgo, K. R. Harris, & M. Braaksma (Eds.), *Design principles for teaching effective writing: Theoretical and empirical grounded principles* (in press). Hershey, PA: Brill.

Harris, M. A., Wetzel, E., Robins, R. W., Donnellan, M. B., & Trzesniewski, K. H. (2017). The development of global and domain self-esteem from ages 10 to 16 for Mexican-origin youth. *International Journal of Behavioral Development*.

Harrison, K., Bost, K. K., McBride, B. A., Donovan, S. M. Grigsby-Toussaint, D. S., Kim, J., et al., (2011). Toward a developmental conceptualization of contributors to overweight and obesity in childhood: The Six-Cs model. *Child Development Perspectives, 5*, 50–58.

Harrist, A. W., Zaia, A. F., Bates, J. E., Dodge, K. A., & Pettit, G. S. (1997). Subtypes of social withdrawal in early childhood: Sociometric status and social-cognitive differences across four years. *Child Development, 68*, 278–294.

Harrist, A., Topham, G., Hubbs-Tait, L., Shriver, L., & Swindle, T. (2017). Psychosocial factors in children's obesity: Examples from an innovative line of inquiry. *Child Development Perspectives, 11*.

Hart, W., Adams, J., & Tullett, A. (2016). "It's complicated"—Sex differences in perceptions of cross-sex friendships. *Journal of Social Psychology, 156*, 190–201. doi:10.1080/00224545.2015.1076762

Harter, S. (1994). Developmental changes in self-understanding across the 5 to 7 shift. In A. Sameroff & M. M. Haith (Eds.), *Reason and responsibility: The passage through childhood*. Chicago: University of Chicago Press.

Harter, S. (2006). The self. In W. Damon & R. M. Lerner (Eds.), *Handbook of child psychology* (6th ed., Vol. 3). New York: Wiley.

Harter, S. (2012). *The construction of the self: Developmental and sociocultural foundations* (2nd ed.). New York: Guilford.

Harter, S., Waters, P., & Whitesell, N. R. (1998). Relational self-worth: Differences in perceived worth as a person across interpersonal contexts among adolescents. *Child Development, 69*, 756–766.

Harter, S., Whitesell, N. R., & Kowalski, P. S. (1992). Individual differences in the effects of educational transitions on young adolescents' perceptions of competence and motivational orientation. *American Educational Research Journal, 29*, 777–807.

Hartung, P. J., & Santilli, S. (2017). The theory and practice of career construction. In M. McMahon (Ed.), *Career counselling: Constructivist approaches* (2nd ed., pp. 174–184). Abingdon, UK: Routledge.

Hartup, W. W. (1983). Peer relations. In P. H. Mussen (Ed.), *Handbook of child psychology* (Vol. 4). New York: Wiley.

Hartup, W. W. (1992). Friendships and their developmental significance. In H. McGurk (Ed.), *Contemporary issues in childhood social development*. (pp. 175–205). London: Routledge.

Hartup, W. W., & Stevens, N. (1999). Friendships and adaptation across the life span. *Current Directions in Psychological Science, 8*, 76–79.

Harvard School of Public Health. (2010). *The nutrition source: Alcohol: Balancing risks and benefits*. Retrieved from www.hsph.harvard.edu/nutritionsource/alcohol-full-story.

Harvey, I. S., Johnson, L., & Heath, C. (2013). Womanism, spirituality, and self-health management behaviors of African American older women. *Women, Gender, and Families of Color, 1*, 59–84. doi:10.1353/wgf.2013.0002

Haselton, M. G., & Galperin, A. (2013). Error management in relationships. In J. A. Simpson & L. Campbell (Eds.), *The Oxford handbook of close relationships* (pp. 234–254). New York: Oxford University Press.

Hashimoto, K. (2013). Understanding depression: Linking brain-derived neurotrophic factor, transglutaminase 2 and serotonin. *Expert Review of Neurotherapeutics, 13*, 5–7.

Hatania, R., & Smith, L. B. (2010). Selective attention and attention switching: Toward a unified developmental approach. *Developmental Science, 13*, 622–635.

Hawley, P. H. (2016). Eight myths of child social development: An evolutionary approach to power, aggression, and social competence. In D. C. Geary & D. B. Berch (Eds.), *Evolutionary perspectives on child development and education* (pp. 145–166). Cham, Switzerland: Springer International Publishing.

Haworth, J., & Lewis, S. (2005). Work, leisure and well-being. *British Journal of Guidance & Counselling, 33*, 67–78. doi:10.1080/03069880412 331335902

Hay, D. F. (2017). The early development of human aggression. *Child Development Perspectives, 11*, 102–106.

Hayden, E. C. (2016). Should you edit your children's genes? *Nature, 530*, 402–405.

Hayflick, L. (1996). *How and why we age* (2nd ed.). New York: Ballantine.

Hayslip Jr, B., & Blumenthal, H. (2016). Grandparenthood: A developmental perspective. In M. H. Meyer & E. A. Daniele (Eds.), *Gerontology: Changes, challenges, and solutions* (Vol.1, pp. 271–298). Santa Barbara, CA: Praeger.

Hayslip, B., Jr., Caballero, D., Ward-Pinson, M., & Riddle, R. R. (2013). Sensitizing young adults to their biases about middle-aged and older persons: A pedagogical approach. *Educational Gerontology, 39,* 37–44. doi:10.1080/03601277.2012.660865

Hayward, R. D., Krause, N., Ironson, G., Hill, P. C., & Emmons, R. (2016). Health and well-being among the non-religious: Atheists, agnostics, and no preference compared with religious group members. *Journal of Religion and Health, 55,* 1024–1037. doi:10.1007/s10943-015-0179-2

Hazell, P. L. (2009). Eight-year follow-up of the MTA sample. *Journal of the American Academy of Child & Adolescent Psychiatry, 48,* 461–462.

Health.gov. (2015). *Dietary guidelines for Americans 2015–2020* (8th ed.). Retrieved from health.gov/dietaryguidelines/2015/resources/2015-2020_Dietary_Guidelines.pdf.

Heathcote, D. (2016). Working memory and performance limitations. In D. Groome & M. W. Eysenck (Eds.), *An introduction to applied cognitive psychology* (2nd ed., pp. 99–123). New York: Routledge.

Hechtman, L., Swanson, J. M., Sibley, M. H., Stehli, A., Owens, E. B., Mitchell, J. T. et al. (2016). Functional adult outcome 16 years after childhood diagnosis of attention-deficit/hyperactivity disorder: MTA results. *Journal of the American Academy of Child and Adolescent Psychiatry, 55,* 945–952.

Heck, A., Hock, A., White, H., Jubran, R., & Bhatt, R. S. (2016). The development of attention to dynamic facial emotions. *Journal of Experimental Child Psychology, 147,* 100–110.

Heckhausen, J., Wrosch, C., & Schulz, R. (2010). A motivational theory of life-span development. *Psychological Review, 117,* 32–60. doi:10.1037/a0017668

Hegewisch, A., & Hartman, H. (2014). *Occupational segregation and the gender wage gap: A job half done.* Retrieved from www.dol.gov/wb/resources/occupational_segregation_and_wage_gap.pdf.

Heilman, K. M. (2016). Possible brain mechanisms of creativity. *Archives of Clinical Neuropsychology, 31,* 285–296. doi:10.1093/arclin/acw009

Heine, S. J., & Buchtel, E. E. (2009). Personality: The universal and the culturally specific. *Annual Review of Psychology, 60,* 369–394. doi:10.1146/annurev.psych.60.110707.163655.

Heinzel, S., Lorenz, R. C., Brockhaus, W.-R., Wüstenberg, T., Kathmann, N., Heinz, A., et al. (2014). Working memory load-dependent brain response predicts behavioral training gains in older adults. *Journal of Neuroscience, 34,* 1224–1233. doi:10.1523/JENUROSCI.2463-13.2014

Heller, S. B. (2014). Summer jobs reduce violence among disadvantaged youth. *Science, 346,* 1219–1223.

Helpguide.org. (2016). *Adult day care services.* Retrieved from www.helpguide.org/articles/caregiving/adult-day-care-services.htm.

Helson, R., Kwan, V. S. Y., John, O. P., & Jones, C. (2002). The growing evidence for personality change in adulthood: Findings from research with personality inventories. *Journal of Research in Personality, 36,* 287–306. doi:10.1016/S0092-6566(02)00010-7

Hemer, S. R. (2010). Grief as social experience: Death and bereavement in Lahir, Papua, New Guinea. *TAJA: The Australian Journal of Anthropology, 21,* 281–297. doi:10.1111/j.1757-6547.2010.00097.x

Henderson, H. A., & Wachs, T. D. (2007). Temperament theory and the study of cognition-emotion interactions across development. *Developmental Review, 27,* 396–427.

Henderson, N. D. (2010). Predicting long-term firefighter performance from cognitive and physical ability measures. *Personnel Psychology, 63,* 999–1039.

Henderson, S., & Gilding, M. (2004). "I've never clicked this much with anyone in my life": Trust and hyperpersonal communication in online friendships. *New Media & Society, 6,* 487–506. doi:10.1177/146144804044331

Hendriks, G.-J., Keijsers, G. P. J., Kampman, M., Hoogduin, C. A. L., & Voshaar, R. C. O. (2012). Predictors of outcome of pharmacological and psychological treatment of late-life panic disorder with agoraphobia. *International Journal of Geriatric Psychiatry, 27,* 146–150. doi:10.1002/gps.2700

Hendry, M., Pasterfield, D., Lewis, R., Carter, B., Hodgson, D., & Wilkinson, C. (2013). Why do we want the right to die? A systematic review of the international literature on the views of patients, careers and the public on assisted dying. *Palliative Medicine, 27,* 13–26. doi:10.1177/0269216312463623

Henrie, J. A. (2010). *Religiousness, future time perspective, and death anxiety among adults.* Dissertation submitted to West Virginia University.

Henry J. Kaiser Family Foundation. (2016). *10 FAQs: Medicare's role in end-of-life care.* Retrieved from kff.org/medicare/fact-sheet/10-faqs-medicares-role-in-end-of-life-care/.

Heo, J., Lee, Y., McCormick, B. P., & Pedersen, P. M. (2010). Daily experience of serious leisure, flow and subjective well-being of older adults. *Leisure Studies, 29,* 207–225. doi:10.1080/02614360903434092

Hepper, P. (2015). Behavior during the prenatal period: Adaptive for development and survival. *Child Development Perspectives, 9,* 38–43.

Heppner, R. S. (2013). *The lost leaders: How corporate America loses women leaders.* New York: Palgrave Macmillan.

Herlitz, A., & Lovén, J. (2013). Sex differences and the own-gender bias in face recognition: A meta-analytic review. *Visual Cognition, 21,* 1306–1336.

Herman, M. (2004). Forced to choose: Some determinants of racial identification in multiracial adolescents. *Child Development, 75,* 730–748.

Heron, M. (2016). *Deaths: Leading causes for 2014.* National Vital Statistics Reports, 65, no 5. Hyattsville, MD: National Center for Health Statistics. Retrieved from www.cdc.gov/nchs/data/nvsr/nvsr65/nvsr65_05.pdf.

Herrenbrueck, L., Xia, X., Eastwick, P., Finkel, E., & Hui, C. M. (2016). *Smart-dating in speed-dating: How a simple search model can explain matching decisions.* Retrieved from www.sfu.ca/econ-research/RePEc/sfu/sfudps/dp16-02.pdf.

Herrnstein, R. J., & Murray, C. (1994). *The bell curve: Intelligence and class structure in American life.* New York: Free Press.

Hershey, D. A., & Henkens, K. (2014). Impact of different types of retirement transitions on perceived satisfaction with life. *The Gerontologist, 54,* 232–244. doi:10/1093/geront/gnt006

Hertzog, C., Kramer, A. F., Wilson, R. S., & Lindenberger, U. (2009). Fit body, fit mind? *Scientific American Mind, 20,* 24–31. doi:10.1038/scientific-americanmind0709-24

Hespos, S. J., & van Marle, K. (2012). Physics for infants: Characterizing the origins of knowledge about objects, substances, and number. *WIREs Cognitive Science, 3,* 19–27.

Hess, T. M., & Pullen, S. M. (1994). Adult age differences in impression change processes. *Psychology and Aging, 9,* 237–250. doi:10.1037/0882-7974.9.2.237

Heyman, G. D. (2009). Children's reasoning about traits. In P. Bauer (Ed.), *Advances in child development and behavior* (Vol. 37, pp. 105–143). London: Elsevier.

Heyman, G. D., & Legare, C. H. (2004). Children's beliefs about gender differences in the academic and social domains. *Sex Roles, 50,* 227–239.

Hiatt, K., Stelle, C., Mulsow, M., & Scott, J. P. (2007). The importance of perspective: Evaluation of hospice care from multiple stakeholders. *American Journal of Hospice & Palliative Medicine, 24,* 376–382. doi:10.1177/1049909107300760

Hill, J. L., Brooks-Gunn, J., & Waldfogel, J. (2003). Sustained effects of high participation in an early intervention for low-birth-weight premature infants. *Developmental Psychology, 39,* 730–744.

Hill, P. L., Duggan, P. M., & Lapsley, D. K. (2012). Subjective invulnerability, risk behavior, and adjustment in early adolescence. *Journal of Early Adolescence, 32,* 489–501.

Hill, R. T., Thomas, C., English, L., & Callaway, K. (2016). The importance and impact of child care on a woman's transition to motherhood. In C. Spitzmueller & R. A. Matthews (Eds.), *Research perspectives on work and the transition to motherhood* (pp. 241–265). New York: Springer.

Hills, L. (2013). Why legacy matters more in midlife. In *Lasting female educational leadership: Leadership legacies of women leaders* (pp. 15–26). New York: Springer.

Hills, W. E. (2010). Grandparenting roles in the evolving American family. In D. Wiseman (Ed.), *The American family: Understanding its changing dynamics and place in society* (pp. 65–78.) Springfield, IL: Charles C. Thomas.

Hillsdon, M., Brunner, E., Guralnik, J., & Marmot, M. (2005). Prospective study of physical activity and physical function in early old age.

American Journal of Preventive Medicine, 28, 245–250. doi:10.1016/j.amepre.2004.12.008

Hines, M. (2015). Gendered development. In R. M. Lerner (Ed.), *Handbook of child psychology and developmental science* (7th ed., Vol. 3, 20:1–486). Hoboken, NJ: Wiley.

Hinton, A., & Chirgwin, S. (2010). Nursing education: Reducing reality shock for graduate indigenous nurses—It's all about time. *Australian Journal of Advanced Nursing, 28,* 60–66. Retrieved from search.informit.com.au/documentSummary;dn=053211061337305;res=IELHEA.

Hipp, L., Morrissey, T. W., & Warner, M. E. (in press). Who participates and who benefits from employer-provided child-care assistance? *Journal of Marriage and Family.* doi:10.1111/momf.12359

Hipwell, A. E., Keenan, K., Loeber, R., & Battista, D. (2010). Early predictors of sexually intimate behaviors in an urban sample of young girls. *Developmental Psychology, 46,* 366–378.

Hirsh-Pasek, K., & Golinkoff, R. M. (2008). King Solomon's take on word learning: An integrative account from the radical middle. In R. V. Kail (Ed.), *Advances in child development and behavior* (Vol. 36, pp. 1–29). San Diego, CA: Elsevier.

Hodnett, E. D., Gates, S., Hofmeyr, G.J., & Sakala, C. (2012). Continuous support for women during childbirth. *Cochrane Database of Systematic Reviews,* Issue 10.

Hoeppner, B. B., Paskausky, A. L., Jackson, K. M., & Barnett, N. P. (2013). Sex differences in college student adherence to NIAAA drinking guidelines. *Alcoholism: Clinical and Experimental Research, 37,* 1779–1786. doi:10.1111/acer.12159

Hofer, J., Busch, H., Chasiotis, A., Kärtner, J., & Campos, D. (2008). Concern for generativity and its relation to implicit pro-social power motivation, generative goals, and satisfaction with life: A cross-cultural investigation. *Journal of Personality, 76,* 1–30. doi:10.1111/j.1467-6494.2007.00478.x

Hofer, M. A. (2006). Psychobiological roots of early attachment. *Current Directions in Psychological Science, 15,* 84–88.

Hoff-Ginsberg, E. (1997). *Language development.* Pacific Grove, CA: Brooks/Cole.

Hoff, E. L. (2014). *Language development* (5th ed.). Belmont, CA: Wadsworth, Cengage Learning.

Hoff, E., & Naigles, L. (2002). How children use input to acquire a lexicon. *Child Development, 73,* 418–433.

Hoff, E., Core, C., Rumiche, R., Señor, M., & Parra, M. (2012). Dual language exposure and early bilingual development. *Journal of Child Language, 39,* 1–27.

Hoffman, E., Kaneshiro, S., & Compton, W. C. (2012). Peak-experiences among Americans in midlife. *Journal of Humanistic Psychology, 52,* 479–503. doi:10.1177/0022167811433851

Hoffman, M. L. (1988). Moral development. In M. H. Bornstein and M. E. Lamb (Eds.), *Developmental psychology: An advanced*

textbook (2nd ed., pp. 497–538). Hillsdale, NJ: Erlbaum.

Hoffman, M. L. (1994). Discipline and internalization. *Developmental Psychology, 30,* 26–28.

Hofhuis, J., van der Rijt, P. G. A., & Vlug, M. (2016). Diversity climate enhances work outcomes through trust and openness in workgroup communication. *SpringerPlus, 5,* 714. doi:s40064-016-2499-4

Hogan, A. M., de Haan, M., Datta, A., & Kirkham, F. J. (2006). Hypoxia: An acute, intermittent and chronic challenge to cognitive development. *Developmental Science, 9,* 335–337.

Hogge, W. A. (1990). Teratology. In I. R. Merkatz & J. E. Thompson (Eds.), *New perspectives on prenatal care.* New York: Elsevier.

Holden, G. W., & Miller, P. C. (1999). Enduring and different: A meta-analysis of the similarity in parents' child rearing. *Psychological Bulletin, 125,* 223–254.

Holland, J. L. (1985). *Making vocational choices: A theory of vocational personalities and work environments* (2nd ed.). Englewood Cliffs, NJ: Prentice Hall.

Holland, J. L. (1987). Current status of Holland's theory of careers: Another perspective. *Career Development Quarterly, 36,* 24–30.

Holland, J. L. (1996). Exploring careers with a typology: What we have learned and some new directions. *American Psychologist, 51,* 397–406.

Holland, J. M. (1997). *Making vocational choices: A theory of vocational personalities and work environments* (3rd ed.). Baltimore, MD: Johns Hopkins University Press.

Holland, J. M., & Neimeyer, R. A. (2010). An examination of stage theory of grief among individuals bereaved by natural and violent causes: A meaning-oriented contribution. *OMEGA: Journal of Death and Dying, 61,* 103–120. doi:10.2190/OM.61.2.b

Holland, J. M., Thompson, K. L., Rozalski, V., & Lichtenthal, W. G. (2014). Bereavement-related regret trajectories among widowed older adults. *Journals of Gerontology: Psychological Sciences and Social Sciences, 69B,* 40–47. doi:10.1093/geronb/gbt050

Holland, K. J., & Cortina, L. M. (2016). Sexual harassment: Undermining the wellbeing of working women. In M. L. Connerley & J. Wu (Eds.), *Handbook on well-being of working women* (pp. 83–101). New York: Springer.

Hollich, G. J., Golinkoff, R. M., & Hirsh-Pasek, K. (2007). Young children associate novel words with complex objects rather than salient parts. *Developmental Psychology, 43,* 1051–1061.

Hollich, G. J., Hirsh-Pasek, K., & Golinkoff, R. M. (2000). Breaking the language barrier: An emergentist coalition model for the origins of word learning. *Monographs of the Society for Research in Child Development, 65* (Serial No. 262).

Holowka, S., & Petitto, L. A. (2002). Left hemisphere cerebral specialization for babies while babbling. *Science, 297,* 1515.

Holtzer, R., Verghese, J., Allali, G., Izzetoglu, M., Wang, C., & Mahoney, J. R. (2016). Neurological

gait abnormalities moderate the functional brain signature of the posture first hypothesis. *Brain Topography, 29,* 334–343. doi:10.1007/s10548-015-0465-z

Hom, P. W., & Kinicki, A. J. (2001). Toward a greater understanding of how dissatisfaction drives employee turnover. *Academy of Management Journal, 44,* 975–987. doi:10.2307/3069441

Honda-Howard, M., & Homma, M. (2001). Job satisfaction of Japanese career women and its influence on turnover intention. *Asian Journal of Social Psychology, 4,* 23–38. doi:10.1111/1467-839X.00073

Hong, J. S., Lee, J., Espelage, D. L., Hunter, S. C., Patton, D. U., & Rivers, T. (2016). Understanding the correlates of face-to-face and cyberbullying victimization among U.S. adolescents: A social-ecological analysis. *Violence and Victims, 31,* 638–663.

Hooker, K. (1999). Possible selves in adulthood. In T. M. Hess & F. Blanchard-Fields (Eds.), *Social cognition and aging* (pp. 97–122). San Diego, CA: Academic Press.

Hooker, K., Fiese, B. H., Jenkins, L., Morfei, M. Z., & Schwagler, J. (1996). Possible selves among parents of infants and preschoolers. *Developmental Psychology, 32,* 542–550. doi:10.1037/0012-1649.32.3.542

Hopkins, B., & Westra, T. (1988). Maternal handling and motor development: An intercultural study. *Genetic, Social, & General Psychology Monographs, 14,* 377–420.

Horn, J. L. (1982). The aging of human abilities. In B. B. Wolman (Ed.), *Handbook of developmental psychology* (pp. 847–870). Englewood Cliffs, NJ: Prentice Hall.

Horn, J. L., & Hofer, S. M. (1992). Major abilities and development in the adult period. In R. J. Sternberg & C. A. Berg (Eds.), *Intellectual development* (pp. 44–99). Cambridge, UK: Cambridge University Press.

Horwitz, B. N., Reynolds, C. A., Walum, H., Ganiban, J., Spotts, E. L., Reiss, D., et al. (2016). Understanding the role of mate selection processes in couples' pair-bonding behavior. *Behavior Genetics, 46,* 143–149. doi:10.1007/s10519-015-9766-y

Horwood, S., & Beanland, V. (2016). Inattentional blindness in older adults: Effects of attentional set and to-be-ignored distractors. *Attention, Perception, & Psychophysics, 78,* 818-828. doi:10.3758/s13414-015-1057-4

Hospice Foundation of America. (2016a). *What is hospice?* Retrieved from http://hospicefoundation.org/End-of-Life-Support-and-Resources/Coping-with-Terminal-Illness/Hospice-Services.

Hospice Foundation of America. (2016b). *A caregiver's guide to the dying process.* Retrieved from http://hospicefoundation.org/hfa/media/Files/Hospice_TheDyingProcess_Docutech-READERSPREADS.pdf.

Hostetler, A. J., & Paterson, S. E. (2017). Toward a community psychology of aging: A lifespan perspective. In M. A. Bond, I. Serrano-Garcia, C. B. Keys, & M. Shinn (Eds.), *APA handbook of* community psychology: Methods for community research and action for diverse groups and issues (Vol. S, pp. 605–622). Washington, DC: American Psychological Association.

Hotz, V. J., & Pantano, J. (2013). Strategic parenting, birth order and school performance. *IZA Working Paper 7680*.

Houston, D. M., & Jusczyk, P. W. (2003). Infants' long-term memory for the sound patterns of words and voices. *Journal of Experimental Psychology: Human Perception & Performance, 29*, 1143–1154.

Howard, D. V., & Howard, J. H., Jr. (2012). Dissociable forms of implicit learning in aging. In M. Naveh-Benjamin & N. Ohta (Eds.). *Memory and aging: Current issues and future directions* (pp. 125–151). New York: Psychology Press.

Howard, D. V., & Howard, J. H., Jr. (2016). Implicit learning and memory. In S. K. Whitbourne (Ed.), *The encyclopedia of adulthood and aging* (pp. 631–635). Malden, MA: Wiley.

Howard, J. H., Jr., & Howard, D. V. (2013). Aging mind and brain: Is implicit learning spared in healthy aging? *Frontiers in Psychology, November 7*. doi: 10.3389/fpsyg.2013.00817. Retrieved from journal.frontiersin.org/ article/10.3389/fpsyg.2013.00817/full.

Howard, L. W., & Cordes, C. L. (2010). Flight from unfairness: Effects of perceived injustice on emotional exhaustion and employee withdrawal. *Journal of Business and Psychology, 25*, 409–428. doi:10.1007/s10869-010-9158-5

Howe, M. L. (2014). The co-emergence of the self and autobiographical memory: An adaptive view of early memory. In P J. Bauer & R. Fivush (Eds.), *The Wiley handbook on the development of children's memory* (pp. 545–567). Chichester, UK: Wiley.

Howe, N., & Ross, H. S. (1990). Socialization, perspective taking and the sibling relationship. *Developmental Psychology, 26*, 160–165.

Howes, C., & Matheson, C. C. (1992). Sequences in the development of competent play with peers: Social and social pretend play. *Developmental Psychology, 28*, 961–974.

Howes, C., Unger, O., & Seidner, L. B. (1990). Social pretend play in toddlers: Parallels with social play and with solitary pretend. *Child Development, 60*, 77–84.

Hoyt, A. T., Canfield, M. A., Romitti, P. A., Botto, L. D., Anderka, M. T., Krikov, S., et al. (2016). Association between maternal periconceptional exposure to secondhand tobacco smoke and major birth defects. *American Journal of Obstetrics and Gynecology, 215*, 613.e1–613.e11.

Hsu, H.-C. (2005). Gender disparity of successful aging in Taiwan. *Women and Health, 42*, 1–21. doi:10.1300/J013v42n01_01

Huang, G. C., Unger, J. B., Soto, D., Fujimoto, K., Pentz, M. A., Jordan-Marsh, M., et al. (2014). Peer influences: the impact of online and offline friendship networks on adolescent smoking and alcohol use. *Journal of Adolescent Health, 54*, 508–514.

Hubbard, R. R. (2010). *Afro-German biracial identity development*. Retrieved from digarchive .library.vcu.edu/bitstream/10156/2804/1/ Afro-German%20HEMBAGI%20%28F3%29 .pdf.

Hughes, C., White, N., & Ensor, R. (2014). How does talk about thoughts, desires, and feelings foster children's socio-cognitive development? Mediators, moderators and implications for intervention. In K. H. Lagattuta (Ed.), *Children and emotion: New insights into developmental affective sciences* (pp. 95–105). Basel, Switzerland: Karger.

Hughes, J. M., Bigler, R. S., & Levy, S. R. (2007). Consequences of learning about historical racism among European American and African American children. *Child Development, 78*, 1689–1705.

Huisman, M., Read, S., Towriss, C. A., Deeg, D. J. H., & Grundy, E. (2013). Socioeconomic inequalities in mortality rates in old age in the World Health Organization Europe region. *Epidemiologic Reviews, 35*, 84–97. doi:10.1093/epirev/mxs010

Hull, T.H. (2009). Caught in transit: Questions about the future of Indonesian fertility. *Population Bulletin of the United Nations, Special Issue Nos. 48/49*, 375–387.

Hulme, C., & Melby-Lervåg, M. (2015). Educational interventions for children's learning difficulties. In A. Thapar, D. S. Pine, J. F. Leckman, S. Scott, M. J. Snowling, & E. Taylor (Eds.), *Rutter's child and adolescent psychiatry* (6th ed., pp. 533–544). Chichester, UK: Wiley.

Hulme, C., & Snowling, M. J. (2011). Children's reading comprehension difficulties: Nature, causes, and treatments. *Current Directions in Psychological Science, 20*, 139–142.

Hulme, C., & Snowling, M. (2016). Reading disorders and dyslexia. *Current Opinion and Pediatrics, 28*, 731–735.

Human Genome Project. (2003). *Genomics and its impact on science and society: A 2003 primer*. Washington, DC: U.S. Department of Energy.

Hunt, E., & Carlson, J. (2007). Considerations relating to the study of group differences in intelligence. *Perspectives on Psychological Science, 2*, 194–213.

Hunt, J. B., & Fitzgerald, M. (2013). The relationship between emotional intelligence and transformational leadership: An investigation and review of competing claims in the literature. *American International Journal of Social Science, 2*, 30–38. Retrieved from www.researchgate.net/profile/ James_Hunt11/publication/264311660_ The_Relationship_between_Emotional_ Intelligence_and_Transformational_ Leadership_An_Investigation_and_Review_ of_Competing_Claims_in_the_Literature/ links/56b15d5408ae795dd5c505a0.pdf.

Hunt, J. B., & Fitzgerald, M. (2014). An evidence-based assessment of the relationship between emotional intelligence and transformational leadership. *International Journal of Arts and Commerce, 3*, 85–100. Retrieved from www .researchgate.net/profile/James_Hunt11/ publication/292802393_An_Evidence-based_ Assessment_of_the_Relationship_Between_ Emotional_Intelligence_and_Transformational_ Leadership/links/56b16e2208ae56d7b06a0f5c. pdf.

Hunt, J. M., & Weintraub, J. R. (2016). *The coaching manager: Developing top talent* (3rd ed.). Thousand Oaks, CA: Sage Publications.

Huston, A. C., & Wright, J. C. (1998). Mass media and children's development. In W. Damon (Ed.), *Handbook of child psychology* (Vol. 4). New York: Wiley.

Huston, A. C., Bobbitt, K. C., & Bentley, A. (2015). Time spent in child care: How and why does it affect social development? *Developmental Psychology, 51*, 621–634.

Huth-Bocks, A.C., Levendosky, A. A., Bogat, G. A., & von Eye, A. (2004). The impact of maternal characteristics and contextual variables on infant–mother attachment. *Child Development, 75*, 480–496.

Huttenlocher, J., Waterfall, H., Vasilyeva, M., Vevea, J., & Hedges, L. V. (2010). Sources of variability in children's language growth. *Cognitive Psychology, 61*, 343–365.

Hwang, M. J. (2007). Asian social workers' perceptions of glass ceiling, organizational fairness and career prospects. *Journal of Social Service Research, 33*, 13–24. doi:10.1300/ J079v33n04_02

Hwang, N., & Domina, T. (2017). The links between youth employment and educational attainment across racial groups. *Journal of Research on Adolescence*, in press.

Hyde, J. S. (2014). Gender similarities and differences. *Annual Review of Psychology, 65*, 373–398.

Hyer, L., Mullen, C. M., & Jackson, K. (2017). The unfolding of unique problems in later life families. In G. L. Welch & A. W. Harrist (Eds.), *Family resilience and chronic illness: interdisciplinary and translational perspectives* (pp. 197–224). New York: Springer.

Iarocci, G., Yager, J., Rombough, A., McLaughlin, J. (2008). The development of social competence among persons with Down syndrome: From survival to social inclusion. *International Review of Research in Mental Retardation, 35*, 87–119.

Ibrahim, R., & Hassan, Z. (2009). Understanding singlehood from the experiences of never-married Malay Muslim women in Malaysia: Some preliminary findings. *European Journal of Social Sciences, 8*, 395–405. Retrieved from server1.doc-foc.us/uploads/Z2016/01/12/w29wSDYY47/ 40f707fa034e0fea7894a419dea90541.pdf.

Iervolino, A. C., Hines, M., Golombok, S. E., Rust, J., & Plomin, R. (2005). Genetic and environmental influences on sex-typed behavior during the preschool years. *Child Development, 76*, 826–840.

Igarashi, H., Hooker, K. Coehlo, D. P., & Manoogian, M. M. (2013). "My nest is full:" Intergenerational relationships at midlife. *Journal of Aging Studies, 27*, 102–112. doi:10.1016/j. jaging.2012.12.004

Imuta, K., Henry, J. D., Slaughter, V., Selcuk, B., & Ruffman, T. (2016). Theory of mind and prosocial behavior in childhood:

A meta-analytic review. *Developmental Psychology, 52*, 1192–1205.

Inhelder, B., & Piaget, J. (1958). *The growth of logical thinking from childhood to adolescence.* New York: Basic Books.

International Labour Organization. (2013). *When work becomes a sexual battleground.* Retrieved from www.ilo.org/global/about-the-ilo/newsroom/features/WCMS_205996/lang–en/index.htm.

Intuit. (2016). *Intuit 2020 report: Twenty trends that will shape the next decade.* Retrieved from http-download.intuit.com/http.intuit/CMO/intuit/futureofsmallbusiness/intuit_2020_report.pdf.

Irish, L. S. (2009). *Modern tribal tattoo designs.* East Petersburg, PA: Fox Chapel Publishing.

Irwin, N. (2016). With "gigs" instead of jobs, workers bear new burdens. *New York Times* (March 31). Retrieved from www.nytimes.com/2016/03/31/upshot/contractors-and-temps-accounted-for-all-of-the-growth-in-employment-in-the-last-decade.html.

Isaacowitz, D. M. (2014). Change in perceptions of personality disorder in late life: The view from socioemotional aging. *Journal of Personality, 28*, 166–171. doi:10.1521/pedi.2014.28.1.166

Ismail, Z., Smith, E. E., Geda, Y., Sultzer, D., Brodaty, H., Smith, G., et al. (2016). Neuropsychiatric symptoms as early manifestations of emergent dementia: Provisional diagnostic criteria for mild behavioral impairment. *Alzheimer's & Dementia, 12*, 195–202. doi:10.1016/j.jalz.2015.05.107

Iverson, J. M., & Goldin-Meadow, S. (2005). Gesture paves the way for language development. *Psychological Science, 16*, 367–371.

Ivory, B. T. (2004). A phenomenological inquiry into the spiritual qualities and transformational themes associated with a self-styled rite of passage into adulthood. *Dissertation Abstracts International. Section A. Humanities & Social Sciences, 65(2-A)*, 429.

Iwarsson, S., Slaug, B., & Fänge, A. M. (2012). The Housing Enabler Screening Tool: Feasibility and interrater agreement in a real estate company practice context. *Journal of Applied Gerontology, 31*, 641–660. doi:10.1177/0733464810397354

Izard, C. E. (2007). Basic emotions, natural kinds, emotion schemas, and a new paradigm. *Perspectives on Psychological Science, 2*, 260–280.

Izumi, S., & Son, C. V. (2016). "I didn't know he was dying": Missed opportunities for making end-of-life decisions for older family members. *Journal of Hospice & Palliative Nursing, 18*, 74–81. doi:10.1097/0000000000000215

Jackson, M. A. (2013). Counseling older workers confronting ageist stereotypes and discrimination. In P. Brownell & J. J. Kelly (Eds.), *Ageism and mistreatment of older workers* (pp. 135–144). New York: Springer.

Jacobson, J. L., & Jacobson, S. W. (1996). Intellectual impairment in children exposed to polychlorinated biphenyls in utero. *New England Journal of Medicine, 335*, 783–789.

Jacobson, J. L., Jacobson, S. W., & Humphrey, H. E. B. (1990). Effects of in utero exposure to polychlorinated biphenyls and related contaminants on cognitive functioning in young children. *Journal of Pediatrics, 116*, 38–45.

Jacobson, S. W., & Jacobson, J. L. (2000). Teratogenic insult and neurobehavioral function in infancy and childhood. In C. A. Nelson (Ed.), *The Minnesota Symposium on Child Psychology: Vol. 31. The effects of early adversity on neurobehavioral development* (pp. 61–112). Mahwah, NJ: Erlbaum.

Jainer, A. K., Kamatchi, R., Marzanski, M., & Somashekar, B. (2013). Current advances in the treatment of major depression: Shift towards receptor specific drugs. In R. Woolfolk & L. Allen (Eds.), *Mental disorders: Theoretical and empirical perspectives* (pp. 269–288). doi:10.5772/46217. Retrieved from cdn.intechopen.com/pdfs/41703/InTech-Current_advances_in_the_treatment_of_major_depression_shift_towards_receptor_specific_drugs.pdf.

James, J. B., Matz-Costa, C., & Smyer, M. A. (2016). Retirement security: It's not just about the money. *American Psychologist, 71*, 334–344. doi:10.1037/a0040220

James, J., Ellis, B. J., Schlomer, G. L., & Garber, J. (2012). Sex-specific pathways to early puberty, sexual debut, and sexual risk taking: Tests of an integrated evolutionary-developmental model. *Developmental Psychology, 48*, 687–702.

James, W. (1890). *The principles of psychology.* New York: Holt.

Janson, H., & Mathiesen, K. S. (2008). Temperament profiles from infancy to middle childhood: Development and associations with behavioral problems. *Developmental Psychology, 44*, 1314–1328.

Janssen I, R. R. (2005). Linking age-related changes in skeletal muscle mass and composition with metabolism and disease. *Journal of Nutrition, Health and Aging, 9*, 408–419. Retrieved from www.researchgate.net/profile/Ian_Janssen/publication/7375203_Linking_age-related_changes_in_skeletal_muscle_mass_and_composition_with_metabolism_and_disease/links/00b7d535a3066571fa000000.pdf.

Jaswal, V. K., & Kondrad, R. L. (2016). Why children are not always epistemically vigilant: Cognitive limits and social considerations. *Child Development Perspectives, 10*, 240–244.

Jenkins, C. L. (Ed.). (2003). *Widows and divorcees in later life: On their own again.* Binghamton, NY: Haworth Press.

Jenkins, J. A. (2016). *Disrupt aging: A bold new path to living your best life at every age.* New York: PublicAffairs Publishing.

Jernigan, T. L., & Stiles, J. (2017). Construction of the human forebrain. *WIRES Cognitive Science, 8*, e1409.

Jeste, D. V., & Palmer, B. W. (2013). A call for a new positive psychiatry of ageing. *British Journal of Psychiatry, 202*, 81–83. doi:10.1192/bjp. bp.112.110643

Jiang, W., Zhao, F., Guderley, N., & Manchaiah, V. (2016). Daily music exposure dose and hearing problems using personal listening devices in adolescents and young adults: A systematic review. *International Journal of Audiology, 55*, 197–205. doi:10.3109/14992027.2015.1122237

Jiang, Z. (2016). The relationship between career adaptability and job content plateau: The mediating roles of fit perceptions. *Journal of Vocational Behavior, 95*, 1–10. doi:10.1016/j.jvb.2016.06.001

Jiao, Z. (1999, April). *Which students keep old friends and which become new friends across a school transition?* Paper presented at the 1999 meeting of the Society for Research in Child Development, Albuquerque, New Mexico.

Jipson, J. L., & Gelman, S. A. (2007). Robots and rodents: Children's inferences about living and nonliving kinds. *Child Development, 78*, 1675–1688.

John, O. P., & Gross, J. J. (2007). Individual differences in emotion regulation. In J. J. Gross (Ed.), *Handbook of emotion regulation* (pp. 351–372). New York: Guilford.

Johnson, H. A., Zabriskie, R. B., & Hill, B. (2006). The contribution of couple leisure involvement, leisure time, and leisure satisfaction to marital satisfaction. *Marriage & Family Review, 40*, 69–91. doi:10.1300/ J002v40n01_05

Johnson, K. J., & Mutchler, J. E. (2014). The emergence of a positive gerontology: From disengagement to social involvement. *The Gerontologist, 54*, S93–S100. doi:10.1093/geront/gnt099

Johnson, M. D. (2016). Online dating. In M. D. Johnson (Ed.), *Great myths of intimate relationships: Dating, sex, and marriage* (pp. 52–70). New York: Wiley.

Johnson, M. H., Grossman, T., & Cohen Kadosh, K. (2009). Mapping functional brain development: Building a social brain through interactive specialization. *Developmental Psychology, 45*, 151–159.

Johnson, R. M., LaValley, M., Schneider, K. E., Musci, R. J., Pettoruto, K., & Rothman, E. F. (2017). Marijuana use and physical dating violence among adolescents and emerging adults: A systematic review and meta-analysis. *Drug and Alcohol Dependence. 174*, 47–57.

Johnson, R. M., Miller, M., Vriniotis, M., Azrael, D., & Hemenway, D. (2006). Are household firearms stored less safely in home with adolescents? Analysis of a national random sample of parents. *Archives of Pediatrics and Adolescent Medicine, 160*, 788–792.

Johnson, S. C., Dweck, C. S., Chen, F. S., Stern, H. L., Ok, S-J., & Barth, M. (2010). At the intersection of social and cognitive development: Internal working models of attachment in infancy. *Cognitive Science, 34*, 807–825.

Johnson, S. P. (2001). Visual development in human infants: Binding features, surfaces, and objects. *Visual Cognition, 8*, 565–578.

Johnson, S. P. (2013). Development of the visual system. In J. L. R. Rubenstein & P Rakic (Eds.), *Neural circuit development and function in the brain* (Vol 3., pp. 249–269). Amsterdam: Elsevier.

Johnston, K. E., Swim, J. K., Saltsman, B. M., Deater-Deckard, K., & Petrill, S. A. (2007). Mothers' racial, ethnic, and cultural socialization of transracially adopted Asian children. *Family Relations, 56,* 390–402. doi:10.1111/j.1741-3729.2007.00468.x

Johnston, L. D., O'Malley, P. M., Miech, R. A., Bachman, J. G., & Schulenberg, J. E. (2017). *Monitoring the future national survey results on drug use, 1975–2016: Overview, key findings on adolescent drug use.* Ann Arbor: Institute for Social Research, The University of Michigan.

Joiner, T. (2010). *Myths about suicide.* Cambridge, MA: Harvard University Press.

Jolie, A. (2013). *My medical choice.* Retrieved from www.nytimes.com/2013/05/14/opinion/my-medical-choice.html.

Jolie, A. (2015). *Diary of a surgery.* Retrieved from mobile.nytimes.com/2015/03/24/opinion/angelina-jolie-pitt-diary-of-a-surgery.html?referrer=&_r=0.

Jones, B. F. (2010). Age and great invention. *Review of Economics and Statistics, 92,* 1–14. Retrieved from www.mitpressjournals.org/doi/pdfplus/10.1162/rest.2009.11724.

Jones, L., Bellis, M. A., Wood, S., Hughes, K., McCoy, E., Eckley, L. et al. (2012). Prevalence and risk of violence against children with disabilities: A systematic review and meta-analysis of observational studies. *The Lancet, 380,* 889–907.

Jonsson, T., Stefansson, H., Steinberg, S., Jonsdottir, I., Jonsson, P. V., Snaedal, J., et al. (2013). Variant of *TREM2* associated with the risk of Alzheimer's disease. *New England Journal of Medicine, 368,* 107–116. doi:10.1056/NEJMoa1211103

Jopp, D. S., & Hertzog, C. (2010). Assessing adult leisure activities: An extension of a self-report activity questionnaire. *Psychological Assessment, 22,* 108–120. doi:10.1037/a0017662

Jordan, N. C., Kaplan, D., Ramineni, C., & Locuniak, M. N. (2008). Development of number combination skill in the early school years: When do fingers help? *Developmental Science, 11,* 662–668.

Joseph, D. L., & Newman, D. A. (2010). Emotional intelligence: An integrative meta-analysis and cascading model. *Journal of Applied Psychology, 95,* 54–78.

Joyner, M. J., & Barnes, J. N. (2013). I am 80 going on 18: Exercise and the fountain of youth. *Journal of Applied Physiology, 114,* 1–2. doi:10.1152/japplphysiol.01313.2012

Juffer, F. (2006). Children's awareness of adoption and their problem behavior in families with 7-year-old internationally adopted children. *Adoption Quarterly, 9,* 1–22. doi:10.1300/J145v09n02_01

Jung, C. G. (1960/1933). The stages of life. In G. Adler, M. Fordham, & H. Read (Eds.), *The collected works of C. J. Jung: Vol. 8. The structure and dynamics of the psyche.* London: Routledge & Kegan Paul.

Jung, R. E., & Haier, R. J. (2007). The parieto-frontal integration theory (P-FIT) of intelligence: Converging neuroimaging evidence. *Behavioral and Brain Sciences, 30,* 135–154. doi:10.1017/S0140525X07001185

Jung, R. E., Flores, R. A., & Hunter, D. (2016). A new measure of imagination ability: Anatomical brain imaging correlates. *Frontiers in Psychology, 7,* 496. doi:10.3389/fpsyq.2016.00496. Available at www.ncbi.nlm.nih.gov/pmc/articles/PMC4834344/.

Jusczyk, P. W. (1995). Language acquisition: Speech sounds and phonological development. In J. L. Miller & P. D. Eimas (Eds.), *Handbook of perception and cognition: Vol. 11. Speech, language, and communication* (pp. 263–301). Orlando, FL: Academic Press.

Jusczyk, P. W. (2002). How infants adapt speech-processing capacities to native-language structure. *Current Directions in Psychological Science, 11,* 15–18.

Justice, L. M., Pullen, P. C., & Pence, K. (2008). Influence of verbal and nonverbal references to print on preschoolers' visual attention to print during storybook reading. *Developmental Psychology, 44,* 855–866.

Juvonen, J., & Graham, S. (2014). Bullying in schools: The power of bullies and the plight of victims. *Annual Review of Psychology, 65,* 159–185.

Kahana, E., & Kahana, B. (2003). Patient proactivity enhancing doctor-patient-family communication in cancer prevention and care among the aged. *Patient Education and Counseling, 50,* 67–73. doi:10.1016/S0738-3991(03)00083-1

Kahana, E., Kahana, B., & Zhang, J. (2005). Motivational antecedents of preventive proactivity in late life: Linking future orientation and exercise. *Motivation and Emotion, 29,* 438–459 (Figure 1). doi:10.1007/s11031-006-9012-2.

Kahana, E., Kelley-Moore, J., & Kahana, B. (2012). Proactive aging: A longitudinal study of stress, resources, and well-being in late life. *Aging and Mental Health, 16,* 438–451. doi:10.1080/13607863.20 11.644519

Kahn, P. H., Gary, H. E., & Shen, S. (2013). Children's social relationships with current and near-future robots. *Child Development Perspectives, 7,* 32–37.

Kaijura, H., Cowart, B. J., & Beauchamp, G. K. (1992). Early developmental change in bitter taste responses in human infants. *Developmental Psychobiology, 25,* 375–386.

Kail, R. (2004). Cognitive development includes global and domain-specific processes. *Merrill-Palmer Quarterly, 50,* 445–455.

Kail, R. V. (2013). Influences of credibility of testimony and strength of statistical evidence on children's and adolescents' reasoning. *Journal of Experimental Child Psychology, 116,* 747–754.

Kail, R., & Bisanz, J. (1992). The information-processing perspective on cognitive development in childhood and adolescence. In R. J. Sternberg & C. A. Berg (Eds.), *Intellectual development.* (pp. 229–260). New York: Cambridge University Press.

Kaiser Family Foundation. (2016). *Total number of Medicare beneficiaries.* Retrieved from http://kff.org/medicare/state-indicator/total-medicare-beneficiaries/?currentTimeframe=0&sortModel=%7B%22colId%22:%22Location%22,%22sort%22:%22asc%22%7D.

Kalanithi, L. (2016). *My marriage didn't end when I became a widow.* Retrieved from opinionator.blogs.nytimes.com/2016/01/06/my-marriage-didnt-end-when-i-became-a-widow/.

Kalish, E. (2016). *Millennials are the least wealthy, but most optimistic, generation.* Retrieved from www.urban.org/research/publication/millennials-are-least-wealthy-most-optimistic-generation.

Kalish, R. A. (1984). *Death, grief, and caring relationships* (2nd ed.). Pacific Grove, CA: Brooks/Cole.

Kalish, R. A. (1987). Death and dying. In P. Silverman (Ed.), *The elderly as modern pioneers* (pp. 320–334). Bloomington: Indiana University Press.

Kalish, R. A., & Reynolds, D. (1976). *Death and ethnicity: A psychocultural study.* Los Angeles: University of Southern California Press.

Kalmijn, M. (2013). Adult children's relationships with married parents, divorced parents, and stepparents: Biology, marriage, or residence? *Journal of Marriage and Family, 75,* 1181–1193. doi:10.1111 /jomf.12057

Kalmijn, M., & Flap, H. (2001). Assortative meeting and mating: Unintended consequences of organized settings for partner choices. *Social Forces, 79,* 1289–1312. doi:10.1353/sof.2001.0044

Kan, D., & Yu, X. (2016). Occupational stress, work-family conflict and depressive symptoms among Chinese bank employees: The role of psychological capital. *International Journal of Environmental Research and Public Health, 13,* 134. doi:10.3390/ijerp13010134

Kaplan, H., & Dove, H. (1987). Infant development among the Ache of eastern Paraguay. *Developmental Psychology, 23,* 190–198.

Kaplan, S. (2015). When are you dead? It may depend on which hospital makes the call. *Washington Post.* Retrieved from www.washingtonpost.com/news/morning-mix/wp/2015/12/29/when-are-you-dead-it-may-depend-on-which-hospital-makes-the-call/.

Kapoor, U., Pfost, K. S., House, A. E., & Pierson, E. (2010). Relation of success and nontraditional career choice to selection for dating and friendship. *Psychological Reports, 107,* 177–184. doi:10.2466/07.17.PR0.107.4.177-184

Karam, E., Kypri, K., & Salamoun, M. (2007). Alcohol use among college students: An international perspective. *Current Opinion in Psychiatry, 20,* 213–221. doi:10.1097/YCO.0b013e3280fa836c

Karasik, L B., Tamis-LeMonda, C. S., & Adolph, K. E. (2016). Decisions at the brink: Locomotor experience affects infants' use of social information on an adjustable drop-off. *Frontiers in Psychology, 7,* 797.

Karasik, L. B., Tamis-LeMonda, C. S., & Adolph, K. E. (2011). Transition from crawling to walking and infants' actions with objects and people. *Child Development, 82,* 1199–1209.

Kärnä, A., Voeten, M., Little, T. D., Alanen, E., Poskiparta, E., & Salmivalli, C. (2013). Effectiveness of the KiVa antibullying program: Grades 1–3 and 7–9. *Journal of Educational Psychology, 105,* 535–551.

Karney, B. R. (2010). *Keeping marriages healthy, and why it's so difficult.* Retrieved from www.apa.org/science/about/psa/2010/02/sci-brief.aspx.

Karney, B. R., & Bradbury, T. N. (1995). The longitudinal course of marital quality and stability: A review of theory, method, and research. *Psychological Bulletin, 118,* 3–34. doi:10.1037/0033-2909.1881.1.3

Karney, B. R., & Crown, J. S. (2007). *Families under stress: An assessment of data, theory, and research on marriage and divorce in the military* (MG-599-OSD). Santa Monica, CA: RAND Corporation.

Karniol, R. (1989). The role of manual manipulative states in the infant's acquisition of perceived control over objects. *Developmental Review, 9,* 205–233.

Karniol, R. (2016). A language-based, three-stage, social-interactional model of social pretend play: Acquiring *pretend* as an epistemic operator, *pretending that,* and *pretending with (the P-PT-PW model). Developmental Review, 41,* 1–37.

Karp, N., & Wood, E. (2012). Choosing home for someone else: Guardian residential decision-making. *Utah Law Review, 2012,* 1445–1490. Retrieved from http://epubs.utah.edu/index.php/ulr/article/view/837/646.

Karraker, K. H., Vogel, D. A., & Lake, M. A. (1995). Parents' gender-stereotyped perceptions of newborns: The eye of the beholder revisited. *Sex Roles, 33,* 687–701.

Kassim, P. N. J., & Alias, F. (2016). Religious, ethical and legal considerations in end-of-life issues: Fundamental requisites for medical decision making. *Journal of Religion and Health, 55,* 119–134. doi:10.1007/210943-014-9995-z

Kast, N. R., Eisenberg, M. E., & Sieving, R. E. (2016), The role of parent communication and connectedness in dating violence victimization among Latino adolescents. *Journal of Interpersonal Violence, 31,* 1932–1955.

Kastenbaum, R. (1999). Dying and bereavement. In J. C. Cavanaugh & S. K. Whitbourne (Eds.), *Gerontology: An interdisciplinary perspective.* New York: Oxford University Press.

Kastenbaum, R., & Thuell, S. (1995). Cookies baking, coffee brewing: Toward a contextual theory of dying. *Omega: The Journal of Death and Dying, 31,* 175–187. doi:10.2190/LQPX-71DE-V5AA-EPFT

Katz-Wise, S. L., Priess, H. A., & Hyde, J. S. (2010). Gender-role attitudes and behavior across the transition to parenthood. *Developmental Psychology, 46,* 18–28.

Katz, L. F., & Woodin, E. M. (2002). Hostility, hostile detachment, and conflict engagement in marriages: Effects on child and family functioning. *Child Development, 73,* 636–652.

Kaufman, J. C. (2016). *Creativity 101* (2nd ed.). New York: Springer.

Kaufman, J. C., Kaufman, S. B., & Plucker, J. A. (2013). Contemporary theories of intelligence. In D. Reisberg (Ed.), *The Oxford handbook of cognitive psychology.* New York: Oxford University Press.

Kavsek, M., & Bornstein, M. H. (2010). Visual habituation and dishabituation in preterm infants: A review and meta-analysis. *Research in Developmental Disabilities, 31,* 951–975.

Kavšek, M., & Braun, S. K. (2016). Binocular vision in infancy: Responsiveness to uncrossed horizontal disparity. *Infant Behavior and Development, 44,* 219–226.

Kavšek, M., Yonas, A., & Granrud, C. E. (2012). Infants' sensitivity to pictorial depth cues: A review and meta-analysis of looking studies. *Infant Behavior and Development, 35,* 109–128.

Kawabata, Y., & Crick, N. R. (2011). The significance of cross-racial/ethnic friendships: Associations with peer victimization, peer support, sociometric status, and classroom diversity. *Developmental Psychology, 47,* 1763–1775.

Kawabata, Y., & Crick, N. R. (2016). Differential associations between maternal and paternal parenting and physical and relational aggression. *Asian Journal of Social Psychology, 19,* 254–263.

Kayser, K. (2010). Couples therapy. In J. R. Brandell (Ed.), *Theory and practice in clinical social work* (2nd ed., pp. 259–288). Thousand Oaks, CA: Sage Publications.

Kearney, C. A., & Spear, M. (2013). Assessment of selective mutism and school refusal behavior. In D. McKay & E. A. Storch (Eds.), *Handbook of assessing variants and complications in anxiety disorders* (pp. 29–42). New York: Spring Science+Business Media.

Keel, P. K. Bulimia nervosa. In K. D. Brownell & B. T. Walsh (Eds.), *Eating disorders and obesity* (3rd ed., pp. 187–191). New York: Guilford.

Keitel, A., & Daum, M. M. (2015). The use of intonation for turn anticipation in observed conversations without visual signals as a source of information. *Frontiers in Psychology, 6,* Article 108.

Keith, J. (1990). Age in social and cultural context: Anthropological perspectives. In R. H. Binstock & L. K. George (Eds.), *Handbook of aging and the social sciences* (3rd ed., pp. 91–111). San Diego, CA: Academic Press.

Kelemen, D. (2003). British and American children's preferences for teleo-functional explanations of the natural world. *Cognition, 88,* 201–221.

Kelemen, D., & DiYanni, C. (2005). Intuitions about origins: Purpose and intelligent design in children's reasoning about nature. *Journal of Cognition & Development, 6,* 3–31.

Kellman, P. J., & Arterberry, M. E. (2006). Infant visual perception. In W. Damon & R. M. Lerner (Eds.), *Handbook of child psychology: Vol. 2. Cognition, perception, and language* (6th ed., pp. 109–160). Hoboken, NJ: Wiley.

Kelly, D., Xie, H., Nord, C. W., Jenkins, F., Chan, J. Y., & Kastberg, D. (2013). *Performance of U.S. 15-year-old students in mathematics, science, and reading literacy in an international context: First look at PISA 2012.* Washington DC: National Center for Education Statistics.

Kelly, P. (2011). Corporal punishment and child maltreatment in New Zealand. *Acta Paediatrica, 100,* 14–20.

Kendall, J., & Hatton, D. (2002). Racism as a source of health disparity in families with children with attention deficit hyperactivity disorder. *Advances in Nursing Science, 25,* 22–39.

Kersting, A., & Nagl, M. (2016). Grief after perinatal loss. In A. Milunsky & J. M. Milunsky (Eds.), *Genetic disorders and the fetus: Diagnosis, prevention, and treatment* (Vol. 7, pp. 1048–1062). Hoboken, NJ: Wiley. doi:10.1002/9781118981559.ch31

Kersting, A., Brähler, E., Glaesmer, H., & Wagner, B. (2011). Prevalence of complicated grief in a representative population-based sample. *Journal of Affective Disorders, 131,* 339–343. doi: 10.1016/j.jad.2010.11.032

Khalil, A., Syngelaki, A., Maiz, N., Zinevich, Y., & Nicolaides, K. H. (2013). Maternal age and adverse pregnancy outcomes: A cohort study. *Ultrasound in Obstetrics and Gynecology, 42,* 634–643.

Khashan, A. S., Baker, P. N., & Kenny, L. C. (2010). Preterm birth and reduced birthweight in first and second teenage pregnancies: A register-based cohort study. *BMC Pregnancy and Childbirth, 10,* 36.

Khurana, A., Romer, D., Betancourt, L. M., Brodsky, N. L., Giannetta, J. M., & Hurt, H. (2012). Early adolescent sexual debut: The mediating role of working memory ability, sensation seeking, and impulsivity. *Developmental Psychology, 48,* 1416–1428.

Kiang, L., Yip, T., Gonzales-Backen, M., Witkow, M., & Fuligni, A. J. (2006). Ethnic identity and the daily psychological well-being of adolescents from Mexican and Chinese backgrounds. *Child Development, 77,* 1338–1350.

Kiaye, R. E., & Singh, A. M. (2013). The glass ceiling: A perspective of women working in Durban. *Gender in Management: An International Journal, 28,* 28–42. doi:10.1108/17542411311301556

Kidd, E. (2012). Implicit statistical learning is directly associated with the acquisition of syntax. *Developmental Psychology, 48,* 171–184.

Kievit, R. A., Scholte, H. S., Waldorp, L. J., & Borsboom, D. (2016). Inter- and intra-individual differences in fluid reasoning show distinct cortical responses. *bioRxiv.* doi:10.1101/039412. Retrieved from http://biorxiv.org/content/biorxiv/early/2016/02/10/039412.full.pdf.

Kilson, M., & Ladd, F. (2009). *Is that your child? Mothers talking about rearing biracial children.* Lanham, MD: Lexington Books.

Kim, H. K., Capaldi, D. M., & Crosby, L. (2007). Generalizability of Gottman and Colleagues' affective process models of couples' relationship outcomes. *Journal of Marriage and Family, 69,* 55–72. doi:10.1111/j.1741-3737.2006.00343.x

Kim, H.-J., & Fredriksen-Goldsen, K. I. (2016). Living arrangement and loneliness among lesbian, gay, and bisexual older adults. *The Gerontologist, 56,* 548–558. doi:10.1093/geront/gnu083

Kim, J.-Y., McHale, S. M., Crouter, A. C., & Osgood, D. (2007). Longitudinal linkages between sibling relationships and adjustment from middle childhood through adolescence. *Developmental Psychology, 43,* 960–973.

Kim, J.-Y., McHale, S. M., Osgood, D., & Crouter, A. C. (2006). Longitudinal course and family correlates of sibling relationships from childhood through adolescence. *Child Development, 77,* 1746–1761.

Kim, P., Strathearn, L., & Swain, J. E. (2016). The maternal brain and its plasticity in humans. *Hormones and Behavior, 77,* 113–123. doi:10.1016/j.yhbeh.2015.08.001

Kim, S., & Hill, N. E. (2015). Including fathers in the picture: A meta-analysis of parental involvement and students' academic achievement. *Journal of Educational Psychology, 107,* 919–934.

Kimmel, D. (2014). Lesbian, gay, bisexual, and transgender aging concerns. *Clinical Gerontologist, 37,* 49–63. doi:10.1080/07317115.2014.847310

King, A. (2016). *Older lesbian, gay, and bisexual adults: Identities, intersections, and institutions.* New York: Routledge.

King, P. E., & Furrow, J. L. (2008). Religion as a resource for positive youth development: Religion, social capital, and moral outcomes. *Psychology of Religion and Spirituality, S,* 34–49.

King, P. M., & Kitchener, K. S. (2002). The reflective judgment model: Twenty years of research on epistemic cognition. In B. K. Hofer & P. R. Pintrich (Eds.), *Personal epistemology: The psychology of beliefs about knowledge and knowing* (pp. 37–61). Mahwah, NJ: Erlbaum.

King, P. M., & Kitchener, K. S. (2004). Reflective judgment: Theory and research on the development of epistemic assumptions through adulthood. *Educational Psychologist, 39,* 5–18. doi:10.1207/ s15326985ep3901_2

King, P. M., & Kitchener, K. S. (2015). Cognitive development in the emerging adult: The emergence of complex cognitive skills. In J. J. Arnett (Ed.), *The Oxford handbook of emerging adulthood* (pp. 105–125). New York: Oxford University Press.

King, S. V., Burgess, E. O., Akinyela, M., Counts-Spriggs, M., & Parker, N. (2006). The religious dimensions of the grandparent role in three-generation African American households. *Journal of Religion, Spirituality & Aging, 19,* 75–96. doi:10.1300/ J496v19n01_06

King, S., Dancause, K., Turcotte-Tremblay, A-M., Veru, F., & Laplante, D. P. (2012). Using natural disasters to study the effects of prenatal maternal stress on child health and human development. *Birth Defects Research (Part C), 96,* 273–288.

Kinney, J. M., & Cavanaugh, J. C. (1993 November). *Until death do us part: Striving to find meaning while caring for a spouse with dementia.* Paper presented at the meeting of the Gerontological Society of America, New Orleans.

Kinney, J. M., Ishler, K. J., Pargament, K. I., & Cavanaugh, J. C. (2003). Coping with the uncontrollable: The use of general and religious coping by caregivers to spouses with dementia. *Journal of Religious Gerontology, 14,* 171–188. doi:10.1300/ J078v14n02_06

Kippen, R., Chapman, B., & Yu, P. (2009). *What's love got to do with it? Homogamy and dyadic approaches to understanding marital instability.* Retrieved from www.cbe.anu.edu .au/researchpapers/cepr/DP631.pdf.

Kisilevsky, B. S. (2016). Fetal auditory processing: Implications for language development? In N. Reissland & B. S. Kisilevsky (Eds.), *Fetal development: Research on brain and behavior, environmental influences, and emerging technologies* (pp. 133–152). New York: Springer.

Kisker, E. E., Lipka, J., Adams, B. L., Rickard, A., Andrew-Ihrke, D., Yanez, E. E., et al. (2012). The potential of culturally based supplemental mathematics curriculum to improve the mathematics performance of Alaska native and other students. *Journal for Research in Mathematics Education, 43,* 75–113. doi:10.5951/ jresematheduc.43.1.0075

Kivett, V. R. (1991). Centrality of the grandfather role among older rural black and white men. *Journal of Gerontology: Social Sciences, 46,* S250–S258. doi:10.1093/ geronb/46.5.S250

Klackl, J., Jonas, E., & Kronbichler, M. (2013). Existential neuroscience: Neurophysiological correlates of proximal defenses against death-related thoughts. *Social Cognitive and Affective Neuroscience, 8,* 333–340. doi:10.1093/scan/ nss003

Klaczynski, P. (2013). Culture and developments in heuristics and biases from preschool through adolescence (pp. 150–192). In P. Barrouillet & C. Gauffroy (Eds.), *The development of thinking and reasoning.* Hove, UK: Psychology Press.

Klaczynski, P. A., & Lavallee, K. L. (2005). Domain-specific identity, epistemic regulation, and intellectual ability as predictors of belief-biased reasoning: A dual-process perspective. *Journal of Experimental Child Psychology, 92,* 1–24.

Klahr, A. M., & Burt, S. A. (2014). Elucidating the etiology of individual differences in parenting: A meta-analysis of behavioral genetic research. *Psychological Bulletin, 140,* 544–586.

Kleiber, D. A. (2013). Redeeming leisure in later life. In T. Freire (Ed.), *Positive leisure science* (pp. 21–38). New York: Springer.

Kleiber, D. A., Hutchinson, S. L., & Williams, R. (2002). Leisure as a resource in transcending negative life events: Self-protection, self-restoration, and personal transformation. *Leisure Sciences, 24,* 219–235. doi:10.1080/ 01490400252900167

Klimczuk, A. (2017). *Economic foundations for creative ageing policy: Putting theory into practice* (Vol. II). New York: Springer.

Klimstra, T. A., Luyckx, K., Branje, S., Teppers, E., Goossens, L., & Meeus, W. H. J. (2013). Personality traits, interpersonal identity, and relationship stability: Longitudinal linkages in late adolescence and young adulthood. *Journal of Youth and Adolescence, 42,* 1661–1673.

Knafo-Noam, A., Uzefovsky, Israel, S., Davidov, M., & Zahn-Waxler, C. (2015). The prosocial personality and its facets: Genetic and environmental architecture of mother-reported behavior of 7-year-old twins. *Frontiers in Psychology, 6,* 112.

Knee, D. O. (2010). Hospice care for the aging population in the United States. In J. C. Cavanaugh & C. K. Cavanaugh (Eds.), *Aging in America: Vol. 3: Societal issues* (pp. 203–221). Santa Barbara, CA: Praeger Perspectives.

Knight, G. P., & Carlo, G. (2012). Prosocial development among Mexican American youth. *Child Development Perspectives, 6,* 258–263.

Knipscheer, K., & van Tilburg, T. (2013). Generational contact and support among late adult siblings within a verticalized family. In M. Silverstein & R. Giarusso (Eds.), *Kinship and cohort in an aging society: From generation to generation* (pp. 59–76). Baltimore, MD: Johns Hopkins University Press.

Knowles, M. S., Holton, E. F., III, & Swanson, R. A. (2015). *The adult learner* (8th ed.). New York: Routledge.

Ko, H.-J., Mejia, S., & Hooker, K. (2014). Social possible selves, self-regulation, and social goal progress in older adulthood. *International Journal of Behavioral Development, 38,* 219–227. doi:10.1177/0165025413512063

Kochanska, G., Aksan, N., & Joy, M. E. (2007). Children's fearfulness as a moderator of parenting in early socialization: Two longitudinal studies. *Developmental Psychology, 43,* 222–237.

Kochanska, G., Gross, J. N., Lin, M-H., & Nichols, K. E. (2002). Guilt in young children: Development, determinants, and relations with a broader system of standards. *Child Development, 73,* 461–482.

Koenig, B. L., Kirkpatrick, L. A., & Ketelaar, T. (2007). Misperception of sexual and romantic interests in opposite-sex friendships: Four hypotheses. *Personal Relationships, 14,* 411–429. doi:10.1111/j.1475-6811.2007.00163.x

Koepke, S., & Denissen, J. A. (2012). Dynamics of identity development and separation-individuation in parent-child relationships during adolescence and emerging adulthood. *Developmental Review, 32,* 67–88.

Koestenbaum, P. (1976). *Is there an answer to death?* Englewood Cliffs, NJ: Prentice Hall.

Kohlberg, L. (1966). A cognitive-developmental analysis of children's sex-role concepts and attitudes. In E. E. Maccoby (Ed.), *The development of sex differences.* Stanford, CA: Stanford University Press.

Kohlberg, L. (1969). Stage and sequence: The cognitive-developmental approach to socialization. In D. Goslin (Ed.), *Handbook of socialization theory and research* (pp. 347–480). Chicago: Rand McNally.

Kohlberg, L., & Ullian, D. Z. (1974). Stages in the development of psychosexual concepts and attitudes. In R. C. Friedman, R. M. Richart, & R. L. Van Wiele (Eds.), *Sex differences in behavior.* New York: Wiley.

Kohn, J. (2015). *Top tips for eating right during pregnancy.* Available at www.eatright.org/resource/health/pregnancy/what-to-eat-when-expecting/eating-right-during-pregnancy.

Kojima, G., Iliffe, S., Jivraj, S., & Walters, K. (2017). Association between frailty and quality of life among community-dwelling older people: A systematic review and meta-analysis. *Journal of Epidemiology & Community Health, 70,* 716–721. doi:10.1136/jech-2015-206717

Kojola, E., & Moen, P. (2016). No more lock-step retirement: Boomers' shifting meanings of work and retirement. *Journal of Aging Studies, 36,* 59–70. doi:10.1016/j.jaging.2015.12.003

Kolb, B., & Teskey, G. C. (2012). Age, experience, injury, and the changing brain. *Developmental Psychobiology, 54,* 311–325.

Kolb, D. M., Williams, J., & Frohlinger, C. (2010). *Her place at the table: A woman's guide to negotiating five key challenges to leadership success.* San Francisco, CA: Jossey-Bass.

Kolberg, K. J. S. (1999). Environmental influences on prenatal development and health. In T. L. Whitman & T. V. Merluzzi (Eds.), *Life-span perspectives on health and illness* (pp. 87–103). Mahwah, NJ: Erlbaum.

Kolko, J. (2016). *Trump was stronger where the economy was weaker.* Retrieved from fivethirtyeight.com/features/trump-was-stronger-where-the-economy-is-weaker/.

Kornadt, A. E., Hess, T. M., Voss, P., & Rothermund, K. (in press). Subjective age across the life span: A differentiated, longitudinal approach. *Journal of Gerontology: Psychological Sciences.* doi:10.1093/geronb/gbw072

Kornhaber, M., Fierros, E., & Veenema, S. (2004). *Multiple intelligences: Best ideas from research and practice.* Boston, MA: Allyn & Bacon.

Koropeckyj-Cox T., & Call, V. R. A. (2007). Characteristics of older childless persons and parents: Cross-national comparisons. *Journal of Family Issues, 28,* 1362–1414. doi:10.1177/0192513X07303837

Koss, C., & Ekerdt, D. J. (in press). Residential reasoning and the tug of the Fourth Age. *The Gerontologist.* doi:10.1093/geront/gnw010

Kost, K., & Maddow-Zimet, I. (2016). *U.S. Teenage pregnancies, births and abortions, 2011: National trends by age, race and ethnicity.* New York: Guttmacher Institute.

Kotre, J. N. (2005). Generativity: Reshaping the past into the future. *Science and Theology News, September,* 42–43. Retrieved from www.johnkotre.com/images/generativity_s_t_news_2005.pdf.

Kotter-Grühn, D. (2016). Aging self. In S. K. Whitbourne (Ed.), *The encyclopedia of adulthood and aging* (pp. 55–59). Malden, MA: Wiley.

Kouros, C. D., Papp, L. M., Goeke-Morey, M. C., & Cummings, E. M. (2014). Spillover between marital quality and parent-child relationship quality: Parental depressive symptoms as moderators. *Journal of Family Psychology, 28,* 315–325.

Koutamanis, M., Vossen, H. G. M., Peter, J., & Valkenburg, P. M. (2013). Practice makes perfect: The longitudinal effect of adolescents' instant messaging on their ability to initiate offline friendships. *Computers in Human Behavior, 29,* 2265–2272.

Kowal, A., & Kramer, L. (1997). Children's understanding of parental differential treatment. *Child Development, 68,* 113–126.

Kowalski, R. M., Giumetti, G. W., Schroeder, A. N., & Lattanner, M. R. (2014). Bullying in the digital age: A critical review and meta-analysis of cyberbullying research among youth. *Psychological Bulletin, 140,* 1073–1137.

Kowalski, S. D., & Bondmass, M. D. (2008). Physiological and psychological symptoms of grief in widows. *Research in Nursing & Health, 31,* 23–30. doi:10.1002/nur.20228

Kozbelt, A., & Durmysheva, Y. (2007). Lifespan creativity in a non-Western artistic tradition: A study of Japanese Ukiyo-e printmakers. *International Journal of Aging & Human Development, 65,* 23–51. doi:10.2190/166N-6470-1325-T341

Kramer, L. (2010). The essential ingredients of successful sibling relationships: An emerging framework for advancing theory and practice. *Child Development Perspectives, 4,* 80–86.

Krassner, A. M., Gartstein, M. A., Park, C., Dragan, W. L., Lecannelier, F., & Putnam, S. P. (2017). East-west, collectivist-individualist: A cross-cultural examination of temperament in toddlers from Chile, Poland, South Korea, and the U.S. *European Journal of Development Psychology, 14,* 449–464.

Kratzer, J. M. W., & Stevens Aubrey, J. (2016). Is the actual ideal?: A content analysis of college students' descriptions of ideal and actual hookups. *Sexuality and Culture, 20,* 236–254. doi:10.1007/s12119-015-9318-x

Krause, N. (2006). Religion and health in late life. In J. E. Birren & K. W. Schaie (Eds.), *Handbook of the psychology of aging* (6th ed., pp. 499–518). Amsterdam, The Netherlands: Elsevier.

Krause, N. (2012). Feelings of gratitude toward God among older whites, older African Americans, and older Mexican Americans. *Research on Aging, 34,* 156–173. doi:10.1177/0164027511417884

Krause, N. (2016). Assessing the relationships among wisdom, humility, and life satisfaction. *Journal of Adult Development, 23,* 140–149. doi:10.1007/s10804-016-9230-0

Krause, N., & Bastida, E. (2011). Prayer to the saints or the Virgin and health among older Mexican Americans. *Hispanic Journal of Behavioral Sciences, 33,* 71–87. doi:10.1177/0739986310393628

Krebs, D., & Gillmore, J. (1982). The relationships among the first stages of cognitive development, role-taking abilities, and moral development. *Child Development, 53,* 877–886.

Kreppner, J. M., Rutter, M., Beckett, C., Castle, J., Colvert, E., Groothues, C., et al. (2007). Normality and impairment following profound early institutional deprivation: A longitudinal follow-up into early adolescence. *Developmental Psychology, 43,* 931–946.

Kretch, K. S., & Adolph, K. E. (2013a). Cliff or step? Posture-specific learning at the edge of a drop-off. *Child Development, 84,* 226–240.

Kretch, K. S., & Adolph, K. E. (2013b). No bridge too high: Infants decide whether to cross based on the probability of falling not the severity of the potential fall. *Developmental Science, 16,* 336–351.

Krispin, O., Sternberg, K. J., & Lamb, M. E. (1992). The dimensions of peer evaluation in Israel: A cross-cultural perspective. *International Journal of Behavioral Development, 15,* 299–314.

Krull, A. C. (2013). Health care professionals, friends, family, and God: Interactions contributing to caregivers' long-term care decisions. *Sociological Spectrum, 33,* 329–340. doi:10.1080/02732173.2013.732886

Kübler-Ross, E. (1969). *On death and dying.* New York: Macmillan.

Kübler-Ross, E. (1974). *Questions and answers on death and dying.* New York: Macmillan.

Kuhl, J., & Keller, H. (2008). Affect-regulation, self-development and parenting: A function-design approach to cross-cultural differences. In R. Sorrentino & S. Yamaguchi (Eds.), *Handbook of motivation and cognition across cultures* (pp. 19–47). San Diego, CA: Academic Press.

Kuhn, L. J., Willoughby, M. T., Wilbourn, M. P., Vernon-Feagons, L., Blair, C. B., & the Family Life Project Key Investigators. (2014). Early communicative gestures prospectively predict language development and executive function in early childhood. *Child Development, 85,* 1898–1914.

Kukutai, T. H. (2007). White mothers, brown children: Ethnic identification of Maori-European children in New Zealand. *Journal of Marriage and Family, 69,* 1150–1161. doi:10.1111/j.1741-3737.2007.00438.x

Kulik, L. (2011). Developments in spousal power relations: Are we moving toward equality? *Marriage and Family Review, 47,* 419–435. doi:10.1 080/01494929.2011.619297

Kulik, L. (2016). Long-term marriages. In S. K. Whitbourne (Ed.), *The encyclopedia of adulthood and aging* (pp. 820–823). New York: Wiley.

Kumar, V., Abbas, A. K., Aster, J. C., & Fausto, N. (2010). *Robbins and Cotran pathologic basis of disease, professional edition* (8th ed.). Philadelphia: W. B. Saunders.

Kunz, J. A. (2007). Older adult development. In J. A. Kunz & F. G. Soltys (Eds.), *Transformational reminiscence: Life story work* (pp. 19–39). New York: Springer.

Kurdek, L. A. (2004). Are gay and lesbian cohabiting couples really different from heterosexual married couples? *Journal of Marriage and Family, 66,* 880–900. doi:10.1111/j.0022-2445.2004.00060.x

Kurtz-Costes, B., Copping, K. E., Rowley, S. J., & Kinlaw, C. R. (2014). Gender and age differences in awareness and endorsement of gender stereotypes about academic abilities. *European Journal of Psychology and Education, 29*, 603–618.

Kurup, R. K., & Kurup, P. A. (2003). Hypothalamic digoxin, hemispheric dominance, and neurobiology of love and affection. *International Journal of Neuroscience, 113*, 721–729. doi:10.1080/00207450390200026

Kurzban, R., Burton-Chellew, M. N., & West, S. A. (2015). The evolution of altruism in humans. *Annual Review of Psychology, 66*, 575–599.

Kypri, K., Paschall, M. J., Langley, J., Baxter, J., Cashell-Smith, M., & Bourdeau, B. (2009). Drinking and alcohol-related harm among New Zealand university students: Findings from a national web-based survey. *Alcoholism: Clinical and Experimental Research, 33*, 307–314. doi:10.1111/j.1530-0277.2008.00834.x

LaBotz, M., & Griesemer, B. A. (2016). Use of performance-enhancing substances. *Pediatrics, 138*, e20161300.

Labouvie-Vief, G. (2015). *Integrating emotions and cognition throughout the lifespan.* New York: Springer.

Labouvie-Vief, G., Grühn, D., & Mouras, H. (2009). Dynamic emotion–cognition interactions in development: Arousal, stress, and the processing of affect. In H. B. Bosworth & C. Hertzog (Eds.), *Aging and cognition: Research methodologies and empirical advances* (pp. 181–196). Washington, DC: American Psychological Association.

Lachman, M. E. (2004). Development in midlife. *Annual Review of Psychology, 55*, 305–331. doi:10.1146/ annurev.psych.55.090902.141521

Lacourse, E., Boivin, M., Brendgen, A., Petitclerc, A., Girard, A., Vitaro, F., et al. (2014). A longitudinal twin study of physical aggression during early childhood: Evidence for a developmentally dynamic genome. *Psychological Medicine, 44*, 2617–2627.

Ladd, G. W. (2003). Probing the adaptive significance of children's behavior and relationships in the school context: A child by environment perspective. In R. V. Kail (Ed.), *Advances in child development and behavior* (Vol. 31, pp. 44–104). San Diego, CA: Academic Press.

Ladd, G. W. (2006). Peer rejection, aggressive or withdrawn behavior, and psychological maladjustment from ages 5 to 12: An examination of four predictive models. *Child Development, 77*, 822–846.

Ladd, G. W., & Ladd, B. K. (1998). Parenting behaviors and parent–child relationships: Correlates of peer victimization in kindergarten? *Developmental Psychology, 34*, 1450–1458.

Ladd, G. W., & Pettit, G. S. (2002). Parents and children's peer relationships. In M. Bornstein (Ed.), *Handbook of parenting: Vol. 4* (2nd ed., pp. 377–409). Hillsdale, NJ: Erlbaum.

Ladd, G. W., Herald-Brown, S. L., & Reiser, M. (2008). Does chronic classroom peer rejection predict the development of children's classroom participation during the grade school years? *Child Development, 79*, 1001–1015.

LaFreniere, P., & MacDonald, K. (2013). A postgenomic view of behavioral development and adaptation to the environment. *Developmental Review, 33*, 89–109.

Lagattuta, K. H., & Wellman, H. M. (2002). Differences in early parent–child conversations about negative versus positive emotions: Implications for the development of psychological understanding. *Developmental Psychology, 38*, 564–580.

Lahey, J. N. (2010). International comparison of age discrimination laws. *Research on Aging, 32*, 679–697. doi:10.1177/0164027510379348

Lahti, J., Sabia, S., Singh-Manoux, A., Kivimäki, M., Tatsuse, T., Yamada, M. et al. (2016). Leisure time physical activity and subsequent physical and mental health functioning among midlife Finnish, British, and Japanese employees: A follow-up study in three occupational cohorts. *BMJ Open, 6*, e009788. doi:10.1136/ bmjopen-2015-009788

Lai, D. W. L. (2010). Filial piety, caregiving appraisal, and caregiving burden. *Research on Aging, 32*, 200–223. doi:10.1177/0164027509351475

Laible, D. J., & Carlo, G. (2004). The differential relations of maternal and paternal support and control to adolescent social competence, self-worth, and sympathy. *Journal of Adolescent Research, 19*, 759–782.

Lam, J. (2015). Picky eating in children. *Frontiers in Pediatrics, 3*, 41.

Lamanna, M. A., Riedmann, A., & Stewart, S. D. (2015). *Marriages, families, and relationships: Making choices in a diverse society* (12th ed.). Stamford, CT: Cengage Learning.

Lamaze, F. (1958). *Painless childbirth.* London: Burke.

Lamb, M. E. (2012). Mothers, fathers, families, and circumstances: Factors affecting children's adjustment. *Applied Developmental Science, 16*, 98–111.

Lamb, M. E., & Lewis, C. (2010). The development and significance of father-child relationships in two-parent families. In M. E. Lamb (Ed.), *The role of the father in child development* (5th ed., pp. 94–153). Hoboken, NJ: Wiley.

Lamb, S. (2014). Permanent personhood or meaningful decline? Toward a critical anthropology of successful aging. *Journal of Aging Studies, 29*, 41–52. doi:10.1016/j. jaging.2013.12.006

Lambert, B. L., & Bauer, C. R. (2012). Developmental and behavioral consequences of prenatal cocaine exposure: A review. *Journal of Perinatology, 32*, 819–828.

Lamela, D., Figueiredo, B., & Bastos, A. (2014). The Portuguese version of the Psychological Adjustment to Separation Test—Part A (PAST—A): A study with recently and non-recently divorced adults. *Journal of Happiness Studies. 15*, 387–406. doi:10.1007/ s10902-013-9427-x

Lamela, D., Figueiredo, B., Bastos, A., & Feinberg, M. (2016). Typologies of post-divorce coparenting and parental well-being, parenting quality and children's psychological adjustment. *Child Psychiatry & Human development, 47*, 716–728. doi:10.1007/s10578-015-0604-S

Lampkin-Hunter, T. (2010). *Single parenting.* Bloomington, IN: Xlibris.

Landis, M., Peter-Wright, M., Martin, M., & Bodenmann, G. (2013). Dyadic coping and marital satisfaction of older spouses in long-term marriages. *GeroPsych: The Journal of Gerontopsychology and Geriatric Psychiatry, 26*, 39–47. doi:10.1024/1662-9647/a000077

Lang, F. R., & Heckhausen, J. (2001). Perceived control over development and subjective well-being: Differential benefits across adulthood. *Journal of Personality and Social Psychology, 81*, 509–523. doi:10.1037/0022-3514 .81.3.509

Lang, F. R., & Heckhausen, J. (2006). Motivation and interpersonal regulation across adulthood: Managing the challenges and constraints of social contexts. In C. Hoare (Ed.), *Handbook of adult development and learning* (pp. 149–166). New York: Oxford University Press.

Lang, J. C., & Lee, C. H. (2005). Identity accumulation, others' acceptance, job-search self-efficacy, and stress. *Journal of Organizational Behavior, 26*, 293–312. doi:10.1002/job.309

Langer, N., Pedroni, A., Gianotti, L. R. R., Hänggi, J., Knoch, D., & Jäncke, L. (2012). Functional brain network efficiency predicts intelligence. *Human Brain Mapping, 33*, 1393–1406. doi:10.1002/hbm.21297

Langeslag, S. J. E., van der Veen, F. M., & Fekkes, D. (2012). Blood levels of serotonin are differentially affected by romantic love in men and women. *Journal of Psychophysiology, 26*, 92–98. doi:10.1027/0269-8803/a000071

Langlais, M. R., Anderson, E. R., & Greene, S. M. (2016). Consequences of dating for post-divorce maternal well-being. *Journal of Marriage and Family, 78*, 1032–1046. doi:10.1111/ jomf.12319

Lansford, J. E. (2009). Parental divorce and children's adjustment. *Perspectives on Psychological Science, 4*, 140–152.

Lansford, J. E., Bornstein, M. H., Deater-Deckard, K., Dodge, K. A., Al-Hassan, S. M., Bacchini, D. et al. (2016). How international research on parenting advances understanding of child development. *Child Development Perspectives, 10*, 202–207.

Larson, R., Csikszentmihalyi, M., & Graef, R. (2014). Mood variability and the psychosocial adjustment of adolescents. In M. Csikszentmihalyi (Ed.)., *Applications of flow in human development and education* (pp. 285–304). Dordrecht, the Netherlands: Springer Science+Business Media.

Laurent, H. K., Lucas, T., Pierce, J., Goetz, S., & Granger, D. A. (2016). Coordination of cortisol response to social evaluative threat with autonomic and inflammatory responses is moderated by stress appraisals and affect. *Biological Psychology, 118*, 17–24. doi:10.1016/j. biopsycho.2016.04.066

Laursen, B., & Collins, W. A. (1994). Interpersonal conflict during adolescence. *Psychological Bulletin, 115*, 197–209.

Lavelli, M., & Fogel, A. (2013). Interdyad differences in early mother-infant face-to-face communication: Real-time dynamics and developmental pathways. *Developmental Psychology, 49*, 2257–2271.

Lavner, J. A., & Bradbury, T. N. (2017). Protecting relationships from stress. *Current Opinion in Psychology, 13*, 11–14. doi:10.1016/j.copsyc.2016.03.003

Lavner, J. A., Karney, B. R., & Bradbury, T. N. (2016). Does couples' communication predict marital satisfaction, or does marital satisfaction predict communication? *Journal of Marriage and Family, 78*, 680–694. doi:10.1111/jomf.12301

Lavner, J. A., Lamkin, J., Miller, J. D., Campbell, W. K., & Karney, B. R. (2016). Narcissism and newlywed marriage: Partner characteristics and marital trajectories. *Personality Disorders: Theory, Research, and Treatment, 7*, 169–179. doi:10.1037/per0000137

Lawton, L. E., & Tulkin, D. O. (2010). *Work-family balance, family structure and family-friendly employer programs.* Paper presented at the annual meeting of the Population Association of America, Dallas. Retrieved from paa2010.princeton.edu/download.aspx?submissionId=100573.

Lawton, M. P. (1982). Competence, environmental press, and the adaptation of old people. In M. P. Lawton, P. G. Windley, & T. O. Byerts (Eds.), *Aging and the environment: Theoretical approaches* (pp. 33–59). New York: Springer.

Lawton, M. P. (1989). Environmental proactivity in older people. In V. L. Bengtson & K. W. Schaie (Eds.), *The course of later life: Research and reflections* (pp. 15–23). New York: Springer.

Lawton, M. P., & Nahemow, L. (1973). Ecology of the aging process. In C. Eisdorfer & M. P. Lawton (Eds.), *The psychology of adult development and aging* (pp. 619–674). Washington, DC: American Psychological Association.

Lazarus, R. S. (1984). Puzzles in the study of daily hassles. *Journal of Behavioral Medicine, 7*, 375–389. doi:10.1007/BF00845271

Lazarus, R. S., & Folkman, S. (1984). *Stress, appraisal, and coping.* New York: Springer.

Lazarus, R. S., DeLongis, A., Folkman, S., & Gruen, R. (1985). Stress and adaptational outcomes: The problem of confounded measures. *American Psychologist, 40*, 770–779. 10.1037/0003-066X.40.7.770

LeanIn.org. (2016). *Women in the workplace 2016.* Retrieved from womenintheworkplace.com.

Leaper, C. (2015). Gender and social-cognitive development. In R. M. Lerner (Ed.), *Handbook of child psychology and developmental science* (7th ed., Vol. 2, 19:1–48). Hoboken, NJ: Wiley.

Leaper, C., & Smith, T. E. (2004). A meta-analytic review of gender variations in children's language use: Talkativeness, affiliative speech, and assertive speech. *Developmental Psychology, 40*, 993–1027.

Lebo, P. B., Quehenberger, F., Kamolz, L.-P., & Lumenta, D. B. (2015). The Angelina Jolie effect revisited: Exploring a media-related impact on public awareness. *Cancer, 121*, 3959–3964. doi:10.1002/cncr.29461

Ledebt, A. (2000). Changes in arm posture during the early acquisition of walking. *Infant Behavior & Development, 23*, 79–89.

Ledebt, A., van Wieringen, P. C. W., & Savelsbergh, G. J. P. (2004). Functional significance of foot rotation in early walking. *Infant Behavior & Development, 27*, 163–172.

LeDoux, J. E., & Gorman, J. M. (2001). A call to action: Overcoming anxiety through active coping. *American Journal of Psychiatry, 158*, 1953–1955. doi:10.1176/appi.ajp.158.12.1953.

Lee, G. R. (2014). Current research on widowhood: Devastation and human resilience. *Journals of Gerontology: Psychological Sciences and Social Sciences, 69B*, 2–3. doi:10.1093/geronb/gbt111

Lee, H. J., Macbeth, A. H., Pagani, J. H., & Young, W. S. (2009). Oxytocin: The great facilitator of life. *Progress in Neurobiology, 88*, 127–151. doi:10.1016/j.pneurobio.2009.04.001

Lee, K. S. (2010). Gender, care work, and the complexity of family membership in Japan. *Gender & Society, 24*, 647–671. doi:10.1177/0891243210382903

Lee, M.-D. (2007). Correlates of consequences of intergenerational caregiving in Taiwan. *Journal of Advanced Nursing, 59*, 47–56. doi:10.1111/j.1365-2648.2007.04274.x

Lee, P. C. B. (2003). Going beyond career plateau: Using professional plateau to account for work outcomes. *Journal of Management Development, 22*, 538–551. doi:10.1108/02621710310478503

Lee, S. J., Altschul, I., & Gershoff, E. T. (2013). Does warmth moderate longitudinal associations between spanking and child aggression in early childhood? *Developmental Psychology, 49*, 2017–2028.

Lee, T.-Y. (2010). The loss and grief in immigration: Pastoral care for immigrants. *Pastoral Psychology, 59*, 159–169. doi:10.1007/s11089-009-0261-3

Leekam, S. (2016). Social cognitive impairment and autism: What are we trying to explain? *Philosophical Transactions of the Royal Society B, 371*, 20150082.

Leerkes, E. M., Blankson, A. M., & O'Brien, M. (2009). Differential effects of maternal sensitivity to infant distress and nondistress on social-emotional functioning. *Child Development, 80*, 762–775.

Lefkowitz, E. S., Vukman, S. N., & Loken, E. (2012). Young adults in a wireless world. In A. Booth, S. L. Brown, N. S. Landale, W. D. Manning, & S. M. McHale (Eds.), *Early adulthood in a family context* (pp. 45–56). New York: Springer.

Legare, C. H., Wellman, H. M., & Gelman, S. A. (2009). Evidence for an explanation advantage in naïve biological reasoning. *Cognitive Psychology, 58*, 177–194.

Leichtentritt, R. D., Leichtentritt, J., Barzllal, Y., & Pedatsur-Sukenik, N. (2013). Unanticipated death of a partner: The loss experience of bereaved girlfriends of fallen Israeli soldiers. *Death Studies, 37*, 803–829. doi:10.1080/07481187.2012.699907

Lemery, K. S., Goldsmith, H. H., Klinnert, M. D., & Mrazek, D. A. (1999). Developmental models of infant and childhood temperament. *Developmental Psychology, 35*, 189–204.

Lemieux, A. (2012). Post-formal thought in gerontagogy or beyond Piaget. *Journal of Behavioral and Brain Science, 2*, 399–406. doi:10.4236/jbbs.2012.23046

Lenhart, A. (2015). *Teen, social media and technology overview 2015.* Washington, DC: Pew Research Center.

Lent, R. W. (2005). A social cognitive view of career development and counseling. In S. D. Brown & R. W. Lent (Eds.), *Career development and counseling: Putting theory and research to work* (pp. 101–127). Hoboken, NJ: Wiley.

Lent, R. W. (2013). Career-life preparedness: Revisiting career planning and adjustment in the new workplace. *Career Development Quarterly, 61*, 2–14. doi:10.1002/j.2161-0045.2013.00031.x

Leon, G. R., Gillum, B., Gillum, R., & Gouze, M. (1979). Personality stability and change over a 30-year period: Middle to old age. *Journal of Consulting and Clinical Psychology, 47*, 517–524. doi:10.1037/0022-006X.47.3.517

LeRoux, H., & Fisher, J. E. (2006). Strategies for enhancing medication adherence in the elderly. In W. T. O'Donohue & E. R. Levensky (Eds.). *Promoting treatment adherence: A practical handbook for health care providers* (pp. 353–362). Thousand Oaks, CA: Sage.

Leshikar, E. D., Cassidy, B. S., & Gutchess, A. H. (2016). *Cognitive, Affective, & Behavioral Neuroscience, 16*, 302–314. doi:10.3758/s13415-015-1-0390-3

Lesnoff-Caravaglia, G. (2010). Technology and aging: The herald of a new age. In J. C. Cavanaugh & C. K. Cavanaugh (Eds.), *Aging in America: Volume 3: Societal issues* (pp. 247–277). Santa Barbara, CA: ABC-CLIO.

Leung, R. K., Toumbourou, J. W., & Hemphill, S. A. (2014). The effects of peer influence and selection processes on adolescent alcohol use: A systematic review of longitudinal studies. *Health Psychology Review, 8*, 426–457.

Leuty, M. E., Hansen, J.-I. C., & Speaks, S. Z. (2016). Vocational and leisure interests: A profile-level approach to examining interests. *Journal of Career Assessment, 24*, 215–239. doi:10.1177/1069072715580321

Levete, S. (2010). *Coming of age.* New York: Wayland/The Rosen Publishing Group.

Levine, I. S. (2009). *Best friends forever: Surviving a breakup with your best friend.* New York: Penguin.

Levine, L. E. (1983). *Mine:* Self-definition in 2-year-old boys. *Developmental Psychology, 19*, 544–549.

Levine, L. J., Kaplan, R. L., & Davis, E. L. (2013). How kids keep their cool: Young children's use of cognitive strategies to regulate emotion. In D. Hermans, B. Rimé, & B. Mesquita (Eds.), *Changing emotions* (pp. 3–9). Hove, UK: Psychology Press.

Levine, S. C., Foley, A., Lourenco, S., Ehrlich, S., & Ratliff, K. (2016). Sex differences in spati-

cognition: Advancing the conversation. *WIREs Cognitive Science, 7,* 127–155.

Levinger, G. (1980). Toward the analysis of close relationships. *Journal of Experimental Social Psychology, 16,* 510–544. doi:10.1016/0022-1031(80)90056-6

Levinger, G. (1983). Development and change. In H. H. Kelley, E. Berscheid, A. Christensen, J. H. Harvey, T. L. Hutson, G. Levinger, et al. (Eds.), *Close relationships* (pp. 315–359). New York: Freeman.

Levitt, A. G., & Utman, J. A. (1992). From babbling towards the sound systems of English and French: A longitudinal two-case study. *Journal of Child Language, 19,* 19–49.

Levy, B. A., Gong, Z., Hessels, S., Evans, M. A., & Jared, D. (2006). Understanding print: Early reading development and the contributions of home literacy experiences. *Journal of Experimental Child Psychology, 93,* 63–93.

Levy, B. R., & Bavishi, A. (in press). Survival advantage mechanism: Inflammation as a mediator of self-perceptions of aging on longevity. *Journals of Gerontology: Psychological Sciences.* doi:10.1093/geronb/gbw035

Levy, G. D., Taylor, M. G., & Gelman, S. A. (1995). Traditional and evaluative aspects of flexibility in gender roles, social conventions, moral rules, and physical laws. *Child Development, 66,* 515–531.

LeWine, H. (2013). *Alcohol: A heart disease-cancer balancing act.* Retrieved from www.health.harvard.edu/blog/alcohol-a-heart-disease-cancer-balancing-act-201302155909.

Lewinsohn, P. M. (1975). The behavioral study and treatment of depression. In M. Hersen, R. M. Eisler, & P. M. Miller (Eds.), *Progress in behavior modification* (Vol. 1, pp. 19–64). New York: Academic Press.

Lewis, D. C., Seponski, D. M., & Camp, T. G. (2011). Religious and spiritual values transactions: A constant-comparison analysis of grandmothers and adult-granddaughters. *Journal of Religion, Spirituality & Aging, 23,* 184–205. doi:10.1080/15528030.2011.533407

Lewis, J. L., & Groh, A. (2016). It's about the people...: Seniors' perspectives on age-friendly communities. In T. Moulaert & S. Garon (Eds.), *Age-friendly communities in international comparison* (pp. 81–98). New York: Springer. doi:10.1007/978-3-319-24031-2_6

Lewis, J. R. (2013). Hair-pulling, culture, and unmourned death. *International Journal of Psychoanalytic Self Psychology, 8,* 202–217. doi:10.1080/1 5551024.2013.768749

Lewis, M. (1997). The self in self-conscious emotions. In J. G. Snodgrass & R. L. Thompson (Eds.), *The self across psychology: Self-awareness, self-recognition, and the self-concept* (pp. 119–142). New York: New York Academy of Science.

Lewis, M. (2011). The origins and uses of self-awareness or the mental representations of me. *Consciousness and Cognition, 20,* 120–129.

Lewis, M. (2016). The emergence of human emotions. In L. F. Barrett, M. Lewis, & J. M. Haviland-Jones (Eds.), *Handbook of emotions* (4th ed., pp. 272–292). New York: Guilford.

Lewis, M., & Brooks-Gunn, J. (1979). *Social cognition and the acquisition of self.* New York: Plenum.

Lewis, M., Lamson, A., & White, M. (2016). The state of dyadic methodology: An Analysis of the literature on interventions for military couples. *Journal of Couple & Relationship therapy, 15,* 135–157. doi:10.1080/15332691.2015.1106998

Lewis, M., Takai-Kawakami, K., Kawakami, K., & Sullivan, M. W. (2010). Cultural differences in emotional responses to success and failure. *International Journal of Behavioral Development, 34,* 53–61.

Lewkowicz, D. J. (2000). Infants' perception of the audible, visible, and bimodal attributes of multimodal syllables. *Child Development, 71,* 1241–1257.

Lewontin, R. (1976). Race and intelligence. In N. J. Block & G. Dworkin (Eds.), *The IQ controversy* (pp. 78–92). New York: Pantheon.

Leys, D., Murao, K., & Pasquier, F. (2014). Vascular cognitive impairment and dementia. In B. Norrving (Ed.), *Oxford textbook of stroke and cerebrovascular disorders* (pp. 215–224). New York: Oxford University Press.

Li-Korotky, H.-S. (2012). Age-related hearing loss: Quality of care for quality of life. *The Gerontologist, 52,* 265–271. doi:10.1093/geront/gnr159

Li, C. M., Zhang, X., Hoffman, H. J., Cotch, M. F., Themann, C. L., & Wilson, M. R. (2014). Hearing impairment associated with depression in US adults, National Health and Nutrition Examination Survey, 2005-2010. *JAMA Otolaryngology—Head & Neck Surgery, 140,* 293–302. doi:10.1001/jamaoto.2014.42

Li, J., & Prigerson, H. G (2016). Assessment and associated features of prolonged grief disorder among Chinese bereaved individuals. *Comprehensive Psychiatry, 66,* 9–16. doi:10.1016/j.comppsych.2015.12.001

Li, K. Z. H., Lindenberger, U., Freund, A. M., & Baltes, P. B. (2001). Walking while memorizing: Age-related differences in compensatory behavior. *Psychological Science, 12,* 230–237. doi:10.1111/1467-9280.00341

Li, Y., Anderson, R. C., Nguyen-Jahiel, K., Dong, T., Archodidou, A., Kim, I.-H., et al. (2007). Emergent leadership in children's discussion groups. *Cognition & Instruction, 25,* 75–111.

Liang, H., & Eley, T. C. (2005). A monozygotic twin differences study of nonshared environmental influence on adolescent depressive symptoms. *Child Development, 76,* 1247–1260.

Liben, L. S. (2016). We've come a long way, baby (But we're not there yet): Gender past, present, and future. *Child Development, 87,* 5–28.

Liben, L. S., & Bigler, R. S. (2002). The developmental course of gender differentiation. *Monographs of the Society for Research in Child Development, 67* (Serial No. 269).

Libertus, K., & Needham, A. (2010). Teach to reach: The effects of active versus passive reaching experiences on action and perception. *Vision Research, 50,* 2750–2757.

Libertus, K., Joh, A. S., & Needham, A. W. (2016). Motor training at 3 months affects object exploration 12 months later. *Developmental Science, 19,* 1058–1066.

Lichtenberg, P. (2016). Financial exploitation, financial capacity, and Alzheimer's disease. *American Psychologist, 71,* 312–320. doi:10.1037/a0040192

Lichtenthal, W. G., & Sweeney, C. (2014). Families "at risk" of complicated bereavement. In D. W. Kissane & F. Parnes (Eds.), *Bereavement care for families* (pp. 249–265). New York: Routledge.

Lichter, D. T., & Carmalt, J. H. (2009). Religion and marital quality among low-income couples. *Social Science Research, 38,* 168–187. doi:10.1016 /j.ssresearch.2008.07.003

Liddle, H. A. (2016). Multidimensional family therapy: Evidence base for transdiagnostic treatment outcomes, change mechanisms, and implementation in community settings. *Family Process, 55,* 558–576.

Liebal, K., Behne, T., Carpenter, M., & Tomasello, M. (2009). Infants use shared experience to interpret pointing gestures. *Developmental Science, 12,* 264–271.

Lieber, J. (2001, October 10). Widows of tower disaster cope, but with quiet fury. *USA Today,* pp. A1–A2.

Light, L. L. (2012). Dual-process theories of memory in old age: An update. In M. Naveh-Benjamin & N. Ohta (Eds.). *Memory and aging: Current issues and future directions* (pp. 97–124). New York: Psychology Press.

Lighthouse International. (2014). *Age-related macular degeneration (AMD).* Retrieved from lighthouse.org/about-low-vision-blindness/vision-disorders/age-related-macular-degeneration-amd/.

Lilgendahl, J. P., & McAdams, D. P. (2011). Constructing stories of self-growth: How individual differences in patterns of autobiographical reasoning relate to well-being in midlife. *Journal of Personality, 79,* 391–428. doi:10.1111/j.1467-6494.2010.00688.x

Lillard, A. S., Lerner, M. D., Hopkins, E. J., Dore, R. A., Smith, E. D., & Palmquist, C. M. (2013). The impact of pretend play on children's development: A review of the evidence. *Psychological Bulletin, 139,* 1–34.

Limb, G. E., & Shafer, K. (2014, January). *The impact of kin support on American Indian families.* Paper presented at the annual meeting of the Society for Social Work and Research, San Antonio, TX.

Limb, G. E., Shafer, K., & Sandoval, K. (2014). The impact of kin support on urban American Indian families. *Child & Family Social Work, 19,* 423–442. doi:10.1111/cfs.12041

Lin, C. C., & Fu, V. R. (1990). A comparison of childrearing practices among Chinese, immigrant Chinese, and Caucasian-American parents. *Child Development, 61,* 429–433.

Lindberg, S. M., Hyde, J. S., Petersen, J. L., & Linn, M. C. (2010). New trends in gender and mathematics performance: A meta-analysis. *Psychological Bulletin, 136,* 1123–1135.

Lindbergh, C. A., Dishman, R. K., & Miller, L. S. (2016). Functional disability I mild cognitive impairment: A systematic review and meta-analysis. *Neuropsychology Review, 26,* 129–159. doi:10.1007/s11065-016-9321-5

Linden, D. E. J. (2016). *Neuroimaging and neurophysiology in psychiatry.* Oxford, UK: Oxford University Press.

Linden, J. A., & Olshaker, J. S. (2014). Elder mistreatment. In J. H. Kahn, B. G. Magauran, Jr., & J. S. Olshaker (Eds.), *Geriatric emergency medicine: Principles and practice* (pp. 355–360). New York: Cambridge University Press.

Lindgren, L., Bergdahl, J., & Nyberg, L. (2016). Longitudinal evidence for smaller hippocampus volume as a vulnerability factor for perceived stress. *Cerebral Cortex, 26,* 3527–3533. doi:10.1093/cercor/bhw154

Lindsey, E. W., Cremeens, P. R., & Caldera, Y. M. (2010). Mother-child and father-child mutuality in two contexts: Consequences for young children's peer relationships. *Infant and Child Development, 19,* 142–160.

Linebarger, D. L., & Vaala, S. E. (2010). Screen media and language development in infants and toddlers: An ecological perspective. *Developmental Review, 30,* 176–202.

Linver, M. R., Roth, J. L., & Brooks-Gunn, J. (2009). Patterns of adolescents' participation in organized activities: Are sports best when combined with other activities? *Developmental Psychology, 45,* 354–367.

Lipp, I., Benedek, M., Fink, A., Koschutnig, K., Reishofer, G., Bergner, S. et al. (2012). Investigating neural efficiency in the visuo-spatial domain: An fMRI study. *PLoS ONE, 7,* e51316. doi:10.1371/journal. pone.0051316. Retrieved from www.plosone.org/article/info%3Adoi%2F10.1371%2Fjournal.pone.0051316.

Lips-Wiersma, M., Wright, S., & Dik. B. (2016). Meaningful work: Differences among blue-, pink-, and white-collar occupations. *Career Development International, 21,* 534–551. doi:10.1108/DCI-04-2016-0052

Lips, H. M. (2016). The gender pay gap and the wellbeing of working women. In M. L. Connerley & J. Wu (eds.), *Handbook on well-being of working women* (pp. 141–157). New York: Springer.

Lipsitt, L. P. (1990). Learning and memory in infants. *Merrill-Palmer Quarterly, 36,* 53–66.

Lipsitt, L. P. (2003). Crib death: A biobehavioral phenomenon. *Psychological Science, 12,* 164–170.

Lipton, A., Costa, L., Sieber, P., Dougall, W. C., & Braun, A. (2014). New targeted therapies for bone metastases. In V. Vassiliou, E. Chow, & D. Kardamakis (Eds.), *Bone metastases* (pp. 235–246). New York: Springer.

Litovsky, R. (2015). Development of the auditory system. In G. G. Celesia & G. Hickok (Eds.), *Handbook of clinical neurology* (Vol. 129, The human auditory system, pp. 55–72). Amsterdam: Elsevier.

Littlecott, H. J., Moore, G. F., Moore, L., Lyons, R. A., & Murphy, S. (2016). Associations between breakfast consumption and educational outcomes in 9- to11-year-old children. *Public Health Nutrition, 19,* 1575–1582.

Liu, C.-C., Kanekiyo, T., Xu, H., & Bu, G. (2013). Apolipoprotein E and Alzheimer's disease: Risk, mechanisms and therapy. *Nature Reviews Neurology, 9,* 106–118. doi:10.1038/nrneurol.2012.263

Liu, D., Gelman, S. A., & Wellman, H. M. (2007). Components of young children's trait understanding: Behavior-to-trait and trait-to-behavior predictions. *Child Development, 78,* 1543–1558.

Liu, G., Dupre, M. E., Gu, D., Mair, C. A., & Chen, F. (2012). Psychological well-being of the institutionalized and community-residing oldest old in China: The role of children. *Social Science and Medicine, 75,* 1874–1882. doi:10.1016/j.socscimed.2012.07.019

Liu, R X., Lin, W., & Chen, Z. Y. (2010). School performance, peer association, psychological and behavioral adjustments: A comparison between Chinese adolescents with and without siblings. *Journal of Adolescence, 33,* 411–417.

Livesley, W. J., & Bromley, D. B. (1973). *Person perception in childhood and adolescence.* New York: Wiley.

Livingston, G. (2014). *Four-in-ten couples are saying "I do," again.* Retrieved from www.pewsocialtrends.org/2014/11/14/four-in-ten-couples-are-saying-i-do-again/.

Lo, M., & Aziz, T. (2009). Muslim marriage goes online: The use of Internet matchmaking by American Muslims. *Journal of Religion and Popular Culture, 2*(3). doi:10.3138/jrpc.21.3.005

Lobo, M. A., & Galloway, J. C. (2012). Enhanced handling and positioning in early infancy advances development throughout the first year. *Child Development, 83,* 1290–1302.

LoBue, V., & DeLoache, J. S. (2010). Superior detection of threat-relevant stimuli in infancy. *Developmental Science, 13,* 221–228.

Lochman, J. E. Baden, R. E., Boxmeyer, C. L., Powell, N. P., Qu, L., Salekin, K. L. et al. (2014). Does a booster intervention augment the preventive effects of an abbreviated version of the coping power program for aggressive children? *Journal of Abnormal Child Psychology, 42,* 367–381.

Loheswaran, G., Barr, M. S., Rajji, T. K., Blumberger, D. M., Le Foll, B., & Daskalakis, Z. J. (2016). Alcohol intoxication by binge drinking impairs neuroplasticity. *Brain Stimulation, 9,* 27–32. doi:10.1016/j.brs.2015.08.011

Lomanowska, A. M., & Guitton, M. J. (2016). Online intimacy and well-being in the digital age. *Internet Interventions, 4*(Part2), 138–144. doi:10.1016/j.invent.2016.06.005. Retrieved from www.sciencedirect.com/science/article/pii/S2214782916300021.

LongTermCare.gov. (2016). *How much care will you need?* Retrieved from longtermcare.gov/the-basics/how-much-care-will-you-need/.

Lopata, H. Z. (1996). Widowhood and husband sanctification. In D. Klass, P. R. Silverman, & S. L. Nickman (Eds.), *Continuing bonds: New understandings of grief* (pp. 149–162). Washington, DC: Taylor & Francis.

Lopez, A. B., Huynh, V. W., & Fuligni, A. J. (2011). A longitudinal study of religious identity and participation during adolescence. *Child Development, 82,* 1297–1309.

Lord, K., Livingston, G., Robertson, S., & Cooper, C. (2016). How people with dementia and their families decide about moving to a care home and support their needs: Development of a decision aid, a qualitative study. *BMC Geriatrics, 16,* 68. doi:10.1186/s12877-016-0242-1. Retrieved from bmcgeriatr.biomedcentral.com/articles/10.1186/s12877-016-0242-1.

Loretto, W., & Vickerstaff, S. (2013). The domestic and gendered context for retirement. *Human Relations, 66,* 65–86. doi:10.1177/0018726712455832

Lovinger, D. M., & Roberto, M. (2013). Synaptic effects induced by alcohol. *Behavioral Neurobiology of Alcohol Addiction, 13,* 31–86. doi:10.1007/7854_2011_143

Lozoff, B., Wolf, A. W., & Davis, N. S. (1985). Sleep problems seen in pediatric practice. *Pediatrics, 75,* 477–483.

Lu, F. J. H., Lee, W. P., Chang, Y-K., Chou, C-C., Hsu, Y-W., Lin, J-H. et al. (2016). Interaction of athletes' resilience and coaches' social support on the stress-burnout relationship: A conjunctive moderation perspective. *Psychology of Sport and Exercise, 22,* 202–209.

Lubans, D., Richards, J., Hillman, C., Faulkner, G., Beauchamp, M., Nilsson, M. et al. (2016). Physical activity for cognitive and mental health in youth: A systematic review of mechanisms. *Pediatrics, 38*(3), e20161642.

Lubinski, D., Benbow, C. P, Webb, R. M., & Bleske-Rechek, A. (2006). Tracking exceptional human capital over two decades. *Psychological Science, 17,* 194–199.

Lucero-Liu, A. A. (2007). Exploring intersections in the intimate lives of Mexican origin women. *Dissertation Abstracts International. Section A. Humanities and Social Sciences, 68*(3-A), 1175.

Lucette, A., Ironson, G., Pargament, K. I., & Krause, N. (2016). Spirituality and religiousness are associated with fewer depressive symptoms in individuals with medical conditions. *Psychosomatics, 57,* 505–513. doi:10.1016/j.psym.2016.03.005

Luders, E. (2014). Exploring age-related brain degeneration in meditation practitioners. *Annals of the New York Academy of Sciences, 1307,* 82–88. doi:10.1111/nyas.12217

Luders, E., & Cherbuin, N. (2016). Searching for the philosopher's stone: Promising links between meditation and brain preservation. *Annals of the New York Academy of Sciences, 1373,* 38–44. doi:10.1111/nyas.13082

...ke, R. L., & Smucker, D. R. (2007). Racial differences in the willingness to use hospice services. *Journal of Palliative Medicine, 10,* 1329–1337. doi:10.1089/jpm.2007.0077

Luhmann, M., Hofmann, W., Eid, M., & Lucas, R. E. (2012). Subjective well-being and adaptation to life events: A meta-analysis. *Journal of Personality and Social Psychology, 102,* 592–615. doi:10.1037/a0025948

Luke, B., Gopal, D., Cabral, H., Diop, H., & Stern, J. (2016). Perinatal outcomes of singleton siblings: The effects of changing maternal fertility status. *Journal of Assisted Reproduction and Genetics, 9,* 1203–1213.

Lukowski, A. F., & Bauer, P. J. (2014). Long-term memory in infancy and early childhood. In P. J. Bauer & R. Fivush (Eds.), *The Wiley handbook on the development of children's memory* (pp. 230–254). Chichester, UK: Wiley.

Lundström, J. N., & Jones-Gotman, M. (2009). Romantic love modulates women's identification of men's body odors. *Hormones and Behavior, 55,* 280–284. doi:10.1016/j.yhbeh.2008.11.009

Lung, F-W., & Shu, B-C. (2011). Sleeping position and health status of children at six-, eighteen-, and thirty-six-month development. *Research in Developmental Disabilities, 32,* 713–718.

Luo, R., & Tamis-LeMonda, C. S. (2016). Mothers' verbal and nonverbal strategies in relation to infants' object-directed actions in real time and across the first three years in ethnically diverse families. *Infancy, 21,* 65–89.

Luo, S., & Zhang, G. (2009). What leads to romantic attraction: Similarity, reciprocity, security, or beauty? Evidence from a speed-dating study. *Journal of Personality, 77,* 933–964. doi:10.1111/j.1467-6494.2009.00570.x

Luong, G., Charles, S. T., & Fingerman, K. L. (2011). Better with age: Social relationships across adulthood. *Journal of Social and Personal Relationships, 28,* 9–23. doi:10.1177/0265407510391362

Lushington, K., Pamula, Y., Martin, J., & Kennedy, J. D. (2013). Developmental changes in sleep: Infancy and preschool years. In A. R. Wolfson and H. W. Montgomery-Downs (Eds.), *The Oxford handbook of infant, child, and adolescent sleep and behavior* (pp. 34–47). Oxford, UK: Oxford University Press.

Luthans, F., Avolio, B. J., Avey, J. B., & Norman, S. M. (2007). Positive psychological capital: Measurement and relationship with performance and satisfaction. *Personnel Psychology, 60,* 541–572. doi:10.1111/j.1744-6570.2007.00083.x

Luxenberg, S. (2014). Welcoming love at an older age, but not necessarily marriage. *New York Times (April 25).* Retrieved from www.nytimes.com/2014/04/26/your-money/welcoming-love-at-an-older-age-but-not-necessarily-marriage.html?_r=0.

Lyall, K., Croen, L. A., Daniels, J., Fallin, M. D., Ladd-Ascota, C., Lee, B. K., et al. (2017). The changing epidemiology of autism spectrum disorders. *Annual Review of Public Health, 38,* 9.1–9.22.

Lyng, S. (2012). Existential transcendence in late modernity: Edgework and hermeneutic reflexivity. *Human Studies, 35,* 401–414. doi:10.1007 /s10746-012-9242-0

Lyster, S-A Halaas, Lervåg, A. O., & Hulme, C. (2016). Preschool morphological training produces long-term improvements in reading comprehension. *Reading and Writing, 29,* 1269–1288.

Lytton, H. (2000). Toward a model of family-environmental and child-biological influences on development. *Developmental Review, 20,* 150–179.

Lytton, H., & Romney, D. M. (1991). Parents' differential socialization of boys and girls: A meta-analysis. *Psychological Bulletin, 109,* 267–296.

Maatz, L., & Hedgepath, A. (2013). *Women and work: 50 years of change since the American Women Report.* Retrieved from www.dol.gov/wb/resources/women_and_work.pdf.

MacArthur, C. A. (2015). Instruction in evaluation and revision. In C. A. MacArthur, S. Graham, & J. Fitzgerald (Eds.), *Handbook of writing research* (2nd ed., pp. 272–287). New York: Guilford.

Maccoby, E. E. (1990). Gender and relationships: A developmental account. *American Psychologist, 45,* 513–520.

Maccoby, E. E. (1998). *The two sexes: Growing up apart, coming together.* Cambridge, MA: Belknap Press.

Maccoby, E. E., & Jacklin, C. N. (1974). *The psychology of sex differences.* Stanford, CA: Stanford University Press.

Mace, J. H., & Clevinger, A. M. (2013). Priming voluntary autobiographical memories: Implications for the organization of autobiographical memory and voluntary recall processes. *Memory, 21,* 524–536. doi:10.1080/09658211.2012.744422

Maciejewski, P. K., Zhang, B, Block, S. D., & Prigerson, H. G. (2007). An empirical examination of the stage theory of grief. *JAMA, 297,* 716–723. doi:10.1001/jama.297.7.716

Mackenzie, P. (2012). Normal changes of ageing. *InnovAiT.* doi:10.1093/ innovait/ins099

Macnamara, B. N., Hambrick, D. Z., & Oswald, F. L. (2014). Deliberate practice and performance in music, games, sports, education, and professions: A meta-analysis. *Psychological Science, 25,* 1608–1618. doi:10.1177/0956797614535810

MacWhinney, B. (1998). Models of the emergence of language. *Annual Review of Psychology, 49,* 199–227.

Magai, C. (2008). Long-lived emotions: A life course perspective on emotional development. In M. Lewis, J. M. Haviland-Jones, & L. F. Barrett (Eds.), *Handbook of emotions* (3rd ed., pp. 376–392). New York: Guilford.

Magee, L., & Hale, L. (2012). Longitudinal associations between sleep duration and subsequent weight gain: A systematic review. *Sleep Medicine Reviews, 16,* 231–241.

Magnuson, K., & Duncan, G. (2006). The role of family socioeconomic resources in black and white test score gaps among young children. *Developmental Review, 26,* 365–399.

Maguire, E. A., Woollett, K., & Spiers, H. J. (2006). London taxi drivers and bus drivers: A structural MRI and neuropsychological analysis. *Hippocampus, 16,* 1091–1101.

Mahady, G. B., Locklear, T. D., Doyle, B. J., Huang, Y., Perez, A. L., & Caceres, A. (2008). Menopause, a universal female experience: Lessons from Mexico and Central America. *Current Women's Health Reviews, 4,* 3–8. doi:10.2174/157340408783572033

Mahon, N. E., Yarcheski, A., Yarcheski, T., Cannella, B. L., & Hanks, M. M. (2006). A meta-analytic study of predictors for loneliness during adolescence. *Nursing Research, 55,* 308–315.

Maitre, N. L., Slaughter, J. C., Aschner, J. L., & Key, A. P. (2014). Hemispheric differences in speech-sound event-related potentials in intensive care neonates: Associations and predictive value for development in infancy. *Journal of Child Neurology, 29,* 903–911.

Makel, M. C., Kell, H. J., Lubinski, D., Putallaz, M., & Benbow, C. P. (2016). When lightning strikes twice: Profoundly gifted, profoundly accomplished. *Psychological Science, 27,* 1004–1018.

Malberg, N. T. (2014). Revisiting, repairing, and restoring: The developmental journey of a bereaved adolescent. In P. Cohen, K. M. Sossin, & R. Ruth (Eds.), *Healing after parent loss in childhood and adolescence* (pp. 135–158). Lanham, MD: Rowman & Littlefield.

Malkinson, R., & Bar-Tur, L. (2004–2005). Long term bereavement processes of older parents: The three phases of grief. *Omega: The Journal of Death and Dying, 50,* 103–129. doi:10.2190/W346-UP8T-RER6-BBD1

Malone, M. L., & Camp, C. J. (2007). Montessori-Based Dementia Programming®: Providing tools for engagement. *Dementia: The International Journal of Social Research and Practice, 6,* 150–157. doi:10.1177/1471301207079099

Mandara, J., Gaylord-Harden, N. K., Richard, M. H., & Ragsdale, B. L. (2009). The effects of changes in racial identity and self-esteem on changes in African American adolescents' mental health. *Child Development, 80,* 1660–1675.

Mandel, D. R., Jusczyk, P. W., & Pisoni, D. B. (1995). Infants' recognition of the sound patterns of their own names. *Psychological Science, 6,* 314–317.

Mandemakers, J. J., & Monden, C. W. S. (2013). Does the effect of job loss on psychological distress differ by educational level? *Work, Employment and Society, 27,* 73–93. doi:10.1177/0950017012460312

Mange, A. P., & Mange, E. J. (1990). *Genetics: Human aspects* (2nd ed.). Sunderland, MA: Sinhauer Associates.

Mangelsdorf, S. C. (1992). Developmental changes in infant–stranger interaction. *Infant Behavior & Development, 15,* 191–208.

Mankus, A. M., Boden, M. T., & Thompson, R. J. (2016). Sources of variation in emotional awareness: Age, gender, and socioeconomic status. *Personality and Individual Differences, 89,* 28–33. doi:10.1016/j.paid.2015.09.043

Mantler, J., Matejicek, A., Matheson, K., & Anisman, H. (2005). Coping with employment uncertainty: A comparison of employed and unemployed workers. *Journal of Occupational Health Psychology, 10,* 200–209. doi:10.1037/1076-8998.10.3.200

Maple, M., Edwards, H. E., Minichiello, V., & Plummer, D. (2013). Still part of the family: The importance of physical, emotional and spiritual memorial places and spaces for parents bereaved through the suicide death of their son or daughter. *Mortality, 18,* 54–71. doi:10.1080/13576275.2012.755158

Maple, M., Edwards, H., Plummer, D., & Minichiello, V. (2010). Silenced voices: Hearing the stories of parents bereaved through the suicide death of a young adult child. *Health and Social Care in the Community, 18,* 241–248. doi:10.1111/j.1365-2524.2009.00886.x

Maratsos, M. (1998). The acquisition of grammar. In W. Damon (Ed.), *Handbook of child psychology.* New York: Wiley.

Marcia, J. E. (1980). Identity in adolescence. In J. Adelson (Ed.), *Handbook of adolescent psychology.* New York: Wiley.

Marcia, J., & Josselson, R. (2013). Eriksonian personality research and its implications for psychotherapy. *Journal of Personality, 81,* 617–629. doi:10.1111/ jopy.12014

Marcus, G. F., Pinker, S., Ullman, M., Hollander, M., Rosen, T. J., & Xu, F. (1992). Overregularization in language acquisition. *Monographs of the Society for Research in Child Development, 58* (Serial No. 228).

Marcus, R. (2013). *Denouncing binge drinking is not victim-blaming.* Opinion article appearing in the *Washington Post.* Retrieved from www.washingtonpost.com/opinions/ruth-marcus-missing-the-point-on-binge-drinking/2013/10/24/56c8a70a-3ce0-11e3-a94f-b58017bfee6c_story.html.

Mares, M-L., & Pan, Z. (2013). Effects of Sesame Street: A meta-analysis of children's learning in 15 countries. *Journal of Applied Developmental Psychology, 34,* 140–151.

Margett, T. E., & Witherington, D. C. (2011). The nature of preschoolers' concept of living and artificial objects. *Child Development, 82,* 2067–2082.

Margrett, J. A., Allaire, J. C., Johnson, T. L., Daugherty, K. E., & Weatherbee, S. R. (2010). Everyday problem solving. In J. C. Cavanaugh & C. K. Cavanaugh (Eds.), *Aging in America: Vol. 1: Psychological aspects* (pp. 79–101). Santa Barbara, CA: Praeger Perspectives.

Markovits, H., Benenson, J., & Dolenszky, E. (2001). Evidence that children and adolescents have internal models of peer interactions that are gender differentiated. *Child Development, 72,* 879–886.

Marks, A. K., Patton, F., & García Coll, C. (2011). Being bicultural: A mixed-methods study of adolescents' implicitly and explicitly measured multiethnic identities. *Developmental Psychology, 47,* 270–288.

Markus, H., & Nurius, P. (1986). Possible selves. *American Psychologist, 41,* 954–969. doi:10.1037/0003-066X.41.9.954

Marschik, P. B., Einspieler, C., Strohmeier, A., Plienegger, J., Garzarolli, B., & Prechtl, H. F. R. (2008). From the reaching behavior at 5 months of age to hand preference at preschool age. *Developmental Psychobiology, 50,* 511–518.

Marsh, H. W., & Martin, A. J. (2011). Academic self-concept and academic achievement: Relations and causal ordering. *British Journal of Educational Psychology, 81,* 59–77.

Marsh, K., & Musson, G. (2008). Men at work and at home: Managing emotion in telework. *Gender, Work & Organization, 15,* 31–48. doi:10.1111/j.1468-0432.2007

Marsiglio, W., & Roy, K. (2013). Fathers' nurturance of children over the life course. In G. W. Peterson & K. R. Bush (Eds.), *Handbook of marriage and the family* (3rd ed., pp. 353–376). New York: Springer.

Martens, A., Goldenberg, J. L., & Greenberg, J. (2005). A terror management perspective on ageism. *Journal of Social Issues, 61,* 223–239. doi:10.1111/j.1540-4560.2005.00403.x

Martin-Storey, A. (2016). Gender, sexuality, and gender nonconformity: Understanding variation in functioning. *Child Development Perspectives, 10,* 257–262.

Martin-Uzzi, M., & Duval-Tsioles, D. (2013). The experience of remarried couples in blended families. *Journal of Divorce & Remarriage, 54,* 43–57. doi:10.1080/10502556.2012.743828

Martin, C. L., & Halverson, C. F. (1987). The roles of cognition in sex role acquisition. In D. B. Carter (Ed.), *Current conceptions of sex roles and sex typing: Theory and research* (pp. 123–137). New York: Praeger.

Martin, C. L., & Ruble, D. (2004). Children's search for gender cues: Cognitive perspectives on gender development. *Current Directions in Psychological Science, 13,* 67–70.

Martin, C. L., Fabes, R. A., Evans, S. M., & Wyman, H. (1999). Social cognition on the playground: Children's beliefs about playing with girls versus boys and their relationships to sex-segregated play. *Journal of Social & Personal Relationships, 16,* 751–772.

Martin, C. L., Kornienko, O., Schaefer, D. R., Hanish, L. D., Fabes, R. A., & Goble, P. (2013). The role of sex of peers and gender-typed activities in young children's peer affiliative networks: A longitudinal analysis of selection and influence. *Child Development, 84,* 921–937.

Martin, J. A., Hamilton, B. E., Ventura, S. J., Osterman, M. J. K., & Mathews, T. J. (2013). Births: Final data for 2011. *National Vital Statistics Reports, 62*(1). Hyattsville, MD: National Center for Health Statistics.

Martin, J., & Ross, H. (2005). Sibling aggression: Sex differences and parents' reactions. *International Journal of Behavioral Development, 29,* 129–138.

Martin, M., Long, M. V., & Poon, L. W. (2002). Age changes and differences in personality traits and states of the old and very old. *Journals*

of Gerontology: Psychological Sciences, 57B, P144–P152. doi:10.1093/ geronb/57.2.P144

Martin, S. P., Astone, N. M., & Peters, H. E. (2014). *Fewer marriages, more divergence: Marriage projections for millennials to age 40.* Retrieved from www.urban.org/research/publication/fewer-marriages-more-divergence-marriage-projections-millennials-age-40/view/full_report.

Mash, H. B. H., Fullerton, C. S., & Ursano, R. J. (2013). Complicated grief and bereavement in young adults following close friend and sibling loss. *Depression and Anxiety, 30*(12), 1202–1210. doi:10.1002/da.22068

Masunaga, H., & Horn, J. (2001). Expertise and age-related changes in components of intelligence. *Psychology and Aging, 16,* 293–311. doi:10.1037/0882-7974.16.2.293

Masur, E. F. (1995). Infants' early verbal imitation and their later lexical development. *Merrill-Palmer Quarterly, 41,* 286–306.

Materne, C. J., Luszcz, M. A., & Goodwin-Smith, I. (2014). Increasing constructive engagement and positive affect for residents with severe and very severe dementia through group-based activities. *Australasian Journal on Ageing.* doi:10.1111/ajag.12127

Mather, M. (2016). The affective neuroscience of aging. *Annual Review of Psychology, 67,* 213–238. doi:10.1146/annurev-psych-122414-033540

Mathur, M. B., Epel, E., Kind, S., Manisha, D., Parks, C. G., Sandler, D. P. et al., (2016). Perceived stress and telomere length: A systematic review, meta-analysis, and methodologic considerations for advancing the field. *Brain, Behavior, and Immunity, 54,* 158–169. doi:10.1016/j.bbi.2016.02.002

Mattis, J., & Sehgal, A. (2016). Circadian rhythms, sleep, and disorders of aging. *Trends in Endocrinology & Metabolism, 27,* 192–203. doi:10.1016/j.tem.2016.02.003

Mattys, S. L., & Jusczyk, P. W. (2001). Phonotactic cues for segmentation of fluent speech by infants. *Cognition, 78,* 91–121.

Mauno, S., Cheng, T., & Lim, V. (2017). The far-reaching consequences of job insecurity: A review on family-related outcomes. *Marriage and Family Review,* doi: 10.1080/01494929.2017.1283382

Maxfield, M., Solomon, S., Pyszczynski, T., & Greenberg, J. (2010). Mortality salience effects on the life expectancy estimates of older adults as a function of neuroticism. *Journal of Aging Research.* doi: 10.4061/2010/260123. Retrieved from www.hindawi.com/journals/jar/2010/260123/.

May, P. A., Blankenship, J., Marais, A-S., Gossage, J. P., Kalberg, W. O., Joubert, B., et al. (2013). Maternal alcohol consumption producing fetal alcohol spectrum disorders (FASD): Quantity, frequency, and timing of drinking. *Drug and Alcohol Dependence, 133,* 502–512.

Mayer, R. E. (2014). What problem solvers know: Cognitive readiness for adaptive problem solving. In H. F. O'Neil, R. S. Perez, & E. L. Baker (Eds.), *Teaching and measuring cognitive readiness* (pp. 149–160). New York: Springer.

Maynard, A. E. (2002). Cultural teaching: The development of teaching skills in Maya sibling interactions. *Child Development, 73,* 969–982.

Mayo Clinic. (2015). *Aerobic exercise.* Retrieved from www.mayoclinic.org/healthy-lifestyle/fitness/basics/aerobic-exercise/hlv-20049447.

Mayo Clinic. (2016). *Managing your cholesterol.* Retrieved from www.mayoclinic.org/cholesterol-site/scs-20089333.

Mazur, E., & Li, Y. (2016). Identity and self-presentation on social networking web sites: A comparison of online profiles of Chinese and American emerging adults. *Psychology of Popular Media Culture, 5,* 101–118. doi:10.1037/ppm0000054

McAdams, D. P. (2001). The psychology of life stories. *Review of General Psychology, 5,* 100–122. doi:10.1037/1089-2680.5.2.100

McAdams, D. P. (2015). *The art and science of personality development.* New York: Guilford.

McAdams, D. P., & Guo, J. (2015). Narrating the generative life. *Psychological Science, 26,* 475–483. doi:10.1177/0956797614568318

McAdams, T. A., Rijsdijk, F. V., Narusyte, J., Ganiban, J. M., Reiss, D., Spotts, E., et al. (2017). Associations between the parent–child relationship and adolescent self-worth: A genetically informed study of twin parents and their adolescent children. *Journal of Child Psychology and Psychiatry, 58,* 46–54.

McAlaney, J., Bewick, B., & Hughes, C. (2011). The international development of the "social norms" approach to drug education and prevention. *Drugs: Education, Prevention, and Policy, 18,* 81–89. doi:10.3109/09687631003610977

McCall, R. B. (1979). *Infants.* Cambridge, MA: Harvard University Press.

McCarty, W. P., & Skogan, W. G. (2013). Job-related burnout among civilian and sworn police personnel. *Police Quarterly, 16,* 66–84. doi:10.1177/1098611112457357

McClinton, B. E. (2010). *Preparing for the third age: A retirement planning course outline for lifelong learning programs.* Master's thesis from California State University, Long Beach. Retrieved from gradworks.umi.com/1486345.pdf.

McClung, M. R., Grauer, A., Boonen, S., Bolognese, M. A., Brown, J. P., Diez-Perez, A., et al. (2014). Romosozumab in postmenopausal women with low bone mineral density. *New England Journal of Medicine, 370,* 412–420. doi:10.1056/NEJMoa1305224.

McCollum, L., & Pincus, T. (2009). A biopsychosocial model to complement a biomedical model: Patient questionnaire data and socioeconomic status usually are more significant than laboratory tests and imaging studies in prognosis of rheumatoid arthritis. *Rheumatoid Disease Clinics of North America, 35,* 699–712. doi:10.1016/j.rdc.2009.10.003

McCormick, C. B. (2003). Metacognition and learning. In I. B. Weiner (Editor-in-Chief) and W. M. Reynolds & G. E. Miller (Vol. Eds.), *Handbook of psychology: Vol. 7. Educational Psychology* (pp. 79–102). New York: Wiley.

McCoyd, J. L. M., & Walter, C. A. (2016). *Grief and loss across the lifespan: A biopsychosocial perspective* (2nd ed.). New York: Springer.

McCrae, R. R. (2016). Integrating trait and process approaches to personality: A sketch of an agenda. In U. Kumar (Ed.), *The Wiley handbook of personality assessment* (pp. 3–18). Malden, MA: Wiley.

McCrae, R. R., & Costa, P. T., Jr. (2003). *Personality in adulthood: A five-factor theory perspective* (2nd ed.). New York: Guilford.

McCrae, R. R., & Terracciano, A. (2005). Universal features of personality traits from the observer's perspective: Data from 50 cultures. *Journal of Personality & Social Psychology, 88,* 547–561. doi:10.1037/0022-3514.88.3.547

McCutchen, D., Covill, A., Hoyne, S. H, & Mildes, K. (1994). Individual differences in writing: Implications of translating fluency. *Journal of Educational Psychology, 86,* 256–266.

McDonald, K. L., Bowker, J. C., Rubin, K. H., Laursen, B., & Duchene, M. S. (2010). Interactions between rejection sensitivity and supportive relationships in the prediction of adolescents' internalizing difficulties. *Journal of Youth & Adolescence, 39,* 563–574.

McElwain, N. L., Booth-LaForce, C., & Wu, X. (2011). Infant-mother attachment and children's friendship quality: Maternal mental-state talk as an intervening mechanism. *Developmental Psychology, 47,* 1295–1311.

McGarry, K., & Schoeni, R. F. (2005). Widow(er) poverty and out-of-pocket medical expenditures near the end of life. *Journal of Gerontology: Social Sciences, 60,* S160–S168. doi:10.1093/geronb/60.3.S160

McGinley, M., Lipperman-Kreda, S., Byrnes, H. F., & Carlo, G. (2010). Parental, social and dispositional pathways to Israeli adolescents' volunteering. *Journal of Applied Developmental Psychology, 31,* 386–394.

McGraw, M. B. (1935). *Growth: A study of Johnny and Jimmy.* East Norwalk, CT: Appleton-Century-Crofts.

McGuire, S., & Shanahan, L. (2010). Sibling experiences in diverse family contexts. *Child Development Perspectives, 4,* 72–79.

McHale, J. P., Laurette, A., Talbot, J., & Pourquette, C. (2002). Retrospect and prospect in the psychological study of coparenting and family group process. In J. P. McHale & W. Grolnick (Eds.), *Retrospect and prospect in the psychological study of families* (pp. 127–165). Mahwah, NJ: Erlbaum.

McHale, S. M., Kim, J. Y., Whiteman, S. D., & Crouter, A. C. (2004). Links between sex-typed activities in middle childhood and gender development in early adolescence. *Developmental Psychology, 40,* 868–881.

McHale, S. M., Updegraff, K. A., & Whiteman, S. D. (2012). Sibling relationships and influences in childhood and adolescence. *Journal of Marriage and Family, 74,* 913–930.

McHale, S. M., Updegraff, K. A., & Whiteman, S. D. (2013). Sibling relationships. In G. W. Peterson & K. R. Bush (Eds.), *Handbook of marriage and the family* (pp. 329–351). New York: Springer Science+Business Media.

McHale, S. M., Whiteman, S. D., Kim, J.-Y., & Crouter, A. C. (2007). Characteristics and correlates of sibling relationships in two-parent African American families. *Journal of Family Psychology, 21,* 227–235.

McKay, B. (2016). A cholesterol conundrum. *Wall Street Journal, February 9,* D1–D2.

McKee-Ryan, F., Song, Z., Wanberg, C. R., & Kinicki, A. J. (2005). Psychological and physical well-being during unemployment: A meta-analytic study. *Journal of Applied Psychology, 90,* 53–76. doi:10.1037/0021-9010.90.1.53

McKee, A. C., Cairns, N. J., Dickson, D. W., Folkerth, R. D., Keene, C. D., Litvan, I., et al. (2016). The first NINDS/NIBIB consensus meeting to define neuropathological criteria for the diagnosis of chronic traumatic encephalopathy. *Acta Neuropathologica, 131,* 75–86. doi:10.1007/s00401-015-1515-z

McKee, K. J., & Schüz, B. (2015). Psychosocial factors in healthy aging. *Psychology & Health, 30,* 607–626. doi:10.1080/08870446.2015.1026905

McLanahan, S., & Jencks, C. (2015). Was Moynihan right? What happens to children of unmarried mothers. *Education Next, 15,* 14–21.

McLaughlin, K. A., Sheridan, M. A., & Lambert, H. K. (2014). Childhood adversity and neural development: Deprivation and threat as distinct dimensions of early experience. *Neuroscience and Biobehavioral Reviews, 47,* 578–591.

McLean, K. C. (2016). *The co-authored self: Family stories and the construction of personal identity.* New York: Oxford University Press.

McLean, K. C., & Pasupathi, M. (2012). Processes of identity development: Where I am and how I got there. *Identity, 12,* 8–28. doi:10.1080/15283488.2011.632363

McLymont, R. (2016). State of women-owned businesses. *The Network Journal, (Spring),* 18–19.

McNutt, B., & Yakushko, O. (2013). Disenfranchised grief among lesbian and gay bereaved individuals. *Journal of LGBT Issues in Counseling, 7,* 87–116. doi:10.1080/15538605.2013.758345

McQuade, J. D. (2017). Peer victimization and changes in physical and relational aggression: The moderating role of executive functioning abilities. *Aggressive Behavior,* in press.

Meaney, M. J. (2010) Epigenetics and the biological definition of gene X environment interactions. *Child Development, 81,* 41–79.

Medicare.gov. (2016). *What's Medicare supplemental insurance (Medigap)?* Retrieved from www.medicare.gov/supplement-other-insurance/medigap/whats-medigap.html.

MedlinePlus. (2014). *Aging changes in the female reproductive system.* Retrieved from www.nlm.nih.gov/medlineplus/ency/article/004016.htm.

Medwell, J., & Wray, D. (2014). Handwriting automaticity: The search for performance thresholds. *Language and Education, 28,* 34–51.

Meeker, J. D., & Benedict, M. D. (2013). Infertility, pregnancy loss and adverse birth outcomes in relation to maternal secondhand tobacco smoke exposure. *Current Women's Health Reviews, 9*, 41–49.

Meeus, W., van de Schoot, R., Keijsers, L., Schwartz, S. J., & Branje, S. (2010). On the progression and stability of adolescent identity formation: A five-wave longitudinal study in early-to-middle and middle-to-late adolescence. *Child Development, 81*, 1565–1581.

Mehta, C. M., & Strough, J. (2009). Sex segregation in friendships and normative contexts across the life span. *Developmental Review, 29*, 201–220.

Meijer A. M., & van den Wittenboer, G. L. H. (2007). Contribution of infants' sleep and crying to marital relationship of first-time parent couples in the 1st year after childbirth. *Journal of Family Psychology, 21*, 49–57. doi:10.1037/0893-3200.21.1.49

Meilaender, G. (2013). *Bioethics: A primer for Christians* (3rd ed.). Grand Rapids, MI: Eerdmans Publishing.

Melby-Lervåg, M., & Lervåg, A. (2014). Effects of educational interventions targeting reading comprehension and underlying components. *Child Development Perspectives, 8*, 96–100.

Melby-Lervåg, M., Lyster, S. H., & Hulme, C. (2012). Phonological skills and their role in learning to read: A meta-analytic review. *Psychological Bulletin, 138*, 322–352.

Melby, J. N., Conger, R. D., Fang, S., Wickrama, K. A. S., & Conger, K. J. (2008). Adolescent family experiences and educational attainment during early adulthood. *Developmental Psychology, 44*, 1519–1536.

Melson, G. F. (2003). Child development and the human-companion animal bond. *American Behavioral Scientist, 47*, 31–39.

Melson, G. F. (2010). Play between children and domestic animals. In E. Enwokah, (Ed.), *Play as engagement and communication* (pp. 23–39). Lanham, MD: University Press of America.

Meltzoff, A. N., & Moore, M. K. (1994). Imitation, memory, and the representation of persons. *Infant Behavior and Development, 17*, 83–99.

Ménard, C., Hodes, G. E., & Russo, S. J. (2016). Pathogenesis of depression: Insights from human and rodent studies. *Neuroscience, 321*, 138–162. doi:10.1016/j.neuroscience.2015.05.053

Mendez-Luck, C. A., Geldhof, G. J., Anthony, K. P., Steers, W. N., Mangione, C. M., & Hays, R. D. (2016). Orientation to the caregiver role among Latinas of Mexican origin. *The Gerontologist, 56*, e99–e108. doi:10.1093/geront/gnw087

Mendle, J., & Ferrero, J. (2012). Detrimental psychological outcomes associated with pubertal timing in adolescent boys. *Developmental Review, 32*, 49–66.

Mendle, J., Turkheimer, E., & Emery, R. E. (2007). Detrimental psychological outcomes associated with early pubertal timing in adolescent girls. *Developmental Review, 27*, 151–171.

Mennella, J. A., & Beauchamp, G. K. (1996). The human infant's response to vanilla flavors in mother's milk and formula. *Infant Behavior and Development, 19*, 13–19.

Mennella, J. A., Jagnow, C. P., & Beauchamp, G. K. (2001). Prenatal and postnatal flavor learning by human infants. *Pediatrics, 107*, e88.

Mennella, J., & Beauchamp, G. K. (1997). The ontogeny of human flavor perception. In G. K. Beauchamp & L. Bartoshuk (Eds.), *Tasting and smelling: Handbook of perception and cognition*. San Diego, CA: Academic Press.

Mensch, B. S., Singh, S., & Casterline, J. B. (2006). Trends in the timing of first marriage among men and women in the developing world. In C. B. Lloyd, J. R. Behrman, N. P. Stromquist, & B. Cohen (Eds.), *The changing transitions to adulthood in developing countries: Selected studies* (pp. 180–171). Washington, DC: National Research Council.

Mercer, T. (2016). Technology-assisted memory. In A. Attrill & C. Fullwood (Eds.), *Applied cyberpsychology* (pp. 74–88). New York: Springer. doi:10.1057/9781137517036_5

Merianos, A. L., King, K. A., Vidourek, R. A., & Nabors, L. A. (2015). Recent alcohol use and binge drinking based on authoritative parenting among Hispanic youth nationwide. *Journal of Child and Family Studies, 24*, 1966–1976.

Merton, T. (1949). *Seeds of contemplation.* Norfolk, CT: New Directions.

Merton, T. (1955). *No man is an island.* San Diego: Harvest Books.

Merton, T. (1962). *New seeds of contemplation.* New York: New Directions.

Mervis, C. B., & Johnson, K. E. (1991). Acquisition of the plural morpheme: A case study. *Developmental Psychology, 27*, 222–235.

Merz, E.-M., & De Jong Gierveld, J. (2016). Childhood memories, family ties, sibling support and loneliness in ever-widowed older adults: Quantitative and qualitative results. *Ageing and Society, 36*, 534–561. doi:10.1017/S0144686X14001329

Meunier, D., Stamatakis, E. A., & Tyler, L. K. (2014). Age-related functional reorganization, structural changes, and preserved cognition. *Neurobiology of Aging, 35*, 42–54. doi:10.1016/j.neurobiolaging.2013.07.003

Meyer, M., Gelman, S. A., Roberts, S. O., & Leslie, S.-J. (2016). My heart made me do it: Children's essentialist belief about heart transplants. *Cognitive Science, 1–19.*

Michel, A. (2016). Burnout and the brain. *Observer, 29* (February). Retrieved from www.psychologicalscience.org/index.php/publications/observer/2016/february-16/burnout-and-the-brain.html.

Midgette, E., Haria, P., & MacArthur, C. (2008). The effects of content and audience awareness goals for revision on the persuasive essays of fifth- and eighth-grade students. *Reading and Writing, 21*, 131–151.

Midlarsky, E., Kahana, E., & Belser, A. (2015). Prosocial behavior in late life. In D. A Schroeder & W. G. Graziano (Eds.), *The Oxford handbook of prosocial behavior* (pp. 415–432). New York: Oxford University Press.

Miething, A., Almquist, Y. B., Rostila, M., Edling, C., & Rydgren, J. (2016). Friendship networks and psychological well-being from late adolescence to young adulthood: A gender-specific structural equation modeling approach. *BMC Psychology, 4*, 34. doi:10.1186/s40359-016-0143-2. Retrieved from bmcpsychology.biomedcentral.com/articles/10.1186/s40359-016-0143-2.

Mietkiewicz, M.-C., & Venditti, L. (2004). Les arrière-grands-pères le point de vue de leurs arrière-petits-enfants [Great-grandfathers from their great-grandchildren's point of view]. *Psychologie & NeuroPsychiatrie du Vieillissement, 2*, 275–283.

Miga, E. M., Gdula, J. A., & Allen, J. P. (2012). Fighting fair: Adaptive marital conflict strategies as predictors of future adolescent peer and romantic relationship quality. *Social Development, 21*, 443–460.

Miles, J. (2009). *Autobiographical reflection and perspective transformation in adult learners returning to study: Research in progress.* Retrieved from www.avetra.org.au/papers-2009/papers/37.00.pdf.

Mileva-Seitz, V. R., Bakermans-Kranenburg, M. J., Battaini, C., & Luijk, M. P. C. M. (2017). Parent-child bed-sharing: The good, the bad, and the burden of evidence. *Sleep Medicine Reviews, 32*, 4–27.

Miller, A. B., Wall, C., Baines, C. J., Sun, P., To, T., & Narod, S. A. (2014). Twenty-five year follow-up for breast cancer incidence and mortality of the Canadian National Breast Screening study: Randomised screening trial. *BMJ, 348*, g366. doi:10.1136/bmj.g366

Miller, A. C. (2016). Opinions on the legitimacy of brain death among Sunni and Shi'a scholars. *Journal of Religion and Health, 55*, 394–402. doi:10.1007/s10943-015-0157-8

Miller, D. I., & Halpern, D. F. (2014). The new science of cognitive sex differences. *Trends in Cognitive Sciences, 18*, 37–45.

Miller, D. T., & Prentice, D. A. (2016). Changing norms to change behavior. *Annual Review of Psychology, 67*, 339–361. doi:10.1146/annurev-psych-010814-015013

Miller, G. E., & Chen, E. (2010). Harsh family climate in early life presages the emergence of proinflammatory phenotype in adolescence. *Psychological Science, 21*, 848–856.

Miller, J. G., & Bersoff, D. M. (1992). Culture and moral judgment: How are conflicts between justice and interpersonal responsibilities resolved? *Journal of Personality & Social Psychology, 62*, 541–554.

Miller, K. I., Shoemaker, M. M., Willyard, J., & Addison, P. (2008). Providing care for elderly parents: A structurational approach to family caregiver identity. *Journal of Family Communication, 8*, 19–43. doi:10.1080/15267430701389947

Miller, L. C., Johnson, A., Duggan, L., & Behm, M. (2011). Consequences of the "Back to Sleep" program in infants. *Journal of Pediatric Nursing, 26*, 364–368.

Miller, P. H. (2011). Piaget's theory: Past, present, and future. In U. Goswami (Ed.),

The Wiley-Blackwell handbook of childhood cognitive development (2nd ed., pp. 649–672). West Sussex, UK: Wiley-Blackwell.

Miller, P. J., & Rosengren, K. S. (2014). Final thoughts. *Monographs of the Society for Research in Child Development, 79*, 113–124. doi:10.1111/mono.12082

Miller, P. J., Rosengren, K. S., & Gutiérrez, I. T. (2014). Introduction. *Monographs of the Society for Research in Child Development, 79*, 1–18. doi:10.1111/mono.12076

Miller, P. M., Danaher, D. L., & Forbes, D. (1986). Sex-related strategies of coping with interpersonal conflict in children aged five to seven. *Developmental Psychology, 22*, 543–548.

Miller, S. A. (2009). Children's understanding of second-order mental states. *Psychological Bulletin, 135*, 749–773.

Miller, T. W., Nigg, J. T., & Miller, R. L. (2009). Attention deficit hyperactivity disorder in African American children: What can be learned from the past ten years? *Clinical Psychology Review, 29*, 77–86.

Miller-Martinez, D., & Wallace, S. P. (2007). Structural contexts and life-course processes in the social networks of older Mexican immigrants in the United States. In S. Carmel, C. Morse, & F. Torres-Gil (Eds.), *Lessons on aging from three nations: Volume I. The art of aging well* (pp. 141–154). Amityville, NY: Baywood.

Milligan, C., Turner, M., Blake, S., Brearley, S., Seamark, D., Thomas, C. et al. (2016). Unpacking the impact of older adults' home death on family care-givers' experiences of home. *Health & Place, 38*, 103–111. doi:10.1016/j.healthplace.2016.01.005

Minnotte, K. L. (2010). *Methodologies of assessing marital success.* Retrieved from workfamily.sas.upenn.edu/wfrn-repo/object/w2yp4p7if8lm7q4k.

Mischel, W. (1970). Sex-typing and socialization. In P. H. Mussen (Ed.), *Carmichael's manual of child psychology* (Vol. 2). New York: Wiley.

Mitchell, B. A. (2006). *The boomerang age: Transitions to adulthood in families.* New Brunswick, NJ: AldineTransaction.

Mitchell, B. A. (2010). Happiness in midlife parental roles: A contextual mixed methods analysis. *Family Relations, 59*, 326–339. doi:10.1111/ j.1741-3729.2010.00605.x

Mitchell, T. B., Amaro, C. M., & Steele, R. G. (2016). Pediatric weight management interventions in primary care settings: A meta-analysis. *Health Psychology, 35*, 704–713.

Mitteldorf, J. (2016). An epigenic clock controls aging. *Biogerontology, 17*, 257–265. doi:10.1007/s10522-015-9617-5

Mize, J., & Pettit, G. S. (1997). Mothers' social coaching, mother-child relationship style, and children's peer competence: Is the medium the message? *Child Development, 68*, 312–332.

Mize, J., Pettit, G. S., & Brown, E. G. (1995). Mothers' supervision of their children's peer play: Relations with beliefs, perceptions, and knowledge. *Developmental Psychology, 31*, 311–321.

Modecki, K. L., Hagan, M., Sandler, I., & Wolchik, S. (2015). Latent profiles of non-residential father engagement six years after divorce predict long term offspring outcomes. *Journal of Clinical Child and Adolescent Psychology, 44*, 123–136.

Moeller, J. R., Lewis, M. M., & Werth, J. L., Jr. (2010). End of life issues. In J. C. Cavanaugh & C. K. Cavanaugh (Eds.), *Aging in America: Vol. 1: Psychological aspects* (pp. 202–231). Santa Barbara, CA: Praeger Perspectives.

Moen, P. (2016a). *Encore adulthood: Boomers on the edge of risk, renewal, & purpose.* New York: Oxford University Press.

Moen, P. (2016b). Work over the gendered life course. In M. J. Shanahan, J. T. Mortimer, & M. K. Johnson (Eds.), *Handbook of the life course* (pp. 249–275). New York: Springer.

Moen, P., & Roehling, P. (2005). *The career mystique: Cracks in the American dream.* Oxford, UK: Rowman & Littlefield.

Moerk, E. L. (2000). *The guided acquisition of first language skills.* Westport, CT: Ablex.

Molin, P., & Rockwood, K. (2016). The new criteria for Alzheimer's disease—Implications for geriatricians. *Canadian Geriatrics Journal, 19*, 66–73. doi:10.5770/cgj.19.207

Molina, B. S. G., Hinshaw, S. P., Swanson, J. M., Arnold, L. E., Vitiello, B., Jensen, P. S., et al. (2009). The MTA at 8 years: Prospective follow-up of children treated for combined-type ADHD in a multisite study. *Journal of the American Academy of Child & Adolescent Psychiatry, 48*, 484–500.

Molina, L. C. (2012). *A qualitative exploration of the effect of age at migration on the acculturative process of Filipino immigrants: Implications for public health studies.* Dissertation in partial fulfillment of the doctor of philosophy degree in public health, University of California Los Angeles. Retrieved from escholarship.org/uc/item/09t9b4g1.

Mollborn, S. (2017). Teenage mothers today: What we know and how it matters. *Child Development Perspectives, 11*, 63–69.

Monahan, A. (2017). When a promise is not a promise: Chicago-style pensions. *UCLA Law Review, 64*. Retrieved from ssrn.com/abstract=2777736.

Monahan, K. C., Steinberg, L., & Cauffman, E. (2013). Age differences in the impact of employment on antisocial behavior. *Child Development, 84*, 791–801.

Monahan, K., Steinberg, L., & Piquero, A. R. (2015). Juvenile justice policy and practice: A developmental perspective. *Crime and Justice, 44*, 577–619.

Mondloch, C. J., Lewis, T. L., Budreau, D. R., Maurer, D., Dannemiller, J. L. Stephens, B. R., et al. (1999). Face perception during early infancy. *Psychological Science, 10*, 419–422.

Monk, C., Fifer, W. P., Myers, M. M., Sloan, R. P., Trien, L., & Hurtando, A. (2000). Maternal stress responses and anxiety during pregnancy: Effects on fetal heart rate. *Developmental Psychology, 36*, 67–77.

Monk, C., Spicer, J., & Champagne, F. A. (2012). Linking prenatal adversity to developmental outcomes in infants: The role of epigenetic pathways. *Development and Psychopathology, 24*, 1361–1376.

Montague, D. P., & Walker-Andrews, A. S. (2001). Peekaboo: A new look at infants' perception of emotion expressions. *Developmental Psychology, 37*, 826–838.

Moon, P. J., (2017). Hospice admission assessment: A narrative view. *American Journal of Hospice & Palliative Care, 34*, 201–204. doi:10.1177/1049909115624375

Moore, K. L., & Persaud, T. V. N. (1993). *Before we are born* (4th ed.). Philadelphia: Saunders.

Moorman, S. M., & Greenfield, E. A. (2010). Personal relationships in later life. In J. C. Cavanaugh & C. K. Cavanaugh (Eds.), *Aging in America: Vol. 3: Societal issues* (pp. 20–52). Santa Barbara, CA: ABC-CLIO.

Moorman, S. M., & Inoue, M. (2013). Persistent problems in end-of-life planning among young- and middle-aged American couples. *Journal of Gerontology: Social Sciences, 68*, 97–106. doi:10.1093/geronb/gbs103

Morfei, M. Z., Hooker, K., Fiese, B. H., & Cordeiro, A. M. (2001). Continuity and change in parenting possible selves: A longitudinal follow-up. *Basic and Applied Social Psychology, 23*, 217–223. doi:10.1207/153248301750433777

Morgan, B., & Gibson, K. R. (1991). Nutritional and environmental interactions in brain development. In K. R. Gibson & A. C. Peterson (Eds.), *Brain maturation and cognitive development: Comparative and cross-cultural perspectives* (pp. 91–106). New York: Aldine de Gruyter.

Morgan, J. P., & Roberts, J. E. (2010). Helping bereaved children and adolescents: Strategies and implications for counselors. *Journal of Mental Health Counseling, 32*, 206–217.

Morgan, P. L., Staff, J., Hillemeier, M. M., Farkas, G., & Maczuga, S. (2013). Racial and ethnic disparities in ADHD diagnosis from kindergarten to eighth grade. *Pediatrics, 132*, 85–93.

Morris, W. L., Sinclair, S., & DePaulo, B. M. (2007). No shelter for singles: The perceived legitimacy of marital status discrimination. *Group Processes & Intergroup Relation, 10*, 457–470. doi:10.1177/1368430207081535

Mortimer, J. T., & Staff, J. (2004). Early work as a source of developmental discontinuity during the transition to adulthood. *Development & Psychopathology, 16*, 1047–1070.

Morton, J., & Johnson, M. H. (1991). CONSPEC and CONLERN: A two-process theory of infant face recognition. *Psychological Review, 98*, 164–181.

Moses, L. J., Baldwin, D. A., Rosicky, J. G., & Tidball, G. (2001). Evidence for referential understanding in the emotions domain at twelve and eighteen months. *Child Development, 72*, 718–735.

Mosten, F. S. (2009). *Collaborative divorce handbook: Helping families without going to court.* San Francisco, CA: Jossey-Bass.

Mõttus, R., Johnson, W., & Deary, I. J. (2012). Personality traits in old age: Measurement and rank-order stability and some mean-level change. *Psychology and Aging, 27*(1), 243–249. doi:10.1037/a0023690

Mountain, G., Cahill, J., & Thorpe, H. (2017). Sensitivity and attachment interventions in early childhood: A systematic review and meta-analysis. *Infant Behavior and Development, 46,* 14–32.

Mounts, N. S. (2011). Parental management of peer relationships and early adolescents' social skills. *Journal of Youth and Adolescence, 40,* 416–427.

Moye, J., Sabatino, C. P., & Brendel, R. W. (2013). Evaluation of the capacity to appoint a health-care proxy. *American Journal of Geriatric Psychiatry, 21,* 326–336. doi:10.1016/j.jagp.2012.09.001

Moyer, A. M., Miller, V. M., & Faubion, S. S. (2016). Could personalized management of menopause based on genomics become a reality? *Future Medicine, 17,* 659–662. doi:10.2217/pgs.16.17

Mozaffarian, D., Benjamin, E. J., Go, A. S., Arnett, D. K., Blaha, M. J., Cushman, M. et al. (2016). Heart disease and stroke statistics—2016 Update. *Circulation, 133,* e38–e360. doi:10.1161/CIR.0000000000000350. Retrieved from circ.ahajournals.org/content/early/2015/12/16/CIR.0000000000000350.

Mühlig-Versen, A., Bowen, C. E., & Staudinger, U. M. (2012). Personality plasticity in later adulthood: Contextual and personal resources are needed to increase openness to new experiences. *Psychology and Aging, 27,* 855–866. doi:10.1037/a0029357

Muise, A., Impett, E. A., Kogan, A., & Desmarais, S. (2013). Keeping the spark alive: Being motivated to meet a partner's sexual needs sustains sexual desire in long-term romantic relationships. *Social Psychological and Personality Science, 4,* 267–273. doi:10.1177/1948550612457185

Muller, E. D., & Thompson, C. L. (2003). The experience of grief after bereavement: A phenomenological study with implications for mental health counseling. *Journal of Mental Health Counseling, 25,* 183–203. doi.org/10.17744/mehc.25.3.wu4n7dljyekuh4ef

Mulvey, K. L. (2016). Children's reasoning about social exclusion: Balancing many factors. *Child Development Perspectives, 10,* 22–27.

Munoz, R. T., & Fox, M. D. (2013). Legal aspects of brain death and organ donorship. In D. Novitzky & D. K. C. Cooper (Eds.), *The brain-dead organ donor* (pp. 21–35). New York: Springer.

Murphy, N., & Messer, D. (2000). Differential benefits from scaffolding and children working alone. *Educational Psychology, 20,* 17–31.

Mussolin, C., Nys, J., Leybaert, J., & Content, A. (2016). How approximate and exact number skills are related to each other across development: A review. *Developmental Review, 39,* 1–15.

Mustanski, B. S., Viken, R. J., Kaprio, J., Pulkkinen, L., & Rose, R. J. (2004). Genetic and environmental influences on pubertal development: Longitudinal data from Finnish twins at ages 11 and 14. *Developmental Psychology, 40,* 1188–1198.

Mutchler, J. E., Baker, L. A., & Lee, S. A. (2007). Grandparents responsible for grandchildren in Native-American families. *Social Science Quarterly, 88,* 990–1009. doi:10.1111/j.1540-6237.2007.00514.x

Muter V., Hulme, C., Snowling, M. J., & Stevenson, J. (2004). Phonemes, rimes, vocabulary, and grammatical skills as foundations of early reading development: Evidence from a longitudinal study. *Developmental Psychology, 40,* 663–681.

Mwanyangala, M. A., Mayombana, C., Urassa, H., Charles, J., Mahutanga, C., Abdullah, S., et al. (2010). Health status and quality of life among older adults in rural Tanzania. *Global Health Action, 3.* Retrieved from journals.sfu.ca/coaction/index.php/gha/article/viewArticle/2142/6055.

Nadig, A. S., & Sedivy, J. C. (2002). Evidence of perspective-taking constraints in children's online reference resolution. *Psychological Science, 13,* 329–336.

Naef, R., Ward, R., Mahrer-Imhof, R., & Grande, G. (2013). Characteristics of the bereavement experience of older persons after spousal loss: An integrative review. *International Journal of Nursing Studies, 50,* 1108–1121. doi:10.1016/j.ijnurstu.2012.11.026

Nagaratnam, N., Nagaratnam, K., & Cheuk, G. (2016). Ear-related problems in the elderly. In N. Nagaratnam, K. Nagaratnam, & G. Cheuk (Eds.), *Diseases in the elderly* (pp. 357–371). New York: Springer. doi:10.1007/978-3-319-25787-7_17

Nahemow, L. (2000). The ecological theory of aging: Powell Lawton's legacy. In R. L. Rubinstein & M. Moss (Eds.), *The many dimensions of aging* (pp. 22–40). New York: Springer.

Naigles, L. G., & Gelman, S. A. (1995). Overextensions in comprehension and production revisited: Preferential-looking in a study of dog, cat, and cow. *Journal of Child Language, 22,* 19–46.

Nánez, J., Sr., & Yonas, A. (1994). Effects of luminance and texture motion on infants' defensive reactions to optical collision. *Infant Behavior & Development, 17,* 165–174.

Narayan, A. J., Englund, M. M., & Egeland, B. (2013). Developmental timing and continuity of exposure to interparental violence and externalizing behavior as prospective predictors of dating violence. *Development and Psychopathology, 25,* 973–990.

Nation, K., Adams, J. W., Bowyer-Crane, C. A., & Snowling, M. J. (1999). Working memory deficits in poor comprehenders reflect underlying language impairments. *Journal of Experimental Child Psychology, 73,* 139–158.

Nation, K., Clark, P., Marshall, C., & Durand, M. (2004). Hidden language impairments in children: Parallels between poor reading comprehension and specific language impairment? *Journal of Speech, Language and Hearing Research, 47,* 199–211.

National Academy of Social Insurance. (2016). *Social Security benefits, finances, and policy options: A primer.* Retrieved from www.nasi.org/socialsecurityprimer.

National Alliance for Caregiving and AARP. (2015). *Caregiving in the U.S.: 2015 report.* Retrieved from www.caregiving.org/wp-content/uploads/2015/05/2015_CaregivingintheUS_Final-Report-June-4_WEB.pdf.

National Association for the Education of Young Children. (2016). *What to look for in a program.* Retrieved from families.naeyc.org/what-to-look-for-in-a-program.

National Cancer Institute. (2006). *DES: Questions and answers.* Washington DC: Author.

National Center for Assisted Living. (2016). *Choosing an assisted living residence: A consumer's guide.* Retrieved from: www.ahcancal.org/ncal/resources/Documents/Choosing%20An%20Assisted%20Living%20Residence%202013.pdf.

National Center for Educational Statistics. (2016). *Immediate college enrollment rate.* Retrieved from nces.ed.gov/programs/coe/indicator_cpa.asp.

National Center for Health Statistics. (2016a). *Health, United States, 2015.* Retrieved from www.cdc.gov/nchs/data/hus/hus15.pdf.

National Center for Health Statistics. (2016b). *Changes in life expectancy by race and Hispanic origin in the United States, 2013–2014.* Retrieved from www.cdc.gov/nchs/products/databriefs/db244.htm.

National Center for Health Statistics. (2016c). *Mean age of mothers is on the rise: United States 2000–2014.* Retrieved from www.cdc.gov/nchs/products/databriefs/db232.htm.

National Center for Health Statistics. (2016d). *Unmarried childbearing.* Retrieved from www.cdc.gov/nchs/fastats/unmarried-childbearing.htm.

National Center for State Courts. (2016). *Elder abuse resource guide.* Retrieved from www.ncsc.org/Topics/Children-Families-and-Elders/Elder-Abuse/Resource-Guide.aspx.

National Eye Institute. (2015). *Facts about diabetic eye disease.* Retrieved from nei.nih.gov/health/diabetic/retinopathy.

National Federation of State High School Associations. (2017). *2015–2016 High school athletics participation survey results.* Retrieved from www.nfhs.org/ParticipationStatistics/ParticipationStatistics.

National Heart, Lung, and Blood Institute. (2010). *Women's health initiative.* Retrieved from www.nhlbi.nih.gov/whi/.

National Institute of Arthritis and Musculoskeletal and Skin Diseases. (2014a). *What is osteoarthritis?* Retrieved from www.niams.nih.gov/Health_Info/Osteoarthritis/osteoarthritis_ff.asp.

National Institute of Arthritis and Musculoskeletal and Skin Diseases. (2014b). *What is rheumatoid arthritis?* Retrieved from www.niams.nih.gov/Health_Info/Rheumatic_Disease/rheumatoid_arthritis_ff.pdf.

National Institute of Arthritis and Musculoskeletal and Skin Diseases. (2015a). *Osteoporosis: Peak bone mass in women.* Retrieved from www.niams.nih.gov/Health_Info/Bone/Osteoporosis/bone_mass.asp.

National Institute of Arthritis and Musculoskeletal and Skin Diseases. (2015b). *Bone mass measurement: What the numbers mean.* Retrieved from www.niams.nih.gov/health_info/bone/bone_health/bone_mass_measure.asp.

National Institute of Mental Health. (2016a). *Major depression among adults.* Retrieved from www.nimh.nih.gov/health/statistics/prevalence/major-depression-among-adults.shtml.

National Institute of Mental Health. (2016b). *Mental health medications.* Retrieved from www.nimh.nih.gov/health/topics/mental-health-medications/index.shtml#part_149856.

National Institute of Mental Health. (2016c). *Anxiety disorders.* Retrieved from www.nimh.nih.gov/health/topics/anxiety-disorders/index.shtml.

National Institute of Mental Health. (2016d). *Obsessive-compulsive disorder.* Retrieved from www.nimh.nih.gov/health/topics/obsessive-compulsive-disorder-ocd/index.shtml.

National Institute of Mental Health. (2016e). *Any anxiety disorder among adults.* Retrieved from www.nimh.nih.gov/health/statistics/prevalence/any-anxiety-disorder-among-adults.shtml.

National Institute of Mental Health. (2016f). *Post-traumatic stress disorder.* Retrieved from www.nimh.nih.gov/health/topics/post-traumatic-stress-disorder-ptsd/index.shtml.

National Institute of Neurological Disorders and Stroke. (2013). *Spina bifida fact sheet.* NIH Publication No. 13-309. Author: Bethesda, MD.

National Institute on Aging. (2012) *Longer lives and disability.* Retrieved from www.nia.nih.gov/research/publication/global-health-and-aging/longer-lives-and-disability.

National Institute on Aging. (2015a). *Aging hearts and arteries: A scientific quest.* Retrieved from d2cauhfh6h4x0p.cloudfront.net/s3fs-public/hearts_and_arteries.pdf.

National Institute on Aging. (2015b). *Alzheimer's disease: Unraveling the mystery. The hallmarks of AD.* Retrieved from www.nia.nih.gov/alzheimers/publication/part-2-what-happens-brain-ad/hallmarks-ad.

National Institute on Alcohol Abuse and Alcoholism (NIAAA). (2002). *A call to action: Changing the culture of drinking at U.S. colleges. Final report of the Task Force on College Drinking.* NIH Pub. No. 02–5010. Rockville, MD: Author.

National Institute on Alcohol Abuse and Alcoholism (NIAAA). (2007). *What colleges need to know now: An update on college drinking research.* Washington, DC: National Institutes of Health.

National Institute on Alcohol Abuse and Alcoholism (NIAAA). (2014). *Treatment of alcohol problems: Finding and getting help.* Retrieved from http://pubs.niaaa.nih.gov/publications/Treatment/treatment.htm.

National Institute on Alcohol Abuse and Alcoholism (NIAAA). (2015). *College drinking.* Retrieved from http://pubs.niaaa.nih.gov/publications/CollegeFactSheet/CollegeFactSheet.pdf.

National Institute on Minority Health and Health Disparities. (2016). *Overview.* Retrieved from www.nimhd.nih.gov/about/overview/.

National Institutes of Health. (2015). *Autism spectrum disorder.* Bethesda, MD: Author.

National Osteoporosis Foundation. (2016a). *Bone health basics: Get the facts.* Retrieved from www.nof.org/prevention/general-facts/.

National Osteoporosis Foundation. (2016b). *Food and your bones: Osteoporosis nutrition guidelines.* Retrieved from www.nof.org/patients/treatment/nutrition/.

National Osteoporosis Foundation. (2016c). *Calcium/Vitamin D.* Retrieved from www.nof.org/patients/treatment/calciumvitamin-d/.

National Women's Law Center. (2016). *The wage gap: The who, how, why, and what to do.* Retrieved from nwlc.org/resources/the-wage-gap-the-who-how-why-and-what-to-do/.

Nawijn, J., De Bloom, J., & Geurts, S. (2013). Pre-vacation time: Blessing or burden? *Leisure Sciences, 35,* 33–44. doi:10.1080/01490400.2013.739875

Nayernouri, T. (2011). Euthanasia, terminal illness and quality of life. *Archives of Iranian Medicine, 14,* 54–55. Retrieved from http://sid.ir/En/VEWSSID/J_pdf/86920110109.pdf.

Neal, M. B., & Hammer, L. B. (2007). *Working couples caring for children and aging parents: Effects on work and well-being.* Mahwah, NJ: Erlbaum.

Neblett, E. W., Rivas-Drake, D., & Umaña-Taylor, A. J. (2012). The promise of racial and ethnic protective factors in promoting ethnic minority youth development. *Child Development Perspectives, 6,* 295–303.

Neft, N., & Levine, A. D. (1997). *Where women stand: An international report on the status of women in over 140 countries, 1997–1998.* New York: Random House.

Nehamas, A. (2016). *On friendship.* New York: Basic Books.

Neimeyer, R. A., & Wogrin, C. (2008). Psychotherapy for complicated bereavement: A meaning-oriented approach. *Illness, Crisis, and Loss, 16,* 1–20. doi:10.2190/IL.16.1.a

Neiss, M., B., Sedikides, C., & Stevenson, J. (2006). Genetic influences on level and stability of self-esteem. *Self and Identity, 5,* 247–266.

Nell, V. (2002). Why young men drive dangerously: Implications for injury prevention. *Current Directions in Psychological Science, 11,* 75–79.

Nelson, E. L., Campbell, J. M., & Michel, G. F. (2013). Unimanual to bimanual: Tracking the development of handedness from 6 to 24 months. *Infant Behavior and Development, 36,* 181–188.

Nelson, K. (1973). Structure and strategy in learning to talk. *Monographs of the Society for Research in Child Development, 38* (Serial No. 149).

Nelson, K. (2001). Language and the self: From the "Experiencing I" to the "Continuing Me." In C. Moore & K. Lemmon (Eds.), *The self in time: Developmental perspectives* (pp. 15–33). Mahwah, NJ: Erlbaum.

Nelson, L. J., Badger, S., & Wu, B. (2004). The influence of culture in emerging adulthood: Perspectives of Chinese college students. *International Journal of Behavioral Development, 28,* 26–36. doi:10.1080/01650250344000244

Nelson, M. A. (1996). Protective equipment. In O. Bar-Or (Ed.), *The child and adolescent athlete* (pp. 214–223). Oxford, UK: Blackwell.

Nerenberg, L. (2010). Elder abuse prevention: A review of the field. In J. C. Cavanaugh & C. K. Cavanaugh (Eds.), *Aging in America: Vol.3: Societal issues* (pp. 53–80). Santa Barbara, CA: Praeger Perspectives.

Nesdale, D. (2001). The development of prejudice in children. In M. A. Augoustinos & K. J. Reynolds (Eds.), *Understanding prejudice, racism, and social conflict* (pp. 57–73). London: Sage.

Neugarten, B. L., & Weinstein, K. K. (1964). The changing American grandparent. *Journal of Marriage and Family, 26,* 299–304. doi:10.2307/349727

Neville, H. J., Stevens, C., Pakulak, E., Bell, T. A., Fanning, J., Klein, S., et al. (2013). Family-based training program improves brain function, cognition, and behavior in lower socioeconomic status preschoolers. *PNAS, 110,* 12138–12143.

New York Times. (2016). *No kegs, no liquor: College crackdown targets drinking and sexual assault.* Retrieved from www.nytimes.com/2016/10/30/us/college-crackdown-drinking-sexual-assault.html.

Newberg, A. B., Serruya, M., Wintering, N., Moss, A. S., Reibel, D. & Monti, D. A. (2014). Meditation and neurodegenerative diseases. *Annals of the New York Academy of Sciences, 1307,* 112–123. doi:10.1111/nyas.12187. Retrieved from onlinelibrary.wiley.com/doi/10.1111/nyas.12187/full

Newbury, J., Klee, T., Stokes, S. F., & Moran, C. (2016). Interrelationships between working memory, processing speed, and language development in the age range 2–4 years. *Journal of Speech, Language, and Hearing Research, 59,* 1146–1158.

Newcombe, N. (2013). Cognitive development: Changing views of cognitive change. *WIREs Cognitive Science, 4,* 479–491.

Newman, A., Thompson, J., & Chandler, E. M. (2013). Continuous care: A home hospice benefit. *Clinical Journal of Oncology Nursing, 17,* 19–20. doi:10.1188/13.CJON.19-20

Newman, B. M., & Newman, P. R. (2015). *Theories of human development* (2nd ed.). New York: Psychology Press.

Newman, R. S., Rowe, M. L., & Ratner, N. B. (2016). Input and uptake at 7 months predicts toddler vocabulary: The role of child-directed speech and infant processing skills in language development. *Journal of Child Language, 43,* 1158–1173.

Newsom, J. T. (1999). Another side to caregiving: Negative reactions to being helped. *Current Directions in Psychological Science, 8,* 183–187. doi:10.1111/1467-8721.00043

Newton, E. K., Thompson, R. A., & Goodman, M. (2016). Individual differences in toddlers' prosociality: Experiences in early relationships explain variability in prosocial behavior. *Child Development, 87,* 1715–1726.

Newton, N. J., & Jones, B. K. (2016). Passing on: Personal attributes associated with midlife expressions of intended legacies. *Developmental Psychology, 52,* 341–353. doi:10.1037/a0039905

Newton, N. J., & Stewart, A. J. (2012). Personality development in adulthood. In S. K. Whitbourne & M. J. Sliwinski (Eds.), *The Wiley-Blackwell handbook of adulthood and aging* (pp. 209–235). Oxford, UK: Wiley-Blackwell.

Ng, R., Allore, H. G., Monin, J. K., & Levy, B. R. (2016). Retirement as meaningful: Positive retirement stereotypes associated with longevity. *Journal of Social Issues, 72,* 69–85. doi:10.1111/josi.12156

Ni, Y., Chiu, M. M., & Cheng, Z-J. (2010). Chinese children learning mathematics: From home to school. In M. H. Bond (Ed.), *Oxford handbook of Chinese psychology* (pp. 143–154). New York: Oxford University Press.

NICHD Early Child Care Research Network. (2001). Child-care and family predictors of preschool attachment and stability from infancy. *Developmental Psychology, 37,* 847–862.

NICHD. (2004). *The NICHD community connection.* Washington DC: Author.

Nickerson, C. J., & Thurkettle, M. A. (2013). Cognitive maturity and readiness for evidence-based nursing practice. *Journal of Nursing Education, 52,* 17–23. doi:10.3928/01484834-20121121-04

Nicolas, G., Wallon, D., Charbonnier, C., Quenez, O., Rousseau, S., Richard, A.-C., et al. (2016). Screening of dementia genes by whole-exome sequencing in early-onset Alzheimer disease: Input and lessons. *European Journal of Human Genetics, 24,* 710–716. doi:10.1038/ejhg.2015.173

Nielsen, M. K., Neergaard, M. A., Jensen, A. B., Bro, F., & Guldin, M.-B. (2016). Do we need to change our understanding of anticipatory grief in caregivers? A systematic review of caregiver studies during end-of-life caregiving and bereavement. *Clinical Psychology Review, 44,* 75–93. doi:10.1016/j.cpr.2016.01.002

Nigro, N., & Christ-Crain, M. (2012). Testosterone treatment in the aging male: Myth or reality? *Swiss Medical Weekly.* doi:10.4414/smw.2012.13539. Retrieved from www.smw.ch/content/smw -2012-13539/.

NIHSeniorHealth.gov. (2016). *Depression.* Retrieved from nihseniorhealth.gov/depression/aboutdepression/01.html.

Nikolaidis, A., Baniqued, P. L., Kranz, M. B., Scavuzzo, C. J., Barbey, A. K., Kramer, A. F. et al. (2017). Multivariate associations of fluid intelligence and NAA. *Cerebral Cortex, 17*(4): 2607-2616. doi:10.1093/cercor/bhw070

Nilsen, E. S., & Graham, S. A. (2012). The development of preschoolers' appreciation of communicative ambiguity. *Child Development, 83,* 1400–1415.

Nimrod, G. (2007a). Retirees' leisure: Activities, benefits, and their contribution to life satisfaction. *Leisure Studies, 26,* 65–80. doi:10.1080/02614360500333937

Nimrod, G. (2007b). Expanding, reducing, concentrating and diffusing: Post retirement leisure behavior and life satisfaction. *Leisure Sciences, 29,* 91–111. doi:10.1080/01490400600983446

Nisbett, R. E., Aronson, J., Clair, C., Dickens, W., Flynn, J., Halpern, D. F., et al. (2012). Intelligence: New findings and theoretical developments. *American Psychologist, 67,* 130–159.

Norris, D. R. (2016). *Job loss, identity, and mental health.* New Brunswick, NJ: Rutgers University Press.

North American Menopause Society. (2016). *The experts do agree about hormone therapy.* Retrieved from www.menopause.org/for-women/menopauseflashes/menopause-symptoms-and-treatments/the-experts-do-agree-about-hormone-therapy.

Norton, M. I., & Gino, F. (2014). Rituals alleviate grieving for loved ones, lovers, and lotteries. *Journal of Experimental Psychology: General, 143,* 266–272. doi:10.1037/a0031772

Nosek, M., Kennedy, H. P., & Gudmundsdottir, M. (2012). Distress during the menopause transition: A rich contextual analysis of midlife women's narratives. *Sage Open, 2.* 10.1177/2158244012455178

NotAlone.gov. (2016). *Not alone: Together against sexual assault.* Retrieved from www.notalone.gov/.

Nunes, T., Bryant, P., & Barros, R. (2012). The development of word recognition and its significance for comprehension and fluency. *Journal of Educational Psychology, 104,* 959–973.

Nurmsoo, E., & Bloom, P. (2008). Preschoolers' perspective taking in word learning: Do they blindly follow eye gaze? *Psychological Science, 19,* 211–215.

Nuzum, D., Meaney, S., O'Donoghue, K., & Morris, H. (2015). The spiritual and theological issues raised in stillbirth for healthcare chaplains. *Journal of Pastoral Care & Counseling, 69,* 163–170. doi:10.1177/1542305015602714

Nyaradi, A., Li, J., Hickling, S., Foster, J., & Oddy, W. H. (2013). The role of nutrition in children's neurocognitive development, from pregnancy through childhood. *Frontiers in Human Neuroscience, 7,* Article 97.

Nye, C. D., Su, R., Rounds, J., & Drasgow, F. (2012). Vocational interests and performance: A quantitative summary of over 60 years of research. *Perspectives on Psychological Science, 7,* 384–403.

O'Donoghue, M. (2005). White mothers negotiating race and ethnicity in the mothering of biracial, Black-White adolescents. *Journal of Ethnic & Cultural Diversity in Social Work, 14*(3), 125–156. doi:10.1300 /J051v14n03_07

O'Hara, M. W. (2009). Postpartum depression: What we know. *Journal of Clinical Psychology, 65,* 1258–1269.

O'Hara, M. W., & McCabe, J. E. (2013). Postpartum depression: Current status and future directions. *Annual Review of Clinical Psychology, 9,* 379–407.

O'Leary, K. D. (1993). Through a psychological lens: Personality traits, personality disorders, and levels of violence. In R. J. Gelles & D. R. Loseke (Eds.), *Current controversies on family violence* (pp. 7–30). Newbury Park, CA: Sage.

O'Neill, D. K. (1996). Two-year-old children's sensitivity to a parent's knowledge state when making requests. *Child Development, 67,* 659–677.

O'Rourke, L., Humphris, G., & Baldacchino, A. (2016). Electronic communication based interventions for hazardous young drinkers: A systematic review. *Neuroscience & Biobehavioral Reviews, 68,* 880–890. doi:10.1016/j.neurobiorev.2016.07.021

O'Rourke, N., & Cappeliez, P. (2005). Marital satisfaction and self-deception: Reconstruction of relationship histories among older adults. *Social Behavior and Personality, 33,* 273–282. doi:10.2224/sbp.2005.33.3.273

Oakhill, J. V., & Cain, K. (2012). The precursors of reading ability in young readers: Evidence from a four-year longitudinal study. *Scientific Studies of Reading, 16,* 91–121.

Oaten, M., Stevenson, R. J., & Case, T. I. (2009). Disgust as a disease-avoidance mechanism. *Psychological Bulletin, 135,* 303–321.

Oburu, P. O., & Palmérus, K. (2005). Stress related factors among primary and part-time caregiving grandmothers of Kenyan grandchildren. *International Journal of Aging & Human Development, 60,* 273–282. doi:10.2190/XLQ2-UJEMTAQR-4944

Ochs, E., & Kremer-Sadlik, T. (2013). *Fast-forward family: Home, work, and relationships in middle-class America.* Berkeley, CA: University of California Press.

Ocklenburg, S., Beste, C., & Güntürkün, O. (2013). Handedness: A neurogenetic shift of perspective. *Neuroscience and Biobehavioral Reviews, 37,* 2788–2793.

OECD. (2006). *Starting strong II: Early childhood education and care.* Paris: OECD Publishing.

OECD. (2016). *Balancing paid work, unpaid work and leisure.* Retrieved from www.oecd.org/gender/data/balancingpaidworkunpaidworkandleisure.htm.

Oedekoven, C. S. H., Jansen, A., Kircher, T. T., & Leube, D. T. (2013). Age-related changes in parietal lobe activation during an episodic memory retrieval task. *Journal of Neural Transmission, 120,* 799–806. doi:10.1007/s00702-012-0904-x

Ogden, C. L., Carroll, M. D., Fryar, C. D., & Flegal, K. M. (2015). Prevalence of obesity among adults and youth: United States, 2011–2014. *NCHS data brief,* no. 219. Hyattsville, MD: National Center for Health Statistics.

Ojanen, T., & Perry, D. G. (2007). Relational schemas and the developing self: Perceptions of mother and of self as joint predictors of early adolescents' self-esteem. *Developmental Psychology, 43,* 1474–1483.

Okonski, B. (1996, May 6). Just say something. *Newsweek,* 14.

Olinghouse, N. G. (2008). Student- and instruction-level predictors of narrative writing in third-grade students. *Reading and Writing, 21,* 3–26.

Olinghouse, N. G., Graham, S., & Gillespie, A. (2015). The relationship of discourse and topic knowledge to fifth graders' writing performance. *Journal of Educational Psychology, 107,* 391–406.

Oliveira, B. S., Zunzunegui, M. V., Quinlan, J., Fahmi, H., Tu, M. T., & Guerra, R. O. (2016). Systematic review of the association between chronic social stress and telomere length: A life course perspective. *Aging Research Reviews, 26,* 37–52. doi:10.1016/j.arr.2015.12.006

Olson, D. H., & McCubbin, H. (1983). *Families: What makes them work.* Newbury Park, CA: Sage.

Olson, I. R., & Newcombe, N. S. (2014). Binding together the elements of episodes: Relational memory and the developmental trajectory of the hippocampus. In P J. Bauer & R. Fivush (Eds.), *The Wiley handbook on the development of children's memory* (pp. 285–308). Chichester, UK: Wiley.

Olson, K. R. (2016). Prepubescent transgender children: what we do and do not know. *Journal of the American Academy of Child and Adolescent Psychiatry, 55,* 155–156.

Olson, K. R., Durwood, L., DeMeules, M., & McLaughlin, K. A. (2016). Mental health of transgender children who are supported in their identities. *Pediatrics, 137*(3):e20153223.

Olson, S. L., Lopez-Duran, N., Lunkenheimer, E. S., Chang, H., & Sameroff, A. J. (2011). Individual differences in the development of early peer aggression: Integrating contributions of self-regulation, theory of mind, and parenting. *Development and Psychopathology, 23,* 253–266.

Olson, S. L., Sameroff, A. J., Kerr, D. C. R., Lopez, N. L., & Wellman, H. M. (2005). Developmental foundations of externalizing problems in young children: The role of effortful control. *Development & Psychopathology, 17,* 25–45.

Olszewski-Kubilius, P., Subotnik, R. F., & Worrell, F. C. (2017). The role of domains in the conceptualization of talent. *Roeper Review, 39,* 59–69.

Oltjenbruns, K. A., & Balk, D. E. (2007). Life span issues and loss, grief, and mourning: Part 1. The importance of a developmental context: Childhood and adolescence as an example; Part 2. Adulthood. In D. Balk, C. Wogrin, G. Thornton, & D. Meagher (Eds.), *Handbook of thanatology: The essential body of knowledge for the study of death, dying, and bereavement* (pp. 143–163). New York: Routledge/Taylor & Francis.

Omori, M., & Smith, D. T. (2009). The impact of occupational status on household chore hours among dual earner couples. *Sociation Today, 7.* Retrieved from www.ncsociology.org/sociationtoday/v71/chore.htm.

Oostenbroek, J., Slaughter, V., Nielson, M., & Suddendorf, T. (2013). Why the confusion around neonatal imitation? A review. *Journal of Reproductive and Infant Psychology, 31,* 328–341.

Oostenbroek, J., Suddendorf, T., Nielsen, M., Redshaw, J., Kennedy-Constantini, S., Davis, J., et al. (2016). Comprehensive longitudinal study challenges the existence of neonatal imitation in humans. *Current Biology, 26,* 1334–1338.

Operskalski, J. T., Paul, E. J., Colom, R., Barbey, A. K., & Grafman, J. (2015). Lesion mapping the four-factor structure of emotional intelligence. *Frontiers in Human Neuroscience, 9,* 649. doi:10.3389/fnhum.2015.00649

Opfer, J. E., & Gelman, S. A. (2011). Development of the animate-inanimate distinction. In U. Goswami (Ed.), *The Wiley-Blackwell handbook of childhood cognitive development* (2nd ed., pp. 213–238). West Sussex, UK: Wiley-Blackwell.

Opfer, J. E., & Siegler, R. S. (2004). Revisiting preschoolers' living things concept: A microgenetic analysis of conceptual change in basic biology. *Cognitive Psychology, 49,* 301–332.

Opfer, J. E., & Siegler, R. S. (2012). Development of quantitative thinking. In K. Holyoak and R. Morrison (Eds.), *Oxford handbook of thinking and reasoning* (pp. 585–605). New York: Oxford University Press.

Orel, N. A., & Coon, D. W. (2016). The challenges of change: How can we meet the care needs of the ever-evolving LGBT family? *Generations, 40,* 41–45.

Orel, N. A., & Fruhauf, C. A. (2013). Lesbian, gay, bisexual, and transgender grandparents. In A. E. Goldberg & K. R. Allen (Eds.), *LGBT-parent families* (pp. 177–192). New York: Springer.

Organisation for Economic Co-operation and Development. (2016). *2015 PISA results in focus.* Paris: OECD Publishing.

Oriña, M. M., Collins, W. A., Simpson, J. A., Salvatore, J. E., Haydon, K. C., & Kim, J. S. (2011). Developmental and dyadic perspectives on commitment in adult romantic relationships. *Psychological Science, 22,* 908–915.

Ornstein, P. A., Coffman, J., Grammer, J., San Souci, P., & McCall, L. (2010). Linking the classroom context and the development of children's memory skills. In J. L. Meece & J. S. Eccles (Eds.), *Handbook of research on schools, schooling, and human development* (pp. 42–59). New York: Routledge.

Ortiz-Walters, R., & Gilson, L. L. (2013). Mentoring programs for under-represented groups. In J. Passmore, D. B. Peterson, & T. Freire (Eds.), *The Wiley-Blackwell handbook of coaching and mentoring* (pp. 266–282). Oxford, UK: Wiley-Blackwell.

Ostrov, J. M., & Godleski, S. A. (2010). Toward an integrated gender-linked model of aggression subtypes in early and middle childhood. *Psychological Review, 117,* 233–242.

Oswald, A. J., & Wu, S. (2010). Objective confirmation of subjective measures of human well-being: Evidence from the USA. *Science, 327,* 576–579. doi:10.1126/science.1180606

Oswald, F. L., & Hough, L. (2012). I-O 2.0 from Intelligence 1.5: Staying (just) behind the cutting edge of intelligence theories. *Industrial and Organizational Psychology: Perspectives on Science and Practice, 5,* 172–175.

Ottaway, A. J. (2010). The impact of parental divorce on the intimate relationships of adult offspring: A review of the literature. *Graduate Journal of Counseling Psychology, 2*(1), Article 5. Retrieved from epublications.marquette.edu/cgi/viewcontent.cgi?article=1037&context=gjcp.

Oudekerk, B. A., Allen, J. P., Hessel, E. T., & Molloy, L. E. (2015). The cascading development of autonomy and relatedness from adolescence to adulthood. *Child Development, 86,* 472–485. doi:10.1111/cdev.12313

Over, H., & Carpenter, M. (2009). Eighteen-month-old infants show increased helping following priming with affiliation. *Psychological Science, 20,* 1189–1193.

Owen, C. J. (2005). The empty nest transition: The relationship between attachment style and women's use of this period as a time for growth and change. *Dissertation Abstracts International. Section B. Sciences and Engineering, 65*(7-B), 3747.

Ownby, R. L., Hertzog, C., & Czaja, S. J. (2012). Relations between cognitive status and medication adherence in patients treated for memory disorders. *Ageing Research.* doi:10.4081/ar.2012.e2. Retrieved from www.pagepress.org/journals/index.php/ar/article/viewArticle/2729.

Pace, A., Luo, R., Hirsh-Pasek, K., & Golinkoff, R. M. (2017). Identifying pathways between socioeconomic status and language development. *Annual Reviews of Linguistics, 3,* 285–308.

Paech, J., Luszczynska, A., & Lippke, S. (2016). A rolling stone gathers no moss—The long way from good intentions to physical activity mediated by planning, social support, and self-regulation. *Frontiers in Psychology, 7,* 1024. doi:10.3389/fpsyg.2016.01024

Paggi, M. E., Jopp, D., & Hertzog, C. (2016). The importance of leisure activities in the relationship between physical health and well-being in a life span sample. *Gerontology, 62,* 450–458. doi:10.1159/000444415

Palkovitz, R., & Palm, G. (2009). Transitions within fathering. *Fathering, 7,* 3–22. doi:10.3149/fth.0701.3

Panay, N. (2016). Body identical hormone replacement: The way forward? In A. R. Genazzani & B. C. Tarlatzis (Eds.), *Frontiers in gynecological endocrinology* (pp. 203–208). New York: Springer. doi:10.1007/978-3-319-23865-4_24

Papa, A., & Litz, B. (2011). Grief. In W. T. O'Donohue & C. Draper (Eds.), *Stepped care and e-health: Practical applications to behavioral disorders* (pp. 223–245). New York: Springer.

Parault, S. J., & Schwanenflugel, P. J. (2000). The development of conceptual categories of attention during the elementary school years. *Journal of Experimental Child Psychology, 75*, 245–262.

Pargament, K. I. (2013). Searching for the sacred: Toward a nonreductionistic theory of spirituality. In K. I., Pargament, J. J. Exline, & J. W. Jones (Eds.), *APA handbook of psychology, religion, and spirituality (Vol. 1): Context, theory, and research* (pp. 257–273). Washington, DC: American Psychological Association.

Park, C. L. (2007). Religiousness/spirituality and health: A meaning systems perspective. *Journal of Behavioral Medicine, 30*, 319–328. doi:10.1007 /s10865-007-9111-x

Park, C. L. (2013). The Meaning Making Model: A framework for understanding meaning, spirituality, and stress-related growth in health psychology. *The European Health Psychologist, 15*, 40–47. Retrieved from openhealthpsychology. net/ehp/issues/2013/v15iss2_June2013/EHP_June_2013.pdf#page=13.

Park, C. L., Edmondson, D., & Hale-Smith, A. (2013). Why religion? Meaning as motivation. In K. I., Pargament, J. J. Exline, & J. W. Jones (Eds.), *APA handbook of psychology, religion, and spirituality (Vol. 1): Context, theory, and research* (pp. 151–171). Washington, DC: American Psychological Association.

Park, D. C., & Festini, S. B. (2017). Theories of memory and aging: A look at the past and a glimpse of the future. *Journal of Gerontology: Psychological Sciences, 72*, 82–90. doi:10.1093/geronb/gbw066

Park, G., Lubinski, D., & Benbow, C. P. (2008). Ability differences among people who have commensurate degrees matter for scientific creativity. *Psychological Science, 19*, 957–961.

Park, J., Kitayama, S., Karasawa, M., Curhan, K., Markus, H. R., Kawakami, N., et al. (2013). Clarifying the links between social support and health: Culture, stress, and neuroticism matter. *Journal of Health Psychology, 18*, 226–235. doi:10.1177/1359105312439731

Park, Y. C., & Pyszczynski, T. (2016). Cultural universals and differences in dealing with death. In L. A. Harvell & G. S. Nisbett (Eds.), *Denying death: An interdisciplinary approach to terror management theory* (pp. 193–214). New York: Routledge.

Parke, R. D., & Buriel, R. (1998). Socialization in the family: Ethnic and ecological perspectives. In W. Damon (Ed.), *Handbook of child psychology* (Vol. 3, pp. 463–552). New York: Wiley.

Parke, R. D., & O'Neil, R. (2000). The influence of significant others on learning about relationships: From family to friends. In R. S. L. Mills & S. Duck (Eds.), *The developmental psychology of personal relationships* (pp. 15–47). New York: Wiley.

Parker, J. G., & Seal, J. (1996). Forming, losing, renewing, and replacing friendships: Applying temporal parameters to the assessment of children's friendship experiences. *Child Development, 67*, 2248–2268.

Parker, L. D. (2008). A study about older African American spousal caregivers of persons with Alzheimer's disease. *Dissertation Abstracts International: Section B: The Sciences and Engineering, 68(10-B)*, 6589.

Parkes, C. M. (2013). Elisabeth Kübler-Ross, *On death and dying*: A reappraisal. *Mortality, 18*, 94–97. doi:10.1 080/13576275.2012.758629

Parkinson's Disease Foundation. (2016a). *What is Parkinson's disease?* Retrieved from www.pdf .org/about_pd.

Parkinson's Disease Foundation. (2016b). *Prescription medications.* Retrieved from www .pdf.org/parkinson_prescription_meds.

Parkman, A. M. (2007). *Smart marriage: Using your (business) head as well as your heart to find wedded bliss.* Westport, CT: Praeger.

Parrella, N., & Vormittag, K. (2017). Health promotion and wellness. In A. A., Paulman & L. S. Nasir (Eds.), *Family medicine* (pp. 99–111). New York: Springer.

Parritz, R. H. (1996). A descriptive analysis of toddler coping in challenging circumstances. *Infant Behavior & Development, 19*, 171–180.

Parten, M. (1932). Social participation among preschool children. *Journal of Abnormal and Social Psychology, 27*, 243–269.

Pascalis, O., de Haan, M., & Nelson, C. A. (2002). Is face processing species-specific during the first year of life? *Science, 296*, 1321–1323.

Pascalis, O., Loevenbruck, H., Quinn, P., Kandel, S., Tanaka, J., & Lee, K. (2014). On the linkage between face processing, language processing, and narrowing during development. *Child Development Perspectives, 8*, 65–70.

Pascual, B., Aguardo, G., Sotillo, M., & Masdeu, J. C. (2008). Acquisition of mental state language in Spanish children: A longitudinal study of the relationship between the production of mental verbs and linguistic development. *Developmental Science, 11*, 454–466.

Passarino, G., De Rango, F., & Montesanto, A. (2016). Human longevity: Genetics or lifestyle? It takes two to tango. *Immunity & Ageing, 13*, 12. doi:10.1186/s12979-016-0066-z. Retrieved from immunityageing.biomedcentral.com/articles/10.1186/s12979-016-0066-z.

Pasupathi, M. (2013). Making meaning for the good life: A commentary on the special issue. *Memory, 21*, 143–149. doi:10.1080/09658211.2012.744843

Patrick, S., Sells, J. N., Giordano, F. G., & Tollerud, T. R. (2007). Intimacy, differentiation, and personality variables as predictors of marital satisfaction. *The Family Journal, 15*, 359–367. doi:10.1177/1066480707303754

Patry, D. A., Blanchard, C. M., & Mask, L. (2007). Measuring university students' regulatory leisure coping styles: Planned breathers or avoidance? *Leisure Sciences, 29*, 247–265. doi:10.1080/01490400701257963

Patterson, C. J. (2013). Family lives of lesbian and gay adults. In G. W. Peterson & K. R. Bush (Eds.), *Handbook of marriage and the family* (3rd ed., pp. 659–681). New York: Springer.

Patterson, G. R. (1980). Mothers: The unacknowledged victims. *Monographs of the Society for Research in Child Development, 45*(5, Serial No. 186).

Patterson, M. M., & Bigler, R. S. (2006). Preschool children's attention to environmental messages about groups: Social categorization and the origins of intergroup bias. *Child Development, 77*, 847–860.

Patton, L. D., Renn, K. A., Guido, F. M., & Quaye, S. J. (2016). *Student development in college* (3rd ed.). San Francisco, CA: Jossey-Bass.

Pauker, K., Ambady, N., & Apfelbaum, E. P. (2010). Race salience and essentialist thinking in racial stereotype development. *Child Development, 81*, 1799–1813.

Paulson, D., Bassett, R., Kitsmiller, E., Luther, K., & Conner, N. (2016). When employment and caregiving collide: Predictors of labor force participation in prospective and current caregivers. *Clinical Gerontologist*. doi:10.1080/07317115.2016.1198856

Paus, T. (2010). Growth of white matter in the adolescent brain: Myelin or axon? *Brain & Cognition, 72*, 26–35.

Pearlin, L. I., Mullan, J. T., Semple, S. J., & Skaff, M. M. (1990). Caregiving and the stress process: An overview of concepts and their measures. *The Gerontologist, 30*, 583–594. doi:10.1093/geront/30.5.583

Pears, K. C., Kim, H. K., Fisher, P. A., & Yoerger, K. (2013). Early school engagement and late elementary outcomes for maltreated children in foster care. *Developmental Psychology, 49*, 2201–2211.

Pelham, W. E., Fabiano, G. A., Waxmonsky, J. G., Greiner, A. R., Gnagy, E. M., Pelham, W. E. et al. (2016). Treatment sequencing for childhood ADHD: A multiple-randomization study of adaptive medication and behavioral interventions. *Journal of Clinical Child & Adolescent Psychology, 45*, 396–415.

Pellegrino, J. W., & Kail, R. (1982). Process analyses of spatial aptitude. In R. J. Sternberg (Ed.), *Advances in the psychology of human intelligence*, Vol. 1. Hillsdale, NJ: Lawrence Erlbaum Associates.

Pellicano, E. (2013). Testing the predictive power of cognitive atypicalities in autistic children: Evidence from a 3-year follow-up study. *Autism Research, 6*, 258–267.

Penson, R. T. (2004). Bereavement across cultures. In R. J. Moore & D. Spiegel (Eds.), *Cancer, culture, and communication* (pp. 241–279). New York: Kluwer/Plenum.

Perrone, K. M., Tschopp, K. M., Snyder, E. R., Boo, J. N., & Hyatt, C. (2010). A longitudinal examination of career expectations and outcomes of academically talented students 10 and 20 years post-high school graduation. *Journal of Career Development, 36*, 291–309. doi:10.1177/0894845309359347

Perry, W. I. (1970). *Forms of intellectual and ethical development in the college years.* New York: Holt, Rinehart & Winston.

Peters, A. M. (1995). Strategies in the acquisition of syntax. In P. Fletcher & B. MacWhinney (Eds.), *The handbook of child language* (pp. 462–483). Oxford, UK: Blackwell.

Peterson, L. (1983). Role of donor competence, donor age, and peer presence on helping in an emergency. *Developmental Psychology, 19,* 873–880.

PetersonLund, R. R. (2013). Living on the edge: A review of the literature. *Nursing Science Quarterly, 26,* 303–310. doi:10.1177/0894318413500311

Petrill, S. A. (2016). Behavioural genetic studies of reading and mathematics skills. In Y. Kovas & S. Malykh (Eds.), *Behavioural genetics for education* (pp. 60–76). Houndmills, Basingstoke, Hampshire, UK: Palgrave Macmillan.

Pettit, G. S., Bates, J. E., & Dodge, K. A. (1997). Supportive parenting, ecological context, and children's adjustment: A seven-year longitudinal study. *Child Development, 68,* 908–923.

Pew Research Center. (2013a). *Living to 120 and beyond: Americans' views on aging, medical advances and radical life extension.* Retrieved from www.pewforum.org/2013/08/06/living-to-120-and-beyond-americans-views-on-aging-medical-advances-and-radical-life-extension/.

Pew Research Center. (2013b). *Religious leaders' views on radical life extension.* Retrieved from www.pewforum.org/2013/08/06/religious-leaders-views-on-radical-life-extension/.

Pew Research Center. (2015). *Median age in years, by sex, race and ethnicity: 2013.* Retrieved from www.pewhispanic.org/2016/04/19/statistical-portrait-of-hispanics-in-the-united-states/ph_2015-03_statistical-portrait-of-hispanics-in-the-united-states-2013_current-09/.

Pfaff, D. W., & Fisher, H. (2012). Generalized brain arousal mechanisms and other biological, environmental and psychological mechanisms that contribute to libido. In A. Fotopoulou, D. W. Pfaff, & M. A. Conway (Eds.), *From the couch to the lab: Trends in neuropsychoanalysis* (pp. 65–84). New York: Cambridge University Press.

Pfoff, M. K., Zarotney, J. R., & Monk, T. H. (2014). Can a function-based therapy for spousally bereaved seniors accrue benefits in both functional and emotional domains? *Death Studies, 38,* 381–386. doi:10.1080/07481187.2013.766658

Phinney, J. S. (2005). Ethnic identity development in minority adolescents. In C. B. Fisher & R. M. Lerner (Eds.), *Encyclopedia of applied developmental science* (Vol. 1, pp. 420–423). Thousand Oaks, CA: Sage.

Phipps, M. G., Rosengard, C., Weitzen, S., Meers, A., & Billinkoff, Z. (2008). Age group differences among pregnant adolescents: Sexual behavior, health habits, and contraceptive use. *Journal of Pediatric & Adolescent Gynecology, 21,* 9–15.

Piaget, J. (1929). *The child's conception of the world.* New York: Harcourt Brace.

Piaget, J. (1951). *Plays, dreams, and imitation in childhood.* New York: Norton.

Piaget, J. (1952). *The origins of intelligence in children.* New York: International Universities Press.

Piaget, J. (1954). *The construction of reality in the child.* New York: Basic Books.

Piaget, J., & Inhelder, B. (1956). *The child's conception of space.* Boston: Routledge & Kegan Paul.

Pickering, C. E. Z., & Phillips, L. R. (2014). Development of a causal model for elder mistreatment. *Public Health Nursing, 31,* 363–372. doi:10.1111 /phn.12108

Piehler, T. F., & Dishion, T. J. (2007). Interpersonal dynamics within adolescent friendships: Dyadic mutuality, deviant talk, and patterns of antisocial behavior. *Child Development, 78,* 1611–1624.

Pienta, A. M., Hayward, M. D., & Jenkins, K. R. (2000). Health consequences of marriage for the retirement years. *Journal of Family Issues, 21,* 559–586. doi:10.1177/019251300021005003

Pillay, H., Kelly, K., & Tones, M. (2006). Career aspirations of older workers: An Australian study. *International Journal of Training and Development, 10,* 298–305. doi:10.1111/j.1468-2419.2006.00263.x

Pineda-Pardo, J. A., Martinez, K., Román, F. J., & Colom, R. (2016). Structural efficiencies within a parieto-frontal network and cognitive differences. *Intelligence, 54,* 105–116. doi:10.1016/j.intell.2015.12.002

Pinto, K. M., & Coltrane, S. (2009). Division of labor in Mexican origin and Anglo families: Structure and culture. *Sex Roles, 60,* 482–495. doi:10.1007/s11199-008-9549-5

Pioneer Network. (2017). *Mission, vision, values.* Retrieved from pioneernetwork.net/AboutUs/Values/.

Piquero, A. R., & Moffitt, T. E. (2014). Moffitt's developmental taxonomy of antisocial behavior. In G. Bruinsma & D. Weisburd (Eds.), *Encyclopedia of criminology and criminal justice* (pp. 3121–3127). New York: Spring Science+Business Media.

Piquet, B. J. (2007). That's what friends are for. *Dissertation Abstracts International. Section B. Sciences and Engineering, 67(7-B),* 4114.

Place, S., & Hoff, E. (2011). Properties of dual language exposure that influence 2-year-olds' bilingual proficiency. *Child Development, 82,* 1834–1849.

Plomin, R. (1990). *Nature and nurture.* Pacific Grove, CA: Brooks/Cole.

Plomin, R. (2013). Child development and molecular genetics: 14 years later. *Child Development, 84,* 104–120.

Plomin, R., & Deary, I. J. (2015). Genetics and intelligence differences: Five special findings. *Molecular Psychiatry, 20,* 98–108.

Plomin, R., & Spinath, F. (2004). Intelligence: Genes, genetics, and genomics. *Journal of Personality and Social Psychology, 86,* 112–129.

Plunkett, K. (1996). *Connectionism and development: Neural networks and the study of change.* New York: Oxford University Press.

Poehlmann, J., Schwichtenberg, A. J., Bolt, D. M., Hane, A., Burnson, C., & Winters, J. (2011). Infant physiological regulation and maternal risks as predictors of dyadic interaction trajectories in families with a preterm infant. *Developmental Psychology, 47,* 91–105.

Poldrack, R. A. (2012). The future of fMRI in cognitive neuroscience. *NeuroImage, 62,* 1216–1220. doi:10.1016/j.neuroimage.2011.08.007

Polivka, L. (2010). Neoliberalism and the new politics of aging and retirement security. In J. C. Cavanaugh & C. K. Cavanaugh (Eds.), *Aging in America: Vol. 3: Societal issues* (pp. 161–202). Santa Barbara, CA: ABC-CLIO.

Polivka, L., & Luo, B. (2015). The neoliberal political economy and erosion of retirement security. *The Gerontologist, 55,* 183–190. doi:10.1083/geront/gnv006

Pomerantz, E. M., Ng, F, F., Chung, C. S., & Qu, Y. (2014). Raising happy children who succeed in school: Lessons from China and the United States. *Child Development Perspectives, 8,* 71–76.

Poole, D. A., & Bruck, M. (2012). Divining testimony? The impact of interviewing props on children's reports of touching. *Developmental Review, 32,* 165–180.

Poole, D. A., & Lindsay, D. S. (1995). Interviewing preschoolers: Effects of nonsuggestive techniques, parental coaching, and leading questions on reports of nonexperienced events. *Journal of Experimental Child Psychology, 60,* 129–154.

Pope, T. M. (2017). Certified patient decision aids: Solving persistent problems with informed consent law. *Journal of Law, Medicine, & Ethics, 45,* 12–40. doi:10.1177/1073110517703097

Popenoe, D. (2009). Cohabitation, marriage, and child well-being: A cross-national perspective. *Society: Social Science and Public Policy, 46,* 429–436. doi:10.1007/s12115-009-9242-5

Porter, K. E., Brennan-Ing, M., Chang, S. C., dickey, l. m., Singh, A. A., Bower, K. L. et al. (2016). Providing competent and affirming services for transgender and gender nonconforming older adults. *Clinical Gerontologist, 39,* 366–388. doi:10.1080/07317115.2016.1203383

Porter, R. H., & Winburg, J. (1999). Unique salience of maternal breast odors for newborn infants. *Neuroscience & Biobehavioral Reviews, 23,* 439–449.

Portnoy, A., Rana, P., Zimmerman, C., & Rodin, G. (2015). The use of palliative sedation to treat existential suffering: A reconsideration. In P. Taboada (Ed.), *Sedation at the end-of-life: An interdisciplinary approach* (pp. 41–54). New York: Springer. doi:10.1007/978-94-017-9106-9_4

Potočnik, K., Tordera, N., & Peiró, J. M. (2013). Truly satisfied with your retirement or just resigned? Pathways toward different patterns of retirement satisfaction. *Journal of Applied Gerontology, 32,* 164–187. doi:10.1177/0733464811405988

Poulson, C. L., Kymissis, E., Reeve, K. F., Andreatos, M., & Reeve, L. (1991). Generalized vocal imitation in infants. *Journal of Experimental Child Psychology, 51,* 267–279.

Power, T. L., & Smith, S. M. (2008). Predictors of fear of death and self-mortality: An Atlantic

Canadian perspective. *Death Studies, 32*, 252–272. doi:10.1080/07481180701880935

Pratt, H. D. (2010). Perspectives from a non-traditional mentor. In C. A. Rayburn, F. L. Denmark, M. E. Reuder, & A.M. Austria, (Eds.), *A handbook for women mentors: Transcending barriers of stereotype, race, and ethnicity* (pp. 223–232). Santa Barbara, CA: ABC-CLIO.

President's Council on Fitness, Sports & Nutrition. (2012). *Physical activity guidelines for Americans midcourse report: Strategies to increase physical activity among youth.* Washington, DC: U.S. Department of Health and Human Services.

President's Council on Physical Fitness and Sports. (2004). Physical activity for children: Current patterns and guidelines. *Research Digest* (Series 5, No. 2).

Pressley, M. (2002). *Reading instruction that works: The case for balanced teaching* (2nd ed.). New York: Guilford Press.

Pressley, M., & Hilden, K. (2006). Cognitive strategies. In D. Kuhn & R. S. Siegler (Eds.), *Handbook of child psychology* (6th ed., Vol. 2, pp. 511–556). Hoboken, NJ: Wiley.

Preston, C., Goldring, E., Guthrie, J. E., Ramsey, R., & Huff, J. (2017). Conceptualizing essential components of effective high schools. *Leadership and Policy in Schools, 16*, in press.

Priaulx, N. (2013). The troubled identity of the bioethicist. *Health Care Analysis, 21*, 6–19. doi:10.1007/ s10728-012-0229-9

Price, T. S., Grosser, T., Plomin, R., & Jaffee, S. R. (2010). Fetal genotype for the xenobiotic metabolizing enzyme NQO1 influences intrauterine growth among infants whose mothers smoked during pregnancy. *Child Development, 81*, 101–114.

Price, V. (2016). Women in non-traditional work fields. In N. A. Naples, r. c. hoogland, M. Wickramasing, & W. C. A. Wong (Eds.), *The Wiley Blackwell encyclopedia of gender and sexuality studies.* Malden, MA: Wiley. doi:10.1002/9781118663219.wbegss546

Prince-Paul, M., & Daly, B. J. (2016). Ethical considerations in palliative care. In N. Coyle (ed.), *Legal and ethical aspects of care* (pp. 1–28). New York: Oxford University Press.

Prot, S., Gentile, D. A., Anderson, C. A., Suzuki, K., Swing, E., Lim, K. M., et al. (2014). Long-term relations among prosocial-media use, empathy, and prosocial behavior. *Psychological Science, 25*, 358–368.

Proulx, C. M. (2016). Marital trajectories. In S. K. Whitbourne (Ed.), *The encyclopedia of adulthood and aging* (pp. 842–845). New York: Wiley.

Provins, K. A. (1997). Handedness and speech: A critical reappraisal of the role of genetic and environmental factors in the cerebral lateralization of function. *Psychological Review, 104*, 554–571.

Pruett, M. K., Insabella, G. M., & Gustafson, K. (2005). The collaborative divorce project: A court-based intervention for separating parents with young children. *Family Court Review, 43*, 38–51. doi:10.1111/j.1744-1617.2005.00006.x

Pryor, L., Brendgen, M., Boivin, M., Dubois, L., Japel, C. Fallissard, B. et al. (2016). Overweight during childhood and internalizing symptoms in early adolescence: The mediating role of peer victimization and the desire to be thinner. *Journal of Affective Disorders, 202*, 203–209.

Puhl, R. M., & Brownell, K. D. (2005). Bulimia nervosa. In C. B. Fisher & R. M. Lerner (Eds.), *Encyclopedia of applied developmental science* (Vol. 1, pp. 192–195). Thousand Oaks, CA: Sage.

Pynoos, J. Caraviello, R., & Cicero, C. (2010). Housing in an aging America. In J. C. Cavanaugh & C. K. Cavanaugh (Eds.), *Aging in America: Vol. 3: Societal issues* (pp. 129–159). Santa Barbara, CA: Praeger Perspectives.

Queen, T. L., Berg, C. A., & Lowrance, W. (2015). A framework for decision making in couples across adulthood. In T. M. Hess, J. Strough, & C. E. Löckenhoff (Eds.), *Aging and decision making: Empirical and applied perspectives* (pp. 371–392). San Diego, CA: Academic Press.

Quinn, J. F., & Cahill, K. E. (2016). The new world of retirement income security in America. *American Psychologist, 71*, 321–333. doi:10.1037/a0040276

Quinn, P. C., Lee, K., Pascalis, O., & Tanaka, J. W. (2016). Narrowing in categorical responding to other-race face classes by infants. *Developmental Science, 19*, 362–371.

Quirin, M., Loktyushin, A., Arndt, J., Küstermann, E., Lo, Y.-Y., Kuhl, J. et al. (2012). Existential neuroscience: A functional magnetic resonance imaging investigation of neural responses to reminders of one's mortality. *Social Cognitive and Affective Neuroscience, 7*, 193–198. doi:10.1093/scan/nsq106

Raabe, T., & Beelmann, A. (2011). Development of ethnic, racial, and national prejudice in childhood and adolescence: A multinational meta-analysis of age differences. *Child Development, 82*, 1715–1737.

Racz, S. J., & McMahon, R. J. (2011). The relationship between parental knowledge and monitoring and child and adolescent conduct problems: A 10-year update. *Clinical Child and Family Psychology Review, 14*, 377–398.

Raikes, H., Luze, G., Brooks-Gunn, J., Raikes, H., Pan, B. A., Tamis-LeMonda, C. S., et al. (2006). Mother–child bookreading in low-income families: Correlates and outcomes during the first three years of life. *Child Development, 77*, 924–953.

Rakic, P. (1995). Corticogenesis in humans and nonhuman primates. In M. S. Gazzaniga (Ed.), *The cognitive neurosciences.* Cambridge, MA: MIT Press.

Ralph, L. J., & Brindis, C. D. (2010). Access to reproductive healthcare for adolescents: Establishing healthy behaviors at a critical juncture in the lifecourse. *Current Opinion in Obstetrics & Gynecology, 22*, 369–374.

Ramalingam, M., Durgadevi, P., & Mahmood, T. (2016). In vitro fertilization. *Obstetrics, Gynaecology, and Reproductive Medicine, 26*, 200–209.

Randall, A. K., & Bodenmann, G. (2017). Stress and its associations with relationship satisfaction. *Current Opinion in Psychology, 13*, 96–106. doi:10.1016/j.copsyc.2016.05.010

Rangul, V., Bauman, A., Holmen, T. L., & Midthjell, K. (2012). Is physical activity maintenance from adolescence to young adulthood associated with reduced CVD risk factors, improved mental health and satisfaction with life: The HUNT Study, Norway. *International Journal of Behavioral Nutrition and Physical Activity, 9*, 103.

Rape, Abuse, and Incest National Network. (2016). *Statistics.* Retrieved from www.rainn.org/statistics.

Raschick, M., & Ingersoll-Dayton, B. (2004). The costs and rewards of caregiving among aging spouses and adult children. *Family Relations: Interdisciplinary Journal of Applied Family Studies, 53*, 317–325. doi:10.1111/j.0022-2445.2004.0008.x

Rawlins, W. K. (2004). Friendships in later life. In J. F. Nussbaum & J. Coupland (Eds.), *Handbook of communication and aging research* (2nd ed., pp. 273–299). Mahwah, NJ: Erlbaum.

Reardon, S. (2016). First CRISPR clinical trial gets green light from US panel. *Nature News,* doi:10.1038/nature.2016.20137.

Redzanowski, U., & Glück, J. (2013). Who knows who is wise? Self and peer ratings of wisdom. *Journal of Gerontology: Psychological Sciences, 68*, 391–394. doi:10.1093/geronb/ gbs079

Reed, A. E., & Carstensen, L. L. (2012). The theory behind the age-related positivity effect. *Frontiers in Psychology.* doi:10.3389/fpsyg.2012.00339

Reese, E., & Cox, A. (1999). Quality of adult book reading affects children's emergent literacy. *Developmental Psychology, 35*, 20–28.

Rehan, W., Antfolk, J., Johansson, A., & Santtila, P. (2017). Do single experiences of childhood abuse increase psychopathology symptoms in adulthood? *Journal of Interpersonal Violence,* in press.

Reich, P. A. (1986). *Language development.* Englewood Cliffs, NJ: Prentice Hall.

Reimer, M. S. (1996). "Sinking into the ground": The development and consequences of shame in adolescence. *Developmental Review, 16*, 321–363.

Remedios, J. D., Chasteen, A. L., & Packer, D. J. (2010). Sunny side up: The reliance on positive age stereotypes in descriptions of future older selves. *Self and Identity, 9*, 257–275. doi:10.1080/15298860903054175

Ren, Q., & Treiman, D. J. (2014). *Living arrangements of the elderly in China and consequences for their emotional well-being.* Population Studies Center Research Report 14-814, University of Michigan. Retrieved from www.psc.isr.umich.edu/pubs/pdf/rr14-814.pdf.

Renshaw, K. D., Rodrigues, C., & Jones, D. H. (2008). Psychological symptoms and marital satisfaction in spouses of operation Iraqi freedom veterans: Relationships with spouses' perceptions of veterans' experiences and symptoms. *Journal of Family Psychology, 22*, 586–594. doi:10.1037/0893-3200.22.3.586

Repacholi, B. M. (1998). Infants' use of attentional cues to identify the referent of another person's emotional expression. *Developmental Psychology, 34*, 1017–1025.

Repacholi, B. M., & Meltzoff, A. N. (2007). Emotional eavesdropping: Infants selectively respond to indirect emotional signals. *Child Development, 78*, 503–521.

Repacholi, B. M., Meltzoff, A. N., & Olsen, B. (2008). Infants' understanding of the link between visual perception and emotion: "If she can't see me doing it, she won't get angry." *Developmental Psychology, 44*, 561–574.

Repetti, R., & Wang, S-w. (2017). Effects of job stress on family relationships. *Current Opinion in Psychology, 13*, 15–18. doi:10.1017/j.copsyc.2016.03.010

Revenson, T. A., Griva, K., Luszczynska, A., Morrison, V., Panagopoulou, E., Vilchinsky, N. et al. (2016). *Caregiving in the illness context.* New York: Palgrave Macmillan.

Rhea, S-A., Bricker, J. B., Wadsworth, S. J., & Corley, R. P. (2013). The Colorado Adoption Project. *Twin Research and Human Genetics, 16*, 358–365.

Rhoades, K. A. (2008). Children's responses to interparental conflict: A meta-analysis of their associations with child adjustment. *Child Development, 79*, 1942–1956.

Rhodes, M. (2013). How two intuitive theories shape the development of social categorization. *Child Development Perspectives, 7*, 12–16.

Rideout, V. (2016). Measuring time spent with media: The Common Sense census of media use by U.S. 8- to 18-year-olds. *Journal of Children and Media, 10*, 138–144.

Ridings, C., & Gefen, D. (2004). Virtual community attraction: Why people hang out online. *Journal of Computer-Mediated Communication, 10.* doi:10.1111/j.1083-6101.2004.tb00229.x.

Rijken, A. J. (2009). *Happy families, high fertility? Childbearing choices in the context of family and partner relationships.* Dissertation submitted in partial fulfillment of the doctor of philosophy degree, University of Utrecht.

Rijken, A. J., & Knijn, T. (2009). Couples' decisions to have a first child: Comparing pathways to early and late parenthood. *Demographic Research, 21*, 765–802. doi:10.4054/DemRes.2009.21.26. Retrieved from core.ac.uk/download/pdf/6405965.pdf.

Riley, M. W. (1979). Introduction. In M. W. Riley (Ed.), *Aging from birth to death: Interdisciplinary perspectives* (pp. 3–14). Boulder, CO: Westview Press.

Rindermann, H., & Thompson, J. (2013). Ability rise in NAEP and narrowing ethnic gaps? *Intelligence, 41*, 821–831.

Ripp, J., Jones, E., & Zhang, M. (2016). Common functional problems. In J. L. Hayashi & B. Leff (Eds.), *Geriatric home-based medical care* (pp. 151–172). New York: Springer. doi:10.1007/978-3-319-23365-9_8

Ritchie, K. L. (1999). Maternal behaviors and cognitions during discipline episodes: A comparison of power bouts and single acts of noncompliance. *Developmental Psychology, 35*, 580–589.

Rittle-Johnson, B. (2017). Developing mathematics knowledge. *Child Development Perspectives, 11*, in press.

Rittle-Johnson, B., & Schneider, M. (2015). Developing conceptual and procedural knowledge of mathematics. In R. Cohen Kadosh & A. Dowker (Eds.), *Oxford handbook of numerical cognition* (pp. 1118–1134). Oxford, UK: Oxford University Press.

Rivas-Drake, D., Seaton, E. K., Markstrom, C., Quintana, S., Syed, M., Lee, R. M., et al. (2014). Ethnic and racial identity in adolescence: Implications for psychosocial, academic, and health outcomes. *Child Development, 85*, 40–57.

Rizzuto, T. E., Cherry, K. E., & LeDoux, J. A. (2012). The aging process and cognitive capabilities. In J. W. Hedge & W. C. Borman (Eds.), *The Oxford handbook of work and aging* (pp. 236–255). New York: Oxford University Press.

Robbins, A., & Wilner, A. (2001). *Quarterlife crisis: The unique challenges of life in your twenties.* New York: Putnam.

Roberto, K. A. (2016). The complexities of elder abuse. *American Psychologist, 71*, 302–311. doi:10.1037/a0040259

Roberto, K. A., & Skoglund, R. R. (1996). Interactions with grandparents and great-grandparents: A comparison of activities, influences, and relationships. *International Journal of Aging & Human Development, 43*, 107–117. doi:10.2190/8F1D-9A4D-h)QY-W9DD

Roberto, K. A., McPherson, M. C., & Brossoie, N. (2013). Intimate partner violence in late life: A review of the empirical literature. *Violence Against Women, 19*, journals.sagepub.com/doi/full/10.1177/1077801213517564. doi:10.1177/1077801213517564

Roberts, B. W., & DelVecchio, W. F. (2000). The rank-order consistency of personality traits from childhood to old age: A quantitative review of longitudinal studies. *Psychological Bulletin, 126*, 3–25. doi:10.1037/0033-2909.126.1.3

Roberts, B. W., Walton, K., Bogg, T., & Caspi, A. (2006). De-investment in work and non-normative personality trait change in young adulthood. *European Journal of Personality, 20*, 461–474. doi:10.1002/per.607

Roberts, K. P., Evans, A. D., & Duncanson, S. (2016). Binding an event to its source at encoding improves children's source monitoring. *Developmental Psychology, 52*, 2191–2201.

Robertson, C. E., Ratai, E., & Kanwisher, N. (2016). Reduced GABAergic action in the autistic brain. *Current Biology, 26*, 1–6.

Robinaugh, D. J., & McNally, R. J. (2013). Remembering the past and envisioning the future in bereaved adults with and without complicated grief. *Clinical Psychological Science, 1*, 290–300. doi:10.1177/2167702613476027

Robins, S., Treiman, R., & Rosales, N. (2014). Letter knowledge in parent-child conversations. *Reading and Writing, 27*, 407–429.

Robinson-Wood, T., & Weber, A. (2016). Deconstructing multiple oppressions among LGBT older adults. In D. A. Harley & P. B. Teaster (Eds.), *Handbook of LGBT elders* (pp. 65–81). New York: Springer.

Robinson, O. C., & Smith, J. A. (2010). Investigating the form and dynamics of crisis episodes in early adulthood: The application of a composite qualitative method. *Qualitative Research in Psychology, 7*, 170–191. doi:10.1080/14780880802699084

Robinson, O. C., & Wright, G. R. T. (2013). The prevalence, types and perceived outcomes of crisis episodes in early adulthood and midlife: A structured retrospective autobiographical study. *International Journal of Behavioural Development, 37*, 407–416. doi:10.1177/0165025413492464

Robinson, O. C., Wright, G. R. T., & Smith, J. A. (2013). The holistic phase model of early adult crisis. *Journal of Adult Development, 20*, 27–37. doi:10.1007/s10804-013-9153-y

Robinson, O.C. (2015). Emerging adulthood, early adulthood and quarter-life crisis: Updating Erikson for the twenty-first century. In R. Žukauskiene (Ed.) *Emerging adulthood in a European context* (pp. 17–30). New York: Routledge.

Robson, S. M., Hansson, R. O., Abalos, A., & Booth, M. (2006). Successful aging: Criteria for aging well in the workplace. *Journal of Career Development, 33*, 156–177. doi:10.1177/0894845306292533

Roby, A. C., & Kidd, E. (2008). The referential communication skills of children with imaginary companions. *Developmental Science, 11*, 531–540.

Rockwood, K. (2016). Conceptual models of frailty: Accumulation of deficits. *Canadian Journal of Cardiology, 32*, 1046–1050. doi:10.1016/j.cjca.2016.03.020

Rocque, G. B., & Cleary, J. F. (2013). Palliative care reduces morbidity and mortality in cancer. *Nature Reviews Clinical Oncology, 10*, 80–89. doi:10.1038/nrclinonc.2012.211

Rodeck, C. H., & Whittle, M. J. (Eds.). (2009). *Fetal medicine: Basic science and clinical practice.* London: Churchill Livingstone.

Rodriguez-Galán, M. B. (2014). The ethnography of ethnic minority families and aging: Familism and beyond. In K. E. Whitfield & T. A. Baker (Eds.), *Handbook of minority aging* (pp. 435–453). New York: Springer.

Roffwarg, H. P., Muzio, J. N., & Dement, W. C. (1966). Ontogenetic development of the human sleep-dream cycle. *Science, 152*, 604–619.

Rogers, L. A., & Graham, S. (2008). A meta-analysis of single subject design writing intervention research. *Journal of Educational Psychology, 100*, 879–906.

Rogoff, B. (2003). *The cultural nature of human development.* New York: Oxford University Press.

Rohmann, E., Führer, A., & Bierhoff, H.-W. (2016). Relationship satisfaction across European cultures: The role of love styles. *Cross-Cultural Research, 50*, 178–211. doi:10.1177/1069397116630950

Rohr, R. (2011). *Falling upward: A spirituality for the two halves of life.* San Francisco, CA: Jossey-Bass.

Rohr, R. (2013). *Immortal diamond: The search for our true self.* San Francisco, CA: Jossey-Bass.

Rollins, N. C., Bhandari, N., Hajeebhoy, N., Horton, S., Lutter, C. K., Martines, J., et al. (2016). Breastfeeding 2: Why invest, and what will it take to improve breastfeeding practices? *Lancet, 387,* 491–504.

Roosevelt, F. D. (1935). *Statement on signing the Social Security Act.* Retrieved from www.ssa.gov/history/fdrstmts.html#signing.

Rose, A. J., & Asher, S. R. (1999). Children's goals and strategies in response to conflicts within a friendship. *Developmental Psychology, 35,* 69–79.

Rose, A. J., & Asher, S. R. (2017). The social tasks of friendships: Do boys and girls excel in different tasks? *Child Development Perspectives, 11,* 3–8.

Rose, A. J., & Rudolph, K. D. (2006). A review of sex differences in peer relationship processes: Potential trade-offs for the emotional and behavioral development of girls and boys. *Psychological Bulletin, 132,* 98–131.

Rose, D. M., & Gordon, R. (2010). Retention practices for engineering and technical professionals in an Australian public agency. *Australian Journal of Public Administration, 69,* 314–325. doi:10.1111/j.1467-8500.2010.00693.x

Rosenbaum, J. L., Smith, J. R., & Zollfrank, B. C. C. (2011). Neonatal end-of-life support care. *Perinatal and Neonatal Nursing, 25,* 61–69. doi:10.1097 /JPN.0b013e318209e1d2

Rosenblatt, P. C. (1996). Grief that does not end. In D. Klass, P. R. Silverman, & S. L. Nickman (Eds.), *Continuing bonds: New understandings of grief* (pp. 45–58). Washington, DC: Taylor & Francis.

Rosengren, K. S., Gutiérrez, I. T., & Schein, S. S. (2014a). Cognitive dimensions of death in context. *Monographs of the Society for Research in Child Development, 79,* 62–82. doi:10.1111/ mono.12079

Rosengren, K. S., Miller, P. J., Gutiérrez, I. T., Chow, P. I., Schein, S. S., & Anderson, K. N. (2014b). Children's understanding of death: Toward a contextualized and integrated account. *Monographs of the Society for Research in Child Development, 79,* 1–162.

Ross, J., Yilmaz, M., Dale, R., Cassidy, R., Yildirim, I., & Zeedyk, M. S. (2017). Cultural differences in self-recognition: the early development of autonomous and related selves? *Developmental Science, 20*(3). doi:10.1111/desc.12387

Ross, N. A., Garner, R., Bernier, J., Feeny, D. H., Kaplan, M. S., McFarland, B., et al. (2012). Trajectories of health-related quality of life by socioeconomic status in a nationally representative Canadian cohort. *Journal of Epidemiology and Community Health, 66,* 593–598. doi:10.1136/jech.2010.115378

Rosso, B. D., Dekas, K. H., & Wrzesniewski, A. (2010). On the meaning of work: A theoretical integration and review. *Research in Organizational Behavior, 30,* 91–127. doi:10.1016/j.riob.2010.09.001

Rostila, M., Saarela, J., Kawachi, I., & Hjern, A. (2015). Testing the anniversary reaction: Causal effects of bereavement in a nationwide follow-up study from Sweden. *Psychiatric Epidemiology, 30,* 239–247. doi:10.1007/ s10654-015-9989-5

Roszko, E. (2010). Commemoration and the state: Memory and legitimacy in Vietnam. *Sojourn: Journal of Social Issues in Southeast Asia, 25,* 1–28. doi:10.1353/soj.0.0041

Rothbart, M. K. (2011). *Becoming who we are: Temperament and personality in development.* New York: Guilford.

Rothbart, M. K., & Rueda, M. R. (2005). The development of effortful control. In U. Mayr, E. Awh, & S. W. Keele (Eds.), *Developing individuality in the human brain: A tribute to Michael I. Posner* (pp. 167–188). Washington, DC: American Psychological Association.

Rovee-Collier, C. (1987). Learning and memory in infancy. In J. D. Osofsky (Ed.), *Handbook of infant development* (2nd ed., pp. 98–148). New York: Wiley.

Rovee-Collier, C. (1997). Dissociations in infant memory: Rethinking the development of implicit and explicit memory. *Psychological Review, 104,* 467–498.

Rovee-Collier, C. (1999). The development of infant memory. *Current Directions in Psychological Science, 8,* 80–85.

Rowe, M. L. (2012). A longitudinal investigation of the role of quantity and quality of child-directed speech in vocabulary development. *Child Development, 83,* 1762–1774.

Rowe, M. L., Radebe's, S. W., & Goldin-Meadow, S. (2012). The pace of vocabulary growth helps predict later vocabulary skill. *Child Development, 83,* 508–525.

Rowe, M. M., & Sherlock, H. (2005). Stress and verbal abuse in nursing: Do burned out nurses eat their young? *Journal of Nursing Management, 13,* 242–248. doi:10.1111/j.1365-2834.2004.00533.x

Rowles, G. D. (2006). Commentary: A house is not a home: But can it become one? In H. W. Wahl et al. (Eds.), *The many faces of health, competence and well-being in old age* (pp. 25–32). New York: Springer.

Rowles, G. D., & Watkins, J. F. (2003). History, habit, heart, and hearth: On making spaces into places. In K. W. Schaie, H.-W. Wahl, H. Mollenkopf, & F. Oswald (Eds.), *Aging independently: Living arrangements and mobility* (pp. 77–96). New York: Springer.

Roxburgh, S. (2002). Racing through life. The distribution of time pressures by roles and roles resources among full-time workers. *Journal of Family and Economic Issues, 23,* 121–145. doi:10.1023/A:1015734516575

Rubin, K. H., Bukowski, W. M., & Bowker, J. C. (2015). Children in peer groups. In R. M. Lerner (Ed.), *Handbook of child psychology and developmental science* (7th ed., Vol 4., pp. 175–222). Hoboken, NJ: Wiley.

Rubin, K. H., Coplan, R. J., Chen, X., Bowker, J. C., McDonald, K. L., & Heverly-Fitt, S. (2015). Peer relationships. In M. H. Bornstein & M. E. Lamb (Eds.), *Developmental science: An advanced textbook* (7th ed., pp. 587–644). New York: Psychology Press.

Rubin, S. S., & Malkinson, R. (2001). Parental response to child loss across the life cycle: Clinical and research perspectives. In M. S. Stroebe, R. O. Hansson, W. Stroebe, & H. Schut (Eds.), *Handbook of bereavement research: Consequences, coping, and care* (pp. 169–197). Washington, DC: American Psychological Association.

Ruble, D. N., Martin, C. L., & Berenbaum, S. A. (2006). Gender development. In N. Eisenberg, W. Damon, & R. M. Lerner (Eds.), *Handbook of child psychology: Vol. 3, Social, emotional, and personality development* (6th ed., pp. 858–932). Hoboken, NJ: Wiley.

Rudd, M. D., Berman, A. L., Joiner, T. E., Nock, M. K., Silverman, M. M., Mandrusiak, M., et al. (2006). Warning signs for suicide: Theory, research, and clinical applications. *Suicide and Life-Threatening Behavior, 36,* 255–262.

Rueger, S. Y., Chen, P., Jenkins, L. N., & Choe, H. J. (2014). Effects of perceived support from mothers, father, and teachers on depressive symptoms during the transition to middle school. *Journal of Youth and Adolescence, 43,* 655–670.

Ruiz, M. E., Phillips, L. R., Kim, H., & Woods, D. L. (2016). Older Latinos: Applying the ethnocultural gerontological nursing model. *Journal of Transcultural Nursing, 27,* 8–17. doi:10.1177/1043695615569539

Ruppanner, L., & Maume, D. J. (2016). Shorter work hours and work-to-family interference: Surprising findings from 32 countries. *Social Forces, 95,* 693–720. doi:10.1093/sf/sow057

Rushton, J. P., & Bons, T. A. (2005). Mate choice and friendship in twins. *Psychological Science, 16,* 555–559.

Russell, A., & Finnie, V. (1990). Preschool children's social status and maternal instructions to assist group entry. *Developmental Psychology, 26,* 603–611.

Rutland, A., & Killen, M. (2017). Fair resource allocation among children and adolescents: The role of group and developmental processes. *Child Development Perspectives, 11,* 56–62.

Ryan, E. G. (2013). *How to write about rape prevention without sounding like an asshole.* Jezebel blog. Retrieved from http://jezebel .com/how-to-write-about-rape-prevention-without-sounding-lik-1446529386.

Ryan, M. K., Haslam, S. A., & Kulich, C. (2010). Politics and the glass cliff: Evidence that women are preferentially selected to contest hard-to-win seats. *Psychology of Women Quarterly, 34,* 56–64. doi:10.1111/j.1471-6402.2009.01541.x

Ryan, M. K., Haslam, S. A., Morgenroth, T., Rink, F., Stoker, J., & Peters, K. (2016). Getting on top of the glass cliff: Reviewing a decade of evidence, explanations, and impact. *The Leadership Quarterly, 27,* 446–455. doi:10.1016/j.leaqua.2015.10.008

Rye, M. S., Folck, C. D., Heim, T. A., Olszewski, B. T., & Traina, E. (2004). Forgiveness of an ex-spouse:

How does it relate to mental health following a divorce? *Journal of Divorce & Remarriage, 41,* 31–51. doi:10.1300/ J087v41n03_02

Saarento, S., & Salmivalli, C. (2015). The role of classroom peer ecology and bystanders' responses in bullying. *Child Development Perspectives, 9,* 201–205.

Saewyc, E. M. (2011). Research on adolescent sexual orientation: Development, health disparities, stigma, and resilience. *Journal of Research on Adolescence, 21,* 256–272.

Saffran, J. R., Aslin, R. N., & Newport, E. L. (1996). Statistical learning by 8-month-old infants. *Science, 274,* 1926–1928.

Sagi, A., Koren-Karie, N., Gini, M., Ziv, Y., & Joels, T. (2002). Shedding further light on the effects of various types and quality of early child care on infant–mother attachment relationship: The Haifa study of early child care. *Child Development, 73,* 1166–1186.

Sahni, R., Fifer, W. P., & Myers, M. M. (2007). Identifying infants at risk for sudden infant death syndrome. *Current Opinion in Pediatrics, 19,* 145–149.

Saint-Georges, C., Chetouani, M., Cassel, R., Apicella, F., Mahdhaoui, A., Muratori, F., et al. (2013). Motherese in interaction: At the crossroad of emotion and cognition? (A systematic review). *PLoS ONE, 8*(10): e78103.

Sakaki, M., Nga, L., & Mather, M. (2013). Amygdala functional connectivity with medial prefrontal context at rest predicts the positivity effect in older adults' memory. *Journal of Cognitive Neuroscience, 25,* 1206–1224. doi:10.1162/jocn_a_00392

Sakraida, T. J. (2005). Divorce transition differences of midlife women. *Issues in Mental Health Nursing, 26,* 225–249. doi:10.1080/01612840590901699

Sakyi, K. S., Surkan, P. J., Fombonne, E., Chollet, A., & Melchior, M. (2015). Childhood friendships and psychological difficulties in young adulthood: An 18-year follow-up study. *European Child and Adolescent Psychiatry, 24,* 815–826.

Sala Frigerio, C., & De Strooper, B. (2016). Alzheimer's disease mechanisms and emerging roads to novel therapeutics. *Annual Review of Neuroscience, 39,* 57–79. doi:10.1146/annurev-neuro-070815-014015

Salomaa, R. (2014). Coaching of key talents in multinational companies. In A. Al Ariss (Ed.), *Global talent management* (pp. 43–63). New York: Springer.

Salovey, P., & Mayer, J. D. (1990). *Emotional intelligence. Imagination, cognition, and personality, 9,* 185–211. doi:10.2190/DUGG-P24E-52WK-6CDG

Salthouse, T. A. (2014a). Relations between running memory and fluid intelligence. *Intelligence, 43,* 1–7. doi:10.1016/j.intell.2013.12.002

Salthouse, T. A. (2014b). Correlates of cognitive change. *Journal of Experimental Psychology: General.* doi:10.1037/a0034847

Samanta, T. (2017). Bridging the gap: Theory and research in social gerontology. In T. Samanta (Ed.), *Cross-cultural and cross-disciplinary perspectives in social gerontology* (pp. 3–22). New York: Springer.

Samuelson, L. K., & McMurray, B. (2017). What does it take to learn a word? *WIREs Cognitive Science, 8,* e1421.

Sánchez-Álvarez, N., Extremera, N., & Fernández-Berrocal, P. (2016). The relation between emotional intelligence and subjective well-being: A meta-analytic investigation. *The Journal of Positive Psychology, 11,* 276–285.

Sanders, M. (2014). *A public health approach to improving parenting and promoting children's well-being.* Unpublished manuscript.

Sandler, I. N., Wolchik, S. A. Ayers, T. S., Tein, J.-Y., & Luecken, L. (2013). Family bereavement program (FBP) approach to promoting resilience following the death of a parent. *Family Science, 4,* 87–94. doi:10.1080/194246 20.2013.821763

Sandler, I. N., Wolchik, S. A., & Ayers, T. S. (2007). Resilience rather than recovery: A contextual framework on adaptation following bereavement. *Death Studies, 32,* 59–73. doi:10.1080/07481180701741343

Sandler, I., Ingram, A., Wolchik, S., Tein, J.-Y., & Winslow, E. (2015). Long-term effects of parenting-focused preventive interventions to promote resilience of children and adolescents. *Child Development Perspectives, 9,* 164–171.

Sanford, L. (2014). *Why lighting is important for the aging eye.* Retrieved from www.lighthouse .org/eye-health/the-basics-of-the-eye/the-aging-eye /lighting/.

Sangrigoli, S., Pallier, C., Argenti, A.-M., Ventureyra, V. A. G., & de Schonen, S. (2005). Reversibility of the other-race effect in face recognition during childhood. *Psychological Science, 16,* 440–444.

Sann, C., & Streri, A. (2007). Perception of object shape and texture in human newborns: Evidence from cross-modal transfer tasks. *Developmental Science, 10,* 399–410.

Sanson, A., Prior, M., Smart, D., & Oberklaid, F. (1993). Gender differences in aggression in childhood: Implications for a peaceful world. *Australian Psychologist, 28,* 86–92.

Sargent, C. S., & Borthick, A. F. (2013). Evidence for insisting on cognitive conflict tasks: Impact on accounting majors in upper level courses. *Issues in Accounting Education, 28* 759–777. doi:10.2308/iace-50518

Sargent, L. D., Lee, M. D., Martin, B., & Zikic, J. (2013). Reinventing retirement: New pathways, new arrangements, new meanings. *Human Relations, 66,* 3–21. doi:10.1177/0018726712465658

Saroglou, V., Pichon, I., Trompette, L., Verschueren, M., & Dernelle, R. (2005). Prosocial behavior and religion: New evidence based on projective measures and peer ratings. *Journal for the Scientific Study of Religion, 44,* 323–348.

Saudino, K. J. (2009). Do different measures tap the same genetic influences? A multi-method study of activity level in young twins. *Developmental Science, 12,* 626–633.

Saudino, K. J., & Micalizzi, L. (2015). Emerging trends in behavioral genetic studies of child temperament. *Child Development Perspectives, 9,* 144–148.

Savela, S., Saijonmaa, O., Strandberg, T. E., Koistinen, P., Strandberg, A. Y., Tilvis, R. S., et al. (2013). Physical activity in midlife and telomere length measured in old age. *Experimental Gerontology, 48,* 81–84. doi:10.1016 /j/exger.2012.02.003

Savickas, M. L. (2013). Career construction theory and practice. In S. D. Brown & R. W. Lent (Eds.), *Career development and counseling: Putting theory and research to work* (pp. 147–183). New York: Wiley.

Saxe, G. B. (1988). The mathematics of child street vendors. *Child Development, 59,* 1415–1425.

Sbarra, D. A. (2015). Divorce and health: Current trends and future directions. *Psychosomatic Medicine, 77,* 227–236. doi:10.1097/0000000000000168

Scantlebury, N., Cunningham, T., Dockstader, C., & Laughlin, S. (2014). Relations between white matter maturation and reaction time in childhood. *Journal of the International Neuropsychological Society, 20,* 99–112.

Scarr, S. (1992). Developmental theories for the 1990s: Development and individual differences. *Child Development, 63,* 1–19.

Scarr, S., & McCartney, K. (1983). How people make their own environments: A theory of genotype environment effects. *Child Development, 54,* 424–435.

Schaal, B., Marlier, L., & Soussignan, R. (1998). Olfactory function in the human fetus: Evidence from selective neonatal responsiveness to the odor of amniotic fluid. *Behavioral Neuroscience, 112,* 1438–1449.

Schaie, K. W., & Zanjani, F. (2006). Intellectual development across adulthood. In C. Hoare (Ed.), *Oxford handbook of adult development and learning* (pp. 99–122). New York: Oxford University Press.

Scharlach, A. E. & Lehning, A. J. (2016). *Creating aging-friendly communities.* New York: Oxford University Press.

Scheele, D., Wille, A., Kendrick, K. M., Stoffel-Wagner, B., Becker, B., Güntürkün, O., et al. (2013). Oxytocin enhances brain reward system responses in men viewing the face of their female partner. *Proceedings of the National Academy of Science.* doi:10.1073/pnas.1314190110. Article available at www .pnas.org/content/110/50/20308.full.

Scheff, S. W., Neltner, J. H., & Nelson, P. T. (2014). Is synaptic loss a unique hallmark of Alzheimer's disease? *Biochemical Pharmacology, 88,* 517–528. doi:10.1016/j.bcp.2013.12.028

Scheibe, S., Kunzmann, U., & Baltes, P. B. (2007). Wisdom, life longings, and optimal development. In J. A. Blackburn & C. N. Dulmus (Eds.), *Handbook of gerontology: Evidence-based approaches to theory, practice, and policy* (pp. 117–142). Hoboken, NJ: Wiley.

Scheidt, R. J., & Schwarz, B. (2010). Environmental gerontology: A sampler of issues and application. In J. C. Cavanaugh & C. K. Cavanaugh (Eds.), *Aging in America: Vol. 1: Psychological aspects* (pp. 156–176). Santa Barbara, CA: Praeger Perspectives.

Schermerhorn, A. C., & Cummings, E. M. (2008). Transactional family dynamics: A new framework for conceptualizing family influence processes. In R. V. Kail (Ed.), *Advances in child development and behavior* (Vol. 36, pp. 187–250). Amsterdam, Netherlands: Academic Press.

Schermerhorn, A. C., Chow, S., & Cummings, E. M. (2010). Developmental family processes and interparental conflict: Patterns of microlevel influences. *Developmental Psychology, 46,* 869–885.

Schlabach, S. (2013). The importance of family, race, and gender for multiracial adolescent well-being. *Family Relations, 62,* 154–174. doi:10.1111/j.1741-3729.2012.—758.x

Schlomer, G. L., & Belsky, J. (2012). Maternal age, investment, and parent-child conflict: A mediational test of the terminal investment hypothesis. *Journal of Family Psychology, 26,* 443–452. doi:10.1037/a0027859

Schmidt, F. L., & Hunter, J. E. (2004). General mental ability in the world of work: Occupational attainment and job performance. *Journal of Personality and Social Psychology, 86,* 162–173.

Schmidt, F. L., & Hunter, J. E. (2014). *Methods of meta-analysis: Correcting error and bias in research findings.* Thousand Oaks, CA: Sage.

Schmitt, D. P., Alcalay, L., Allensworth, M., Allik, J., Ault, L., Austers, I., et al. (2004). Patterns and universals of adult romantic attachment across 62 cultural regions: Are models of self and of other pancultural constructs? *Journal of Cross-Cultural Psychology, 35,* 367–402. doi:10.1177/0022022104266105

Schneider, J. (2013). The death of an adult child: Contemporary psychoanalytic models of mourning. In S. Arbiser & G. Saragnano (Eds.), *On Freud's inhibitions, symptoms, and anxiety* (pp. 219–230). London, UK: Karnac Books.

Schneider, W. (2015). *Memory development from early childhood through emerging adulthood.* Cham, Switzerland: Springer International.

Schneiders, J., Nicolson, N. A., Berkhof, J., Feron, F. J., van Os., J., & deVries, M. W. (2006). Mood reactivity to daily negative events in early adolescence: Relationship to risk for psychopathology. *Developmental Psychology, 42,* 543–554.

Schoklitsch, A., & Bauman, U. (2012). Generativity and aging: A promising future research topic? *Journal of Aging Studies, 26,* 262–272. doi:10.1016/jaging.2012.01.002

Schoon, I. (2001). Teenage job aspirations and career attainment in adulthood: A 17-year follow-up study of teenagers who aspired to become scientists, health professionals, or engineers. *International Journal of Behavioral Development, 25,* 124–132. doi:10.1080/01650250042000186

Schoulte, J. (2011). Bereavement among African Americans and Latino/a Americans. *Journal of Mental Health Counseling, 33,* 11–20. doi:10.17744/mehc.33.1.r4971657p7176307

Schuetze, P., Molnar, D. S., & Eiden, R. D. (2012). Profiles of reactivity in cocaine-exposed children. *Journal of Applied Developmental Psychology, 33,* 282–293.

Schultz, D. P., & Schultz, S. E. (2017). *Theories of personality* (11th ed.). Boston: Cengage Learning.

Schulz-Helk, R. J., Poole, J. H., Dahdah, M. N., Sullivan, C., Date, E. S., Salerno, R. M. et al. (2016). Long-term outcomes after moderate-to-severe traumatic brain injury among military veterans: Successes and challenges. *Brain Injury, 30,* 271–279. doi:10.3109/02699052.2015.1113567

Schulz, D. J., & Enslin, C. (2014). The female executive's perspective on career planning and advancement in organizations. *Sage Open.* doi:10.1172/2158244014558040

Schulz, R., & Morycz, R. (2013). Psychosocial actors, health, and quality of life. In M. D. Miller & L. K. Salai (Eds.), *Geriatric psychiatry* (pp. 343–371). New York: Oxford University Press.

Schwab, A. K., & Greitemeyer, T. (2015). The world's biggest salad bowl: Facebook connecting cultures. *Journal of Applied Social Psychology, 45,* 243–252. doi:10.1111/jasp.12291

Schwartz-Mette, R. A., & Rose, A. J. (2012). Co-rumination mediates contagion of internalizing symptoms within youths' friendships. *Developmental Psychology, 48,* 1355–1365.

Schwartz, A. E., Leos-Urbel, J., & Wiswall, M. (2015). *Making summer matter: The impact of youth employment on academic performance.* National Bureau of Economic Research, Working Paper No. 21470.

Schwartz, B. (2015) *Why we work.* New York: TED Books.

Schwartz, C. E., Wright, C. I., Shin, L. M., Kagan, J., & Rauch, S. L. (2003). Inhibited and uninhibited infants "grow up": Adult amygdalar response to novelty. *Science, 300,* 1952–1953.

Schwartz, C., Issanchou, S., & Nicklaus, S. (2009). Developmental changes in the acceptance of the five basic tastes in the first year of life. *British Journal of Nutrition, 102,* 1375–1385.

Schwartz, D., Dodge, K. A., Pettit, G. S., Bates, J. E., & The Conduct Problems Prevention Research Group. (2000). Friendship as a moderating factor in the pathway between early harsh home environment and later victimization in the peer group. *Developmental Psychology, 36,* 646–662.

Schwarzer, R. (2008). Modeling health behavior change: How to predict and modify the adoption and maintenance of health behaviors. *Applied Psychology, 57,* 1–29. doi:10.1111/j.1464-0597.2007.00325.x

Schwerdtfeger, A., & Friedrich-Mai, P. (2009). Social interaction moderates the relationship between depressive mood and heart rate variability: Evidence from an ambulatory monitoring study. *Health Psychology, 28,* 501–509. doi:10.1037/a0014664

Scott, W. A., Scott, R., & McCabe, M. (1991). Family relationships and children's personality: A cross-cultural, cross-source comparison. *British Journal of Social Psychology, 30,* 1–20.

Scrimgeour, M. B., Blandon, A. Y., Stifter, C. A., & Buss, K. A. (2013). Cooperative coparenting moderates the association between parenting practices and children's prosocial behavior. *Journal of Family Psychology, 27,* 506–511.

Seaman, P. M. (2012). Time for my life now: Early boomer women's anticipation of volunteering in retirement. *The Gerontologist, 52,* 245–254. doi:10.1093/geront/gns001

Segal, D. L., Qualls, S. H., & Smyer, M. A. (2011). *Aging and mental health* (2nd ed.). Malden, MA: Wiley-Blackwell.

Seidl, A., & Johnson, E. L. (2006). Infants' word segmentation revisited: Edge alignment facilitates target extraction. *Developmental Science, 9,* 565–573.

Selkoe, D. J. (2016). The amyloid hypothesis of Alzheimer's disease at 25 years. *EMBO Molecular Medicine, 8,* 595–608. doi:10.15252/emmm.201606210

Selman, R. L. (1980). *The growth of interpersonal understanding: Development and clinical analyses.* New York: Academic Press.

Selman, R. L. (1981). The child as a friendship philosopher: A case study in the growth of interpersonal understanding. In S. R. Asher & J. M. Gottman (Eds.), *The development of children's friendships.* Cambridge, UK: Cambridge University Press.

Sénéchal, M. (2012). Child language and literacy development at home. In B. H. Wasik & B. Van Horn (Eds.), *Handbook on family literacy* (pp. 38–50). New York: Routledge.

Seward, R. R., & Stanley-Stevens, L. (2014). Fathers, fathering, and fatherhood across cultures. In H. Selin (Ed.), *Parenting across cultures* (pp. 459–474). New York: Springer.

Seychell, A. (2016). *Keeping your happy marriage: Tips for dealing with marriage issues.* Retrieved from positivepsychologyprogram.com/marriage-fulfillment-lifelong-relationship/.

Seyda, B. A., & Fitzsimons, A. M. (2010). Infant deaths. In C. A. Corr & D. A. Balk (Eds.), *Children's encounters with death, bereavement, and coping* (pp. 83–107). New York: Springer.

Shahaeian, A., Peterson, C. C., Slaughter, V., & Wellman, H. M. (2011). Culture and the sequence of steps in theory of mind development. *Developmental Psychology, 47,* 1239–1247.

Shanafelt, T. D., Mungo, M., Schmitgen, J., Storz, K. A., Reeves, D., Hayes, S. N., et al. (2016). Longitudinal study evaluating the association between physician burnout and changes in professional work effort. *Mayo Clinic Proceedings, 91,* 422–431. doi:10.1016/j.mayocp.2016.02.001

Shanahan, L., McHale, S. M., Crouter, A. C., & Osgood, D. (2007). Warmth with mothers and fathers from middle childhood to late adolescence: Within- and between-families comparisons. *Developmental Psychology, 43,* 551–563.

Shanahan, M. J., Elder, G. H., Burchinal, M., & Conger, R. D. (1996). Adolescent earnings and relationships with parents: The work-family nexus in urban and rural ecologies. In J. T. Mortimer & M. D. Finch (Eds.), *Adolescents, work, and family: An intergenerational developmental analysis.* Thousand Oaks, CA: Sage.

Shao, J., Li, D., Zhang, D., Zhang, L., Zhang, Q., & Qi, X. (2013). Birth cohort changes in the depressive symptoms of Chinese older adults: A cross-temporal meta-analysis. *International Journal of Geriatric Psychiatry, 28,* 1101–1108. doi:10.1002/gps.3942

Share, D. L. (2008). Orthographic learning, phonological recoding, and self-teaching. In R. V. Kail (Ed.), *Advances in child development and behavior* (Vol. 36, pp. 31–84). San Diego, CA: Elsevier.

Shariff, A. F., & Tracy, J. L. (2011). What are emotion expressions for? *Current Directions in Psychological Science, 20,* 395–399.

Sharma, A., & Sharma, V. (2012). The psycho-cultural analysis of sex discrimination. *Advances in Asian Social Science, 2,* 411–414. Retrieved from www.worldsciencepublisher.org/journals/index.php/AASS/article/viewFile/380/362.

Sharma, M. (2014). Yoga as an alternative and complementary approach for stress management: A systematic review. *Journal of Evidence-Based Complementary and Alternative Medicine, 19,* 59–67. doi:10.1177/2156587213503344

Shaw, D. S., & Shelleby, E. C. (2014). Early-starting conduct problems: Intersection of conduct problems and poverty. *Annual Review of Clinical Psychology, 10,* 503–528.

Shaw, S. S. (2007). Losing a parent twice. *American Journal of Alzheimer's Disease and Other Dementias, 21,* 389–390. doi:10.1177/1533317506292860

Shayshon, B., & Popper-Giveon, A. (in press). "These are not the realities I imagined": An inquiry into the lost hopes and aspirations of beginning teachers. *Cambridge Journal of Education.* doi:10.1080/0305764X.2016.1214238

Shen, H. (2016). Why women earn less: Just two factors explain post-PhD pay gap. *Nature,* May 20. doi:10.1038/nature.2016.19950 Retrieved from www.nature.com/news/why-women-earn-less-just-two-factors-explain-post-phd-pay-gap-1.19950.

Sherman, D. K., Hartson, K. A., Binning, K. R., Purdie-Vaughns, V., Garcia, J., Taborsky-Barba, S., et al. (2013). Deflecting the trajectory and changing the narrative: How self-affirmation affects academic performance and motivation under identity threat. *Journal of Personality and Social Psychology, 104,* 591–618.

Sherwin, S. (2011). Looking backwards, looking forward: Hope for *Bioethics'* next twenty-five years. *Bioethics, 25,* 75–82. doi:10.1111/j.1467-8519.2010.01866.x

Sheu, H., Lent, R. W., Brown, S. D., Miller, M. J., Hennessy, K. D., & Duffy, R. D. (2010). Testing the choice model of social cognitive career theory across Holland themes: A meta-analytic path analysis. *Journal of Vocational Behavior, 76,* 252–264. doi:10.1016/j.jvb.2009.10.015

Shi, R. (2014). Functional morphemes and early language acquisition. *Child Development Perspectives, 8,* 6–11.

Shi, R., & Werker, J. F. (2001). Six-month old infants' preference for lexical words. *Psychological Science, 12,* 70–75.

Shim, H. S. (2014). Vascular cognitive impairment and post-stroke cognitive deficits. *Current Neurology and Neuroscience Reports, 14.* doi:10.1007 /s11910-013-0418-4

Shin, H., & Ryan, A. M. (2014). Early adolescent friendships and academic adjustment: Examining selection and influence processes with longitudinal social network analysis. *Developmental Psychology, 50,* 2462–2472.

Shipp, A. J., Furst-Holloway, S., Harris, T. B., & Rosen, B. (2014). Gone today but here tomorrow: Extending the unfolding model of turnover to consider boomerang employees. *Personnel Psychology, 67,* 421–462. doi:10.1111/peps.12039

Shirley, M. M. (1931). *The first two years: A study of twenty-five babies: Vol 1. Postural and locomotor development.* Westport, CT: Greenwood Press.

Shoji, K., Cieslak, R., Smoktunowicz, E., Rogala, A., Benight, C. C., & Luszczynska, A. (2016). Associations between job burnout and self-efficacy: A meta-analysis. *Anxiety, Stress, & Coping, 29,* 367–386. doi:10.1080/10615806.2015.1058369

Shonkoff, J. P., Garner, A. S., the Committee on Psychosocial Aspects of Child and Family Health, Committee on Early Childhood, Adoption, and Dependent Care, and Section on Developmental and Behavioral Pediatrics, et al. (2012). The lifelong effects of early childhood adversity and toxic stress. *Pediatrics, 129,* e232–e246. doi:10.1542/peds.2011-2668

Shore, J. C., Gelber, M. W., Koch, L. M., & Sower, E. (2016). Anticipatory grief: An evidence-based approach. *Journal of Hospice & Palliative Nursing, 18,* 15–19. doi:10.1097/NJH.0000000000000208

Shulman, S., & Kipnis, O. (2001). Adolescent romantic relationships: A look from the future. *Journal of Adolescence, 24,* 337–351.

Shutts, K. (2015). Young children's preferences: Gender, race, and social status. *Child Development Perspectives, 9,* 262–266.

Shutts, K., Banaji, M. R., & Spelke, E. S. (2010). Social categories guide young children's preferences for novel objects. *Developmental Science, 13,* 599–610.

Sidebotham, P., Heron, J., & the ALSPAC Study Team. (2003). Child maltreatment in the "children of the nineties": The role of the child. *Child Abuse and Neglect, 27,* 337–352.

Siegler, R. S. (1981). Developmental sequences within and between concepts. *Monographs of the Society for Research in Child Development, 46* (Serial No. 189).

Siegler, R. S. (1986). Unities in strategy choices across domains. In M. Perlmutter (Ed.), *Minnesota symposia on child development* (Vol. 19, pp. 1–48). Hillsdale, NJ: Erlbaum.

Siegler, R. S., & Alibali, M. W. (2005). *Children's thinking* (4th ed.). Upper Saddle River, NJ: Prentice Hall.

Siegler, R. S., & Jenkins, E. (1989). *How children discover new strategies.* Hillsdale, NJ: Erlbaum.

Siegler, R. S., & Robinson, M. (1982). The development of numerical understanding. In H. W. Reese & L. P. Lipsitt (Eds.), *Advances in child development and behavior* (Vol. 16). New York: Academic Press.

Siegler, R. S., & Shrager, J. (1984). Strategy choices in addition and subtraction: How do children know what to do? In C. Sophian (Ed.), *Origins of cognitive skills.* Hillsdale, NJ: Erlbaum.

Silk, J. S., Morris, A. S., Kanaya, T., & Steinberg, L. D. (2003). Psychological control and autonomy granting: Opposite ends of a continuum or distinct constructs? *Journal of Research on Adolescence, 13,* 113–128.

Silva, L. C. R., de Araújo, A. L., Fernandes, J. R., Matias, M. de S. T., Silva, P. R., Duarte, A. J. S. et al. (2016). Moderate and intense exercise lifestyles attenuate the effects of aging on telomere length and the survival and composition of T cell subpopulations. *AGE, 38,* 24. doi:10.1007/s11357-016-9879-0

Silver, M. P. (2016). An inquiry into self-identification with retirement. *Journal of Women & Aging, 28,* 477–488. doi:10.1080/08952841.2015.1018068

Silverman, W. K., La Greca, A. M., & Wasserstein, S. (1995). What do children worry about? Worries and their relations to anxiety. *Child Development, 66,* 671–686.

Silvers, J. A., Buhle, J. T., & Ochsner, K. N. (2014). The neuroscience of emotion regulation: Basic mechanisms and their role in development, aging and psychopathology. In K. N. Ochsner & S. M. Kosslyn (Eds.), *The Oxford handbook of cognitive neuroscience* (pp. 53–78). Oxford, UK: Oxford University Press.

Simons, B. S., Foltz, P. A., Chalupa, R. L., Hylden, C. M., Dowd, T. C., & Johnson, A. E. (2016). Burnout in U.S. military orthopaedic residents and staff physicians. *Military Medicine, 181,* 835–838. doi:10.7205/MILMED-D-15-00325

Simons, L. G., Wickrama, K. A. S., Lee, T. K., Landers-Potts, M., Cutrona, C., & Conger, R. D. (2016). Testing family stress and family investment explanations for conduct problems among African American adolescents. *Journal of Marriage and Family, 78,* 498–515.

Simonton, D. K. (in press). Defining creativity: Don't we also need to define what is *not* creative? *Journal of Creative Behavior.* doi:10.1002/jocb.137

Simonton, D. K., & Song, A. V. (2009). Eminence, IQ, physical and mental health, and achievement domain: Cox's 282 geniuses revisited. *Psychological Science, 20,* 429–434.

Simpson, J. M. (2001). Infant stress and sleep deprivation as an aetiological basis for the sudden infant death syndrome. *Early Human Development, 61,* 1–43.

Sinclair, R. R., Sears, L. E., Zajack, M., & Probst, T. (2010). A multilevel model of economic stress and employee well-being. In J. Houdmont & S. Leka (Eds.), *Contemporary occupational health psychology: Global perspectives on research and practice* (Vol. 1, pp. 1–20). Malden, MA: Wiley-Blackwell.

Singh, J. A., Saag, K. G., Bridges, S. L., Jr., Akl, E. A., Bannuru, R. R., Sullivan, M. C., et al. (2016). 2015 American College of Rheumatology Guideline for the treatment of rheumatoid arthritis. *Arthritis & Rheumatology, 68*, 1–26. doi:10.1002/art.39480

Sinnott, J. D. (2014). *Adult development: Cognitive aspects of thriving close relationships.* New York: Oxford University Press.

Skinner, B. F. (1957). *Verbal behavior.* New York: Appleton-Century-Crofts.

Skinner, E. A. (1985). Determinants of mother-sensitive and contingent-responsive behavior: The role of childbearing beliefs and socioeconomic status. In I. E. Sigel (Ed.), *Parental belief systems: The psychological consequences for children* (pp. 51–82). Hillsdale, NJ: Erlbaum.

Skoog, T., & Stattin, H. (2014). Why and under what contextual conditions do early-maturing girls develop problem behaviors? *Child Development Perspectives, 8*, 158–162.

Skouteris, H., McNaught, S., & Dissanayake, C. (2007). Mothers' transition back to work and infants' transition to child care: Does work-based child care make a difference? *Child Care in Practice, 13*, 33–47. doi:10.1080/13575270601103432

Slater, A., Bremner, G., Johnson, S. P., Sherwood, P., Hayes, R., & Brown, E. (2000). Newborn infants' preference for attractive faces: The role of internal and external facial features. *Infancy, 1*, 265–274.

Slaughter, V. (2015). Theory of mind in infants and young children: A review. *Australian Psychologist, 50*, 169–172.

Slaughter, V., Imuta, K., Peterson, C. C., & Henry, J. D. (2015). Meta-analysis of theory of mind and peer popularity in the preschool and early school years. *Child Development, 86*, 1159–1174.

Sleddens, E. F. C., Gerards, M. P. L., Thijs, C., de Vries, N. K., & Kremers, S. P. J. (2011). General parenting, childhood overweight and obesity-inducing behaviors: A review. *International Journal of Pediatric Obesity, 6*, e12–e27.

Sleeter, C. E. (2016). Ethnicity and curriculum. In D. Wyse, L. Hayward, & J. Pandya (Eds.), *The SAGE handbook of curriculum, pedagogy, and assessment* (pp. 231–246). Thousand Oaks, CA: Sage.

Slobin, D. I. (1985). Cross-linguistic evidence for the language-making capacity. In D. I. Slobin (Ed.), *The cross-linguistic study of language acquisition: Vol. 2. Theoretical issues.* Hillsdale, NJ: Erlbaum.

Smith-Bynum, M. A. (2013). African American families: Research progress and potential in the age of Obama. In G. W. Peterson & K. R. Bush (Eds.), *Handbook of marriage and the family* (3rd ed., pp. 683–704). New York: Springer.

Smith-Howell, E. R., Hickman, S. E., Meghani, S. H., Perkins, S. M., & Rawl, S. M. (2016). End-of-life decision making and communication of bereaved family members of African Americans with serious illness. *Journal of Palliative Medicine, 19*, 174–182. doi:10.1089/jpm.2015.0314

Smith, E. R., Mackie, D. M., & Claypool, H. M. (2015). *Social psychology* (4th ed.). New York: Psychology Press.

Smith, L. B. (2000). How to learn words: An associative crane. In R. Golinkoff & K. Hirsch-Pasek (Eds.), *Breaking the word learning barrier* (pp. 51–80). Oxford, UK: Oxford University Press.

Smith, L. B. (2009). From fragments to geometric shape: Changes in visual object recognition between 18 and 24 months. *Current Directions in Psychological Science, 18*, 290–294.

Smith, W. J., Howard, J. T., & Harrington, K. V. (2005). Essential formal mentor characteristics and functions in governmental and non-governmental organizations from the program administrator's and the mentor's perspective. *Public Personnel Management, 34*, 31–58.

Smits, S. J., & Bowden, D. E. (2013). Leveraging psychological assets for the development and maintenance of leadership capabilities. *International Leadership Journal, 5*, 3–26. Available at www.tesu.edu/documents/ILJ_Winter_2013.pdf.

Smoll, F. L., & Schutz, R. W. (1990). Quantifying gender differences in physical performance: A developmental perspective. *Developmental Psychology, 26*, 360–369.

Smyke, A. T., Zeanah, C. H. Fox, N. A., Nelson, C. A., & Guthrie, D. (2010). Placement in foster care enhances quality of attachment among young institutionalized children. *Child Development, 81*, 212–223. doi:10.1111/j.1467-8624.2009.01390.x

Snow, C. W. (1998). *Infant development* (2nd ed.). Upper Saddle River, NJ: Prentice Hall.

Snow, D. (2006). Regression and reorganization of intonation between 6 and 23 months. *Child Development, 77*, 281–296.

Snow, M. E., Jacklin, C. N., & Maccoby, E. E. (1983). Sex-of-child differences in father–child interaction at one year of age. *Child Development, 54*, 227–232.

Snowling, M. J., & Hulme, C. (2015). Disorders of reading, mathematical, and motor development. In A. Thapar, D. S. Pine, J. F. Leckman, S. Scott, M. J. Snowling, & E. Taylor (Eds.). *Rutter's child and adolescent psychiatry* (6th ed., pp. 702–718). Chichester, UK: Wiley.

Social Security and Medicare Boards of Trustees. (2016). *A summary of the 2016 annual reports.* Retrieved from www.ssa.gov/oact/trsum/.

Solomon, G. E. A., & Zaitchik, D. (2012). Folkbiology. *WIREs Cognitive Science, 3*, 105–115.

Sommer, S., Plumm, K. M., Terrance, C. A., & Tubré, T. (2013). Perceptions of younger single adults as a function of their gender and number of children. *Journal of General Psychology, 140*, 87–109. doi:10.1080 /00221309.2013.769931

Song, S., Georgiou, G. K., Su, M., & Hua, S. (2016). How well do phonological awareness and rapid automatized naming correlate with Chinese reading accuracy and fluency? A meta-analysis. *Reading and Writing, 20*, 99–123.

Sonuga-Barke, E. J. S., & Taylor, E. (2015). ADHD and hyperkinetic disorder. In A. Thapar, D. S. Pine, J. F. Leckman, S. Scott, M. J. Snowling, & E. Taylor (Eds.), *Rutter's child and adolescent psychiatry* (6th ed., pp. 738–756). Chichester, UK: Wiley.

Sorg, S. F., Delano-Wood, L., Luc, N., Schiehser, D., Hanson, K. L., Nation, D. A., et al. (2014). White matter integrity in veterans with mild traumatic brain injury: Associations with executive function and loss of consciousness. *Journal of Head Trauma Rehabilitation, 29*, 21–32. doi:10.1097 /HTR.0b013e31828a1aa4

Spector, F., & Maurer, D. (2009). Synesthesia: A new approach to understanding the development of perception. *Developmental Psychology, 45*, 175–189.

Spector, P. E., Allen, T. D., Poelmans, S., Cooper, C. L., Bernin, P., Hart, P., et al. (2005). An international comparative study of work-family stress and occupational strain. In S. A. Y. Poelmans (Ed.), *Work and family: An international research perspective* (pp. 71–84). Mahwah, NJ: Erlbaum.

Spelke, E. S., & Kinzler, K. D. (2007). Core knowledge. *Developmental Science, 10*, 89–96.

Spivak, I. M., Mikhelson, V. M., & Spivak, D. L. (2016). Telomere length, telomerase activity, stress, and aging. *Advances in Gerontology, 6*, 29–35. doi:10.1134/S2079057016010136

Sritharan, R., Heilpern, K., Wilbur, C. J., & Gawronski, B. (2010). I think I like you: Spontaneous and deliberate evaluations of potential romantic partners in an online dating context. *European Journal of Social Psychology, 40*, 1062–1077. doi:10.1002/ejsp.703

Srivastava, S., John, O. P., Gosling, S. D., & Potter, J. (2003). Development of personality in early and middle adulthood: Set like plaster or persistent change? *Journal of Personality and Social Psychology, 84*, 1041–1053. doi:10.1037/0022-3514.84.5.1041

St. George, I. M., Williams, S., & Silva, P. A. (1994). Body size and menarche: The Dunedin study. *Journal of Adolescent Health, 15*, 573–576.

St. James-Roberts, I. (2007). Helping parents to manage infant crying and sleeping: A review of the evidence and its implications for services. *Child Abuse Review, 16*, 47–69.

St. James-Roberts, I., & Plewis, I. (1996). Individual differences, daily fluctuations, and developmental changes in amounts of infant waking, fussing, crying, feeding, and sleeping. *Child Development, 67*, 2527–2540.

Staff, J., Mont'Alvao, A., & Mortimer, J. (2015). Children at work. In R. M. Lerner (Ed.), *Handbook of child psychology and developmental science* (Vol 4., pp. 345–375). Hoboken, NJ: Wiley.

Stafford, L., Kline, S. L., & Rankin, C. T. (2004). Married individuals, cohabiters, and cohabiters who marry: A longitudinal study of relational and individual well-being. *Journal of Social & Personal Relationships, 21*, 231–248. doi:10.1177/0265407504041385

Stalp, M. C., & Conti, R. (2011). Serious leisure in the home: Professional quilters negotiate family space. *Gender, Work and Organization, 18*, 399–414. doi:10.1111/j.1468-0432.2009.0044.x

Staneva, A., Bogossian, F., Pritchard, M., & Wittkowski, A. (2015). The effects of maternal depression, anxiety, and perceived stress during pregnancy on preterm birth: A systematic review. *Women and Birth, 28*, 179–193.

Stanik, C. E., Riina, E. M., & McHale, S. M. (2013). Parent-adolescent relationship qualities and adolescent adjustment in two-parent African American families. *Family Relations, 62*, 597–608.

Staudinger, U. (2015). Images of aging: Outside and inside perspectives. *Annual Review of Gerontology and Geriatrics, 35*, 187–209. doi:10.1891/0198-8794.35.187

Staudinger, U. M., & Glück, J. (2011). Psychological wisdom research: Commonalities and differences in a growing field. *Annual Review of Psychology, 62*, 215–241. doi:10.1146/ annurev.psych.121208.131659

Staudinger, U. M., Dörner, J., & Mickler, C. (2005). Wisdom and personality. In R. J. Sternberg & J. Jordan (Eds.), *A handbook of wisdom: Psychological perspectives* (pp. 191–219). New York: Cambridge University Press.

Steck, A., & Steck, B. (2016). *Brain and mind: Subjective experience and scientific objectivity.* New York: Springer.

Steeger, C. M., & Gondoli, D. M. (2013). Mother-adolescent conflict as a mediator between adolescent problem behaviors and maternal psychological control. *Developmental Psychology, 49*, 804–814.

Steele, C. M. (1997). A threat in the air: How stereotypes shape intellectual identity and performance. *American Psychologist, 52*, 613–629.

Steele, C. M., & Aronson, J. (1995). Stereotype threat and the intellectual test performance of African Americans. *Journal of Personality and Social Psychology, 69*, 797–811.

Stein, D. J., & Vythilingum, B. (2009). Love and attachment: The psychobiology of social bonding. *CNS Spectrums, 14*, 239–242. Retrieved from 66.199.228.237/boundary/Sexual_Addiction/love_and_attachment_neurobiology.pdf.

Stein, J. H., & Reiser, L. W. (1994). A study of White middle-class adolescent boys' responses to "semenarche" (the first ejaculation). *Journal of Youth and Adolescence, 23*, 373–384.

Steinberg, L. (2001). We know some things: Parent-adolescent relationships in retrospect and prospect. *Journal of Research on Adolescence, 11*, 1–19.

Steinberg, L. D. (1999). *Adolescence* (5th ed.). Boston, MA: McGraw-Hill.

Steinberg, L., & Monahan, K. C. (2007). Age differences in resistance to peer influence. *Developmental Psychology, 43*, 1531–1543.

Steinberg, L., & Silk, J. (2002). Parenting adolescents. In M. Bornstein (Ed.), *Handbook of parenting: Vol. 1* (2nd ed., pp. 103–133). Hillsdale, NJ: Erlbaum.

Stenberg, G. (2013). Do 12-month-old infants trust a competent adult? *Infancy, 18*, 873–904.

Sternberg, R. J. (1985). *Beyond IQ: A triarchic theory of human intelligence.* Cambridge, England: Cambridge University Press.

Sternberg, R. J. (1999). The theory of successful intelligence. *Review of General Psychology, 3*, 292–316.

Sternberg, R. J. (2006). A duplex theory of love. In R. J. Sternberg & K. Weis (Eds.), *The new psychology of love* (pp. 184–199). New Haven, CT: Yale University Press.

Sternberg, R. J. (2008). The triarchic theory of successful intelligence. In N. Salkind (Ed.), *Encyclopedia of educational psychology* (pp. 988–994). Thousand Oaks, CA: Sage.

Sternberg, R. J. (2015). Multiple intelligences in the new age of thinking. In S. Goldstein, D. Princiotta, & J. A. Naglieri (Eds.), *Handbook of intelligence: Evolutionary theory* (pp. 229–241). New York: Springer Verlag.

Sternberg, R. J., & Kaufman, J. C. (1998). Human abilities. *Annual Review of Psychology, 49*, 479–502.

Sternberg, R. J., & Sternberg, K. (2017). *Cognitive psychology* (7th ed.). Boston: Cengage Learning.

Sternberg, R. J., Grigorenko, E. L, & Kidd, K. K. (2005). Intelligence, race, and genetics. *American Psychologist, 60*, 46–59.

Sternberg, R. J., Jarvin, L., & Grigorenko, E. L. (2009). *Teaching for wisdom, intelligence, creativity, and success.* Thousand Oaks, CA: Corwin.

Sterns, H. L., & Chang, B. (2010). Workforce issues and retirement. In J. C. Cavanaugh & C. K. Cavanaugh (Eds.), *Aging in America: Vol. 3: Societal issues* (pp. 81–105). Santa Barbara, CA: ABC-CLIO.

Sterns, H. L., & Spokus, D. M. (2013). Lifelong learning and the world of work. In P. Taylor (Ed.), *Older workers in an ageing society: Critical topics in research and policy* (pp. 89–108). Northampton, MA: Edward Elgar Publishing.

Steuerle, C. E., & Quakenbush, C. (2015). *Social Security and Medicare lifetime benefits and taxes.* Retrieved from www.urban.org/research/publication/social-security-and-medicare-lifetime-benefits-and-taxes/view/full_report.

Stevens, H. (2016, August 12). Part-time work during the school year? Why it can be a good thing. *Chicago Tribune.* Retrieved from www.chicagotribune.com/lifestyles/stevens/ct-back-to-school-job-stevens-0814-20160812-column.html.

Stevenson-Hinde, J., & Shouldice, A. (2009). Wariness to strangers: A behavior systems perspective revisited. In K. H. Rubin & J. B. Asendorpf (Eds.), *Social withdrawal, inhibition, and shyness in childhood* (pp. 101–116). New York: Psychology Press.

Stevenson, H. W., & Lee, S. (1990). Contexts of achievement. *Monographs of the Society for Research in Child Development, 55* (Serial No. 221).

Stevenson, H. W., & Stigler, J. W. (1992). *The learning gap.* New York: Summit Books.

Stevenson, R. J., Oaten, M. J., Case, T. I., Repacholi, B. M., & Wagland, P. (2010). Children's response to adult disgust elicitors: Development and acquisition. *Developmental Psychology, 46*, 165–177.

Stewart, J. S., Goad Oliver, E., Cravens, K. S., & Oishi, S. (2017). Managing millennials: Embracing generational differences. *Business Horizons, 60*, 45–54. doi:10.1016/j.bushor.2016.08.011

Stice, E., Rohde, P., Gau, J., & Shaw, H. (2009). An effectiveness trial of a dissonance-based eating disorder prevention program for high-risk adolescent girls. *Journal of Consulting and Clinical Psychology, 77*, 825–834.

Stice, E., South, K., & Shaw, H. (2012). Future directions in etiologic, prevention, and treatment research for eating disorders. *Journal of Clinical Child and Adolescent Psychology, 41*, 845–855.

Stiles, J. (2008). *Fundamentals of brain development.* Cambridge MA: Harvard University Press.

Stokes, J. (2016). The influence of intergenerational relationships on marital quality following the death of a parent in adulthood. *Journal of Social and Personal Relationships, 33*, 3–22. doi:10.1177/0265407514558962

Stoltz, K. B. (2016). Midlife adults: At 40, the eyes had it, now at 50, the career does! When career vision begins to blur. In W. K. Killam, S. Degges-White, & R. E. Michel (Eds.), *Career counseling interventions: Practice with diverse clients* (pp. 59–66). New York: Springer.

Stoner, S., O'Riley, A., & Edelstein, B. (2010). Assessment of mental health. In J. C. Cavanaugh & C. K. Cavanaugh (Eds.), *Aging in America: Volume 2: Physical and mental health* (pp. 141–170). Santa Barbara, CA: ABC-CLIO.

Strawbridge, W. J., Shema, S. J., Balfour, J. L., Higby, H. R., & Kaplan, G. A. (1998). Antecedents of frailty over three decades in an older cohort. *Journal of Gerontology: Social Sciences, 53B*, S9–S16. doi:10.1093/geronb/53B.1.S9

Strenze, T. (2015). Intelligence and success. In S. Goldstein, D. Princiotta, & J. A. Naglieri (Eds.), *Handbook of intelligence: Evolutionary theory* (pp. 405–413). New York: Springer Verlag.

Strinic, V. (2015). Arguments in support and against euthanasia. *British Journal of Medicine & Medical Research, 9*, 1–12. doi:10.9734/BJMMR/2015/19151

Stroebe, M. S., & Archer, J. (2013). Origins of modern ideas on love and loss: Contrasting forerunners of attachment theory. *Review of General Psychology, 17*, 28–39. doi:10.1037/ a0030030

Stroebe, M., Finkenauer, C., Wijngaards-de Meij, L., Schut, H., van den Bout, J., & Stroebe, W. (2013). Partner-oriented self-regulation among bereaved parents: The costs of holding in grief for the partner's sake. *Psychological Science.* doi:10.1177/0956797612457383

Stroebe, M., Schut, H., & Boerner, K. (2010). Continuing bonds in adaptation to bereavement: Toward theoretical integration. *Clinical Psychology Review, 30,* 259–268. doi:10.1016/j.cpr.2009.11.007

Stroebe, M., Schut, H., & Stroebe, W. (2005). Attachment in coping with bereavement: A theoretical integration. *Review of General Psychology, 9,* 48–66. doi:10.1037/1089-2680.9.1.48

Stroebe, M., Schut, H., & Stroebe, W. (2007). Health outcomes of bereavement. *Lancet, 370,* 1960–1973. doi:10.1016/S0140-6736(07)61816-9

Stroebe, M., Schut, H., & van den Bout, J. (Eds.). (2012). *Complicated grief: Scientific foundations for health care professionals.* New York: Routledge.

Stroebe, W., Abakoumkin, G., & Stroebe, M. (2010). Beyond depression: Yearning for the loss of a loved one. *OMEGA: Journal of Death and Dying, 61,* 85–101. doi:10.2190/ OM.61.2.a

Strohmeier, D., Kärnä, A., & Salmivalli, C. (2011). Intrapersonal and interpersonal risk factors for peer victimization in immigrant youth in Finland. *Developmental Psychology, 47,* 248–258.

Strohschein, L. (2012). Parental divorce and child mental health: Understanding predisruption effects. *Journal of Divorce and Remarriage, 53,* 489–502.

Strong, C., Juon, H-S., & Ensminger, M. E. (2016). Effect of adolescent cigarette smoking on adult substance use and abuse: The mediating role of educational attainment. *Substance Use and Misuse, 51,* 141–154.

Strough, J., & Berg, C. A. (2000). Goals as a mediator of gender differences in high-affiliation dyadic conversations. *Developmental Psychology, 36,* 117–125.

Sturaro, C, van Lier, P. A. C., Cuijpers, P., & Koot, H. M. (2011). The role of peer relationships in the development of early school-age externalizing problems. *Child Development, 82,* 758–765.

Sturge-Apple, M. L., Davies, P. T., & Cummings, E. M. (2010). Typologies of family functioning and children's adjustment during the early school years. *Child Development, 81,* 1320–1335.

Sturman, D. A., & Moghaddam, B. (2012). Striatum processes reward differently in adolescents versus adults. *Proceedings of the National Academy of Sciences, 109,* 1719–1724.

Su, J., & Supple, A. J. (2016). School substance use norms and racial composition moderate parental and peer influences on adolescent substance use. *American Journal of Community Psychology, 57,* 280–290.

Subotnik, R. F., Olszewski-Kubilius, P., & Worrell, F. C. (2011). Rethinking giftedness and gifted education: A proposed direction forward based on psychological science. *Psychological Science in the Public Interest, 12,* 3–54.

Sugimoto-Matsuda, J. J., & Guerrero, A. P. S. (2016). Violence and abuse. In D. Alicata, N. Jacobs, A. Guerrero, & M. Piasecki (Eds.), *Problem-based behavioral science and psychiatry* (pp. 113–133). New York: Springer.

Sugiura, M. (2016). Functional neuroimaging of normal aging: Declining brain, adapting brain. *Ageing Research Reviews, 30,* 61–72. doi:10.1016/j.arr.2016.006

Suja, C., Shuhaib, B., Khathoom, H., & Simi, K. (2016). A review on dietary antioxidants. *Research Journal of Pharmacy and Technology, 9*(2), 196–202. doi:10.5958/0974-360X.2016.00035.4

Sullivan, L., & Meschede, T. (2016). Race, gender, and senior economic well-being: How financial vulnerability over the life course shapes retirement for older women of color. *Public Policy & Aging Report, 26,* 58–62. doi:10.1093/ppar/prw001

Sullivan, M. W., & Lewis, M. (2003). Contextual determinants of anger and other negative expressions in young infants. *Developmental Psychology, 39,* 693–705.

Sulloway, F. J., & Zweigenhaft, R. L. (2010). Birth order and risk taking in athletics: A meta-analysis and study of major league baseball. *Personality and Social Psychology Review, 14,* 402–416.

Sumter, S. R., Vandenbosch, L., & Ligtenberg, L. (2017). Love me Tinder: Untangling emerging adults' motivations for using the dating application Tinder. *Telematics and Informatics, 34,* 67–78.

Sung, S., Simpson, J. A., Griskevicius, V., Kuo, S. I., S chlomer, G. L., & Belsky, J. (2016). Secure infant-mother attachment buffers the effect of early-life stress on age of menarche. *Psychological Science, 27,* 667–674.

Suo, C., Singh, M. F., Gates, N., Wen, W., Sachev, P., Brodaty, H. et al. (2016). Therapeutically relevant structural and functional mechanisms triggered by physical and cognitive exercise. *Molecular Psychiatry, 21,* 1633–1642. doi:10.1038/mp.2016.19

Super, C. M. (1981). Cross-cultural research on infancy. In H. C. Triandis & A. Heron (Eds.), *Handbook of cross-cultural psychology: Vol. 4. Developmental psychology.* Boston, MA: Allyn & Bacon.

Super, C. M., Herrera, M. G., & Mora, J. O. (1990). Long-term effects of food supplementation and psychosocial intervention on the physical growth of Colombian infants at risk of malnutrition. *Child Development, 61,* 29–49.

Super, D. E. (1957). *The psychology of careers.* New York: Harper & Row.

Super, D. E. (1976). *Career education and the meanings of work.* Washington, DC: U.S. Offices of Education.

Super, D. E. (1980). A life-span, life-space approach to career development. *Journal of Vocational Behavior, 16,* 282–298. doi:10.1016/0001 -8791(80)90056-1

Super, D., Savickas, M., & Super, C. (1996). The life-span, life-space approach to careers. In D. Brown, L. Brooks, & Associates (Eds.), *Career choice & development* (3rd ed., pp. 121–178). San Francisco: Jossey-Bass.

Suri, R., Lin, A. S., Cohen, L. S., & Atlshuler, L. L. (2014). Acute and long-term behavioral outcome of infants and children exposed in utero to either maternal depression or antidepressants: A review of the literature. *Journal of Clinical Psychiatry, 75,* e1142–e1152.

Suzuki, L., & Aronson, J. (2005). The cultural malleability of intelligence and its impact on the racial/ethnic hierarchy. *Psychology, Public Policy, and Law, 11,* 320–327.

Sweeney, M. M. (2010). Remarriage and stepfamilies: Strategic sites for family scholarship in the 21st century. *Journal of Marriage and Family, 72,* 667–684.

Sweeper, S. (2012). Children's adjustment after parental separation. In Patricia Noller & Gery C. Karantzas (Eds.), *The Wiley-Blackwell handbook of couples and family relationships* (pp. 345–360). Chichester, UK: Wiley-Blackwell.

Swindell, R. (2012). Successful ageing and international approaches to later-life learning. In G. Boulton-Lewis & M. Tam (Eds.), *Active ageing, active learning* (pp. 35–63). New York: Springer.

Swingle, A. L.-V. (2013). *College student parents: Stress, role conflict, and coping.* Unpublished doctoral dissertation, Indiana University of Pennsylvania. Retrieved from dspace.iup.edu/bitstream/handle/2069/2047/Amy%20Louise-Vannurded%20Swingle.pdf?sequence=1.

Symonds, W. C., Schwartz, R. B., & Ferguson, R. (2011). *Pathways to prosperity: Meeting the challenge of preparing young Americans for the 21st century.* Cambridge, MA: Harvard Graduate School of Education.

Tabor, J. (2016). Adjustment to divorce (children). In C. L. Shehan (Ed.), *The Wiley Blackwell encyclopedia of family studies* (Vol 1., pp. 25–30). Chichester, UK: Wiley.

Tach, L., & Halpern-Meekin, S. (2009). How does premarital cohabitation affect trajectories of marital quality? *Journal of Marriage and Family, 71,* 298–317. doi:10.1111/j.1741-3737.2009.00600.x

Tager-Flusberg, H. (1993). Putting words together: Morphology and syntax in the preschool years. In J. Berko Gleason (Ed.), *The development of language* (3rd ed.). New York: Macmillan.

Tahiroglu, D., Mannering, A. M., & Taylor, M. (2011). Visual and auditory imagery associated with children's imaginary companions. *Imagination, Cognition, and Personality, 31,* 99–112.

Talbot, L. A., Morrell, C. H., Fleg, J. L., & Metter, E. J. (2007). Changes in leisure time physical activity and risk of all-cause mortality in men and women: The Baltimore longitudinal study of aging. *Preventive Medicine, 45,* 169–176. doi:10.1016/j. ypmed.2007.05.014

Tam, K.-P. (2013). Existential motive underlying cosmetic surgery: A terror management analysis. *Journal of Applied Social Psychology, 43,* 947–955. doi:10.1111/jasp.12059

Tamayo, G. J., Broxson, A., Munsell, M., & Cohen, M Z. (2010). Caring for the caregiver. *Oncology Nursing Forum, 37,* E50–E57. doi:10.1188/10. ONF.E50-E57

Tamis-LeMonda, C. S., & Bornstein, M. H. (1996). Variation in children's exploratory, nonsymbolic, and symbolic play: An explanatory multi-dimensional framework. In C. Rovee-Collier & L. P. Lipsitt (Eds.), *Advances in infancy research* (Vol. 10, pp. 37–78). Norwood, NJ: Ablex.

Tamis-LeMonda, C. S., Kuchirko, Y., & Song, L. (2014). Why is infant language learning facilitated by parental responsiveness? *Current Directions in Psychological Science, 23,* 121–126.

Tan, K. L. (2009). Bed sharing among mother-infant pairs in Kiang District, Peninsular Malaysia and its relationship to breast-feeding. *Journal of Developmental and Behavioral Pediatrics, 30,* 420–425.

Tang, F., Morrow-Howell, N., & Choi, E. (2010). Why do older adult volunteers stop volunteering? *Ageing and Society, 30,* 859–878. doi:10.1017/ S0144686X10000140

Tang, P.-L., Chiou, C.-P., Lin, H.-S., Wang, C., & Liand, S.-L. (2011). Correlates of death anxiety among Taiwanese cancer patients. *Cancer Nursing, 34,* 286–292. doi:10.1097/ NCC.0b013e31820254c6

Tang, Y.-Y., & Posner, M. I. (2012). Tools of the trade: Theory and method in mindfulness neuroscience. *Social Cognitive and Affective Neuroscience, 8,* 118–120. doi:10.1093/scan/nss112

Tanner, J. M. (1970). Physical growth. In P. H. Mussen (Ed.), *Carmichael's manual of child psychology* (3rd ed., pp. 77–155). New York: Wiley.

Tanner, J. M. (1990). *Fetus into man: Physical growth from conception to maturity* (2nd ed.). Cambridge, MA: Harvard University Press.

Tardif, T., Fletcher, P., Liang, W., Zhang, Z., Kaciroti, N., & Marchman, V. A. (2008). Baby's first 10 words. *Developmental Psychology, 44,* 929–938.

Taylor, J. L., O'Hara, R., Mumenthaler, M. S., Rosen, A. C., & Yesavage, J. A. (2005). Cognitive ability, expertise, and age differences in following air-traffic control instructions. *Psychology and Aging, 20,* 117–133. doi:10.1037/0882-7974.20.1.117

Taylor, M. G., Rhodes, M., & Gelman, S. A. (2009). Boys will be boys; cows will be cows: Children's essentialist reasoning about gender categories and animal species. *Child Development, 80,* 461–481.

Taylor, M., Carlson, S. M., Maring, B. L., Gerow, L., & Charley, C. M. (2004). The characteristics of fantasy in school-age children: Imaginary companions, impersonation, and social understanding. *Developmental Psychology, 40,* 1173–1187.

Taylor, M., Hulette, A. C., & Dishion, T. J. (2010). Longitudinal outcomes of young high-risk adolescents with imaginary companions. *Developmental Psychology, 46,* 632–1636.

Taylor, M., Sachet, A. B., Maring, B. L., & Mannering, A. M. (2013). The assessment of elaborated role-play in young children: Invisible friends, personified objects, and pretend identities. *Social Development, 22,* 75–93.

Taylor, S. E. (2006). Tend and befriend: Biobehavioral bases of affiliation under stress. *Current Directions in Psychological Science, 15,* 273–277. doi:10.1111/j.1467-8721.2006.00451.x

Teachman, J. (2008). Complex life course patterns and the risk of divorce in second marriages. *Journal of Marriage and Family, 70,* 294–305.

Teachman, J., Tedrow, L., & Kim, G. (2013). The demography of families. In G. W. Peterson & K. R. Bush (Eds.), *Handbook of marriage and the family* (3rd ed., pp. 39–63). New York: Springer.

Teaster, P. B., Harley, D. A., & Kettaneh, A. (2014). Aging and mistreatment: Victimization of older adults in the United States. In H. F. Ofahengaue Vakalahi, G. M. Simpson, & N. Giunta (Eds.), *The collective spirit of aging across cultures* (pp. 41–64). New York: Springer.

Tegethoff, M., Greene, N., Olsen, J., Meyer, A. H., & Meinlschmidt, G. (2010). Maternal psychosocial adversity is associated with length of gestation and offspring size at birth: Evidence from a population-based cohort study. *Psychosomatic Medicine, 72,* 419–426.

Tenenbaum, H. R., & Leaper, C. (2002). Are parents' gender schemas related to their children's gender-related cognitions? A meta-analysis. *Developmental Psychology, 38,* 615–630.

Terkel, S. (1974). *Working.* New York: Pantheon.

Thelen, E., & Smith, L. B. (1998). Dynamic systems theories. In W. Damon (Ed.), *Handbook of child psychology* (Vol. 1). New York: Wiley.

Thelen, E., & Ulrich, B. D. (1991). Hidden skills. *Monographs of the Society for Research in Child Development, 56* (Serial No. 223).

Therborn, G. (2010). Families in global perspective. In A. Giddens & P. W. Sutton (Eds.), *Sociology: Introductory readings* (3rd ed., pp. 119–124). Malden, MA: Polity Press.

Thiessen, E. D., & Saffran, J. R. (2003). When cues collide: Use of stress and statistical cues to word boundaries by 7- to 9-month-old infants. *Developmental Psychology, 39,* 706–716.

Thomas, A., & Chess, S. (1977). *Temperament and development.* New York: Brunner/Mazel.

Thomas, A., Chess, S., & Birch, H. G. (1968). *Temperament and behavior disorders in children.* New York: NYU Press.

Thomas, F. (2008). Remarriage after spousal death: Options facing widows and implications for livelihood security. *Gender and Development, 16,* 73–83. doi:10.1080/13552070701876235

Thomas, J. R., Alderson, J. A., Thomas, K. T., Campbell, A. C., & Elliot, B. C. (2010). Developmental gender differences for overhand throwing in Aboriginal Australian children. *Research Quarterly for Exercise & Sport, 81,* 432–441.

Thomas, M. L., Bangen, K. J., Ardelt, M., & Jeste, D. V. (2017). Development of a 12-item Abbreviated Three-Dimensional Wisdom Scale (3D-WS-12). *Assessment, 24,* 71-82. doi:10.1177/107319115595714

Thomas, R., & Zimmer-Gembeck, M. J. (2011). Accumulating evidence for parent-child interaction therapy in the prevention of child maltreatment. *Child Development, 82,* 177–192.

Thompson, A. E., & Voyer, D. (2014). Sex differences in the ability to recognise non-verbal displays of emotion: A meta-analysis. *Cognition and Emotion, 28,* 1164–1195.

Thompson, G. E., Cameron, R. E., & Fuller-Thompson, E. (2013). Walking the red road: The role of First Nations grandparents in promoting cultural well-being. *International Journal of Aging and Human development, 76,* 55–78. doi:10.2190/AG.76.1.c

Thompson, R. A. (2000). The legacy of early attachments. *Child Development, 71,* 145–152.

Thompson, R. A. (2006). The development of the person: Social understanding, relationships, conscience, self. In N. Eisenberg (Ed.), *Handbook of child psychology: Vol. 3. Social, emotional, and personality development* (6th ed.). Hoboken, NJ: Wiley.

Thompson, R. A., & Limber, S. (1991). "Social anxiety" in infancy: Stranger wariness and separation distress. In H. Leitenberg (Ed.), *Handbook of social and evaluation anxiety.* New York: Plenum.

Thompson, R. A., Laible, D. J., & Ontai, L. L. (2003). Early understandings of emotion, morality, and self: Developing a working model. *Advances in Child Development & Behavior, 31,* 137–172.

Thornton, W. L., Paterson, T. S. E., & Yeung, S. E. (2013). Age differences in everyday problem solving: The role of problem context. *International Journal of Behavioral Development, 37,* 13–20. doi:10.1177/0165025412454028

Tiffany, D. W., & Tiffany, P. G. (1996). Control across the life span: A model for understanding self-direction. *Journal of Adult Development, 3,* 93–108. doi:10.1007/BF02278775.

Tincoff, R., & Jusczyk, P. W. (1999). Some beginnings of word comprehension in 6-month-olds. *Psychological Science, 10,* 172–175.

Tobin, D. J. (2017). Introduction to skin aging. *Journal of Tissue Viability, 26,* 37–46. doi:10.1016/j.jtv.2016.03.022

Tolkko, T. (2016). Becoming an expert by experience: An analysis of service users' learning process. *Social Work in Mental Health, 14,* 292–312. doi:10.1080/15332985 .2015.1038411

Tomasello, M., Carpenter, M., & Liszkowski, U. (2007). A new look at infant pointing. *Child Development, 78,* 705–722.

Tong, C., & Kram, K. E. (2013). The efficacy of mentoring—the benefits for mentees, mentors, and organizations. In J. Passmore, D. B. Peterson, & T. Freire (Eds.), *The Wiley-Blackwell handbook of coaching and mentoring* (pp. 217–242). Oxford, UK: Wiley-Blackwell.

Tooby, J., & Cosmides, L. (2008). The evolutionary psychology of emotions and their relationship to internal regulatory variables. In M. Lewis, J. M. Haviland-Jones, & L. F. Barrett (Eds.), *Handbook of emotions* (3rd ed., pp. 114–137). New York: Guilford.

Torges, C. M., Stewart, A. J., & Duncan, L. E. (2008). Achieving ego integrity: Personality development in late midlife. *Journal of Research in Personality, 42,* 1004–1019. doi:10.1016/ j.jrp.2008.02.006

Toril, P., Reales, J. M., Mayas, J., & Ballesteros, S. (2016). Video game training enhances visuospatial working memory and episodic memory in older adults. *Frontiers in*

Human Neuroscience, 10, 206. doi:10.3389/fnhum.2016.00206. Retrieved from www.ncbi.nlm.nih.gov/pmc/articles/PMC4859063/.

Torres, L., Lindstrom, K., Hannah, L., & Webb, F. (2016). Exploring barriers among primary care providers in referring patients to hospice. *Journal of Hospice & Palliative Nursing, 18*, 167–172. doi:10.1097/NJH.0000000000000233

Tracy, B., Reid, R., & Graham, S. (2009). Teaching young students strategies for planning and drafting stories: The impact of self-regulated strategy development. *Journal of Educational Research, 102*, 323–331.

Trainor, L. J., & Heinmiller, B. M. (1998). The development of evaluative responses to music: Infants prefer to listen to consonance over dissonance. *Infant Behavior & Development, 21*, 77–88.

Treiman, R., & Kessler, B. (2003). The role of letter names in acquisition of literacy. *Advances in Child Development & Behavior, 31*, 105–135.

Tremblay, R. E., Schall, B., Boulerice, B., Arsonault, L., Soussignan, R. G., & Paquette, D. (1998). Testosterone, physical aggression, and dominance and physical development in adolescence. *International Journal of Behavioral Development, 22*, 753–777.

Trim, R. S., Meehan, B. T., King, K. M., & Chassin, L. (2007). The relation between adolescent substance use and young adult internalizing symptoms: Findings from a high-risk longitudinal sample. *Psychology of Addictive Behaviors, 21*, 97–107.

Troutman, M., Nies, M. A., & Mavellia, H. (2011). Perceptions of successful aging in Black older adults. *Journal of Psychosocial Nursing and Mental Health Services, 49*, 28–34. doi:10.3928/02793695-20101201-01

Trzaskowski, M., Harlaar, N., Arden, R., Krapohl, E., Rimfield, K., McMillan, A., et al. (2014). Genetic influence on family socioeconomic status and children's intelligence. *Intelligence, 42*, 83–88.

Trzesniewski, K., H., & Donnellan, M. B. (2010). Rethinking "Generation Me": A study of cohort effects from 1976–2006. *Perspective on Psychological Science, 5*, 58–75. doi:10.1177/1745691609356789

Tsuno, N., & Homma, A. (2009). Aging in Asia—The Japan experience. *Ageing International, 34*, 1–14. doi:10.1007/s12126-009-9032-9

Tu, M. C.-H. (2006). *Culture and job satisfaction: A comparative study between Taiwanese and Filipino caregivers working in Taiwan's long-term care industry.* Unpublished dissertation, Nova Southeastern University.

Tucker-Drob, E. M., Briley, D. A., & Harden, K. P. (2013). Genetic and environmental influences on cognition across development and context. *Current Directions in Psychological Science, 22*, 349–355.

Tucker, M. S. (2011). *Surpassing Shanghai: An agenda for American education built on the world's leading systems.* Cambridge, MA: Harvard Education Press.

Turiel, E. (2006). The development of morality. In W. Damon & R. M. Lerner (Eds.), *Handbook of child psychology* (6th ed., Vol. 3, pp. 789–857). Hoboken, NJ: Wiley.

Turner, R. N., & Cameron, L. (2016). Confidence in contact: A new perspective on promoting cross-group friendship among children and adolescents. *Social Issues and Policy Review, 10*, 212–246.

Twenge, J. M., & Crocker, J. (2002). Race and self-esteem: Meta-analysis comparing Whites, Blacks, Hispanics, and American Indians and comment on Gray-Little and Hafdahl (2000). *Psychological Bulletin, 128*, 371–408.

Tynes, B. M. (2007). Role taking in online "classrooms": What adolescents are learning about race and ethnicity. *Developmental Psychology, 43*, 1312–1320.

Tynes, B. M., Umaña-Taylor, A. J., Rose, C. A., Lin, J., & Anderson, C. J. (2012). Online racial discrimination and the protective function of ethnic identity and self-esteem for African American adolescents. *Developmental Psychology, 48*, 343–355.

U.S. Department of Agriculture. (2017). *Expenditures on children by families, 2015.* Retrieved from www.cnpp.usda.gov/sites/default/files/crc2015_March2017.pdf.

U.S. Department of Health & Human Services. (2016). *Child maltreatment 2014.* Retrieved from www.acf.hhs.gov/programs/cb/research-data-technology/statistics-research/child-maltreatment.

U.S. Department of Health and Human Services. (2010). *The Surgeon General's vision for a healthy and fit nation.* Rockville, MD: Author.

U.S. Department of Labor Women's Bureau. (2016a). *Data and statistics.* Retrieved from www.dol.gov/wb/stats/stats_data.htm.

U.S. Department of Labor Women's Bureau. (2016b). *Women's earnings by race and ethnicity as a percentage of white, non-Hispanic men's earnings, March 1987–2014.* Retrieved from www.dol.gov/wb/stats/earnings_race_ethnic_percent_white_nonhisp_mens_earn_87_14_txt.htm.

U.S. Department of Labor. (2016) *Nontraditional occupations.* Retrieved from www.dol.gov/wb/stats/Nontraditional%20Occupations.pdf.

Uchino, B. N., Cawthon, R. M., Smith, T. W., Light, K. C., McKenzie, J., Carlisle, M., et al. (2012). Social relationships and health: Is feeling positive, negative, or both (ambivalent) about your social ties related to telomeres? *Health Psychology, 31*, 789–796. doi:10.1037/a0026836

Ukraintseva, S. V., Yashin, A., Arbeev, K. G., Kulminski, A., Akushevich, I., Wu, D., et al. (2016). Puzzling role of genetic risk factors in human longevity: "Risk alleles" as prolongevity variants. *Biogerontology, 17*, 109–127. doi:10.1007/s10522-015-9600-1

Umaña-Taylor, A., Diversi, M., & Fine, M. (2002). Ethnic identity and self-esteem among Latino adolescents: Distinctions among Latino populations. *Journal of Adolescent Research, 17*, 303–327.

UNICEF-WHO-The World Bank. (2016). Levels and trends in child malnutrition. New York: Author.

UNICEF. (2007). *The state of the world's children, 2008.* New York: Author.

UNICEF. (2016). Breastfeeding. Retrieved from www.unicef.org/nutrition/index_24824.html.

University of Massachusetts Medical School Center for Mindfulness. (2017). *Stress reduction program.* Retrieved from www.umassmed.edu/cfm/mindfulness-based-programs/ .

Updegraff, K. A., McHale, S. M., Whiteman, S. D., Thayer, S. M., & Delgado, M. Y. (2005). Adolescent sibling relationships in Mexican American families: Exploring the role of familism. *Journal of Family Psychology, 19*, 512–522.

Updegraff, K. A., Thayer, S. M., Whiteman, S. D., Denning, D. J., & McHale, S. M. (2005). Aggression in adolescents' sibling relationships: Links to sibling and parent–adolescents relationship quality. *Family Relations: Interdisciplinary Journal of Applied Family Studies, 54*, 373–385.

Usher, E. L., & Pajares, F. (2009). Sources of self-efficacy in mathematics: A validation study. *Contemporary Educational Psychology, 34*, 89–101.

Utz, R.L., & Pascoe, A. (2016). Bereavement/widowhood. In S. K. Whitbourne (Ed.), *Encyclopedia of adulthood and aging* (Vol. 1, pp. 118–121). Malden, MA: Wiley-Blackwell.

Vacha-Haase, T., Donaldson, W. V., & Foster, A. (2014). Race-ethnicity and gender in older adults. In M. L. Minville & A. D. Ferguson (Eds.), *Handbook of race-ethnicity and gender in psychology* (pp. 65–83). New York: Springer.

Vaillancourt, T., Brittain, H. L., McDougall, P., & Duku, E. (2013). Longitudinal links between childhood peer victimization, internalizing and externalizing problems, and academic functioning: Developmental cascades. *Journal of Abnormal Child Psychology, 41*, 1203–1215.

Vaish, A., Carpenter, M., & Tomasello, M. (2009). Sympathy through affective perspective taking and its relation to prosocial behavior in toddlers. *Developmental Psychology, 45*, 534–543.

Vaish, A., Woodward, A., & Grossmann, T. (2008). Not all emotions are created equal: The negativity bias in social-emotional development. *Psychological Bulletin, 134*, 383–403.

Valenza, E., & Bulf, H. (2011). Early development of object unity: Evidence for perceptual completion in newborns. *Developmental Science, 14*, 799–808.

Valkenburg, P. M., & Peter, J. (2011). Adolescents' online communication: An integrated model of its attraction, opportunities, and risks. *Journal of Adolescent Health, 48*, 121–127.

Vallerand, R. J. (2008). On the psychology of passion: In search of what makes people's lives most worth living. *Canadian Psychology, 49*, 1–13. doi:10.1037/0708-5591.49.1.1

Vallerand, R. J. (2015). *The psychology of passion: A dualistic model.* New York: Oxford University Press.

Vallerand, R. J., Paquet, Y., Philippe, F. L., & Charest, J. (2010). On the role of passion for work in burnout: A process model. *Journal of Personality, 78,* 289–312. doi:10.1111/j.1467-6494.2009.00616.x

van den Wijngaart, M. A. G., Vernooij-Dassen, M. J. F. J., & Felling, A. J. A. (2007). The influence of stressors, appraisal and personal conditions on the burden of spousal caregivers of persons with dementia. *Aging & Mental Health, 11,* 626–636. doi:10.1080/13607860701368463

van der Geest, S. (2004). Dying peacefully: Considering good death and bad death in Kwahu-Tafo, Ghana. *Social Science and Medicine, 58,* 899–911. doi:10.1016/j.socscimed.2003.10.041

van der Pas, S., & Koopman-Boyden, P. (2010). Leisure and recreation activities and wellbeing among midlife New Zealanders. In C. Waldegrave & P. Koopman-Boyden (Eds.), *Midlife New Zealanders aged 40–64 in 2008: Enhancing well-being in an aging society* (pp. 111–128). Hamilton, New Zealand: Family Centre Social Policy Research Unit, Lower Hutt, Wellington and the Population Studies Centre, University of Waikato. Retrieved from www.familycentre.org.nz/Publications/PDF's/EWAS_M2.pdf.

Van Duijvenvoorde, A. C., Huizenga, H. M., & Jansen, B. R. J. (2014). What is and what could have been: Experiencing regret and relief across childhood. *Cognition and Emotion, 28,* 926–935.

van Goozen, S. H. M. (2015). The role of early emotion impairments in the development of persistent antisocial behavior. *Child Development Perspectives, 9,* 206–210.

van Hof, P., van der Kamp, J., & Savelsbergh, G. J. P. (2002). The relation of unimanual and bimanual reaching to crossing the midline. *Child Development, 73,* 1352–1362.

Van IJzendoorn, M. H., Bakermans-Kranenburg, M. J., & Ebstein, R. P. (2011). Methylation matters in child development: Toward developmental behavioral epigenetics. *Child Development Perspectives, 5,* 305–310.

van Klaveren, C., van den Brink, H. M., & van Praag, B. (2013). Intrahousehold work timing: the effect on joint activities and the demand for child care. *European Sociological Review, 29,* 1–18. doi:10.1093/esr/jcr035

van Muijden, J., Band, G. P. H., & Hommel, B. (2012). Online games training aging brains: Limited transfer to cognitive control functions. *Frontiers in Human Neuroscience, 6.* doi:10.3389/fnhum.2012.00221. Retrieved from www.ncbi.nlm.nih.gov/pmc/articles/PMC3421963/.

Van Rijsewijk, L., Dijkstra, J. K., Pattiselanno, K., Steglich, C., & Veenstra, R. (2016). Who helps whom? Investigating the development of adolescent prosocial relationships. *Developmental Psychology, 52,* 894–908.

van Wanrooy, B. (2013). Couple strategies: Negotiating working time over the life course. In A. Evans, & J. Baxter (Eds.), *Negotiating the life course: Stability and change in life pathways* (pp. 175–190). New York: Springer.

Vance, J. D. (2016). *Hillbilly elegy: A memoir of a family and culture in crisis.* New York: HarperCollins.

Vander Wal, J. S., & Thelen, M. H. (2000). Eating and body image concerns among obese and average-weight children. *Addictive Behaviors, 25,* 775–778.

Vansteenkiste, S., Deschacht, N., & Sels, L. (2015). Why are unemployed aged fifty and over less likely to find a job? A decomposition analysis. *Journal of Vocational Behavior, 90,* 55–65. doi:10.1016/j.jvb.2015.07.004

Varkal, M. D., Yalvac, D., Tufan, F., Turan, S., Cengiz, M., & Emul, M. (2013). Metacognitive differences between elderly and adult outpatients with generalized anxiety disorder. *European Geriatric Medicine, 4,* 150–153. doi:10.1016/j.eurger.2012.12.001

Vazire, S., & Doris, J. M. (2009). Personality and personal control. *Journal of Research in Personality, 43,* 274–275. doi:10.1016/j.jrp.2008.12.033

Vélez, C. E., Wolchik, S. A., & Sandler, I. N. (2014). Divorce effects on adolescents (pp. 1076–1085). In T. P. Gullotta & M. Bloom (Eds.), *Encyclopedia of primary prevention and health promotion.* New York: Springer Science+Business Media.

Verbrugge, L. M., & Jette, A. M. (1994). The disablement process. *Social Science and Medicine, 38,* 1–14. doi: 10.1016/0277-9536(94)90294-1

Verbrugge, L. M., Brown, D. C., & Zajacova, A. (2017). Disability rises gradually for a cohort of older Americans, *Journals of Gerontology: Psychological Sciences, 72,* 151–161. doi:10.1093/geronb/gbw002

Victora, C. G., Bahl, R., Barros, A. J. D., França, G. V. A., Horton, S., Krasevec, J., et al. (2016). Breastfeeding 1: Breastfeeding in the 21st century: Epidemiology, mechanisms, and lifelong effect. *Lancet, 387,* 475–490.

Vieno, A., Nation, M., Pastore, M., & Santinello, M. (2009). Parenting and antisocial behavior: A model of the relationship between adolescent self-disclosure, parental closeness, parental control, and adolescent antisocial behavior. *Developmental Psychology, 45,* 1509–1519.

Villar, F., & Serrat, R. (2017). Changing the culture of long-term care through *narrative* care: Individual, interpersonal, and institutional dimensions. *Journal of Aging Studies, 40,* 44–48. doi:10.1016/j.jaging.2016.12.007

Volling, B. L. (2012). Family transitions following the birth of a sibling: An empirical review of changes in the firstborn's adjustment. *Psychological Bulletin, 138,* 497–528.

Volpe, U., Fiorillo, A., Jovanovic, N., & Bhugra, D. (2016). Mentoring and career coaching. In A. Fiorillo, U. Volpe, & D. Bhugra (Eds.), *Psychiatry in practice: Education, experience, and expertise* (pp. 83–95). New York: Oxford University Press.

von Ranson, K. M., & Wallace, L. M. (2014). Eating disorders. In R. A. Barkley & E. J. Mash (Eds.), *Child psychopathology* (3rd ed., pp. 801–847) New York: Guilford.

Vorhees, C. V., & Mollnow, E. (1987). Behavior teratogenesis: Long-term influences on behavior. In J. D. Osofsky (Ed.), *Handbook of infant development* (2nd ed.). New York: Wiley.

Voss, M. W., Vivar, C., Kramer, A. F., & van Praag, H. (2013). Bridging animal and human models of exercise-induced brain plasticity. *Trends in Cognitive Science, 17,* 525–544. doi:10.1016/j.tics.2013.08.001

Vouloumanos, A., Hauser, M. D., Werker, J. F., & Martin, A. (2010). The tuning of human neonates' preference for speech. *Child Development, 81,* 517–527.

Voyer, D., Postma, A., Brake, B., & Imperato-McGinley, J. (2007). Gender differences in object location memory: A meta-analysis. *Psychonomic Bulletin & Review, 14,* 23–38.

Vraneković, J., Božović, I. B., Grubić, Z., Wagner, J., Pavlinić, D., Dahoun, S., Bena, F., Čulić, V., & Brajenović-Milić, B. (2012). Down syndrome: Parental origin, recombination, and maternal age. *Genetic Testing and Molecular Biomarkers, 16,* 70–73.

Vygotsky, L. S. (1978). *Mind in society: The development of higher psychological processes.* M. Cole, V. John-Steiner, S. Scribner, & E. Souberman (Eds.). Cambridge, MA: Harvard University Press.

Wachs, T. D., & Bates, J. E. (2001). Temperament. In G. Bremner & A. Fogel (Eds.), *Blackwell handbook of infant development* (pp. 465–501). Malden, MA: Blackwell.

Wadlington, W. (2005). Family law in America. *Family Court Review, 43,* 178–179.

Wadsworth, S. M., Hughes-Kirchubel, L., & Riggs, D. S. (2014). Research and training about military families: Where are we? In S. M. Wadsworth & D. S. Riggs (Eds.), *Military deployment and its consequences for families* (pp. 1–17). New York: Springer.

Wahl, H.-W. (2015). Theories of environmental influences on aging and behavior. In N. A. Pachana (Ed.), *Encyclopedia of geropsychology* (pp. 1–8). New York: Springer. doi:10.1007/978-981-287-080-3_132-1

Waites, C. (2009). Building on strengths: Intergenerational practice with African-American families. *Social Work, 54,* 278–287. doi:10.1093/ sw/54.3.278

Walberg, H. J. (1995). General practices. In G. Cawelti (Ed.), *Handbook of research on improving student achievement.* Arlington, VA: Educational Research Service.

Walker, A. C., & Balk, D. E. (2007). Bereavement rituals in the Muscogee Creek tribe. *Death Studies, 31,* 633–652. doi:10.1080/07481180701405188

Walker, L. E. A. (1984). *The battered woman syndrome.* New York: Springer.

Walker, L. J. (1980). Cognitive and perspective-taking prerequisites for moral development. *Child Development, 51,* 131–139.

Walker, L. J., & Taylor, J. H. (1991). Family interactions and the development of moral reasoning. *Child Development, 62,* 264–283.

Walker, L. J., Hennig, K. H., & Krettenauer, T. (2000). Parent and peer contexts for children's moral reasoning development. *Child Development, 71,* 1033–1048.

Walker, P., Bremner, J. G., Mason, U., Spring, J., Mattock, K., Slater, A., et al. (2010). Preverbal infants' sensitivity to synaesthetic cross-modality correspondences. *Psychological Science, 21,* 21–25.

Wallerstein, J. S., & Lewis, J. M. (2004). The unexpected legacy of divorce: Report of a 25-year study. *Psychoanalytic Psychology, 21,* 353–370. doi:10.1037/0736-9735.21.3.353

Walther, A. N. (1991). *Divorce hangover.* New York: Pocket Books.

Wang, Q. (2014). The cultured self and remembering. In P. J. Bauer & R. Fivush (Eds.), *The Wiley handbook on the development of children's memory* (pp. 605–625). Chichester, UK: Wiley.

Wang, S-w., & Repetti, R. L. (2016). Who gives to whom? Testing the support gap hypothesis with naturalistic observations of couple interactions. *Journal of Family Psychology, 30,* 492–502. doi:10.1037/fam0000196

Wang, S.-H., Zhang, Y., & Baillargeon, R. (2016). Young infants view physically possible support events as unexpected: New evidence for rule learning. *Cognition, 157,* 100–105.

Wang, W. (2015). *The link between a college education and a lasting marriage.* Retrieved from www.pewresearch.org/fact-tank/2015/12/04/education-and-marriage/.

Wang, W.-C., & Giovanello, K. S. (2016). The role of medial temporal lobe regions in incidental and intentional retrieval of item and relational information in aging. *Hippocampus, 26,* 693–699. doi:10.1002/hipo.22578

Wansink, B., & Sobal, J. (2007). Mindless eating: The 200 daily food decisions we overlook. *Environment & Behavior, 39,* 106–123.

Wanzer, S. H., & Glenmullen, J. (2007). *To die well: Your right to comfort, calm, and choice in the last days of life.* Cambridge, MA: Da Capo Press.

Waren, W., & Pals, H. (2013). Comparing characteristics of voluntarily childless men and women. *Journal of Population Research, 30,* 151–170. doi:10.1007/s12546-012-9103-8

Warner, B., Altimier, L., & Crombleholme, T. M. (2007). Fetal surgery. *Newborn & Infant Nursing Reviews, 7,* 181–188.

Warner, S. C., & Valdes, A. M. (2016). The genetics of osteoarthritis: A review. *Journal of Functional Morphology and Kinesiology, 1,* 140–153. doi:10.3390/jfmk1010140

Warnock, F. F., Craig, K., Bakeman, R., & Castral, T. (2014). Self-regulation (recovery) from pain: Association between time-based measures of infant pain behavior and prenatal exposure to maternal depression and anxiety. *Clinical Journal of Pain, 30,* 663–671.

Warr, P., Butcher, V., & Robertson, I. (2004). Activity and psychological well-being in older people. *Aging & Mental Health, 8,* 172–183. doi:10.10 80/13607860410001649662

Warren-Findlow, J., & Issel, I. M. (2010). Stress and coping in African American women with chronic heart disease: A cultural cognitive coping model. *Journal of Transcultural Nursing, 21,* 45–54. doi:10.1177/1043659609348622

Wasik, B. A., Hindman, A. H., & Snell, E. K. (2016). Book reading and vocabulary development: A systematic review. *Early Childhood Research Quarterly, 37,* 39–57.

Waterhouse, L. (2006). Multiple intelligences, the Mozart effect, and emotional intelligence: A critical review. *Educational Psychologist, 41,* 207–225.

Waters, E., & Cummings, E. M. (2000). A secure base from which to explore close relationships. *Child Development, 71,* 164–172.

Waters, H. S. (1980). "Class news": A single-subject longitudinal study of prose production and schema formation during childhood. *Journal of Verbal Learning and Verbal Behavior, 19,* 152–167.

Watson, R. W. (2013). *Frisky 60s flower children are still making love not war.* Retrieved from www.psychologytoday.com/blog/love-and-gratitude/201302/frisky-60s-flower-children-are-still-making-love-not-war.

Wax, J. R., Pinette, M. G., & Cartin, A. (2010). Home versus hospital birth: Process and outcome. *Obstetrical & Gynecological Survey, 65,* 132–140.

Waxman, S., Fu, X., Arunachalam, S., Leddon, E., Geraghty, K., & Song, H.-J. (2013). Are nouns learned before verbs? Infants provide insights into a long-standing debate. *Child Development Perspectives, 7,* 155–159.

Wayland, S., Maple, M., McKay, K., & Glassock, G. (2016). Holding onto hope: A review of the literature exploring missing persons, hope and ambiguous loss. *Death Studies, 40,* 54–60. doi:10.1080/07481187.2015.1068245

Weaver, C. C., Leffingwell, T. R., Lombardi, N. J., Claborn, K. R. Miller, M. E., & Martens, M. P. (2014). A computer-based feedback only interaction with and without a moderation skills component. *Journal of Substance Abuse Treatment, 46,* 22–28. doi:10.1016/j.sat.2013.08.011

Weaver, D. A. (2010). Widows and Social Security. *Social Security Bulletin, 70,* 89–109. Retrieved from heinonline.org/HOL/LandingPage?collection=journals&handle=hein.journals/ssbul70&div=20&id=&page.

Weaver, J., & Schofield, T. (2015). Mediation and moderation of divorce effects on children's behavior problems. *Journal of Family Psychology, 29,* 39–48.

Webb, N. B. (2010a). The child and death. In N. B. Webb (Ed.), *Helping bereaved children: A handbook for practitioners* (3rd ed., pp. 3–21). New York: Guilford Press.

Webb, N. B. (2010b). Assessment of the bereaved child. In N. B. Webb (Ed.), *Helping bereaved children: A handbook for practitioners* (3rd ed., pp. 22–47). New York: Guilford Press.

Webb, S. J., Monk, C. S., & Nelson, C. A. (2001). Mechanisms of postnatal neurobiological development: Implications for human development. *Developmental Neuropsychology, 19,* 147–171.

Weber, D., Dekhtyar, S., & Herlitz, A. (2017). The Flynn effect in Europe—Effects of sex and region. *Intelligence, 60,* 39–45.

Webster-Marketon, J., & Glaser, R. (2008). Stress hormones and immune function. *Cellular Immunology, 252,* 16–26. doi:10.1016/j.cellimm.2007.09.006

Wechsler, H., Davenport, A., Dowdall, G., Moeykens, B., & Castillo, S. (1994). Health and behavioral consequences of binge drinking in college. *Journal of the American Medical Association, 272,* 1672–1677. doi:10.1001/jama.1994.03520210056032

Wegman, L. A., Hoffman, B. J., Carter, N. T., Twenge, J. M., & Guenole, N. (in press). Placing job characteristics in context: Cross-temporal meta-analysis of changes in job characteristics since 1975. *Journal of Management.* doi:10.1177/149206316654545

Wegman, M. E. (1994). Annual summary of vital statistics—1993. *Pediatrics, 95,* 792–803.

Wei, W., Lu, H., Zhao, H., Chen, C., Dong, Q., & Zhou, X. (2012). Gender differences in children's arithmetic performance are accounted for by gender differences in language abilities. *Psychological Science, 23,* 320–330.

Weichold, K., & Silbereisen, R. K. (2005). Puberty. In C. B. Fisher & R. M. Lerner (Eds.), *Encyclopedia of applied developmental science* (Vol. 2, pp. 893–898). Thousand Oaks, CA: Sage.

Weinstock, M. P., Neuman, Y., & Glassner, A. (2006). Identification of informal reasoning fallacies as a function of epistemological level, grade level, and cognitive ability. *Journal of Educational Psychology, 89,* 327–341.

Weis, R., & Cerankosky, B. C. (2010). Effects of video-game ownership on young boys' academic and behavioral functioning: A randomized, controlled study. *Psychological Science, 21,* 463–470.

Weisgram, E. S., Bigler, R. S., & Liben, L. S. (2010). Gender, values, and occupational interests among children, adolescents, and adults. *Child Development, 81,* 778–796.

Weisner, T. S., & Wilson-Mitchell, J. E. (1990). Nonconventional family lifestyles and sex typing in six-year-olds. *Child Development, 61,* 1915–1933.

Weisner, T. S., Garnier, H., & Loucky, J. (1994). Domestic tasks, gender egalitarian values and children's gender typing in conventional and nonconventional families. *Sex Roles, 30,* 23–54.

Weiss, D. (2016). On the inevitability of aging: Essentialist beliefs moderate the impact of negative age stereotypes on older adults' memory performance and physiological reactivity. *Journal of Gerontology: Psychological Sciences.* doi:10.1093/geronb/gbw087

Wellman, H. M. (2012). Theory of mind: Better methods, clearer findings, more development. *European Journal of Developmental Psychology, 9,* 313–330.

Wellman, H. M. (2014). *Making minds: How theory of mind develops.* New York: Oxford.

Wellman, H. M., & Gelman, S. A. (1998). Knowledge acquisition in foundational domains. In W. Damon (Ed.), *Handbook of child psychology* (Vol. 2, pp. 523–573). New York: Wiley.

Wellman, H. M., Fang, F., & Peterson, C. C. (2011). Sequential progressions in a theory-of-mind scale. *Child Development, 82,* 780–792.

Weltzin, T. E. (2017). Eating disorders in males. In K. D. Brownell & B. T. Walsh (Eds.), *Eating disorders and obesity* (3rd ed., pp. 209–213). New York: Guilford.

Wentkowski, G. (1985). Older women's perceptions of greatgrandparenthood: A research note. *The Gerontologist, 25,* 593–596. doi:10.1093 /geront/25.6.593

Wentzel, K. R., Filisetti, L., & Looney, L. (2007). Adolescent prosocial behavior: The role of self-processes and contextual cues. *Child Development, 78,* 895–910.

Werker, J. F., & Hensch, T. K. (2015). Critical periods in speech perception: New directions. *Annual Review of Psychology, 66,* 173–196.

Werner, E. (1994). Overcoming the odds. *Journal of Developmental & Behavioral Pediatrics, 15,* 131–136.

Werner, E. E. (1989). Children of Garden Island. *Scientific American, 260,* 106–111.

Werner, E. E. (1995). Resilience in development. *Current Directions in Psychological Science, 4,* 81–85.

Werner, E. E., & Smith, R. S. (1992). *Overcoming the odds: High risk children from birth to adulthood.* Ithaca, NY: Cornell University Press.

Werner, H. (1948). *Comparative psychology of mental development.* Chicago: Follet.

Werner, N. E., Eaton, A. D., Lyle, K., Tseng, H., & Holst, B. (2014). Maternal social coaching quality interrupts the development of relational aggression during early childhood. *Social Development, 23,* 470–486.

Werner, T. L., & Shannon C. S. (2013). Doing more with less: Women's leisure during their partners' military deployment. *Leisure Sciences, 35,* 63–80. doi:10.1080/01490400. 2013.739897

Wertsch, J. V., & Tulviste, P. (1992). L. S. Vygotsky and contemporary developmental psychology. *Developmental Psychology, 28,* 548–557.

West, M. D. (2010). Embryonic stem cells: Prospects of regenerative medicine for the treatment of human aging. In G. M. Fahy, M. D. West, L. S. Coles, & S. B. Harris (Eds.), *The future of aging* (pp. 451–487). New York: Springer.

Westerhof, G. J., Bohlmeijer, E., & Webster, J. D. (2010). Reminiscence and mental health: A review of recent progress in theory, research and interventions. *Ageing and Society, 30,* 697–721. doi: 10.1017/s0144686x09990328

Westrate, N. M., Ferrari, M., & Ardelt, M. (2016). The many faces of wisdom: An investigation of cultural-historical wisdom exemplars reveals practical, philosophical, and benevolent prototypes. *Personality and Social Psychology Bulletin, 42,* 662–676. doi:10.1177/0146167216638075

Wettstein, R. M. (2013). Legal issues geriatric psychiatrists should understand. In M. D. Miller & L. K. Salai (Eds.), *Geriatric psychiatry* (pp. 55–77). New York: Oxford University Press.

Whalley, L. J. (2015). *Understanding brain aging and dementia: A lifecourse approach.* New York: Columbia University Press.

White, H., & Venkatesh, B. (2016). Traumatic brain injury. In M. Smith, G. Citerio, & W. A. Kofke (Eds.), *Oxford textbook of neurocritical care* (pp. 210–224). New York: Oxford University Press.

White, K. D. (2010). Covenant marriage: An unnecessary second attempt at fault-based divorce. *Alabama Law Review, 61,* 869. Retrieved from www.law.ua.edu/pubs/ lrarticles/Volume%2061/Issue%204/white.pdf.

White, L., & Gilbreth, J. G. (2001). When children have two fathers: Effects of relationships with stepfathers and noncustodial fathers on adolescent outcomes. *Journal of Marriage and the Family, 63,* 155–167.

Whitehurst, G. J., & Vasta, R. (1975). Is language acquired through imitation? *Journal of Psycholinguistic Research, 4,* 37–59.

Whiting, B. B., & Edwards, P. E. (1988). *Children of different worlds.* Cambridge, MA: Harvard University Press.

Whitty, M. T., & Buchanan, T. (2009). Looking for love in so many places: Characteristics of online daters and speed daters. *Interpersona: An International Journal on Personal Relationships, 3*(Suppl. 2), 63–86. Retrieved from crawl.prod.proquest.com.s3.amazonaws. com/fpcache/4228bb2686d8dc3cecf9ca4d31bc b15f.pdf?AWSAccessKeyId=AKIAJF7V7KNV 2KKY2NUQ&Expires=1476657636&Signatur e=LXYaIQm21fOgAwRDo40NnvcuCm8%3D.

Wickrama, K. A. S., O'Neal, C. W., & Lorenz, F. O. (2013). Marital functioning from middle to later years: A life course-stress process framework. *Journal of Family Theory and Review,5,* 15–34. doi:10.1111/jftr.12000

Wicks-Nelson, R., & Israel, A. C. (2015). *Abnormal child and adolescent psychology* (8th ed.). Upper Saddle River, NJ: Pearson.

Widen, S. C., & Russell, J. A. (2013). Children's recognition of disgust in others. *Psychological Bulletin, 139,* 271–299.

Widman, L., Choukas-Bradley, S., Noar, S. M., Nesi, J., & Garrett, K. (2016). Parent-adolescent sexual communication and adolescent safer sex behavior: A meta-analysis. *JAMA Pediatrics, 170,* 52–61.

Widom, C. S., Czaja, S. J., & DuMont, K. A. (2015). Intergenerational transmission of child abuse and neglect: Real or detection bias? *Science, 347,* 1480–1485.

Wijdicks, E. F. M., Varelas, P. N., Gronseth, G. S., & Greer, D. M. (2010). Evidence-based guideline update: Determining brain death in adults. Report of the Quality Standards Subcommittee of the American Academy of Neurology. *Neurology, 74,* 1911–1918. doi:10.1212/ WNL.0b013e3181e242a8

Wiles, J. L., & Jayasinha, R. (2013). Care for place: The contributions older people make to their communities. *Journal of Aging Studies, 27,* 93–101. doi:10.1016/j.jaging.2012.12.001

Wilhelm-Leen, E. R., Hall, Y. N., Horwitz, R. I., & Chertow, G. M. (2014). Phase angle, frailty and mortality in older adults. *Journal of General Internal Medicine, 29,* 147–154. doi:10.1007/ s11606-013-2585-z

Williams, J. C., Phillips, K. W., & Hall, E. V. (2014). *Double jeopardy? Gender bias against women of color in science.* Retrieved from www .uchastings.edu/news/articles/2015/01/double-jeopardy-report.pdf.

Williams, S. T., Conger, K. J., & Blozis, S. A. (2007). The development of interpersonal aggression during adolescence: The importance of parents, siblings, and family economics. *Child Development, 78,* 1526–1542.

Wilson, R. D. (2000). Amniocentesis and chorionic villus sampling. *Current Opinion in Obstetrics & Gynecology, 12,* 81–86.

Wilt, J., Cox, K. S., & McAdams, D. P. (2010). The Eriksonian life story: Developmental scripts and psychosocial adaptation. *Journal of Adult Development, 17,* 156–161. doi:10.1007/ s10804-010-9093-8

Winecoff, A., LaBar, K. S. Madden, D. J., Cabeza, R., & Huettel, S. A. (2011). Cognitive and neural contributions to emotion regulation in aging. *Social Cognitive and Affective Neuroscience, 6,* 165–176. doi:10.1093/scan/nsq030

Winneke, G. (2011). Developmental aspects of environmental neurotoxicology: Lessons from lead and polychlorinated biphenyls. *Journal of the Neurological Sciences, 308,* 9–15.

Winner, E. (2000). Giftedness: Current theory and research. *Current Directions in Psychological Science, 9,* 153–156.

Winslow, M., & Meldrum, M. (2013). A history of hospice and palliative care. In S. Lutz, E. Chow, & P. Hoskin (Eds.), *Radiation oncology in palliative cancer care* (pp. 63–71). New York: Wiley.

Wise, D. (2017). *Social Security programs and retirement around the world.* Chicago, IL: University of Chicago Press.

Witten, T. M. (2016). The intersectional challenges of aging and of being a gender non-conforming adult. *Generations, 40,* 63–70.

Wojtunik-Kulesza, K. A., Oniszczuk, A., Oniszczuk, T., & Waksmundzka-Hajnos, M. (2016). The influence of common free radicals and antioxidants on development of Alzheimer's disease. *Biomedicine & Pharmacotherapy, 78,* 39–49. doi: 10.1016/j. biopha.2015.12.024

Wolff, P. H. (1987). *The development of behavioral states and the expression of emotions in early infancy.* Chicago: University of Chicago Press.

Wolke, D., Copeland, W. E., Angold, A., & Costello, E. J. (2013). Impact of bullying on adult health, wealth, crime, and social outcomes. *Psychological Science, 24,* 1958–1970.

Women's Health Research Institute. (2016). *How hormone depletion affects you.* Retrieved from menopause.northwestern.edu/content/ how-hormone-depletion-affects-you.

WomensHealth.gov. (2010). *Menopause basics.* Retrieved from www.omenshealth.gov/menopause/menopause-basics/index.html.

Wong, D. R., & Rothenhaus, T. C. (2014). Management of trauma in the elderly. In J. H. Kahn, B. G. Magauran, Jr., & J. S. Olshaker (Eds.), *Geriatric emergency medicine: Principles and practice* (pp. 59–68). New York: Cambridge University Press.

Wong, P. T. P. (2015). *The meaning hypothesis of living a good life: Virtue, happiness and meaning.* Retrieved from www.drpaulwong.com/the-meaning-hypothesis-of-living-a-good-life-virtue-happiness-and-meaning/.

Woodbridge, S. (2008). Sustaining families in the 21st century: The role of grandparents. *International Journal of Environmental, Cultural, Economic and Social Sustainability.* Retrieved from www98.griffith.edu.au/dspace/bitstream/10072/27417/1/50932_1.pdf.

Worden, W. (1991). *Grief counseling and grief therapy: A handbook for the mental health practitioner* (2nd ed.). New York: Springer.

World Health Organization. (2010). *Population-based prevention strategies for childhood obesity.* Geneva, Switzerland: Author.

World Health Organization. (2012). *Seniors and disabilities.* Retrieved from new.paho.org/hq/index.php?option=com_content&view=article&id=7316%3Aseniors-a-disabilities-april-2012&catid=4684%3Afchldisabilities-and-rehabilitation&Itemid=936&lang=en.

World Health Organization. (2013). *Responding to intimate partner violence and sexual violence against women.* Retrieved from www.who.int/reproductivehealth/publications/violence/9789241548595/en/.

World Health Organization. (2015). *10 facts on dementia.* Retrieved from www.who.int/features/factfiles/dementia/en/.

Wray-Lake, L., Crouter, A. C., & McHale, S. M. (2010). Developmental patterns in decision-making autonomy across middle childhood and adolescence: European American parents perspectives. *Child Development, 81,* 636–651.

Wrenn, R. L. (1999). The grieving college student. In J. D. Davidson & K. J. Doka (Eds.), *Living with grief: At work, at school, at worship* (pp. 131–141). Levittown, PA: Brunner/Mazel.

Wright, J. C., Huston, A. C., Murphy, K. C., St. Peters, M., Piñon, M., Scantlin, R., et al. (2001). The relations of early television viewing to school readiness and vocabulary of children from low-income families: The Early Window Project. *Child Development, 72,* 1347–1366.

Wrzus, C., & Roberts, B. W. (2017). Processes of personality development in adulthood: The TESSERA framework. *Personality and Social Psychology Review, 21*(3): 253–277. doi:10.1177/1088868316652279

Wu, L., & Zhao, L. (2016). ApoE2 and Alzheimer's disease: Time to take a closer look. *Neural Regeneration Research, 11,* 412–413. doi:10.4103/1673-5374.179044

Wyman, E. (2014). Language and collective fiction: From children's pretence to social institutions. In D. Dor, C. Knight, & J. Lewis (Eds.), *The social origins of language* (pp. 171–183). Oxford: Oxford University Press.

Wynn, K. (1992). Addition and subtraction by human infants. *Nature, 358,* 749–750.

Xia, Y. R., Do, K. A., & Xie, X. (2013). The adjustment of Asian American families to the U.S. context: The ecology of strengths and stress. In G. W. Peterson & K. R. Bush (Eds.), *Handbook of marriage and the family* (3rd ed., pp. 723–747). New York: Springer.

Xu, X., Zhu, F., O'Campo, P., Koenig, M. A., Mock, V., & Campbell, J. (2005). Prevalence of and risk factors for intimate partner violence in China. *American Journal of Public Health, 95,* 78–85. doi:10.2105/ AJPH.2003.023978

Yaakobi, E. (2015). Desire to work as a death anxiety buffer mechanism. *Experimental Psychology, 62,* 110–122. doi:10.1027/1618-3169/a000278

Yang, J., Kanazawa, S., Yamaguchi, M. K., & Kuriki, I. (2016). Cortical response to categorical color perception in infants investigated by near-infrared spectroscopy. *Proceedings of the National Academy of Sciences of the United States of America, 113,* 2370–2375.

Yang, T., Yang, X. Y., Cottrell, R. R., Wu, D., Jiang, S., & Anderson, J. G. (2016). Violent injuries and regional correlates among women in China: Results from 21 cities study in China. *The European Journal of Public Health, 26,* 513–517. doi:10.1093/eurpub/ckv193

Yap, M. B. H., Pilkington, P. d., Ryan, S. B., & Jorm, A. F. (2014). Parental factors associated with depression and anxiety in young people: A systematic review and meta-analysis. *Journal of Affective Disorders, 156,* 8–23.

Yárnoz-Yaben, S. (2010). Attachment style and adjustment to divorce. *Spanish Journal of Psychology, 13,* 210–219. doi:10.1017/S1138741600003796

Yarwood, A., Huizinga, T. W. J., & Worthington, J. (2016). The genetics of rheumatoid arthritis: Risk and protection in different stages of the evolution of RA. *Rheumatology, 55,* 1990209. doi:10.1093/rheumatology/keu323

Yngvesson, B. (2010). *Belonging in an adopted world: Race, identity, and transnational adoption.* Chicago: University of Chicago Press.

Yoffe, E. (2013). *College women: Stop getting drunk.* Retrieved from www.slate.com/articles/double_x/doublex/2013/10/sexual_assault_and_drinking_teach_women_the_connection.html.

Yoon, S. M. (2005). The characteristics and needs of Asian-American grandparent caregivers: A study of Chinese-American and Korean-American grandparents in New York City. *Journal of Gerontological Social Work, 44,* 75–94. doi:10.1300/ J083v44n03_06

Young, K. (2013). Adult friendships in the Facebook era. *Webology, 10.* Retrieved from pirate.24nieuwe.nl/www.webology.org/2013/v10n1/a103.html.

Young, S. K., Fox, N. A., & Zahn-Waxler, C. (1999). The relations between temperament and empathy in 2-year-olds. *Developmental Psychology, 35,* 1189–1197.

Yousafzai, A. K., Obradović, J., Rasheed, M. A., Rizvi, A., Portilla, X. A., Tirado-Strayer, N., et al. (2016). Effects of responsive stimulation and nutrition interventions on children's development and growth at age 4 years in a disadvantaged population in Pakistan: A longitudinal follow-up of a cluster-randomised factorial effectiveness trial. *Lancet Global Health, 4,* e548–558.

Youssef-Morgan, C. M., & Luthans, F. (2013). Psychological capital theory: Toward a positive holistic model. In A. B. Bakker (Ed.), *Advances in positive organizational psychology* (Vol. 1, pp. 145–166). Bingley, UK: Emerald Group Publishing.

Yu, T., Pettit, G. S., Lansford, J. E., Dodge, K. A., & Bates, J. E. (2010). The interactive effects of marital conflict and divorce on parent-adult children's relationships. *Journal of Marriage and Family, 72,* 282–292. doi:10.1111/j.1741-3737.2010.00699.x

Yuan, S., & Fisher, C. (2009). "Really? She blicked the baby?": Two-year-olds learn combinatorial facts about verbs by listening. *Psychological Science, 20,* 619–626.

Yuen, H. K., & Vogtle, L. K. (2016). Multi-morbidity, disability and adaptation strategies among community-dwelling adults aged 75 years and older. *Disability and Health Journal, 9,* 593–599. doi:10.1016/j.dhjo.2016.03.004

Yumoto, C., Jacobson, S. W., & Jacobson, J. L. (2008). Fetal substance exposure and cumulative environmental risk in an African American cohort. *Child Development, 79,* 1761–1776.

Zabriskie, R. B., & Kay, T. (2013). Positive leisure science: Leisure in family contexts. In T. Freire (Ed.), *Positive leisure science* (pp. 81–99). New York: Springer.

Zahn-Waxler, C., Radke-Yarrow, M., Wagner, E., & Chapman, M. (1992). Development of concern for others. *Developmental Psychology, 28,* 126–136.

Zalewski, M., Lengua, L. J., Wilson, A. C., Trancik, A., & Bazinet, A. (2011). Emotion regulation profiles, temperament, and adjustment problems in preadolescents. *Child Development, 82,* 951–966.

Zarrett, N., Fay, K., Li, Y., Carrano, J., Phelps, E., & Lerner, R. M. (2009). More than child's play: Variable- and pattern-centered approaches for examining effects of sports participation on youth development. *Developmental Psychology, 45,* 368–382.

Zaslow, M. J., & Hayes, C. D. (1986). Sex differences in children's responses to psychosocial stress: Toward a cross-context analysis. In M. E. Lamb, A. L. Brown, & B. Rogoff (Eds.), *Advances in developmental psychology* (Vol. 4, pp. 285–337). Hillsdale, NJ: Erlbaum.

Zelazo, P. R. (1993). The development of walking: New findings and old assumptions. *Journal of Motor Behavior, 15,* 99–137.

Zetumer, S., Young, I., Shear, M. K., Skritskaya, N., Lebowitz, B., Simon, N. et al. (2015). The impact of losing a child on the clinical presentation of complicated grief. *Journal of Affective Disorders, 170,* 15–21. doi:10.1016/j.jad.2014.08.021

Zhai, F., Waldfogel, J., & Brooks-Gunn, J. (2013). Estimating the effects of Head Start on parenting and child maltreatment. *Child and Youth Services Review, 35,* 1119–1129.

Zhan, H. J. (2006). Joy and sorrow: Explaining Chinese caregivers' reward and stress. *Journal of Aging Studies, 20,* 27–38. doi:10.1016/j.aging.2005.01.002

Zheng, Z., Shemmassian, S., Wijekoon, C., Kim, W., Bookheimer, S. Y., & Pouratian, N. (2014). DTI correlates of distinct cognitive impairments in Parkinson's disease. *Human Brain Mapping. 35,* 1325–1333. doi:10.1002 / hbm.22256

Zhou, L., Lu, J., Chen, G., & Yao, Y. (2017). Is there a paradox of aging: When the negative aging stereotype meets the positivity effect in older adults. *Experimental Aging Research, 43,* 80–93. doi:10.1080/0361073X.2017.1258254

Zhou, Q., Eisenberg, N., Losoya, S. H., Fabes, R. A., Reiser, M., Guthrie, I. K., et al. (2002). The relations of parental warmth and positive expressiveness to children's empathy-related responding and social functioning: A longitudinal study. *Child Development, 73,* 893–915.

Zhou, Q., Wang, Y., Eisenberg, N., Wolchik, S., Tein, J-W., & Deng, X. (2008). Relations of parenting and temperament to Chinese children's experience of negative life events, coping efficacy, and externalizing problems. *Child Development, 79,* 493–513.

Zhu, W., Chen, Q., Tang, C., Cao, G., Hou, Y., & Qiu, J. (2016). Brain structure links everyday creativity to creative achievement. *Brain and Cognition, 103,* 70–76. doi:10.1016/j.bandc.2015.09.008

Zigler, E., & Finn-Stevenson, M. (1992). Applied developmental psychology. In M. H. Bornstein & M. E. Lamb (Eds.), *Developmental psychology: An advanced textbook* (pp. 677–729). Hillsdale, NJ: Erlbaum.

Zimmer-Gembeck, M. J., & Helfand, M. (2008). Ten years of longitudinal research on U.S. adolescent sexual behavior: Developmental correlates of sexual intercourse, and the importance of age, gender and ethnic background. *Developmental Review, 28,* 153–224.

Zimmer-Gembeck, M. J., & Skinner, E. A. (2011). The development of coping across childhood and adolescence: An integrative review and critique of research. *International Journal of Behavioral Development, 35,* 1–17.

Zimmerman, B. J. (2001). Theories of self-regulated learning and academic achievement: An overview and analysis. In B. J. Zimmerman & D. H. Schunk (Eds.), *Self-regulated learning and academic achievement: Theoretical perspectives* (2nd ed., pp. 1–37). Mahwah, NJ: Erlbaum.

Zinar, S. (2000). The relative contributions of word identification skill and comprehension-monitoring behavior to reading comprehension ability. *Contemporary Educational Psychology, 25,* 363–377.

Zinn, J. O. (2016). Risk taking. In A. Burgess, A. Alemanno, & J. O. Zinn (Eds.), *Routledge handbook of risk studies* (pp. 344–355). New York: Routledge.

Zosh, J. M., Lytle, S. R., Golinkoff, R. M., & Hirsh-Pasek, K. (2017). Putting the education back in educational apps: How content and context interact to promote learning. In R. Barr & D. N. Linebarger (Eds.), *Media exposure during infancy and early childhood* (pp. 259–282). Cham, Switzerland: Springer.

Zukow-Goldring, P. (2002). Sibling caregiving. In M. H. Bornstein (Ed.), *Handbook of parenting: Vol. 3. Status and social conditions of parenting* (2nd ed., pp. 253–286). Mahwah, NJ: Erlbaum.

Name Index

Luong, G., 519
Lushington, K., 83
Luszcz, M. A., 495
Luszczynska, A., 435
Luthans, F., 394
Lütkenhaus, P., 110
Luxenberg, S., 366
Lyall, K., 112
Lyng, S., 320
Lyon, T. D., 134
Lyster, S-A. H., 206–207
Lyster, S. H., 210
Lytton, H., 50, 181

Ma, Y-Y., 197
Maatz, L., 402
MacArthur, C. A., 212, 213
Maccoby, E. E., 170–171, 179, 181
MacDonald, K., 47
Mace, J. H., 483
Maciejewski, P. K., 564
Mackenzie, P., 467
Mackenzie, S. H., 320
Mackie, D. M., 177
Macnamara, B. N., 486
MacWhinney, B., 148
Maddow-Zimet, I., 299
Magai, C., 521
Magee, L., 271
Magilvy, J. K., 575
Magnuson, K., 201
Maguire, E. A., 95
Mahady, G. B., 428
Mahmood, T., 52
Mahon, N. E., 309
Maitre, N. L., 94
Makel, M. C., 204
Makhijani, M. G., 179
Malberg, N. T., 572
Malkinson, R., 573, 574
Malone, M. L., 484, 495
Malone, P. S., 312
Mancini, A. D., 562
Mandara, J., 293
Mandel, D. R., 104
Mandela, N., 543
Mandemakers, J. J., 407
Mange, A. P., 43
Mange, E. J., 43
Mangelsdorf, S. C., 165
Mankus, A. M., 343
Mannering, A. M., 170
Mantler, J., 405
Manuti, A., 395
Mao, D., 271
Maple, M., 573
Maratsos, M., 148
Marcia, J., 393
Marcus, G. F., 147
Marcus, R., 327
Mares, M-L., 250
Margett, T. E., 128
Margrett, J. A., 437
Markman, E. M., 90
Markovits, H., 243
Marks, A. K., 294
Marks, N. F., 517
Markus, H., 347
Marlier, L., 103
Marschik, P. B., 102
Marsh, H. W., 294
Marsh, K., 394
Marshall, S., 575
Marsiglio, W., 374

Martens, A., 552
Martin, A. J., 294
Martin, C. L., 171, 177, 182, 183
Martin, J., 181
Martin, J. A., 59, 69
Martin, M., 442
Martin, N., 90
Martin, S. P., 366
Martinez, M. E., 73
Martínez, M. L., 234
Martin-Storey, A., 300
Martin-Uzzi, M., 383
Mash, H. B. H., 572
Mask, L., 415
Masunaga, H., 439
Masur, E. F., 145
Materne, C. J., 495
Materstvedt, L. J., 545
Mather, M., 469, 509, 510
Matheson, C. C., 169
Mathiesen, K. S., 86
Mathur, M. B., 431
Matthews, D., 148
Mattis, J., 476
Mattys, S. L., 140
Matz-Costa, C., 514
Maume, D. J., 412
Mauno, S., 234
Maurer, D., 108
Mavellia, H., 516
Maxfield, M., 550
May, P. A., 60
Maybery, M. T., 112
Mayer, H. U., 20
Mayer, J. D., 343
Mayer, R. E., 437
Maynard, A. E., 235
Maynard, B., 546, 547
Mayo Clinic, 331, 435
Mazur, E., 319
McAdams, D. P., 346, 347, 444–445
McAdams, T. A., 231
McAlaney, J., 328
McCabe, J. E., 69, 70
McCabe, M., 295
McCall, R. B., 87
McCartney, K., 49
McCarty, W. P., 395
McClinton, B. E., 514
McClung, M. R., 425
McCollum, L., 332–333
McCormick, C. B., 193
McCormick, C. M., 311
McCoy, J. K., 236
McCoyd, J. L. M., 524, 563, 572, 573
McCrae, R. R., 441, 442
McCubbin, H., 370
McCullough, B. M., 520
McCutchen, D., 213
McDaniel, M. A., 301
McDermott, J. M., 236–237
McDonald, K. L., 245
McElwain, N. L., 160
McGarry, K., 524
McGinley, M., 175
McGinty, T., 547
McGraw, M. B., 96
McGuire, S., 236
McHale, J. P., 233
McHale, S. M., 171, 234, 235, 236, 296
McKay, B., 433
McKee, A. C., 497
McKee, K. J., 330, 477
McKee-Ryan, F., 405, 406, 407

McLanahan, S., 376
McLaughlin, K. A., 95
McLean, K. C., 347
McLeod, K., 192
McLymont, R., 398
McMahon, R. J., 228
McMurray, B, 143
McMurray, B., 139, 144
McNally, R. J., 565
McNulty, M., 490, 491
McNutt, B., 575
McPherson, M. C., 532
McQuade, J. D., 311
Meck, E., 135
Medart, P., 474
Medicare.gov, 534
MedlinePlus, 428
Medwell, J., 213
Meeker, J. D., 60
Meeus, W., 291
Mehta, C. M., 244
Meijer, A. M., 371, 373
Meilaender, G., 545
Meins, E., 170
Mejia, S., 347
Melby, J. N., 231
Melby-Lervåg, M., 206, 207, 210
Meldrum, M., 556
Mellor, D., 508
Melson, G. F., 170
Meltzoff, A. N., 132, 167, 177
Menaker, R., 394
Ménard, C., 489
Mendez-Luck, C. A., 449
Mendle, J., 269, 298
Mennella, J. A., 56, 103
Mensch, B. S., 319
Mercer, T., 484
Merianos, A. L., 230
Merten, M. J., 234
Merton, T., 512
Mertz, M. E., 524, 525
Mervis, C. B., 147
Merz, E.-M., 357–358
Merz, M. Y., 555
Meschede, T., 516
Mesquita, B., 163
Messer, D., 138
Meunier, D., 483
Meyer, M., 129
Micalizzi, L., 85
Michel, A., 395
Michel, G. F., 102
Mickler, C., 443
Midgette, E., 212
Midlarsky, E., 505
Miethi, A., 356
Mietkiewicz, M.-C., 525
Miga, E. M., 233
Mikhelson, V. M., 466
Miklowski, C., 20
Miles, J., 322, 323
Mileva-Seitz, V. R., 83
Miller, A. B., 476
Miller, A. C., 544, 545
Miller, D. I., 179
Miller, D. T., 328
Miller, G. E., 233
Miller, J. G., 282
Miller, K. I., 449
Miller, L. C., 99
Miller, L. S., 503
Miller, M. M., 180
Miller, P. C., 228

Miller, P. H., 125
Miller, P. J., 570, 571
Miller, P. M., 179
Miller, R. L., 208
Miller, S. A., 256
Miller, T. W., 208
Miller, V. M., 429
Miller-Martinez, D., 519
Milligan, C., 549
Mills, T. L., 525
Minnotte, K. L., 368
Miranda, J., 310
Miranda, L-M., 486
Mischel, W., 181
Mishra, G. D., 528
Mitchell, B. A., 447, 448
Mitchell, T. B., 272
Mitteldorf, J., 467
Mize, J., 172, 231
Modecki, K. L., 238
Moeller, J. R., 545, 554
Moen, P., 393, 515, 516
Moerk, E. L., 147
Moffitt, T. E., 311
Moghaddam, B., 265
Mokdad, C., 90
Molin, P., 493
Molina, B. S. G., 208
Molina, L. C., 519
Mollborn, S., 59
Mollnow, E., 62
Molnar, D. S., 64
Monahan, A., 514, 515
Monahan, K. C., 246, 305, 313
Monden, C. W. S., 407
Mondloch, C. J., 107
Monk, C., 58
Monk, C. S., 93
Monk, T. H., 575
Montague, D. P., 166
Mont'Alvao, A., 306
Montesanto, A., 462
Moon, P. J., 558
Moone, R. P., 523
Moore, K. L., 44, 63
Moore, M. K., 132
Moorman, S. M., 357–358, 520, 523, 524, 560
Morais, M. L. S., 169
Morfei, M. Z., 347
Morgan, B., 91
Morgan, J. L., 140
Morgan, J. P., 572
Morgan, P. L., 208
Morris, P., 228
Morris, W. L., 365
Morrissey, T. W., 410
Morrow-Howell, N., 517
Mortimer, J. T., 306
Morton, J., 107
Morycz, R., 520
Moses, L. J., 167
Mosten, F. S., 382
Mõttus, R., 442
Mount, M. K., 392
Mountain, G., 161
Mounts, N. S., 172
Mouras, H., 342, 446
Moye, J., 560
Moyer, A. M., 429
Mozaffarian, D., 470
Mrayyan, M. T., 558
Mühlig-Versen, A., 443
Muise, A., 371

molecular genetics, research in, 47, 48
monoamine oxidase (MAO)
    inhibitors, 490
monozygotic twins, defined, 46, *47*
mood
    altruism and, 174
    exercise for improving, *435*
    pubertal changes and, 268
moral reasoning, 279–284
    Kohlberg's theory of moral
        development, 280–283
    promoting, 283–284
    religion and, 283–285
moratorium, 291, *291*
Moray House Test, 29
Moro reflex, *81*
motion parallax, defined, 105
motor skills
    assessing, 81
    defined, 96
    fine, 100–102
    gender differences in, 220
    in infants, 96–102
    locomotion, 96–99
    in middle childhood, *219*, 219–221
    physical fitness and, 220
    sports participation and, 220–221
mourning, defined, 561
    See also grief
multichannel encephalography, 470
multidimensional, defined, 334
multidirectionality
    defined, 334
    in life-span perspective, 19
multiethnic families, *375*, 375–376
multiple causation, in life-span
    perspective, 19
multiple intelligences, Gardner's theory
    of, *196*, 196–197
musical intelligence, 196, *196*, 197
Muslims, 4, 8
myelin, defined, 92

naïve theories of children, 126–130
    naïve biology, 128–129
    naïve physics, *127*, 127–128
naltrexone, 330
narrative
    defined, 445
    grief and, 563
NASA, 507
National Academy of Social
    Insurance, 534
National Adult Reading Test, 29
National Alliance for Caregiving &
    AARP, 449
National Association for the Education
    of Young Children, 409
National Cancer Institute, 64
National Center for Assisted Living,
    529–530
National Center for Education Statistics,
    321, 322
National Center for Health Statistics,
    373, 376, 461, 462, 463, 475, 476,
    528, 542
National Center for State Courts, 532
National Eye Institute, 473
National Federation of State High
    School Associations, 274
National Heart, Lung, and Blood
    Institute, 429
National Institute of Arthritis and
    Musculoskeletal and Skin
    Diseases, 423, 424, 426, 427

National Institute of Biomedical and
    Bioengineering, 497
National Institute of Child Health and
    Human Development, 84–85
National Institute of Mental Health,
    434, 488, 489, 490–491
National Institute of Neurological
    Disorders and Stroke (NINDS),
    57, 497
National Institute on Aging, 468, 470,
    528
National Institute on Alcohol Abuse
    and Alcoholism (NIAAA),
    327, 328
National Institute on Minority Health
    and Health Disparities, 332
National Institutes of Health (NIH), 32,
    84–85, 113
National Osteoporosis Foundation,
    423, 424
National Women's Law Center, 401
Native Americans
    Apache menarche celebration,
        267, *268*
    binge drinking and, 328
    cardiovascular disease and, 470
    career preferences of, 304
    ethnic identity and, 293, 294
    grandparenthood and, 451
    nutrition and, 330
    parenting and, 375
    sudden infant death syndrome and,
        84–85
    swaddling and, 82
    teen suicide and, 310
    terms for describing, 9
Native Hawaiians, 470, *489*
naturalistic intelligence, 196, *196*
naturalistic observation
    defined, 23
    summarized, *25*
nature–nurture issue, defined, 6
near infrared spectroscopic imaging
    (NIRSI), 470
negative reinforcement, 14
negative reinforcement trap,
    defined, 232
neglect
    of children, 239
    in elder abuse, 532
neglected children, defined, 247
Neonatal Behavioral Assessment Scale
    (NBAS), 81–82
nervous system, of infants, 91–95
    brain structures, *92*, 92–93
    specialized brain, growth of, 93–95
neural efficiency hypothesis,
    defined, 340
neural network connections, 483
neural plate, defined, 92
neuritic plaques, 468, 493, 495
neurochemicals, love and, 362
neurofibrillary tangles, defined, 468
neuroimaging
    brain–behavior relations and, *25*,
        469–470
    functional, 470
    neuroscience and intelligence and,
        339, 339–340
    response to threat and, 357
    structural, 470
neurons
    beta-amyloids, 468–469, *469*
    changes in, age-related, 468–470
    defined, 91

neuroimaging, 469–470
neurotransmitters, 469
    structure of, *468*
neuropsychological tests, 471–472, 483
neuroscience
    defined, 10–11
    romantic relationships and, 362–363
neuroscience research, 339–340
    on binge drinking, 329
    emotion-focused, 509–510
    neural efficiency hypothesis, 340
    P-FIT, 339–340
neurostimulator, 496
neuroticism, defined, 441
neurotransmitters, defined, 91, 469
New York Times, 328
newborns, 80–86
    alert inactivity and, 82
    assessing, 80, 81–82
    crying and, 82–83
    infant mortality and, 72–73, *73*
    preterm *or* premature, 71–72
    reflexes of, 80–82, *81*
    sleeping and, 82, 83–84
    small-for-date babies, 72, *72*
    states of, 82–85
    temperament and, 85–86
    waking inactivity and, 82
    well-being of, 81
NIAAA, 328, 329
NICHD Early Child Care Research
    Network, 161
niche-picking, defined, 49
nicotine. *See* cigarette smoking
NIHSeniorHealth, 488, 489
non-invasive prenatal testing (NIPT),
    defined, 66
nonshared environmental influences,
    defined, 50
North American Menopause Society,
    428, 429
Not Alone campaign, 363
NotAlone.gov, 363
nuclear family, defined, 372
number skills, learning, 134–136, *135*
    approximate number system,
        134–135
    counting, 135
nursing home, defined, 530
nutrition
    in adolescence, 270–273
    breastfeeding and, 83, 89, 90
    cancer and, 10, 332, 477
    cardiovascular disease and, 10,
        332, 477
    diabetes mellitus and, 332, 476, 477
    *Dietary Guidelines for Americans
        2015–2020*, 477
    eating disorders and, 272–273
    ethnicity and, 330
    infant growth and, 89–90
    in late adulthood, 477, *478*
    obesity and, 271–272, 332, *332*
    in prenatal development, 57
    in young and middle adulthood,
        330–332

obedience orientation, defined, 280
obesity, 271–272
    body mass index and, 271, 332, *332*
    breastfed babies and, 89
    causes of, 271–272
    in middle childhood, 271–272
    weight-loss programs for, 272
    in young and middle adulthood, 332

object permanence, defined, 121
objects
    perception of, 106–107, *107*, *108*
    understanding, in sensorimotor
        period, 121
observational learning, imitation/
    counterimitation and, 231
occipital cortex, *92*
occupational choice, 389–391
    ethnicity and, 399–400
    gender differences in, 397, *398*
    theories, *390*, 390–391
    vocational maturity and, 390
occupational development, 392–394
    crystallization and, 302
    developmental coaches and, 393–394
    ethnicity and, 399–400
    expectations in, 392–393
    implementation and, 303
    mentors and, 393–394
    in middle childhood, 302–305
    personality-type theory and,
        303–304
    social cognitive career theory and,
        304–305, *305*
    specification and, 303
    women and, 398–399, *399*
occupational transitions, 404–407
    advice for adults trying to
        manage, 407
    occupational insecurity and, 405
    retraining workers and, 404–405
    unemployment and, 405–407
OECD, 73, 410, 411
older adults. *See* late adulthood
one-to-one principle, defined, 135
online dating, 359–360
online friendships, 357
open adoption, defined, 237
openness to experience, defined, 442
operant conditioning
    defined, 13, 132
    Skinner's, 13, 14
opioid peptides, 329
opioids for pain management, 558
optimization, 20
    See also selective optimization with
        compensation (SOC) model
Organisation for Economic
    Co-operation and Development
    (OECD), 214, 463–464
organization, defined, 192
orienting response, defined, 131
osteoarthritis, defined, 426, *426*
    See also arthritis
osteoporosis
    defined, 423–425
    estrogen and, 428
    medications for, 425
    osteoarthritis and rheumatoid
        arthritis compared to, *427*
    vitamin D and calcium intake and,
        424, *425*
others, understanding, 253–257
    describing others, 253–254
    prejudiced against others, 256–257
    Selman's theory of perspective taking
        and, 254–255, *255*
    thoughts of, 254–256
outcome expectations, 304, 390
ovarian cancer, 476, 477
overextension, defined, 144
overregularization, defined, 147
overweight. *See* obesity
oxytocin, 174

sensorimotor period, *120,* 120–122
  defined, 120
  environment and, adapting to and
      exploring, 120–121
  objects and, understanding, 121
  symbols and, using, 121–122
sensorimotor stage, 15, *15*
sensory changes, age-related, 472–475
  hearing, 473–475, *474*
  vision, *472,* 472–473
sensory information, integrating,
      108–109
sentence cues, 144
sentences, speaking in, 146–148
  grammar, acquisition of, 147–148
  from two words to complex
      sentences, 146–147
separation distress, defined, 567
sequential design
  defined, 30
  five-factor trait model and, 441
  in research design, 30–31
  summarized, *31*
serotonin, 329, 362, 469, 495
Sex, Romance, and Relationships study
      (AARP), 429
sex chromosomes, defined, 40
Sex in America study (AARP), 429
sexual abuse
  of children, 239
  in elder abuse, 532
sexual behavior, 298–301
  contraception and, 300
  dating violence and, 300–301
  sexual minority youth and, 300
  STIs and, 298–299, *299*
  teen pregnancy and, 299–300
sexually transmitted infections (STIs),
      298–299, *299*
sexual maturation, 266
  See also puberty
sexual minority youth, 300
sexual orientation, 300
shyness. *See* inhibition (shyness)
siblings, 235–238
  adopted children and, 236–237
  birth order and, 237–238
siblings, in late adulthood, 520
sickle-cell trait
  CRISPR and, 66
  defined, 42
  genetic mechanism responsible for,
      41–43, *42*
  preimplantation genetic screening
      and, 52
  recessive alleles for, 42, 43, 66
  red blood cells of, 40, *40,* 41
simple social play, defined, 169
Sinemet°, 495, 496
singlehood, 365–366
single parents, *376,* 376–377
single photon emission computerized
      tomography (SPECT), 470
skeletal maturity, defined, 423
skin cancer, 424
Skinner's operant conditioning, 13, 14
sleep, in late adulthood, 476, 477
sleeping, defined, 82
  newborns and, 82, 83–84
  nonREM sleep, 83–84
  REM sleep, 83–84
  sudden infant death syndrome and,
      84–85
small-for-date babies, 72, *72*
smell, sense of, 103

smoking. *See* cigarette smoking
social clock, defined, 346
social cognitive career theory (SCCT)
  career development and,
      304–305, *305*
  defined, 390, *390*
social contract, defined, 281
social convoy, defined, 519
social directors, parents as, 172
social influences, gender-related
      differences in, 179
social-informational stage, 255, *255*
social issues, in late adulthood, 525–535
  elder abuse and neglect, 532–533
  frail older adults, 526–528, *527*
  housing options, 528–532
  Medicare, 534–535
  Social Security, 533–534
socialization, defined, 227, 228
social learning theory, 14, *21*
social media, 251
  cyberbullying and, 248, 252
social personality type, *304*
social policy, developmental research
      and, 33
social referencing, defined, 167
social role, defined, 177
Social Security, 533–534
Social Security and Medicare Boards of
      Trustees, 534
social smiles, defined, 164
social system, assessing, 81
social system morality, defined, 281
societal stage, 255, *255*
sociocultural definitions of death,
      543–544
sociocultural forces
  in alcohol use, 327
  in biopsychosocial framework, 7, 8–9
  death and, 575–576
  defined, 7
  grammatical development and, 147
  human development created by,
      summary of, *21*
  identity and, 347
  life-course perspective and, 20
  life span and, 4
  low birth weight and, 72
  malnutrition and, 91
  neuroscience and, 11
  in occupational selection, 391
  pragmatics of intelligence and, 438
  in romantic relationships, 362–363
socioeconomic status
  birth complications and, 71
  delinquency and, 312
  health and, 330–331
  intelligence and, 201–203
  parenting styles and, 230–231
  prenatal risk and, 64
  puberty and, 267
socioemotional development
  in adolescence, 289–313
  attachment and, 157–162
  delinquency and, 310–313
  depression and, 308–310
  drug use and, 307–308
  electronic media and, 249–252
  emotions and, 163–168
  Erikson's psychosocial theory and,
      156, 156–157
  family relationships and, 228–242
  gender identity and, 176–184
  gender roles and, 176–184
  identity and, 290–296

  in infancy and early childhood,
      154–184
  interacting with others and, 168–176
  in middle childhood, 227–257
  peers and, 243–249
  romantic relationships and, 297–298
  self-esteem and, 294–295
  sexual behavior and, 298–301
  storm and stress and, myth of, 296
  understanding others and, 253–257
  work and, 296–306
socioemotional selectivity
  defined, 520–521
  in late adulthood, 520–521
software for nonexperts, 440
spatial ability, gender-related differences
      in, 179, *180*
spatial intelligence, 196, *196,* 197
special needs, children with, 204–209
  ADHD and, 208–209
  children with disability, 204–207
  gifted children, 204
specification, defined, 303
speech, 139–142
  identifying words and, 140–141
  language exposure and, impact of,
      139–140
  perceiving, 139–141
  private, 138
  speaking in sentences and, 146–148
  steps to, 141–142
speed dating, 359
speed of processing, defined, 480
spermarche
  defined, 266
  response to, 268
spina bifida, defined, 57
spirituality
  grief and, 563
  hospice and, 557
  in late adulthood, 512–513
  See also religion
spiritual support, defined, 513
sports participation
  in adolescence, 274–275
  in middle childhood, 220–221
stable-order principle, defined, 135
stagnation, defined, 444
Stalevo°, 495, 496
Stanford-Binet test, 199, 205
states, of newborn, 82–85
  alert inactivity, 82
  assessing, 81
  crying, 82–83
  sleeping, 82, 83–84
  waking inactivity, 82
statins, 331–332
stem cell research, 33, 468
step-parenting, 377–378
stepping, 98
stepping reflex, 80, *81*
stereotype threat, defined, 203
Sternberg's theory of successful
      intelligence, 197–198
storm and stress, myth of, 296
stranger wariness, defined, 164
Strange Situation, 158, *159*
strength, in young adulthood, 325
stress
  appraisals of, 423
  of caring for aging parents, 449–450
  coping and, 423–433
  defined, 58
  divorce and, 238, 382
  first pregnancy and, 373, 374, 375

  friendship networks and, 357
  hormones released in response
      to, 329
  leisure and, 415, 416
  in LGBTQ relationships, 367
  marriage and, 370, 371
  in middle adulthood, 430–434
  physical effects of, 433
  as physiological response, 430–431
  prenatal development and, 58
  psychological effects of, 434
  PTSD, 371, 434
  remarriage and, 383
  of single parenthood, 377
  storm and, myth of, 296
  transactional model of, *431*
  vulnerability–stress–adaptation
      model and, 370, *370*
  of work-family-school conflict, 322
  work-related, 234, *364,* 430
stress and coping paradigm,
      defined, 431
stress urinary incontinence, 428
strokes, or cerebral vascular accidents
      (CVAs), defined, 470
structural neuroimaging, defined, 470
structured life review, 508–509
structured observations
  defined, 23
  summarized, *25*
  in systematic observation, 23–24
structure of intelligence, defined, 335
subjective well-being, defined, 509
successful intelligence, Sternberg's
      theory of, 197–198
sucking reflex, 80, *81*
sudden infant death syndrome (SIDS),
      defined, 84–85
suicide
  depression and, 310
  in middle childhood, 275
  physician-assisted, 546, 547
Super's theory of occupational
      development, 390–391, *391*
swaddling, 82
symbols
  using, 121–122
  words as, 142
synaptic pruning, defined, 93
syphilis
  features of, *299*
  prenatal development and, 61, *61*
systematic observation
  defined, 23
  in human development research,
      23–24
  summarized, *25*
systems view of family, 228–229

taste, sense of, 103, *103*
tau proteins, *469*
teacher-based influences on student
      achievement, 216–217
teenagers. *See* adolescence; middle
      childhood
telegraphic speech, defined, 147
teleological explanations, defined, 128
television programs, 250
telomerase, defined, 466
telomeres, defined, 466, *467*
temperament
  attachment and, 157
  defined, 85
  depression and, 309
  environmental contributions to, 86

temperament (continued)
 genetic influence on, 174, 176
 hereditary contributions to, 85
 of newborns, 85–86
 stability of, 86
 theory of, 85
teratogens, 59–64
 defined, 59
 diseases, 60–61, 61
 drugs, 59–60, 60
 environmental hazards, 61–62
 harm associated with, challenges in
  determining, 64
 influence of, on prenatal
  development, 62–64, 63
terminal buttons, defined, 91
terror management theory, defined, 552
TESSERA model, 443, 444
testicular cancer, 64
testosterone
 aggression and, 311
 decline in, 430
 gender typing and, 183
 performance-enhancing drugs and, 274
 puberty and, 266
texture gradient, defined, 106
thalidomide, 59, 62
thanatology, defined, 542
theory, defined, 12
theory of mind, 111, 111–113
 in children with autism, 112–113
 cultural differences in, 111–112
 defined, 111
thinking
 adolescent, characteristics of,
  291–292, 292
 in adulthood, 340–342
 onset of, 118–130 (See also cognitive
  development)
 postformal thought, 341
 preschooler, essentialist, 129
 reflective judgment and, 341,
  341–342
 See also information processing
Third Age, 464–465
third-person stage, 255, 255
time-out, defined, 232–233
tissue plasminogen activator (tPA), 471
tobacco. See cigarette smoking
toddler, defined, 96
toddling, defined, 96
touch, sense of, 103, 103
toxoplasmosis, prenatal development
 and, 61
transgender and gender nonconforming
 (TGNC), 522
transgender youth, 300
transient ischemic attacks (TIAs),
 defined, 471
traumatic brain injury (TBI), 496
traumatic distress, defined, 567
true attachment, 158
trust
 vs. mistrust, 156, 156
 secure attachment and, 158, 160
Turner's syndrome, 45
type 1 diabetes, defined, 475
type 2 diabetes, defined, 475

ultrasound, defined, 65, 65
umbilical cord, defined, 54

underextension, defined, 144
undifferentiated stage, 255, 255
unemployment, 405–407
 advice for adults trying to
  manage, 407
 effects of, 406, 407, 407
 financial support and, 406
 politics of, 406
UNICEF, 73, 89
UNICEF-WHO-The World Bank, 90
uninvolved parenting, defined, 230
universal and context-specific-
 development issue, defined, 6–7
universal ethical principles, defined, 281
urinary incontinence, 428
U.S. Bureau of Labor Statistics, 380
U.S. Department of Agriculture, 330,
 373
U.S. Department of Health and Human
 Services, 240, 271
U.S. Department of Labor, 397, 398, 407
U.S. Department of Labor Women's
 Bureau, 397, 400, 401
U.S. Public Health Service, 84
University of Massachusetts
 Medical School Center for
 Mindfulness, 434

validity
 defined, 25
 in human development research, 25
Van Gogh, V., 3
vascular dementia, defined, 471
verbal ability, gender-related differences
 in, 179
vernix, defined, 55
very low birth weight, defined, 72
video games, 251–252
 visual-spatial skills and, 251
Vietnam War, 11, 438
violence
 continuum of progressive behaviors
  and, 364
 dating, 300–301
 on television, 250
 in young and middle adulthood
  relationships, 363–364
vision
 age-related changes in, 472, 472–473
 in fetal development, 55
 See also seeing
visual acuity, defined, 104
visual cliff, defined, 105
visual expansion, defined, 105
visual organization, 338
visual-spatial skills, video games
 and, 251
vocational maturity, defined, 390
volunteering, in late life, 517–518
vulnerability-stress-adaptation model,
 defined, 370, 370
Vygotsky's theory of social
 development, 16–17, 136–138
 private speech and, 138
 scaffolding and, 137–138
 summarized, 21
 zone of proximal development
  and, 137

waking activity, defined, 82
Watson's view of behaviorism, 13, 21

Wechsler Intelligence Scale for
 Children-V (WISC-V), 199, 200
Wechsler Logical Memory Test, 29
weight-loss programs, 272
well-being
 in adolescence, 275
 in late adulthood, 509
 in newborns, 81
 unemployment and, 406, 407
whole-brain death, defined, 544
widowhood, 523–524
will, defined, 157
Winehouse, Amy, 541, 541
Winfrey, Oprah, 196
wisdom, in late adulthood, 486, 487
women
 bias and discrimination in workplace
  and, 400–402
 conception and, 52
 equal pay for equal work and,
  401, 401
 first pregnancy and, 59
 glass ceiling and, 400
 glass cliff and, 400
 occupational selection and
  development and, 397, 398,
  399–400
 reproductive changes in, age-related,
  428–430
 sexual harassment and, 402
Women's Health Initiative (WHI), 429
Women's Health Research Institute,
 428, 429
WomensHealth.gov, 428
word recognition, defined, 210
words
 bilingualism and, 145
 developmental change in
  learning, 144
 fast mapping and, 143–144
 first, 142–146
 identifying, 140–141
 individual differences in learning,
  144–145
 language growth and,
  encouraging, 146
 learning styles and, 146–147
 phonological memory and, 145
 reading comprehension and,
  206–207, 207, 210
 as symbols, 142
 from two words to complex sentences
  and, 146–147
work, 302–306, 388–413
 age discrimination and, 403
 career development and, 302–305
 child care and, 161–162
 dependent care and, 409–410
 employed caregivers and, 408–409
 family and, 408–413
 gender bias discrimination and,
  400–402
 in late life, 516–517, 517
 meaning of, 388–4389
 occupational choice and, 389–391
 occupational success predicted by IQ
  scores and, 199–200
 part-time employment and, 305–306
 possible selves and, 347–348
 sexual harassment and, 402
 stress related to, 234, 430

See also job satisfaction; occupational
 choice; occupational
 development; occupational
 transitions
work–family conflict, defined, 410
working memory, defined, 192, 482
World Health Organization, 90, 271,
 363, 364, 491, 528
writing skills, 212–213
 contributing to improved writing,
  212–213
 knowledge-telling strategy and, 212
 knowledge-transforming strategy
  and, 212
 mechanical requirements and, 213
 revising, 213
 teaching effectively, 213

X chromosomes, 40, 44, 45
X-rays, 44, 62, 470
XXX syndrome, 45
XYY complement, 45

Y chromosomes, 40, 41, 44, 45
young adulthood, 356–383
 abusive relationships in, 363–364
 alcohol use in, 326–330
 becoming rich and famous in, 324
 cigarette smoking in, 326, 326
 cognitive development in,
  334–345
 crystallized intelligence in, 337, 338,
  339, 339
 death of child in, 573
 divorce in, 379–382
 emotion in, 342–345
 family in, 372–383
 fluid intelligence in, 337, 338,
  339, 339
 friendships in, 356–358
 grief expressed by, 572–573
 growth in, 325
 health in, 325–333
 intelligence in, 334–340
 LGBTQ, 367–368
 lifestyle and, 365–372
 logic in, 342–345
 memory in, 338, 347
 mental abilities in, 335–337, 337
 nutrition in, 330–332
 obesity in, 332
 parents/parenting in, 372–376
 personality in, 243–247
 physical development in, 325
 relationships in, 356–383
 romantic relationships, 297–298,
  358–363
 strength in, 325
 thinking in, 340–342
 violence in relationships, 363–364
 See also emerging adulthood

zone of maximum comfort,
 defined, 504
zone of maximum performance
 potential, defined, 504
zone of proximal development,
 defined, 137
zygote
 defined, 52
 period of, 51–52, 53, 53